The CRICKETER DIGEST of a SEASON

1990

The
CRICKETER
DIGEST
of a
SEASON
1990

Compiled by Richard Lockwood

Macdonald
Queen Anne Press

A QUEEN ANNE PRESS BOOK

© Lennard Associates Ltd 1990

First published in 1990 by
Queen Anne Press, a division of
Macdonald & Co (Publishers) Ltd
Orbit House
1 New Fetter Lane
London EC4A 1AR

A member of the Maxwell Macmillan Pergamon Publishing Corporation

British Library Cataloguing in Publication Data
The Cricketer digest of a season
1990 –
1. England. First-class cricket
796.3586
ISBN 0–356–20016–7

Made by Lennard Associates Ltd
Mackerye End, Harpenden
Herts AL5 5DR

Photograhs by David Munden Photography
Designed by Forest Publication Services
Cover design by Pocknell & Co
Typesetting by Leaside Graphics
Printed and bound in England by
The Bath Press, Bath, Avon

CONTENTS

FOREWORD

The Cricketer Digest of a Season, an impressively detailed statistical account of the English cricket season, has been produced as a direct result of the creation, at the start of the year, of the TCCB/Bull Computer Statistics Service. This new service was developed so that, for the first time, *official* records could be maintained of all first-class and major one-day matches played in England.

Before this season, the Test and County Cricket Board never had any control over, nor access to, the statistics of the game. They felt that an official, accurate computer record of an English season, made available to all media outlets, would provide a valuable service for all followers of cricket.In its first year it has already been of great help to the England Committee in providing valuable information to supplement the regular selection meetings.

The establishment of a computer-based service was also a most appropriate venture for Bull Computers, the company who have developed on-screen statistics for the BBC over the last decade and now provide the same service for both satellite stations. 1990 has also marked the first year of Bull's sponsorship of the Development of Excellence programme, which hopes to prepare the best cricketers at Under 15, Under 17 and Under 19 levels for a career in first-class cricket.

The Cricketer Digest of a Season with its scorecards, averages and player records, all taken from the TCCB/Bull official database, represents a triumph for computer technology. That so much information could be gathered together so quickly and with such a high level of accuracy is a great endorsement of the decision to proceed with the service.

All those with an interest in cricket are now able, with the help of the Digest to recapture the flavour of an English season in more detail than has ever been available before the onset of winter.

1990 was a memorable season by any standards: many long-standing records were broken and England were able to build on what had been achieved against the odds in the Caribbean. *The Cricketer Digest of a Season* gives readers the opportunity to relive the highlights of an historic summer. I hope that next year's edition will reflect a continuing improvement in cricket at all levels.

Ted Dexter

EDITOR'S PREFACE

**THE TCCB / BULL COMPUTER OFFICIAL
STATISTICS SERVICE**

The Digest of a Season for 1990 is the culmination of my first summer's work as Editor of the TCCB / Bull Computer Official Statistics Service, a service developed to provide all areas of the media, television, radio and newspaper, with the official facts and figures on the English season. All the scorecards that make up the first section of the book have been entered into the computer at the centre of the whole operation in Ted Dexter's office; the county scorers have contributed greatly by checking every detail to ensure the highest possible level of accuracy; the computer has then used the information contained in the scorecards to calculate all the averages and to compile the player performance charts. The scorecards, averages and player breakdowns have then all been typeset direct from computer discs, enabling a book of this complexity to be produced with such speed, and thankfully reducing proofreading to a minimum.

It has been a very rewarding summer - being given the opportunity to produce the official statisitcs and then to see them gathered together in a book of this magnitude and many people deserve credit and my thanks for their help and guidance in setting up the whole project: Gordon Vince who has been able to interpret my ideas and tocreate the computer programme, and dedicated many many hours to ensure that all ran smoothly; Ted Dexter and Ivo Longfield for all their support in setting up the service and for tolerating the presence of myself and the computer in the office; the TCCB for giving the project their blessing; Bull Computers for providing the much-appreciated financial backing and the computer technology; the county scorers for their invaluable assistance; Adrian Stephenson for his vision in agreeing to produce the book and for spending so much time at his own computer to see that it actuallyreached publication; all at *The Cricketer* for the four years I spent in the editorial office which helped turn my hobby into my livelihood; my parents for, above all else, instilling in me the confidence that I could make a successful career out of cricket-watching; and, finally, to all the cricketers who have helped to make 1990 such a memorable season.

Richard Lockwood

INTRODUCTION

The Members stand to applaud Graham Gooch as he returns
to the Pavilion after his record-breaking innings at Lord's.

1990 - A SUMMER OF RUN-MAKING AND RECORD-BREAKING

In many ways the summer of 1990 belonged to one man - England captain Graham Gooch who reached the zenith of his career both as a batsman and as a captain. His outstanding performances placed his name indeliably in cricket's record books and helped England to win Test series against New Zealand and India and remain unbeaten in a home season for the first time since 1979.

In a summer blessed with good weather and a rich diversity of record-breaking achievement, the Lord's Test against India must be regarded as the pinnacle, with Gooch's own efforts giving him a permanent place in cricket's hall of fame. He became the 11th man to score a triple century in Tests and went on to make the sixth highest score in Test history. When he scored another century in the second innings he became the first batsman to make a triple hundred and a hundred in the same match, Test or first- class. With 456 runs in the match, he created a new record aggregate for a Test match, eclipsing Greg Chappell's 380 for Australia against New Zealand in 1974-75; it was also the second best in all first-class cricket. All this and the wicket of Sanjay Manjrekar and the run out that won the match for England.

At Old Trafford, Gooch made his third 100 in successive innings as he and Michael Atherton shared their second opening stand of over 200 in succession, so that when he arrived at the Oval for the final Test of the summer, Sir Donald Bradman's record aggregate for Test runs in an English season (974 in 1930) was in sight. Nor did Gooch disappoint: he overtook Bradman's aggregate when he had made five in the second innings and finished the summer with a total of 1,058 Test runs to his credit in 11 innings. His 752 runs in the series

INTRODUCTION

against India was a new record for a three-match rubber, and helped England to their second series victory of the summer, something they last managed in 1978.

The England captain also broke new ground in first-class cricket in 1990: although a broken thumb deprived him of the chance to reach 3,000 first-class runs in a season, his final aggregate of 2,746 was the best since 1961, and he became only the fourth man to finish an English season with a first-class average better than 100 after Bradman, Bill Johnston and Geoff Boycott.

Nor was Graham Gooch alone in rewriting the record books: indeed, hardly a day of the season went past without a career best or a new record of some sort. In the Test arena three performances deserve special attention: Sir Richard Hadlee (after deservedly being knighted in the Birthday Honours List) finished his Test career on a high note at Edgbaston, by taking his world record tally of Test wickets to 431 with his 36th haul of five or more wickets in a Test innings. Devon Malcolm was his final victim, dismissed with the last ball of Hadlee's Test career; Sachin Tendulkar is more than 20 years his junior and wasn't born when Sir Richard played his first Test match, yet the youngster confirmed his reputation as a great player of the future by becoming the second youngest (at 17 years 112 days) ever to score a Test 100 and the youngest to do so in England with a magnificently composed 119* to save India in the Old Trafford Test; finally, Kapil Dev's incredible Houdini-like escape act at Lord's will live in the memory for many years. With India needing 24 to save the follow on and the last pair at the wicket, Kapil hit the last four balls of Eddie Hemmings's over for enormous straight sixes to claim a unique achievement for himself.

David Gower's immaculate 157* against India at The Oval put the seal on a series that had seen a feast of runs: England made their highest total against India at Lord's; India responded with their highest against England at The Oval; over 1,600 runs were scored at both Lord's and Old Trafford and series produced a total of 15 individual 100s, a new record for any three-match series.

County cricket also saw the pendulum swing violently in favour of the batsmen, as bowlers were forced to toil away with a reduced-seam ball on better quality pitches, often with clear skies and a hot sun offering no comfort. Ten batsmen, Graham Gooch, Jimmy Cook, Desmond Haynes, Graeme Hick, Hugh Morris, Chris Broad, Alan Butcher, Mark Waugh, David Ward and Ashley Metcalfe completed 2,000 first-class runs, and 76 reached the 1,000 mark, compared to 65 in 1989. In all first-class cricket 428 individual 100s were recorded, a dramatic increase on 1989 (248), and the most ever made in a single English season. The prevailing batsman-friendly conditions also produced 32 scores of more than 200, another new record. Neil Fairbrother (366), Graham Gooch (333) and Jimmy Cook (313*) went on to record triple centuries. Only six double hundreds had been scored in 1989.

The pre-eminence of batsmen across the country is emphasied by the final national averages: 48 finished the season with a first-class average better than 50.00 when only 15 managed that level in 1989. By contrast, only 25 bowlers with 20 or more wickets could average less than 30.00, compared to 76 in the previous season. Essex's Neil Foster was leading wicket-taker with 94 wickets, but was the only bowler to capture more than 80.

23 totals of more than 500 were recorded in county cricket, compared to four in 1989, as Essex, Lancashire, and Northamptonshire established new record scores. Lancashire's 863 against Surrey at The Oval was the second highest total in the history of the County Championship, while Northants improved their best in successive matches, both against Essex.

Record aggregates were posted both for three-day and four-day matches: Glamorgan and Worcestershire managed a total of 1,641 in a three-day match at Abergavenny, while Surrey and Lancashire scored 1,650 runs in their four-day match at The Oval.

INTRODUCTION

As well as becoming the youngest player ever to complete 50 first-class 100s, Graeme Hick scored 645 runs without being dismissed to set a new record for Enlish cricket, beating Everton Weekes's 575 for the West Indians on tour in 1950; only K.C.Ibrahim (709 runs for Hindus in 1947-48) has done better in first-class cricket.

Australian Tom Moody also deserves individual recognition for what he has achieved in his first season of county cricket. He hit 100s in his first three first-class matches for Warwickshire, reached 98 in his fourth, and added 100s in each of his next four. The fourth of these made against Glamorgan at Cardiff was the fastest century ever recorded in first-class cricket having taken him only 26 minutes. Moody's innings was made against declaration bowling and is perhaps one of several instances in 1990 when run-making was just too easy.

But the excitement and the record-breaking flavour of the 1990 season was sustained right to the last. Middlesex only beat off Essex's challenge for the County Championship on the season's penultimate day, and Hampshire brought the summer to a close by achieving the second highest total ever to win a Championship match against Gloucestershire at Southampton to move into third place. A fitting finale to a run-filled season.

Sir Richard Hadlee's farewell to Lord's.

THE
SCORECARDS

THE OPENING FIRST-CLASS MATCHES

CAMBRIDGE UNIV vs. NORTHANTS

at Fenner's on 14th, 15th, 16th April 1990
Toss : Cambridge Univ.   Umpires : B.Hassan and R.Julian
Match drawn

NORTHANTS

G.Cook	c James b Johnson	87			
A.Fordham	c Morris b Johnson	17	(1) c Johnson b Pyman	54
N.A.Felton	b Pyman	26	(2) lbw b Jenkins	3
D.J.Wild	c Hooper b Lowrey	20	(3) c Turner b Lowrey	43
A.L.Penberthy	not out	101		
D.Ripley +	lbw b Pyman	22		
J.G.Thomas	not out	13	(6) c James b Lowrey	8
J.W.Govan			(4) lbw b Pyman	3
N.G.B.Cook *			(5) not out	0
S.J.Brown				
M.A.Robinson				
Extras	(lb 6,nb 5)	11		0
TOTAL	(for 5 wkts dec)	297	(for 5 wkts dec)	111

CAMBRIDGE UNIV

S.P.James	lbw b Thomas	39	lbw b Brown	6
R.Heap	c Felton b Govan	18	c Thomas b Wild	37
M.J.Lowrey	run out	8	not out	23
J.C.M.Atkinson *	c Cook N.G.B. b Robinson	2	not out	47
M.J.Morris	b Brown	5		
A.M.Hooper	c Thomas b Robinson	0		
R.A.Pyman	b Govan	4		
R.J.Turner +	c Brown b Penberthy	21		
D.H.Shufflebotham	not out	16		
R.H.J.Jenkins	lbw b Penberthy	0		
S.W.Johnson	c Brown b Penberthy	0		
Extras	(b 1,lb 13,w 1)	15	(lb 3)	3
TOTAL		128	(for 2 wkts)	116

CAMBRIDGE U	O	M	R	W	O	M	R	W
Johnson	21	2	86	2	4	0	17	0
Jenkins	23.5	2	59	0	11	1	52	1
Pyman	36	12	62	2	12	6	29	2
Shufflebotham	5	0	26	0				
Lowrey	24	7	58	1	4.1	1	13	2

NORTHANTS	O	M	R	W	O	M	R	W
Brown	12	6	18	1	9	4	11	1
Thomas	10	1	47	1	7	1	26	0
Govan	11	7	12	2	3	2	10	0
Robinson	16	6	24	2	6	0	18	0
Cook N.G.B.	2	1	2	0	2	2	0	0
Penberthy	8.4	5	11	3	3	1	12	0
Wild					9	2	32	1
Fordham					1	0	4	0

FALL OF WICKETS

	NOR	CAM	NOR	CAM
1st	37	54	26	28
2nd	79	66	88	46
3rd	110	74	103	
4th	197	74	103	
5th	254	75	111	
6th		88		
7th		90		
8th		123		
9th		126		
10th		128		

OXFORD UNIV vs. GLAMORGAN

at The Parks on 14th, 16th, 17th April 1990
Toss : Oxford Univ.   Umpires : J.D.Bond and A.G.T.Whitehead
Match drawn

GLAMORGAN

A.R.Butcher *	c Lunn b Crawley	60		
H.Morris	c & b Crawley	103		
G.C.Holmes	c van der Merwe b Turner	62		
M.P.Maynard	b Crawley	40	(2) not out	32
I.Smith	c van der Merwe b Crawley	17	(1) not out	18
H.A.Anthony	c Gerrans b Crawley	19		
N.G.Cowley	c & b Crawley	13		
M.L.Roberts +	not out	5		
S.J.Dennis				
M.Frost				
S.R.Barwick				
Extras	(b 9,lb 9,w 5,nb 10)	33	(lb 2,nb 3)	5
TOTAL	(for 7 wkts dec)	352	(for 0 wkts)	55

OXFORD UNIV

D.A.Hagan	c Holmes b Cowley	47	
R.E.Morris *	c Cowley b Dennis	16	
M.J.Kilborn	c Roberts b Holmes	83	
G.J.Turner	lbw b Barwick	5	
M.A.Crawley	not out	103	
P.D.Lunn	lbw b Dennis	5	
W.M.van der Merwe	lbw b Anthony	1	
P.S.Gerrans	b Anthony	0	
S.D.Weale	not out	7	
J.McGrady +			
I.M.Henderson			
Extras	(b 2,lb 9,w 2,nb 9)	22	
TOTAL	(for 7 wkts dec)	289	

OXFORD UNIV	O	M	R	W	O	M	R	W
van der Merwe	15	3	43	0	2	0	24	0
Henderson	9	2	36	0	4	1	8	0
Gerrans	27	7	80	0				
Crawley	27.3	4	92	6				
Turner	16	3	52	1	2	0	21	0
Weale	10	3	31	0				

GLAMORGAN	O	M	R	W	O	M	R	W
Anthony	20.4	5	72	2				
Frost	20	5	33	0				
Cowley	20	6	49	1				
Barwick	15	6	16	1				
Dennis	24	6	51	2				
Smith	6	0	24	0				
Holmes	8	2	33	1				

FALL OF WICKETS

	GLA	OXF	GLA	OXF
1st	123	41		
2nd	226	54		
3rd	278	165		
4th	301	239		
5th	325	262		
6th	337	263		
7th	352	263		
8th				
9th				
10th				

HEADLINES

14th-16th April

● The first first-class century of the season was completed by 20-year-old Cornishman Tony Penberthy for Northants against Cambridge University at Fenner's. It was his maiden 100 in his ninth first-class innings and he followed by improving his best bowling figures with 3 for 11 in the University's first innings.

● Mark Crawley, in his fourth year of University cricket, produced his best bowling figures for Oxford against Glamorgan at The Parks and then proceeded to make the second first-class 100 of his career.

● First-class debuts: M.J.Lowrey, R.H.J.Jenkins, S.W.Johnson(Cambridge U); P.S.Gerrans, J.McGrady (Oxford U).

17th-20th April

● 19-year-old Chris Adams made his maiden first-class 100 for Derbyshire v Cambridge University at Fenner's, while new SouthAfrican Adrian Kuiper passed 50 on his first appearance for the county.

● Derbyshire captain Kim Barnett produced match figures of 7 for 37 in his side's 243 run victory.

● The first day of the season lost to the weather was the last day of the MCC v Worcestershire match at Lord's.

● First-class debut: R.P.Lefebvre (Somerset).

MCC vs. WORCESTERSHIRE

at Lord's on 17th, 18th, 19th, 20th (no play) April 1990
Toss : Worcestershire.   Umpires : B.Dudleston and K.J.Lyons
Match drawn

MCC

M.D.Moxon	c Rhodes b McEwan	12
M.R.Benson	c Newport b Radford	52
P.W.G.Parker *	b Botham	93
M.A.Atherton	lbw b Botham	19
J.E.Morris	lbw b Botham	15
D.A.Reeve	c Hick b Radford	39
W.K.Hegg +	c Rhodes b Radford	57
D.V.Lawrence	c McEwan b Radford	4
S.L.Watkin	c Hick b McEwan	14
N.G.Cowans	not out	46
P.C.R.Tufnell	b Botham	12
Extras	(lb 11,w 3,nb 8)	22
TOTAL		385

WORCESTERSHIRE

T.S.Curtis	lbw b Watkin	81
G.J.Lord	b Lawrence	20
G.A.Hick	c Parker b Lawrence	72
R.K.Illingworth	c Atherton b Watkin	6
I.T.Botham	c Hegg b Cowans	19
P.A.Neale *	not out	22
D.B.D'Oliveira	b Watkin	12
S.J.Rhodes +	c Hegg b Watkin	19
P.J.Newport	not out	1
N.V.Radford		
S.M.McEwan		
Extras	(b 4,lb 5,w 1,nb 27)	37
TOTAL	(for 7 wkts)	289

WORCS	O	M	R	W	O	M	R	W
Radford	34	7	116	4				
McEwan	31	9	101	2				
Botham	20	4	68	4				
Newport	18	0	85	0				
Illingworth	1	0	4	0				

MCC	O	M	R	W	O	M	R	W
Lawrence	25.1	1	105	2				
Cowans	18	5	39	1				
Reeve	13	3	40	0				
Watkin	29	7	83	4				
Tufnell	7	2	13	0				

FALL OF WICKETS

	MCC	WOR	MCC	WOR
1st	13	81		
2nd	151	165		
3rd	184	181		
4th	191	213		
5th	216	237		
6th	285	258		
7th	299	288		
8th	319			
9th	349			
10th	385			

THE OPENING FIRST-CLASS MATCHES

Tony Penberthy of Northants on his way to the first century of the season against Cambridge University at Fenner's

OXFORD UNIV vs. SOMERSET

at The Parks on 18th, 19th, 20th April 1990
Toss : Oxford Univ.   Umpires : J.D.Bond and A.G.T.Whitehead
Match drawn

SOMERSET

S.J.Cook	lbw b Gerrans	28
P.M.Roebuck	c Crawley b van der Merwe	26
J.J.E.Hardy	c Almaer b Gerrans	0
C.J.Tavare *	c Almaer b Henderson	83
R.J.Harden	c & b Henderson	99
N.D.Burns +	not out	28
G.D.Rose	c Crawley b Turner	32
R.Lefebvre		
I.G.Swallow		
N.A.Mallender		
A.N.Jones		
Extras	(b 10,lb 8,w 3,nb 11)	32
TOTAL	(for 6 wkts dec)	328

OXFORD UNIV

D.A.Hagan	c Cook b Jones	7
S.A.Almaer	b Rose	4
M.J.Kilborn	c & b Swallow	37
G.J.Turner	b Jones	0
M.A.Crawley *	b Lefebvre	33
P.D.Lunn	not out	19
W.M.van der Merwe	not out	18
S.D.Weale		
P.S.Gerrans		
J.McGrady +		
I.M.Henderson		
Extras	(b 2,lb 15,w 1,nb 8)	26
TOTAL	(for 5 wkts)	144

OXFORD UNIV	O	M	R	W	O	M	R	W
van der Merwe	17	5	44	1				
Henderson	17	1	92	2				
Gerrans	24	8	56	2				
Turner	11.2	4	41	1				
Crawley	13	0	63	0				
Weale	4	1	14	0				

SOMERSET	O	M	R	W	O	M	R	W
Jones	16	8	17	2				
Mallender	16	2	30	0				
Rose	14	2	37	1				

FALL OF WICKETS

	SOM	OXF	SOM	OXF
1st	57	8		
2nd	57	14		
3rd	58	14		
4th	246	83		
5th	277	95		
6th	328			
7th				
8th				
9th				
10th				

CAMBRIDGE UNIV vs. DERBYSHIRE

at Fenner's on 18th, 19th, 20th April 1990
Toss : Cambridge Univ.   Umpires : B.Hassan and R.Julian
Derbyshire won by 243 runs

DERBYSHIRE

K.J.Barnett *	c Atkinson b Buzza	62			
T.J.G.O'Gorman	c Heap b Pyman	55			
C.J.Adams	not out	111			
A.P.Kuiper	lbw b Pyman	51			
B.Roberts	b Buzza	12	(1) c Lowrey b Buzza	33
A.M.Brown	not out	34			
S.C.Goldsmith			(2) lbw b Atkinson	51
G.Miller			(3) not out	25
M.Jean-Jacques			(4) not out	13
B.J.M.Maher +					
O.H.Mortensen					
Extras	(b 3,lb 4)	7	(lb 2,w 3)	5
TOTAL	(for 4 wkts dec)	332	(for 2 wkts dec)	127

CAMBRIDGE UNIV

S.P.James	b Jean-Jacques	21	c Adams b Kuiper	7
R.Heap	lbw b Mortensen	4	c Brown b Miller	0
M.J.Lowrey	c Adams b Mortensen	4	lbw b Jean-Jacques	1
J.C.M.Atkinson *	lbw b Miller	36	b Roberts	23
M.J.Morris	c Miller b Jean-Jacques	2	c Miller b Barnett	45
A.M.Hooper	lbw b Mortensen	0	b Barnett	5
R.A.Pyman	c O'Gorman b Roberts	5	b Miller	2
R.J.Turner +	c Miller b Barnett	18	c Goldsmith b Barnett	0
G.A.Pointer	lbw b Barnett	7	b Barnett	9
A.J.Buzza	c Goldsmith b Barnett	0	not out	9
R.H.J.Jenkins	not out	0	lbw b Miller	1
Extras	(lb 5,w 3,nb 1)	9	(b 5,lb 3)	8
TOTAL		106		110

CAMBRIDGE U	O	M	R	W	O	M	R	W
Jenkins	13	3	47	0	8	2	37	0
Pointer	8	0	35	0	9	3	32	0
Pyman	28	3	94	2	4.3	2	2	0
Buzza	32	5	117	2	10	2	27	1
Lowrey	9	1	32	0				
Atkinson					7	1	27	1

DERBYSHIRE	O	M	R	W	O	M	R	W
Mortensen	15	3	21	3				
Jean-Jacques	14	4	31	2	10	3	23	1
Miller	10	4	9	1	23.4	16	14	3
Barnett	8.2	5	9	3	18	7	28	4
Goldsmith	7	2	15	0	9	1	21	0
Roberts	6	2	16	1	3	3	0	1
Kuiper					7	2	16	1

FALL OF WICKETS

	DER	CAM	DER	CAM
1st	78	22	86	1
2nd	156	32	86	8
3rd	241	32		8
4th	268	36		70
5th		39		82
6th		58		89
7th		90		89
8th		105		92
9th		105		103
10th		106		110

REFUGE ASSURANCE LEAGUE

HEADLINES

22nd April

- Six sides won away from home as Nottinghamshire were the only county to win on their home territory.

- Highest innings of the day was Tim Curtis's 124 for Worcestershire v Somerset at Taunton. It was his highest score in the Sunday League and only his second 100. In the same match Steve Rhodes took five catches and a stumping.

- Graeme Fowler and Desmond Haynes both passed the 100 mark in the Lancashire v Middlesex match at Old Trafford. Fowler hit his fourth Sunday League century while Haynes made his first one-day 100 for Middlesex.

- Martin Speight's 77 was his highest Sunday League score but it was countered by Simon Base who produced his best figures in the competition (4 for 28) and by Adrian Kuiper and Chris Adams who added 81 in 8 overs to take Derbyshire to a six wicket victory over Sussex.

- Neil Foster returned the best figures of the day (4 for 21) but Essex lost to Kent as Tony Merrick took 4 for 24 in his first match for Kent.

LEICESTERSHIRE vs. NORTHANTS

at Leicester on 22nd April 1990
Toss : Northants. Umpires : J.W.Holder and B.J.Meyer
Northants won by 6 wickets. (Leics 0pts Northants 4pts)

LEICESTERSHIRE

T.J.Boon	b Capel	9
N.E.Briers *	c Lamb b Cook	10
J.J.Whitaker	c Ripley b Robinson	32
P.Willey	c Bailey b Cook	5
J.D.R.Benson	b Thomas	8
C.C.Lewis	b Thomas	9
P.Whitticase +	c Lamb b Thomas	38
M.I.Gidley	c Capel b Brown	10
J.P.Agnew	b Brown	1
A.D.Mullally	not out	0
L.B.Taylor	lbw b Brown	0
Extras	(lb 9,w 5,nb 3)	17
TOTAL	(40 overs)	139

NORTHANTS

R.J.Bailey	c Lewis b Gidley	70
W.Larkins	c Whitticase b Lewis	17
A.J.Lamb *	c Whitaker b Lewis	4
D.J.Capel	not out	47
D.J.Wild	lbw b Lewis	5
A.L.Penberthy	not out	0
D.Ripley +		
J.G.Thomas		
N.G.B.Cook		
M.A.Robinson		
S.J.Brown		
Extras	(w 5)	5
TOTAL	(37.1 overs)(for 4 wkts)	143

NORTHANTS	O	M	R	W	FALL OF WICKETS		
						LEI	NOR
Capel	6	2	18	1	1st	20	39
Brown	8	0	26	3	2nd	35	53
Robinson	8	4	8	1	3rd	43	138
Cook	8	1	31	2	4th	66	139
Thomas	7	1	27	3	5th	80	
Penberthy	3	0	20	0	6th	97	
LEICS	O	M	R	W	7th	134	
Taylor	7	1	34	0	8th	137	
Mullally	6	0	33	0	9th	138	
Lewis	8	0	18	3	10th	139	
Agnew	8	1	25	0			
Gidley	6.1	0	28	1			
Willey	2	0	5	0			

LANCASHIRE vs. MIDDLESEX

at Old Trafford on 22nd April 1990
Toss : Middlesex. Umpires : J.H.Hampshire and B.White
Middlesex won by 8 wickets. (Lancs 0pts Middx 4pts)

LANCASHIRE

G.Fowler	lbw b Williams	101
M.A.Atherton	b Emburey	63
N.H.Fairbrother	run out	1
G.D.Lloyd	run out	7
M.Watkinson	c Emburey b Williams	7
P.A.J.DeFreitas	c Brown b Williams	6
T.E.Jesty	lbw b Williams	10
I.D.Austin	not out	8
D.P.Hughes *		
P.J.W.Allott		
W.K.Hegg +		
Extras	(lb 6,w 5,nb 1)	12
TOTAL	(40 overs)(for 7 wkts)	215

MIDDLESEX

D.L.Haynes	not out	107
M.A.Roseberry	lbw b Watkinson	73
M.R.Ramprakash	run out	22
K.R.Brown	not out	2
M.W.Gatting *		
J.D.Carr		
P.R.Downton +		
J.E.Emburey		
N.F.Williams		
J.R.Hemstock		
P.N.Weekes		
Extras	(lb 9,w 4,nb 2)	15
TOTAL	(38.2 overs)(for 2 wkts)	219

MIDDLESEX	O	M	R	W	FALL OF WICKETS		
						LAN	MID
Williams	8	0	49	4	1st	141	176
Hemstock	8	0	43	0	2nd	148	213
Emburey	8	1	35	1	3rd	181	
Carr	3.4	0	20	0	4th	187	
Weekes	4	0	21	0	5th	190	
Haynes	7.2	0	34	0	6th	196	
Ramprakash	1	0	7	0	7th	215	
					8th		
LANCASHIRE	O	M	R	W	9th		
DeFreitas	8	0	35	0	10th		
Allott	8	1	20	0			
Austin	6	0	45	0			
Watkinson	7.2	0	50	1			
Jesty	2	0	16	0			
Atherton	4	0	24	0			
Hughes	3	0	20	0			

ESSEX vs. KENT

at Chelmsford on 22nd April 1990
Toss : Essex. Umpires : D.O.Oslear and N.T.Plews
Kent won by 27 runs. (Essex 0pts Kent 4pts)

KENT

S.G.Hinks	b Childs	50
N.R.Taylor	c Pringle b Childs	58
T.R.Ward	c Garnham b Foster	13
C.S.Cowdrey *	b Foster	11
G.R.Cowdrey	c Garnham b Foster	6
R.M.Ellison	lbw b Foster	0
M.V.Fleming	not out	24
S.A.Marsh +	not out	27
M.A.Ealham		
C.Penn		
T.A.Merrick		
Extras	(b 1,lb 14,w 8,nb 3)	26
TOTAL	(40 overs)(for 6 wkts)	215

ESSEX

G.A.Gooch *	c Ealham b Merrick	3
B.R.Hardie	run out	56
M.E.Waugh	c Taylor b Fleming	50
P.J.Prichard	c Ealham b Ellison	18
D.R.Pringle	b Ellison	15
J.P.Stephenson	b Penn	5
A.W.Lilley	b Merrick	10
M.A.Garnham +	b Merrick	10
N.A.Foster	c Ellison b Merrick	6
T.D.Topley	not out	3
J.H.Childs	b Penn	2
Extras	(lb 8,w 2)	10
TOTAL	(39 overs)	188

ESSEX	O	M	R	W	FALL OF WICKETS		
						KEN	ESS
Foster	8	1	21	4	1st	98	5
Topley	8	0	38	0	2nd	122	116
Waugh	5	0	32	0	3rd	145	121
Gooch	5	0	28	0	4th	153	151
Pringle	8	0	43	0	5th	153	152
Childs	6	0	38	2	6th	155	159
					7th		171
KENT	O	M	R	W	8th		181
Penn	8	1	30	2	9th		183
Merrick	7	0	24	4	10th		188
Ealham	8	0	29	0			
Fleming	8	0	43	1			
Cowdrey C.S.	1	0	9	0			
Ellison	7	0	45	2			

GLOUCESTERSHIRE vs. GLAMORGAN

at Bristol on 22nd April 1990
Toss : Gloucestershire. Umpires : B.Hassan and R.Palmer
Glamorgan won by 5 runs. (Glos 0pts Glamorgan 4pts)

GLAMORGAN

G.C.Holmes	c Russell b Curran	8
H.Morris	st Russell b Graveney	46
A.Dale	c Wright b Alleyne	42
M.P.Maynard	c Athey b Alleyne	11
A.R.Butcher *	b Lawrence	8
I.Smith	b Lawrence	46
N.G.Cowley	c Russell b Lawrence	17
C.P.Metson +	not out	0
S.J.Dennis		
S.L.Watkin		
S.R.Barwick		
Extras	(lb 5,w 2,nb 3)	10
TOTAL	(40 overs)(for 7 wkts)	188

GLOUCESTERSHIRE

A.J.Wright *	c Maynard b Cowley	30
C.W.J.Athey	c Butcher b Dale	15
G.D.Hodgson	c Dale b Cowley	28
K.M.Curran	run out	37
P.W.Romaines	c Holmes b Watkin	22
M.W.Alleyne	c Maynard b Dennis	11
R.C.Russell +	c Watkin b Barwick	28
E.T.Milburn	not out	5
D.A.Graveney		
D.V.Lawrence		
K.B.S.Jarvis		
Extras	(lb 6,w 1)	7
TOTAL	(40 overs)(for 7 wkts)	183

GLOUCS	O	M	R	W	FALL OF WICKETS		
						GLA	GLO
Curran	8	0	22	1	1st	10	33
Jarvis	8	1	45	0	2nd	82	58
Milburn	2	0	11	0	3rd	114	84
Lawrence	7	0	40	3	4th	116	134
Graveney	8	1	20	1	5th	133	145
Alleyne	7	0	45	2	6th	180	151
					7th	188	183
GLAMORGAN	O	M	R	W	8th		
Dennis	8	1	35	1	9th		
Watkin	8	2	24	1	10th		
Barwick	8	2	24	1			
Dale	6	0	41	1			
Cowley	8	1	36	2			
Smith	2	0	17	0			

SUSSEX vs. DERBYSHIRE

at Hove on 22nd April 1990
Toss : Derbys Umpires : A.G.T.Whitehead and P.B.Wight
Derbyshire won by 6 wickets. (Sussex 0pts Derbys 4pts)

SUSSEX

N.J.Lenham	c Bowler b Base	0
P.W.G.Parker *	lbw b Mortensen	0
A.P.Wells	c Kuiper b Malcolm	57
M.P.Speight	c Bowler b Base	77
C.M.Wells	c Mortensen b Kuiper	8
I.J.Gould	b Kuiper	0
A.C.S.Pigott	c Bowler b Base	11
A.I.C.Dodemaide	not out	24
P.Moores +	c Bowler b Base	0
A.R.Hansford	not out	5
I.D.K.Salisbury		
Extras	(lb 17,w 2,nb 4)	23
TOTAL	(40 overs)(for 8 wkts)	205

DERBYSHIRE

K.J.Barnett *	c Moores b Pigott	60
P.D.Bowler +	c & b Salisbury	51
J.E.Morris	run out	5
A.P.Kuiper	not out	53
T.J.G.O'Gorman	lbw b Pigott	0
C.J.Adams	not out	30
B.Roberts		
G.Miller		
D.E.Malcolm		
S.J.Base		
O.H.Mortensen		
Extras	(lb 6,w 2,nb 2)	10
TOTAL	(38.5 overs)(for 4 wkts)	209

DERBYSHIRE	O	M	R	W	FALL OF WICKETS		
						SUS	DER
Mortensen	8	0	23	1	1st	1	117
Base	8	0	28	4	2nd	3	125
Miller	6	0	38	0	3rd	140	128
Malcolm	8	0	47	1	4th	153	128
Kuiper	6	0	30	2	5th	160	
Barnett	4	0	22	0	6th	164	
					7th	183	
SUSSEX	O	M	R	W	8th	183	
Wells C.M.	7.5	1	41	0	9th		
Dodemaide	8	0	38	0	10th		
Salisbury	8	1	29	1			
Hansford	7	0	35	0			
Pigott	8	0	60	2			

REFUGE ASS. LEAGUE | BENSON & HEDGES CUP

NOTTINGHAMSHIRE vs. YORKSHIRE
at Trent Bridge on 22nd April 1990
Toss : Notts. Umpires : J.D.Bond and B.Leadbeater
Nottinghamshire won by 5 wickets. (Notts 4pts Yorks 0pts)

YORKSHIRE

M.D.Moxon *	lbw b Pick	37
A.A.Metcalfe	lbw b Saxelby	11
R.J.Blakey +	b Hemmings	30
P.E.Robinson	c Robinson b Hemmings	4
D.Byas	c French b Saxelby	7
C.White	not out	26
P.Carrick	run out	1
A.Sidebottom	c French b Stephenson	1
P.W.Jarvis	not out	28
D.Gough		
S.D.Fletcher		
Extras	(lb 9,w 6,nb 1)	16
TOTAL	(40 overs)(for 7 wkts)	161

NOTTINGHAMSHIRE

B.C.Broad	c Blakey b Jarvis	4
P.Pollard	b Jarvis	3
R.T.Robinson *	lbw b Sidebottom	1
P.Johnson	c Blakey b Carrick	39
D.W.Randall	not out	54
F.D.Stephenson	c Blakey b Gough	42
B.N.French +	not out	15
E.E.Hemmings		
K.E.Cooper		
R.A.Pick		
K.Saxelby		
Extras	(b 1,lb 3)	4
TOTAL	(39.1 overs)(for 5 wkts)	162

NOTTS	O	M	R	W	FALL OF WICKETS	YOR	NOT
Stephenson	8	2	28	1			
Cooper	8	2	24	0	1st	38	8
Saxelby	8	0	49	2	2nd	61	9
Hemmings	8	0	28	2	3rd	76	9
Pick	8	0	23	1	4th	96	67
					5th	102	129
YORKSHIRE	O	M	R	W	6th	104	
Jarvis	8	1	26	2	7th	107	
Sidebottom	8	3	22	1	8th		
Fletcher	7.1	0	31	0	9th		
Gough	5	0	29	1	10th		
Carrick	6	0	27	1			
Byas	5	0	23	0			

SOMERSET vs. WORCESTERSHIRE
at Taunton on 22nd April 1990
Toss : Somerset. Umpires : K.E.Palmer and D.R.Shepherd
Worcestershire won by 33 runs. (Somerset 0pts Worcs 4pts)

WORCESTERSHIRE

T.S.Curtis	c Cook b Roebuck	124
I.T.Botham	st Burns b Swallow	24
G.A.Hick	not out	78
D.B.D'Oliveira	not out	0
P.A.Neale *		
M.J.Weston		
S.J.Rhodes +		
R.K.Illingworth		
P.J.Newport		
N.V.Radford		
S.M.McEwan		
Extras	(lb 6,w 5)	11
TOTAL	(40 overs)(for 2 wkts)	237

SOMERSET

S.J.Cook	c Rhodes b Newport	18
P.M.Roebuck	c Rhodes b McEwan	39
R.J.Bartlett	c Rhodes b Newport	2
C.J.Tavare *	c Rhodes b Botham	3
R.J.Harden	c Rhodes b Botham	35
N.D.Burns +	run out	19
G.D.Rose	not out	41
R.P.Lefebvre	c & b Illingworth	11
A.N.Jones	st Rhodes b Illingworth	10
I.G.Swallow	not out	6
N.A.Mallender		
Extras	(lb 11,w 6,nb 3)	20
TOTAL	(40 overs)(for 8 wkts)	204

SOMERSET	O	M	R	W	FALL OF WICKETS	WOR	SOM
Jones	8	0	40	0			
Mallender	8	1	26	0	1st	86	30
Rose	8	0	54	0	2nd	236	35
Swallow	7	0	47	1	3rd		45
Lefebvre	8	0	54	0	4th		102
Roebuck	1	0	10	1	5th		121
					6th		139
WORCS	O	M	R	W	7th		175
Newport	8	1	17	2	8th		197
Weston	3	0	22	0	9th		
Botham	8	0	39	2	10th		
McEwan	8	0	49	1			
Radford	5	0	20	0			
Illingworth	8	0	46	2			

GLOUCESTERSHIRE vs. WORCS
at Bristol on 24th April 1990
Toss : Glos. Umpires : A.A.Jones and M.J.Kitchen
Worcestershire won by 3 wickets. (Glos 0pts Worcs 2pts)

GLOUCESTERSHIRE

A.J.Wright *	c Newport b Botham	97
A.W.Stovold	c D'Oliveira b Dilley	8
G.D.Hodgson	c Botham b Illingworth	1
C.W.J.Athey	c Neale b Radford	49
K.M.Curran	c Rhodes b Dilley	55
R.C.Russell +	c Hick b Dilley	10
M.W.Alleyne	not out	23
P.Bainbridge	not out	0
D.A.Graveney		
E.T.Milburn		
D.V.Lawrence		
Extras	(lb 6,w 3,nb 2)	11
TOTAL	(55 overs)(for 6 wkts)	254

WORCESTERSHIRE

T.S.Curtis	c Lawrence b Curran	2
G.J.Lord	c Athey b Graveney	26
G.A.Hick	c Lawrence b Milburn	2
I.T.Botham	not out	138
P.A.Neale *	c & b Curran	30
D.B.D'Oliveira	b Lawrence	2
S.J.Rhodes +	run out	1
R.K.Illingworth	c Alleyne b Curran	5
P.J.Newport	not out	22
N.V.Radford		
G.R.Dilley		
Extras	(b 1,lb 7,w 14,nb 6)	28
TOTAL	(54.1 overs)(for 7 wkts)	256

WORCS	O	M	R	W	FALL OF WICKETS	GLO	WOR
Dilley	11	0	43	3			
Radford	11	1	45	1	1st	34	3
Newport	7	0	23	0	2nd	37	20
Illingworth	10	0	43	1	3rd	148	87
Hick	5	0	25	0	4th	186	184
Botham	11	0	69	1	5th	207	187
					6th	250	190
GLOUCS	O	M	R	W	7th		220
Curran	11	0	53	3	8th		
Lawrence	11	3	36	1	9th		
Milburn	5	1	23	1	10th		
Bainbridge	8	0	37	0			
Graveney	11	0	40	1			
Alleyne	8.1	0	59	0			

Man of the match: I.T.Botham

LEICESTERSHIRE vs. NORTHANTS
at Leicester on 24th April 1990
Toss : Leicestershire. Umpires : P.J.Eele and R.Palmer
Northants won by 5 runs. (Leics 0pts Northants 2pts)

NORTHANTS

G.Cook	run out	6
W.Larkins	c Lewis b Taylor	46
R.J.Bailey	not out	92
A.J.Lamb *	b Mullally	34
D.J.Capel	b Lewis	33
D.J.Wild	c Whitticase b Lewis	0
D.Ripley +	not out	1
J.G.Thomas		
C.E.L.Ambrose		
N.G.B.Cook		
M.A.Robinson		
Extras	(b 1,lb 11,w 1,nb 1)	14
TOTAL	(55 overs)(for 5 wkts)	226

LEICESTERSHIRE

T.J.Boon	c Cook G. b Thomas	84
N.E.Briers *	b Ambrose	7
J.J.Whitaker	b Capel	46
P.Willey	b Ambrose	49
L.Potter	c Cook N.G.B. b Ambrose	6
C.C.Lewis	run out	5
J.D.R.Benson	b Thomas	1
P.Whitticase +	not out	7
J.P.Agnew		
A.D.Mullally		
L.B.Taylor		
Extras	(lb 13,w 2,nb 1)	16
TOTAL	(55 overs)(for 7 wkts)	221

LEICS	O	M	R	W	FALL OF WICKETS	NOR	LEI
Lewis	11	2	42	2			
Mullally	10	2	47	1	1st	14	9
Taylor	9	1	32	1	2nd	81	138
Agnew	11	1	49	0	3rd	155	171
Willey	11	0	36	0	4th	218	195
Potter	3	0	8	0	5th	218	206
					6th		211
NORTHANTS	O	M	R	W	7th		221
Ambrose	11	4	19	3	8th		
Capel	11	1	38	1	9th		
Thomas	11	0	59	2	10th		
Robinson	11	0	47	0			
Cook N.G.B.	11	1	45	0			

Man of the match: R.J.Bailey

WARWICKSHIRE vs. GLAMORGAN
at Edgbaston on 24th April 1990
Toss : Warwicks. Umpires : B.Hassan and B.Leadbeater
Glamorgan won by 3 runs. (Warwicks 0pts Glam 2pts)

GLAMORGAN

A.R.Butcher *	c Humpage b Munton	11
H.Morris	c Humpage b Small	1
G.C.Holmes	c Asif Din b Munton	11
M.P.Maynard	c Lloyd b Small	77
I.V.A.Richards	c Booth	21
P.A.Cottey	lbw b Booth	2
N.G.Cowley	b Donald	19
C.P.Metson +	c Booth b Small	20
S.J.Dennis	c Lloyd b Small	2
S.L.Watkin	not out	2
S.R.Barwick		
Extras	(b 4,lb 20,w 4,nb 2)	30
TOTAL	(55 overs)(for 9 wkts)	196

WARWICKSHIRE

A.J.Moles	run out	52
T.A.Lloyd *	c Richards b Barwick	10
Asif Din	b Cowley	50
A.I.Kallicharran	c Holmes b Richards	13
P.A.Smith	lbw b Richards	13
G.W.Humpage +	c Butcher b Barwick	15
D.A.Reeve	lbw b Richards	14
G.C.Small	run out	1
P.A.Booth	not out	13
A.A.Donald		
T.A.Munton		
Extras	(lb 5,w 7)	12
TOTAL	(55 overs)(for 8 wkts)	193

WARWICKS	O	M	R	W	FALL OF WICKETS	GLA	WAR
Donald	11	1	42	1			
Small	11	2	22	4	1st	2	20
Munton	7	0	28	2	2nd	21	117
Reeve	10	0	26	0	3rd	28	123
Smith P.A.	5	0	15	0	4th	97	143
Booth	11	1	39	2	5th	111	162
					6th	139	164
GLAMORGAN	O	M	R	W	7th	175	165
Watkin	11	2	35	0	8th	182	193
Dennis	6	0	20	0	9th	196	
Barwick	11	0	44	2	10th		
Richards	11	1	38	3			
Cowley	11	0	23	1			
Holmes	5	0	28	0			

Man of the match: M.P.Maynard

DERBYSHIRE vs. SUSSEX
at Derby on 24th April 1990
Toss : Sussex. Umpires : D.O.Oslear and D.R.Shepherd
Sussex won by 5 wickets. Derbys 0pts Sussex 2pts

DERBYSHIRE

K.J.Barnett *	run out	94
P.D.Bowler +	st Moores b Lenham	61
J.E.Morris	b Dodemaide	23
A.P.Kuiper	not out	41
T.J.G.O'Gorman	b Pigott	8
C.J.Adams	not out	2
B.Roberts		
G.Miller		
A.E.Warner		
S.J.Base		
O.H.Mortensen		
Extras	(lb 8,w 11,nb 1)	20
TOTAL	(55 overs)(for 4 wkts)	249

SUSSEX

N.J.Lenham	c Bowler b Warner	22
P.W.G.Parker *	c Mortensen b Base	8
A.P.Wells	c & b Warner	53
M.P.Speight	c Adams b Mortensen	71
C.M.Wells	not out	36
I.J.Gould	c Miller b Warner	7
A.C.S.Pigott	not out	38
A.I.C.Dodemaide		
P.Moores +		
A.R.Hansford		
I.D.K.Salisbury		
Extras	(b 1,lb 7,w 5,nb 2)	15
TOTAL	(53.4 overs)(for 5 wkts)	250

SUSSEX	O	M	R	W	FALL OF WICKETS	DER	SUS
Pigott	11	2	38	1			
Dodemaide	11	3	37	1	1st	169	17
Wells C.M.	11	1	44	0	2nd	169	59
Hansford	11	0	58	0	3rd	206	142
Salisbury	6	0	32	0	4th	238	167
Lenham	5	0	32	1	5th		178
					6th		
DERBYSHIRE	O	M	R	W	7th		
Base	10	3	46	1	8th		
Mortensen	11	1	43	1	9th		
Kuiper	10.4	0	64	0	10th		
Warner	11	0	47	3			
Miller	11	0	42	0			

Man of the match: M.P.Speight

BENSON & HEDGES CUP

HAMPSHIRE vs. YORKSHIRE

at Southampton on 24th April 1990
Toss : Yorks. Umpires : A.G.T.Whitehead and P.B.Wight
Yorkshire won by 7 wickets. (Hants 0pts Yorks 2pts)

HAMPSHIRE

V.P.Terry *	c Metcalfe b Byas	15
R.J.Scott	c Metcalfe b Carrick	47
K.D.James	run out	2
C.L.Smith	b Fletcher	44
M.D.Marshall	run out	24
J.R.Wood	not out	43
J.R.Ayling	b Fletcher	14
R.J.Parks +	not out	6
R.J.Maru		
C.A.Connor		
K.J.Shine		
Extras	(lb 7,w 4)	11
TOTAL	(55 overs)(for 6 wkts)	206

YORKSHIRE

M.D.Moxon *	c Parks b James	11
A.A.Metcalfe	c Parks b Ayling	36
R.J.Blakey +	b Connor	66
P.E.Robinson	not out	73
C.White	not out	17
D.Byas		
P.Carrick		
A.Sidebottom		
P.W.Jarvis		
S.D.Fletcher		
P.Berry		
Extras	(lb 4,nb 1)	5
TOTAL	(53.2 overs)(for 3 wkts)	208

YORKSHIRE	O	M	R	W	FALL OF WICKETS		
						HAM	YOR
Jarvis	11	2	48	0			
Sidebottom	11	4	37	0	1st	28	37
Fletcher	11	0	42	2	2nd	41	49
Byas	6	1	13	1	3rd	106	179
Carrick	11	1	31	1	4th	121	
Berry	5	0	28	0	5th	149	
					6th	189	
HAMPSHIRE	O	M	R	W	7th		
Marshall	10	0	28	0	8th		
Shine	9.2	1	53	0	9th		
Connor	11	1	25	1	10th		
James	11	3	34	1			
Ayling	7	0	41	1			
Maru	5	0	23	0			

Man of the match: P.E.Robinson

MIDDLESEX vs. MINOR COUNTIES

at Lord's on 24th April 1990
Toss : Minor Counties. Umpires : J.W.Holder and K.J.Lyons
Middx won by 4 wickets. (Middx 2pts Minor Counties 0pts)

MINOR COUNTIES

S.N.V.Waterton +	c Haynes b Hemstock	6
M.J.Roberts	c Emburey b Tufnell	57
G.K.Brown	lbw b Emburey	32
N.A.Folland	not out	53
S.G.Plumb *	c Downton b Williams	5
T.A.Lester	b Hemstock	4
S.Greensword	b Emburey	3
R.A.Evans	not out	5
N.R.Taylor		
R.C.Green		
A.J.Mack		
Extras	(lb 10,w 13,nb 1)	24
TOTAL	(55 overs)(for 6 wkts)	189

MIDDLESEX

D.L.Haynes	c Waterton b Taylor	80
M.A.Roseberry	b Taylor	4
M.R.Ramprakash	c Brown b Mack	2
K.R.Brown	b Mack	56
R.O.Butcher	c Roberts b Evans	23
P.R.Downton +	not out	17
J.E.Emburey *	b Green	0
N.F.Williams	not out	1
P.N.Weekes		
P.C.R.Tufnell		
J.R.Hemstock		
Extras	(lb 5,w 2,nb 3)	10
TOTAL	(49.5 overs)(for 6 wkts)	193

MIDDLESEX	O	M	R	W	FALL OF WICKETS		
						MIN	MID
Hemstock	10	1	37	2	1st	16	16
Williams	11	2	27	1	2nd	96	37
Haynes	5	0	19	0	3rd	125	129
Weekes	7	1	27	0	4th	145	157
Tufnell	11	0	42	1	5th	160	188
Emburey	11	0	27	2	6th	176	188
MIN COUNTIES	O	M	R	W	7th		
Taylor	11	2	26	2	8th		
Green	10.5	1	49	1	9th		
Mack	11	2	47	2	10th		
Greensword	7	2	30	0			
Evans	10	1	36	1			

Man of the match: D.L.Haynes

HEADLINES

24th April

● Two former team-mates at Somerset who are well used to making the headlines caught the eye in the first round of Benson & Hedges matches.

● Ian Botham made his first 100 in English cricket since 1987 to guide Worcestershire to victory over Gloucestershire at Bristol. His 138* was his highest score in the Benson & Hedges Cup and included six sixes, the last of which ended the match.

● Viv Richards, returning to county cricket after an absence of three seasons, secured his new county, Glamorgan, a win over Warwicks at Edgbaston by dismissing Dermot Reeve with the final ball of the match. His figures of 3 for 38 were his best in the competition.

● Essex gained revenge over Notts for their defeat in last year's final as Graham Gooch announced his return to fitness with his ninth B & H 100 (and his 17th Gold Award).

● Desmond Haynes made his highest score in the Benson & Hedges Cup in Middlesex's match against Minor Counties, while two others just back from the Caribbean Northamptonshire's Curtly Ambrose (3 for19) and Warwickshire's Gladstone Small (4 for 22) both produced their best B & H bowling figures.

● Others to record their best performances in the competition on an action packed day were Gloucestershire's new captain Tony Wright (97), Yorkshire's Richard Blakey (66) and Phil Robinson (73*), Leicestershire's Tim Boon (84), and Lancashire's Ian Austin (4 for 25).

LANCASHIRE vs. SURREY

at Old Trafford on 24th April 1990
Toss : Surrey. Umpires : J.C.Balderstone and B.J.Meyer
Lancashire won by 76 runs. (Lancs 2pts Surrey 0pts)

LANCASHIRE

G.D.Mendis	c & b Bullen	40
G.Fowler	c & b Bicknell M.P.	9
M.A.Atherton	c Bicknell M.P. b Bullen	44
N.H.Fairbrother	not out	95
M.Watkinson	b Thorpe	23
P.A.J.DeFreitas	c Lynch b Bicknell M.P.	20
I.D.Austin	not out	1
D.P.Hughes *		
P.J.W.Allott		
W.K.Hegg +		
B.P.Patterson		
Extras	(lb 4,w 4,nb 2)	10
TOTAL	(55 overs)(for 5 wkts)	242

SURREY

D.J.Bicknell	c Hegg b Patterson	9
G.S.Clinton	c Hegg b Austin	40
A.J.Stewart	c Hegg b Atherton	31
M.A.Lynch	b Austin	0
G.P.Thorpe	c Hegg b Austin	8
D.M.Ward +	st Hegg b Atherton	18
I.A.Greig *	c & b Atherton	1
M.A.Feltham	b Austin	4
C.K.Bullen	not out	17
M.P.Bicknell	not out	27
A.H.Gray		
Extras	(lb 4,w 3,nb 4)	11
TOTAL	(55 overs)(for 8 wkts)	166

SURREY	O	M	R	W	FALL OF WICKETS		
						LAN	SUR
Gray	11	1	52	0	1st	10	11
Bicknell M.P.	11	4	48	2	2nd	71	78
Feltham	6	0	28	0	3rd	124	78
Greig	11	0	45	0	4th	188	89
Bullen	11	1	35	2	5th	231	100
Thorpe	5	0	30	1	6th		101
LANCASHIRE	O	M	R	W	7th		117
Patterson	8	2	6	1	8th		121
Allott	10	1	35	0	9th		
DeFreitas	9	0	33	0	10th		
Watkinson	6	0	31	0			
Atherton	11	1	32	3			
Austin	11	3	25	4			

Man of the match: N.H.Fairbrother

ESSEX vs. NOTTINGHAMSHIRE

at Chelmsford on 24th April 1990
Toss : Essex. Umpires : B.Dudleston and D.S.Thompsett
Essex won by 4 wickets. (Essex 2pts Nottinghamshire 0pts)

NOTTINGHAMSHIRE

B.C.Broad	b Topley	22
P.Pollard	c Garnham b Pringle	5
R.T.Robinson *	c Childs b Waugh	56
P.Johnson	not out	104
D.W.Randall	c Garnham b Foster	25
F.D.Stephenson	not out	22
B.N.French +		
E.E.Hemmings		
R.A.Pick		
K.E.Cooper		
J.A.Afford		
Extras	(b 1,lb 3,w 2,nb 1)	7
TOTAL	(55 overs)(for 4 wkts)	241

ESSEX

G.A.Gooch *	c Hemmings b Stephenson	102
B.R.Hardie	c Robinson b Cooper	20
P.J.Prichard	run out	17
M.E.Waugh	c Johnson b Afford	16
D.R.Pringle	not out	55
J.P.Stephenson	b Hemmings	0
A.W.Lilley	b Pick	7
M.A.Garnham +	not out	12
N.A.Foster		
T.D.Topley		
J.H.Childs		
Extras	(lb 7,w 4,nb 2)	13
TOTAL	(52 overs)(for 6 wkts)	242

ESSEX	O	M	R	W	FALL OF WICKETS		
						NOT	ESS
Foster	11	0	46	1	1st	8	48
Pringle	11	0	57	1	2nd	51	80
Gooch	11	2	51	0	3rd	103	131
Topley	6	1	16	1	4th	194	207
Childs	10	0	42	0	5th		210
Waugh	6	0	25	1	6th		229
NOTTS	O	M	R	W	7th		
Stephenson	11	1	49	1	8th		
Cooper	10	2	37	1	9th		
Pick	9	0	37	1	10th		
Hemmings	11	0	49	1			
Afford	11	1	63	1			

Man of the match: G.A.Gooch

OTHER FIRST-CLASS MATCH

REFUGE ASS. LEAGUE

Neil Fairbrother in aggressive mood against Surrey in Lancashire's Benson & Hedges win at Old Trafford.

WARWICKSHIRE vs. NORTHANTS

at Edgbaston on 29th April 1990
Toss : Warwicks.   Umpires : J.C.Balderstone and H.D.Bird
Warwicks won by 7 wkts. (Warwicks 4 pts Northants 0 pts)

NORTHANTS

R.J.Bailey	c Reeve b Smith N.M.K.	58
W.Larkins	c Smith N.M.K. b Munton	0
A.J.Lamb *	b Moody	70
D.J.Capel	c Small b Moody	20
A.Fordham	not out	29
D.J.Wild	c sub b Reeve	0
D.Ripley +	not out	3
J.G.Thomas		
C.E.L.Ambrose		
N.G.B.Cook		
M.A.Robinson		
Extras	(lb 9,w 7)	16
TOTAL	(40 overs)(for 5 wkts)	196

WARWICKSHIRE

Asif Din	hit wicket b Capel	23
A.I.Kallicharran	b Robinson	76
T.M.Moody	b Cook	56
G.W.Humpage +	not out	22
D.A.Reeve	not out	17
T.A.Lloyd *		
P.A.Smith		
N.M.K.Smith		
R.G.Twose		
G.C.Small		
T.A.Munton		
Extras	(lb 4,w 2)	6
TOTAL	(37.3 overs)(for 3 wkts)	200

WARWICKS	O	M	R	W	FALL OF WICKETS		
						NOR	WAR
Small	8	1	27	0			
Munton	6	1	22	1	1st	0	39
Reeve	8	1	45	1	2nd	128	153
Smith N.M.K.	7	0	34	1	3rd	145	171
Smith P.A.	3	0	17	0	4th	177	
Moody	8	0	42	2	5th	177	
					6th		
NORTHANTS	O	M	R	W	7th		
Ambrose	7	1	31	0	8th		
Robinson	7.3	0	53	1	9th		
Capel	8	0	35	1	10th		
Thomas	7	0	37	0			
Cook	8	0	40	1			

CAMBRIDGE UNIV vs. WARWICKSHIRE

at Fenner's on 26th, 27th, 28th April 1990
Toss : Cambridge Univ. Umpires : B.Dudleston and P.J.Eele
Match drawn

WARWICKSHIRE

A.J.Moles	c Atkinson b Johnson	1	lbw b Shufflebotham	29
T.M.Moody	b Buzza	147		
G.W.Humpage	c Turner b Pyman	17	not out	4
A.I.Kallicharran	c James b Buzza	43		
D.A.Reeve *	not out	102		
Asif Din	c Turner b Buzza	0	(2) not out	100
K.J.Piper +	run out	10		
N.M.K.Smith	b Buzza	47		
P.A.Booth	not out	3		
J.E.Benjamin				
T.A.Munton				
Extras	(lb 2,nb 6)	8	(lb 8,nb 2)	10
TOTAL	(for 7 wkts dec)	378	(for 1 wkt dec)	143

CAMBRIDGE UNIV

S.P.James	c Humpage b Benjamin	19	(7) c Smith b Munton	8
R.Heap	lbw b Benjamin	0	(1) c Humpage b Munton	17
M.J.Lowrey	b Benjamin	1	c Smith b Reeve	24
J.C.M.Atkinson *	c Reeve b Smith	41	c Reeve b Asif Din	17
M.J.Morris	lbw b Benjamin	0	lbw b Reeve	19
G.B.A.Dyer	b Asif Din	19	not out	20
R.J.Turner +	c Booth b Asif Din	12	(2) lbw b Reeve	28
R.A.Pyman	run out	21	not out	23
D.H.Shufflebotham	c Reeve b Asif Din	24		
A.J.Buzza	b Benjamin	1		
S.W.Johnson	not out	14		
Extras	(lb 10,w 1)	11	(b 13,lb 9,nb 3)	25
TOTAL		163	(for 6 wkts)	181

CAMBRIDGE U	O	M	R	W	O	M	R	W
Johnson	9	2	43	1	6	0	41	0
Pyman	20	4	109	1	6	1	43	0
Shufflebotham	17	1	76	0	5	0	29	1
Buzza	22	1	108	4	1	0	4	0
Atkinson	8	1	40	0				
Lowrey					3.1	0	18	0

FALL OF WICKETS	WAR	CAM	WAR	CAM
1st	2	2	105	19
2nd	41	6		74
3rd	188	44		95
4th	214	44		101
5th	214	72		122
6th	231	95		133
7th	366	106		
8th		135		
9th		142		
10th		163		

WARWICKS	O	M	R	W	O	M	R	W
Munton	8	3	17	0	16	4	40	2
Benjamin	18	8	29	5	12	5	12	0
Moody	8	1	33	0	10	7	6	0
Smith	10	4	25	1	10	2	18	0
Asif Din	10.5	3	17	3	15	3	49	1
Booth	8	1	23	0				
Reeve	6	3	9	0	19	7	34	3

HEADLINES

26th - 28th April

● Australian Tom Moody hit 147 in his first innings for Warwickshire against Cambridge University at Fenner's, while Joey Benjamin returned career best figures.

● First-class debut: G.B.A.Dyer (Cambridge U).

29th April

● Derbyshire, Glamorgan, Kent and Middlesex each made it two wins out of two in Sunday cricket.

● Simon Base took four wickets for the second week in a row as Derbyshire restricted Essex to a total of just 158.

● Viv Richards continued his impressive start for Glamorgan with 59 on his Sunday debut for the county.

● Neil Taylor's 95 was a competition best as Kent overcame Hampshire, for whom David Gower was making his first appearance.

● Mike Atherton (3 for 33) and Graham Lloyd (47) both recorded Sunday bests for Lancashire, while Alan Wells (86) and Ian Salisbury (3 for 40) did so for Sussex.

● 56 and two wickets from Tom Moody got Warwickshire off to a winning start against Northamptonshire.

REFUGE ASSURANCE LEAGUE

DERBYSHIRE vs. WORCESTERSHIRE

at Derby on 29th April 1990
Toss : Worcs. Umpires : J.H.Hampshire and B.J.Meyer
Derbyshire won by 35 runs. (Derbys 4 pts Worcs 0 pts)

DERBYSHIRE

K.J.Barnett *	st Rhodes b Illingworth	66
P.D.Bowler +	lbw b Illingworth	40
J.E.Morris	run out	3
A.P.Kuiper	c Leatherdale b Newport	17
C.J.Adams	b Illingworth	26
B.Roberts	b Radford	9
G.Miller	not out	14
A.E.Warner	run out	5
D.E.Malcolm	not out	0
S.J.Base		
O.H.Mortensen		
Extras	(lb 5,w 8)	13
TOTAL	(40 overs)(for 7 wkts)	193

WORCESTERSHIRE

T.S.Curtis	c Morris b Mortensen	7
I.T.Botham	c Bowler b Mortensen	15
G.A.Hick	c Adams b Kuiper	46
D.B.D'Oliveira	c Adams b Base	10
P.A.Neale *	c Warner b Base	40
D.A.Leatherdale	lbw b Warner	2
S.J.Rhodes +	c Roberts b Miller	2
N.V.Radford	c Adams b Miller	0
R.K.Illingworth	c Bowler b Base	8
P.J.Newport	not out	12
S.M.McEwan	b Base	5
Extras	(lb 6,w 5)	11
TOTAL	(37.5 overs)	158

WORCS	O	M	R	W	FALL OF WICKETS		
						DER	WOR
Newport	8	0	30	1	1st	97	11
Botham	8	0	27	0	2nd	117	40
Radford	6	0	26	1	3rd	117	57
Illingworth	8	0	41	3	4th	162	95
McEwan	8	0	42	0	5th	166	98
Hick	2	0	22	0	6th	178	105
DERBYSHIRE	O	M	R	W	7th	189	105
Malcolm	7	0	32	0	8th		141
Mortensen	8	3	15	2	9th		144
Warner	8	0	28	1	10th		158
Base	5.5	0	32	4			
Kuiper	4	0	23	1			
Miller	5	2	22	2			

MIDDLESEX vs. ESSEX

at Lord's on 29th April 1990
Toss : Essex. Umpires : B.Hassan and A.G.T.Whitehead
Middlesex won by 12 runs. (Middlesex 4 pts Essex 0 pts)

MIDDLESEX

D.L.Haynes	b Pringle	31
M.A.Roseberry	c Foster b Pringle	16
M.W.Gatting *	c Garnham b Pringle	7
M.R.Ramprakash	c Waugh b Topley	40
K.R.Brown	c Garnham b Topley	50
R.O.Butcher	not out	44
P.R.Downton +	c Garnham b Pringle	6
J.E.Emburey	not out	10
N.F.Williams		
S.P.Hughes		
N.G.Cowans		
Extras	(lb 12,w 2,nb 2)	16
TOTAL	(40 overs)(for 6 wkts)	220

ESSEX

G.A.Gooch *	c Downton b Williams	3
B.R.Hardie	c & b Emburey	16
M.E.Waugh	c Brown b Williams	44
P.J.Prichard	run out	35
D.R.Pringle	b Hughes	18
J.P.Stephenson	st Downton b Emburey	5
A.W.Lilley	c Butcher b Emburey	10
M.A.Garnham +	run out	26
N.A.Foster	c Roseberry b Cowans	19
T.D.Topley	c Downton b Cowans	10
J.H.Childs	not out	3
Extras	(lb 11,w 4,nb 4)	19
TOTAL	(39.5 overs)	208

ESSEX	O	M	R	W	FALL OF WICKETS		
						MID	ESS
Foster	8	0	51	0	1st	42	4
Topley	8	0	37	2	2nd	58	54
Pringle	8	3	27	4	3rd	59	91
Gooch	8	0	44	0	4th	145	129
Waugh	4	0	25	0	5th	156	133
Childs	4	0	24	0	6th	202	140
MIDDLESEX	O	M	R	W	7th		157
Hughes	8	1	37	1	8th		184
Williams	8	0	33	2	9th		200
Cowans	8	1	40	2	10th		208
Emburey	7.5	1	49	3			
Gatting	8	0	38	0			

SUSSEX vs. SURREY

at Hove on 29th April 1990
Toss : Surrey. Umpires : D.J.Constant and D.S.Thompsett
Sussex won by 3 wickets. (Sussex 4 pts Surrey 0 pts)

SURREY

D.J.Bicknell	c Moores b Clarke	21
A.J.Stewart	b Salisbury	64
M.A.Lynch	lbw b Clarke	9
G.P.Thorpe	run out	53
D.M.Ward +	b Salisbury	7
I.A.Greig *	c Moores b Salisbury	2
K.T.Medlycott	b Hansford	17
M.A.Feltham	not out	7
C.K.Bullen	b Hansford	3
M.P.Bicknell	not out	4
A.J.Murphy		
Extras	(lb 6,w 1)	7
TOTAL	(40 overs)(for 8 wkts)	194

SUSSEX

N.J.Lenham	run out	12
I.J.Gould	run out	9
A.P.Wells	not out	86
M.P.Speight	c Ward b Feltham	18
C.M.Wells	b Bullen	5
P.W.G.Parker *	b Murphy	28
A.I.C.Dodemaide	b Lynch	17
P.Moores +	b Lynch	0
A.R.Clarke	not out	0
I.D.K.Salisbury		
A.R.Hansford		
Extras	(b 8,lb 14,w 1)	23
TOTAL	(39.4 overs)(for 7 wkts)	198

SUSSEX	O	M	R	W	FALL OF WICKETS		
						SUR	SUS
Wells C.M.	8	1	34	0	1st	50	31
Dodemaide	8	0	43	0	2nd	64	51
Clarke	8	0	23	2	3rd	131	89
Hansford	8	0	48	2	4th	141	107
Salisbury	8	0	40	3	5th	145	165
SURREY	O	M	R	W	6th	169	190
Bicknell M.P.	7	0	33	0	7th	183	190
Murphy	7.4	0	41	1	8th	187	
Bullen	8	0	40	1	9th		
Medlycott	8	0	30	0	10th		
Feltham	8	0	30	1			

GLAMORGAN vs. LEICESTERSHIRE

at Cardiff on 29th April 1990
Toss : Leics. Umpires : M.J.Kitchen and B.Leadbeater
Glamorgan won by 32 runs. (Glam 4 pts Leics 0 pts)

GLAMORGAN

A.Dale	b Benjamin	3
H.Morris	c Boon b Benjamin	13
M.P.Maynard	c Whitticase b Taylor	22
I.V.A.Richards	b Taylor	59
A.R.Butcher *	c Potter b Agnew	17
I.Smith	run out	35
N.G.Cowley	c Whitticase b Taylor	0
C.P.Metson +	c Briers b Mullally	11
S.J.Dennis	run out	7
S.R.Barwick	not out	0
M.Frost		
Extras	(lb 8,w 5,nb 2)	15
TOTAL	(40 overs)(for 9 wkts)	182

LEICESTERSHIRE

T.J.Boon	c Smith b Frost	2
N.E.Briers *	c Richards b Cowley	37
J.J.Whitaker	c Morris b Frost	72
L.Potter	lbw b Cowley	6
J.D.R.Benson	c Richards b Barwick	3
P.Whitticase +	run out	2
W.K.M.Benjamin	c Morris b Dale	5
G.J.Parsons	c Richards b Barwick	12
J.P.Agnew	c Barwick b Frost	1
A.D.Mullally	c & b Richards	2
L.B.Taylor	not out	0
Extras	(lb 6,w 2)	8
TOTAL	(38.1 overs)	150

LEICS	O	M	R	W	FALL OF WICKETS		
						GLA	LEI
Parsons	8	0	53	0	1st	15	4
Benjamin	8	1	26	2	2nd	39	79
Taylor	8	0	34	3	3rd	43	87
Agnew	8	1	20	1	4th	90	96
Mullally	8	0	41	1	5th	131	114
GLAMORGAN	O	M	R	W	6th	131	121
Frost	8	0	30	3	7th	165	137
Dennis	6	0	13	0	8th	180	142
Barwick	6.1	0	30	2	9th	182	150
Cowley	8	0	26	2	10th		150
Dale	4	0	22	1			
Richards	6	1	23	1			

KENT vs. HAMPSHIRE

at Canterbury on 29th April 1990
Toss : Kent. Umpires : J.W.Holder and K.J.Lyons
Kent won by 53 runs. (Kent 4 pts Hampshire 0 pts)

KENT

S.G.Hinks	c Terry b James	1
N.R.Taylor	st Parks b Scott	95
T.R.Ward	c Connor b Maru	24
C.S.Cowdrey *	c Connor b Tremlett	18
G.R.Cowdrey	st Parks b Scott	22
S.A.Marsh +	c Terry b Connor	15
M.V.Fleming	not out	29
R.M.Ellison	not out	3
M.A.Ealham		
R.P.Davis		
T.A.Merrick		
Extras	(lb 3,w 3)	6
TOTAL	(40 overs)(for 6 wkts)	213

HAMPSHIRE

V.P.Terry *	b Ellison	9
R.J.Scott	lbw b Merrick	0
R.A.Smith	c Cowdrey C.S. b Fleming	22
D.I.Gower	c Fleming b Davis	32
C.L.Smith	not out	47
K.D.James	c Marsh b Davis	4
M.D.Marshall	c Fleming b Davis	3
R.J.Parks +	b Davis	4
T.M.Tremlett	c Cowdrey C.S. b Fleming	18
R.J.Maru	not out	12
C.A.Connor		
Extras	(lb 6,w 2,nb 1)	9
TOTAL	(40 overs)(for 8 wkts)	160

HAMPSHIRE	O	M	R	W	FALL OF WICKETS		
						KEN	HAM
James	8	0	33	1	1st	3	12
Connor	8	2	49	1	2nd	51	12
Tremlett	5	0	22	1	3rd	87	61
Maru	6	0	29	1	4th	134	71
Marshall	8	0	41	0	5th	173	78
Scott	5	0	36	2	6th	186	93
KENT	O	M	R	W	7th		98
Ellison	8	0	23	1	8th		133
Merrick	8	0	32	1	9th		
Ealham	8	0	35	0	10th		
Davis	8	0	25	4			
Fleming	8	0	39	2			

NOTTINGHAMSHIRE vs. LANCS

at Trent Bridge on 29th April 1990
Toss : Lancs. Umpires : D.O.Oslear and D.R.Shepherd
Lancashire won by 5 wickets. (Notts 0 pts Lancs 4 pts)

NOTTINGHAMSHIRE

B.C.Broad	lbw b Allott	13
P.Pollard	lbw b DeFreitas	8
R.T.Robinson *	c Fairbrother b Atherton	61
P.Johnson	c Atherton b Jesty	15
D.W.Randall	b Austin	14
F.D.Stephenson	c Fowler b Allott	23
B.N.French +	c Watkinson b Atherton	11
K.P.Evans	st Hegg b Atherton	0
E.E.Hemmings	c Fowler b DeFreitas	12
K.E.Cooper	c Jesty b DeFreitas	21
R.A.Pick	not out	0
Extras	(b 1,lb 6,w 7,nb 1)	15
TOTAL	(39.3 overs)	193

LANCASHIRE

G.Fowler	c Robinson b Hemmings	52
M.A.Atherton	c Robinson b Pick	5
G.D.Lloyd	b Hemmings	47
N.H.Fairbrother	c French b Evans	19
T.E.Jesty	c Broad b Stephenson	15
M.Watkinson	not out	33
P.A.J.DeFreitas	not out	7
I.D.Austin		
D.P.Hughes *		
W.K.Hegg +		
P.J.W.Allott		
Extras	(b 1,lb 10,w 4,nb 1)	16
TOTAL	(38.4 overs)(for 5 wkts)	194

LANCASHIRE	O	M	R	W	FALL OF WICKETS		
						NOT	LAN
Allott	8	0	29	2	1st	14	14
DeFreitas	7.3	0	36	3	2nd	28	100
Watkinson	7	0	41	0	3rd	54	126
Jesty	2	0	9	1	4th	107	139
Austin	8	0	38	1	5th	128	166
Atherton	7	0	33	3	6th	148	
NOTTS	O	M	R	W	7th	149	
Cooper	8	0	32	0	8th	162	
Pick	8	0	43	1	9th	186	
Evans	7	0	42	1	10th	193	
Stephenson	7.4	1	48	1			
Hemmings	8	2	18	2			

BRITANNIC ASSURANCE CHAMPIONSHIP

LANCASHIRE vs. WORCESTERSHIRE

at Old Trafford on 26th (no play),27th,28th,30th April 1990
Toss : Worcestershire. Umpires : J.C.Balderstone and H.D.Bird
Match drawn. (Lancashire 7 pts (Bt: 4, Bw: 3) Worcestershire 5 pts (Bt: 4, Bw: 1))

WORCESTERSHIRE

T.S.Curtis	c DeFreitas b Patterson	7	b Patterson		37
G.J.Lord	c Hegg b Patterson	9	c Hegg b Jesty		19
G.A.Hick	b Watkinson	23	not out		106
I.T.Botham	c Hegg b DeFreitas	17	not out		50
P.A.Neale *	lbw b DeFreitas	10			
D.B.D'Oliveira	c Fairbrother b Hughes	155			
S.J.Rhodes +	b Hughes	72			
R.K.Illingworth	not out	35			
P.J.Newport	not out	5			
N.V.Radford					
G.R.Dilley					
Extras	(b 8,lb 6,nb 13)	27	(b 3,lb 5,w 1,nb 10)		19
TOTAL	(for 7 wkts dec)	360	(for 2 wkts dec)		231

LANCASHIRE

G.D.Mendis	b Illingworth	80	not out	35
G.Fowler	c Botham b Illingworth	16	not out	35
M.A.Atherton	b Illingworth	50		
N.H.Fairbrother	not out	74		
T.E.Jesty	b Illingworth	54		
M.Watkinson	not out	0		
D.P.Hughes *				
W.K.Hegg +				
P.A.J.DeFreitas				
J.D.Fitton				
B.P.Patterson				
Extras	(lb 17,w 5,nb 4)	26	(b 1,lb 6,nb 1)	8
TOTAL	(for 4 wkts dec)	300	(for 0 wkts)	78

LANCASHIRE	O	M	R	W	O	M	R	W
Patterson	22.1	5	55	2	10	0	27	1
DeFreitas	26	11	62	2	15	5	51	0
Watkinson	21	1	96	1	9	3	19	0
Atherton	6	0	32	0	8	0	36	0
Fitton	21	2	79	0	14	1	70	0
Hughes	8	1	22	2				
Jesty					5	1	20	1

WORCS	O	M	R	W	O	M	R	W
Dilley	16	1	80	0	3	0	9	0
Radford	19	6	66	0	6	0	15	0
Newport	19	3	61	0	5	2	14	0
Illingworth	35.3	17	46	4	6	2	5	0
Botham	7	1	24	0				
Hick	1	0	6	0	12	4	11	0
D'Oliveira					5	1	12	0
Curtis					2	1	5	0

FALL OF WICKETS				
	WOR	LAN	WOR	LAN
1st	17	47	48	
2nd	25	155	114	
3rd	49	160		
4th	65	296		
5th	86			
6th	312			
7th	341			
8th				
9th				
10th				

SOMERSET vs. GLOUCESTERSHIRE

at Taunton on 26th, 27th, 28th, 29th April 1990
Toss : Somerset. Umpires : K.E.Palmer and N.T.Plews
Somerset won by 10 wkts. (Somerset 24 pts (Bt: 4, Bw: 4) Gloucestershire 5 pts (Bt: 1, Bw: 4))

GLOUCESTERSHIRE

A.J.Wright *	c Tavare b Lefebvre	25	c Hardy b Rose	37
A.W.Stovold	b Mallender	4	st Burns b Swallow	74
G.D.Hodgson	lbw b Lefebvre	8	lbw b Jones	25
C.W.J.Athey	c Rose b Lefebvre	68	b Jones	39
K.M.Curran	c Burns b Lefebvre	41	c Burns b Rose	13
J.W.Lloyds	b Mallender	0	c Lefebvre b Jones	93
R.C.Russell +	lbw b Rose	12	(8) c Tavare b Jones	18
C.A.Walsh	c Burns b Mallender	26	(9) c Harden b Jones	0
D.V.Lawrence	lbw b Mallender	3	(7) c Lefebvre b Rose	9
D.A.Graveney	b Lefebvre	0	c Rose b Jones	5
K.B.S.Jarvis	not out	0	not out	1
Extras	(lb 6,nb 2)	8	(b 1,lb 21,nb 3)	25
TOTAL		197		339

SOMERSET

S.J.Cook	c Russell b Walsh	16	not out	62
P.M.Roebuck	c Graveney b Curran	40	(2) not out	30
J.J.E.Hardy	c Walsh b Lawrence	4		
C.J.Tavare *	c Lloyds b Jarvis	18		
R.J.Harden	c Athey b Walsh	46		
N.D.Burns +	c Athey b Curran	166		
G.D.Rose	c Russell b Walsh	85		
R.P.Lefebvre	lbw b Walsh	3		
I.G.Swallow	not out	7		
N.A.Mallender	c Russell b Walsh	0		
A.N.Jones	c Wright b Walsh	9		
Extras	(b 3,lb 15,w 4,nb 22)	44	(b 4,lb 1,nb 2)	7
TOTAL		438	(for 0 wkts)	99

SOMERSET	O	M	R	W	O	M	R	W
Jones	14	1	68	0	27.1	5	75	6
Mallender	19	4	46	4	26	6	55	0
Rose	15	5	46	1	25	5	64	3
Lefebvre	15.1	7	30	5	24	6	66	0
Swallow	1	0	1	0	34	13	57	1

GLOUCS	O	M	R	W	O	M	R	W
Lawrence	14	1	77	1	2	0	21	0
Walsh	26.1	2	112	6	5	0	31	0
Jarvis	12	1	61	1				
Curran	18	3	91	2	2	0	8	0
Graveney	19	3	62	0	11	4	12	0
Lloyds	5	1	17	0	6.2	0	22	0

FALL OF WICKETS				
	GLO	SOM	GLO	SOM
1st	16	30	84	
2nd	38	38	141	
3rd	39	75	149	
4th	133	101	178	
5th	134	196	228	
6th	148	409	250	
7th	192	419	301	
8th	192	419	305	
9th	197	420	338	
10th	197	438	339	

SUSSEX vs. SURREY

at Hove on 26th, 27th, 28th, 30th April 1990
Toss : Sussex. Umpires : D.J.Constant and D.S.Thompsett
Sussex won by 5 wickets. (Sussex 21 pts (Bt: 4, Bw: 1) Surrey 4 pts (Bt: 3, Bw: 1))

SURREY

D.J.Bicknell	lbw b Dodemaide	65	c Speight b Dodemaide	2
G.S.Clinton	b Hansford	43	run out	98
A.J.Stewart	c Wells A.P. b Salisbury	77	c Speight b Hansford	15
M.A.Lynch	c Lenham b Wells C.M.	70	b Wells C.M.	46
G.P.Thorpe	c Gould b Salisbury	9	not out	23
D.M.Ward +	c Parker b Pigott	38	not out	18
I.A.Greig *	c Salisbury b Pigott	9		
K.T.Medlycott	c Lenham b Salisbury	29		
M.P.Bicknell	not out	50		
A.H.Gray	run out	11		
A.J.Murphy	not out	4		
Extras	(b 5,lb 15)	20	(lb 6,w 1)	7
TOTAL	(for 9 wkts dec)	425	(for 4 wkts dec)	209

SUSSEX

N.J.Lenham	c Lynch b Murphy	85	run out	44
P.Moores +	b Gray	1	c Stewart b Medlycott	30
P.W.G.Parker *	b Murphy	100	b Murphy	42
A.P.Wells	not out	44	c Ward b Murphy	16
M.P.Speight	not out	50	c Lynch b Medlycott	75
C.M.Wells			c Lynch b Medlycott	37
I.J.Gould			not out	62
A.I.C.Dodemaide				
A.C.S.Pigott				
I.D.K.Salisbury				
A.R.Hansford				
Extras	(b 5,lb 8,nb 7)	20	(b 8,lb 21,w 1,nb 1)	31
TOTAL	(for 3 wkts dec)	300	(for 5 wkts)	337

SUSSEX	O	M	R	W	O	M	R	W
Pigott	30	8	77	2	5	1	17	0
Dodemaide	26	3	96	1	13	3	38	1
Wells C.M.	27	8	59	1	9	2	16	1
Hansford	25.5	3	84	1	10	2	41	1
Salisbury	32	7	89	3	11	0	26	0
Wells A.P.					9	0	39	0
Lenham					4	0	16	0
Gould					3	0	10	0

SURREY	O	M	R	W	O	M	R	W
Gray	15	0	58	1				
Bicknell M.P.	24	5	71	0	15	2	59	0
Murphy	19	4	68	2	17	2	76	2
Medlycott	29	9	67	0	14.2	1	101	2
Greig	5	0	19	0	10	2	45	0
Lynch	2	1	4	0	7	1	27	0

FALL OF WICKETS				
	SUR	SUS	SUR	SUS
1st	57	9	9	52
2nd	193	197	37	123
3rd	201	198	110	130
4th	221		180	154
5th	282			215
6th	304			
7th	355			
8th	367			
9th	393			
10th				

NOTTINGHAMSHIRE vs. DERBYSHIRE

at Trent Bridge on 26th, 27th, 28th, 30th April 1990
Toss : Nottinghamshire. Umpires : B.J.Meyer and D.O.Oslear
Match drawn. (Nottinghamshire 5 pts (Bt: 3, Bw: 2) Derbyshire 3 pts (Bt: 2, Bw: 1))

NOTTINGHAMSHIRE

B.C.Broad	c Miller b Base	180	c Bowler b Base	5
P.Pollard	c Bowler b Mortensen	40	lbw b Mortensen	27
R.T.Robinson *	b Kuiper	11	b Barnett	86
P.Johnson	c Bowler b Warner	45	b Barnett	54
D.W.Randall	c Brown b Barnett	6	c & b Barnett	23
F.D.Stephenson	sub b Warner	18	b Miller	12
B.N.French +	c Brown b Mortensen	25	not out	1
E.E.Hemmings	c Adams b Mortensen	15		
K.E.Cooper	b Miller	12		
R.A.Pick	not out	14		
J.A.Afford	c Bowler b Mortensen	2		
Extras	(b 4,lb 12,w 4,nb 13)	33	(b 5,lb 7,w 3,nb 2)	17
TOTAL		401	(for 6 wkts dec)	225

DERBYSHIRE

P.D.Bowler +	c Broad b Pick	20	lbw b Afford	11
A.M.Brown	c Johnson b Cooper	54	c Cooper b Hemmings	20
J.E.Morris	lbw b Cooper	66	not out	16
A.P.Kuiper	c Randall b Afford	25	c Pollard b Afford	10
C.J.Adams	c French b Cooper	3	not out	11
B.Roberts	st French b Hemmings	46		
K.J.Barnett *	c Johnson b Hemmings	73		
G.Miller	b Hemmings	10		
A.E.Warner	lbw b Pick	11		
S.J.Base	st French b Afford	34		
O.H.Mortensen	not out	5		
Extras	(lb 9,nb 4)	13	(b 2,lb 4,nb 1)	7
TOTAL		360	(for 3 wkts)	75

DERBYSHIRE	O	M	R	W	O	M	R	W
Mortensen	26.5	6	67	4	7	3	14	1
Base	28	5	89	1	12.3	2	56	1
Warner	30	6	78	2	4	1	14	0
Kuiper	13	2	60	1	7	2	20	0
Miller	45	16	84	1	18	3	60	1
Barnett	2	0	7	1	17	2	49	3

NOTTS	O	M	R	W	O	M	R	W
Stephenson	27	7	92	0	4	0	9	0
Cooper	35	9	75	3	6	1	17	0
Pick	25	4	81	2				
Hemmings	39	17	64	3	21	12	22	1
Afford	19.5	8	39	2	22	17	21	2

FALL OF WICKETS				
	NOT	DER	NOT	DER
1st	127	50	12	32
2nd	153	122	62	34
3rd	266	170	180	53
4th	293	170	195	
5th	308	175	221	
6th	323	280	225	
7th	366	299		
8th	378	320		
9th	384	326		
10th	401	360		

BRITANNIC ASSURANCE CHAMPIONSHIP

MIDDLESEX vs. ESSEX

at Lord's on 26th, 27th, 28th, 30th April 1990
Toss : Essex.   Umpires : B.Hassan and A.G.T.Whitehead
Match drawn. (Middlesex 5 pts (Bt: 3, Bw: 2) Essex 6 pts (Bt: 4, Bw: 2))

MIDDLESEX

D.L.Haynes	c Garnham b Foster	24	c Foster b Shahid	116
M.A.Roseberry	c Waugh b Andrew	12	c Stephenson b Foster	1
M.W.Gatting *	b Andrew	41	retired hurt	32
M.R.Ramprakash	c Topley b Pringle	12	c Garnham b Foster	1
K.R.Brown	lbw b Topley	141	c Waugh b Andrew	12
P.R.Downton +	lbw b Topley	47	not out	42
J.E.Emburey	b Andrew	41	not out	21
N.F.Williams	c Garnham b Waugh	26		
N.G.Cowans	b Waugh	2		
S.P.Hughes	not out	14		
P.C.R.Tufnell	not out	7		
Extras	(lb 6,nb 3)	9	(b 2,lb 5,nb 4)	11
TOTAL	(for 9 wkts dec)	376	(for 4 wkts dec)	236

ESSEX

G.A.Gooch *	c Downton b Williams	137	c Downton b Williams	39
J.P.Stephenson	c Downton b Hughes	14	c Roseberry b Tufnell	59
P.J.Prichard	c Downton b Williams	10	not out	49
M.E.Waugh	b Tufnell	34	run out	0
B.R.Hardie	c Emburey b Williams	21	not out	0
N.Shahid	not out	34		
M.A.Garnham +	not out	36		
D.R.Pringle				
N.A.Foster				
T.D.Topley				
S.J.W.Andrew				
Extras	(b 1,lb 6,w 1,nb 2)	14	(b 4,lb 6,nb 6)	16
TOTAL	(for 5 wkts dec)	300	(for 3 wkts)	163

ESSEX	O	M	R	W	O	M	R	W		FALL OF WICKETS			
											MID	ESS	MID	ESS
Foster	30	7	86	1	17	4	39	2	1st	32	44	11	67
Pringle	30	10	79	1	5	3	12	0	2nd	36	75	88	141
Andrew	29	5	93	3	20	2	79	1	3rd	61	146	126	141
Topley	36	4	79	2	10	2	42	0	4th	111	223	210	
Shahid	1	0	12	0	8	0	33	1	5th	217	227		
Waugh	8	1	21	2	3	1	17	0	6th	296			
Gooch					1	1	0	0	7th	346			
Stephenson					2	0	7	0	8th	349			
									9th	356			
MIDDLESEX	O	M	R	W	O	M	R	W	10th				
Williams	18	4	69	3	6	0	26	1					
Cowans	17	3	43	0	5	1	32	0					
Hughes	16	3	60	1	7	0	29	0					
Emburey	19	3	53	0	16	7	23	0					
Tufnell	21.5	5	68	1	13	4	35	1					
Ramprakash					1	0	8	0					

GLAMORGAN vs. LEICESTERSHIRE

at Cardiff on 26th, 27th, 28th, 30th April 1990
Toss : Glamorgan.   Umpires : M.J.Kitchen and B.Leadbeater
Leics won by 9 wkts. (Glamorgan 3 pts (Bt: 0, Bw: 3) Leics 24 pts (Bt: 4, Bw: 4))

LEICESTERSHIRE

T.J.Boon	c Holmes b Dennis	72	not out	61
N.E.Briers *	c Maynard b Frost	21	c Maynard b Watkin	10
J.J.Whitaker	b Dennis	32	not out	31
L.Potter	lbw b Frost	50		
J.D.R.Benson	lbw b Frost	9		
C.C.Lewis	lbw b Dennis	39		
P.Whitticase +	c Metson b Dennis	11		
M.I.Gidley	c Dennis b Croft	73		
G.J.F.Ferris	lbw b Frost	24		
J.P.Agnew	c Metson b Dennis	0		
A.D.Mullally	not out	16		
Extras	(lb 9,w 3,nb 2)	14	(lb 4,nb 3)	7
TOTAL		361	(for 1 wkt)	109

GLAMORGAN

A.R.Butcher *	b Lewis	10	c Agnew b Ferris	4
H.Morris	c Whitticase b Lewis	33	c Whitticase b Agnew	32
G.C.Holmes	lbw b Ferris	14	c Gidley b Mullally	11
M.P.Maynard	c Gidley b Ferris	6	run out	92
I.V.A.Richards	b Lewis	3	lbw b Lewis	119
M.J.Cann	c Whitticase b Lewis	11	c Potter b Ferris	17
R.D.B.Croft	c Whitticase b Ferris	5	not out	27
C.P.Metson +	c Boon b Lewis	8	c Benson b Lewis	5
S.J.Dennis	c Whitticase b Lewis	3	c Whitticase b Lewis	2
S.L.Watkin	not out	21	c Briers b Lewis	5
M.Frost	c Boon b Ferris	1	lbw b Agnew	0
Extras	(lb 5,nb 7)	12	(lb 7,w 3,nb 15)	25
TOTAL		127		339

GLAMORGAN	O	M	R	W	O	M	R	W		FALL OF WICKETS			
										LEI	GLA	GLA	LEI
Watkin	30	3	94	0	10.4	0	60	1	1st	57	14	7	26
Frost	33	3	117	4	7	0	26	0	2nd	109	34	51	
Dennis	37	15	76	5	3	0	16	0	3rd	135	45	53	
Croft	9.3	0	42	1	3	2	3	0	4th	150	48	239	
Richards	5	2	9	0					5th	230	86	287	
Holmes	5	2	14	0					6th	230	87	309	
									7th	252	101	320	
LEICS	O	M	R	W	O	M	R	W	8th	320	101	330	
Lewis	24	7	55	6	25	3	64	4	9th	322	116	336	
Ferris	11.2	1	44	4	16	3	57	2	10th	361	127	339	
Mullally	4	2	10	0	24	6	67	1					
Gidley	2	1	1	0	14	7	31	0					
Agnew	10	5	12	0	23.5	3	92	2					
Potter					5	2	14	0					

KENT vs. HAMPSHIRE

at Canterbury on 26th, 27th, 28th, 30th April 1990
Toss : Hampshire.   Umpires : J.W.Holder and K.J.Lyons
Hampshire won by 6 runs. (Kent 4 pts (Bt: 4, Bw: 0) Hampshire 21 pts (Bt: 3, Bw: 2))

HAMPSHIRE

V.P.Terry *	c Ward b Fleming	107	c Hinks b Merrick	17
T.C.Middleton	lbw b Penn	127	b Fleming	23
K.D.James	b Penn	50	not out	104
C.L.Smith	c & b Davis	16	c Cowdrey C.S. b Hinks	52
R.J.Scott	lbw b Penn	0	not out	1
J.R.Wood	c Ellison b Merrick	17		
R.J.Parks +	not out	19		
L.A.Joseph	not out	25		
R.J.Maru				
C.A.Connor				
K.J.Shine				
Extras	(b 1,lb 14,w 1,nb 2)	18	(b 1,w 1,nb 1)	3
TOTAL	(for 6 wkts dec)	379	(for 3 wkts dec)	200

KENT

S.G.Hinks	c Middleton b Shine	31	c Maru b James	82
N.R.Taylor	c Terry b Joseph	0	c Terry b Shine	6
T.R.Ward	c Parks b Connor	21	c Middleton b Connor	11
C.S.Cowdrey *	b Connor	79	c Connor b Scott	107
G.R.Cowdrey	b Scott	87	st Parks b Scott	30
S.A.Marsh +	not out	61	b Shine	4
M.V.Fleming	not out	6	b Maru	20
R.M.Ellison			c Smith b Connor	0
T.A.Merrick			b Connor	0
C.Penn			not out	0
R.P.Davis			run out	1
Extras	(b 3,lb 5,w 6,nb 3)	17	(lb 8,w 1,nb 1)	10
TOTAL	(for 5 wkts dec)	302		271

KENT	O	M	R	W	O	M	R	W		FALL OF WICKETS			
										HAM	KEN	HAM	KEN
Merrick	29	4	83	1	13	3	24	1	1st	183	2	32	11
Penn	28	8	79	3	6	2	6	0	2nd	289	45	57	25
Fleming	20	3	50	1	7	3	23	1	3rd	300	74	179	187
Ellison	22	6	43	0	4	1	12	0	4th	300	197		222
Davis	31	8	96	1	21	3	63	0	5th	325	290		237
Cowdrey C.S.	2	0	13	0	5	2	14	0	6th	337			253
Ward					10	3	41	0	7th				258
Hinks					3	1	16	1	8th				258
									9th				270
HAMPSHIRE	O	M	R	W	O	M	R	W	10th				271
Shine	19	4	70	1	13	1	48	2					
Joseph	17	3	76	1									
Connor	19	5	38	2	12.1	2	44	3					
James	17	6	31	0	11	2	43	1					
Maru	17	2	64	0	20	5	87	1					
Scott	5	1	15	1	8	1	41	2					

YORKSHIRE vs. NORTHANTS

at Headingley on 26th, 27th, 28th, 30th April 1990
Toss : Northants.   Umpires : J.H.Hampshire and D.R.Shepherd
Northants won by an innings and 50 runs.
(Yorks 1 pts (Bt: 1, Bw: 0) Northants 24 pts (Bt: 4, Bw: 4))

YORKSHIRE

S.A.Kellett	c Fordham b Ambrose	0	lbw b Thomas	63
A.A.Metcalfe *	c Fordham b Robinson	38	lbw b Capel	45
R.J.Blakey +	b Ambrose	25	(10) b Robinson	0
P.E.Robinson	c Ripley b Ambrose	30	b Thomas	22
C.White	c Thomas b Ambrose	9	(3) lbw b Ambrose	9
D.Byas	b Robinson	0	(5) c Ripley b Thomas	0
P.Carrick	b Capel	37	(6) c Lamb b Robinson	23
A.Sidebottom	c Fordham b Ambrose	16	(7) c Ripley b Capel	31
P.W.Jarvis	b Capel	29	(8) c Ripley b Robinson	0
P.Berry	not out	4	(9) not out	31
S.D.Fletcher	c Robinson b Thomas	1	b Capel	19
Extras	(b 4,lb 5)	9	(b 4,lb 2,w 1)	7
TOTAL		198		250

NORTHANTS

W.Larkins	b Jarvis	0		
A.Fordham	not out	206		
R.J.Bailey	c Byas b Sidebottom	16		
A.J.Lamb *	c White b Berry	235		
D.J.Capel	not out	21		
G.Cook				
D.Ripley +				
J.G.Thomas				
C.E.L.Ambrose				
N.G.B.Cook				
M.A.Robinson				
Extras	(b 3,lb 16,nb 1)	20		
TOTAL	(for 3 wkts dec)	498		

NORTHANTS	O	M	R	W	O	M	R	W		FALL OF WICKETS			
										YOR	NOR	YOR	NOR
Ambrose	22	9	49	5	21	5	70	1	1st	0		69	
Thomas	12.2	2	45	1	13	1	47	3	2nd	44	41	93	
Capel	16	4	40	2	23	6	72	3	3rd	98	434	136	
Robinson	22	12	47	2	20	5	47	3	4th	98		138	
Cook N.G.B.	5	2	8	0	7	2	8	0	5th	98		141	
									6th	124		191	
YORKSHIRE	O	M	R	W	O	M	R	W	7th	144		191	
Jarvis	23	3	90	1					8th	188		201	
Sidebottom	26	5	67	1					9th	197		201	
Fletcher	28	6	109	0					10th	198		250	
Byas	8	2	23	0									
Carrick	23	4	89	0									
Berry	21.5	1	101	1									

BRIT. ASS. C'SHIP	**BENSON & HEDGES CUP**

HEADLINES

26th - 30th April

- Northamptonshire, Somerset and Leicestershire all gained the maximum 24 points from the opening round of Championship matches

- Northamptonshire's Alan Fordham with a career best 206* and Allan Lamb with 235, his highest score in county cricket, added 393 for the third wicket, the biggest partnership in the county's history, as Northants beat Yorkshire by an innings at Headingley

- Chris Lewis returned match figures of 10 for 119, his best in the County Championship, as Leicestershire beat Glamorgan, despite 119 from Viv Richards on his Championship debut for the Welsh county

- Somerset defeated Gloucestershire thanks to a career best 166 from wicket-keeper Neil Burns and 5 for 30 from Roland Lefebvre in his first Championship match

- There were also wins for Hampshire, for whom Tony Middleton made a maiden first-class century, and Sussex, reaching a victory target of 337 in 64 overs

- Nottinghamshire's Chris Broad (180), Worcestershire's Damian D'Oliveira (155) and Middlesex's Keith Brown (141) also took advantage of the early season four-day games to post career best scores.

SCOTLAND vs. ESSEX

at Glasgow on 1st May 1990
Toss : Essex. Umpires : B.Hassan and A.G.T.Whitehead
Essex won by 83 runs. (Scotland 0 pts Essex 2 pts)

ESSEX

G.A.Gooch *	run out	2
B.R.Hardie	c Henry b Parfitt	34
P.J.Prichard	run out	107
M.E.Waugh	b Bee	62
D.R.Pringle	not out	77
M.A.Garnham +	run out	5
J.P.Stephenson	not out	4
A.W.Lilley		
N.A.Foster		
T.D.Topley		
J.H.Childs		
Extras	(b 1,lb 7,w 5,nb 5)	18
TOTAL	(55 overs)(for 5 wkts)	309

SCOTLAND

I.L.Philip	c Garnham b Pringle	29
C.G.Greenidge	b Childs	50
O.Henry	c Childs b Foster	24
B.M.W.Patterson	b Gooch	42
R.G.Swan *	b Childs	11
A.B.Russell	b Foster	9
A.W.Bee	lbw b Childs	0
D.Cowan	b Stephenson	7
D.J.Haggo +	not out	18
J.D.Moir	lbw b Stephenson	5
C.L.Parfitt	not out	1
Extras	(b 4,lb 13,w 11,nb 2)	30
TOTAL	(55 overs)(for 9 wkts)	226

SCOTLAND	O	M	R	W		FALL OF WICKETS	
						ESS	SCO
Moir	11	2	50	0			
Cowan	11	0	80	0	1st	2	93
Bee	10	0	67	1	2nd	105	101
Parfitt	11	1	41	1	3rd	185	131
Henry	10	1	54	0	4th	250	179
Russell	2	0	9	0	5th	304	188
					6th		188
ESSEX	O	M	R	W	7th		195
Foster	11	1	44	2	8th		213
Pringle	8	3	28	1	9th		223
Topley	11	0	35	0	10th		
Gooch	9	0	44	1			
Childs	11	1	37	3			
Stephenson	3	0	14	2			
Lilley	2	0	7	0			

Man of the match: P.J.Prichard

COMBINED UNIV vs. LANCASHIRE

at Fenner's on 1st May 1990
Toss : Comb. Univ. Umpires : D.J.Constant and K.J.Lyons
Lancs won by 22 runs. (Combined Univ 0 pts Lancs 2 pts)

LANCASHIRE

G.D.Mendis	c James b van der Merwe	6
G.Fowler	c Turner b van der Merwe	18
M.A.Atherton	not out	69
N.H.Fairbrother	c Turner b Dale	25
M.Watkinson	lbw b Crawley	3
P.A.J.DeFreitas	c & b Boiling	12
I.D.Austin	not out	61
D.P.Hughes *		
W.K.Hegg +		
P.J.W.Allott		
B.P.Patterson		
Extras	(lb 8,w 7)	15
TOTAL	(55 overs)(for 5 wkts)	209

COMBINED UNIV

S.P.James	c Allott b Patterson	0
N.V.Knight	c Hegg b Austin	9
M.A.Crawley *	c Fairbrother b Watkinson	46
C.M.Tolley	lbw b Allott	77
J.I.Longley	run out	4
J.C.M.Atkinson	c Hughes b Allott	10
A.Dale	c Mendis b Watkinson	2
W.M.van der Merwe	b DeFreitas	10
R.J.Turner +	not out	12
M.Smith	not out	4
J.Boiling		
Extras	(b 1,lb 8,w 4)	13
TOTAL	(55 overs)(for 8 wkts)	187

COMBINED U	O	M	R	W		FALL OF WICKETS	
						LAN	COM
van der Merwe	10	4	42	2			
Tolley	8	1	26	0	1st	23	0
Crawley	11	3	18	1	2nd	26	22
Dale	8	1	21	1	3rd	65	114
Boiling	8	0	37	1	4th	74	126
Smith	10	0	57	0	5th	96	154
					6th		159
LANCASHIRE	O	M	R	W	7th		161
Patterson	11	3	24	1	8th		180
Allott	11	3	23	2	9th		
Austin	11	1	42	1	10th		
DeFreitas	11	0	38	1			
Watkinson	11	0	51	2			

Man of the match: C.M.Tolley

SOMERSET vs. DERBYSHIRE

at Taunton on 1st May 1990
Toss : Somerset. Umpires : B.Leadbeater and R.Palmer
Somerset won by 7 runs. (Somerset 2 pts Derbyshire 0 pts)

SOMERSET

S.J.Cook	st Bowler b Miller	66
J.J.E.Hardy	b Mortensen	109
G.D.Rose	c Morris b Base	64
C.J.Tavare *	not out	47
R.J.Harden	not out	3
P.M.Roebuck		
N.D.Burns +		
A.N.Hayhurst		
R.P.Lefebvre		
I.G.Swallow		
J.C.Hallett		
Extras	(lb 12,w 9)	21
TOTAL	(55 overs)(for 3 wkts)	310

DERBYSHIRE

K.J.Barnett *	c Hardy b Rose	0
P.D.Bowler +	b Hayhurst	109
J.E.Morris	c Harden b Hallett	123
A.P.Kuiper	run out	22
C.J.Adams	b Lefebvre	8
B.Roberts	c Hardy b Hayhurst	4
S.C.Goldsmith	c Cook b Rose	4
S.J.Base	not out	15
D.E.Malcolm	not out	0
G.Miller		
O.H.Mortensen		
Extras	(lb 13,w 4,nb 1)	18
TOTAL	(55 overs)(for 7 wkts)	303

DERBYSHIRE	O	M	R	W		FALL OF WICKETS	
						SOM	DER
Malcolm	11	1	54	0			
Base	11	1	54	1	1st	126	0
Mortensen	10	0	55	1	2nd	234	210
Miller	11	0	46	1	3rd	298	250
Kuiper	11	0	80	0	4th		270
Barnett	1	0	9	0	5th		275
					6th		285
SOMERSET	O	M	R	W	7th		291
Rose	11	0	58	2	8th		
Hallett	9	0	52	1	9th		
Lefebvre	11	1	55	1	10th		
Swallow	11	0	45	0			
Roebuck	8	0	57	0			
Hayhurst	5	0	23	2			

Man of the match: G.D.Rose

SURREY vs. HAMPSHIRE

at The Oval on 1st May 1990
Toss : Hants. Umpires : N.T.Plews and D.S.Thompsett
Surrey won by 87 runs. (Surrey 2 pts Hampshire 0 pts)

SURREY

D.J.Bicknell	c Gower b Shine	119
G.S.Clinton	c Terry b James	9
A.J.Stewart	c Parks b Shine	76
M.A.Lynch	c Terry b Shine	8
G.P.Thorpe	not out	50
D.M.Ward +	c Parks b Shine	38
I.A.Greig *	not out	9
K.T.Medlycott		
M.A.Feltham		
M.P.Bicknell		
A.J.Murphy		
Extras	(lb 8,w 6,nb 8)	22
TOTAL	(55 overs)(for 5 wkts)	331

HAMPSHIRE

V.P.Terry *	st Ward b Medlycott	24
D.I.Gower	c & b Bicknell M.P.	6
R.A.Smith	c Greig b Murphy	132
C.L.Smith	c Ward b Greig	3
K.D.James	b Medlycott	2
R.J.Scott	run out	7
M.D.Marshall	c Ward b Bicknell M.P.	31
R.J.Parks +	not out	20
R.J.Maru	c & b Greig	9
C.A.Connor	c Ward b Murphy	3
K.J.Shine	run out	0
Extras	(lb 5,w 2)	7
TOTAL	(46.2 overs)	244

HAMPSHIRE	O	M	R	W		FALL OF WICKETS	
						SUR	HAM
Marshall	11	1	52	0			
Shine	10	0	68	4	1st	20	9
James	5	0	36	1	2nd	164	68
Connor	11	0	71	0	3rd	174	75
Maru	7	0	40	0	4th	262	82
Scott	11	0	56	0	5th	322	100
					6th		161
SURREY	O	M	R	W	7th		222
Bicknell M.P.	8	1	48	2	8th		233
Murphy	9	3	36	2	9th		239
Feltham	3	0	24	0	10th		244
Medlycott	11	0	44	2			
Greig	6.2	0	35	2			
Lynch	9	0	52	0			

Man of the match: D.J.Bicknell

BENSON & HEDGES CUP

GLAMORGAN vs. GLOUCESTERSHIRE

at Cardiff on 1st May 1990
Toss : Glamorgan. Umpires : P.J.Eele and R.Julian
Glamorgan won by 9 runs. (Glam 2 pts Gloucs 0 pts)

GLAMORGAN

A.R.Butcher *	c Russell b Curran	95
H.Morris	lbw b Curran	23
M.P.Maynard	c Graveney b Alleyne	33
I.V.A.Richards	c Russell b Alleyne	28
G.C.Holmes	c Russell b Walsh	9
I.Smith	c Russell b Alleyne	0
N.G.Cowley	lbw b Alleyne	1
C.P.Metson +	c Athey b Curran	14
S.J.Dennis	not out	2
S.R.Barwick	b Walsh	1
M.Frost		
Extras	(lb 10,w 1,nb 2)	13
TOTAL	(55 overs)(for 9 wkts)	219

GLOUCESTERSHIRE

A.J.Wright *	c Holmes b Barwick	10
A.W.Stovold	b Frost	1
P.Bainbridge	b Dennis	55
C.W.J.Athey	b Holmes	20
K.M.Curran	b Holmes	14
J.W.Lloyds	lbw b Richards	6
M.W.Alleyne	b Frost	30
R.C.Russell +	not out	46
C.A.Walsh	lbw b Cowley	1
D.A.Graveney	not out	12
K.B.S.Jarvis		
Extras	(b 4,lb 9,w 1,nb 1)	15
TOTAL	(55 overs)(for 8 wkts)	210

GLOUCS	O	M	R	W	FALL OF WICKETS	GLA	GLO
Jarvis	10	1	32	0			
Walsh	11	1	32	2	1st	65	5
Curran	9	1	29	3	2nd	115	17
Graveney	11	1	55	0	3rd	157	65
Bainbridge	3	0	19	0	4th	172	87
Alleyne	11	1	42	4	5th	173	104
					6th	181	129
GLAMORGAN	O	M	R	W	7th	215	159
Frost	8	4	12	2	8th	215	164
Barwick	9	1	37	1	9th	219	
Dennis	10	2	38	1	10th		
Cowley	11	0	40	1			
Holmes	8	0	27	2			
Richards	9	0	41	1			

Man of the match: A.R.Butcher

MINOR COUNTIES vs. SUSSEX

at Marlow on 1st May 1990
Toss : Sussex. Umpires : J.W.Holder and A.A.Jones
Sussex won by 5 wickets. (Min Counties 0 pts Sussex 2 pts)

MINOR COUNTIES

G.K.Brown	c Speight b Lenham	46
M.J.Roberts	c Dodemaide b Clarke	121
N.A.Folland	not out	78
S.Sharp	not out	11
S.G.Plumb *		
T.A.Lester		
S.Greensword		
A.R.Fothergill +		
N.R.Taylor		
R.C.Green		
A.J.Mack		
Extras	(b 4,lb 7,w 6)	17
TOTAL	(55 overs)(for 2 wkts)	273

SUSSEX

N.J.Lenham	b Mack	37
P.Moores +	c Brown b Greensword	41
P.W.G.Parker *	not out	85
A.P.Wells	c Fothergill b Mack	0
M.P.Speight	run out	40
C.M.Wells	c Taylor b Green	33
I.J.Gould	not out	16
A.I.C.Dodemaide		
A.C.S.Pigott		
A.R.Clarke		
A.R.Hansford		
Extras	(lb 17,w 3,nb 2)	22
TOTAL	(51.4 overs)(for 5 wkts)	274

SUSSEX	O	M	R	W	FALL OF WICKETS	MIN	SUS
Pigott	9	2	38	0			
Dodemaide	11	0	52	0	1st	118	70
Wells C.M.	9	1	30	0	2nd	252	106
Clarke	11	1	53	1	3rd		106
Hansford	11	0	70	1	4th		177
Gould	3	0	16	0	5th		232
Lenham	1	0	3	1	6th		
					7th		
MIN COUNTIES	O	M	R	W	8th		
Taylor	9	1	37	0	9th		
Green	10.4	2	51	1	10th		
Mack	11	2	36	2			
Greensword	9	0	53	1			
Plumb	9	0	54	0			
Sharp	3	0	26	0			

Man of the match: M.J.Roberts

NOTTINGHAMSHIRE vs. LEICS

at Trent Bridge on 1st May 1990
Toss : Notts. Umpires : H.D.Bird and D.R.Shepherd
Nottinghamshire won by 4 wickets. (Notts 2 pts Leics 0 pts)

LEICESTERSHIRE

T.J.Boon	c French b Cooper	4
N.E.Briers *	c Randall b Pick	10
J.J.Whitaker	c Johnson b Cooper	7
L.Potter	c French b Cooper	0
J.D.R.Benson	c Cooper b Pick	43
C.C.Lewis	b Afford	23
P.Whitticase +	c Broad b Pick	45
M.I.Gidley	not out	20
W.K.M.Benjamin	c Cooper b Stephenson	2
J.P.Agnew	not out	1
L.B.Taylor		
Extras	(b 2,lb 1,w 6)	9
TOTAL	(55 overs)(for 8 wkts)	164

NOTTINGHAMSHIRE

B.C.Broad	run out	49
M.Newell	lbw b Agnew	13
P.Johnson	c Lewis b Potter	39
D.W.Randall	c Whitaker b Taylor	6
F.D.Stephenson	c Whitticase b Benjamin	10
B.N.French +	not out	14
E.E.Hemmings	b Benjamin	5
R.T.Robinson *	not out	25
K.E.Cooper		
R.A.Pick		
J.A.Afford		
Extras	(b 1,w 2,nb 4)	7
TOTAL	(46.4 overs)(for 6 wkts)	168

NOTTS	O	M	R	W	FALL OF WICKETS	LEI	NOT
Stephenson	11	1	39	1			
Cooper	11	2	25	3	1st	10	46
Pick	11	0	50	3	2nd	19	66
Hemmings	11	5	10	0	3rd	23	83
Afford	11	3	37	1	4th	23	119
					5th	79	126
LEICS	O	M	R	W	6th	103	136
Benjamin	9	3	29	2	7th	157	
Lewis	9	2	28	0	8th	163	
Agnew	6	0	34	1	9th		
Taylor	9.4	0	34	1	10th		
Gidley	5	0	16	0			
Potter	8	1	26	1			

Man of the match: K.E.Cooper

WORCESTERSHIRE vs. KENT

at Worcester on 1st May 1990
Toss : Kent. Umpires : M.J.Kitchen and R.A.White
Worcestershire won by 27 runs. (Worcs 2 pts Kent 0 pts)

WORCESTERSHIRE

T.S.Curtis	lbw b Ealham	11
S.J.Rhodes +	c Cowdrey G.R. b Ealham	8
G.A.Hick	c Marsh b Ealham	41
I.T.Botham	c Ellison b Cowdrey C.S.	37
P.A.Neale *	c Hinks b Cowdrey C.S.	13
D.B.D'Oliveira	c Marsh b Davis	7
S.R.Lampitt	c Ward b Fleming	6
R.K.Illingworth	not out	36
P.J.Newport	c Ward b Ealham	28
N.V.Radford	not out	1
G.R.Dilley		
Extras	(lb 8,w 4,nb 7)	19
TOTAL	(55 overs)(for 8 wkts)	207

KENT

S.G.Hinks	c Hick b Dilley	1
N.R.Taylor	c D'Oliveira b Dilley	8
T.R.Ward	c Hick b Newport	94
C.S.Cowdrey *	c Hick b Newport	6
G.R.Cowdrey	c Rhodes b Newport	0
S.A.Marsh +	run out	17
R.M.Ellison	lbw b Dilley	12
M.V.Fleming	c Radford b Lampitt	6
M.A.Ealham	c Hick b Dilley	5
T.A.Merrick	b Newport	14
R.P.Davis	not out	0
Extras	(lb 5,w 6,nb 6)	17
TOTAL	(49 overs)	180

KENT	O	M	R	W	FALL OF WICKETS	WOR	KEN
Merrick	11	0	46	0			
Ellison	6	2	14	0	1st	19	11
Ealham	11	1	57	4	2nd	32	12
Fleming	9	1	27	1	3rd	91	40
Davis	11	1	36	1	4th	117	46
Cowdrey C.S.	7	1	19	2	5th	130	86
					6th	134	120
WORCS	O	M	R	W	7th	147	132
Dilley	9	1	48	4	8th	203	141
Radford	7	3	13	0	9th		176
Newport	8	0	25	4	10th		180
Lampitt	11	1	47	1			
Illingworth	8	1	23	0			
Botham	6	2	19	0			

Man of the match: T.R.Ward

HEADLINES

1st May

● There were runs galore in idyllic conditions for batting as four counties passed 300 and seven individual 100s were scored.

● Surrey made a record score (331 for 5) in a B & H match between two counties, as Darren Bicknell made his first 100 in the competition and Alec Stewart, Graham Thorpe and David Ward also improved their competition bests. Robin Smith announced his return to fitness with 132 in Hampshire's forlorn reply.

● Somerset and Derbyshire created a new record aggregate for the B & H Cup by sharing 613 runs, as Somerset scored 310 for 3 and scraped home by just seven runs. Somerset's Jonathan Hardy (109) and Derbyshire's Peter Bowler (109) and John Morris (123) all made their first B & H centuries.

● Essex also passed 300 in their match against Scotland, Paul Prichard making his first 100 in the competition and Derek Pringle (77*) his highest score.

● The Minor Counties compiled their highest B & H total (273 for 2) as Malcolm Roberts hit 121, but it wasn't enough to prevent a Sussex victory, Paul Parker improving his best score with 86*.

● Mike Atherton (B & H best 69*) and Ian Austin (61*) rescued Lancashire with a sixth wicket stand of 113* against Combined Universities for whom Chris Tolley impressed with 77.

● Alan Butcher (95) and Jack Russell (46*) both posted their B & H bests in Glamorgan's win over Gloucestershire.

● Bowlers to be spared from punishment on a difficult day were Phil Newport (4 for 25) in Worcestershire's victory over Kent and Kevin Cooper (3 for 25) as Notts beat Leicestershire.

BRITANNIC ASSURANCE CHAMPIONSHIP

NORTHANTS vs. DERBYSHIRE

at Northampton on 3rd, 4th May 1990
Toss : Northants.   Umpires : J.H.Harris and R.A.White
Derby won by an inns and 51 runs. (Northants 6 pts (Bt: 2, Bw: 4) Derby 23 pts (Bt: 4, Bw: 3))

NORTHANTS

W.Larkins *	c Krikken b Malcolm	1	b Bishop	0
A.Fordham	c Krikken b Bishop	10	c & b Bishop	32
R.J.Bailey	c Adams b Griffith	30	b Malcolm	8
A.J.Lamb	retired hurt	14	absent hurt	
D.J.Capel	c Roberts b Jean-Jacques	11	lbw b Bishop	2
G.Cook	run out	44	(4) b Bishop	3
D.Ripley +	c Roberts b Malcolm	17	absent hurt	
J.W.Govan	lbw b Goldsmith	17	(6) c Adams b Malcolm	4
W.W.Davis	c Barnett b Malcolm	23	(7) b Malcolm	0
N.G.B.Cook	retired hurt	9	absent hurt	
M.A.Robinson	not out	1	(8) not out	1
Extras	(b 4,lb 9,w 6,nb 6)	25	(w 1)	1
TOTAL		202		50

DERBYSHIRE

P.D.Bowler	lbw b Robinson	24
A.M.Brown	c Fordham b Govan	44
C.J.Adams	c Larkins b Capel	24
K.J.Barnett *	c & b Capel	58
B.Roberts	lbw b Robinson	44
S.C.Goldsmith	b Robinson	34
F.A.Griffith	c sub b Capel	1
K.M.Krikken +	lbw b Capel	0
I.R.Bishop	b Davis	19
M.Jean-Jacques	run out	4
D.E.Malcolm	not out	20
Extras	(b 5,lb 19,nb 7)	31
TOTAL		303

DERBYSHIRE	O	M	R	W	O	M	R	W		FALL OF WICKETS				
Bishop	17	2	48	1	9	1	25	4			NOR	DER	NOR	DER
Malcolm	22.4	5	60	3	8	2	25	3	1st	5	37	0	
Jean-Jacques	17	2	39	1					2nd	24	71	9	
Griffith	11	2	20	1					3rd	62	142	20	
Goldsmith	11	2	21	1					4th	79	183	40	
Barnett	3	2	1	0					5th	119	234	48	
									6th	161	253	48	
NORTHANTS	O	M	R	W	O	M	R	W	7th	166	253	50	
Davis	24.3	5	85	1					8th	202	254		
Capel	27	7	83	4					9th		258		
Robinson	28	8	80	3					10th		303		
Govan	14	5	19	1									
Bailey	5	2	12	0									

GLAMORGAN vs. SOMERSET

at Cardiff on 3rd, 4th, 5th, 6th May 1990
Toss : Somerset. Umpires : P.J.Eele and J.W.Holder
Match drawn. (Glamorgan 3 pts (Bt: 3, Bw: 0) Somerset 5 pts (Bt: 4, Bw: 1))

SOMERSET

S.J.Cook	not out	313		
P.M.Roebuck	lbw b Dennis	69		
J.J.E.Hardy	b Holmes	7	(2) lbw b Dennis	0
C.J.Tavare *	not out	120	(3) c Richards b Smith	64
R.J.Harden			(1) not out	110
A.N.Hayhurst			(4) c sub b Barwick	28
N.D.Burns +			(5) not out	31
I.G.Swallow				
G.D.Rose				
R.P.Lefebvre				
A.N.Jones				
Extras	(b 8,lb 16,nb 2)	26	(lb 6,w 1,nb 4)	11
TOTAL	(for 2 wkts dec)	535	(for 3 wkts dec)	244

GLAMORGAN

M.J.Cann	c Harden b Jones	64	c Swallow b Hayhurst	54
H.Morris	c Hardy b Jones	52	b Lefebvre	19
G.C.Holmes	not out	125	c Burns b Lefebvre	44
M.P.Maynard	c Roebuck b Swallow	19	c Cook b Lefebvre	64
I.Smith	c Jones b Swallow	56	(6) c Cook b Roebuck	16
I.V.A.Richards	c Burns b Rose	16	(5) c Swallow b Roebuck	16
N.G.Cowley	run out	43	not out	8
C.P.Metson +			not out	4
S.J.Dennis				
S.R.Barwick *				
S.L.Watkin				
Extras	(b 6,lb 22,w 4,nb 5)	37	(b 3,lb 7,w 3,nb 1)	14
TOTAL	(for 6 wkts dec)	412	(for 6 wkts)	239

GLAMORGAN	O	M	R	W	O	M	R	W		FALL OF WICKETS			
Watkin	27	6	84	0							SOM	GLA	SOM	GLA
Dennis	27	3	125	1	7	1	16	1	1st	210	120	4	61
Barwick	29	7	107	0	16	1	56	1	2nd	250	127	138	80
Cowley	41	5	88	0					3rd		159	181	188
Smith	3	0	19	0	11	1	43	1	4th		270		205
Richards	9	1	22	0	22	2	68	0	5th		296		218
Holmes	12	1	44	1					6th		412		227
Cann	6	1	22	0	15	2	44	0	7th				
Maynard					3	0	11	0	8th				
SOMERSET	O	M	R	W	O	M	R	W	9th				
Jones	18	1	80	2	7	0	24	0	10th				
Rose	22	6	50	1	9	4	23	0					
Swallow	45	11	117	2	21	6	57	0					
Lefebvre	26	8	45	0	17	2	52	3					
Hayhurst	16	2	37	0	8	0	39	1					
Roebuck	20	6	33	0	14.3	5	34	2					
Harden	7	1	21	0									
Tavare	0.3	0	1	0									

SURREY vs. LANCASHIRE

at The Oval on 3rd, 4th, 5th, 7th May 1990
Toss : Surrey. Umpires : B.Dudleston and A.A.Jones
Match drawn. (Surrey 4 pts (Bt: 4, Bw: 0) Lancashire 6 pts (Bt: 4, Bw: 2))

SURREY

R.I.Alikhan	st Hegg b Fitton	55	c Watkinson b Atherton	15
G.S.Clinton	c Patterson b DeFreitas	8	(1) not out	54
A.J.Stewart	c Fowler b Patterson	70	(3) not out	6
M.A.Lynch	c & b Watkinson	95		
G.P.Thorpe	c Atherton b Fitton	27		
D.M.Ward +	c Hughes b Fitton	36		
I.A.Greig *	c Jesty b Hughes	291		
K.T.Medlycott	c Fairbrother b Patterson	33		
M.P.Bicknell	c Hegg b Hughes	42		
N.M.Kendrick	not out	18		
A.J.Murphy				
Extras	(b 6,lb 16,nb 10)	32	(b 2,lb 1,nb 2)	5
TOTAL	(for 9 wkts dec)	707	(for 1 wkt)	80

LANCASHIRE

G.D.Mendis	run out	102
G.Fowler	run out	20
M.A.Atherton	c Greig b Kendrick	191
N.H.Fairbrother	c Kendrick b Greig	366
T.E.Jesty	retired hurt	18
M.Watkinson	b Greig	46
W.K.Hegg +	c Ward b Bicknell	45
P.A.J.DeFreitas	b Murphy	31
D.P.Hughes *	not out	8
J.D.Fitton	c Stewart b Murphy	3
B.P.Patterson	c Greig b Medlycott	0
Extras	(b 8,lb 15,w 1,nb 9)	33
TOTAL		863

LANCASHIRE	O	M	R	W	O	M	R	W		FALL OF WICKETS			
Patterson	27	4	108	2							SUR	LAN	SUR	LAN
DeFreitas	26	4	99	1	4	0	10	0	1st	10	45	57	
Watkinson	23	2	113	1					2nd	118	184		
Fitton	45	6	185	3	16	4	42	0	3rd	187	548		
Atherton	22	5	75	0	13	5	25	1	4th	261	745		
Hughes	22.1	0	105	2					5th	275	774		
									6th	316	844		
SURREY	O	M	R	W	O	M	R	W	7th	401	848		
Murphy	44	6	160	2					8th	606	862		
Bicknell	43	2	175	1					9th	707	863		
Kendrick	56	10	192	1					10th				
Medlycott	50.5	4	177	1									
Lynch	5	2	17	0									
Greig	19	3	73	2									
Thorpe	7	1	46	0									

WORCESTERSHIRE vs. NOTTINGHAMSHIRE

at Worcester on 3rd, 4th, 5th, 7th May 1990
Toss : Worcestershire. Umpires : B.Leadbeater and K.J.Lyons
Worcs won by an innings and 6 runs. (Worcs 23 pts (Bt: 3, Bw: 4) Notts 2 pts (Bt: 0, Bw: 2))

WORCESTERSHIRE

T.S.Curtis	c French b Cooper	46
G.J.Lord	b Pick	12
G.A.Hick	b Stephenson	97
D.B.D'Oliveira	c Evans R.J. b Pick	9
P.A.Neale *	b Hemmings	122
S.R.Lampitt	st French b Hemmings	1
R.K.Illingworth	b Stephenson	117
P.J.Newport	c Newell b Pick	35
G.R.Dilley	b Hemmings	8
S.R.Bevins +	not out	6
S.M.McEwan	lbw b Pick	0
Extras	(b 10,lb 9,w 2,nb 7)	28
TOTAL		481

NOTTINGHAMSHIRE

B.C.Broad	c Newport b Dilley	2	c Hick b Dilley	16
M.Newell	c Curtis b Lampitt	6	c Curtis b Lampitt	30
R.J.Evans	c Lampitt b Newport	11	(4) lbw b McEwan	4
R.T.Robinson *	c Bevins b Newport	15	(3) c Lampitt b McEwan	48
P.Johnson	c Dilley b Newport	3	lbw b McEwan	83
D.W.Randall	b Lampitt	6	c Bevins b Dilley	87
B.N.French +	b Newport	10	(8) c Bevins b Dilley	0
F.D.Stephenson	lbw b McEwan	13	(7) not out	12
E.E.Hemmings	lbw b Lampitt	24	retired hurt	4
K.E.Cooper	c & b McEwan	1	b Dilley	1
R.A.Pick	not out	27	b Dilley	5
Extras	(b 8,lb 3,w 4,nb 1)	16	(b 15,lb 26,w 11,nb 4)	56
TOTAL		134		341

NOTTS	O	M	R	W	O	M	R	W		FALL OF WICKETS			
Stephenson	35	4	112	2							WOR	NOT	NOT	WOR
Cooper	37	11	113	1					1st	24	3	22	
Pick	36.5	5	119	4					2nd	133	24	99	
Hemmings	61	21	117	3					3rd	154	24	121	
Newell	1	0	1	0					4th	193	27	122	
									5th	206	36	309	
WORCS	O	M	R	W	O	M	R	W	6th	426	49	309	
Dilley	8	2	13	1	23.2	4	62	5	7th	432	77	309	
McEwan	13	2	26	2	23	5	57	3	8th	451	77	341	
Newport	18	4	44	4	13	4	42	0	9th	481	79	341	
Illingworth	1	1	0	0	30	15	47	0	10th	481	134		
Lampitt	11.2	1	40	3	19	6	60	1					
Hick					8	1	32	0					

BRITANNIC ASSURANCE CHAMPIONSHIP

ESSEX vs. LEICESTERSHIRE

at Chelmsford on 3rd, 4th, 5th, 7th May 1990
Toss : Leicestershire. Umpires : K.E.Palmer and D.R.Shepherd
Match drawn. (Essex 5 pts (Bt: 4, Bw: 1) Leicestershire 3 pts (Bt: 3, Bw: 0))

LEICESTERSHIRE

T.J.Boon	lbw b Such	90	c Waugh b Childs	89
N.E.Briers *	c Garnham b Such	65	c Garnham b Such	104
J.J.Whitaker	c & b Such	31	b Stephenson	15
L.Potter	c Prichard b Waugh	62	not out	16
J.D.R.Benson	c Shahid b Foster	8	not out	10
C.C.Lewis	not out	189		
P.Whitticase +	lbw b Waugh	0		
M.I.Gidley	c & b Shahid	9		
J.P.Agnew	lbw b Shahid	37		
G.J.F.Ferris	c Waugh b Foster	11		
A.D.Mullally	b Foster	3		
Extras	(b 1,lb 9,w 4,nb 1)	15	(b 5,lb 3,w 1,nb 6)	15
TOTAL		520	(for 3 wkts)	249

ESSEX

G.A.Gooch *	c Whitticase b Lewis	215		
J.P.Stephenson	c Lewis b Mullally	35		
P.J.Prichard	c Briers b Mullally	245		
M.E.Waugh	b Lewis	43		
B.R.Hardie	not out	74		
M.A.Garnham +	b Lewis	0		
N.A.Foster	run out	101		
N.Shahid				
J.H.Childs				
S.J.W.Andrew				
P.M.Such				
Extras	(b 9,lb 20,w 3,nb 16)	48		
TOTAL	(for 6 wkts dec)	761		

ESSEX	O	M	R	W	O	M	R	W		FALL OF WICKETS			
										LEI	ESS	LEI	ESS
Foster	41	8	102	3	8	2	30	0	1st	145	82	170	
Andrew	20	3	72	0	9	1	31	0	2nd	178	485	205	
Waugh	23	5	76	2					3rd	197	551	236	
Childs	41	14	88	0	33	10	93	1	4th	214	587		
Such	43	7	118	3	19	9	29	1	5th	303	589		
Shahid	13	1	54	2	11	3	42	0	6th	309	761		
Stephenson					9	5	16	1	7th	458			
									8th	460			
LEICS	O	M	R	W	O	M	R	W	9th	498			
Mullally	31	3	124	2					10th	520			
Agnew	35.5	4	170	0									
Ferris	23	2	100	0									
Lewis	28	3	115	3									
Potter	14	0	91	0									
Gidley	25	3	121	0									
Benson	2	0	11	0									

WARWICKSHIRE vs. YORKSHIRE

at Edgbaston on 3rd, 4th, 5th May 1990
Toss : Yorkshire. Umpires : R.Palmer and P.B.Wight
Warwickshire won by 7 wickets. (Warwicks 23 pts (Bt: 3, Bw: 4) Yorks 5 pts (Bt: 1, Bw: 4))

YORKSHIRE

M.D.Moxon *	c Humpage b Small	12	(5) c Kallicharran b Booth	0
A.A.Metcalfe	c Reeve b Donald	33	b Smith	24
R.J.Blakey +	c Booth b Reeve	6	c Moles b Booth	24
S.A.Kellett	lbw b Small	1	(1) c Humpage b Booth	31
P.E.Robinson	run out	1	(4) lbw b Reeve	59
C.White	b Small	1	c Asif Din b Booth	6
P.Carrick	c Reeve b Munton	7	b Small	14
A.Sidebottom	c Asif Din b Munton	38	c Moles b Munton	19
P.W.Jarvis	c Humpage b Small	0	c Humpage b Reeve	6
D.Gough	c Humpage b Donald	4	not out	3
S.D.Fletcher	not out	11	b Donald	0
Extras	(b 9,lb 11,w 2,nb 1)	23	(b 17,lb 12,w 2,nb 2)	33
TOTAL		167		219

WARWICKSHIRE

A.J.Moles	lbw b Sidebottom	6	c Blakey b White	32
T.A.Lloyd *	b Fletcher	31	b Carrick	30
Asif Din	c Blakey b Sidebottom	0	c Blakey b Carrick	23
A.I.Kallicharran	lbw b Fletcher	2	not out	11
G.W.Humpage +	lbw b Sidebottom	52	not out	19
D.A.Reeve	c Moxon b Fletcher	29		
N.M.K.Smith	not out	83		
P.A.Booth	lbw b Jarvis	15		
G.C.Small	b Jarvis	0		
A.A.Donald	c Sidebottom b Carrick	16		
T.A.Munton	lbw b Fletcher	0		
Extras	(b 10,lb 6,w 5,nb 4)	25	(b 8,lb 5)	13
TOTAL		259	(for 3 wkts)	128

WARWICKS	O	M	R	W	O	M	R	W		FALL OF WICKETS			
										YOR	WAR	YOR	WAR
Donald	19	5	56	2	17.4	4	41	1	1st	35	11	57	60
Small	18	5	40	4	19	9	29	1	2nd	60	11	61	96
Munton	15.5	3	41	2	8	3	21	1	3rd	74	38	100	102
Reeve	17	12	6	1	5	3	2	2	4th	102	43	104	
Booth	2	1	4	0	33	9	55	4	5th	104	127	120	
Smith					12	2	36	1	6th	105	134	149	
Asif Din					2	1	6	0	7th	119	162	199	
									8th	121	162	213	
YORKSHIRE	O	M	R	W	O	M	R	W	9th	139	242	216	
Jarvis	16	1	52	2	6	2	22	0	10th	167	259	219	
Sidebottom	18	4	54	3									
Fletcher	20.5	6	47	4	4	0	18	0					
Gough	14	1	53	0									
Carrick	10	3	31	1	12.2	2	35	2					
White	2	0	6	0	11	2	40	1					

KENT vs. SUSSEX

at Folkestone on 3rd, 4th, 5th, 7th May 1990
Toss : Sussex. Umpires : D.J.Constant and N.T.Plews
Kent won by 5 wickets. (Kent 20 pts (Bt: 3, Bw: 1) Sussex 4 pts (Bt: 3, Bw: 1))

SUSSEX

N.J.Lenham	c Fleming b De Villiers	63	c Ward b Igglesden	18
P.Moores +	c Marsh b Igglesden	0	c Benson b Davis	46
P.W.G.Parker *	c Ward b Davis	107	c Ward b Davis	19
A.P.Wells	b Ellison	69	lbw b Davis	13
M.P.Speight	b Davis	12	lbw b Davis	22
C.M.Wells	c Ward b Igglesden	14	c Marsh b Davis	0
I.J.Gould	c Marsh b Ellison	0	c De Villiers b Ward	33
I.D.K.Salisbury	not out	30	(10) not out	5
A.I.C.Dodemaide	c Cowdrey b Igglesden	9	(8) c & b Davis	13
J.A.North	b Igglesden	9	(9) b De Villiers	6
A.R.Hansford	c Marsh b Ellison	19	lbw b De Villiers	2
Extras	(b 5,lb 16,w 1,nb 2)	24	(b 6,lb 6)	12
TOTAL		356		189

KENT

S.G.Hinks	c North b Wells C.M.	48	c Moores b Dodemaide	4
M.R.Benson	c Speight b Dodemaide	109	c Moores b Dodemaide	13
N.R.Taylor	c Speight b Hansford	57	(4) c Speight b Dodemaide	20
T.R.Ward	c Moores b Hansford	13	(5) lbw b Dodemaide	0
C.S.Cowdrey *	lbw b Dodemaide	24	(6) not out	0
S.A.Marsh +	b Dodemaide	10	(7) not out	4
M.V.Fleming	c Moores b Hansford	53	(3) b Salisbury	39
R.M.Ellison	b Dodemaide	81		
P.S.De Villiers	c Dodemaide b Wells C.M.	37		
R.P.Davis	run out	3		
A.P.Igglesden	not out	2		
Extras	(b 2,lb 19,w 1,nb 6)	28	(lb 4)	4
TOTAL		465	(for 5 wkts)	84

KENT	O	M	R	W	O	M	R	W		FALL OF WICKETS			
										SUS	KEN	SUS	KEN
De Villiers	29	4	84	1	12.1	4	37	2	1st	4	115	35	4
Igglesden	31	9	86	4	17	1	44	1	2nd	133	210	64	23
Ellison	24.4	8	70	3	6	4	10	0	3rd	225	236	102	79
Davis	42	14	75	2	26	10	59	6	4th	257	265	105	79
Fleming	14	8	20	0	11	5	21	0	5th	269	268	105	80
Ward					2	0	6	1	6th	274	297	160	
									7th	286	348	160	
SUSSEX	O	M	R	W	O	M	R	W	8th	296	412	175	
Dodemaide	43.1	10	105	4	7	1	29	4	9th	318	436	187	
Hansford	35	11	91	3	7	0	31	0	10th	356	465	189	
Wells C.M.	30	9	67	2									
Salisbury	60	15	135	0	5	1	20	1					
North	15	6	30	0									
Gould	2	0	8	0									
Lenham	2	1	8	0									

HIGHEST INDIVIDUAL SCORES IN COUNTY CRICKET

424	A.C.MacLaren	Lancashire v Somerset	Taunton	1895
405*	G.A.Hick	Worcestershire v Somerset	Taunton	1988
366	N.H.Fairbrother	Lancashire v Surrey	The Oval	1990
357*	R.Abel	Surrey v Somerset	The Oval	1899
343*	P.A.Perrin	Essex v Derbyshire	Chesterfield	1904
341	G.H.Hirst	Yorkshire v Leicestershire	Leicester	1905
333	K.S.Duleepsinhji	Sussex v Northamptonshire	Hove	1930
332	W.H.Ashdown	Kent v Essex	Brentwood	1934
331*	J.D.B.Robertson	Middlesex v Worcestershire	Worcester	1949
322	E.Paynter	Lancashire v Sussex	Hove	1937
322	I.V.A.Richards	Somerset v Warwickshire	Taunton	1985
318*	W.G.Grace	Gloucestershire v Yorkshire	Cheltenham	1876
317	W.R.Hammond	Gloucestershire v Notts	Gloucester	1936
316*	J.B.Hobbs	Surrey v Middlesex	Lord's	1926
316	R.H.Moore	Hampshire v Warwickshire	Bournemouth	1937
315*	T.W.Hayward	Surrey v Lancashire	The Oval	1898
315*	P.Holmes	Yorkshire v Middlesex	Lord's	1925
313*	S.J.Cook	Somerset v Glamorgan	Cardiff	1990
313	H.Sutcliffe	Yorkshire v Essex	Leyton	1932

HIGHEST TOTALS IN COUNTY CRICKET

887	Yorkshire v Warwickshire	Edgbaston	1896
863	Lancashire v Surrey	The Oval	1990
811	Surrey v Somerset	The Oval	1899
803-4 dec	Kent v Sussex	Brentwood	1934
801	Lancashire v Somerset	Taunton	1895
761-6 dec	Essex v Leicestershire	Chelmsford	1990
742	Surrey v Hampshire	The Oval	1909
739-7 dec	Notts v Leicestershire	Trent Bridge	1903
726	Notts v Sussex	Trent Bridge	1895
707-9 dec	Surrey v Lancashire	The Oval	1990
706-4 dec	Surrey v Notts	Trent Bridge	1947
705-8 dec	Sussex v Surrey	Hastings	1902
704	Yorkshire v Surrey	The Oval	1899
701-4	Leicestershire v Worcestershire	Worcester	1906

BRITANNIC ASS. CHAMPIONSHIP	OTHER FIRST-CLASS MATCHES

HEADLINES

3rd - 7th May

● Record books were consulted continuously in the course of an extraordinary four days' play as events at Cardiff, The Oval and Chelmsford in particular unfolded.

● Those three venues alone produced three of the top 10 Championship totals of all time, two individual triple centuries, three more double centuries and the highest ever aggregate in a Championship match.

● Somerset's Jimmy Cook was the first to catch the eye with a career best 313* against Glamorgan. He was only nine runs short of Viv Richards's record score for Somerset when Chris Tavare declared on 535 for two.

● Meanwhile at The Oval Ian Greig reached 291, almost doubling his previous highest score, in Surrey's total of 707 for nine declared against Lancashire. It was the first time since 1947 that 700 had been made in a Championship match.

● On Saturday attention turned first to Chelmsford, and the second wicket partnership of 403 between Graham Gooch (215) and Paul Prichard (a career best 245) - which was an Essex record for any wicket - and then back to the Oval where Mike Atherton (191) and Neil Fairbrother (311* at the close of play) both sailed past their previous career bests during a stand of 364 for the third wicket. Fairbrother actually managed to score more than 100 in each session.

● On Monday more records were in the air with Lancashire starting the day on 665 for 3 and Essex on 712 for 5: Fairbrother's innings ended at 366 (504 mins, 47 fours and 5 sixes), the third highest score ever made in English cricket, and Lancashire reached 863, the second highest total ever made in the County Championship. The match produced an aggregate of 1650 runs - a new Championship record. Essex's final total of 761 for six declared is now the sixth best Championship score.

● That summary still does not do full justice to the landmarks achieved in a remarkable trio of matches: at Chelmsford Chris Lewis and Neil Foster both made maiden 100s and Leicester openers Nigel Briers and Tim Boon shared century opening stands in both innings; at Cardiff Andy Hayhurst scored 110* on his Championship debut for Somerset.

● The remaining four matches, although less eye-catching, at least all ended in positive results: Derbyshire, Warwickshire, Worcestershire and Kent all gaining their first Championship successes of the season. In a round of matches dominated by the batsmen, Ian Bishop and Devon Malcolm needed less than two days to dismantle an injury-hit Northants.

● The shift in the balance of power between bat and ball is well illustrated by the fact that the first two rounds of Championship matches produced seven individual scores of more than 200, when only three double centuries were scored in the Championship in the whole of the 1989 season.

● Hampshire's Chris Smith and Paul Terry did not miss out at The Parks. They shared an opening stand of 264 against Oxford University.

● Middlesex's Mark Ramprakash made the second first-class 100 of his career against Cambridge University at Fenner's.

● First-class debuts: J.North (Sussex), H.Davies, M.J.Russell and A.Winchester (Oxford University).

OXFORD UNIV vs. HAMPSHIRE

at The Parks on 3rd, 4th, 5th May 1990
Toss : Hampshire. Umpires : H.D.Bird and R.Julian
Match drawn

HAMPSHIRE

V.P.Terry	c & b Turner	112			
C.L.Smith	st McGrady b Turner	148			
D.I.Gower	c & b Crawley	72	(1) c van der Merwe b Turner	46	
R.A.Smith	c van der Merwe b Lunn	44	(2) c Kilborn b Davies	47	
M.C.J.Nicholas *	not out	37	(3) c Kilborn b Davies	8	
R.J.Parks +	not out	5	(4) b Davies	1	
R.J.Maru			(5) not out	69	
L.A.Joseph			(6) c Russell b Turner	14	
I.J.Turner			(7) not out	24	
K.J.Shine					
C.A.Connor					
Extras	(b 9,lb 4,nb 6)	19	(b 1,lb 4,nb 1)	6	
TOTAL	(for 4 wkts dec)	437	(for 5 wkts dec)	215	

OXFORD UNIV

D.A.Hagan	c Smith R.A. b Maru	14
R.E.Morris *	c Parks b Shine	61
M.J.Kilborn	c Smith C.L. b Turner	17
G.J.Turner	c & b Smith C.L.	59
M.A.Crawley	c & b Maru	9
P.D.Lunn	c Maru b Turner	16
W.M.van der Merwe	c Smith C.L. b Maru	84
M.J.Russell	b Shine	4
H.Davies	c Nicholas b Smith C.L.	24
J.McGrady +	c Gower b Maru	14
A.Winchester	not out	0
Extras	(b 4,lb 12,nb 6)	22
TOTAL		324

OXFORD UNIV	O	M	R	W	O	M	R	W
van der Merwe	22	5	77	0	6	2	9	0
Winchester	10	0	50	0	3	0	31	0
Crawley	20	1	100	1	3	0	16	0
Turner	32	4	148	2	23	5	61	2
Lunn	13	2	49	1				
Davies					23	4	93	3

HAMPSHIRE	O	M	R	W	O	M	R	W
Shine	27	13	51	2				
Joseph	10	2	28	0				
Maru	46.3	16	89	4				
Turner	40	11	98	2				
Nicholas	7	2	21	0				
Smith C.L.	6	1	21	2				

FALL OF WICKETS

	HAM	OXF	HAM	OXF
1st	264	39	57	
2nd	275	80	82	
3rd	383	104	86	
4th	427	142	125	
5th		171	164	
6th		197		
7th		243		
8th		302		
9th		324		
10th		324		

CAMBRIDGE UNIV vs. MIDDLESEX

at Fenner's on 3rd, 4th, 5th May 1990
Toss : Middlesex. Umpires : V.A.Holder and M.J.Kitchen
Match drawn

MIDDLESEX

M.A.Roseberry	st Turner b Buzza	85	(9) not out	2	
J.C.Pooley	b Pyman	8	b Jenkins	13	
M.W.Gatting *	c Morris b Buzza	19			
M.R.Ramprakash	not out	118	(8) not out	13	
K.R.Brown	b Jenkins	42			
R.O.Butcher	not out	29	(1) c Buzza b Jenkins	32	
P.Farbrace +			(3) c Pyman b Buzza	79	
S.P.Hughes			(4) b Jenkins	2	
J.E.Emburey			(5) lbw b Jenkins	4	
N.F.Williams			(6) c Turner b Jenkins	20	
P.C.R.Tufnell			(7) c James b Buzza	36	
Extras	(lb 7,w 5,nb 7)	19	(lb 2,nb 1)	3	
TOTAL	(for 4 wkts dec)	320	(for 7 wkts dec)	204	

CAMBRIDGE UNIV

S.P.James	c Butcher b Hughes	54	c Roseberry b Tufnell	46	
R.Heap	c Emburey b Williams	15	b Tufnell	23	
M.J.Lowrey	c Brown b Williams	6	(5) c Emburey b Tufnell	12	
J.C.M.Atkinson *	c Farbrace b Hughes	6	c Butcher b Brown	17	
M.J.Morris	lbw b Emburey	9	(6) not out	32	
G.B.A.Dyer	c Farbrace b Williams	23	(7) not out	9	
R.J.Turner +	c Tufnell b Emburey	26	(3) c Pooley b Roseberry	34	
R.A.Pyman	c Brown b Emburey	10			
D.H.Shufflebotham	c Brown b Tufnell	1			
A.J.Buzza	c Gatting b Emburey	0			
R.H.J.Jenkins	not out	0			
Extras	(b 4,lb 5,w 3)	12	(b 4,lb 17,w 6)	27	
TOTAL		162	(for 5 wkts)	200	

CAMBRIDGE U	O	M	R	W	O	M	R	W
Jenkins	20	1	96	1	26	3	100	5
Pyman	20	8	54	1	7	2	31	0
Shufflebotham	14	3	50	0	9	1	17	0
Buzza	26	5	55	2	11.1	2	25	2
Lowrey	16	1	58	0	9	2	29	0

MIDDLESEX	O	M	R	W	O	M	R	W
Williams	18	5	35	3	1	0	5	0
Hughes	20	5	30	2	4	2	11	0
Emburey	26.3	13	33	4	14	8	13	0
Tufnell	17	6	36	1	27	11	57	3
Gatting	8	3	19	0	3	0	6	0
Ramprakash					7	2	17	0
Brown					10	2	16	1
Roseberry					11	2	41	1
Pooley					2	0	11	0
Butcher					2	0	2	0

FALL OF WICKETS

	MID	CAM	MID	CAM
1st	26	24	35	43
2nd	76	30	52	91
3rd	166	38	58	126
4th	264	61	70	138
5th		95	132	157
6th		135	183	
7th		153	200	
8th		162		
9th		162		
10th		162		

REFUGE ASSURANCE LEAGUE

KENT vs. MIDDLESEX

at Folkestone on 6th May 1990
Toss : Middlesex. Umpires : D.J.Constant and N.T.Plews
Middlesex won by 6 wickets. (Kent 0 pts Middlesex 4 pts)

KENT

Batsman	Dismissal	Runs
S.G.Hinks	run out	86
N.R.Taylor	b Emburey	28
T.R.Ward	lbw b Taylor	24
C.S.Cowdrey *	c Roseberry b Cowans	20
G.R.Cowdrey	st Downton b Gatting	28
S.A.Marsh +	st Downton b Emburey	18
R.M.Ellison	not out	11
T.A.Merrick	not out	1
C.Penn		
M.A.Ealham		
R.P.Davis		
Extras	(lb 8)	8
TOTAL	(40 overs)(for 6 wkts)	224

MIDDLESEX

Batsman	Dismissal	Runs
D.L.Haynes	c Cowdrey G.R. b Davis	67
M.A.Roseberry	lbw b Ealham	52
M.R.Ramprakash	c Ealham b Ellison	32
K.R.Brown	c Marsh b Ward	20
R.O.Butcher	not out	27
P.R.Downton +	not out	9
M.W.Gatting *		
J.E.Emburey		
N.F.Williams		
N.R.Taylor		
N.G.Cowans		
Extras	(lb 15,w 3)	18
TOTAL	(37.5 overs)(for 4 wkts)	225

MIDDLESEX	O	M	R	W		FALL OF	WICKETS
						KEN	MID
Williams	7	0	51	0	1st	72	122
Cowans	8	2	29	1	2nd	129	134
Taylor	8	0	47	1	3rd	155	180
Emburey	8	1	36	2	4th	170	204
Gatting	7	0	41	1	5th	202	
Haynes	2	0	12	0	6th	222	
					7th		
KENT	O	M	R	W	8th		
Penn	3	0	22	0	9th		
Merrick	7.5	0	39	0	10th		
Ellison	7	0	32	1			
Davis	8	0	29	1			
Ealham	7	0	47	1			
Cowdrey C.S.	3	0	24	0			
Ward	2	0	17	1			

WORCESTERSHIRE vs. NOTTS

at Worcester on 6th May 1990
Toss : Notts. Umpires : B.Leadbeater and K.J.Lyons
Worcestershire won by 61 runs. (Worcs 4 pts Notts 0 pts)

WORCESTERSHIRE

Batsman	Dismissal	Runs
T.S.Curtis	lbw b Pick	73
R.K.Illingworth	c French b Cooper	3
G.A.Hick	not out	114
D.B.D'Oliveira	b Stephenson	6
P.A.Neale *	b Saxelby	11
S.R.Lampitt	not out	4
D.A.Leatherdale		
P.J.Newport		
N.V.Radford		
S.R.Bevins +		
S.M.McEwan		
Extras	(lb 6,w 1,nb 1)	10
TOTAL	(40 overs)(for 4 wkts)	221

NOTTINGHAMSHIRE

Batsman	Dismissal	Runs
B.C.Broad	c Bevins b Newport	0
P.Pollard	c Leatherdale b Lampitt	13
R.T.Robinson *	run out	0
P.Johnson	c Bevins b McEwan	58
D.W.Randall	c Hick b Radford	12
F.D.Stephenson	c Bevins b McEwan	3
B.N.French +	c Illingworth b Newport	9
E.E.Hemmings	st Bevins b Illingworth	24
K.E.Cooper	c Hick b Newport	4
R.A.Pick	b Lampitt	12
K.Saxelby	not out	6
Extras	(lb 13,w 6)	19
TOTAL	(39.2 overs)	160

NOTTS	O	M	R	W		FALL OF	WICKETS
						WOR	NOT
Stephenson	8	1	41	1	1st	19	0
Cooper	8	1	32	1	2nd	161	1
Saxelby	8	0	54	1	3rd	182	35
Pick	8	0	47	1	4th	217	66
Hemmings	8	0	41	0	5th		76
					6th		99
WORCS	O	M	R	W	7th		115
Newport	8	0	37	3	8th		129
McEwan	8	0	32	2	9th		138
Lampitt	7.2	0	22	2	10th		160
Radford	8	0	30	1			
Illingworth	8	0	26	1			

WARWICKSHIRE vs. YORKSHIRE

at Edgbaston on 6th May 1990
Toss : Yorkshire. Umpires : R.Palmer and P.B.Wight
Warwicks won by 8 wickets. (Warwicks 4 pts Yorks 0 pts)

YORKSHIRE

Batsman	Dismissal	Runs
S.A.Kellett	b Reeve	21
A.A.Metcalfe *	b Moody	56
R.J.Blakey +	b Reeve	9
P.E.Robinson	c Reeve b Booth	22
D.Byas	run out	7
C.White	not out	30
P.Carrick	c Munton b Reeve	22
P.J.Hartley	not out	3
P.W.Jarvis		
D.Gough		
S.D.Fletcher		
Extras	(lb 8,w 7)	15
TOTAL	(40 overs)(for 6 wkts)	185

WARWICKSHIRE

Batsman	Dismissal	Runs
A.I.Kallicharran	c Fletcher b Carrick	65
Asif Din	b Byas	40
T.M.Moody	not out	51
G.W.Humpage +	not out	16
D.A.Reeve		
T.A.Lloyd *		
R.G.Twose		
N.M.K.Smith		
P.A.Booth		
G.C.Small		
T.A.Munton		
Extras	(lb 13,w 3,nb 1)	17
TOTAL	(37.1 overs)(for 2 wkts)	189

WARWICKS	O	M	R	W		FALL OF	WICKETS
						YOR	WAR
Small	8	0	41	0			
Munton	8	2	23	0	1st	47	73
Reeve	8	1	29	3	2nd	62	140
Booth	8	0	46	1	3rd	96	
Moody	8	0	38	1	4th	116	
					5th	129	
YORKSHIRE	O	M	R	W	6th	171	
Jarvis	8	1	21	0	7th		
Fletcher	5.1	0	27	0	8th		
Hartley	4	0	16	0	9th		
Gough	3	0	20	0	10th		
Carrick	7	0	39	1			
Byas	5	0	27	1			
White	5	0	26	0			

SURREY vs. LANCASHIRE

at The Oval on 6th May 1990
Toss : Lancashire. Umpires : B.Dudleston and A.A.Jones
Lancashire won by 7 wickets. (Surrey 0 pts Lancashire 4 pts)

SURREY

Batsman	Dismissal	Runs
A.J.Stewart	c Atherton b DeFreitas	125
G.S.Clinton	c Fairbrother b DeFreitas	26
M.A.Lynch	c Mendis b Watkinson	58
G.P.Thorpe	c Allott b DeFreitas	11
D.M.Ward +	not out	17
I.A.Greig *	not out	21
K.T.Medlycott		
M.A.Feltham		
C.K.Bullen		
M.P.Bicknell		
A.J.Murphy		
Extras	(b 1,lb 6,w 1,nb 1)	9
TOTAL	(39 overs)(for 4 wkts)	267

LANCASHIRE

Batsman	Dismissal	Runs
G.D.Mendis	c & b Medlycott	45
G.Fowler +	c & b Bicknell	84
M.A.Atherton	not out	76
N.H.Fairbrother	c Stewart b Bicknell	51
M.Watkinson	not out	3
G.D.Lloyd		
P.A.J.DeFreitas		
D.P.Hughes *		
I.D.Austin		
P.J.W.Allott		
B.P.Patterson		
Extras	(lb 4,w 5)	9
TOTAL	(37.1 overs)(for 3 wkts)	268

LANCASHIRE	O	M	R	W		FALL OF	WICKETS
						SUR	LAN
Patterson	8	0	55	0			
Allott	8	0	40	0	1st	75	79
DeFreitas	8	0	48	3	2nd	190	194
Austin	7	0	56	0	3rd	213	265
Watkinson	8	0	61	1	4th	232	
					5th		
SURREY	O	M	R	W	6th		
Bicknell	7	0	48	2	7th		
Murphy	7.1	0	63	0	8th		
Bullen	8	0	46	0	9th		
Medlycott	8	0	39	1	10th		
Lynch	4	0	40	0			
Feltham	3	0	28	0			

LEICESTERSHIRE vs. ESSEX

at Leicester on 6th May 1990
Toss : Essex. Umpires : K.E.Palmer and D.R.Shepherd
Leicestershire won by 5 wickets. (Leics 4 pts Essex 0 pts)

ESSEX

Batsman	Dismissal	Runs
G.A.Gooch *	c Nixon b Mullally	65
B.R.Hardie	c Potter b Mullally	2
M.E.Waugh	st Nixon b Benson	84
P.J.Prichard	c Boon b Gidley	8
J.P.Stephenson	not out	38
N.A.Foster	c Potter b Agnew	8
M.A.Garnham +	c Briers b Lewis	4
A.W.Lilley	c Boon b Agnew	2
T.D.Topley	not out	1
M.C.Ilott		
J.H.Childs		
Extras	(b 1,lb 4,w 5,nb 1)	11
TOTAL	(40 overs)(for 7 wkts)	223

LEICESTERSHIRE

Batsman	Dismissal	Runs
T.J.Boon	b Ilott	56
N.E.Briers *	c Garnham b Foster	5
J.J.Whitaker	c Topley b Gooch	44
C.C.Lewis	not out	93
L.Potter	run out	4
J.D.R.Benson	b Ilott	12
M.I.Gidley	not out	6
P.A.Nixon +		
A.D.Mullally		
J.P.Agnew		
L.B.Taylor		
Extras	(lb 3,w 2)	5
TOTAL	(38.3 overs)(for 5 wkts)	225

LEICS	O	M	R	W		FALL OF	WICKETS
						ESS	LEI
Lewis	8	0	42	1			
Mullally	8	0	32	2	1st	5	14
Agnew	8	0	39	2	2nd	131	78
Taylor	8	0	41	0	3rd	140	131
Gidley	6	0	51	1	4th	186	157
Benson	2	0	13	1	5th	197	186
					6th	214	
ESSEX	O	M	R	W	7th	220	
Foster	7.3	0	37	1	8th		
Ilott	8	0	41	2	9th		
Topley	8	0	49	0	10th		
Childs	8	0	29	0			
Gooch	7	0	66	1			

NORTHANTS vs. DERBYSHIRE

at Northampton on 6th May 1990
Toss : Derbyshire. Umpires : J.H.Harris and R.A.White
Derbys won by 4 wickets. (Northants 0 pts Derbys 4 pts)

NORTHANTS

Batsman	Dismissal	Runs
W.Larkins *	c Adams b Malcolm	13
A.Fordham	c Kuiper b Malcolm	0
R.J.Bailey	c Bowler b Kuiper	29
D.J.Capel	c Bowler b Warner	39
N.A.Felton	run out	19
D.J.Wild	not out	48
W.M.Noon +	run out	1
J.G.Thomas	c Barnett b Warner	9
J.W.Govan	c Adams b Malcolm	5
W.W.Davis	not out	4
M.A.Robinson		
Extras	(b 1,lb 6,w 6)	13
TOTAL	(40 overs)(for 8 wkts)	180

DERBYSHIRE

Batsman	Dismissal	Runs
K.J.Barnett *	b Robinson	23
P.D.Bowler +	b Thomas	30
J.E.Morris	b Govan	12
A.P.Kuiper	not out	62
C.J.Adams	b Robinson	5
B.Roberts	c Govan b Capel	15
S.C.Goldsmith	run out	13
A.E.Warner	not out	13
S.J.Base		
D.E.Malcolm		
O.H.Mortensen		
Extras	(lb 4,w 3,nb 1)	8
TOTAL	(38.5 overs)(for 6 wkts)	181

DERBYSHIRE	O	M	R	W		FALL OF	WICKETS
						NOR	DER
Mortensen	8	1	19	0			
Malcolm	8	1	34	3	1st	2	57
Base	8	0	40	0	2nd	13	57
Warner	8	0	34	2	3rd	76	79
Kuiper	8	0	46	1	4th	88	92
					5th	123	122
NORTHANTS	O	M	R	W	6th	126	152
Capel	7.5	0	46	1	7th	155	
Davis	7	1	42	0	8th	175	
Thomas	8	1	39	1	9th		
Robinson	8	1	23	2	10th		
Govan	8	0	27	1			

REFUGE ASS. LEAGUE

BENSON & HEDGES CUP

HAMPSHIRE vs. GLOUCESTERSHIRE

at Southampton on 6th May 1990
Toss : Gloucestershire. Umpires : H.D.Bird and
D.S.Thompsett. (Hampshire 2 pts Gloucestershire 2 pts)
No result

HAMPSHIRE

V.P.Terry	c Lloyds b Walsh	6
D.I.Gower	c Lloyds b Walsh	0
R.A.Smith	c Ball b Bainbridge	85
C.L.Smith	run out	89
M.C.J.Nicholas *	lbw b Bainbridge	15
R.J.Scott	c Ball b Walsh	12
M.D.Marshall	not out	6
J.R.Ayling	not out	2
R.J.Parks +		
R.J.Maru		
C.A.Connor		
Extras	(b 1,lb 3,w 3,nb 2)	9
TOTAL	(40 overs)(for 6 wkts)	224

GLOUCESTERSHIRE

A.J.Wright *		
P.W.Romaines		
P.Bainbridge		
C.W.J.Athey		
K.M.Curran		
J.W.Lloyds		
M.W.Alleyne		
R.C.Russell +		
C.A.Walsh		
E.T.Milburn		
M.C.J.Ball		
Extras		
TOTAL		

GLOUCS	O	M	R	W	FALL OF WICKETS		
						HAM	GLO
Walsh	8	1	30	3	1st	1	
Curran	8	0	41	0	2nd	21	
Alleyne	7	0	41	0	3rd	165	
Milburn	4	0	25	0	4th	201	
Ball	6	0	31	0	5th	209	
Bainbridge	7	0	52	2	6th	221	
					7th		
HAMPSHIRE	O	M	R	W	8th		
					9th		
					10th		

HEADLINES

6th May

- Derbyshire and Middlesex headed the Refuge table after both achieving their third successive wins. Adrian Kuiper hit 62* to take Derbyshire to victory over Northamptonshire, while Desmond Haynes and Mike Roseberry enjoyed an opening stand of 112 in Middlesex's success over Kent.

- There was no respite for the bowlers at The Oval where Surrey and Lancashire shared 535 runs. Alec Stewart's 125 was a Sunday best but Mike Atherton (76 - another career best) and Neil Fairbrother (51 in 29 balls) helped themselves to runs again as Lancashire coasted to victory.

- Graham Gooch completed 6,000 Sunday runs in Essex's match against Leicestershire at Chelmsford but the home side came off second best after Chris Lewis hit 93* in 61 balls with 5 sixes and 7 fours.

- Graeme Hick made his highest score in the Sunday League as Worcestershire beat Notts and Dermot Reeve returned the day's best bowling figures (3 for 29) as Warwickshire defeated Yorkshire.

SOMERSET vs. MINOR COUNTIES

at Taunton on 8th May 1990
Toss : Minor Counties. Umpires : B.Hassan and K.E.Palmer
Somerset won by 6 wickets. (Somerset 2 pts Min Counties 0 pts)

MINOR COUNTIES

G.K.Brown	c Tavare b Rose	4
M.J.Roberts	lbw b Jones	7
N.A.Folland	lbw b Hayhurst	16
S.G.Plumb *	st Burns b Swallow	63
T.A.Lester	c Burns b Lefebvre	14
S.Greensword	c Cook b Swallow	10
D.R.Thomas	not out	49
A.R.Fothergill +	not out	45
N.R.Taylor		
R.C.Green		
A.J.Mack		
Extras	(b 5,lb 11,w 16)	32
TOTAL	(55 overs)(for 6 wkts)	240

SOMERSET

S.J.Cook	b Mack	27
P.M.Roebuck	c Fothergill b Taylor	13
A.N.Hayhurst	lbw b Taylor	76
C.J.Tavare *	c Fothergill b Mack	29
R.J.Harden	not out	53
G.D.Rose	not out	26
N.D.Burns +		
I.G.Swallow		
R.P.Lefebvre		
A.N.Jones		
J.C.Hallett		
Extras	(lb 6,w 6,nb 5)	17
TOTAL	(51.4 overs)(for 4 wkts)	241

SOMERSET	O	M	R	W	FALL OF WICKETS		
						MIN	SOM
Jones	11	1	63	1	1st	9	41
Rose	11	2	31	1	2nd	17	45
Hallett	2	0	18	0	3rd	51	107
Lefebvre	11	0	44	1	4th	77	192
Hayhurst	11	0	36	1	5th	102	
Swallow	9	0	32	2	6th	160	
					7th		
MIN COUNTIES	O	M	R	W	8th		
Taylor	11	2	50	2	9th		
Green	10.4	0	57	0	10th		
Mack	9	0	22	2			
Thomas	5	0	29	0			
Greensword	7	0	34	0			
Plumb	9	0	43	0			

Man of the match: A.N.Hayhurst

NORTHANTS vs. ESSEX

at Northampton on 8th May 1990
Toss : Essex. Umpires : J.H.Harris and R.A.White
Essex won by 8 wickets. (Northants 0 pts Essex 2 pts)

NORTHANTS

W.Larkins *	lbw b Pringle	20
A.Fordham	c Topley b Foster	9
G.Cook	b Childs	28
R.J.Bailey	c Prichard b Stephenson	29
D.J.Capel	c Waugh b Stephenson	12
D.J.Wild	b Stephenson	0
D.Ripley +	c Garnham b Foster	27
J.G.Thomas	c Waugh b Pringle	3
J.W.Govan	c Gooch b Foster	11
C.E.L.Ambrose	run out	12
M.A.Robinson	not out	0
Extras	(lb 10,w 6)	16
TOTAL	(53.3 overs)	167

ESSEX

G.A.Gooch *	not out	94
B.R.Hardie	c Larkins b Robinson	27
P.J.Prichard	c Larkins b Ambrose	26
M.E.Waugh	not out	8
J.P.Stephenson		
M.A.Garnham +		
D.R.Pringle		
N.A.Foster		
T.D.Topley		
M.C.Ilott		
J.H.Childs		
Extras	(b 1,lb 2,w 5,nb 5)	13
TOTAL	(38.3 overs)(for 2 wkts)	168

ESSEX	O	M	R	W	FALL OF WICKETS		
						NOR	ESS
Foster	10	2	18	3	1st	17	82
Ilott	9	1	39	0	2nd	43	151
Topley	11	1	25	0	3rd	79	
Pringle	10.3	1	28	2	4th	100	
Childs	6	0	25	1	5th	107	
Stephenson	7	0	22	3	6th	108	
					7th	116	
NORTHANTS	O	M	R	W	8th	146	
Ambrose	11	0	35	1	9th	161	
Capel	6	0	24	0	10th	167	
Robinson	7.3	0	35	1			
Thomas	8	0	48	0			
Govan	1	0	3	0			
Wild	5	2	20	0			

Man of the match: G.A.Gooch

KENT vs. WARWICKSHIRE

at Canterbury on 8th May 1990
Toss : Kent. Umpires : D.J.Constant and N.T.Plews
Kent won by 70 runs. (Kent 2 pts Warwickshire 0 pts)

KENT

S.G.Hinks	c Humpage b Small	2
M.R.Benson	c Reeve b Smith	85
N.R.Taylor	b Small	90
T.R.Ward	lbw b Small	1
C.S.Cowdrey	c Humpage b Reeve	64
M.V.Fleming	c Twose b Small	0
S.A.Marsh +	c & b Munton	9
M.A.Ealham	run out	0
T.A.Merrick	not out	1
A.P.Igglesden	not out	0
R.P.Davis		
Extras	(b 2,lb 4,w 6,nb 1)	13
TOTAL	(55 overs)(for 8 wkts)	265

WARWICKSHIRE

T.A.Lloyd *	lbw b Cowdrey	72
Asif Din	c Marsh b Ealham	9
T.M.Moody	c Ealham b Davis	33
A.I.Kallicharran	c sub b Ealham	11
G.W.Humpage +	lbw b Merrick	1
D.A.Reeve	c Hinks b Cowdrey	12
N.M.K.Smith	c sub b Davis	11
R.G.Twose	run out	2
P.A.Booth	c Merrick b Cowdrey	5
G.C.Small	lbw b Merrick	22
T.A.Munton	not out	1
Extras	(b 6,lb 8,w 2)	16
TOTAL	(44.4 overs)	195

WARWICKS	O	M	R	W	FALL OF WICKETS		
						KEN	WAR
Small	11	0	38	4	1st	14	26
Munton	10	2	39	1	2nd	142	78
Moody	9	0	50	0	3rd	147	111
Reeve	9	0	52	1	4th	235	120
Smith	10	0	43	1	5th	235	150
Booth	4	0	33	0	6th	259	152
Twose	2	0	4	0	7th	263	153
					8th	264	163
KENT	O	M	R	W	9th		186
Merrick	8.4	2	30	2	10th		195
Igglesden	5	0	31	0			
Ealham	8	0	37	2			
Davis	11	0	40	2			
Fleming	6	1	14	0			
Cowdrey	6	1	29	3			

Man of the match: C.S.Cowdrey

WORCESTERSHIRE vs. GLAMORGAN

at Worcester on 8th May 1990
Toss : Glamorgan. Umpires : H.D.Bird and P.B.Wight
Glamorgan won by 16 runs. (Worcs 0 pts Glamorgan 2 pts)

GLAMORGAN

A.R.Butcher *	b Hick	57
H.Morris	c D'Oliveira b Lampitt	57
M.P.Maynard	b Radford	36
I.V.A.Richards	c & b Radford	25
G.C.Holmes	c & b Newport	8
I.Smith	c Radford b Dilley	21
N.G.Cowley	c Lampitt b Dilley	11
C.P.Metson +	not out	14
S.L.Watkin	not out	1
S.R.Barwick		
M.Frost		
Extras	(lb 18,w 4,nb 3)	25
TOTAL	(55 overs)(for 7 wkts)	255

WORCESTERSHIRE

T.S.Curtis	c Metson b Cowley	36
G.J.Lord	c Morris b Frost	0
G.A.Hick	b Frost	0
D.B.D'Oliveira	c Smith b Frost	57
P.A.Neale *	b Barwick	31
S.R.Lampitt	c Metson b Barwick	41
R.K.Illingworth	c Morris b Frost	6
P.J.Newport	c Butcher b Barwick	4
N.V.Radford	c Holmes b Barwick	40
G.R.Dilley	not out	5
S.R.Bevins +	not out	0
Extras	(lb 10,w 9)	19
TOTAL	(55 overs)(for 9 wkts)	239

WORCS	O	M	R	W	FALL OF WICKETS		
						GLA	WOR
Dilley	11	2	45	2	1st	121	15
Radford	11	0	52	2	2nd	134	17
Lampitt	6	0	43	1	3rd	176	77
Newport	11	1	28	1	4th	185	112
Illingworth	8	0	33	0	5th	223	152
Hick	8	0	36	1	6th	229	170
					7th	248	175
GLAMORGAN	O	M	R	W	8th		229
Barwick	11	0	67	4	9th		239
Watkin	11	1	45	0	10th		
Frost	11	3	25	4			
Cowley	11	0	33	1			
Richards	11	0	59	0			

Man of the match: M.Frost

BENSON & HEDGES CUP

SUSSEX vs. MIDDLESEX

at Hove on 8th May 1990
Toss : Middlesex. Umpires : J.D.Bond and J.H.Hampshire
Middlesex won on faster scoring rate over first 30 overs.
(Sussex 0 pts Middlesex 2 pts)

SUSSEX

N.J.Lenham	c Emburey b Williams	3
P.Moores +	b Haynes	76
P.W.G.Parker *	c Downton b Gatting	7
A.P.Wells	c Ramprakash b Williams	74
M.P.Speight	c Roseberry b Hughes	43
C.M.Wells	c Butcher b Emburey	59
I.J.Gould	not out	12
A.I.C.Dodemaide		
J.A.North		
A.R.Clarke		
A.R.Hansford		
Extras	(b 1,lb 2,w 1,nb 4)	8
TOTAL	(55 overs)(for 6 wkts)	282

MIDDLESEX

D.L.Haynes	c Wells A.P. b Hansford	131
M.A.Roseberry	c Gould b Wells C.M.	1
M.W.Gatting *	c Parker b Hansford	54
M.R.Ramprakash	c Moores b Dodemaide	44
K.R.Brown	b North	12
R.O.Butcher	b Dodemaide	5
P.R.Downton	not out	15
J.E.Emburey +	not out	4
N.F.Williams		
S.P.Hughes		
N.G.Cowans		
Extras	(b 1,lb 11,w 2,nb 2)	16
TOTAL	(55 overs)(for 6 wkts)	282

MIDDLESEX	O	M	R	W	FALL OF WICKETS		
						SUS	MID
Cowans	11	0	66	0			
Williams	10	1	45	2	1st	39	14
Gatting	8	0	41	1	2nd	64	110
Hughes	11	0	47	1	3rd	98	210
Emburey	11	0	57	1	4th	197	229
Haynes	4	0	23	1	5th	249	254
					6th	282	269
SUSSEX	O	M	R	W	7th		
Dodemaide	11	0	36	2	8th		
Wells C.M.	11	2	45	1	9th		
North	8	0	48	1	10th		
Hansford	11	0	55	2			
Clarke	11	0	70	0			
Lenham	3	0	16	0			

Man of the match: D.L.Haynes

LANCASHIRE vs. HAMPSHIRE

at Old Trafford on 8th, 9th May 1990
Toss : Hampshire. Umpires : D.O.Oslear and
D.S.Thompsett
No result. (The original match was abandoned and an 18-over a side replacement contest started.) (Lancashire 1 pt Hampshire 1 pt)

LANCASHIRE

G.D.Mendis	c Parks b Connor	9
G.Fowler	c Nicholas b Connor	1
N.H.Fairbrother	c Terry b Ayling	8
M.A.Atherton	c Smith C.L. b Ayling	2
M.Watkinson	st Parks b Maru	40
P.A.J.DeFreitas	not out	75
I.D.Austin	not out	9
W.K.Hegg +		
D.P.Hughes *		
P.J.W.Allott		
B.P.Patterson		
Extras	(lb 1,w 1,nb 1)	3
TOTAL	(18 overs)(for 5 wkts)	147

HAMPSHIRE

D.I.Gower	not out	44
V.P.Terry	c Fairbrother b DeFreitas	7
R.A.Smith	not out	45
C.L.Smith		
M.C.J.Nicholas *		
J.R.Ayling		
M.D.Marshall		
R.J.Parks +		
R.J.Maru		
K.J.Shine		
C.A.Connor		
Extras	(w 2,nb 1)	3
TOTAL	(12 overs)(for 1 wkt)	99

HAMPSHIRE	O	M	R	W	FALL OF WICKETS		
						LAN	HAM
Connor	3	0	26	2	1st	4	24
Shine	4	0	13	0			
Ayling	3	0	22	2	2nd	20	
Marshall	4	0	45	0	3rd	22	
Maru	4	0	40	1	4th	23	
					5th	106	
LANCASHIRE	O	M	R	W	6th		
Patterson	2	0	10	0	7th		
Allott	3	0	29	0	8th		
DeFreitas	2	0	14	1	9th		
Austin	3	0	26	0	10th		
Watkinson	2	0	20	0			

SCOTLAND vs. NOTTINGHAMSHIRE

at Glasgow on 8th, 9th May 1990
Toss : Notts. Umpires : B.Leadbeater and K.J.Lyons
Nottinghamshire won by 4 wickets. (Scot 0 pts Notts 2 pts)

SCOTLAND

I.L.Philip	lbw b Pick	16
C.G.Greenidge	c Cooper b Stephenson	1
B.M.W.Patterson	run out	22
R.G.Swan	c Pick b Saxelby	53
M.J.Smith	lbw b Saxelby	7
O.Henry	not out	62
D.R.Brown	b Stephenson	24
D.J.Haggo +	not out	2
D.Cowan		
J.D.Moir		
C.L.Parfitt		
Extras	(b 1,lb 10,w 9,nb 1)	21
TOTAL	(55 overs)(for 6 wkts)	208

NOTTINGHAMSHIRE

B.C.Broad	b Cowan	14
P.Pollard	c Greenidge b Moir	5
R.T.Robinson *	not out	70
P.Johnson	b Parfitt	52
D.W.Randall	lbw b Parfitt	7
F.D.Stephenson	b Parfitt	5
B.N.French +	c Brown b Parfitt	25
K.E.Cooper	not out	11
R.A.Pick		
K.Saxelby		
J.A.Afford		
Extras	(b 3,lb 5,w 14)	22
TOTAL	(54.2 overs)(for 6 wkts)	211

NOTTS	O	M	R	W	FALL OF WICKETS		
						SCO	NOT
Stephenson	11	0	49	2			
Cooper	11	1	33	0	1st	7	20
Pick	11	0	45	1	2nd	46	20
Saxelby	11	3	39	2	3rd	46	95
Afford	11	2	31	0	4th	61	114
					5th	151	133
SCOTLAND	O	M	R	W	6th	204	173
Cowan	10.2	0	51	1	7th		
Moir	11	2	43	1	8th		
Brown	11	0	43	0	9th		
Henry	1	0	5	0	10th		
Smith	10	0	45	0			
Parfitt	11	3	16	4			

Man of the match: R.T.Robinson

YORKSHIRE vs. COMBINED UNIV

at Headingley on 8th, 9th May 1990
Toss : Comb U. Umpires : J.C.Balderstone and B.J.Meyer
Combined U won by 2 wickets. (Yorks 0 pts Comb U 2 pts)

YORKSHIRE

M.D.Moxon *	run out	4
A.A.Metcalfe	c Boiling b Crawley	11
R.J.Blakey +	run out	65
S.A.Kellett	c Boiling b Smith	29
P.E.Robinson	c Tolley b van der Merwe	57
C.White	run out	1
P.Carrick	c James b Smith	8
A.Sidebottom	not out	9
P.J.Hartley	c Orrell b van der Merwe	0
P.W.Jarvis	not out	2
S.D.Fletcher		
Extras	(lb 9,w 2)	11
TOTAL	(55 overs)(for 8 wkts)	197

COMBINED UNIV

S.P.James	b Sidebottom	63
M.A.Crawley *	c Blakey b Jarvis	9
A.Dale	c Sidebottom b Hartley	16
C.M.Tolley	c Sidebottom b Hartley	6
J.C.M.Atkinson	lbw b Hartley	16
J.I.Longley	c Blakey b Jarvis	14
T.M.Orrell	run out	15
W.M.van der Merwe	run out	27
R.J.Turner +	not out	12
M.Smith	not out	4
J.Boiling		
Extras	(b 1,lb 11,w 3,nb 3)	18
TOTAL	(53.5 overs)(for 8 wkts)	200

COMBINED U	O	M	R	W	FALL OF WICKETS		
						YOR	COM
van der Merwe	11	3	34	2			
Tolley	11	3	38	0	1st	14	17
Crawley	11	2	21	1	2nd	17	50
Dale	8	1	38	0	3rd	76	65
Smith	11	0	46	2	4th	166	85
Boiling	3	0	11	0	5th	167	121
					6th	180	145
YORKSHIRE	O	M	R	W	7th	190	176
Jarvis	10	0	29	2	8th	190	195
Sidebottom	11	1	41	1	9th		
Fletcher	10.5	1	44	0	10th		
Hartley	11	2	34	3			
Carrick	11	0	40	0			

Man of the match: W.M.van der Merwe

BENSON & HEDGES CUP

WARWICKSHIRE vs. WORCS

at Edgbaston on 10th May 1990
Toss : Worcs. Umpires : D.O.Oslear and D.S.Thompsett
Worcs won by 32 runs. (Warwicks 0 pts Worcs 2 pts)

WORCESTERSHIRE

T.S.Curtis	c Lloyd b Benjamin	97
M.J.Weston	b Reeve	36
G.A.Hick	c Twose b Small	64
N.V.Radford	run out	31
D.B.D'Oliveira	c Benjamin b Small	3
P.A.Neale *	not out	5
S.R.Lampitt	not out	1
R.K.Illingworth		
P.J.Newport		
S.R.Bevins +		
G.R.Dilley		
Extras	(lb 13,w 5)	18
TOTAL	(55 overs)(for 5 wkts)	255

WARWICKSHIRE

T.A.Lloyd *	b Radford	8
Asif Din	c Bevins b Hick	37
T.M.Moody	lbw b Hick	41
A.I.Kallicharran	c Neale b Lampitt	32
G.W.Humpage +	st Bevins b Hick	6
D.A.Reeve	c Bevins b Radford	6
R.G.Twose	c Weston b Radford	17
N.M.K.Smith	not out	30
G.C.Small	c Radford b Illingworth	5
J.E.Benjamin	run out	20
T.A.Munton	c Lampitt b Dilley	0
Extras	(lb 12,w 7,nb 2)	21
TOTAL	(51.5 overs)	223

WARWICKS	O	M	R	W		FALL OF WICKETS	
						WOR	WAR
Small	11	1	36	2	1st	78	16
Benjamin	11	4	40	1	2nd	206	87
Moody	5	0	29	0	3rd	217	109
Munton	11	0	35	0	4th	239	120
Reeve	11	1	70	1	5th	250	136
Smith	5	0	20	0	6th		151
Twose	1	0	12	0	7th		166
WORCS	O	M	R	W	8th		173
Dilley	8.5	0	36	1	9th		219
Radford	9	0	41	3	10th		223
Newport	3	0	21	0			
Illingworth	9	0	42	1			
Hick	11	0	36	3			
Lampitt	11	0	35	1			

Man of the match: G.A.Hick

YORKSHIRE vs. LANCASHIRE

at Headingley on 10th May 1990
Toss : Yorkshire. Umpires : B.J.Meyer and R.A.White
Lancashire won by 5 wickets. (Yorks 0 pts Lancs 2 pts)

YORKSHIRE

M.D.Moxon *	c Hegg b Allott	9
S.A.Kellett	lbw b DeFreitas	22
R.J.Blakey	b Austin	2
A.A.Metcalfe	lbw b DeFreitas	28
P.E.Robinson	c Allott b DeFreitas	0
D.L.Bairstow +	c Hegg b Watkinson	9
P.Carrick	b Watkinson	3
A.Sidebottom	run out	2
P.J.Hartley	c Fowler b Watkinson	1
P.W.Jarvis	b Patterson	42
S.D.Fletcher	not out	15
Extras	(lb 5,w 3)	8
TOTAL	(53.1 overs)	141

LANCASHIRE

G.D.Mendis	run out	25
G.Fowler	c Jarvis b Fletcher	36
M.A.Atherton	lbw b Sidebottom	3
N.H.Fairbrother	lbw b Fletcher	12
M.Watkinson	not out	43
P.A.J.DeFreitas	b Jarvis	10
I.D.Austin	not out	0
W.K.Hegg +		
D.P.Hughes *		
P.J.W.Allott		
B.P.Patterson		
Extras	(b 1,lb 5,w 6,nb 3)	15
TOTAL	(36.1 overs)(for 5 wkts)	144

LANCASHIRE	O	M	R	W		FALL OF WICKETS	
						YOR	LAN
Allott	11	2	22	1	1st	22	49
Patterson	10.1	4	33	1	2nd	31	68
Austin	11	6	14	1	3rd	35	86
DeFreitas	10	1	36	3	4th	35	88
Watkinson	11	1	31	3	5th	49	138
YORKSHIRE	O	M	R	W	6th	68	
Jarvis	11	1	51	1	7th	77	
Sidebottom	7.1	0	35	1	8th	80	
Fletcher	9	3	23	2	9th	88	
Hartley	9	1	29	0	10th	141	

Man of the match: M.Watkinson

COMBINED UNIV vs. SURREY

at The Parks on 10th May 1990
Toss : Surrey. Umpires : B.Hassan and A.G.T.Whitehead
Surrey won by 6 wickets. (Combined U 0 pts Surrey 2 pts)

COMBINED UNIV

S.P.James	b Medlycott	59
M.A.Crawley *	c Lynch b Bicknell M.P.	9
A.Dale	c Clinton b Greig	40
J.C.M.Atkinson	c Bicknell M.P. b Bullen	9
C.M.Tolley	run out	14
W.M.van der Merwe	c Stewart b Medlycott	14
J.I.Longley	st Ward b Medlycott	9
T.M.Orrell	c Ward b Bicknell M.P.	0
R.J.Turner +	not out	25
M.Smith	not out	15
J.Boiling		
Extras	(b 8,lb 11,w 10,nb 5)	34
TOTAL	(55 overs)(for 8 wkts)	228

SURREY

D.J.Bicknell	st Turner b Crawley	32
G.S.Clinton	lbw b van der Merwe	61
A.J.Stewart	not out	84
M.A.Lynch	lbw b van der Merwe	1
G.P.Thorpe	run out	8
D.M.Ward +	not out	33
I.A.Greig *		
K.T.Medlycott		
C.K.Bullen		
M.P.Bicknell		
A.H.Gray		
Extras	(lb 3,w 4,nb 3)	10
TOTAL	(53.4 overs)(for 4 wkts)	229

SURREY	O	M	R	W		FALL OF WICKETS	
						COM	SUR
Gray	10	1	20	0	1st	17	56
Bicknell M.P.	11	2	27	2	2nd	120	137
Greig	10	0	51	1	3rd	133	149
Thorpe	2	0	15	0	4th	144	165
Bullen	11	1	48	1	5th	164	
Medlycott	11	0	48	3	6th	178	
COMBINED U	O	M	R	W	7th	179	
van der Merwe	10.4	0	50	2	8th	179	
Tolley	11	2	43	0	9th		
Crawley	11	1	34	1	10th		
Boiling	11	1	33	0			
Smith	8	0	53	0			
Dale	2	0	13	0			

Man of the match: A.J.Stewart

ESSEX vs LEICESTERSHIRE

at Chelmsford on 10th, 11th May 1990
No result. (The original match was abandoned and a replacement contest could not be started.)
(Essex 1pt Leicestershire 1pt)

MIDDLESEX vs. SOMERSET

at Lord's on 10th, 11th May 1990
Toss : Somerset. Umpires : J.D.Bond and J.H.Hampshire
Middlesex won by 8 runs. (Middlesex 2 pts Somerset 0 pts)

MIDDLESEX

D.L.Haynes	lbw b Mallender	28
M.A.Roseberry	b Mallender	30
M.W.Gatting *	run out	66
M.R.Ramprakash	c Burns b Hayhurst	4
K.R.Brown	b Hayhurst	31
R.O.Butcher	run out	3
P.R.Downton +	c Mallender b Jones	15
J.E.Emburey	c Roebuck b Rose	12
N.F.Williams	not out	22
N.G.Cowans	not out	10
S.P.Hughes		
Extras	(b 6,lb 15,w 5)	26
TOTAL	(55 overs)(for 8 wkts)	247

SOMERSET

S.J.Cook	c Downton b Cowans	6
P.M.Roebuck	c Butcher b Hughes	8
A.N.Hayhurst	c Emburey b Gatting	20
C.J.Tavare *	c Downton b Gatting	93
R.J.Harden	c Haynes b Williams	5
N.D.Burns +	c Butcher b Cowans	21
G.D.Rose	c sub b Williams	15
I.G.Swallow	b Emburey	0
R.P.Lefebvre	run out	37
A.N.Jones	c Brown b Gatting	7
N.A.Mallender	not out	3
Extras	(lb 11,w 13)	24
TOTAL	(54.2 overs)	239

SOMERSET	O	M	R	W		FALL OF WICKETS	
						MID	SOM
Jones	11	0	49	1	1st	56	13
Rose	11	4	47	1	2nd	95	17
Mallender	11	2	32	2	3rd	115	78
Lefebvre	11	1	46	0	4th	160	108
Swallow	1	0	9	0	5th	175	153
Hayhurst	10	0	43	2	6th	181	178
MIDDLESEX	O	M	R	W	7th	205	178
Hughes	11	0	39	1	8th	226	197
Cowans	11	0	35	2	9th		226
Williams	11	0	52	2	10th		239
Emburey	10.2	2	37	1			
Gatting	11	0	65	3			

Man of the match: : M.W.Gatting

NORTHANTS vs. SCOTLAND

at Northampton on 10th May 1990
Toss : Northants. Umpires : H.D.Bird and P.B.Wight
Scotland won by 2 runs. (Northants 0 pts Scotland 2 pts)

SCOTLAND

I.L.Philip +	lbw b Ambrose	95
C.G.Greenidge	lbw b Capel	32
B.M.W.Patterson	b Govan	8
R.G.Swan *	c Ripley b Ambrose	44
A.C.Storie	c Larkins b Robinson	8
A.B.Russell	b Robinson	0
D.R.Brown	c Capel	16
A.W.Bee	b Ambrose	0
D.Cowan	not out	4
J.D.Moir	not out	3
C.L.Parfitt		
Extras	(b 2,lb 7,w 12)	21
TOTAL	(55 overs)(for 8 wkts)	231

NORTHANTS

W.Larkins *	c Bee b Moir	111
A.Fordham	lbw b Moir	0
G.Cook	lbw b Cowan	6
R.J.Bailey	b Cowan	1
D.J.Capel	b Brown	0
D.J.Wild	c Parfitt b Brown	15
D.Ripley +	b Brown	9
J.G.Thomas	c Patterson b Cowan	32
J.W.Govan	run out	30
C.E.L.Ambrose	not out	11
M.A.Robinson	not out	0
Extras	(b 1,lb 7,w 4,nb 2)	14
TOTAL	(55 overs)(for 9 wkts)	229

NORTHANTS	O	M	R	W		FALL OF WICKETS	
						SCO	NOR
Ambrose	11	3	26	3	1st	54	11
Thomas	9	0	52	0	2nd	81	55
Robinson	10	0	47	2	3rd	166	57
Capel	11	0	29	2	4th	195	76
Govan	11	2	55	1	5th	195	105
Wild	3	0	13	0	6th	213	137
SCOTLAND	O	M	R	W	7th	213	159
Moir	11	0	51	2	8th	221	212
Bee	11	1	58	0	9th		226
Parfitt	11	1	26	0	10th		
Cowan	11	1	36	3			
Brown	11	2	50	3			

Man of the match: I.L.Philip

BENSON & HEDGES CUP

MINOR COUNTIES vs. DERBYSHIRE
at Wellington on 10th May 1990
Toss : Minor Counties. Umpires : P.J.Eele and K.E.Palmer
Derbys won by 43 runs. (Min Counties 0 pts Derbys 2 pts)

DERBYSHIRE
K.J.Barnett *	b Taylor	8
P.D.Bowler +	c Folland b Thomas	16
J.E.Morris	lbw b Mack	6
A.P.Kuiper	c Fothergill b Taylor	16
C.J.Adams	c Fothergill b Greensword	44
B.Roberts	c Plumb b Greensword	46
S.J.Base	lbw b Greensword	0
S.C.Goldsmith	not out	45
A.E.Warner	c Sharp b Mack	16
D.E.Malcolm	b Taylor	5
O.H.Mortensen	not out	2
Extras	(lb 6,w 3,nb 5)	14
TOTAL	(55 overs)(for 9 wkts)	218

MINOR COUNTIES
M.J.Roberts	lbw b Goldsmith	31
G.K.Brown	c Barnett b Warner	16
N.A.Folland	c Bowler b Goldsmith	25
S.Sharp	b Goldsmith	0
S.G.Plumb *	c Kuiper b Malcolm	16
S.Greensword	b Base	28
D.R.Thomas	b Warner	14
A.R.Fothergill +	b Base	3
N.R.Taylor	b Warner	3
R.C.Green	not out	5
A.J.Mack	b Base	6
Extras	(lb 16,w 7,nb 5)	28
TOTAL	(50.4 overs)	175

MIN COUNTIES	O	M	R	W	FALL OF WICKETS		
						DER	MIN
Taylor	10	0	52	3			
Mack	10	1	49	2	1st	9	43
Green	8	1	26	0	2nd	18	79
Thomas	11	3	24	1	3rd	42	79
Greensword	11	0	38	3	4th	74	99
Plumb	5	0	23	0	5th	131	115
					6th	134	146
DERBYSHIRE	O	M	R	W	7th	165	151
Mortensen	8	3	15	0	8th	192	164
Malcolm	8	1	22	1	9th	207	164
Warner	11	1	31	3	10th		175
Base	8.4	0	33	3			
Kuiper	5	0	20	0			
Goldsmith	10	0	38	3			

Man of the match: S.C.Goldsmith

KENT vs. GLOUCESTERSHIRE
at Canterbury on 10th, 11th May 1990
Toss : Kent. Umpires : B.Dudleston and J.H.Harris
No result. (The original match was abandoned and a
replacement 13-over a side contest started.) (Kent 1 pt
Gloucestershire 1 pt)

KENT
S.G.Hinks	c Bainbridge b Jarvis	3
T.R.Ward	not out	60
C.S.Cowdrey *	not out	67
M.R.Benson		
N.R.Taylor		
G.R.Cowdrey		
S.A.Marsh +		
M.V.Fleming		
T.A.Merrick		
C.Penn		
M.A.Ealham		
Extras	(lb 2,w 3,nb 3)	8
TOTAL	(10 overs)(for 1 wkt)	138

GLOUCESTERSHIRE
A.J.Wright *		
A.W.Stovold		
P.Bainbridge		
K.M.Curran		
C.W.J.Athey		
M.W.Alleyne		
R.C.Russell +		
J.W.Lloyds		
C.A.Walsh		
M.C.J.Ball		
K.B.S.Jarvis		
Extras		
TOTAL		

GLOUCS	O	M	R	W	FALL OF WICKETS		
						KEN	GLO
Bainbridge	2	0	21	0			
Jarvis	2	0	30	1	1st	7	
Ball	2	0	28	0	2nd		
Alleyne	1	0	22	0	3rd		
Curran	2	0	23	0	4th		
Walsh	1	0	12	0	5th		
					6th		
KENT	O	M	R	W	7th		
					8th		
					9th		
					10th		

HEADLINES

10th - 11th May

● Rain and the rulebook again intervened as two more matches were twice abandoned affairs.

● Gloucestershire's total of 268 for 7 and Tony Wright's 134 (his first B & H 100) counted for nothing after their first match with Kent at Canterbury was abandoned with the home side on 49 for 2 after 19 overs. Only 10 overs had been bowled when the replacement game (which counts in the record books) was also abandoned, ensuring that Worcestershire and Glamorgan qualified for the quarter-finals from Group A.

● Leicestershire reached 162 for 6 in 45 overs against Essex at Chelmsford when that match was abandoned but, although the replacement game did not even get under way, all performances were ruled invalid. Essex, heading Group D, gained a place in the quarter-finals.

● Lancashire qualified at the top of Group C after a convincing victory over Yorkshire at Headingley, while Middlesex's eight-run win over Somerset at Lord's guaranteed them a place in the quarter-finals from Group B.

● Scotland achieved only their second win in the competition by beating Northants by two runs at Northampton. Ian Philip hit a career best 95 and even Wayne Larkins's 111 could not save the home side from defeat.

● Steve Goldsmith produced B & H best batting and bowling performances as Derbyshire held off Minor Counties' challenge, while Graeme Hick's all-round contribution accounted for Warwickshire.

HAMPSHIRE vs. COMBINED UNIV
at Southampton on 12th May 1990
Toss : Hampshire. Umpires : R.Julien and D.R.Shepherd
Hampshire won by 99 runs. (Hants 2 pts Combined U 0 pts)

HAMPSHIRE
V.P.Terry	c van der Merwe b Smith	134
C.L.Smith	not out	154
D.I.Gower	c Smith b van der Merwe	0
R.A.Smith	not out	8
M.C.J.Nicholas *		
L.A.Joseph		
R.J.Parks +		
R.J.Maru		
K.J.Shine		
C.A.Connor		
P.J.Bakker		
Extras	(lb 1)	1
TOTAL	(55 overs)(for 2 wkts)	297

COMBINED UNIV
S.P.James	b Maru	46
N.V.Knight	c Parks b Bakker	16
A.Dale	c Maru b Connor	2
C.M.Tolley	c Smith C.L. b Connor	74
M.A.Crawley *	b Maru	26
J.C.M.Atkinson	lbw b Connor	0
J.I.Longley	run out	1
W.M.van der Merwe	run out	4
R.J.Turner +	b Maru	0
M.Smith	not out	7
J.Boiling	lbw b Nicholas	2
Extras	(lb 16,w 4)	20
TOTAL	(52 overs)	198

COMBINED U	O	M	R	W	FALL OF WICKETS		
						HAM	COM
Smith	11	2	49	1			
van der Merwe	11	0	53	1	1st	252	33
Crawley	11	1	40	0	2nd	252	38
Boiling	11	0	71	0	3rd		104
Dale	3	0	21	0	4th		171
Tolley	8	0	62	0	5th		172
					6th		179
HAMPSHIRE	O	M	R	W	7th		184
Shine	9	0	33	0	8th		184
Bakker	10	3	21	1	9th		190
Joseph	11	1	38	0	10th		198
Connor	9	0	40	3			
Maru	11	2	46	3			
Smith C.L.	1	0	2	0			
Nicholas	1	0	2	1			

Man of the match: C.L.Smith

SUSSEX vs. SOMERSET
at Hove on 12th May 1990
Toss : Somerset. Umpires : B.Dudleston and P.B.Wight
Somerset won by 107 runs. (Sussex 0 pts Somerset 2 pts)

SOMERSET
S.J.Cook	c Smith b Dodemaide	177
P.M.Roebuck	b Pigott	91
G.D.Rose	b Salisbury	14
C.J.Tavare *	b Pigott	5
R.J.Harden	b Dodemaide	15
A.N.Hayhurst	not out	5
N.D.Burns +	not out	6
I.G.Swallow		
R.P.Lefebvre		
N.A.Mallender		
A.N.Jones		
Extras	(b 1,lb 6,nb 1)	8
TOTAL	(55 overs)(for 5 wkts)	321

SUSSEX
D.M.Smith	c Burns b Jones	3
P.Moores +	c Mallender b Rose	13
P.W.G.Parker *	lbw b Jones	1
A.P.Wells	c Tavare b Swallow	23
M.P.Speight	b Rose	6
C.M.Wells	c Mallender b Rose	101
I.J.Gould	c Swallow b Hayhurst	6
A.I.C.Dodemaide	c Cook b Rose	32
A.C.S.Pigott	b Lefebvre	12
I.D.K.Salisbury	lbw b Lefebvre	2
A.R.Hansford	not out	2
Extras	(b 1,lb 4,w 8)	13
TOTAL	(46.2 overs)	214

SUSSEX	O	M	R	W	FALL OF WICKETS		
						SOM	SUS
Pigott	11	1	33	2			
Dodemaide	11	1	68	2	1st	194	17
Wells C.M.	11	0	71	0	2nd	222	20
Hansford	11	0	82	0	3rd	280	23
Salisbury	11	0	60	1	4th	309	40
					5th	310	87
SOMERSET	O	M	R	W	6th		96
Jones	7	2	22	2	7th		194
Rose	9	0	37	4	8th		206
Lefebvre	9.2	0	39	2	9th		211
Mallender	6	0	14	0	10th		214
Hayhurst	8	0	42	1			
Swallow	7	0	55	1			

Man of the match: S.J.Cook

BENSON & HEDGES CUP

DERBYSHIRE vs. MIDDLESEX

at Derby on 12th May 1990
Toss : Derbyshire. Umpires : H.D.Bird and R.Palmer
Derbyshire won by 8 runs. (Derbys 2 pts Middlesex 0 pts)

DERBYSHIRE

K.J.Barnett *	c Downton b Williams	22
P.D.Bowler +	c Haynes b Hughes	77
J.E.Morris	c Downton b Williams	0
A.P.Kuiper	not out	106
C.J.Adams	b Williams	26
A.E.Warner	b Emburey	7
B.Roberts	not out	5
S.C.Goldsmith		
S.J.Base		
D.E.Malcolm		
O.H.Mortensen		
Extras	(lb 1,w 4,nb 3)	8
TOTAL	(55 overs)(for 5 wkts)	251

MIDDLESEX

D.L.Haynes	c Mortensen b Kuiper	64
M.R.Ramprakash	c Bowler b Malcolm	7
M.W.Gatting *	b Malcolm	6
K.R.Brown	b Kuiper	34
R.O.Butcher	c Barnett b Warner	9
P.R.Downton +	c Adams b Base	40
J.E.Emburey	c Roberts b Kuiper	1
N.F.Williams	b Warner	28
S.P.Hughes	b Base	22
N.G.Cowans	b Malcolm	12
P.C.R.Tufnell	not out	7
Extras	(b 1,lb 7,w 4,nb 1)	13
TOTAL	(54.2 overs)	243

MIDDLESEX	O	M	R	W	FALL OF WICKETS		
						DER	MID
Williams	11	3	37	3			
Cowans	11	2	48	0	1st	29	16
Tufnell	7	0	36	0	2nd	29	26
Hughes	11	0	64	1	3rd	187	89
Emburey	9	0	41	1	4th	227	110
Gatting	6	0	24	0	5th	236	138
					6th		141
DERBYSHIRE	O	M	R	W	7th		186
Malcolm	11	0	55	3	8th		204
Mortensen	11	5	18	0	9th		230
Base	10.2	0	43	2	10th		243
Kuiper	11	0	71	3			
Warner	11	1	48	2			

Man of the match: A.P.Kuiper

SURREY vs. YORKSHIRE

at The Oval on 12th May 1990
Toss : Yorkshire. Umpires : J.H.Harris and D.O.Oslear
Yorkshire won by 6 wickets. (Surrey 0 pts Yorkshire 2 pts)

SURREY

D.J.Bicknell	lbw b Sidebottom	55
G.S.Clinton	run out	30
A.J.Stewart	b Fletcher	76
M.A.Lynch	c Bairstow b Jarvis	0
G.P.Thorpe	lbw b White	14
D.M.Ward +	not out	46
I.A.Greig *	c White b Jarvis	15
J.D.Robinson	not out	2
K.T.Medlycott		
M.P.Bicknell		
A.J.Murphy		
Extras	(b 5,lb 8,w 9,nb 2)	24
TOTAL	(55 overs)(for 6 wkts)	262

YORKSHIRE

S.A.Kellett	b Robinson	45
A.A.Metcalfe *	c Medlycott b Robinson	38
R.J.Blakey	c Bicknell D.J. b Bicknell M.P.	79
D.Byas	c Robinson b Bicknell M.P.	36
P.E.Robinson	not out	43
D.L.Bairstow +	not out	1
C.White		
A.Sidebottom		
P.W.Jarvis		
D.Gough		
S.D.Fletcher		
Extras	(b 6,lb 10,w 2,nb 3)	21
TOTAL	(53.5 overs)(for 4 wkts)	263

YORKSHIRE	O	M	R	W	FALL OF WICKETS		
						SUR	YOR
Jarvis	11	0	58	2			
Sidebottom	11	2	43	1	1st	71	82
Fletcher	11	0	53	1	2nd	116	104
Gough	6	0	27	0	3rd	117	178
Byas	7	0	37	0	4th	157	258
White	9	0	31	1	5th	222	-
					6th	242	
SURREY	O	M	R	W	7th		
Bicknell M.P.	10.5	0	53	2	8th		
Murphy	9	1	41	0	9th		
Greig	9	0	45	0	10th		
Robinson	11	0	41	2			
Medlycott	11	0	53	0			
Lynch	3	0	14	0			

Man of the match: R.J.Blakey

HEADLINES

12th May

● The three remaining quarter-final places were claimed by Somerset, Surrey and Nottinghamshire

● Somerset's batting line-up overpowered Sussex at Hove, Jimmy Cook's 177 creating a new record for a Somerset batsman in one-day cricket as the visitors compiled their highest total (321 for 5) in the B & H Cup. Somerset's phenomenal run-scoring enabled them them to finish top of Group B ahead of Middlesex who lost their 100 % record to Derbyshire, the prolific Adrian Kuiper hitting his first 100 for the county

● Surrey qualified in second place in Group C despite losing to Yorkshire at The Oval who successfully chased a target of 262, Richard Blakey again improving his highest score in the B & H

● Nottinghamshire were again indebted to their captain Tim Robinson who made 106* against Northamptonshire to take Notts into the quarter-finals from Group D

● Mark Benson's B & H best of 118 helped Kent end Glamorgan's sequence of five one-day victories, while Nigel Briers brought Leicestershire their first success with a career best 93* against Scotland

● Hampshire also saved their best until last, Chris Smith (154*) and Paul Terry (134) both recording competition bests against the Combined Universities as they shared an opening stand of 252, the best ever in the B & H Cup. Warwickshire recorded their first victory at the expense of Gloucestershire

GLAMORGAN vs. KENT

at Swansea on 12th May 1990
Toss : Kent. Umpires : J.C.Balderstone and K.J.Lyons
Kent won by 18 runs. (Glamorgan 0 pts Kent 2 pts)

KENT

S.G.Hinks	c Morris b Frost	1
M.R.Benson	c Richards b Frost	118
N.R.Taylor	c Metson b Dennis	19
T.R.Ward	c Morris b Cowley	36
G.R.Cowdrey	c Cowley b Frost	12
C.S.Cowdrey *	c Morris b Watkin	35
S.A.Marsh +	c Morris b Holmes	9
M.A.Ealham	not out	17
P.S.De Villiers	run out	0
C.Penn	not out	8
R.P.Davis		
Extras	(b 1,lb 5,w 4)	10
TOTAL	(55 overs)(for 8 wkts)	265

GLAMORGAN

A.R.Butcher *	b De Villiers	6
H.Morris	run out	16
G.C.Holmes	c Cowdrey G.R. b Cowdrey C.S.	62
M.P.Maynard	c Davis b De Villiers	84
I.V.A.Richards	c sub b Ealham	27
I.Smith	c Hinks b Ealham	9
N.G.Cowley	c Cowdrey G.R. b Cowdrey C.S.	4
C.P.Metson +	b Penn	23
S.J.Dennis	c De Villiers b Cowdrey C.S.	1
S.L.Watkin	b Penn	6
M.Frost	not out	1
Extras	(lb 3,w 4,nb 1)	8
TOTAL	(53.5 overs)	247

GLAMORGAN	O	M	R	W	FALL OF WICKETS		
						KEN	GLA
Frost	11	1	56	3			
Dennis	9	1	37	1	1st	8	8
Watkin	11	2	51	1	2nd	48	36
Cowley	9	0	55	1	3rd	103	161
Richards	11	0	30	0	4th	135	202
Holmes	4	0	30	1	5th	195	204
					6th	215	214
KENT	O	M	R	W	7th	243	219
De Villiers	10	0	37	2	8th	243	228
Penn	10.5	1	40	2	9th		246
Davis	8	0	45	0	10th		247
Ealham	11	0	47	2			
Cowdrey C.S.	9	0	52	3			
Cowdrey G.R.	5	0	23	0			

Man of the match: M.R.Benson

GLOUCESTERSHIRE vs. WARWICKS

at Bristol on 12th May 1990
Toss : Warwickshire. Umpires : A.A.Jones and B.Leadbeater
Warwicks won by 6 wickets. (Gloucs 0 pts Warwicks 2 pts)

GLOUCESTERSHIRE

A.J.Wright *	c Small b Reeve	15
A.W.Stovold	c Humpage b Benjamin	5
P.Bainbridge	c Humpage b Reeve	10
C.W.J.Athey	not out	83
K.M.Curran	c Humpage b Munton	0
M.W.Alleyne	c Smith b Small	11
R.C.Russell +	c Humpage b Benjamin	20
J.W.Lloyds	not out	53
C.A.Walsh		
M.C.J.Ball		
K.B.S.Jarvis		
Extras	(lb 7,w 3)	10
TOTAL	(55 overs)(for 6 wkts)	207

WARWICKSHIRE

A.J.Moles	run out	57
Asif Din	c Alleyne b Curran	27
T.M.Moody	c Alleyne b Bainbridge	16
A.I.Kallicharran	c & b Bainbridge	21
G.W.Humpage +	not out	30
D.A.Reeve *	not out	29
R.G.Twose		
N.M.K.Smith		
G.C.Small		
J.E.Benjamin		
T.A.Munton		
Extras	(b 4,lb 14,w 7,nb 3)	28
TOTAL	(49.4 overs)(for 4 wkts)	208

WARWICKS	O	M	R	W	FALL OF WICKETS		
						GLO	WAR
Small	11	1	27	1			
Benjamin	11	2	32	2	1st	14	77
Reeve	11	3	27	2	2nd	31	109
Munton	11	1	41	1	3rd	34	141
Moody	11	0	73	0	4th	36	141
					5th	69	
GLOUCS	O	M	R	W	6th	99	
Walsh	11	1	30	0	7th		
Jarvis	5	0	25	0	8th		
Curran	10	1	36	1	9th		
Alleyne	4.4	0	28	0	10th		
Ball	8	0	40	0			
Bainbridge	11	3	31	2			

Man of the match: C.W.J.Athey

BENSON & HEDGES CUP

LEICESTERSHIRE vs. SCOTLAND ——

at Leicester on 12th May 1990
Toss : Leicestershire. Umpires : J.D.Bond and K.E.Palmer
Leicestershire won by 7 wickets. (Leics 2 pts Scotland 0 pts)

SCOTLAND

I.L.Philip +	c Whitticase b Agnew	29
C.G.Greenidge	c Whitticase b Taylor	34
B.M.W.Patterson	c Lewis b Agnew	4
R.G.Swan *	c Potter b Agnew	40
A.C.Storie	b Mullally	19
O.Henry	run out	48
D.R.Brown	c Potter b Taylor	17
D.Cowan	b Taylor	3
J.D.Moir	not out	7
A.W.Bee		
C.L.Parfitt		
Extras	(lb 4,w 8,nb 2)	14
TOTAL	(55 overs)(for 8 wkts)	215

LEICESTERSHIRE

T.J.Boon	run out	39
N.E.Briers *	not out	93
J.J.Whitaker	c Henry b Moir	46
L.Potter	c Philip b Cowan	10
C.C.Lewis	not out	20
P.Whitticase +		
M.I.Gidley		
G.J.Parsons		
J.P.Agnew		
A.D.Mullally		
L.B.Taylor		
Extras	(b 1,lb 2,w 7,nb 1)	11
TOTAL	(51.3 overs)(for 3 wkts)	219

LEICS	O	M	R	W	FALL OF WICKETS		
						SCO	LEI
Lewis	11	0	49	0			
Parsons	4	1	26	0	1st	43	75
Agnew	11	3	20	3	2nd	70	159
Taylor	11	0	65	3	3rd	72	182
Mullally	11	3	28	1	4th	128	
Gidley	7	1	23	0	5th	134	
					6th	184	
SCOTLAND	O	M	R	W	7th	189	
Bee	3	0	21	0	8th	215	
Moir	11	3	35	1	9th		
Brown	8.3	0	47	0	10th		
Cowan	7	0	45	1			
Parfitt	11	1	39	0			
Henry	11	1	29	0			

Man of the match: N.E.Briers

NOTTINGHAMSHIRE vs. NORTHANTS ——

at Trent Bridge on 12th May 1990
Toss : Notts. Umpires : J.W.Holder and M.J.Kitchen
Notts won by 3 wickets. (Notts 2 pts Northants 0 pts)

NORTHANTS

A.Fordham	c Johnson b Pick	67
N.A.Felton	c Pollard b Hemmings	16
R.J.Bailey *	st French b Afford	18
R.G.Williams	b Stephenson	17
A.L.Penberthy	run out	10
D.Ripley +	c French b Cooper	7
J.G.Thomas	c French b Stephenson	0
J.W.Govan	b Cooper	1
C.E.L.Ambrose	not out	11
A.Walker	b Stephenson	5
M.A.Robinson	b Pick	1
Extras	(lb 8,w 17)	25
TOTAL	(54.4 overs)	178

NOTTINGHAMSHIRE

B.C.Broad	c Bailey b Thomas	8
P.Pollard	c Ambrose b Thomas	5
R.T.Robinson *	not out	106
P.Johnson	lbw b Thomas	9
F.D.Stephenson	c Ambrose b Thomas	2
D.W.Randall	c Thomas b Ambrose	2
B.N.French +	c Ripley b Ambrose	24
E.E.Hemmings	c Ambrose b Robinson	6
K.E.Cooper	not out	8
R.A.Pick		
J.A.Afford		
Extras	(lb 2,w 8)	10
TOTAL	(54.1 overs)(for 7 wkts)	180

NOTTS	O	M	R	W	FALL OF WICKETS		
						NOR	NOT
Cooper	11	1	41	2	1st	64	11
Stephenson	11	1	33	3	2nd	113	16
Pick	10.4	1	47	2	3rd	114	34
Hemmings	11	2	30	1	4th	137	40
Afford	11	3	19	1	5th	146	54
					6th	146	127
NORTHANTS	O	M	R	W	7th	156	159
Ambrose	11	2	20	2	8th	157	
Walker	11	1	39	0	9th	166	
Thomas	11	0	45	4	10th	178	
Robinson	10.1	1	47	1			
Govan	11	2	27	0			

Man of the match: R.T.Robinson

BENSON AND HEDGES CUP
FINAL GROUP TABLES

GROUP A

		P	W	L	T	NR	Pts	Run Rate
1	Worcestershire	4	3	1	0	0	6	72.77
2	Glamorgan	4	3	1	0	0	6	69.47
3	Kent	4	2	1	0	1	5	71.71
4	Warwickshire	4	1	3	0	0	2	63.58
5	Gloucestershire	4	0	3	0	1	1	67.77

GROUP B

		P	W	L	T	NR	Pts	Run Rate
1	Somerset	4	3	1	0	0	6	85.46
2	Middlesex	4	3	1	0	0	6	74.86
3	Sussex	4	2	2	0	0	4	78.94
4	Derbyshire	4	2	2	0	0	4	77.34
5	Minor Counties	4	0	4	0	0	0	66.43

GROUP C

		P	W	L	T	NR	Pts	Run Rate
1	Lancashire	4	3	0	0	1	7	67.84
2	Surrey	4	2	2	0	0	4	75.30
3	Yorkshire	4	2	2	0	0	4	62.08
4	Hampshire	4	1	2	0	1	3	75.45
5	Combined Univ	4	1	3	0	0	2	61.91

GROUP D

		P	W	L	T	NR	Pts	Run rate
1	Essex	4	3	0	0	1	7	82.36
2	Nottinghamshire	4	3	1	0	0	6	63.44
3	Leicestershire	4	1	2	0	1	3	62.33
4	Scotland	4	1	3	0	0	2	66.66
5	Northants	4	1	3	0	0	2	60.60

REFUGE ASSURANCE LEAGUE

SOMERSET vs. HAMPSHIRE

at Taunton on 13th May 1990
Toss : Hampshire. Umpires : A.A.Jones and B.Leadbeater
Somerset won by 5 wickets. (Somerset 4 pts Hamps 0 pts)

HAMPSHIRE

D.I.Gower	c Tavare b Jones	12
V.P.Terry	not out	113
R.A.Smith	c Hayhurst b Cleal	51
C.L.Smith	b Lefebvre	25
M.C.J.Nicholas *	not out	33
M.D.Marshall		
J.R.Ayling		
R.J.Parks +		
R.J.Maru		
C.A.Connor		
P.J.Bakker		
Extras	(b 1,lb 6,w 5)	12
TOTAL	(40 overs)(for 3 wkts)	246

SOMERSET

S.J.Cook	c Smith R.A. b Bakker	132
P.M.Roebuck	b Bakker	1
A.N.Hayhurst	c & b Maru	38
G.D.Rose	c Terry b Marshall	32
C.J.Tavare *	c Parks b Marshall	9
R.J.Harden	not out	13
N.D.Burns +	not out	13
I.G.Swallow		
R.P.Lefebvre		
M.W.Cleal		
A.N.Jones		
Extras	(b 4,lb 2,w 1,nb 2)	9
TOTAL	(37 overs)(for 5 wkts)	247

SOMERSET	O	M	R	W	FALL OF WICKETS		
						HAM	SOM
Jones	6	1	40	1	1st	23	2
Rose	8	0	49	0	2nd	125	130
Lefebvre	8	0	50	1	3rd	181	195
Hayhurst	8	0	35	0	4th		211
Swallow	4	0	24	0	5th		220
Cleal	6	0	41	1	6th		
					7th		
HAMPSHIRE	O	M	R	W	8th		
Marshall	8	0	53	2	9th		
Bakker	6	1	42	2	10th		
Connor	8	0	48	0			
Ayling	5	0	38	0			
Maru	8	0	38	1			
Nicholas	2	0	22	0			

YORKSHIRE vs. DERBYSHIRE

at Headingley on 13th May 1990
Toss : Yorkshire. Umpires : H.D.Bird and R.Palmer
Yorkshire won by 6 wickets. (Yorks 4 pts Derbyshire 0 pts)

DERBYSHIRE

K.J.Barnett *	c White b Byas	29
P.D.Bowler	c Bairstow b Sidebottom	5
B.Roberts	c Sidebottom b Jarvis	53
A.P.Kuiper	c Blakey b Jarvis	5
C.J.Adams	c Bairstow b Byas	7
S.C.Goldsmith	c Byas b Sidebottom	7
K.M.Krikken +	b Jarvis	14
A.E.Warner	c Kellett b Jarvis	5
S.J.Base	b Fletcher	0
D.E.Malcolm	b Jarvis	0
O.H.Mortensen	not out	0
Extras	(lb 11,w 5,nb 2)	18
TOTAL	(38.1 overs)	143

YORKSHIRE

S.A.Kellett	run out	32
A.A.Metcalfe *	b Base	41
R.J.Blakey	c Krikken b Base	1
D.Byas	not out	30
P.E.Robinson	c Krikken b Barnett	21
D.L.Bairstow +	not out	1
C.White		
A.Sidebottom		
P.W.Jarvis		
D.Gough		
S.D.Fletcher		
Extras	(b 1,lb 9,w 11)	21
TOTAL	(39 overs)(for 4 wkts)	147

YORKSHIRE	O	M	R	W	FALL OF WICKETS		
						DER	YOR
Sidebottom	8	0	18	2	1st	14	71
Jarvis	7	1	18	5	2nd	71	78
Fletcher	7.1	0	37	1	3rd	79	85
Gough	8	0	26	0	4th	106	140
Byas	8	0	33	2	5th	121	
					6th	122	
DERBYSHIRE	O	M	R	W	7th	143	
Mortensen	8	0	26	0	8th	143	
Malcolm	8	1	28	0	9th	143	
Warner	8	0	28	0	10th	143	
Base	8	2	33	2			
Goldsmith	3	0	10	0			
Barnett	4	0	12	1			

MIDDLESEX vs. NOTTINGHAMSHIRE

at Lord's on 13th May 1990
Toss : Middlesex. Umpires : J.H.Harris and D.O.Oslear
Notts won by 12 runs. (Middlesex 0 pts Notts 4 pts)

NOTTINGHAMSHIRE

B.C.Broad	c Emburey b Cowans	72
R.T.Robinson *	run out	6
P.Johnson	c Ramprakash b Williams	100
D.W.Randall	not out	30
M.Saxelby	c Taylor b Haynes	20
F.D.Stephenson	not out	5
B.N.French +		
E.E.Hemmings		
K.E.Cooper		
K.Saxelby		
J.A.Afford		
Extras	(lb 13,w 5)	18
TOTAL	(40 overs)(for 4 wkts)	251

MIDDLESEX

D.L.Haynes	lbw b Stephenson	10
M.A.Roseberry	lbw b Hemmings	80
M.W.Gatting *	c Hemmings b Stephenson	0
M.R.Ramprakash	st French b Afford	17
K.R.Brown	lbw b Hemmings	56
R.O.Butcher	c Randall b Hemmings	7
P.R.Downton +	b Hemmings	10
N.F.Williams	c & b Stephenson	3
J.E.Emburey	st French b Hemmings	4
N.G.Cowans	c Afford b Saxelby K.	27
N.R.Taylor	not out	4
Extras	(b 4,lb 8,w 7,nb 2)	21
TOTAL	(37.5 overs)	239

MIDDLESEX	O	M	R	W	FALL OF WICKETS		
						NOT	MID
Taylor	8	0	34	0			
Williams	8	1	30	1	1st	15	24
Cowans	8	1	52	1	2nd	183	25
Emburey	8	0	53	0	3rd	192	80
Gatting	5	0	52	0	4th	244	171
Haynes	3	0	17	1	5th		180
					6th		187
NOTTS	O	M	R	W	7th		199
Stephenson	7	0	29	3	8th		207
Cooper	8	0	40	0	9th		208
Saxelby K.	4.5	0	51	1	10th		239
Afford	6	0	41	1			
Saxelby M.	4	0	33	0			
Hemmings	8	0	33	5			

ESSEX vs. GLOUCESTERSHIRE

at Chelmsford on 13th May 1990
Toss : Gloucs. Umpires : P.J.Eele and A.G.T.Whitehead
Gloucestershire won by 7 wickets. (Essex 0 pts Gloucs 4 pts)

ESSEX

G.A.Gooch *	lbw b Bainbridge	56
B.R.Hardie	st Russell b Alleyne	42
M.E.Waugh	b Bainbridge	1
P.J.Prichard	c Wright b Alleyne	21
D.R.Pringle	c Romaines b Alleyne	21
J.P.Stephenson	run out	23
M.A.Garnham +	not out	24
N.A.Foster	not out	11
T.D.Topley		
J.H.Childs		
M.C.Ilott		
Extras	(b 1,lb 6,w 5)	12
TOTAL	(40 overs)(for 6 wkts)	211

GLOUCESTERSHIRE

R.C.Russell +	c Topley b Foster	62
C.W.J.Athey	not out	101
J.W.Lloyds	c & b Foster	10
A.J.Wright *	b Prichard b Pringle	20
K.M.Curran	not out	5
P.W.Romaines		
P.Bainbridge		
M.W.Alleyne		
C.A.Walsh		
M.C.J.Ball		
K.B.S.Jarvis		
Extras	(lb 9,w 5,nb 3)	17
TOTAL	(39.1 overs)(for 3 wkts)	215

GLOUCS	O	M	R	W	FALL OF WICKETS		
						ESS	GLO
Walsh	8	0	42	0			
Jarvis	6	0	30	0	1st	94	137
Curran	8	0	43	0	2nd	97	158
Alleyne	6	1	25	3	3rd	120	208
Bainbridge	8	0	46	2	4th	144	
Ball	4	0	18	0	5th	153	
					6th	182	
ESSEX	O	M	R	W	7th		
Ilott	8	0	34	0	8th		
Foster	8	0	22	2	9th		
Pringle	7.1	0	49	1	10th		
Topley	8	0	51	0			
Childs	6	0	35	0			
Stephenson	2	0	15	0			

GLAMORGAN vs. KENT

at Llanelli on 13th May 1990
Toss : Glam. Umpires : J.C.Balderstone and K.J.Lyons
Kent won by 2 wickets. (Glamorgan 0 pts Kent 4 pts)

GLAMORGAN

G.C.Holmes	c Merrick b Fleming	57
H.Morris	c Marsh b Penn	0
M.P.Maynard	c Cowdrey G.R. b Fleming	20
I.V.A.Richards	c Ealham b Fleming	55
A.R.Butcher *	c Taylor b Cowdrey C.S.	38
I.Smith	not out	39
N.G.Cowley	not out	0
C.P.Metson +		
S.J.Dennis		
S.L.Watkin		
M.Frost		
Extras	(b 5,lb 2,w 4)	11
TOTAL	(40 overs)(for 5 wkts)	220

KENT

S.G.Hinks	c Metson b Watkin	74
N.R.Taylor	c Metson b Richards	27
T.R.Ward	b Richards	0
C.S.Cowdrey *	c Holmes b Cowley	3
G.R.Cowdrey	c Dennis b Holmes	5
M.V.Fleming	run out	18
S.A.Marsh +	b Frost	14
M.A.Ealham	not out	29
T.A.Merrick	b Frost	8
C.Penn	not out	20
R.P.Davis		
Extras	(b 1,lb 15,w 10)	26
TOTAL	(39.5 overs)(for 8 wkts)	224

KENT	O	M	R	W	FALL OF WICKETS		
						GLA	KEN
Penn	8	0	51	1	1st		65
Merrick	8	1	32	0	2nd	41	65
Davis	4	0	27	0	3rd	132	77
Fleming	7	0	30	3	4th	132	124
Ealham	7	1	37	0	5th	200	131
Cowdrey C.S.	6	0	36	1	6th		162
					7th		164
GLAMORGAN	O	M	R	W	8th		177
Frost	8	0	45	2	9th		
Watkin	7.5	1	48	1	10th		
Dennis	8	0	28	0			
Richards	8	0	28	2			
Cowley	3	0	27	1			
Holmes	5	0	32	1			

HEADLINES
13th May

• Derbyshire, Glamorgan, and Middlesex all suffered their first Sunday League defeats, leaving Warwickshire as the only unbeaten side.

• Yorkshire gained their second win in two days as Paul Jarvis (5 for 18) destroyed Derbyshire with the best one-day figures of the season.

• Kent's ninth wicket pair, Mark Ealham and Chris Penn, took 23 off the last over to gain an improbable two wicket win over Glamorgan.

• Paul Johnson (a maiden Sunday League 100) and Eddie Hemmings (5 for 33) combined to overcome Middlesex.

• The runs continued to flow at Taunton, where Jimmy Cook made 132 (the highest of his four Sunday hundreds) to take his tally of runs for the weekend to 309 and his season's aggregate to 845. Somerset needed Cook's contribution to overcome a Hampshire total of 246 for 3 based upon Paul Terry's 113 - he also hit 100s in successive days.

• Bill Athey's 101* gained Gloucestershire their first victory of the season and condemned Essex to their fourth consecutive Refuge defeat.

ONE-DAY TOUR MATCHES

D. NORFOLK'S XI vs. NEW ZEALAND
at Arundel Castle on 6th May 1990
Toss : D. Norfolk's XI. Umpires : C.Cook and J.G.Langridge
New Zealand won by 7 wickets

D. NORFOLK'S XI
I.J.F.Hutchinson	b Priest	19
A.I.C.Dodemaide	c sub b Snedden	131
P.W.G.Parker *	c Priest b Millmow	90
A.P.Wells	c Crowe M.D. b Millmow	16
M.P.Speight +	lbw b Snedden	0
C.M.Wells	run out	2
I.J.Gould	not out	1
V.J.Marks		
J.K.Lever		
A.R.Hansford		
J.Boiling		
Extras	(lb 16,w 1,nb 1)	18
TOTAL	(50 overs)(for 6 wkts)	277

NEW ZEALAND
J.J.Crowe	b Hansford	43
T.J.Franklin	b Lever	82
M.J.Greatbatch	c Hansford b Boiling	20
M.D.Crowe *	not out	89
K.R.Rutherford	not out	32
S.A.Thomson		
M.W.Priest		
J.G.Bracewell		
A.C.Parore +		
M.C.Snedden		
J.P.Millmow		
Extras	(b 1,lb 11)	12
TOTAL	(47.2 overs)(for 3 wkts)	278

NEW ZEALAND	O	M	R	W	FALL OF WICKETS		
						D.N	NZ
Millmow	10	2	55	2			
Thomson	10	2	58	0	1st	59	81
Priest	10	1	42	1	2nd	239	114
Snedden	10	1	42	2	3rd	262	182
Bracewell	9	0	57	0	4th	263	
Rutherford	1	0	7	0	5th	274	
					6th	277	
NORFOLK	O	M	R	W	7th		
Lever	9	1	48	1	8th		
Wells C.M.	10	1	39	0	9th		
Marks	10	0	63	0	10th		
Boiling	9	0	57	1			
Hansford	9	0	58	1			
Parker	0.2	0	1	0			

MCC vs. NEW ZEALAND
at Lord's on 7th May 1990
Toss : MCC. Umpires : J.D.Bond and R.Julian
MCC won by 6 wickets

NEW ZEALAND
T.J.Franklin	c Tufnell b Tremlett	29
J.J.Crowe	c & b Lever	1
A.H.Jones	st Parks b Bainbridge	49
M.J.Greatbatch	c Wright b Jarvis	52
S.A.Thomson	b Bainbridge	5
M.D.Crowe *	c Parks b Tremlett	26
M.W.Priest	c Bainbridge b Jarvis	28
A.C.Parore +	run out	6
M.C.Snedden	not out	8
D.K.Morrison		
J.P.Millmow		
Extras	(b 1,lb 2,w 15)	18
TOTAL	(55 overs)(for 8 wkts)	222

MCC
A.J.Wright	c Parore b Snedden	8
V.P.Terry	b Millmow	4
D.I.Gower *	c Parore b Snedden	97
M.R.Ramprakash	c Crowe M.D. b Snedden	6
K.R.Brown	not out	79
P.Bainbridge	not out	19
R.J.Parks +		
T.M.Tremlett		
J.K.Lever		
P.C.R.Tufnell		
K.B.S.Jarvis		
Extras	(b 4,lb 3,w 4)	11
TOTAL	(50.5 overs)(for 4 wkts)	224

MCC	O	M	R	W	FALL OF WICKETS		
						NZ	MCC
Jarvis	11	1	49	2			
Lever	11	1	45	1	1st	8	8
Tufnell	11	1	42	0	2nd	44	46
Tremlett	11	0	50	2	3rd	129	62
Bainbridge	11	1	33	2	4th	135	171
					5th	164	
NEW ZEALAND	O	M	R	W	6th	178	
Morrison	5	1	33	0	7th	206	
Millmow	10	0	43	1	8th	222	
Snedden	10	3	28	3	9th		
Thomson	9.5	1	40	0	10th		
Priest	11	0	40	0			
Jones	5	0	33	0			

IRELAND vs. NEW ZEALAND
at Downpatrick on 9th May 1990
Toss : New Zealand. Umpires : L.Hogan and M.Moore
New Zealand won by 7 wickets

IRELAND
M.F.Cohen	c Hadlee b Millmow	8
R.Lamba	c Smith b Hadlee	52
M.A.F.Nulty	c Franklin b Millmow	1
S.J.S.Warke	c Smith b Hadlee	23
G.D.Harrison	lbw b Millmow	6
D.A.Lewis	b Snedden	19
T.J.T.Patterson	run out	9
N.E.Thompson	b Snedden	2
P.B.Jackson *+	b Hadlee	6
P.McCrum	not out	1
P.O'Reilly	not out	1
Extras	(b 2,lb 8,w 4,nb 9)	23
TOTAL	(55 overs)(for 9 wkts)	151

NEW ZEALAND
T.J.Franklin	c O'Reilly b Thompson	26
J.G.Wright *	run out	49
M.D.Crowe	c Jackson b McCrum	48
K.R.Rutherford	not out	13
S.A.Thomson	not out	1
A.H.Jones		
R.J.Hadlee		
M.W.Priest		
I.D.S.Smith +		
M.C.Snedden		
J.P.Millmow		
Extras	(lb 3,w 8,nb 4)	15
TOTAL	(36.3 overs)(for 3 wkts)	152

NEW ZEALAND	O	M	R	W	FALL OF WICKETS		
						IRE	NZ
Hadlee	11	1	25	3			
Millmow	11	1	28	3	1st	25	71
Snedden	11	1	27	2	2nd	30	89
Thomson	11	3	30	0	3rd	99	150
Priest	11	1	31	0	4th	100	
					5th	120	
IRELAND	O	M	R	W	6th	138	
McCrum	7.3	2	26	1	7th	138	
O'Reilly	4	0	22	0	8th	149	
Thompson	7	0	23	1	9th	149	
Harrison	11	3	42	0	10th		
Lamba	6	1	27	0			
Lewis	1	0	9	0			

IRELAND vs. NEW ZEALAND
at Belfast on 10th May 1990
Toss : Ireland. Umpires : B.Arlow and H.Henderson
New Zealand won by 40 runs

NEW ZEALAND
J.G.Wright *	c Thompson b Harrison	44
J.J.Crowe	st Jackson b Harrison	19
A.H.Jones	b Thompson	32
M.J.Greatbatch	b O'Reilly	32
K.R.Rutherford	c Lamba b O'Reilly	2
R.J.Hadlee	b McCrum	20
I.D.S.Smith	c Patterson b Lamba	19
M.W.Priest	not out	18
A.C.Parore +	not out	4
M.C.Snedden		
D.K.Morrison		
Extras	(b 1,lb 4,w 2,nb 6)	13
TOTAL	(50 overs)(for 7 wkts)	203

IRELAND
M.F.Cohen	b Hadlee	2
R.Lamba	c Hadlee b Snedden	5
M.A.F.Nulty	lbw b Hadlee	6
S.J.S.Warke	run out	44
G.D.Harrison	c Hadlee b Priest	17
D.A.Lewis	c Crowe J. b Rutherford	18
T.J.T.Patterson	b Rutherford	23
N.E.Thompson	b Rutherford	8
P.B.Jackson *+	st Parore b Smith	17
P.McCrum	not out	9
P.O'Reilly	not out	2
Extras	(b 9,lb 2,w 1)	12
TOTAL	(50 overs)(for 9 wkts)	163

IRELAND	O	M	R	W	FALL OF WICKETS		
						NZ	IRE
McCrum	10	1	42	1			
Lamba	10	1	40	1	1st	61	2
Harrison	10	2	25	2	2nd	72	12
O'Reilly	10	0	56	2	3rd	135	20
Thompson	10	0	35	1	4th	139	57
					5th	142	104
NEW ZEALAND	O	M	R	W	6th	173	104
Hadlee	6	2	13	2	7th	191	112
Morrison	8	1	20	0	8th		143
Snedden	5	2	4	1	9th		160
Priest	10	1	39	1	10th		
Rutherford	10	1	38	3			
Jones	8	1	22	0			
Smith	2	0	8	1			
Greatbatch	1	0	3	0			

SUSSEX vs. ZIMBABWE
at Hove on 13th May 1990
Toss : Zimbabwe. Umpires : B.Dudleston and P.B.Wight
Sussex won by 95 runs

SUSSEX
N.J.Lenham	b Jarvis	1
J.W.Hall	c Briant b Brandes	53
K.Greenfield	b Jarvis	10
M.P.Speight	c Butchart b Traicos	76
C.C.Remy	not out	0
P.W.G.Parker *	lbw b Shah	10
P.Moores +	c Robertson b Brandes	39
I.D.K.Salisbury	run out	0
R.A.Bunting	lbw b Traicos	6
P.W.Threlfall	not out	17
A.M.Babington		
Extras	(b 7,lb 6,w 3,nb 5)	21
TOTAL	(55 overs)(for 8 wkts)	233

ZIMBABWE
K.J.Arnott	lbw b Threlfall	11
G.A.Paterson	b Salisbury	18
C.M.Robertson	b Threlfall	9
A.J.Pycroft *	run out	10
G.A.Briant +	run out	7
A.H.Shah	b Salisbury	21
I.P.Butchart	lbw b Babington	24
E.A.Brandes	c Bunting b Salisbury	23
A.J.Traicos	b Salisbury	0
M.P.Jarvis	b Threlfall	4
E.Dube	not out	0
Extras	(lb 10,w 7,nb 3)	20
TOTAL	(40.3 overs)	138

ZIMBABWE	O	M	R	W	FALL OF WICKETS		
						SUS	ZIM
Brandes	11	0	39	2			
Jarvis	9	3	30	2	1st	1	32
Dube	8	0	43	0	2nd	23	38
Shah	11	1	36	1	3rd	145	50
Traicos	11	0	42	2	4th	158	55
Butchart	5	0	30	0	5th	177	106
					6th	182	108
SUSSEX	O	M	R	W	7th	190	108
Babington	9	2	20	1	8th	232	114
Threlfall	10	2	40	3	9th		127
Lenham	7	0	13	0	10th		138
Bunting	7	1	30	0			
Salisbury	7.3	2	25	4			

ESSEX vs. ZIMBABWE
at Chelmsford on 14th May 1990
Toss : Essex. Umpires : P.J.Eele and A.G.T.Whitehead
Essex won by 71 runs

ESSEX
J.P.Stephenson	c Arnott b Jarvis	105
A.C.Seymour	lbw b Brandes	6
A.W.Lilley	run out	12
M.E.Waugh	b Duers	0
M.A.Garnham +	c Robertson b Duers	14
G.A.Gooch *	c Briant b Jarvis	105
P.J.Prichard	not out	3
N.A.Foster	not out	4
T.D.Topley		
J.H.Childs		
S.J.W.Andrew		
Extras	(lb 12,nb 4)	16
TOTAL	(55 overs)(for 6 wkts)	265

ZIMBABWE
K.J.Arnott	c Garnham b Andrew	6
A.H.Shah	c Garnham b Andrew	0
W.James	b Andrew	27
A.J.Pycroft *	c Prichard b Stephenson	62
C.M.Robertson	c Seymour b Andrew	3
G.A.Briant +	b Childs	17
J.P.Brent	lbw b Stephenson	32
E.A.Brandes	c Prichard b Stephenson	7
M.P.Jarvis	c Waugh b Foster	5
A.J.Traicos	not out	8
K.G.Duers	b Foster	1
Extras	(lb 8,w 12,nb 6)	26
TOTAL	(51.1 overs)	194

ZIMBABWE	O	M	R	W	FALL OF WICKETS		
						ESS	ZIM
Brandes	11	2	58	1			
Jarvis	10	1	44	2	1st	7	1
Shah	6	0	20	0	2nd	49	21
Duers	11	0	52	2	3rd	50	46
Traicos	11	0	45	0	4th	83	60
Brent	6	0	34	0	5th	258	95
					6th	258	170
ESSEX	O	M	R	W	7th		173
Foster	8.1	2	19	2	8th		180
Andrew	11	1	36	4	9th		184
Gooch	7	1	17	0	10th		194
Topley	5	0	29	0			
Childs	11	1	37	1			
Waugh	5	0	22	0			
Stephenson	4	0	26	3			

TOUR MATCH

WORCESTERSHIRE vs. NEW ZEALAND

at Worcester on 12th, 13th, 14th May 1990
Toss : New Zealand.   Umpires : J.H.Hampshire and B.J.Meyer
New Zealand won by 6 wickets

WORCESTERSHIRE

P.Bent	b Morrison	22	lbw b Hadlee		9
M.J.Weston	c Rutherford b Hadlee	3	c Priest b Morrison		7
G.A.Hick	retired hurt	2	absent hurt		
D.B.D'Oliveira	c Greatbatch b Hadlee	48	(3) c Morrison b Hadlee		24
P.A.Neale *	b Millmow	5	(4) lbw b Millmow		15
S.R.Lampitt	b Hadlee	40	(7) b Millmow		30
R.K.Illingworth	c Rutherford b Hadlee	0	(5) c Crowe J. b Morrison		74
P.J.Newport	c Greatbatch b Morrison	7	(6) c Rutherford b Priest		98
N.V.Radford	c Priest b Millmow	13	(8) c & b Morrison		1
S.R.Bevins +	lbw b Hadlee	10	(9) lbw b Millmow		1
S.M.McEwan	not out	1	(10) not out		0
Extras	(lb 12,w 1,nb 7)	20	(b 1,lb 8,nb 6)		15
TOTAL		171			274

NEW ZEALAND

T.J.Franklin	c sub b McEwan	28	c sub b McEwan	50
J.G.Wright *	lbw b Newport	8	hit wicket b Illingworth	99
A.H.Jones	c Bevins b Newport	1	c Radford b Illingworth	9
M.J.Greatbatch	c sub b Newport	1	c Radford b Illingworth	19
K.R.Rutherford	lbw b Weston	4	not out	26
J.J.Crowe	c Bevins b McEwan	13		
M.W.Priest	c sub b Newport	13	(6) not out	16
R.J.Hadlee	c Bevins b McEwan	90		
I.D.S.Smith +	c sub b Newport	2		
D.K.Morrison	lbw b Newport	5		
J.P.Millmow	not out	2		
Extras	(b 8,lb 12,w 10,nb 4)	34	(b 4,lb 15,w 4,nb 3)	26
TOTAL		201	(for 4 wkts)	245

NEW ZEALAND	O	M	R	W	O	M	R	W
Hadlee	15	7	27	5	20	3	72	2
Morrison	20	5	46	2	16	2	60	3
Millmow	16	2	59	2	20.2	3	66	3
Rutherford	8	2	25	0	7	0	27	0
Priest	2	1	2	0	22	7	40	1

WORCS	O	M	R	W	O	M	R	W
Newport	26	8	54	6	19	4	56	0
McEwan	16.3	2	49	3	17.5	3	69	1
Weston	7	1	32	1	7	1	19	0
Illingworth	12	6	13	0	17	5	35	3
Radford	10	1	33	0	13	3	47	0

FALL OF WICKETS	WOR	NZ	WOR	NZ
1st	11	16	9	164
2nd	46	20	21	172
3rd	90	25	55	196
4th	102	29	59	203
5th	102	68	238	
6th	109	69	238	
7th	133	111	241	
8th	170	113	269	
9th	171	152	274	
10th		201		

HEADLINES

New Zealand Tour

6th - 14th May

- The New Zealand touring party made a confident start by winning three of their four one-day warm-up matches and then defeating county champions Worcestershire in their opening first-class fixture.

- Richard Hadlee began his farewell tour by making a successful first visit to Ireland and then taking five wickets in an innings for the 101st time in first-class cricket with 5 for 27 at Worcester - followed by a robust 90.

- Phil Newport responded with figures of 6 for 54 and a career best 98 as Worcestershire recovered from losing their prime asset Graeme Hick with a broken finger.

- New Zealand's one reverse came against MCC at Lord's where David Gower stroked an elegant 97.

Zimbabwe Tour

13th - 14th May

- Zimbabwe started their two-week tour of England with one-day defeats by Sussex and Essex.

Tony Dodemaide (left) and Paul Parker of Sussex who both enjoyed the festive atmosphere at Arundel Castle, where they represented Lavinia, Duchess of Norfolk's XI against the New Zealanders.

BRITANNIC ASSURANCE CHAMPIONSHIP

MIDDLESEX vs. KENT
at Lord's on 15th, 16th, 17th May 1990
Toss : Middlesex. Umpires : J.H.Hampshire and M.J.Kitchen
Middlesex won by 8 wickets. (Middlesex 23 pts (Bt: 3, Bw: 4) Kent 4 pts (Bt: 1, Bw: 3))

KENT
S.G.Hinks	b Williams	16	c Haynes b Fraser		5
M.R.Benson	b Cowans	24	c Emburey b Williams		24
N.R.Taylor	c Emburey b Williams	12	c Emburey b Hughes		91
T.R.Ward	b Williams	0	lbw b Fraser		13
C.S.Cowdrey *	c Haynes b Williams	47	c Gatting b Fraser		44
M.V.Fleming	c Downton b Cowans	69	b Williams		12
S.A.Marsh +	c Downton b Williams	15	b Gatting		38
M.A.Ealham	c Downton b Williams	0	not out		13
C.Penn	c Ramprakash b Williams	3	c Gatting		0
T.A.Merrick	c Emburey b Hughes	10	c Ramprakash b Gatting		0
R.P.Davis	not out	6	lbw b Gatting		0
Extras	(b 4,lb 3,nb 11)	18	(b 11,lb 8,nb 6)		25
TOTAL		196			265

MIDDLESEX
D.L.Haynes	st Marsh b Cowdrey	36	lbw b Ealham		25
M.A.Roseberry	c Ward b Merrick	50	c Marsh b Ealham		37
M.W.Gatting *	b Merrick	58	not out		87
M.R.Ramprakash	c Ward b Penn	9	not out		36
K.R.Brown	c Taylor b Davis	58			
P.R.Downton +	c Marsh b Ealham	19			
N.F.Williams	c Taylor b Penn	18			
J.E.Emburey	c Marsh b Merrick	3			
S.P.Hughes	c Davis b Penn	4			
A.R.C.Fraser	lbw b Merrick	0			
N.G.Cowans	not out	0			
Extras	(b 1,lb 6,nb 10)	17	(b 4,lb 3,nb 1)		8
TOTAL		272	(for 2 wkts)		193

MIDDLESEX	O	M	R	W	O	M	R	W
Fraser	17	3	30	0	26	4	79	3
Cowans	16	6	41	2	11	4	39	0
Williams	22	4	61	7	20	0	67	2
Hughes	19.3	5	50	1	17	4	43	1
Emburey	3	2	7	0	14	6	16	0
Gatting					2	1	2	4

KENT	O	M	R	W	O	M	R	W
Merrick	26	7	66	4	10	2	44	0
Penn	22	5	45	3	7	1	46	0
Fleming	21	7	49	0	7	1	23	0
Ealham	11	2	39	1	11	1	33	2
Davis	12	4	25	1	7	2	23	0
Cowdrey	12	2	41	1	2	1	2	0
Ward					4.3	1	15	0

FALL OF WICKETS	KEN	MID	KEN	MID
1st	0	86	24	60
2nd	20	96	63	79
3rd	20	145	83	
4th	33	202	172	
5th	155	247	198	
6th	166	247	220	
7th	166	267	265	
8th	174	272	265	
9th	183	272	265	
10th	196	272	265	

HAMPSHIRE vs. SUSSEX
at Southampton on 15th, 16th, 17th May 1990
Toss : Sussex. Umpires : J.C.Balderstone and A.A.Jones
Hants won by an innings and 157 runs. (Hants 24 pts (Bt: 4, Bw: 4) Sx 2 pts (Bt: 1, Bw: 1))

SUSSEX
N.J.Lenham	c Gower b Marshall	0	b Maru		121
D.M.Smith	retired hurt	5	absent hurt		
P.Moores +	c Nicholas b Bakker	8	(2) c Smith C.L. b Bakker		5
A.P.Wells	lbw b Bakker	0	retired hurt		22
M.P.Speight	c Gower b Bakker	7	c Parks b Maru		3
C.M.Wells *	c Turner b Connor	22	c Maru b Turner		25
I.J.Gould	c Smith C.L. b Marshall	6	c Marshall b Turner		1
A.I.C.Dodemaide	c Parks b Bakker	10	not out		37
A.C.S.Pigott	c Parks b Turner	50	c Marshall b Maru		19
I.D.K.Salisbury	c Terry b Maru	37	(3) c Parks b Connor		19
A.R.Hansford	not out	3	(10) b Connor		29
Extras	(nb 5)	5	(b 1,lb 14,w 2,nb 9)		26
TOTAL		152			291

HAMPSHIRE
V.P.Terry	c Moores b Dodemaide	40
C.L.Smith	b Salisbury	35
D.I.Gower	c Wells A.P. b Dodemaide	145
R.A.Smith	c Moores b Wells C.M.	181
M.D.Marshall	c Gould b Hansford	85
M.C.J.Nicholas *	c Gould b Hansford	12
R.J.Parks +	c Speight b Wells C.M.	36
R.J.Maru	not out	54
I.J.Turner	st Moores b Salisbury	1
C.A.Connor		
P.J.Bakker		
Extras	(b 1,lb 8,nb 2)	11
TOTAL	(for 8 wkts dec)	600

HAMPSHIRE	O	M	R	W	O	M	R	W
Marshall	15	3	26	2	24	10	66	0
Bakker	20	4	51	4	16	9	21	1
Connor	12	3	52	1	21	3	80	2
Turner	5	1	13	1	27	10	60	2
Maru	7.2	3	10	1	22	11	49	3
Smith C.L.					2	2	0	0

SUSSEX	O	M	R	W	O	M	R	W
Pigott	20	2	87	0				
Dodemaide	37	6	161	2				
Salisbury	28.3	2	159	2				
Hansford	26	2	102	2				
Wells C.M.	25	1	73	2				
Lenham	3	1	9	0				

FALL OF WICKETS	SUS	HAM	SUS	HAM
1st	0	68	20	
2nd	7	112	140	
3rd	7	368	192	
4th	21	453	207	
5th	29	496	219	
6th	48	507	222	
7th	66	593	225	
8th	142	600	291	
9th	152			
10th				

LEICESTERSHIRE vs. NOTTINGHAMSHIRE
at Leicester on 15th, 16th, 17th May 1990
Toss : Leicestershire. Umpires : B.J.Meyer and N.T.Plews
Nottinghamshire won by 5 wickets. (Leics 7 pts (Bt: 3, Bw: 4) Notts 22 pts (Bt: 4, Bw: 2))

LEICESTERSHIRE
T.J.Boon	c Randall b Pick	1	(3) c Randall b Stephenson		27
N.E.Briers *	not out	157	b Pick		22
J.J.Whitaker	lbw b Pick	43	(4) lbw b Pick		13
P.Willey	c Robinson b Hemmings	30	(5) c Randall b Hemmings		1
L.Potter	b Pick	24	(1) c French b Stephenson		50
C.C.Lewis	lbw b Pick	1	c Hemmings b Pick		2
P.Whitticase +	retired hurt	2	absent hurt		
M.I.Gidley	st French b Afford	8	(7) not out		21
J.P.Agnew	c Afford b Pick	36	b Stephenson		4
G.J.F.Ferris	lbw b Pick	35	(8) b Hemmings		0
A.D.Mullally	c French b Pick	0	(10) b Stephenson		0
Extras	(b 2,lb 6,w 3,nb 11)	22	(b 4,lb 5,nb 2,nb 7)		18
TOTAL		359			158

NOTTINGHAMSHIRE
B.C.Broad	c Boon b Agnew	3	lbw b Willey		23
D.J.R.Martindale	c sub b Lewis	9	c Whitaker b Mullally		43
R.T.Robinson *	lbw b Agnew	8	lbw b Mullally		8
P.Johnson	c sub b Lewis	4	lbw b Mullally		11
D.W.Randall	c Whitaker b Ferris	120	c Mullally b Willey		11
M.Saxelby	b Agnew	11	not out		18
F.D.Stephenson	c Boon b Agnew	0	not out		13
B.N.French +	b Mullally	37			
E.E.Hemmings	c Whitaker b Agnew	83			
R.A.Pick	b Ferris	22			
J.A.Afford	not out	1			
Extras	(b 33,lb 26,w 2,nb 10)	71	(b 21,lb 7,nb 2)		30
TOTAL		361	(for 5 wkts)		157

NOTTS	O	M	R	W	O	M	R	W
Stephenson	27	4	98	0	20.5	4	33	4
Pick	34.5	5	128	7	17	2	56	3
Saxelby	10	2	39	0	6	0	30	0
Hemmings	22	6	58	1	12	9	3	2
Afford	29	17	28	1	13	5	27	0

LEICS	O	M	R	W	O	M	R	W
Lewis	22	1	92	2	10	2	34	0
Agnew	22	4	85	5				
Mullally	14	2	65	1	17.2	5	27	3
Ferris	11	1	37	2	5	0	19	0
Gidley	5	1	23	0	6	3	9	0
Willey	1	1	0	0	18	4	40	2

FALL OF WICKETS	LEI	NOT	LEI	NOT
1st	3	11	55	49
2nd	67	11	100	66
3rd	107	21	119	98
4th	171	22	120	101
5th	173	99	126	139
6th	185	43	133	
7th	301	99	134	
8th	357	262	158	
9th	359	358	158	
10th		361		

GLOUCESTERSHIRE vs. GLAMORGAN
at Bristol on 15th, 16th, 17th May 1990
Toss : Glamorgan. Umpires : J.D.Bond and K.E.Palmer
Glamorgan won by 145 runs. (Gloucs 4 pts (Bt: 1, Bw: 3) Glam 23 pts (Bt: 3, Bw: 4))

GLAMORGAN
A.R.Butcher *	c Wright b Alleyne	83	c Wright b Lloyds		53
H.Morris	c Athey b Walsh	7	c Russell b Lawrence		1
G.C.Holmes	c Lawrence b Walsh	12	absent hurt		
M.P.Maynard	retired hurt	55	absent hurt		
I.V.A.Richards	c & b Bainbridge	32	(3) lbw b Walsh		1
I.Smith	c Russell b Curran	19	(4) c Athey b Lawrence		14
N.G.Cowley	not out	51	(5) c Athey b Walsh		61
C.P.Metson +	lbw b Alleyne	0	(6) b Walsh		4
S.J.Dennis	c Ball b Alleyne	6	(7) b Walsh		0
S.L.Watkin	c Athey b Walsh	1	(8) c Curran b Walsh		10
M.Frost	lbw b Walsh	1	(9) not out		4
Extras	(b 1,lb 7,w 2,nb 14)	24	(b 4,lb 5,nb 13)		22
TOTAL		291			170

GLOUCESTERSHIRE
M.C.J.Ball	c Richards b Frost	5	(10) lbw b Cowley		15
A.J.Wright *	b Frost	3	(1) lbw b Frost		5
A.W.Stovold	c Metson b Frost	7	(2) c Metson b Watkin		19
P.Bainbridge	b Watkin	35	(3) b Frost		0
C.W.J.Athey	c Smith b Dennis	8	(4) b Frost		0
K.M.Curran	c Metson b Watkin	47	(5) c Richards b Watkin		44
J.W.Lloyds	c Metson b Frost	0	(6) c Metson b Frost		14
M.W.Alleyne	b Frost	0	(7) b Dennis		6
R.C.Russell +	c Metson b Dennis	33	(9) b Watkin		31
C.A.Walsh	not out	19	not out		1
D.V.Lawrence	b Cowley	1	(8) b Dennis		0
Extras	(b 1,lb 2,nb 1)	4	(lb 5,w 2,nb 2)		9
TOTAL		171			145

GLOUCS	O	M	R	W	O	M	R	W
Walsh	22.4	4	62	4	17.2	3	48	5
Lawrence	17	0	65	0	10	0	40	2
Bainbridge	17	7	36	1	3	1	12	0
Curran	16	5	39	1	13	0	35	0
Ball	12	3	34	0	3	2	4	0
Alleyne	16	5	47	3	3	2	4	0
Athey					3	2	4	0
Lloyds					5	3	9	1

GLAMORGAN	O	M	R	W	O	M	R	W
Frost	14	4	42	5	14	2	40	5
Watkin	18	5	55	2	13	3	51	3
Dennis	15	5	46	2	11	3	35	1
Cowley	14.3	6	25	1	5.5	2	14	1

FALL OF WICKETS	GLA	GLO	GLA	GLO
1st	20	3	4	17
2nd	47	11	11	29
3rd	170	28	51	29
4th	203	43	136	29
5th	253	75	153	50
6th	253	98	156	51
7th	275	98	157	61
8th	283	134	170	124
9th	291	168		129
10th		171		145

BRITANNIC ASSURANCE CHAMPIONSHIP

NORTHANTS vs. WARWICKSHIRE

at Northampton on 15th, 16th, 17th, 18th May 1990
Toss : Northants.   Umpires : B.Dudleston and D.O.Oslear
Warwicks won by an innings and 30 runs.
(Northants 4 pts (Bt: 2, Bw: 2) Warwicks 23 pts (Bt: 3, Bw: 4))

WARWICKSHIRE

A.J.Moles	lbw b Thomas	13
T.A.Lloyd *	c Ripley b Ambrose	21
Asif Din	lbw b Penberthy	3
A.I.Kallicharran	c & b Penberthy	72
G.W.Humpage +	c Ripley b Thomas	13
D.A.Reeve	not out	202
N.M.K.Smith	b Penberthy	8
G.C.Small	c Felton b Robinson	55
A.A.Donald	c Felton b Robinson	24
J.E.Benjamin	b Penberthy	14
T.A.Munton	not out	1
Extras	(b 4,lb 28,w 7,nb 8)	47
TOTAL	(for 9 wkts dec)	473

NORTHANTS

A.Fordham	c Kallicharran b Munton	37	c Humpage b Munton	18
N.A.Felton	c Moles b Small	8	c Small b Asif Din	75
R.J.Bailey *	c Kallicharran b Small	0	c Humpage b Munton	31
A.L.Penberthy	run out	0	lbw b Reeve	12
G.Cook	lbw b Munton	33	c Humpage b Reeve	13
R.G.Williams	c Smith b Donald	8	b Smith	9
D.J.Wild	c Humpage b Small	17	b Reeve	0
D.Ripley +	c Humpage b Munton	36	c Reeve b Munton	6
J.G.Thomas	c Asif Din b Munton	30	not out	14
C.E.L.Ambrose	not out	11	c Moles b Donald	16
M.A.Robinson	c Kallicharran b Munton	1	lbw b Munton	0
Extras	(b 17,lb 8,w 7,nb 5)	38	(b 8,lb 9,w 9,nb 4)	30
TOTAL		219		224

NORTHANTS	O	M	R	W	O	M	R	W
Ambrose	30	8	80	1				
Thomas	28	5	84	2				
Robinson	35.1	9	91	2				
Penberthy	29.5	5	91	4				
Wild	12.5	4	42	0				
Williams	5	1	38	0				
Bailey	8	1	15	0				

WARWICKSHIRE	O	M	R	W	O	M	R	W
Donald	20	5	51	1	14	2	45	1
Small	20	3	72	3	7	1	34	0
Munton	25.1	10	33	5	19.5	7	44	4
Benjamin	12	2	16	0	9	2	23	0
Smith	13	4	17	0	12	7	22	1
Asif Din	2	1	5	0	4	1	13	1
Reeve					17	7	26	3

FALL OF WICKETS

	WAR	NOR	NOR	WAR
1st	29	18	43	
2nd	38	18	127	
3rd	47	29	160	
4th	75	46	169	
5th	174	58	181	
6th	198	94	181	
7th	317	140	187	
8th	419	184	193	
9th	458	198	223	
10th		219	224	

DERBYSHIRE vs. LANCASHIRE

at Derby on 15th, 16th, 17th, 18th May 1990
Toss : Lancashire. Umpires : H.D.Bird and R.Palmer
Lancashire won by 60 runs. (Derbyshire 3 pts (Bt: 3, Bw: 0) Lancashire 21 pts (Bt: 2, Bw: 3))

LANCASHIRE

G.D.Mendis	c Roberts b Miller	90	c & b Jean-Jacques	4
G.Fowler	b Barnett	25	c Roberts b Jean-Jacques	23
M.A.Atherton	b Barnett	93	run out	51
N.H.Fairbrother	c Kuiper b Jean-Jacques	63	not out	65
T.E.Jesty	not out	55	not out	15
P.A.J.DeFreitas	st Krikken b Barnett	79		
W.K.Hegg +				
D.P.Hughes *				
J.D.Fitton				
P.J.W.Allott				
P.J.Martin				
Extras	(b 17,lb 18,w 1,nb 4)	40	(b 3,lb 11)	14
TOTAL	(for 5 wkts dec)	445	(for 3 wkts dec)	172

DERBYSHIRE

K.J.Barnett *	c Hegg b Fitton	69	c Allott b Fitton	33
J.E.Morris	c Hegg b Atherton	27	b Fitton	52
S.J.Base	c Fitton b Atherton	54	(9) not out	16
M.Jean-Jacques	b Martin	18	(10) c Jesty b Hughes	2
A.P.Kuiper	c Fowler b Fitton	48	(3) b Atherton	13
C.J.Adams	c Fairbrother b Atherton	9	(5) lbw b Hughes	36
B.Roberts	lbw b Atherton	8	(6) b Atherton	0
S.C.Goldsmith	b Atherton	24	(7) c Mendis b Hughes	4
P.D.Bowler	c Mendis b DeFreitas	24	(4) c Fairbrother b Fitton	54
K.M.Krikken +	b Allott	11	(8) b Hughes	26
G.Miller	not out	3	lbw b DeFreitas	1
Extras	(b 4,lb 8,nb 2)	14	(b 4,lb 6,nb 1)	11
TOTAL		309		248

DERBYSHIRE	O	M	R	W	O	M	R	W
Base	39	8	67	0	8	1	30	0
Jean-Jacques	34	5	112	1	19	2	55	2
Miller	59	17	111	1	19	5	45	0
Goldsmith	11	2	39	0				
Barnett	33.3	4	81	3	8	0	28	0

LANCASHIRE	O	M	R	W	O	M	R	W
DeFreitas	24.3	4	70	1	7.1	3	36	1
Allott	13	3	40	1	7	0	26	0
Fitton	36	10	82	2	24	4	69	3
Atherton	38	11	95	5	24	5	82	2
Martin	8	4	10	1				
Hughes					24	12	25	4

FALL OF WICKETS

	LAN	DER	LAN	DER
1st	79	93	10	64
2nd	171	105	45	99
3rd	267	155	141	103
4th	325	183		154
5th	445	206		155
6th		216		160
7th		255		223
8th		275		229
9th		301		243
10th		309		248

HEADLINES

15th - 18th May

● The third round of Championship matches provided the perfect illustration of the advantages of four-day cricket - all six matches ended in positive results with the winning side bowling out the opposition twice on each occasion.

● Warwickshire went to the top of the Championship table after their innings win over Northants - Dermot Reeve becoming the eighth batsman in the 1990 season to pass 200 with a career best 202*.

● David Gower made 145 on his Championship debut for Hampshire, adding 256 for the third wicket with Robin Smith (181) as Hampshire reached 600 against Sussex. Neil Lenham's career best 121 could not prevent a hefty innings defeat.

● Bowlers at last got a share of the limelight as Neil Williams returned the season's best figures so far with 7 for 61 against Kent at Lord's, Middlesex gaining their first Championship victory.

● Nottinghamshire's Andy Pick achieved career best figures of 7 for 128 and finished with 10 wickets in the match as Notts overcame Leicestershire.

● Mark Frost continued his fine start with Glamorgan by returning his best ever match figures, 10 for 82, in his county's 145 run victory over Gloucestershire.

● Other fast bowlers to make an impression were Warwickshire's Tim Munton (9 for 77) and Gloucestershire's Courtney Walsh (9 for 110).

● Batsmen to suffer from this fast bowling revival included Geoff Holmes, Matthew Maynard, Phil Whitticase, David Smith and Alan Wells who all broke bones in their hands.

● But spin won the day for Lancashire at Derby, Michael Atherton's 5 for 95 in Derbyshire's first innings being a career best, after the country's most in form batting line-up had earlier reached 447 for 5.

OTHER FIRST-CLASS MATCHES

TOUR MATCHES

OXFORD UNIV vs. SURREY

at The Parks on 16th, 17th, 18th May 1990
Toss : Oxford Univ.   Umpires : P.J.Eele and V.A.Holder
Match drawn

OXFORD UNIV

D.A.Hagan	c Thorpe b Greig	17	c Ward b Medlycott		12
R.E.Morris *	c Ward b Bicknell M.P.	96	c Stewart b Kendrick		31
M.J.Kilborn	c Ward b Thorpe	11	(7) not out		36
G.J.Turner	c Clinton b Kendrick	34	b Medlycott		3
M.A.Crawley	c Lynch b Bicknell M.P.	60	c Ward b Kendrick		47
P.D.Lunn	not out	44	st Ward b Kendrick		20
H.Davies	lbw b Bicknell M.P.	2	(8) not out		1
P.S.Gerrans	b Robinson	0			
S.D.Weale	c Ward b Bicknell M.P.	13			
I.M.Henderson			(3) c Ward b Medlycott		44
J.McGrady +					
Extras	(b 9,lb 15,w 16,nb 5)	45	(b 7,lb 5,nb 1)		13
TOTAL	(for 8 wkts dec)	322	(for 6 wkts dec)		207

SURREY

D.J.Bicknell	b Crawley	33	b Gerrans		63
G.S.Clinton	c & b Turner	29			
A.J.Stewart	c Crawley b Gerrans	24			
M.A.Lynch	not out	81			
G.P.Thorpe	not out	46	(7) not out		2
D.M.Ward +			(2) c Turner b Crawley		181
J.D.Robinson			(3) c & b Crawley		24
I.A.Greig *			(4) c Crawley b Gerrans		17
K.T.Medlycott			(5) c Kilborn b Gerrans		4
M.P.Bicknell			(6) not out		1
N.M.Kendrick					
Extras	(b 1,lb 3,w 5)	9	(b 4,lb 5,w 1,nb 3)		13
TOTAL	(for 3 wkts dec)	222	(for 5 wkts)		305

SURREY	O	M	R	W	O	M	R	W
Bicknell M.P.	35.2	11	80	4	7	1	18	0
Robinson	26	7	69	1	2	0	14	0
Greig	12	1	38	1	5	1	15	0
Thorpe	14	6	30	1				
Medlycott	33	13	61	0	25	7	69	3
Kendrick	10	3	20	1	25	4	79	3

OXFORD UNIV	O	M	R	W	O	M	R	W
Henderson	9	1	24	0	4	1	23	0
Gerrans	13	1	50	1	15	1	86	3
Crawley	19	5	29	1	13	0	83	2
Turner	16	4	54	1	10	2	53	0
Davies	7	1	25	0				
Weale	5	0	36	0	6	0	51	0

FALL OF WICKETS

	OXF	SUR	OXF	SUR
1st	33	64	55	256
2nd	81	64	62	256
3rd	158	99	72	278
4th	187		141	289
5th	271		151	302
6th	280		196	
7th	284			
8th	322			
9th				
10th				

CAMBRIDGE UNIV vs. ESSEX

at Fenner's on 16th, 17th, 18th May 1990
Toss : Essex.   Umpires : G.I.Burgess and J.W.Holder
Essex won by 120 runs

ESSEX

J.P.Stephenson	c Buzza b Lowrey	58	(1) b Pyman		89
A.C.Seymour	lbw b Jenkins	28			
P.J.Prichard	c Heap b Pyman	116			
M.A.Garnham +	c James b Jenkins	26			
B.R.Hardie	not out	22	(2) not out		56
D.R.Pringle *	c Morris b Pyman	58			
T.D.Topley			(3) lbw b Pyman		0
M.C.Ilott					
J.H.Childs					
S.J.W.Andrew					
P.M.Such					
Extras	(lb 7,nb 4)	11	(b 5,lb 4,w 1)		10
TOTAL	(for 5 wkts dec)	319	(for 2 wkts dec)		155

CAMBRIDGE UNIV

S.P.James	c Topley b Andrew	5	lbw b Ilott		12
R.Heap	c Seymour b Pringle	50	lbw b Ilott		2
R.A.Pyman	c Stephenson b Andrew	0	b Ilott		10
A.J.Buzza	b Ilott	21	(9) c Hardie b Ilott		0
J.C.M.Atkinson *	run out	51	(4) c Pringle b Ilott		0
M.J.Lowrey	c Hardie b Pringle	6	(5) lbw b Such		69
M.J.Morris	c Prichard b Pringle	2	(6) c Garnham b Andrew		1
G.B.A.Dyer	c Hardie b Topley	17	(7) c Pringle b Topley		14
J.Arscott +	lbw b Childs	9	(8) c Hardie b Pringle		10
R.H.J.Jenkins	c Garnham b Topley	6	lbw b Such		11
S.W.Johnson	not out	10	not out		2
Extras	(b 7,lb 5,w 2,nb 10)	24	(b 4,lb 8,w 3,nb 7)		22
TOTAL		201			153

CAMBRIDGE U	O	M	R	W	O	M	R	W
Johnson	8	0	59	0	4	1	23	0
Jenkins	25	7	68	2	14	3	48	0
Pyman	22.1	7	46	2	16	5	36	2
Buzza	21	2	90	0	5	1	17	0
Atkinson	2	0	23	0				
Lowrey	9	1	26	1	6	0	22	0

ESSEX	O	M	R	W	O	M	R	W
Andrew	20	3	39	2	12	1	34	1
Ilott	17	3	42	1	16	2	43	5
Childs	16	7	39	1	16	9	18	0
Topley	12	4	25	2	11	2	29	1
Such	12	4	67	0	8.1	5	6	2
Pringle	9	2	16	3	9	3	11	1
Stephenson	2	1	10	0				

FALL OF WICKETS

	ESS	CAM	ESS	CAM
1st	36	13	155	13
2nd	197	17	155	23
3rd	235	53		24
4th	239	137		30
5th	319	146		32
6th		148		76
7th		153		97
8th		173		100
9th		188		150
10th		201		153

SOMERSET vs. NEW ZEALAND

at Taunton on 16th, 17th, 18th May 1990
Toss : Somerset.   Umpires : D.J.Constant and D.R.Shepherd
New Zealand won by 5 wickets

SOMERSET

S.J.Cook	c Parore b Thomson	31	not out		117
P.M.Roebuck	lbw b Snedden	17	lbw b Snedden		6
J.J.E.Hardy	c Parore b Snedden	13	c Parore b Millmow		5
C.J.Tavare *	b Snedden	156			
R.J.Harden	c Millmow b Priest	104			
N.D.Burns +	c Parore b Snedden	1	(5) c Crowe J.J. b Priest		59
A.N.Hayhurst	not out	3	(4) run out		2
G.D.Rose			(6) not out		59
I.G.Swallow					
A.N.Jones					
J.C.Hallett					
Extras	(lb 5,nb 1)	6	(lb 6,nb 2)		8
TOTAL	(for 6 wkts dec)	343	(for 4 wkts dec)		256

NEW ZEALAND

T.J.Franklin	lbw b Swallow	103	(2) lbw b Hallett		30
J.J.Crowe	c & b Jones	0	(1) c Hardy b Hallett		30
A.C.Parore +	c Jones b Swallow	43	(3) c Tavare b Roebuck		53
A.H.Jones	not out	57	(4) b Jones		64
M.D.Crowe *	not out	55	(5) b Rose		85
M.J.Greatbatch			(6) not out		46
K.R.Rutherford			(7) not out		4
S.A.Thomson					
M.W.Priest					
M.C.Snedden					
J.P.Millmow					
Extras	(b 9,lb 9,w 1,nb 1)	20	(b 4,lb 4,w 1,nb 1)		10
TOTAL	(for 3 wkts dec)	278	(for 5 wkts)		322

NEW ZEALAND	O	M	R	W	O	M	R	W
Millmow	16	4	55	0	8	1	35	1
Snedden	30	7	79	4	18	3	49	1
Thomson	17	2	104	1				
Priest	27	8	79	1	28.3	11	80	1
Rutherford	3	0	13	0	10	1	62	0
Jones	2	0	8	0	4	0	8	0
Crowe M.D.					5	1	16	0

SOMERSET	O	M	R	W	O	M	R	W
Jones	9	2	20	1	8	1	28	1
Rose	16	4	33	0	11	0	74	1
Hayhurst	17	3	55	0	13	1	58	0
Hallett	14	2	52	0	11.3	0	51	2
Swallow	19	5	52	2	15	0	68	0
Roebuck	11	3	26	0	6	0	35	1
Harden	3	0	22	0				

FALL OF WICKETS

	SOM	NZ	SOM	NZ
1st	44	9	23	57
2nd	48	122	34	64
3rd	70	201	84	174
4th	326		148	201
5th	328			312
6th	329			
7th				
8th				
9th				
10th				

YORKSHIRE vs. ZIMBABWE

at Headingley on 16th, 17th, 18th May 1990
Toss : Zimbabwe.   Umpires : B.Leadbeater and K.J.Lyons
Match drawn

YORKSHIRE

M.D.Moxon *	c Pycroft b Shah	130			
A.A.Metcalfe	c Brandes b Duers	49	c Pycroft b Butchart		30
R.J.Blakey +	c James b Brandes	5	not out		58
S.A.Kellett	lbw b Brandes	0	(1) retired out		39
P.E.Robinson	b Flower	13			
C.White	c & b Flower	9	(4) not out		12
D.Byas	c Flower b Shah	3			
P.Grayson	c James b Brandes	10			
C.S.Pickles	not out	54			
P.J.Hartley	b Duers	3			
D.Gough	not out	7			
Extras	(b 6,lb 8,w 1)	15	(b 5,lb 1,nb 2)		8
TOTAL	(for 9 wkts dec)	298	(for 2 wkts dec)		147

ZIMBABWE

G.W.Flower	c Robinson b Hartley	0	c Hartley b Gough		12
A.H.Shah	c Blakey b Hartley	10	lbw b Gough		20
W.James +	b Hartley	16	lbw b Gough		0
A.J.Pycroft *	lbw b Byas	18	(6) b White		23
C.M.Robertson	lbw b White	18	c Kellett b White		15
G.A.Briant	c Byas b Pickles	5	(4) c Moxon b Pickles		35
J.P.Brent	b White	17	not out		34
I.P.Butchart	c White b Pickles	18	not out		15
E.A.Brandes	b Gough	22			
K.G.Duers	not out	11			
E.Dube	c Robinson b Hartley	1			
Extras	(b 2,lb 8,w 1)	11	(lb 5)		5
TOTAL		147	(for 6 wkts)		159

ZIMBABWE	O	M	R	W	O	M	R	W
Brandes	21	5	75	3	6	1	23	0
Dube	4	1	19	0	6	1	22	0
Butchart	7	1	19	0	10	1	39	1
Duers	18	5	63	2	13	3	48	0
Shah	26	7	46	2				
Brent	6	1	29	0	2	0	9	0
Flower	16	4	33	2				

YORKSHIRE	O	M	R	W	O	M	R	W
Hartley	9.5	1	27	4				
Gough	10	1	21	1	13	5	32	3
Pickles	17	6	29	2	12	7	27	1
Byas	12	4	40	1	7	1	20	0
White	8	2	12	2	22	7	40	2
Grayson	4	2	8	0	13	4	35	0

FALL OF WICKETS

	YOR	ZIM	YOR	ZIM
1st	93	0	57	28
2nd	126	20	93	32
3rd	126	31		33
4th	188	59		82
5th	218	64		84
6th	220	74		134
7th	225	85		
8th	261	114		
9th	290	146		
10th		147		

REFUGE ASSURANCE LEAGUE

HEADLINES

16th - 18th May

● Three Somerset batsmen made centuries against the New Zealanders at Taunton, but ended on the losing side as the tourists reached a target of 321 to gain an impressive five-wicket victory.

● Zimbabwe held on for the draw against Yorkshire at Headingley after conceding a first-innings lead of 151.

● There were career best scores for Oxford University captain Russell Morris (96) and Surrey's David Ward (181) at The Parks and career best bowling figures (5 for 43) for Essex's Mark Ilott at Fenner's.

● First-class debuts: J.C.Hallett (Somerset); P.A.Grayson (Yorkshire); G.A.Briant and E.Dube (Zimbabwe); J.Arscott (Cambridge U)

20th May

● In the Sunday League Adrian Kuiper took Derbyshire to a table-topping fourth victory over Somerset at Taunton with a six off the last ball of the 40th over as the visitors achieved the necessary 6.5 runs an over.

● During his innings of 53 Somerset's Jimmy Cook became the first player to complete 1,000 runs in all competitions for the season.

● John Morris's 134 was the highest Sunday League score ever made by a Deryshire batsman as he and Kim Barnett launched the innings with a county record stand of 232.

● Kent also recorded their fourth win as their total of 245 for 5 proved too much for Yorkshire.

● Former England openers Chris Broad and Graeme Fowler both hit 100s as Notts and Lancashire enjoyed their third victories of the season.

● Essex gained their first Sunday win of the year as Derek Pringle hit 48 in 24 balls against Worcestershire.

● Kevin Curran made a Sunday best 77 as Gloucestershire ended Warwickshire's unbeaten run, while Ian Salisbury again improved his best figures in Sussex's win over Glamorgan.

SOMERSET vs. DERBYSHIRE

at Taunton on 20th May 1990
Toss : Derbyshire. Umpires : K.E.Palmer and D.S.Thompsett
Derbyshire won by 7 wickets. (Somerset 0 pts Derbys 4 pts)

SOMERSET

S.J.Cook	b Malcolm	53
P.M.Roebuck	b Barnett	85
A.N.Hayhurst	lbw b Miller	13
G.D.Rose	c Goldsmith b Kuiper	5
C.J.Tavare *	run out	7
R.J.Harden	c Barnett b Malcolm	30
N.D.Burns +	run out	30
R.P.Lefebvre	not out	16
M.W.Cleal	not out	13
I.G.Swallow		
A.N.Jones		
Extras	(lb 2,w 4)	6
TOTAL	(40 overs)(for 7 wkts)	258

DERBYSHIRE

K.J.Barnett *	b Lefebvre	100
J.E.Morris	b Rose	134
A.P.Kuiper	not out	21
A.E.Warner	c Harden b Jones	4
C.J.Adams	not out	0
B.Roberts		
S.C.Goldsmith		
K.M.Krikken +		
G.Miller		
D.E.Malcolm		
O.H.Mortensen		
Extras	(lb 3,w 2)	5
TOTAL	(40 overs)(for 3 wkts)	264

DERBYSHIRE	O	M	R	W		FALL OF WICKETS	
						SOM	DER
Mortensen	8	0	42	0			
Miller	8	0	37	1	1st	91	232
Warner	2	0	26	0	2nd	119	240
Malcolm	8	0	48	2	3rd	124	258
Kuiper	8	0	48	1	4th	135	
Barnett	6	0	55	1	5th	183	
					6th	210	
SOMERSET	O	M	R	W	7th	230	
Jones	6	0	38	1	8th		
Rose	8	0	45	1	9th		
Hayhurst	8	0	47	0	10th		
Lefebvre	8	0	44	1			
Swallow	5	0	38	0			
Cleal	3	0	27	0			
Roebuck	2	0	22	0			

NOTTINGHAMSHIRE vs. SURREY

at Trent Bridge on 20th May 1990
Toss : Notts. Umpires : J.H.Hampshire and A.A.Jones
Notts won by 8 wickets. (Notts 4 pts Surrey 0 pts)

SURREY

A.J.Stewart	lbw b Saxelby K.	10
G.S.Clinton	c Broad b Afford	40
M.A.Lynch	b Hemmings	20
G.P.Thorpe	c Afford b Hemmings	0
D.M.Ward +	c Afford b Saxelby M.	34
I.A.Greig *	b Hemmings	12
K.T.Medlycott	c Saxelby M. b Hemmings	2
M.A.Feltham	c Hemmings b Saxelby K.	14
C.K.Bullen	not out	23
M.P.Bicknell	not out	11
A.J.Murphy		
Extras	(b 1,lb 9,w 5)	15
TOTAL	(40 overs)(for 8 wkts)	181

NOTTINGHAMSHIRE

B.C.Broad	not out	106
R.T.Robinson *	c Ward b Bicknell	2
P.Johnson	b Bicknell	63
D.W.Randall	not out	9
M.Saxelby		
F.D.Stephenson		
B.N.French +		
E.E.Hemmings		
K.E.Cooper		
K.Saxelby		
J.A.Afford		
Extras	(lb 3,w 2)	5
TOTAL	(38.1 overs)(for 2 wkts)	185

NOTTS	O	M	R	W		FALL OF WICKETS	
						SUR	NOT
Stephenson	8	1	21	0	1st	32	5
Cooper	6	0	19	0	2nd	64	144
Saxelby K.	6	0	44	2	3rd	68	
Afford	8	1	24	1	4th	84	
Hemmings	8	0	48	4	5th	107	
Saxelby M.	4	0	15	1	6th	130	
					7th	132	
SURREY	O	M	R	W	8th	154	
Bicknell	8	1	23	2	9th		
Murphy	8	0	41	0	10th		
Feltham	8	1	34	0			
Medlycott	4	0	35	0			
Bullen	8	0	36	0			
Lynch	2	0	9	0			
Stewart	0.1	0	4	0			

LANCASHIRE vs. LEICESTERSHIRE

at Old Trafford on 20th May 1990
Toss : Leicestershire. Umpires : B.Hasssan and R.Palmer
Lancashire won by 23 runs. (Lancashire 4 pts Leics 0 pts)

LANCASHIRE

G.Fowler	c Boon b Taylor	108
M.A.Atherton	b Willey	33
N.H.Fairbrother	c & b Willey	27
G.D.Lloyd	c Nixon b Lewis	10
T.E.Jesty	b Lewis	19
Wasim Akram	b Benson	5
P.A.J.DeFreitas	b Lewis	7
I.D.Austin	c Whitaker b Agnew	2
W.K.Hegg +	lbw b Lewis	0
D.P.Hughes *	not out	0
P.J.W.Allott		
Extras	(lb 9,w 5)	14
TOTAL	(39 overs)(for 9 wkts)	225

LEICESTERSHIRE

T.J.Boon	c Hegg b Austin	46
N.E.Briers *	run out	26
J.J.Whitaker	c Allott b Austin	34
P.Willey	c Atherton b Austin	18
C.C.Lewis	c Hughes b DeFreitas	10
L.Potter	not out	32
J.D.R.Benson	b DeFreitas	21
P.A.Nixon +	not out	1
W.K.M.Benjamin		
J.P.Agnew		
L.B.Taylor		
Extras	(b 1,lb 10,w 2,nb 1)	14
TOTAL	(39 overs)(for 6 wkts)	202

LEICS	O	M	R	W		FALL OF WICKETS	
						LAN	LEI
Benjamin	5	0	23	0			
Lewis	8	1	34	4	1st	117	66
Agnew	7	0	39	1	2nd	157	94
Taylor	8	0	65	1	3rd	173	131
Willey	8	0	39	2	4th	186	143
Benson	3	0	16	1	5th	200	145
					6th	212	197
LANCASHIRE	O	M	R	W	7th	217	
DeFreitas	7	0	40	2	8th	224	
Allott	8	0	46	0	9th	225	
Atherton	8	0	40	0	10th		
Wasim Akram	8	0	32	0			
Austin	8	0	33	3			

SUSSEX vs. GLAMORGAN

at Hove on 20th May 1990
Toss : Sussex. Umpires : M.J.Kitchen and R.A.White
Sussex won by 6 wickets. (Sussex 4 pts Glamorgan 0 pts)

GLAMORGAN

H.Morris	c Pigott b Salisbury	68
P.A.Cottey	lbw b Clarke	36
I.V.A.Richards	c Pigott b Salisbury	31
A.R.Butcher *	c Dodemaide b Salisbury	6
I.Smith	not out	33
M.L.Roberts +	not out	12
N.G.Cowley		
S.J.Dennis		
S.L.Watkin		
S.R.Barwick		
M.Frost		
Extras	(lb 9,w 3)	12
TOTAL	(40 overs)(for 4 wkts)	198

SUSSEX

N.J.Lenham	b Richards	62
I.J.Gould	c Butcher b Dennis	41
M.P.Speight	b Richards	26
C.M.Wells	c Butcher b Richards	14
A.I.C.Dodemaide	not out	25
A.C.S.Pigott	not out	24
P.W.G.Parker *		
P.Moores +		
A.R.Clarke		
I.D.K.Salisbury		
A.M.Babington		
Extras	(lb 5,w 3,nb 1)	9
TOTAL	(38.4 overs)(for 4 wkts)	201

SUSSEX	O	M	R	W		FALL OF WICKETS	
						GLA	SUS
Wells C.M.	8	0	21	0			
Babington	4	0	21	0	1st	76	71
Pigott	8	1	32	0	2nd	126	120
Clarke	8	0	47	1	3rd	140	150
Dodemaide	7	0	32	0	4th	156	153
Salisbury	5	0	36	3	5th		
					6th		
GLAMORGAN	O	M	R	W	7th		
Watkin	6	0	28	0	8th		
Frost	7.4	0	51	0	9th		
Dennis	8	0	25	1	10th		
Cowley	3	0	15	0			
Barwick	7	0	40	0			
Richards	7	0	37	3			

REFUGE ASSURANCE LEAGUE

WORCESTERSHIRE vs. ESSEX

at Worcester on 20th May 1990
Toss : Worcs. Umpires : B.Dudleston and P.B.Wight
Essex won by 2 wickets. (Worcestershire 0 pts Essex 4 pts)

WORCESTERSHIRE

T.S.Curtis	c Prichard b Topley	34
M.J.Weston	b Pringle	90
I.T.Botham	c Garnham b Foster	5
D.B.D'Oliveira	c Hardie b Pringle	41
N.V.Radford	not out	26
P.A.Neale *	run out	1
S.R.Lampitt		
S.J.Rhodes +		
R.K.Illingworth		
P.J.Newport		
S.M.McEwan		
Extras	(b 2,lb 11,w 5)	18
TOTAL	(40 overs)(for 5 wkts)	215

ESSEX

G.A.Gooch *	b Weston	30
B.R.Hardie	c Newport b Illingworth	54
M.E.Waugh	c & b Weston	4
P.J.Prichard	c Neale b Botham	47
D.R.Pringle	not out	48
J.P.Stephenson	c McEwan b Botham	9
M.A.Garnham +	c Weston b Botham	5
N.A.Foster	run out	0
T.D.Topley	lbw b Botham	0
J.H.Childs	not out	5
M.C.Ilott		
Extras	(lb 12,w 2)	14
TOTAL	(39.3 overs)(for 8 wkts)	216

ESSEX	O	M	R	W		FALL OF WICKETS	
						WOR	ESS
Foster	8	1	38	1	1st	78	50
Ilott	8	0	28	0	2nd	116	55
Gooch	6	0	35	0	3rd	164	148
Topley	8	0	39	1	4th	209	148
Pringle	8	0	48	2	5th	215	172
Childs	2	0	14	0	6th		181
					7th		181
WORCS	O	M	R	W	8th		188
Newport	6	0	33	0	9th		
Weston	8	0	33	2	10th		
Radford	7	0	39	0			
Illingworth	8	0	41	1			
Lampitt	4.3	0	33	0			
Botham	6	1	25	4			

KENT vs. YORKSHIRE

at Canterbury on 20th May 1990
Toss : Kent. Umpires : P.J.Eele and J.W.Holder
Kent won by 69 runs. (Kent 4 pts Yorkshire 0 pts)

KENT

S.G.Hinks	b Fletcher	89
N.R.Taylor	c Gough b White	35
T.R.Ward	c Gough b White	37
C.S.Cowdrey *	c sub b Gough	18
G.R.Cowdrey	not out	31
M.V.Fleming	b Fletcher	13
S.A.Marsh +	not out	2
M.A.Ealham		
T.A.Merrick		
C.Penn		
R.P.Davis		
Extras	(b 1,lb 11,w 8)	20
TOTAL	(40 overs)(for 5 wkts)	245

YORKSHIRE

M.D.Moxon *	c Davis b Fleming	43
A.A.Metcalfe	b Davis	32
R.J.Blakey	b Davis	9
D.Byas	c Ward b Ealham	25
P.E.Robinson	c Taylor b Ealham	17
D.L.Bairstow +	c Marsh b Merrick	10
C.White	retired hurt	20
C.S.Pickles	c Cowdrey C.S. b Merrick	0
P.W.Jarvis	c Marsh b Merrick	1
D.Gough	b Penn	4
S.D.Fletcher	not out	1
Extras	(b 4,lb 8,w 2)	14
TOTAL	(36.3 overs)	176

YORKSHIRE	O	M	R	W		FALL OF WICKETS	
						KEN	YOR
Pickles	8	0	42	0	1st	74	59
Jarvis	8	0	37	0	2nd	156	75
Fletcher	8	1	32	2	3rd	195	105
Gough	8	0	54	1	4th	196	122
White	6	0	49	2	5th	229	135
Byas	2	0	19	0	6th		152
					7th		152
KENT	O	M	R	W	8th		156
Penn	6.3	0	28	1	9th		176
Merrick	7	0	22	3	10th		
Fleming	8	1	47	1			
Ealham	4	0	25	2			
Davis	8	0	30	2			
Cowdrey C.S.	3	0	12	0			

GLOUCESTERSHIRE vs. WARWICKS

at Moreton-in-Marsh on 20th May 1990
Toss : Gloucestershire. Umpires : J.D.Bond and R.Julian
Gloucs won by 48 runs. (Gloucs 4 pts Warwicks 0 pts)

GLOUCESTERSHIRE

R.C.Russell +	c Humpage b Munton	7
C.W.J.Athey	lbw b Benjamin	4
A.J.Wright *	b Munton	40
K.M.Curran	c Smith b Munton	75
J.W.Lloyds	c Twose b Munton	0
P.Bainbridge	not out	41
P.W.Romaines	c Humpage b Munton	5
M.W.Alleyne	not out	13
M.W.Pooley		
C.A.Walsh		
M.C.J.Ball		
Extras	(lb 15,w 2)	17
TOTAL	(40 overs)(for 6 wkts)	202

WARWICKSHIRE

Asif Din	c Athey b Walsh	59
A.I.Kallicharran	c Wright b Pooley	0
T.M.Moody	b Walsh	1
G.W.Humpage +	c Wright b Alleyne	11
T.A.Lloyd *	c & b Bainbridge	13
N.M.K.Smith	c Alleyne b Ball	5
R.G.Twose	b Alleyne	13
D.P.Ostler	not out	24
G.C.Small	lbw b Pooley	1
J.E.Benjamin	c Russell b Alleyne	1
T.A.Munton	lbw b Curran	3
Extras	(b 3,lb 5,w 14,nb 1)	23
TOTAL	(34.2 overs)	154

WARWICKS	O	M	R	W		FALL OF WICKETS	
						GLO	WAR
Benjamin	8	1	21	1	1st	13	1
Munton	8	1	23	5	2nd	21	6
Moody	8	1	33	0	3rd	127	39
Small	8	0	50	0	4th	127	71
Twose	2	0	14	0	5th	159	83
Smith	6	0	46	0	6th	176	116
					7th		127
GLOUCS	O	M	R	W	8th		132
Walsh	6	1	14	2	9th		141
Pooley	7	0	29	2	10th		154
Curran	5.2	0	22	1			
Alleyne	7	0	40	3			
Bainbridge	5	0	24	1			
Ball	4	0	17	1			

Stuart Lampitt, who established a regular place in the Worcestershire attack.

HEADLINES

19th - 22nd May

● Desmond Haynes scored 100s in both innings for Middlesex against New Zealand at Lord's but, although the visitors again flexed their impressive batting muscles, they were denied a third first-class victory.

● Dean Hodgson made his maiden first-class 100 for Gloucestershire against Zimbabwe at Bristol, but after a career best from Ali Shah the Zimbabweans finished only 17 runs short of victory.

● First-class debuts: P.N.Weekes and M.J.Thursfield (Middlesex); S.N.Barnes (Gloucs).

● Back to three-day Championship cricket and a return to declarations and unlikely run-chases – three matches were drawn and only Essex and Nottinghamshire bowled the opposition out twice

● Notts took over at the top of the table after a dramatic five-run win over Warwickshire at Edgbaston as the home side narrowly missed a third successive victory

● Graham Gooch made his third 100 in three Championship matches and the familiar trio of Foster, Pringle and Topley shared the wickets as Essex outplayed Worcestershire at New Road

● John Morris scored 100s in each innings (and another in the Sunday game) and Karl Krikken made a career best 77* to set Derbyshire on the road to victory over Somerset at Taunton

● There was deadlock elsewhere as county batsmen continued to prosper - the matches at The Oval and Old Trafford both produced three individual century-makers and only 19 wickets

● Viv Richards made the season's fastest 100 at Hove in just 73 balls but Glamorgan could not force victory over Sussex as Martin Speight made his maiden first-class century despite batting with a runner

● First-class debut: J.W.Hall (Sussex)

TOUR MATCHES

BRITANNIC ASS. CHAMPIONSHIP

GLOUCESTERSHIRE vs. ZIMBABWE

at Bristol on 19th, 21st, 22nd May 1990
Toss : Gloucestershire. Umpires : J.D.Bond and R.Julian
Match drawn

GLOUCESTERSHIRE

I.P.Butcher	c Robertson b Brent	78	(6) not out		26
G.D.Hodgson	c Traicos b Brent	126	(7) c James b Traicos		6
M.W.Alleyne	b Shah	37	(4) b Traicos		54
C.W.J.Athey *	not out	8	(9) lbw b Brandes		2
P.Bainbridge	not out	4	(1) b Traicos		23
J.W.Lloyds			(2) b Jarvis		31
K.M.Curran			(3) c Briant b Jarvis		6
G.A.Tedstone +			(5) c Traicos b Dolphin		23
D.A.Graveney			(8) b Brandes		7
D.V.Lawrence			b Brandes		0
S.N.Barnes			b Brandes		0
Extras	(b 4,lb 8,nb 2)	14	(b 10,lb 15,nb 3)		28
TOTAL	(for 3 wkts dec)	267			206

ZIMBABWE

W.James	c Graveney b Lawrence	36	lbw b Curran		23
A.H.Shah	c Alleyne b Graveney	185			
C.M.Robertson	c Tedstone b Curran	4	(2) c Tedstone b Lawrence		6
A.J.Pycroft *	st Tedstone b Graveney	9	retired hurt		15
G.A.Briant +	c Graveney b Curran	69			
J.P.Brent	b Alleyne	23	(3) not out		27
I.P.Butchart	lbw b Curran	6	(5) run out		5
E.A.Brandes	lbw b Lawrence	10	(6) not out		8
A.J.Traicos	lbw b Lawrence	1			
M.P.Jarvis	not out	1			
D.F.Dolphin					
Extras	(b 10,lb 12,w 1,nb 1)	24	(b 3,lb 1,nb 1)		5
TOTAL	(for 9 wkts dec)	368	(for 3 wkts)		89

ZIMBABWE	O	M	R	W	O	M	R	W
Brandes	12	3	32	0	10.2	3	35	4
Jarvis	9	1	40	0	21	6	61	2
Butchart	7	1	23	0				
Dolphin	13	2	58	0	16	7	29	1
Traicos	17	8	30	0	25	10	43	3
Shah	15	4	44	1				
Brent	13	2	28	2	5	3	13	0

GLOUCS	O	M	R	W	O	M	R	W
Lawrence	18.1	5	45	3	10.4	0	43	1
Barnes	26	8	80	0				
Curran	27	4	80	3	10	2	42	1
Graveney	23	11	44	2				
Alleyne	10	2	42	1				
Bainbridge	5	0	29	0				
Lloyds	5	0	26	0				

FALL OF WICKETS

	GLO	ZIM	GLO	ZIM
1st	170	60	52	14
2nd	255	78	60	36
3rd	255	103	90	78
4th		281	138	
5th		340	158	
6th		351	176	
7th		359	188	
8th		366	198	
9th		368	202	
10th			206	

MIDDLESEX vs. NEW ZEALAND

at Lord's on 19th, 20th, 21st May 1990
Toss : Middlesex. Umpires : J.C.Balderstone and N.T.Plews
Match drawn

MIDDLESEX

D.L.Haynes	lbw b Hadlee	181	c & b Jones		129
M.A.Roseberry	c Rutherford b Snedden	9	c Hadlee b Morrison		0
M.R.Ramprakash	c Hadlee b Snedden	21	c Priest b Snedden		62
K.R.Brown	lbw b Snedden	23	not out		24
R.O.Butcher	lbw b Snedden	0	not out		22
P.R.Downton *+	not out	57			
P.N.Weekes	lbw b Snedden	22			
S.P.Hughes					
M.J.Thursfield					
N.G.Cowans					
P.C.R.Tufnell					
Extras	(lb 14,nb 5)	19	(b 1,lb 9,nb 4)		14
TOTAL	(for 6 wkts dec)	332	(for 3 wkts dec)		251

NEW ZEALAND

J.J.Crowe	c Downton b Cowans	14	lbw b Cowans		20
J.G.Wright *	c Weekes b Hughes	54	c Butcher b Thursfield		18
A.H.Jones	lbw b Hughes	41	run out		70
M.D.Crowe	c Downton b Tufnell	13	(9) not out		13
M.J.Greatbatch	b Hughes	34	(4) b Weekes		52
K.R.Rutherford	not out	68	st Downton b Tufnell		2
M.W.Priest	not out	51	b Tufnell		19
I.D.S.Smith +			(5) c Weekes b Tufnell		34
R.J.Hadlee			(8) c Roseberry b Tufnell		7
M.C.Snedden			not out		0
D.K.Morrison					
Extras	(b 7,lb 1,nb 1)	9	(b 4,lb 3,w 1)		8
TOTAL	(for 5 wkts dec)	284	(for 8 wkts)		243

NEW ZEALAND	O	M	R	W	O	M	R	W
Hadlee	22	3	78	1	11	2	25	0
Morrison	22	1	100	0	17	1	67	1
Snedden	27.5	7	63	5	8	2	22	1
Priest	22	7	77	0	19	3	73	0
Jones					5	0	28	1
Rutherford					6	0	26	0

MIDDLESEX	O	M	R	W	O	M	R	W
Cowans	21	4	56	1	6	0	25	1
Hughes	23.2	6	87	3	6	0	38	0
Tufnell	20	5	64	1	17	3	76	4
Thursfield	16	7	41	0	9	0	44	1
Weekes	13	6	28	0	13	3	53	1

FALL OF WICKETS

	MID	NZ	MID	NZ
1st	48	44	4	34
2nd	96	77	143	40
3rd	159	103	226	144
4th	161	148		150
5th	286	170		173
6th	332			213
7th				223
8th				242
9th				
10th				

SOMERSET vs. DERBYSHIRE

at Taunton on 19th, 21st, 22nd May 1990
Toss : Somerset. Umpires : K.E.Palmer and D.S.Thompsett
Derbyshire won by 146 runs. (Somerset 5 pts (Bt: 3, Bw: 2) Derbyshire 21 pts (Bt: 4, Bw: 1))

DERBYSHIRE

K.J.Barnett *	c Hayhurst b Jones	94	(7) lbw b Swallow		25
P.D.Bowler	c Harden b Rose	6	(1) b Harden		109
J.E.Morris	c Burns b Lefebvre	122	(5) c Hayhurst b Cook		19
A.P.Kuiper	b Jones	5	(2) c Burns b Rose		23
C.J.Adams	c Roebuck b Swallow	58	(3) lbw b Roebuck		4
B.Roberts	lbw b Jones	37	(4) not out		77
K.M.Krikken +	lbw b Lefebvre	24	(6) lbw b Cook		1
A.E.Warner	lbw b Swallow	1			
D.E.Malcolm	lbw b Swallow	10	(8) not out		2
O.H.Mortensen	not out	2			
G.Miller					
Extras	(b 1,lb 9,nb 3)	13	(nb 5)		5
TOTAL	(for 9 wkts dec)	372	(for 6 wkts dec)		265

SOMERSET

S.J.Cook	c Kuiper b Warner	1	c Adams b Malcolm		5
J.J.E.Hardy	c Krikken b Warner	4	c sub b Malcolm		91
A.N.Hayhurst	c Mortensen b Miller	90	lbw b Mortensen		0
C.J.Tavare *	b Kuiper	64	c Kuiper b Malcolm		9
R.J.Harden	not out	69	c Mortensen b Warner		42
P.M.Roebuck	not out	34	lbw b Miller		6
N.D.Burns +			c Kuiper b Barnett		10
G.D.Rose			c Krikken b Malcolm		31
R.P.Lefebvre			st Krikken b Miller		13
I.G.Swallow			lbw b Miller		0
A.N.Jones			not out		8
Extras	(b 1,lb 6,nb 3)	10	(b 1,w 1,nb 2)		4
TOTAL	(for 4 wkts dec)	272			219

SOMERSET	O	M	R	W	O	M	R	W
Jones	17	1	85	3	4	0	26	0
Rose	16	0	75	1	5	1	24	1
Lefebvre	24.3	6	67	2	3	1	5	0
Hayhurst	16	5	42	0				
Swallow	40	7	89	3	20	4	51	1
Roebuck	3	2	4	0	12	3	23	1
Harden					16	2	60	1
Tavare					5	0	43	0
Cook					5	0	25	2
Burns					0.3	0	8	0

DERBYSHIRE	O	M	R	W	O	M	R	W
Malcolm	12.4	4	20	0	17	2	88	4
Warner	11	3	30	2	9	1	34	1
Mortensen	10	3	17	0	7	0	25	1
Kuiper	12	1	46	1				
Miller	19	3	69	1	23.5	5	57	3
Barnett	25	3	83	0	4	0	14	1

FALL OF WICKETS

	DER	SOM	DER	SOM
1st	18	3	52	6
2nd	189	25	81	7
3rd	217	152	178	25
4th	237	189	201	118
5th	317		204	138
6th	335		249	153
7th	338			174
8th	360			201
9th	372			211
10th				219

WORCESTERSHIRE vs. ESSEX

at Worcester on 19th, 21st, 22nd May 1990
Toss : Essex. Umpires : B.Dudleston and P.B.Wight
Essex won by 10 wickets. (Worcestershire 4 pts (Bt: 3, Bw: 1) Essex 24 pts (Bt: 4, Bw: 4))

ESSEX

G.A.Gooch *	c Rhodes b Newport	121	not out		42
J.P.Stephenson	c Curtis b Radford	4	not out		6
P.J.Prichard	run out	45			
M.E.Waugh	not out	166			
B.R.Hardie	c D'Oliveira b Botham	59			
N.Shahid	not out	35			
D.R.Pringle					
M.A.Garnham +					
N.A.Foster					
T.D.Topley					
J.H.Childs					
Extras	(lb 7,nb 10)	17			0
TOTAL	(for 4 wkts dec)	447	(for 0 wkts)		48

WORCESTERSHIRE

T.S.Curtis	c Shahid b Pringle	48	lbw b Foster		2
M.J.Weston	c Gooch b Foster	0	c Gooch b Foster		14
R.K.Illingworth	b Pringle	89	(7) c Gooch b Topley		9
P.A.Neale *	b Pringle	9	(3) c Hardie b Pringle		4
I.T.Botham	c Foster b Topley	53	(4) b Pringle		5
D.B.D'Oliveira	c Hardie b Topley	32	(5) c Stephenson b Pringle		25
S.R.Lampitt	lbw b Topley	1	(6) c Stephenson b Foster		1
S.J.Rhodes +	b Foster	0	(11) not out		5
P.J.Newport	c Waugh b Topley	18	(8) c & b Pringle		96
N.V.Radford	b Foster	10	(9) lbw b Pringle		10
G.R.Dilley	not out	0	(10) c Garnham b Foster		40
Extras	(lb 6,w 2,nb 5)	13	(lb 4,nb 3)		7
TOTAL		273			218

WORCS	O	M	R	W	O	M	R	W
Dilley	10	1	76	0	5	1	33	0
Radford	16	1	95	1				
Newport	19	2	88	1	5	1	7	0
Lampitt	15	5	55	0				
Botham	19	2	58	1				
Illingworth	14	3	45	0				
Weston	7	1	23	0				
Curtis					0.3	0	8	0

ESSEX	O	M	R	W	O	M	R	W
Foster	22.1	5	70	3	23	5	64	4
Pringle	21	2	67	3	24.1	6	66	5
Topley	19	4	67	4	8	1	44	1
Waugh	13	4	63	0	3	0	21	0
Childs					8	6	9	0
Stephenson					3	1	10	0

FALL OF WICKETS

	ESS	WOR	WOR	ESS
1st	37	5	12	
2nd	135	104	19	
3rd	226	152	21	
4th	392	163	25	
5th		223	32	
6th		223	58	
7th		226	66	
8th		254	82	
9th		267	202	
10th		273	218	

BRITANNIC ASSURANCE CHAMPIONSHIP

WARWICKSHIRE vs. NOTTINGHAMSHIRE

at Edgbaston on 19th, 21st, 22nd May 1990
Toss : Nottinghamshire. Umpires : J.H.Hampshire and A.A.Jones
Nottinghamshire won by 5 runs. (Warwicks 5 pts (Bt: 3, Bw: 2) Notts 24 pts (Bt: 4, Bw: 4))

NOTTINGHAMSHIRE

B.C.Broad	b Smith	119	c Reeve b Benjamin	30
D.J.R.Martindale	c Humpage b Munton	73	lbw b Munton	10
R.T.Robinson *	c Smith b Small	41	lbw b Small	47
P.Johnson	c sub b Munton	2	c Benjamin b Munton	73
D.W.Randall	c Humpage b Small	5	lbw b Benjamin	17
M.Saxelby	not out	32	c Asif Din b Smith	13
F.D.Stephenson	c Munton b Donald	15	c Moles b Smith	12
B.N.French +	not out	1	not out	25
E.E.Hemmings			not out	16
K.E.Cooper				
R.A.Pick				
Extras	(lb 14,nb 1)	15	(lb 5,w 2,nb 2)	9
TOTAL	(for 6 wkts dec)	303	(for 7 wkts dec)	252

WARWICKSHIRE

A.J.Moles	b Cooper	13	lbw b Cooper	35
T.A.Lloyd *	lbw b Stephenson	4	(7) run out	10
T.A.Munton	lbw b Cooper	13	(11) b Stephenson	0
Asif Din	c Randall b Hemmings	41	(2) lbw b Hemmings	61
A.I.Kallicharran	st French b Hemmings	20	(3) c Saxelby b Hemmings	58
G.W.Humpage +	c Randall b Pick	74	(4) run out	62
D.A.Reeve	c French b Stephenson	34	(5) c Saxelby b Hemmings	26
N.M.K.Smith	c French b Pick	6	(6) c Robinson b Stephenson	14
G.C.Small	c Randall b Cooper	0	(8) c French b Pick	0
A.A.Donald	not out	24	(9) not out	9
J.E.Benjamin	b Stephenson	14	(10) b Stephenson	1
Extras	(b 1,lb 7,nb 1)	9	(b 4,lb 18)	22
TOTAL		252		298

WARWICKS	O	M	R	W	O	M	R	W		FALL OF WICKETS				
											NOT	WAR	NOT	WAR
Donald	16	5	38	1	3	0	5	0	1st		176	8	30	88
Small	19	3	34	2	12	1	39	1	2nd		247	28	54	120
Munton	25	5	85	2	18	3	57	2	3rd		247	45	135	185
Smith	23.5	0	82	1	17	1	76	2	4th		254	79	176	253
Benjamin	14	2	41	0	18	1	55	2	5th		255	134	195	259
Asif Din	2	1	9	0	2	0	15	0	6th		295	178	197	284
									7th			190	217	285
NOTTS	O	M	R	W	O	M	R	W	8th			198		287
Pick	20	4	46	2	11	0	56	1	9th			234		298
Stephenson	19.3	1	69	3	14.4	2	69	3	10th			252		298
Hemmings	15	3	46	2	23	0	108	3						
Cooper	23	6	72	3	16	3	43	1						
Saxelby	4	1	11	0										

SURREY vs. HAMPSHIRE

at The Oval on 19th, 21st, 22nd May 1990
Toss : Hampshire. Umpires : P.J.Eele and J.W.Holder
Match drawn. (Surrey 5 pts (Bt: 4, Bw: 1) Hampshire 5 pts (Bt: 3, Bw: 2))

SURREY

D.J.Bicknell	retired hurt	41		
G.S.Clinton	c Maru b Connor	73	retired hurt	37
A.J.Stewart	c Maru b Connor	17	(1) not out	100
M.A.Lynch	c Gower b Marshall	11	(3) c Gower b Shine	2
G.P.Thorpe	c Parks b Marshall	2	(4) lbw b Maru	18
D.M.Ward +	not out	129	(5) b Turner	23
I.A.Greig *	c Terry b Marshall	34	(6) c Maru b Turner	4
K.T.Medlycott	not out	30	(7) c Parks b Maru	8
M.A.Feltham			(8) not out	3
M.P.Bicknell				
A.J.Murphy				
Extras	(b 4,lb 15,w 2,nb 16)	37	(b 2,lb 4,w 1,nb 2)	9
TOTAL	(for 5 wkts dec)	374	(for 5 wkts dec)	204

HAMPSHIRE

V.P.Terry	lbw b Murphy	8	c Medlycott b Bicknell M.P.	0
C.L.Smith *	run out	71	c Medlycott b Murphy	84
D.I.Gower	b Feltham	4	c sub b Bicknell M.P.	69
R.A.Smith	not out	114	c Feltham b Bicknell M.P.	1
T.C.Middleton	lbw b Greig	1	(6) b Medlycott	20
M.D.Marshall	not out	47	(5) not out	51
R.J.Parks +			not out	5
R.J.Maru				
I.J.Turner				
K.J.Shine				
C.A.Connor				
Extras	(b 2,lb 2,nb 1)	5	(b 6,lb 1,w 1)	8
TOTAL	(for 4 wkts dec)	250	(for 5 wkts)	238

HAMPSHIRE	O	M	R	W	O	M	R	W		FALL OF WICKETS				
											SUR	HAM	SUR	HAM
Marshall	20	4	65	3	7	1	14	0	1st		148	19	73	0
Shine	16	2	75	0	9	0	55	1	2nd		151	26	111	158
Connor	25	4	84	2	5	0	13	0	3rd		166	163	154	161
Turner	13	0	45	0	14.3	4	60	2	4th		173	179	158	167
Maru	36	12	86	0	21	5	47	2	5th		308		187	197
Smith C.L.					1	0	9	0	6th					
									7th					
SURREY	O	M	R	W	O	M	R	W	8th					
Bicknell M.P.	15	5	43	0	16	5	39	3	9th					
Murphy	22	6	65	1	12	1	65	1	10th					
Feltham	19	7	51	1	8	0	31	0						
Greig	8	1	40	1										
Medlycott	21.1	8	47	0	20	3	84	1						
Lynch					3	0	12	0						

SUSSEX vs. GLAMORGAN

at Hove on 19th, 21st, 22nd May 1990
Toss : Glamorgan. Umpires : M.J.Kitchen and R.A.White
Match drawn. (Sussex 3 pts (Bt: 2, Bw: 1) Glamorgan 8 pts (Bt: 4, Bw: 4))

GLAMORGAN

A.R.Butcher *	c Moores b Pigott	139
H.Morris	c Moores b Dodemaide	73
M.J.Cann	c Moores b Wells C.M.	13
I.V.A.Richards	not out	118
P.A.Cottey	not out	43
I.Smith		
N.G.Cowley		
C.P.Metson +		
S.J.Dennis		
S.L.Watkin		
M.Frost		
Extras	(b 6,lb 7,nb 3)	16
TOTAL	(for 3 wkts dec)	402

SUSSEX

N.J.Lenham	lbw b Dennis	34	c Cowley b Watkin	18
J.W.Hall	lbw b Frost	8	c Metson b Dennis	7
A.I.C.Dodemaide	c Cottey b Watkin	3	c Richards b Dennis	45
M.P.Speight	c Richards b Frost	60	c Cann b Dennis	131
C.M.Wells	c & b Watkin	1	c Frost b Watkin	94
I.J.Gould	lbw b Frost	9	c Morris b Butcher	11
P.Moores +	lbw b Richards	3	not out	106
A.C.S.Pigott	c Metson b Richards	8	c Morris b Cann	54
P.W.G.Parker *	not out	57	(9) not out	10
I.D.K.Salisbury	c Metson b Frost	3		
A.M.Babington	c & b Cowley	20		
Extras	(b 10,lb 3,nb 3)	16	(b 4,lb 4,w 5,nb 3)	16
TOTAL		222	(for 7 wkts dec)	492

SUSSEX	O	M	R	W	O	M	R	W		FALL OF WICKETS			
											GLA	SUS	SUS	GLA
Pigott	17	1	86	1					1st		188	12	15
Dodemaide	24	4	81	1					2nd		241	29	27
Babington	20	5	57	0					3rd		241	76	163
Wells C.M.	22	2	90	1					4th			91	279
Lenham	6	1	18	0					5th			118	295
Salisbury	13	2	57	0					6th			121	350
GLAMORGAN	O	M	R	W	O	M	R	W	7th			121	443
Frost	18	2	62	4	24	0	96	0	8th			138	
Watkin	19	2	66	2	30	4	94	2	9th			157	
Dennis	11	2	36	1	25	3	83	3	10th			222	
Richards	15	4	27	2	9	2	14	0					
Cowley	8.4	1	18	1	13	5	28	0					
Smith					8	0	49	0					
Cottey					9	0	44	0					
Cann					7	0	39	1					
Butcher					3	0	16	1					
Morris					3	0	21	0					

LANCASHIRE vs. LEICESTERSHIRE

at Old Trafford on 19th, 21st, 22nd May 1990
Toss : Leicestershire. Umpires : B.Hassan and R.Palmer
Match drawn. (Lancashire 6 pts (Bt: 3, Bw: 3) Leicestershire 3 pts (Bt: 3, Bw: 0))

LEICESTERSHIRE

T.J.Boon	c & b Atherton	84	run out	30
N.E.Briers *	c Hegg b DeFreitas	0	not out	81
J.J.Whitaker	c Mendis b Patterson	8	not out	107
P.Willey	c Hegg b Fitton	43		
L.Potter	c & b Atherton	55		
C.C.Lewis	c Hegg b Atherton	32		
M.I.Gidley	st Hegg b Atherton	2		
W.K.M.Benjamin	run out	65		
P.A.Nixon +	not out	33		
J.P.Agnew	c Fairbrother b Patterson	6		
A.D.Mullally	c sub b Patterson	2		
Extras	(lb 2,nb 4)	6	(b 2,lb 5,nb 4)	11
TOTAL		336	(for 1 wkt dec)	229

LANCASHIRE

G.D.Mendis	c Boon b Willey	113	c & b Agnew	82
G.Fowler	not out	115	b Willey	22
M.A.Atherton	not out	10	c Briers b Willey	3
N.H.Fairbrother			c Mullally b Agnew	46
T.E.Jesty			b Lewis	0
P.A.J.DeFreitas			not out	19
W.K.Hegg +			c & b Lewis	1
D.P.Hughes *			c sub b Potter	6
J.D.Fitton			not out	0
P.J.Martin				
B.P.Patterson				
Extras	(lb 7,w 1,nb 4)	12	(b 5,lb 10,w 4,nb 3)	22
TOTAL	(for 1 wkt dec)	250	(for 7 wkts)	201

LANCASHIRE	O	M	R	W	O	M	R	W		FALL OF WICKETS			
											LEI	LAN	LEI	LAN
Patterson	21	2	68	3	6	2	27	0	1st		4	231	49	78
DeFreitas	26	3	78	1	7	0	23	0	2nd		17		88	
Martin	19	4	45	0	5	0	17	0	3rd		113		158	
Fitton	22	8	54	1	24	4	54	0	4th		158		159	
Atherton	27	5	89	4	15	3	55	0	5th		227		163	
Hughes					13	1	46	0	6th		228		167	
									7th		251		189	
LEICS	O	M	R	W	O	M	R	W	8th		319			
Lewis	6	0	21	0	17	8	20	2	9th		326			
Agnew	18	3	76	0	11	1	43	2	10th		336			
Mullally	22.2	5	60	0	11	1	61	0					
Willey	19	6	43	1	11	1	54	2					
Gidley	9	0	43	0									
Potter					4.4	3	8	1					

BRITANNIC ASSURANCE CHAMPIONSHIP

MIDDLESEX vs. SURREY

at Lord's on 23rd, 24th, 25th May 1990
Toss : Middlesex. Umpires : K.J.Lyons and R.A.White
Match drawn. (Middlesex 7 pts (Bt: 4, Bw: 3) Surrey 6 pts (Bt: 2, Bw: 4))

MIDDLESEX

D.L.Haynes	c Lynch b Gray	33	b Bicknell		0
M.A.Roseberry	c Greig b Murphy	122	c Ward b Murphy		0
M.W.Gatting *	c Ward b Gray	20	(4) c Medlycott b Bicknell		13
M.R.Ramprakash	c Alikhan b Kendrick	30	(5) b Medlycott		10
K.R.Brown	c Murphy b Medlycott	16	(6) c & b Medlycott		56
P.R.Downton +	b Murphy	3	(7) st Ward b Kendrick		55
N.F.Williams	c Alikhan b Medlycott	40	(8) c Kendrick b Medlycott		18
J.E.Emburey	c Ward b Medlycott	10	(3) b Bicknell		17
N.G.Cowans	c Kendrick b Medlycott	6	(10) c Bicknell b Kendrick		5
S.P.Hughes	c Greig b Bicknell	0	(9) not out		23
P.C.R.Tufnell	not out	14	b Medlycott		1
Extras	(b 4,lb 8,w 1,nb 3)	16	(b 16,lb 8,nb 2)		26
TOTAL		310			224

SURREY

R.I.Alikhan	b Hughes	20	not out	0
P.D.Atkins	c Gatting b Hughes	23	not out	0
G.P.Thorpe	c Tufnell b Emburey	16		
D.M.Ward +	c Downton b Hughes	46		
M.A.Lynch	b Tufnell	46		
I.A.Greig *	b Williams	44		
K.T.Medlycott	c Downton b Williams	0		
M.P.Bicknell	not out	26		
N.M.Kendrick	not out	52		
A.H.Gray				
A.J.Murphy				
Extras	(lb 11,nb 2)	13		0
TOTAL	(for 7 wkts dec)	286	(for 0 wkts)	0

SURREY	O	M	R	W	O	M	R	W
Gray	22	3	68	2				
Bicknell	25	7	72	1	25	14	25	3
Murphy	22	8	50	2	25	7	75	1
Greig	1	0	5	0	3	0	8	0
Medlycott	26.1	5	91	4	32	14	65	4
Kendrick	4	0	12	1	14	4	25	2
Alikhan					1	0	2	0

MIDDLESEX	O	M	R	W	O	M	R	W
Williams	22	5	57	2				
Cowans	21	8	36	0				
Tufnell	24	11	57	1	2	2	0	0
Emburey	24.1	8	58	1				
Hughes	16	2	57	3				
Gatting	2	0	6	0				
Haynes	1	0	4	0	3	3	0	0

FALL OF WICKETS				
	MID	SUR	MID	SUR
1st	75	42	0	
2nd	103	53	0	
3rd	165	77	24	
4th	206	124	31	
5th	220	206	85	
6th	241	206	137	
7th	258	208	167	
8th	266		201	
9th	275		221	
10th	310		224	

GLAMORGAN vs. KENT

at Swansea on 23rd, 24th, 25th May 1990
Toss : Kent. Umpires : J.H.Harris and P.B.Wight
Kent won by 6 runs. (Glamorgan 4 pts (Bt: 3, Bw: 1) Kent 19 pts (Bt: 3, Bw: 0))

KENT

S.G.Hinks	b Watkin	107	c Morris b Dennis	4
M.R.Benson *	lbw b Watkin	17	c Morris b Dennis	96
N.R.Taylor	lbw b Watkin	106		
T.R.Ward	c Cann b Watkin	3	b Cowley	7
G.R.Cowdrey	not out	68	not out	80
M.V.Fleming	not out	10	not out	45
R.P.Davis			(3) run out	12
S.A.Marsh +				
M.A.Ealham				
C.Penn				
P.S.De Villiers				
Extras	(b 6,lb 7,w 3,nb 1)	17	(b 1,lb 2)	3
TOTAL	(for 4 wkts dec)	328	(for 4 wkts dec)	247

GLAMORGAN

A.R.Butcher *	not out	151	b Davis	50
H.Morris	not out	100	c & b Davis	29
I.V.A.Richards			c Cowdrey b Davis	21
M.J.Cann			c Fleming b Davis	10
P.A.Cottey			c sub b Ward	21
I.Smith			run out	66
N.G.Cowley			b De Villiers	76
C.P.Metson +			b De Villiers	21
S.J.Dennis			lbw b De Villiers	6
S.L.Watkin			c Davis b De Villiers	1
S.R.Barwick			not out	0
Extras	(lb 2,nb 2)	4	(b 8,lb 1,nb 4)	13
TOTAL	(for 0 wkts dec)	255		314

GLAMORGAN	O	M	R	W	O	M	R	W
Watkin	28	5	77	4	10	1	27	0
Dennis	11	0	39	0	12	0	53	2
Barwick	28.2	9	72	0	8	3	18	0
Richards	13	4	34	0				
Cowley	33	7	75	0	22	4	67	1
Cann	1	0	1	0	6	0	56	0
Butcher	3	1	17	0				
Cottey					3	0	23	0

KENT	O	M	R	W	O	M	R	W
De Villiers	17	5	39	0	15.3	3	69	4
Penn	14	5	44	0	7	0	39	0
Fleming	16	1	48	0	3	0	20	0
Ealham	12.2	2	48	0				
Davis	24	4	74	0	25	5	97	4
Ward					9	0	52	1
Benson					3	0	28	0

FALL OF WICKETS				
	KEN	GLA	KEN	GLA
1st	33		23	60
2nd	194		92	87
3rd	210		112	108
4th	297		132	139
5th				145
6th				267
7th				297
8th				308
9th				314
10th				314

DERBYSHIRE vs. YORKSHIRE

at Chesterfield on 23rd, 24th, 25th May 1990
Toss : Derbyshire. Umpires : P.J.Eele and A.A.Jones
Derbyshire won by 144 runs. (Derbyshire 24 pts (Bt: 4, Bw: 4) Yorkshire 8 pts (Bt: 4, Bw: 4))

DERBYSHIRE

K.J.Barnett *	c Byas b Fletcher	38	c Blakey b Hartley	141
J.E.Morris	c Byas b Hartley	60	c Blakey b Fletcher	5
B.Roberts	c Byas b Jarvis	49	not out	124
P.D.Bowler	lbw b Fletcher	29		
C.J.Adams	run out	12	c Metcalfe b Byas	10
S.C.Goldsmith	c Byas b Hartley	0	c Moxon b Byas	8
K.M.Krikken +	c Bairstow b Hartley	0		
G.Miller	not out	47		
I.R.Bishop	c Berry b Fletcher	0		
A.E.Warner	c Moxon b Jarvis	1	(4) c Blakey b Hartley	10
S.J.Base	c Hartley b Berry	58	(7) c Robinson b Byas	7
Extras	(lb 16,w 1,nb 6)	23	(b 1,lb 9,w 3,nb 3)	16
TOTAL		317	(for 6 wkts dec)	321

YORKSHIRE

M.D.Moxon *	b Warner	45	c Krikken b Warner	15
A.A.Metcalfe	c Krikken b Bishop	32	c Roberts b Bishop	5
R.J.Blakey	c Bowler b Goldsmith	9	c Goldsmith b Miller	25
S.A.Kellett	b Barnett	22	lbw b Miller	55
P.E.Robinson	c Roberts b Base	12	lbw b Miller	4
D.L.Bairstow +	lbw b Base	19	b Miller	21
D.Byas	c Krikken b Bishop	67	c Goldsmith b Bishop	6
P.J.Hartley	c Goldsmith b Warner	75	c Bowler b Miller	11
P.W.Jarvis	c Base b Bishop	15	c Adams b Bishop	8
P.Berry	not out	6	not out	4
S.D.Fletcher	c Bowler b Bishop	2	b Miller	0
Extras	(lb 12,w 3,nb 13)	28	(lb 2,w 2,nb 7)	11
TOTAL		332		162

YORKSHIRE	O	M	R	W	O	M	R	W
Jarvis	29	5	88	2	12	0	59	0
Hartley	23	4	80	3	14	0	74	2
Fletcher	24	9	57	3	14	1	100	1
Byas	8	3	28	0	11	0	55	3
Berry	13.4	1	48	1	9	2	23	0

DERBYSHIRE	O	M	R	W	O	M	R	W
Bishop	21.2	6	62	4	18	3	42	3
Base	15	0	72	2	7	1	29	0
Warner	24	1	90	2	10	4	32	1
Barnett	9	1	37	1	6	1	12	0
Goldsmith	7	1	21	1				
Miller	11	2	38	0	20.3	6	45	6

FALL OF WICKETS				
	DER	YOR	DER	YOR
1st	44	64	10	16
2nd	119	80	259	26
3rd	180	118	272	78
4th	201	131	292	82
5th	201	143	308	114
6th	201	157	321	135
7th	207	297		141
8th	207	308		158
9th	210	319		158
10th	317	332		162

NOTTINGHAMSHIRE vs. NORTHANTS

at Trent Bridge on 23rd, 24th, 25th May 1990
Toss : Northants. Umpires : J.W.Holder and A.G.T.Whitehead
Nottinghamshire won by 8 wickets. (Notts 22 pts (Bt: 3, Bw: 3) Northants 8 pts (Bt: 4, Bw: 4))

NORTHANTS

A.Fordham	c Johnson b Pick	21	c French b Pick	74
N.A.Felton	lbw b Pick	11	not out	119
R.J.Bailey *	run out	65	not out	54
G.Cook	b Pick	49		
D.J.Capel	c Randall b Cooper	4		
A.L.Penberthy	not out	67		
J.G.Thomas	c French b Afford	5		
D.Ripley +	st French b Afford	55		
W.W.Davis	b Cooper	4		
A.R.Roberts	b Afford	5		
J.W.Govan	b Saxelby	17		
Extras	(lb 12,nb 10)	22	(b 6,lb 11,nb 1)	18
TOTAL		325	(for 1 wkt dec)	265

NOTTINGHAMSHIRE

B.C.Broad	b Govan	49	run out	0
D.J.R.Martindale	c Fordham b Thomas	0	not out	108
R.T.Robinson *	c Thomas b Capel	30	lbw b Davis	56
P.Johnson	c Thomas b Govan	27	not out	165
D.W.Randall	run out	37		
M.Saxelby	b Penberthy	42		
F.D.Stephenson	b Roberts	11		
B.N.French +	c & b Penberthy	33		
K.E.Cooper	c Ripley b Penberthy	4		
R.A.Pick	c Penberthy b Davis	3		
J.A.Afford	not out	0		
Extras	(lb 3,w 2,nb 9)	14	(b 4,lb 4,w 1,nb 6)	15
TOTAL		250	(for 2 wkts)	344

NOTTS	O	M	R	W	O	M	R	W
Stephenson	16	5	23	0	13	0	52	0
Cooper	25	6	65	2	22	1	59	0
Pick	19	1	64	3	17	4	40	1
Saxelby	13.4	1	71	1	5	1	23	0
Afford	33	6	90	3	17	4	74	0

NORTHANTS	O	M	R	W	O	M	R	W
Davis	13	1	50	1	14.4	1	63	1
Thomas	7	1	41	0	12	1	54	0
Govan	13	0	56	2	6	0	45	0
Capel	14	2	45	1	13	1	60	0
Penberthy	6	0	28	3	10	1	57	0
Roberts	15	8	27	1	9	0	57	0

FALL OF WICKETS				
	NOR	NOT	NOR	NOT
1st	24	6	147	0
2nd	47	82		95
3rd	150	94		
4th	157	150		
5th	170	153		
6th	178	176		
7th	273	233		
8th	278	237		
9th	301	246		
10th	325	250		

BRITANNIC ASSURANCE CHAMPIONSHIP

HEADLINES

23rd - 25th May

- There was no sign of relief for the bowlers as 17 centuries and a succession of big partnerships were made in the six Championship matches

- Paul Johnson led the way with an explosive career best 165* from just 120 balls as an unbeaten third wicket stand of 249 with Duncan Martindale (career best 108*) brought Notts to victory over Northants to keep them at the top of the table

- Derbyshire moved to second place with a comfortable victory over Yorkshire which owed much to a stand of 249 between Kim Barnett and Bruce Roberts and six wickets from Geoff Miller

- Spin also played its part in Kent's six run victory over Glamorgan, Richard Davis taking four second innings wickets after the Welshmen had declared at 255 for no wicket in their first innings, Alan Butcher and Hugh Morris proving inseperable

- A welcome return to wicket-taking ways by Keith Medlycott was not enough to breathe interest into Surrey's match against Middlesex for whom Mike Roseberry had earlier made a career best 122

- There was no chance of a positive result at Southampton as 100s from Essex's Brian Hardie and Mark Waugh and Hampshire's Chris Smith and Tony Middleton cancelled each other out

- Somerset's Jimmy Cook took his first-class aggregate to 770 runs with 197 against Sussex and Andy Hayhurst improved his best score to 170 in a first day score of 500 for five but Neil Lenham and Martin Speight again came to Sussex's rescue

SOMERSET vs. SUSSEX

at Taunton on 23rd, 24th, 25th May 1990
Toss : Somerset. Umpires : K.E.Palmer and D.S.Thompsett
Match drawn. (Somerset 7 pts (Bt: 4, Bw: 3) Sussex 4 pts (Bt: 3, Bw: 1))

SOMERSET

S.J.Cook	c Gould b Wells C.M.	197	
P.M.Roebuck	c Moores b Babington	27	
A.N.Hayhurst	c Babington b Dodemaide	170	
C.J.Tavare *	c & b Babington	28	
R.J.Harden	c & b Pigott	51	
N.D.Burns +	not out	14	
G.D.Rose	not out	4	
R.P.Lefebvre			
I.G.Swallow			
N.A.Mallender			
A.N.Jones			
Extras	(b 1,lb 3,w 1,nb 4)	9	
TOTAL	(for 5 wkts dec)	500	

SUSSEX

N.J.Lenham	lbw b Roebuck	51	run out	108
J.W.Hall	lbw b Mallender	6	c Tavare b Jones	1
A.I.C.Dodemaide	lbw b Rose	0	b Lefebvre	20
A.P.Wells	c Burns b Roebuck	18	b Mallender	23
M.P.Speight	c Rose b Lefebvre	73	not out	83
C.M.Wells *	not out	99	not out	6
I.J.Gould	c sub b Rose	30		
P.Moores +	b Rose	1		
A.C.S.Pigott	c Rose b Swallow	2		
I.D.K.Salisbury	c Harden b Jones	5		
A.M.Babington	c Burns b Jones	8		
Extras	(b 4,lb 2,nb 14)	20	(b 5,lb 7,w 3)	15
TOTAL		313	(for 4 wkts dec)	256

SUSSEX	O	M	R	W	O	M	R	W
Pigott	22	2	117	1				
Dodemaide	25	2	115	1				
Babington	23	2	109	2				
Wells C.M.	21	1	72	1				
Salisbury	17	4	66	0				
Lenham	2	0	17	0				

SOMERSET	O	M	R	W	O	M	R	W
Jones	18.5	1	71	2	8	5	11	1
Mallender	16	6	21	1	13	2	24	1
Swallow	24	8	62	1	14	4	28	0
Rose	17	4	52	3	8	2	21	0
Roebuck	21	4	63	2	12	1	38	0
Lefebvre	18	4	38	1	12	2	33	1
Harden					11	1	43	0
Hayhurst					5	0	22	0
Tavare					3	0	12	0
Cook					2	0	12	0

FALL OF WICKETS

	SOM	SUS	SUS	SOM
1st	76	30	4	
2nd	319	30	45	
3rd	364	64	107	
4th	477	108	219	
5th	487	206		
6th		268		
7th		270		
8th		277		
9th		291		
10th		313		

HAMPSHIRE vs. ESSEX

at Southampton on 23rd, 24th, 25th May 1990
Toss : Essex. Umpires : R.Julian and M.J.Kitchen
Match drawn. (Hampshire 4 pts (Bt: 3, Bw: 1) Essex 4 pts (Bt: 4, Bw: 0))

ESSEX

B.R.Hardie *	b Connor	125	c Parks b Maru	31
J.P.Stephenson	c Parks b Shine	2	retired hurt	4
P.J.Prichard	c Maru b Shine	23	b Connor	4
M.E.Waugh	c Parks b Marshall	125	c Maru b Shine	39
N.Shahid	not out	19	(6) b Marshall	0
A.C.Seymour	not out	10	(7) c Parks b Marshall	0
T.D.Topley			(5) c Parks b Shine	23
M.A.Garnham +			not out	62
N.A.Foster			b Maru	40
J.H.Childs			c Connor b Maru	0
S.J.W.Andrew			c Turner b Maru	0
Extras	(b 4,lb 5,nb 2)	11	(b 2,lb 2,w 1,nb 2)	7
TOTAL	(for 4 wkts dec)	315		210

HAMPSHIRE

V.P.Terry	c Stephenson b Foster	14	c Topley b Andrew	12
T.C.Middleton	not out	104	(3) b Childs	11
C.L.Smith	c Garnham b Waugh	128	(2) st Garnham b Childs	31
R.J.Parks +	not out	3		
M.C.J.Nicholas *			(4) not out	32
R.J.Scott			not out	7
M.D.Marshall			(5) b Foster	9
R.J.Maru				
I.J.Turner				
K.J.Shine				
C.A.Connor				
Extras	(b 4,lb 3,nb 4)	11		0
TOTAL	(for 2 wkts dec)	260	(for 4 wkts)	102

HAMPSHIRE	O	M	R	W	O	M	R	W
Marshall	21	3	49	1	15	5	18	2
Shine	15	1	56	2	16	6	52	2
Connor	28	6	95	1	17	1	71	1
Turner	14	2	48	0	9	3	18	0
Maru	20	5	45	0	18.3	2	47	4
Scott	2	0	13	0				

ESSEX	O	M	R	W	O	M	R	W
Foster	19	5	43	1	15	4	33	1
Andrew	15	5	50	0	13	4	42	1
Topley	15	3	53	0	2	0	3	0
Childs	23	6	49	0	17	10	24	2
Waugh	9	0	33	1				
Shahid	5	1	25	0				

FALL OF WICKETS

	ESS	HAM	ESS	HAM
1st	16	20	18	27
2nd	67	257	78	42
3rd	270		81	59
4th	294		82	88
5th			86	
6th			126	
7th			201	
8th			208	
9th			210	
10th				

OTHER FIRST-CLASS MATCHES

TOUR MATCH

OXFORD UNIV vs. LEICESTERSHIRE

at The Parks on 23rd, 24th, 25th May 1990
Toss : Oxford Univ.   Umpires : R.Palmer and H.J.Rhodes
Match drawn

OXFORD UNIV

D.A.Hagan	b Millns	0	c Parsons b Ferris	6
R.E.Morris *	lbw b Ferris	0	c Whitaker b Ferris	11
D.Curtis	lbw b Millns	0	c Benson b Willey	19
G.J.Turner	c Ferris b Willey	51	lbw b Gidley	9
M.A.Crawley	c Nixon b Millns	50	not out	105
P.Gerrans	c Nixon b Millns	0	lbw b Millns	22
W.M.van der Merwe	lbw b Parsons	24	not out	39
S.Chauhan	c Boon b Parsons	25		
M.J.Russell	c Benson b Parsons	4		
H.Davies	not out	9		
J.McGrady +	lbw b Millns	1		
Extras	(b 6,lb 4,w 5)	15	(lb 7,nb 1)	8
TOTAL		179	(for 5 wkts)	219

LEICESTERSHIRE

J.D.R.Benson	b van der Merwe	94
P.Willey	b Chauhan	177
B.Smith	lbw b Crawley	4
J.J.Whitaker	not out	124
P.A.Nixon +	not out	16
T.J.Boon		
N.E.Briers *		
G.J.Parsons		
M.I.Gidley		
D.J.Millns		
G.J.F.Ferris		
Extras	(b 12,lb 10,w 5,nb 5)	32
TOTAL	(for 3 wkts dec)	447

LEICS	O	M	R	W	O	M	R	W		FALL OF WICKETS			
											OXF	LEI	OXF	LEI
Millns	22.3	8	47	5	20	8	47	1	1st	0	165	16	
Ferris	20	6	45	1	17	7	33	2	2nd	0	189	17	
Parsons	24	11	34	3	15	6	35	0	3rd	1	380	33	
Gidley	14	4	27	0	19	8	54	1	4th	106		71	
Willey	5	4	4	1	22	9	29	1	5th	107		138	
Benson	4	2	12	0					6th	114			
Boon					3	0	14	0	7th	154			
									8th	165			
OXFORD UNIV	O	M	R	W	O	M	R	W	9th	170			
van der Merwe	16	1	52	1					10th	179			
Gerrans	19	3	73	0									
Crawley	19	4	50	1									
Turner	21	3	72	0									
Davies	20	1	112	0									
Chauhan	15	1	58	1									
Curtis	1	0	8	0									

CAMBRIDGE UNIV vs. GLOUCESTERSHIRE

at Fenner's on 23rd, 24th, 25th May 1990
Toss : Gloucestershire.   Umpires : D.R.Shepherd and R.C.Tolchard
Gloucestershire won by 70 runs

GLOUCESTERSHIRE

A.J.Wright *	st Arscott b Buzza	44	run out	58
G.D.Hodgson	lbw b Shufflebotham	51	(4) not out	39
I.P.Butcher	c Atkinson b Lowrey	79	(5) b Jenkins	8
P.Bainbridge	st Arscott b Lowrey	61	(6) not out	2
J.W.Lloyds	not out	73	(2) c Atkinson b Buzza	95
P.W.Romaines	not out	15	(3) c Morris b Buzza	23
G.A.Tedstone +				
M.W.Pooley				
S.N.Barnes				
M.C.J.Ball				
K.B.S.Jarvis				
Extras	(b 7,lb 11,w 2,nb 10)	30	(lb 3,w 1,nb 1)	5
TOTAL	(for 4 wkts dec)	353	(for 4 wkts dec)	230

CAMBRIDGE UNIV

S.P.James	c Tedstone b Pooley	116	lbw b Jarvis	6
R.Heap	c Butcher b Barnes	11	c Wright b Barnes	0
A.J.Buzza	c Ball b Pooley	6	(9) b Barnes	1
J.C.M.Atkinson *	c Hodgson b Ball	72	b Ball	34
M.J.Lowrey	c Tedstone b Bainbridge	20	run out	45
M.J.Morris	c Butcher b Barnes	18	lbw b Bainbridge	17
G.B.A.Dyer	c Ball b Barnes	1	(3) c Tedstone b Jarvis	4
J.Arscott +	c Lloyds b Barnes	13	(7) not out	43
D.H.Shufflebotham	not out	25	(8) c Tedstone b Barnes	29
R.H.J.Jenkins	not out	3	c Butcher b Barnes	1
S.W.Johnson			c Wright b Ball	1
Extras	(b 12,lb 9,nb 8)	29	(b 6,lb 7,w 1,nb 4)	18
TOTAL	(for 8 wkts dec)	314		199

CAMBRIDGE U	O	M	R	W	O	M	R	W		FALL OF WICKETS			
										GLO	CAM	GLO	CAM
Jenkins	20	3	61	0	23.3	3	68	1	1st	107	23	103	7
Johnson	14	1	44	0	13	5	25	0	2nd	107	38	179	12
Shufflebotham	17	2	65	1	11	3	37	0	3rd	198	146	198	13
Buzza	27	6	97	1	20	1	91	2	4th	312	190	220	81
Atkinson	4	1	9	0					5th		226		115
Lowrey	14	2	59	2	2	0	6	0	6th		241		121
									7th		257		173
GLOUCS	O	M	R	W	O	M	R	W	8th		304		184
Barnes	24	9	65	4	14	2	51	4	9th				186
Jarvis	15	2	50	0	7	0	31	2	10th				199
Ball	15	4	50	1	13	4	37	2					
Pooley	13	1	51	2	3	0	16	0					
Bainbridge	12	3	33	1	8	3	27	1					
Lloyds	22	5	44	0	11	2	24	0					

LANCASHIRE vs. ZIMBABWE

at Old Trafford on 23rd, 24th, 25th May 1990
Toss : Lancashire.   Umpires : G.I.Burgess and D.O.Oslear
Match drawn

LANCASHIRE

N.J.Speak	c & b Traicos	138	c sub b Duers	74
G.D.Lloyd	c Traicos b Butchart	78	c Flower b Shah	76
S.P.Titchard	c Flower b Duers	15	b Flower	80
J.P.Crawley	run out	1	not out	76
M.Watkinson	c Traicos b Shah	48		
Wasim Akram	c James b Duers	18		
I.D.Austin	not out	11		
G.Yates	not out	2		
I.Folley				
R.Irani				
J.Stanworth *+				
Extras	(lb 5,w 6,nb 4)	15	(b 1,lb 3)	4
TOTAL	(for 6 wkts dec)	326	(for 3 wkts dec)	310

ZIMBABWE

K.J.Arnott *	c Stanworth b Wasim Akram	0	(2) lbw b Irani	2
G.W.Flower	c Crawley b Folley	65	(1) not out	20
D.F.Dolphin	c Lloyd b Austin	25		
C.M.Robertson	c sub b Yates	125	not out	0
I.P.Butchart	c Speak b Irani	71		
A.J.Pycroft	b Austin	55		
W.James +	not out	16	(3) lbw b Folley	52
A.H.Shah				
A.J.Traicos				
K.G.Duers				
E.Dube				
Extras	(lb 4,w 1,nb 14)	19	(w 2,nb 2)	4
TOTAL	(for 6 wkts dec)	376	(for 2 wkts)	78

ZIMBABWE	O	M	R	W	O	M	R	W		FALL OF WICKETS			
										LAN	ZIM	LAN	ZIM
Dube	11	1	48	0	4	1	18	0	1st	154	0	133	6
Duers	23	5	96	2	20	4	59	1	2nd	188	39	165	76
Butchart	12	3	48	1	5	1	27	0	3rd	204	228	310	
Dolphin	8	3	28	0	2	0	19	0	4th	284	228		
Shah	23	5	57	1	11	1	46	1	5th	294	342		
Traicos	15	0	44	1	27	4	69	0	6th	319	376		
Flower					13.5	0	68	1	7th				
									8th				
LANCASHIRE	O	M	R	W	O	M	R	W	9th				
Wasim Akram	13	1	46	1					10th				
Watkinson	5	2	6	0									
Irani	15	3	61	1	7	4	12	1					
Austin	19	5	93	2	8	4	10	0					
Yates	28	5	88	1	11	3	26	0					
Folley	27	7	78	1	11	3	30	1					

HEADLINES

23rd - 25th May

• Zimbabwe's short tour ended with their third draw in first-class matches. Lancashire's second string openers Nick Speak and Graham Lloyd shared century stands in both innings, Speak making his maiden 100. Colin Robertson responded with his first first-class 100 as the Zimbabweans again demonstrated their depth in batting

• Leicestershire's Peter Willey and James Whitaker helped themselves to centuries at The Parks after David Millns had taken a career best 5 for 47 on his debut for the county

• Nor did the students miss out on the flood of run-making: Cambridge's Steve James made 116 against Gloucestershire and Oxford's Mark Crawley hit 105* against Leicestershire.

• First-class debuts: D.Curtis (Oxford U.); B.Smith (Leicestershire) S.P.Titchard, J.P.Crawley, G.Yates and R.Irani (Lancashire). Irani replaced P.J.Martin who injured himself before taking any part in the game

TEXACO TROPHY

REFUGE ASS. LEAGUE

ENGLAND vs. NEW ZEALAND

at Headingley on 23rd May 1990
Toss : New Zealand. Umpires : B.J.Meyer and N.T.Plews
New Zealand won by 4 wickets

ENGLAND

G.A.Gooch *	c Millmow b Pringle	55
D.I.Gower	c Smith b Hadlee	1
R.A.Smith	c Crowe b Hadlee	128
A.J.Lamb	run out	18
A.J.Stewart	lbw b Morrison	33
D.R.Pringle	not out	30
R.C.Russell +	c Crowe b Pringle	13
P.A.J.DeFreitas	not out	1
C.C.Lewis		
G.C.Small		
E.E.Hemmings		
Extras	(lb 10,w 1,nb 5)	16
TOTAL	(55 overs)(for 6 wkts)	295

NEW ZEALAND

J.G.Wright *	c Stewart b Gooch	52
A.H.Jones	st Russell b Gooch	51
M.D.Crowe	c Russell b Lewis	46
M.J.Greatbatch	not out	102
K.R.Rutherford	lbw b Lewis	0
R.J.Hadlee	c Lamb b Lewis	12
M.W.Priest	c Gower b Small	2
I.D.S.Smith +	not out	17
C.Pringle		
D.K.Morrison		
J.P.Millmow		
Extras	(b 5,lb 7,w 3,nb 1)	16
TOTAL	(54.5 overs)(for 6 wkts)	298

NEW ZEALAND	O	M	R	W	FALL OF WICKETS		
						ENG	NZ
Hadlee	11	4	46	2			
Pringle	11	2	45	2	1st	5	97
Morrison	11	0	70	1	2nd	118	106
Millmow	11	0	65	0	3rd	168	224
Priest	11	0	59	0	4th	225	224
					5th	261	254
ENGLAND	O	M	R	W	6th	274	259
Small	11	1	43	1	7th		
DeFreitas	10.5	0	70	0	8th		
Pringle	7	0	45	0	9th		
Lewis	11	0	54	3	10th		
Hemmings	11	0	51	0			
Gooch	4	0	23	2			

Man of the match: M.J.Greatbatch

ENGLAND vs. NEW ZEALAND

at The Oval on 25th May 1990
Toss : England. Umpires : D.J.Constant and J.H.Hampshire
England won by 6 wickets

NEW ZEALAND

J.G.Wright *	c Small b Malcolm	15
A.H.Jones	run out	15
M.D.Crowe	c Russell b Lewis	7
M.J.Greatbatch	c Smith b Malcolm	111
K.R.Rutherford	retired hurt	0
R.J.Hadlee	retired hurt	9
M.W.Priest	c Smith b DeFreitas	24
I.D.S.Smith +	not out	25
C.Pringle	b Small	1
J.P.Millmow		
D.K.Morrison		
Extras	(lb 2,w 3)	5
TOTAL	(55 overs)(for 6 wkts)	212

ENGLAND

G.A.Gooch *	not out	112
D.I.Gower	b Hadlee	4
R.A.Smith	c Smith b Hadlee	5
A.J.Lamb	lbw b Pringle	4
A.J.Stewart	c Morrison b Priest	28
R.C.Russell +	not out	47
C.C.Lewis		
P.A.J.DeFreitas		
G.C.Small		
E.E.Hemmings		
D.E.Malcolm		
Extras	(lb 7,w 5,nb 1)	13
TOTAL	(49.3 overs)(for 4 wkts)	213

ENGLAND	O	M	R	W	FALL OF WICKETS		
						NZ	ENG
DeFreitas	11	1	47	0			
Malcolm	11	5	19	2	1st	25	5
Lewis	11	1	51	1	2nd	33	15
Small	11	0	59	1	3rd	53	29
Hemmings	11	2	34	0	4th	174	104
					5th	202	
NEW ZEALAND	O	M	R	W	6th	212	
Hadlee	11	2	34	2	7th		
Pringle	9.3	0	53	1	8th		
Millmow	9	1	47	0	9th		
Morrison	9	0	38	0	10th		
Priest	11	2	34	1			

Man of the match: D.E.Malcolm

HEADLINES

England vs New Zealand
Texaco Trophy

Headingley: 23rd May

● New Zealand quickly confirmed the power of their batting at Headingley by making the highest score ever made by a side batting second in One-Day Internationals as they beat England by four wickets with one ball to spare, reaching 298 for six.

● After John Wright and Andrew Jones had opened with a stand of 97, Mark Greatbatch took over, completing his first One-Day International 100 and dominating a stand of 118 for the third wicket with Martin Crowe.

● Robin Smith had earlier made his first century in One-Day Internationals

● Four consecutive boundaries by Derek Pringle off Richard Hadlee's final over had carried England to 295 for 5 but even Chris Lewis's best figures for England could not prevent a record-breaking New Zealand victory

● New Zealand's injury problems had forced them to call in Chris Pringle straight from the Bradford League

The Oval: 25th May

● England squared the series and took the Texaco Trophy for the fourth consecutive time with a hard-earned six wicket win at The Oval

● After Devon Malcolm had started his One-Day International career with four consecutive maidens to put New Zealand on the defensive, the visitors were rocked by two serious injuries: Ken Rutherford ducked into a Chris Lewis bouncer and Richard Hadlee broke a bone in his right hand after being struck by the same bowler – both had to retire hurt

● Mark Greatbatch made his second successive 100 and, ably supported by Mark Priest and Ian Smith, lifted the total to 212 for six which was made to look a formidable score when Hadlee returned to reduce England to 29 for 3

● Graham Gooch stood firm, making his eighth 100 in One-Day Internationals and his fifth in the Texaco Trophy and the Prudential Trophy that preceded it, and a stand of of 109* for the fifth wicket with Jack Russell who hit a career best 47* took England to victory with 33 balls to spare - enough to win the Texaco Trophy on run-rate

WORCESTERSHIRE vs. WARWICKS

at Worcester on 27th May 1990
Toss : Worcs. Umpires : B.Leadbeater and N.T.Plews
Warwicks won by 6 wickets. (Worcs 0 pts Warwicks 4 pts)

WORCESTERSHIRE

T.S.Curtis	run out	61
M.J.Weston	c Humpage b Reeve	15
I.T.Botham	c Ostler b Smith	29
D.B.D'Oliveira	b Smith	3
P.A.Neale *	run out	23
D.A.Leatherdale	run out	3
S.R.Lampitt	not out	16
N.V.Radford	c Munton b Small	4
P.J.Newport	run out	8
S.J.Rhodes +		
S.M.McEwan		
Extras	(lb 13,w 7)	20
TOTAL	(40 overs)(for 8 wkts)	182

WARWICKSHIRE

Asif Din	not out	86
T.A.Lloyd *	c Rhodes b Weston	0
T.M.Moody	c Rhodes b Radford	29
A.I.Kallicharran	lbw b McEwan	5
D.A.Reeve	c Botham b Lampitt	11
G.W.Humpage +	not out	40
N.M.K.Smith		
D.P.Ostler		
G.C.Small		
J.E.Benjamin		
T.A.Munton		
Extras	(b 2,lb 2,w 7,nb 3)	14
TOTAL	(39.4 overs)(for 4 wkts)	185

WARWICKS	O	M	R	W	FALL OF WICKETS		
						WOR	WAR
Munton	8	0	36	0			
Benjamin	8	0	27	0	1st	42	2
Reeve	8	2	45	1	2nd	111	45
Smith	8	1	39	2	3rd	115	67
Small	8	0	22	1	4th	135	104
					5th	139	
WORCS	O	M	R	W	6th	163	
Newport	8	2	20	0	7th	169	
Weston	3	0	12	1	8th	182	
Radford	8	0	34	1	9th		
Botham	6	0	43	0	10th		
McEwan	6.4	0	39	1			
Lampitt	8	0	33	1			

NORTHANTS vs. KENT

at Northampton on 27th May 1990
Toss : Kent. Umpires : B.J.Meyer and D.S.Thompsett
Kent won by 55 runs. (Northants 0 pts Kent 4 pts)

KENT

S.G.Hinks	c Penberthy b Capel	11
N.R.Taylor	c Capel b Robinson	73
T.R.Ward	c Felton b Penberthy	71
C.S.Cowdrey *	not out	45
G.R.Cowdrey	not out	70
S.A.Marsh +		
M.V.Fleming		
M.A.Ealham		
T.A.Merrick		
C.Penn		
R.P.Davis		
Extras	(b 1,lb 10,w 6)	17
TOTAL	(40 overs)(for 3 wkts)	287

NORTHANTS

A.Fordham	run out	28
N.A.Felton	c Marsh b Cowdrey C.S.	64
A.J.Lamb *	c Penn b Cowdrey C.S.	27
R.J.Bailey	lbw b Fleming	11
D.J.Capel	c Davis b Cowdrey C.S.	38
A.L.Penberthy	c Ealham b Cowdrey C.S.	6
J.G.Thomas	c Cowdrey C.S. b Merrick	1
D.Ripley +	c Taylor b Merrick	6
J.W.Govan	not out	9
W.W.Davis	c Cowdrey C.S. b Penn	19
M.A.Robinson	b Merrick	0
Extras	(b 2,lb 16,w 5)	23
TOTAL	(37.4 overs)	232

NORTHANTS	O	M	R	W	FALL OF WICKETS		
						KEN	NOR
Davis	8	1	49	0			
Capel	8	1	40	1	1st	17	67
Thomas	8	1	46	0	2nd	137	116
Govan	4	0	28	0	3rd	172	135
Robinson	8	0	73	1	4th		145
Penberthy	4	0	40	1	5th		161
					6th		178
KENT	O	M	R	W	7th		189
Penn	7	1	33	1	8th		196
Merrick	7.4	0	37	3	9th		223
Ealham	5	0	33	0	10th		232
Davis	4	0	29	0			
Fleming	6	0	25	1			
Cowdrey C.S.	8	0	57	4			

REFUGE ASSURANCE LEAGUE

YORKSHIRE vs. HAMPSHIRE

at Headingley on 27th May 1990
Toss : Yorkshire. Umpires : D.O.Oslear and A.G.T.Whitehead
Hampshire won by 36 runs. (Yorks 0 pts Hants 4 pts)

HAMPSHIRE		
D.I.Gower	c Byas b Hartley	12
V.P.Terry	b Byas	56
R.A.Smith	b Hartley	44
M.D.Marshall	b Byas	10
R.J.Scott	c Robinson b Carrick	1
M.C.J.Nicholas *	c Blakey b Byas	8
J.R.Ayling	b Fletcher	13
A.N Aymes +	not out	15
T.M.Tremlett	not out	2
R.J.Maru		
C.A.Connor		
Extras	(lb 14,w 8,nb 1)	23
TOTAL	(40 overs)(for 7 wkts)	184

YORKSHIRE		
C.S.Pickles	c Maru b Marshall	6
A.A.Metcalfe *	b Connor	0
S.A.Kellett	run out	7
R.J.Blakey	c Gower b Tremlett	22
P.E.Robinson	c Maru b Scott	26
D.Byas	lbw b Tremlett	2
D.L.Bairstow +	c Smith b Scott	21
P.Carrick	c Nicholas b Ayling	14
P.J.Hartley	b Connor	14
D.Gough	not out	17
S.D.Fletcher	c Nicholas b Connor	6
Extras	(b 1,lb 10,nb 2)	13
TOTAL	(39 overs)	148

YORKSHIRE	O	M	R	W	FALL OF WICKETS		
						HAM	YOR
Fletcher	8	1	34	1			
Pickles	8	0	30	0	1st	34	7
Hartley	8	1	24	2	2nd	113	7
Carrick	8	1	39	1	3rd	129	23
Gough	2	0	17	0	4th	131	49
Byas	6	0	26	3	5th	146	55
					6th	149	71
HAMPSHIRE	O	M	R	W	7th	180	100
Connor	8	1	31	3	8th		116
Marshall	7	1	32	1	9th		125
Tremlett	8	0	19	2	10th		148
Ayling	8	2	16	1			
Scott	8	0	39	2			

LEICESTERSHIRE vs. SOMERSET

at Leicester on 27th May 1990
Toss : Somerset. Umpires : D.J.Constant and B.Dudleston
Somerset won by 3 wickets. (Leics 0 pts Somerset 4 pts)

LEICESTERSHIRE		
T.J.Boon	c Burns b Cleal	18
N.E.Briers *	c Lefebvre b Rose	6
J.J.Whitaker	c Tavare b Rose	83
P.Willey	c Cook b Rose	52
L.Potter	run out	1
J.D.R.Benson	not out	17
P.A.Nixon +	not out	9
J.P.Agnew		
G.J.F.Ferris		
A.D.Mullally		
D.J.Millns		
Extras	(lb 5)	5
TOTAL	(40 overs)(for 5 wkts)	191

SOMERSET		
S.J.Cook	b Millns	60
P.M.Roebuck	b Ferris	28
A.N.Hayhurst	lbw b Ferris	1
C.J.Tavare *	b Agnew	26
R.J.Harden	not out	31
N.D.Burns +	b Willey	3
G.D.Rose	c Briers b Millns	20
R.P.Lefebvre	lbw b Willey	0
M.W.Cleal	not out	8
I.G.Swallow		
N.A.Mallender		
Extras	(b 1,lb 4,w 11)	16
TOTAL	(38.3 overs)(for 7 wkts)	193

SOMERSET	O	M	R	W	FALL OF WICKETS		
						LEI	SOM
Rose	8	0	36	3			
Cleal	5	0	27	1	1st	17	54
Lefebvre	8	0	42	0	2nd	31	62
Mallender	8	0	28	0	3rd	156	124
Swallow	5	0	20	0	4th	163	126
Hayhurst	6	0	33	0	5th	166	131
					6th		166
LEICS	O	M	R	W	7th		169
Agnew	7	2	20	1	8th		
Millns	8	1	71	2	9th		
Mullally	7.3	1	36	0	10th		
Ferris	8	1	28	2			
Willey	8	0	33	2			

GLAMORGAN vs. LANCASHIRE

at Colwyn Bay on 27th May 1990
Toss : Lancashire. Umpires : J.H.Harris and P.B.Wight
Lancashire won by 4 wickets. (Glamorgan 0 pts Lancs 4 pts)

GLAMORGAN		
A.R.Butcher *	b Wasim Akram	38
H.Morris	c Austin b DeFreitas	6
M.P.Maynard	c Austin b Wasim Akram	100
I.V.A.Richards	c Atherton b Austin	77
I.Smith	b Hughes	6
N.G.Cowley	b Austin	1
C.P.Metson +	not out	5
J.Derrick		
S.J.Dennis		
S.R.Barwick		
M.Frost		
Extras	(lb 5,w 3,nb 1)	9
TOTAL	(40 overs)(for 6 wkts)	242

LANCASHIRE		
G.Fowler	c Metson b Dennis	2
M.A.Atherton	c Maynard b Richards	74
G.D.Lloyd	c Metson b Frost	3
N.H.Fairbrother	run out	27
T.E.Jesty	c Butcher b Barwick	25
Wasim Akram	c Cowley b Frost	50
P.A.J.DeFreitas	not out	35
I.D.Austin	not out	10
W.K.Hegg +		
D.P.Hughes *		
P.J.W.Allott		
Extras	(b 5,lb 7,w 8)	20
TOTAL	(37.5 overs)(for 6 wkts)	246

LANCASHIRE	O	M	R	W	FALL OF WICKETS		
						GLA	LAN
Allott	8	1	28	0			
DeFreitas	8	0	42	1	1st	26	5
Atherton	7	0	66	0	2nd	73	20
Wasim Akram	8	0	46	2	3rd	216	113
Austin	8	0	51	2	4th	224	114
Hughes	1	0	4	1	5th	227	183
					6th	242	211
GLAMORGAN	O	M	R	W	7th		
Frost	8	0	39	2	8th		
Dennis	8	0	38	1	9th		
Barwick	8	1	54	1	10th		
Derrick	3	0	26	0			
Richards	6.5	0	42	1			
Cowley	4	0	35	0			

MIDDLESEX vs. GLOUCESTERSHIRE

at Lord's on 27th May 1990
Toss : Gloucestershire. Umpires : K.J.Lyons and R.A.White
Middlesex won by 7 wickets. (Middlesex 4 pts Gloucs 0 pts)

GLOUCESTERSHIRE		
R.C.Russell +	b Cowans	17
C.W.J.Athey	c Gatting b Emburey	29
A.J.Wright *	run out	58
K.M.Curran	c Roseberry b Gatting	13
P.Bainbridge	b Gatting	18
J.W.Lloyds	not out	36
P.W.Romaines	c Downton b Cowans	11
M.W.Alleyne	b Emburey	1
C.A.Walsh	b Williams	1
D.V.Lawrence	b Hughes	1
M.C.J.Ball	run out	1
Extras	(lb 9,w 6)	15
TOTAL	(40 overs)	201

MIDDLESEX		
D.L.Haynes	lbw b Alleyne	50
M.A.Roseberry	b Lawrence	0
M.W.Gatting *	c Wright b Walsh	5
M.R.Ramprakash	not out	88
K.R.Brown	not out	39
R.O.Butcher		
P.R.Downton +		
J.E.Emburey		
N.F.Williams		
S.P.Hughes		
N.G.Cowans		
Extras	(lb 10,w 11)	21
TOTAL	(37.4 overs)(for 3 wkts)	203

MIDDLESEX	O	M	R	W	FALL OF WICKETS		
						GLO	MID
Cowans	8	2	27	2			
Hughes	8	0	43	1	1st	29	4
Gatting	8	0	48	2	2nd	80	17
Williams	8	0	44	1	3rd	115	105
Emburey	8	1	30	2	4th	137	
					5th	152	
GLOUCS	O	M	R	W	6th	179	
Walsh	7.4	2	22	1	7th	186	
Lawrence	8	0	39	1	8th	195	
Curran	7	0	37	0	9th	198	
Bainbridge	7	0	40	0	10th	201	
Ball	2	0	20	0			
Alleyne	6	0	35	1			

Refuge Assurance League Table at 27th May 1990

		P	W	L	T	NR	Away wins	Pts	Run rate
1	Kent (12)	6	5	1	0	0	3	20	97.84
2	Lancashire (1)	5	4	1	0	0	3	16	99.30
3	Derbyshire (5)	5	4	1	0	0	3	16	83.47
4	Middlesex (9)	5	4	1	0	0	2	16	95.09
5	Nottinghamshire (4)	5	3	2	0	0	1	12	80.32
6	Warwickshire (15)	4	3	1	0	0	1	12	78.61
7	Gloucestershire (16)	5	2	2	0	1	1	10	83.87
8	Somerset (10)	4	2	2	0	0	1	8	96.67
9	Glamorgan (17)	5	2	3	0	0	1	8	85.83
10	Worcestershire (2)	5	2	3	0	0	1	8	84.41
11	Sussex (13)	3	2	1	0	0	0	8	85.07
12	Hampshire (6)	4	1	2	0	1	1	6	84.79
13	Essex (3)	5	1	4	0	0	1	4	87.38
14	Northants (8)	4	1	3	0	0	1	4	79.63
15	Leicestershire (14)	5	1	4	0	0	0	4	76.54
16	Yorkshire (11)	5	1	4	0	0	0	4	68.42
17	Surrey (7)	3	0	3	0	0	0	0	89.91

| TOUR MATCH | BRITANNIC ASS. CHAMPIONSHIP |

SUSSEX vs. NEW ZEALAND

at Hove on 26th, 27th, 28th May 1990
Toss : Sussex. Umpires : B.Hassan and D.R.Shepherd
New Zealand won by 7 wickets

SUSSEX

N.J.Lenham	b Morrison	64	c Parore b Pringle	6
J.W.Hall	not out	120	run out	40
A.I.C.Dodemaide	b Morrison	4	not out	110
A.P.Wells	c Parore b Thomson	86		
C.M.Wells *	c Greatbatch b Pringle	8	(4) not out	113
I.J.Gould	not out	6		
P.Moores +				
I.D.K.Salisbury				
B.T.P.Donelan				
R.A.Bunting				
A.M.Babington				
Extras	(b 1,lb 5,w 1,nb 5)	12	(lb 1)	1
TOTAL	(for 4 wkts dec)	300	(for 2 wkts dec)	270

NEW ZEALAND

T.J.Franklin	b Dodemaide	0	b Bunting	78
J.J.Crowe	b Salisbury	48	(3) not out	81
M.W.Priest	c Moores b Donelan	72		
M.J.Greatbatch	c Wells C.M. b Bunting	26	(5) not out	51
M.D.Crowe	c Donelan b Babington	65	(4) c Gould b Salisbury	24
J.G.Wright *	not out	10	(2) c Wells C.M. b Dodemaide	82
S.A.Thomson	not out	3		
J.G.Bracewell				
A.C.Parore +				
C.Pringle				
D.K.Morrison				
Extras	(b 3,lb 1,nb 2)	6	(b 15,lb 7,nb 3)	25
TOTAL	(for 5 wkts dec)	230	(for 3 wkts)	341

NEW ZEALAND	O	M	R	W	O	M	R	W
Morrison	10	2	35	2				
Pringle	19	3	66	1	20	5	61	1
Thomson	18.4	6	52	1				
Bracewell	34.2	9	99	0	34	5	138	0
Priest	16	4	42	0	20	3	66	0
Crowe M.D.					3	2	4	0

SUSSEX	O	M	R	W	O	M	R	W
Dodemaide	14	2	56	1	19	6	57	1
Bunting	14	3	42	1	7	0	45	1
Wells C.M.	5	1	22	0	3	0	20	0
Babington	9	0	36	1	11	0	54	0
Salisbury	16	2	55	1	14	0	80	1
Donelan	9	3	15	1	14	0	62	0
Gould					0.4	0	1	0

FALL OF WICKETS

	SUS	NZ	SUS	NZ
1st	99	0	12	147
2nd	103	114	82	204
3rd	269	139		268
4th	294	193		
5th		223		
6th				
7th				
8th				
9th				
10th				

HEADLINES

26th- 28th May

● New Zealand gained their third
first-class victory of their tour
as they successfully chased a target
of 341 in 69 overs on a perfect
Hove pitch.

● The Sussex batsmen also gave
a good account of themselves as 1141 runs
were scored for the loss of 14 wickets,
Jamie Hall and Tony Dodemaide both
compiling their maiden
first-class 100s

MIDDLESEX vs. GLOUCESTERSHIRE

at Lord's on 26th, 28th, 29th May 1990
Toss : Middlesex. Umpires : K.J.Lyons and R.A.White
Middlesex won by 10 runs (Middlesex 21 pts (Bt: 4, Bw: 1) Gloucs 6 pts (Bt: 3, Bw: 3))

MIDDLESEX

D.L.Haynes	c Wright b Curran	24	c Bainbridge b Lloyds	49
M.A.Roseberry	c Russell b Curran	50	lbw b Lawrence	1
M.W.Gatting *	c & b Curran	16	lbw b Walsh	4
M.R.Ramprakash	c Bainbridge b Graveney	64	b Lloyds	0
K.R.Brown	b Graveney	5	c Russell b Athey	60
P.R.Downton +	lbw b Curran	63	c Russell b Athey	25
N.F.Williams	b Lloyds	0	not out	50
J.E.Emburey	not out	38	not out	30
S.P.Hughes	not out	12		
N.G.Cowans				
P.C.R.Tufnell				
Extras	(b 1,lb 14,nb 14)	29	(lb 9,nb 2)	11
TOTAL	(for 7 wkts dec)	301	(for 6 wkts dec)	230

GLOUCESTERSHIRE

A.J.Wright *	retired hurt	24	b Cowans	8
G.D.Hodgson	c Emburey b Tufnell	65	b Hughes	25
I.P.Butcher	c Roseberry b Emburey	102	st Downton b Tufnell	31
C.W.J.Athey	c Gatting b Tufnell	31	c Ramprakash b Emburey	69
P.Bainbridge	st Downton b Tufnell	2	(6) c Roseberry b Emburey	22
K.M.Curran	not out	9	(7) not out	53
J.W.Lloyds	not out	10	(5) c Roseberry b Tufnell	19
R.C.Russell +			(9) c & b Tufnell	1
C.A.Walsh			(8) b Emburey	16
D.A.Graveney			c Emburey b Tufnell	3
D.V.Lawrence			c Hughes b Emburey	0
Extras	(b 1,lb 10,nb 6)	17	(b 9,lb 4,nb 1)	14
TOTAL	(for 4 wkts dec)	260		261

GLOUCS	O	M	R	W	O	M	R	W
Walsh	17	6	59	0	5	2	25	1
Lawrence	16	4	46	0	4	0	13	1
Curran	22.4	7	64	4				
Graveney	32	7	89	2	27	6	61	0
Bainbridge	5	2	9	0				
Lloyds	5	0	19	1	20.2	3	109	2
Athey					7	2	13	2

MIDDLESEX	O	M	R	W	O	M	R	W
Williams	17	5	32	0	5	2	10	0
Cowans	16	5	36	0	9	4	24	1
Emburey	32	10	63	1	22.4	4	69	4
Tufnell	27	6	68	3	22	0	111	4
Hughes	10	2	37	0	6	3	16	1
Gatting	4	1	13	0				
Brown					1	0	18	0

FALL OF WICKETS

	MID	GLO	MID	GLO
1st	61	155	30	27
2nd	94	231	39	33
3rd	97	241	44	87
4th	124	241	77	127
5th	210		136	169
6th	211		157	194
7th	261			229
8th				232
9th				260
10th				261

WARWICKSHIRE vs. WORCESTERSHIRE

at Edgbaston on 26th, 28th, 29th May 1990
Toss : Warwickshire. Umpires : B.Leadbeater and N.T.Plews
Match drawn. (Warwickshire 6 pts (Bt: 3, Bw: 3) Worcestershire 5 pts (Bt: 2, Bw: 3))

WARWICKSHIRE

A.J.Moles	c Rhodes b Illingworth	76	c Rhodes b Illingworth	56
T.A.Lloyd *	c Illingworth b Dilley	9	lbw b Newport	9
Asif Din	c D'Oliveira b Botham	70	(7) c Radford b Illingworth	1
G.W.Humpage +	c Curtis b Illingworth	9	c Weston b Illingworth	12
D.A.Reeve	lbw b Botham	21	not out	49
D.P.Ostler	c Rhodes b Lampitt	26	b Lampitt	14
N.M.K.Smith	c Dilley b Lampitt	33	(8) c D'Oliveira b Lampitt	0
P.A.Booth	lbw b Lampitt	3	(3) c Rhodes b Radford	43
A.A.Donald	not out	10	b Lampitt	0
J.E.Benjamin	not out	12	not out	12
T.A.Munton				
Extras	(b 2,lb 16,w 4,nb 4)	26	(lb 4,nb 1)	5
TOTAL	(for 8 wkts dec)	295	(for 8 wkts dec)	201

WORCESTERSHIRE

T.S.Curtis	b Benjamin	34	not out	47
M.J.Weston	c Humpage b Donald	6	c Reeve b Booth	11
P.A.Neale *	c Humpage b Donald	29	not out	39
I.T.Botham	b Munton	48		
D.B.D'Oliveira	c Humpage b Munton	29		
S.R.Lampitt	c Humpage b Munton	0		
P.J.Newport	lbw b Munton	9		
S.J.Rhodes +	c Reeve b Booth	2		
N.V.Radford	not out	43		
G.R.Dilley	not out	32		
R.K.Illingworth				
Extras	(b 2,lb 12,w 4,nb 3)	21	(lb 8,nb 1)	9
TOTAL	(for 8 wkts dec)	253	(for 1 wkt)	106

WORCS	O	M	R	W	O	M	R	W
Dilley	10	2	34	1	11	3	33	0
Radford	12	2	49	0	8	1	32	1
Newport	11	2	38	0	7	1	26	1
Botham	22	6	46	2				
Lampitt	14	3	44	3	10.1	1	39	3
Illingworth	33	9	66	2	22	4	67	3

WARWICKS	O	M	R	W	O	M	R	W
Donald	21	4	54	2	4	2	10	0
Benjamin	19	5	52	1	3	1	6	0
Munton	21.5	6	45	4	2.3	0	12	0
Booth	38	18	67	1	11	2	36	1
Smith	1	1	0	0	8	2	34	0
Reeve	10	4	21	0				

FALL OF WICKETS

	WAR	WOR	WAR	WOR
1st	18	12	16	29
2nd	169	60	109	
3rd	169	87	118	
4th	193	151	129	
5th	203	152	168	
6th	251	153	169	
7th	257	162	169	
8th	281	164	169	
9th				
10th				

BRITANNIC ASSURANCE CHAMPIONSHIP

DERBYSHIRE vs. NOTTINGHAMSHIRE

at Derby on 26th, 27th, 28th May 1990
Toss : Derbyshire.   Umpires : P.J.Eele and A.A.Jones
Match drawn. (Derbyshire 7 pts (Bt: 3, Bw: 4) Nottinghamshire 6 pts (Bt: 2, Bw: 4))

NOTTINGHAMSHIRE

B.C.Broad	c Adams b Warner	45	lbw b Mortensen	50
D.J.R.Martindale	lbw b Mortensen	12	c Krikken b Malcolm	2
R.T.Robinson *	c Adams b Malcolm	69	lbw b Bishop	15
P.Johnson	c Mortensen b Bishop	20	c Roberts b Malcolm	2
D.W.Randall	c Krikken b Bishop	12	c Roberts b Mortensen	88
M.Saxelby	c Krikken b Warner	6	c Roberts b Bishop	14
B.N.French +	c Krikken b Malcolm	9	not out	105
G.W.Mike	c Krikken b Warner	11	b Barnett	7
K.E.Cooper	c Warner b Bishop	16	not out	35
R.A.Pick	not out	1		
J.A.Afford	c Roberts b Malcolm	0		
Extras	(b 4,lb 12,w 3,nb 2)	21	(b 12,lb 21,w 12,nb 6)	51
TOTAL		222	(for 7 wkts dec)	369

DERBYSHIRE

K.J.Barnett *	c Randall b Cooper	29	not out	46
P.D.Bowler	c Randall b Pick	8	(4) c French b Cooper	23
J.E.Morris	c French b Saxelby	103	(2) c & b Cooper	7
B.Roberts	b Pick	15	(5) c French b Afford	7
C.J.Adams	c Randall b Mike	14	(6) not out	4
S.C.Goldsmith	c French b Cooper	30		
K.M.Krikken +	b Cooper	31		
I.R.Bishop	lbw b Cooper	8		
A.E.Warner	run out	8	(3) c Mike b Pick	1
O.H.Mortensen	not out	0		
D.E.Malcolm	b Cooper	12		
Extras	(lb 4,w 1,nb 11)	16	(b 4,lb 3,nb 8)	15
TOTAL		274	(for 4 wkts)	103

DERBYSHIRE	O	M	R	W	O	M	R	W
Bishop	18	3	60	3	24	7	57	2
Malcolm	16.2	2	46	3	31	3	106	2
Warner	23	4	64	3	20	3	72	0
Mortensen	24	12	36	1	19	5	73	2
Barnett					6	0	28	1

NOTTS	O	M	R	W	O	M	R	W
Pick	24	3	97	2	11	1	38	1
Cooper	25	6	72	5	12	4	36	2
Mike	14	2	59	1	4	1	9	0
Afford	18	9	21	0	11	7	13	1
Saxelby	3	0	21	1				

FALL OF WICKETS

	NOT	DER	NOT	DER
1st	53	32	10	8
2nd	77	42	46	21
3rd	120	97	55	73
4th	134	141	99	91
5th	147	191	145	
6th	162	235	234	
7th	179	243	287	
8th	216	258		
9th	222	262		
10th	222	274		

YORKSHIRE vs. HAMPSHIRE

at Headingley on 26th, 28th, 29th May 1990
Toss : Yorkshire.   Umpires : D.O.Oslear and A.G.T.Whitehead
Hampshire won by 5 wickets. (Yorkshire 7 pts (Bt: 4, Bw: 3) Hampshire 23 pts (Bt: 4, Bw: 3))

YORKSHIRE

S.A.Kellett	c Gower b Connor	56	c sub b Turner	26
A.A.Metcalfe *	c Maru b Connor	22	c Smith C.L. b Connor	35
R.J.Blakey	c Parks b Shine	17	b Connor	20
P.E.Robinson	lbw b Shine	60	b Connor	24
D.Byas	b Shine	29	c Maru b Connor	0
D.L.Bairstow +	c Connor b Turner	37	lbw b Marshall	9
P.Carrick	c Maru b Marshall	23	c Gower b Marshall	32
P.J.Hartley	c Terry b Shine	3	c Terry b Nicholas	5
C.S.Pickles	not out	13	not out	57
D.Gough	not out	7	c Shine b Marshall	8
S.D.Fletcher			c Gower b Connor	6
Extras	(lb 19,w 1,nb 13)	33	(b 10,lb 11,w 1,nb 7)	29
TOTAL	(for 8 wkts dec)	300		251

HAMPSHIRE

V.P.Terry	lbw b Pickles	23	b Fletcher	18
C.L.Smith	c Kellett b Hartley	28	c Bairstow b Gough	58
D.I.Gower	lbw b Hartley	64	c Robinson b Gough	33
R.A.Smith	b Pickles	15	not out	51
M.D.Marshall	c Blakey b Carrick	117	b Gough	28
M.C.J.Nicholas *	lbw b Fletcher	0	c Gough b Hartley	15
R.J.Maru	c Bairstow b Gough	25		
R.J.Parks +	not out	36	(7) not out	1
D.R.Turner	not out	0		
K.J.Shine				
C.A.Connor				
Extras	(b 3,lb 19,w 1,nb 6)	29	(lb 11)	11
TOTAL	(for 7 wkts dec)	337	(for 5 wkts)	215

HAMPSHIRE	O	M	R	W	O	M	R	W
Marshall	22	7	44	1	22	5	51	3
Shine	19	2	52	4	8	0	50	0
Maru	21	9	43	0				
Connor	21	2	79	2	27.5	3	96	5
Turner	16.5	3	63	1	9	5	19	1
Nicholas					6	1	14	1

YORKSHIRE	O	M	R	W	O	M	R	W
Hartley	23	6	68	2	15	3	52	1
Fletcher	20	5	57	1	14	1	66	1
Carrick	15.4	6	46	1				
Pickles	14	1	64	2	4	0	25	0
Gough	13	3	67	1	12.5	1	61	3
Byas	7	1	13	0				

FALL OF WICKETS

	YOR	HAM	YOR	HAM
1st	56	53	45	37
2nd	93	61	84	103
3rd	130	99	100	113
4th	200	178	100	181
5th	225	182	113	206
6th	259	281	138	
7th	279	337	153	
8th	288		186	
9th			230	
10th			251	

John Morris (left) and Ian Bishop, leading contributors with bat and ball in Derbyshire's drawn match against local rivals Nottinghamshire at Derby.

BRITANNIC ASSURANCE CHAMPIONSHIP

GLAMORGAN vs. LANCASHIRE

at Colwyn Bay on 26th, 28th, 29th May 1990
Toss : Glamorgan.   Umpires : J.H.Harris and P.B.Wight
Match drawn. (Glamorgan 5 pts (Bt: 2, Bw: 3) Lancashire 8 pts (Bt: 4, Bw: 4))

GLAMORGAN

M.J.Cann	c Hughes b DeFreitas	4	c Hegg b DeFreitas	7
H.Morris	lbw b Patterson	3	lbw b Patterson	1
P.A.Cottey	c Hegg b Allott	8	c Mendis b DeFreitas	13
A.R.Butcher *	c Hegg b Patterson	46	not out	66
I.Smith	c Atherton b DeFreitas	10	not out	112
M.L.Roberts	c Jesty b Allott	13		
N.G.Cowley	c Allott b Patterson	4		
H.A.Anthony	c Fairbrother b DeFreitas	39		
C.P.Metson +	c & b Allott	34		
S.L.Watkin	not out	25		
M.Frost	c Hegg b Allott	0		
Extras	(b 9,lb 4,nb 6)	19	(lb 3,nb 1)	4
TOTAL		205	(for 3 wkts)	203

LANCASHIRE

G.D.Mendis	c Metson b Watkin	90
G.Fowler	c Butcher b Watkin	22
M.A.Atherton	lbw b Cowley	15
N.H.Fairbrother	c & b Cowley	60
T.E.Jesty	b Anthony	30
P.A.J.DeFreitas	lbw b Anthony	21
W.K.Hegg +	not out	82
D.P.Hughes *	b Cowley	33
J.D.Fitton	not out	25
P.J.W.Allott		
B.P.Patterson		
Extras	(b 4,lb 11,nb 6)	21
TOTAL	(for 7 wkts dec)	399

LANCASHIRE	O	M	R	W	O	M	R	W	FALL OF WICKETS			
										GLA	LAN	GLA	LAN
Patterson	19	4	88	3	17	5	41	1				
DeFreitas	24	7	53	3	22	6	61	2	1st	5	60	5
Allott	15	8	23	4	20	6	54	0	2nd	11	92	22
Fitton	4	1	17	0	15	6	25	0	3rd	26	169	29
Atherton	5	1	11	0	8	5	19	0	4th	39	210	
									5th	60	237	
GLAMORGAN	O	M	R	W	O	M	R	W	6th	68	252	
Frost	21	3	81	0					7th	114	345	
Anthony	20	2	99	2					8th	139		
Watkin	25	4	84	2					9th	205		
Cowley	28	8	84	3					10th	205		
Butcher	3	1	17	0								
Smith	3	0	19	0								

LEICESTERSHIRE vs. SOMERSET

at Leicester on 26th, 28th, 29th May 1990
Toss : Leicestershire.   Umpires : D.J.Constant and B.Dudleston
Match drawn. (Leicestershire 6 pts (Bt: 4, Bw: 2) Somerset 5 pts (Bt: 4, Bw: 1))

LEICESTERSHIRE

T.J.Boon	c Harden b Swallow	128	lbw b Mallender	10
N.E.Briers *	lbw b Hayhurst	39	c Harden b Jones	5
J.J.Whitaker	c Burns b Lefebvre	89	lbw b Mallender	18
P.Willey	c Rose b Lefebvre	15	lbw b Rose	29
L.Potter	not out	41	c Harden b Rose	2
J.D.R.Benson	not out	29	c Tavare b Rose	13
P.A.Nixon +			c Cook b Rose	33
J.P.Agnew			b Rose	36
G.J.F.Ferris			lbw b Swallow	33
A.D.Mullally			not out	12
D.J.Millns			not out	1
Extras	(b 4,lb 3,w 2,nb 2)	11	(b 5,lb 2,nb 1)	8
TOTAL	(for 4 wkts dec)	352	(for 9 wkts dec)	200

SOMERSET

S.J.Cook	c Nixon b Mullally	42	c Benson b Agnew	8
P.M.Roebuck	c Potter b Willey	63	not out	23
A.N.Hayhurst	c Whitaker b Mullally	34	not out	22
C.J.Tavare *	c Willey b Millns	88		
R.J.Harden	c Nixon b Millns	44		
N.D.Burns +	not out	2		
G.D.Rose	not out	3		
R.P.Lefebvre				
I.G.Swallow				
N.A.Mallender				
A.N.Jones				
Extras	(b 2,lb 6,w 1,nb 15)	24	(b 1,lb 3,w 2,nb 3)	9
TOTAL	(for 5 wkts dec)	300	(for 1 wkt)	62

SOMERSET	O	M	R	W	O	M	R	W	FALL OF WICKETS			
										LEI	SOM	LEI	SOM
Jones	9	3	34	0	12	6	26	1				
Mallender	19	2	51	0	21	8	62	2	1st	97	64	11	9
Rose	17	0	85	0	20	6	52	5	2nd	258	121	15	
Lefebvre	24	3	61	2	10	5	26	0	3rd	272	170	61	
Hayhurst	14	2	35	1	4	1	10	0	4th	284	293	65	
Swallow	17	2	47	1	10	3	16	1	5th		296	66	
Roebuck	10	3	32	0	4	3	1	0	6th			103	
									7th			122	
LEICS	O	M	R	W	O	M	R	W	8th			167	
Agnew	24	6	84	0	7	3	18	1	9th			193	
Ferris	15	4	55	0	4	1	15	0	10th				
Mullally	23	6	57	2	4	1	9	0					
Millns	15.1	1	57	2									
Willey	11	5	23	1	4	1	4	0					
Potter	3	1	16	0	7	3	5	0					
Benson					4.5	1	7	0					

HEADLINES

26th - 29th May

● East Midland rivals Derbyshire and Notinghamshire enjoyed a top of the table encounter at Derby, Notts holding on to first place thanks to Bruce French's maiden first-class century. John Morris had earlier made his fourth 100 in nine days as Derbyshire gained a useful first innings advantage

● Hampshire moved up to third place in the Championship table with their third win of the season, Malcolm Marshall weighing in with a career best 117, as Yorkshire suffered their fourth successive Championship defeat

● Middlesex spinners John Emburey and Philip Tufnell shared eight second innings wickets as Gloucestershire were defeated by 10 runs at Lord's

● Rain returned to halt Worcestershire's chase for victory at Edgbaston and also came to Glamorgan's aid at Colwyn Bay. Ian Smith had reached 112 as Glamorgan clawed back a first innings deficit of 194 against Lancashire

● Jimmy Cook ended the month of May with 820 first-class runs to his credit as Somerset drew with Leicestershire. He remained the most prolific of the many batsmen to enjoy the favourable start of season conditions

Britannic Assurance Championship Table
at 29th May 1990

		P	W	L	D	T	Bt	Bl	Pts
1	Nottinghamshire (11)	6	3	1	2	0	16	17	81
	Derbyshire (7)	6	3	1	2	0	20	13	81
3	Hampshire (6)	5	3	0	2	0	17	12	77
4	Warwickshire (8)	4	2	1	1	0	12	13	57
5	Middlesex (3)	4	2	0	2	0	14	10	56
6	Lancashire (4)	5	1	0	4	0	17	15	48
7	Kent (15)	4	2	2	0	0	11	4	47
8	Somerset (14)	5	1	1	3	0	19	11	46
	Glamorgan (17)	6	1	2	3	0	15	15	46
10	Leicestershire (13)	5	1	1	3	0	17	10	43
11	Northants (5)	4	1	3	0	0	12	14	42
12	Essex (2)	4	1	0	3	0	16	7	39
13	Worcestershire (1)	4	1	1	2	0	12	9	37
14	Sussex (10)	5	1	2	2	0	13	5	34
15	Yorkshire (16)	4	0	4	0	0	10	11	21
16	Surrey (12)	4	0	1	3	0	13	6	19
17	Gloucestershire (9)	3	0	3	0	0	5	10	15

BENSON & HEDGES CUP QUARTER-FINALS

SOMERSET vs. MIDDLESEX

at Taunton on 30th May 1990
Toss : Middlesex. Umpires : K.J.Lyons and B.J.Meyer
Somerset won by 22 runs

SOMERSET

S.J.Cook	c Downton b Williams	4
P.M.Roebuck	b Cowans	17
A.N.Hayhurst	b Hughes	17
C.J.Tavare *	c Gatting b Hughes	49
R.J.Harden	c Downton b Emburey	23
N.D.Burns +	c Haynes b Cowans	12
G.D.Rose	b Emburey	12
R.P.Lefebvre	c Downton b Williams	8
I.G.Swallow	c Emburey b Hughes	18
A.N.Jones	b Williams	3
N.A.Mallender	not out	6
Extras	(lb 5,w 6,nb 3)	14
TOTAL	(53.5 overs)	183

MIDDLESEX

D.L.Haynes	c Roebuck b Jones	23
M.A.Roseberry	run out	38
M.W.Gatting *	b Lefebvre	16
M.R.Ramprakash	lbw b Mallender	21
K.R.Brown	run out	8
R.O.Butcher	c Roebuck b Jones	22
P.R.Downton +	lbw b Jones	15
N.F.Williams	lbw b Roebuck	4
J.E.Emburey	not out	6
S.P.Hughes	b Roebuck	2
N.G.Cowans	b Jones	1
Extras	(lb 2,w 1,nb 2)	5
TOTAL	(51.5 overs)	161

MIDDLESEX	O	M	R	W	FALL OF WICKETS		
						SOM	MID
Williams	11	1	40	3			
Cowans	11	3	22	2	1st	9	34
Hughes	10.5	0	37	3	2nd	35	60
Gatting	8	1	28	0	3rd	53	87
Emburey	10	1	36	2	4th	103	100
Haynes	3	0	15	0	5th	123	122
					6th	142	144
SOMERSET	O	M	R	W	7th	146	150
Mallender	9	1	25	1	8th	154	153
Jones	8.5	0	41	4	9th	160	158
Lefebvre	8	1	15	1	10th	183	161
Rose	3	0	23	0			
Swallow	11	2	26	0			
Hayhurst	6	0	16	0			
Roebuck	6	0	13	2			

Man of the match: A.N.Jones

ESSEX vs. NOTTINGHAMSHIRE

at Chelmsford on 30th May 1990
Toss : Notts. Umpires : J.C.Balderstone and D.J.Constant
Nottinghamshire won by 6 wickets

ESSEX

G.A.Gooch *	c French b Cooper	87
B.R.Hardie	b Pick	0
P.J.Prichard	lbw b Afford	25
M.E.Waugh	st French b Hemmings	4
D.R.Pringle	b Afford	19
J.P.Stephenson	c & b Hemmings	4
A.W.Lilley	b Stephenson	23
M.A.Garnham +	not out	21
N.A.Foster	run out	8
T.D.Topley	not out	10
J.H.Childs		
Extras	(lb 8,w 5,nb 2)	15
TOTAL	(55 overs)(for 8 wkts)	216

NOTTINGHAMSHIRE

B.C.Broad	c Garnham b Gooch	38
D.W.Randall	c Hardie b Childs	16
R.T.Robinson *	not out	72
P.Johnson	c & b Stephenson	50
M.Saxelby	st Garnham b Stephenson	0
F.D.Stephenson	not out	25
B.N.French +		
E.E.Hemmings		
K.E.Cooper		
R.A.Pick		
J.A.Afford		
Extras	(b 11,w 7)	18
TOTAL	(52.1 overs)(for 4 wkts)	219

NOTTS	O	M	R	W	FALL OF WICKETS		
						ESS	NOT
Pick	11	0	60	1			
Cooper	11	4	34	1	1st	2	51
Afford	11	0	47	2	2nd	65	73
Stephenson	11	1	34	1	3rd	84	165
Hemmings	11	1	33	2	4th	117	165
					5th	132	
ESSEX	O	M	R	W	6th	169	
Foster	11	3	37	0	7th	172	
Pringle	9.1	0	35	0	8th	184	
Gooch	8	1	27	1	9th		
Childs	11	2	40	1	10th		
Topley	3	0	25	0			
Stephenson	10	0	44	2			

Man of the match: P.Johnson

HEADLINES

Benson & Hedges Cup
Quarter-finals

30th May

● All four quarter-finals were re-runs of earlier group matches - and three of the losing sides did better second time around

● Nottinghamshire repeated their 1989 victory at Lord's, beating Essex by six wickets at Chelmsford

● In a unexpectedly low-scoring contest against Middlesex at Taunton, Somerset were able to defend a total of 183 thanks to four wickets from Adrian Jones

● Worcestershire beat Glamorgan by six wickets at New Road to record their first victory over them in the B & H Cup despite the day's only 100 from Hugh Morris

● Lancashire's Mike Atherton and Neil Fairbrother again took heavy toll of Surrey's attack in their match at Old Trafford, despite the surprise inclusion of Pakistani Waqar Younis: Atherton made a competition best 74 during a second wicket stand of 172 with Graeme Fowler; Fairbrother hit 61 in 36 balls to take his aggregate of runs against Surrey this season towards 500

LANCASHIRE vs. SURREY

at Old Trafford on 30th May 1990
Toss : Surrey. Umpires : J.H.Harris and A.G.T.Whitehead
Lancashire won by 46 runs

LANCASHIRE

G.D.Mendis	c & b Bicknell	9
G.Fowler	c Bullen b Waqar Younis	96
M.A.Atherton	c Lynch b Murphy	74
N.H.Fairbrother	not out	61
M.Watkinson	c Lynch b Murphy	4
Wasim Akram	c Lynch b Waqar Younis	2
P.A.J.DeFreitas	run out	
W.K.Hegg +	not out	10
D.P.Hughes *		
I.D.Austin		
P.J.W.Allott		
Extras	(b 4,lb 8,w 6,nb 5)	23
TOTAL	(55 overs)(for 6 wkts)	279

SURREY

M.A.Lynch	c Fowler b Allott	24
G.S.Clinton	c Atherton b DeFreitas	77
A.J.Stewart	b Watkinson	67
D.M.Ward +	b Austin	10
I.A.Greig *	b DeFreitas	9
G.P.Thorpe	c Fairbrother b Allott	9
K.T.Medlycott	b DeFreitas	1
C.K.Bullen	b Watkinson	10
M.P.Bicknell	c Allott b Watkinson	8
Waqar Younis	c Mendis b Watkinson	4
A.J.Murphy	not out	0
Extras	(b 1,lb 5,w 7,nb 1)	14
TOTAL	(51.4 overs)	233

SURREY	O	M	R	W	FALL OF WICKETS		
						LAN	SUR
Bicknell	11	2	61	1			
Waqar Younis	11	0	55	2	1st	26	37
Bullen	11	2	37	0	2nd	198	160
Murphy	11	1	61	2	3rd	203	185
Medlycott	11	0	53	0	4th	235	190
					5th	246	203
LANCASHIRE	O	M	R	W	6th	249	207
DeFreitas	11	2	40	3	7th		208
Allott	11	3	25	2	8th		219
Wasim Akram	9	0	39	0	9th		233
Watkinson	10.4	1	58	4	10th		233
Atherton	3	0	20	0			
Austin	7	0	45	1			

Man of the match: N.H.Fairbrother

WORCESTERSHIRE vs. GLAMORGAN

at Worcester on 30th May 1990
Toss : Glamorgan. Umpires : R.Julian and K.E.Palmer
Worcestershire won by 7 wickets

GLAMORGAN

A.R.Butcher *	c D'Oliveira b Dilley	16
H.Morris	c D'Oliveira b Newport	106
G.C.Holmes	c Rhodes b Botham	19
M.P.Maynard	c Rhodes b Botham	0
I.V.A.Richards	lbw b Radford	3
I.Smith	b Radford	2
N.G.Cowley	c Newport b Weston	0
C.P.Metson +	c Lampitt b Newport	7
S.L.Watkin	c Rhodes b Radford	5
S.R.Barwick	not out	13
M.Frost	c Curtis b Radford	3
Extras	(lb 7,w 5,nb 5)	17
TOTAL	(54.3 overs)	191

WORCESTERSHIRE

T.S.Curtis	not out	76
M.J.Weston	lbw b Barwick	25
P.A.Neale *	lbw b Watkin	50
I.T.Botham	b Richards	22
D.B.D'Oliveira	not out	12
D.A.Leatherdale		
S.R.Lampitt		
P.J.Newport		
S.J.Rhodes +		
N.V.Radford		
G.R.Dilley		
Extras	(lb 6,w 3,nb 1)	10
TOTAL	(52.2 overs)(for 3 wkts)	195

WORCS	O	M	R	W	FALL OF WICKETS		
						GLA	WOR
Newport	11	3	34	2			
Dilley	11	0	39	1	1st	30	48
Radford	10.3	4	26	4	2nd	119	146
Botham	11	3	29	2	3rd	119	176
Lampitt	5	0	35	0	4th	132	
Weston	6	1	21	1	5th	138	
					6th	139	
GLAMORGAN	O	M	R	W	7th	159	
Frost	9.2	0	51	0	8th	168	
Watkin	11	2	32	1	9th	181	
Barwick	10	2	45	1	10th	191	
Cowley	11	2	22	0			
Richards	9	0	32	1			
Holmes	2	0	7	0			

Man of the match: H.Morris

TOUR MATCHES

OTHER FIRST-CLASS MATCH

WARWICKSHIRE vs. NEW ZEALAND

at Edgbaston on 30th, 31st May, 1st June 1990
Toss : New Zealand. Umpires : M.J.Kitchen and R.C.Tolchard
Match drawn

WARWICKSHIRE

J.D.Ratcliffe	c Crowe J.J. b Watson	29	c & b Bracewell		43
R.G.Twose	c Pringle b Watson	64	c Wright b Millmow		21
T.M.Moody	c Jones b Snedden	44	b Bracewell		106
A.I.Kallicharran	c Smith b Millmow	3			
G.W.Humpage *+	c Smith b Pringle	9	(4) b Pringle		46
D.P.Ostler	c & b Snedden	19	(5) b Pringle		0
N.M.K.Smith	c Franklin b Bracewell	24	(6) c Pringle b Bracewell		41
P.A.Booth	not out	51	(7) b Millmow		1
A.A.Donald	not out	25	(8) not out		3
J.E.Benjamin			(9) b Bracewell		4
T.A.Munton					
Extras	(b 4,lb 9,w 2,nb 14)	29	(lb 5,nb 4)		9
TOTAL	(for 7 wkts dec)	297	(for 8 wkts dec)		274

NEW ZEALAND

T.J.Franklin	b Benjamin	2			
J.G.Wright *	c sub b Twose	51	not out		2
M.C.Snedden	b Benjamin	2			
A.H.Jones	b Benjamin	82			
M.D.Crowe	c sub b Smith	52			
J.J.Crowe	not out	9	(1) not out		10
J.G.Bracewell	not out	31			
I.D.S.Smith +					
C.Pringle					
W.Watson					
J.P.Millmow					
Extras	(b 3,lb 6,w 6,nb 2)	17	(w 3)		3
TOTAL	(for 5 wkts dec)	246	(for 0 wkts)		15

NEW ZEALAND	O	M	R	W	O	M	R	W
Millmow	18	2	64	1	11	1	47	2
Pringle	13	1	57	1	15	3	67	2
Snedden	24	3	69	2	5	0	32	0
Watson	22	6	67	2	12	0	57	0
Bracewell	17	5	27	1	10.2	1	66	4

WARWICKS	O	M	R	W	O	M	R	W
Donald	13	3	24	0	2	0	9	0
Benjamin	18	4	45	3	1	0	2	0
Munton	15	3	33	0	2.4	0	3	0
Twose	14	6	44	1				
Smith	24	8	63	1				
Moody	3	0	28	0				
Humpage					2	1	1	0

FALL OF WICKETS	WAR	NZ	WAR	NZ
1st	69	7	52	
2nd	133	25	93	
3rd	154	109	186	
4th	167	203	200	
5th	171	207	259	
6th	218		267	
7th	218		269	
8th			274	
9th				
10th				

DERBYSHIRE vs. NEW ZEALAND

at Derby on 2nd, 3rd, 4th June 1990
Toss : Derbyshire. Umpires : M.J.Kitchen and R.A.White
New Zealand won by 82 runs

NEW ZEALAND

T.J.Franklin	c Bowler b Cork	19	(2) c & b Adams		9
J.J.Crowe	lbw b Jean-Jacques	1	(1) c Morris b Roberts		47
A.H.Jones	not out	121			
M.D.Crowe *	c Krikken b Kuiper	32			
M.J.Greatbatch	c & b Kuiper	3			
M.W.Priest	c Bowler b Jean-Jacques	20	(4) c Krikken b Cork		10
J.G.Bracewell	not out	40	(5) not out		3
A.C.Parore +			(3) lbw b Jean-Jacques		37
M.C.Snedden					
D.K.Morrison					
J.P.Millmow					
Extras	(lb 11,w 1,nb 4)	16	(lb 2,w 1,nb 1)		4
TOTAL	(for 5 wkts dec)	252	(for 4 wkts dec)		110

DERBYSHIRE

K.J.Barnett *	not out	14	lbw b Morrison		0
P.D.Bowler	not out	11	lbw b Snedden		9
J.E.Morris			b Millmow		20
B.Roberts			c Crowe M.D. b Morrison		25
A.P.Kuiper			lbw b Bracewell		68
C.J.Adams			c Crowe J.J. b Priest		21
K.M.Krikken +			c Crowe M.D. b Snedden		62
M.Jean-Jacques			b Snedden		14
I.R.Bishop			c Greatbatch b Bracewell		7
D.E.Malcolm			lbw b Snedden		0
D.G.Cork			not out		2
Extras	(lb 1,nb 4)	5	(lb 15,nb 7)		22
TOTAL	(for 0 wkts dec)	30			250

DERBYSHIRE	O	M	R	W	O	M	R	W
Bishop	12	3	37	0				
Malcolm	12	1	36	0				
Jean-Jacques	14	2	67	2	0.4	0	2	1
Cork	14	2	49	1	1	0	4	1
Kuiper	10	2	52	2				
Morris					7	0	47	0
Adams					6	1	20	1
Bowler					3	0	25	0
Roberts					3	0	10	1

NEW ZEALAND	O	M	R	W	O	M	R	W
Morrison	4	0	16	0	9	2	40	2
Millmow	4	1	13	0	8	0	36	1
Snedden					18	4	55	4
Priest					10	1	46	1
Bracewell					15.2	3	58	2

FALL OF WICKETS	NZ	DER	NZ	DER
1st	11	20	0	
2nd	55	83	24	
3rd	123	104	36	
4th	132	110	79	
5th	191		159	
6th			169	
7th			233	
8th			248	
9th			248	
10th			250	

OXFORD UNIV vs. GLAMORGAN

at The Parks on 2nd, 4th, 5th June 1990
Toss : Oxford Univ. Umpires : P.J.Eele and A.A.Jones
Match drawn

GLAMORGAN

M.J.Cann	c Gerrans b Henderson	19	c Trevelyan b Henderson		7
P.A.Cottey	run out	156			
G.C.Holmes	b Henderson	39	(2) not out		12
M.P.Maynard	c Turner b Gerrans	59			
N.R.Pook	lbw b Gerrans	0	(3) not out		0
M.L.Roberts +	c Trevelyan b Henderson	14			
H.A.Anthony	c Gerrans b Crawley	30			
J.Derrick	not out	28			
M.Davies	not out	5			
S.Bastien					
S.R.Barwick *					
Extras	(b 6,lb 14,w 2,nb 16)	38	(lb 3,nb 2)		5
TOTAL	(for 7 wkts dec)	388	(for 1 wkt)		24

OXFORD UNIV

D.A.Hagan	c Cottey b Barwick		43
R.E.Morris *	c Roberts b Bastien		0
P.D.Lunn	c Roberts b Bastien		11
G.J.Turner	c Roberts b Bastien		13
M.A.Crawley	c Davies b Anthony		67
P.S.Gerrans	c Roberts b Barwick		18
D.Curtis	lbw b Holmes		43
M.J.Russell	c Roberts b Barwick		2
S.Chauhan	run out		4
I.M.Henderson	not out		1
B.W.D.Trevelyan +	c Roberts b Bastien		0
Extras	(lb 8,w 3,nb 5)		16
TOTAL			218

OXFORD UNIV	O	M	R	W	O	M	R	W
Henderson	28	1	102	3	4.2	0	17	1
Gerrans	26	3	94	2	5	2	4	0
Crawley	26	6	94	1				
Turner	19	4	78	0				

GLAMORGAN	O	M	R	W	O	M	R	W
Anthony	18	7	29	1				
Bastien	20.2	3	51	4				
Barwick	19	10	29	3				
Derrick	9	2	58	0				
Davies	8	1	16	0				
Pook	8	3	19	0				
Holmes	7	4	8	1				

FALL OF WICKETS	GLA	OXF	GLA	OXF
1st	37	2	21	
2nd	141	31		
3rd	233	66		
4th	233	77		
5th	284	152		
6th	343	187		
7th	380	204		
8th		212		
9th		217		
10th		218		

HEADLINES

30th May - 1st June

- Rain prevented New Zealand chasing a victory target of 326 against Warwickshire at Edgbaston

- Tom Moody made his second 100 in his second first-class match for Warwickshire

2nd - 5th June

- New Zealand completed their preparations for the First Test with their fourth first-class victory, as two declarations early on the last day revived their match with Derbyshire

- Derbyshire's Dominic Cork dismissed Trevor Franklin with his third ball in first-class cricket but New Zealand went on to record their fourth first-class victory of the tour

- Glamorgan's Tony Cottey made his maiden first-class 100 against Oxford University at The Parks in a match curtailed by the weather

- First-class debuts: M.Davies (Glamorgan) D.G.Cork (Derbyshire) and B.W.D.Trevelyan (Oxford U)

REFUGE ASSURANCE LEAGUE

LEICESTERSHIRE vs. HAMPSHIRE

at Leicester on 3rd June 1990
Toss : Hampshire. Umpires : J.H.Hampshire and P.B.Wight
Hampshire won by 5 wickets. (Leics 0 pts Hants 4 pts)

LEICESTERSHIRE

T.J.Boon	c Parks b Ayling	6
N.E.Briers *	run out	9
J.J.Whitaker	b Connor	0
P.Willey	not out	68
L.Potter	lbw b Tremlett	23
J.D.R.Benson	c Maru b Tremlett	7
P.A.Nixon +	c Maru b Ayling	10
J.P.Agnew	b Connor	5
G.J.F.Ferris	lbw b Marshall	6
A.D.Mullally	not out	10
L.B.Taylor		
Extras	(b 5,lb 2,w 12,nb 3)	22
TOTAL	(40 overs)(for 8 wkts)	166

HAMPSHIRE

V.P.Terry	c Briers b Agnew	2
R.J.Scott	b Mullally	4
R.A.Smith	c Nixon b Mullally	0
D.I.Gower	c Nixon b Taylor	53
M.D.Marshall	c Mullally b Benson	44
M.C.J.Nicholas *	not out	28
J.R.Ayling	not out	23
R.J.Parks +		
R.J.Maru		
T.M.Tremlett		
C.A.Connor		
Extras	(lb 4,w 9,nb 2)	15
TOTAL	(38.2 overs)(for 5 wkts)	169

HAMPSHIRE	O	M	R	W		FALL OF WICKETS	
						LEI	HAM
Marshall	8	1	23	1			
Connor	8	1	35	2	1st	13	8
Ayling	8	1	28	2	2nd	13	8
Tremlett	8	1	28	2	3rd	17	8
Maru	2	0	14	0	4th	75	104
Scott	6	0	31	0	5th	86	118
					6th	114	
LEICS	O	M	R	W	7th	129	
Agnew	7.2	1	35	1	8th	138	
Mullally	8	0	27	2	9th		
Taylor	8	1	35	1	10th		
Ferris	5	0	27	0			
Willey	8	0	25	0			
Benson	2	0	16	1			

MIDDLESEX vs. WARWICKSHIRE

at Lord's on 3rd June 1990
Toss : Middlesex. Umpires : P.J.Eele and A.A.Jones
Middlesex won by 9 wickets. (Mx 4 pts Warwicks 0 pts)

WARWICKSHIRE

T.M.Moody	b Taylor	17
P.A.Smith	b Williams	2
A.I.Kallicharran	not out	41
G.W.Humpage +	c Haynes b Hughes	13
D.A.Reeve	c Ramprakash b Emburey	5
Asif Din	run out	17
N.M.K.Smith	c Williams b Emburey	10
T.A.Lloyd *	not out	0
G.C.Small		
J.E.Benjamin		
T.A.Munton		
Extras	(lb 3,w 7)	10
TOTAL	(17 overs)(for 6 wkts)	115

MIDDLESEX

D.L.Haynes	c Asif Din b Benjamin	50
M.A.Roseberry	not out	51
M.W.Gatting *	not out	6
M.R.Ramprakash		
K.R.Brown		
R.O.Butcher		
P.R.Downton +		
N.F.Williams		
J.E.Emburey		
S.P.Hughes		
N.R.Taylor		
Extras	(w 3,nb 6)	9
TOTAL	(13 overs)(for 1 wkt)	116

MIDDLESEX	O	M	R	W		FALL OF WICKETS	
						WAR	MID
Taylor	4	0	16	1			
Williams	4	0	22	1	1st	13	107
Gatting	1	0	13	0	2nd	29	
Hughes	3	0	32	1	3rd	53	
Emburey	3	0	21	2	4th	62	
Haynes	2	0	8	0	5th	91	
					6th	112	
WARWICKS	O	M	R	W	7th		
Munton	3	0	19	0	8th		
Benjamin	3	0	31	1	9th		
Small	2	0	28	0	10th		
Smith N.M.K.	3	0	26	0			
Smith P.A.	2	0	12	0			

WORCESTERSHIRE vs. YORKSHIRE

at Worcester on 3rd June 1990
Toss : Worcestershire. Umpires : J.H.Harris and K.J.Lyons
Yorkshire won by 16 runs. (Worcs 0 pts Yorks 4 pts)

YORKSHIRE

K.Sharp	run out	71
A.A.Metcalfe *	c D'Oliveira b Newport	0
R.J.Blakey	c Rhodes b McEwan	79
P.E.Robinson	c Rhodes b McEwan	13
D.Byas	b Lampitt	14
D.L.Bairstow +	not out	5
C.S.Pickles	c Rhodes b McEwan	0
P.J.Hartley	run out	7
P.Carrick	not out	0
P.W.Jarvis		
S.D.Fletcher		
Extras	(lb 8,w 8)	16
TOTAL	(37 overs)(for 7 wkts)	205

WORCESTERSHIRE

T.S.Curtis	b Hartley	76
M.J.Weston	c Jarvis b Hartley	4
P.A.Neale *	c Metcalfe b Hartley	18
D.B.D'Oliveira	c Jarvis b Carrick	1
D.A.Leatherdale	c Blakey b Pickles	35
S.J.Rhodes +	c Metcalfe b Jarvis	2
I.T.Botham	c Jarvis b Hartley	12
P.J.Newport	c Carrick b Hartley	8
S.R.Lampitt	c Hartley b Jarvis	8
R.D.Stemp	b Fletcher	1
S.M.McEwan	not out	18
Extras	(lb 6)	6
TOTAL	(36.1 overs)	189

WORCS	O	M	R	W		FALL OF WICKETS	
						YOR	WOR
Newport	8	0	32	1			
Weston	8	0	36	0	1st	4	6
Botham	1	0	4	0	2nd	161	34
McEwan	8	0	44	3	3rd	177	37
Lampitt	8	0	53	1	4th	193	106
Stemp	4	0	28	0	5th	193	109
					6th	193	137
YORKSHIRE	O	M	R	W	7th	204	152
Jarvis	7.1	0	26	2	8th		164
Hartley	8	0	38	5	9th		165
Carrick	8	0	34	1	10th		189
Fletcher	7	0	42	1			
Pickles	6	0	43	1			

SURREY vs. NORTHANTS

at The Oval on 3rd June 1990
Toss : Surrey. Umpires : D.O.Oslear and R.Palmer
Surrey won by 4 wickets. (Surrey 4 pts Northants 0 pts)

NORTHANTS

A.Fordham	c & b Bicknell	7
N.A.Felton	c Waqar Younis b Feltham	10
A.J.Lamb *	b Murphy	0
R.J.Bailey	lbw b Bullen	20
D.J.Capel	c & b Feltham	0
D.J.Wild	c Greig b Bullen	10
W.M.Noon +	c Feltham b Waqar Younis	21
J.G.Thomas	c & b Bullen	0
A.L.Penberthy	c Bullen b Waqar Younis	4
W.W.Davis	c Bicknell b Murphy	9
N.G.B.Cook	not out	7
Extras	(b 2,lb 4,w 6,nb 1)	13
TOTAL	(18.4 overs)	101

SURREY

A.J.Stewart	c Penberthy b Thomas	20
M.A.Lynch	c Davis b Wild	37
G.P.Thorpe	c Noon b Wild	2
D.M.Ward +	c Fordham b Wild	7
I.A.Greig *	c Cook b Thomas	19
J.D.Robinson	c Capel b Thomas	4
M.A.Feltham	not out	1
C.K.Bullen	not out	1
M.P.Bicknell		
Waqar Younis		
A.J.Murphy		
Extras	(lb 8,w 2,nb 1)	11
TOTAL	(18.1 overs)(for 6 wkts)	102

SURREY	O	M	R	W		FALL OF WICKETS	
						NOR	SUR
Bicknell	4	0	21	1			
Murphy	3.4	0	15	2	1st	11	32
Feltham	3	0	23	2	2nd	14	56
Bullen	4	0	13	3	3rd	43	72
Waqar Younis	4	1	23	2	4th	46	77
					5th	50	100
NORTHANTS	O	M	R	W	6th	72	101
Davis	3.1	0	13	0	7th	72	
Capel	4	0	22	0	8th	84	
Thomas	4	0	21	3	9th	84	
Penberthy	3	0	19	0	10th	101	
Cook	1	0	11	0			
Wild	3	0	8	3			

ESSEX vs. GLAMORGAN

at Ilford on 3rd June 1990
Toss : Essex. Umpires : B.Leadbeater and B.J.Meyer
Essex won by 6 wickets. (Essex 4 pts Glamorgan 0 pts)

GLAMORGAN

M.P.Maynard	b Topley	75
H.Morris	c & b Pringle	18
I.V.A.Richards	c & b Topley	0
I.Smith	c Gooch b Pringle	8
A.R.Butcher *	c Stephenson b Foster	1
G.C.Holmes	c & b Waugh	14
C.P.Metson +	b Waugh	1
S.J.Dennis	b Waugh	3
S.L.Watkin	not out	1
S.R.Barwick		
M.Frost		
Extras	(w 4,nb 6)	10
TOTAL	(15 overs)(for 7 wkts)	131

ESSEX

G.A.Gooch *	run out	58
B.R.Hardie	c Butcher b Barwick	30
M.E.Waugh	b Frost	12
P.J.Prichard	not out	23
D.R.Pringle	run out	9
N.A.Foster	not out	0
J.P.Stephenson		
A.W.Lilley		
M.A.Garnham +		
T.D.Topley		
S.J.W.Andrew		
Extras	(lb 2,w 1)	3
TOTAL	(15 overs)(for 4 wkts)	135

ESSEX	O	M	R	W		FALL OF WICKETS	
						GLA	ESS
Andrew	3	0	38	0			
Foster	3	0	33	1	1st	95	75
Topley	3	0	23	2	2nd	95	97
Waugh	3	0	19	2	3rd	104	106
Pringle	3	0	18	2	4th	111	129
					5th	115	
GLAMORGAN	O	M	R	W	6th	119	
Frost	3	0	26	1	7th	123	
Watkin	3	0	19	0	8th		
Dennis	3	0	23	0	9th		
Richards	3	0	31	0	10th		
Barwick	3	0	34	1			

SUSSEX vs LANCASHIRE

at Hove on 3rd June 1990
Match abandoned. (Sussex 2pts Lancashire 2pts)

GLOUCESTERSHIRE vs. SOMERSET

at Bristol on 3rd June 1990
Toss : Gloucs. Umpires : J.C.Balderstone and N.T.Plews
Gloucestershire won by 8 wickets. (Gloucs 4 pts Som 0 pts)

SOMERSET

S.J.Cook	c Walsh b Lawrence	10
P.M.Roebuck	b Curran	4
A.N.Hayhurst	c Russell b Lawrence	4
C.J.Tavare *	c Wright b Lawrence	4
R.J.Harden	c Wright b Lawrence	3
N.D.Burns +	c Lloyds b Walsh	20
G.D.Rose	c Bainbridge b Lawrence	14
M.W.Cleal	c Wright b Alleyne	0
I.G.Swallow	c Wright b Bainbridge	19
N.A.Mallender	b Bainbridge	24
J.C.Hallett	not out	4
Extras	(b 1,lb 4,w 6,nb 1)	12
TOTAL	(39.3 overs)	118

GLOUCESTERSHIRE

R.C.Russell +	b Cleal	13
C.W.J.Athey	not out	53
A.J.Wright *	c Rose b Hayhurst	17
K.M.Curran	not out	29
P.Bainbridge		
J.W.Lloyds		
P.W.Romaines		
M.W.Alleyne		
C.A.Walsh		
D.V.Lawrence		
S.N.Barnes		
Extras	(lb 5,w 2)	7
TOTAL	(25.5 overs)(for 2 wkts)	119

GLOUCS	O	M	R	W		FALL OF WICKETS	
						SOM	GLO
Walsh	8	1	14	1			
Curran	8	0	22	1	1st	12	39
Lawrence	8	1	18	5	2nd	20	67
Barnes	5	0	26	0	3rd	21	
Alleyne	8	0	26	1	4th	25	
Bainbridge	2.3	0	7	2	5th	32	
					6th	61	
SOMERSET	O	M	R	W	7th	63	
Mallender	8	0	25	0	8th	69	
Hallett	5.5	1	28	0	9th	103	
Rose	5	0	34	0	10th	118	
Cleal	3	0	14	1			
Hayhurst	4	0	13	1			

BRITANNIC ASSURANCE CHAMPIONSHIP

HEADLINES

3rd June

- There were pyrotechnics amongst the puddles as all but one match in the Refuge Assurance League were badly rain affected

- Desmond Haynes (50 in 36 balls) and Mike Roseberry (50 in 41 balls) blasted Middlesex to their fifth win in six matches to join Kent at the top of the table

- Matthew Maynard made 75 in 43 balls but Graham Gooch countered with a fifty from 30 balls as Essex beat Glamorgan, while David Gower hit 53 as his new county beat his old county at Grace Road

- Peter Hartley and David Lawrence both took five wickets in an innings in the Sunday League for the first time as Yorkshire and Gloucestershire gained unexpectedly comfortable wins

- 1989 champions Lancashire were confined to third place after their match with Sussex at Horsham was the first of the season to be completely washed out

2nd - 5th June

- Lancashire were the only side to win as all the other matches in the Britannic Assurance Championship were badly affected by rain. Phil DeFreitas and Patrick Patterson combined to bowl Sussex out for 108 in their second innings as the Lancastrians claimed maximum points

- On an opening day that was again full of runs Chris Broad and Desmond Haynes both made double centuries. Broad passed 200 for the first time in his long county career as he and Derek Randall added 285 for Notts's fourth wicket against Kent. Haynes also recorded a career best for Middlesex against Essex and shared an opening stand of 306 with Mike Roseberry, who was another to improve his best score

- Notts and Middlesex retained the initiative in their matches, both forcing the opposition to follow on, but Essex captain, Graham Gooch, with his fourth 100 in four Championship matches, and Kent's Matthew Fleming, with his maiden first-class 100, led successful rearguard actions

- Hampshire forced Leicestershire to follow on but their attempt to go top of the table was foiled by the loss of the last day's play, while Worcestershire remained in the lower half of the table as the last day of their match with Yorkshire was also lost

- Jack Russell made his first Championship 100 as Gloucestershire gained a first innings lead over Somerset, while Warwickshire just held off Northants

- First-class debut: R.D.Stemp (Worcestershire)

GLOUCESTERSHIRE vs. SOMERSET

at Bristol on 2nd, 4th, 5th June 1990
Toss : Somerset.   Umpires : J.C.Balderstone and N.T.Plews
Match drawn. (Gloucs 7 pts (Bt: 3, Bw: 4) Som 4 pts (Bt: 2, Bw: 2)).

SOMERSET

S.J.Cook	c Wright b Lawrence	40	lbw b Lawrence	81
P.M.Roebuck	c Russell b Walsh	3		
A.N.Hayhurst	b Curran	15	not out	17
C.J.Tavare *	c Lloyds b Graveney	30	not out	1
R.J.Harden	c Lawrence b Curran	81		
N.D.Burns +	c Russell b Graveney	16	(2) c Athey b Walsh	38
G.D.Rose	c Athey b Lawrence	0		
I.G.Swallow	lbw b Graveney	10		
N.A.Mallender	b Walsh	8		
J.C.Hallett	c Athey b Graveney	0		
A.N.Jones	not out	0		
Extras	(b 3,lb 11,nb 8)	22	(lb 10,nb 11)	21
TOTAL		225	(for 2 wkts)	158

GLOUCESTERSHIRE

A.J.Wright *	c Roebuck b Mallender	4
G.D.Hodgson	b Jones	24
I.P.Butcher	c Harden b Hallett	41
C.W.J.Athey	c Cook b Rose	37
P.Bainbridge	c Burns b Rose	29
K.M.Curran	not out	103
J.W.Lloyds	c & b Rose	3
R.C.Russell +	c Burns b Rose	120
C.A.Walsh		
D.V.Lawrence		
D.A.Graveney		
Extras	(b 6,lb 8,w 2,nb 4)	20
TOTAL	(for 7 wkts dec)	381

GLOUCS	O	M	R	W	O	M	R	W
Walsh	14.5	1	43	2	17	3	53	1
Lawrence	14	2	65	2	12	1	41	1
Curran	16	4	41	2	4	2	14	0
Graveney	27	7	53	4	18	7	38	0
Athey	1	0	9	0	0.5	0	2	0

SOMERSET	O	M	R	W	O	M	R	W
Jones	25	2	96	1				
Mallender	26	7	69	1				
Rose	24.3	7	78	4				
Swallow	19	5	43	0				
Hallett	21	3	63	1				
Hayhurst	7	1	18	0				

FALL OF WICKETS

	SOM	GLO	SOM	GLO
1st	37	9	111	
2nd	58	31	148	
3rd	70	134		
4th	143	142		
5th	174	149		
6th	175	152		
7th	197	381		
8th	215			
9th	221			
10th	225			

KENT vs. NOTTINGHAMSHIRE

at Tunbridge Wells on 2nd, 4th, 5th June 1990
Toss : Nottinghamshire.   Umpires : D.O.Oslear and R.Palmer
Match drawn. (Kent 4 pts (Bt: 3, Bw: 1) Notts 8 pts (Bt: 4, Bw: 4)).

NOTTINGHAMSHIRE

B.C.Broad	not out	227	c Marsh b Merrick	1
D.J.R.Martindale	lbw b Davis	23		
R.T.Robinson *	b Davis	2	(5) not out	1
P.Johnson	c Wells b Davis	25	(3) c Davis b Merrick	3
D.W.Randall	c Benson b Merrick	178	(2) c Marsh b Merrick	6
B.N.French +	c Marsh b Igglesden	0		
F.D.Stephenson	c Fleming b Igglesden	4	(4) not out	1
E.E.Hemmings				
K.E.Cooper				
R.A.Pick				
J.A.Afford				
Extras	(b 5,lb 12,w 1)	18	(lb 3,w 2)	5
TOTAL	(for 6 wkts dec)	477	(for 3 wkts)	17

KENT

S.G.Hinks	b Stephenson	6	c Afford b Pick	14
M.R.Benson *	c French b Cooper	34	lbw b Stephenson	1
N.R.Taylor	c Stephenson b Pick	1	c Martindale b Hemmings	21
G.R.Cowdrey	c French b Stephenson	27	(5) c French b Stephenson	51
V.J.Wells	c French b Pick	2	(6) c Hemmings b Stephenson	20
M.V.Fleming	c Broad b Cooper	1	(7) b Stephenson	102
S.A.Marsh +	not out	114	(8) c French b Stephenson	4
R.P.Davis	lbw b Afford	9	(4) c French b Pick	13
C.Penn	b Pick	23	b Pick	17
T.A.Merrick	c Martindale b Afford	35	c Martindale b Stephenson	15
A.P.Igglesden	c Johnson b Afford	0	not out	1
Extras	(b 2,lb 17,nb 4)	23	(b 4,lb 4,w 1,nb 8)	17
TOTAL		275		276

KENT	O	M	R	W	O	M	R	W
Merrick	23	2	60	1	3	0	10	3
Igglesden	20.3	2	62	2	2	0	4	0
Penn	19	1	105	0				
Davis	37	3	155	3				
Fleming	10	0	78	0				

NOTTS	O	M	R	W	O	M	R	W
Stephenson	24	5	77	2	21	3	84	6
Cooper	20	9	40	2	18	1	57	0
Hemmings	12	2	52	0	18	12	15	1
Afford	13	4	30	3	10	3	21	0
Pick	22	7	57	3	28	6	91	3

FALL OF WICKETS

	NOT	KEN	KEN	NOT
1st	115	19	4	3
2nd	121	20	28	11
3rd	177	52	50	16
4th	462	65	50	
5th	467	72	104	
6th	477	103	142	
7th		129	185	
8th		171	210	
9th		265	258	
10th		275	276	

BRITANNIC ASSURANCE CHAMPIONSHIP

ESSEX vs. MIDDLESEX

at Ilford on 2nd, 4th, 5th June 1990
Toss : Middlesex.   Umpires : B.Leadbeater and B.J.Meyer
Match drawn. (Essex 3 pts (Bt: 3,Bw: 0) Middx 8 pts (Bt: 4, Bw: 4)).

MIDDLESEX

D.L.Haynes	not out	220		
M.A.Roseberry	c Prichard b Foster	135		
M.W.Gatting *	b Pringle	34		
M.R.Ramprakash	not out	30		
K.R.Brown				
P.R.Downton +				
N.F.Williams				
J.E.Emburey				
S.P.Hughes				
M.J.Thursfield				
P.C.R.Tufnell				
Extras	(b 4,lb 11,w 3,nb 5)	23		
TOTAL	(for 2 wkts dec)	442		

ESSEX

G.A.Gooch *	c Downton b Hughes	0	c Brown b Tufnell	120
J.P.Stephenson	c Downton b Williams	16	c Brown b Tufnell	31
P.J.Prichard	c Downton b Thursfield	7	(4) not out	56
M.E.Waugh	c Haynes b Emburey	39	(5) not out	59
B.R.Hardie	c Downton b Hughes	74		
M.A.Garnham +	lbw b Emburey	36		
D.R.Pringle	c Downton b Emburey	8		
N.A.Foster	c Brown b Emburey	0	(3) c Gatting b Williams	13
S.J.W.Andrew	c Roseberry b Emburey	15		
J.H.Childs	not out	10		
P.M.Such	b Williams	27		
Extras	(lb 17,nb 8)	25	(b 8,lb 8,nb 10)	26
TOTAL		257	(for 3 wkts dec)	305

ESSEX	O	M	R	W	O	M	R	W
Foster	18	6	60	1				
Pringle	22	8	66	1				
Andrew	14	3	61	0				
Gooch	9	2	36	0				
Childs	17	1	58	0				
Stephenson	10	2	36	0				
Such	9	2	41	0				
Waugh	15	2	69	0				

MIDDLESEX	O	M	R	W	O	M	R	W
Williams	19.5	4	58	2	18	4	57	1
Hughes	14	2	43	2	12	2	58	0
Thursfield	8	2	24	1	9	2	21	0
Tufnell	27	7	54	0	33	12	73	2
Emburey	24	7	61	5	32	9	80	0

FALL OF WICKETS				
	MID	ESS	ESS	MID
1st	306	2	88	
2nd	369	19	112	
3rd		31	201	
4th		83		
5th		153		
6th		168		
7th		170		
8th		205		
9th		213		
10th		257		

LEICESTERSHIRE vs. HAMPSHIRE

at Leicester on 2nd, 4th, 5th (no play) June 1990
Toss : Hampshire.   Umpires : J.H.Hampshire and P.B.Wight
Match drawn. (Leicestershire 4 pts (Bt: 1, Bw: 3) Hampshire 8 pts (Bt: 4, Bw: 4))

HAMPSHIRE

V.P.Terry	c Nixon b Ferris	7
C.L.Smith	not out	80
D.I.Gower	c Whitaker b Lewis	25
R.A.Smith	c Potter b Mullally	1
M.D.Marshall	b Mullally	112
M.C.J.Nicholas *	b Mullally	13
R.J.Parks +	c Willey b Agnew	2
R.J.Maru	c Boon b Agnew	59
T.M.Tremlett	not out	25
C.A.Connor		
P.J.Bakker		
Extras	(lb 8,w 1,nb 16)	25
TOTAL	(for 7 wkts dec)	349

LEICESTERSHIRE

T.J.Boon	c Connor b Marshall	6	lbw b Bakker	1
N.E.Briers *	c sub b Bakker	0	c Terry b Connor	29
P.A.Nixon +	b Bakker	0		
J.J.Whitaker	b Bakker	6	(3) b Marshall	62
P.Willey	c Connor b Marshall	42	(4) c Terry b Marshall	23
L.Potter	b Tremlett	43	(5) b Marshall	0
J.D.R.Benson	lbw b Tremlett	11	(6) not out	29
C.C.Lewis	not out	36	(7) not out	40
J.P.Agnew	c Parks b Tremlett	0		
G.J.F.Ferris	c Marshall b Bakker	1		
A.D.Mullally	b Connor	29		
Extras	(lb 4)	4	(lb 3,nb 2)	5
TOTAL		178	(for 5 wkts)	189

LEICS	O	M	R	W	O	M	R	W
Agnew	32	2	115	2				
Ferris	16	4	77	1				
Lewis	14	2	56	1				
Mullally	20	4	68	3				
Willey	12	3	25	0				

HAMPSHIRE	O	M	R	W	O	M	R	W
Marshall	13	2	44	2	15	4	44	3
Bakker	15	4	51	4	10	2	46	1
Connor	10.5	2	46	1	17	4	54	1
Tremlett	15	4	33	3	9	4	16	0
Maru					7	1	26	0

FALL OF WICKETS				
	HAM	LEI	LEI	HAM
1st	21	2	2	
2nd	69	2	81	
3rd	73	8	111	
4th	119	26	111	
5th	144	87	130	
6th	220	111		
7th	295	111		
8th		123		
9th		124		
10th		178		

SUSSEX vs. LANCASHIRE

at Horsham on 2nd, 4th, 5th June 1990
Toss : Sussex.   Umpires : B.Hassan and D.R.Shepherd
Lancashire won by 9 wickets. (Sussex 6 pts (Bt: 2, Bw: 4) Lancashire 24 pts (Bt: 4, Bw: 4))

SUSSEX

N.J.Lenham	c Mendis b Watkinson	8	c Hughes b DeFreitas	24
J.W.Hall	c Watkinson b Allott	24	c Allott b Patterson	15
A.I.C.Dodemaide	c Hegg b Watkinson	70	c Hughes b DeFreitas	14
A.P.Wells	c Fairbrother b Fitton	33	lbw b DeFreitas	0
M.P.Speight	c Hughes b Patterson	11	lbw b DeFreitas	21
C.M.Wells *	c Hegg b Patterson	0	(8) c Atherton b DeFreitas	13
P.Moores +	c Fairbrother b Allott	28	(6) c Mendis b DeFreitas	2
A.C.S.Pigott	c Fairbrother b Atherton	14	(7) c Hegg b Patterson	6
I.D.K.Salisbury	c Hughes b Atherton	15	not out	0
B.T.P.Donelan	c Atherton b Watkinson	8	b Patterson	0
R.A.Bunting	not out	10	c Hegg b Patterson	0
Extras	(b 3,lb 9,nb 2)	14	(b 1,lb 2,nb 10)	13
TOTAL		235		108

LANCASHIRE

G.D.Mendis	lbw b Dodemaide	9	c Moores b Bunting	11
M.A.Atherton	c Pigott b Dodemaide	76	not out	0
J.D.Fitton	c Pigott b Dodemaide	25		
N.H.Fairbrother	c Wells A.P. b Bunting	22	(3) not out	10
M.Watkinson	c Donelan b Salisbury	51		
P.A.J.DeFreitas	c Moores b Pigott	26		
W.K.Hegg +	c Dodemaide b Salisbury	10		
D.P.Hughes *	c Moores b Dodemaide	0		
G.Fowler	not out	54		
P.J.W.Allott	b Dodemaide	42		
B.P.Patterson	b Dodemaide	0		
Extras	(b 4,lb 4,nb 1)	9	(lb 1)	1
TOTAL		324	(for 1 wkt)	22

LANCASHIRE	O	M	R	W	O	M	R	W
Patterson	17	3	37	2	18.4	2	52	4
DeFreitas	13	4	27	0	19	8	39	6
Watkinson	14	8	26	3				
Allott	14	4	30	2	4	2	10	0
Fitton	19	6	56	1				
Atherton	20.1	8	47	2	3	2	4	0

SUSSEX	O	M	R	W	O	M	R	W
Pigott	14	2	60	1				
Dodemaide	28.4	2	106	6				
Salisbury	24	7	46	2				
Wells C.M.	7	1	16	0				
Bunting	13	1	61	1	3	0	20	1
Donelan	5	1	27	0	2	1	1	0

FALL OF WICKETS				
	SUS	LAN	SUS	LAN
1st	21	11	21	12
2nd	47	54	58	
3rd	108	111	58	
4th	127	185	62	
5th	127	187	72	
6th	161	224	87	
7th	197	224	106	
8th	207	224	108	
9th	219	324	108	
10th	235	324	108	

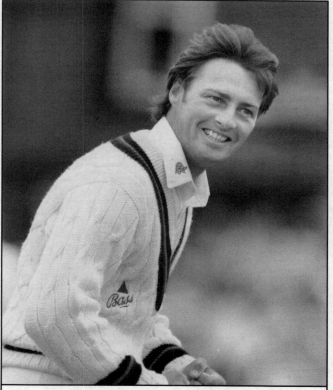

Graeme Fowler, who set up Lancashire's win over Sussex with a century partnership with Paul Allott after going in to bat at No 9.

BRITANNIC ASS. CHAMPIONSHIP

OTHER FIRST-CLASS MATCH

WORCESTERSHIRE vs. YORKSHIRE

at Worcester on 2nd, 4th, 5th (no play) June 1990
Toss : Yorkshire. Umpires : J.H.Harris and K.J.Lyons
Match drawn. (Worcs 7 pts (Bt: 3, Bw: 4) Yorks 6 pts (Bt: 2, Bw: 4)).

YORKSHIRE

M.D.Moxon *	c Botham b Lampitt	23	c D'Oliveira b McEwan	28
A.A.Metcalfe	c Rhodes b Lampitt	20	not out	56
R.J.Blakey	lbw b Botham	0	c McEwan b Stemp	8
S.A.Kellett	c Rhodes b Lampitt	0	not out	4
P.E.Robinson	c Rhodes b Botham	28		
D.L.Bairstow +	c D'Oliveira b Lampitt	61		
P.Carrick	c D'Oliveira b Botham	2		
C.S.Pickles	c D'Oliveira b Newport	30		
P.J.Hartley	b Lampitt	36		
P.W.Jarvis	c Stemp b Botham	17		
S.D.Fletcher	not out	0		
Extras	(lb 1,nb 4)	5	(b 2,lb 3,w 3,nb 2)	10
TOTAL		222	(for 2 wkts)	106

WORCESTERSHIRE

T.S.Curtis	lbw b Fletcher	13
P.Bent	c Blakey b Jarvis	39
P.A.Neale *	c Jarvis b Fletcher	1
D.B.D'Oliveira	c Hartley b Pickles	41
I.T.Botham	lbw b Carrick	86
S.M.McEwan	c Bairstow b Jarvis	54
M.J.Weston	lbw b Jarvis	3
P.J.Newport	c Bairstow b Carrick	17
S.J.Rhodes +	c Bairstow b Hartley	13
S.R.Lampitt	b Hartley	10
R.D.Stemp	not out	3
Extras	(lb 6,nb 2)	8
TOTAL		288

WORCS	O	M	R	W	O	M	R	W
Newport	17	2	55	1				
McEwan	13	3	47	0	15	4	35	1
Botham	16.5	3	65	4				
Lampitt	20	5	54	5	17	6	34	0
Stemp					19	6	32	1

YORKSHIRE	O	M	R	W	O	M	R	W
Jarvis	25	5	59	3				
Hartley	20.1	4	92	2				
Fletcher	11	2	31	2				
Carrick	36	12	70	2				
Pickles	8	3	30	1				

FALL OF WICKETS				
	YOR	WOR	YOR	WOR
1st	44	19	78	
2nd	45	27	95	
3rd	45	95		
4th	45	108		
5th	85	233		
6th	87	245		
7th	127	246		
8th	197	266		
9th	216	276		
10th	222	288		

WARWICKSHIRE vs. NORTHANTS

at Edgbaston on 2nd, 4th, 5th June 1990
Toss : Northants. Umpires : D.J.Constant and B.Dudleston
Match drawn. (Warwickshire 5 pts (Bt: 2, Bw: 3) Northants 8 pts (Bt: 4, Bw: 4))

WARWICKSHIRE

A.J.Moles	lbw b Ambrose	40	lbw b Ambrose	13
T.A.Lloyd *	lbw b Capel	65	b Thomas	10
Asif Din	b Capel	5	c Fordham b Thomas	9
A.I.Kallicharran	b Capel	2	lbw b Thomas	0
G.W.Humpage +	c Fordham b Ambrose	13	b Ambrose	42
D.A.Reeve	c Fordham b Capel	5	lbw b Ambrose	0
P.A.Smith	b Ambrose	23	run out	41
G.C.Small	lbw b Capel	24	c & b Thomas	0
A.A.Donald	c Capel b Ambrose	0	(10) run out	1
A.R.K.Pierson	not out	5	(9) not out	9
T.A.Munton	b Ambrose	0	not out	10
Extras	(b 11,lb 8,w 1)	20	(lb 7)	7
TOTAL		202	(for 9 wkts)	142

NORTHANTS

A.Fordham	c Lloyd b Munton	33
N.A.Felton	c Kallicharran b Small	8
R.J.Bailey	c Humpage b Munton	40
A.J.Lamb *	run out	48
D.J.Capel	lbw b Smith	89
G.Cook	b Munton	34
A.L.Penberthy	c Humpage b Donald	17
J.G.Thomas	c Asif Din b Pierson	9
C.E.L.Ambrose	not out	23
D.Ripley +	not out	2
N.G.B.Cook		
Extras	(b 1,lb 13,w 1)	15
TOTAL	(for 8 wkts dec)	318

NORTHANTS	O	M	R	W	O	M	R	W
Ambrose	21	8	53	5	25	6	55	3
Thomas	6	0	29	0	23	6	53	4
Capel	21	5	74	5	7	3	21	0
Penberthy	7	2	27	0	2	0	6	0
Cook N.G.B.					4	4	0	0

WARWICKS	O	M	R	W	O	M	R	W
Donald	23	5	56	1				
Small	17	2	44	1				
Munton	33	8	92	3				
Smith	15	4	63	1				
Pierson	8	1	49	1				

FALL OF WICKETS				
	WAR	NOR	WAR	NOR
1st	104	14	20	
2nd	113	57	30	
3rd	123	134	32	
4th	140	134	42	
5th	141	263	42	
6th	153	267	115	
7th	171	289	118	
8th	171	304	122	
9th	201		132	
10th	202			

OXFORD UNIV vs. NOTTINGHAMSHIRE

at The Parks on 6th, 7th, 8th (no play) June 1990
Toss : Nottinghamshire. Umpires : K.J.Lyons and H.J.Rhodes
Match drawn

NOTTINGHAMSHIRE

M.Newell +	retired not out	20
D.J.R.Martindale	c Morris b Crawley	15
R.J.Evans	c sub b Gerrans	1
P.Johnson *	not out	112
D.R.Laing	b van der Merwe	2
K.P.Evans	not out	43
G.W.Mike		
M.G.Field-Buss		
R.A.Pick		
K.Saxelby		
J.A.Afford		
C.W.Scott		
Extras	(b 4,lb 3,nb 1)	8
TOTAL	(for 3 wkts dec)	201

OXFORD UNIV

D.A.Hagan	c Mike b Evans K.P.	15
R.E.Morris *	not out	73
P.D.Lunn	not out	22
D.Curtis		
M.A.Crawley		
W.M.van der Merwe		
P.Gerrans		
H.Davies		
M.J.Russell		
S.Chauhan		
B.W.D.Trevelyan +		
Extras	(b 2,lb 5,w 1)	8
TOTAL	(for 1 wkt dec)	118

OXFORD UNIV	O	M	R	W	O	M	R	W
van der Merwe	20	5	69	1				
Gerrans	19	4	58	1				
Crawley	15.5	4	36	1				
Davies	4	0	31	0				

NOTTS	O	M	R	W	O	M	R	W
Pick	3	0	20	0				
Saxelby	2	0	10	0				
Mike	6	1	33	0				
Evans K.P.	6	4	13	1				
Afford	8	4	9	0				
Laing	5	1	21	0				
Field-Buss	2.1	1	5	0				

FALL OF WICKETS				
	NOT	OXF	NOT	OXF
1st	27	33		
2nd	32			
3rd	92			
4th				
5th				
6th				
7th				
8th				
9th				
10th				

HEADLINES

6th - 8th June

● The last day of Oxford University's match against Notts was lost to the elements. Earlier Mike Newell had retired not out on 20 when he was called to act as twelfth man in the Test match. He was replaced by Chris Scott

● Rain intervened on the last day in all six Championship matches to ensure all were drawn

● Mark Waugh hit a career best 204 for Essex against Gloucestershire at Ilford, sharing a third wicket partnership of 242 with Brian Hardie who announced he would be retiring at the end of the season

● On 7th June, Jimmy Cook became the first man to complete 1,000 first-class runs for the season with his unbeaten 59 in Somerset's abbreviated first innings against Hampshire at Basingstoke. It was the second year in succession he had achieved the feat

● Andy Moles was undefeated in both innings and on the field for the whole match as Warwickshire had the better of a draw with Middlesex at Lord's. Joey Benjamin took five wickets in an innings for the first time in the County Championship

● Leicestershire's Justin Benson made a career best 86 against Northants, while Derbyshire and Surrey's openers both shared century stands on the last day, before rain brought another early finish. Nor could Kent's forfeiture of their second innings bring a positive conclusion to their match against Yorkshire

BRITANNIC ASSURANCE CHAMPIONSHIP

ESSEX vs. GLOUCESTERSHIRE

at Ilford on 6th, 7th, 8th June 1990
Toss : Essex.   Umpires : B.Leadbeater and B.J.Meyer
Match drawn (Essex 6 pts (Bt: 4,Bw: 2) Gloucestershire 4 pts (Bt: 3, Bw: 1))

ESSEX

J.P.Stephenson	b Lawrence	1	(2) not out	35
A.C.Seymour	retired hurt	4		
P.J.Prichard	c Curran b Bainbridge	45		
M.E.Waugh	b Graveney	204		
B.R.Hardie *	not out	110	(1) c Tedstone b Walsh	13
N.Shahid	c Lawrence b Curran	15	(3) not out	14
M.A.Garnham +	not out	20		
D.R.Pringle				
N.A.Foster				
J.H.Childs				
P.M.Such				
Extras	(b 8,lb 6,w 1,nb 11)	26	(lb 1,w 3,nb 1)	5
TOTAL	(for 4 wkts dec)	425	(for 1 wkt)	67

GLOUCESTERSHIRE

A.J.Wright *	b Foster	92
G.D.Hodgson	c sub b Foster	27
I.P.Butcher	c Waugh b Foster	5
C.W.J.Athey	run out	9
P.Bainbridge	run out	64
K.M.Curran	c Garnham b Childs	39
J.W.Lloyds	not out	29
G.A.Tedstone +	c Garnham b Foster	13
D.A.Graveney	not out	0
C.A.Walsh		
D.V.Lawrence		
Extras	(b 6,lb 4,nb 10)	20
TOTAL	(for 7 wkts dec)	298

GLOUCS	O	M	R	W	O	M	R	W		FALL OF WICKETS			
										ESS	GLO	ESS	GLO
Walsh	16	2	60	0	9	6	8	1	1st	2	58	23	
Lawrence	11	0	57	1	6	1	17	0	2nd	105	88		
Curran	19	2	93	1					3rd	347	111		
Graveney	27	2	101	1					4th	388	170		
Bainbridge	18	2	65	1	4	0	11	0	5th		235		
Lloyds	11	1	35	0	2	1	4	0	6th		264		
Athey					7	1	25	0	7th		298		
Tedstone					2	1	1	0	8th				
									9th				
ESSEX	O	M	R	W	O	M	R	W	10th				
Foster	32.4	5	104	4									
Pringle	18	2	52	0									
Childs	32	16	48	1									
Such	9	2	34	0									
Waugh	7	3	17	0									
Stephenson	7	1	33	0									

HAMPSHIRE vs. SOMERSET

at Basingstoke on 6th, 7th, 8th June 1990
Toss : Hampshire.   Umpires : D.R.Shepherd and A.G.T.Whitehead
Match drawn (Hampshire 3 pts (Bt: 3,Bw: 0) Somerset 2 pts (Bt: 0, Bw: 2)

HAMPSHIRE

V.P.Terry	lbw b Mallender	64	lbw b Rose	6
C.L.Smith	lbw b Rose	25	not out	73
T.C.Middleton	c Burns b Rose	90	c Swallow b Rose	1
D.I.Gower	lbw b Jones	1	c & b Swallow	26
M.C.J.Nicholas *	retired ill	23	b Swallow	23
R.J.Parks +	c Mallender b Rose	11	not out	15
L.A.Joseph	lbw b Hayhurst	13		
R.J.Maru	not out	17		
T.M.Tremlett	not out	3		
C.A.Connor				
P.J.Bakker				
Extras	(b 4,lb 3,w 2,nb 1)	10	(b 4,w 1,nb 3)	8
TOTAL	(for 6 wkts dec)	257	(for 4 wkts dec)	152

SOMERSET

S.J.Cook	not out	59	c Parks b Connor	29
J.J.E.Hardy	not out	30	not out	23
A.N.Hayhurst			not out	31
C.J.Tavare *				
R.J.Harden				
N.D.Burns +				
G.D.Rose				
I.G.Swallow				
H.R.J.Trump				
N.A.Mallender				
A.N.Jones				
Extras		0	(nb 1)	1
TOTAL	(for 0 wkts dec)	89	(for 1 wkt)	84

SOMERSET	O	M	R	W	O	M	R	W		FALL OF WICKETS			
										HAM	SOM	HAM	SOM
Jones	20	2	56	1					1st	69		6	36
Mallender	26	7	50	1	5	1	9	0	2nd	117		13	
Rose	25	1	84	3	9	4	21	2	3rd	118		50	
Swallow	8	2	24	0	25	8	54	2	4th	218		99	
Hayhurst	11	5	12	1	6	2	18	0	5th	233			
Trump	8	1	24	0	9.2	0	46	0	6th	254			
									7th				
HAMPSHIRE	O	M	R	W	O	M	R	W	8th				
Bakker	4	1	24	0	6	1	35	0	9th				
Joseph	5	1	40	0					10th				
Connor	5.2	1	23	0	7	1	20	1					
Maru	4	2	2	0									
Middleton					1	0	10	0					
Terry					1	0	19	0					

MIDDLESEX vs. WARWICKSHIRE

at Lord's on 6th, 7th, 8th June 1990
Toss : Middlesex.   Umpires : D.J.Constant and R.Julian
Match drawn (Middlesex 2 pts (Bt: 0, Bw: 2) Warwickshire 8 pts (Bt:4, Bw: 4))

WARWICKSHIRE

A.J.Moles	not out	128	not out	65
T.A.Lloyd *	retired hurt	70		
Asif Din	c Emburey b Tufnell	49	(2) c Williams b Roseberry	44
A.I.Kallicharran	c Emburey b Tufnell	10		
G.W.Humpage +	c Gatting b Emburey	73		
D.A.Reeve	b Hughes	12	(3) not out	31
P.A.Smith	not out	0		
N.M.K.Smith				
A.A.Donald				
J.E.Benjamin				
T.A.Munton				
Extras	(b 11,lb 16,w 1,nb 2)	30	(b 1,lb 1,nb 1)	3
TOTAL	(for 4 wkts dec)	372	(for 1 wkt dec)	143

MIDDLESEX

D.L.Haynes	c Humpage b Donald	67	b Donald	0
M.A.Roseberry	lbw b Benjamin	64	retired hurt	19
M.W.Gatting *	c sub b Smith P.A.	23		
M.R.Ramprakash	lbw b Benjamin	0	(3) c Reeve b Munton	38
K.R.Brown	c Reeve b Benjamin	15	(4) not out	41
P.R.Downton +	lbw b Smith P.A.	4	(5) lbw b Munton	11
N.F.Williams	c Humpage b Donald	17		
J.E.Emburey	c Benjamin b Donald	18	(6) not out	5
S.P.Hughes	c sub b Benjamin	2		
P.C.R.Tufnell	not out	11		
A.R.C.Fraser	b Benjamin	7		
Extras	(b 8,lb 7)	15	(b 4,lb 4)	8
TOTAL		243	(for 3 wkts)	122

MIDDLESEX	O	M	R	W	O	M	R	W		FALL OF WICKETS			
										WAR	MID	WAR	MID
Williams	22	2	77	0	5	2	12	0	1st	206	130	94	0
Fraser	19	9	18	0	8	1	23	0	2nd	222	142		90
Hughes	16	5	48	1	4	1	20	0	3rd	351	142		116
Gatting	11	3	43	0					4th	371	178		
Tufnell	28	4	111	2					5th		178		
Emburey	14	3	48	1					6th		191		
Roseberry					6	0	58	1	7th		204		
Ramprakash					4	0	28	0	8th		219		
WARWICKSHIRE	O	M	R	W	O	M	R	W	9th		221		
Donald	25	5	60	3	7	3	26	1	10th		243		
Benjamin	22.5	5	71	5	7	0	30	0					
Munton	18	7	36	0	8	1	21	2					
Smith P.A.	11	3	46	2									
Smith N.M.K.	5	1	15	0									
Reeve					7.4	1	37	0					

NORTHANTS vs. LEICESTERSHIRE

at Northampton on 6th, 7th, 8th (no play) June 1990
Toss : Northants.   Umpires : J.D.Bond and P.B.Wight
Match drawn (Northants 4 pts (Bt: 0, Bw: 4) Leicestershire 3 pts (Bt: 3,Bw: 0))

LEICESTERSHIRE

T.J.Boon	c Capel b Thomas	4	not out	18
N.E.Briers *	b Thomas	6	b Capel	5
J.J.Whitaker	c Cook N.G.B. b Penberthy	35	c & b Capel	3
P.Willey	c Noon b Ambrose	34	not out	20
L.Potter	c Noon b Ambrose	14		
J.D.R.Benson	c Capel b Penberthy	86		
W.K.M.Benjamin	b Capel	33		
P.A.Nixon +	b Ambrose	27		
J.P.Agnew	c Noon b Capel	8		
A.D.Mullally	not out	1		
D.J.Millns	c Capel b Penberthy	1		
Extras	(b 3,lb 3,w 3,nb 3)	12		0
TOTAL		261	(for 2 wkts)	46

NORTHANTS

A.Fordham	not out	59
N.A.Felton	c Benjamin b Mullally	22
G.Cook	not out	8
R.J.Bailey		
D.J.Capel		
R.G.Williams		
A.L.Penberthy		
W.M.Noon +		
J.G.Thomas		
C.E.L.Ambrose		
N.G.B.Cook *		
Extras	(lb 2,w 2,nb 2)	6
TOTAL	(for 1 wkt dec)	95

NORTHANTS	O	M	R	W	O	M	R	W		FALL OF WICKETS			
										LEI	NOR	LEI	NOR
Ambrose	23	6	54	3					1st	6	44	13	
Thomas	22	5	74	2	4	0	12	0	2nd	13		17	
Capel	22	7	49	2	6	3	4	2	3rd	81			
Cook N.G.B.	6	1	17	0	7	3	11	0	4th	83			
Penberthy	15.2	2	61	3					5th	112			
Williams					9	3	19	0	6th	182			
LEICS	O	M	R	W	O	M	R	W	7th	223			
Benjamin	11	2	33	0					8th	259			
Agnew	7	1	23	0					9th	259			
Mullally	5	0	17	1					10th	261			
Willey	1	0	1	0									
Millns	2	0	19	0									

BRITANNIC ASSURANCE CHAMPIONSHIP

SURREY vs. DERBYSHIRE
at The Oval on 6th, 7th, 8th June 1990
Toss : Surrey. Umpires : J.H.Harris and J.W.Holder
Match drawn (Surrey 5 pts (Bt: 1, Bw: 4) Derbyshire 3 pts (Bt: 3, Bw: 0))

DERBYSHIRE

K.J.Barnett *	c Greig b Waqar Younis	1	not out	51
P.D.Bowler	c Ward b Waqar Younis	75	not out	85
J.E.Morris	lbw b Waqar Younis	25		
B.Roberts	c Clinton b Feltham	17		
A.P.Kuiper	lbw b Feltham	37		
C.J.Adams	lbw b Feltham	3		
K.M.Krikken +	c Feltham b Medlycott	35		
M.Jean-Jacques	c Greig b Medlycott	25		
A.E.Warner	c sub b Medlycott	17		
S.J.Base	b Medlycott	0		
G.Miller	not out	10		
Extras	(b 6,lb 14,w 6,nb 4)	30	(b 4,lb 4)	8
TOTAL		275	(for 0 wkts dec)	144

SURREY

R.I.Alikhan	c Bowler b Miller	39	not out	82
K.T.Medlycott	run out	6		
G.P.Thorpe	not out	58		
D.M.Ward +	not out	37		
G.S.Clinton			(2) not out	70
M.A.Lynch				
I.A.Greig *				
M.A.Feltham				
M.P.Bicknell				
Waqar Younis				
A.J.Murphy				
Extras	(lb 3,w 2,nb 7)	12	(lb 6,w 2,nb 1)	9
TOTAL	(for 2 wkts dec)	152	(for 0 wkts)	161

SURREY	O	M	R	W	O	M	R	W
Waqar Younis	30	4	77	4	4	0	16	0
Bicknell	20	4	64	0				
Murphy	22	4	59	0	4	2	7	0
Feltham	19	7	40	2				
Medlycott	10.1	4	14	4	11	2	21	0
Alikhan	1	0	1	0	5	0	29	0
Greig					9	1	36	0
Lynch					4	0	27	0

DERBYSHIRE	O	M	R	W	O	M	R	W
Jean-Jacques	14.1	3	47	0	8	0	49	0
Base	12	1	38	0	9	2	33	0
Warner	11	2	36	0	9	0	30	0
Kuiper	7	1	15	0	1.3	0	13	0
Miller	8	2	13	1	9	2	30	0

FALL OF WICKETS

	DER	SUR	DER	SUR
1st	9	9		
2nd	57	88		
3rd	95			
4th	163			
5th	168			
6th	186			
7th	239			
8th	242			
9th	242			
10th	275			

KENT vs. YORKSHIRE
at Tunbridge Wells on 6th, 7th, 8th June 1990
Toss : Kent. Umpires : D.O.Oslear and R.Palmer
Match drawn (Kent 4 pts (Bt: 4,Bw: 0) Yorkshire 2 pts (Bt: 0, Bw: 2))

KENT

S.G.Hinks	c Bairstow b Jarvis	6
M.R.Benson *	c Metcalfe b Hartley	57
N.R.Taylor	not out	124
G.R.Cowdrey	c Kellett b Moxon	67
V.J.Wells	c Bairstow b Hartley	4
M.V.Fleming	c Kellett b Hartley	18
S.A.Marsh +	not out	41
R.M.Ellison		
R.P.Davis		
P.S.De Villiers		
A.P.Igglesden		
Extras	(b 4,lb 12)	16
TOTAL	(for 5 wkts dec)	333

YORKSHIRE

M.D.Moxon *	not out	24	not out	6
A.A.Metcalfe	c Davis b Benson	0	c Marsh b De Villiers	14
R.J.Blakey	not out	9	not out	1
S.A.Kellett				
P.E.Robinson				
D.L.Bairstow +				
C.White				
P.Carrick				
P.J.Hartley				
P.W.Jarvis				
D.Gough		0	(lb 2)	2
Extras				
TOTAL	(for 1 wkt dec)	33	(for 1 wkt)	23

YORKSHIRE	O	M	R	W	O	M	R	W
Jarvis	8	4	16	1				
Hartley	36	8	105	3				
Gough	23	3	94	0				
Carrick	25	9	40	0				
White	10	0	33	0				
Moxon	10	2	29	1				

KENT	O	M	R	W	O	M	R	W
Benson	2	0	14	1				
Cowdrey	1.3	0	19	0				
De Villiers					4.1	0	10	1
Igglesden					4	1	11	0

FALL OF WICKETS

	KEN	YOR	KEN	YOR
1st	42	1		21
2nd	84			
3rd	230			
4th	243			
5th	277			
6th				
7th				
8th				
9th				
10th				

Neil Taylor, who scored a century for Kent in their rain-affected match against Yorkshire at Tunbridge Wells.

REFUGE ASSURANCE LEAGUE

NORTHANTS vs. GLAMORGAN

at Northampton on 10th June 1990
Toss : Northants. Umpires : J.D.Bond and P.B.Wight
Northants won by 10 runs (Northants 4 pts Glam 0 pts)

NORTHANTS

A.Fordham	c Metson b Frost	0
N.A.Felton	c Cowley b Watkin	21
R.J.Bailey	b Frost	71
D.J.Capel	c Morris b Frost	121
D.J.Wild	c Metson b Frost	4
R.G.Williams	not out	1
W.M.Noon +	c Morris b Dennis	11
J.G.Thomas	not out	0
W.W.Davis		
N.G.B.Cook *		
M.A.Robinson		
Extras	(b 2,lb 6,w 7)	15
TOTAL	(40 overs)(for 6 wkts)	244

GLAMORGAN

A.R.Butcher *	b Williams	40
H.Morris	lbw b Cook	40
M.P.Maynard	c Williams b Cook	13
I.V.A.Richards	c Cook b Robinson	45
G.C.Holmes	not out	50
P.A.Cottey	c Noon b Davis	28
N.G.Cowley	not out	2
C.P.Metson +		
S.J.Dennis		
S.L.Watkin		
M.Frost		
Extras	(b 1,lb 10,w 5)	16
TOTAL	(40 overs)(for 5 wkts)	234

GLAMORGAN	O	M	R	W		FALL OF WICKETS	NOR	GLA
Frost	8	1	30	4				
Watkin	8	0	37	1	1st		0	77
Cowley	7	0	43	0	2nd		27	102
Dennis	8	0	63	1	3rd		218	105
Richards	7	0	45	0	4th		228	172
Holmes	2	0	18	0	5th		232	218
					6th		243	
NORTHANTS	O	M	R	W	7th			
Capel	6	0	34	0	8th			
Davis	8	1	39	1	9th			
Thomas	8	0	42	0	10th			
Williams	8	0	34	1				
Cook	6	1	40	2				
Robinson	4	0	34	1				

KENT vs. SOMERSET

at Canterbury on 10th June 1990
Toss : Kent. Umpires : D.J.Constant and B.J.Meyer
Kent won by 6 wickets (Kent 4 pts Somerset 0 pts)

SOMERSET

S.J.Cook	c Cowdrey C.S. b Fleming	50
P.M.Roebuck	c Benson b Cowdrey C.S.	29
G.D.Rose	b Merrick	29
C.J.Tavare *	c Benson b Cowdrey C.S.	11
R.J.Harden	not out	21
N.D.Burns +	b Igglesden	14
A.N.Hayhurst	b Merrick	3
M.W.Cleal	run out	0
I.G.Swallow	not out	0
N.A.Mallender		
A.N.Jones		
Extras	(lb 6,w 2)	8
TOTAL	(40 overs)(for 7 wkts)	165

KENT

S.G.Hinks	c Cook b Mallender	1
M.R.Benson	c Roebuck b Rose	55
N.R.Taylor	c Cook b Jones	59
C.S.Cowdrey *	not out	26
G.R.Cowdrey	c Cook b Jones	6
M.V.Fleming	not out	11
S.A.Marsh +		
M.A.Ealham		
T.A.Merrick		
R.P.Davis		
A.P.Igglesden		
Extras	(b 1,lb 6,w 4)	11
TOTAL	(37.5 overs)(for 4 wkts)	169

KENT	O	M	R	W		FALL OF WICKETS	SOM	KEN
Igglesden	8	0	27	1				
Merrick	8	2	26	2	1st		80	1
Fleming	8	0	27	1	2nd		89	121
Ealham	8	0	42	0	3rd		125	127
Davis	3	0	17	0	4th		127	150
Cowdrey C.S.	5	0	20	2	5th		156	
					6th		163	
SOMERSET	O	M	R	W	7th		163	
Jones	8	0	25	2	8th			
Mallender	7.5	0	29	1	9th			
Rose	8	0	29	1	10th			
Cleal	2	0	9	0				
Hayhurst	5	0	34	0				
Swallow	3	0	12	0				
Roebuck	4	0	24	0				

HAMPSHIRE vs. MIDDLESEX

at Basingstoke on 10th June 1990
Toss : Middlesex. Umpires : K.E.Palmer and R.Palmer
Middlesex won by 7 wickets (Hants 0 pts Middx 4 pts)

HAMPSHIRE

R.J.Scott	c Haynes b Hughes	0
V.P.Terry	c Downton b Williams	4
D.I.Gower	c Hughes b Fraser	23
M.D.Marshall	c Butcher b Hughes	46
J.R.Wood	b Emburey	18
M.C.J.Nicholas *	b Emburey	1
J.R.Ayling	c Brown b Williams	9
R.J.Parks +	b Fraser	11
R.J.Maru	c Gatting b Hughes	9
C.A.Connor	b Hughes	3
P.J.Bakker	not out	0
Extras	(lb 6,w 6,nb 4)	16
TOTAL	(39.5 overs)	140

MIDDLESEX

D.L.Haynes	b Ayling	19
M.A.Roseberry	b Connor	17
M.W.Gatting *	c & b Maru	27
M.R.Ramprakash	not out	52
K.R.Brown	not out	13
R.O.Butcher		
P.R.Downton +		
N.F.Williams		
J.E.Emburey		
S.P.Hughes		
A.R.C.Fraser		
Extras	(b 5,lb 5,w 5,nb 1)	16
TOTAL	(37.5 overs)(for 3 wkts)	144

MIDDLESEX	O	M	R	W.		FALL OF WICKETS	HAM	MID
Hughes	6.5	1	19	4				
Williams	8	0	29	2	1st		2	41
Fraser	8	1	26	2	2nd		12	41
Gatting	3	0	20	0	3rd		47	93
Haynes	6	1	21	0	4th		101	
Emburey	8	2	19	2	5th		102	
					6th		112	
HAMPSHIRE	O	M	R	W	7th		118	
Marshall	8	0	19	0	8th		134	
Bakker	4	0	23	0	9th		137	
Connor	8	1	18	1	10th		140	
Ayling	7	0	27	1				
Maru	7.5	0	40	1				
Scott	3	0	7	0				

DERBYSHIRE vs. NOTTINGHAMSHIRE

at Derby on 10th June 1990
Toss : Notts. Umpires : J.W.Holder and N.T.Plews
Notts won on faster scoring rate (Derbys 0 pts Notts 4 pts)

DERBYSHIRE

K.J.Barnett *	c French b Evans	63
P.D.Bowler +	b Saxelby M.	45
J.E.Morris	c Evans b Saxelby K.	32
A.P.Kuiper	c French b Stephenson	46
B.Roberts	not out	26
C.J.Adams	b Stephenson	0
S.C.Goldsmith	not out	0
A.E.Warner		
G.Miller		
M.Jean-Jacques		
S.J.Base		
Extras	(lb 13,w 2)	15
TOTAL	(40 overs)(for 5 wkts)	227

NOTTINGHAMSHIRE

B.C.Broad	c Bowler b Jean-Jacques	11
D.W.Randall	c Kuiper b Warner	21
P.Johnson	c Bowler b Base	0
R.T.Robinson *	run out	116
M.Saxelby	c Kuiper b Jean-Jacques	34
F.D.Stephenson	c Kuiper b Jean-Jacques	6
B.N.French +	not out	17
K.E.Cooper	not out	1
K.P.Evans		
K.Saxelby		
J.A.Afford		
Extras	(lb 7,w 6)	13
TOTAL	(38 overs)(for 6 wkts)	219

NOTTS	O	M	R	W		FALL OF WICKETS	DER	NOT
Saxelby K.	8	0	53	1				
Cooper	8	1	29	0	1st		112	23
Stephenson	8	0	43	2	2nd		116	25
Evans	8	0	39	1	3rd		189	50
Afford	3	0	26	0	4th		214	151
Saxelby M.	5	0	24	1	5th		216	158
					6th			214
DERBYSHIRE	O	M	R	W	7th			
Jean-Jacques	8	0	47	3	8th			
Base	8	0	52	1	9th			
Warner	6	0	39	1	10th			
Miller	8	0	34	0				
Barnett	8	0	40	0				

YORKSHIRE vs. SURREY

at Hull on 10th June 1990
Toss : Surrey. Umpires : J.C.Balderstone & D.S.Thompsett
Surrey won by 6 wickets (Yorkshire 0 pts Surrey 4 pts)

YORKSHIRE

K.Sharp	c Ward b Bicknell	0
A.A.Metcalfe	lbw b Feltham	16
R.J.Blakey	b Medlycott	38
P.E.Robinson	b Medlycott	22
M.D.Moxon *	c Ward b Medlycott	9
D.Byas	b Waqar Younis	2
D.L.Bairstow +	not out	21
P.Carrick	b Murphy	7
P.J.Hartley	b Waqar Younis	8
P.W.Jarvis	c Bicknell b Murphy	3
A.Sidebottom	not out	0
Extras	(lb 10,w 5)	15
TOTAL	(40 overs)(for 9 wkts)	144

SURREY

G.S.Clinton	c Metcalfe b Byas	28
M.A.Feltham	c Sharp b Sidebottom	16
G.P.Thorpe	not out	46
D.M.Ward +	b Hartley	22
M.A.Lynch	c Metcalfe b Jarvis	8
I.A.Greig *	not out	2
K.T.Medlycott		
C.K.Bullen		
M.P.Bicknell		
Waqar Younis		
A.J.Murphy		
Extras	(b 3,lb 13,w 4,nb 3)	23
TOTAL	(37.5 overs)(for 4 wkts)	145

SURREY	O	M	R	W		FALL OF WICKETS	YOR	SUR
Bicknell	6	1	20	1				
Murphy	8	1	29	2	1st		0	39
Feltham	4	0	10	1	2nd		39	68
Bullen	6	0	21	0	3rd		78	112
Medlycott	8	1	20	3	4th		91	131
Waqar Younis	8	0	34	2	5th		92	
					6th		102	
YORKSHIRE	O	M	R	W	7th		114	
Jarvis	8	1	19	1	8th		131	
Sidebottom	8	1	31	1	9th		136	
Hartley	8	2	22	1	10th			
Byas	6	0	22	1				
Carrick	4	0	22	0				
Moxon	3.5	0	15	0				

LEICESTERSHIRE vs. SUSSEX

at Leicester on 10th June 1990
Toss : Leicestershire. Umpires : P.J.Eele and D.O.Oslear
Leicestershire won by 7 wickets (Leics 4 pts Sussex 0 pts)

SUSSEX

N.J.Lenham	c Benson b Willey	32
I.J.Gould	c Potter b Agnew	8
P.W.G.Parker *	c Nixon b Lewis	2
A.P.Wells	c Willey b Lewis	2
M.P.Speight	c Lewis b Mullally	21
C.M.Wells	c Nixon b Lewis	16
A.I.C.Dodemaide	c Briers b Benjamin	26
C.C.Remy	not out	12
P.Moores +	not out	17
A.R.Clarke		
I.D.K.Salisbury		
Extras	(lb 6,w 5,nb 5)	16
TOTAL	(40 overs)(for 7 wkts)	152

LEICESTERSHIRE

T.J.Boon	c Lenham b Dodemaide	29
N.E.Briers *	c Speight b Salisbury	31
J.J.Whitaker	not out	53
P.Willey	c Moores b Salisbury	4
C.C.Lewis	not out	25
L.Potter		
J.D.R.Benson		
P.A.Nixon +		
W.K.M.Benjamin		
J.P.Agnew		
A.D.Mullally		
Extras	(b 4,lb 7,w 1,nb 2)	14
TOTAL	(37.4 overs)(for 3 wkts)	156

LEICS	O	M	R	W		FALL OF WICKETS	SUS	LEI
Benjamin	8	3	13	1				
Agnew	8	1	25	1	1st		8	65
Lewis	8	0	36	3	2nd		21	87
Mullally	8	0	28	1	3rd		26	91
Willey	8	0	44	1	4th		70	
					5th		86	
SUSSEX	O	M	R	W	6th		95	
Wells C.M.	7	0	30	0	7th		126	
Dodemaide	8	3	20	1	8th			
Remy	6.4	0	34	0	9th			
Clarke	8	0	40	0	10th			
Salisbury	8	1	21	2				

REFUGE ASSURANCE LEAGUE

LANCASHIRE vs. GLOUCESTERSHIRE

at Old Trafford on 10th June 1990
Toss : Gloucs. Umpires : M.J.Kitchen and K.J.Lyons
Gloucestershire won by 2 wickets (Lancs 0 pts Gloucs 4 pts)

LANCASHIRE
G.D.Mendis	c & b Lawrence	32
G.Fowler	run out	6
G.D.Lloyd	run out	85
T.E.Jesty	c Lawrence b Alleyne	22
M.Watkinson	c Bainbridge b Alleyne	23
Wasim Akram	b Walsh	37
W.K.Hegg +	not out	2
I.D.Austin	not out	1
D.P.Hughes *		
J.D.Fitton		
P.J.W.Allott		
Extras	(b 2,lb 11,w 9)	22
TOTAL	(40 overs)(for 6 wkts)	230

GLOUCESTERSHIRE
I.P.Butcher	c Fowler b Watkinson	13
C.W.J.Athey	c Hegg b Watkinson	6
A.J.Wright *	c Mendis b Watkinson	68
K.M.Curran	c Hegg b Wasim Akram	7
P.Bainbridge	b Wasim Akram	39
J.W.Lloyds	lbw b Wasim Akram	0
P.W.Romaines	not out	45
M.W.Alleyne	st Hegg b Fitton	18
C.A.Walsh	b Wasim Akram	12
G.A.Tedstone +	not out	1
D.V.Lawrence		
Extras	(lb 14,w 7,nb 1)	22
TOTAL	(39.4 overs)(for 8 wkts)	231

GLOUCS	O	M	R	W		FALL OF WICKETS	
						LAN	GLO
Walsh	8	0	46	1			
Curran	8	0	52	0	1st	22	15
Bainbridge	8	0	39	0	2nd	68	30
Lawrence	8	0	38	1	3rd	109	49
Alleyne	8	0	42	2	4th	162	139
					5th	220	139
LANCASHIRE	O	M	R	W	6th	229	166
Watkinson	8	0	22	3	7th		188
Allott	8	0	46	0	8th		225
Wasim Akram	8	0	39	4	9th		
Fitton	8	0	53	1	10th		
Austin	7.4	0	57	0			

WARWICKSHIRE vs. ESSEX

at Edgbaston on 10th June 1990
Toss : Essex. Umpires : B.Dudleston and R.A.White
Essex won by 7 wickets (Warwickshire 0 pts Essex 4 pts)

WARWICKSHIRE
Asif Din	lbw b Foster	4
T.M.Moody	c Shahid b Childs	54
P.A.Smith	lbw b Topley	2
G.W.Humpage +	c Stephenson b Pringle	5
R.G.Twose	st Garnham b Stephenson	4
D.A.Reeve *	b Foster	28
D.P.Ostler	b Waugh	18
N.M.K.Smith	c Stephenson b Pringle	10
J.E.Benjamin	not out	10
G.Smith	b Pringle	5
T.A.Munton	not out	2
Extras	(lb 7,w 3,nb 3)	13
TOTAL	(40 overs)(for 9 wkts)	155

ESSEX
B.R.Hardie	b Smith G.	54
P.J.Prichard	lbw b Benjamin	8
M.E.Waugh	b Smith G.	60
D.R.Pringle *	not out	17
A.W.Lilley	not out	9
J.P.Stephenson		
N.Shahid		
M.A.Garnham +		
N.A.Foster		
T.D.Topley		
J.H.Childs		
Extras	(lb 4,w 3,nb 3)	10
TOTAL	(35.3 overs)(for 3 wkts)	158

ESSEX	O	M	R	W		FALL OF WICKETS	
						WAR	ESS
Topley	8	1	27	1			
Foster	8	0	35	2	1st	19	19
Childs	8	0	19	1	2nd	29	121
Pringle	8	1	29	3	3rd	43	149
Stephenson	3	0	20	1	4th	65	
Waugh	5	0	18	1	5th	82	
					6th	118	
WARWICKS	O	M	R	W	7th	135	
Munton	8	1	23	0	8th	137	
Benjamin	6	1	18	1	9th	153	
Moody	4	1	18	0	10th		
Reeve	3	0	12	0			
Smith N.M.K.	6.3	0	40	0			
Smith G.	5	0	20	2			
Smith P.A.	1	0	6	0			
Asif Din	2	0	17	0			

More runs for Mark Waugh to see Essex safely home against Warwickshire in the Refuge Assurance League.

HEADLINES

10th June

● Kent and Middlesex achieved their sixth wins in seven attempts both thanks to impressive performances in the field, restricting Somerset and Hampshire to 165 for seven and 140 all out respectively. Middlesex's Simon Hughes returned the best figures of the day with 4 for 19

● Similar virtues accounted for victories for Essex, Surrey and Hampshire, even a full complement of three Smiths and eight bowlers not being able to save Warwickshire from defeat by Essex

● David Capel, having made a Championship 100 the day before, hit his maiden Refuge 100 as Northants beat Glamorgan by 10 runs.

● Viv Richards completed 5,000 runs in the Sunday League when he reached 33 and Mark Frost produced career best bowling figures

● Tim Robinson's 116 not out against Derbyshire was his highest score and second 100 in the Sunday League as Notts reached a target reduced after two overs had been lost to the weather at the start of their innings

● Lancashire lost ground on the leaders with a surprising defeat at the hands of Gloucestershire - even after Graham Lloyd had recorded a career best 85 and Wasim Akram taken 4 for 39

BRITANNIC ASSURANCE CHAMPIONSHIP

NORTHANTS vs. GLAMORGAN

at Northampton on 9th, 11th, 12th June 1990
Toss : Northants.   Umpires : J.D.Bond and P.B.Wight
Glamorgan won by 6 wickets (Northants 8 pts (Bt: 4, Bw: 4) Glamorgan 22 pts (Bt: 3, Bw: 3))

NORTHANTS

A.Fordham	lbw b Frost	27	lbw b Barwick	45
N.A.Felton	c Richards b Barwick	122	c Metson b Frost	44
G.Cook	lbw b Frost	7	(4) c Metson b Frost	0
R.J.Bailey	c Metson b Barwick	38	(5) not out	47
D.J.Capel	c Metson b Frost	113	(6) not out	64
A.L.Penberthy	c Watkin b Barwick	1		
R.G.Williams	c Metson b Frost	34		
W.M.Noon +	run out	2	(3) lbw b Frost	2
J.G.Thomas	not out	0		
C.E.L.Ambrose				
N.G.B.Cook *				
Extras	(lb 4,nb 2)	6	(b 6,lb 4,w 3)	13
TOTAL	(for 8 wkts dec)	350	(for 4 wkts dec)	215

GLAMORGAN

A.R.Butcher *	b Williams	43	st Noon b Williams	36
H.Morris	lbw b Thomas	80	c Noon b Williams	24
P.A.Cottey	c Bailey b Cook N.G.B.	11	lbw b Capel	2
I.V.A.Richards	lbw b Thomas	25	(5) c Fordham b Williams	109
N.G.Cowley	lbw b Thomas	0		
C.P.Metson +	b Thomas	0		
M.P.Maynard	lbw b Thomas	74	(4) not out	125
G.C.Holmes	c Bailey b Cook N.G.B.	9	(6) not out	0
S.L.Watkin	b Thomas	3		
S.R.Barwick	not out	2		
M.Frost	c Capel b Thomas	4		
Extras	(b 2,lb 5,nb 1)	8	(b 3,lb 4,w 5,nb 1)	13
TOTAL		259	(for 4 wkts)	309

GLAMORGAN	O	M	R	W	O	M	R	W
Frost	23.2	6	82	4	13	0	58	3
Watkin	26	2	93	0	13	1	66	0
Barwick	24	4	76	3	19.2	3	67	1
Cowley	12	1	65	0	6	0	14	0
Richards	11	3	30	0				

NORTHANTS	O	M	R	W	O	M	R	W
Ambrose	20	4	65	0	14	4	58	0
Thomas	25	7	75	7	10	0	68	0
Penberthy	5	0	33	0				
Williams	19	5	42	1	13	2	51	3
Capel	6	0	20	0	7	2	17	1
Cook N.G.B.	11	2	17	2	19.4	1	108	0

FALL OF WICKETS

	NOR	GLA	NOR	GLA
1st	50	102	89	58
2nd	62	131	91	61
3rd	149	137	91	71
4th	267	137	124	308
5th	283	145		
6th	342	178		
7th	350	208		
8th	350	248		
9th		253		
10th		259		

LANCASHIRE vs. GLOUCESTERSHIRE

at Old Trafford on 9th (no play), 11th, 12th June 1990
Toss : Lancashire.   Umpires : M.J.Kitchen and K.J.Lyons
Lancashire won by 5 wickets (Lancashire 18 pts (Bt: 0, Bw: 2) Gloucs 3 pts (Bt: 3, Bw: 0))

GLOUCESTERSHIRE

A.J.Wright *	c Hegg b Patterson	15
G.D.Hodgson	c & b Hughes	72
P.W.Romaines	retired hurt	12
C.W.J.Athey	c Hegg b Patterson	33
P.Bainbridge	b Austin	72
K.M.Curran	c Allott b Fitton	48
J.W.Lloyds	lbw b Austin	0
G.A.Tedstone +	b Austin	6
D.A.Graveney	not out	19
C.A.Walsh	not out	33
D.V.Lawrence		
Extras	(b 2,lb 8,nb 1)	11
TOTAL	(for 7 wkts dec)	321

LANCASHIRE

G.Fowler			c Lloyds b Curran	126
G.D.Mendis			c Hodgson b Graveney	23
N.J.Speak			c Tedstone b Lawrence	30
T.E.Jesty			not out	84
M.Watkinson			b Lawrence	4
W.K.Hegg +			lbw b Lawrence	0
I.D.Austin			not out	26
D.P.Hughes *				
J.D.Fitton				
P.J.W.Allott				
B.P.Patterson				
Extras			(b 5,lb 14,w 1,nb 11)	31
TOTAL			(for 5 wkts)	324

LANCASHIRE	O	M	R	W	O	M	R	W
Patterson	18	4	43	2				
Allott	16	2	39	0				
Austin	21	3	42	3				
Watkinson	12	3	33	0				
Fitton	36	7	111	1				
Hughes	17.5	5	43	1				

GLOUCS	O	M	R	W	O	M	R	W
Walsh					20	1	66	0
Lawrence					18	2	86	3
Bainbridge					11	1	32	0
Curran					14	0	68	1
Graveney					19	3	39	1
Lloyds					2	0	7	0
Wright					0.5	0	7	0

FALL OF WICKETS

	GLO	LAN	GLO	LAN
1st	26			94
2nd	127			146
3rd	161			247
4th	236			277
5th	236			277
6th	240			
7th	273			
8th				
9th				
10th				

KENT vs. SOMERSET

at Canterbury on 9th, 11th, 12th June 1990
Toss : Somerset.   Umpires : D.J.Constant and B.J.Meyer
Match drawn (Kent 4 pts (Bt: 2, Bw: 2) Somerset 8 pts (Bt: 4, Bw: 4))

SOMERSET

S.J.Cook	c & b Davis	36		
J.J.E.Hardy	c Marsh b Hinks	42	not out	47
A.N.Hayhurst	lbw b Igglesden	55	c Benson b Igglesden	9
C.J.Tavare *	c Hinks b Igglesden	82		
R.J.Harden	not out	52	(4) not out	50
N.D.Burns +	c Ellison b Davis	31	(1) run out	40
G.D.Rose	not out	8		
I.G.Swallow				
N.A.Mallender				
A.N.Jones				
J.C.Hallett				
Extras	(lb 15,w 1)	16	(lb 3,w 1)	4
TOTAL	(for 5 wkts dec)	322	(for 2 wkts dec)	150

KENT

S.G.Hinks	lbw b Hallett	30	b Swallow	55
M.R.Benson	b Jones	0	c Burns b Rose	116
N.R.Taylor	c Hardy b Mallender	9	c Hardy b Swallow	5
G.R.Cowdrey	b Hayhurst	42	c Cook b Mallender	10
C.S.Cowdrey *	b Hallett	0	b Rose	14
M.V.Fleming	c Swallow b Rose	37	b Rose	6
S.A.Marsh +	c Burns b Rose	5	c Tavare b Hallett	8
R.M.Ellison	not out	31	not out	6
R.P.Davis	lbw b Rose	0	(10) not out	8
P.S.De Villiers	c Burns b Rose	15	(9) lbw b Rose	0
A.P.Igglesden	not out	19		
Extras	(b 1,lb 11,w 1,nb 2)	15	(lb 4)	4
TOTAL	(for 9 wkts dec)	203	(for 8 wkts)	232

KENT	O	M	R	W	O	M	R	W
Igglesden	20	2	85	2	7	1	42	1
De Villiers	23	7	51	0	2	0	7	0
Ellison	25	2	101	0	7	0	38	0
Hinks	5	1	15	1				
Davis	19	7	50	2	5	0	18	0
Fleming	4	0	5	0				
Cowdrey C.S.					4	2	9	0
Taylor					6	1	29	0
Benson					3	2	4	0

SOMERSET	O	M	R	W	O	M	R	W
Jones	8.4	1	24	1				
Mallender	19	6	32	1	10	2	34	1
Rose	19	4	59	4	10.5	0	55	4
Hallett	12.2	4	40	2	7	0	32	1
Hayhurst	14	1	36	1	8	0	48	0
Swallow					9	1	59	2

FALL OF WICKETS

	SOM	KEN	SOM	KEN
1st	85	1	50	121
2nd	85	12	59	135
3rd	211	61		162
4th	230	61		198
5th	299	114		209
6th		129		210
7th		130		222
8th		130		224
9th		153		
10th				

HEADLINES

9th - 12th June

- Exciting finishes were contrived despite more bad weather after which only two points seperated the top four teams

- Lancashire became the new leaders with a five wicket win over Gloucestershire after both sides had forfeited an innings, David Hughes's side reaching 324 in 85 overs

- Warwickshire also gained their third win of the season to move into third place one point behind Notts and level with Hampshire, achieving a target of 291 in the 81st over after Essex had forfeited their second innings. Mark Waugh had earlier made his fourth 100 of the season

- Viv Richards and Matthew Maynard's exhilarating fourth wicket stand of 227 carried Glamorgan to victory over Northants at Northampton after Greg Thomas had returned career best figures against his old county and David Capel and Nigel Felton both hit centuries

- Surrey forfeited their first innings to revive interest in their match against Yorkshire at Harrogate and the gesture almost paid dividends as the visitors fell one short of victory with nine wickets down. Career best figures from Chris White were in vain as Surrey gained eight points for levelling the scores after four results were possible from the last ball

- Kent and Somerset both had hopes of victory during a last afternoon of of fluctuating fortunes at Canterbury. Kent finished 38 short with two wickets left

BRITANNIC ASS. CHAMPIONSHIP

CORNHILL TEST MATCH

WARWICKSHIRE vs. ESSEX

at Edgbaston on 9th, 11th, 12th June 1990
Toss : Essex. Umpires : B.Dudleston and R.A.White
Warwickshire won by 5 wickets (Warwicks 18 pts (Bt: 0, Bw: 2) Essex 3 pts (Bt: 3, Bw: 0))

ESSEX

B.R.Hardie	lbw b Benjamin	2
J.P.Stephenson	c Humpage b Benjamin	85
P.J.Prichard	c & b Munton	29
M.E.Waugh	c Humpage b Munton	103
A.W.Lilley	lbw b Donald	1
N.Shahid	not out	75
M.A.Garnham +	not out	26
D.R.Pringle *		
N.A.Foster		
J.H.Childs		
S.J.W.Andrew		
Extras	(b 6,w 1,nb 3)	10
TOTAL	(for 5 wkts dec)	331

WARWICKSHIRE

A.J.Moles	not out	14	lbw b Pringle		97
J.D.Ratcliffe	not out	27	run out		22
Asif Din			run out		42
G.W.Humpage +			run out		43
D.A.Reeve *			not out		33
P.A.Smith			lbw b Pringle		2
N.M.K.Smith			not out		30
A.A.Donald					
A.R.K.Pierson					
J.E.Benjamin					
T.A.Munton					
Extras		0	(b 1,lb 12,w 1,nb 11)		25
TOTAL	(for 0 wkts dec)	41	(for 5 wkts)		294

WARWICKSHIRE	O	M	R	W	O	M	R	W
Donald	25	7	53	1				
Benjamin	22	2	79	2				
Munton	35	8	72	2				
Pierson	26.1	2	86	0				
Smith N.M.K.	12	2	35	0				

ESSEX	O	M	R	W	O	M	R	W
Waugh	6	2	7	0	3	0	24	0
Stephenson	6	2	54	0	3	1	7	0
Lilley	1	0	7	0				
Prichard	0.4	0	2	0				
Foster					14	2	68	0
Pringle					23	6	72	2
Childs					25.3	7	66	0
Andrew					12	1	44	0

FALL OF WICKETS

	ESS	WAR	ESS	WAR
1st	11			56
2nd	60			148
3rd	194			212
4th	197			245
5th	244			253
6th				
7th				
8th				
9th				
10th				

YORKSHIRE vs. SURREY

at Harrogate on 9th (no play), 11th, 12th June 1990
Toss : Surrey. Umpires : J.C.Balderstone and D.S.Thompsett
Match drawn (Yorkshire 3 pts (Bt: 3, Bw: 0) Surrey 12 pts (Bt: 0, Bw: 4))

YORKSHIRE

M.D.Moxon *	lbw b Waqar Younis	10	not out		23
A.A.Metcalfe	c Lynch b Bicknell	6	c Lynch b Medlycott		1
R.J.Blakey	b Waqar Younis	1	not out		2
S.A.Kellett	lbw b Feltham	24			
P.E.Robinson	c Lynch b Medlycott	85			
D.L.Bairstow +	c Ward b Bicknell	32			
C.White	b Waqar Younis	2			
C.S.Pickles	c & b Bicknell	0			
P.Carrick	c Bicknell b Medlycott	64			
P.W.Jarvis	b Feltham	7			
D.Gough	not out	1			
Extras	(b 7,lb 8,w 7)	22			0
TOTAL		254	(for 1 wkt dec)		26

SURREY

R.I.Alikhan	lbw b Pickles	31
G.S.Clinton	c Robinson b White	5
G.P.Thorpe	c Blakey b White	44
D.M.Ward +	c Blakey b Pickles	71
M.A.Lynch	c Bairstow b Jarvis	11
I.A.Greig *	c Pickles b White	72
K.T.Medlycott	b White	6
M.A.Feltham	c Jarvis b White	21
M.P.Bicknell	run out	0
Waqar Younis	not out	1
A.J.Murphy	not out	0
Extras	(b 6,lb 6,w 6)	18
TOTAL	(for 9 wkts)	280

SURREY	O	M	R	W	O	M	R	W
Waqar Younis	24	6	56	3				
Bicknell	25	11	40	3				
Feltham	18	4	45	2	3	0	21	0
Murphy	13	4	45	0				
Medlycott	16	0	53	2	3.4	2	5	1

YORKSHIRE	O	M	R	W	O	M	R	W
Jarvis					17	4	60	1
Gough					6	1	24	0
Pickles					12	2	45	2
White					18	2	74	5
Carrick					20	6	65	0

FALL OF WICKETS

	YOR	SUR	YOR	SUR
1st	14		9	41
2nd	19			45
3rd	29			147
4th	55			166
5th	101			183
6th	110			204
7th	114			270
8th	245			270
9th	252			279
10th	254			

ENGLAND vs. NEW ZEALAND

at Trent Bridge on 7th, 8th, 9th, 11th, 12th June
Toss : New Zealand. Umpires : H.D.Bird and J.H.Hampshire
Match drawn

NEW ZEALAND

T.J.Franklin	b Malcolm	33	not out		22
J.G.Wright *	c Stewart b Small	8	c Russell b Small		1
A.H.Jones	c Stewart b Malcolm	39	c Russell b DeFreitas		13
M.D.Crowe	b DeFreitas	59			
M.J.Greatbatch	b Hemmings	1			
M.W.Priest	c Russell b DeFreitas	26			
M.C.Snedden	c Gooch b DeFreitas	0			
J.G.Bracewell	c Gooch b Small	28			
R.J.Hadlee	b DeFreitas	0			
I.D.S.Smith +	not out	2			
D.K.Morrison	lbw b DeFreitas	0	(4) not out		0
Extras	(b 1,lb 10,w 1)	12			0
TOTAL		208	(for 2 wkts)		36

ENGLAND

G.A.Gooch *	lbw b Hadlee	0
M.A.Atherton	c Snedden b Priest	151
A.J.Stewart	c Smith b Hadlee	27
A.J.Lamb	b Hadlee	0
R.A.Smith	c Smith b Bracewell	55
N.H.Fairbrother	c Franklin b Snedden	19
R.C.Russell +	c Snedden b Morrison	28
P.A.J.DeFreitas	lbw b Bracewell	14
G.C.Small	c Crowe b Hadlee	26
E.E.Hemmings	not out	13
D.E.Malcolm	not out	4
Extras	(b 2,lb 3,nb 3)	8
TOTAL	(for 9 wkts dec)	345

ENGLAND	O	M	R	W	O	M	R	W
Small	29	9	49	2	6	2	14	1
Malcolm	19	7	48	2	7	2	22	0
Hemmings	19	6	47	1	2	2	0	0
DeFreitas	22	6	53	5	2	2	0	1

NEW ZEALAND	O	M	R	W	O	M	R	W
Hadlee	33	6	89	4				
Morrison	22	3	96	1				
Snedden	36	17	54	1				
Bracewell	35	8	75	2				
Priest	12	4	26	1				

FALL OF WICKETS

	NZ	ENG	NZ	ENG
1st	16	0	8	
2nd	75	43	36	
3rd	110	45		
4th	121	141		
5th	170	168		
6th	174	260		
7th	191	302		
8th	191	306		
9th	203	340		
10th	208			

Man of the match: M.A.Atherton (England)

HEADLINES

England vs New Zealand: First Cornhill Test Match

7th - 12th June

- The rain and bad light which affected all five days play prevented the First Test from developing into a meaningful contest but England were able to gain a useful psychological advantage

- Phillip DeFreitas, certain of his place only after an injury to Chris Lewis, produced his best Test figures to restrict New Zealand's first innings to 208

- Fellow Lancastrian Mike Atherton, playing in his third Test and opening for England for the first time, made an accomplished maiden Test 100. He batted almost eight hours for his 151 which has been bettered only by John Edrich for England v New Zealand at Trent Bridge

- Richard Hadlee marked his last appearance at Trent Bridge by dismissing Graham Gooch with his first ball of his farewell series and also removing Allan Lamb without scoring on the way to figures of 4 for 83

- England declared at tea on the final day with a lead of 137 and captured two more New Zealand wickets before the close

- Test debut: M.W.Priest (New Zealand)

B & H SEMI-FINALS

TILCON TROPHY

NOTTS vs. WORCESTERSHIRE

at Trent Bridge on 13th June 1990
Toss : Worcestershire. Umpires : D.O.Oslear and R.Palmer
Worcestershire won by 9 wickets

NOTTINGHAMSHIRE

B.C.Broad	c Lampitt b Botham	32
D.J.R.Martindale	b McEwan	0
R.T.Robinson *	c D'Oliveira b Lampitt	26
P.Johnson	c Hick b Botham	4
D.W.Randall	c Rhodes b McEwan	39
F.D.Stephenson	not out	98
B.N.French +	run out	4
E.E.Hemmings	not out	12
K.E.Cooper		
R.A.Pick		
J.A.Afford		
Extras	(lb 9,w 5,nb 1)	15
TOTAL	(55 overs)(for 6 wkts)	230

WORCESTERSHIRE

T.S.Curtis *	b Stephenson	61
M.J.Weston	not out	99
G.A.Hick	not out	57
I.T.Botham		
D.B.D'Oliveira		
S.R.Lampitt		
D.A.Leatherdale		
S.J.Rhodes +		
P.J.Newport		
R.D.Stemp		
S.M.McEwan		
Extras	(lb 10,w 3,nb 2)	15
TOTAL	(53.2 overs)(for 1 wkt)	232

WORCS	O	M	R	W	FALL OF WICKETS		
						NOT	WOR
Newport	11	3	28	0			
McEwan	11	0	53	2	1st	5	141
Lampitt	11	0	47	1	2nd	56	
Botham	11	2	43	2	3rd	65	
Stemp	8	1	38	0	4th	70	
Hick	3	0	12	0	5th	162	
					6th	171	
NOTTS	O	M	R	W	7th		
Pick	11	1	45	0	8th		
Cooper	10.2	1	29	0	9th		
Stephenson	11	0	45	1	10th		
Afford	11	0	43	0			
Hemmings	10	0	60	0			

Man of the match: M.J.Weston

SURREY vs. WARWICKSHIRE

at Harrogate on 13th June 1990
Toss : Warwickshire. Umpires: J.C.Balderstone and
D.S.Thompsett. Warwickshire won by 2 wickets

SURREY

G.S.Clinton	c Asif Din b Moody	32
M.A.Feltham	c Moody b Donald	10
A.J.Stewart	c Reeve b Benjamin	20
G.P.Thorpe	c Reeve b Smith	0
D.M.Ward +	c Asif Din b Moody	40
I.A.Greig *	run out	39
K.T.Medlycott	c Benjamin b Munton	1
C.K.Bullen	run out	22
M.P.Bicknell	c Donald b Moody	10
A.H.Gray	not out	9
A.J.Murphy	not out	6
Extras	(b 5,lb 10,w 8)	23
TOTAL	(55 overs)(for 9 wkts)	212

WARWICKSHIRE

A.J.Moles	c & b Medlycott	51
Asif Din	c Ward b Gray	0
T.M.Moody	lbw b Feltham	31
G.W.Humpage +	b Gray	2
D.A.Reeve *	c & b Murphy	13
T.L.Penney	b Bicknell	36
R.G.Twose	not out	36
N.M.K.Smith	c Ward b Bicknell	23
A.A.Donald	c Medlycott b Bicknell	0
J.E.Benjamin	not out	7
T.A.Munton		
Extras	(b 6,lb 1,w 7)	14
TOTAL	(54 overs)(for 8 wkts)	213

WARWICKS	O	M	R	W	FALL OF WICKETS		
Donald	11	0	41	1		SUR	WAR
Benjamin	11	2	25	1	1st	16	15
Munton	11	1	36	1	2nd	47	58
Moody	11	3	49	3	3rd	75	62
Smith	11	2	46	1	4th	77	78
					5th	127	121
SURREY	O	M	R	W	6th	132	159
Gray	11	1	55	2	7th	173	197
Bicknell	9	0	48	3			
Feltham	3	0	16	1			
Murphy	9	0	23	1			
Medlycott	11	0	40	1			
Bullen	11	1	24	0			

Man of the match: T.M.Moody

YORKSHIRE vs. SUSSEX

at Harrogate on 14th June 1990
Toss : Yorkshire. Umpires : J.C.Balderstone and
D.S.Thompsett. Yorkshire won by 7 wickets

SUSSEX

N.J.Lenham	c Jarvis b Carrick	52
K.Greenfield	c Robinson b Jarvis	10
P.W.G.Parker *	c Bairstow b Jarvis	0
A.P.Wells	c Byas b Moxon	5
M.P.Speight	c White b Carrick	30
C.C.Remy	c Robinson b White	3
P.Moores +	c Moxon b Pickles	40
J.A.North	c Byas b Carrick	6
I.D.K.Salisbury	not out	14
B.T.P.Donelan	c White b Pickles	4
R.A.Bunting	not out	5
Extras	(lb 7)	7
TOTAL	(55 overs)(for 9 wkts)	176

YORKSHIRE

M.D.Moxon *	c Wells b Lenham	22
A.A.Metcalfe	c Parker b Remy	64
R.J.Blakey	run out	21
K.Sharp	not out	37
P.E.Robinson	not out	24
D.L.Bairstow +		
D.Byas		
C.White		
P.Carrick		
C.S.Pickles		
P.W.Jarvis		
Extras	(b 2,lb 6,w 4)	12
TOTAL	(53.3 overs)(for 3 wkts)	180

YORKSHIRE	O	M	R	W	FALL OF WICKETS		
Jarvis	11	4	29	2		SUS	YOR
Pickles	11	2	26	2	1st	19	56
Moxon	11	4	26	1	2nd	19	111
White	9	1	42	1	3rd	27	119
Carrick	11	3	39	3	4th	68	
Byas	2	0	7	0	5th	81	
					6th	135	
SUSSEX	O	M	R	W	7th	151	
Remy	11	2	38	1	8th	157	
Bunting	10.3	1	28	0	9th	162	
Donelan	11	2	25	0	10th		
Salisbury	11	1	44	0			
Lenham	5	2	16	1			
North	4	0	17	0			
Parker	1	0	4	0			

Man of the match: A.A.Metcalfe

LANCASHIRE vs. SOMERSET

at Old Trafford on 13th June 1990
Toss : Lancashire. Umpires : B.Dudleston and J.W.Holder
Lancashire won by 6 wickets

SOMERSET

S.J.Cook	c Hegg b Austin	49
J.J.E.Hardy	c Allott b Wasim Akram	19
A.N.Hayhurst	c Hegg b Wasim Akram	1
C.J.Tavare *	c Hughes b Austin	10
R.J.Harden	c Hegg b DeFreitas	16
N.D.Burns +	c Hughes b Watkinson	21
G.D.Rose	run out	32
R.P.Lefebvre	not out	25
I.G.Swallow	b Wasim Akram	8
N.A.Mallender	run out	3
A.N.Jones	not out	1
Extras	(b 5,lb 12,w 6,nb 4)	27
TOTAL	(55 overs)(for 9 wkts)	212

LANCASHIRE

G.D.Mendis	c & b Swallow	37
G.Fowler	b Jones	14
M.A.Atherton	not out	56
N.H.Fairbrother	c Burns b Rose	78
M.Watkinson	c Harden b Rose	11
Wasim Akram	not out	8
P.A.J.DeFreitas		
W.K.Hegg +		
I.D.Austin		
D.P.Hughes *		
P.J.W.Allott		
Extras	(lb 4,w 5,nb 1)	10
TOTAL	(44.5 overs)(for 4 wkts)	214

LANCASHIRE	O	M	R	W	FALL OF WICKETS		
Allott	11	2	34	0		SOM	LAN
DeFreitas	11	0	51	1	1st	50	34
Wasim Akram	11	0	29	3	2nd	55	74
Watkinson	11	1	33	1	3rd	81	185
Austin	11	0	48	2	4th	109	203
					5th	113	
SOMERSET	O	M	R	W	6th	163	
Jones	9	0	48	1	7th	174	
Mallender	9	3	31	0	8th	202	
Rose	10	0	44	2	9th	208	
Lefebvre	8	1	31	0	10th		
Swallow	6.5	1	40	1			
Hayhurst	2	0	16	0			

Man of the match: N.H.Fairbrother

HEADLINES

13th June

● Worcestershire and Lancashire won through to the B & H Final at Lord's with comfortable victories

● Despite being well below full strength, Worcs beat Notts, by nine wickets with 1.4 overs in hand. Martin Weston ended one short of his first B & H century but could be content with a new career best and the Gold Award. Earlier, only Franklyn Stephenson's highest B & H score had kept Notts in the contest

● Lancashire beat Somerset by six wickets with 10.1 overs to spare. Having been contained by Wasim Akram Somerset were put to the sword by Neil Fairbrother (78 in 53 balls) and Michael Atherton who added 111 in 18 overs

13th - 15th June

● Warwickshire became the 1990 winners of the annual Tilcon Trophy in a high-scoring final

● Trevor Penney, a young Zimbabwean qualifying for England, impressed in his first appearances for Warwickshire

YORKSHIRE vs. WARWICKSHIRE

at Harrogate on 15th June 1990
Toss : Warwickshire. Umpires: J.C.Balderstone and
D.S.Thompsett. Warwickshire won by 4 runs

WARWICKSHIRE

A.J.Moles	not out	102
Asif Din	c Metcalfe b Pickles	10
T.M.Moody	c Moxon b Carrick	67
G.W.Humpage +	c Bairstow b Carrick	11
D.A.Reeve *	lbw b Carrick	2
R.G.Twose	b Pickles	2
T.L.Penney	not out	64
N.M.K.Smith		
A.A.Donald		
J.E.Benjamin		
T.A.Munton		
Extras	(b 4,lb 6,w 4)	14
TOTAL	(55 overs)(for 5 wkts)	272

YORKSHIRE

M.D.Moxon *	c Smith b Asif Din	77
A.A.Metcalfe	c Moody b Asif Din	76
R.J.Blakey	run out	54
K.Sharp	c Reeve b Smith	34
P.E.Robinson	c Moody b Smith	3
D.L.Bairstow +	c Reeve b Donald	1
D.Byas	not out	4
P.Carrick	not out	7
C.S.Pickles		
P.W.Jarvis		
S.D.Fletcher		
Extras	(b 4,lb 2,w 5,nb 1)	12
TOTAL	(55 overs)(for 6 wkts)	268

YORKSHIRE	O	M	R	W	FALL OF WICKETS		
Jarvis	11	1	53	0		WAR	YOR
Pickles	11	1	51	2	1st	20	133
Fletcher	10	0	59	0	2nd	126	194
Carrick	11	1	41	3	3rd	142	240
Byas	11	0	55	0	4th	152	254
Moxon	1	0	3	0	5th	156	254
					6th		257
WARWICKS	O	M	R	W	7th		
Donald	11	0	53	1	8th		
Benjamin	11	2	35	0	9th		
Munton	11	0	49	0	10th		
Smith	10	0	52	2			
Moody	2	0	15	0			
Asif Din	10	0	58	2			

Man of the match: A.J.Moles

TOUR MATCH	REFUGE ASSURANCE LEAGUE

LEICESTERSHIRE vs. NEW ZEALAND

at Leicester on 14th June 1990
Toss : Leicestershire.   Umpires : V.A.Holder and A.A.Jones
Leicestershire won by 4 wickets

NEW ZEALAND

J.G.Wright *	c Potter b Mullally	62
J.J.Crowe	b Mullally	7
M.J.Greatbatch	b Mullally	0
K.R.Rutherford	b Mullally	19
M.D.Crowe	b Agnew	20
S.A.Thomson	c Nixon b Benjamin	25
M.W.Priest	c Lewis b Mullally	1
A.C.Parore +	not out	19
M.C.Snedden	c Potter b Mullally	1
D.K.Morrison	lbw b Willey	2
J.P.Millmow	not out	2
Extras	(lb 1,w 3,nb 3)	7
TOTAL	(55 overs)(for 9 wkts)	165

LEICESTERSHIRE

T.J.Boon	c Crowe M.D. b Priest	40
N.E.Briers *	b Morrison	7
J.J.Whitaker	c Rutherford b Millmow	9
P.Willey	c Parore b Snedden	4
C.C.Lewis	c Crowe J.J. b Thomson	51
L.Potter	not out	27
J.D.R.Benson	run out	19
W.K.M.Benjamin	not out	0
P.A.Nixon +		
J.P.Agnew		
A.D.Mullally		
Extras	(lb 10,w 3,nb 1)	14
TOTAL	(52.4 overs)(for 6 wkts)	171

LEICS	O	M	R	W	FALL OF WICKETS		
Benjamin	11	1	27	1		NZ	LEI
Agnew	11	1	21	1	1st	23	8
Lewis	11	1	57	0	2nd	23	23
Mullally	11	3	38	6	3rd	50	29
Willey	11	3	21	1	4th	76	115
					5th	128	119
NEW ZEALAND	O	M	R	W	6th	139	165
Morrison	11	1	27	1	7th	141	
Millmow	11	4	28	1	8th	142	
Snedden	9	2	32	1	9th	149	
Thomson	10	0	42	1	10th		
Priest	11	3	26	1			
Crowe M.D.	0.4	0	6	0			

Man of the match: A.D.Mullally

HEADLINES

14th June

- Leicestershire became the first county to beat the New Zealanders with a four-wicket win in a one-day match at Leicester after Alan Mullally had taken six wickets and Chris Lewis confirmed his fitness with 51

17th June

- Kent and Middlesex continued their battle at the top of the Refuge table, each recording their seventh win in eight attempts

- Middlesex owed their victory over Leicestershire to Mike Gatting's best ever score in the Sunday League. Their total of 259 for 5 proved 16 too many for Leicestershire

- By contrast, Kent were able to defend a modest score of 178 for 9 against Notts, Alan Igglesden managing figures of 4 for 24

SUSSEX vs. YORKSHIRE

at Hove on 17th June 1990
Toss : Sussex.   Umpires : J.D.Bond and R.Palmer
Yorkshire won by 40 runs (Sussex 0 pts Yorkshire 4 pts)

YORKSHIRE

K.Sharp	b Pigott	34
A.A.Metcalfe	c Moores b Wells C.M.	16
R.J.Blakey	c Moores b Lenham	23
D.Byas	c Parker b Remy	26
M.D.Moxon *	c Dodemaide b Remy	39
P.E.Robinson	c Moores b Dodemaide	1
D.L.Bairstow +	c Wells A.P. b Pigott	14
P.Carrick	not out	24
P.J.Hartley	not out	5
C.S.Pickles		
P.W.Jarvis		
Extras	(lb 6,w 4)	10
TOTAL	(40 overs)(for 7 wkts)	192

SUSSEX

N.J.Lenham	c Robinson b Jarvis	16
I.J.Gould	run out	0
P.W.G.Parker *	lbw b Moxon	36
A.P.Wells	c Blakey b Moxon	6
M.P.Speight	b Moxon	24
C.M.Wells	c & b Carrick	2
A.I.C.Dodemaide	c Pickles b Carrick	20
A.C.S.Pigott	st Bairstow b Carrick	19
P.Moores	c Byas b Jarvis	8
C.C.Remy	c Moxon b Hartley	7
I.D.K.Salisbury	not out	3
Extras	(b 4,lb 6,w 1)	11
TOTAL	(36.5 overs)	152

SUSSEX	O	M	R	W	FALL OF WICKETS		
Wells C.M.	8	1	17	1		YOR	SUS
Remy	8	0	45	2	1st	33	1
Dodemaide	8	2	32	1	2nd	77	24
Salisbury	4	0	36	0	3rd	79	38
Pigott	8	0	35	2	4th	132	76
Lenham	4	0	21	1	5th	133	83
					6th	157	93
YORKSHIRE	O	M	R	W	7th	175	122
Pickles	7	0	24	0	8th		131
Jarvis	5	0	19	2	9th		143
Hartley	6.5	0	26	1	10th		152
Moxon	8	0	29	3			
Byas	2	0	16	0			
Carrick	8	2	28	3			

SOMERSET vs. ESSEX

at Bath on 17th June 1990
Toss : Somerset.   Umpires : R.Julian and K.J.Lyons
Essex won by 101 runs (Somerset 0 pts Essex 4 pts)

ESSEX

G.A.Gooch *	b Hayhurst	34
B.R.Hardie	b Mallender	7
M.E.Waugh	b Rose	3
P.J.Prichard	c & b Rose	64
D.R.Pringle	b Mallender	37
J.P.Stephenson	b Rose	1
A.W.Lilley	c Bartlett b Jones	10
N.A.Foster	not out	39
M.A.Garnham +	not out	12
T.D.Topley		
J.H.Childs		
Extras	(b 5,lb 2,w 3)	10
TOTAL	(40 overs)(for 7 wkts)	217

SOMERSET

S.J.Cook	lbw b Pringle	23
P.M.Roebuck	c Hardie b Foster	0
R.J.Bartlett	run out	16
C.J.Tavare *	b Childs	5
R.J.Harden	run out	13
A.N.Hayhurst	run out	20
G.D.Rose	b Topley	20
N.D.Burns +	b Foster	0
I.G.Swallow	c Gooch b Topley	3
A.N.Jones	b Stephenson	0
N.A.Mallender	not out	7
Extras	(lb 6,w 3)	9
TOTAL	(34.5 overs)	116

SOMERSET	O	M	R	W	FALL OF WICKETS		
Jones	7	0	47	1		ESS	SOM
Mallender	8	0	30	2	1st	32	32
Rose	8	0	33	3	2nd	38	33
Swallow	5	0	32	0	3rd	79	48
Hayhurst	7	0	41	1	4th	149	48
Roebuck	5	0	27	0	5th	150	80
					6th	159	104
ESSEX	O	M	R	W	7th	179	104
Topley	7.5	1	22	2	8th		106
Foster	6	0	16	2	9th		108
Childs	8	2	14	1	10th		116
Pringle	6	0	23	1			
Waugh	6	1	32	0			
Stephenson	1	0	3	1			

SURREY vs. WORCESTERSHIRE

at The Oval on 17th June 1990
Toss : Surrey.   Umpires : H.D.Bird and J.H.Harris
Surrey won by 7 wickets (Surrey 4 pts Worcs 0 pts)

WORCESTERSHIRE

T.S.Curtis	c Ward b Bicknell	0
M.J.Weston	c Ward b Murphy	5
G.A.Hick	c Stewart b Murphy	16
I.T.Botham	b Waqar Younis	27
D.B.D'Oliveira	c & b Medlycott	53
P.A.Neale *	run out	3
P.J.Newport	c Waqar Younis b Medlycott	3
S.J.Rhodes +	not out	35
S.R.Lampitt	b Waqar Younis	11
S.M.McEwan	b Waqar Younis	0
R.D.Stemp	not out	3
Extras	(b 2,lb 10,w 8,nb 1)	21
TOTAL	(40 overs)(for 9 wkts)	177

SURREY

A.J.Stewart	lbw b Newport	0
M.A.Feltham	c Stemp b Hick	56
G.P.Thorpe	c & b Hick	55
D.M.Ward +	not out	27
M.A.Lynch	not out	21
I.A.Greig *		
K.T.Medlycott		
C.K.Bullen		
M.P.Bicknell		
Waqar Younis		
A.J.Murphy		
Extras	(lb 6,w 15)	21
TOTAL	(38.5 overs)(for 3 wkts)	180

SURREY	O	M	R	W	FALL OF WICKETS		
Bicknell	6	0	19	1		WOR	SUR
Murphy	7	0	38	2	1st	0	0
Feltham	3	0	19	0	2nd	23	120
Bullen	8	1	29	0	3rd	23	133
Waqar Younis	8	0	27	3	4th	81	
Medlycott	8	0	33	2	5th	90	
					6th	103	
WORCS	O	M	R	W	7th	131	
Newport	8	2	31	1	8th	164	
Weston	3	0	15	0	9th	166	
McEwan	4	0	15	0	10th		
Botham	7	0	32	0			
Stemp	8	0	37	0			
Lampitt	2	0	15	0			
Hick	6.5	1	29	2			

KENT vs. NOTTINGHAMSHIRE

at Canterbury on 17th June 1990
Toss : Kent.   Umpires : B.Leadbeater and R.A.White
Kent won by 24 runs (Kent 4 pts Nottinghamshire 0 pts)

KENT

S.G.Hinks	c Saxelby b Stephenson	12
M.A.Ealham	c Evans b Stephenson	2
N.R.Taylor	c & b Hemmings	28
C.S.Cowdrey *	c Broad b Saxelby	13
G.R.Cowdrey	c Broad b Stephenson	46
M.V.Fleming	b Saxelby	21
S.A.Marsh +	run out	20
R.M.Ellison	b Stephenson	9
T.A.Merrick	not out	12
A.P.Igglesden	run out	0
R.P.Davis	not out	0
Extras	(lb 6,w 6,nb 3)	15
TOTAL	(40 overs)(for 9 wkts)	178

NOTTINGHAMSHIRE

B.C.Broad	c Marsh b Igglesden	8
D.W.Randall	run out	49
P.Johnson	c Marsh b Merrick	3
R.T.Robinson *	b Fleming	3
M.Saxelby	c Cowdrey G.R. b Davis	25
F.D.Stephenson	lbw b Cowdrey C.S.	9
B.N.French +	c & b Davis	0
K.P.Evans	c Ellison b Igglesden	30
E.E.Hemmings	c Ealham b Igglesden	15
K.E.Cooper	c Taylor b Igglesden	1
J.A.Afford	not out	0
Extras	(lb 7,w 4)	11
TOTAL	(38.3 overs)	154

NOTTS	O	M	R	W	FALL OF WICKETS		
Stephenson	8	0	28	4		KEN	NOT
Cooper	8	1	33	0	1st	10	20
Saxelby	8	0	48	2	2nd	17	23
Evans	7	1	34	0	3rd	54	28
Afford	4	1	12	0	4th	73	93
Hemmings	5	0	17	1	5th	124	93
					6th	148	97
KENT	O	M	R	W	7th	154	111
Igglesden	6.3	1	24	4	8th	171	144
Merrick	7	0	26	1	9th	171	154
Fleming	8	0	21	1	10th		154
Ellison	2	0	18	0			
Ealham	3	0	18	0			
Davis	8	0	25	2			
Cowdrey C.S.	4	0	15	1			

REFUGE ASSURANCE LEAGUE

HAMPSHIRE vs. GLAMORGAN

at Bournemouth on 17th June 1990
Toss : Glamorgan. Umpires : J.W.Holder and B.J.Meyer
Hampshire won by 64 runs (Hants 4 pts Glamorgan 0 pts)

HAMPSHIRE

V.P.Terry	lbw b Watkin	2
R.J.Scott	c Dennis b Cowley	61
R.A.Smith	c Maynard b Frost	122
D.I.Gower	lbw b Richards	1
M.D.Marshall	c Metson b Watkin	1
M.C.J.Nicholas *	b Frost	16
J.R.Ayling	not out	5
R.J.Maru	not out	4
R.J.Parks +		
C.A.Connor		
P.J.Bakker		
Extras	(b 1,lb 14,w 7)	22
TOTAL	(37 overs)(for 6 wkts)	234

GLAMORGAN

A.R.Butcher *	c Nicholas b Ayling	52
H.Morris	c Smith b Bakker	7
M.P.Maynard	c Nicholas b Maru	34
I.V.A.Richards	c Terry b Maru	8
I.Smith	c Terry b Maru	2
N.G.Cowley	b Bakker	7
C.P.Metson +	not out	30
J.Derrick	c sub b Bakker	19
S.J.Dennis	not out	1
S.L.Watkin		
M.Frost		
Extras	(lb 8,w 2)	10
TOTAL	(37 overs)(for 7 wkts)	170

GLAMORGAN	O	M	R	W		FALL OF WICKETS	
						HAM	GLA
Frost	8	0	49	2	1st	6	12
Watkin	8	0	46	2	2nd	165	82
Dennis	8	0	43	0	3rd	181	98
Cowley	8	1	43	1	4th	184	104
Richards	5	0	38	1	5th	215	113
					6th	228	116
HAMPSHIRE	O	M	R	W	7th		166
Connor	6	0	26	0	8th		
Bakker	8	1	33	3	9th		
Marshall	5	0	23	0	10th		
Ayling	8	0	39	1			
Maru	8	0	38	3			
Nicholas	2	0	3	0			

DERBYSHIRE vs. WARWICKSHIRE

at Derby on 17th June 1990
Toss : Warwicks. Umps: J.H.Hampshire and A.G.T.Whitehead
Derbyshire won by 1 run (Derbyshire 4 pts Warwicks 0 pts)

DERBYSHIRE

K.J.Barnett *	c Asif Din b Pierson	19
P.D.Bowler +	c Pierson b Twose	0
J.E.Morris	c Ostler b Twose	4
A.P.Kuiper	c Ostler b Pierson	37
B.Roberts	lbw b Small	9
C.J.Adams	not out	58
S.C.Goldsmith	b Smith	50
A.E.Warner	c Munton b Smith	6
D.E.Malcolm	c Moles b Moody	0
S.J.Base	not out	0
G.Miller		
Extras	(lb 15,w 1,nb 4)	20
TOTAL	(40 overs)(for 8 wkts)	203

WARWICKSHIRE

A.J.Moles	b Malcolm	81
Asif Din	c Bowler b Base	11
T.M.Moody	run out	45
G.W.Humpage +	c Bowler b Kuiper	0
D.A.Reeve *	b Base	31
D.P.Ostler	not out	7
R.G.Twose	c Bowler b Kuiper	9
G.C.Small	not out	4
G.Smith		
A.R.K.Pierson		
T.A.Munton		
Extras	(b 2,lb 9,w 3)	14
TOTAL	(40 overs)(for 6 wkts)	202

WARWICKS	O	M	R	W		FALL OF WICKETS	
						DER	WAR
Munton	8	0	25	0	1st	2	27
Twose	8	2	11	2	2nd	10	129
Pierson	8	0	24	2	3rd	36	130
Small	8	1	53	1	4th	58	181
Smith	4	0	37	2	5th	77	181
Moody	4	0	38	1	6th	184	198
DERBYSHIRE	O	M	R	W	7th	191	
Base	8	1	32	2	8th	191	
Malcolm	8	0	33	1	9th		
Miller	8	0	38	0	10th		
Warner	8	0	35	0			
Kuiper	8	0	53	2			

LEICESTERSHIRE vs. MIDDLESEX

at Leicester on 17th June 1990
Toss : Leicestershire. Umpires : B.Hassan and K.E.Palmer
Middlesex won by 16 runs (Leics 0 pts Middlesex 4 pts)

MIDDLESEX

D.L.Haynes	c & b Lewis	49
M.A.Roseberry	lbw b Agnew	18
M.W.Gatting *	not out	124
M.R.Ramprakash	c & b Willey	22
K.R.Brown	c Nixon b Willey	8
R.O.Butcher	lbw b Agnew	22
J.E.Emburey	not out	5
P.Farbrace +		
N.F.Williams		
S.P.Hughes		
A.R.C.Fraser		
Extras	(b 1,lb 6,w 3,nb 1)	11
TOTAL	(40 overs)(for 5 wkts)	259

LEICESTERSHIRE

T.J.Boon	st Farbrace b Emburey	84
N.E.Briers *	c Farbrace b Hughes	46
J.J.Whitaker	c Gatting b Haynes	4
C.C.Lewis	c Roseberry b Fraser	14
P.Willey	c Butcher b Williams	39
L.Potter	c & b Williams	8
J.D.R.Benson	not out	36
W.K.M.Benjamin	not out	2
P.A.Nixon +		
J.P.Agnew		
A.D.Mullally		
Extras	(lb 3,w 3,nb 4)	10
TOTAL	(40 overs)(for 6 wkts)	243

LEICS	O	M	R	W		FALL OF WICKETS	
						MID	LEI
Benjamin	8	0	59	0	1st	34	119
Agnew	8	3	35	2	2nd	88	128
Lewis	8	0	64	1	3rd	125	148
Mullally	8	0	36	0	4th	164	168
Willey	8	0	58	2	5th	226	191
MIDDLESEX	O	M	R	W	6th		227
Fraser	8	0	34	1	7th		
Williams	8	1	55	2	8th		
Haynes	5	0	29	1	9th		
Gatting	3	0	18	0	10th		
Hughes	8	0	52	1			
Emburey	8	0	52	1			

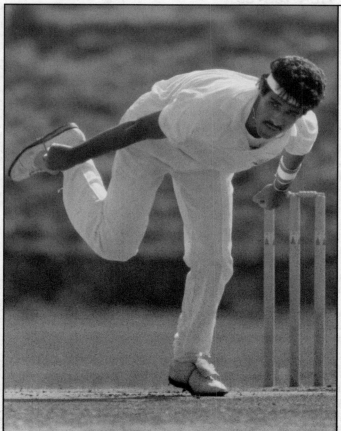

Waqar Younis, whose genuine pace surprised a number of batsmen throughout the season.

TOUR MATCH | BRITANNIC ASS. CHAMPIONSHIP

NORTHANTS vs. NEW ZEALAND

at Northampton on 16th, 17th, 18th June 1990
Toss : Northants.   Umpires : B.Dudleston and D.S.Thompsett
Match drawn

NORTHANTS

A.Fordham	lbw b Bracewell	20	run out		23
N.A.Felton	c Rutherford b Morrison	3	c sub b Bracewell		22
R.J.Bailey	c & b Millmow	0	lbw b Morrison		22
A.J.Lamb *	lbw b Morrison	21	c Parore b Thomson		42
D.J.Capel	c & b Priest	123	not out		65
R.G.Williams	c Wright b Priest	73	not out		11
W.M.Noon +	lbw b Morrison	2			
N.G.B.Cook	b Priest	10			
W.W.Davis	not out	5			
C.E.L.Ambrose	lbw b Bracewell	0			
M.A.Robinson					
Extras	(b 13,lb 4,w 1,nb 4)	22	(b 2,lb 6,w 1,nb 2)		11
TOTAL	(for 9 wkts dec)	279	(for 4 wkts)		196

NEW ZEALAND

T.J.Franklin	c Noon b Ambrose	92
J.G.Wright *	b Davis	31
A.H.Jones	lbw b Ambrose	46
M.J.Greatbatch	c Capel b Ambrose	0
K.R.Rutherford	not out	42
M.W.Priest	run out	32
S.A.Thomson	not out	4
A.C.Parore +		
J.G.Bracewell		
D.K.Morrison		
J.P.Millmow		
Extras	(b 1,lb 5,w 2,nb 10)	18
TOTAL	(for 5 wkts dec)	265

NEW ZEALAND	O	M	R	W	O	M	R	W
Morrison	21	4	68	3	11	2	49	1
Millmow	3.4	0	16	1				
Bracewell	30	9	78	2	23	13	27	1
Thomson	13	0	65	0	21	3	97	1
Priest	27	10	35	3	7.5	1	14	0
Rutherford					1	0	1	0

NORTHANTS	O	M	R	W	O	M	R	W
Davis	21	2	65	1				
Ambrose	20	3	60	3				
Robinson	17	1	53	0				
Williams	15	3	39	0				
Cook	16	5	42	0				

FALL OF WICKETS

	NOR	NZ	NOR	NZ
1st	22	67	45	
2nd	23	176	50	
3rd	33	182	92	
4th	73	186	139	
5th	240	249		
6th	253			
7th	267			
8th	274			
9th	279			
10th				

HEADLINES

16th - 19th June

● Northamptonshire's David Capel hit 123 and 65 not out to press for a recall to the Test team before rain ended any hopes of another New Zealand run chase

● Warwickshire returned to the top of the Championship table with a two wicket win at Derby, as rain around the country once more forced captains to reach agreement to gain results.

● After Derbyshire had forfeited their second innings, Warwickshire were left a target of 350 in 83 overs which they achieved largely thanks to Tom Moody's 168 on his Championship debut. (He had now scored 100s in each of his first three first-class matches for the county.)

● Glamorgan had all of the third day to make 364 to beat Hampshire but achieved victory only when Viv Richards took 14 off the first four balls of the final available over bowled by Malcolm Marshall. Richards's unbeaten 164, his fourth 100 in seven matches, contained five sixes and 16 fours. Robin Smith had earlier made 153 in Hampshire's first innings

● Ian Botham made his first first-class 100 for three years when he hit 113 for Worcestershire against Surrey at The Oval, while Desmond Haynes became the second man to reach 1,000 first-class runs in 1990 as Middlesex beat Leicestershire by 103 runs

● John Stephenson made his first ever double century as Essex piled up 431 for three declared on the first day of their match against Somerset at Bath, before a thunderstom brought proceedings to an early close on the last day

---

DERBYSHIRE vs. WARWICKSHIRE

at Derby on 16th, 18th, 19th June 1990
Toss : Warwickshire. Umpires : J.H.Hampshire and A.G.T.Whitehead
Warwickshire won by 2 wickets (Derbys 4 pts (Bt: 4, Bw: 0) Warwicks 16 pts (Bt: 0, Bw: 0))

DERBYSHIRE

K.J.Barnett *	c Small b Munton	131
P.D.Bowler	c Reeve b Moody	120
J.E.Morris	not out	103
B.Roberts	c Reeve b Twose	86
A.P.Kuiper	c Reeve b Munton	11
C.J.Adams	not out	6
K.M.Krikken +		
G.Miller		
A.E.Warner		
D.E.Malcolm		
S.J.Base		
Extras	(b 5,lb 8,w 2,nb 3)	18
TOTAL	(for 4 wkts dec)	475

WARWICKSHIRE

A.J.Moles	not out	70	c Krikken b Malcolm		4
J.D.Ratcliffe	c & b Bowler	38	c Roberts b Base		25
Asif Din	not out	17	c Miller b Base		30
T.M.Moody			c Base b Malcolm		168
G.W.Humpage +			b Barnett		34
D.A.Reeve *			c Krikken b Malcolm		25
R.G.Twose			lbw b Malcolm		1
D.P.Ostler			not out		42
G.C.Small			run out		8
T.A.Munton			not out		0
A.R.K.Pierson					
Extras	(lb 1)	1	(lb 8,w 3,nb 5)		16
TOTAL	(for 1 wkt dec)	126	(for 8 wkts)		353

WARWICKS	O	M	R	W	O	M	R	W
Small	14	3	44	0				
Munton	29.2	4	105	2				
Pierson	37	9	84	0				
Twose	17	1	82	1				
Moody	7	0	43	1				
Asif Din	19	1	85	0				
Moles	7	2	19	0				

DERBYSHIRE	O	M	R	W	O	M	R	W
Miller	7	4	11	0	12	0	71	0
Warner	3	1	9	0	17	4	66	0
Barnett	4	2	5	0	10	1	39	1
Morris	6	0	52	0				
Bowler	6	0	48	1				
Malcolm					19	1	63	4
Base					18	2	88	2
Kuiper					6	1	18	0

FALL OF WICKETS

	DER	WAR	DER	WAR
1st	249	74		9
2nd	281			54
3rd	437			80
4th	452			152
5th				261
6th				271
7th				334
8th				349
9th				
10th				

SURREY vs. WORCESTERSHIRE

at The Oval on 16th, 18th, 19th June 1990
Toss : Surrey. Umpires : H.D.Bird and J.H.Harris
Match drawn (Surrey 4 pts (Bt: 0, Bw: 4) Worcestershire 4 pts (Bt: 4, Bt: 0))

WORCESTERSHIRE

T.S.Curtis	c Ward b Bicknell	0	not out		31
M.J.Weston	c Gray b Bicknell	6	not out		38
G.A.Hick	c Ward b Bicknell	59			
D.B.D'Oliveira	c Lynch b Bicknell	0			
I.T.Botham	c Stewart b Medlycott	113			
P.A.Neale *	b Gray	36			
P.J.Newport	c Ward b Medlycott	41			
S.J.Rhodes +	c Lynch b Medlycott	4			
S.R.Lampitt	not out	21			
S.M.McEwan	c Bicknell b Medlycott	2			
R.D.Stemp	not out	0			
Extras	(b 5,lb 11,w 1,nb 1)	18	(b 4,lb 9,w 2)		15
TOTAL	(for 9 wkts dec)	300	(for 0 wkts dec)		84

SURREY

R.I.Alikhan	run out	23	c Rhodes b Lampitt		21
G.S.Clinton	not out	33	c Lampitt b Newport		80
A.J.Stewart	not out	7	c Rhodes b McEwan		55
G.P.Thorpe			c D'Oliveira b McEwan		0
D.M.Ward +			c Curtis b Hick		21
M.A.Lynch			c Botham b Hick		21
I.A.Greig *			c Lampitt b Hick		6
K.T.Medlycott			not out		16
M.P.Bicknell			not out		15
A.H.Gray					
A.J.Murphy					
Extras	(lb 2,nb 2)	4	(lb 7,w 1,nb 1)		9
TOTAL	(for 1 wkt dec)	67	(for 7 wkts)		244

SURREY	O	M	R	W	O	M	R	W
Gray	26	8	41	1	6	3	8	0
Bicknell	22	4	70	4	5	0	15	0
Murphy	19	4	64	0	5	1	12	0
Medlycott	29	8	92	4	5	1	19	0
Greig	4	0	17	0				
Alikhan					1	0	17	0

WORCS	O	M	R	W	O	M	R	W
Newport	9	7	6	0	13	1	35	1
McEwan	6	2	26	0	17	4	40	2
Stemp	9	3	13	0	17	5	78	0
Lampitt	6.2	1	20	0	13	4	40	1
Botham					10.4	2	24	0
Hick					6	1	20	3

FALL OF WICKETS

	WOR	SUR	WOR	SUR
1st	11	46		42
2nd	16			155
3rd	22			155
4th	94			163
5th	187			199
6th	257			212
7th	263			219
8th	282			
9th	284			
10th				

BRITANNIC ASSURANCE CHAMPIONSHIP

SOMERSET vs. ESSEX

at Bath on 16th, 18th, 19th June 1990
Toss : Essex.   Umpires : R.Julian and K.J.Lyons
Match drawn (Somerset 3 pts (Bt: 2, Bw: 1) Essex 4 pts (Bt: 4, Bw: 0))

ESSEX

G.A.Gooch *	c Hardy b Swallow	72			
J.P.Stephenson	not out	202	not out		63
P.J.Prichard	c Burns b Mallender	115	c Hayhurst b Harden		4
M.E.Waugh	c Burns b Mallender	0	not out		73
B.R.Hardie	not out	22			
M.A.Garnham +			(1) c Hayhurst b Harden		10
D.R.Pringle					
N.A.Foster					
T.D.Topley					
J.H.Childs					
P.M.Such					
Extras	(b 1,lb 14,nb 5)	20	(lb 1,nb 1)		2
TOTAL	(for 3 wkts dec)	431	(for 2 wkts dec)		152

SOMERSET

S.J.Cook	c Childs b Foster	32	not out		19
J.J.E.Hardy	lbw b Topley	42	not out		13
A.N.Hayhurst	not out	65			
C.J.Tavare *	not out	78			
P.M.Roebuck					
R.J.Harden					
N.D.Burns +					
G.D.Rose					
I.G.Swallow					
N.A.Mallender					
A.N.Jones					
Extras	(b 1,lb 10,nb 3)	14			0
TOTAL	(for 2 wkts dec)	231	(for 0 wkts)		32

SOMERSET	O	M	R	W	O	M	R	W
Jones	17	2	59	0				
Mallender	20	2	74	2				
Rose	18	1	78	0				
Swallow	35	8	140	1				
Hayhurst	12	1	39	0	2	0	11	0
Roebuck	8	2	26	0				
Harden					9	1	54	2
Tavare					7.5	0	86	0

ESSEX	O	M	R	W	O	M	R	W
Pringle	15	6	28	0	6	3	7	0
Foster	14	2	56	1	6.5	2	25	0
Topley	14	1	48	1				
Childs	16	8	21	0				
Such	12	2	29	0				
Waugh	6	0	38	0				

FALL OF WICKETS	ESS	SOM	ESS	SOM
1st	106	52	13	
2nd	331	100	17	
3rd	331			
4th				
5th				
6th				
7th				
8th				
9th				
10th				

SUSSEX vs. GLOUCESTERSHIRE

at Hove on 16th, 18th, 19th June 1990
Toss : Sussex.   Umpires : J.D.Bond and R.Palmer
Match drawn (Sussex 4 pts (Bt: 0, Bw: 4) Gloucestershire 5 pts (Bt: 4, Bw: 1))

GLOUCESTERSHIRE

A.J.Wright *	c Moores b Dodemaide	17	not out		45
G.D.Hodgson	c Salisbury b Dodemaide	0	b Remy		33
I.P.Butcher	c Speight b Wells C.M.	42	not out		3
C.W.J.Athey	st Moores b Salisbury	131			
P.Bainbridge	c Salisbury b Wells C.M.	3			
K.M.Curran	c & b Bunting	15			
J.W.Lloyds	b Bunting	43			
R.C.Russell +	c Moores b Dodemaide	98			
C.A.Walsh	c & b Salisbury	9			
D.A.Graveney	c Dodemaide b Salisbury	0			
D.V.Lawrence	not out	0			
Extras	(b 4,lb 9,w 1,nb 2)	16	(lb 6)		6
TOTAL		374	(for 1 wkt dec)		87

SUSSEX

N.J.Lenham	c Russell b Lawrence	37	c Wright b Curran		84
J.W.Hall	b Walsh	19	c Russell b Walsh		17
P.W.G.Parker *	not out	48	c Wright b Lloyds		53
A.P.Wells	b Walsh	8	c Lloyds b Curran		22
M.P.Speight	not out	0	run out		59
C.M.Wells			c Walsh b Curran		55
P.Moores +			run out		6
A.I.C.Dodemaide			c Lawrence b Walsh		11
C.C.Remy			not out		4
I.D.K.Salisbury			not out		3
R.A.Bunting					
Extras	(lb 2,nb 6)	8	(lb 8,nb 3)		11
TOTAL	(for 3 wkts dec)	120	(for 8 wkts)		325

SUSSEX	O	M	R	W	O	M	R	W
Dodemaide	22	3	95	3	3	0	6	0
Bunting	23	6	91	2	4	0	21	0
Wells C.M.	20	3	59	2				
Remy	12	0	54	0	5	0	37	1
Salisbury	20	6	62	3				
Wells A.P.					4	0	17	0

GLOUCS	O	M	R	W	O	M	R	W
Lawrence	9	3	30	1	10	0	56	0
Walsh	13	3	40	2	21	1	79	2
Graveney	4.4	2	9	0	16	3	48	0
Curran	11	1	33	0	19	3	64	3
Bainbridge	3	0	6	0				
Lloyds					18	2	70	1

FALL OF WICKETS	GLO	SUS	GLO	SUS
1st	3	57	73	35
2nd	49	69		132
3rd	69	117		183
4th	73			190
5th	117			295
6th	177			306
7th	346			314
8th	368			321
9th	368			
10th	374			

HAMPSHIRE vs. GLAMORGAN

at Southampton on 16th, 18th, 19th June 1990
Toss : Hampshire.   Umpires : J.W.Holder and B.J.Meyer
Glamorgan won by 4 wickets (Hants 4 pts (Bt: 4, Bw: 0) Glamorgan 19 pts (Bt: 0, Bw: 3))

HAMPSHIRE

V.P.Terry	c Metson b Richards	52	not out		25
C.L.Smith	c Metson b Watkin	48	not out		39
D.I.Gower	c Metson b Watkin	41			
R.A.Smith	c Metson b Frost	153			
M.D.Marshall	c Metson b Dennis	4			
M.C.J.Nicholas *	c Cowley b Watkin	30			
R.J.Parks +	c Metson b Watkin	0			
R.J.Maru	c Maynard b Cowley	9			
T.M.Tremlett	not out	14			
C.A.Connor					
P.J.Bakker					
Extras	(lb 10,w 1,nb 1)	12	(lb 5,w 1,nb 1)		7
TOTAL	(for 8 wkts dec)	363	(for 0 wkts dec)		71

GLAMORGAN

A.R.Butcher *	c Terry b Bakker	7	c Connor b Maru		51
H.Morris	not out	38	c Maru b Connor		44
M.P.Maynard	not out	20	(4) c Gower b Connor		1
G.C.Holmes			(3) c Terry b Marshall		14
I.V.A.Richards			not out		164
I.Smith			c Parks b Marshall		0
N.G.Cowley			c & b Maru		58
C.P.Metson +			not out		14
S.J.Dennis					
S.L.Watkin					
M.Frost					
Extras	(b 1,lb 1,w 1,nb 3)	6	(b 5,lb 11,nb 5)		21
TOTAL	(for 1 wkt dec)	71	(for 6 wkts)		367

GLAMORGAN	O	M	R	W	O	M	R	W
Frost	24	4	107	1				
Watkin	30	9	84	4				
Dennis	20	5	83	1				
Cowley	17.5	6	47	1				
Richards	8	3	32	1				
Smith					8	2	27	0
Maynard					6	1	22	0
Butcher					1.5	0	17	0

HAMPSHIRE	O	M	R	W	O	M	R	W
Marshall	3	1	9	0	22.4	7	63	2
Bakker	4	0	14	1	23	6	54	0
Tremlett	5	2	19	0	24	7	80	0
Nicholas	4.1	0	27	0				
Connor					18	1	86	2
Maru					14	2	68	2

FALL OF WICKETS	HAM	GLA	HAM	GLA
1st	73	31		90
2nd	127			104
3rd	177			106
4th	182			135
5th	336			139
6th	340			305
7th	341			
8th	363			
9th				
10th				

LEICESTERSHIRE vs. MIDDLESEX

at Leicester on 16th, 18th, 19th June 1990
Toss : Middlesex.   Umpires : B.Hassan and K.E.Palmer
Middlesex won by 103 runs (Leics 4 pts (Bt: 0, Bw: 4) Middlesex 19 pts (Bt: 3, Bw: 0))

MIDDLESEX

D.L.Haynes	b Benjamin	85	not out		68
M.A.Roseberry	c Lewis b Benjamin	15	b Lewis		0
M.W.Gatting *	lbw b Lewis	4	not out		41
M.R.Ramprakash	not out	87			
K.R.Brown	lbw b Benjamin	0			
J.E.Emburey	c Nixon b Mullally	16			
P.Farbrace +	c Potter b Agnew	5			
N.F.Williams	c & b Lewis	1			
P.C.R.Tufnell	b Lewis	37			
S.P.Hughes	c Benson b Benjamin	4			
A.R.C.Fraser	c Potter b Benjamin	12			
Extras	(b 4,lb 10,nb 15)	29	(lb 1,nb 6)		7
TOTAL		295	(for 1 wkt dec)		116

LEICESTERSHIRE

T.J.Boon	c Farbrace b Hughes	10	c Brown b Fraser		51
N.E.Briers *	c Farbrace b Fraser	23	c Farbrace b Tufnell		34
J.J.Whitaker	not out	42	lbw b Fraser		0
P.Willey	not out	5	lbw b Williams		11
L.Potter			c Brown b Emburey		7
J.D.R.Benson			b Williams		45
C.C.Lewis			b Tufnell		21
W.K.M.Benjamin			c Roseberry b Emburey		1
P.A.Nixon +			c Gatting b Emburey		22
J.P.Agnew			c Roseberry b Emburey		0
A.D.Mullally			not out		0
Extras	(lb 1,nb 10)	11	(lb 4,nb 21)		25
TOTAL	(for 2 wkts dec)	91			217

LEICS	O	M	R	W	O	M	R	W
Benjamin	24.1	10	73	5				
Agnew	15	2	60	1	11	1	62	0
Mullally	19	6	34	1				
Lewis	21	3	98	3	6	0	11	1
Willey	8	0	14	0				
Potter	1	0	2	0	5.2	0	42	0

MIDDLESEX	O	M	R	W	O	M	R	W
Williams	12	1	34	0	12.4	2	49	2
Fraser	13	1	34	1	20	2	45	2
Emburey	2	1	2	0	26	7	57	4
Hughes	3	1	5	1	7	1	23	0
Tufnell	6	2	15	0	16	5	39	2

FALL OF WICKETS	MID	LEI	MID	LEI
1st	38	25	2	82
2nd	60	65		82
3rd	129			113
4th	129			113
5th	148			126
6th	173			159
7th	174			162
8th	253			210
9th	264			212
10th	295			217

OTHER FIRST-CLASS MATCHES | BRITANNIC ASS. CHAMPIONSHIP

CAMBRIDGE UNIV vs. NOTTINGHAMSHIRE

at Fenner's on 16th, 18th, 19th June 1990
Toss: Nottinghamshire. Umpires: B.Leadbeater and R.A.White
Match drawn

NOTTINGHAMSHIRE

P.Pollard	lbw b Jenkins	13			
D.J.R.Martindale	st Turner b Lowrey	138			
M.Newell	c Atkinson b Jenkins	60			
P.Johnson *	lbw b Pyman	4	(1) run out	49	
M.Saxelby	not out	30	(2) c Atkinson b Lowrey	73	
R.J.Evans	not out	21	(4) not out	0	
C.W.Scott +			(3) not out	67	
K.P.Evans					
R.A.Pick					
J.A.Afford					
M.G.Field-Buss					
Extras	(b 2,lb 2,nb 6)	10	(b 4,lb 3,nb 2)	9	
TOTAL	(for 4 wkts dec)	276	(for 2 wkts dec)	198	

CAMBRIDGE UNIV

S.P.James	b Pick	1	not out	104	
R.Heap	c Evans K.P. b Field-Buss	4	lbw b Evans K.P.	31	
R.H.J.Jenkins	lbw b Evans K.P.	12			
R.J.Turner +	c Evans K.P. b Afford	32	(3) c Scott b Evans K.P.	0	
J.C.M.Atkinson *	c Evans K.P. b Afford	0	(4) c Pick b Afford	5	
M.J.Lowrey	c Pick b Evans K.P.	19	(5) b Newell	25	
M.J.Morris	b Evans K.P.	4	(6) not out	0	
G.Hutchinson	b Evans K.P.	29			
R.A.Pyman	b Field-Buss	11			
D.H.Shufflebotham	not out	4			
A.J.Buzza	b Field-Buss	0			
Extras	(b 4,lb 13,nb 2)	19	(b 3,lb 4,w 1,nb 1)	9	
TOTAL		135	(for 4 wkts)	174	

CAMB UNIV	O	M	R	W	O	M	R	W
Jenkins	21	1	51	2	11	0	49	0
Pyman	21	3	72	1	9	0	50	0
Shufflebotham	11	2	38	0	5	0	37	0
Lowrey	20	6	55	1	3	0	5	1
Buzza	18	5	54	0	10	1	50	0
Atkinson	2	0	2	0				

FALL OF WICKETS				
	NOT	CAM	NOT	CAM
1st	29	5	79	63
2nd	212	9	172	67
3rd	220	43		80
4th	226	44		173
5th		57		
6th		75		
7th		88		
8th		112		
9th		130		
10th		135		

NOTTS	O	M	R	W	O	M	R	W
Pick	13	6	31	1	5	1	12	0
Evans K.P.	23	8	50	4	15	6	27	2
Afford	14	8	13	2	17	6	44	1
Field-Buss	15.4	9	14	3	21	4	37	0
Saxelby M.	5	1	10	0				
Newell					5	2	22	1
Evans R.J.					6	1	24	0
Johnson					1	0	1	0

OXFORD UNIV vs. LANCASHIRE

at The Parks on 16th, 18th, 19th June 1990
Toss: Oxford Univ. Umpires: G.I.Burgess and N.T.Plews
Match drawn

OXFORD UNIV

D.A.Hagan	c Atherton b Gallian	1	c Stanworth b Folley	5	
R.E.Morris *	lbw b DeFreitas	61			
M.J.Kilborn	c DeFreitas b Atherton	95			
G.J.Turner	run out	48			
M.A.Crawley	not out	91			
P.D.Lunn	c Stanworth b Folley	3	(3) not out	9	
W.M.van der Merwe	not out	56			
S.D.Weale			(4) lbw b Atherton	0	
P.S.Gerrans			(2) c DeFreitas b Folley	39	
I.M.Henderson			(5) not out	1	
J.McGrady +					
Extras	(b 1,lb 5,w 1,nb 4)	11	(b 1,lb 9)	10	
TOTAL	(for 5 wkts dec)	366	(for 3 wkts)	64	

LANCASHIRE

N.J.Speak	c Hagan b Turner	61	
M.A.Atherton	c Henderson b Weale	117	
N.H.Fairbrother *	c Kilborn b Turner	105	
P.A.J.DeFreitas	st McGrady b Turner	102	
S.P.Titchard	b Crawley	22	
J.P.Crawley	b Lunn	26	
G.D.Lloyd	not out	78	
J.Gallian	not out	17	
G.Yates			
I.Folley			
J.Stanworth +			
Extras	(b 12,lb 3,w 2,nb 13)	30	
TOTAL	(for 6 wkts dec)	558	

LANCASHIRE	O	M	R	W	O	M	R	W
DeFreitas	17	3	39	1	4	1	7	0
Gallian	18	8	50	1	3	0	15	0
Folley	24	1	120	1	10	3	18	2
Yates	27	7	52	0	4	2	4	0
Atherton	31	5	99	1	8	5	10	1

FALL OF WICKETS				
	OXF	LAN	OXF	LAN
1st	3	115	28	
2nd	118	248	58	
3rd	189	383	58	
4th	257	416		
5th	280	446		
6th		474		
7th				
8th				
9th				
10th				

OXFORD UNIV	O	M	R	W	O	M	R	W
Henderson	25	2	146	0				
Gerrans	20	1	80	0				
Crawley	17	2	64	1				
Turner	27	7	100	3				
Weale	25	4	119	1				
Lunn	8	1	34	1				

LANCASHIRE vs. MIDDLESEX

at Old Trafford on 20th, 21st, 22nd June 1990
Toss: Middlesex. Umpires: H.D.Bird and P.J.Eele
Middlesex won by 5 wickets. (Lancashire 2 pts (Bt: 2, Bw: 0) Middlesex 18 pts (Bt: 0, Bw: 2))

LANCASHIRE

G.Fowler	b Williams	24
G.D.Mendis	b Emburey	114
G.D.Lloyd	c Emburey b Fraser	21
T.E.Jesty	c Emburey b Tufnell	5
M.Watkinson	c Roseberry b Tufnell	37
W.K.Hegg +	c Haynes b Tufnell	14
I.D.Austin	not out	45
J.D.Fitton	not out	13
D.P.Hughes *		
P.J.W.Allott		
B.P.Patterson		
Extras	(b 3,lb 5,nb 20)	28
TOTAL	(for 6 wkts dec)	301

MIDDLESEX

D.L.Haynes	c Mendis b Watkinson	49
M.A.Roseberry	hit wicket b Patterson	79
M.W.Gatting *	c Hegg b Watkinson	95
M.R.Ramprakash	c Hegg b Watkinson	8
K.R.Brown	not out	21
J.E.Emburey	c Hegg b Watkinson	6
P.Farbrace +	not out	17
N.F.Williams		
S.P.Hughes		
P.C.R.Tufnell		
A.R.C.Fraser		
Extras	(b 8,lb 11,nb 9)	28
TOTAL	(for 5 wkts)	303

MIDDLESEX	O	M	R	W	O	M	R	W
Williams	15	4	53	1				
Fraser	24	5	52	1				
Hughes	13	4	32	0				
Tufnell	44	12	90	3				
Emburey	18	4	35	1				
Ramprakash	2	0	17	0				
Roseberry	1	0	14	0				

FALL OF WICKETS				
	LAN	MID	LAN	MID
1st	41	100		
2nd	77	216		
3rd	104	255		
4th	182	258		
5th	219	282		
6th	262			
7th				
8th				
9th				
10th				

LANCASHIRE	O	M	R	W	O	M	R	W
Patterson					13	0	74	1
Allott					7	0	32	0
Austin					13.1	1	58	0
Watkinson					13	0	61	4
Fitton					8	0	35	0
Hughes					5	0	24	0

HEADLINES

16th - 19th June

● Steve James's 104 not out steered Cambridge University to safety at Fenner's after Nottinghamshire had bowled them out for 135 in their first innings

● Lancashire's three England players, Mike Atherton, Neil Fairbrother and Phil DeFreitas, all made 100s against Oxford University at The Parks as the visitors reached 558 for six before declaring. DeFreitas reached his 100 in 69 balls to post the fastest century of the season so far

● First-class debuts: G.Hutchinson (Cambridge U); J.Gallian(Lancashire)

20th - 22nd June

● Middlesex moved up to second place in the Championship table with a five-wicket win over Lancashire at Lord's after both captains had forfeited an innings. Mike Gatting made his highest first-class score of the season so far as Middlesex reached their target in the 62nd over

● Leaders Warwickshire narrowly lost out to Yorkshire at Sheffield who moved off the bottom of the table with their first win. Dominic Ostler made his maiden first-class fifty in Warwickshire's first innings, and Keith Piper just missed out on his; while for Yorkshire Peter Hartley returned career best bowling figures against his former county and Simon Kellett improved his highest score with 75*

BRITANNIC ASSURANCE CHAMPIONSHIP

SOMERSET vs. GLAMORGAN

at Bath on 20th, 21st, 22nd June 1990
Toss : Somerset. Umpires : R.Julian and N.T.Plews
Match drawn. (Somerset 4 pts (Bt: 4, Bw: 0) Glamorgan 1 pt (Bt: 0, Bw: 1))

SOMERSET

S.J.Cook	c Metson b Watkin	61
J.J.E.Hardy	lbw b Bastien	10
A.N.Hayhurst	c Butcher b Watkin	48
N.D.Burns +	not out	71
G.D.Rose	not out	97
C.J.Tavare *		
R.J.Harden		
I.G.Swallow		
N.A.Mallender		
H.R.J.Trump		
A.N.Jones		
Extras	(lb 7,w 2,nb 5)	14
TOTAL	(for 3 wkts dec)	301

GLAMORGAN

A.R.Butcher *	not out	83
H.Morris	c Harden b Jones	2
G.C.Holmes	lbw b Mallender	1
M.P.Maynard	c Harden b Swallow	33
I.V.A.Richards	b Swallow	21
R.D.B.Croft	not out	17
N.G.Cowley		
C.P.Metson +		
S.J.Dennis		
S.L.Watkin		
S.Bastien		
Extras	(lb 2,nb 6)	8
TOTAL	(for 4 wkts)	165

GLAMORGAN	O	M	R	W	O	M	R	W
Watkin	26	9	53	2				
Bastien	25	9	64	1				
Dennis	8	1	20	0				
Cowley	1	0	4	0				
Croft	4	1	12	0				
Holmes	4	0	27	0				
Morris	3	0	41	0				
Butcher	7	0	45	0				
Maynard	5	0	28	0				
SOMERSET	O	M	R	W	O	M	R	W
Jones					7	3	15	1
Mallender					9	1	27	1
Swallow					19	3	63	2
Rose					9	0	35	0
Trump					4	2	11	0
Harden					3	0	12	0

FALL OF WICKETS	SOM	GLA	SOM	GLA
1st	22			8
2nd	108			27
3rd	141			87
4th				113
5th				
6th				
7th				
8th				
9th				
10th				

GLOUCESTERSHIRE vs. HAMPSHIRE

at Gloucester on 20th, 21st (no play), 22nd (no play) June 1990
Toss : Hampshire. Umpires : A.A.Jones and D.S.Thompsett
Match drawn (Gloucestershire 0 pts (Bt: 0, Bt: 0) Hampshire 0 pts (Bt: 0, Bw: 0))

GLOUCESTERSHIRE

A.J.Wright *	c Connor b Marshall	9
G.D.Hodgson	not out	22
I.P.Butcher	b Connor	4
C.W.J.Athey	not out	14
K.M.Curran		
J.W.Lloyds		
M.W.Alleyne		
G.A.Tedstone +		
C.A.Walsh		
D.A.Graveney		
D.V.Lawrence		
Extras	(lb 2,w 1,nb 2)	5
TOTAL	(for 2 wkts)	54

HAMPSHIRE

V.P.Terry		
C.L.Smith		
T.C.Middleton		
D.I.Gower		
M.D.Marshall		
M.C.J.Nicholas *		
R.J.Parks +		
R.J.Maru		
T.M.Tremlett		
K.J.Shine		
C.A.Connor		
Extras		
TOTAL		

HAMPSHIRE	O	M	R	W	O	M	R	W
Marshall	6	0	20	1				
Connor	6	1	17	1				
Tremlett	4.1	0	9	0				
Shine	3	1	6	0				
Maru	1	1	0	0				
GLOUCS	O	M	R	W	O	M	R	W

FALL OF WICKETS	GLO	HAM	GLO	HAM
1st	19			
2nd	25			
3rd				
4th				
5th				
6th				
7th				
8th				
9th				
10th				

WORCESTERSHIRE vs. SUSSEX

at Worcester on 20th, 21st, 22nd June 1990
Toss : Sussex. Umpires : D.J.Constant and J.W.Holder
Match drawn. (Worcestershire 1 pt (Bt: 0, Bw: 1) Sussex 3 pts (Bt: 3, Bw: 0))

SUSSEX

N.J.Lenham	b Illingworth	66
J.W.Hall	lbw b Botham	72
P.W.G.Parker *	c Hick b Botham	14
A.P.Wells	not out	59
M.P.Speight	not out	60
C.M.Wells		
P.Moores +		
A.I.C.Dodemaide		
A.C.S.Pigott		
I.D.K.Salisbury		
R.A.Bunting		
Extras	(lb 8,w 2,nb 9)	19
TOTAL	(for 3 wkts dec)	290

WORCESTERSHIRE

T.S.Curtis	c Parker b Bunting	27
P.Bent	b Bunting	5
G.A.Hick	c Moores b Pigott	28
D.B.D'Oliveira	st Moores b Salisbury	79
I.T.Botham	c Wells A.P. b Salisbury	50
P.A.Neale *	c Pigott b Salisbury	8
P.J.Newport	st Moores b Salisbury	2
S.J.Rhodes +	not out	9
S.R.Lampitt	c & b Salisbury	3
R.K.Illingworth	not out	0
S.M.McEwan		
Extras	(lb 6,w 1,nb 1)	8
TOTAL	(for 8 wkts)	219

WORCS	O	M	R	W	O	M	R	W
Newport	22	3	64	0				
McEwan	6	2	12	0				
Lampitt	14	2	55	0				
Botham	15	4	32	2				
Illingworth	23	6	82	1				
Hick	6	0	37	0				
SUSSEX	O	M	R	W	O	M	R	W
Dodemaide					14.5	6	32	0
Pigott					15	2	68	1
Bunting					10	2	40	2
Wells C.M.					5	0	41	0
Salisbury					10	2	32	5

FALL OF WICKETS	SUS	WOR	SUS	WOR
1st	126			21
2nd	155			43
3rd	183			71
4th				193
5th				197
6th				207
7th				210
8th				217
9th				
10th				

NOTTINGHAMSHIRE vs. SURREY

at Trent Bridge on 20th, 21st, 22nd June 1990
Toss : Surrey. Umpires : J.C.Balderstone and J.H.Hampshire
Match drawn (Nottinghamshire 1 pt (Bt: 0, Bw: 1) Surrey 8 pts (Bt: 4, Bw: 4))

NOTTINGHAMSHIRE

B.C.Broad	c Thorpe b Robinson	30	b Medlycott	30
D.J.R.Martindale	lbw b Bicknell	0	b Medlycott	33
R.T.Robinson *	lbw b Waqar Younis	5	lbw b Medlycott	72
P.Johnson	b Murphy	10	b Medlycott	78
D.W.Randall	c Ward b Bicknell	24	c Ward b Bicknell	26
F.D.Stephenson	b Waqar Younis	9	c & b Medlycott	2
B.N.French +	b Waqar Younis	0	not out	14
M.G.Field-Buss	lbw b Bicknell	0	c Alikhan b Medlycott	0
K.E.Cooper	c Ward b Bicknell	7	lbw b Bicknell	1
K.Saxelby	c Thorpe b Bicknell	0	lbw b Medlycott	8
J.A.Afford	not out	0	lbw b Bicknell	0
Extras	(b 1,lb 13,w 1)	15	(b 26,lb 14,w 3)	43
TOTAL		100		307

SURREY

R.I.Alikhan	c Robinson b Stephenson	88
G.S.Clinton	lbw b Stephenson	1
G.P.Thorpe	c Randall b Afford	20
D.M.Ward +	not out	154
M.A.Lynch *	not out	18
I.A.Greig		
K.T.Medlycott		
J.D.Robinson		
M.P.Bicknell		
Waqar Younis		
A.J.Murphy		
Extras	(b 5,lb 11,nb 6)	22
TOTAL	(for 3 wkts dec)	303

SURREY	O	M	R	W	O	M	R	W
Waqar Younis	15	3	29	3	22	3	86	0
Bicknell	14.2	4	34	5	19.3	6	46	3
Murphy	4	1	9	1	9	2	34	0
Robinson	4	2	14	1				
Medlycott					33	4	92	7
Greig					1	0	9	0
NOTTS	O	M	R	W	O	M	R	W
Stephenson	27.5	7	66	2				
Cooper	25	8	52	0				
Saxelby	14	5	42	0				
Afford	22	3	84	1				
Field-Buss	10	2	43	0				

FALL OF WICKETS	NOT	SUR	NOT	SUR
1st	5	3	76	
2nd	22	40	77	
3rd	54	262	218	
4th	54		263	
5th	73		269	
6th	79		287	
7th	80		292	
8th	97		293	
9th	97		306	
10th	100		307	

BRITANNIC ASS. CHAMPIONSHIP | OTHER FIRST-CLASS MATCH

YORKSHIRE vs. WARWICKSHIRE

at Sheffield on 20th, 21st, 22nd June 1990
Toss : Yorkshire.   Umpires : B.Leadbeater and D.O.Oslear
Yorkshire won by 2 wickets. (Yorkshire 20 pts (Bt: 0, Bw: 4) Warwicks 4 pts (Bt: 2, Bw: 2))

WARWICKSHIRE

A.J.Moles	c Blakey b Hartley	21	not out	60
J.D.Ratcliffe	b Gough	9	run out	16
Asif Din	lbw b Hartley	0	lbw b Jarvis	0
G.W.Humpage	lbw b Gough	23	b Jarvis	12
D.A.Reeve *	lbw b Moxon	30	not out	42
R.G.Twose	c Blakey b Hartley	15		
D.P.Ostler	c Carrick b Gough	61		
K.J.Piper +	c Moxon b Hartley	49		
A.A.Donald	c Blakey b Hartley	4		
J.E.Benjamin	c Moxon b Hartley	1		
T.A.Munton	not out	1		
Extras	(lb 8,w 2,nb 7)	17	(lb 2,w 1,nb 1)	4
TOTAL		231	(for 3 wkts dec)	134

YORKSHIRE

M.D.Moxon *	c Ratcliffe b Donald	3	c Piper b Benjamin	46
A.A.Metcalfe	c & b Munton	53	c Moles b Benjamin	45
S.A.Kellett	c Benjamin b Asif Din	18	not out	75
R.J.Blakey +	b Munton	1	(5) c Piper b Benjamin	8
P.E.Robinson	c Piper b Benjamin	14	(6) c Humpage b Benjamin	28
K.Sharp	not out	22	(4) c Humpage b Munton	8
P.Carrick	not out	1	(8) run out	3
P.J.Hartley			(7) b Donald	13
C.S.Pickles			b Benjamin	1
P.W.Jarvis			not out	7
D.Gough				
Extras	(lb 8,nb 3)	11	(b 3,lb 5,nb 1)	9
TOTAL	(for 5 wkts dec)	123	(for 8 wkts)	243

YORKSHIRE	O	M	R	W	O	M	R	W
Jarvis	22	6	52	0	8	0	43	2
Hartley	21.3	3	57	6	6	1	21	0
Gough	18	5	36	3	8	0	34	0
Pickles	9	5	33	0	9.3	0	34	0
Moxon	8	2	16	1				
Carrick	13	5	29	0				

WARWICKS	O	M	R	W	O	M	R	W
Donald	12	3	30	1	13	0	65	1
Benjamin	16	4	37	1	20.4	2	83	5
Munton	18.3	6	34	2	15	1	63	1
Twose	4	0	9	0				
Asif Din	3	1	5	1				
Reeve					6	0	24	0

FALL OF WICKETS	WAR	YOR	WAR	YOR
1st	33	14	36	70
2nd	33	64	38	135
3rd	33	75	52	148
4th	88	88		161
5th	97	105		197
6th	118			219
7th	199			234
8th	212			235
9th	222			
10th	231			

LEICESTERSHIRE vs. DERBYSHIRE

at Leicester on 20th, 21st, 22nd June 1990
Toss : Leicestershire.   Umpires : B.Hassan and K.E.Palmer
Leicestershire won by 140 runs. (Leics 20 pts (Bt: 4, Bw: 0) Derbyshire 2 pts (Bt: 0, Bw: 2))

LEICESTERSHIRE

T.J.Boon	b Warner	8	not out	5
N.E.Briers *	c Krikken b Jean-Jacques	29	not out	14
J.J.Whitaker	b Warner	116		
P.Willey	c Miller b Goldsmith	4		
L.Potter	lbw b Miller	16		
J.D.R.Benson	c Adams b Miller	9		
W.K.M.Benjamin	not out	101		
P.A.Nixon +	not out	20		
J.P.Agnew				
A.D.Mullally				
L.B.Taylor				
Extras	(b 3,lb 5,nb 9)	17	(nb 1)	1
TOTAL	(for 6 wkts dec)	320	(for 0 wkts dec)	20

DERBYSHIRE

K.J.Barnett *	not out	31	c Potter b Benjamin	0
P.D.Bowler	not out	36	c Potter b Agnew	0
J.E.Morris			not out	63
B.Roberts			c Nixon b Agnew	1
A.P.Kuiper			c & b Agnew	3
C.J.Adams			c Nixon b Mullally	5
S.C.Goldsmith			lbw b Mullally	8
K.M.Krikken +			b Willey	30
G.Miller			c Nixon b Benjamin	1
M.Jean-Jacques			lbw b Benjamin	4
A.E.Warner			c Whitaker b Willey	2
Extras	(nb 3)	3	(b 2,lb 9,nb 2)	13
TOTAL	(for 0 wkts dec)	70		130

DERBYSHIRE	O	M	R	W	O	M	R	W
Warner	28.5	8	72	2				
Jean-Jacques	21	3	93	1				
Goldsmith	13	5	24	1				
Barnett	8	0	25	0				
Miller	32	10	98	2				
Bowler					2	0	8	0
Adams					1.3	0	12	0

LEICS	O	M	R	W	O	M	R	W
Benjamin	4	0	17	0	16	5	35	3
Agnew	4	0	25	0	9	2	33	3
Taylor	4	0	18	0	5	1	16	0
Mullally	4	2	10	0	12	3	28	2
Willey	2	2	0	0	8	4	7	2

FALL OF WICKETS	LEI	DER	LEI	DER
1st	22			0
2nd	67			0
3rd	73			2
4th	148			12
5th	163			29
6th	249			43
7th				110
8th				113
9th				117
10th				130

CAMBRIDGE UNIV vs. KENT

at Fenner's on 20th, 21st, 22nd June 1990
Toss : Cambridge Univ.   Umpires : G.I.Burgess and B.J.Meyer
Kent won by 92 runs

KENT

S.G.Hinks	lbw b Lowrey	42	
N.R.Taylor	c Pyman b Buzza	120	
G.R.Cowdrey	st Turner b Lowrey	34	
C.S.Cowdrey *	not out	102	
M.V.Fleming	not out	19	
S.A.Marsh +			
R.M.Ellison			
T.A.Merrick			
R.P.Davis			
N.J.Llong			
A.P.Igglesden			
Extras	(b 1,lb 5,w 5,nb 1)	12	
TOTAL	(for 3 wkts dec)	329	

CAMBRIDGE UNIV

S.P.James	c Marsh b Igglesden	3	b Merrick	57
R.Heap	not out	27	b Davis	17
R.J.Turner +	b Fleming	22	c & b Merrick	35
J.C.M.Atkinson *	not out	0	b Merrick	0
M.J.Lowrey			b Davis	4
M.J.Morris			b Davis	24
G.Hutchinson			c & b Davis	2
R.A.Pyman			c Cowdrey G.R. b Davis	0
D.H.Shufflebotham			c Marsh b Igglesden	16
R.H.J.Jenkins			c Llong b Davis	1
A.J.Buzza			not out	1
Extras	(lb 5)	5	(b 12,lb 8,w 1,nb 2)	23
TOTAL	(for 2 wkts dec)	57		180

CAMB UNIV	O	M	R	W	O	M	R	W
Jenkins	19	5	43	0				
Pyman	26	8	60	0				
Shufflebotham	8	0	42	0				
Buzza	26	7	106	1				
Lowrey	28	12	72	2				

KENT	O	M	R	W	O	M	R	W
Merrick	7	5	7	0	10	6	13	3
Igglesden	6	2	12	1	14	3	45	1
Fleming	5.3	1	13	1	9	5	14	0
Ellison	5	0	20	0	24	3	24	0
Davis					28.1	15	40	6
Llong					7	1	24	0

FALL OF WICKETS	KEN	CAM	KEN	CAM
1st	91	3		27
2nd	144	53		122
3rd	225			122
4th				125
5th				129
6th				137
7th				141
8th				172
9th				175
10th				180

HEADLINES

20th - 22nd June

● Leicestershire were the only other winners in a round of matches again badly disrupted by the weather. Derbyshire could manage only 130 after they had been left 271 to win despite 63* from John Morris. Leicester's Winston Benjamin had earlier made his first first-class 100

● Surrey could not quite press home their advantage over Notts at Trent Bridge, despite 154* from David Ward and 7 for 92 from Keith Medlycott, while a career best 5 for 32 from Sussex's Ian Salisbury stopped Worcestershire from pressing for victory at Worcester

● Even two forfeitures and a quickfire career best 97* from Somerset's Graham Rose could not provide a bright end to the Bath festival as Glamorgan's attempt to reach a target of 304 was quickly aborted, while only 75 minutes play was possible at all in Gloucestershire's match with Hampshire at Gloucester

● 100s from Neil Taylor and Chris Cowdrey and career best figures from Richard Davis helped Kent to a 92 run victory over Cambridge at Fenner's

● First-class debut: N.J.Llong (Kent)

REFUGE ASSURANCE LEAGUE

NORTHANTS vs. MIDDLESEX

at Luton on 24th June 1990
Toss : Middlesex. Umpires : N.T.Plews and R.A.White
Middlesex won by 9 wickets (Northants 0 pts Middx 4 pts)

NORTHANTS

A.Fordham	c Hughes b Williams	4
N.A.Felton	c Haynes b Gatting	10
R.J.Bailey	c Butcher b Emburey	60
D.J.Capel	st Farbrace b Emburey	46
D.J.Wild	run out	8
R.G.Williams	run out	1
D.Ripley +	st Farbrace b Emburey	3
J.G.Thomas	c Ramprakash b Fraser	2
W.W.Davis	c Ramprakash b Hughes	7
N.G.B.Cook *	b Emburey	1
M.A.Robinson	not out	0
Extras	(lb 1,w 3,nb 5)	9
TOTAL	(37.2 overs)	151

MIDDLESEX

M.W.Gatting *	not out	76
M.A.Roseberry	run out	50
M.R.Ramprakash	not out	8
D.L.Haynes		
K.R.Brown		
R.O.Butcher		
J.E.Emburey		
P.Farbrace +		
N.F.Williams		
S.P.Hughes		
A.R.C.Fraser		
Extras	(lb 7,w 8,nb 4)	19
TOTAL	(25.4 overs)(for 1 wkt)	153

MIDDLESEX	O	M	R	W	FALL OF WICKETS		
						NOR	MID
Fraser	7	2	16	1	1st	8	112
Williams	8	1	39	1	2nd	32	
Gatting	8	1	34	1	3rd	113	
Hughes	7	0	35	1	4th	127	
Emburey	7.2	0	26	4	5th	131	
					6th	137	
NORTHANTS	O	M	R	W	7th	140	
Davis	5	0	19	0	8th	143	
Capel	4	0	31	0	9th	151	
Thomas	2	0	20	0	10th	151	
Robinson	7	0	32	0			
Cook	3	0	13	0			
Wild	4.4	0	31	0			

SURREY vs. DERBYSHIRE

at The Oval on 24th June 1990
Toss : Derbyshire. Umpires : J.H.Harris and B.J.Meyer
Derbyshire won by 3 wickets (Surrey 0 pts Derbys 4 pts)

SURREY

G.S.Clinton	c Bowler b Kuiper	45
M.A.Feltham	lbw b Miller	42
G.P.Thorpe	c & b Kuiper	27
D.M.Ward +	b Jean-Jacques	25
M.A.Lynch	c Miller b Jean-Jacques	48
I.A.Greig *	not out	8
K.T.Medlycott	not out	4
C.K.Bullen		
A.Robson		
Waqar Younis		
A.J.Murphy		
Extras	(lb 5,w 6)	11
TOTAL	(40 overs)(for 5 wkts)	210

DERBYSHIRE

K.J.Barnett *	c Ward b Murphy	0
P.D.Bowler +	run out	50
J.E.Morris	b Waqar Younis	45
A.P.Kuiper	c Bullen b Medlycott	34
B.Roberts	b Waqar Younis	13
C.J.Adams	b Waqar Younis	19
S.C.Goldsmith	not out	14
G.Miller	c Ward b Robson	2
A.E.Warner	not out	11
M.Jean-Jacques		
O.H.Mortensen		
Extras	(b 5,lb 14,w 3,nb 3)	25
TOTAL	(38.3 overs)(for 7 wkts)	213

DERBYSHIRE	O	M	R	W	FALL OF WICKETS		
						SUR	DER
Jean-Jacques	8	0	51	2	1st	64	0
Mortensen	8	0	27	0	2nd	113	77
Warner	8	0	56	0	3rd	130	136
Miller	8	0	39	1	4th	167	143
Kuiper	8	0	32	2	5th	204	173
					6th		178
SURREY	O	M	R	W	7th		186
Murphy	7.3	0	26	1	8th		
Robson	7	0	37	1	9th		
Feltham	3	0	15	0	10th		
Bullen	8	0	38	0			
Waqar Younis	7	0	41	3			
Medlycott	6	0	37	1			

WORCESTERSHIRE vs. SUSSEX

at Worcester on 24th June 1990
Toss : Sussex. Umpires : B.Hassan and A.G.T.Whitehead
Worcestershire won by 2 runs (Worcs 4 pts Sussex 0 pts)

WORCESTERSHIRE

T.S.Curtis	c & b Pigott	58
I.T.Botham	b Wells C.M.	19
G.A.Hick	c Pigott b Dodemaide	75
D.B.D'Oliveira	b Clarke	16
P.A.Neale *	c Pigott b Lenham	8
D.A.Leatherdale	run out	6
P.J.Newport	c Salisbury b Dodemaide	3
S.J.Rhodes +	c & b Dodemaide	0
S.R.Lampitt	not out	0
R.K.Illingworth		
S.M.McEwan		
Extras	(lb 12,w 3)	15
TOTAL	(40 overs)(for 8 wkts)	200

SUSSEX

P.W.G.Parker *	lbw b McEwan	42
I.J.Gould	b Lampitt	12
A.P.Wells	c Illingworth b Newport	34
M.P.Speight	lbw b Illingworth	15
C.M.Wells	c Neale b Botham	29
A.C.S.Pigott	b Botham	4
A.I.C.Dodemaide	run out	24
P.Moores +	c & b Botham	13
N.J.Lenham	not out	3
I.D.K.Salisbury	c Rhodes b Lampitt	0
A.R.Clarke	not out	1
Extras	(lb 11,w 5,nb 5)	21
TOTAL	(40 overs)(for 9 wkts)	198

SUSSEX	O	M	R	W	FALL OF WICKETS		
						WOR	SUS
Wells C.M.	8	0	21	1	1st	46	48
Dodemaide	8	0	27	3	2nd	153	83
Clarke	8	0	42	1	3rd	177	111
Pigott	8	0	43	1	4th	182	130
Salisbury	7	0	50	0	5th	195	155
Lenham	1	0	5	1	6th	200	155
					7th	200	171
WORCS	O	M	R	W	8th	200	196
Newport	8	0	33	1	9th		197
McEwan	8	0	55	1	10th		
Botham	8	0	40	3			
Lampitt	8	1	24	2			
Illingworth	8	0	35	1			

WARWICKSHIRE vs. KENT

at Edgbaston on 24th June 1990
Toss : Warwickshire. Umpires : J.D.Bond and K.E.Palmer
Warwicks won by 3 wickets (Warwicks 4 pts Kent 0 pts)

KENT

S.G.Hinks	c Moody b Munton	6
M.A.Ealham	b Twose	25
N.R.Taylor	st Piper b Pierson	18
C.S.Cowdrey *	b Benjamin	46
G.R.Cowdrey	run out	16
M.V.Fleming	lbw b Moody	2
S.A.Marsh +	run out	9
R.M.Ellison	run out	8
P.S.De Villiers	b Benjamin	10
R.P.Davis	not out	2
A.P.Igglesden	b Reeve	1
Extras	(b 6,lb 3,w 4,nb 3)	16
TOTAL	(39.1 overs)	159

WARWICKSHIRE

A.J.Moles	c Ealham b Cowdrey C.S.	24
A.I.Kallicharran	c Ealham b Cowdrey C.S.	23
T.M.Moody	c & b Davis	29
D.A.Reeve *	b Cowdrey C.S.	25
Asif Din	not out	19
R.G.Twose	c Igglesden b Davis	5
D.P.Ostler	c Davis b De Villiers	3
K.J.Piper +	run out	4
J.E.Benjamin	not out	14
A.R.K.Pierson		
T.A.Munton		
Extras	(b 4,lb 6,w 4)	14
TOTAL	(39 overs)(for 7 wkts)	160

WARWICKSHIRE	O	M	R	W	FALL OF WICKETS		
						KEN	WAR
Munton	6	0	9	1	1st	11	46
Twose	8	1	35	1	2nd	45	58
Benjamin	8	0	29	2	3rd	68	107
Pierson	5	2	18	1	4th	89	115
Moody	6	0	27	1	5th	95	122
Reeve	6.1	0	32	1	6th	128	127
					7th	137	138
KENT	O	M	R	W	8th	152	
Igglesden	8	0	37	0	9th	158	
De Villiers	7	1	17	1	10th	159	
Fleming	8	0	39	0			
Ellison	8	0	27	0			
Cowdrey C.S.	4	0	19	3			
Davis	4	0	11	2			

GLOUCESTERSHIRE vs. LEICS

at Gloucester on 24th June 1990
Toss : Gloucs. Umpires : A.A.Jones and D.S.Thompsett
Leics won on faster scoring rate (Gloucs 0 pts Leics 4 pts)

LEICESTERSHIRE

T.J.Boon	c Wright b Bainbridge	15
N.E.Briers *	not out	90
J.J.Whitaker	c Lloyds b Alleyne	31
P.Willey	c Lloyds b Lawrence	1
C.C.Lewis	c Hodgson b Curran	30
L.Potter	b Curran	2
J.D.R.Benson	not out	8
P.A.Nixon +		
W.K.M.Benjamin		
J.P.Agnew		
A.D.Mullally		
Extras	(lb 7,w 2,nb 1)	10
TOTAL	(40 overs)(for 5 wkts)	187

GLOUCESTERSHIRE

A.J.Wright *	c Nixon b Agnew	0
J.W.Lloyds	c Nixon b Benjamin	10
P.Bainbridge	b Benjamin	20
K.M.Curran	c Willey b Lewis	14
C.W.J.Athey	b Willey	15
P.W.Romaines	c Briers b Benjamin	13
M.W.Alleyne	run out	14
C.A.Walsh	b Willey	0
G.D.Hodgson	lbw b Mullally	12
G.A.Tedstone +	c Willey b Mullally	25
D.V.Lawrence	not out	1
Extras	(b 4,lb 4,w 7)	15
TOTAL	(31 overs)	139

GLOUCS	O	M	R	W	FALL OF WICKETS		
						LEI	GLO
Curran	8	0	38	2	1st	26	0
Walsh	8	1	38	0	2nd	95	27
Bainbridge	8	0	21	1	3rd	98	32
Lawrence	8	0	47	1	4th	153	53
Alleyne	8	0	36	1	5th	166	83
					6th		85
LEICS	O	M	R	W	7th		85
Agnew	6	0	22	1	8th		102
Benjamin	7	0	36	3	9th		134
Lewis	8	0	41	1	10th		139
Mullally	7	0	20	2			
Willey	3	0	12	2			

LANCASHIRE vs. HAMPSHIRE

at Old Trafford on 24th June 1990
Toss : Hampshire. Umpires : H.D.Bird and P.J.Eele
No result (Lancashire 2 pts Hampshire 2 pts)

LANCASHIRE

G.D.Mendis	not out	1
G.Fowler	not out	1
G.D.Lloyd		
T.E.Jesty		
M.Watkinson		
Wasim Akram		
I.D.Austin		
D.P.Hughes *		
J.D.Fitton		
P.J.W.Allott		
J.Stanworth +		
Extras	(w 1)	1
TOTAL	(1 over)(for 0 wkts)	3

HAMPSHIRE

V.P.Terry		
R.J.Scott		
D.I.Gower		
C.L.Smith		
M.D.Marshall		
M.C.J.Nicholas *		
J.R.Ayling		
R.J.Maru		
R.J.Parks +		
T.M.Tremlett		
C.A.Connor		
Extras		
TOTAL		

HAMPSHIRE	O	M	R	W	FALL OF WICKETS		
						LAN	HAM
Marshall	1	0	3	0	1st		
					2nd		
LANCASHIRE	O	M	R	W	3rd		
					4th		
					5th		
					6th		
					7th		
					8th		
					9th		
					10th		

REFUGE ASSURANCE LEAGUE	BRIT. ASS. C'SHIP

SOMERSET vs. NOTTINGHAMSHIRE ▬

at Bath on 24th June 1990
Toss : Nottinghamshire. Umpires : K.J.Lyons and R.Palmer
Somerset won by 29 runs (Somerset 4 pts Notts 0 pts)

SOMERSET

S.J.Cook	lbw b Stephenson	3
R.J.Bartlett	run out	50
C.J.Tavare *	b Cooper	86
N.D.Burns +	b Saxelby K.	10
G.D.Rose	b Stephenson	45
R.J.Harden	c Cooper b Evans	2
A.N.Hayhurst	run out	8
M.W.Cleal	not out	12
I.G.Swallow	not out	3
N.A.Mallender		
J.C.Hallett		
Extras	(b 4,lb 14,w 8)	26
TOTAL	(40 overs)(for 7 wkts)	245

NOTTINGHAMSHIRE

B.C.Broad	c Burns b Mallender	18
M.Newell	c Cleal b Hayhurst	85
P.Johnson	c Burns b Hallett	1
R.T.Robinson *	c Tavare b Swallow	12
M.Saxelby	c Burns b Rose	19
F.D.Stephenson	c Rose b Hallett	34
B.N.French +	c Bartlett b Rose	1
K.P.Evans	not out	18
K.E.Cooper	b Hayhurst	9
K.Saxelby	not out	6
J.A.Afford		
Extras	(b 4,lb 5,w 4)	13
TOTAL	(40 overs)(for 8 wkts)	216

NOTTS	O	M	R	W	FALL OF WICKETS		
						SOM	NOT
Cooper	8	0	32	1			
Stephenson	8	0	34	2	1st	11	26
Saxelby K.	8	0	51	1	2nd	120	27
Evans	6	0	40	1	3rd	145	60
Afford	4	0	25	0	4th	202	93
Saxelby M.	6	0	45	0	5th	218	155
					6th	224	170
SOMERSET	O	M	R	W	7th	236	180
Mallender	8	0	34	1	8th		207
Hallett	8	0	39	2	9th		
Swallow	8	0	35	1	10th		
Cleal	4	0	17	0			
Rose	8	0	61	2			
Hayhurst	4	0	21	2			

GLAMORGAN vs YORKSHIRE

at Newport on 24th June 1990.
Match abandoned without a ball being bowled.
(Glamorgan 2pts, Yorkshire 2pts)

HEADLINES

24th June

● The deadlock at the top of the table was finally broken, with Middlesex beating Northants at Northampton and Kent losing to Warwickshire at Edgbaston

● Middlesex had 14.2 overs to spare as they cruised past Northants' modest 151 to secure their eighth victory, but Kent could not do likewise after Warwickshire's bowlers had restricted them to a total of 159

● Derbyshire kept in touch with a three wicket victory over Surrey at The Oval, and Worcestershire just held off Sussex's challenge at Worcester

● Somerset's batsmen resumed their heavy scoring against Notts at Bath as Mike Newell's best Sunday score proved in vain for the visitors, while Leicestershire's bowling attack proved too formidable for Gloucestershire

● Lancashire's attempt to defend their title successfully was again hampered by the weather, only one over being bowled in their match with Hampshire at Old Trafford, while Glamorgan's contest with Yorkshire at Newport was completely washed out

HEADLINES

23rd - 26th June

● Middlesex, who took over from Warwicks as Championship leaders, Yorkshire and Leicestershire were again the only successful teams

● Middlesex were grateful to spinners Philip Tufnell (match figures of 8 for 137) and John Emburey (match figures 7 for 135) for their victory over Northants at Luton

● Yorkshire, growing in confidence, gained their second successive victory thanks to season's bests from Richard Blakey and David Byas as they gained a five wicket win over Glamorgan at Cardiff

● Leicestershire's seam bowlers this time demolished Gloucestershire's second innings batting, reducing them to 13 for 5 before claiming a 111 run victory

● Warwickshire's Allan Donald ensured that Kent would not run away with a closely contested match at Edgbaston after the visitors had been left 233 for victory. Earlier 19-year-old Dominic Ostler had again improved his career best

● At Old Trafford, Lancashire were content to draw with Hampshire after they could make little progress towards a stiff victory target

Refuge Assurance League Table
at 24th June 1990

		P	W	L	T	NR	Away wins	Pts	Run rate
1	Middlesex (9)	9	8	1	0	0	5	32	94.87
2	Kent (12)	9	7	2	0	0	3	28	89.18
3	Derbyshire (5)	8	6	2	0	0	4	24	86.08
4	Lancashire (1)	8	4	2	0	2	3	20	98.50
5	Gloucs (16)	8	4	3	0	1	2	18	83.11
6	Essex (3)	8	4	4	0	0	3	16	89.42
7	Nottinghamshire (4)	8	4	4	0	0	2	16	81.39
8	Warwickshire (15)	8	4	4	0	0	1	16	78.07
9	Hampshire (6)	8	3	3	0	2	2	16	82.14
10	Yorkshire (11)	9	3	5	0	1	2	14	71.62
11	Surrey (7)	7	3	4	0	0	1	12	83.97
12	Worcestershire (2)	8	3	5	0	0	1	12	83.01
13	Somerset (10)	8	3	5	0	0	1	12	81.66
14	Leicestershire (14)	9	3	6	0	0	1	12	77.85
15	Glamorgan (17)	9	2	6	0	1	1	10	89.32
16	Sussex (13)	7	2	4	0	1	1	10	77.34
17	Northamptonshire (8)	7	2	5	0	0	1	8	81.13

BRITANNIC ASSURANCE CHAMPIONSHIP

GLOUCESTERSHIRE vs. LEICESTERSHIRE
at Gloucester on 23rd, 25th, 26th June 1990
Toss : Gloucestershire.   Umpires : A.A.Jones and D.S.Thompsett
Leicestershire won by 111 runs (Gloucs 3 pts (Bt: 0, Bw: 3) Leics 20 pts (Bt: 4, Bw: 0))

LEICESTERSHIRE

T.J.Boon	b Lloyds	138
N.E.Briers *	b Lawrence	67
J.J.Whitaker	c Lloyds b Curran	37
P.Willey	c Tedstone b Curran	8
L.Potter	b Walsh	11
J.D.R.Benson	c Graveney b Curran	45
C.C.Lewis	lbw b Lloyds	6
W.K.M.Benjamin	c Athey b Curran	16
P.A.Nixon +	not out	24
J.P.Agnew	not out	46
A.D.Mullally		
Extras	(b 1,lb 11,w 1,nb 15)	28
TOTAL	(for 8 wkts dec)	426

GLOUCESTERSHIRE

G.D.Hodgson	not out	23	b Agnew		4
A.J.Wright *	not out	51	lbw b Agnew		2
I.P.Butcher			c Potter b Benjamin		0
C.W.J.Athey			c Potter b Agnew		5
P.Bainbridge			c Nixon b Mullally		74
K.M.Curran			c Nixon b Agnew		0
J.W.Lloyds			c Whitaker b Benjamin		26
G.A.Tedstone +			c Benjamin b Lewis		23
D.A.Graveney			not out		46
C.A.Walsh			b Mullally		12
D.V.Lawrence			c Whitaker b Agnew		29
Extras	(lb 1)	1	(b 5,lb 9,w 3,nb 2)		19
TOTAL	(for 0 wkts dec)	75			240

GLOUCS	O	M	R	W	O	M	R	W
Walsh	21	2	97	1				
Curran	28	3	100	4				
Lawrence	19	1	84	1				
Bainbridge	7	4	16	0				
Graveney	28	6	96	0				
Lloyds	7	1	21	2				

LEICS	O	M	R	W	O	M	R	W
Willey	7	0	25	0	2	1	2	0
Potter	7	0	49	0				
Benjamin					23	11	44	2
Agnew					25.5	10	70	5
Mullally					16	5	37	2
Lewis					17	3	73	1

FALL OF WICKETS	LEI	GLO	LEI	GLO
1st	146			6
2nd	209			7
3rd	217			11
4th	267			13
5th	289			13
6th	314			102
7th	342			135
8th	361			173
9th				187
10th				240

GLAMORGAN vs. YORKSHIRE
at Cardiff on 23rd, 25th, 26th June 1990
Toss : Yorkshire.   Umpires : D.J.Constant and R.Julian
Yorkshire won by 5 wickets (Glamorgan 5 pts (Bt: 4, Bw: 1) Yorkshire 19 pts (Bt: 1, Bw: 2))

GLAMORGAN

A.R.Butcher *	c Kellett b Carrick	50	c Robinson b Hartley	17
H.Morris	c Blakey b Hartley	102	c Blakey b Moxon	28
P.A.Cottey	c Kellett b Hartley	18	not out	36
M.P.Maynard	c & b Hartley	54	not out	26
I.V.A.Richards	b Gough	38		
G.C.Holmes	not out	30		
C.P.Metson +	b Gough	14		
S.J.Dennis				
S.L.Watkin				
S.Bastien				
M.Frost				
Extras	(w 1,nb 2)	3	(lb 1,nb 5)	6
TOTAL	(for 6 wkts dec)	309	(for 2 wkts dec)	113

YORKSHIRE

M.D.Moxon *	c Cottey b Dennis	27	b Frost	10
A.A.Metcalfe	c Morris b Bastien	5	c Dennis b Watkin	37
S.A.Kellett	b Bastien	2	c Butcher b Bastien	8
K.Sharp	not out	53	b Dennis	24
P.E.Robinson	not out	53	not out	21
R.J.Blakey +			not out	71
D.Byas			c Metson b Frost	79
P.Carrick				
P.J.Hartley				
P.W.Jarvis				
D.Gough				
Extras	(b 4,lb 4,w 4)	12	(b 9,lb 8,w 2,nb 2)	21
TOTAL	(for 3 wkts dec)	152	(for 5 wkts)	271

YORKSHIRE	O	M	R	W	O	M	R	W
Jarvis	20	3	83	0				
Hartley	24	7	51	3	10	1	35	1
Moxon	13	4	36	0	5	0	10	1
Gough	21	2	72	2	7	0	44	0
Carrick	22	6	67	1				
Byas					8	4	23	0

GLAMORGAN	O	M	R	W	O	M	R	W
Frost	13	2	23	0	15.5	1	64	2
Watkin	13	2	38	0	14	1	46	1
Bastien	11	1	49	2	16	0	67	1
Dennis	7	0	34	1	15	2	58	1
Richards					5	0	19	0

FALL OF WICKETS	GLA	YOR	GLA	YOR
1st	107	12	31	28
2nd	196	18	75	40
3rd	209	76		70
4th	255			102
5th	276			223
6th	309			
7th				
8th				
9th				
10th				

LANCASHIRE vs. HAMPSHIRE
at Old Trafford on 23rd, 25th, 26th June 1990
Toss : Lancashire.   Umpires : H.D.Bird and P.J.Eele
Match drawn (Lancashire 2 pts (Bt: 0, Bw: 2) Hampshire 4 pts (Bt: 4, Bw: 0))

HAMPSHIRE

V.P.Terry	lbw b Watkinson	15	c Hegg b Wasim Akram	0
C.L.Smith	c Jesty b Wasim Akram	25	not out	53
T.C.Middleton	b Watkinson	20	not out	34
D.I.Gower	c Speak b Wasim Akram	49		
M.D.Marshall	c Mendis b Watkinson	86		
M.C.J.Nicholas *	not out	58		
R.J.Parks +	not out	14		
R.J.Maru				
T.M.Tremlett				
K.J.Shine				
C.A.Connor				
Extras	(b 11,lb 10,w 1,nb 11)	33		0
TOTAL	(for 5 wkts dec)	300	(for 1 wkt dec)	87

LANCASHIRE

G.D.Mendis	not out	37	c Parks b Marshall	23
G.Fowler	not out	15	c Middleton b Maru	17
G.D.Lloyd			c Tremlett b Maru	6
N.J.Speak			c Parks b Marshall	6
T.E.Jesty			not out	26
M.Watkinson			not out	41
Wasim Akram				
W.K.Hegg +				
I.D.Austin				
J.D.Fitton				
P.J.W.Allott *				
Extras	(lb 1,nb 5)	6	(b 6,lb 2,nb 4)	12
TOTAL	(for 0 wkts dec)	58	(for 4 wkts)	131

LANCASHIRE	O	M	R	W	O	M	R	W
Wasim Akram	29	3	106	2	4	0	5	1
Allott	17	8	26	0	5	1	10	0
Watkinson	22	8	54	3	4	0	10	0
Fitton	21.4	5	75	0	11	1	34	0
Austin	10	5	18	0	8	1	28	0

HAMPSHIRE	O	M	R	W	O	M	R	W
Marshall	5	0	28	0	14	2	42	2
Shine	5	0	22	0	6.4	0	15	0
Connor	1	0	1	0	5.2	1	12	0
Tremlett	1	0	6	0	5	1	13	0
Maru					20	12	22	2
Nicholas					5	0	11	0
Smith					5	3	8	0

FALL OF WICKETS	HAM	LAN	HAM	LAN
1st	32		0	31
2nd	64			47
3rd	104			50
4th	168			60
5th	247			
6th				
7th				
8th				
9th				
10th				

NORTHANTS vs. MIDDLESEX
at Luton on 23rd, 25th, 26th June 1990
Toss : Middlesex.   Umpires : N.T.Plews and R.A.White
Middlesex won by 79 runs (Northants 3 pts (Bt: 1, Bw: 2) Middlesex 23 pts (Bt: 3, Bw: 4))

MIDDLESEX

D.L.Haynes	c Cook G. b Ambrose	9	not out	69
M.A.Roseberry	c & b Cook N.G.B.	115	c Fordham b Ambrose	36
M.W.Gatting *	c Felton b Ambrose	62	c Ripley b Ambrose	0
M.R.Ramprakash	b Williams	26	not out	0
K.R.Brown	c Cook N.G.B.	69		
P.Farbrace +	c Robinson b Williams	0		
J.E.Emburey	st Ripley b Williams	13		
N.F.Williams	st Ripley b Williams	14		
P.C.R.Tufnell	c Williams b Cook N.G.B.	8		
A.R.C.Fraser	not out	1		
S.P.Hughes	c Cook G. b Cook N.G.B.	1		
Extras	(b 2,lb 9,nb 15)	26	(w 1,nb 1)	2
TOTAL		344	(for 2 wkts)	107

NORTHANTS

A.Fordham	c Farbrace b Williams	4	c & b Fraser	7
N.A.Felton	lbw b Williams	19	c Brown b Tufnell	11
G.Cook	c Roseberry b Emburey	8	c Farbrace b Fraser	1
R.J.Bailey	c Roseberry b Emburey	73	b Tufnell	87
D.J.Capel	c Gatting b Tufnell	12	s Farbrace b Tufnell	15
R.G.Williams	c Roseberry b Emburey	4	c Gatting b Emburey	11
D.Ripley +	run out	17	c Roseberry b Emburey	5
J.G.Thomas	lbw b Emburey	0	b Emburey	5
N.G.B.Cook *	c Roseberry b Tufnell	18	c Brown b Tufnell	0
C.E.L.Ambrose	b Tufnell	6	c & b Tufnell	3
M.A.Robinson	not out	0	not out	0
Extras	(b 10,lb 8,w 1,nb 20)	39	(b 6,lb 6,nb 15)	27
TOTAL		200		172

NORTHANTS	O	M	R	W	O	M	R	W
Ambrose	18	4	53	2	11	2	38	2
Thomas	17	3	40	0	6	0	38	0
Robinson	19	6	46	0	0.3	0	0	0
Cook N.G.B.	28.4	9	79	4	4	0	31	0
Capel	6	0	21	0				
Williams	35	6	94	4				

MIDDLESEX	O	M	R	W	O	M	R	W
Williams	9	1	23	2	5	1	12	0
Fraser	10	1	22	0	5	2	11	2
Emburey	44.1	17	55	4	33	5	80	3
Tufnell	38	8	80	3	30.1	7	57	5
Ramprakash	1	0	2	0				

FALL OF WICKETS	MID	NOR	MID	NOR
1st	17	5	107	7
2nd	147	34	107	9
3rd	191	40		36
4th	277	72		94
5th	278	86		118
6th	302	113		133
7th	328	126		150
8th	339	178		155
9th	342	194		166
10th	344	200		172

| BRITANNIC ASS. CHAMPIONSHIP | CORNHILL TEST MATCH |

WARWICKSHIRE vs. KENT

at Edgbaston on 23rd, 25th, 26th June 1990
Toss : Warwickshire.   Umpires : J.D.Bond and K.E.Palmer
Match drawn (Warwickshire 6 pts (Bt: 2, Bw: 4) Kent 6 pts (Bt: 2, Bw: 4))

WARWICKSHIRE

A.J.Moles	b Merrick	12	run out		11
J.D.Ratcliffe	c Marsh b Ellison	28	b Davis		43
Asif Din	c & b Igglesden	19	c Davis b Fleming		14
R.G.Twose	c Cowdrey C.S. b Ellison	51	c Cowdrey G.R. b Davis		12
D.A.Reeve *	c Marsh b Igglesden	30	not out		59
D.P.Ostler	c & b Davis	71	b Taylor		8
K.J.Piper +	c Wells b Cowdrey C.S.	9	c Wells b Davis		10
A.R.K.Pierson	c Marsh b Igglesden	2	lbw b Marsh		6
A.A.Donald	c Wells b Davis	0	c Igglesden b Marsh		1
J.E.Benjamin	not out	3	not out		15
T.A.Munton	c Cowdrey C.S. b Igglesden	4			
Extras	(b 4,lb 7,w 1,nb 1)	13	(b 4,lb 6,w 1)		11
TOTAL		242	(for 8 wkts dec)		190

KENT

S.G.Hinks	lbw b Donald	66	lbw b Benjamin		15
V.J.Wells	c Twose b Benjamin	5	lbw b Pierson		25
N.R.Taylor	lbw b Pierson	25	b Donald		28
G.R.Cowdrey	c Reeve b Munton	20	not out		22
C.S.Cowdrey *	not out	56	lbw b Donald		0
M.V.Fleming	lbw b Reeve	3	b Donald		0
S.A.Marsh +	c Reeve b Benjamin	5			
R.M.Ellison	lbw b Benjamin	6	(7) not out		8
R.P.Davis	c Twose b Pierson	5			
A.P.Igglesden	c Munton b Asif Din	5			
T.A.Merrick	not out	0			
Extras	(lb 2,w 2)	4	(lb 1,nb 3)		4
TOTAL	(for 9 wkts dec)	200	(for 5 wkts)		102

KENT	O	M	R	W	O	M	R	W
Merrick	9	2	19	1				
Igglesden	27.3	4	79	4	6	0	23	0
Fleming	13	7	22	0	7	1	21	1
Ellison	18	7	36	2	7	3	23	0
Davis	26	8	70	2	26	5	61	3
Cowdrey C.S.	2	1	5	1				
Taylor					11	4	19	1
Cowdrey G.R.					2	0	13	0
Marsh					5	0	20	2

WARWICKS	O	M	R	W	O	M	R	W
Donald	14	5	19	1	10.5	2	28	3
Benjamin	16	4	31	3	8	1	34	1
Munton	13	4	46	1	7	4	6	0
Pierson	21	5	68	2	14	5	19	1
Reeve	7	3	16	1				
Asif Din	1.5	0	18	1	3	0	14	0

FALL OF WICKETS

	WAR	KEN	WAR	KEN
1st	14	10	17	15
2nd	51	47	51	68
3rd	68	90	70	76
4th	127	133	84	76
5th	166	136	105	76
6th	202	154	118	
7th	223	160	155	
8th	224	177	173	
9th	237	192		
10th	242			

ENGLAND vs. NEW ZEALAND

at Lord's on 21st, 22nd, 23rd, 25th, 26th June 1990
Toss : New Zealand.   Umpires : M.J.Kitchen and D.R.Shepherd
Match drawn

ENGLAND

G.A.Gooch *	c & b Bracewell	85	b Hadlee		37
M.A.Atherton	b Morrison	0	c Bracewell b Jones		54
A.J.Stewart	lbw b Hadlee	54	c sub b Bracewell		42
A.J.Lamb	lbw b Snedden	39	not out		84
R.A.Smith	c Bracewell b Morrison	64	hit wicket b Bracewell		0
N.H.Fairbrother	c Morrison b Bracewell	2	not out		33
R.C.Russell +	b Hadlee	13			
P.A.J.DeFreitas	c Franklin b Morrison	38			
G.C.Small	b Morrison	3			
E.E.Hemmings	b Hadlee	0			
D.E.Malcolm	not out	0			
Extras	(lb 13,w 1,nb 22)	36	(b 8,lb 8,nb 6)		22
TOTAL		334	(for 4 wkts dec)		272

NEW ZEALAND

T.J.Franklin	c Russell b Malcolm		101
J.G.Wright *	c Stewart b Small		98
A.H.Jones	c Stewart b Malcolm		49
M.D.Crowe	c Russell b Hemmings		1
M.J.Greatbatch	b Malcolm		47
K.R.Rutherford	c Fairbrother b Malcolm		0
R.J.Hadlee	b Hemmings		86
J.G.Bracewell	run out		4
I.D.S.Smith +	c Small b Malcolm		27
M.C.Snedden	not out		13
D.K.Morrison	not out		2
Extras	(b 12,lb 15,w 2,nb 5)		34
TOTAL	(for 9 wkts dec)		462

NEW ZEALAND	O	M	R	W	O	M	R	W
Hadlee	29	5	113	3	13	2	32	1
Morrison	18.4	4	64	4	16	0	81	0
Snedden	21	4	72	1				
Bracewell	21	3	72	2	34	13	85	2
Jones					12	3	40	1
Rutherford					3	0	18	0

ENGLAND	O	M	R	W	O	M	R	W
Malcolm	43	14	94	5				
Small	35	4	127	1				
DeFreitas	35.4	1	122	0				
Hemmings	30	13	67	2				
Gooch	13	7	25	0				
Atherton	1	1	0	0				

FALL OF WICKETS

	ENG	NZ	ENG	NZ
1st	3	185	68	
2nd	151	278	135	
3rd	178	281	171	
4th	216	284	175	
5th	226	285		
6th	255	408		
7th	319	415		
8th	322	425		
9th	332	448		
10th	334			

Man of the match: Sir Richard Hadlee (New Zealand)

Britannic Assurance Championship Table
at 26th June 1990

		P	W	L	D	T	Bt	Bl	Pts
1	Middlesex (3)	9	5	0	4	0	26	20	126
2	Warwickshire (8)	10	4	2	4	0	22	28	114
3	Hampshire (6)	10	3	1	6	0	32	16	96
4	Lancashire (4)	9	3	1	5	0	23	23	94
	Leicestershire (13)	10	3	2	5	0	29	17	94
6	Glamorgan (17)	10	3	3	4	0	22	23	93
7	Derbyshire (7)	9	3	3	3	0	27	15	90
	Nottinghamshire (11)	8	3	1	4	0	20	22	90
9	Yorkshire (16)	9	2	4	3	0	16	23	71
10	Somerset (14)	10	1	1	8	0	31	20	67
11	Kent (15)	8	2	2	4	0	22	11	65
12	Northants (5)	8	1	5	2	0	21	28	65
13	Essex (2)	8	1	1	6	0	30	9	55
14	Worcestershire (1)	7	1	1	5	0	19	14	49
15	Surrey (12)	8	0	1	7	0	18	22	48
16	Sussex (10)	8	1	3	4	0	18	13	47
17	Gloucestershire (9)	9	0	5	4	0	18	19	37

HEADLINES

England vs New Zealand: Second Cornhill Test Match

22nd - 26th June

● This time New Zealand had the better of a drawn match once more badly affected by the weather as Sir Richard Hadlee, the first cricketing knight to play in a Test match, held centre stage as he made his last appearance at Lord's

● England did not take full advantage of a second wicket partnership of 148 between Graham Gooch and Alec Stewart who made the first 50 of his Test career, although Robin Smith completed 1,000 runs in Tests during his innings of 64.

● New Zealand's reply was based on an opening stand of 185 (their best ever in Tests in England) between John Wright and Trevor Franklin, who took almost seven hours to complete his maiden Test 100, and, after the initiative had briefly been regained by England, Hadlee launched a blistering counter-attack eventually falling 14 short of what would have been his first 100 against England.

● Devon Malcolm took five wickets in an innings for the second time in his Test career but could not prevent New Zealand's first innings lead stretching to 128 at their declaration early on the final morning

● England had few problems batting out for the draw, Neil Fairbrother making sure of another chance with his first score above 20 in his 7th Test innings

NATWEST TROPHY – 1st ROUND

MIDDLESEX vs. BERKSHIRE
at Lord's on 27th June 1990
Toss : Middlesex. Umpires : J.A.Jameson and K.E.Palmer
Middlesex won by 4 wickets

BERKSHIRE
G.E.Loveday	c Roseberry b Gatting	36
M.G.Lickley	lbw b Cowans	12
M.L.Simmons *	c Haynes b Cowans	30
G.T.Hedley	c Butcher b Emburey	13
D.Shaw	run out	36
B.S.Jackson	c Farbrace b Fraser	10
P.Oxley	not out	33
M.G.Stear	not out	5
M.E.Stevens +		
J.H.Jones		
D.J.Hartley		
Extras	(lb 9,w 8,nb 12)	29
TOTAL	(60 overs)(for 6 wkts)	204

MIDDLESEX
D.L.Haynes	b Hedley	50
M.A.Roseberry	lbw b Jones	3
M.W.Gatting *	not out	79
M.R.Ramprakash	run out	3
K.R.Brown	lbw b Stear	16
R.O.Butcher	c Jackson b Hartley	22
P.Farbrace +	b Hartley	17
J.E.Emburey	not out	4
N.F.Williams		
A.R.C.Fraser		
N.G.Cowans		
Extras	(b 2,lb 6,w 5,nb 1)	14
TOTAL	(50.3 overs)(for 6 wkts)	208

MIDDLESEX	O	M	R	W	FALL OF WICKETS		
						BER	MID
Cowans	10	3	25	2			
Williams	12	1	67	0	1st	24	3
Fraser	12	0	37	1	2nd	68	100
Gatting	6	0	31	1	3rd	99	117
Haynes	8	3	18	0	4th	114	149
Emburey	12	2	17	1	5th	135	186
					6th	178	204
BERKSHIRE	O	M	R	W	7th		
Jones	9	2	32	1	8th		
Jackson	10	1	46	0	9th		
Hedley	12	1	35	1	10th		
Stear	9	0	39	1			
Lickley	1	0	13	0			
Hartley	9.3	1	35	2			

Man of the match: M.W.Gatting

HERTFORDSHIRE vs. WARWICKSHIRE
at St Albans on 27th June 1990
Toss : Herts. Umpires : V.A.Holder and A.G.T.Whitehead
Warwickshire won by 128 runs

WARWICKSHIRE
A.J.Moles	b Surridge	60
Asif Din	c Evans b Needham	66
T.M.Moody	c Smith T.S. b Needham	58
A.I.Kallicharran	c Maclaurin b Surridge	41
G.W.Humpage +	b Surridge	43
D.A.Reeve *	not out	36
R.G.Twose	c Vartan b Merry	1
G.C.Small	c Surridge b Merry	0
J.E.Benjamin	not out	1
A.R.K.Pierson		
T.A.Munton		
Extras	(b 5,lb 22,w 3)	30
TOTAL	(60 overs)(for 7 wkts)	336

HERTFORDSHIRE
B.G.Evans	b Munton	27
N.P.G.Wright	run out	17
R.N.R.Vartan +	c Moody b Munton	10
A.Needham	c Benjamin b Asif Din	35
N.R.C.Maclaurin	c Moles b Munton	21
I.Fletcher	c & b Asif Din	1
D.M.Smith	st Humpage b Moody	39
T.S.Smith	c Twose b Asif Din	15
W.G.Merry	c Moody b Asif Din	11
G.A.R.Harris	c Moles b Asif Din	0
D.Surridge *	not out	3
Extras	(b 4,lb 12,w 13)	29
TOTAL	(53.1 overs)	208

HERTS	O	M	R	W	FALL OF WICKETS		
						WAR	HER
Harris	12	0	61	0	1st	133	52
Surridge	12	0	61	3	2nd	147	65
Smith T.S.	12	1	57	0	3rd	229	74
Merry	11	0	62	2	4th	292	106
Needham	12	0	50	2	5th	304	125
Smith D.M.	1	0	12	0	6th	321	134
WARWICKS	O	M	R	W	7th	321	163
Small	6	0	21	0	8th		189
Benjamin	6	1	9	0	9th		189
Reeve	8	1	20	0	10th		208
Munton	12	1	46	3			
Pierson	12	1	49	0			
Asif Din	8	2	40	5			
Moody	1.1	0	7	1			

Man of the match: Asif Din

DEVON vs. SOMERSET
at Torquay on 27th June 1990
Toss : Somerset. Umpires : D.Halfyard and R.Julian
Somerset won by 346 runs

SOMERSET
S.J.Cook	run out	42
P.M.Roebuck	c & b Woodman	43
A.N.Hayhurst	c Pugh b Folland	51
C.J.Tavare *	not out	162
G.D.Rose	c Pugh b Dawson	110
R.J.Harden		
N.D.Burns +		
I.G.Swallow		
R.P.Lefebvre		
N.A.Mallender		
A.N.Jones		
Extras	(w 5)	5
TOTAL	(60 overs)(for 4 wkts)	413

DEVON
J.H.Edwards	lbw b Jones	4
K.G.Rice *	b Mallender	0
N.A.Folland	c Burns b Mallender	0
A.J.Pugh	b Lefebvre	12
P.A.Brown	lbw b Lefebvre	12
R.C.Turpin +	c Rose b Lefebvre	4
R.I.Dawson	lbw b Lefebvre	0
K.Donohue	not out	18
J.K.Tierney	b Lefebvre	0
M.C.Woodman	b Lefebvre	1
R.S.Yeabsley	lbw b Lefebvre	2
Extras	(lb 5,w 9)	14
TOTAL	(30.3 overs)	67

DEVON	O	M	R	W	FALL OF WICKETS		
						SOM	DEV
Donohue	12	2	101	0	1st	79	4
Woodman	12	3	50	1	2nd	88	4
Tierney	11	2	62	0	3rd	224	11
Yeabsley	12	0	77	0	4th	413	35
Rice	6	0	34	0	5th		41
Dawson	4	0	37	1	6th		41
Folland	3	0	52	1	7th		44
					8th		44
SOMERSET	O	M	R	W	9th		63
Jones	6	1	20	1	10th		67
Mallender	6	3	4	2			
Rose	5	1	11	0			
Lefebvre	9.3	6	15	7			
Swallow	4	0	12	0			

Man of the match: C.J.Tavare

IRELAND vs. SUSSEX
at Downpatrick on 27th June 1990
Toss : Ireland. Umpires : J.C.Balderstone and B.Dudleston
Sussex won by 9 wickets

IRELAND
A.Dunlop	b Dodemaide	1
R.Lamba	b Dodemaide	5
M.P.Rea	c Moores b Pigott	5
S.J.S.Warke *	c Speight b Dodemaide	22
D.A.Lewis	b Wells C.M.	1
S.Smyth	c Clarke b Lenham	15
G.D.Harrison	c Moores b Lenham	3
P.McCrum	not out	4
P.B.Jackson +	b Dodemaide	0
A.N.Nelson	b Dodemaide	3
A.Johnston	b Dodemaide	0
Extras	(b 3,lb 3,w 7)	13
TOTAL	(49 overs)	72

SUSSEX
N.J.Lenham	not out	41
I.J.Gould	c Lamba b Nelson	26
P.W.G.Parker *	not out	4
A.P.Wells		
M.P.Speight		
C.M.Wells		
P.Moores +		
A.I.C.Dodemaide		
A.C.S.Pigott		
A.R.Clarke		
I.D.K.Salisbury		
Extras	(w 2)	2
TOTAL	(15.1 overs)(for 1 wkt)	73

SUSSEX	O	M	R	W	FALL OF WICKETS		
						IRE	SUS
Pigott	8	1	14	1	1st	1	58
Dodemaide	11	7	9	6			
Wells C.M.	9	6	6	1	2nd	10	
Salisbury	5	2	19	0	3rd	18	
Clarke	10	7	6	0	4th	19	
Lenham	6	0	12	2	5th	47	
					6th	58	
IRELAND	O	M	R	W	7th	61	
McCrum	3	0	16	0	8th	64	
Johnston	4	0	21	0	9th	72	
Nelson	5	0	27	1	10th	72	
Harrison	3.1	0	9	0			

Man of the match: A.I.C.Dodemaide

SUFFOLK vs. WORCESTERSHIRE
at Bury St Edmonds on 27th June 1990
Toss : Worcs. Umpires : D.O.Oslear and R.A.White
Worcestershire won by 8 wickets

SUFFOLK
M.S.A.McEvoy	c Illingworth b Lampitt	55
C.Gladwin	c & b Lampitt	5
J.W.Edrich	c Rhodes b D'Oliveira	52
P.J.Caley	not out	39
S.M.Clements	c Weston b D'Oliveira	11
M.J.Peck	b Botham	0
I.D.Graham	lbw b Lampitt	3
A.K.Golding	c Neale b Botham	0
A.D.Brown +	b Lampitt	4
M.D.Bailey *	b Botham	0
R.C.Green	lbw b Lampitt	0
Extras	(lb 3,w 3,nb 2)	8
TOTAL	(59.4 overs)	177

WORCESTERSHIRE
T.S.Curtis	b Golding	16
M.J.Weston	c & b Golding	40
G.A.Hick	not out	78
D.B.D'Oliveira	not out	33
I.T.Botham		
P.A.Neale *		
D.A.Leatherdale		
S.J.Rhodes +		
S.R.Lampitt		
R.K.Illingworth		
S.M.McEwan		
Extras	(b 2,lb 2,w 7,nb 3)	14
TOTAL	(48 overs)(for 2 wkts)	181

WORCS	O	M	R	W	FALL OF WICKETS		
						SFK	WOR
Botham	12	2	44	3			
Lampitt	11.4	1	22	5	1st	10	39
Illingworth	12	5	26	0	2nd	117	98
Hick	12	2	30	0	3rd	121	
D'Oliveira	5	0	17	2	4th	138	
McEwan	3	0	15	0	5th	146	
Weston	4	0	20	0	6th	163	
					7th	164	
SUFFOLK	O	M	R	W	8th	169	
Green	11	1	38	0	9th	176	
Graham	9	1	37	0	10th	177	
Golding	12	4	29	2			
Bailey	6	0	18	0			
Caley	9	0	49	0			
Gladwin	1	0	6	0			

Man of the match: S.R.Lampitt

DERBYSHIRE vs. SHROPSHIRE
at Chesterfield on 27th June 1990
Toss : Derbyshire. Umpires : J.D.Bond and J.W.Holder
Derbyshire won by 7 wickets

SHROPSHIRE
J.Foster *	lbw b Kuiper	20
J.B.R.Jones	c Bowler b Warner	26
J.Abrahams	b Mortensen	47
T.Parton	lbw b Mortensen	2
M.R.Davies	c Bowler b Warner	20
J.Weaver +	lbw b Mortensen	0
P.B.Wormwald	b Warner	16
D.Page	b Warner	0
A.B.Byram	not out	20
B.K.Shantry	not out	4
A.S.Barnard		
Extras	(lb 11,w 18)	29
TOTAL	(60 overs)(for 8 wkts)	184

DERBYSHIRE
K.J.Barnett *	c Weaver b Shantry	1
P.D.Bowler +	c Weaver b Shantry	14
J.E.Morris	not out	94
A.P.Kuiper	c Parton b Wormwald	49
B.Roberts	not out	14
C.J.Adams		
S.C.Goldsmith		
A.E.Warner		
G.Miller		
D.E.Malcolm		
O.H.Mortensen		
Extras	(lb 6,w 5,nb 3)	14
TOTAL	(38.1 overs)(for 3 wkts)	186

DERBYSHIRE	O	M	R	W	FALL OF WICKETS		
						SHR	DER
Malcolm	12	3	31	0	1st	33	9
Mortensen	11	2	29	3	2nd	97	45
Warner	12	1	39	4	3rd	112	162
Goldsmith	5	0	23	0	4th	114	
Miller	10	0	31	0	5th	114	
Kuiper	10	0	20	1	6th	147	
					7th	149	
SHROPSHIRE	O	M	R	W	8th	169	
Page	5	0	24	0	9th		
Shantry	10	1	47	2	10th		
Barnard	6	1	19	0			
Wormwald	5.1	1	24	1			
Byram	6	0	35	0			
Abrahams	6	0	31	0			

Man of the match: J.E.Morris

NATWEST TROPHY – 1st ROUND

LANCASHIRE vs. DURHAM

at Old Trafford on 27th June 1990
Toss : Lancashire.   Umpires : D.B.Harrison and
B.Leadbeater
Lancashire won by 8 wickets

DURHAM

G.K.Brown	lbw b Wasim Akram	42
J.Glendenen	b Allott	14
P.Burn	c Wasim Akram b Atherton	26
P.V.Simmons	c Hegg b Austin	14
J.F.Sykes	lbw b DeFreitas	4
A.S.Patel	not out	31
N.A.Riddell *	b Austin	16
S.Greensword	lbw b Allott	0
P.G.Newman	lbw b Allott	0
A.R.Fothergill +	b Austin	2
I.Young	b Wasim Akram	0
Extras	(lb 11,w 1,nb 3)	15
TOTAL	(55.2 overs)	164

LANCASHIRE

G.D.Mendis	not out	62
G.Fowler	b Newman	31
M.A.Atherton	c Burn b Sykes	4
N.H.Fairbrother	not out	50
M.Watkinson		
Wasim Akram		
P.A.J.DeFreitas		
W.K.Hegg +		
I.D.Austin		
D.P.Hughes *		
P.J.W.Allott		
Extras	(b 5,lb 4,w 8,nb 1)	18
TOTAL	(34.1 overs)(for 2 wkts)	165

LANCASHIRE	O	M	R	W	FALL OF	WICKETS	
						DUR	LAN
Allott	10	4	24	3			
DeFreitas	10	2	22	1	1st	17	70
Wasim Akram	9.2	1	19	2	2nd	76	90
Watkinson	12	1	45	0	3rd	108	
Austin	12	0	36	3	4th	114	
Atherton	2	1	7	1	5th	116	
					6th	157	
DURHAM	O	M	R	W	7th	160	
Newman	10	0	30	1	8th	160	
Young	6.1	0	47	0	9th	163	
Simmons	4	0	28	0	10th	164	
Sykes	6	0	16	1			
Greensword	6	1	23	0			
Patel	2	0	12	0			

Man of the match: N.H.Fairbrother

BUCKINGHAMSHIRE vs. NOTTS

at Marlow on 27th June 1990
Toss : Bucks.   Umpires : P.J.Eele and D.S.Thompsett
Nottinghamshire won by 192 runs

NOTTINGHAMSHIRE

B.C.Broad	b Black	115
M.Newell	b Scriven	35
F.D.Stephenson	c Harwood b Burrow	29
R.T.Robinson *	c & b Percy	30
P.Johnson	c Harwood b Lynch	14
M.Saxelby	c Lynch b Black	41
B.N.French +	c Black b Barry	7
E.E.Hemmings	b Barry	3
K.E.Cooper	c Percy b Barry	10
R.A.Pick	not out	4
J.A.Afford	not out	2
Extras	(b 4,lb 10,w 6,nb 2)	22
TOTAL	(60 overs)(for 9 wkts)	312

BUCKINGHAMSHIRE

A.R.Harwood	c French b Cooper	13
M.J.Roberts	retired hurt	17
T.Butler	c Johnson b Cooper	5
S.Burrow	c Hemmings b Pick	19
T.J.A.Scriven	c Robinson b Cooper	1
N.G.Hames *	c French b Hemmings	4
B.S.Percy	b Pick	0
G.R.Black	lbw b Pick	6
S.G.Lynch	c Newell b Hemmings	46
T.J.Barry	c Saxelby b Hemmings	5
D.J.Goldsmith +	not out	0
Extras	(lb 2,w 2)	4
TOTAL	(40.3 overs)	120

BUCKS	O	M	R	W	FALL OF	WICKETS	
						NOT	BUC
Barry	12	2	49	3			
Black	11	2	52	2	1st	97	32
Burrow	12	1	42	1	2nd	140	42
Scriven	12	0	73	1	3rd	187	44
Lynch	7	0	52	1	4th	206	55
Percy	6	0	30	1	5th	277	56
					6th	288	63
NOTTS	O	M	R	W	7th	293	70
Stephenson	5	2	12	0	8th	305	95
Pick	9	2	22	3	9th	308	120
Cooper	8	3	16	3	10th		
Afford	11	6	26	0			
Hemmings	7.3	2	42	3			

Man of the match: B.C.Broad

HEADLINES

27th - 28th June

● There were no surprises as the 15 counties matched against non-first-class opposition progressed comfortably through to the second round

● Torquay was the setting for the most one-sided contest: Somerset amassed the record score in 60-over cricket when they reached 413 for 4 against Devon and also created a new record for the biggest margin of victory – 346 runs. Chris Tavare made a career best 162 and Graham Rose completed his first 100 for Somerset in 36 balls, then Roland Lefebvre took 7 for 15 on his debut in the competition

● Alan Fordham hit 130 in his first match in the competition as Northants raced to 360 for 2 against Staffs, while Chris Broad made his first NatWest 100 as Notts reached 312 for 9 against Bucks

● Sussex's Tony Dodemaide returned a career best 6 for 9 as Ireland were dismissed for 72 , and Stuart Lampitt also produced career best figures as Worcs beat Suffolk by eight wickets

● After champions Warwickshire had made 336 for 7 against Herts, Asif Din took 5 for 40 after managing just 2 wickets in his previous 21 NatWest matches. Phil Carrick's career best 3 for 8 in 12 overs was too much for Norfolk as Yorkshire won by 10 wickets

● Vince Wells was another to impress on his debut in the NatWest Trophy, hitting 100* to ensure a safe passage for Kent against Oxfordshire, while Surrey's Chris Bullen, promoted to open against Wiltshire at Trowbridge, surpassed himself with 93* in a nine-wicket victory

● Alan Warner (4 for 39) and John Morris (94*) both recorded NatWest bests in Derbyshire's eight-wicket win over Shropshire, as did Tony Wright (92) in Gloucs' 195-run success over Lincs

● Graham Gooch's fourth 100 in the competition was enough to ensure an Essex victory over Scotland, while the round's two other century-makers were Hugh Morris and Viv Richards as Glamorgan reached 295 for 4 against Dorset. Andrew Wingfield Digby's team replied with the highest score ever made by a minor county in the competition, finishing only 34 runs short of victory

● Leics were the only first-class casualties of the first round, losing out by one run to Hampshire

OXFORDSHIRE vs. KENT

at Christ Church, Oxford on 27th June 1990
Toss : Oxfordshire.   Umpires : D.J.Constant and S.Cook
Kent won by 102 runs

KENT

S.G.Hinks	c Garner b Hartley	43
V.J.Wells +	not out	100
N.R.Taylor	retired hurt	13
G.R.Cowdrey	c Hartley b Curtis	3
C.S.Cowdrey *	c Jobson b Evans	6
M.V.Fleming	b Evans	7
D.J.M.Kelleher	c Evans b Curtis	21
P.S.De Villiers	st Waterton b Evans	10
A.P.Igglesden	not out	12
R.P.Davis		
M.M.Patel		
Extras	(b 2,lb 9,w 8)	19
TOTAL	(60 overs)(for 6 wkts)	234

OXFORDSHIRE

G.C.Ford	b Davis	26
S.N.V.Waterton +	c Cowdrey C.S. b Igglesden	0
J.Hartley	lbw b Igglesden	7
T.A.Lester	lbw b Kelleher	13
P.J.Garner *	lbw b Patel	4
P.M.Jobson	b Patel	7
G.P.Savin	lbw b Fleming	23
R.A.Evans	b Fleming	24
D.A.Hale	lbw b Kelleher	6
K.A.Arnold	b Kelleher	2
I.J.Curtis	not out	0
Extras	(b 4,lb 11,w 5)	20
TOTAL	(49 overs)	132

OXFORDSHIRE	O	M	R	W	FALL OF	WICKETS	
						KEN	OSH
Hale	4	0	15	0			
Arnold	12	3	48	0	1st	70	8
Savin	12	0	35	0	2nd	110	22
Hartley	8	1	26	1	3rd	124	41
Curtis	12	0	53	2	4th	140	58
Evans	12	1	46	3	5th	188	66
					6th	206	66
KENT	O	M	R	W	7th		119
De Villiers	7	3	28	0	8th		120
Igglesden	6	1	13	2	9th		131
Kelleher	9	3	16	3	10th		132
Patel	12	6	29	2			
Davis	12	3	27	1			
Fleming	3	1	4	2			

Man of the match: V.J.Wells

GLOUCESTERSHIRE vs. LINCS

at Gloucester on 27th June 1990
Toss : Gloucs.   Umpires : J.H.Harris and C.T.Spencer
Gloucestershire won by 195 runs

GLOUCESTERSHIRE

G.D.Hodgson	c McKeown b Airey	42
A.J.Wright *	st Priestley b Marshall	92
P.Bainbridge	lbw b Marshall	13
C.W.J.Athey	not out	81
K.M.Curran	b Pont	2
J.W.Lloyds	not out	73
M.W.Alleyne		
R.C.Russell +		
C.A.Walsh		
D.A.Graveney		
D.V.Lawrence		
Extras	(lb 13,w 5,nb 4)	22
TOTAL	(60 overs)(for 4 wkts)	325

LINCOLNSHIRE

N.Priestley *+	c Graveney b Alleyne	54
D.B.Storer	lbw b Walsh	0
J.D.Love	b Walsh	1
N.C.J.Gandon	b Alleyne	31
I.L.Pont	b Graveney	1
R.Bates	b Graveney	5
S.N.Warman	lbw b Alleyne	3
N.French	c Wright b Alleyne	7
J.R.Airey	st Russell b Alleyne	0
P.D.McKeown	not out	3
D.Marshall	b Lloyds	5
Extras	(b 5,lb 6,w 7,nb 2)	20
TOTAL	(49 overs)	130

LINCOLNSHIRE	O	M	R	W	FALL OF	WICKETS	
						GLO	LIN
Pont	12	0	52	1			
French	12	1	42	0	1st	113	6
McKeown	12	1	84	0	2nd	142	17
Airey	10	0	60	1	3rd	124	79
Marshall	12	0	63	2	4th	178	80
Love	2	0	11	0	5th		98
					6th		108
GLOUCS	O	M	R	W	7th		112
Walsh	7	1	16	2	8th		112
Curran	8	3	11	0	9th		117
Lawrence	5	0	15	0	10th		130
Bainbridge	6	0	15	0			
Graveney	12	0	26	2			
Alleyne	10	2	30	5			
Lloyds	1	0	6	1			

Man of the match: A.J.Wright

NATWEST TROPHY – 1st ROUND

ESSEX vs. SCOTLAND

at Chelmsford on 27th June 1990
Toss : Scotland. Umpires : J.H.Hampshire and H.J.Rhodes
Essex won by 9 wickets

SCOTLAND

I.L.Philip +	c Waugh b Andrew	1
C.G.Greenidge	b Foster	15
B.M.W.Patterson	b Andrew	19
R.G.Swan *	c Pringle b Childs	26
A.B.Russell	run out	37
O.Henry	c Hardie b Pringle	53
W.Morton	c Garnham b Foster	5
P.G.Duthie	lbw b Foster	0
J.D.Moir	not out	4
A.W.Bee	run out	14
C.L.Parfitt	b Pringle	0
Extras	(b 2,lb 15,w 9)	26
TOTAL	(59.3 overs)	200

ESSEX

G.A.Gooch *	not out	103
B.R.Hardie	b Bee	31
P.J.Prichard	not out	37
M.E.Waugh		
D.R.Pringle		
J.P.Stephenson		
M.A.Garnham +		
N.A.Foster		
T.D.Topley		
J.H.Childs		
S.J.W.Andrew		
Extras	(b 2,lb 17,w 11,nb 1)	31
TOTAL	(42.4 overs)(for 1 wkt)	202

ESSEX	O	M	R	W		FALL OF WICKETS	
						SCO	ESS
Andrew	12	2	34	2			
Foster	12	4	26	3	1st	5	105
Topley	7	0	32	0	2nd	33	
Pringle	11.3	2	30	2	3rd	37	
Childs	12	1	44	1	4th	82	
Waugh	5	1	17	0	5th	164	
					6th	170	
SCOTLAND	O	M	R	W	7th	176	
Moir	10	3	34	0	8th	180	
Duthie	8	0	37	0	9th	199	
Parfitt	9.4	3	29	0	10th	200	
Bee	10	4	27	1			
Henry	3	0	21	0			
Morton	2	0	35	0			

Man of the match: G.A.Gooch

LEICESTERSHIRE vs. HAMPSHIRE

at Leicester on 27th June 1990
Toss : Leicestershire. Umpires : H.D.Bird and B.Hassan
Hampshire won by 1 run

HAMPSHIRE

V.P.Terry	c Lewis b Willey	21
C.L.Smith	c Willey b Benjamin	52
R.A.Smith	c Nixon b Lewis	35
D.I.Gower	c Willey b Mullally	28
M.D.Marshall	c Briers b Agnew	6
M.C.J.Nicholas *	b Mullally	19
J.R.Ayling	b Agnew	29
R.J.Parks +	not out	14
R.J.Maru	not out	6
C.A.Connor		
P.J.Bakker		
Extras	(lb 4,w 8,nb 4)	16
TOTAL	(60 overs)(for 7 wkts)	226

LEICESTERSHIRE

T.J.Boon	c Parks b Maru	19
N.E.Briers *	b Bakker	8
J.J.Whitaker	c Smith R.A. b Maru	24
P.Willey	not out	72
C.C.Lewis	lbw b Maru	32
L.Potter	run out	19
J.D.R.Benson	c Nicholas b Ayling	11
W.K.M.Benjamin	c Gower b Ayling	7
P.A.Nixon +	run out	12
J.P.Agnew		
A.D.Mullally		
Extras	(b 1,lb 12,w 6,nb 2)	21
TOTAL	(60 overs)(for 8 wkts)	225

LEICS	O	M	R	W		FALL OF WICKETS	
						HAM	LEI
Benjamin	12	4	34	1	1st	65	16
Agnew	12	1	44	2	2nd	91	55
Lewis	12	1	35	1	3rd	129	56
Willey	12	2	54	1	4th	151	118
Mullally	12	0	55	2	5th	151	157
					6th	188	185
HAMPSHIRE	O	M	R	W	7th	213	195
Marshall	12	2	32	0	8th		225
Bakker	12	0	51	1	9th		
Connor	12	1	49	0	10th		
Ayling	12	3	34	2			
Maru	12	1	46	3			

Man of the match: P.Willey

NORTHANTS vs. STAFFORDSHIRE

at Northampton on 27th June 1990
Toss : Staffs. Umpires : D.Fawkner-Corbett and N.T.Plews
Northants won by 216 runs

NORTHANTS

A.Fordham	c Cartledge b Blank	130
N.A.Felton	c Humphries b Blank	70
R.J.Bailey	not out	72
A.J.Lamb *	not out	68
D.J.Capel		
R.G.Williams		
D.Ripley +		
J.G.Thomas		
C.E.L.Ambrose		
N.G.B.Cook		
M.A.Robinson		
Extras	(lb 14,w 6)	20
TOTAL	(60 overs)(for 2 wkts)	360

STAFFORDSHIRE

S.J.Dean	c Williams b Ambrose	8
D.Cartledge	run out	19
J.P.Addison	c Thomas b Robinson	10
P.R.Oliver	lbw b Thomas	28
N.J.Archer *	b Williams	26
A.J.Dutton	c Lamb b Cook	32
M.Humphries +	not out	5
J.P.Taylor	c Capel b Bailey	5
D.C.Blank	not out	1
R.J.Dyer		
R.Grant		
Extras	(lb 1,w 6,nb 3)	10
TOTAL	(60 overs)(for 7 wkts)	144

STAFFS	O	M	R	W		FALL OF WICKETS	
						NOR	STA
Taylor	12	0	92	0	1st	166	29
Grant	12	2	56	0	2nd	242	30
Blank	12	0	74	2	3rd		66
Dyer	8	0	49	0	4th		73
Dutton	12	1	52	0	5th		133
Cartledge	4	0	23	0	6th		133
					7th		142
NORTHANTS	O	M	R	W	8th		
Ambrose	10	2	15	1	9th		
Thomas	10	2	21	1	10th		
Cook N.G.B.	12	4	31	1			
Robinson	12	1	39	1			
Williams	12	3	32	1			
Fordham	2	1	3	0			
Bailey	2	1	2	1			

Man of the match: A.Fordham

WILTSHIRE vs. SURREY

at Trowbridge on 27th June 1990
Toss : Surrey. Umpires : K.J.Lyons and R.C.Tolchard
Surrey won by 9 wickets

WILTSHIRE

B.H.White *	c Lynch b Waqar Younis	0
P.A.C.Bail	run out	66
D.R.Turner	c Ward b Bullen	18
K.N.Foyle	b Waqar Younis	16
S.Williams	b Murphy	11
D.P.Simpkins	c Thorpe b Bicknell	18
J.Thompson	run out	7
N.Shardlow	b Waqar Younis	6
A.Mildenhall	run out	3
S.J.Malone	not out	5
M.Holland	not out	0
Extras	(b 3,lb 9,w 4)	16
TOTAL	(60 overs)(for 9 wkts)	166

SURREY

G.S.Clinton	c Shardlow b Mildenhall	50
C.K.Bullen	not out	93
G.P.Thorpe	not out	15
A.J.Stewart		
D.M.Ward +		
M.A.Lynch		
I.A.Greig *		
K.T.Medlycott		
M.P.Bicknell		
Waqar Younis		
A.J.Murphy		
Extras	(lb 5,w 6,nb 1)	12
TOTAL	(36.1 overs)(for 1 wkt)	170

SURREY	O	M	R	W		FALL OF WICKETS	
						WIL	SUR
Waqar Younis	12	3	23	3	1st	0	111
Bicknell	12	3	16	1	2nd	55	
Murphy	12	1	46	1	3rd	102	
Bullen	12	1	41	1	4th	116	
Medlycott	12	1	27	0	5th	131	
					6th	148	
WILTSHIRE	O	M	R	W	7th	158	
Malone	9.1	0	54	0	8th	159	
Thompson	8	0	42	0	9th	161	
Simpkins	6	2	29	0	10th		
Mildenhall	8	2	32	1			
Holland	5	2	10	0			

Man of the match: C.K.Bullen

GLAMORGAN vs. DORSET

at Swansea on 27th, 28th June 1990
Toss : Dorset. Umpires : D.J.Dennis and A.A.Jones
Glamorgan won by 34 runs

GLAMORGAN

A.R.Butcher *	st Fitzgerald b Stone	41
H.Morris	c Calway b Merriman	116
M.P.Maynard	st Fitzgerald b Stone	8
I.V.A.Richards	c Hall b Merriman	118
P.A.Cottey	not out	2
A.Dale	not out	4
N.G.Cowley		
C.P.Metson +		
S.J.Dennis		
S.L.Watkin		
M.Frost		
Extras	(lb 2,w 4)	6
TOTAL	(60 overs)(for 4 wkts)	295

DORSET

R.P.Merriman	c Cottey b Frost	25
G.D.Reynolds	c Dennis b Watkin	60
J.Graham-Brown	c Metson b Richards	58
G.S.Calway	c Butcher b Frost	32
P.V.Lewis	b Watkin	0
C.Stone	b Richards	25
J.R.Hall	c Metson b Frost	12
N.R.Taylor	run out	7
A.Wingfield Digby *	not out	23
S.M.Fitzgerald +	not out	2
J.H.Shackleton		
Extras	(b 2,lb 11,w 4)	17
TOTAL	(60 overs)(for 8 wkts)	261

DORSET	O	M	R	W		FALL OF WICKETS	
						GLA	DOR
Taylor	10	0	55	0	1st	76	35
Shackleton	12	1	44	0	2nd	90	127
Hall	6	2	26	0	3rd	266	165
Stone	12	2	44	2	4th	288	166
Wingfield Digby	12	0	60	0	5th		211
Calway	4	0	29	0	6th		215
Merriman	3	0	32	2	7th		225
Graham-Brown	1	0	3	0	8th		252
					9th		
GLAMORGAN	O	M	R	W	10th		
Frost	12	3	50	3			
Watkin	12	0	56	2			
Cowley	12	2	31	0			
Dennis	6	0	28	0			
Dale	6	1	28	0			
Richards	12	0	55	2			

Man of the match: I.V.A.Richards

YORKSHIRE vs. NORFOLK

at Headingley on 27th June 1990
Toss : Yorkshire. Umpires : B.J.Meyer and T.G.Wilson
Yorkshire won by 10 wickets

NORFOLK

S.G.Plumb *	c Byas b Hartley	20
F.L.Q.Handley	c Sharp b Hartley	0
D.M.Stamp	lbw b Moxon	18
R.J.Finney	c Blakey b Moxon	25
S.B.Dixon	c Sharp b Gough	1
D.R.Thomas	b Carrick	5
M.S.Taylor	b Carrick	0
J.C.M.Lewis	c Blakey b Carrick	9
R.Kingshott	b Gough	9
D.E.Mattocks +	lbw b Hartley	2
M.T.Ellis	not out	0
Extras	(b 5,lb 1,w 5,nb 4)	15
TOTAL	(47.5 overs)	104

YORKSHIRE

M.D.Moxon *	not out	56
A.A.Metcalfe	not out	46
S.A.Kellett		
K.Sharp		
P.E.Robinson		
R.J.Blakey +		
D.Byas		
P.Carrick		
P.J.Hartley		
A.Sidebottom		
D.Gough		
Extras	(lb 1,w 3)	4
TOTAL	(20.2 overs)(for 0 wkts)	106

YORKSHIRE	O	M	R	W		FALL OF WICKETS	
						NFK	YOR
Hartley	8.5	1	28	3	1st	7	
Sidebottom	10	1	21	0	2nd	29	
Moxon	7	2	19	2	3rd	55	
Gough	10	2	22	2	4th	72	
Carrick	12	9	8	3	5th	81	
					6th	81	
NORFOLK	O	M	R	W	7th	81	
Lewis	8	2	37	0	8th	92	
Taylor	4	0	32	0	9th	103	
Kingshott	6	2	24	0	10th	104	
Ellis	2.2	0	12	0			

Man of the match: P.Carrick

TOUR MATCH	REFUGE ASSURANCE LEAGUE

LEAGUE CRICKET CONF. vs. INDIA

at Sunderland on 28th June 1990
Toss : India. Umpires : W.Atkinson and R.Smith
India won by 40 runs

INDIA

W.V.Raman	b Walcott	0
N.S.Sidhu	b Day	17
S.R.Tendulkar	c Wunkde b Holmes	19
D.B.Vengsarkar	c Borthwick b Day	28
M.Azharuddin *	b Wundke	20
Kapil Dev	c Tuckwell b Wundke	0
K.S.More +	b Wundke	51
Venkatapathy Raju	not out	37
S.K.Sharma	c Lambert b Walcott	6
A.Wasson	c Ingham b McLeod	10
A.Kumble	not out	2
Extras	(b 7,lb 9,w 19,nb 6)	41
TOTAL	(55 overs)(for 9 wkts)	231

LEAGUE CRICKET CONFERENCE

C.B.Lambert	c Kapil Dev b Sharma	22
D.Lampitt	c Vengsarkar b Sharma	15
D.Tuckwell	c Vengsarkar b Wasson	17
N.Heaton *	st More b Kumble	41
M.Ingham	lbw b Sharma	26
S.Wundke	c More b Kumble	3
K.I.McLeod	not out	46
D.Borthwick +	lbw b Kapil Dev	1
V.de C.Walcott	b Kapil Dev	0
A.Day	c More b Sharma	1
B.Holmes	not out	0
Extras	(b 10,w 3,nb 6)	19
TOTAL	(55 overs)(for 9 wkts)	191

LEAGUE	O	M	R	W	FALL OF WICKETS		
						IND	LCC
McLeod	11	1	44	1			
Walcott	11	2	37	2	1st	1	41
Holmes	11	3	22	1	2nd	51	48
Day	11	1	71	2	3rd	51	82
Wundke	11	0	41	3	4th	87	119
					5th	106	127
INDIA	O	M	R	W	6th	128	189
Kapil Dev	10	3	29	2	7th	195	190
Sharma	10	2	25	4	8th	216	190
Wasson	7	0	39	1	9th	227	191
Tendulkar	6	1	16	0	10th		
Kumble	11	4	32	2			
Venkatapathy	11	0	40	0			

Man of the match: K.S.More

MIDDLESEX vs. WORCESTERSHIRE

at Lord's on 1st July 1990
Toss : Worcs. Umpires : R.Palmer and D.R.Shepherd
Middlesex won by 99 runs (Middlesex 4 pts Worcs 0 pts)

MIDDLESEX

D.L.Haynes	c Neale b Lampitt	11
M.A.Roseberry	lbw b Botham	73
M.W.Gatting *	b Lampitt	9
M.R.Ramprakash	not out	147
K.R.Brown	c & b Lampitt	14
R.O.Butcher	c & b Lampitt	1
P.Farbrace +	b Lampitt	3
J.E.Emburey	not out	8
N.F.Williams		
A.R.C.Fraser		
N.G.Cowans		
Extras	(lb 19,w 5)	24
TOTAL	(40 overs)(for 6 wkts)	290

WORCESTERSHIRE

T.S.Curtis	c Farbrace b Gatting	16
M.J.Weston	c Williams b Gatting	7
G.A.Hick	c Haynes b Cowans	45
I.T.Botham	c Williams b Emburey	35
D.B.D'Oliveira	c Williams b Cowans	2
P.A.Neale *	c Williams b Emburey	13
D.A.Leatherdale	b Emburey	0
S.J.Rhodes +	st Farbrace b Emburey	16
R.K.Illingworth	not out	16
S.R.Lampitt	not out	25
S.M.McEwan		
Extras	(lb 14,w 1,nb 1)	16
TOTAL	(40 overs)(for 8 wkts)	191

WORCS	O	M	R	W	FALL OF WICKETS		
						MID	WOR
Botham	8	0	42	1	1st	43	28
Weston	4	0	30	0	2nd	64	33
Illingworth	8	1	28	0	3rd	196	86
Lampitt	8	1	67	5	4th	230	98
McEwan	3	0	33	0	5th	232	125
Hick	3	0	31	0	6th	238	126
Leatherdale	6	0	40	0	7th		137
					8th		152
MIDDLESEX	O	M	R	W	9th		
Fraser	5	1	15	0	10th		
Williams	4	0	17	0			
Haynes	4	0	21	0			
Gatting	8	0	29	2			
Emburey	8	1	39	4			
Cowans	8	0	43	2			
Ramprakash	2	0	9	0			
Brown	1	0	4	0			

KENT vs. LANCASHIRE

at Maidstone on 1st July 1990
Toss : Kent. Umpires : J.C.Balderstone and B.Dudleston
Lancashire won by 77 runs (Kent 0 pts Lancashire 4 pts)

LANCASHIRE

G.Fowler	c Wells b Cowdrey C.S.	59
M.A.Atherton	c Marsh b Fleming	13
G.D.Lloyd	not out	100
N.H.Fairbrother	c Ealham b De Villiers	45
M.Watkinson	not out	33
Wasim Akram		
P.A.J.DeFreitas		
W.K.Hegg +		
I.D.Austin		
D.P.Hughes *		
P.J.W.Allott		
Extras	(lb 3,w 6)	9
TOTAL	(40 overs)(for 3 wkts)	259

KENT

S.G.Hinks	b Allott	17
M.A.Ealham	lbw b Allott	3
V.J.Wells	c Fowler b DeFreitas	13
C.S.Cowdrey *	b Watkinson	33
G.R.Cowdrey	c Hegg b Allott	0
M.V.Fleming	c Fairbrother b Wasim Akram	8
S.A.Marsh +	c Hughes b Watkinson	38
R.M.Ellison	b Wasim Akram	43
P.S.De Villiers	c Watkinson b DeFreitas	1
R.P.Davis	b Austin	14
A.P.Igglesden	not out	0
Extras	(b 2,lb 9,w 1)	12
TOTAL	(37.1 overs)	182

KENT	O	M	R	W	FALL OF WICKETS		
						LAN	KEN
Igglesden	8	0	39	0	1st	33	11
De Villiers	8	0	53	1	2nd	112	34
Ellison	4	0	24	0	3rd	201	36
Fleming	8	0	51	1	4th		38
Ealham	3	0	21	0	5th		69
Davis	5	0	33	0	6th		90
Cowdrey C.S.	4	0	35	1	7th		148
					8th		151
LANCASHIRE	O	M	R	W	9th		182
Allott	7	1	28	3	10th		182
DeFreitas	8	0	48	2			
Watkinson	8	0	37	2			
Wasim Akram	7.1	0	31	2			
Austin	7	0	27	1			

LEADING FIRST-CLASS AVERAGES
at 29th June 1990

BATTING AVERAGES Qualifying requirements : 6 completed innings

Name	M	I	NO	Runs	HS	Avge	100s	50s
N.H.Fairbrother	9	12	4	865	366	108.12	2	4
D.M.Ward	9	11	4	754	181	107.71	3	1
M.E.Waugh	8	12	3	885	204	98.33	4	2
R.J.Harden	12	11	3	702	104	87.75	1	7
B.R.Hardie	9	13	6	609	125	87.00	2	4
G.A.Gooch	7	11	1	868	215	86.80	4	2
C.J.Tavare	12	12	3	757	156	84.11	2	5
S.J.Cook	12	19	5	1177	313 *	84.07	3	4
A.J.Lamb	6	8	2	483	235	80.50	1	1
D.L.Haynes	10	18	3	1184	220 *	78.93	4	4
M.A.Crawley	9	11	3	617	105 *	77.12	2	4
M.D.Marshall	8	9	2	539	117	77.00	2	3
C.L.Smith	11	17	4	994	148	76.46	2	7
P.W.G.Parker	6	9	2	533	107	76.14	2	3
R.A.Smith	8	11	2	679	181	75.44	3	3
A.N.Hayhurst	10	15	6	671	170	74.55	2	3
M.P.Maynard	9	15	5	700	125 *	70.00	1	6
D.A.Reeve	12	18	7	769	202 *	69.90	2	1
M.A.Atherton	10	14	2	830	191	69.16	3	5
P.J.Prichard	9	13	2	748	245	68.00	3	1

BOWLING AVERAGES Qualifying requirements : 10 wickets taken

Name	O	M	R	W	Avge	Best	5wI	10wM
I.R.Bishop	119.2	25	331	17	19.47	4-25	-	-
W.K.M.Benjamin	78.1	28	202	10	20.20	5-73	1	-
C.White	71	13	205	10	20.50	5-74	1	-
O.H.Mortensen	108.5	32	253	12	21.08	4-67	-	-
D.A.Reeve	107.4	43	215	10	21.50	3-26	-	-
J.E.Benjamin	236.3	48	646	28	23.07	5-29	3	-
T.A.Merrick	130	31	326	14	23.28	4-66	-	-
D.E.Malcolm	207.4	43	608	26	23.38	5-94	1	-
I.T.Botham	110.3	22	317	13	24.38	4-65	-	-
P.J.Hartley	202.3	38	662	27	24.51	6-57	1	-
K.J.Barnett	161.5	28	446	18	24.77	4-28	-	-
A.L.Penberthy	86.5	16	326	13	25.07	4-91	-	-
D.J.Capel	168	40	506	20	25.30	5-74	1	-
C.E.L.Ambrose	225	59	635	25	25.40	5-49	2	-
T.A.Munton	354.4	90	906	35	25.88	5-33	1	-
M.C.Snedden	187.5	47	495	19	26.05	5-63	1	-
Waqar Younis	95	16	264	10	26.40	4-77	-	-
M.D.Marshall	224.4	54	583	22	26.50	3-44	-	-
J.E.Emburey	364.3	114	753	28	26.89	5-61	1	-
P.J.Bakker	98	27	296	11	26.90	4-51	-	-

HEADLINES

28th June

● The Indians started their tour with a 40-run victory in a one-day match against the League Cricket Conference at Sunderland, Kiran More reviving their innings after an uncertain start

1st July

● Middlesex increased their lead in the Refuge Assurance League with an overwhelming victory over Worcestershire at Lord's. Mark Ramprakash hammered a career best 147*, the highest score in the Sunday League by a Middlesex batsman, as they reached 290 for 6, the season's highest total

● Lancashire, perhaps Middlesex's main rivals, were convincing winners over early pace-setters, Kent, as Graham Lloyd made his first Sunday 100 on his 21st birthday.

REFUGE ASSURANCE LEAGUE

NOTTINGHAMSHIRE vs. LEICS
at Trent Bridge on 1st July 1990
Toss : Notts.   Umpires : R.Julian and D.S.Thompsett
Nottinghamshire won by 8 wickets (Notts 4 pts Leics 0 pts)

LEICESTERSHIRE

T.J.Boon	c French b Evans	13
N.E.Briers *	c & b Saxelby K.	33
J.J.Whitaker	c Cooper b Evans	4
P.Willey	b Evans	41
C.C.Lewis	c & b Stephenson	36
J.D.R.Benson	b Stephenson	2
G.J.Parsons	not out	11
P.A.Nixon +	b Evans	6
J.P.Agnew	c Saxelby M. b Stephenson	1
A.D.Mullally	run out	4
L.B.Taylor		
Extras	(lb 3,w 1)	4
TOTAL	(38 overs)(for 9 wkts)	155

NOTTINGHAMSHIRE

B.C.Broad	c Whitaker b Mullally	57
M.Newell	not out	60
P.Johnson	c Nixon b Taylor	35
R.T.Robinson *	not out	0
M.Saxelby		
F.D.Stephenson		
B.N.French +		
K.P.Evans		
E.E.Hemmings		
K.E.Cooper		
K.Saxelby		
Extras	(lb 4,w 1)	5
TOTAL	(31.4 overs)(for 2 wkts)	157

NOTTS	O	M	R	W	FALL OF WICKETS		
						LEI	NOT
Stephenson	8	1	21	3	1st	28	104
Cooper	8	2	21	0	2nd	38	144
Evans	8	0	30	4	3rd	72	
Hemmings	7	0	33	0	4th	127	
Saxelby K.	5	0	27	1	5th	131	
Saxelby M.	2	0	20	0	6th	136	
					7th	145	
LEICS	O	M	R	W	8th	148	
Agnew	5	0	25	0	9th	155	
Mullally	6.4	1	25	1	10th		
Lewis	5	1	27	0			
Taylor	7	0	35	1			
Willey	2	0	17	0			
Parsons	6	1	24	0			

SOMERSET vs. NORTHANTS
at Taunton on 1st July 1990
Toss : Somerset.   Umpires : K.J.Lyons and D.O.Oslear
Somerset won by 7 wickets (Som 4 pts Northants 0 pts)

NORTHANTS

A.Fordham	b Lefebvre	53
N.A.Felton	b Swallow	41
R.J.Bailey	run out	6
A.J.Lamb *	c Lefebvre b Hayhurst	41
D.J.Capel	c & b Mallender	11
R.G.Williams	c Burns b Lefebvre	1
J.G.Thomas	not out	19
D.Ripley +	c Burns b Rose	3
W.W.Davis	b Lefebvre	3
S.J.Brown	c Burns b Rose	0
N.G.B.Cook	c Burns b Lefebvre	5
Extras	(lb 6,w 4)	10
TOTAL	(40 overs)	193

SOMERSET

S.J.Cook	run out	88
N.J.Pringle	c Ripley b Thomas	1
C.J.Tavare *	c Felton b Williams	56
R.J.Harden	not out	22
G.D.Rose	not out	22
A.N.Hayhurst		
N.D.Burns +		
I.G.Swallow		
R.P.Lefebvre		
N.A.Mallender		
J.C.Hallett		
Extras	(lb 3,w 2)	5
TOTAL	(37.4 overs)(for 3 wkts)	194

SOMERSET	O	M	R	W	FALL OF WICKETS		
						NOR	SOM
Mallender	8	1	24	1	1st	75	10
Hallett	3	0	27	0	2nd	89	124
Lefebvre	8	0	35	4	3rd	118	161
Rose	6	0	40	2	4th	154	
Swallow	8	1	19	1	5th	158	
Hayhurst	7	1	42	1	6th	163	
					7th	170	
NORTHANTS	O	M	R	W	8th	178	
Davis	6.4	0	25	0	9th	183	
Thomas	7	0	38	1	10th	193	
Cook	8	0	42	0			
Brown	8	0	55	0			
Williams	8	0	31	1			

HEADLINES

1st July

• Derbyshire kept in touch with the league leaders with a six-wicket win over Gloucestershire at Derby in a 27-over match

• Sussex managed 244 for 5 in 33 overs against Hampshire at Hove, as Neil Lenham hit his best Sunday score in an opening stand of 135 with Ian Gould.

• Chris Broad and Mike Newell opened with 104 as Nottinghamshire beat Leicestershire by eight wickets at Trent Bridge

• Roland Lefebvre produced his best Sunday figures in Somerset's win over Northamptonshire at Taunton, while Viv Richards saw Glamorgan home against Surrey in a 10-over match at Cardiff

GLAMORGAN vs. SURREY
at Cardiff on 1st July 1990
Toss : Glam.   Umpires : R.A.White and A.G.T.Whitehead
Glamorgan won by 8 wickets (Glam 4 pts Surrey 0 pts)

SURREY

D.M.Ward +	c Butcher b Watkin	5
M.A.Feltham	c & b Watkin	12
M.A.Lynch	c Cottey b Frost	38
I.A.Greig *	c Richards b Dennis	23
G.P.Thorpe	not out	11
D.J.Bicknell	c Richards b Frost	6
G.S.Clinton		
C.K.Bullen		
Waqar Younis		
M.P.Bicknell		
A.J.Murphy		
Extras	(lb 2,w 1)	3
TOTAL	(10 overs)(for 5 wkts)	98

GLAMORGAN

M.P.Maynard	b Bullen	11
H.Morris	b Waqar Younis	48
I.V.A.Richards	not out	34
A.R.Butcher *	not out	0
P.A.Cottey		
A.Dale		
J.Derrick		
C.P.Metson +		
S.J.Dennis		
S.L.Watkin		
M.Frost		
Extras	(b 2,lb 2,w 2)	6
TOTAL	(9.5 overs)(for 2 wkts)	99

GLAMORGAN	O	M	R	W	FALL OF WICKETS		
						SUR	GLA
Derrick	1	0	12	0	1st	18	29
Dennis	2	0	14	1	2nd	21	94
Watkin	2	0	18	2	3rd	73	
Dale	2	0	16	0	4th	86	
Richards	1	0	14	0	5th	98	
Frost	2	0	22	2	6th		
					7th		
SURREY	O	M	R	W	8th		
Murphy	2	0	9	0	9th		
Bicknell M.P.	2	0	16	0	10th		
Feltham	2	0	25	0			
Bullen	2	0	28	1			
Waqar Younis	1.5	0	17	1			

SUSSEX vs. HAMPSHIRE
at Hove on 1st July 1990
Toss : Hampshire.   Umpires : J.H.Harris and A.A.Jones
Sussex won on faster scoring rate (Sussex 4 pts Hants 0 pts)

SUSSEX

N.J.Lenham	c Connor b Maru	72
I.J.Gould	c Smith R.A. b Nicholas	68
P.W.G.Parker *	c Nicholas b Bakker	12
A.P.Wells	not out	44
M.P.Speight	c Smith R.A. b Ayling	21
C.M.Wells	b Marshall	1
A.I.C.Dodemaide	not out	1
A.C.S.Pigott		
P.Moores +		
C.C.Remy		
A.R.Clarke		
Extras	(b 1,lb 13,w 9,nb 2)	25
TOTAL	(33 overs)(for 5 wkts)	244

HAMPSHIRE

V.P.Terry	c Lenham b Wells C.M.	25
M.D.Marshall	c Lenham b Wells C.M.	19
R.A.Smith	b Dodemaide	24
D.I.Gower	c Speight b Pigott	10
C.L.Smith	c Moores b Pigott	3
M.C.J.Nicholas *	b Dodemaide	27
J.R.Ayling	not out	17
R.J.Parks +	c Wells C.M. b Pigott	4
R.J.Maru	c Clarke b Dodemaide	2
C.A.Connor	c Lenham b Pigott	4
P.J.Bakker	st Moores b Clarke	9
Extras	(lb 3,w 4)	7
TOTAL	(27.3 overs)	151

HAMPSHIRE	O	M	R	W	FALL OF WICKETS		
						SUS	HAM
Marshall	7	0	50	1	1st	135	37
Bakker	7	0	48	1	2nd	172	53
Connor	5	0	18	0	3rd	176	79
Ayling	7	0	52	1	4th	217	82
Maru	5	0	39	1	5th	228	88
Nicholas	2	0	23	1	6th		114
					7th		119
SUSSEX	O	M	R	W	8th		123
Wells C.M.	7	0	30	2	9th		133
Dodemaide	8	0	50	3	10th		151
Clarke	5.3	0	26	1			
Pigott	7	0	42	4			

DERBYSHIRE vs. GLOUCESTERSHIRE
at Derby on 1st July 1990
Toss : Derbyshire.   Umpires : J.W.Holder and B.Leadbeater
Derbyshire won by 6 wickets (Derbys 4 pts Gloucs 0 pts)

GLOUCESTERSHIRE

R.C.Russell +	c Roberts b Mortensen	5
C.W.J.Athey	c Bowler b Mortensen	17
A.J.Wright *	c Goldsmith b Mortensen	17
P.Bainbridge	run out	21
K.M.Curran	run out	4
P.W.Romaines	run out	2
J.W.Lloyds	c & b Kuiper	21
M.W.Alleyne	lbw b Base	7
G.D.Hodgson	not out	5
C.A.Walsh	not out	15
D.V.Lawrence		
Extras	(b 5,lb 10,w 4)	19
TOTAL	(27 overs)(for 8 wkts)	133

DERBYSHIRE

K.J.Barnett *	c Hodgson b Lloyds	57
P.D.Bowler +	c Lawrence b Curran	5
J.E.Morris	run out	57
A.P.Kuiper	c Hodgson b Lloyds	0
B.Roberts	not out	5
C.J.Adams	not out	2
S.C.Goldsmith		
G.Miller		
D.E.Malcolm		
S.J.Base		
O.H.Mortensen		
Extras	(b 1,lb 4,w 3)	8
TOTAL	(26.3 overs)(for 4 wkts)	134

DERBYSHIRE	O	M	R	W	FALL OF WICKETS		
						GLO	DER
Malcolm	5	0	16	0	1st	12	18
Mortensen	6	0	16	3	2nd	42	125
Miller	5	0	26	0	3rd	48	125
Base	6	0	25	1	4th	55	126
Kuiper	5	1	35	1	5th	59	
					6th	89	
GLOUCS	O	M	R	W	7th	105	
Walsh	6	0	19	0	8th	106	
Lawrence	2	0	18	0	9th		
Curran	6	0	20	1	10th		
Bainbridge	5	0	27	0			
Alleyne	5	0	32	0			
Lloyds	2.3	0	13	2			

TOUR MATCHES

COMBINED UNIV vs. NEW ZEALAND

at Fenner's on 27th, 28th, 29th June 1990
Toss : Combined Univ. Umpires : G.I.Burgess and R.Palmer
Combined Univ won by 2 wickets

NEW ZEALAND

Batsman	1st innings		2nd innings	
J.J.Crowe	c Crawley b Gerrans	132	c Turner G.J. b Crawley	64
T.J.Franklin	c Kilborn b Gerrans	19		
M.J.Greatbatch	c van der Merwe b Crawley	62	(3) c & b Buzza	38
K.R.Rutherford	c van der Merwe b Buzza	21	(6) c Gerrans b Buzza	31
M.W.Priest	not out	55	(2) b Gerrans	20
S.A.Thomson	not out	1	(4) c Turner R.J. b Buzza	15
A.C.Parore +			(5) c Turner R.J. b Buzza	38
J.G.Bracewell			(7) not out	17
W.Watson			(8) c Atkinson b Crawley	6
C.Pringle				
I.D.S.Smith *				
Extras	(lb 8,w 1,nb 2)	11	(b 4,lb 2,nb 3)	9
TOTAL	(for 4 wkts dec)	301	(for 7 wkts dec)	238

COMBINED UNIV

Batsman	1st innings		2nd innings	
S.P.James	c Thomson b Bracewell	67	not out	131
P.S.Gerrans	c Parore b Pringle	0	(8) b Bracewell	7
M.J.Kilborn	c Parore b Watson	27	run out	3
M.A.Crawley	c Smith b Bracewell	47	(5) lbw b Bracewell	5
R.E.Morris *	c Thomson b Bracewell	75	(2) c Greatbatch b Bracewell	53
J.C.M.Atkinson	c Bracewell b Priest	10	b Bracewell	4
G.J.Turner	c Crowe J.J. b Priest	14	(4) c Crowe J.J. b Bracewell	26
W.M.van der Merwe	b Priest	24	(7) c Parore b Bracewell	14
R.J.Turner +	b Bracewell	5	b Bracewell	10
R.A.Pyman	c Thomson b Bracewell	4	not out	0
A.J.Buzza	not out	0		
Extras	(lb 4)	4	(b 2,lb 8,nb 3)	13
TOTAL		277	(for 8 wkts)	266

COMBINED U	O	M	R	W	O	M	R	W
van der Merwe	11	3	28	0	8	1	30	0
Gerrans	18	6	59	2	9	3	18	1
Pyman	17	3	56	0	6	2	12	0
Turner G.J.	21	3	76	0	14	0	63	0
Buzza	13	5	44	1	17	0	87	4
Crawley	14	5	30	1	6.3	0	22	2

NEW ZEALAND	O	M	R	W	O	M	R	W
Pringle	10	2	28	1	6	2	16	0
Watson	13	3	26	1	7	1	27	0
Priest	36	16	93	3	25.2	7	79	0
Bracewell	38.3	10	107	5	33	6	120	7
Thomson	6	0	19	0	5	1	14	0

FALL OF WICKETS

	NZ	COM	NZ	COM
1st	33	5	47	93
2nd	130	74	124	106
3rd	199	121	145	164
4th	297	154	146	178
5th		177	205	184
6th		199	224	220
7th		237	238	230
8th		264		262
9th		276		
10th		277		

ESSEX vs. NEW ZEALAND

at Chelmsford on 30th June, 1st, 2nd July 1990
Toss : New Zealand. Umpires : P.J.Eele and K.E.Palmer
Match drawn

NEW ZEALAND

Batsman	1st innings		2nd innings	
T.J.Franklin	c Gooch b Topley	74		
J.G.Wright *	lbw b Childs	121		
A.H.Jones	c Garnham b Topley	3	not out	66
M.D.Crowe	not out	123		
K.R.Rutherford	st Garnham b Stephenson	42	(4) not out	40
J.J.Crowe	not out	9	(1) c Hussain b Topley	15
A.C.Parore +			(2) lbw b Pringle	4
M.W.Priest				
S.A.Thomson				
C.Pringle				
D.K.Morrison				
Extras	(b 2,lb 3,w 1,nb 10)	16	(lb 2,w 2,nb 12)	16
TOTAL	(for 4 wkts dec)	388	(for 2 wkts)	141

ESSEX

G.A.Gooch *	retired hurt	102
J.P.Stephenson	c Thomson b Priest	147
P.J.Prichard	c Crowe M.D. b Priest	15
N.Hussain	c Crowe M.D. b Jones	1
M.E.Waugh	c Priest b Pringle	63
D.R.Pringle	c Thomson b Priest	67
M.A.Garnham +	lbw b Pringle	0
T.D.Topley	not out	23
K.O.Thomas	c Priest b Thomson	2
S.J.W.Andrew	b Thomson	0
J.H.Childs		
Extras	(lb 25,w 1,nb 3)	29
TOTAL	(for 8 wkts dec)	449

ESSEX	O	M	R	W	O	M	R	W
Andrew	14	3	45	0	8	1	16	0
Pringle	9	4	25	0	6	0	15	1
Thomas	16	3	76	0	2.2	0	5	0
Topley	12	2	57	2	10	0	45	1
Childs	23	6	76	1	5.4	0	22	0
Hussain	7	1	28	0	1	0	5	0
Waugh	5	0	24	0	3	0	16	0
Stephenson	8	0	52	1	5	1	15	0

NEW ZEALAND	O	M	R	W	O	M	R	W
Morrison	19	2	57	0				
Pringle	42	15	103	2				
Thomson	25.4	6	84	2				
Priest	38	7	155	3				
Jones	2	1	1	1				
Rutherford	4	0	24	0				

FALL OF WICKETS

	NZ	ESS	NZ	ESS
1st	169	209	9	
2nd	180	218	53	
3rd	205	315		
4th	322	404		
5th		408		
6th		438		
7th		449		
8th		449		
9th				
10th				

YORKSHIRE vs. INDIA

at Headingley on 30th June, 1st, 2nd July 1990
Toss : India. Umpires : H.D.Bird and J.H.Hampshire
Match drawn

INDIA

Batsman	1st innings		2nd innings	
W.V.Raman	c Byas b Fletcher	12	b Houseman	0
N.S.Sidhu	c Blakey b Fletcher	61	c Blakey b Houseman	3
S.V.Manjrekar	not out	158		
D.B.Vengsarkar	not out	47		
R.J.Shastri			(3) not out	53
M.Azharuddin *			(4) not out	75
Kapil Dev				
K.S.More +				
M.Prabhakar				
A.Wasson				
N.D.Hirwani				
Extras	(lb 3,nb 13)	16	(lb 2,nb 3)	5
TOTAL	(for 2 wkts dec)	294	(for 2 wkts)	136

YORKSHIRE

Batsman	1st innings		2nd innings	
M.D.Moxon *	not out	45	c Kapil Dev b Hirwani	93
A.A.Metcalfe	not out	40	b Shastri	74
K.Sharp			c Shastri b Hirwani	2
S.A.Kellett			not out	36
R.J.Blakey +			b Kapil Dev	2
D.Byas			not out	8
M.Doidge				
C.White				
A.Sidebottom				
I.J.Houseman				
S.D.Fletcher				
Extras	(lb 1,nb 2)	3	(b 1,lb 8,w 1)	10
TOTAL	(for 0 wkts dec)	88	(for 4 wkts)	225

YORKSHIRE	O	M	R	W	O	M	R	W
Houseman	13	2	43	0	7	1	26	2
Sidebottom	12.5	1	46	0	4	1	23	0
Fletcher	18	2	82	2	6	0	17	0
Byas	5	0	29	0	3	0	16	0
White	7	2	37	0				
Doidge	14	2	54	0	10	3	52	0

INDIA	O	M	R	W	O	M	R	W
Kapil Dev	8	2	13	0	10	3	37	1
Prabhakar	8	1	38	0	8	0	48	0
Wasson	5	0	31	0	6	2	24	0
Shastri	3	2	5	0	16	2	54	1
Hirwani					13	1	45	2
Raman					3	1	8	0

FALL OF WICKETS

	IND	YOR	IND	YOR
1st	25	0		152
2nd	135	12		161
3rd				192
4th				208

HEADLINES

27th - 29th June

● New Zealand suffered their first first-class defeat of their tour at Fenner's when the combined forces of Oxford and Cambridge Universities gained a two-wicket victory to confirm the improving standards of Varsity cricket. Steve James followed his first innings 67 with an unbeaten 131 to guide the students to victory despite the efforts of John Bracewell who recorded match figures of 12 for 227, the best of the season so far

30th June - 2nd July

● New Zealand ensured they retained their unbeaten record against the counties with a draw against Essex at Chelmsford. John Wright and Martin Crowe hit centuries for the tourists, Graham Gooch and John Stephenson responded for Essex

● India's batsmen made an impressive start in the first first-class fixture of their tour against Yorkshire at Headingley, Sanjay Manjrekar contributing 158* in his first innings in England, but their bowlers struggled to break through, Martyn Moxon and Ashley Metcalfe adding a total of 240 before being separated

● First-class debut: M.Doidge (Yorkshire)

BRITANNIC ASSURANCE CHAMPIONSHIP

SOMERSET vs. NORTHANTS

at Taunton on 30th June, 2nd, 3rd July 1990
Toss : Somerset.   Umpires : K.J.Lyons and D.O.Oslear
Northants won by 7 wickets (Somerset 5 pts (Bt: 4, Bw: 1) Northants 21 pts (Bt: 4, Bw: 1))

SOMERSET

S.J.Cook	c Fordham b Williams	65	retired hurt		112
P.M.Roebuck	c Ripley b Thomas	60	lbw b Davis		44
A.N.Hayhurst	c Davis b Cook	81	(7) not out		28
C.J.Tavare *	c Felton b Williams	39			
R.J.Harden	b Williams	23	(3) b Robinson		28
G.D.Rose	not out	33	(4) c sub b Robinson		8
N.D.Burns +	b Thomas	0	(6) c Bailey b Cook		7
R.P.Lefebvre	not out	0	(5) c Bailey b Cook		53
I.G.Swallow			(8) run out		9
N.A.Mallender					
A.N.Jones					
Extras	(lb 8,w 1,nb 14)	23	(lb 3,nb 13)		16
TOTAL	(for 6 wkts dec)	324	(for 6 wkts dec)		305

NORTHANTS

A.Fordham	c Tavare b Mallender	6	c Burns b Rose		128
N.A.Felton	c Rose b Jones	101	c Rose b Lefebvre		7
J.G.Thomas	c Roebuck b Rose	48			
R.J.Bailey	not out	80	(3) b Jones		101
A.J.Lamb *	c Mallender b Swallow	40	(4) not out		64
D.J.Capel	not out	13	(5) not out		21
R.G.Williams					
D.Ripley +					
W.W.Davis					
N.G.B.Cook					
M.A.Robinson					
Extras	(b 1,lb 5,w 1,nb 6)	13	(b 5,lb 3,nb 3)		11
TOTAL	(for 4 wkts dec)	301	(for 3 wkts)		332

NORTHANTS	O	M	R	W	O	M	R	W
Davis	18	1	45	0	14	2	72	1
Thomas	20	5	76	2				
Cook	25	8	69	1	20	3	63	2
Robinson	18	1	62	0	15	1	76	2
Williams	22	6	64	3	21	5	54	0
Bailey					4	0	37	0

SOMERSET	O	M	R	W	O	M	R	W
Jones	14	0	48	1	12	2	63	1
Mallender	14	1	70	1	12	2	33	0
Lefebvre	14	4	49	0	10	2	41	1
Rose	7	1	15	1	13	0	77	1
Swallow	21	5	84	1	13.3	0	76	0
Roebuck	6	2	17	0	4	0	21	0
Hayhurst	5	0	12	0	1	0	13	0

FALL OF WICKETS

	SOM	NOR	SOM	NOR
1st	128	13	126	26
2nd	134	92	196	211
3rd	254	215	211	287
4th	278	263	254	
5th	309		279	
6th	317		305	
7th				
8th				
9th				
10th				

DERBYSHIRE vs. GLOUCESTERSHIRE

at Derby on 30th June, 2nd, 3rd July 1990
Toss : Derbyshire.   Umpires : J.W.Holder and B.Leadbeater
Match drawn (Derbyshire 4 pts (Bt: 0, Bw: 4) Gloucestershire 4 pts (Bt: 0, Bw: 4))

DERBYSHIRE

K.J.Barnett *	b Lawrence	7	c Curran b Walsh		107
P.D.Bowler	b Walsh	5	lbw b Walsh		23
J.E.Morris	c Athey b Walsh	9	c Athey b Lloyds		66
B.Roberts	c Barnes b Lawrence	2	b Barnes		59
C.J.Adams	b Barnes	7	lbw b Barnes		48
S.C.Goldsmith	lbw b Lawrence	5	not out		7
K.M.Krikken +	c Lloyds b Barnes	9	c Russell b Curran		1
M.Jean-Jacques	b Lawrence	7	not out		3
I.R.Bishop	b Walsh	10			
D.E.Malcolm	not out	0			
O.H.Mortensen	b Walsh	4			
Extras	(nb 7)	7	(b 3,lb 13,w 1,nb 15)		32
TOTAL		72	(for 6 wkts dec)		346

GLOUCESTERSHIRE

G.D.Hodgson	c Morris b Bishop	13	c Krikken b Bishop		52
A.J.Wright *	c Morris b Malcolm	3	c Krikken b Jean-Jacques		44
I.P.Butcher	c Krikken b Malcolm	0	(8) not out		0
C.W.J.Athey	lbw b Bishop	12	(3) b Bishop		21
P.Bainbridge	lbw b Bishop	6	(4) lbw b Barnett		40
K.M.Curran	b Bishop	24	(5) c Morris b Jean-Jacques		3
J.W.Lloyds	not out	28	(6) not out		25
R.C.Russell +	b Mortensen	2	(7) c Krikken b Barnett		15
C.A.Walsh	b Mortensen	1			
D.V.Lawrence	c Krikken b Mortensen	8			
S.N.Barnes	lbw b Mortensen	6			
Extras	(b 3,lb 5,w 3)	11	(b 1,lb 3)		4
TOTAL		114	(for 6 wkts)		204

GLOUCS	O	M	R	W	O	M	R	W
Walsh	14	2	32	4	26.4	2	86	2
Lawrence	10	1	27	4	3	0	20	0
Curran	3	1	3	0	20.2	2	75	1
Barnes	6	2	10	2	23	2	75	2
Lloyds					29	6	74	1

DERBYSHIRE	O	M	R	W	O	M	R	W
Bishop	19	4	38	4	14	1	44	2
Malcolm	18	5	46	2	17	4	49	0
Mortensen	15	7	22	4	17	2	52	0
Jean-Jacques					8	0	26	2
Barnett					11	6	19	2
Morris					1	0	10	0

FALL OF WICKETS

	DER	GLO	DER	GLO
1st	11	7	74	81
2nd	13	7	202	116
3rd	23	33	213	137
4th	26	34	328	146
5th	31	43	337	170
6th	44	71	338	198
7th	49	74		
8th	68	78		
9th	68	96		
10th	72	114		

KENT vs. LANCASHIRE

at Maidstone on 30th June, 2nd, 3rd July 1990
Toss : Kent.   Umpires : J.C.Balderstone and B.Dudleston
Lancashire won by 3 wickets (Kent 6 pts (Bt: 2, Bw: 4) Lancashire 22 pts (Bt: 2, Bw: 4))

KENT

S.G.Hinks	c Atherton b DeFreitas	29	c Fowler b Atherton		49
M.C.Dobson	run out	0	b Allott		6
V.J.Wells	lbw b Wasim Akram	9	lbw b Watkinson		11
G.R.Cowdrey	c Fowler b Allott	40	b Atherton		14
C.S.Cowdrey *	b Watkinson	6	c Hegg b DeFreitas		28
S.A.Marsh +	run out	11	(7) c & b DeFreitas		8
D.J.M.Kelleher	b Wasim Akram	0	(9) lbw b Wasim Akram		0
R.M.Ellison	c Hegg b DeFreitas	41	not out		12
P.S.De Villiers	b Allott	0	(10) lbw b Atherton		33
R.P.Davis	c Allott b Wasim Akram	59	(6) c Hegg b Wasim Akram		19
A.P.Igglesden	not out	16	c Fowler b Atherton		0
Extras	(lb 14,nb 12)	26	(b 5,lb 12,w 1,nb 3)		21
TOTAL		237			201

LANCASHIRE

G.Fowler	c & b De Villiers	3	c sub b De Villiers		13
M.A.Atherton	lbw b Kelleher	101	c Marsh b Davis		44
J.D.Fitton	c Kelleher b Igglesden	0			
T.E.Jesty	b Cowdrey C.S.	98	(3) b Ellison		4
N.H.Fairbrother	c Cowdrey G.R. b Davis	6	(4) c Marsh b De Villiers		47
M.Watkinson	b Davis	4	(5) c Marsh b Davis		66
Wasim Akram	st Marsh b Cowdrey C.S.	1	(6) c & b Davis		9
P.A.J.DeFreitas	c & b De Villiers	6	(7) not out		7
W.K.Hegg +	not out	20	(8) lbw b Davis		0
D.P.Hughes *	c Cowdrey C.S. b Davis	1	(9) not out		0
P.J.W.Allott	b Davis	0			
Extras	(b 2,lb 8,w 1,nb 2)	13	(lb 2,w 1)		3
TOTAL		249	(for 7 wkts)		193

LANCASHIRE	O	M	R	W	O	M	R	W
Wasim Akram	22	6	86	3	21	6	58	2
Allott	23	10	55	2	9	5	16	1
DeFreitas	19	6	43	2	23	7	55	2
Watkinson	18	6	38	1	11	3	32	1
Atherton	1	0	1	0	10.3	3	23	4

KENT	O	M	R	W	O	M	R	W
Igglesden	8	2	29	1				
De Villiers	19	6	73	2	11	0	58	2
Davis	23	7	49	4	17	6	54	4
Kelleher	8	2	30	1	6	1	21	0
Ellison	8	1	38	0	12	1	41	1
Cowdrey C.S.	12	3	20	2	1	0	10	0
Dobson					3.1	1	7	0

FALL OF WICKETS

	KEN	LAN	KEN	LAN
1st	11	5	38	28
2nd	34	6	53	37
3rd	45	174	83	97
4th	54	185	98	151
5th	72	185	139	174
6th	76	188	152	189
7th	125	210	154	189
8th	126	247	154	
9th	194	249	201	
10th	237	249	201	

NOTTINGHAMSHIRE vs. LEICESTERSHIRE

at Trent Bridge on 30th June, 2nd, 3rd July 1990
Toss : Leicestershire.   Umpires : R.Julian and D.S.Thompsett
Match drawn (Nottinghamshire 5 pts (Bt: 3, Bw: 2) Leicestershire 6 pts (Bt: 2, Bw: 4))

NOTTINGHAMSHIRE

B.C.Broad	lbw b Benjamin	40	not out		112
M.Newell	lbw b Benjamin	7	lbw b Potter		26
R.T.Robinson *	lbw b Agnew	0	not out		69
P.Johnson	c Benson b Benjamin	4			
D.J.R.Martindale	c Nixon b Benjamin	7			
F.D.Stephenson	c Lewis b Willey	121			
E.E.Hemmings	c Nixon b Agnew	17			
B.N.French +	c Nixon b Mullally	27			
K.E.Cooper	c Benson b Benjamin	29			
R.A.Pick	c Nixon b Mullally	34			
J.A.Afford	not out	0			
Extras	(lb 5,w 1)	6	(b 3,lb 4)		7
TOTAL		292	(for 1 wkt dec)		214

LEICESTERSHIRE

T.J.Boon	s French b Afford	40	lbw b Cooper		8
N.E.Briers *	c French b Stephenson	30	c Johnson b Cooper		8
J.J.Whitaker	c Cooper b Hemmings	43	c French b Stephenson		83
P.Willey	not out	73	c Broad b Afford		2
L.Potter	lbw b Cooper	0	(6) c & b Cooper		48
J.D.R.Benson	c Afford b Cooper	11	(7) c French b Cooper		62
C.C.Lewis	not out	28	(5) run out		3
W.K.M.Benjamin			lbw b Cooper		0
P.A.Nixon +			lbw b Stephenson		0
J.P.Agnew			not out		8
A.D.Mullally			not out		2
Extras	(b 3,lb 6,nb 2)	11	(b 10,lb 6,nb 2)		18
TOTAL	(for 5 wkts dec)	236	(for 9 wkts)		242

LEICS	O	M	R	W	O	M	R	W
Benjamin	32	5	109	5	3	0	12	0
Agnew	27	5	97	2				
Lewis	6	1	23	0	14	5	28	0
Mullally	17	1	43	2	7	1	17	0
Willey	8.4	3	15	1	10	3	24	0
Potter					18	0	78	1
Benson					11	0	43	0
Boon					0.5	0	5	0

NOTTS	O	M	R	W	O	M	R	W
Stephenson	16	4	53	1	15	5	36	2
Pick	14	1	52	0	2	0	12	0
Cooper	21	6	47	2	15	2	56	5
Hemmings	13	3	52	1	14	1	60	0
Afford	11	4	23	1	15	4	62	1

FALL OF WICKETS

	NOT	LEI	NOT	LEI
1st	13	56	79	17
2nd	16	94		20
3rd	27	146		42
4th	47	150		49
5th	64	170		195
6th	109			230
7th	186			232
8th	230			232
9th	292			232
10th	292			

BRITANNIC ASS. CHAMPIONSHIP

OTHER FIRST-CLASS MATCH

MIDDLESEX vs. WORCESTERSHIRE

at Lord's on 30th June, 2nd, 3rd July 1990
Toss : Middlesex. Umpires : R.Palmer and D.R.Shepherd
Match drawn (Middlesex 8 pts (Bt: 4, Bw: 4) Worcestershire 4 pts (Bt: 1, Bw: 3))

MIDDLESEX

D.L.Haynes	b McEwan	40
M.A.Roseberry	c Botham b Illingworth	43
M.W.Gatting *	c Rhodes b McEwan	26
M.R.Ramprakash	c D'Oliveira b Lampitt	69
K.R.Brown	c Rhodes b Illingworth	52
P.Farbrace +	c Curtis b Illingworth	14
J.E.Emburey	lbw b Lampitt	9
N.F.Williams	not out	49
P.C.R.Tufnell	b Lampitt	3
A.R.C.Fraser	b Botham	27
N.G.Cowans	c Hick b Botham	1
Extras	(b 4,lb 10,nb 1)	15
TOTAL		348

WORCESTERSHIRE

T.S.Curtis	c Emburey b Williams	30	lbw b Cowans		0
P.Bent	b Cowans	7	b Fraser		13
G.A.Hick	b Cowans	0	(4) c Roseberry b Tufnell		80
D.B.D'Oliveira	s Farbrace b Emburey	13	(5) not out		87
I.T.Botham	c Haynes b Williams	4	(6) c Emburey b Fraser		0
P.A.Neale *	c Farbrace b Fraser	16	(7) not out		41
M.J.Weston	c & b Emburey	2			
S.J.Rhodes +	c Emburey b Cowans	26			
R.K.Illingworth	lbw b Fraser	0			
S.R.Lampitt	lbw b Williams	5			
S.M.McEwan	not out	27	(3) b Fraser		7
Extras	(b 3,lb 25,nb 12)	40	(b 1,lb 7,nb 9)		17
TOTAL		170	(for 5 wkts dec)		245

WORCS	O	M	R	W	O	M	R	W
Botham	18.1	3	71	2				
Lampitt	32	1	119	3				
McEwan	14	1	51	2				
Illingworth	37	12	65	3				
Hick	8	1	28	0				

MIDDLESEX	O	M	R	W	O	M	R	W
Fraser	22	7	40	2	23	6	53	3
Cowans	10	5	23	3	15	6	36	1
Williams	17	4	27	3	11	3	28	0
Emburey	19	9	27	2	22	6	52	0
Tufnell	14	7	25	0	31	12	68	1

FALL OF WICKETS				
	MID	WOR	WOR	MID
1st	57	21	0	
2nd	85	21	11	
3rd	130	48	30	
4th	201	68	153	
5th	225	70	154	
6th	256	77		
7th	269	95		
8th	281	95		
9th	344	122		
10th	348	170		

GLAMORGAN vs. SURREY

at Cardiff on 30th June, 2nd, 3rd July 1990
Toss : Surrey. Umpires : R.A.White and A.G.T.Whitehead
Match drawn (Glamorgan 3 pts (Bt: 3, Bw: 0) Surrey 5 pts (Bt: 1, Bw: 4))

GLAMORGAN

A.R.Butcher *	c & b Medlycott	67	c sub b Feltham		21
H.Morris	lbw b Bicknell M.P.	62	c sub b Gray		8
P.A.Cottey	c Ward b Bicknell M.P.	19	not out		35
M.P.Maynard	c Ward b Feltham	22	c Thorpe b Feltham		5
I.V.A.Richards	lbw b Feltham	0	lbw b Bicknell M.P.		14
A.Dale	lbw b Bicknell M.P.	25	lbw b Bicknell M.P.		4
R.D.B.Croft	c Lynch b Medlycott	35	not out		20
C.P.Metson +	st Ward b Medlycott	21			
S.J.Dennis	c Gray b Bicknell M.P.	2			
S.L.Watkin	not out	3			
M.Frost	c Clinton b Medlycott	0			
Extras	(b 10,lb 9,w 4,nb 20)	43	(b 4,lb 7,nb 9)		20
TOTAL		299	(for 5 wkts dec)		127

SURREY

D.J.Bicknell	not out	59			
G.S.Clinton	b Watkin	41	c Morris b Croft		22
G.P.Thorpe	not out	40	c Watkin b Croft		4
K.T.Medlycott			(1) lbw b Frost		4
D.M.Ward +			(4) c Butcher b Frost		29
M.A.Lynch *			(5) c Metson b Watkin		7
I.A.Greig			(6) c Dale b Croft		25
M.A.Feltham			(7) not out		30
M.P.Bicknell			(8) not out		0
R.I.Alikhan					
A.H.Gray					
Extras	(lb 9,nb 1)	10	(b 6,lb 6,w 2,nb 4)		18
TOTAL	(for 1 wkt dec)	150	(for 6 wkts)		139

SURREY	O	M	R	W	O	M	R	W
Gray	21	5	42	0	11	2	29	1
Bicknell M.P.	28	4	87	4	10	0	36	2
Feltham	21	5	60	2	7	1	32	2
Medlycott	26.5	3	77	4	7	3	19	0
Greig	3	1	14	0				

GLAMORGAN	O	M	R	W	O	M	R	W
Frost	13	2	48	0	14	2	33	2
Watkin	14	3	36	1	17	3	33	1
Dennis	8	1	11	0	2	0	5	0
Croft	20.1	6	46	0	24	7	46	3
Richards					2	1	10	0

FALL OF WICKETS				
	GLA	SUR	GLA	SUR
1st	136	90	37	6
2nd	148		37	20
3rd	188		45	68
4th	192		70	68
5th	192		84	84
6th	252			117
7th	291			
8th	296			
9th	299			
10th	299			

SUSSEX vs. CAMBRIDGE UNIV

at Hove on 30th June, 2nd, 3rd July 1990
Toss : Cambridge Univ. Umpires : J.H.Harris and A.A.Jones
Cambridge Univ won by 3 wickets

SUSSEX

N.J.Lenham	b Shufflebotham	70	b Pyman		22
J.W.Hall	c Heap b Jenkins	3	c Turner b Buzza		49
K.Greenfield	not out	102	not out		54
A.P.Wells	c Shufflebotham b Pyman	137	not out		27
P.W.G.Parker *	not out	10			
M.P.Speight					
P.Moores +					
C.C.Remy					
J.A.North					
B.T.P.Donelan					
R.A.Bunting					
Extras	(b 5,lb 1,nb 11)	17	(b 1,lb 9,nb 2)		12
TOTAL	(for 3 wkts dec)	339	(for 2 wkts dec)		164

CAMBRIDGE UNIV

S.P.James	c Wells b Remy	61	c Speight b North		102
R.Heap	b Bunting	63	(7) not out		20
R.J.Turner +	c Moores b Wells	38	(2) c Moores b Bunting		14
J.C.M.Atkinson *	c Parker b Wells	2	run out		0
M.J.Lowrey	lbw b North	6	(3) lbw b Lenham		72
M.J.Morris	c Hall b Remy	12	(5) lbw b Lenham		7
R.A.Pyman	b Remy	0	(6) run out		8
D.H.Shufflebotham	b Remy	0	b North		6
R.H.J.Jenkins	not out	19	not out		4
A.J.Buzza	c Moores b Bunting	10			
S.W.Johnson	not out	8			
Extras	(b 8,lb 20,w 1)	29	(b 9,lb 12,w 1,nb 3)		25
TOTAL	(for 9 wkts dec)	248	(for 7 wkts)		258

CAMB UNIV	O	M	R	W	O	M	R	W
Johnson	12	1	48	0	6	1	18	0
Jenkins	22.2	5	94	1	4	0	18	0
Pyman	26	7	60	1	14	1	59	1
Shufflebotham	12	2	36	1	6	1	25	0
Buzza	12	2	65	0	7.5	1	34	1
Lowrey	4	0	30	0				

SUSSEX	O	M	R	W	O	M	R	W
Bunting	27	4	60	2	14	0	54	1
North	22	5	46	1	11.5	2	43	2
Remy	22	6	63	4	15	0	70	0
Donelan	11	2	26	0	12	1	44	0
Wells	10	4	25	2				
Lenham					7	1	26	2

FALL OF WICKETS				
	SUS	CAM	SUS	CAM
1st	15	88	40	28
2nd	124	171	114	170
3rd	316	181		178
4th		185		206
5th		202		223
6th		202		229
7th		202		245
8th		205		
9th		238		
10th				

HEADLINES

30th June - 3rd July

● Worcs, after following on, batted through the last day to deny leaders Middlesex, while Lancs moved up to second place by beating Kent. Mike Atherton made 101, his fourth 100 of the summer, and took 4 for 23

● Northants returned to winning ways against Somerset, a second-wicket stand of 185 between Alan Fordham and Rob Bailey putting them well on the way towards a target of 329. Nigel Felton made a century against his former county and Jimmy Cook hit his fourth 100 of the season

● Wickets tumbled at Derby as the first innings of Derbyshire and Gloucestershire produced a combined total of only 186.

● After recovering from 64 for 5 in their first innings, Notts held the upper hand in their match against Leics, but were denied victory by last-wicket pair, Jonathan Agnew and Tony Mullally

● Alan Butcher of Glamorgan became the first Englishman to complete 1,000 first-class runs for the season

● Cambridge University gained their first victory over a county since 1982 when they beat Sussex by three wickets at Hove. Keith Greenfield had earlier hit his maiden first-class 100 in Sussex's first innings

BRITANNIC ASSURANCE CHAMPIONSHIP

YORKSHIRE vs. NOTTINGHAMSHIRE

at Scarborough on 4th (no play), 5th, 6th July 1990
Toss : Nottinghamshire.   Umpires : H.D.Bird and R.Julian
Nottinghamshire won by 5 wickets (Yorks 4 pts (Bt: 4, Bw: 0) Notts 17 pts (Bt: 0, Bw: 1))

YORKSHIRE

M.D.Moxon *	c Robinson b Evans	123
A.A.Metcalfe	c Pick b Evans	75
K.Sharp	c Robinson b Afford	17
P.E.Robinson	not out	73
R.J.Blakey +	not out	46
D.Byas		
C.White		
P.Carrick		
P.J.Hartley		
D.Gough		
I.J.Houseman		
Extras	(lb 13,nb 4)	17
TOTAL	(for 3 wkts dec)	351

NOTTINGHAMSHIRE

B.C.Broad	c Robinson b White	126
M.Newell	b Hartley	0
R.T.Robinson *	c Sharp b Carrick	43
P.Johnson	c & b White	149
D.J.R.Martindale	b Carrick	4
F.D.Stephenson	not out	4
K.P.Evans	not out	12
B.N.French +		
K.E.Cooper		
R.A.Pick		
J.A.Afford		
Extras	(b 8,lb 2,nb 6)	16
TOTAL	(for 5 wkts)	354

NOTTS	O	M	R	W	O	M	R	W	FALL OF WICKETS				
										YOR	NOT	YOR	NOT
Stephenson	6	1	23	0					1st	175			15
Cooper	25	5	69	0					2nd	223			111
Pick	20	2	74	0					3rd	223			298
Evans	22	4	73	2					4th				334
Afford	29	7	87	1					5th				334
Newell	1.2	0	12	0					6th				
YORKSHIRE	O	M	R	W	O	M	R	W	7th				
Hartley					18	2	75	1	8th				
Houseman					12	5	40	0	9th				
Carrick					23.3	4	69	2	10th				
Gough					8	0	46	0					
White					22	3	99	2					
Byas					4	0	15	0					

SURREY vs. NORTHANTS

at The Oval on 4th (no play), 5th, 6th July 1990
Toss : Northants.   Umpires : M.J.Kitchen and R.Palmer
Surrey won by 147 runs (Surrey 20 pts (Bt; 4, Bw: 0) Northants 0 pts (Bt: 0, Bw: 0))

SURREY

D.J.Bicknell	b Williams	169
G.S.Clinton	b Robinson	146
G.P.Thorpe	not out	15
D.M.Ward +	not out	4
M.A.Lynch		
I.A.Greig *		
J.D.Robinson		
K.T.Medlycott		
M.A.Feltham		
M.P.Bicknell		
Waqar Younis		
Extras	(lb 3,nb 10)	13
TOTAL	(for 2 wkts dec)	347

NORTHANTS

A.Fordham	c Greig b Bicknell M.P.	3
N.A.Felton	lbw b Bicknell M.P.	2
R.J.Bailey	c Ward b Waqar Younis	33
D.J.Capel	b Waqar Younis	19
W.Larkins *	b Waqar Younis	107
R.G.Williams	b Waqar Younis	0
D.Ripley +	b Bicknell M.P.	9
J.Hughes	c Ward b Bicknell M.P.	1
W.W.Davis	b Waqar Younis	9
N.G.B.Cook	b Waqar Younis	0
M.A.Robinson	not out	0
Extras	(b 4,lb 6,nb 7)	17
TOTAL		200

NORTHANTS	O	M	R	W	O	M	R	W	FALL OF WICKETS				
										SUR	NOR	SUR	NOR
Davis	22	5	70	0					1st	321			3
Robinson	20	4	57	1					2nd	331			6
Hughes	12	0	84	0					3rd				58
Williams	25	8	65	1					4th				83
Cook	9	2	34	0					5th				83
Bailey	7	1	34	0					6th				107
SURREY	O	M	R	W	O	M	R	W	7th				153
Waqar Younis					18.2	9	36	6	8th				187
Bicknell M.P.					16	3	58	4	9th				199
Feltham					13	1	42	0	10th				200
Medlycott					16	4	54	0					

KENT vs. ESSEX

at Maidstone on 4th (no play), 5th, 6th July 1990
Toss : Essex.   Umpires : J.C.Balderstone and B.Dudleston
Essex won by 4 wickets (Kent 4 pts (Bt: 4, Bw: 0) Essex 17 pts (Bt: 0, Bw: 1))

KENT

S.G.Hinks	c Topley b Pringle	1
M.R.Benson	lbw b Pringle	159
N.R.Taylor	c Hardie b Pringle	6
G.R.Cowdrey	run out	116
C.S.Cowdrey *	not out	3
M.V.Fleming	not out	0
S.A.Marsh +		
R.M.Ellison		
P.S.De Villiers		
C.Penn		
R.P.Davis		
Extras	(lb 8,nb 15)	23
TOTAL	(for 4 wkts dec)	308

ESSEX

B.R.Hardie	c Hinks b De Villiers	12
J.P.Stephenson	b Davis	67
P.J.Prichard	c Marsh b Fleming	55
M.E.Waugh	c Marsh b Davis	3
N.Hussain	c Cowdrey C.S. b De Villiers	41
N.Shahid	run out	63
D.R.Pringle *	not out	40
M.A.Garnham +	not out	17
N.A.Foster		
T.D.Topley		
J.H.Childs		
Extras	(b 2,lb 6,nb 3)	11
TOTAL	(for 6 wkts)	309

ESSEX	O	M	R	W	O	M	R	W	FALL OF WICKETS				
										KEN	ESS	KEN	ESS
Foster	33	2	107	0					1st	4			18
Pringle	31	9	54	3					2nd	30			124
Topley	25	4	60	0					3rd	298			140
Childs	10	1	41	0					4th	308			140
Stephenson	7	1	38	0					5th				238
KENT	O	M	R	W	O	M	R	W	6th				269
De Villiers					19	2	84	2	7th				
Penn					22	6	68	0	8th				
Davis					18	5	76	2	9th				
Ellison					12	0	46	0	10th				
Fleming					10	1	23	1					
Cowdrey C.S.					2	0	4	0					

GLAMORGAN vs. GLOUCESTERSHIRE

at Swansea on 4th (no play), 5th, 6th July 1990
Toss : Glamorgan.   Umpires : R.A.White and A.G.T.Whitehead
Match drawn (Glamorgan 4 pts (Bt: 4, Bw: 0) Gloucestershire 3 pts (Bt: 0, Bw: 3))

GLAMORGAN

A.R.Butcher *	b Bell	19
H.Morris	c Williams b Curran	21
P.A.Cottey	lbw b Curran	12
M.P.Maynard	c & b Curran	63
I.V.A.Richards	run out	41
R.D.B.Croft	b Curran	68
N.G.Cowley	b Lloyds	44
C.P.Metson +	b Barnes	30
S.L.Watkin	not out	19
S.J.Dennis	not out	4
M.Frost		
Extras	(b 5,lb 7,nb 1)	13
TOTAL	(for 8 wkts dec)	334

GLOUCESTERSHIRE

G.D.Hodgson	lbw b Watkin	23
A.J.Wright *	lbw b Dennis	19
I.P.Butcher	not out	25
C.W.J.Athey	not out	35
P.Bainbridge		
K.M.Curran		
J.W.Lloyds		
M.W.Alleyne		
R.C.J.Williams +		
M.W.Bell		
S.N.Barnes		
Extras	(lb 2,w 2,nb 2)	6
TOTAL	(for 2 wkts)	108

GLOUCS	O	M	R	W	O	M	R	W	FALL OF WICKETS				
										GLA	GLO	GLA	GLO
Curran	30	4	92	4					1st	39			44
Barnes	21	4	47	1					2nd	45			44
Bell	27	3	76	1					3rd	55			
Bainbridge	3	0	17	0					4th	134			
Alleyne	2	0	14	0					5th	182			
Lloyds	25	6	76	1					6th	262			
GLAMORGAN	O	M	R	W	O	M	R	W	7th	302			
Frost					8	1	31	0	8th	314			
Dennis					12	4	23	1	9th				
Watkin					6	1	23	1	10th				
Croft					8	2	23	0					
Cowley					5	2	6	0					

BRITANNIC ASSURANCE CHAMPIONSHIP

SUSSEX vs. DERBYSHIRE

at Hove on 4th, (no play), 5th, 6th July 1990
Toss : Sussex. Umpires : J.H.Harris and A.A.Jones
Derbyshire won by 18 runs (Sussex 3 pts (Bt: 0, Bw: 3) Derbyshire 20 pts (Bt: 4, Bw: 0))

DERBYSHIRE

K.J.Barnett *	c Salisbury b Pigott	123
P.D.Bowler	b Bunting	50
J.E.Morris	c Hall b Pigott	21
B.Roberts	c Moores b Pigott	47
C.J.Adams	st Moores b Salisbury	91
S.C.Goldsmith	c Moores b Pigott	11
K.M.Krikken +	c Lenham b Salisbury	12
M.Jean-Jacques	not out	0
I.R.Bishop	not out	0
S.J.Base		
O.H.Mortensen		
Extras	(lb 6,w 2)	8
TOTAL	(for 7 wkts dec)	363

SUSSEX

N.J.Lenham		lbw b Mortensen	12
J.W.Hall		c Morris b Bishop	6
P.Moores +		c Goldsmith b Mortensen	13
A.P.Wells		c sub b Jean-Jacques	18
M.P.Speight		lbw b Base	43
C.M.Wells		c Morris b Goldsmith	51
A.I.C.Dodemaide		c & b Bishop	33
A.C.S.Pigott		c Roberts b Bishop	12
P.W.G.Parker *		c Krikken b Bishop	35
I.D.K.Salisbury		c Adams b Bishop	68
R.A.Bunting		not out	24
Extras		(b 5,lb 8,w 2,nb 15)	30
TOTAL			345

SUSSEX	O	M	R	W	O	M	R	W		FALL OF WICKETS			
Dodemaide	22.1	1	81	0							DER	SUS	DER	SUS
Pigott	18	4	69	4					1st	126		16
Bunting	20	1	100	1					2nd	185		33
Wells C.M.	13	1	58	0					3rd	214		47
Salisbury	11	4	49	2					4th	265		68
									5th	291		152
DERBYSHIRE	O	M	R	W	O	M	R	W	6th	338		166
Bishop					27.1	6	90	5	7th	361		185
Mortensen					27	5	77	2	8th			243
Jean-Jacques					13	3	60	1	9th			256
Base					20	5	65	1	10th			345
Goldsmith					8	0	40	1				

SOMERSET vs. WARWICKSHIRE

at Taunton on 4th, 5th, 6th July 1990
Toss : Warwickshire. Umpires : K.J.Lyons and D.O.Oslear
Match drawn (Somerset 4 pts (Bt: 3, Bw: 1) Warwickshire 5 pts (Bt: 1, Bw: 4))

SOMERSET

S.J.Cook	c Piper b Reeve	35	c Ostler b Moles	137
P.M.Roebuck	not out	114	not out	90
A.N.Hayhurst	c Humpage b Reeve	6	c Reeve b Moles	3
C.J.Tavare *	c Piper b Benjamin	23		
R.J.Harden	lbw b Benjamin	9		
N.D.Burns +	c Piper b Benjamin	0	(4) not out	3
G.D.Rose	c Piper b Donald	14		
N.A.Mallender	c Piper b Benjamin	0		
R.P.Lefebvre	c Humpage b Reeve	22		
I.G.Swallow	c Reeve b Pierson	32		
A.N.Jones	st Piper b Pierson	0		
Extras	(lb 3,w 1,nb 11)	15	(b 1,lb 2,w 1,nb 1)	5
TOTAL		270	(for 2 wkts dec)	238

WARWICKSHIRE

A.J.Moles	c Harden b Jones	14	c Burns b Mallender	6
J.D.Ratcliffe	lbw b Rose	7	not out	16
Asif Din	c Rose b Lefebvre	45	lbw b Mallender	0
G.W.Humpage	not out	67	not out	0
D.A.Reeve *	b Jones	4		
D.P.Ostler	not out	11		
K.J.Piper +				
A.A.Donald				
A.R.K.Pierson				
J.E.Benjamin				
T.A.Munton				
Extras	(lb 2,nb 2)	4	(lb 1,nb 1)	2
TOTAL	(for 4 wkts dec)	152	(for 2 wkts)	24

WARWICKSHIRE	O	M	R	W	O	M	R	W		FALL OF WICKETS			
Donald	23	9	58	1	8	1	27	0			SOM	WAR	SOM	WAR
Benjamin	27	3	86	4	8	1	31	0	1st	77	16	223	22
Munton	21	2	65	0	6	0	35	0	2nd	97	46	231	22
Reeve	20	8	47	3	5	0	19	0	3rd	129	106		
Pierson	1.5	0	11	2	9	2	23	0	4th	146	117		
Asif Din					10	0	41	0	5th	152			
Moles					8	0	56	2	6th	173			
Humpage					2	1	3	0	7th	181			
									8th	226			
SOMERSET	O	M	R	W	O	M	R	W	9th	268			
Jones	11	3	38	2	6	1	19	0	10th	270			
Mallender	10.2	2	24	0	5	4	4	2					
Lefebvre	11	5	31	1									
Rose	9	0	57	1									

HEADLINES

4th - 6th July

● The first day's play was lost in five of the six Championship fixtures, but a series of forfeitures kept interest alive and batsmen continued to enjoy themselves

● Nottinghamshire were asked to make 352 by Yorkshire at Scarborough and got them in 87.3 overs as Chris Broad made his fifth first-class 100 of the season and Paul Johnson his second in a stand of 187 for the third wicket. Martyn Moxon and Ashley Metcalfe had earlier shared an opening stand of 175

● Kent's Mark Benson and Graham Cowdrey added 266 together for the third wicket against Essex at Maidstone, but still finished on the losing side

● Surrey's Grahame Clinton and Darren Bicknell did even better, sharing an opening stand of 321 against Northamptonshire at The Oval, Bicknell improving his career best to 169. Waqar Younis was too much for Northants as Surrey gained their first Championship victory of the season

● Kim Barnett became the leading century-maker in the history of Derbyshire with his 123 against Sussex at Hove, but then had to watch the home side's last wicket pair, Ian Salisbury and Rodney Bunting, add 89 of the 108 they needed when they came together. Salisbury made his maiden first-class fifty before becoming Ian Bishop's fifth victim

● Although play survived on the first day at Taunton, Somerset's match against Warwicks eventually came to grief midway through the last. Peter Roebuck returned to form with a combined total of 194 runs without being dismissed, sharing an opening stand of 223 with Jimmy Cook in the second innings, Cook passing 1500 first-class runs during his fifth first-class 100 of the summer

● Rain returned to Swansea as Gloucestershire were chasing a total of 335 after Glamorgan's Robert Croft had made his highest first-class score

● First-class debuts: R.C.J.Williams and M.W.Bell (Gloucestershire); J.Hughes (Northants)

VARSITY MATCH

TOUR MATCH

CAMBRIDGE UNIV vs. OXFORD UNIV

at Lord's on 4th (no play), 5th, 6th July 1990
Toss : Cambridge Univ. Umpires : D.J.Constant and K.E.Palmer
Match drawn

OXFORD UNIV

D.A.Hagan	c James b Jenkins	8
R.E.Morris *	c Turner b Jenkins	21
P.D.Lunn	b Shufflebotham	35
G.J.Turner	c Jenkins b Shufflebotham	36
M.A.Crawley	c Johnson b Buzza	55
D.M.Curtis	run out	27
W.M.van der Merwe	st Turner b Buzza	50
P.S.Gerrans	c James b Shufflebotham	16
S.D.Weale	not out	4
I.M.Henderson	not out	0
B.W.D.Trevelyan +		
Extras	(b 3,lb 12,nb 2)	17
TOTAL	(for 8 wkts dec)	269

CAMBRIDGE UNIV

S.P.James	c Hagan b Crawley	56
R.Heap	b Crawley	37
R.J.Turner +	run out	7
J.C.M.Atkinson *	b Crawley	7
M.J.Lowrey	not out	18
M.J.Morris	not out	9
R.A.Pyman		
D.H.Shufflebotham		
R.H.J.Jenkins		
A.J.Buzza		
S.W.Johnson		
Extras	(b 3,lb 7,nb 2)	12
TOTAL	(for 4 wkts)	146

CAMB UNIV	O	M	R	W	O	M	R	W
Johnson	16	1	48	0				
Jenkins	20	2	68	2				
Pyman	18	7	63	0				
Shufflebotham	19	5	60	3				
Buzza	8	1	15	2				
OXFORD UNIV	O	M	R	W	O	M	R	W
van der Merwe					14	2	23	0
Henderson					5	0	21	0
Gerrans					13	0	37	0
Crawley					17	4	46	3
Lunn					2	1	9	0

FALL OF WICKETS

	OXF	CAM	OXF	CAM
1st	13			87
2nd	41			110
3rd	95			111
4th	108			118
5th	175			
6th	238			
7th	263			
8th	265			
9th				
10th				

HAMPSHIRE vs. INDIA

at Southampton on 4th (no play), 5th, 6th July 1990
Toss : India. Umpires : N.T.Plews and D.R.Shepherd
Hampshire won by 7 wickets

INDIA

W.V.Raman	c Terry b Joseph	26	c Maru b Connor	22
N.S.Sidhu	c Terry b Joseph	6	not out	58
S.R.Tendulkar	c Terry b Bakker	32	not out	58
D.B.Vengsarkar	c Parks b Connor	21		
M.Azharuddin *	b Ayling	74		
M.Prabhakar	c & b Maru	76		
N.R.Mongia +	not out	14		
Venkatapathy Raju	c Parks b Maru	18		
S.K.Sharma				
A.R.Kumble				
N.D.Hirwani				
Extras	(b 6,lb 3,w 2)	11	(b 1,lb 3,nb 1)	5
TOTAL	(for 7 wkts dec)	278	(for 1 wkt dec)	143

HAMPSHIRE

V.P.Terry	c Raman b Prabhakar	5	lbw b Sharma	11
C.L.Smith	c Raman b Hirwani	24	lbw b Prabhakar	36
M.C.J.Nicholas *	not out	37	b Prabhakar	104
D.I.Gower	not out	44	not out	126
J.R.Ayling			not out	21
T.C.Middleton				
L.A.Joseph				
R.J.Parks +				
R.J.Maru				
C.A.Connor				
P.J.Bakker				
Extras	(lb 1,nb 6)	7	(b 2,lb 7,nb 1)	10
TOTAL	(for 2 wkts dec)	117	(for 3 wkts)	308

HAMPSHIRE	O	M	R	W	O	M	R	W
Bakker	22	1	84	1	13	2	37	0
Joseph	10	2	28	2				
Connor	14	4	43	1	8	3	28	1
Ayling	15	2	45	1	8	1	26	0
Maru	16.4	1	69	2	6	0	31	0
Nicholas					4	0	17	0
INDIA	O	M	R	W	O	M	R	W
Prabhakar	8	1	20	1	19	0	102	2
Sharma	8	0	34	0	16	3	79	1
Hirwani	7	1	25	1	8	0	39	0
Venkatapathy	9	2	28	0	13	1	56	0
Kumble	2	0	9	0	5	0	23	0

FALL OF WICKETS

	IND	HAM	IND	HAM
1st	22	13	38	26
2nd	39	55		85
3rd	78			240
4th	92			
5th	240			
6th	246			
7th	278			
8th				
9th				
10th				

HEADLINES

4th - 6th July

● The weather again had the decisive say as the students' annual visit to Lord's was ruined by the loss of over half its playing time, but both universities could reflect on their much improved record against the counties in 1990

● The Indians came to grief against a David Gower anxious to impress as they lost to Hampshire at Southampton by seven wickets. Gower made an exhilarating 126* as Hampshire reached their target in 61 overs

Willem van der Merwe, a regular wicket-taker for Oxford University, but who had more success with the bat in a Varsity Match marred by the weather.

REFUGE ASSURANCE LEAGUE

LANCASHIRE vs. DERBYSHIRE

at Old Trafford on 8th July 1990
Toss : Lancashire. Umpires : R.Julian and D.O.Oslear
Derbyshire won by 5 runs (Lancashire 0 pts Derbyshire 4 pts)

DERBYSHIRE

K.J.Barnett *	c Wasim Akram b Watkinson	85
P.D.Bowler +	c Allott b Watkinson	40
J.E.Morris	c Lloyd b DeFreitas	55
A.P.Kuiper	c Allott b DeFreitas	7
B.Roberts	b Allott	28
C.J.Adams	b Wasim Akram	14
S.C.Goldsmith	not out	7
G.Miller		
A.E.Warner		
S.J.Base		
O.H.Mortensen		
Extras	(lb 8,w 3,nb 2)	13
TOTAL	(40 overs)(for 6 wkts)	249

LANCASHIRE

G.D.Mendis	c Barnett b Kuiper	71
G.D.Lloyd	c Bowler b Base	1
W.K.Hegg +	run out	10
T.E.Jesty	b Miller	20
G.Fowler	lbw b Warner	57
M.Watkinson	c & b Base	8
Wasim Akram	c Adams b Kuiper	7
P.A.J.DeFreitas	c Kuiper b Base	17
I.D.Austin	c Bowler b Kuiper	3
D.P.Hughes *	not out	21
P.J.W.Allott	run out	12
Extras	(b 1,lb 12,w 4)	17
TOTAL	(39.5 overs)	244

LANCASHIRE	O	M	R	W	FALL OF WICKETS		
						DER	LAN
Allott	8	0	34	1			
DeFreitas	8	0	53	2	1st	108	6
Watkinson	8	0	42	2	2nd	175	30
Wasim Akram	8	0	59	1	3rd	198	81
Austin	8	0	53	0	4th	198	134
					5th	230	147
DERBYSHIRE	O	M	R	W	6th	249	158
Mortensen	8	1	25	0	7th		189
Base	7.5	0	49	3	8th		203
Miller	8	0	50	1	9th		207
Warner	8	0	57	1	10th		244
Kuiper	8	0	50	3			

SURREY vs. WARWICKSHIRE

at The Oval on 8th July 1990
Toss : Warwickshire. Umpires : D.J.Constant and R.Palmer
Surrey won by 15 runs (Surrey 4 pts Warwickshire 0 pts)

SURREY

D.J.Bicknell	c Piper b Twose	0
M.A.Feltham	b Reeve	61
G.P.Thorpe	c Moody b Munton	35
D.M.Ward +	c & b Reeve	0
M.A.Lynch	c Reeve b Smith P.A.	25
I.A.Greig *	c Humpage b Reeve	43
K.T.Medlycott	run out	27
C.K.Bullen	c & b Reeve	0
M.P.Bicknell	b Benjamin	0
N.M.Kendrick	not out	2
Waqar Younis	not out	1
Extras	(b 1,lb 6,w 4)	11
TOTAL	(37 overs)(for 9 wkts)	205

WARWICKSHIRE

T.A.Lloyd *	run out	5
P.A.Smith	c Waqar Younis b Feltham	9
T.M.Moody	b Bicknell M.P.	3
G.W.Humpage	b Medlycott	33
D.A.Reeve	st Ward b Medlycott	25
N.M.K.Smith	c Greig b Medlycott	12
R.G.Twose	c & b Feltham	40
D.P.Ostler	run out	30
K.J.Piper +	b Waqar Younis	2
J.E.Benjamin	not out	8
T.A.Munton	not out	6
Extras	(b 4,lb 3,w 10)	17
TOTAL	(37 overs)(for 9 wkts)	190

WARWICKS	O	M	R	W	FALL OF WICKETS		
						SUR	WAR
Twose	4	0	29	1	1st	0	8
Benjamin	8	0	38	1	2nd	90	11
Moody	3	0	27	0	3rd	93	27
Smith N.M.K.	6	0	35	0	4th	114	76
Munton	6	1	25	1	5th	142	90
Reeve	8	0	36	4	6th	191	91
Smith P.A.	2	1	8	1	7th	192	162
					8th	193	172
SURREY	O	M	R	W	9th	200	175
Bicknell M.P.	8	0	34	1	10th		
Feltham	8	1	23	2			
Bullen	4	0	22	0			
Waqar Younis	8	0	41	1			
Medlycott	6	0	43	3			
Kendrick	3	0	20	0			

MIDDLESEX vs. SOMERSET

at Lord's on 8th July 1990
Toss : Middlesex. Umpires : J.H.Harris and D.S.Thompsett
Somerset won by 24 runs (Middlesex 0 pts Somerset 4 pts)

SOMERSET

S.J.Cook	b Williams	58
R.J.Bartlett	c Gatting b Emburey	54
C.J.Tavare *	not out	72
R.J.Harden	not out	41
A.N.Hayhurst		
G.D.Rose		
N.D.Burns +		
R.P.Lefebvre		
I.G.Swallow		
N.A.Mallender		
J.C.Hallett		
Extras	(b 2,lb 7,w 11,nb 3)	23
TOTAL	(40 overs)(for 2 wkts)	248

MIDDLESEX

D.L.Haynes	c Harden b Mallender	82
M.A.Roseberry	b Mallender	16
M.W.Gatting *	b Hayhurst	24
M.R.Ramprakash	b Hayhurst	9
K.R.Brown	c Harden b Mallender	15
R.O.Butcher	c Lefebvre b Swallow	12
P.Farbrace +	b Mallender	0
N.F.Williams	c Bartlett b Swallow	12
J.E.Emburey	c & b Rose	32
A.R.C.Fraser	b Lefebvre	6
N.G.Cowans	not out	0
Extras	(b 4,lb 12)	16
TOTAL	(39.3 overs)	224

MIDDLESEX	O	M	R	W	FALL OF WICKETS		
						SOM	MID
Williams	8	0	39	1	1st	116	32
Fraser	8	0	49	0	2nd	143	87
Haynes	7	0	41	0	3rd		107
Gatting	2	0	11	0	4th		141
Cowans	7	0	59	0	5th		166
Emburey	8	1	40	1	6th		166
					7th		170
SOMERSET	O	M	R	W	8th		190
Rose	5.3	0	42	1	9th		204
Mallender	8	1	32	4	10th		224
Lefebvre	7	0	37	1			
Hallett	5	0	23	0			
Hayhurst	6	0	30	2			
Swallow	8	0	44	2			

HAMPSHIRE vs. ESSEX

at Southampton on 8th July 1990
Toss : Essex. Umpires : B.Hassan and D.R.Shepherd
Hampshire won by 7 wickets (Hampshire 4 pts Essex 0 pts)

ESSEX

B.R.Hardie	c Parks b Marshall	4
J.P.Stephenson	c Gower b Tremlett	28
M.E.Waugh	c Gower b Ayling	17
P.J.Prichard	c Parks b Maru	12
D.R.Pringle *	c Gower b Tremlett	63
N.Hussain	b Ayling	12
M.A.Garnham +	not out	40
N.A.Foster	c Gower b Marshall	4
T.D.Topley	c Terry b Bakker	2
M.C.Ilott	not out	1
J.H.Childs		
Extras	(b 1,lb 8,w 4)	13
TOTAL	(40 overs)(for 8 wkts)	196

HAMPSHIRE

V.P.Terry	c Hardie b Foster	52
R.J.Scott	lbw b Foster	7
D.I.Gower *	c Childs b Topley	66
M.D.Marshall	not out	43
C.L.Smith	not out	22
J.R.Ayling		
T.C.Middleton		
R.J.Parks +		
R.J.Maru		
T.M.Tremlett		
P.J.Bakker		
Extras	(b 2,lb 4,w 2,nb 2)	10
TOTAL	(39 overs)(for 3 wkts)	200

HAMPSHIRE	O	M	R	W	FALL OF WICKETS		
						ESS	HAM
Bakker	8	2	30	1			
Marshall	8	0	33	2	1st	7	23
Ayling	8	0	40	2	2nd	49	130
Tremlett	8	1	43	2	3rd	53	132
Maru	8	0	41	1	4th	75	
					5th	120	
ESSEX	O	M	R	W	6th	161	
Foster	8	0	43	2	7th	180	
Ilott	7	1	34	0	8th	186	
Childs	8	2	36	0	9th		
Topley	8	0	32	1	10th		
Pringle	7	0	42	0			
Waugh	1	0	7	0			

NOTTINGHAMSHIRE vs. SUSSEX

at Trent Bridge on 8th July 1990
Toss : Sussex. Umpires : H.D.Bird and K.E.Palmer
Nottinghamshire won by 8 runs (Notts 4 pts Sussex 0 pts)

NOTTINGHAMSHIRE

B.C.Broad	c Salisbury b Pigott	61
M.Newell	c Moores b Lenham	15
P.Johnson	lbw b Clarke	104
F.D.Stephenson	b Pigott	32
G.W.Mike	lbw b Pigott	13
R.T.Robinson *	not out	15
K.P.Evans	not out	7
B.N.French +		
K.E.Cooper		
K.Saxelby		
J.A.Afford		
Extras	(b 1,lb 10,w 5)	16
TOTAL	(40 overs)(for 5 wkts)	263

SUSSEX

N.J.Lenham	b Afford	60
I.J.Gould	c French b Cooper	6
A.P.Wells	run out	98
M.P.Speight	run out	2
C.M.Wells *	b Mike	25
A.I.C.Dodemaide	lbw b Mike	22
A.C.S.Pigott	c Johnson b Mike	17
P.Moores +	run out	10
C.C.Remy	run out	1
I.D.K.Salisbury	b Stephenson	0
A.R.Clarke	not out	0
Extras	(lb 12,w 2)	14
TOTAL	(39.2 overs)	255

SUSSEX	O	M	R	W	FALL OF WICKETS		
						NOT	SUS
Wells C.M.	8	0	45	0			
Dodemaide	6	0	46	0	1st	51	34
Clarke	7	0	37	1	2nd	128	93
Lenham	8	0	36	1	3rd	202	98
Pigott	8	0	55	3	4th	224	150
Salisbury	3	0	33	0	5th	245	201
					6th		229
NOTTS	O	M	R	W	7th		251
Saxelby	6	0	49	0	8th		254
Cooper	4	0	18	1	9th		254
Stephenson	7.2	0	48	1	10th		255
Afford	6	0	40	1			
Evans	8	0	46	0			
Mike	8	0	42	3			

NORTHANTS vs. YORKSHIRE

at Tring on 8th July 1990
Toss : Northants. Umpires : J.C.Balderstone and A.A.Jones
Yorkshire won by 61 runs (Northants 0 pts Yorkshire 4 pts)

YORKSHIRE

S.A.Kellett	run out	10
A.A.Metcalfe *	lbw b Wild	55
R.J.Blakey +	st Ripley b Wild	42
P.E.Robinson	not out	58
P.J.Hartley	b Davis	51
D.Byas	not out	18
C.White		
C.Chapman		
P.Carrick		
A.Sidebottom		
S.D.Fletcher		
Extras	(b 5,lb 7,w 4,nb 1)	17
TOTAL	(40 overs)(for 4 wkts)	251

NORTHANTS

A.Fordham	b Sidebottom	28
W.Larkins *	c Hartley b Sidebottom	12
R.J.Bailey	b Hartley	18
D.J.Capel	c Robinson b Carrick	25
N.A.Felton	st Blakey b Carrick	9
D.J.Wild	c Fletcher b White	19
R.G.Williams	b Hartley	35
W.W.Davis	c Carrick b Byas	20
D.Ripley +	c Chapman b Hartley	17
N.G.B.Cook	b White	1
M.A.Robinson	not out	0
Extras	(b 1,lb 2,w 1,nb 2)	6
TOTAL	(37.1 overs)	190

NORTHANTS	O	M	R	W	FALL OF WICKETS		
						YOR	NOR
Davis	8	1	38	1			
Capel	8	0	26	0	1st	18	40
Cook	8	0	60	0	2nd	113	53
Robinson	6	0	53	0	3rd	118	72
Williams	4	0	36	0	4th	200	94
Wild	6	0	26	2	5th		97
					6th		124
YORKSHIRE	O	M	R	W	7th		146
Sidebottom	8	1	21	2	8th		187
Hartley	7	0	37	3	9th		190
Fletcher	5	0	34	0	10th		190
Carrick	8	2	22	2			
White	7.1	0	56	2			
Byas	2	0	17	1			

REFUGE ASSURANCE LEAGUE

WORCESTERSHIRE vs. GLOUCS ────────

at Worcester on 8th July 1990
Toss : Worcestershire. Umpires : P.J.Eele and P.B.Wight
Worcestershire won by 8 wickets (Worcs 4 pts Gloucs 0 pts)

GLOUCESTERSHIRE

G.D.Hodgson	c Leatherdale b Weston	10
C.W.J.Athey	c Leatherdale b Lampitt	63
A.J.Wright *	c Leatherdale b Tolley	24
K.M.Curran	c Curtis b Botham	56
P.Bainbridge	lbw b Lampitt	15
P.W.Romaines	not out	27
J.W.Lloyds	b Botham	2
M.W.Alleyne	not out	8
R.C.J.Williams +		
C.A.Walsh		
D.A.Graveney		
Extras	(lb 9,w 6)	15
TOTAL	(40 overs)(for 6 wkts)	220

WORCESTERSHIRE

T.S.Curtis	not out	93
M.J.Weston	b Walsh	4
G.A.Hick	c Williams b Alleyne	67
I.T.Botham	not out	41
P.A.Neale *		
D.B.D'Oliveira		
S.J.Rhodes +		
D.A.Leatherdale		
C.M.Tolley		
S.R.Lampitt		
S.Herzberg		
Extras	(lb 8,w 7,nb 1)	16
TOTAL	(38.4 overs)(for 2 wkts)	221

WORCS	O	M	R	W		FALL OF WICKETS		
Weston	7	0	26	1			GLO	WOR
Tolley	8	0	26	1	1st		19	20
Botham	8	0	40	2	2nd		53	146
Lampitt	6	0	56	2	3rd		155	
Hick	4	0	23	0	4th		171	
Herzberg	5	0	28	0	5th		198	
Leatherdale	2	0	12	0	6th		205	
					7th			
GLOUCS	O	M	R	W	8th			
Curran	7.4	0	39	0	9th			
Walsh	7	0	28	1	10th			
Bainbridge	5	0	25	0				
Graveney	8	0	42	0				
Alleyne	7	0	51	1				
Lloyds	4	0	28	0				

HEADLINES

8th July

● Middlesex's progress to their first Sunday League title was checked by Somerset as the long time leaders were defeated by 24 runs at Lord's

● Derbyshire just got the better of Lancashire to move within four points of Middlesex, Kim Barnett and Peter Bowler again laying the base for a formidable total

● Mark Feltham's Sunday best 61 helped Surrey to a 15-run victory over Warwicks, while Malcolm Marshall completed the Sunday double of 1000 runs and 100 wickets in Hampshire's win over Essex

● Notts had to survive a spirited effort from Sussex to overtake their total of 263 for 5 at Trent Bridge. Paul Johnson and Alan Wells both posted new personal Sunday bests

● Yorkshire defeated Northants at Tring as Peter Hartley followed his first Sunday 50 with 3 for 37

A Sunday best for Nottinghamshire's Paul Johnson against Sussex at Trent Bridge.

CORNHILL TEST MATCH	TOUR MATCH

ENGLAND vs. NEW ZEALAND

at Edgbaston on 5th, 6th, 7th, 9th, 10th July 1990
Toss : New Zealand.   Umpires : J.W.Holder and B.J.Meyer
England won by 114 runs

ENGLAND

G.A.Gooch *	c Hadlee b Morrison	154	b Snedden	30
M.A.Atherton	lbw b Snedden	82	c Rutherford b Bracewell	70
A.J.Stewart	c Parore b Morrison	9	lbw b Bracewell	15
A.J.Lamb	c Parore b Hadlee	2	st Parore b Bracewell	4
R.A.Smith	c Jones b Bracewell	19	c & b Hadlee	14
N.H.Fairbrother	lbw b Snedden	2	lbw b Bracewell	3
R.C.Russell +	b Snedden	43	c sub b Hadlee	0
C.C.Lewis	c Rutherford b Bracewell	32	c Parore b Hadlee	1
G.C.Small	not out	44	not out	11
E.E.Hemmings	c Parore b Hadlee	20	b Hadlee	0
D.E.Malcolm	b Hadlee	0	b Hadlee	0
Extras	(b 4,lb 15,nb 9)	28	(lb 6,nb 4)	10
TOTAL		435		158

NEW ZEALAND

T.J.Franklin	c Smith b Hemmings	66	lbw b Malcolm	5
J.G.Wright *	c Russell b Malcolm	24	c Smith b Lewis	46
A.H.Jones	c Russell b Malcolm	2	c Gooch b Small	40
M.D.Crowe	lbw b Lewis	11	lbw b Malcolm	25
M.J.Greatbatch	b Malcolm	45	c Atherton b Hemmings	22
K.R.Rutherford	c Stewart b Hemmings	29	c Lamb b Lewis	18
R.J.Hadlee	c Atherton b Hemmings	8	b Malcolm	13
J.G.Bracewell	b Hemmings	25	(9) c Atherton b Malcolm	0
A.C.Parore +	not out	12	(8) c Lamb b Lewis	20
M.C.Snedden	lbw b Hemmings	1	not out	21
D.K.Morrison	b Hemmings	1	b Malcolm	6
Extras	(b 9,lb 11,w 2,nb 2)	24	(lb 9,w 1,nb 4)	14
TOTAL		249		230

NEW ZEALAND	O	M	R	W	O	M	R	W
Hadlee	37.5	8	97	3	21	3	53	5
Morrison	26	7	81	2	3	1	29	0
Snedden	35	9	106	3	9	0	32	1
Bracewell	42	12	130	2	16	5	38	4
Jones	1	0	2	0				

ENGLAND	O	M	R	W	O	M	R	W
Small	18	7	44	0	16	5	56	1
Malcolm	25	7	59	3	24.4	8	46	5
Lewis	19	5	51	1	22	3	76	3
Hemmings	27.3	10	58	6	29	13	43	1
Atherton	9	5	17	0				

FALL OF WICKETS

	ENG	NZ	ENG	NZ
1st	170	45	50	25
2nd	193	67	87	85
3rd	198	90	99	111
4th	245	161	129	125
5th	254	163	136	155
6th	316	185	141	163
7th	351	223	146	180
8th	381	230	157	180
9th	435	243	158	203
10th	435	249	158	230

Man of the match: D.E.Malcolm (England)

KENT vs. INDIA

at Canterbury on 7th, 8th, 9th July 1990
Toss : Kent.   Umpires : M.J.Kitchen and N.T.Plews
India won by 7 wickets

KENT

S.G.Hinks	b Venkatapathy	62		
M.R.Benson	b Hirwani	90		
N.R.Taylor	not out	107	(6) not out	27
G.R.Cowdrey	c More b Wasson	44	(4) c Tendulkar b Hirwani	12
C.S.Cowdrey *	not out	20	(1) c Sharma b Venkatapathy	44
S.A.Marsh +			(2) c Hirwani b Wasson	21
M.V.Fleming			(3) not out	29
R.M.Ellison			(5) b Hirwani	6
T.A.Merrick				
C.Penn				
R.P.Davis				
Extras	(b 7,lb 8,w 2,nb 10)	27	(b 4,lb 5)	9
TOTAL	(for 3 wkts dec)	350	(for 4 wkts dec)	148

INDIA

K.S.More +	c Taylor b Fleming	32	c Penn b Fleming	27
S.R.Tendulkar	c Davis b Merrick	92	st Marsh b Davis	70
S.V.Manjrekar	c Davis b Penn	20	c Marsh b Fleming	9
D.B.Vengsarkar	not out	50	not out	83
Kapil Dev	c Ellison b Davis	17	not out	59
Venkatapathy Raju	lbw b Penn	4		
S.K.Sharma	not out	13		
R.J.Shastri *				
M.Prabhakar				
A.Wasson				
N.D.Hirwani				
Extras	(lb 3,nb 3)	6	(b 8,lb 9,nb 2)	19
TOTAL	(for 5 wkts dec)	234	(for 3 wkts)	267

INDIA	O	M	R	W	O	M	R	W
Kapil Dev	21	6	58	0	8	3	20	0
Prabhakar	10	1	34	0				
Sharma	11	3	37	0	3	0	11	0
Wasson	24	3	101	1	3	0	19	1
Shastri	10	2	37	0				
Hirwani	14	2	41	1	16	4	48	2
Venkatapathy	14	7	27	1	17.3	5	41	1

FALL OF WICKETS

	KEN	IND	KEN	IND
1st	126	75	44	66
2nd	196	125	82	96
3rd	295	154	96	130
4th		189	104	
5th		204		
6th				
7th				
8th				
9th				
10th				

KENT	O	M	R	W	O	M	R	W
Merrick	17	2	75	1	4.1	1	17	0
Penn	16	2	40	2	12	0	61	0
Davis	23	4	66	1	17.5	0	90	1
Cowdrey G.R.	1	1	0	0	2	0	12	0
Ellison	11	2	27	0	8	1	23	0
Fleming	8.3	2	23	1	11	5	28	2
Cowdrey C.S.					4	0	19	0

HEADLINES

England vs New Zealand: Third Cornhill Test Match

5th - 10th July

- England won a Test series at home for the first time in five years with only their second Test win on home soil in 26 attempts, but Sir Richard Hadlee stole the show by taking a wicket with the last ball of his Test career

- After a delayed start Graham Gooch and Mike Atherton set England on their way with an opening stand of 170. Gooch made his ninth Test 100 and his second against New Zealand, also becoming the 11th Englishman to score 5000 Test runs.

- After a steady start New Zealand were made to struggle by Eddie Hemmings, who produced his best Test figures.

- John Bracewell became the second New Zealander (after Sir Richard) to complete the Test double of 1000 runs and 100 wickets when he dismissed Allan Lamb. Hadlee then took over as England collapsed from 129 for three to 158 all out. Devon Malcolm became the great man's 431st and last Test victim, also providing him with his 36th haul of five or more wickets in an innings in Tests

- New Zealand needed 358 to win in more than four sessions, and when they were 101 for two at the close of the fourth day, the match was evenly balanced. However, Devon Malcolm brought victory to England with figures of five for 46

- Test debuts: C.C.Lewis (England); A.C.Parore (NewZealand).

- Men of the series: M.A.Atherton (England); Sir Richard Hadlee (New Zealand)

HEADLINES

7th - 9th July

- India continued their preparations for the internationals with the first first-class victory of their tour, beating Kent by seven wickets at Canterbury.

- Sachin Tendulkar, on his first tour of England, and Dilip Vengsarkar, on his sixth, caught the eye with the bat

BRITANNIC ASSURANCE CHAMPIONSHIP

LEICESTERSHIRE vs. GLAMORGAN

at Hinckley on 7th, 8th, 9th July 1990
Toss : Glamorgan. Umpires : J.H.Hampshire and K.J.Lyons
Match drawn (Leicestershire 6 pts (Bt: 4, Bw: 2) Glamorgan 6 pts (Bt: 4, Bw: 2))

GLAMORGAN

A.R.Butcher *	c Nixon b Benjamin	115	c Mullally b Willey	30
H.Morris	c Potter b Agnew	53	c Nixon b Benjamin	0
P.A.Cottey	c Nixon b Agnew	3	c Smith b Willey	125
M.P.Maynard	c Nixon b Agnew	59	c Potter b Benson	47
I.V.A.Richards	c Nixon b Agnew	14	not out	68
R.D.B.Croft	not out	25	not out	0
N.G.Cowley	c Nixon b Agnew	13		
C.P.Metson +	c Potter b Willey	2		
S.L.Watkin	c & b Potter	2		
S.J.Dennis	st Nixon b Potter	0		
M.Frost	not out	0		
Extras	(b 6,lb 11,w 1,nb 8)	26	(lb 6,w 1)	7
TOTAL	(for 9 wkts dec)	312	(for 4 wkts dec)	277

LEICESTERSHIRE

T.J.Boon	c Cowley b Watkin	51	not out	75
N.E.Briers *	c Richards b Frost	80	b Croft	22
J.J.Whitaker	c Cowley b Watkin	94	c Cottey b Cowley	45
P.Willey	c & b Frost	4	not out	0
L.Potter	c Butcher b Croft	13		
J.D.R.Benson	not out	35		
B.Smith	not out	15		
W.K.M.Benjamin				
P.A.Nixon +				
J.P.Agnew				
A.D.Mullally				
Extras	(b 1,lb 7,nb 1)	9	(lb 7,nb 3)	10
TOTAL	(for 5 wkts dec)	301	(for 2 wkts)	152

LEICS	O	M	R	W	O	M	R	W		FALL OF WICKETS			
											GLA	LEI	GLA	LEI
Benjamin	25	6	59	1	5	0	17	1	1st	112	105	3	60
Agnew	29	4	89	5	3	0	8	0	2nd	127	186	71	152
Mullally	29	8	84	0	10	2	26	0	3rd	218	196	150	
Willey	19	4	60	1	16	3	69	2	4th	258	228	272	
Benson	1	0	1	0	17	0	83	1	5th	261	271		
Potter	2	0	2	2	7	0	48	0	6th	292			
Boon					3	0	20	0	7th	304			
									8th	307			
GLAMORGAN	O	M	R	W	O	M	R	W	9th	309			
Frost	16	5	56	2	6	0	31	0	10th				
Watkin	22.5	6	53	2	10	1	34	0					
Dennis	19	4	79	0	8	1	28	0					
Richards	4	1	13	0									
Cowley	18	3	46	0	4.4	0	19	1					
Croft	13	3	46	1	10	2	33	1					

SURREY vs. WARWICKSHIRE

at The Oval on 7th, 9th, 10th July 1990
Toss : Warwickshire. Umpires : D.J.Constant and R.Palmer
Surrey won by 168 runs (Surrey 24 pts (Bt: 4, Bw: 4) Warwickshire 3 pts (Bt: 1, Bw: 2))

SURREY

D.J.Bicknell	c Ratcliffe b Benjamin	1	lbw b Benjamin	9
G.S.Clinton	c Humpage b Munton	18	b Benjamin	33
G.P.Thorpe	c Humpage b Donald	9	c Piper b Munton	3
D.M.Ward +	c Ostler b Reeve	126	c Benjamin b Munton	15
M.A.Lynch	c Piper b Munton	92	c Piper b Benjamin	46
J.D.Robinson	c Piper b Reeve	11	(7) b Feltham	27
I.A.Greig *	not out	30	(6) b Munton	34
K.T.Medlycott	not out	4	c sub b Benjamin	23
M.A.Feltham			not out	22
M.P.Bicknell			not out	6
Waqar Younis				
Extras	(b 2,lb 8,w 1,nb 1)	12	(lb 14,nb 4)	18
TOTAL	(for 6 wkts dec)	303	(for 8 wkts dec)	236

WARWICKSHIRE

A.J.Moles	b Waqar Younis	16	b Waqar Younis	1
J.D.Ratcliffe	lbw b Waqar Younis	15	(7) lbw b Bicknell M.P.	19
Asif Din	c Lynch b Bicknell M.P.	22	(2) c Lynch b Waqar Younis	4
G.W.Humpage	b Waqar Younis	0	c sub b Waqar Younis	4
D.P.Ostler	b Waqar Younis	30	(3) b Medlycott	59
K.J.Piper +	c Clinton b Bicknell M.P.	28	(5) b Feltham	14
D.A.Reeve *	c Medlycott b Bicknell M.P.	11	(6) lbw b Waqar Younis	17
A.R.K.Pierson	c Ward b Waqar Younis	0	not out	10
J.E.Benjamin	not out	28	c Bicknell M.P. b Feltham	41
A.A.Donald	b Waqar Younis	0	c Lynch b Feltham	3
T.A.Munton	b Waqar Younis	6	c Thorpe b Feltham	3
Extras	(b 3,lb 11,w 7)	21	(b 9,lb 3,w 1,nb 6)	19
TOTAL		177		194

WARWICKSHIRE	O	M	R	W	O	M	R	W		FALL OF WICKETS			
										SUR	WAR	SUR	WAR
Donald	12	1	31	1					1st	2	34	22	9
Benjamin	17	4	37	1	24	2	72	5	2nd	13	44	31	10
Munton	33	4	85	2	27	3	107	3	3rd	47	44	55	21
Reeve	24	6	64	2	12	3	43	0	4th	255	74	100	56
Pierson	7	0	39	0					5th	255	124	115	78
Asif Din	2	0	6	0					6th	293	138	173	128
Humpage	5	1	31	0					7th		141	185	128
									8th		143	210	185
SURREY	O	M	R	W	O	M	R	W	9th		151		188
Waqar Younis	21.1	2	73	7	14	0	55	4	10th		177		194
Bicknell M.P.	24	7	56	3	16	7	32	1					
Feltham	10	3	15	0	15.4	2	59	4					
Robinson	2	0	9	0									
Medlycott	2	0	10	0	8	0	36	1					

WORCESTERSHIRE vs. GLOUCESTERSHIRE

at Worcester on 7th, 9th, 10th July 1990
Toss : Worcestershire. Umpires : P.J.Eele and P.B.Wight
Worcestershire won by 148 runs (Worcs 22 pts (Bt: 2, Bw: 4) Gloucs 5 pts (Bt: 2, Bw: 3))

WORCESTERSHIRE

T.S.Curtis	lbw b Curran	4	b Graveney	21
P.Bent	c Athey b Barnes	44	b Curran	22
G.A.Hick	c Williams b Bell	0	b Bainbridge	79
D.B.D'Oliveira	c Williams b Bell	69	b Bainbridge	26
I.T.Botham	c Wright b Barnes	2	c Barnes b Bainbridge	16
P.A.Neale *	c Wright b Curran	14	not out	3
S.J.Rhodes +	b Graveney	55		
R.K.Illingworth	run out	50		
C.M.Tolley	b Curran	29		
S.R.Lampitt	not out	20		
G.R.Dilley	not out	17		
Extras	(b 1,lb 11,w 1,nb 2)	15	(lb 6,nb 3)	9
TOTAL	(for 9 wkts dec)	319	(for 5 wkts dec)	176

GLOUCESTERSHIRE

G.D.Hodgson	lbw b Hick	77	c D'Oliveira b Dilley	22
A.J.Wright *	lbw b Botham	13	(3) lbw b Dilley	5
I.P.Butcher	b Dilley	27	(2) c D'Oliveira b Dilley	0
C.W.J.Athey	c D'Oliveira b Hick	15	c Botham b Illingworth	32
P.Bainbridge	not out	31	c Botham b Illingworth	7
K.M.Curran	b Illingworth	7	b Hick	19
J.W.Lloyds	c Rhodes b Hick	28	st Rhodes b Hick	40
D.A.Graveney	c & b Illingworth	1	b Hick	0
R.C.J.Williams +	c Curtis b Illingworth	0	st Rhodes b Hick	1
S.N.Barnes	b Hick	0	c D'Oliveira b Illingworth	0
M.W.Bell	c Curtis b Hick	0	not out	0
Extras	(b 10,lb 7,w 3,nb 1)	21	(b 1)	1
TOTAL		220		127

GLOUCS	O	M	R	W	O	M	R	W		FALL OF WICKETS			
										WOR	GLO	WOR	GLO
Curran	33	6	76	3	12	2	37	1	1st	16	44	46	15
Barnes	22	4	74	2	1	0	6	0	2nd	17	96	46	26
Bell	17	4	38	2					3rd	60	133	126	27
Graveney	46	24	64	1	11	2	67	1	4th	62	140	173	49
Bainbridge	13	1	42	0	3	0	23	3	5th	94	155	176	80
Lloyds	2	0	13	0	3	0	37	0	6th	168	208		120
									7th	214	215		121
WORCS	O	M	R	W	O	M	R	W	8th	274	215		126
Dilley	9	1	26	1	7	2	16	3	9th	279	218		127
Lampitt	11	0	38	0					10th		220		127
Tolley	3	1	7	0	2	0	20	0					
Botham	10	3	20	1									
Illingworth	32	10	75	3	18	4	47	3					
Hick	16.3	5	37	5	14.3	1	43	4					

NOTTINGHAMSHIRE vs. SUSSEX

at Trent Bridge on 7th, 9th, 10th July 1990
Toss : Nottinghamshire. Umpires : H.D.Bird and K.E.Palmer
Match drawn (Nottinghamshire 5 pts (Bt: 1, Bw: 4) Sussex 8 pts (Bt: 4, Bw: 4))

SUSSEX

N.J.Lenham	c French b Pick	0	c French b Pick	27
J.W.Hall	b Cooper	125	not out	59
I.J.Gould	c Newell b Pick	4		
A.P.Wells	c French b Evans	23	(3) c & b Saxelby	25
M.P.Speight	lbw b Pick	55	(4) c Broad b Afford	30
C.M.Wells *	c Evans b Saxelby	5	(5) c Saxelby b Afford	44
A.I.C.Dodemaide	c French b Evans	72	(6) c & b Pick	7
P.Moores +	c Johnson b Evans	22	(7) not out	7
A.C.S.Pigott	lbw b Cooper	3		
I.D.K.Salisbury	not out	0		
R.A.Bunting				
Extras	(lb 9,w 1,nb 3)	13	(lb 9,nb 1)	10
TOTAL	(for 9 wkts dec)	322	(for 5 wkts dec)	209

NOTTINGHAMSHIRE

B.C.Broad	c Moores b Pigott	12	b Dodemaide	34
M.Newell	c Salisbury b Pigott	8	b Wells C.M.	85
R.T.Robinson *	c Gould b Pigott	6	c Pigott b Wells C.M.	52
P.Johnson	c Salisbury b Dodemaide	68	c Speight b Wells C.M.	14
D.W.Randall	c Moores b Wells C.M.	34	lbw b Salisbury	9
K.P.Evans	c Salisbury b Dodemaide	29	not out	21
B.N.French +	c Moores b Dodemaide	0	not out	17
K.E.Cooper	c Gould b Salisbury	0		
R.A.Pick	not out	13		
K.Saxelby	b Bunting	5		
J.A.Afford	b Bunting	0		
Extras	(lb 4,w 1)	5	(lb 7,w 4,nb 1)	12
TOTAL		185	(for 5 wkts)	244

NOTTS	O	M	R	W	O	M	R	W		FALL OF WICKETS			
										SUS	NOT	SUS	NOT
Pick	21	5	49	3	13	1	40	2	1st	0	14	43	64
Saxelby	14	3	44	1	10	2	29	1	2nd	4	23	80	175
Cooper	19.4	2	79	2	10	1	37	0	3rd	34	34	136	186
Evans	13	2	69	3	8	2	47	0	4th	135	111	190	201
Afford	19	2	72	0	9	2	47	2	5th	146	147	197	201
									6th	279	166		
SUSSEX	O	M	R	W	O	M	R	W	7th	311	166		
Pigott	14	4	47	3	9	2	18	0	8th	320	166		
Dodemaide	15	4	43	3	14	4	39	1	9th	322	185		
Bunting	13	3	42	2	9	0	46	0	10th		185		
Wells C.M.	9	1	20	1	14	3	48	3					
Salisbury	9	2	28	1	23	6	86	1					

BRITANNIC ASSURANCE CHAMPIONSHIP

NORTHANTS vs. YORKSHIRE

at Northampton on 7th, 9th, 10th July 1990
Toss : Yorkshire.   Umpires : J.C.Balderstone and A.A.Jones
Match drawn (Northants 6 pts (Bt: 4, Bw: 2) Yorkshire 7 pts (Bt: 4, Bw: 3))

YORKSHIRE

R.J.Blakey +	c Felton b Ambrose	17	c Bailey b Cook	57
A.A.Metcalfe *	b Cook	48	c & b Bailey	79
K.Sharp	retired hurt	40		
P.E.Robinson	b Cook	58	not out	76
D.Byas	lbw b Cook	28	c Ripley b Fordham	35
C.Chapman	c Felton b Williams	5	(3) c Fordham b Bailey	17
C.White	c Felton b Cook	38	(6) not out	29
P.Carrick	c Capel b Robinson	27		
P.J.Hartley	c Fordham b Williams	40		
S.D.Fletcher	lbw b Cook	0		
I.J.Houseman	not out	0		
Extras	(b 2,lb 8,w 1,nb 6)	17	(b 4,w 1,nb 4)	9
TOTAL		318	(for 4 wkts dec)	302

NORTHANTS

A.Fordham	c Blakey b Hartley	12	c Metcalfe b Fletcher	59
N.A.Felton	c Fletcher b Carrick	66	b Carrick	106
R.J.Bailey	b Hartley	0	c & b Carrick	6
D.J.Capel	c Metcalfe b Fletcher	64	b Fletcher	83
W.Larkins *	c Hartley b Fletcher	15	c & b Carrick	4
R.G.Williams	run out	69	st Blakey b Carrick	2
A.L.Penberthy	c & b Carrick	8	c & b Fletcher	1
D.Ripley +	not out	34	c Blakey b Fletcher	16
N.G.B.Cook	run out	30	(10) not out	1
C.E.L.Ambrose			(9) b Fletcher	14
M.A.Robinson			not out	0
Extras	(lb 5,nb 4)	9	(b 2,lb 4,nb 2)	8
TOTAL	(for 8 wkts dec)	307	(for 9 wkts)	300

NORTHANTS	O	M	R	W	O	M	R	W
Ambrose	12	0	42	1				
Capel	5	0	24	0	6	1	17	0
Robinson	22	3	67	1	12	2	50	0
Cook	25	10	44	5	14	6	25	1
Penberthy	12	2	32	0	6	0	29	0
Williams	27.2	5	99	2	4	1	6	0
Bailey					24.2	3	81	2
Felton					12	0	65	0
Fordham					5	0	25	1

YORKSHIRE	O	M	R	W	O	M	R	W
Hartley	15.2	2	56	2	11	0	66	0
Fletcher	17	6	44	2	18	0	94	5
Houseman	12	1	53	0	6	0	36	0
Carrick	37	6	91	2	20	1	98	4
White	10	1	39	0				
Byas	9	1	19	0				

FALL OF WICKETS

	YOR	NOR	YOR	NOR
1st	50	52	143	115
2nd	97	52	143	125
3rd	203	107	187	252
4th	204	156	260	264
5th	222	169		268
6th	263	200		269
7th	318	257		271
8th	318	307		299
9th	318			300
10th				

LANCASHIRE vs. DERBYSHIRE

at Liverpool on 7th, 9th, 10th July 1990
Toss : Lancashire. Umpires : R.Julian and D.O.Oslear
Match drawn (Lancashire 4 pts (Bt: 4, Bw: 0) Derbyshire 6 pts (Bt: 3, Bw: 3))

LANCASHIRE

G.D.Mendis	c Kuiper b Base	7	b Kuiper	25
G.Fowler	c Roberts b Jean-Jacques	19	(8) c G'smith b Jean-Jacques	31
G.D.Lloyd	lbw b Kuiper	62	(5) c Krikken b Kuiper	26
T.E.Jesty	c Krikken b Base	27	c Adams b Base	4
M.Watkinson	b Kuiper	4	(6) c G'smith b Jean-Jacques	63
P.A.J.DeFreitas	c Adams b Kuiper	16	(7) c Kuiper b Base	11
W.K.Hegg +	lbw b Miller	83	(3) c Krikken b Kuiper	34
I.D.Austin	c Roberts b Miller	29	(9) not out	27
D.P.Hughes *	not out	25	(10) not out	36
J.D.Fitton	not out	6	(2) b Kuiper	4
P.J.W.Allott				
Extras	(lb 11,w 4,nb 8)	23	(lb 2,w 1,nb 10)	13
TOTAL	(for 8 wkts dec)	301	(for 8 wkts dec)	274

DERBYSHIRE

K.J.Barnett *	c Hegg b Watkinson	109	not out	90
P.D.Bowler	not out	115	(5) c sub b Watkinson	30
J.E.Morris	c sub b Hughes	14	(2) c Hegg b Austin	22
B.Roberts	not out	4	(6) not out	1
A.P.Kuiper			(3) c Lloyd b DeFreitas	8
S.C.Goldsmith			(4) lbw b DeFreitas	7
C.J.Adams				
K.M.Krikken +				
G.Miller				
M.Jean-Jacques				
S.J.Base				
Extras	(b 2,lb 4,nb 2)	8	(b 8,lb 3)	11
TOTAL	(for 2 wkts dec)	250	(for 4 wkts)	169

DERBYSHIRE	O	M	R	W	O	M	R	W
Base	24	2	79	2	24	5	79	2
Jean-Jacques	25	3	104	1	16.3	0	90	2
Goldsmith	6	1	24	0	2	0	8	0
Kuiper	19	6	42	0	24	4	69	4
Barnett	1	0	9	0				
Miller	18	5	32	2	11	4	26	0

LANCASHIRE	O	M	R	W	O	M	R	W
DeFreitas	13	1	44	0	10	2	35	2
Watkinson	14.2	0	56	1	13	5	47	1
Austin	12	0	33	0	7	2	18	1
Fitton	23	5	66	0	11	3	43	0
Hughes	15	3	45	1	7	1	15	0

FALL OF WICKETS

	LAN	DER	LAN	DER
1st	10	200	12	55
2nd	53	240	58	81
3rd	111		71	89
4th	122		84	152
5th	138		112	
6th	146		139	
7th	234		206	
8th	284		207	
9th				
10th				

HEADLINES

7th - 10th July

● Victory for either Lancashire or Derbyshire in their match at Liverpool would have taken them to the top of the table, but the contest didn't live up to its star billing, as Kim Barnett gave up the chase 10 short of his second 100 of the match and what would have been his fourth in successive first-class innings

● Surrey continued to make up lost ground on the leaders in impressive style as Waqar Younis demolished Warwickshire at The Oval. His first innings analysis of 7 for 73 was a career best and he finished with match figures of 11 for 128. David Ward and Monte Lynch had earleir rescued Surrey from a sticky start with a stand of 208

● Worcestershire began to make up for a bad start with a comfortable victory over Gloucestershire at Worcester, Graeme Hick taking the honours with the ball - a career best 5 for 37 in the first innings and match figures of 9 for 80

● Jamie Hall made his maiden Championship 100 for Sussex against Nottinghamshire at Trent Bridge, but the visitors could not press home the advantage of a first innings lead of 137

● Northamptonshire made a valiant attempt to achieve a target of 314 in 55 overs against Yorkshire at Northampton, finishing 14 runs short with the last pair at the crease, after Nigel Felton and David Capel had put them in contention at 252 for two

● Leicestershire's match with Glamorgan at Hinckley was curtailed by rain. Tony Cottey became another to reach his maiden Championship 100 in the Glamorgan second innings in a summer rich in personal bests

● First-class debut: C.Chapman (Yorkshire)

NATWEST TROPHY – 2nd ROUND

YORKSHIRE vs. WARWICKSHIRE

at Headingley on 11th July 1990
Toss : Yorkshire. Umpires : H.D.Bird and R.A.White
Yorkshire won by 10 wickets

WARWICKSHIRE

A.J.Moles	c Blakey b Gough	27
T.A.Lloyd *	c Byas b Sidebottom	15
T.M.Moody	c Metcalfe b Carrick	51
G.W.Humpage +	c Sidebottom b Gough	2
D.A.Reeve	c Robinson b Carrick	0
D.P.Ostler	c Blakey b Carrick	4
Asif Din	c Gough b Byas	58
N.M.K.Smith	c Robinson b Hartley	52
G.C.Small	b Hartley	8
J.E.Benjamin	not out	2
T.A.Munton	not out	1
Extras	(lb 9,w 7,nb 5)	21
TOTAL	(60 overs)(for 9 wkts)	241

YORKSHIRE

M.D.Moxon *	not out	107
A.A.Metcalfe	not out	127
S.A.Kellett		
P.E.Robinson		
R.J.Blakey +		
D.Byas		
P.Carrick		
P.J.Hartley		
A.Sidebottom		
D.Gough		
S.D.Fletcher		
Extras	(lb 3,w 3,nb 2)	8
TOTAL	(55 overs)(for 0 wkts)	242

YORKSHIRE	O	M	R	W	FALL OF WICKETS	WAR	YOR
Hartley	12	0	62	2			
Sidebottom	12	4	20	1	1st	33	
Fletcher	12	1	56	0	2nd	79	
Carrick	12	0	26	3	3rd	85	
Gough	9	1	45	2	4th	86	
Byas	3	0	23	1	5th	97	
					6th	138	
WARWICKS	O	M	R	W	7th	211	
Benjamin	8	1	40	0	8th	236	
Small	9	1	37	0	9th	236	
Reeve	12	1	42	0	10th		
Munton	6	0	31	0			
Smith	8	0	41	0			
Moody	9	0	34	0			
Asif Din	3	0	14	0			

Man of the match: M.D.Moxon

MIDDLESEX vs. SURREY

at Uxbridge on 11th July 1990
Toss : Middlesex. Umpires : N.T.Plews and D.S.Thompsett
Middlesex won by 5 wickets

SURREY

D.J.Bicknell	b Cowans	12
G.S.Clinton	lbw b Fraser	33
A.J.Stewart *	c Farbrace b Fraser	48
M.A.Lynch	run out	59
D.M.Ward +	b Brown b Haynes	11
G.P.Thorpe	c Cowans b Fraser	16
M.A.Feltham	c Farbrace b Fraser	5
K.T.Medlycott	c Farbrace b Cowans	38
C.K.Bullen	not out	20
M.P.Bicknell	not out	4
Waqar Younis		
Extras	(b 1,lb 19,w 16,nb 6)	42
TOTAL	(60 overs)(for 8 wkts)	288

MIDDLESEX

D.L.Haynes	c Ward b Waqar Younis	0
M.A.Roseberry	c Bicknell M.P. b Waqar Younis	48
M.R.Ramprakash	c Ward b Bicknell M.P.	104
K.R.Brown	not out	103
R.O.Butcher	c Stewart b Medlycott	1
M.W.Gatting *	c Ward b Feltham	3
J.E.Emburey	not out	15
P.Farbrace +		
N.F.Williams		
A.R.C.Fraser		
N.G.Cowans		
Extras	(b 8,lb 6,w 1,nb 2)	17
TOTAL	(59.4 overs)(for 5 wkts)	291

MIDDLESEX	O	M	R	W	FALL OF WICKETS	SUR	MID
Cowans	11	2	45	2			
Williams	11	2	42	0	1st	18	0
Haynes	12	0	41	1	2nd	113	94
Gatting	2	0	20	0	3rd	114	220
Fraser	12	1	44	4	4th	175	223
Emburey	12	0	76	0	5th	215	241
					6th	221	
SURREY	O	M	R	W	7th	221	
Waqar Younis	12	2	39	2	8th	274	
Bicknell M.P.	12	0	63	1	9th		
Feltham	11.4	0	65	1	10th		
Medlycott	12	0	64	1			
Bullen	12	0	46	0			

Man of the match: K.R.Brown

ESSEX vs. HAMPSHIRE

at Chelmsford on 11th July 1990
Toss : Hampshire. Umpires : J.D.Bond and J.H.Harris
Hampshire won by losing fewer wickets

ESSEX

G.A.Gooch *	b Connor	144
J.P.Stephenson	run out	44
P.J.Prichard	c Gower b Marshall	21
M.E.Waugh	c Parks b Marshall	47
D.R.Pringle	c Nicholas b Bakker	33
N.A.Foster	c Gower b Connor	0
N.Hussain	not out	2
M.A.Garnham +	not out	1
T.D.Topley		
J.H.Childs		
M.C.Ilott		
Extras	(b 5,lb 3,w 3,nb 4)	15
TOTAL	(60 overs)(for 6 wkts)	307

HAMPSHIRE

V.P.Terry	c Gooch b Ilott	76
C.L.Smith	c Gooch b Stephenson	106
D.I.Gower	c Topley b Foster	19
R.A.Smith	c Topley b Pringle	59
M.D.Marshall	b Pringle	9
M.C.J.Nicholas *	not out	9
J.R.Ayling	not out	10
R.J.Parks +		
R.J.Maru		
C.A.Connor		
P.J.Bakker		
Extras	(lb 13,w 6)	19
TOTAL	(60 overs)(for 5 wkts)	307

HAMPSHIRE	O	M	R	W	FALL OF WICKETS	ESS	HAM
Marshall	12	0	45	2			
Bakker	12	3	60	1	1st	93	173
Connor	12	0	71	2	2nd	143	195
Ayling	12	0	57	0	3rd	240	233
Maru	12	0	66	0	4th	304	253
					5th	304	289
ESSEX	O	M	R	W	6th	304	
Foster	12	4	35	1	7th		
Ilott	9	0	45	1	8th		
Pringle	12	1	64	2	9th		
Childs	12	0	60	0	10th		
Topley	11	0	66	0			
Stephenson	4	0	24	1			

Man of the match: C.L.Smith

GLOUCESTERSHIRE vs. KENT

at Bristol on 11th July 1990
Toss : Kent. Umpires : B.Hassan and K.J.Lyons
Gloucestershire won by 6 wickets

KENT

M.R.Benson	c Russell b Walsh	7
S.G.Hinks	c Graveney b Curran	15
N.R.Taylor	b Walsh	0
G.R.Cowdrey	c Bainbridge b Alleyne	37
T.R.Ward	lbw b Walsh	47
C.S.Cowdrey *	b Walsh	5
S.A.Marsh +	b Walsh	0
R.M.Ellison	not out	27
P.S.De Villiers	b Curran	14
R.P.Davis	c Russell b Walsh	12
A.P.Igglesden	not out	2
Extras	(lb 9,w 4,nb 2)	15
TOTAL	(60 overs)(for 9 wkts)	181

GLOUCESTERSHIRE

A.J.Wright *	c Ellison b Davis	45
G.D.Hodgson	c Davis b De Villiers	39
P.Bainbridge	not out	56
C.W.J.Athey	c Marsh b Ellison	22
K.M.Curran	c Taylor b Cowdrey G.R.	1
J.W.Lloyds	not out	4
M.W.Alleyne		
R.C.Russell +		
C.A.Walsh		
D.A.Graveney		
S.N.Barnes		
Extras	(lb 3,w 11,nb 1)	15
TOTAL	(48.3 overs)(for 4 wkts)	182

GLOUCS	O	M	R	W	FALL OF WICKETS	KEN	GLO
Walsh	12	3	21	6			
Curran	12	2	30	2	1st	11	88
Barnes	6	0	29	0	2nd	13	94
Bainbridge	11.1	1	38	0	3rd	30	175
Graveney	6.5	0	21	0	4th	93	178
Alleyne	12	2	33	1	5th	120	
					6th	123	
KENT	O	M	R	W	7th	124	
De Villiers	9	1	29	1	8th	156	
Igglesden	8	0	34	0	9th	175	
Ellison	12	6	18	1	10th		
Cowdrey C.S.	5	0	29	0			
Davis	9	0	33	1			
Hinks	3	0	23	0			
Cowdrey G.R.	2.3	0	13	1			

Man of the match: C.A.Walsh

SOMERSET vs. WORCESTERSHIRE

at Taunton on 11th July 1990
Toss : Somerset. Umpires : B.Dudleston and D.R.Shepherd
Worcestershire won by 7 wickets

SOMERSET

S.J.Cook	lbw b Lampitt	45
P.M.Roebuck	b Lampitt	20
A.N.Hayhurst	c Lampitt b Newport	46
C.J.Tavare *	not out	99
G.D.Rose	c Neale b Botham	16
R.J.Harden	b Botham	12
N.D.Burns +	not out	25
R.P.Lefebvre		
I.G.Swallow		
N.A.Mallender		
A.N.Jones		
Extras	(b 6,lb 7,w 6,nb 1)	20
TOTAL	(60 overs)(for 5 wkts)	283

WORCESTERSHIRE

T.S.Curtis	c Swallow b Rose	112
M.J.Weston	c Cook b Lefebvre	98
G.A.Hick	c Burns b Lefebvre	2
D.B.D'Oliveira	not out	51
I.T.Botham	not out	0
P.A.Neale *		
C.M.Tolley		
S.J.Rhodes +		
R.K.Illingworth		
P.J.Newport		
S.R.Lampitt		
Extras	(lb 12,w 7,nb 2)	21
TOTAL	(57.2 overs)(for 3 wkts)	284

WORCS	O	M	R	W	FALL OF WICKETS	SOM	WOR
Botham	12	0	65	2			
Newport	10	0	54	1	1st	64	188
Lampitt	12	1	48	2	2nd	71	195
Illingworth	12	3	22	0	3rd	171	279
Tolley	6	0	32	0	4th	200	
Hick	8	0	49	0	5th	230	
					6th		
SOMERSET	O	M	R	W	7th		
Jones	10	0	64	0	8th		
Mallender	10	2	29	0	9th		
Lefebvre	12	0	46	2	10th		
Rose	9	0	40	1			
Hayhurst	2	0	14	0			
Swallow	9	0	57	0			
Roebuck	5.2	0	22	0			

Man of the match: T.S.Curtis

DERBYSHIRE vs. LANCASHIRE

at Derby on 11th July 1990
Toss : Lancashire. Umpires : M.J.Kitchen and K.E.Palmer
Lancashire won by 3 wickets

DERBYSHIRE

K.J.Barnett *	b Wasim Akram	59
P.D.Bowler +	b Wasim Akram	2
J.E.Morris	c Fairbrother b Atherton	74
A.P.Kuiper	c Atherton b Austin	25
B.Roberts	b DeFreitas	31
C.J.Adams	c Hegg b Austin	0
S.C.Goldsmith	c Watkinson b DeFreitas	21
G.Miller	b DeFreitas	0
A.E.Warner	not out	1
D.E.Malcolm	b Wasim Akram	0
O.H.Mortensen	b Wasim Akram	0
Extras	(lb 12,w 12,nb 4)	28
TOTAL	(56.5 overs)	241

LANCASHIRE

G.D.Mendis	c Bowler b Mortensen	42
M.A.Atherton	b Miller	55
G.D.Lloyd	c Adams b Warner	36
N.H.Fairbrother	c Miller b Malcolm	39
M.Watkinson	b Malcolm	5
Wasim Akram	b Goldsmith	9
P.A.J.DeFreitas	c Roberts b Malcolm	1
I.D.Austin	not out	13
W.K.Hegg +	not out	13
D.P.Hughes *		
P.J.Martin		
Extras	(b 6,lb 14,w 6,nb 3)	29
TOTAL	(59.2 overs)(for 7 wkts)	242

LANCASHIRE	O	M	R	W	FALL OF WICKETS	DER	LAN
Wasim Akram	10.5	0	34	4			
DeFreitas	11	4	34	3	1st	18	64
Watkinson	5	0	31	0	2nd	123	134
Martin	5	0	28	0	3rd	161	184
Austin	10	0	46	2	4th	180	194
Atherton	12	0	37	1	5th	180	209
Hughes	3	0	19	0	6th	239	214
					7th	239	215
DERBYSHIRE	O	M	R	W	8th	240	
Malcolm	12	1	54	3	9th	241	
Mortensen	12	4	22	1	10th	241	
Warner	12	1	45	1			
Miller	12	1	56	1			
Kuiper	6	1	25	0			
Goldsmith	5.2	0	20	1			

Man of the match: M.A.Atherton

NATWEST TROPHY – 2nd ROUND

GLAMORGAN vs. SUSSEX

at Cardiff on 11th July 1990
Toss : Sussex. Umpires : P.J.Eele and R.Palmer
Glamorgan won by 34 runs

GLAMORGAN

A.R.Butcher *	c Pigott b Dodemaide	30
H.Morris	c Salisbury b Dodemaide	58
P.A.Cottey	lbw b Clarke	27
M.P.Maynard	c Speight b Lenham	24
I.V.A.Richards	not out	74
I.Smith	st Moores b Clarke	22
N.G.Cowley	not out	32
C.P.Metson +		
S.J.Dennis		
S.L.Watkin		
M.Frost		
Extras	(b 2,lb 12,w 2)	16
TOTAL	(60 overs)(for 5 wkts)	283

SUSSEX

N.J.Lenham	lbw b Smith	47
J.W.Hall	run out	0
P.W.G.Parker *	b Richards	83
A.P.Wells	c Smith b Cowley	85
M.P.Speight	c Butcher b Cowley	4
A.I.C.Dodemaide	lbw b Richards	1
A.C.S.Pigott +	b Watkin	1
P.Moores	run out	0
C.C.Remy	b Watkin	1
I.D.K.Salisbury	not out	2
A.R.Clarke	lbw b Watkin	0
Extras	(b 1,lb 18,w 5,nb 1)	25
TOTAL	(55.5 overs)	249

SUSSEX	O	M	R	W		FALL OF WICKETS		
							GLA	SUS
Pigott	11	1	56	0		1st	33	2
Dodemaide	12	1	70	2		2nd	97	101
Remy	10	1	30	0		3rd	144	229
Salisbury	12	1	47	0		4th	160	233
Lenham	3	0	13	1		5th	206	236
Clarke	12	0	53	2		6th		243
						7th		243
GLAMORGAN	O	M	R	W		8th		247
Frost	10	1	34	0		9th		249
Watkin	11.5	5	18	3		10th		249
Dennis	8	0	44	0				
Richards	10	0	43	2				
Cowley	12	0	71	2				
Smith	4	0	20	1				

Man of the match: I.V.A.Richards

NORTHANTS vs. NOTTINGHAMSHIRE

at Northampton on 11th July 1990
Toss : Notts. Umpires : J.H.Hampshire and P.B.Wight
Northants won by 24 runs

NORTHANTS

A.Fordham	c French b Cooper	23
N.A.Felton	b Hemmings	32
R.J.Bailey	c French b Evans	7
A.J.Lamb *	c Evans b Stephenson	61
D.J.Capel	b Evans	101
W.Larkins	c French b Stephenson	21
R.G.Williams	not out	9
D.Ripley +	not out	1
C.E.L.Ambrose		
N.G.B.Cook		
M.A.Robinson		
Extras	(b 1,lb 14,w 3,nb 1)	19
TOTAL	(60 overs)(for 6 wkts)	274

NOTTINGHAMSHIRE

B.C.Broad	c Robinson b Williams	13
M.Newell	run out	4
R.T.Robinson *	b Bailey	61
P.Johnson	b Robinson	48
D.W.Randall	c Ambrose b Bailey	56
F.D.Stephenson	c Ambrose b Bailey	4
B.N.French +	c Fordham b Ambrose	35
K.P.Evans	run out	0
E.E.Hemmings	c & b Cook	0
K.E.Cooper	run out	0
R.A.Pick	not out	5
Extras	(lb 3,w 10,nb 11)	24
TOTAL	(57.1 overs)	250

NOTTS	O	M	R	W		FALL OF WICKETS		
							NOR	NOT
Stephenson	12	1	40	2		1st	33	24
Cooper	12	0	49	1		2nd	66	119
Pick	12	1	64	0		3rd	72	149
Evans	12	3	53	2		4th	226	163
Hemmings	12	2	53	1		5th	258	171
						6th	264	235
NORTHANTS	O	M	R	W		7th		239
Ambrose	10.1	1	30	1		8th		240
Robinson	11	0	46	1		9th		240
Cook	12	1	42	1		10th		250
Capel	6	0	43	0				
Williams	8	1	39	1				
Bailey	10	1	47	3				

Man of the match: D.J.Capel

A first Refuge century for David Capel against Nottinghamshire at Northampton.

TOUR MATCH

B & H CUP FINAL

Mike Watkinson, man of the match in Lancashire's Benson & Hedges Cup Final success.

LANCASHIRE vs. WORCESTERSHIRE

at Lord's on 14th July 1990
Toss : Worcs.   Umpires : J.H.Hampshire and N.T.Plews
Lancashire won by 69 runs

LANCASHIRE

G.D.Mendis	c Neale b Botham	19
G.Fowler	c Neale b Newport	11
M.A.Atherton	run out	40
N.H.Fairbrother	b Lampitt	11
M.Watkinson	c & b Botham	50
Wasim Akram	c Radford b Newport	28
P.A.J.DeFreitas	b Lampitt	28
I.D.Austin	run out	17
W.K.Hegg +	not out	31
D.P.Hughes *	not out	1
P.J.W.Allott		
Extras	(lb 4,nb 1)	5
TOTAL	(55 overs)(for 8 wkts)	241

WORCESTERSHIRE

T.S.Curtis	c Hegg b Wasim Akram	16
M.J.Weston	b Watkinson	19
G.A.Hick	c Hegg b Wasim Akram	1
D.B.D'Oliveira	b Watkinson	23
I.T.Botham	b DeFreitas	38
P.A.Neale *	c Hegg b Austin	0
S.J.Rhodes +	lbw b Allott	5
N.V.Radford	not out	26
R.K.Illingworth	lbw b DeFreitas	16
P.J.Newport	b Wasim Akram	3
S.R.Lampitt	b Austin	4
Extras	(lb 9,w 8,nb 4)	21
TOTAL	(54 overs)	172

WORCS	O	M	R	W	FALL OF WICKETS	
					LAN	WOR
Newport	11	1	47	2		
Botham	11	0	49	2	1st 25	27
Lampitt	11	3	43	2	2nd 33	38
Radford	8	1	41	0	3rd 47	41
Illingworth	11	0	41	0	4th 135	82
Hick	3	0	16	0	5th 136	87
					6th 191	112
LANCASHIRE	O	M	R	W	7th 199	114
Allott	10	1	22	1	8th 231	154
DeFreitas	11	2	30	2	9th	164
Wasim Akram	11	0	30	3	10th	172
Watkinson	11	0	37	2		
Austin	11	1	44	2		

Man of the match: M.Watkinson

MINOR COUNTIES vs. INDIA

at Trowbridge on 11th, 12th, 13th July 1990
Toss : Minor Counties. Umpires : D.J.Halfyard and G.A.Stickley
Match drawn

MINOR COUNTIES

G.K.Brown	s Mongia b Kumble	103	not out		89
M.J.Roberts	b Shastri	85	c Azharuddin b Sharma		1
P.Burn	c Mongia b Sharma	0	(4) not out		47
N.A.Folland	lbw b Kumble	26	(3) b Venkatapathy		82
T.A.Lester	c Raman b Kumble	4			
D.R.Thomas	c Shastri b Kumble	27			
S.Greensword *	c Mongia b Kapil Dev	1			
A.R.Fothergill +	b Kumble	3			
R.A.Evans	not out	4			
N.R.Taylor	b Kumble	0			
K.A.Arnold					
Extras	(b 8,lb 17,w 6,nb 9)	40	(b 20,lb 2,nb 2)		24
TOTAL	(for 9 wkts dec)	293	(for 2 wkts)		243

INDIA

R.J.Shastri	b Evans	105
W.V.Raman	c Greensword b Arnold	55
S.V.Manjrekar	run out	40
M.Azharuddin *	c Arnold b Taylor	105
Kapil Dev	c Arnold b Evans	47
S.R.Tendulkar	lbw b Brown	65
N.R.Mongia +	not out	43
Venkatapathy Raju	not out	33
S.K.Sharma		
A.Wasson		
A.R.Kumble		
Extras	(b 5,lb 4,w 3,nb 7)	19
TOTAL	(for 6 wkts dec)	512

INDIA	O	M	R	W	O	M	R	W	FALL OF WICKETS				
										MIN	IND	MIN	IND
Kapil Dev	14	6	27	1	16	9	20	0	1st	178	102	6	
Sharma	15	4	43	1	15	4	47	1	2nd	183	201	163	
Wasson	9	1	36	0	9	0	42	0	3rd	245	238		
Venkatapathy	21	4	67	0	18	4	58	1	4th	246	312		
Kumble	18	3	49	6	16	4	54	0	5th	250	426		
Shastri	20	4	43	1					6th	253	449		
Tendulkar	1	0	3	0					7th	264			
									8th	293			
M. COUNTIES	O	M	R	W	O	M	R	W	9th	293			
Taylor	23	2	87	1					10th				
Arnold	28	6	113	1									
Evans	28	1	147	2									
Thomas	15	1	65	0									
Greensword	19	6	52	0									
Brown	9	1	39	1									

HEADLINES

11th - 13th July

● The Minor Counties batsmen distinguished themselves against the Indians at Trowbridge, as they comfortably held on for a draw. Gary Brown, who played one first-class match for Middlesex, hit a miden 100 in the first innings and was only 11 short of another in the second. Anil Kumble returned career best figures in the Minor Counties first innings, while Ravi Shastri and Mohammed Azharuddin both made 100s as the Indians raced to 512 for 6

● First-class debuts: P.Burn, R.A.Evans, N.A.Folland, A.R.Fothergill, T.A.Lester, M.J.Roberts, N.R.Taylor and D.R.Thomas (Minor Counties)

Benson & Hedges Cup Final

14th July

● Worcestershire's dismal record in Lord's finals continued as Lancashire won the Benson and Hedges Cup for the second time, all-round contributions from Mike Watkinson, who won the Gold Award, Wasim Akram and Phil DeFreitas swaying the balance of what should have been an even contest decisively in their favour

TOUR MATCHES	REFUGE ASSURANCE LEAGUE

SCOTLAND vs. INDIA

at Glasgow on 14th July 1990
Toss : India. Umpires : J.van Geloven and A.Wood
India won by 7 wickets

SCOTLAND

I.L.Philip	run out	14
C.G.Greenidge	lbw b Sharma	34
B.M.W.Patterson	c Manjrekar b Venkatapathy	0
G.Salmond	c Manjrekar b Venkatapathy	0
O.Henry *	c Raman b Kapil Dev	74
D.J.Haggo +	c Tendulkar b Venkatapathy	6
A.B.Russell	c & b Kapil Dev	48
D.Cowan	not out	1
A.W.Bee	not out	2
C.T.McKnight		
J.D.Moir		
Extras	(lb 13,w 3,nb 1)	17
TOTAL	(55 overs)(for 7 wkts)	196

INDIA

N.S.Sidhu	c McKnight b Henry	50
W.V.Raman	c Haggo b Bee	89
S.V.Manjrekar	c Greenidge b Bee	31
S.R.Tendulkar	not out	10
Kapil Dev	not out	11
M.Azharuddin *		
M.Prabhakar		
K.S.More +		
Venkatapathy Raju		
S.K.Sharma		
A.R.Kumble		
Extras	(b 2,lb 2,w 1,nb 4)	9
TOTAL	(51.3 overs)(for 3 wkts)	200

INDIA	O	M	R	W	FALL OF WICKETS		
						SCO	IND
Kapil Dev	10	2	25	2	1st	44	98
Prabhakar	10	2	43	0	2nd	45	159
Sharma	11	1	27	1	3rd	45	183
Tendulkar	3	1	9	0	4th	56	
Venkatapathy	11	3	22	3	5th	71	
Kumble	10	0	57	0	6th	193	
					7th	194	
SCOTLAND	O	M	R	W	8th		
Moir	9	1	34	0	9th		
Cowan	9.3	0	48	0	10th		
Bee	11	1	35	2			
McKnight	11	2	29	0			
Henry	11	0	50	1			

DERBYSHIRE vs. INDIA

at Chesterfield on 16th July 1990
Toss : Derbyshire. Umpires : H.D.Bird and M.J.Kitchen
India won by 2 wickets

DERBYSHIRE

K.J.Barnett *	c Sidhu b Kapil Dev	115
P.D.Bowler +	b Venkatapathy	59
J.E.Morris	c sub b Kapil Dev	37
B.Roberts	c Azharuddin b Kapil Dev	8
C.J.Adams	run out	0
S.C.Goldsmith	run out	3
K.M.Krikken +	not out	0
G.Miller		
I.R.Bishop		
S.J.Base		
O.H.Mortensen		
Extras	(lb 7,w 4,nb 2)	13
TOTAL	(55 overs)(for 6 wkts)	235

INDIA

W.V.Raman	b Base	17
N.S.Sidhu	lbw b Bishop	0
S.R.Tendulkar	not out	105
M.Azharuddin *	lbw b Miller	7
Kapil Dev	c Barnett b Mortensen	1
M.Prabhakar	run out	31
K.S.More +	c Barnett b Miller	6
D.B.Vengsarkar	st Krikken b Miller	28
Venkatapathy Raju	c Roberts b Miller	1
S.K.Sharma	not out	8
A.R.Kumble		
Extras	(lb 2,w 17,nb 16)	35
TOTAL	(54.4 overs)(for 8 wkts)	239

INDIA	O	M	R	W	FALL OF WICKETS		
						DER	IND
Kapil Dev	11	1	76	3	1st	137	5
Prabhakar	11	2	29	0	2nd	208	59
Sharma	11	0	51	0	3rd	223	80
Kumble	11	1	26	0	4th	224	81
Venkatapathy	11	0	46	1	5th	235	134
					6th	235	144
DERBYSHIRE	O	M	R	W	7th		210
Mortensen	11	1	31	1	8th		212
Bishop	11	2	44	1	9th		
Base	11	0	45	1	10th		
Goldsmith	10.4	0	71	0			
Miller	11	0	46	4			

DERBYSHIRE vs. LEICESTERSHIRE

at Knypersley on 15th July 1990
Toss : Derbyshire. Umpires : D.O.Oslear and R.A.White
Derbyshire won by 118 runs (Derbyshire 4 pts Leics 0 pts)

DERBYSHIRE

K.J.Barnett *	c Nixon b Mullally	39
P.D.Bowler +	c Nixon b Benjamin	4
J.E.Morris	c Nixon b Lewis	21
A.P.Kuiper	c Benjamin b Agnew	42
B.Roberts	not out	77
C.J.Adams	b Benjamin	9
S.C.Goldsmith	not out	4
A.E.Warner		
D.E.Malcolm		
S.J.Base		
O.H.Mortensen		
Extras	(lb 13,w 10,nb 3)	26
TOTAL	(40 overs)(for 5 wkts)	222

LEICESTERSHIRE

T.J.Boon	c Bowler b Base	2
N.E.Briers *	lbw b Warner	29
J.J.Whitaker	c Roberts b Malcolm	12
P.Willey	c Bowler b Malcolm	24
C.C.Lewis	run out	0
L.Potter	b Barnett	6
J.D.R.Benson	c Morris b Warner	1
W.K.M.Benjamin	b Malcolm	11
P.A.Nixon +	c Adams b Warner	4
J.P.Agnew	b Malcolm	0
A.D.Mullally	not out	5
Extras	(lb 4,w 5,nb 1)	10
TOTAL	(28 overs)	104

LEICS	O	M	R	W	FALL OF WICKETS		
						DER	LEI
Benjamin	8	0	32	2	1st	16	6
Agnew	8	1	52	1	2nd	66	33
Lewis	8	0	43	1	3rd	71	55
Mullally	8	1	37	1	4th	158	58
Willey	8	0	45	0	5th	206	79
					6th		81
DERBYSHIRE	O	M	R	W	7th		83
Base	5	0	20	1	8th		98
Mortensen	6	0	18	0	9th		98
Malcolm	6	0	21	4	10th		104
Warner	5	0	18	3			
Goldsmith	3	0	14	0			
Barnett	3	0	9	1			

LANCASHIRE vs. WORCESTERSHIRE

at Old Trafford on 15th July 1990
Toss : Lancashire. Umpires : B.Hassan and J.W.Holder
Lancashire won by 7 wickets (Lancashire 4 pts Worcs 0 pts)

WORCESTERSHIRE

T.S.Curtis *	lbw b Watkinson	32
M.J.Weston	c Fowler b Watkinson	31
G.A.Hick	b Wasim Akram	42
D.B.D'Oliveira	c Hegg b Watkinson	3
D.A.Leatherdale	c Hughes b Watkinson	4
S.J.Rhodes	b Austin	12
N.V.Radford +	c Atherton b Wasim Akram	2
P.J.Newport	not out	16
S.R.Lampitt	c DeFreitas b Austin	0
C.M.Tolley	not out	1
S.M.McEwan		
Extras	(lb 8,w 6)	14
TOTAL	(40 overs)(for 8 wkts)	157

LANCASHIRE

G.Fowler	c Curtis b Lampitt	33
M.A.Atherton	c Rhodes b Tolley	1
G.D.Lloyd	not out	65
N.H.Fairbrother	run out	36
M.Watkinson	not out	15
Wasim Akram		
P.A.J.DeFreitas		
I.D.Austin		
W.K.Hegg +		
D.P.Hughes *		
P.J.W.Allott		
Extras	(lb 5,w 4,nb 1)	10
TOTAL	(30.1 overs)(for 3 wkts)	160

LANCASHIRE	O	M	R	W	FALL OF WICKETS		
						LAN	
Allott	8	0	31	0		WOR	LAN
DeFreitas	8	1	28	0	1st	68	4
Watkinson	8	0	34	4	2nd	68	71
Wasim Akram	8	0	34	2	3rd	80	125
Austin	8	1	26	2	4th	92	
					5th	117	
WORCS	O	M	R	W	6th	125	
Newport	7	0	31	0	7th	148	
Tolley	6	0	20	1	8th	149	
Radford	4	0	24	0	9th		
Lampitt	7.1	0	34	1	10th		
McEwan	3	0	23	0			
Hick	2	0	17	0			
Leatherdale	1	0	6	0			

SURREY vs. MIDDLESEX

at The Oval on 15th July 1990
Toss : Middlesex. Umpires : P.J.Eele and D.R.Shepherd
Surrey won by 68 runs (Surrey 4 pts Middlesex 0 pts)

SURREY

D.J.Bicknell	b Emburey	75
M.A.Feltham	c Brown b Williams	4
G.P.Thorpe	c Gatting b Haynes	41
D.M.Ward +	c Haynes b Cowans	60
M.A.Lynch	lbw b Emburey	25
I.A.Greig *	not out	4
A.Brown	run out	2
K.T.Medlycott	not out	0
C.K.Bullen		
M.P.Bicknell		
Waqar Younis		
Extras	(lb 6,w 10,nb 1)	17
TOTAL	(40 overs)(for 6 wkts)	228

MIDDLESEX

D.L.Haynes	c Ward b Bicknell M.P.	4
M.A.Roseberry	b Medlycott	48
M.W.Gatting *	b Bicknell M.P.	2
M.R.Ramprakash	c Thorpe b Waqar Younis	60
K.R.Brown	c Greig b Medlycott	12
R.O.Butcher	b Waqar Younis	3
J.E.Emburey	c Bullen b Bicknell M.P.	15
P.Farbrace +	b Waqar Younis	2
N.F.Williams	lbw b Waqar Younis	1
A.R.C.Fraser	not out	4
N.G.Cowans	c & b Bicknell M.P.	0
Extras	(lb 3,w 5,nb 1)	9
TOTAL	(33.2 overs)	160

MIDDLESEX	O	M	R	W	FALL OF WICKETS		
						SUR	MID
Cowans	8	0	46	1	1st	6	4
Williams	8	1	42	1	2nd	77	18
Emburey	8	1	39	2	3rd	182	99
Brown	2	0	16	0	4th	215	125
Fraser	8	0	40	0	5th	222	134
Haynes	6	0	39	1	6th	224	136
					7th		142
SURREY	O	M	R	W	8th		156
Bicknell M.P.	4.2	0	14	4	9th		160
Feltham	4	0	23	0	10th		160
Greig	3	0	16	0			
Bullen	8	0	38	0			
Waqar Younis	6	0	27	4			
Medlycott	8	0	39	2			

ESSEX vs. NORTHANTS

at Chelmsford on 15th July 1990
Toss : Essex. Umpires : M.J.Kitchen and D.S.Thompsett
Essex won by 6 wickets (Essex 4 pts Northants 0 pts)

NORTHANTS

A.Fordham	run out	74
W.Larkins	c Gooch b Foster	6
D.J.Capel	c Garnham b Ilott	56
A.J.Lamb *	c Prichard b Pringle	34
R.J.Bailey	c Hussain b Topley	26
D.J.Wild	c & b Pringle	20
W.W.Davis	c Ilott b Waugh	2
D.Ripley +	not out	3
N.G.B.Cook		
M.A.Robinson		
S.J.Brown		
Extras	(lb 7,w 5)	12
TOTAL	(40 overs)(for 7 wkts)	233

ESSEX

G.A.Gooch *	run out	0
J.P.Stephenson	c Fordham b Wild	66
M.E.Waugh	b Cook	53
N.Hussain	b Bailey	22
D.R.Pringle	not out	61
M.A.Garnham +	not out	29
P.J.Prichard		
N.A.Foster		
T.D.Topley		
J.H.Childs		
M.C.Ilott		
Extras	(lb 7,w 1)	8
TOTAL	(38.2 overs)(for 4 wkts)	239

ESSEX	O	M	R	W	FALL OF WICKETS		
						NOR	ESS
Foster	8	1	36	1	1st	15	0
Ilott	8	0	17	1	2nd	141	111
Topley	5	0	34	1	3rd	147	139
Childs	6	0	38	0	4th	188	158
Pringle	8	0	59	2	5th	226	
Waugh	5	0	42	1	6th	227	
					7th	233	
NORTHANTS	O	M	R	W	8th		
Robinson	7	1	46	0	9th		
Davis	8	0	38	0	10th		
Cook	8	0	42	1			
Brown	5.2	0	39	0			
Wild	5	0	36	1			
Bailey	5	0	31	1			

REFUGE ASSURANCE LEAGUE

WARWICKSHIRE vs. GLAMORGAN

at Edgbaston on 15th July 1990
Toss : Warwickshire.   Umpires : A.A.Jones and B.J.Meyer
Glamorgan won by 7 wickets (Warwicks 0 pts Glam 4 pts)

WARWICKSHIRE

T.A.Lloyd *	c Dale b Watkin	12
Asif Din	run out	46
T.M.Moody	b Dale	4
G.W.Humpage	c Watkin b Cowley	11
D.P.Ostler	b Cowley	15
D.A.Reeve	b Watkin	28
K.J.Piper +	b Richards	1
G.C.Small	b Watkin	4
J.E.Benjamin	b Watkin	5
A.R.K.Pierson	c Metson b Watkin	1
T.A.Munton	not out	2
Extras	(b 1,lb 6,w 5)	12
TOTAL	(39.4 overs)	141

GLAMORGAN

M.P.Maynard	not out	61
H.Morris	b Benjamin	19
I.V.A.Richards	c Pierson b Reeve	31
I.Smith	c Moody b Pierson	10
A.R.Butcher *	not out	6
A.Dale		
N.G.Cowley		
C.P.Metson +		
S.J.Dennis		
S.L.Watkin		
M.Frost		
Extras	(b 1,lb 4,w 10)	15
TOTAL	(34 overs)(for 3 wkts)	142

GLAMORGAN	O	M	R	W	FALL OF WICKETS		
						WAR	GLA
Frost	6	0	21	0			
Watkin	7.4	0	23	5	1st	19	45
Dale	8	0	29	1	2nd	32	92
Dennis	6	0	24	0	3rd	63	125
Cowley	8	1	17	2	4th	93	
Richards	4	0	20	1	5th	95	
					6th	97	
WARWICKS	O	M	R	W	7th	118	
Small	8	1	17	0	8th	130	
Munton	6	2	14	0	9th	133	
Benjamin	6	1	34	1	10th	141	
Reeve	6	0	28	1			
Pierson	7	1	38	1			
Moody	1	0	6	0			

YORKSHIRE vs. SOMERSET

at Scarborough on 15th July 1990
Toss : Somerset. Umpires : H.D.Bird and J.D.Bond
Yorkshire won by 16 runs (Yorkshire 4 pts Somerset 0 pts)

YORKSHIRE

M.D.Moxon *	c Tavare b Mallender	105
A.A.Metcalfe	c Harden b Hallett	14
R.J.Blakey	c Harden b Rose	52
P.J.Hartley	c Burns b Lefebvre	27
P.E.Robinson	b Hayhurst	15
D.Byas	not out	6
C.S.Pickles	not out	1
C.White		
P.Carrick		
A.Sidebottom		
S.D.Fletcher		
Extras	(b 1,lb 4,w 2)	7
TOTAL	(40 overs)(for 5 wkts)	227

SOMERSET

S.J.Cook	c Blakey b Carrick	52
R.J.Bartlett	c Robinson b Pickles	21
C.J.Tavare *	c & b Pickles	8
R.J.Harden	c White b Pickles	28
G.D.Rose	c Moxon b White	6
N.D.Burns +	run out	1
A.N.Hayhurst	b Pickles	16
R.P.Lefebvre	b Fletcher	28
I.G.Swallow	c Carrick b Fletcher	31
N.A.Mallender	b Hartley	3
J.C.Hallett	not out	0
Extras	(lb 16,nb 1)	17
TOTAL	(39.4 overs)	211

SOMERSET	O	M	R	W	FALL OF WICKETS		
						YOR	SOM
Mallender	8	0	51	1			
Rose	8	0	45	1	1st	46	55
Lefebvre	8	0	35	1	2nd	157	69
Hallett	5	0	23	1	3rd	198	95
Hayhurst	7	0	43	1	4th	217	110
Swallow	4	0	25	0	5th	226	119
					6th		147
YORKSHIRE	O	M	R	W	7th		147
Hartley	7	0	42	1	8th		194
Sidebottom	5	0	25	0	9th		205
Fletcher	7.4	0	40	2	10th		211
Pickles	6	0	36	4			
Carrick	8	0	18	1			
White	6	0	34	1			

HAMPSHIRE vs. NOTTINGHAMSHIRE

at Southampton on 15th July 1990
Toss : Notts. Umpires : J.H.Harris and A.G.T.Whitehead
Hampshire won by 7 runs (Hampshire 4 pts Notts 0 pts)

HAMPSHIRE

V.P.Terry	c Robinson b Cooper	3
R.J.Scott	b Saxelby	55
R.A.Smith	c Newell b Afford	77
D.I.Gower	not out	66
M.D.Marshall	run out	7
M.C.J.Nicholas *	not out	46
J.R.Ayling		
R.J.Parks +		
R.J.Maru		
C.A.Connor		
P.J.Bakker		
Extras	(lb 5,w 7,nb 1)	13
TOTAL	(40 overs)(for 4 wkts)	267

NOTTINGHAMSHIRE

B.C.Broad	b Connor	86
P.Johnson	c Parks b Marshall	9
R.T.Robinson *	b Maru	44
M.Saxelby	b Ayling	24
F.D.Stephenson	c Nicholas b Ayling	14
G.W.Mike	c Scott b Ayling	10
B.N.French +	c Terry b Ayling	9
K.E.Cooper	b Marshall	1
M.Newell	not out	11
E.E.Hemmings	not out	32
J.A.Afford		
Extras	(b 5,lb 9,w 3,nb 3)	20
TOTAL	(40 overs)(for 8 wkts)	260

NOTTS	O	M	R	W	FALL OF WICKETS		
						HAM	NOT
Cooper	8	0	44	1			
Stephenson	8	1	43	0	1st	15	34
Hemmings	7	0	36	0	2nd	134	142
Mike	4	0	26	0	3rd	154	155
Afford	8	0	74	1	4th	162	182
Saxelby	5	0	39	1	5th		196
					6th		205
HAMPSHIRE	O	M	R	W	7th		213
Bakker	7	0	52	0	8th		214
Marshall	8	0	36	2	9th		
Connor	7	0	49	1	10th		
Ayling	8	0	37	4			
Maru	5	0	38	1			
Scott	5	0	34	0			

GLOUCESTERSHIRE vs. SUSSEX

at Swindon on 15th July 1990
Toss : Gloucs. Umpires : D.J.Constant and R.Palmer
Gloucestershire won by 1 wicket (Gloucs 4 pts Sussex 0 pts)

SUSSEX

N.J.Lenham	run out	65
P.W.G.Parker *	b Curran	7
A.P.Wells	c Russell b Barnes	17
M.P.Speight	c Romaines b Barnes	60
C.M.Wells	b Bainbridge	9
A.I.C.Dodemaide	c Alleyne b Curran	23
A.C.S.Pigott	run out	10
J.A.North	run out	1
P.Moores +	not out	4
C.C.Remy	run out	2
A.R.Clarke	b Walsh	0
Extras	(b 4,lb 5,w 1,nb 2)	12
TOTAL	(34.5 overs)	210

GLOUCESTERSHIRE

R.C.Russell +	c Moores b Dodemaide	2
C.W.J.Athey	c Dodemaide b Pigott	23
A.J.Wright *	c Remy b Dodemaide	3
K.M.Curran	b Pigott	52
P.Bainbridge	c Speight b Pigott	0
P.W.Romaines	c Parker b Lenham	47
J.W.Lloyds	not out	38
M.W.Alleyne	st Moores b Clarke	20
C.A.Walsh	c North b Lenham	11
G.D.Hodgson	st Moores b Clarke	1
S.N.Barnes	not out	0
Extras	(b 1,lb 4,w 12)	17
TOTAL	(40 overs)(for 9 wkts)	214

GLOUCS	O	M	R	W	FALL OF WICKETS		
						SUS	GLO
Walsh	5.5	0	33	1			
Curran	5	0	21	2	1st	26	10
Bainbridge	8	0	52	1	2nd	60	16
Barnes	8	0	46	2	3rd	136	32
Alleyne	8	0	49	0	4th	163	32
					5th	175	130
SUSSEX	O	M	R	W	6th	198	146
Dodemaide	8	0	22	2	7th	199	179
Wells C.M.	8	0	17	0	8th	205	202
Pigott	8	2	35	3	9th	210	204
Clarke	7	0	58	2	10th	210	
Remy	2	0	23	0			
Lenham	7	0	54	2			

HEADLINES

14th - 16th June

● India warmed up for the Texaco Trophy with one-day wins over Scotland in Glasgow and Derbyshire at Chesterfield, the most significant performance coming from 17-year-old Sachin Tendulkar who made his first 100 of the tour, 105*, against Derbyshire

15th July

● Middlesex's position at the head of the Refuge table continued to look vulnerable as they suffered their second successive defeat, losing by 68 runs to Surrey at The Oval. Darren Bicknell made a career best 75, then his brother Martin and Waqar Younis both improved their best bowling figures with four wickets apiece

● Derbyshire were impressive victors over Leicestershire at Knypersley to join Middlesex on 36 points, Devon Malcolm returning another personal best

● Lancashire repeated their success of the day before over Worcestershire at Old Trafford, Mike Watkinson taking the first four wickets, as the Lancastrians moved up to third place

● Hampshire stayed in contention for at least a play-off place with a seven-run win over Nottinghamshire at Southampton, their total of 267 for 4 being based on century partnerships for the second and fifth wickets. Jonathan Ayling's best Sunday figures ensured Notts finished just short of their required total

● Martyn Moxon's first Sunday League century and career best figures from Chris Pickles helped Yorkshire to a 16-run win over Somerset at Scarborough, while Steve Watkin's 5 for 23, another career best, was too much for Warwickshire at Edgbaston as Glamorgan won by seven wickets

● Northamptonshire's miserable Sunday form continued at Chelmsford, where Essex's batsmen proved too formidable a proposition, while Sussex's batting line-up again managed to self-destruct against Gloucestershire at Swindon. The visitors were unable to capitalise on a position of 136 for 2 in 20 overs and Gloucestershire scraped home by one wicket from the last ball

TEXACO TROPHY

ENGLAND vs. INDIA

at Headingley on 18th July 1990
Toss : India.   Umpires : J.H.Hampshire and J.W.Holder
India won by 6 wickets

ENGLAND

G.A.Gooch *	c & b Shastri	45
M.A.Atherton	lbw b Prabhakar	7
D.I.Gower	b Kumble	50
A.J.Lamb	c Prabhakar b Kapil Dev	56
R.A.Smith	c More b Kumble	6
R.C.Russell +	c Manjrekar b Kapil Dev	14
P.A.J.DeFreitas	b Sharma	11
C.C.Lewis	lbw b Prabhakar	6
E.E.Hemmings	b Sharma	3
A.R.C.Fraser	not out	4
D.E.Malcolm	c Kapil Dev b Prabhakar	4
Extras	(b 6,lb 8,w 9)	23
TOTAL	(54.3 overs)	229

INDIA

W.V.Raman	c Atherton b DeFreitas	0
N.S.Sidhu	lbw b Lewis	39
S.V.Manjrekar	c Gower b Lewis	82
S.R.Tendulkar	b Malcolm	19
M.Azharuddin *	not out	55
R.J.Shastri	not out	23
Kapil Dev		
M.Prabhakar		
K.S.More +		
S.K.Sharma		
A.R.Kumble		
Extras	(lb 5,w 9,nb 1)	15
TOTAL	(53 overs)(for 4 wkts)	233

INDIA	O	M	R	W		FALL OF WICKETS	
						ENG	IND
Kapil Dev	11	1	49	2			
Prabhakar	10.3	1	40	3	1st	22	1
Sharma	11	1	57	2	2nd	86	76
Shastri	11	0	40	1	3rd	134	115
Kumble	11	2	29	2	4th	142	183
					5th	186	
ENGLAND	O	M	R	W	6th	196	
DeFreitas	10	1	40	1	7th	211	
Malcolm	11	0	57	1	8th	221	
Fraser	11	3	37	0	9th	224	
Lewis	10	0	58	2	10th	229	
Hemmings	11	0	36	0			

Man of the match: A.R.Kumble

ENGLAND vs. INDIA

at Trent Bridge on 20th July 1990
Toss : India.   Umpires : M.J.Kitchen and D.R.Shepherd
India won by 5 wickets

ENGLAND

G.A.Gooch *	b Prabhakar	7
M.A.Atherton	c More b Prabhakar	59
D.I.Gower	run out	25
A.J.Lamb	run out	3
R.A.Smith	b Shastri	103
R.C.Russell +	c Azharuddin b Kapil Dev	50
P.A.J.DeFreitas	c Vengsarkar b Sharma	1
C.C.Lewis	lbw b Prabhakar	7
G.C.Small	c Azharuddin b Kapil Dev	4
E.E.Hemmings	run out	0
A.R.C.Fraser	not out	0
Extras	(b 1,lb 12,w 8,nb 1)	22
TOTAL	(55 overs)	281

INDIA

R.J.Shastri	c Atherton b Hemmings	33
N.S.Sidhu	b Small	23
S.V.Manjrekar	st Russell b Hemmings	59
D.B.Vengsarkar	b Lewis	54
M.Azharuddin *	not out	63
S.R.Tendulkar	b Fraser	31
Kapil Dev	not out	5
M.Prabhakar		
K.S.More +		
S.K.Sharma		
A.R.Kumble		
Extras	(lb 5,w 9)	14
TOTAL	(53 overs)(for 5 wkts)	282

INDIA	O	M	R	W		FALL OF WICKETS	
						ENG	IND
Kapil Dev	11	2	40	2			
Prabhakar	11	0	58	3	1st	12	42
Sharma	10	0	50	1	2nd	47	69
Shastri	11	0	52	1	3rd	62	166
Kumble	11	1	58	0	4th	173	186
Tendulkar	1	0	10	0	5th	246	249
					6th	254	
ENGLAND	O	M	R	W	7th	275	
Small	10	0	73	1	8th	280	
DeFreitas	11	0	59	0	9th	281	
Fraser	11	1	38	1	10th	281	
Hemmings	11	1	53	2			
Lewis	10	0	54	1			

Man of the match: R.A.Smith

HEADLINES

England vs India Texaco Trophy

Headingley: 18th July

● India's spinners, Ravi Shastri and Anil Kumble, tied England's batsmen in knots after Gooch and Gower, making exactly 50 on his return to international cricket, had looked to be building a formidable total

● A target of 230 proved a formality for India as Sanjay Manjrekar made his highest score in One-Day Internationals

● One-day International debut: M.A.Atherton (England)

Trent Bridge: 20th July

● India gained their second victory to win the Texaco Trophy despite an improved batting performance from England. Mike Atherton and Jack Russell both made their first 50s in One-Day Internationals, but it was Robin Smith with his second Texaco Trophy 100 of the summer who took the initiative away from the spinners

● India's batsmen made the required run-rate of over five an over look almost a formality with an inspired display: Manjrekar made 59, Dilip Vengsarkar 54, Mohammed Azharuddin his second unbeaten 50 and Sachin Tendulkar an explosive 31 and the visitors had secured victory with two overs to spare

● Men of the series: R.C.Russell (England); M.Azharuddin (India)

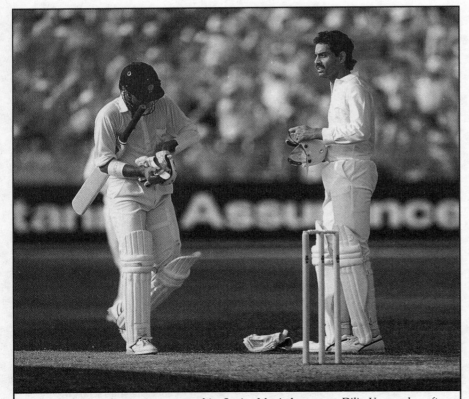

The end of a match-winning partnership: Sanjay Manjrekar passes Dilip Vengsarkar after being stumped by Jack Russell off Eddie Hemmings, but not before the partnership had contributed 97 runs for the 3rd wicket.

BRITANNIC ASSURANCE CHAMPIONSHIP

ESSEX vs. DERBYSHIRE

at Colchester on 18th, 19th, 20th July 1990
Toss : Derbyshire.   Umpires : P.J.Eele and N.T.Plews
Essex won by 9 wickets (Essex 24 pts (Bt: 4, Bw: 4) Derbyshire 7 pts (Bt: 3, Bw: 4))

DERBYSHIRE

K.J.Barnett *	c Stephenson b Foster	38	c Shahid b Foster	0
P.D.Bowler	b Childs	33	b Foster	4
A.M.Brown	c Garnham b Foster	3	c Garnham b Foster	0
B.Roberts	c Shahid b Andrew	56	c Hardie b Andrew	26
C.J.Adams	c Hussain b Andrew	33	lbw b Foster	7
S.C.Goldsmith	c Hardie b Such	11	lbw b Foster	24
K.M.Krikken +	c Hardie b Andrew	4	b Childs	43
I.R.Bishop	lbw b Foster	26	c Such b Foster	9
A.E.Warner	c Shahid b Such	0	lbw b Andrew	2
G.Miller	not out	24	not out	18
S.J.Base	c Garnham b Andrew	26	b Such	4
Extras	(b 1,lb 8,nb 5)	14	(lb 2,w 4,nb 2)	8
TOTAL		268		145

ESSEX

B.R.Hardie	c Brown b Warner	24	not out	41
J.P.Stephenson	c Krikken b Bishop	1	c Krikken b Bishop	4
N.Shahid	c Krikken b Goldsmith	42	not out	4
M.E.Waugh	c Krikken b Miller	126		
N.Hussain	c Krikken b Bishop	60		
M.A.Garnham +	c Krikken b Bishop	16		
D.R.Pringle *	b Miller	30		
N.A.Foster	b Barnett	32		
J.H.Childs	c Base b Barnett	2		
S.J.W.Andrew	c Roberts b Miller	1		
P.M.Such	not out	0		
Extras	(lb 9,w 6,nb 17)	32	(lb 1,w 1)	2
TOTAL		366	(for 1 wkt)	51

ESSEX	O	M	R	W	O	M	R	W
Foster	24	4	75	3	15	2	49	6
Andrew	15.5	4	60	4	9	2	49	2
Childs	19	7	57	1	7	4	7	1
Pringle	6	1	31	0	8	1	31	0
Such	17	3	36	2	2	0	7	1

DERBYSHIRE	O	M	R	W	O	M	R	W
Bishop	23	7	41	3	5	2	21	1
Warner	24	2	76	1				
Base	17	2	90	0	4.3	0	29	0
Miller	25	0	113	3				
Goldsmith	7	0	25	1				
Barnett	4	0	12	2				

FALL OF WICKETS	DER	ESS	DER	ESS
1st	67	5	1	32
2nd	71	72	1	
3rd	85	109	26	
4th	170	237	34	
5th	176	267	53	
6th	188	310	66	
7th	198	359	84	
8th	203	363	94	
9th	231	366	132	
10th	268	366	145	

HAMPSHIRE vs. NOTTINGHAMSHIRE

at Portsmouth on 18th, 19th, 20th July 1990
Toss : Hampshire. Umpires : J.C.Balderstone and D.J.Constant
Hampshire won by 8 wickets (Hampshire 24 pts (Bt: 4, Bw: 4) Notts 4 pts (Bt: 0, Bw: 4))

HAMPSHIRE

V.P.Terry	c Cooper b Stephenson	0		
C.L.Smith	c Pollard b Stephenson	85	not out	46
T.C.Middleton	c Evans b Saxelby	37	(1) b Afford	5
M.C.J.Nicholas *	c Robinson b Cooper	70	(3) c Afford b Cooper	9
M.D.Marshall	c Newell b Afford	5	(4) not out	23
J.R.Wood	c French b Evans	11		
J.R.Ayling	lbw b Evans	61		
R.J.Parks +	c Evans b Cooper	0		
R.J.Maru	c Robinson b Evans	19		
C.A.Connor	not out	2		
P.J.Bakker	not out	1		
Extras	(lb 9,w 1)	10	(lb 1)	1
TOTAL	(for 9 wkts dec)	301	(for 2 wkts)	84

NOTTINGHAMSHIRE

B.C.Broad	b Maru	8	c Parks b Connor	13
P.Pollard	b Bakker	21	c Wood b Maru	21
K.P.Evans	c Terry b Marshall	8	(9) c Parks b Marshall	7
M.Newell	run out	13	(3) c Parks b Marshall	34
R.T.Robinson *	c Maru b Connor	3	(4) c Marshall b Ayling	7
P.Johnson	c Terry b Maru	34	(5) b Maru	8
M.Saxelby	b Connor	0	(6) c Smith b Bakker	51
F.D.Stephenson	lbw b Marshall	10	(7) not out	88
B.N.French +	lbw b Marshall	0	(8) lbw b Marshall	21
K.E.Cooper	b Marshall	6	c Maru b Marshall	7
J.A.Afford	not out	0	c Parks b Marshall	1
Extras	(b 4,lb 2,w 1)	7	(b 4,lb 7,w 2,nb 3)	16
TOTAL		110		274

NOTTS	O	M	R	W	O	M	R	W
Stephenson	23	6	78	2	8	1	26	0
Cooper	24	7	49	2	8	3	15	1
Evans	21	3	76	3				
Afford	21	6	58	1	9	3	38	1
Saxelby	11	3	31	1	1	0	4	0

HAMPSHIRE	O	M	R	W	O	M	R	W
Bakker	9	4	28	1	18	3	57	1
Marshall	16.1	4	30	4	21.1	4	64	5
Maru	8	6	5	2	30	6	87	2
Ayling	7	3	12	0	9	4	14	1
Connor	7	2	29	2	14	3	41	1

FALL OF WICKETS	HAM	NOT	NOT	HAM
1st	0	10	27	25
2nd	109	41	43	50
3rd	149	47	54	
4th	170	55	63	
5th	198	63	118	
6th	257	63	176	
7th	257	99	216	
8th	285	104	228	
9th	298	110	259	
10th		110	274	

WORCESTERSHIRE vs. SOMERSET

at Worcester on 18th, 19th, 20th July 1990
Toss : Somerset. Umpires : A.A.Jones and D.S.Thompsett
Match drawn (Worcestershire 4 pts (Bt: 4, Bw: 0) Somerset 5 pts (Bt: 4, Bw: 1))

SOMERSET

S.J.Cook	c & b Tolley	6	c Neale b Tolley	39
P.M.Roebuck	not out	201	lbw b Lampitt	68
A.N.Hayhurst	run out	119	(5) c Rhodes b Tolley	16
C.J.Tavare *	c & b Newport	54	b Lampitt	10
R.J.Harden	not out	0	(3) c Rhodes b Lampitt	29
N.D.Burns +			not out	27
G.D.Rose			not out	44
R.P.Lefebvre				
I.G.Swallow				
N.A.Mallender				
A.N.Jones				
Extras	(b 5,lb 7,w 1,nb 5)	18	(b 2,lb 4,nb 2)	8
TOTAL	(for 3 wkts dec)	398	(for 5 wkts dec)	241

WORCESTERSHIRE

T.S.Curtis	lbw b Mallender	6	lbw b Mallender	24
P.Bent	c Rose b Jones	1	c & b Lefebvre	36
G.A.Hick	c sub b Swallow	171	not out	69
D.B.D'Oliveira	c sub b Swallow	55	c & b Swallow	24
P.A.Neale *	not out	49	not out	22
C.M.Tolley				
S.J.Rhodes +				
R.K.Illingworth				
P.J.Newport				
N.V.Radford				
S.R.Lampitt				
Extras	(b 7,lb 10,w 1)	18	(lb 4,nb 2)	6
TOTAL	(for 3 wkts dec)	300	(for 3 wkts)	181

WORCS	O	M	R	W	O	M	R	W
Newport	19	1	70	1	11	2	46	0
Tolley	24	4	84	1	18	2	66	2
Radford	18	0	78	0	12	0	49	0
Lampitt	16	2	70	0	13.2	1	46	3
Illingworth	30	8	72	0	7	1	28	0
Hick	3	0	12	0				

SOMERSET	O	M	R	W	O	M	R	W
Jones	8	3	17	1	5	0	25	0
Mallender	13	5	35	1	5	1	13	1
Rose	13	1	49	0	10	1	29	0
Lefebvre	17	4	49	0	11	2	33	1
Swallow	23	5	84	1	15	0	69	1
Roebuck	5	1	20	0	2	1	8	0
Hayhurst	5.4	0	29	0				

FALL OF WICKETS	SOM	WOR	SOM	WOR
1st	9	3	85	40
2nd	267	13	137	94
3rd	398	152	144	127
4th			152	
5th			189	
6th				
7th				
8th				
9th				
10th				

MIDDLESEX vs. YORKSHIRE

at Uxbridge on 18th, 19th, 20th July 1990
Toss : Yorkshire. Umpires : J.D.Bond and B.Dudleston
Middlesex won by 7 wickets (Middlesex 24 pts (Bt: 4, Bw: 4) Yorkshire 5 pts (Bt: 2, Bw: 3))

YORKSHIRE

M.D.Moxon *	c Roseberry b Williams	12	c Gatting b Williams	23
C.Chapman	c Farbrace b Williams	20	lbw b Emburey	5
R.J.Blakey +	c Farbrace b Williams	0	c Farbrace b Williams	42
P.E.Robinson	c Emburey b Hughes	3	c Emburey b Williams	40
D.Byas	c Gatting b Emburey	83	c Brown b Tufnell	17
C.White	c Haynes b Williams	12	c Brown b Emburey	0
P.Carrick	b Emburey	52	c & b Emburey	10
C.S.Pickles	c Roseberry b Tufnell	17	c Brown b Tufnell	18
P.J.Hartley	c Farbrace b Tufnell	11	not out	9
D.Gough	b Emburey	11	c Brown b Tufnell	2
S.D.Fletcher	not out	0	b Williams	0
Extras	(b 6,lb 5,nb 11)	22	(b 10,lb 8,w 1,nb 7)	26
TOTAL		243		192

MIDDLESEX

D.L.Haynes	c Robinson b Hartley	18	c Hartley b Carrick	26
M.A.Roseberry	c Blakey b Gough	36	c Moxon b Hartley	9
M.W.Gatting *	c Carrick b Fletcher	86	b White	28
M.R.Ramprakash	c Chapman b Hartley	9	not out	15
K.R.Brown	not out	109	not out	12
J.E.Emburey	st Blakey b Carrick	45		
N.F.Williams	b Pickles	2		
P.Farbrace +	c Chapman b Carrick	2		
P.C.R.Tufnell	c White b Carrick	10		
S.P.Hughes	st Blakey b Carrick	4		
N.G.Cowans	c Pickles b Carrick	2		
Extras	(lb 7,nb 10)	17	(lb 2,nb 4)	6
TOTAL		340	(for 3 wkts)	96

MIDDLESEX	O	M	R	W	O	M	R	W
Williams	19	5	55	3	18.5	2	43	4
Cowans	11	3	21	0	3	1	7	0
Emburey	27	10	51	4	27	8	62	3
Hughes	9	3	38	1	5	1	9	0
Tufnell	24	7	67	2	24	7	49	3
Haynes					1	0	4	0

YORKSHIRE	O	M	R	W	O	M	R	W
Hartley	20	3	76	2	5	0	24	1
Fletcher	17	7	29	1	4	0	10	0
Gough	13	5	40	1				
Carrick	31	4	99	5	10.3	2	22	1
White	12	1	59	0	9	0	38	1
Pickles	10	3	30	1				

FALL OF WICKETS	YOR	MID	YOR	MID
1st	31	30	20	13
2nd	31	104	77	60
3rd	39	125	84	76
4th	56	180	122	
5th	106	266	123	
6th	195	281	140	
7th	204	290	161	
8th	229	318	187	
9th	239	338	191	
10th	243	340	192	

BRITANNIC ASSURANCE CHAMPIONSHIP

SURREY vs. SUSSEX

at Guildford on 18th, 19th, 20th July 1990
Toss : Surrey.   Umpires : B.J.Meyer and K.E.Palmer
Sussex won by 7 wickets (Surrey 7 pts (Bt: 3, Bw: 4) Sussex 21 pts (Bt: 4, Bw: 1))

SURREY

D.J.Bicknell	b Pigott	143	b Donelan	6
G.S.Clinton	c Parker b Dodemaide	1	b Dodemaide	93
G.P.Thorpe	c Speight b Wells C.M.	33	c & b Salisbury	79
D.M.Ward +	b Salisbury	40	not out	36
M.A.Lynch	c Dodemaide b Salisbury	52	not out	1
I.A.Greig *	run out	37		
M.A.Feltham	lbw b Dodemaide	0		
K.T.Medlycott	c Wells A.P. b Dodemaide	16		
M.P.Bicknell	c & b Pigott	8		
N.M.Kendrick	c Parker b Dodemaide	2		
Waqar Younis	not out	1		
Extras	(b 2,lb 9,w 1)	12	(lb 4,w 1,nb 1)	6
TOTAL		345	(for 3 wkts dec)	221

SUSSEX

N.J.Lenham	run out	46	not out	109
J.W.Hall	c & b Medlycott	16	c Bicknell M.P. b Medlycott	21
P.W.G.Parker *	b Waqar Younis	11	c Ward b Feltham	64
A.P.Wells	c Kendrick b Medlycott	0	c Kendrick b Medlycott	42
M.P.Speight	c Greig b Waqar Younis	108	not out	0
C.M.Wells	c Ward b Waqar Younis	0		
A.I.C.Dodemaide	b Medlycott	11		
P.Moores +	lbw b Feltham	24		
A.C.S.Pigott	c Feltham b Medlycott	33		
I.D.K.Salisbury	b Medlycott	21		
B.T.P.Donelan	not out	11		
Extras	(b 19,lb 9,w 1,nb 3)	32	(b 7,lb 10,nb 1)	18
TOTAL		313	(for 3 wkts)	254

SUSSEX	O	M	R	W	O	M	R	W
Pigott	22.3	0	68	2	7	1	26	0
Dodemaide	27	2	84	4	10	3	23	1
Wells C.M.	22	10	47	1	6.3	0	21	0
Donelan	21	7	42	0	22	3	70	1
Salisbury	26	4	84	2	15	0	77	1
Lenham	2	0	9	0				

SURREY	O	M	R	W	O	M	R	W
Waqar Younis	21	4	65	3	8	0	45	0
Bicknell M.P.	18	5	32	0	12.4	3	52	0
Feltham	17	5	44	1	4	0	36	1
Medlycott	27.1	3	121	5	14	3	61	2
Kendrick	8	2	23	0	5	0	43	0

FALL OF WICKETS	SUR	SUS	SUR	SUS
1st	2	54	9	69
2nd	67	76	140	159
3rd	152	76	220	251
4th	228	80		
5th	293	80		
6th	296	111		
7th	314	193		
8th	340	263		
9th	343	290		
10th	345	313		

WARWICKSHIRE vs. LANCASHIRE

at Coventry & North Warwicks CC on 18th, 19th, 20th July 1990
Toss : Warwickshire.   Umpires : R.Palmer and R.A.White
Match drawn (Warwickshire 7 pts (Bt: 4, Bw: 3) Lancashire 7 pts (Bt: 4, Bw: 3))

WARWICKSHIRE

A.J.Moles	b Wasim Akram	31	not out	100
T.A.Lloyd *	lbw b Allott	1	b Wasim Akram	8
Asif Din	c Mendis b Watkinson	45	lbw b Wasim Akram	1
T.M.Moody	c Hegg b Wasim Akram	30	c Hegg b Hughes	96
D.P.Ostler	lbw b Wasim Akram	3	c Mendis b Hughes	18
D.A.Reeve	run out	78		
P.A.Smith	c Hughes b Fitton	82	(6) not out	7
K.J.Piper +	not out	40		
J.E.Benjamin	not out	28		
A.R.K.Pierson				
T.A.Munton				
Extras	(b 13,lb 18,w 2,nb 3)	36	(b 5,lb 7,nb 14)	26
TOTAL	(for 7 wkts dec)	374	(for 4 wkts dec)	256

LANCASHIRE

G.D.Mendis	c Piper b Munton	5	(6) not out	20
G.Fowler	c Piper b Munton	0	(1) c sub b Pierson	30
J.D.Fitton	c Ostler b Benjamin	10		
T.E.Jesty	c Ostler b Benjamin	17	(5)lbw b Asif Din	6
N.H.Fairbrother	not out	203	(4) b Pierson	50
M.Watkinson	lbw b Smith	14	(2) lbw b Benjamin	5
Wasim Akram	c Ostler b Smith	7	(3) c sub b Pierson	32
W.K.Hegg +	c Pierson b Benjamin	9	(7) not out	20
I.D.Austin	lbw b Munton	9		
D.P.Hughes *	not out	29		
P.J.W.Allott				
Extras	(b 12,lb 5,w 3,nb 9)	29	(b 1,lb 7,nb 2)	10
TOTAL	(for 8 wkts dec)	332	(for 5 wkts)	173

LANCASHIRE	O	M	R	W	O	M	R	W
Wasim Akram	26	6	76	3	18	7	51	2
Allott	14	1	45	1	10	1	31	0
Austin	16	5	48	0	10	3	19	0
Watkinson	15	3	53	1	17	3	38	0
Hughes	17	0	73	0	15.4	2	54	2
Fitton	15	3	48	1	15	2	44	0
Jesty					1	0	7	0

WARWICKS	O	M	R	W	O	M	R	W
Munton	22	7	75	3	3	0	30	0
Benjamin	21	4	97	3	7	0	42	1
Pierson	24	8	70	0	14	1	56	3
Smith	10	2	37	2				
Moody	5	0	25	0				
Asif Din	4.3	2	11	0	10	3	37	1

FALL OF WICKETS	WAR	LAN	WAR	LAN
1st	2	7	29	25
2nd	71	12	31	44
3rd	105	26	189	86
4th	114	49	235	107
5th	117	107		131
6th	247	116		
7th	332	181		
8th		203		
9th				
10th				

NORTHANTS vs. KENT

at Northampton on 18th, 19th, 20th July 1990
Toss : Northants.   Umpires : B.Hassan and B.Leadbeater
Match drawn (Northants 8 pts (Bt: 4, Bw: 4) Kent 4 pts (Bt: 3, Bw: 1))

NORTHANTS

A.Fordham	c Marsh b Igglesden	2
W.Larkins *	c Marsh b De Villiers	12
N.A.Felton	b Patel	90
D.J.Capel	c Taylor b Igglesden	85
R.J.Bailey	not out	138
R.G.Williams	c Ellison b De Villiers	96
D.Ripley +	b Ellison	7
S.J.Brown	b Ellison	2
N.G.B.Cook	c Cowdrey C.S. b Ellison	1
C.E.L.Ambrose	not out	0
M.A.Robinson		
Extras	(lb 12)	12
TOTAL	(for 8 wkts dec)	445

KENT

S.G.Hinks	c Capel b Ambrose	5	b Cook	83
M.R.Benson	c Ripley b Ambrose	10	b Bailey	36
N.R.Taylor	c Fordham b Cook	97	c Felton b Ambrose	4
G.R.Cowdrey	c Larkins b Ambrose	0	not out	107
C.S.Cowdrey *	c Fordham b Ambrose	0	not out	25
S.A.Marsh +	c Felton b Brown	29		
R.M.Ellison	c Ripley b Robinson	24		
R.P.Davis	c Capel b Bailey	43	(2) c Bailey b Cook	41
P.S.De Villiers	c & b Williams	0		
M.M.Patel	not out	41		
A.P.Igglesden	b Ambrose	24		
Extras	(lb 2,w 1,nb 7)	10	(b 4,lb 2,nb 3)	9
TOTAL		283	(for 4 wkts dec)	305

KENT	O	M	R	W	O	M	R	W
De Villiers	20	2	78	2				
Igglesden	14	2	41	2				
Ellison	21	1	85	3				
Cowdrey C.S.	9	0	39	0				
Davis	24	4	109	0				
Patel	22	4	81	1				

NORTHANTS	O	M	R	W	O	M	R	W
Ambrose	19	4	59	5	18	7	47	1
Brown	15	1	81	1	8	2	22	0
Robinson	19	3	75	1	10	2	19	0
Cook	25	17	33	1	28	13	59	2
Williams	18	7	28	1	22	8	67	0
Bailey	3	2	5	1	19	3	71	1
Fordham					4	0	14	0

FALL OF WICKETS	NOR	KEN	KEN	NOR
1st	5	15	131	
2nd	29	42	132	
3rd	175	45	151	
4th	207	49	210	
5th	394	94		
6th	409	143		
7th	419	202		
8th	441	203		
9th		230		
10th		283		

REFUGE ASSURANCE LEAGUE

GLAMORGAN vs. SOMERSET

at Neath on 22nd July 1990
Toss : Somerset. Umpires : D.R.Shepherd & D.S.Thompsett
Somerset won by 220 runs (Glam 0 pts Somerset 4 pts)

SOMERSET

S.J.Cook	not out	136
R.J.Bartlett	c Dale b Cowley	11
C.J.Tavare *	c Maynard b Dale	10
G.D.Rose	c Smith b Richards	148
R.J.Harden	not out	32
N.D.Burns +		
A.N.Hayhurst		
R.P.Lefebvre		
I.G.Swallow		
N.A.Mallender		
J.C.Hallett		
Extras	(lb 5,w 17,nb 1)	23
TOTAL	(40 overs)(for 3 wkts)	360

GLAMORGAN

M.P.Maynard	c Swallow b Mallender	0
H.Morris	c Lefebvre b Rose	3
I.V.A.Richards	b Hallett	36
I.Smith	run out	6
A.R.Butcher *	c Tavare b Hayhurst	18
A.Dale	c Tavare b Hallett	14
N.G.Cowley	c Harden b Hallett	10
C.P.Metson +	b Hayhurst	10
S.L.Watkin	b Lefebvre	28
S.J.Dennis	run out	5
M.Frost	not out	2
Extras	(lb 6,w 2)	8
TOTAL	(28.5 overs)	140

GLAMORGAN	O	M	R	W		FALL OF WICKETS	
						SOM	GLA
Watkin	8	0	71	0	1st	35	0
Frost	8	0	46	0	2nd	62	6
Dennis	8	0	67	0	3rd	285	19
Cowley	5	0	44	1	4th		50
Dale	3	0	28	1	5th		81
Richards	7	0	76	1	6th		85
Maynard	1	0	23	0	7th		96
					8th		108
SOMERSET	O	M	R	W	9th		128
Mallender	5	0	19	1	10th		140
Rose	5	1	24	1			
Lefebvre	5.5	0	26	1			
Hallett	8	0	41	3			
Hayhurst	5	0	24	2			

HAMPSHIRE vs. DERBYSHIRE

at Portsmouth on 22nd July 1990
Toss : Derbys. Umpires : J.C.Balderstone and D.J.Constant
Hampshire won by 189 runs (Hants 4 pts Derbyshire 0 pts)

HAMPSHIRE

M.C.J.Nicholas *	c Malcolm b Mortensen	4
R.J.Scott	c Roberts b Malcolm	76
R.A.Smith	c Kuiper b Malcolm	83
D.I.Gower	not out	47
M.D.Marshall	run out	1
C.L.Smith	run out	30
J.R.Ayling	not out	0
R.J.Parks +		
R.J.Maru		
C.A.Connor		
P.J.Bakker		
Extras	(lb 4,w 5)	9
TOTAL	(38 overs)(for 5 wkts)	250

DERBYSHIRE

K.J.Barnett *	c Nicholas b Bakker	5
J.E.Morris	c Parks b Marshall	1
B.Roberts	c Parks b Connor	10
A.P.Kuiper	c Smith C.L. b Bakker	1
C.J.Adams	c Parks b Connor	21
S.C.Goldsmith	c Smith C.L. b Bakker	4
K.M.Krikken +	b Connor	0
S.J.Base	b Ayling	2
D.E.Malcolm	b Connor	9
O.H.Mortensen	not out	2
G.Miller	absent hurt	
Extras	(lb 3,w 3)	6
TOTAL	(19.1 overs)	61

DERBYSHIRE	O	M	R	W		FALL OF WICKETS	
						HAM	DER
Base	7	0	37	0	1st	8	6
Mortensen	7	0	35	1	2nd	155	6
Malcolm	8	0	50	2	3rd	178	14
Miller	8	0	54	0	4th	180	22
Goldsmith	4	0	42	0	5th	245	37
Kuiper	4	0	28	0	6th		38
					7th		42
HAMPSHIRE	O	M	R	W	8th		50
Bakker	6	1	31	3	9th		61
Marshall	4	2	4	1	10th		
Connor	5.1	0	11	4			
Ayling	3	0	9	1			
Scott	1	0	3	0			

ESSEX vs. LANCASHIRE

at Colchester on 22nd July 1990
Toss : Lancashire. Umpires : P.J.Eele and N.T.Plews
Lancashire won by 2 wickets (Essex 0 pts Lancashire 4 pts)

ESSEX

G.A.Gooch *	lbw b Allott	1
J.P.Stephenson	c Hughes b Austin	109
M.E.Waugh	b DeFreitas	111
D.R.Pringle	run out	1
N.Hussain	b Wasim Akram	12
N.A.Foster	not out	4
B.R.Hardie	not out	2
N.Shahid		
M.A.Garnham +		
J.H.Childs		
M.C.Ilott		
Extras	(lb 2,w 3,nb 2)	7
TOTAL	(40 overs)(for 5 wkts)	247

LANCASHIRE

G.Fowler	c Hardie b Ilott	5
M.A.Atherton	b Pringle	111
G.D.Lloyd	c Shahid b Pringle	30
N.H.Fairbrother	run out	23
M.Watkinson	c Garnham b Foster	1
Wasim Akram	b Ilott	3
P.A.J.DeFreitas	c Pringle b Foster	18
I.D.Austin	c Hussain b Pringle	10
W.K.Hegg +	not out	24
D.P.Hughes *	not out	8
P.J.W.Allott		
Extras	(lb 10,w 6)	16
TOTAL	(39.5 overs)(for 8 wkts)	249

LANCASHIRE	O	M	R	W		FALL OF WICKETS	
						ESS	LAN
DeFreitas	8	0	38	1	1st	8	9
Allott	8	0	40	1	2nd	222	84
Watkinson	8	0	47	0	3rd	225	145
Wasim Akram	8	0	53	1	4th	234	156
Austin	8	0	67	1	5th	245	169
					6th		198
ESSEX	O	M	R	W	7th		213
Foster	8	0	42	2	8th		221
Ilott	8	0	44	2	9th		
Gooch	3	0	24	0	10th		
Childs	8	0	37	0			
Pringle	7.5	0	47	3			
Waugh	5	0	45	0			

Jimmy Cook (left) and John Stephenson, two century-makers in the Refuge Assurance League.

REFUGE ASSURANCE LEAGUE

SURREY vs. KENT

at The Oval on 22nd July 1990
Toss : Surrey.   Umpires : B.J.Meyer and K.E.Palmer
Surrey won by 5 wickets (Surrey 4 pts Kent 0 pts)

KENT

S.G.Hinks	run out	41
N.R.Taylor	c Ward b Medlycott	26
T.R.Ward	b Waqar Younis	14
C.S.Cowdrey *	c Sargeant b Waqar Younis	7
G.R.Cowdrey	c Sargeant b Medlycott	14
M.V.Fleming	b Waqar Younis	4
S.A.Marsh +	c Bullen b Waqar Younis	35
R.M.Ellison	c Robinson b Bullen	0
P.S.De Villiers	b Waqar Younis	6
R.P.Davis	c Sargeant b Feltham	0
A.P.Igglesden	not out	3
Extras	(lb 6,w 8)	14
TOTAL	(37.4 overs)	164

SURREY

D.J.Bicknell	b Davis	26
M.A.Feltham	b De Villiers	9
G.P.Thorpe	not out	69
D.M.Ward	b Fleming	4
M.A.Lynch	lbw b Ward	26
J.D.Robinson	c Igglesden b Ellison	16
I.A.Greig *	not out	0
K.T.Medlycott		
C.K.Bullen		
N.F.Sargeant +		
Waqar Younis		
Extras	(lb 11,w 6)	17
TOTAL	(37.1 overs)(for 5 wkts)	167

SURREY	O	M	R	W	FALL OF WICKETS		
						KEN	SUR
Feltham	7	0	26	1			
Robinson	3	0	19	0	1st	54	16
Medlycott	8	0	40	2	2nd	80	53
Greig	4	0	22	0	3rd	93	64
Bullen	8	0	25	1	4th	98	118
Waqar Younis	7.4	0	26	5	5th	107	162
					6th	122	
KENT	O	M	R	W	7th	123	
* Igglesden	8	0	29	0	8th	153	
De Villiers	6.1	1	26	1	9th	157	
Davis	8	0	30	1	10th	164	
Ellison	8	0	33	1			
Fleming	3	0	21	1			
Ward	4	0	17	1			

NORTHANTS vs. SUSSEX

at Wellingborough on 22nd July 1990
Toss : Northants.   Umpires : B.Hassan and B.Leadbeater
Sussex won by 21 runs (Northants 0 pts Sussex 4 pts)

SUSSEX

N.J.Lenham	c Larkins b Robinson	25
I.J.Gould	c Bailey b Cook	55
P.W.G.Parker *	lbw b Williams	34
A.P.Wells	lbw b Cook	2
M.P.Speight	b Cook	32
C.M.Wells	c Williams b Davis	6
A.I.C.Dodemaide	c & b Davis	19
A.C.S.Pigott	c Cook b Robinson	37
J.A.North	not out	15
P.Moores +	not out	6
I.D.K.Salisbury		
Extras	(b 1,lb 14,w 6,nb 1)	22
TOTAL	(40 overs)(for 8 wkts)	253

NORTHANTS

A.Fordham	lbw b North	21
W.Larkins	lbw b Dodemaide	7
A.J.Lamb *	c Parker b Pigott	17
D.J.Capel	c Salisbury b Lenham	115
R.J.Bailey	c Speight b Pigott	4
R.G.Williams	c Gould b North	6
D.Ripley +	c Wells C.M. b Pigott	26
W.W.Davis	b Lenham	24
S.J.Brown	not out	3
N.G.B.Cook	not out	0
M.A.Robinson		
Extras	(lb 2,w 7)	9
TOTAL	(40 overs)(for 8 wkts)	232

NORTHANTS	O	M	R	W	FALL OF WICKETS		
						SUS	NOR
Davis	8	1	32	2			
Brown	8	0	48	0	1st	55	22
Robinson	8	0	59	2	2nd	113	39
Williams	8	0	63	1	3rd	121	61
Cook	8	1	36	3	4th	127	67
					5th	140	88
SUSSEX	O	M	R	W	6th	179	149
Wells C.M.	8	0	28	0	7th	226	204
Dodemaide	8	0	38	1	8th	239	231
Pigott	8	0	60	3	9th		
North	8	0	45	2	10th		
Lenham	8	0	59	2			

WARWICKSHIRE vs. NOTTS

at Edgbaston on 22nd July 1990
Toss : Notts.   Umpires : J.D.Bond and B.Dudleston
Notts won by 10 runs (Warwicks 0 pts Notts 4 pts)

NOTTINGHAMSHIRE

B.C.Broad	c Piper b Munton	1
P.Pollard	b Benjamin	3
P.Johnson	c Munton b Twose	114
R.T.Robinson *	c Moody b Twose	63
F.D.Stephenson	b Munton	4
M.Newell	run out	6
G.W.Mike	run out	4
B.N.French +	not out	34
K.P.Evans	run out	1
E.E.Hemmings	not out	2
K.E.Cooper		
Extras	(lb 6,w 3)	9
TOTAL	(40 overs)(for 8 wkts)	241

WARWICKSHIRE

T.A.Lloyd *	c Pollard b Evans	63
Asif Din	lbw b Hemmings	43
T.M.Moody	lbw b Mike	7
P.A.Smith	st French b Hemmings	19
D.A.Reeve	run out	41
R.G.Twose	not out	30
J.E.Benjamin	not out	3
K.J.Piper +		
G.C.Small		
A.R.K.Pierson		
T.A.Munton		
Extras	(lb 7,w 14,nb 4)	25
TOTAL	(40 overs)(for 5 wkts)	231

WARWICKS	O	M	R	W	FALL OF WICKETS		
						NOT	WAR
Benjamin	8	0	20	1			
Munton	8	2	45	2	1st	1	99
Pierson	3	0	27	0	2nd	7	115
Reeve	7	0	43	0	3rd	176	133
Small	4	0	29	0	4th	187	154
Smith	2	0	21	0	5th	197	224
Twose	8	0	50	2	6th	199	
					7th	222	
NOTTS	O	M	R	W	8th	239	
Cooper	8	0	50	0	9th		
Stephenson	8	0	29	0	10th		
Mike	8	0	54	1			
Evans	8	0	57	1			
Hemmings	8	1	34	2			

GLOUCESTERSHIRE vs. YORKSHIRE

at Cheltenham on 22nd July 1990
Toss : Yorkshire.   Umpires : J.H.Hampshire and R.A.White
Yorkshire won by 7 wickets (Gloucs 0 pts Yorkshire 4 pts)

GLOUCESTERSHIRE

A.J.Wright *	c Sharp b Carrick	57
C.W.J.Athey	c Blakey b Moxon	80
J.W.Lloyds	c Metcalfe b Carrick	0
P.Bainbridge	c & b Moxon	11
K.M.Curran	not out	31
P.W.Romaines	run out	9
R.C.Russell +	c Sharp b Moxon	12
M.W.Alleyne	not out	14
C.A.Walsh		
M.W.Bell		
S.N.Barnes		
Extras	(lb 7,w 3,nb 2)	12
TOTAL	(40 overs)(for 6 wkts)	226

YORKSHIRE

M.D.Moxon *	run out	68
A.A.Metcalfe	c Russell b Curran	0
R.J.Blakey +	not out	100
P.E.Robinson	c Romaines b Alleyne	33
K.Sharp	not out	9
D.Byas		
P.Carrick		
P.J.Hartley		
C.S.Pickles		
A.Sidebottom		
S.D.Fletcher		
Extras	(lb 4,w 11,nb 2)	17
TOTAL	(35.5 overs)(for 3 wkts)	227

YORKSHIRE	O	M	R	W	FALL OF WICKETS		
						GLO	YOR
Hartley	5	0	36	0			
Sidebottom	8	1	27	0	1st	104	1
Fletcher	8	0	36	0	2nd	123	132
Carrick	8	0	47	2	3rd	145	204
Pickles	4	0	21	0	4th	165	
Moxon	7	0	52	3	5th	183	
					6th	203	
GLOUCS	O	M	R	W	7th		
Curran	8	0	31	1	8th		
Walsh	6	0	16	0	9th		
Bell	4	0	38	0	10th		
Barnes	6	0	53	0			
Alleyne	5.5	0	38	1			
Lloyds	6	0	47	0			

HEADLINES

22nd July

● Somerset rewrote the Sunday League record books with their remarkable performance against Glamorgan at Neath: their total of 360 for 3 in 40 overs was the competition's highest; on his way to a career best 148, Graham Rose made the fastest 50 (16 balls) and the fastest 100 (44 balls) in the league's history, as he and Jimmy Cook added 223 for the third wicket; Somerset's margin of victory - 220 runs - was yet another record

● Hampshire's victory over Derbyshire at Portsmouth was almost as conclusive: Cardigan Connor returned career best figures as Derbyshire, who would have moved four points clear at the top of the table had they won, were bowled out for 61

● Lancashire's defence of their title gathered momentum with a two-wicket win over Essex at Colchester, Mike Atherton making his first Sunday century. John Stephenson, who also made his first 100 in the Sunday League, and Mark Waugh had earlier added 214 for the Essex second wicket

● Waqar Younis's latest victims were Kent, as the young Pakistani improved his best figures to 5 for 26 to set up a comfortable Surrey victory at The Oval

● Richard Blakey was another to record his maiden Sunday League 100 as Yorkshire beat Gloucestershire by seven wickets at Cheltenham, while Paul Johnson's best Sunday score helped Nottinghamshire to a narrow win over Warwickshire at Edgbaston

● David Capel's 115 was in vain as Northamptonshire finished 21 short of Sussex's 253 for 8 at Wellingborough School to remain rooted to the bottom of the table

TOUR MATCH

BRITANNIC ASS. CHAMPIONSHIP

LEICESTERSHIRE vs. INDIA

at Leicester on 21st, 22nd, 23rd July 1990
Toss : India.   Umpires : J.H.Harris and J.W.Holder
Match drawn

LEICESTERSHIRE

T.J.Boon	b Sharma	1	c Hirwani b Wasson	16
N.E.Briers *	not out	150		
J.J.Whitaker	b Hirwani	61	(9) not out	7
P.Willey	c Tendulkar b Hirwani	5	b Venkatapathy	76
L.Potter	b Wasson	22	(2) b Hirwani	30
C.C.Lewis	c Manjrekar b Venkatapathy	1	(5) c Prabhakar b V'katapathy	28
J.D.R.Benson	c Sharma b Wasson	0	(3) c Prabhakar b Hirwani	106
W.K.M.Benjamin	c Mongia b Wasson	55	(7) b Venkatapathy	0
P.A.Nixon +	not out	3	(6) hit wicket b Venkatapathy	13
G.J.Parsons			(8) not out	11
A.D.Mullally				
Extras	(b 8,w 1,nb 3)	12	(lb 8,w 1,nb 2)	11
TOTAL	(for 7 wkts dec)	310	(for 7 wkts dec)	298

INDIA

M.Prabhakar	c Potter b Benjamin	2	c Nixon b Lewis	13
N.S.Sidhu	c Nixon b Lewis	25	lbw b Lewis	6
S.V.Manjrekar	c Nixon b Mullally	66	not out	3
S.R.Tendulkar	c Benson b Parsons	30	not out	25
D.B.Vengsarkar	c Whitaker b Potter	80		
M.Azharuddin *	c Mullally b Willey	46		
N.R.Mongia +	not out	63		
Venkatapathy Raju	run out	3		
S.K.Sharma	not out	23		
A.Wasson				
N.D.Hirwani				
Extras	(b 10,lb 9,nb 4)	23	(lb 6,nb 1)	7
TOTAL	(for 7 wkts dec)	361	(for 2 wkts)	54

INDIA	O	M	R	W	O	M	R	W		FALL OF WICKETS			
										LEI	IND	LEI	IND
Prabhakar	10	1	35	0	5	3	6	0	1st	1	8	25	20
Sharma	16	5	41	1	13	2	52	0	2nd	132	76	108	25
Tendulkar	1	0	9	0					3rd	150	131	181	
Wasson	17	1	76	3	15	0	56	1	4th	199	135	234	
Venkatapathy	30	7	62	1	28	6	73	4	5th	216	227	274	
Hirwani	22	1	79	2	21	0	103	2	6th	217	285	274	
									7th	303	302	281	
LEICS	O	M	R	W	O	M	R	W	8th				
Benjamin	20	2	81	1	4	1	8	0	9th				
Lewis	11	3	28	1	8	3	23	2	10th				
Parsons	16	2	73	1	2	2	0	0					
Mullally	18	1	78	1	5	0	17	0					
Willey	17	5	42	1									
Potter	12	1	40	1									

ESSEX vs. LANCASHIRE

at Colchester on 21st, 23rd, 24th July 1990
Toss : Lancashire.   Umpires : P.J.Eele and N.T.Plews
Essex won by 6 wickets (Essex 24 pts (Bt: 4, Bw: 4) Lancashire 8 pts (Bt: 4, Bw: 4))

LANCASHIRE

G.D.Mendis	c Shahid b Andrew	9	lbw b Childs	20
G.Fowler	b Foster	12	c Pringle b Foster	9
M.A.Atherton	c Shahid b Pringle	11	not out	108
N.H.Fairbrother	c Gooch b Pringle	24	not out	109
T.E.Jesty	c Garnham b Childs	66		
M.Watkinson	c Garnham b Pringle	45		
Wasim Akram	b Pringle	0		
P.A.J.DeFreitas	c Foster b Such	41		
W.K.Hegg +	not out	100		
D.P.Hughes *	run out	57		
P.J.W.Allott	not out	10		
Extras	(b 4,lb 6,w 1,nb 9)	20	(b 1,lb 2,nb 3)	6
TOTAL	(for 9 wkts dec)	395	(for 2 wkts dec)	252

ESSEX

G.A.Gooch *	c Hegg b DeFreitas	17	lbw b Atherton	177
J.P.Stephenson	run out	21	c Watkinson b Atherton	60
N.Shahid	c & b Atherton	125	run out	26
M.E.Waugh	c Hegg b DeFreitas	0	c sub b Atherton	58
N.Hussain	c Hegg b Atherton	40	not out	9
M.A.Garnham +	lbw b Allott	17		
D.R.Pringle	c Mendis b Hughes	45	(6) not out	6
N.A.Foster	c & b Atherton	4		
J.H.Childs	not out	13		
S.J.W.Andrew	b Hughes	0		
P.M.Such	not out	13		
Extras	(lb 2,nb 3)	5	(b 3,lb 7,w 2,nb 3)	15
TOTAL	(for 9 wkts dec)	300	(for 4 wkts)	351

ESSEX	O	M	R	W	O	M	R	W		FALL OF WICKETS			
										LAN	ESS	LAN	ESS
Foster	20	1	98	1	11	3	30	1	1st	24	39	24	158
Andrew	20	2	81	1	7	0	51	0	2nd	24	39	32	214
Pringle	17	3	47	4	8	0	38	0	3rd	38	39		331
Such	16	4	57	1	15	3	24	0	4th	70	130		336
Stephenson	2	0	11	0					5th	161	158		
Childs	19.4	3	63	1	23	7	45	1	6th	162	268		
Shahid	6	2	28	0	10	0	46	0	7th	190	270		
Hussain					2	0	15	0	8th	262	274		
									9th	375	276		
LANCASHIRE	O	M	R	W	O	M	R	W	10th				
Wasim Akram	3	0	19	0									
DeFreitas	22.1	4	68	2	12	0	69	0					
Allott	17	2	76	1	12	1	59	0					
Watkinson	6	0	19	0	10	0	64	0					
Atherton	22	3	73	3	14	0	106	3					
Hughes	14	4	43	2	5	0	43	0					

MIDDLESEX vs. SOMERSET

at Uxbridge on 21st, 23rd, 24th July 1990
Toss : Somerset.   Umpires : J.D.Bond and B.Dudleston
Middlesex won by 4 wickets (Middlesex 20 pts (Bt: 4, Bw: 0) Somerset 4 pts (Bt: 3, Bw: 1))

SOMERSET

S.J.Cook	c Farbrace b Tufnell	152	b Ramprakash	85
P.M.Roebuck	b Tufnell	70	b Fraser	9
A.N.Hayhurst	c & b Weekes	15		
C.J.Tavare *	c Haynes b Weekes	57	c Emburey b Tufnell	61
R.J.Harden	c Brown b Tufnell	17	(3) c Farbrace b Emburey	38
N.D.Burns +	not out	37	not out	4
G.D.Rose	b Fraser	57	(5) not out	10
I.G.Swallow	not out	11		
H.R.J.Trump				
N.A.Mallender				
A.N.Jones				
Extras	(lb 22,nb 7)	29	(b 10,lb 2,nb 9)	21
TOTAL	(for 6 wkts dec)	445	(for 4 wkts dec)	228

MIDDLESEX

D.L.Haynes	c Cook b Swallow	41	c Harden b Mallender	108
M.A.Roseberry	c Burns b Mallender	25	lbw b Rose	7
M.W.Gatting *	not out	170	b Mallender	36
M.R.Ramprakash	c Tavare b Mallender	2	not out	146
K.R.Brown	c & b Trump	46	c Burns b Mallender	9
J.E.Emburey	not out	1	b Mallender	11
N.F.Williams			b Jones	22
P.Farbrace +			not out	4
P.C.R.Tufnell				
P.N.Weekes				
A.R.C.Fraser				
Extras	(b 6,lb 4,nb 10)	20	(b 10,lb 14,nb 4)	28
TOTAL	(for 4 wkts dec)	305	(for 6 wkts)	371

MIDDLESEX	O	M	R	W	O	M	R	W		FALL OF WICKETS			
										SOM	MID	SOM	MID
Fraser	23	3	66	1	6	1	11	1	1st	189	67	27	40
Williams	10	0	45	0	5	0	38	0	2nd	234	117	100	110
Emburey	35	11	57	0	20	4	52	1	3rd	274	142	210	215
Tufnell	51	11	140	3	24	4	96	1	4th	302	296	218	238
Weekes	28	2	115	2					5th	349			260
Ramprakash					5	1	19	1	6th	426			353
									7th				
SOMERSET	O	M	R	W	O	M	R	W	8th				
Jones	10	1	47	0	14	2	69	1	9th				
Mallender	11	2	46	2	16.5	1	60	4	10th				
Trump	20.4	3	91	1	15	1	89	0					
Swallow	19	2	100	1	12	0	66	0					
Rose	7	3	11	0	10	1	43	1					
Tavare					1	0	20	0					

HEADLINES

21st - 24th July

- India's last match before the First Test ended in stalemate at Leicester. Leicestershire captain Nigel Briers batted through their first innings for 150*, while in the second Justin Benson made his maiden first-class 100

- Middlesex stretched their lead at the top of the Championship table to 36 points with their seventh win of the season at the expense of Somerset at Uxbridge. Mark Ramprakash with a career best 146 made the decisive contribution as the home side chased a target of 369 in 69 overs

- Essex completed a satisfying week at Colchester with a six-wicket win over Lancashire, Graham Gooch masterminding their chase with an imperious 177. Nadeem Shahid made his maiden first-class 100 in Essex's first innings, while a partnership of 220* between Mike Atherton and Neil Fairbrother had left Essex a seemingly daunting target at almost seven an over

- Batsmen were very much in the ascendancy at Northampton and Cheltenham: Rob Bailey reached 204* for Northants against Sussex, while Ashley Metcalfe and Phil Bainbridge hit 162 and 152 respectively as both Yorks and Gloucs made big first innings scores

BRITANNIC ASSURANCE CHAMPIONSHIP

GLAMORGAN vs. WORCESTERSHIRE

at Abergavenny on 21st, 22nd, 23rd July 1990
Toss : Glamorgan. Umpires : D.R.Shepherd and D.S.Thompsett
Match drawn (Glamorgan 5 pts (Bt: 4, Bw: 1) Worcestershire 6 pts (Bt: 4, Bw: 2))

WORCESTERSHIRE

T.S.Curtis	b Watkin	23	not out	111
P.Bent	c Cowley b Croft	69	c Metson b Watkin	79
G.A.Hick	not out	252	not out	100
D.B.D'Oliveira	c Maynard b Cowley	121		
I.T.Botham	c Morris b Bastien	29		
P.A.Neale *				
S.J.Rhodes +				
R.K.Illingworth				
P.J.Newport				
S.R.Lampitt				
N.V.Radford				
Extras	(b 9,lb 10,nb 1)	20	(lb 9,w 4,nb 4)	17
TOTAL	(for 4 wkts dec)	514	(for 1 wkt dec)	307

GLAMORGAN

A.R.Butcher *	b Lampitt	79	c Neale b Illingworth	130
H.Morris	lbw b Botham	57	c Lampitt b Newport	119
P.A.Cottey	not out	100	(5) c D'Oliveira b Newport	1
M.P.Maynard	c Lampitt b Botham	15	(3) c Hick b Newport	1
I.V.A.Richards	c Rhodes b Radford	41	(4) c & b Illingworth	43
R.D.B.Croft	c D'Oliveira b Illingworth	28	(7) not out	91
N.G.Cowley	not out	2	(6) c Rhodes b Botham	63
C.P.Metson +			not out	12
S.L.Watkin				
S.Bastien				
M.Frost				
Extras	(lb 1,nb 4)	5	(b 10,lb 21,nb 2)	33
TOTAL	(for 5 wkts dec)	327	(for 6 wkts)	493

GLAMORGAN	O	M	R	W	O	M	R	W
Frost	18	0	109	0	11	0	38	0
Watkin	23	3	93	1	19	1	109	1
Bastien	15.2	2	90	1	12.3	2	61	0
Cowley	22	3	101	1	1	0	1	0
Croft	12	0	71	1	10	0	61	0
Richards	7	0	31	0				
Butcher					4	0	28	0

WORCS	O	M	R	W	O	M	R	W
Newport	15	0	72	0	19	4	87	3
Radford	15	1	79	1	12	1	67	0
Illingworth	15.1	3	80	1	24	2	124	2
Lampitt	11	2	40	1	3	1	14	0
Botham	12	1	55	2	12	2	40	1
Hick	1	1	0	0	12	3	61	0
Curtis					3	0	30	0
D'Oliveira					3	0	39	0

FALL OF WICKETS				
	WOR	GLA	WOR	GLA
1st	53	140	132	256
2nd	157	144		257
3rd	421	178		272
4th	514	248		288
5th		317		326
6th				450
7th				
8th				
9th				
10th				

HAMPSHIRE vs. DERBYSHIRE

at Portsmouth on 21st, 23rd, 24th July 1990
Toss : Hampshire. Umpires : J.C.Balderstone and D.J.Constant
Hampshire won by 48 runs (Hampshire 22 pts (Bt: 4, Bw: 2) Derbyshire 8 pts (Bt: 4, Bw: 4))

HAMPSHIRE

T.C.Middleton	c Barnett b Malcolm	6	c Krikken b Warner	59
C.L.Smith	b Malcolm	57	c Krikken b Mortensen	2
D.I.Gower	run out	48	b Bishop	3
R.A.Smith	c Morris b Mortensen	2	c Brown b Bishop	37
M.D.Marshall	c Adams b Bishop	32	c Barnett b Mortensen	60
M.C.J.Nicholas *	c Krikken b Warner	7	(7) c Krikken b Warner	15
J.R.Ayling	c Krikken b Mortensen	31	(8) c Morris b Malcolm	5
R.J.Maru	c Krikken b Bishop	44	(6) c Krikken b Mortensen	0
R.J.Parks +	run out	0	not out	8
C.A.Connor	b Bishop	46	c Barnett b Malcolm	6
P.J.Bakker	not out	16	c Krikken b Warner	10
Extras	(b 4,lb 11,w 2,nb 1)	18	(b 6,lb 9,w 2,nb 5)	22
TOTAL		307		227

DERBYSHIRE

P.D.Bowler	c Parks b Ayling	58	(2) b Marshall	56
A.M.Brown	lbw b Connor	24	(3) b Connor	15
J.E.Morris	not out	157	(4) c & b Marshall	10
B.Roberts	c Parks b Marshall	7	(5) c Parks b Marshall	0
C.J.Adams	c Parks b Marshall	4	(6) c Parks b Marshall	1
K.M.Krikken +	c Nicholas b Bakker	0	(7) lbw b Marshall	0
K.J.Barnett *	b Marshall	13	(1) c Parks b Ayling	63
I.R.Bishop	not out	27	b Connor	31
A.E.Warner			c Parks b Marshall	0
D.E.Malcolm			b Marshall	0
O.H.Mortensen			not out	0
Extras	(b 6,nb 4)	10	(lb 10)	10
TOTAL	(for 6 wkts dec)	300		186

DERBYSHIRE	O	M	R	W	O	M	R	W
Bishop	23.2	6	72	3	15	4	32	2
Malcolm	19	1	90	2	15	2	39	2
Mortensen	18	6	64	2	17	3	47	3
Warner	16	2	63	1	22.4	4	75	3
Roberts	2	0	3	0				
Barnett					4	0	19	0

HAMPSHIRE	O	M	R	W	O	M	R	W
Bakker	13	1	45	1	3	0	24	0
Marshall	21	7	60	3	15	4	47	7
Connor	15	7	58	1	12.1	2	49	2
Maru	22	5	70	0	12	2	33	0
Ayling	12.2	1	61	1	6	1	23	1

FALL OF WICKETS				
	HAM	DER	HAM	DER
1st	11	46	2	91
2nd	85	153	15	140
3rd	93	179	78	150
4th	150	195	172	150
5th	159	200	172	151
6th	167	230	196	151
7th	207		199	156
8th	208		201	160
9th	267		212	186
10th	307		227	186

NORTHANTS vs. SUSSEX

at Northampton on 21st, 23rd, 24th July 1990
Toss : Sussex. Umpires : B.Hassan and B.Leadbeater
Match drawn (Northants 7 pts (Bt: 4, Bw: 3) Sussex 5 pts (Bt: 4, Bw: 1))

NORTHANTS

A.Fordham	c Wells C.M. b Pigott	9	c Lenham b Bunting	26
W.Larkins	b Pigott	61	lbw b Pigott	11
N.A.Felton	c Moores b Dodemaide	78	c Speight b Dodemaide	42
A.J.Lamb *	not out	135	(6) b Wells A.P.	1
D.J.Capel	c Speight b Bunting	12	b Lenham	29
R.J.Bailey	not out	24	(4) not out	204
D.Ripley +			not out	44
W.W.Davis				
S.J.Brown				
N.G.B.Cook				
M.A.Robinson				
Extras	(b 4,lb 6)	10	(b 1,lb 3)	4
TOTAL	(for 4 wkts dec)	329	(for 5 wkts dec)	361

SUSSEX

N.J.Lenham	c Felton b Davis	41	lbw b Robinson	38
J.W.Hall	lbw b Cook	42	b Brown	7
P.W.G.Parker *	lbw b Davis	90	lbw b Robinson	38
A.P.Wells	c Bailey b Marshall	21	not out	102
M.P.Speight	c Bailey b Cook	2	b Bailey	13
C.M.Wells	b Cook	42	c Lamb b Bailey	6
A.I.C.Dodemaide	c Ripley b Robinson	26	c Fordham b Bailey	14
P.Moores +	b Cook	10	c Cook b Robinson	8
A.C.S.Pigott	not out	5	not out	17
I.D.K.Salisbury	not out	0		
R.A.Bunting				
Extras	(lb 9,w 2,nb 12)	23	(b 4,lb 1,nb 3)	8
TOTAL	(for 8 wkts dec)	302	(for 7 wkts)	251

SUSSEX	O	M	R	W	O	M	R	W
Dodemaide	21	4	55	1	12	1	26	1
Pigott	19	2	83	2	5	0	28	1
Wells C.M.	20	6	42	0	4	2	10	0
Bunting	23	6	79	1	15	1	68	1
Salisbury	7	1	30	0				
Lenham	8	3	24	0	13.5	1	78	1
Wells A.P.					16	4	88	1
Parker					8	0	59	0

NORTHANTS	O	M	R	W	O	M	R	W
Davis	21	4	75	2				
Robinson	17.1	3	61	1	17	3	68	3
Cook	31	9	89	4	13	4	21	0
Brown	14	3	46	1	7	0	41	1
Bailey	3	0	22	0	20	2	82	3
Larkins					6	1	21	0
Capel					1	0	13	0

FALL OF WICKETS				
	NOR	SUS	NOR	SUS
1st	11	61	30	25
2nd	136	120	42	78
3rd	179	163	89	89
4th	224	166	178	111
5th		239	183	131
6th		264		174
7th		295		209
8th		299		
9th				
10th				

GLOUCESTERSHIRE vs. YORKSHIRE

at Cheltenham on 21st, 23rd, 24th July 1990
Toss : Yorkshire. Umpires : J.H.Hampshire and R.A.White
Match drawn (Gloucestershire 6 pts (Bt: 4, Bw: 2) Yorkshire 5 pts (Bt: 4, Bw: 1))

YORKSHIRE

M.D.Moxon *	b Walsh	66	c & b Lloyds	18
A.A.Metcalfe	c & b Lawrence	162	c Wright b Lawrence	26
R.J.Blakey +	c Russell b Lawrence	9	c Curran b Lloyds	94
K.Sharp	c Russell b Lawrence	38		
P.E.Robinson	lbw b Walsh	49	(4) not out	70
D.Byas	not out	63	(5) not out	0
P.Carrick	c Russell b Curran	17		
C.S.Pickles	not out	28		
P.J.Hartley				
J.D.Batty				
S.D.Fletcher				
Extras	(b 4,lb 4,w 1,nb 10)	19	(lb 1,w 2,nb 8)	11
TOTAL	(for 6 wkts dec)	451	(for 3 wkts dec)	219

GLOUCESTERSHIRE

G.D.Hodgson	b Batty	65	
A.J.Wright *	c Robinson b Batty	78	
P.W.Romaines	c Byas b Fletcher	46	
C.W.J.Athey	b Batty	68	
P.Bainbridge	c Blakey b Hartley	152	
K.M.Curran	c Moxon b Hartley	8	
J.W.Lloyds	b Batty	38	
R.C.Russell +	b Hartley	16	
C.A.Walsh	not out	63	
D.V.Lawrence	c Blakey b Fletcher	6	
P.A.Owen	run out	1	
Extras	(b 8,lb 17,w 1,nb 7)	33	
TOTAL		574	

GLOUCS	O	M	R	W	O	M	R	W
Walsh	22	5	70	2	11	1	46	0
Lawrence	14	0	94	2	8	0	34	1
Curran	22	4	84	2	10	4	30	0
Bainbridge	7	0	37	0				
Lloyds	14	1	73	0	14	3	61	2
Owen	16	1	72	0	16	3	47	0
Athey	4	0	13	0				

YORKSHIRE	O	M	R	W	O	M	R	W
Hartley	28	5	111	3				
Fletcher	28.1	5	98	2				
Carrick	50	16	144	0				
Pickles	8	0	45	0				
Batty	38	6	137	4				
Byas	1	0	14	0				

FALL OF WICKETS			
	YOR	GLO	YOR
1st	204	126	45
2nd	224	163	51
3rd	286	227	213
4th	297	309	
5th	362	350	
6th	409	452	
7th		489	
8th		498	
9th		554	
10th		574	

BRITANNIC ASSURANCE CHAMPIONSHIP

SURREY vs. KENT

at Guildford on 21st, 23rd, 24th July 1990
Toss : Surrey.   Umpires : B.J.Meyer and K.E.Palmer
Match drawn (Surrey 8 pts (Bt: 4, Bw: 4) Kent 6 pts (Bt: 4, Bw: 2))

KENT

R.P.Davis	c Lynch b Feltham	0	(2) b Gray		4
S.G.Hinks	c Clinton b Gray	120	(1) c & b Feltham		1
N.R.Taylor	c Gray b Kendrick	69	(4) lbw b Gray		26
G.R.Cowdrey	c Lynch b Feltham	71	(6) not out		119
T.R.Ward	b Feltham	10	(3) c Thorpe b Medlycott		88
C.S.Cowdrey *	c Greig b Gray	20	(10) lbw b Medlycott		27
S.A.Marsh +	c Sargeant b Kendrick	7	(5) c Sargeant b Medlycott		11
R.M.Ellison	c & b Kendrick	10	c Sargeant b Medlycott		0
P.S.De Villiers	lbw b Kendrick	32	(5) b Kendrick		28
M.M.Patel	c Lynch b Feltham	2	(9) c Lynch b Medlycott		0
A.P.Igglesden	not out	15	c Ward b Kendrick		6
Extras	(b 2,lb 2,nb 12)	16	(b 1,lb 2,w 2,nb 14)		19
TOTAL		372			329

SURREY

D.J.Bicknell	c Patel b Igglesden	4	not out		9
G.S.Clinton	c Marsh b Igglesden	38	not out		8
G.P.Thorpe	lbw b Igglesden	42			
D.M.Ward	c Marsh b Igglesden	48			
M.A.Lynch	b De Villiers	20			
M.A.Feltham	b Ellison	55			
I.A.Greig *	not out	89			
K.T.Medlycott	b Ellison	28			
N.M.Kendrick					
A.H.Gray					
N.F.Sargeant +					
Extras	(b 1,lb 11,w 4,nb 4)	20			0
TOTAL	(for 7 wkts dec)	344	(for 0 wkts)		17

SURREY	O	M	R	W	O	M	R	W		FALL OF WICKETS				
											KEN	SUR	KEN	SUR
Gray	20	4	54	2	24	2	93	2	1st		4	4	4	
Feltham	22	1	86	4	11	1	32	1	2nd		118	85	10	
Greig	6	0	36	0					3rd		243	114	48	
Thorpe	2	0	23	0					4th		257	148	125	
Medlycott	7	0	59	0	41	13	99	5	5th		298	191	187	
Kendrick	33.2	8	110	4	29.4	7	102	2	6th		301	249	228	
Lynch					1	1	0	0	7th		314	344	234	
									8th		328		234	
KENT	O	M	R	W	O	M	R	W	9th		335		310	
Igglesden	25	1	88	4					10th		372		329	
De Villiers	21	5	57	1										
Davis	24	3	89	0	6	2	9	0						
Patel	17	3	54	0	5	2	6	0						
Ellison	19.3	4	44	2										
Ward					1	0	1	0						
Taylor					1	0	1	0						

DERBYSHIRE vs. WORCESTERSHIRE

at Derby on 25th, 26th, 27th July 1990
Toss : Worcestershire.   Umpires : P.J.Eele and K.J.Lyons
Match drawn (Derbyshire 2 pts (Bt: 1, Bw: 1) Worcestershire 7 pts (Bt: 3, Bw: 4))

WORCESTERSHIRE

T.S.Curtis	c Krikken b Base	17
C.M.Tolley	lbw b Base	16
G.A.Hick	c Adams b Warner	53
D.B.D'Oliveira	b Warner	87
I.T.Botham	c Brown b Barnett	27
P.A.Neale *	c Roberts b Warner	65
S.J.Rhodes +	c Krikken b Base	0
R.K.Illingworth	c Adams b Base	6
P.J.Newport	c Barnett b Base	2
S.R.Lampitt	not out	16
N.V.Radford	c Krikken b Base	14
Extras	(b 12,lb 15,w 5,nb 13)	45
TOTAL		348

DERBYSHIRE

P.D.Bowler	c Botham b Illingworth	36	c Rhodes b Newport		18
A.M.Brown	lbw b Illingworth	32	c Rhodes b Hick		42
T.J.G.O'Gorman	c Radford b Illingworth	0	c Neale b Lampitt		9
C.J.Adams	c Rhodes b Illingworth	32	st Rhodes b Illingworth		63
A.P.Kuiper	c Hick b Lampitt	38	b Hick		41
B.Roberts	c Hick b Lampitt	18	c Rhodes b Illingworth		0
K.J.Barnett *	b Lampitt	9	c Rhodes b Illingworth		23
K.M.Krikken +	lbw b Lampitt	4	c Neale b Newport		13
A.E.Warner	lbw b Lampitt	4	not out		5
S.J.Base	b Illingworth	14	not out		0
O.H.Mortensen	not out	0			
Extras	(lb 2,nb 3)	5	(b 9,lb 12)		21
TOTAL		192	(for 8 wkts)		235

DERBYSHIRE	O	M	R	W	O	M	R	W		FALL OF WICKETS				
											WOR	DER	DER	WOR
Mortensen	3	2	4	0					1st		35	61	24	
Base	39.3	3	105	6					2nd		44	61	50	
Kuiper	19	8	42	0					3rd		136	76	119	
Barnett	32	8	61	1					4th		173	121	181	
Warner	30	5	109	3					5th		275	147	181	
									6th		277	164	201	
WORCS	O	M	R	W	O	M	R	W	7th		295	171	229	
Newport	8	1	23	0	7	1	29	2	8th		310	175	235	
Radford	5	0	23	0	4	2	10	0	9th		323	192		
Botham	7	2	12	0	6	1	26	0	10th		348	192		
Illingworth	38	19	59	5	53	31	52	3						
Hick	14	2	39	0	25	9	45	2						
Lampitt	19.4	6	34	5	19	3	52	1						

HEADLINES

21st - 24th July

- Even in a season with new records almost common place, the events at Abergavenny were extraordinary. Inevitably Graeme Hick held centre stage: he made 100s in both innings for the second time in his career, the second 100 being his 50th in first-class cricket; at 24 he is the youngest to reach this milestone, and needed only 249 innings, giving him a 'strike-rate' bettered only by Sir Donald Bradman; Hick also reached 592 runs in first-class cricket without being dismissed, a record in English cricket

- Phil Neale left Glamorgan a target of 495 to win in 88 overs. Agonisingly, they ended two short. Alan Butcher and Hugh Morris lead the chase with a stand of 256 and Robert Croft almost won the match with a career best 91*. The aggregate of 1641 was a record for 3-day cricket

- Malcolm Marshall returned the best figures of the season, 7 for 47, as Hampshire moved into second place with a win over Derbyshire. John Morris had earlier prepared for his Test debut with his fifth 100 of the season

- With five second innings wickets Keith Medlycott became the first bowler to take 50 first-class wickets in 1990, in Surrey's match against Kent.

- First-class debut: P.A.Owen (Gloucestershire)

LANCASHIRE vs. NOTTINGHAMSHIRE

at Southport on 25th, 26th, 27th July 1990
Toss : Lancashire.   Umpires : J.W.Holder and A.G.T.Whitehead
Lancashire won by 7 wickets (Lancashire 24 pts (Bt: 4, Bw: 4) Notts 4 pts (Bt: 2, Bw: 2))

LANCASHIRE

G.D.Mendis	c Robinson b Stephenson	180	c Evans b Stephenson		21
G.Fowler	c Stephenson b Evans	18	c Robinson b Afford		6
G.D.Lloyd	c Johnson b Afford	39	not out		59
N.H.Fairbrother	c Robinson b Cooper	93	c Johnson b Afford		10
T.E.Jesty	c & b Evans	38	not out		30
M.Watkinson	st French b Afford	47			
J.D.Fitton	c French b Evans	3			
D.P.Hughes *	b Evans	7			
S.N.V.Waterton +	c Broad b Afford	3			
P.J.W.Allott	st French b Afford	5			
P.J.Martin	not out	1			
Extras	(b 2,lb 5,nb 11)	18	(lb 2,w 1,nb 1)		4
TOTAL		452	(for 3 wkts)		130

NOTTINGHAMSHIRE

B.C.Broad	c Mendis b Allott	122	lbw b Allott		46
P.Pollard	lbw b Allott	0	c Waterton b Martin		27
R.T.Robinson *	c Waterton b Martin	0	c Waterton b Hughes		41
P.Johnson	c Mendis b Martin	4	b Allott		82
D.W.Randall	lbw b Allott	0	c & b Martin		68
M.Saxelby	c Waterton b Fitton	13	c Fairbrother b Martin		8
F.D.Stephenson	c Hughes b Fitton	8	run out		18
B.N.French +	lbw b Martin	6	run out		1
K.P.Evans	not out	48	not out		34
K.E.Cooper	b Allott	0	c Fitton b Watkinson		24
J.A.Afford	c Watkinson b Hughes	0	run out		0
Extras	(lb 2,w 1,nb 1)	4	(b 1,lb 18,w 3,nb 2)		24
TOTAL		205			373

NOTTS	O	M	R	W	O	M	R	W		FALL OF WICKETS				
											LAN	NOT	NOT	LAN
Stephenson	23	4	127	1	9	0	44	1	1st		54	16	58	26
Cooper	23	1	94	1	2	1	11	0	2nd		155	17	98	39
Evans	25	10	57	4	4.4	1	15	0	3rd		318	37	172	53
Afford	34	5	137	4	11	2	58	2	4th		378	38	216	
Saxelby	3	0	30	0					5th		432	77	284	
									6th		434	97	295	
LANCASHIRE	O	M	R	W	O	M	R	W	7th		441	112	313	
Martin	14	1	57	3	27	2	110	3	8th		442	196	314	
Allott	16	5	37	4	14	2	52	2	9th		449	202	367	
Watkinson	7	0	36	0	34.3	7	129	1	10th		452	205	373	
Fitton	12	1	61	2	6	0	33	0						
Hughes	5	1	12	1	10	3	30	1						

BRITANNIC ASSURANCE CHAMPIONSHIP

GLOUCESTERSHIRE vs. NORTHANTS

at Cheltenham on 25th, 26th, 27th July 1990
Toss : Northants.   Umpires : J.H.Hampshire and R.A.White
Gloucs won by an innings and 128 runs (Glos 24 pts (Bt: 4, Bw: 4) N'hants 3 pts (Bt: 1, Bw: 2))

NORTHANTS

A.Fordham	c Wright b Curran	13	c Williams b Walsh	1
W.Larkins *	c Williams b Walsh	16	b Walsh	30
N.A.Felton	c Williams b Walsh	6	not out	82
R.J.Bailey	b Curran	36	c Hodgson b Owen	3
D.J.Capel	b Walsh	10	(6) c Romaines b Walsh	4
R.G.Williams	c Williams b Curran	47	(7) b Walsh	0
D.Ripley +	c Williams b Lawrence	6	(8) b Walsh	31
A.R.Roberts	c Lloyds b Curran	0	(9) b Walsh	0
J.Hughes	c Williams b Lawrence	1	(5) hit wicket b Walsh	0
C.E.L.Ambrose	c Wright b Lawrence	8	lbw b Curran	6
M.A.Robinson	not out	0	c Williams b Walsh	0
Extras	(lb 1,nb 6)	7	(b 8,lb 4,nb 8)	20
TOTAL		150		177

GLOUCESTERSHIRE

G.D.Hodgson	c Fordham b Robinson	50
A.J.Wright *	c Ripley b Ambrose	112
P.W.Romaines	b Williams	28
C.W.J.Athey	b Bailey	27
P.Bainbridge	c Capel b Roberts	34
K.M.Curran	c & b Roberts	86
J.W.Lloyds	c Ripley b Ambrose	34
C.A.Walsh	c Larkins b Robinson	12
R.C.J.Williams +	not out	44
D.V.Lawrence	b Williams	0
P.A.Owen		
Extras	(lb 13,w 5,nb 10)	28
TOTAL	(for 9 wkts dec)	455

GLOUCS	O	M	R	W	O	M	R	W
Walsh	12	0	41	3	19.2	6	58	8
Curran	13	4	37	4	16	1	58	1
Lawrence	13.4	1	52	3	6	2	20	0
Owen	5	0	12	0	4	1	13	1
Athey	2	1	7	0				
Lloyds					5	3	16	0

NORTHANTS	O	M	R	W	O	M	R	W
Ambrose	22	7	53	2				
Robinson	36	5	119	2				
Roberts	39	6	123	2				
Hughes	17	4	69	0				
Williams	19.2	7	42	2				
Bailey	9	1	36	1				

FALL OF WICKETS				
	NOR	GLO	NOR	GLO
1st	20	97	40	
2nd	34	159	41	
3rd	39	203	52	
4th	61	271	60	
5th	123	271	72	
6th	136	315	72	
7th	140	343	127	
8th	142	454	127	
9th	142	455	141	
10th	150		177	

KENT vs. MIDDLESEX

at Canterbury on 25th, 26th, 27th July 1990
Toss : Middlesex.   Umpires : A.A.Jones and R.Julian
Match drawn (Kent 5 pts (Bt: 4, Bw: 1) Middlesex 4 pts (Bt: 4, Bw: 0))

KENT

S.G.Hinks	c Farbrace b Hughes	234	b Cowans	2
M.R.Benson *	c Farbrace b Haynes	45	b Emburey	10
N.R.Taylor	not out	152	(8) c Roseberry b Cowans	3
G.R.Cowdrey			(3) lbw b Williams	22
T.R.Ward			(4) c Williams b Emburey	0
R.P.Davis			(5) c Farbrace b Cowans	12
S.A.Marsh +			(6) c Emburey b Williams	61
R.M.Ellison			(7) c Brown b Tufnell	9
P.S.De Villiers			c Haynes b Emburey	9
M.M.Patel			not out	1
A.P.Igglesden			b Williams	1
Extras	(lb 6,w 1,nb 11)	18	(b 1,lb 2,nb 7)	10
TOTAL	(for 2 wkts dec)	449		140

MIDDLESEX

D.L.Haynes	b Igglesden	9	b De Villiers	0
M.A.Roseberry	c Igglesden b Ellison	82	lbw b De Villiers	14
M.W.Gatting *	c Igglesden b Davis	52	b Igglesden	101
M.R.Ramprakash	not out	100	b De Villiers	125
K.R.Brown	not out	57	c Hinks b Igglesden	5
J.E.Emburey			c Marsh b De Villiers	0
N.F.Williams			c Marsh b De Villiers	8
P.Farbrace +			lbw b De Villiers	3
S.P.Hughes			not out	6
N.G.Cowans			not out	2
P.C.R.Tufnell				
Extras	(b 5,lb 1,nb 2)	8	(b 2,lb 10)	12
TOTAL	(for 3 wkts dec)	308	(for 8 wkts)	276

MIDDLESEX	O	M	R	W	O	M	R	W
Williams	15	2	49	0	19.5	1	65	3
Cowans	23	5	57	0	10	2	20	3
Hughes	16.1	1	87	1	2	0	14	0
Emburey	28	4	93	0	7	4	3	3
Tufnell	22	2	69	0	14	5	35	1
Ramprakash	9	0	41	0				
Haynes	10	1	47	1				

KENT	O	M	R	W	O	M	R	W
Igglesden	10	1	53	1	20	0	93	2
De Villiers	11	1	32	0	21	3	70	6
Ellison	9	0	37	1	9	0	45	0
Davis	30	8	104	1	8	1	56	0
Patel	16.2	4	54	0				
Ward	5	0	22	0				

FALL OF WICKETS				
	KEN	MID	KEN	MID
1st	83	12	15	0
2nd	449	121	30	23
3rd		155	30	211
4th			43	231
5th			53	232
6th			75	240
7th			86	250
8th			126	271
9th			138	
10th			140	

YORKSHIRE vs. SOMERSET

at Scarborough on 25th, 26th, 27th July 1990
Toss : Somerset.   Umpires : M.J.Kitchen and P.B.Wight
Match drawn (Yorkshire 6 pts (Bt: 4, Bw: 2) Somerset 6 pts (Bt: 4, Bw: 2))

SOMERSET

S.J.Cook	b Fletcher	21	c Blakey b Gough	53
P.M.Roebuck	b Pickles	11	c Byas b Fletcher	8
A.N.Hayhurst	c Blakey b Gough	170	c Byas b Pickles	24
C.J.Tavare *	c Robinson b Gough	14	b Gough	0
R.J.Harden	c Pickles b Batty	101	b Pickles	24
N.D.Burns +	c Moxon b Pickles	33	c Metcalfe b Robinson	72
G.D.Rose	c Batty b Gough	35	c Blakey b Pickles	0
R.P.Lefebvre	not out	3	not out	25
I.G.Swallow	not out	3	not out	12
A.N.Jones				
N.A.Mallender				
Extras	(b 1,lb 6,w 1,nb 2)	10	(lb 2,nb 1)	3
TOTAL	(for 7 wkts dec)	401	(for 7 wkts dec)	221

YORKSHIRE

M.D.Moxon *	c Burns b Mallender	23	lbw b Jones	4
A.A.Metcalfe	c Jones b Roebuck	102	b Rose	23
R.J.Blakey +	c Hayhurst b Swallow	29	c Swallow b Roebuck	111
S.A.Kellett	c Roebuck b Swallow	15	c Cook b Rose	57
P.E.Robinson	c Burns b Rose	31	c Lefebvre b Hayhurst	44
D.Byas	b Jones	36	b Hayhurst	32
P.Grayson	not out	44	(8) not out	16
C.S.Pickles	not out	9	(7) b Mallender	1
D.Gough			not out	7
J.D.Batty				
S.D.Fletcher				
Extras	(b 1,lb 5,nb 8)	14	(b 8,lb 13)	21
TOTAL	(for 6 wkts dec)	303	(for 7 wkts)	316

YORKSHIRE	O	M	R	W	O	M	R	W
Fletcher	22.5	6	47	1	5	1	12	1
Gough	15	3	77	3	13	3	47	2
Pickles	20	1	82	2	15	1	56	3
Batty	22	3	83	1	8	2	41	0
Moxon	6	0	24	0	3	1	6	0
Grayson	17	2	66	0	4	1	23	0
Byas	2	0	15	0	5	2	14	0
Metcalfe					1.3	0	10	0
Robinson					1	0	10	1

SOMERSET	O	M	R	W	O	M	R	W
Jones	18	1	78	1	12	1	54	1
Mallender	11	2	42	1	15	0	69	1
Lefebvre	15	2	40	0	16	5	52	0
Rose	15	2	41	1	10	2	41	2
Swallow	25.5	6	71	2	7	2	35	0
Roebuck	11	3	25	1	2	0	25	1
Hayhurst					3	0	19	2

FALL OF WICKETS				
	SOM	YOR	SOM	YOR
1st	33	36	21	4
2nd	33	118	85	57
3rd	77	159	85	173
4th	251	202	85	244
5th	302	210	126	274
6th	376	277	126	280
7th	396		206	298
8th				
9th				
10th				

SUSSEX vs. HAMPSHIRE

at Arundel Castle on 25th, 26th, 27th July 1990
Toss : Sussex.   Umpires : B.Dudleston and B.Leadbeater
Match drawn (Sussex 5 pts (Bt: 3, Bw: 2) Hampshire 6 pts (Bt: 3, Bw: 3))

SUSSEX

N.J.Lenham	c Maru b Ayling	15	b Connor	15
J.W.Hall	lbw b Marshall	4	run out	36
P.W.G.Parker *	b Marshall	0	b Ayling	18
A.P.Wells	c Scott b Udal	53	b Maru	32
M.P.Speight	c & b Udal	37	run out	24
C.M.Wells	c Ayling b Udal	107	c Cox b Udal	6
A.I.C.Dodemaide	lbw b Marshall	2	(8) not out	2
P.Moores +	c Smith b Udal	61		
A.C.S.Pigott	not out	64	(7) b Udal	5
I.D.K.Salisbury	run out	0		
B.T.P.Donelan	not out	11		
Extras	(b 1,lb 21,w 4,nb 3)	29	(lb 4,nb 2)	6
TOTAL	(for 9 wkts dec)	383	(for 7 wkts)	144

HAMPSHIRE

T.C.Middleton	b Pigott	50	b Donelan	28
C.L.Smith	not out	132	st Moores b Donelan	61
R.J.Scott	c Dodemaide b Salisbury	13	st Moores b Donelan	16
M.C.J.Nicholas *	run out	0	c Moores b Pigott	1
M.D.Marshall	c Dodemaide b Salisbury	11	c Donelan b Salisbury	34
R.M.F.Cox	c Moores b Dodemaide	9	(7) not out	35
J.R.Ayling	not out	28	(6) c Hall b Salisbury	22
R.J.Parks +			not out	15
R.J.Maru				
S.D.Udal				
C.A.Connor				
Extras	(b 6,lb 4,nb 1)	11	(b 6,nb 2)	8
TOTAL	(for 5 wkts dec)	254	(for 6 wkts)	220

HAMPSHIRE	O	M	R	W	O	M	R	W
Connor	12	4	20	0	8	1	23	1
Marshall	16	4	35	3	9	4	18	0
Ayling	15.4	8	36	1	6.2	0	36	1
Maru	32.2	5	105	0	6	0	51	1
Udal	43	7	144	4	2	0	12	2
Scott	4	1	21	0				

SUSSEX	O	M	R	W	O	M	R	W
Dodemaide	20	9	31	1	10	2	23	0
Pigott	18	7	43	1	8	3	12	1
Wells C.M.	5	0	18	0	11	3	31	0
Donelan	19	5	44	0	19.4	4	79	3
Salisbury	36	5	108	2	16	1	69	2

FALL OF WICKETS				
	SUS	HAM	SUS	HAM
1st	13	96	27	76
2nd	13	131	51	93
3rd	28	144	90	94
4th	105	157	123	141
5th	134	192	134	143
6th	137		141	189
7th	276		144	
8th	319			
9th	324			
10th				

BRITANNIC ASSURANCE CHAMPIONSHIP

HEADLINES

25th - 27th July

● Warwickshire's Tom Moody made the fastest first-class century ever recorded as he took advantage of some declaration bowling served up by Glamorgan's Matthew Maynard and Tony Cottey. He reached his 100 in 26 minutes, bettering the previous record of 35 minutes established by Percy Fender and Steve O'Shaughnessy. Moody's 100 was not the fastest in terms of balls faced as he needed 44 balls to make his 100, 10 more than fellow Australian David Hookes. Moody's innings eclipsed the achievement of Andy Moles (307 runs in the match without being dismissed) but could not prevent a five-wicket victory for Glamorgan

● Derbyshire's Allan Warner ended Graeme Hick's unbeaten sequence of scores at 645 – a new record for English cricket but short of the world's best. Worcestershire were unable to bowl Derbyshire out a second time after asking them to follow on

● There were more records established at Canterbury where leaders Middlesex finished six runs short of victory. Simon Hinks, who made a career best 234, and Neil Taylor shared a second wicket partnership of 366, a new Kent record for any wicket. Middlesex's Mark Ramprakash responded with 100* and 125, giving him three 100s in his last three innings

● Lancashire's challenge for the County Championship gathered momentum with their seven-wicket win over Nottinghamshire, as they moved into second place

● Gloucestershire gained their first success of the season as they beat Northamptonshire by an innings and 128 runs at Cheltenham. Courtney Walsh improved the season's best figures with 8 for 58, but Gloucestershire remained at the foot of the Championship table

● There was a batting feast at Scarborough where Yorkshire finished three runs short of victory over Somerset. Andy Hayhurst equalled his career best score, while Richard Blakey at last joined in the run-making with his first 100 of the season

● Championship cricket made a welcome first appearance at Arundel Castle, one of the most beautiful grounds in the country, as Sussex held Hampshire to a draw

● John Stephenson's determined 131*, and a seventh wicket stand of 132 with Derek Pringle, brought Essex to safety against Leicestershire at Leicester

● First-class debut: R.M.F.Cox (Hampshire)

FASTEST FIRST-CLASS HUNDREDS

26 mins	T.M.Moody	Warwicks v Glamorgan	Swansea	1990
35 mins	P.G.H.Fender	Surrey v Northants	Northampton	1920
35 mins	S.J.O'Shaughnessy	Lancs v Leics	Old Trafford	1983
37 mins	C.M.Old	Yorks v Warwicks	Edgbaston	1977
40 mins	G.L.Jessop	Gloucs v Yorks	Harrogate	1897
41 mins	N.F.M.Popplewell	Somerset v Gloucs	Bath	1983
42 mins	G.L.Jessop	Gentlemen of South v Players of South	Hastings	1907
43 mins	D.W.Hookes	South Aust v Victoria	Adelaide	1982-83

GLAMORGAN vs. WARWICKSHIRE

at Swansea on 25th, 26th, 27th July 1990
Toss : Warwickshire. Umpires : D.R.Shepherd and D.S.Thompsett
Glamorgan won by 5 wickets (Glamorgan 20 pts (Bt: 4, Bw: 0) Warwicks 7 pts (Bt: 4, Bw: 3))

WARWICKSHIRE

A.J.Moles	not out	224	not out	83
T.A.Lloyd *	c Maynard b Croft	101	c Maynard b Bastien	0
Asif Din	c Metson b Watkin	47	lbw b Bastien	6
T.M.Moody	c Dennis b Cowley	40	(5) not out	103
P.A.Smith	not out	14		
T.A.Munton			(4) c Butcher b Cottey	14
D.A.Reeve				
K.J.Piper +				
G.C.Small				
J.E.Benjamin				
A.R.K.Pierson				
Extras	(lb 12,w 2,nb 3)	17	(lb 6)	6
TOTAL	(for 3 wkts dec)	443	(for 3 wkts dec)	212

GLAMORGAN

A.R.Butcher *	c Piper b Munton	33	c Piper b Pierson	116
H.Morris	c Reeve b Pierson	106	c Munton b Small	15
P.A.Cottey	lbw b Pierson	50	run out	2
M.P.Maynard	b Pierson	27	c Piper b Asif Din	56
I.V.A.Richards	c & b Munton	11	not out	65
R.D.B.Croft	not out	74	(7) not out	12
N.G.Cowley	c Moody b Pierson	30	(6) c Moody b Pierson	10
C.P.Metson +	s Piper b Pierson	7		
S.L.Watkin	not out	10		
S.Bastien				
S.J.Dennis				
Extras	(b 6,lb 14,w 2,nb 3)	25	(lb 3,w 1,nb 3)	7
TOTAL	(for 7 wkts dec)	373	(for 5 wkts)	283

GLAMORGAN	O	M	R	W	O	M	R	W		FALL OF WICKETS			
										WAR	GLA	WAR	GLA
Watkin	22	2	94	1	8	1	36	0	1st	220	47	4	42
Dennis	25	3	91	0					2nd	327	163	15	70
Bastien	17	1	81	0	6	1	11	2	3rd	394	201	81	167
Croft	16	2	54	1	7	4	12	0	4th		218		206
Cowley	30	2	111	1	4	2	9	0	5th		267		232
Maynard					6	0	89	0	6th		347		
Cottey					6	0	49	1	7th		355		
WARWICKS	O	M	R	W	O	M	R	W	8th				
Small	12	3	47	0	12.4	2	62	1	9th				
Munton	17	2	65	2	15	1	77	0	10th				
Benjamin	10	1	45	0	6	2	24	0					
Smith	3	0	17	0									
Pierson	35	6	101	5	15	2	78	2					
Asif Din	13	2	50	0	6	0	39	1					
Reeve	7	2	28	0									

LEICESTERSHIRE vs. ESSEX

at Leicester on 25th, 26th, 27th July 1990
Toss : Essex. Umpires : D.J.Constant and B.J.Meyer
Match drawn (Leicestershire 7 pts (Bt: 3, Bw: 4) Essex 5 pts (Bt: 1, Bw: 4))

ESSEX

J.P.Stephenson	c Nixon b Agnew	7	not out	131
N.Shahid	b Agnew	2	hit wicket b Agnew	48
P.J.Prichard	lbw b Benjamin	2	c Potter b Agnew	0
M.E.Waugh	c Boon b Benjamin	69	c Willey b Mullally	31
N.Hussain	c Nixon b Agnew	9	(6) c Nixon b Agnew	0
M.A.Garnham +	c Benjamin b Parsons	8	(7) b Mullally	7
D.R.Pringle *	c Willey b Benjamin	20	(8) c Nixon b Mullally	84
N.A.Foster	lbw b Benjamin	23	(9) not out	32
T.D.Topley	b Agnew	23	(5) c Nixon b Mullally	2
J.H.Childs	run out	13		
S.J.W.Andrew	not out	3		
Extras	(b 6,lb 8,w 2,nb 2)	18	(b 7,lb 3,w 1,nb 3)	14
TOTAL		197	(for 7 wkts dec)	349

LEICESTERSHIRE

T.J.Boon	c Pringle b Andrew	13	c Waugh b Andrew	20
N.E.Briers *	run out	92	lbw b Foster	1
J.J.Whitaker	c Topley b Foster	8	c Hussain b Foster	34
P.Willey	c Shahid b Pringle	7	c Stephenson b Foster	1
L.Potter	c Shahid b Andrew	48	c Stephenson b Andrew	23
J.D.R.Benson	b Pringle	12	not out	34
W.K.M.Benjamin	c Foster b Topley	54	not out	9
P.A.Nixon +	c Garnham b Topley	11		
G.J.Parsons	not out	19		
J.P.Agnew	c Hussain b Topley	5		
A.D.Mullally	b Pringle	0		
Extras	(b 1,lb 17,nb 14)	32	(b 8,lb 2,nb 9)	19
TOTAL		301	(for 5 wkts)	141

LEICS	O	M	R	W	O	M	R	W		FALL OF WICKETS			
										ESS	LEI	ESS	LEI
Benjamin	21	5	51	4	11	1	48	0	1st	10	33	74	11
Agnew	21.3	3	73	4	24	4	106	3	2nd	13	51	76	40
Mullally	17	6	37	0	32	11	131	4	3rd	38	71	150	48
Parsons	7	2	22	1	18	6	54	0	4th	58	150	154	79
Willey					2	2	0	0	5th	127	178	159	96
									6th	136	228	176	
ESSEX	O	M	R	W	O	M	R	W	7th	159	272	308	
Foster	22	3	70	1	21	9	47	3	8th	191	277		
Andrew	24	4	62	2	9	1	39	2	9th	197	294		
Topley	22	3	69	3	3	0	22	0	10th	197	301		
Pringle	20.2	5	51	3	8	3	19	0					
Childs	14	3	31	0									
Waugh					1	0	4	0					

REFUGE ASSURANCE LEAGUE

LANCASHIRE vs. SOMERSET

at Old Trafford on 29th July 1990
Toss : Som. Umpires : J.W.Holder and A.G.T.Whitehead
Lancashire won by 6 wickets (Lancs 4 pts Somerset 0 pts)

SOMERSET

S.J.Cook	c Martin b Wasim Akram	41
R.J.Bartlett	c Lloyd b Watkinson	55
C.J.Tavare *	c Mendis b Austin	17
R.J.Harden	b Wasim Akram	32
G.D.Rose	b Austin	1
N.D.Burns +	b Watkinson	8
A.N.Hayhurst	c Fowler b Austin	17
R.P.Lefebvre	not out	14
I.G.Swallow	not out	7
N.A.Mallender		
J.C.Hallett		
Extras	(lb 2,w 4,nb 5)	11
TOTAL	(40 overs)(for 7 wkts)	203

LANCASHIRE

G.D.Mendis	c Burns b Mallender	7
G.Fowler	c Rose b Swallow	60
G.D.Lloyd	c Hayhurst b Rose	57
N.H.Fairbrother *	c Rose b Hallett	47
T.E.Jesty	not out	13
M.Watkinson	not out	11
Wasim Akram		
P.A.J.DeFreitas		
I.D.Austin		
W.K.Hegg +		
P.J.Martin		
Extras	(lb 7,w 3,nb 2)	12
TOTAL	(37.4 overs)(for 4 wkts)	207

LANCASHIRE	O	M	R	W	FALL OF WICKETS		
						SOM	LAN
DeFreitas	8	0	36	0			
Martin	8	0	38	0	1st	73	12
Wasim Akram	8	0	36	2	2nd	110	103
Watkinson	8	0	57	2	3rd	122	171
Austin	8	1	34	3	4th	124	186
					5th	140	
SOMERSET	O	M	R	W	6th	174	
Mallender	8	1	37	1	7th	188	
Rose	8	0	24	1	8th		
Hallett	4.4	0	31	1	9th		
Lefebvre	6	0	44	0	10th		
Hayhurst	4	0	23	0			
Swallow	7	0	41	1			

KENT vs. WORCESTERSHIRE

at Canterbury on 29th July 1990
Toss : Worcestershire. Umpires : A.A.Jones and R.Julian
Worcestershire won by 5 wickets (Kent 0 pts Worcs 4 pts)

KENT

S.G.Hinks	c Botham b Lampitt	51
M.R.Benson	lbw b Newport	24
V.J.Wells	c Radford b Botham	16
T.R.Ward	c Lampitt b Botham	45
C.S.Cowdrey *	c D'Oliveira b Illingworth	4
M.V.Fleming	b Illingworth	8
S.A.Marsh +	b Illingworth	7
R.M.Ellison	not out	9
T.A.Merrick	c Rhodes b Botham	11
R.P.Davis		
A.P.Igglesden		
Extras	(lb 5,w 3,nb 1)	9
TOTAL	(40 overs)(for 8 wkts)	184

WORCESTERSHIRE

I.T.Botham	b Davis	45
M.J.Weston	c Merrick b Fleming	6
G.A.Hick	b Davis	25
D.B.D'Oliveira	c Merrick b Ellison	35
P.A.Neale *	c Marsh b Merrick	39
D.A.Leatherdale	not out	20
S.J.Rhodes +	not out	1
R.K.Illingworth		
P.J.Newport		
S.R.Lampitt		
N.V.Radford		
Extras	(b 2,lb 13,w 1)	16
TOTAL	(38 overs)(for 5 wkts)	187

WORCS	O	M	R	W	FALL OF WICKETS		
						KEN	WOR
Weston	6	0	26	0	1st	34	31
Newport	8	1	18	1	2nd	85	83
Botham	7	0	54	3	3rd	113	84
Radford	3	0	24	0	4th	123	148
Lampitt	8	0	38	1	5th	141	178
Illingworth	8	1	19	3	6th	159	
					7th	165	
KENT	O	M	R	W	8th	184	
Igglesden	7	1	26	0	9th		
Merrick	7	0	38	1	10th		
Fleming	8	0	32	1			
Ellison	8	0	37	1			
Davis	5	0	30	2			
Cowdrey C.S.	3	0	9	0			

ESSEX vs. SUSSEX

at Chelmsford on 29th July 1990
Toss : Sussex. Umpires : D.O.Oslear and K.E.Palmer
Essex won by 2 wickets (Essex 4 pts Sussex 0 pts)

SUSSEX

D.M.Smith	b Topley	0
I.J.Gould	c & b Such	56
P.W.G.Parker *	c Such b Topley	72
A.P.Wells	c Foster b Such	6
C.M.Wells	c Hussain b Childs	28
A.I.C.Dodemaide	not out	26
A.C.S.Pigott	lbw b Pringle	30
P.Moores +	not out	2
R.A.Bunting		
A.R.Hansford		
B.T.P.Donelan		
Extras	(b 2,lb 7,w 3,nb 6)	18
TOTAL	(39 overs)(for 6 wkts)	238

ESSEX

B.R.Hardie	run out	44
N.Shahid	c Parker b Pigott	31
M.E.Waugh	b Pigott	28
P.J.Prichard	run out	64
D.R.Pringle *	c Moores b Donelan	15
N.Hussain	not out	32
N.A.Foster	c Smith b Dodemaide	5
M.A.Garnham +	c Dodemaide b Hansford	6
T.D.Topley	b Hansford	0
J.H.Childs	not out	4
P.M.Such		
Extras	(lb 4,w 6,nb 2)	12
TOTAL	(39 overs)(for 8 wkts)	241

ESSEX	O	M	R	W	FALL OF WICKETS		
						SUS	ESS
Foster	8	0	43	0			
Topley	8	0	43	2	1st	8	76
Childs	8	2	47	1	2nd	103	93
Such	8	0	43	2	3rd	124	130
Pringle	7	0	53	1	4th	172	171
					5th	187	214
SUSSEX	O	M	R	W	6th	233	225
Dodemaide	8	0	51	1	7th		234
Wells C.M.	6	1	27	0	8th		237
Hansford	8	0	62	2	9th		
Donelan	8	0	43	1	10th		
Pigott	8	0	42	2			
Bunting	1	0	12	0			

YORKSHIRE vs. LEICESTERSHIRE

at Sheffield on 29th July 1990
Toss : Leicestershire. Umpires : K.J.Lyons and P.B.Wight
Yorkshire won by 8 wickets (Yorkshire 4 pts Leics 0 pts)

LEICESTERSHIRE

T.J.Boon	c Carrick b Hartley	88
N.E.Briers *	st Blakey b Carrick	37
J.J.Whitaker	c Metcalfe b Carrick	25
P.Willey	b Jarvis	7
L.Potter	c Sharp b Hartley	0
J.D.R.Benson	not out	18
W.K.M.Benjamin	c Blakey b Jarvis	3
P.A.Nixon +	not out	8
G.J.Parsons		
J.P.Agnew		
A.D.Mullally		
Extras	(b 6,lb 12,w 3)	21
TOTAL	(40 overs)(for 6 wkts)	207

YORKSHIRE

M.D.Moxon *	c Whitaker b Potter	73
A.A.Metcalfe	c Willey b Parsons	71
R.J.Blakey +	not out	30
K.Sharp	not out	26
P.E.Robinson		
D.Byas		
P.Carrick		
C.S.Pickles		
P.J.Hartley		
P.W.Jarvis		
S.D.Fletcher		
Extras	(lb 4,w 3,nb 1)	8
TOTAL	(35.5 overs)(for 2 wkts)	208

YORKSHIRE	O	M	R	W	FALL OF WICKETS		
						LEI	YOR
Jarvis	8	0	25	2			
Pickles	3	0	21	0	1st	104	134
Fletcher	7	0	40	0	2nd	165	155
Hartley	8	0	42	2	3rd	177	
Carrick	8	0	29	2	4th	177	
Moxon	6	0	32	0	5th	177	
					6th	183	
LEICS	O	M	R	W	7th		
Benjamin	6	1	35	0	8th		
Agnew	7.5	0	33	0	9th		
Mullally	7	0	24	0	10th		
Parsons	5	0	36	1			
Willey	3	0	25	0			
Potter	7	0	51	1			

GLAMORGAN vs. DERBYSHIRE

at Swansea on 29th July 1990
Toss : Derbyshire. Umpires : B.Dudleston and B.Hassan
Derbyshire won by 6 wickets (Glam 0 pts Derbyshire 4 pts)

GLAMORGAN

M.P.Maynard	b Warner	30
H.Morris	c Bowler b Mortensen	16
I.V.A.Richards	c Bowler b Warner	22
A.R.Butcher *	c Barnett b Base	28
G.C.Holmes	c Base b Kuiper	21
A.Dale	not out	13
C.P.Metson +	st Bowler b Kuiper	9
S.L.Watkin	not out	2
S.J.Dennis		
S.Bastien		
M.Frost		
Extras	(lb 3,w 8,nb 2)	13
TOTAL	(34 overs)(for 6 wkts)	154

DERBYSHIRE

K.J.Barnett *	c Metson b Bastien	14
P.D.Bowler +	not out	52
B.Roberts	lbw b Watkin	23
A.P.Kuiper	b Watkin	12
T.J.G.O'Gorman	c & b Richards	32
C.J.Adams	not out	9
S.C.Goldsmith		
S.J.Base		
A.E.Warner		
M.Jean-Jacques		
O.H.Mortensen		
Extras	(lb 10,w 4)	14
TOTAL	(32.4 overs)(for 4 wkts)	156

DERBYSHIRE	O	M	R	W	FALL OF WICKETS		
						GLA	DER
Base	8	0	40	1			
Mortensen	8	0	17	1	1st	41	19
Jean-Jacques	8	0	35	0	2nd	62	55
Warner	5	0	26	2	3rd	80	80
Goldsmith	1	0	6	0	4th	125	141
Kuiper	4	0	27	2	5th	143	
					6th	152	
GLAMORGAN	O	M	R	W	7th		
Frost	7	2	26	0	8th		
Bastien	4	0	21	1	9th		
Watkin	8	0	29	2	10th		
Dennis	6.4	0	26	0			
Dale	3	0	17	0			
Richards	4	0	27	1			

WARWICKSHIRE vs. HAMPSHIRE

at Edgbaston on 29th July 1990
Toss : Hampshire. Umpires : D.R.Shepherd and R.A.White
Hampshire won by 3 wickets (Warwicks 0 pts Hants 4 pts)

WARWICKSHIRE

A.J.Moles	c Parks b Marshall	14
T.A.Lloyd *	lbw b Bakker	4
T.M.Moody	b Marshall	5
P.A.Smith	c Parks b Ayling	26
D.A.Reeve	b Bakker	1
Asif Din	not out	77
R.G.Twose	b Udal	5
N.M.K.Smith	not out	38
K.J.Piper +		
J.E.Benjamin		
T.A.Munton		
Extras	(lb 6,w 2,nb 1)	9
TOTAL	(40 overs)(for 6 wkts)	179

HAMPSHIRE

V.P.Terry	c Munton b Smith N.M.K.	53
R.J.Scott	st Piper b Smith N.M.K.	47
M.C.J.Nicholas *	b Benjamin	0
M.D.Marshall	run out	24
C.L.Smith	run out	0
J.R.Ayling	c Lloyd b Munton	25
R.J.Maru	st Piper b Smith N.M.K.	1
R.J.Parks +	not out	23
S.D.Udal	not out	2
C.A.Connor		
P.J.Bakker		
Extras	(b 1,lb 5,w 2)	8
TOTAL	(39.4 overs)(for 7 wkts)	183

HAMPSHIRE	O	M	R	W	FALL OF WICKETS		
						WAR	HAM
Marshall	8	0	36	2			
Bakker	7	1	33	2	1st	6	88
Connor	8	0	45	0	2nd	23	89
Ayling	8	0	27	1	3rd	24	127
Udal	8	0	20	1	4th	25	127
Maru	1	0	12	0	5th	74	139
					6th	102	149
WARWICKS	O	M	R	W	7th		165
Twose	7.4	0	47	0	8th		
Munton	8	1	29	1	9th		
Benjamin	8	1	29	1	10th		
Reeve	8	0	36	0			
Smith N.M.K.	8	0	36	3			

REFUGE ASSURANCE LEAGUE

NOTTINGHAMSHIRE vs. NORTHANTS

at Trent Bridge on 29th July 1990
Toss : Northants. Umpires : J.H.Hampshire and M.J.Kitchen
Notts won by 5 runs (Notts 4 pts Northants 0 pts)

NOTTINGHAMSHIRE

B.C.Broad	lbw b Capel	38
M.Newell	lbw b Capel	16
P.Johnson	c Capel b Larkins	29
R.T.Robinson *	not out	74
M.Saxelby	b Larkins	5
F.D.Stephenson	b Williams	2
K.P.Evans	not out	28
G.W.Mike		
B.N.French +		
K.E.Cooper		
J.A.Afford		
Extras	(lb 4,w 6)	10
TOTAL	(40 overs)(for 5 wkts)	202

NORTHANTS

A.Fordham	c Robinson b Mike	59
W.Larkins *	b Afford	58
D.J.Capel	run out	4
R.J.Bailey	b Cooper	4
N.A.Felton	not out	33
R.G.Williams	c Newell b Mike	20
D.J.Wild	b Evans	2
D.Ripley +	run out	0
J.Hughes	not out	1
N.G.B.Cook		
M.A.Robinson		
Extras	(lb 9,w 7)	16
TOTAL	(40 overs)(for 7 wkts)	197

NORTHANTS	O	M	R	W	FALL OF WICKETS		
						NOT	NOR
Robinson	6	0	34	0	1st	50	113
Hughes	4	0	16	0	2nd	70	123
Capel	8	0	34	2	3rd	115	136
Cook	5	0	21	0	4th	125	138
Wild	5	0	24	0	5th	136	190
Larkins	6	0	34	2	6th		195
Williams	6	0	35	1	7th		195
					8th		
NOTTS	O	M	R	W	9th		
Cooper	8	0	62	1	10th		
Stephenson	8	2	19	0			
Evans	8	0	42	1			
Mike	8	0	41	2			
Afford	8	0	24	1			

GLOUCESTERSHIRE vs. SURREY

at Cheltenham on 29th July 1990
Toss : Gloucs. Umpires : J.C.Balderstone and B.Leadbeater
Gloucs won by 5 wickets (Gloucs 4 pts Surrey 0 pts)

SURREY

A.J.Stewart	c Williams b Barnes	3
M.A.Feltham	c Hodgson b Barnes	47
G.P.Thorpe	c Wright b Barnes	11
D.M.Ward	c Wright b Milburn	51
M.A.Lynch	c Williams b Walsh	3
I.A.Greig *	c Walsh b Alleyne	14
K.T.Medlycott	c Williams b Milburn	2
C.K.Bullen	c Barnes b Curran	25
N.F.Sargeant +	c Romaines b Walsh	22
M.P.Bicknell	not out	4
Waqar Younis	not out	0
Extras	(b 1,lb 4, w 3,nb 2)	10
TOTAL	(40 overs)(for 9 wkts)	192

GLOUCESTERSHIRE

G.D.Hodgson	c Ward b Medlycott	28
C.W.J.Athey	c Ward b Waqar Younis	113
A.J.Wright *	c Ward b Bullen	21
K.M.Curran	c & b Medlycott	23
P.W.Romaines	c & b Medlycott	0
J.W.Lloyds	not out	5
M.W.Alleyne	not out	1
C.A.Walsh		
R.C.J.Williams +		
E.T.Milburn		
S.N.Barnes		
Extras	(lb 2,w 3)	5
TOTAL	(39.5 overs)(for 5 wkts)	196

GLOUCS	O	M	R	W	FALL OF WICKETS		
						SUR	GLO
Barnes	8	1	39	3	1st	10	71
Walsh	8	0	29	2	2nd	49	118
Curran	8	0	50	1	3rd	70	185
Alleyne	8	1	35	1	4th	85	185
Milburn	8	0	34	2	5th	113	190
					6th	118	
SURREY	O	M	R	W	7th	157	
Bicknell	8	0	24	0	8th	176	
Feltham	8	0	44	0	9th	191	
Medlycott	8	0	47	3	10th		
Bullen	8	1	41	1			
Waqar Younis	7.5	0	38	1			

Refuge Assurance League Table
at 29th July 1990

		P	W	L	T	NR	Away wins	Pts	Run rate
1	Derbyshire (5)	13	10	3	0	0	6	40	82.93
2	Middlesex (9)	12	9	3	0	0	5	36	94.52
3	Lancashire (1)	13	8	3	0	2	5	36	98.89
4	Notts (4)	13	8	5	0	0	3	32	87.54
5	Hampshire (6)	13	7	4	0	2	3	32	87.24
6	Yorkshire (11)	13	7	5	0	1	4	30	80.93
7	Kent (12)	12	7	5	0	0	3	28	85.27
8	Gloucs (16)	13	6	6	0	1	2	26	85.26
9	Essex (3)	12	6	6	0	0	3	24	92.36
10	Somerset (10)	13	6	7	0	0	3	24	89.70
11	Surrey (7)	12	6	6	0	0	1	24	86.48
12	Worcs (2)	12	5	7	0	0	2	20	82.16
13	Glamorgan (17)	13	4	8	0	1	2	18	85.40
14	Sussex (13)	12	4	7	0	1	1	18	89.31
15	Warwicks (15)	12	4	8	0	0	1	16	78.27
16	Leics (14)	12	3	9	0	0	1	12	74.85
17	Northants (8)	12	2	10	0	0	1	8	83.74

HEADLINES

29th July

• The race for the League title continued to hot up as Derbyshire overhauled Middlesex with their six-wicket win over Glamorgan at Swansea. Ole Mortensen confirmed his reputation as the League's tightest bowler and Peter Bowler guided Derbyshire to their modest target

• Lancashire overcame Somerset's challenge at Old Trafford with another formidable team performance, and Hampshire kept their heads to beat Warwickshire by three wickets at Edgbaston, as both kept the pressure on Derbyshire and Middlesex

• Yorkshire continued their impressive run of results with an eight-wicket victory over Leicestershire at Sheffield, Martyn Moxon and Ashley Metcalfe setting them on their way with an opening stand of 134; but Kent lost further ground with their defeat against Worcestershire at Canterbury

• John Childs was Essex's unlikely hero as he hit the last ball of the match for four to secure a two-wicket win over Sussex at Chelmsford, while Gloucestershire beat Surrey by five wickets at Cheltenham, Bill Athey making the day's only century

• Nottinghamshire were the only side to win batting first, as Northamptonshire proved unable to win, even after Alan Fordham and Wayne Larkins had contributed an opening stand of 113

CORNHILL TEST MATCH

HEADLINES

England vs India: First Cornhill Test Match

26th - 31st July

● Even in a summer where record-breaking has seemed almost common place, the Lord's Test Match between England and India must be considered the highpoint of the season as Graham Gooch indelibly stamped his name on Test cricket's batting roll of honour

● Invited to bat by Indian captain Mohammed Azharuddin and dropped by wicket-keeper Kiran More on just 36, Gooch finished the first day unbeaten on 194, just two short of his best score in Test cricket. On the second day records were broken hour by hour as Gooch and England's scores mounted

● Eventually, taking a single from the first ball bowled after tea, Gooch became the 11th man to make 300 in a Test innings and the fifth Englishman. His final score of 333, just 33 short of a world record, was the sixth highest individual score in Test history and the third best by an English batsman. It was Gooch's highest first-class score, the highest in Tests against India and the highest first-class score ever made at Lord's

● The third wicket partnership of 306 between Gooch and Allan Lamb was a new record for any wicket for England against India, as Lamb made his highest Test score. Robin Smith also joined in the fun, making his third Test 100, as England reached 653 for 4, their highest total against India

● 100s by Ravi Shastri and Mohammed Azharuddin, who blazed his way to a scintillating century in only 87 balls, set India well on the way to the 454 they needed to avoid the follow on, but this figure was only achieved in the most astonishing fashion by Kapil Dev. When last man Narendra Hirwani joined him at the crease 24 were still needed, and Kapil proceeded to get them with four consecutive sixes off Eddie Hemmings, the first time this has ever been done in Test cricket

● India's 'great escape' only allowed Gooch to resume his batting master-class and he did not disappoint: this time he managed 123 to give himself an aggregate of 456 runs in the match, a record aggregate in Test matches and the second best in all first-class cricket. He became the first man ever to score a triple-century and a century in the same match in and first to score two 100s in a Test for England since Denis Compton in 1947-48. His opening stand of 204 with Mike Atherton was yet another record

● After Gooch's declaration, India needed 472 to win in a minimum of 105 overs, but that particular Test record at least was never in danger as England's bowlers brought Gooch his fourth victory in eight Tests as England captain.

● Angus Fraser's match figures of 8 for 143 could not be under-rated in a match which produced a record aggregate for a Lord's Test of 1603 runs, but it was Gooch, inevitably, who completed victory by running out Sanjeev Sharma with a direct hit from mid-on

● Test debut: J.E.Morris (England)

ENGLAND vs. INDIA

at Lord's on 26th, 27th, 28th, 30th, 31st July 1990
Toss : India.   Umpires : H.D.Bird and N.T.Plews
England won by 247 runs

ENGLAND

G.A.Gooch *	b Prabhakar	333	c Azharuddin b Sharma	123
M.A.Atherton	b Kapil Dev	8	c Vengsarkar b Sharma	72
D.I.Gower	c Manjrekar b Hirwani	40	not out	32
A.J.Lamb	c Manjrekar b Sharma	139	c Tendulkar b Hirwani	19
R.A.Smith	not out	100	b Prabhakar	15
J.E.Morris	not out	4		
R.C.Russell +				
C.C.Lewis				
E.E.Hemmings				
A.R.C.Fraser				
D.E.Malcolm				
Extras	(b 2,lb 21,w 2,nb 4)	29	(lb 11)	11
TOTAL	(for 4 wkts dec)	653	(for 4 wkts dec)	272

INDIA

R.J.Shastri	c Gooch b Hemmings	100	c Russell b Malcolm	12
N.S.Sidhu	c Morris b Fraser	30	c Morris b Fraser	1
S.V.Manjrekar	c Russell b Gooch	18	c Russell b Malcolm	33
D.B.Vengsarkar	c Russell b Fraser	52	c Russell b Hemmings	35
M.Azharuddin *	b Hemmings	121	c Atherton b Lewis	37
S.R.Tendulkar	b Lewis	10	c Gooch b Fraser	27
M.Prabhakar	c Lewis b Malcolm	25	lbw b Lewis	8
Kapil Dev	not out	77	c Lewis b Hemmings	7
K.S.More +	c Morris b Fraser	8	lbw b Fraser	16
S.K.Sharma	c Russell b Fraser	0	run out	38
N.D.Hirwani	lbw b Fraser	0	not out	0
Extras	(lb 1,w 4,nb 8)	13	(b 3,lb 1,nb 6)	10
TOTAL		454		224

INDIA	O	M	R	W	O	M	R	W
Kapil Dev	34	5	120	1	10	0	53	0
Prabhakar	43	6	187	1	11.2	2	45	1
Sharma	33	5	122	1	15	0	75	2
Shastri	22	0	99	0	7	0	38	0
Hirwani	30	1	102	1	11	0	50	1

ENGLAND	O	M	R	W	O	M	R	W
Malcolm	25	1	106	1	10	0	65	2
Fraser	39.1	9	104	5	22	7	39	3
Lewis	24	3	108	1	8	1	26	2
Gooch	6	3	26	1				
Hemmings	20	3	109	2	21	2	79	2
Atherton					1	0	11	0

FALL OF WICKETS

	ENG	IND	ENG	IND
1st	14	63	204	9
2nd	141	102	207	23
3rd	449	191	250	63
4th	641	241	272	114
5th		288		127
6th		348		140
7th		393		158
8th		430		181
9th		430		206
10th		454		224

Man of the match: G.A.Gooch (England)

TRIPLE CENTURIES IN TEST CRICKET

365*	G.St A.Sobers	West Indies v Pakistan	Kingston	1957-58
364	L.Hutton	England v Australia	The Oval	1938
337	Hanif Mohammad	Pakistan v West Indies	Bridgetown	1957-58
336*	W.R.Hammond	England v New Zealand	Auckland	1932-33
334	D.G.Bradman	Australia v England	Headingley	1930
333	G.A.Gooch	England v India	Lord's	1990
325	A.Sandham	England v West Indies	Kingston	1929-30
311	R.B.Simpson	Australia v England	Old Trafford	1964
310*	J.H.Edrich	England v New Zealand	Headingley	1965
307	R.M.Cowper	Australia v England	Melbourne	1965-66
304	D.G.Bradman	Australia v England	Headingley	1964
302	L.G.Rowe	West Indies v England	Bridgetown	1973-74

MOST RUNS IN A MATCH IN FIRST-CLASS CRICKET

499	Hanif Mohammad	Karachi v Bahawalpur	Karachi	1958-59
456	G.A.Gooch	England v India	Lord's	1990
455	D.G.Bradman	NSW v Queensland	Sydney	1929-30
446	A.E.Fagg	Kent v Essex	Colchester	1938
443	B.B.Nimbalkar	Maharashtra v Kathiawar	Poona	1948-49
437	W.H.Ponsford	Victoria v Queensland	Melbourne	1927-28

BRITANNIC ASSURANCE CHAMPIONSHIP

WARWICKSHIRE vs. HAMPSHIRE
at Edgbaston on 28th, 30th, 31st July 1990
Toss : Hampshire. Umpires : D.R.Shepherd and R.A.White
Warwickshire won by 6 wickets (Warwicks 21 pts (Bt: 3, Bw: 2) Hants 3 pts (Bt: 2, Bw: 1))

HAMPSHIRE
T.C.Middleton	c Asif Din b Reeve	10	c Reeve b Asif Din	64
C.L.Smith	c Ratcliffe b Reeve	18	b Smith	29
R.J.Scott	lbw b Reeve	4	c Reeve b Pierson	0
M.C.J.Nicholas *	b Munton	16	not out	78
M.D.Marshall	c Reeve b Pierson	26	c Moody b Pierson	10
V.P.Terry	not out	119	not out	19
R.J.Maru	run out	53		
R.J.Parks +	c Asif Din b Pierson	33		
S.D.Udal	b Pierson	9		
C.A.Connor				
P.J.Bakker				
Extras	(b 4,lb 7,nb 8)	19	(b 11,lb 1,nb 4)	16
TOTAL	(for 8 wkts dec)	307	(for 4 wkts dec)	216

WARWICKSHIRE
A.J.Moles	b Connor	24	b Udal	36
J.D.Ratcliffe	not out	81	st Parks b Maru	46
T.A.Lloyd *	c Terry b Connor	1	b Udal	61
T.M.Moody	c Middleton b Maru	48	not out	101
P.A.Smith	not out	85	c Smith b Maru	5
D.A.Reeve			not out	12
Asif Din				
K.J.Piper +				
A.R.K.Pierson				
J.E.Benjamin				
T.A.Munton				
Extras	(b 4,lb 8,nb 2)	14	(lb 8,nb 5)	13
TOTAL	(for 3 wkts dec)	253	(for 4 wkts)	274

WARWICKS	O	M	R	W	O	M	R	W
Benjamin	12	3	37	0	3	0	7	0
Munton	27	9	50	1	8	1	24	0
Reeve	29	11	58	3				
Smith	7	3	11	0	6	1	16	1
Pierson	30.4	2	73	3	25	5	66	2
Asif Din	14	0	67	0	11	2	62	1
Moody					3	0	23	0
Moles					1	0	6	0

HAMPSHIRE	O	M	R	W	O	M	R	W
Bakker	14	6	44	0	4	1	17	0
Marshall	8	3	17	0	8	1	27	0
Maru	22	2	67	1	24	1	90	2
Connor	10	2	23	2	9	0	39	0
Udal	13	0	66	0	17.3	0	93	2
Nicholas	2.4	0	24	0				

FALL OF WICKETS				
	HAM	WAR	HAM	WAR
1st	28	32	82	79
2nd	34	38	92	103
3rd	37	110	123	234
4th	80		150	251
5th	90			
6th	208			
7th	291			
8th	307			
9th				
10th				

NOTTINGHAMSHIRE vs. MIDDLESEX
at Trent Bridge on 28th, 30th, 31st July 1990
Toss : Nottinghamshire. Umpires : J.H.Hampshire and M.J.Kitchen
Match drawn (Nottinghamshire 7 pts (Bt: 3, Bw: 4) Middlesex 4 pts (Bt:2, Bw: 2))

NOTTINGHAMSHIRE
B.C.Broad	lbw b Cowans	140	b Tufnell	25
P.Pollard	c Brown b Emburey	24	c Haynes b Tufnell	72
R.T.Robinson *	lbw b Cowans	5	(4) c Downton b Williams	2
P.Johnson	c Emburey b Cowans	30	(3) c & b Tufnell	5
D.W.Randall	b Emburey	70	b Cowans	56
F.D.Stephenson	c Downton b Tufnell	8	not out	44
K.P.Evans	not out	28	not out	24
B.N.French +	c Cowans b Emburey	4		
G.W.Mike	c Downton b Tufnell	9		
K.E.Cooper	not out	3		
J.A.Afford				
Extras	(b 2,lb 10,nb 3)	15	(lb 7, w 4,nb 1)	12
TOTAL	(for 8 wkts dec)	336	(for 5 wkts dec)	240

MIDDLESEX
D.L.Haynes	c Pollard b Cooper	21	c French b Cooper	0
M.A.Roseberry	c Mike b Evans	74	c Cooper b Stephenson	0
M.W.Gatting *	c French b Cooper	6	not out	169
M.R.Ramprakash	lbw b Stephenson	46	c Randall b Afford	52
K.R.Brown	c Johnson b Stephenson	4	b Stephenson	55
P.R.Downton +	b Cooper	16	(7) b Evans	20
J.E.Emburey	c Johnson b Cooper	0	(8) b Stephenson	10
N.F.Williams	lbw b Evans	14	(9) lbw b Stephenson	3
P.C.R.Tufnell	c Pollard b Evans	12	(10) not out	5
C.W.Taylor	b Cooper	13		
N.G.Cowans	not out	11	(6) lbw b Stephenson	0
Extras	(lb 5,nb 1)	6	(lb 13,nb 2)	15
TOTAL		223	(for 8 wkts)	329

MIDDLESEX	O	M	R	W	O	M	R	W
Williams	18	6	34	0	15	4	46	1
Cowans	22	3	80	3	17	1	70	1
Taylor	13	1	45	0	6	0	15	0
Emburey	18	0	61	3	8	2	16	0
Tufnell	39	5	104	2	26	6	86	3

NOTTS	O	M	R	W	O	M	R	W
Stephenson	16	6	33	2	20.5	1	82	5
Cooper	25	6	108	5	14	2	41	1
Evans	18	4	54	3	12	2	72	1
Mike	6	3	12	0	9	0	46	0
Afford	5	1	11	0	14	1	75	1

FALL OF WICKETS				
	NOT	MID	NOT	MID
1st	58	27	57	0
2nd	63	39	63	7
3rd	116	129	66	99
4th	254	133	156	244
5th	271	164	171	244
6th	291	173		293
7th	309	178		310
8th	331	198		318
9th		201		
10th		223		

GLOUCESTERSHIRE vs. SURREY
at Cheltenham on 28th, 30th, 31st July 1990
Toss : Surrey. Umpires : J.C.Balderstone and B.Leadbeater
Match drawn (Gloucestershire 5 pts (Bt: 3, Bw: 2) Surrey 5 pts (Bt: 2, Bw: 3))

GLOUCESTERSHIRE
G.D.Hodgson	c Medlycott b Bicknell M.P.	54	c Bicknell M.P. b Medlycott	44
A.J.Wright *	c Greig b Bicknell M.P.	2	c Waqar Younis b Bicknell M.	12
P.Bainbridge	not out	37		
C.W.J.Athey	c Thorpe b Bicknell M.P.	0	(3) not out	86
M.W.Alleyne	c & b Feltham	118	(4) c Lynch b Greig	15
K.M.Curran	lbw b Medlycott	46	(5) c Feltham b Greig	25
J.W.Lloyds	b Medlycott	23	(6) not out	8
R.C.J.Williams +	c Sargeant b Waqar Younis	0		
D.V.Lawrence	c Sargeant b Waqar Younis	2		
S.N.Barnes	c Thorpe b Bicknell M.P.	2		
P.A.Owen	c & b Feltham	1		
Extras	(b 1,lb 7,nb 8)	16	(b 2,lb 6,w 4)	12
TOTAL		301	(for 4 wkts dec)	202

SURREY
D.J.Bicknell	not out	83	c sub b Lloyds	81
G.S.Clinton	c Williams b Lloyds	38	c Williams b Owen	13
G.P.Thorpe	b Lloyds	0	(4) c Williams b Lawrence	0
D.M.Ward	c Hodgson b Barnes	5	(3) c Williams b Lawrence	45
M.A.Lynch	c Lloyds b Owen	33	b Curran	77
I.A.Greig *	st Williams b Owen	1	c Curran b Lawrence	34
M.A.Feltham	c Hodgson b Lloyds	14	b Lawrence	1
K.T.Medlycott	not out	14	not out	18
N.F.Sargeant +			c Wright b Curran	1
M.P.Bicknell			c Williams b Lawrence	7
Waqar Younis			not out	1
Extras	(b 3,lb 7,w 1,nb 1)	12	(b 6,lb 16,nb 2)	24
TOTAL	(for 6 wkts dec)	200	(for 9 wkts)	302

SURREY	O	M	R	W	O	M	R	W
Waqar Younis	23	4	69	2	13	4	36	0
Bicknell M.P.	24	4	63	4	3	0	17	1
Medlycott	35	10	82	2	25.3	7	97	1
Feltham	19.4	2	73	2	6	1	17	0
Greig	2	0	6	0	10	2	27	2

GLOUCS	O	M	R	W	O	M	R	W
Lawrence	7	1	28	0	15	3	54	5
Curran	10	2	26	0	14	1	59	2
Alleyne	5	1	15	0				
Barnes	12	4	19	1	8	1	29	0
Lloyds	19.3	5	65	3	15	0	80	1
Owen	9	2	37	2	7	0	58	1

FALL OF WICKETS				
	GLO	SUR	GLO	SUR
1st	14	83	28	45
2nd	27	83	96	124
3rd	86	90	129	124
4th	169	138	183	194
5th	217	140		259
6th	218	161		262
7th	222			273
8th	283			278
9th	291			301
10th	301			

LANCASHIRE vs. SOMERSET
at Old Trafford on 28th, 30th, 31st July 1990
Toss : Lancashire. Umpires : J.W.Holder and A.G.T.Whitehead
Match drawn (Lancashire 8 pts (Bt: 4, Bw: 4) Somerset 5 pts (Bt:2, Bw: 3))

SOMERSET
S.J.Cook	lbw b Martin	49	c Fairbrother b Watkinson	64
P.M.Roebuck	lbw b Watkinson	26	c Hegg b Patterson	12
A.N.Hayhurst	c Hegg b Watkinson	6	c Hegg b Watkinson	30
C.J.Tavare *	c Fairbrother b Patterson	17	not out	84
R.J.Harden	b Martin	60	(6) c Jesty b Watkinson	2
N.D.Burns +	c Hegg b Patterson	7	(7) c Fowler b Watkinson	10
G.D.Rose	c Mendis b Austin	27	(8) c Lloyd b Martin	76
R.P.Lefebvre	lbw b Austin	4	(9) lbw b Austin	2
I.G.Swallow	c Lloyd b Watkinson	16	(5) b Watkinson	0
N.A.Mallender	not out	3	c Lloyd b Austin	7
H.R.J.Trump	b Patterson	1	not out	4
Extras	(b 8,lb 8,w 1,nb 8)	25	(b 13,lb 12,w 3,nb 5)	33
TOTAL		237	(for 9 wkts dec)	324

LANCASHIRE
G.Fowler	c Burns b Swallow	10	
G.D.Mendis	c & b Swallow	29	
G.D.Lloyd	b Swallow	0	
N.H.Fairbrother *	c Burns b Rose	91	
T.E.Jesty	b Mallender	30	
M.Watkinson	c Cook b Trump	96	
W.K.Hegg +	c Rose b Trump	33	
I.D.Austin	c Swallow b Trump	9	
J.D.Fitton	not out	25	
P.J.Martin	c Trump b Rose	9	
B.P.Patterson	b Mallender	1	
Extras	(b 5,lb 3,w 1,nb 5)	14	
TOTAL		339	

LANCASHIRE	O	M	R	W	O	M	R	W
Patterson	13.5	2	76	3	23	7	68	1
Martin	17	5	55	2	18	4	50	1
Watkinson	18	12	29	3	35	7	97	5
Fitton	4	0	17	0	26	7	65	0
Austin	16	8	44	2	23	14	19	2
Fowler					2	2	0	0

SOMERSET	O	M	R	W	O	M	R	W
Mallender	18	5	63	2				
Rose	18	0	77	2				
Lefebvre	14	5	22	0				
Swallow	28	11	88	3				
Trump	26	10	58	3				
Roebuck	6	0	17	0				
Hayhurst	1	0	6	0				

FALL OF WICKETS				
	SOM	LAN	SOM	LAN
1st	74	42	53	
2nd	86	42	108	
3rd	96	68	133	
4th	138	141	133	
5th	163	212	137	
6th	206	301	166	
7th	206	302	297	
8th	212	307	300	
9th	230	334	312	
10th	237	339		

BRITANNIC ASSURANCE CHAMPIONSHIP

YORKSHIRE vs. LEICESTERSHIRE
at Sheffield on 28th, 30th, 31st July 1990
Toss : Leicestershire. Umpires : K.J.Lyons and P.B.Wight
Leicestershire won by 8 wickets (Yorkshire 5 pts (Bt: 2, Bw: 3) Leics 24 pts (Bt: 4, Bw: 4))

LEICESTERSHIRE
T.J.Boon	lbw b Hartley	76	c Moxon b Pickles	11
N.E.Briers *	c Batty b Hartley	45	b Hartley	21
J.J.Whitaker	c Byas b Hartley	23	not out	38
P.Willey	c Blakey b Hartley	47	not out	18
L.Potter	not out	109		
J.D.R.Benson	lbw b Hartley	0		
W.K.M.Benjamin	c Kellett b Batty	16		
P.A.Nixon +	b Batty	33		
J.P.Agnew	not out	4		
G.J.Parsons				
A.D.Mullally				
Extras	(b 1,lb 10,w 2,nb 10)	23	(nb 2)	2
TOTAL	(for 7 wkts dec)	376	(for 2 wkts)	90

YORKSHIRE
M.D.Moxon *	c Nixon b Benjamin	21	b Mullally	17
A.A.Metcalfe	c Benson b Agnew	1	c Benson b Agnew	1
S.A.Kellett	c Nixon b Mullally	47	(4) c Nixon b Mullally	54
R.J.Blakey +	c Nixon b Agnew	36	(3) c Nixon b Mullally	12
P.E.Robinson	c Potter b Mullally	7	c Nixon b Mullally	4
D.Byas	run out	5	b Willey	81
P.Grayson	not out	36	c Nixon b Parsons	11
C.S.Pickles	lbw b Agnew	14	not out	56
P.J.Hartley	c Nixon b Agnew	0	c Willey b Agnew	7
D.Gough	lbw b Agnew	24	c Briers b Agnew	2
J.D.Batty	b Benjamin	2	run out	0
Extras	(b 1,lb 2,w 1,nb 3)	7	(b 7,lb 7,nb 3)	17
TOTAL		200		262

YORKSHIRE	O	M	R	W	O	M	R	W		FALL OF WICKETS				
											LEI	YOR	YOR	LEI
Hartley	26	2	106	5	7	1	20	1	1st	121	6	1	27
Gough	15	3	53	0	7	1	34	0	2nd	152	34	33	35
Pickles	20	7	65	0	4	0	9	1	3rd	161	107	38	
Batty	32	4	124	2					4th	271	107	50	
Moxon	5	0	12	0	2	0	7	0	5th	271	118	133	
Grayson	1	0	5	0					6th	294	130	156	
Byas					4	0	20	0	7th	372	158	218	
									8th		158	247	
LEICS	O	M	R	W	O	M	R	W	9th		193	249	
Benjamin	19.5	3	78	2	15	5	40	0	10th		200	262	
Agnew	21	4	54	5	22	4	54	3					
Parsons	7	2	20	0	23	7	61	1					
Mullally	15	2	45	2	25	9	59	4					
Willey					16	4	29	1					
Potter					4	2	5	0					

KENT vs. WORCESTERSHIRE
at Canterbury on 28th, 30th, 31st July 1990
Toss : Worcestershire. Umpires : A.A.Jones and R.Julian
Match drawn (Kent 5 pts (Bt: 3, Bw: 2) Worcestershire 7 pts (Bt: 4, Bw: 3))

WORCESTERSHIRE
G.J.Lord	c Benson b Wren	14	c & b Ward	81
C.M.Tolley	c Taylor b Ellison	4	lbw b Ellison	0
G.A.Hick	c Marsh b Ellison	66	c & b Wren	22
D.B.D'Oliveira	c Marsh b Igglesden	21	c Davis b Ward	4
I.T.Botham	c Marsh b Igglesden	4	b Davis	46
P.A.Neale *	not out	119	not out	14
S.J.Rhodes +	c Igglesden b Wren	94	not out	0
R.K.Illingworth	lbw b Igglesden	15		
P.J.Newport	not out	5		
S.R.Lampitt				
N.V.Radford				
Extras	(lb 5,w 3,nb 1)	9	(lb 3)	3
TOTAL	(for 7 wkts dec)	351	(for 5 wkts dec)	170

KENT
S.G.Hinks	b Newport	32	hit wicket b Botham	25
M.R.Benson *	c Rhodes b Newport	10	c Rhodes b Newport	8
S.A.Marsh +	c Hick b Newport	0	(7) lbw b Newport	8
T.R.Ward	c D'Oliveira b Newport	1	(5) c D'Oliveira b Tolley	18
M.V.Fleming	b Radford	59	(6) b Illingworth	42
R.M.Ellison	c Hick b Newport	0	(8) c Radford b Illingworth	1
G.R.Cowdrey	lbw b Newport	57	(4) lbw b Radford	9
N.R.Taylor	not out	64	(3) s Rhodes b Illingworth	73
R.P.Davis	c Rhodes b Botham	8	not out	2
A.P.Igglesden	not out	13	not out	0
T.Wren				
Extras	(lb 4,w 1,nb 1)	6	(b 4,lb 3,nb 1)	8
TOTAL	(for 8 wkts dec)	250	(for 8 wkts)	194

KENT	O	M	R	W	O	M	R	W		FALL OF WICKETS				
											WOR	KEN	WOR	KEN
Igglesden	21	1	97	3	6	1	23	0	1st	12	15	16	23
Ellison	21	4	65	2	5	1	33	1	2nd	40	17	82	33
Wren	24	4	78	2	2	0	17	1	3rd	71	19	88	64
Fleming	18	3	46	0					4th	75	46	133	107
Davis	22	8	54	0	11	1	46	1	5th	132	46	162	161
Ward	3	1	6	0	9.3	0	48	2	6th	317	132		184
									7th	341	197		189
WORCS	O	M	R	W	O	M	R	W	8th		218		192
Newport	27.1	11	73	6	14.5	2	27	2	9th				
Botham	13	2	44	1	6	2	29	1	10th				
Lampitt	21	7	42	0	11	1	45	0					
Illingworth	7	3	19	0	10	3	20	3					
Radford	10	2	33	1	9	2	41	1					
Tolley	8	1	29	0	10	3	25	1					
Hick	2	0	6	0									

ESSEX vs. SUSSEX
at Chelmsford on 28th, 30th, 31st July 1990
Toss : Essex. Umpires : D.O.Oslear and K.E.Palmer
Match drawn (Essex 7 pts (Bt: 3, Bw: 4) Sussex 6 pts (Bt: 4, Bw: 2))

SUSSEX
D.M.Smith	c Pringle b Andrew	3	b Andrew	15
J.W.Hall	c Pringle b Childs	62	c Garnham b Topley	50
P.W.G.Parker *	lbw b Foster	20	(9) c Andrew b Childs	14
A.P.Wells	c Garnham b Topley	19	lbw b Pringle	14
I.J.Gould	c Waugh b Topley	73	c & b Childs	0
C.M.Wells	c Stephenson b Topley	0	lbw b Topley	21
A.I.C.Dodemaide	not out	79	not out	35
P.Moores	c Stephenson b Childs	27	(3) c Topley b Childs	28
A.C.S.Pigott	c Garnham b Andrew	0	(8) c Prichard b Childs	1
B.T.P.Donelan	b Childs	31	not out	12
R.A.Bunting	not out	11		
Extras	(b 4,lb 9,nb 13)	26	(nb 10)	10
TOTAL	(for 9 wkts dec)	351	(for 8 wkts dec)	200

ESSEX
N.Shahid	c Moores b Bunting	55	b Donelan	89
J.P.Stephenson	c Wells A.P. b Pigott	14	c Gould b Pigott	45
P.J.Prichard	lbw b Bunting	11	(4) b Donelan	22
M.E.Waugh	not out	103	(3) b Pigott	11
N.Hussain	lbw b Dodemaide	21	c Moores b Pigott	21
M.A.Garnham +	run out	8	(7) c Dodemaide b Bunting	20
D.R.Pringle *	lbw b Wells C.M.	21	(6) c Smith b Donelan	39
N.A.Foster	not out	2	c Pigott b Bunting	30
T.D.Topley			not out	7
J.H.Childs			run out	0
S.J.W.Andrew			not out	0
Extras	(b 10,lb 2,w 1,nb 2)	15	(b 9,lb 5)	14
TOTAL	(for 6 wkts dec)	250	(for 9 wkts)	298

ESSEX	O	M	R	W	O	M	R	W		FALL OF WICKETS				
											SUS	ESS	SUS	ESS
Foster	26	2	102	1	11	3	23	0	1st	3	37	26	137
Andrew	25	4	108	2	13	0	60	1	2nd	47	65	69	137
Topley	14	2	36	3	10	1	34	2	3rd	78	100	101	168
Pringle	10	2	29	0	4	2	12	1	4th	190	171	102	176
Waugh	2	0	12	0	1	1	0	0	5th	190	196	131	226
Childs	25	11	51	3	30	13	56	4	6th	207	244	143	236
Shahid					3.5	0	15	0	7th	247		145	282
									8th	254		171	292
SUSSEX	O	M	R	W	O	M	R	W	9th	337			294
Pigott	16	2	67	1	14	1	79	3	10th				
Dodemaide	13	2	41	1	8	1	46	0					
Bunting	12	1	53	2	8	2	36	2					
Donelan	4	0	33	0	11	0	86	3					
Wells C.M.	14.3	2	44	1	4	0	37	0					

HEADLINES

28th - 31st July

● Middlesex again just failed to press home their advantage at the top of the table, finishing 25 short of victory at Trent Bridge, despite an unbeaten 169 from Mike Gatting. Chris Broad had earlier made his seventh 100 of the season

● Warwickshire moved to third place after victory over fellow title contenders Hampshire. Tom Moody timed the run-chase to perfection, reaching his fifth 100 in six matches

● First-class debuts: T.Wren (Kent); C.W.Taylor (Middlesex)

Britannic Assurance Championship Table
at 31st July 1990

		P	W	L	D	T	Bt	Bl	Pts
1	Middlesex (3)	14	7	0	7	0	44	30	186
2	Lancashire (4)	15	5	2	8	0	45	42	167
3	Warwickshire (8)	15	5	4	6	0	35	42	157
4	Hampshire (6)	14	5	2	7	0	45	26	151
5	Derbyshire (7)	15	4	5	6	0	42	31	137
	Leicestershire (13)	14	4	2	8	0	42	31	137
7	Nottinghamshire (11)	14	4	3	7	0	29	39	132
	Essex (2)	13	4	1	8	0	42	26	132
9	Glamorgan (17)	15	4	3	8	0	41	26	131
10	Surrey (12)	14	2	2	10	0	36	41	117
11	Northants (5)	14	2	5	7	0	38	40	110
12	Yorkshire (16)	15	2	7	6	0	36	35	103
13	Worcestershire (1)	13	2	1	10	0	37	30	99
14	Somerset (14)	16	1	3	12	0	51	29	96
15	Kent (15)	14	2	4	8	0	42	21	95
	Sussex (10)	14	2	4	8	0	37	26	95
17	Gloucestershire (9)	15	1	6	8	0	31	37	84

NATWEST TROPHY QUARTER-FINALS

LANCASHIRE vs. GLOUCESTERSHIRE
at Old Trafford on 1st August 1990
Toss : Gloucs. Umpires : B.Leadbeater and K.J.Lyons
Lancashire won by 241 runs

LANCASHIRE

G.Fowler	c Russell b Lawrence	52
G.D.Mendis	run out	88
M.A.Atherton	c & b Barnes	25
N.H.Fairbrother	b Walsh	86
M.Watkinson	c Wright b Walsh	90
Wasim Akram	not out	5
P.A.J.DeFreitas		
I.D.Austin		
W.K.Hegg +		
D.P.Hughes *		
P.J.Martin		
Extras	(lb 5,w 20,nb 1)	26
TOTAL	(60 overs)(for 5 wkts)	372

GLOUCESTERSHIRE

A.J.Wright *	c Atherton b DeFreitas	4
G.D.Hodgson	c & b Atherton	52
P.W.Romaines	b Austin	20
C.W.J.Athey	c & b Wasim Akram	8
R.C.Russell +	c & b Atherton	12
K.M.Curran	c Hegg b Watkinson	1
J.W.Lloyds	c Hegg b Watkinson	2
M.W.Alleyne	not out	9
C.A.Walsh	c Hegg b Watkinson	7
D.V.Lawrence	b Wasim Akram	0
S.N.Barnes	b Wasim Akram	0
Extras	(b 4,w 12)	16
TOTAL	(30 overs)	131

GLOUCS	O	M	R	W	FALL OF WICKETS		
						LAN	GLO
Walsh	12	0	69	2	1st	124	21
Curran	12	2	63	0	2nd	176	59
Barnes	12	1	64	1	3rd	180	90
Lawrence	9	0	62	1	4th	349	106
Alleyne	7	0	51	0	5th	372	107
Lloyds	5	0	44	0	6th		113
Athey	3	0	14	0	7th		115
					8th		123
LANCASHIRE	O	M	R	W	9th		131
Martin	3	0	25	0	10th		131
DeFreitas	5	1	22	1			
Austin	7	0	22	1			
Wasim Akram	6	0	29	3			
Watkinson	5	0	14	3			
Atherton	4	0	15	2			

Man of the match: M.Watkinson

HAMPSHIRE vs. YORKSHIRE
at Southampton on 1st August 1990
Toss : Yorkshire. Umpires : R.Julian and R.Palmer
Hampshire won by 111 runs

HAMPSHIRE

V.P.Terry	c Byas b Hartley	16
C.L.Smith	c Blakey b Hartley	30
D.I.Gower	c Moxon b Hartley	26
R.A.Smith	c Byas b Sidebottom	27
M.D.Marshall	c Sidebottom b Hartley	4
M.C.J.Nicholas *	b Hartley	50
J.R.Ayling	s Blakey b Carrick	7
R.J.Parks +	not out	27
R.J.Maru	c Blakey b Fletcher	22
C.A.Connor	c Blakey b Fletcher	13
P.J.Bakker	not out	3
Extras	(lb 3,w 1)	4
TOTAL	(60 overs)(for 9 wkts)	229

YORKSHIRE

M.D.Moxon *	run out	1
A.A.Metcalfe	c Maru b Marshall	2
R.J.Blakey +	b Ayling	21
S.A.Kellett	b Marshall	0
P.E.Robinson	c Terry b Connor	7
D.Byas	b Maru	4
P.Carrick	c Smith R.A. b Ayling	14
P.J.Hartley	c Smith C.L. b Ayling	52
P.W.Jarvis	c Connor b Marshall	6
A.Sidebottom	c Parks b Marshall	1
S.D.Fletcher	not out	6
Extras	(lb 1,w 2,nb 1)	4
TOTAL	(39 overs)	118

YORKSHIRE	O	M	R	W	FALL OF WICKETS		
						HAM	YOR
Jarvis	12	1	58	0	1st	28	1
Sidebottom	12	3	35	1	2nd	63	9
Hartley	12	2	46	5	3rd	76	9
Fletcher	12	0	53	2	4th	80	34
Carrick	12	0	34	1	5th	121	34
					6th	154	40
HAMPSHIRE	O	M	R	W	7th	168	74
Marshall	8	1	17	4	8th	199	105
Bakker	7	1	12	0	9th	223	107
Connor	6	2	10	1	10th		118
Ayling	9	2	30	3			
Maru	9	0	48	1			

Man of the match: P.J.Hartley

HEADLINES

NatWest Trophy
Quarter-Finals

1st August

● Lancashire remained on course to become the first county to win both knockout competitions in the same year by crushing Gloucestershire at Old Trafford by 241 runs. They made a record score in a one-day match between two first-class counties, Mike Watkinson hitting a career best 90 as he shared a fourth wicket stand of 169 with Neil Fairbrother

● Ian Botham narrowly failed to take Worcestershire to victory over Northamptonshire at Northampton. 10 runs were needed off the last over but Mark Robinson conceded only one run from the first five balls to take Northants into the semi-finals

● At Lord's Glamorgan's batsmen never broke free from the stranglehold imposed by Middlesex's spinners John Emburey and Philip Tufnell who took 5 for 49 in their 24 overs, and Alan Butcher's first 100 in the competition was not enough to prevent a nine-wicket victory for Middlesex

● Malcolm Marshall ensured that Hampshire reached the semi-finals for the second year in succession with figures of 4 for 17 as Yorkshire collapsed to 118 all out at Southampton, even though Peter Hartley followed his best figures with a maiden fifty

MIDDLESEX vs. GLAMORGAN
at Lord's on 1st August 1990
Toss : Glamorgan. Umpires : A.A.Jones and D.O.Oslear
Middlesex won by 9 wickets

GLAMORGAN

A.R.Butcher *	not out	104
H.Morris	b Tufnell	26
M.P.Maynard	c Cowans b Emburey	1
I.V.A.Richards	c Gatting b Emburey	9
A.Dale	c Emburey b Tufnell	3
R.D.B.Croft	run out	26
N.G.Cowley	b Cowans	5
C.P.Metson +	c Gatting b Emburey	9
S.L.Watkin	not out	6
S.J.Dennis		
M.Frost		
Extras	(b 10,lb 7,w 1,nb 6)	24
TOTAL	(60 overs)(for 7 wkts)	213

MIDDLESEX

D.L.Haynes	not out	75
M.A.Roseberry	lbw b Dale	48
M.W.Gatting *	not out	70
M.R.Ramprakash		
K.R.Brown		
P.R.Downton +		
J.E.Emburey		
N.F.Williams		
A.R.C.Fraser		
P.C.R.Tufnell		
N.G.Cowans		
Extras	(lb 15,w 8)	23
TOTAL	(50.1 overs)(for 1 wkt)	216

MIDDLESEX	O	M	R	W	FALL OF WICKETS		
						GLA	MID
Cowans	12	2	48	1	1st	40	84
Fraser	12	2	47	0	2nd	50	
Williams	8	0	38	0	3rd	76	
Emburey	12	5	27	3	4th	86	
Tufnell	12	2	22	2	5th	150	
Ramprakash	4	1	14	0	6th	162	
GLAMORGAN	O	M	R	W	7th	187	
Frost	9	1	39	0	8th		
Watkin	11.1	0	28	0	9th		
Dennis	5	0	27	0	10th		
Cowley	8	1	33	0			
Croft	10	0	44	0			
Dale	3	0	14	1			
Richards	4	0	16	0			

Man of the match: A.R.Butcher

NORTHANTS vs. WORCESTERSHIRE
at Northampton on 1st August 1990
Toss : Worcs. Umpires : J.C.Balderstone and M.J.Kitchen
Northants won by 4 runs

NORTHANTS

A.Fordham	lbw b Lampitt	96
N.A.Felton	c Curtis b Newport	12
W.Larkins	b Illingworth	52
A.J.Lamb *	c Rhodes b Illingworth	0
D.J.Capel	c Rhodes b Newport	53
R.J.Bailey	c Weston b Botham	29
R.G.Williams	b Newport	6
D.Ripley +	run out	2
C.E.L.Ambrose	lbw b Newport	0
N.G.B.Cook	run out	1
M.A.Robinson	not out	0
Extras	(lb 11,w 1)	12
TOTAL	(59.1 overs)	263

WORCESTERSHIRE

T.S.Curtis	b Cook	30
M.J.Weston	c Fordham b Robinson	14
G.A.Hick	c Cook b Williams	49
D.B.D'Oliveira	b Cook	2
I.T.Botham	not out	86
P.A.Neale *	c Larkins b Williams	43
S.J.Rhodes +	c & b Williams	2
R.K.Illingworth	b Ambrose	7
N.V.Radford	b Robinson	0
P.J.Newport	b Robinson	0
S.R.Lampitt	not out	3
Extras	(b 2,lb 14,w 7)	23
TOTAL	(60 overs)(for 9 wkts)	259

WORCS	O	M	R	W	FALL OF WICKETS		
						NOR	WOR
Newport	12	0	46	4	1st	46	28
Radford	4	0	23	0	2nd	138	56
Botham	7.1	0	42	1	3rd	140	72
Lampitt	12	0	58	1	4th	205	107
Illingworth	12	1	44	2	5th	231	192
Hick	12	0	39	0	6th	251	195
NORTHANTS	O	M	R	W	7th	259	243
Ambrose	12	3	39	1	8th	261	244
Robinson	12	1	33	3	9th	263	246
Capel	12	0	51	0	10th	263	
Cook	12	2	34	2			
Williams	12	0	86	3			

Man of the match: I.T.Botham

ONE-DAY MATCHES | REFUGE ASSURANCE LEAGUE

ENGLAND XI vs. REST OF WORLD ━━━

at Jesmond on 2nd August 1990
Toss : Rest Of World. Umpires : S.Levison and G.McLean
England XI won by 9 wickets

REST OF WORLD
C.G.Greenidge *	lbw b Munton	27
S.J.Cook	c Hussain b Munton	39
M.D.Crowe	lbw b Munton	16
T.M.Moody	c Stephenson b Hemmings	27
M.J.Greatbatch	c Hussain b Cowans	57
A.I.C.Dodemaide	b Barnett	36
P.R.Sleep	not out	35
F.D.Stephenson	c Munton b Cowans	0
A.C.Parore +	c Munton b Cowans	5
W.K.M.Benjamin	b Munton	1
I.R.Bishop	not out	1
Extras	(b 4,lb 6,w 7,nb 3)	20
TOTAL	(55 overs)(for 9 wkts)	264

ENGLAND XI
G.A.Gooch *	c Sleep b Stephenson	62
B.C.Broad	not out	84
J.E.Morris	not out	87
J.P.Stephenson		
N.Hussain		
K.J.Barnett		
B.N.French +		
E.E.Hemmings		
N.G.Cowans		
A.P.Igglesden		
T.A.Munton		
Extras	(lb 13,w 18,nb 3)	34
TOTAL	(52.4 overs)(for 1 wkt)	267

ENGLAND XI	O	M	R	W	FALL OF WICKETS		
						ROW	EXI
Cowans	10	0	44	3	1st	54	107
Igglesden	10	0	44	1	2nd	80	
Munton	11	1	38	4	3rd	91	
Stephenson	4	0	20	0	4th	121	
Hemmings	11	1	50	1	5th	193	
Barnett	9	0	58	1	6th	240	
R. OF WORLD	O	M	R	W	7th	240	
Bishop	11	1	40	0	8th	252	
Stephenson	9.4	1	41	1	9th	257	
Benjamin	11	1	50	0	10th		
Dodemaide	10	1	67	0			
Sleep	6	0	28	0			
Moody	5	0	28	0			

Man of the match: T.A.Munton

ENGLAND XI vs. REST OF WORLD ━━━

at Jesmond on 3rd August 1990
Toss : Rest Of World. Umpires : S.Levison and G.McLean
Rest Of World won by 10 wickets

ENGLAND XI
B.C.Broad	b Sleep	55
J.P.Stephenson	b Benjamin	7
J.E.Morris	c Parore b Dodemaide	5
N.Hussain	b Moody	26
A.J.Lamb *	c Dodemaide b Sleep	20
K.J.Barnett	b Moody	10
B.N.French +	c Moody b Greenidge	30
E.E.Hemmings	c Parore b Sleep	0
N.G.Cowans	b Sleep	1
A.P.Igglesden	not out	11
T.A.Munton	c Benjamin b Greenidge	0
Extras	(b 4,lb 6,w 4)	14
TOTAL	(50.2 overs)	179

REST OF WORLD
S.J.Cook	not out	70
M.D.Crowe	not out	106
C.G.Greenidge *		
T.M.Moody		
M.J.Greatbatch		
A.I.C.Dodemaide		
P.R.Sleep		
F.D.Stephenson		
A.C.Parore +		
W.K.M.Benjamin		
I.R.Bishop		
Extras	(lb 4,w 1)	5
TOTAL	(25.3 overs)(for 0 wkts)	181

R. OF WORLD	O	M	R	W	FALL OF WICKETS		
						EXI	ROW
Benjamin	5	1	21	1	1st	26	
Bishop	4	0	7	0	2nd	36	
Dodemaide	7	1	32	1	3rd	82	
Stephenson	6	2	17	0	4th	118	
Sleep	10	0	34	4	5th	126	
Moody	8	1	23	2	6th	137	
Crowe	6	0	26	0	7th	138	
Greatbatch	4	0	9	0	8th	146	
Greenidge	0.2	0	0	2	9th	179	
ENGLAND XI	O	M	R	W	10th	179	
Cowans	5	1	22	0			
Munton	7	0	33	0			
Hemmings	6	0	53	0			
Igglesden	3	1	26	0			
Barnett	2	0	10	0			
Stephenson	2	0	21	0			
Hussain	0.3	0	12	0			

Man of the match: P.R.Sleep

YORKSHIRE vs. LANCASHIRE ━━━

at Scarborough on 5th August 1990
Toss : Yorkshire. Umpires : B.Leadbeater and N.T.Plews
Lancashire won by 78 runs (Yorkshire 0 pts Lancs 4 pts)

LANCASHIRE
G.Fowler	c Sidebottom b Fletcher	55
M.A.Atherton	b Fletcher	53
G.D.Lloyd	c & b Fletcher	76
N.H.Fairbrother	lbw b Fletcher	3
M.Watkinson	run out	31
Wasim Akram	not out	35
W.K.Hegg +	not out	1
I.D.Austin		
D.P.Hughes *		
P.J.W.Allott		
P.J.Martin		
Extras	(lb 6,nb 3)	9
TOTAL	(40 overs)(for 5 wkts)	263

YORKSHIRE
M.D.Moxon *	c Watkinson b Allott	31
A.A.Metcalfe	c Fairbrother b Allott	6
R.J.Blakey +	c Hegg b Wasim Akram	35
K.Sharp	c Martin b Atherton	37
P.E.Robinson	b Wasim Akram	0
D.Byas	not out	35
P.J.Hartley	c Watkinson b Atherton	18
P.Carrick	c Hughes b Austin	1
P.W.Jarvis	b Wasim Akram	3
A.Sidebottom	b Wasim Akram	2
S.D.Fletcher	lbw b Austin	2
Extras	(lb 9,w 5,nb 1)	15
TOTAL	(35.3 overs)	185

YORKSHIRE	O	M	R	W	FALL OF WICKETS		
						LAN	YOR
Jarvis	8	0	69	0	1st	106	26
Sidebottom	8	0	33	0	2nd	115	59
Hartley	8	1	44	0	3rd	127	105
Carrick	8	0	48	0	4th	210	105
Fletcher	8	0	63	4	5th	253	138
LANCASHIRE	O	M	R	W	6th		161
Allott	8	1	21	2	7th		169
Martin	6	0	41	0	8th		176
Watkinson	8	0	47	0	9th		182
Wasim Akram	6	0	19	4	10th		185
Austin	4.3	0	21	2			
Atherton	3	0	27	2			

MIDDLESEX vs. GLAMORGAN ━━━

at Lord's on 5th August 1990
Toss : Middlesex. Umpires : D.J.Constant and K.J.Lyons
Middlesex won by 84 runs (Middx 4 pts Glamorgan 0 pts)

MIDDLESEX
D.L.Haynes	c Cottey b Dale	37
M.A.Roseberry	c Frost b Butcher	68
M.W.Gatting *	b Dennis	99
M.R.Ramprakash	b Watkin	47
K.R.Brown	run out	5
J.E.Emburey	not out	6
N.F.Williams	not out	9
P.R.Downton +		
P.C.R.Tufnell		
A.R.C.Fraser		
N.G.Cowans		
Extras	(b 2,lb 14)	16
TOTAL	(40 overs)(for 5 wkts)	287

GLAMORGAN
M.P.Maynard	b Fraser	59
H.Morris	c Haynes b Williams	11
I.V.A.Richards	b Emburey	35
A.R.Butcher *	s Downton b Emburey	52
P.A.Cottey	b Fraser	28
R.D.B.Croft	b Fraser	6
A.Dale	c Ramprakash b Fraser	0
C.P.Metson +	not out	2
S.L.Watkin	b Emburey	1
S.J.Dennis	b Emburey	0
M.Frost	c Roseberry b Ramprakash	6
Extras	(b 1,lb 1,w 1)	3
TOTAL	(39.3 overs)	203

GLAMORGAN	O	M	R	W	FALL OF WICKETS		
						MID	GLA
Watkin	8	1	67	1			
Frost	5	0	40	0	1st	61	30
Dennis	7	0	54	1	2nd	154	83
Dale	8	0	38	1	3rd	264	136
Croft	8	0	52	0	4th	270	176
Butcher	4	0	20	1	5th	272	194
MIDDLESEX	O	M	R	W	6th		194
Williams	6	0	33	1	7th		195
Cowans	8	0	46	0	8th		196
Tufnell	8	0	45	0	9th		196
Emburey	8	2	32	4	10th		203
Fraser	8	0	28	4			
Haynes	1	0	12	0			
Ramprakash	0.3	0	5	1			

HEADLINES

Callers Pegasus Jesmond Festival

2nd - 3rd August

● The 10th staging of the festival that has done so much to foster cricket in the North-East again featured many top players from home and overseas. Tim Munton impressed the watching England selectors with 4 for 38 on his representative debut as the England XI won the first match by nine wickets. But an unbroken opening stand of 181 by Jimmy Cook and Martin Crowe took Rest of the World to victory in the second match

5th August

● The Refuge League continued to boil up to an exciting finish as the top five sides in the table all won. Derbyshire were most impressive, sweeping to victory over Kent at Chesterfield even though they needed to score at almost seven an over. Kim Barnett, who hit his sixth Sunday century, and Peter Bowler shared an opening stand of 146, setting them on course to a victory that kept them four points clear of Middlesex and Lancashire

● Middlesex's 287 for 5 proved too formidable for Glamorgan at Lord's, Angus Fraser recording his best Sunday figures as the home side won by 84 runs, while in the Roses match at Scarborough Yorkshire could make little of Lancashire's 263 for 5 as Wasim Akram collected 4 for 19

● Nottinghamshire and Hampshire remained locked together a further four points behind following their wins over Essex and Northants respectively. Even 139 from Graham Gooch, his 10th Sunday League 100, could not save Essex from defeat at Southend, Mike Newell completing his first Sunday 100 in Notts's six-wicket win. Hampshire enjoyed a comfortable success over their NatWest semi-final opponents at Bournemouth as Paul Terry and Richard Scott added 127 for the first wicket

● There were also wins for Surrey, Warwicks and Worcs, Graeme Hick being denied the chance of a hundred against Leics when a wide ended the match

REFUGE ASSURANCE LEAGUE

SOMERSET vs. SURREY

at Weston-super-Mare on 5th August 1990
Toss : Surrey. Umpires : P.J.Eele and R.A.White
Surrey won by 6 wickets (Somerset 0 pts Surrey 4 pts)

SOMERSET

S.J.Cook	c Stewart b Feltham	21
C.J.Tavare *	c Brown b Waqar Younis	41
R.J.Harden	b Bicknell	53
J.C.M.Atkinson	c Brown b Waqar Younis	8
G.D.Rose	run out	3
R.P.Lefebvre	lbw b Feltham	10
N.D.Burns +	lbw b Waqar Younis	26
A.N.Hayhurst	b Bicknell	2
I.G.Swallow	not out	8
N.A.Mallender	not out	10
A.N.Jones		
Extras	(b 7,lb 4,w 6)	17
TOTAL	(40 overs)(for 8 wkts)	199

SURREY

M.A.Feltham	b Rose	24
A.Brown +	c Hayhurst b Jones	32
G.P.Thorpe	run out	42
D.M.Ward	c Burns b Hayhurst	27
M.A.Lynch	not out	32
I.A.Greig *	not out	27
A.J.Stewart		
K.T.Medlycott		
C.K.Bullen		
M.P.Bicknell		
Waqar Younis		
Extras	(lb 8,w 11)	19
TOTAL	(38.2 overs)(for 4 wkts)	203

SURREY	O	M	R	W	FALL OF WICKETS		
						SOM	SUR
Bicknell	8	1	38	2	1st	41	37
Feltham	8	0	40	2	2nd	98	76
Bullen	8	0	37	0	3rd	113	120
Medlycott	8	0	34	0	4th	119	150
Waqar Younis	8	0	39	3	5th	144	
					6th	161	
SOMERSET	O	M	R	W	7th	177	
Mallender	8	0	44	0	8th	179	
Rose	7	0	41	1	9th		
Lefebvre	3.2	0	19	0	10th		
Jones	8	0	33	1			
Swallow	5	1	26	0			
Hayhurst	7	0	30	1			

SUSSEX vs. WARWICKSHIRE

at Eastbourne on 5th August 1990
Toss : Sussex. Umpires : J.D.Bond and M.J.Kitchen
Warwickshire won by 2 runs (Sussex 0 pts Warwicks 4 pts)

WARWICKSHIRE

A.J.Moles	c Moores b Dodemaide	3
Asif Din	c Smith b Dodemaide	6
T.M.Moody	b Pigott	64
D.A.Reeve	lbw b Clarke	22
P.A.Smith	c Hansford b Pigott	11
T.A.Lloyd *	c Remy b Clarke	48
N.M.K.Smith	s Moores b Hansford	16
R.G.Twose	not out	1
K.J.Piper +	not out	3
G.Smith		
T.A.Munton		
Extras	(lb 4,w 1)	5
TOTAL	(40 overs)(for 7 wkts)	179

SUSSEX

M.P.Speight	b Munton	20
D.M.Smith	b Moody	18
A.P.Wells	c Piper b Munton	0
C.M.Wells *	c Smith N.M.K. b Smith P.A.	64
R.Hanley	b Smith N.M.K.	11
C.C.Remy	b Smith N.M.K.	11
A.I.C.Dodemaide	c Smith N.M.K. b Smith P.A.	3
A.C.S.Pigott	not out	29
P.Moores +	b Munton	6
A.R.Hansford	c Asif Din b Smith P.A.	2
A.R.Clarke	not out	4
Extras	(b 1,lb 6,w 2)	9
TOTAL	(40 overs)(for 9 wkts)	177

SUSSEX	O	M	R	W	FALL OF WICKETS		
						WAR	SUS
Pigott	8	0	46	2	1st	7	30
Dodemaide	8	1	21	2	2nd	9	30
Wells C.M.	8	1	17	0	3rd	65	53
Hansford	8	1	49	1	4th	82	101
Clarke	8	0	42	2	5th	144	121
					6th	174	133
WARWICKSHIRE	O	M	R	W	7th	174	134
Munton	8	1	36	3	8th		146
Smith G.	2	0	8	0	9th		155
Reeve	8	1	20	0	10th		
Moody	7	0	31	1			
Smith N.M.K.	7	0	41	2			
Smith P.A.	8	0	34	3			

LEICESTERSHIRE vs. WORCS

at Leicester on 5th August 1990
Toss : Worcestershire. Umpires : J.W.Holder and R.Palmer
Worcestershire won by 7 wickets (Leics 0 pts Worcs 4 pts)

LEICESTERSHIRE

T.J.Boon	c Lampitt b Weston	16
N.E.Briers *	b Newport	42
B.Smith	c Neale b McEwan	10
C.C.Lewis	c Curtis b Lampitt	13
J.D.R.Benson	b Illingworth	15
L.Potter	c Lampitt b McEwan	33
M.I.Gidley	not out	14
P.A.Nixon +	c Rhodes b McEwan	0
G.J.Parsons	not out	19
D.J.Millns		
A.D.Mullally		
Extras	(lb 14,w 9)	23
TOTAL	(40 overs)(for 7 wkts)	185

WORCESTERSHIRE

I.T.Botham	c Lewis b Millns	1
T.S.Curtis	b Mullally	19
G.A.Hick	not out	98
D.B.D'Oliveira	b Lewis	24
P.A.Neale *	not out	34
M.J.Weston		
S.J.Rhodes +		
R.K.Illingworth		
P.J.Newport		
S.R.Lampitt		
S.M.McEwan		
Extras	(b 1,lb 1,w 7,nb 1)	10
TOTAL	(36.3 overs)(for 3 wkts)	186

WORCS	O	M	R	W	FALL OF WICKETS		
						LEI	WOR
Newport	8	0	36	1	1st	34	3
Weston	8	0	27	1	2nd	49	74
McEwan	8	0	38	3	3rd	81	121
Lampitt	8	1	38	1	4th	100	
Illingworth	8	0	32	1	5th	132	
					6th	156	
LEICS	O	M	R	W	7th	157	
Lewis	7.3	0	34	1	8th		
Millns	5	1	22	1	9th		
Parsons	5	0	27	0	10th		
Mullally	7	0	35	1			
Gidley	8	0	40	0			
Benson	4	0	26	0			

HAMPSHIRE vs. NORTHANTS

at Bournemouth on 5th August 1990
Toss : Northants. Umpires : B.J.Meyer and D.O.Oslear
Hampshire won by 6 wickets (Hants 4 pts Northants 0 pts)

NORTHANTS

A.Fordham	c Scott b Marshall	63
W.Larkins	c Scott b Bakker	7
R.J.Bailey	c Marshall b Maru	33
A.J.Lamb *	b Connor	45
R.G.Williams	not out	34
D.J.Wild	not out	16
D.Ripley +		
J.W.Govan		
S.J.Brown		
N.G.B.Cook		
M.A.Robinson		
Extras	(b 1,lb 2,w 2,nb 5)	10
TOTAL	(40 overs)(for 4 wkts)	208

HAMPSHIRE

V.P.Terry	c Robinson b Brown	84
R.J.Scott	c Ripley b Brown	70
R.A.Smith	c & b Cook	9
D.I.Gower	c Bailey b Cook	18
M.D.Marshall	not out	17
M.C.J.Nicholas *	not out	0
J.R.Ayling		
R.J.Parks +		
R.J.Maru		
C.A.Connor		
P.J.Bakker		
Extras	(lb 9,w 2,nb 1)	12
TOTAL	(37.5 overs)(for 4 wkts)	210

HAMPSHIRE	O	M	R	W	FALL OF WICKETS		
						NOR	HAM
Bakker	7	0	36	1	1st	19	127
Marshall	8	1	33	1	2nd	109	140
Connor	8	0	51	1	3rd	111	188
Ayling	8	0	44	0	4th	180	200
Maru	8	0	28	1	5th		
Scott	1	0	13	0	6th		
					7th		
NORTHANTS	O	M	R	W	8th		
Robinson	7	1	21	0	9th		
Brown	6.5	0	37	2	10th		
Wild	4	0	23	0			
Cook	8	1	42	2			
Govan	3	0	23	0			
Larkins	4	0	26	0			
Williams	5	0	29	0			

DERBYSHIRE vs. KENT

at Chesterfield on 5th August 1990
Toss : Derbyshire. Umpires : J.H.Hampshire and B.Hassan
Derbyshire won by 6 wickets (Derbyshire 4 pts Kent 0 pts)

KENT

S.G.Hinks	c Morris b Miller	50
M.R.Benson	run out	4
N.R.Taylor	c Roberts b Kuiper	78
T.R.Ward	c Warner b Kuiper	80
G.R.Cowdrey	not out	36
M.V.Fleming	not out	15
C.S.Cowdrey *		
S.A.Marsh +		
T.A.Merrick		
R.P.Davis		
A.P.Igglesden		
Extras	(lb 6,nb 7)	13
TOTAL	(40 overs)(for 4 wkts)	276

DERBYSHIRE

K.J.Barnett *	run out	127
P.D.Bowler +	b Fleming	54
J.E.Morris	c Cowdrey C.S. b Igglesden	45
A.P.Kuiper	not out	22
T.J.G.O'Gorman	b Davis	11
B.Roberts	not out	11
C.J.Adams		
A.E.Warner		
G.Miller		
D.E.Malcolm		
O.H.Mortensen		
Extras	(b 4,lb 2,w 1)	7
TOTAL	(38.2 overs)(for 4 wkts)	277

DERBYSHIRE	O	M	R	W	FALL OF WICKETS		
						KEN	DER
Warner	8	0	59	0	1st	8	146
Mortensen	8	2	23	0	2nd	80	232
Malcolm	8	0	55	0	3rd	210	234
Miller	8	0	59	1	4th	249	259
Kuiper	8	0	74	2	5th		
					6th		
KENT	O	M	R	W	7th		
Igglesden	7.2	0	54	1	8th		
Merrick	7	0	43	0	9th		
Cowdrey C.S.	8	0	50	0	10th		
Fleming	8	0	60	1			
Davis	8	0	64	1			

ESSEX vs. NOTTINGHAMSHIRE

at Southend on 5th August 1990
Toss : Notts. Umpires : J.C.Balderstone and J.H.Harris
Nottinghamshire won by 6 wickets (Essex 0 pts Notts 4 pts)

ESSEX

G.A.Gooch *	c Johnson b Cooper	136
J.P.Stephenson	c Randall b Hemmings	50
M.E.Waugh	c Newell b Hemmings	7
P.J.Prichard	c Johnson b Stephenson	4
N.Hussain	c French b Mike	5
N.Shahid	c Mike b Stephenson	8
N.A.Foster	c Newell b Stephenson	10
M.A.Garnham +	b Evans	5
T.D.Topley	b Evans	2
M.C.Ilott	run out	3
J.H.Childs	not out	1
Extras	(lb 6,w 1,nb 1)	8
TOTAL	(38.4 overs)	239

NOTTINGHAMSHIRE

B.C.Broad	b Gooch	35
M.Newell	not out	109
P.Johnson	c Hussain b Topley	48
R.T.Robinson *	c & b Foster	4
D.W.Randall	run out	9
F.D.Stephenson	not out	26
K.P.Evans		
B.N.French +		
G.W.Mike		
E.E.Hemmings		
K.E.Cooper		
Extras	(lb 7,w 1,nb 1)	9
TOTAL	(38.3 overs)(for 4 wkts)	240

NOTTS	O	M	R	W	FALL OF WICKETS		
						ESS	NOT
Cooper	8	0	49	1	1st	147	61
Stephenson	8	0	28	3	2nd	158	154
Evans	7.4	0	52	2	3rd	178	160
Mike	7	0	68	1	4th	192	184
Hemmings	8	0	36	2	5th	212	
					6th	221	
ESSEX	O	M	R	W	7th	228	
Ilott	7.3	0	41	0	8th	233	
Foster	8	0	50	1	9th	238	
Gooch	8	0	34	1	10th	239	
Childs	6	0	43	0			
Topley	7	0	45	1			
Waugh	2	0	20	0			

TOUR MATCHES

SURREY vs. INDIA
at The Oval on 1st, 2nd, 3rd August 1990
Toss : Surrey.   Umpires : A.G.T.Whitehead and P.B.Wight
Match drawn

SURREY

D.J.Bicknell	b Wasson	22			
G.S.Clinton	c Shastri b Kumble	97	c sub b Shastri	74	
A.J.Stewart	b Hirwani	82	lbw b Shastri	22	
D.M.Ward	c Mongia b Kumble	20	b Hirwani	28	
M.A.Lynch	c Raman b Hirwani	94	c Manjrekar b Hirwani	3	
I.A.Greig *	st More b Hirwani	36	not out	76	
M.A.Feltham	c Mongia b Venkatapathy	1	c Vengsarkar b Hirwani	5	
K.T.Medlycott	not out	2	not out	15	
N.F.Sargeant +			(1) c Raman b Hirwani	18	
N.M.Kendrick					
A.H.Gray					
Extras	(b 5,lb 8,w 9,nb 8)	30	(b 2,lb 9,nb 3)	14	
TOTAL	(for 7 wkts dec)	384	(for 6 wkts dec)	255	

INDIA

W.V.Raman	c Gray b Kendrick	127	c sub b Kendrick	58	
N.R.Mongia	c Kendrick b Feltham	10	c Feltham b Kendrick	41	
S.V.Manjrekar	c Kendrick b Gray	9	not out	52	
D.B.Vengsarkar	c Stewart b Gray	55			
R.J.Shastri *	st Sargeant b Medlycott	8			
K.S.More +	c Sargeant b Medlycott	12	(4) not out	12	
Venkatapathy Raju	c & b Medlycott	7			
S.K.Sharma	c Gray b Kendrick	15			
A.R.Kumble	c Kendrick b Gray	19			
A.Wasson	not out	8			
N.D.Hirwani					
Extras	(b 5,lb 7,nb 7)	19	(lb 1,nb 3)	4	
TOTAL	(for 9 wkts dec)	289	(for 2 wkts)	167	

INDIA	O	M	R	W	O	M	R	W	FALL OF WICKETS				
										SUR	IND	SUR	IND
Sharma	10	0	29	0	3	0	7	0	1st	34	18	57	94
Wasson	13	1	81	1	4	0	19	0	2nd	189	46	96	111
Venkatapathy	22	4	64	1	10	1	52	0	3rd	233	183	149	
Hirwani	24.2	0	122	3	15	0	71	4	4th	282	209	149	
Kumble	21	1	75	2	3	0	15	0	5th	351	237	170	
Shastri					27.3	5	80	2	6th	352	242	190	
SURREY	O	M	R	W	O	M	R	W	7th	384		261	
Gray	18.1	0	69	3	9	0	41	0	8th			261	
Feltham	11	2	48	1	4	0	20	0	9th			289	
Medlycott	35	8	102	3	24	7	55	0	10th				
Kendrick	20	4	58	2	20	5	50	2					

GLOUCESTERSHIRE vs. INDIA
at Bristol on 4th, 5th, 6th August 1990
Toss : India.   Umpires : B.Dudleston and D.S.Thompsett
Match drawn

INDIA

R.J.Shastri	b Walsh	5	b Alleyne	133	
N.S.Sidhu	c Williams b Lawrence	31	c Barnes b Lloyds	142	
W.V.Raman	c Williams b Walsh	0	not out	56	
S.R.Tendulkar	c Williams b Milburn	13	c Lawrence b Romaines	47	
M.Azharuddin *	b Alleyne	23			
M.Prabhakar	c Hodgson b Alleyne	12	(5) not out	11	
Kapil Dev	c Butcher b Alleyne	12			
K.S.More	c Williams b Milburn	95			
N.R.Mongia +	c Alleyne b Lawrence	1			
Venkatapathy Raju	not out	40			
N.D.Hirwani	c Williams b Milburn	0			
Extras	(lb 1,nb 6)	7	(lb 1,nb 1)	2	
TOTAL		239	(for 3 wkts dec)	391	

GLOUCESTERSHIRE

G.D.Hodgson	c Hirwani b Tendulkar	16	not out	23	
I.P.Butcher	b Hirwani	41	b Prabhakar	1	
P.W.Romaines	c Mongia b Tendulkar	2	c More b Prabhakar	6	
C.W.J.Athey	c Azharuddin b Hirwani	80			
M.W.Alleyne	c Shastri b Tendulkar	0	(4) c More b Kapil Dev	0	
J.W.Lloyds	c Kapil Dev b Hirwani	8	(5) c More b Kapil Dev	21	
E.T.Milburn	c Mongia b Hirwani	35	(6) not out	11	
R.C.J.Williams +	not out	50			
C.A.Walsh *	c Prabhakar b Hirwani	0			
D.V.Lawrence	c Mongia b Prabhakar	35			
S.N.Barnes	not out	12			
Extras	(b 7,lb 7,w 1,nb 12)	27	(lb 1,nb 3)	4	
TOTAL	(for 9 wkts dec)	306	(for 4 wkts)	66	

GLOUCS	O	M	R	W	O	M	R	W	FALL OF WICKETS				
										IND	GLO	IND	GLO
Walsh	17	4	45	2	11	5	16	0	1st	13	54	251	2
Lawrence	12	1	65	2	13	1	42	0	2nd	19	66	301	14
Barnes	5	1	18	0					3rd	42	71	374	15
Milburn	14.3	3	43	3	11	0	73	0	4th	54	73		42
Alleyne	10	3	41	3	15	1	54	1	5th	79	89		
Lloyds	9	1	24	0	21	0	136	1	6th	86	188		
Athey	1	0	2	0	13	1	39	0	7th	103	211		
Romaines					6	0	30	1	8th	112	219		
INDIA	O	M	R	W	O	M	R	W	9th	239	266		
Prabhakar	18	4	53	1	11	2	26	2	10th	239			
Tendulkar	32	6	79	3	5	1	6	0					
Hirwani	43	9	117	5	4	0	4	0					
Shastri	22	6	36	0									
Raman	1	0	7	0	1	0	1	0					
Kapil Dev					11	1	28	2					

LEADING FIRST-CLASS AVERAGES
at 31st July 1990

BATTING AVERAGES Qualifying requirements : 6 completed innings

Name	M	I	NO	Runs	HS	Avge	100s	50s
G.A.Gooch	11	18	2	1804	333	112.75	9	2
T.M.Moody	6	10	2	883	168	110.37	5	1
G.A.Hick	12	18	6	1279	252 *	106.58	4	8
N.H.Fairbrother	15	23	6	1503	366	88.41	4	7
S.J.Cook	18	31	6	1995	313 *	79.80	6	8
M.E.Waugh	14	21	4	1349	204	79.35	6	5
D.M.Ward	15	20	6	1102	181	78.71	4	1
B.R.Hardie	11	16	7	686	125	76.22	2	4
M.A.Crawley	10	12	3	672	105 *	74.66	2	5
A.J.Lamb	10	16	4	887	235	73.91	3	2
C.L.Smith	16	27	6	1484	148	70.66	3	10
D.J.Bicknell	9	15	4	768	169	69.81	2	5
M.A.Atherton	14	22	3	1326	191	69.78	5	8
A.R.Butcher	15	26	3	1559	151 *	67.78	5	10
N.Shahid	11	16	6	646	125	64.60	1	4
K.J.Barnett	17	28	5	1453	141	63.17	5	8
R.J.Bailey	15	24	6	1136	204 *	63.11	3	5
C.J.Tavare	18	22	4	1116	156	62.00	2	9
R.A.Smith	11	17	3	866	181	61.85	4	3
A.N.Hayhurst	16	26	7	1169	170	61.52	4	4

BOWLING AVERAGES Qualifying requirements : 20 wickets taken

Name	O	M	R	W	Avge	Best	5wI	10wM
I.R.Bishop	245.5	55	669	37	18.08	5-90	1	-
M.D.Marshall	339	84	881	44	20.02	7-47	2	1
Waqar Younis	213.3	39	643	32	20.09	7-73	2	1
O.H.Mortensen	205.5	57	519	23	22.56	4-22	-	-
K.P.Evans	167.4	46	553	23	24.04	4-50	-	-
R.J.Hadlee	201.5	39	586	24	24.41	5-27	2	-
C.E.L.Ambrose	296	77	836	34	24.58	5-49	3	-
K.J.Barnett	213.5	42	566	23	24.60	4-28	-	-
C.A.Walsh	330	52	1116	44	25.36	8-58	3	1
D.E.Malcolm	361.2	71	1108	43	25.76	5-46	2	-
A.R.C.Fraser	277.1	61	627	24	26.12	5-104	1	-
J.E.Benjamin	371.3	68	1124	42	26.76	5-29	4	-
M.C.Snedden	231.5	56	633	23	27.52	5-63	1	-
J.E.Emburey	575.3	172	1227	44	27.88	5-61	1	-
M.P.Bicknell	462.5	114	1284	46	27.91	5-34	1	-
D.J.Capel	180	41	560	20	28.00	5-74	1	-
P.J.Hartley	332.5	53	1196	42	28.47	6-57	2	-
N.F.Williams	396.1	73	1167	40	29.17	7-61	1	-
R.K.Illingworth	465.4	163	1051	36	29.19	5-59	1	-
I.T.Botham	194.4	38	614	21	29.23	4-65	-	-

BRITANNIC ASSURANCE CHAMPIONSHIP

MIDDLESEX vs. GLAMORGAN
at Lord's on 4th, 6th, 7th August 1990
Toss : Middlesex. Umpires : D.J.Constant and K.J.Lyons
Match drawn (Middlesex 7 pts (Bt: 4, Bw: 3) Glamorgan 7 pts (Bt: 4, Bw: 3))

MIDDLESEX
D.L.Haynes	b Croft	173			
M.A.Roseberry	c Metson b Bastien	0	(1) b Croft	62
M.W.Gatting *	b Bastien	89	(2) b Watkin	21
M.R.Ramprakash	lbw b.Watkin	8	(3) c Morris b Frost	18
K.R.Brown	c Metson b Croft	120	(4) c Morris b Frost	4
P.R.Downton +	c Watkin b Croft	4	(5) c Maynard b Bastien	6
J.E.Emburey	c Butcher b Frost	23	(6) c Metson b Watkin	7
N.F.Williams	c Morris b Frost	17	(7) c Cowley b Bastien	1
A.R.C.Fraser	not out	4	(8) c Metson b Frost	23
P.C.R.Tufnell			(9) not out	4
N.G.Cowans			(10) not out	12
Extras	(lb 7,nb 2)	9	(lb 4,nb 1)	5
TOTAL	(for 8 wkts dec)	447	(for 8 wkts dec)	163

GLAMORGAN
A.R.Butcher *	c Brown b Williams	34	lbw b Fraser	54
H.Morris	c Downton b Cowans	100	lbw b Williams	4
P.A.Cottey	c Gatting b Williams	0	b Fraser	33
M.P.Maynard	c Downton b Tufnell	27	c Cowans b Tufnell	20
I.V.A.Richards	c Haynes b Emburey	80	b Fraser	9
R.D.B.Croft	c Brown b Cowans	15	b Tufnell	13
N.G.Cowley	not out	52	c Downton b Fraser	8
C.P.Metson +	lbw b Williams	0	c Gatting b Fraser	0
S.L.Watkin	c Gatting b Williams	9	not out	0
S.Bastien	c & b Williams	11	lbw b Fraser	0
M.Frost	not out	4	not out	0
Extras	(b 9,lb 11,w 1,nb 3)	24	(lb 2,nb 3)	5
TOTAL	(for 9 wkts dec)	360	(for 9 wkts)	146

GLAMORGAN	O	M	R	W	O	M	R	W
Watkin	24	2	85	1	15	4	47	2
Bastien	15.2	1	81	2	21	4	72	2
Frost	19.4	1	110	2	8	0	24	3
Croft	24	4	100	3	2	0	16	1
Cowley	9	1	29	0				
Richards	6	0	22	0				
Butcher	3.4	0	13	0				

MIDDLESEX	O	M	R	W	O	M	R	W
Fraser	21	2	76	0	14	7	30	6
Williams	23	6	59	5	7	2	30	1
Emburey	32	10	88	1	16	7	28	0
Cowans	15	2	50	2	2	1	8	0
Tufnell	24	4	67	1	14	5	48	2

FALL OF WICKETS
	MID	GLA	MID	GLA
1st	0	71	33	7
2nd	171	71	63	86
3rd	196	117	72	101
4th	330	255	83	125
5th	344	266	93	125
6th	413	280	98	146
7th	431	294	147	146
8th	447	324	151	146
9th		346		146
10th				

LEICESTERSHIRE vs. WORCESTERSHIRE
at leicester on 4th, 6th, 7th August 1990
Toss : Worcestershire. Umpires : J.W.Holder and R.Palmer
Worcestershire won by 1 run (Leicestershire 4 pts (Bt: 3, Bw: 1) Worcs 23 pts (Bt: 4, Bw: 3))

WORCESTERSHIRE
T.S.Curtis	not out	151	lbw b Lewis	6
G.J.Lord	lbw b Agnew	19	b Mullally	35
G.A.Hick	c Boon b Agnew	102	(4) not out	88
D.B.D'Oliveira	c Potter b Willey	5	(5) not out	44
I.T.Botham	run out	26		
P.A.Neale *	not out	20	(3) b Lewis	6
S.R.Lampitt				
S.J.Rhodes +				
R.K.Illingworth				
P.J.Newport				
S.M.McEwan				
Extras	(b 6,lb 5,nb 21)	42	(b 4,lb 6,w 1,nb 10)	21
TOTAL	(for 4 wkts dec)	365	(for 3 wkts dec)	200

LEICESTERSHIRE
T.J.Boon	c D'Oliveira b Lampitt	42	st Rhodes b Illingworth	40
N.E.Briers *	c D'Oliveira b Lampitt	111	c & b Newport	17
J.J.Whitaker	c Hick b Illingworth	16	c sub b Newport	62
P.Willey	c Curtis b Illingworth	7	b Lampitt	79
L.Potter	c Newport b Illingworth	20	c Rhodes b McEwan	27
C.C.Lewis	c Neale b Illingworth	27	c sub b Lampitt	16
J.D.R.Benson	not out	28	st Rhodes b Illingworth	2
W.K.M.Benjamin	c D'Oliveira b Newport	10	b Illingworth	6
P.A.Nixon +	c Hick b McEwan	5	run out	3
J.P.Agnew	b McEwan	0	run out	1
A.D.Mullally	lbw b McEwan	0	not out	3
Extras	(b 10,lb 17,w 4,nb 4)	35	(lb 4,nb 3)	7
TOTAL		301		263

LEICS	O	M	R	W	O	M	R	W
Benjamin	9	1	31	0				
Agnew	18	2	73	2				
Lewis	22	2	76	0	13	2	31	2
Mullally	19.4	6	56	0	16	3	78	1
Willey	28	5	96	1	16	2	59	0
Potter	3	0	12	0	7	3	22	0

WORCS	O	M	R	W	O	M	R	W
Newport	26.1	2	84	1	15	4	56	2
McEwan	20	4	62	3	13	5	37	1
Lampitt	17.5	4	43	2	11	0	68	2
Illingworth	42	16	85	4	21	5	98	3

FALL OF WICKETS
	WOR	LEI	WOR	LEI
1st	33	104	7	35
2nd	226	162	30	120
3rd	235	180	105	125
4th	288	198		178
5th		248		242
6th		256		248
7th		282		250
8th		301		258
9th		301		260
10th		301		263

SOMERSET vs. SURREY
at Weston-super-Mare on 4th, 6th, 7th August 1990
Toss : Surrey. Umpires : P.J.Eele and R.A.White
Match drawn (Somerset 6 pts (Bt: 4, Bw: 2) Surrey 6 pts (Bt: 4, Bw: 2))

SOMERSET
S.J.Cook	c Stewart b Waqar Younis	52	not out	116
P.M.Roebuck	c Lynch b Bicknell	49	lbw b Kendrick	39
A.N.Hayhurst	c Stewart b Waqar Younis	40		
C.J.Tavare	b Kendrick	38	(3) b Kendrick	4
R.J.Harden	not out	104	(4) not out	55
N.D.Burns +	b Waqar Younis	25		
G.D.Rose	b Bicknell	85		
R.P.Lefebvre	c Stewart b Bicknell	8		
I.G.Swallow	c Stewart b Bicknell	11		
N.A.Mallender				
A.N.Jones				
Extras	(b 8,lb 9,w 3,nb 9)	29	(b 1,lb 10,nb 4)	15
TOTAL	(for 8 wkts dec)	441	(for 2 wkts dec)	229

SURREY
G.S.Clinton	c Roebuck b Jones	8	(2) c Burns b Jones	16
M.A.Feltham	c Harden b Jones	0	(1) b Jones	0
G.P.Thorpe	run out	9	lbw b Swallow	86
D.M.Ward	b Lefebvre	18	c Lefebvre b Swallow	43
M.A.Lynch	b Swallow	97	b Hayhurst	104
I.A.Greig *	not out	123	lbw b Lefebvre	24
A.J.Stewart +	not out	24	(8) lbw b Rose	0
K.T.Medlycott			(7) c sub b Rose	38
M.P.Bicknell			not out	2
N.M.Kendrick			not out	0
Waqar Younis				
Extras	(b 4,lb 6,w 4,nb 9)	23	(lb 13,w 1)	14
TOTAL	(for 5 wkts dec)	302	(for 8 wkts)	327

SURREY	O	M	R	W	O	M	R	W
Waqar Younis	23	2	80	3	8	1	31	0
Bicknell	23	3	79	4	8	1	15	0
Feltham	6	0	23	0				
Medlycott	25	8	100	0	21	3	99	0
Kendrick	21	3	87	1	21	4	73	2
Greig	12	0	55	0	0.1	0	0	0

SOMERSET	O	M	R	W	O	M	R	W
Jones	16	4	62	2	9	1	36	2
Mallender	13	2	49	0	14	1	47	0
Lefebvre	17	4	47	1	14.5	0	72	1
Rose	13	1	40	0	9	3	26	2
Hayhurst	6	2	11	0	13	0	59	1
Swallow	20.5	3	83	1	11	0	74	2

FALL OF WICKETS
	SOM	SUR	SOM	SUR
1st	99	1	110	0
2nd	110	13	118	37
3rd	194	25		142
4th	194	39		179
5th	277	227		245
6th	401			325
7th	415			325
8th	441			325
9th				
10th				

ESSEX vs. NOTTINGHAMSHIRE
at Southend on 4th, 6th, 7th August 1990
Toss : Nottinghamshire. Umpires : J.C.Balderstone and J.H.Harris
Essex won by 10 wickets (Essex 24 pts (Bt: 4, Bw: 4) Notts 4 pts (Bt: 2, Bw: 2))

NOTTINGHAMSHIRE
B.C.Broad	c Stephenson b Ilott	19	c Garnham b Ilott	84
P.Pollard	c Waugh b Foster	12	c Gooch b Foster	10
R.T.Robinson *	c Waugh b Pringle	6	c & b Childs	26
P.Johnson	run out	34	(5) b Childs	60
D.W.Randall	c Pringle b Ilott	34	(6) not out	36
F.D.Stephenson	c Prichard b Foster	2	(7) c Prichard b Childs	4
K.P.Evans	c Garnham b Foster	51	(8) c sub b Foster	31
B.N.French +	run out	25	(4) b Such	0
E.E.Hemmings	lbw b Foster	32	c Childs b Ilott	12
K.E.Cooper	not out	10	b Childs	4
J.A.Afford	lbw b Such	1	lbw b Ilott	0
Extras	(b 1,lb 1,nb 3)	5	(lb 3)	3
TOTAL		231		270

ESSEX
G.A.Gooch *	c Johnson b Hemmings	87	not out	65
J.P.Stephenson	b Hemmings	46	not out	32
P.J.Prichard	b Hemmings	60		
M.C.Ilott	b Cooper	37		
M.E.Waugh	c Robinson b Hemmings	30		
N.Hussain	c French b Stephenson	64		
M.A.Garnham +	c French b Hemmings	22		
N.A.Foster	b Evans	22		
D.R.Pringle	c French b Evans	15		
J.H.Childs	c French b Stephenson	2		
P.M.Such	not out	2		
Extras	(b 3,lb 8,w 1,nb 4)	16	(b 1,nb 2)	3
TOTAL		403	(for 0 wkts)	100

ESSEX	O	M	R	W	O	M	R	W
Foster	25	5	73	4	30	12	59	2
Ilott	15	2	63	2	19.5	9	48	3
Pringle	15	2	74	1				
Gooch	1	0	4	0				
Childs	8	3	10	0	41	13	104	4
Such	4.3	1	5	1	20	4	56	1

NOTTS	O	M	R	W	O	M	R	W
Stephenson	27.2	2	105	2	6	0	30	0
Cooper	17	3	76	1	3.1	1	19	0
Evans	15	3	53	2				
Hemmings	39	15	99	5	5	0	32	0
Afford	25	7	59	0	4	0	18	0

FALL OF WICKETS
	NOT	ESS	NOT	ESS
1st	26	135	19	
2nd	38	135	73	
3rd	38	190	80	
4th	90	261	175	
5th	100	266	183	
6th	126	336	194	
7th	158	379	235	
8th	219	383	255	
9th	222	401	270	
10th	231	403	270	

BRITANNIC ASSURANCE CHAMPIONSHIP

DERBYSHIRE vs. KENT

at Chesterfield on 4th, 6th, 7th August 1990
Toss : Kent. Umpires : J.H.Hampshire and B.Hassan
Derbyshire won by 10 wickets (Derbyshire 24 pts (Bt: 4, Bw: 4) Kent 5 pts (Bt: 4, Bw: 1))

KENT

S.G.Hinks	c Krikken b Bishop	0	c Roberts b Jean-Jacques	9
M.R.Benson *	c Krikken b Bishop	0	b Malcolm	15
N.R.Taylor	c Krikken b Base	18	c Bowler b Jean-Jacques	12
G.R.Cowdrey	c Krikken b Malcolm	6	c Bowler b Jean-Jacques	21
T.R.Ward	lbw b Base	124	c Krikken b Base	5
S.A.Marsh +	c Adams b Bishop	38	c Krikken b Jean-Jacques	4
R.M.Ellison	c Roberts b Base	41	c Krikken b Jean-Jacques	62
R.P.Davis	c Krikken b Bishop	41	c Brown b Malcolm	26
P.S.De Villiers	c Roberts b Bishop	5	c Base b Bishop	30
M.M.Patel	c Roberts b Bishop	7	not out	25
A.P.Igglesden	not out	1	b Jean-Jacques	2
Extras	(lb 3,w 5,nb 14)	22	(b 4,lb 4,w 1,nb 12)	21
TOTAL		303		232

DERBYSHIRE

K.J.Barnett *	c Davis b De Villiers	64	not out	10
P.D.Bowler	c Cowdrey b Patel	210	not out	13
J.E.Morris	c De Villiers b Davis	32		
A.M.Brown	lbw b Igglesden	6		
C.J.Adams	c Taylor b Patel	52		
B.Roberts	not out	100		
K.M.Krikken +	not out	27		
I.R.Bishop				
M.Jean-Jacques				
D.E.Malcolm				
S.J.Base				
Extras	(b 2,lb 20,w 1)	23	(w 1)	1
TOTAL	(for 5 wkts dec)	514	(for 0 wkts)	24

DERBYSHIRE	O	M	R	W	O	M	R	W
Bishop	22.1	3	71	6	15	4	45	1
Malcolm	18	7	58	1	17	0	57	2
Base	21	3	85	3	19	3	59	1
Jean-Jacques	21	2	84	0	20.4	5	60	6
Barnett	2	1	2	0	1	0	3	0

KENT	O	M	R	W	O	M	R	W
De Villiers	21	3	75	1				
Igglesden	25	4	113	1				
Ellison	6	0	26	0				
Davis	39	8	152	1				
Patel	27	6	97	2				
Hinks	7	0	29	0				
Marsh					3.4	0	16	0
Taylor					3	0	8	0

FALL OF WICKETS	KEN	DER	KEN	DER
1st	2	138	29	
2nd	3	179	35	
3rd	15	191	46	
4th	40	304	58	
5th	133	449	70	
6th	231		89	
7th	245		134	
8th	259		187	
9th	293		214	
10th	303		232	

HAMPSHIRE vs. NORTHANTS

at Bournemouth on 4th, 6th August 1990
Toss : Hampshire. Umpires : B.J.Meyer and D.O.Oslear
Hants won by an innings and 22 runs (Hants 24 pts (Bt: 4, Bw: 4) N'thants 1 pt (Bt: 0, Bw: 1))

HAMPSHIRE

V.P.Terry	st Ripley b Williams	165
T.C.Middleton	b Williams	123
R.A.Smith	lbw b Williams	0
D.I.Gower	not out	28
M.C.J.Nicholas *	not out	19
M.D.Marshall		
J.R.Ayling		
R.J.Parks +		
R.J.Maru		
C.A.Connor		
P.J.Bakker		
Extras	(b 6,lb 10,w 2,nb 7)	25
TOTAL	(for 3 wkts dec)	360

NORTHANTS

A.Fordham	c Parks b Marshall	58	c Parks b Marshall	1
W.Larkins	c Bakker b Maru	5	lbw b Marshall	1
N.A.Felton	c & b Connor	26	c Ayling b Bakker	99
R.J.Bailey	c Parks b Connor	5	lbw b Marshall	6
A.J.Lamb *	c Parks b Maru	9	lbw b Bakker	15
R.G.Williams	b Maru	16	c Gower b Maru	13
D.Ripley +	c Terry b Marshall	0	c Parks b Ayling	5
J.Hughes	c Maru b Marshall	0	c Parks b Ayling	2
N.G.B.Cook	not out	2	(10) not out	7
W.W.Davis	c Gower b Maru	13	(9) c Smith b Maru	47
M.A.Robinson	b Marshall	0	b Bakker	0
Extras	(lb 5,nb 2)	7	(lb 1)	1
TOTAL		141		197

NORTHANTS	O	M	R	W	O	M	R	W
Davis	21	3	61	0				
Robinson	20	0	60	0				
Cook	24	5	73	0				
Hughes	14	5	47	0				
Williams	19	1	82	3				
Bailey	6	1	21	0				

HAMPSHIRE	O	M	R	W	O	M	R	W
Bakker	9	0	26	0	9.2	0	38	3
Marshall	17	4	37	4	10	4	24	3
Maru	12	3	37	4	17	3	64	2
Connor	7	0	21	2	10	2	22	0
Ayling	3	1	15	0	6	0	48	2

FALL OF WICKETS	HAM	NOR	NOR	HAM
1st	292	11	1	
2nd	294	62	8	
3rd	331	78	24	
4th		95	43	
5th		121	57	
6th		121	70	
7th		125	72	
8th		125	167	
9th		140	197	
10th		141	197	

YORKSHIRE vs. LANCASHIRE

at Headingley on 4th, 6th, 7th August 1990
Toss : Lancashire. Umpires : B.Leadbeater and N.T.Plews
Match drawn (Yorkshire 5 pts (Bt: 1, Bw: 4) Lancashire 8 pts (Bt: 4, Bw: 4))

LANCASHIRE

G.D.Mendis	c Metcalfe b Gough	54	lbw b Fletcher	10
G.Fowler	c Moxon b Carrick	43	c Moxon b Fletcher	6
M.A.Atherton	c Kellett b Jarvis	64	(6) st Blakey b Fletcher	25
N.H.Fairbrother	c Fletcher b Carrick	5	c Blakey b Jarvis	7
G.D.Lloyd	c Blakey b Pickles	36	(3) c Pickles b Jarvis	70
M.Watkinson	b Jarvis	33	(5) run out	1
P.A.J.DeFreitas	st Blakey b Carrick	66	b Jarvis	2
W.K.Hegg +	st Blakey b Carrick	29	not out	0
D.P.Hughes *	b Jarvis	14		
P.J.Martin	not out	10		
B.P.Patterson	not out	4		
Extras	(lb 10,nb 1)	11	(b 1,lb 11)	12
TOTAL	(for 9 wkts dec)	369	(for 7 wkts)	133

YORKSHIRE

M.D.Moxon *	c Fowler b Atherton	14	b Patterson	39
A.A.Metcalfe	c Atherton b Patterson	31	c Atherton b Watkinson	146
D.Gough	lbw b Patterson	3	(10) c Fowler b Atherton	13
R.J.Blakey +	c Fairbrother b Atherton	22	(3) b Watkinson	3
S.A.Kellett	b Watkinson	25	(8) run out	15
P.E.Robinson	c Atherton b Watkinson	2	(4) b Martin	11
D.Byas	c Hughes b Atherton	0	(5) c Hegg b Martin	9
P.Carrick	not out	34	(6) b Martin	5
C.S.Pickles	b Martin	21	(7) c Fowler b Watkinson	39
P.W.Jarvis	c Fowler b Atherton	27	(9) not out	20
S.D.Fletcher	c Hegg b Atherton	0	c Patterson b Atherton	0
Extras	(b 1,lb 1,nb 7)	9	(b 3,lb 11,nb 14)	28
TOTAL		188		328

YORKSHIRE	O	M	R	W	O	M	R	W
Jarvis	21	2	91	3	6.4	0	59	3
Fletcher	15	3	55	0	6	0	62	3
Pickles	16	4	69	1				
Gough	12	3	37	1				
Carrick	36	10	107	4				

LANCASHIRE	O	M	R	W	O	M	R	W
Patterson	18	3	77	2	18	0	88	1
Martin	16	2	54	1	18	1	48	3
Atherton	11	4	26	5	27.2	5	71	2
Watkinson	11	4	29	2	38	14	94	3
Hughes					9	6	6	0
DeFreitas					2	0	7	0

FALL OF WICKETS	LAN	YOR	YOR	LAN
1st	94	23	115	15
2nd	116	41	118	26
3rd	123	50	155	49
4th	195	94	167	55
5th	230	98	197	129
6th	253	100	262	131
7th	328	100	283	133
8th	349	154	296	
9th	355	188	328	
10th		188	328	

SUSSEX vs. WARWICKSHIRE

at Eastbourne on 4th, 6th, 7th August 1990
Toss : Sussex. Umpires : J.D.Bond and M.J.Kitchen
Warwickshire won by 6 wickets (Sussex 4 pts (Bt: 1, Bw: 3) Warwicks 24 pts (Bt: 4, Bw: 4))

SUSSEX

D.M.Smith	c Piper b Munton	18	b Smith G.	4
J.W.Hall	b Moody	30	lbw b Munton	12
R.Hanley	lbw b Smith P.A.	2	c & b Munton	28
A.P.Wells	lbw b Smith P.A.	0	not out	144
M.P.Speight	c Piper b Smith G.	22	b Pierson	11
C.M.Wells *	run out	40	(8) c Smith G. b Reeve	19
A.I.C.Dodemaide	b Munton	4	(9) b Smith P.A.	0
P.Moores +	lbw b Munton	10	(10) c Asif Din b Smith P.A.	0
A.C.S.Pigott	lbw b Smith G.	32	(11) c Piper b Smith P.A.	0
B.T.P.Donelan	c Reeve b Smith G.	6	(7) c Piper b Munton	53
R.A.Bunting	not out	1	(6) c Asif Din b Pierson	2
Extras	(b 4,lb 3,w 1,nb 6)	14	(b 10,lb 6,w 2,nb 2)	20
TOTAL		179		294

WARWICKSHIRE

A.J.Moles	b Dodemaide	58	c Moores b Donelan	39
J.D.Ratcliffe	c Moores b Bunting	61	c Moores b Dodemaide	8
T.M.Moody	c Hall b Donelan	110		
T.A.Lloyd *	b Bunting	1	(3) c Moores b Donelan	28
P.A.Smith	b Dodemaide	2	(4) lbw b Dodemaide	13
D.A.Reeve	c & b Pigott	30	(5) not out	7
Asif Din	not out	57	(6) not out	0
K.J.Piper +	lbw b Pigott	5		
A.R.K.Pierson	b Pigott	9		
G.Smith	b Dodemaide	30		
T.A.Munton				
Extras	(b 1,lb 11)	12	(b 4,lb 3)	7
TOTAL	(for 9 wkts dec)	375	(for 4 wkts)	102

WARWICKS	O	M	R	W	O	M	R	W
Munton	20	7	46	3	28	7	63	3
Smith G.	15.5	2	36	3	11	1	45	1
Smith P.A.	13	3	30	2	11.5	2	45	3
Reeve	14	5	28	0	11	1	31	1
Pierson	3	0	8	0	14	3	65	2
Moody	8	5	7	1				
Asif Din	4	1	17	0	9	5	29	0

SUSSEX	O	M	R	W	O	M	R	W
Pigott	30	4	101	3	3	0	21	0
Dodemaide	28.2	6	84	3	11.2	0	45	2
Bunting	21	2	89	2	3	0	10	0
Donelan	12	3	46	1	6	1	19	2
Wells C.M.	17	5	43	0				

FALL OF WICKETS	SUS	WAR	SUS	WAR
1st	33	113	9	24
2nd	48	131	23	73
3rd	48	143	73	88
4th	79	183	120	98
5th	79	271	130	
6th	93	273	242	
7th	109	279	277	
8th	162	297	294	
9th	170	375	294	
10th	179		294	

BRITANNIC ASSURANCE CHAMPIONSHIP

DERBYSHIRE vs. NORTHANTS
at Chesterfield on 8th, 9th, 10th August 1990
Toss : Northants. Umpires : H.D.Bird and B.Hassan
Match drawn (Derbyshire 6 pts (Bt: 3, Bw: 3) Northants 7 pts (Bt: 4, Bw: 3))

DERBYSHIRE
K.J.Barnett *	b Robinson	20	c Ripley b Robinson		3
P.D.Bowler	c Ripley b Robinson	22	b Hughes		40
A.M.Brown	retired hurt	139			
T.J.G.O'Gorman	c Ripley b Hughes	19	(3) c Bailey b Felton		82
C.J.Adams	c Larkins b Robinson	5	(4) c Fordham b Bailey		12
B.Roberts	c Felton b Ambrose	34	(5) not out		56
K.M.Krikken +	c Capel b Ambrose	0	(6) c Robinson b Cook		24
I.R.Bishop	b Williams	34	(7) c & b Cook		0
G.Miller	b Hughes	36	(8) not out		6
A.E.Warner	run out	24			
O.H.Mortensen	not out	0			
Extras	(lb 9,nb 6)	15	(lb 10,nb 1)		11
TOTAL		348	(for 6 wkts dec)		234

NORTHANTS
A.Fordham	c & b Miller	74	c Krikken b Bishop		4
N.A.Felton	c O'Gorman b Mortensen	5	c Warner b Miller		42
W.Larkins *	c sub b Mortensen	16	b O'Gorman b Miller		5
R.J.Bailey	run out	79	not out		134
D.J.Capel	not out	103	c Krikken b Warner		50
R.G.Williams	lbw b Bishop	9	c Adams b Warner		4
D.Ripley +	c Barnett b Warner	12	hit wicket b Bishop		0
J.Hughes	b Warner	0	(9) run out		4
N.G.B.Cook	not out	0	(8) run out		0
C.E.L.Ambrose			not out		0
M.A.Robinson					
Extras	(lb 13,nb 3)	16	(b 1,lb 6)		7
TOTAL	(for 7 wkts dec)	314	(for 8 wkts)		250

NORTHANTS	O	M	R	W	O	M	R	W		FALL OF WICKETS			
											DER	NOR	DER	NOR
Ambrose	33	8	90	2	9	2	20	0	1st	45	16	9	4
Robinson	26	9	96	3	7	1	24	1	2nd	46	38	73	18
Williams	35	19	41	1	3	0	9	0	3rd	99	185	109	91
Hughes	15	2	57	2	8	1	36	1	4th	118	186	153	188
Cook	19	2	55	0	4	1	19	2	5th	181	221	204	211
Bailey					17	4	44	1	6th	181	310	206	211
Larkins					4	0	24	0	7th	248	310		235
Felton					6	0	48	1	8th	344			246
									9th	348			

DERBYSHIRE	O	M	R	W	O	M	R	W					
Bishop	15	6	27	1	13.5	2	43	2	10th				
Mortensen	13	1	43	2	13	2	42	0					
Warner	21	4	68	2	12	0	96	2					
Miller	19.2	2	108	1	12	0	62	2					
Barnett	12	2	32	0									
Roberts	5	0	23	0									

WORCESTERSHIRE vs. LANCASHIRE
at Kidderminster on 8th, 9th, 10th August 1990
Toss : Worcestershire. Umpires : B.Dudleston and K.E.Palmer
Worcestershire won by 10 wickets (Worcs 24 pts (Bt: 4, Bw: 4) Lancs 2 pts (Bt: 1, Bw: 1))

WORCESTERSHIRE
T.S.Curtis *	lbw b Austin	56	not out		4
G.J.Lord	c Martin b Hughes	101	not out		0
G.A.Hick	c Lloyd b Hughes	67			
D.B.D'Oliveira	run out	59			
D.A.Leatherdale	c Fairbrother b Hughes	70			
C.M.Tolley	not out	28			
S.J.Rhodes +	b Austin	22			
R.K.Illingworth	not out	19			
P.J.Newport					
S.R.Lampitt					
S.M.McEwan					
Extras	(b 10,lb 9,nb 10)	29	(w 4)		4
TOTAL	(for 6 wkts dec)	451	(for 0 wkts)		8

LANCASHIRE
G.D.Mendis	b Newport	15	c D'Oliveira b Lampitt		36
G.Fowler	c Rhodes b Newport	9	lbw b Lampitt		18
G.D.Lloyd	b McEwan	2	b Tolley		14
N.H.Fairbrother	c Rhodes b Newport	22	(9) not out		64
T.E.Jesty	b Lampitt	35	(4) b Illingworth		54
M.Watkinson	lbw b Newport	4	(5) c Rhodes b Lampitt		7
Wasim Akram	c Hick b Newport	14	(6) c D'Oliveira b McEwan		23
W.K.Hegg +	c Lord b Illingworth	47	(7) lbw b McEwan		5
I.D.Austin	c D'Oliveira b Illingworth	0	(8) c Lampitt b Hick		58
D.P.Hughes *	lbw b Illingworth	2	c Leatherdale b Hick		1
P.J.Martin	not out	1	b Illingworth		0
Extras	(lb 5,w 2,nb 2)	9	(b 12,lb 4,nb 1)		17
TOTAL		160			297

LANCASHIRE	O	M	R	W	O	M	R	W		FALL OF WICKETS			
											WOR	LAN	LAN	WOR
Wasim Akram	20	4	68	0					1st	152	19	41	
Martin	17	7	39	0					2nd	189	23	68	
Watkinson	20	3	85	0					3rd	279	35	72	
Austin	27	5	105	2					4th	336	51	99	
Hughes	42	12	135	3					5th	398	55	133	
Lloyd					0.1	0	8	0	6th	424	89	157	

WORCS	O	M	R	W	O	M	R	W					
Newport	18	1	59	5	10	0	48	0	7th		144	167	
McEwan	10	1	31	1	14	3	25	2	8th		149	290	
Tolley	9	1	41	0	10	2	39	1	9th		151	296	
Lampitt	6	1	16	1	16	4	58	3	10th		160	297	
Illingworth	4.1	0	8	3	25.3	3	92	2					
Hick					6	2	19	2					

ESSEX vs. GLAMORGAN
at Southend on 8th, 9th, 10th August 1990
Toss : Glamorgan. Umpires : J.C.Balderstone and J.H.Harris
Match drawn (Essex 7 pts (Bt: 4, Bw: 3) Glamorgan 7 pts (Bt: 4, Bw: 3))

GLAMORGAN
A.R.Butcher *	c Foster b Ilott	0	c Garnham b Andrew		59
H.Morris	c Childs b Foster	9	b Such		28
P.A.Cottey	c Garnham b Foster	51	not out		85
M.P.Maynard	c Childs b Such	46	c Shahid b Andrew		0
I.V.A.Richards	c Stephenson b Ilott	111	not out		118
A.Dale	c Waugh b Andrew	92			
R.D.B.Croft	c Hussain b Foster	6			
C.P.Metson +	not out	15			
S.L.Watkin	c Foster b Andrew	7			
S.Bastien	not out	3			
M.Frost					
Extras	(lb 11,w 1,nb 4)	16	(lb 9,nb 2)		11
TOTAL	(for 8 wkts dec)	356	(for 3 wkts dec)		301

ESSEX
N.Shahid	hit wicket b Bastien	1	c Cottey b Bastien		46
J.P.Stephenson	b Watkin	63	c Metson b Bastien		65
M.C.Ilott	c Metson b Frost	9	(8) b Watkin		17
P.J.Prichard	c Metson b Bastien	34	(3) c Metson b Richards		94
M.E.Waugh	c Richards b Watkin	66	(4) lbw b Frost		14
N.Hussain	lbw b Frost	33	(5) c Morris b Richards		29
M.A.Garnham +	not out	84	(6) b Watkin		19
N.A.Foster *	c Cottey b Watkin	18	(7) run out		16
J.H.Childs	not out	8	(10) not out		1
S.J.W.Andrew			(9) not out		12
P.M.Such					
Extras	(b 4,lb 3,nb 2)	9	(b 4,lb 6,w 1,nb 1)		12
TOTAL	(for 7 wkts dec)	325	(for 8 wkts)		325

ESSEX	O	M	R	W	O	M	R	W		FALL OF WICKETS			
											GLA	ESS	GLA	ESS
Foster	23	6	71	3	7	0	46	0	1st	5	1	86	97
Ilott	17	4	62	2	6	0	22	0	2nd	15	20	94	154
Andrew	16	1	66	2	18	1	67	2	3rd	103	66	95	200
Childs	19	4	69	0	9	2	35	0	4th	121	178		252
Such	20	7	43	1	21	4	73	1	5th	281	181		257
Waugh	3	0	11	0	6	1	40	0	6th	297	230		292
Shahid	4	1	23	0					7th	337	311		294
Prichard					1	0	9	0	8th		345		317

GLAMORGAN	O	M	R	W	O	M	R	W					
Watkin	22	2	72	3	18	0	102	2	9th				
Bastien	20	6	60	2	14	0	75	2	10th				
Frost	20	4	73	2	8	1	51	1					
Croft	12	0	63	0	5	0	24	0					
Dale	3	0	18	0									
Richards	11	3	32	0	10	0	63	2					

KENT vs. LEICESTERSHIRE
at Dartford on 8th, 9th, 10th August 1990
Toss : Leicestershire. Umpires : D.S.Thompsett and A.G.T.Whitehead
Kent won by 7 wickets (Kent 21 pts (Bt: 2, Bw: 3) Leicestershire 4 pts (Bt: 1, Bw: 3))

LEICESTERSHIRE
T.J.Boon	c Ward b Davis	18	lbw b Patel		21
N.E.Briers *	c Fleming b Patel	55	b Davis		35
J.J.Whitaker	c Cowdrey b Patel	6	(7) b Patel		0
P.Willey	c Marsh b Davis	61	c sub b Davis		10
G.J.Parsons	st Marsh b Davis	15	(6) c Marsh b Patel		13
L.Potter	c Marsh b Patel	7	(5) c Marsh b Davis		0
J.D.R.Benson	b Davis	9	(3) c & b Davis		25
P.A.Nixon +	lbw b Davis	17	b Patel		14
J.P.Agnew	c Wren b Patel	0	b Patel		12
A.D.Mullally	c Hinks b Davis	7	b Patel		21
D.J.Millns	not out	0	not out		10
Extras	(lb 5,nb 1)	6	(b 6,lb 12,nb 1)		19
TOTAL		201			180

KENT
S.G.Hinks	c Boon b Willey	14	b Willey		37
M.R.Benson *	c Millns b Potter	107	b Potter		18
N.R.Taylor	b Willey	18	c Boon b Parsons		32
G.R.Cowdrey	c Millns b Parsons	39	not out		17
T.R.Ward	b Parsons	14	not out		0
M.V.Fleming	c Benson b Parsons	31			
S.A.Marsh +	b Mullally	0			
R.P.Davis	lbw b Mullally	0			
M.M.Patel	b Parsons	17			
T.Wren	b Parsons	1			
A.P.Igglesden	not out	0			
Extras	(b 19,lb 6,nb 4)	29	(b 5,lb 3)		8
TOTAL		270	(for 3 wkts)		112

KENT	O	M	R	W	O	M	R	W		FALL OF WICKETS			
											LEI	KEN	LEI	KEN
Igglesden	8	3	19	0	2	0	6	0	1st	41	62	36	43
Wren	7	2	18	0					2nd	68	159	95	67
Davis	44.2	18	63	6	39	9	79	4	3rd	115	173	100	106
Patel	44	13	91	4	37.5	15	57	6	4th	136	213	100	
Ward	1	0	5	0					5th	149	230	119	
Fleming					3	0	20	0	6th	162	231	121	

LEICS	O	M	R	W	O	M	R	W					
Agnew	11	3	44	0	2	0	28	0	7th	185	231	121	
Willey	39	12	94	2	12	3	29	1	8th	190	259	135	
Mullally	15	6	31	2					9th	200	261	163	
Potter	33	15	45	1	15	4	29	1	10th	201	270	180	
Parsons	15	5	31	5	5.5	0	18	1					

BRITANNIC ASSURANCE CHAMPIONSHIP

SOMERSET vs. NOTTINGHAMSHIRE

at Weston-super-Mare on 8th, 9th, 10th August 1990
Toss : Nottinghamshire.   Umpires : P.J.Eele and R.A.White
Match drawn (Somerset 8 pts (Bt: 4, Bw: 4) Nottinghamshire 5 pts (Bt: 2, Bw: 3))

NOTTINGHAMSHIRE

B.C.Broad	c Burns b Mallender	4	c Rose b Mallender	7
M.Newell	c Burns b Trump	59	c Hayhurst b Lefebvre	7
R.T.Robinson *	b Lefebvre	79	(4) not out	125
P.Johnson	c Mallender b Trump	4	(5) b Mallender	12
D.W.Randall	b Trump	0	(6) c Burns b Mallender	0
K.P.Evans	lbw b Mallender	0	(7) not out	100
F.D.Stephenson	b Swallow	34		
B.N.French +	not out	24		
K.E.Cooper	c Tavare b Mallender	7		
K.Saxelby	lbw b Mallender	6	(3) c Cook b Trump	20
J.A.Afford	lbw b Mallender	0		
Extras	(b 4,lb 13,w 3,nb 1)	21	(b 10,lb 6,nb 5)	21
TOTAL		238	(for 5 wkts dec)	292

SOMERSET

S.J.Cook	lbw b Cooper	6
P.M.Roebuck	c French b Cooper	0
A.N.Hayhurst	c & b Saxelby	79
C.J.Tavare *	b Stephenson	96
R.J.Harden	c Afford b Stephenson	0
N.D.Burns +	c & b Afford	56
G.D.Rose	b Afford	60
R.P.Lefebvre	lbw b Evans	0
I.G.Swallow	c Johnson b Cooper	27
N.A.Mallender	not out	17
H.R.J.Trump	st French b Afford	4
Extras	(b 4,lb 24,w 1,nb 14)	43
TOTAL		388

SOMERSET	O	M	R	W	O	M	R	W		FALL OF WICKETS			
											NOT	SOM	NOT	SOM
Mallender	20.1	6	46	5	26	6	69	3	1st	12	1	11
Rose	13	4	37	0	13	4	26	0	2nd	116	17	19
Lefebvre	13	6	20	1	13	5	24	1	3rd	120	181	64
Hayhurst	8	2	24	0	4	0	15	0	4th	120	185	96
Swallow	15	6	33	1	16	5	46	0	5th	121	258	96
Trump	21	5	61	3	19	5	56	1	6th	190	288	
Roebuck					8	1	22	0	7th	201	289	
Harden					6	1	13	0	8th	220	355	
Cook					1	0	5	0	9th	230	365	
									10th	238	388	

NOTTS	O	M	R	W	O	M	R	W
Stephenson	27	2	89	2				
Cooper	20	1	57	3				
Saxelby	16	4	55	1				
Afford	38	11	102	3				
Evans	15	5	57	1				

GLOUCESTERSHIRE vs. WARWICKSHIRE

at Bristol on 8th, 9th, 10th August 1990
Toss : Warwickshire.   Umpires : D.R.Shepherd and P.B.Wight
Gloucestershire won by 66 runs (Glouc 21 pts (Bt: 2, Bw: 3) Warwicks 7 pts (Bt: 3, Bw: 4))

GLOUCESTERSHIRE

G.D.Hodgson	c Ostler b Munton	8	b Small	8
A.J.Wright *	c Lloyd b Small	4	c Reeve b Munton	4
P.W.Romaines	c Ostler b Munton	1	c Smith b Pierson	61
C.W.J.Athey	not out	108	c Piper b Lloyd	122
M.W.Alleyne	c Ratcliffe b Small	34	b Pierson	13
K.M.Curran	c Ratcliffe b Small	15	not out	83
J.W.Lloyds	c Piper b Reeve	14	not out	18
R.C.J.Williams +	c Piper b Reeve	2		
C.A.Walsh	lbw b Reeve	8		
D.V.Lawrence	b Small	7		
S.N.Barnes	c Ostler b Small	0		
Extras	(lb 10,w 2)	12	(b 14,lb 10,nb 1)	25
TOTAL		213	(for 5 wkts dec)	334

WARWICKSHIRE

A.J.Moles	c Lloyds b Curran	94	c Athey b Walsh	12
J.D.Ratcliffe	b Lloyds	75	c Athey b Curran	7
T.A.Lloyd *	c Williams b Lloyds	11	(5) c Lloyds b Curran	5
Asif Din	b Walsh	0	(3) c Williams b Lawrence	65
P.A.Smith	run out	4	(4) c Curran b Walsh	21
D.A.Reeve	lbw b Walsh	1	c Williams b Lawrence	20
D.P.Ostler	c Romaines b Curran	54	b Lloyds	23
K.J.Piper +	c Wright b Curran	0	(9) b Lloyds	9
G.C.Small	c Curran b Alleyne	24	(8) s Williams b Lloyds	5
A.R.K.Pierson	not out	16	not out	0
T.A.Munton	c Hodgson b Curran	2	c Curran b Lloyds	0
Extras	(b 3,lb 17,nb 4)	24	(b 1,lb 6,nb 2)	9
TOTAL		305		176

WARWICKS	O	M	R	W	O	M	R	W		FALL OF WICKETS			
											GLO	WAR	GLO	WAR
Small	23	5	57	5	16	6	39	1	1st	11	131	10	21
Munton	23	5	69	2	22	4	40	1	2nd	13	147	24	23
Reeve	25	4	46	3	6	3	9	0	3rd	13	148	179	51
Smith	10	1	31	0	8	2	26	0	4th	94	164	196	90
Pierson					18	4	69	2	5th	114	171	254	139
Asif Din					5	2	17	0	6th	160	203		140
Lloyd					9	1	58	1	7th	174	211		151
Moles					6	0	52	0	8th	184	257		171
									9th	207	302		176
									10th	213	305		176

GLOUCS	O	M	R	W	O	M	R	W
Walsh	32	10	86	2	11	0	51	2
Curran	27.1	9	50	3	9	0	70	2
Lawrence	16	2	56	1	6	0	37	2
Barnes	15	2	38	0				
Lloyds	19	5	51	2	3.4	0	11	4
Alleyne	2	1	4	1				

HEADLINES

8th - 10th August

● Middlesex remained Championship leaders after drawing with Hampshire at Bournemouth as the other counties chasing the title were unable to force victory. Middlesex had looked well placed after managing 430 for 7 declared in their first innings thanks to a John Emburey century, but Phil Tufnell's six wickets could not prevent Hampshire from avoiding the follow on

● Second placed Warwickshire missed a chance to go top when they could not press home their early advantage over Gloucestershire at Bristol. Two centuries in the match from Bill Athey enabled the home side to declare 242 ahead, then, still hinting victory,Warwickshire collapsed in 29.4 overs to present Gloucestershire with their second win of the season

● Lancashire found Worcestershire at their most impressive at Kidderminster, only an eighth-wicket stand of 123 between Ian Austin and Neil Fairbrother saving them from an innings defeat

● Essex, another side attempting to make a late challenge, finished eight short of victory over Glamorgan at Southend, having been asked to make 333 in 55 overs. Viv Richards had earlier hit 100s in both innings for the first time in his county career

● Both Derbyshire and Northamptonshire had visions of victory at Chesterfield as Northants finished 19 short with two wickets left. Derbyshire's Andrew Brown made his maiden first-class 100 before retiring hurt, while Rob Bailey's 134 not out was not enough to bring Northants to their target of 269 in 50 overs

● Kent's two left-arm spinners will remember their visit to Dartford for many years. Bowling in tandem, Richard Davis and Min Patel both took 10 wickets in the match to spin Kent to a seven-wicket win over Leicestershire. Both recorded career best match figures, while Patel also twice improved his best innings figures

● Yorkshire's long trip down to Eastbourne paid dividends as they enjoyed an innings victory over Sussex, Martyn Moxon hitting the first double century of his career and Phil Carrick returning match figures of 9 for 86 in 64 miserly overs

● Somerset could not press home their advantage over Nottinghamshire at Weston, as Tim Robinson and Kevin Evans, who made his first first-class 100, shared an unbroken sixth-wicket stand of 196 in Notts' second innings

BRITANNIC ASS. CHAMPIONSHIP

CORNHILL TEST MATCH

HAMPSHIRE vs. MIDDLESEX
at Bournemouth on 8th, 9th, 10th August 1990
Toss : Middlesex. Umpires : B.J.Meyer and D.O.Oslear
Match drawn (Hampshire 4 pts (Bt: 2, Bw: 2) Middlesex 5 pts (Bt: 3, Bw: 2))

MIDDLESEX
D.L.Haynes	c Scott b Bakker	75	c Parks b Bakker		0
M.A.Roseberry	c Maru b Marshall	84	c Terry b Bakker		6
M.W.Gatting *	b Bakker	3	(5) c Parks b Maru		35
M.R.Ramprakash	c Parks b Bakker	47	(3) lbw b Marshall		0
K.R.Brown	c Maru b Bakker	23	(4) lbw b Marshall		12
P.R.Downton +	c Parks b Bakker	38	c Smith b Scott		38
J.E.Emburey	not out	111	st Parks b Smith		36
S.P.Hughes	c Scott b Bakker	6	b Smith		0
P.C.R.Tufnell	not out	28	c Parks b Smith		12
N.R.Taylor			lbw b Scott		0
N.G.Cowans			not out		4
Extras	(lb 12,w 1,nb 2)	15	(b 2,lb 2,nb 4)		8
TOTAL	(for 7 wkts dec)	430			151

HAMPSHIRE
T.C.Middleton	run out	31
R.J.Scott	c & b Tufnell	71
C.L.Smith	c Emburey b Tufnell	31
V.P.Terry	c Hughes b Tufnell	31
M.D.Marshall	lbw b Tufnell	9
M.C.J.Nicholas *	c Brown b Tufnell	7
J.R.Ayling	c Taylor b Tufnell	41
R.J.Maru	c Ramprakash b Taylor	43
R.J.Parks +	lbw b Taylor	4
C.A.Connor	c Gatting b Taylor	7
P.J.Bakker	not out	7
Extras	(b 4,lb 6,nb 9)	19
TOTAL		296

HAMPSHIRE	O	M	R	W	O	M	R	W
Bakker	35	8	101	5	6	1	19	2
Marshall	25	5	54	2	11	2	28	2
Maru	40	5	153	0	9	3	40	1
Connor	3	0	15	0				
Ayling	25	5	63	0	5	1	12	0
Smith	1	1	0	0	10	2	35	3
Scott	7	1	24	0	2	1	5	2
Nicholas	1	0	8	0	6	2	8	0

MIDDLESEX	O	M	R	W	O	M	R	W
Cowans	17	5	49	0				
Hughes	18	4	51	0				
Taylor	14	5	44	3				
Emburey	34	8	63	0				
Tufnell	38	11	79	6				

FALL OF WICKETS				
	MID	HAM	MID	HAM
1st	139	104	0	
2nd	143	104	1	
3rd	179	163	11	
4th	219	179	23	
5th	253	187	72	
6th	320	199	126	
7th	370	271	134	
8th		281	143	
9th		285	147	
10th		296	151	

SUSSEX vs. YORKSHIRE
at Eastbourne on 8th, 9th, 10th August 1990
Toss : Yorkshire. Umpires : J.D.Bond and M.J.Kitchen
Yorks won by an innings and 5 runs (Sussex 2 pts (Bt: 1, Bw: 1) Yorks 23 pts (Bt: 4, Bw: 3))

YORKSHIRE
M.D.Moxon *	not out	218
A.A.Metcalfe	b Donelan	53
K.Sharp	c Moores b Wells C.M.	42
P.E.Robinson	c Hansford b Donelan	59
R.J.Blakey +	not out	2
D.Byas		
P.Carrick		
C.S.Pickles		
P.J.Hartley		
P.W.Jarvis		
J.D.Batty		
Extras	(b 12,lb 6,nb 8)	26
TOTAL	(for 3 wkts dec)	400

SUSSEX
D.M.Smith	c Blakey b Pickles	29	c Blakey b Pickles		37
J.W.Hall	c Blakey b Carrick	32	c Hartley b Jarvis		38
R.Hanley	b Jarvis	2	c Metcalfe b Pickles		0
A.P.Wells	c Blakey b Carrick	42	c Blakey b Carrick		4
M.P.Speight	lbw b Jarvis	14	c Blakey b Jarvis		53
C.M.Wells *	c Blakey b Carrick	5	b Carrick		15
A.I.C.Dodemaide	c Byas b Pickles	40	lbw b Hartley		0
P.Moores +	c Blakey b Carrick	10	c & b Carrick		2
A.C.S.Pigott	not out	29	lbw b Carrick		0
B.T.P.Donelan	c Blakey b Carrick	9	not out		10
A.R.Hansford	b Jarvis	2	b Jarvis		0
Extras	(b 14,lb 4)	18	(b 9)		9
TOTAL		227			168

SUSSEX	O	M	R	W	O	M	R	W
Dodemaide	20	3	57	0				
Pigott	21	7	76	0				
Hansford	20	3	76	0				
Wells C.M.	14	3	76	1				
Donelan	28	1	97	2				

YORKSHIRE	O	M	R	W	O	M	R	W
Jarvis	21.4	7	56	3	14.1	4	39	3
Hartley	19	7	50	0	16	2	60	1
Carrick	44	22	49	5	20	6	37	4
Pickles	15	5	28	2	6	2	23	2
Batty	9	1	26	0				

FALL OF WICKETS				
	YOR	SUS	SUS	YOR
1st	120	60	62	
2nd	213	70	62	
3rd	375	70	69	
4th		85	91	
5th		92	124	
6th		158	131	
7th		181	140	
8th		197	148	
9th		218	160	
10th		227	168	

ENGLAND vs. INDIA
at Old Trafford on 9th, 10th, 11th, 13th, 14th August 1990
Toss : England. Umpires : J.H.Hampshire and J.W.Holder
Match drawn

ENGLAND
G.A.Gooch *	c More b Prabhakar	116	c More b Prabhakar		7
M.A.Atherton	c More b Hirwani	131	lbw b Kapil Dev		74
D.I.Gower	c Tendulkar b Kapil Dev	38	b Hirwani		16
A.J.Lamb	c Manjrekar b Kumble	38	b Kapil Dev		109
R.C.Russell +	c More b Hirwani	8	(7) not out		16
R.A.Smith	not out	121	(5) not out		61
J.E.Morris	b Kumble	13	(6) retired hurt		15
C.C.Lewis	b Hirwani	3			
E.E.Hemmings	lbw b Hirwani	19			
A.R.C.Fraser	c Tendulkar b Kumble	1			
D.E.Malcolm	b Shastri	13			
Extras	(b 2,lb 9,w 1,nb 6)	18	(lb 15,nb 7)		22
TOTAL		519	(for 4 wkts dec)		320

INDIA
R.J.Shastri	c Gooch b Fraser	25	b Malcolm		12
N.S.Sidhu	c Gooch b Fraser	13	c sub b Fraser		0
S.V.Manjrekar	c Smith b Hemmings	93	c sub b Hemmings		50
D.B.Vengsarkar	c Russell b Fraser	6	b Lewis		32
M.Azharuddin *	c Atherton b Fraser	179	c Lewis b Hemmings		11
S.R.Tendulkar	c Lewis b Hemmings	68	not out		119
M.Prabhakar	c Russell b Malcolm	4	(8) not out		67
Kapil Dev	lbw b Lewis	0	(7) b Hemmings		26
K.S.More +	b Fraser	6			
A.R.Kumble	run out	2			
N.D.Hirwani	not out	15			
Extras	(b 5,lb 4,nb 12)	21	(b 17,lb 3,nb 6)		26
TOTAL		432	(for 6 wkts)		343

INDIA	O	M	R	W	O	M	R	W
Kapil Dev	13	2	67	1	22	4	69	2
Prabhakar	25	2	112	1	18	1	80	1
Kumble	43	7	105	3	17	3	65	0
Hirwani	62	10	174	4	15	0	52	1
Shastri	17.5	2	50	1	9	0	39	0

ENGLAND	O	M	R	W	O	M	R	W
Malcolm	26	3	96	1	14	5	59	1
Fraser	35	5	124	5	21	3	81	1
Hemmings	29.2	8	74	2	31	10	75	3
Lewis	13	1	61	1	20	3	86	1
Atherton	16	3	68	0	4	0	22	0

FALL OF WICKETS				
	ENG	IND	ENG	IND
1st	225	26	15	4
2nd	292	48	46	35
3rd	312	57	180	109
4th	324	246	248	109
5th	366	358		127
6th	392	364		183
7th	404	365		
8th	434	396		
9th	459	401		
10th	519	432		

Man of the match: S.R.Tendulkar (India)

HEADLINES

England vs India: Second Cornhill Test Match

9th - 14th August

● This was another Test match of almost epic proportions, the final aggregate of runs scored, 1614, being even more than had been seen at Lord's, but the match will be remembered most of all for the maiden Test 100 of Sachin Tendulkar

● After Graham Gooch had won the toss, he and Mike Atherton began where they left off at Lord's, becoming the first England opening pair to share two successive double century stands. They improved their record partnership for England v India to 225 as Gooch made his third Test 100 in succession

● The Indian spinners led a determined fightback on the second morning, but Robin Smith, given valuable support by Devon Malcolm in a last wicket stand of 60, reached his fourth Test 100 to take England past the 500 mark

● After Angus Fraser had reduced them to 57 for 3, the Indians captivated the Saturday crowd with their batsmanship. Again it was Mohammed Azharuddin who held centre stage, hitting his 10th Test 100 and his third in successive matches

● With India reduced to 183 for 6 and almost three hours play still to come, England's victory looked a certainty, but Sachin Tendulkar, aged 17 and 112 days, became the second youngest player after Mushtaq Mohammad to make a Test 100

● Test debut: A.R.Kumble (India)

REFUGE ASSURANCE LEAGUE

MIDDLESEX vs. SUSSEX
at Lord's on 12th August 1990
Toss : Middx. Umpires : B.J.Meyer and A.G.T.Whitehead
Sussex won by 7 wickets (Middlesex 0 pts Sussex 4 pts)

MIDDLESEX
D.L.Haynes	b Wells C.M.	7
M.A.Roseberry	run out	4
M.W.Gatting *	run out	5
M.R.Ramprakash	b Pigott	11
K.R.Brown	c Pigott b Hansford	68
P.R.Downton +	b Donelan	23
J.E.Emburey	c Hanley b Dodemaide	27
N.F.Williams	not out	11
P.C.R.Tufnell	not out	0
N.R.Taylor		
N.G.Cowans		
Extras	(lb 4,w 4)	8
TOTAL	(40 overs)(for 7 wkts)	164

SUSSEX
N.J.Lenham	b Tufnell	78
C.M.Wells *	c Emburey b Taylor	10
A.P.Wells	c Gatting b Williams	30
M.P.Speight	not out	16
A.I.C.Dodemaide	not out	19
R.Hanley		
P.Moores +		
A.C.S.Pigott		
B.T.P.Donelan		
I.D.K.Salisbury		
A.R.Hansford		
Extras	(lb 2,w 6,nb 4)	12
TOTAL	(34.5 overs)(for 3 wkts)	165

SUSSEX	O	M	R	W	FALL OF WICKETS		
						MID	SUS
Dodemaide	8	1	24	1	1st	9	36
Wells C.M.	8	0	28	1	2nd	15	129
Pigott	8	0	20	1	3rd	27	135
Donelan	8	2	23	1	4th	31	
Hansford	5	0	46	1	5th	93	
Salisbury	3	0	19	0	6th	149	
					7th	162	
MIDDLESEX	O	M	R	W	8th		
Taylor	6.5	0	38	1	9th		
Williams	8	0	32	1	10th		
Cowans	8	0	23	0			
Tufnell	7	0	40	1			
Emburey	5	0	30	0			

NORTHANTS vs. LANCASHIRE
at Northampton on 12th August 1990
Toss : Lancs. Umpires : J.H.Hampshire and D.S.Thompsett
Lancashire won by 7 wickets (Northants 0 pts Lancs 4 pts)

NORTHANTS
A.Fordham	c Mendis b Watkinson	44
N.A.Felton	run out	8
W.Larkins *	c Lloyd b DeFreitas	104
R.J.Bailey	c Allott b DeFreitas	47
D.J.Capel	c Allott b DeFreitas	4
D.J.Wild	c Lloyd b DeFreitas	0
R.G.Williams +	not out	1
D.Ripley	not out	6
S.J.Brown		
N.G.B.Cook		
M.A.Robinson		
Extras	(b 2,lb 6,w 1)	9
TOTAL	(40 overs)(for 6 wkts)	223

LANCASHIRE
G.D.Mendis	c Felton b Wild	37
G.Fowler	c Cook b Robinson	81
G.D.Lloyd	c Ripley b Wild	0
N.H.Fairbrother	not out	86
M.Watkinson	not out	6
Wasim Akram		
P.A.J.DeFreitas		
I.D.Austin		
W.K.Hegg +		
D.P.Hughes *		
P.J.W.Allott		
Extras	(lb 10,w 5)	15
TOTAL	(36.5 overs)(for 3 wkts)	225

LANCASHIRE	O	M	R	W	FALL OF WICKETS		
						NOR	LAN
Allott	6	1	19	0	1st	13	67
DeFreitas	8	1	22	4	2nd	71	68
Watkinson	6	0	32	1	3rd	203	209
Wasim Akram	8	0	50	0	4th	214	
Hughes	6	0	49	0	5th	214	
Austin	6	0	43	0	6th	215	
					7th		
NORTHANTS	O	M	R	W	8th		
Brown	4.5	0	21	0	9th		
Robinson	7	0	56	1	10th		
Cook	6	0	42	0			
Wild	8	0	31	2			
Williams	8	0	45	0			
Bailey	3	0	20	0			

WORCESTERSHIRE vs. HAMPSHIRE
at Worcester on 12th August 1990
Toss : Worcs. Umpires : B.Dudleston and K.E.Palmer
Hampshire won by 20 runs (Worcs 0 pts Hampshire 4 pts)

HAMPSHIRE
V.P.Terry	run out	17
R.J.Scott	c McEwan b Hick	53
M.C.J.Nicholas *	c Illingworth b McEwan	17
C.L.Smith	c Lampitt b Hick	21
M.D.Marshall	c Newport b Lampitt	38
J.R.Ayling	not out	47
R.J.Parks +	b Hick	4
R.M.F.Cox	not out	2
R.J.Maru		
T.M.Tremlett		
S.D.Udal		
Extras	(b 4,lb 2,w 2)	8
TOTAL	(40 overs)(for 6 wkts)	207

WORCESTERSHIRE
T.S.Curtis *	b Tremlett	13
G.J.Lord	c Terry b Tremlett	17
G.A.Hick	c Terry b Scott	88
D.A.Leatherdale	lbw b Tremlett	0
M.J.Weston	c Terry b Udal	6
C.M.Tolley	c Terry b Udal	1
S.J.Rhodes +	c Udal b Ayling	26
R.K.Illingworth	b Marshall	7
P.J.Newport	run out	7
S.R.Lampitt	b Scott	8
S.M.McEwan	not out	3
Extras	(lb 10,nb 1)	11
TOTAL	(39.4 overs)	187

WORCS	O	M	R	W	FALL OF WICKETS		
						HAM	WOR
Newport	6	1	33	0	1st	42	32
Weston	8	0	32	0	2nd	81	35
Illingworth	8	0	24	0	3rd	115	35
McEwan	3	0	15	1	4th	115	44
Hick	8	0	47	3	5th	191	46
Lampitt	7	0	50	1	6th	200	125
					7th		165
HAMPSHIRE	O	M	R	W	8th		171
Marshall	8	0	22	1	9th		184
Tremlett	8	0	22	3	10th		187
Ayling	8	0	43	1			
Udal	7	0	36	2			
Maru	7	0	46	0			
Scott	1.4	0	8	2			

GLOUCESTERSHIRE vs. KENT
at Bristol on 12th August 1990
Toss : Gloucs. Umpires : D.R.Shepherd and P.B.Wight
Gloucestershire won by 6 wickets (Gloucs 4 pts Kent 0 pts)

KENT
S.G.Hinks	b Barnes	13
N.R.Taylor	c Athey b Alleyne	37
T.R.Ward	c Alleyne b Barnes	3
G.R.Cowdrey	lbw b Walsh	24
M.V.Fleming	c Alleyne b Bainbridge	10
S.A.Marsh +	c Athey b Curran	24
C.S.Cowdrey *	run out	27
D.J.M.Kelleher	b Walsh	2
P.S.De Villiers	run out	4
C.Penn	c Williams b Walsh	0
R.P.Davis	not out	0
Extras	(lb 3,w 1)	4
TOTAL	(39.2 overs)	148

GLOUCESTERSHIRE
G.D.Hodgson	b Fleming	27
C.W.J.Athey	c & b Kelleher	3
P.Bainbridge	not out	59
K.M.Curran	b Fleming	12
A.J.Wright *	run out	3
M.W.Alleyne	not out	39
P.W.Romaines		
C.A.Walsh		
R.C.J.Williams +		
E.T.Milburn		
S.N.Barnes		
Extras	(lb 4,w 1,nb 1)	6
TOTAL	(35.5 overs)(for 4 wkts)	149

GLOUCS	O	M	R	W	FALL OF WICKETS		
						KEN	GLO
Barnes	8	0	25	2	1st	18	20
Walsh	7.2	0	28	3	2nd	22	65
Curran	8	2	24	1	3rd	75	86
Alleyne	8	0	33	1	4th	90	89
Milburn	4	0	24	0	5th	96	
Bainbridge	4	0	11	1	6th	137	
					7th	140	
KENT	O	M	R	W	8th	148	
Kelleher	8	2	20	1	9th	148	
De Villiers	6.5	2	25	0	10th	148	
Cowdrey C.S.	3	0	20	0			
Fleming	8	1	20	2			
Penn	7	0	44	0			
Davis	3	0	16	0			

YORKSHIRE vs. ESSEX
at Middlesbrough on 12th August 1990
Toss : Essex. Umpires : B.Hassan and A.A.Jones
Yorkshire won by 59 runs (Yorkshire 4 pts Essex 0 pts)

YORKSHIRE
M.D.Moxon *	c Garnham b Ilott	12
A.A.Metcalfe	run out	1
R.J.Blakey +	c Stephenson b Waugh	76
K.Sharp	c Hussain b Waugh	30
P.E.Robinson	c Waugh b Stephenson	14
D.Byas	c Hussain b Ilott	18
P.Carrick	c Hussain b Andrew	30
C.S.Pickles	b Andrew	0
P.J.Hartley	not out	9
P.W.Jarvis	b Waugh	7
A.Sidebottom	not out	8
Extras	(lb 12,w 4)	16
TOTAL	(40 overs)(for 9 wkts)	221

ESSEX
B.R.Hardie *	c Sidebottom b Jarvis	5
J.P.Stephenson	b Sidebottom	4
M.E.Waugh	c Pickles b Hartley	19
P.J.Prichard	c Byas b Jarvis	2
N.Hussain	not out	66
N.Shahid	b Carrick	31
M.A.Garnham +	c Blakey b Carrick	0
T.D.Topley	c Pickles b Carrick	4
M.C.Ilott	run out	6
S.J.W.Andrew	c Metcalfe b Pickles	5
P.M.Such	c Metcalfe b Jarvis	5
Extras	(b 5,lb 8,w 1,nb 1)	15
TOTAL	(34.4 overs)	162

ESSEX	O	M	R	W	FALL OF WICKETS		
						YOR	ESS
Ilott	8	2	24	2	1st	4	11
Andrew	8	2	30	2	2nd	23	11
Such	4	0	35	0	3rd	124	15
Topley	7	0	48	0	4th	131	39
Waugh	8	0	37	3	5th	149	105
Stephenson	5	0	35	1	6th	193	105
					7th	194	124
YORKSHIRE	O	M	R	W	8th	194	131
Jarvis	5.4	0	16	3	9th	208	145
Sidebottom	8	1	22	1	10th		162
Hartley	6	0	27	1			
Carrick	8	0	46	3			
Pickles	7	0	38	1			

NOTTINGHAMSHIRE vs. GLAMORGAN
at Trent Bridge on 12th August 1990
Toss : Notts. Umpires : D.J.Constant and D.O.Oslear
Notts won by 8 wickets (Notts 4 pts Glamorgan 0 pts)

GLAMORGAN
M.P.Maynard	lbw b Cooper	7
H.Morris	c Evans b Mike	9
I.V.A.Richards	c & b Afford	54
A.R.Butcher *	c French b Mike	11
P.A.Cottey	not out	50
A.Dale	c Saxelby b Afford	7
R.D.B.Croft	c Robinson b Stephenson	31
C.P.Metson +	not out	17
S.L.Watkin		
S.J.Dennis		
M.Frost		
Extras	(b 1,lb 4,w 2,nb 1)	8
TOTAL	(40 overs)(for 6 wkts)	194

NOTTINGHAMSHIRE
B.C.Broad	b Richards	26
R.T.Robinson *	not out	107
P.Johnson	c Metson b Richards	23
M.Saxelby	not out	28
M.Newell		
F.D.Stephenson		
K.P.Evans		
B.N.French +		
G.W.Mike		
K.E.Cooper		
J.A.Afford		
Extras	(lb 4,w 10)	14
TOTAL	(37 overs)(for 2 wkts)	198

NOTTS	O	M	R	W	FALL OF WICKETS		
						GLA	NOT
Cooper	8	1	25	1	1st	15	95
Stephenson	8	1	40	1	2nd	28	154
Evans	8	0	47	0	3rd	85	
Mike	8	1	38	2	4th	87	
Afford	8	0	39	2	5th	101	
					6th	151	
GLAMORGAN	O	M	R	W	7th		
Watkin	7	0	27	0	8th		
Frost	8	0	48	0	9th		
Croft	8	0	40	0	10th		
Dennis	5	0	32	0			
Richards	8	0	32	2			
Dale	1	0	15	0			

REFUGE ASSURANCE LEAGUE

OTHER FIRST-CLASS

SOMERSET vs. WARWICKSHIRE

at Weston-super-Mare on 12th August 1990
Toss : Warwickshire. Umpires : R.Julian and K.J.Lyons
Somerset won by 7 wickets (Somerset 4 pts Warwicks 0 pts)

WARWICKSHIRE

A.J.Moles	c Cook b Lefebvre	37
Asif Din	c Tavare b Mallender	113
S.J.Green	b Roebuck	25
P.A.Smith	c Pringle b Rose	33
N.M.K.Smith	c Cook b Roebuck	21
T.A.Lloyd *	not out	12
D.A.Reeve	not out	18
G.W.Humpage +		
R.G.Twose		
J.E.Benjamin		
T.A.Munton		
Extras	(b 1,lb 4,w 6)	11
TOTAL	(40 overs)(for 5 wkts)	270

SOMERSET

S.J.Cook	not out	112
P.M.Roebuck	c Humpage b Benjamin	9
C.J.Tavare *	b Smith P.A.	54
G.D.Rose	c Benjamin b Smith N.M.K.	37
R.J.Harden	not out	41
N.J.Pringle		
N.D.Burns +		
R.P.Lefebvre		
N.A.Mallender		
H.R.J.Trump		
J.C.Hallett		
Extras	(b 2,lb 8,w 8)	18
TOTAL	(37.4 overs)(for 3 wkts)	271

SOMERSET	O	M	R	W	FALL OF WICKETS		
						WAR	SOM
Mallender	8	0	57	1			
Rose	8	0	41	1	1st	70	16
Hallett	2	0	16	0	2nd	130	114
Trump	7	0	43	0	3rd	200	176
Lefebvre	8	0	60	1	4th	237	
Roebuck	7	1	48	2	5th	240	
					6th		
WARWICKSHIRE	O	M	R	W	7th		
Munton	7.4	0	42	0	8th		
Benjamin	8	0	46	1	9th		
Reeve	7	0	55	0	10th		
Smith P.A.	5	0	38	1			
Smith N.M.K.	8	0	59	1			
Twose	2	0	21	0			

SURREY vs. LEICESTERSHIRE

at The Oval on 12th August 1990
Toss : Surrey. Umpires : J.D.Bond and B.Leadbeater
Surrey won by 69 runs (Surrey 4 pts Leicestershire 0 pts)

SURREY

M.A.Feltham	c Nixon b Parsons	0
A.Brown	c Mullally b Gidley	56
G.P.Thorpe	c Millns b Mullally	85
D.M.Ward +	b Gidley	6
M.A.Lynch	c Millns b Gidley	23
I.A.Greig *	c Boon b Benson	26
J.D.Robinson	c Benson b Millns	13
K.T.Medlycott	not out	44
C.K.Bullen	not out	12
M.P.Bicknell		
Waqar Younis		
Extras	(b 2,lb 3,w 5,nb 3)	13
TOTAL	(40 overs)(for 7 wkts)	278

LEICESTERSHIRE

J.J.Whitaker	c Bullen b Bicknell	8
N.E.Briers *	c Bullen b Bicknell	5
B.Smith	c Bullen b Bicknell	10
T.J.Boon	c Thorpe b Bullen	59
L.Potter	run out	6
J.D.R.Benson	c Brown b Bicknell	67
G.J.Parsons	c sub b Waqar Younis	18
P.A.Nixon +	b Waqar Younis	1
M.I.Gidley	not out	5
A.D.Mullally	c Bicknell b Feltham	5
D.J.Millns	b Waqar Younis	0
Extras	(b 5,lb 10,w 10)	25
TOTAL	(40 overs)	209

LEICS	O	M	R	W	FALL OF WICKETS		
						SUR	LEI
Parsons	8	0	70	1			
Millns	8	0	47	1	1st	0	15
Mullally	8	0	57	1	2nd	112	26
Gidley	8	0	45	3	3rd	121	29
Benson	8	1	54	1	4th	163	45
					5th	185	160
SURREY	O	M	R	W	6th	213	193
Bicknell	8	0	26	4	7th	216	196
Feltham	7	0	29	1	8th		196
Bullen	8	0	35	1	9th		208
Medlycott	6	0	39	0	10th		209
Waqar Younis	8	0	43	3			
Robinson	3	0	22	0			

HEADLINES

11th - 13th August

● The annual encounter between Scotland and Ireland was given extra flavour this year by the performance of Ireland's Garfield Harrison who returned career best figures of 9 for 113, the best achieved in first-class cricket in 1990.

● Veterans of the fixture, Iain Philip and Stephen Warke both made 100s as the match ended in a draw

HEADLINES

12th August

● Middlesex suffered a suprise defeat at the hands of Sussex at Lord's to deal their hopes of their first Sunday title a severe blow. Mike Gatting's men could not defend a modest total of 164 for 7

● Lancahire remained in contention with a seven-wicket win over Northants, Graeme Fowler and Neil Fairbrother adding 141 for the third wicket after David Capel had made his second Sunday 100 for Northants

● Hampshire and Notts kept up their hopes of a place in the Refuge Cup with victories over Worcestershire and Glamorgan respectively. Tim Robinson hit his third Sunday League 100 in Notts' eight-wicket win

● Surrey's 278 for 7, based upon a career best 85 from Graham Thorpe, was enough to guarantee victory over Leicestershire, while Gloucestershire and Yorkshire also stayed in the top half of the table with comfortable victories over Kent and Essex

● Somerset gave another demonstration of their formidable batting power, successfully overcoming Warwickshire at Weston. Asif Din had made his highest Sunday score for Warwickshire, but he was eclipsed by Jimmy Cook who made yet another 100 to better Clive Rice's record aggregate for a Sunday League season

SCOTLAND vs. IRELAND

at Edinburgh on 11th, 12th, 13th August 1990
Toss : Ireland. Umpires : J.Breslin and D.N.Herd
Match drawn

IRELAND

M.F.Cohen	b McKnight	60	(2) b Mahmood	15	
M.P.Rea	st Haggo b Russell	22	(3) not out	21	
A.R.Dunlop	c & b Mahmood	56			
S.J.S.Warke *	c Storie b Mahmood	4	(1) not out	100	
D.A.Lewis	c Patterson b McKnight	6			
T.J.T.Patterson	c Patterson b Henry	84			
G.D.Harrison	c Patterson b Mahmood	1			
P.B.Jackson +	st Haggo b Moir	59			
P.McCrum	b Henry	0			
N.Nelson	c Moir b McKnight	0			
A.N.Nelson	not out	23			
Extras	(b 6,lb 4,w 2)	12	(b 2)	2	
TOTAL		327	(for 1 wkt)	138	

SCOTLAND

I.L.Philip	b Harrison	100
B.M.W.Patterson	b Harrison	60
A.C.Storie	b Harrison	32
R.G.Swan *	c sub b Harrison	9
O.Henry	st Jackson b Harrison	47
A.B.Russell	c Nelson N. b Nelson A.N.	47
D.J.Haggo +	lbw b Harrison	34
C.T.McKnight	c Warke b Harrison	0
A.W.Bee	not out	29
J.D.Moir	c Dunlop b Harrison	12
M.Mahmood	c Patterson b Harrison	3
Extras	(lb 8,w 2,nb 7)	17
TOTAL		366

SCOTLAND	O	M	R	W	O	M	R	W	FALL OF WICKETS			
										IRE	SCO	IRE	SCO
Moir	26.3	8	76	1					1st	44	147	51
Bee	19	7	53	0	9	4	20	0	2nd	129	175	
Russell	6	1	23	1					3rd	137	193	
Henry	18	0	54	2	15.4	3	52	0	4th	155	209	
Mahmood	18	5	63	3	13	4	40	1	5th	156	241	
McKnight	16	5	48	3	7	0	24	0	6th	179	316	
									7th	289	316	
IRELAND	O	M	R	W	O	M	R	W	8th	291	324	
McCrum	12	3	28	0					9th	292	353	
Nelson A.N.	33	8	74	1					10th	327	366	
Nelson N.	15	0	51	0								
Harrison	43.2	11	113	9								
Lewis	11	0	55	0								
Dunlop	10	0	37	0								

BRITANNIC ASSURANCE CHAMPIONSHIP

WORCESTERSHIRE vs. HAMPSHIRE

at Worcester on 11th, 13th, 14th August 1990
Toss : Worcestershire.   Umpires : B.Dudleston and K.E.Palmer
Match drawn (Worcestershire 5 pts (Bt: 4, Bw: 1) Hampshire 5 pts (Bt: 4, Bw: 1))

WORCESTERSHIRE

Batsman	How out	Runs	How out	Runs
T.S.Curtis *	c Scott b Joseph	71	not out	38
G.J.Lord	c Middleton b Udal	190	c Joseph b Maru	19
G.A.Hick	c Parks b Joseph	72	not out	50
D.B.D'Oliveira	lbw b Tremlett	30		
D.A.Leatherdale	c Maru b Tremlett	13		
C.M.Tolley	c Parks b Tremlett	2		
S.J.Rhodes +	not out	33		
R.K.Illingworth	not out	9		
P.J.Newport				
S.R.Lampitt				
S.M.McEwan				
Extras	(b 7,lb 15,w 1,nb 6)	29	(b 2,lb 5,nb 4)	11
TOTAL	(for 6 wkts dec)	449	(for 1 wkt dec)	118

HAMPSHIRE

Batsman	How out	Runs	How out	Runs
R.J.Scott	c Rhodes b Newport	17	c D'Oliveira b McEwan	15
C.L.Smith	c Rhodes b Newport	5	c Leatherdale b McEwan	12
T.C.Middleton	not out	117	c D'Oliveira b McEwan	2
V.P.Terry	c Rhodes b Illingworth	40	c D'Oliveira b Illingworth	42
M.C.J.Nicholas *	lbw b Lampitt	6	c & b Lampitt	35
R.M.F.Cox	not out	104	run out	15
L.A.Joseph			not out	43
R.J.Maru			c Tolley b Illingworth	7
R.J.Parks +			c Hick b Illingworth	0
S.D.Udal			not out	0
T.M.Tremlett				
Extras	(lb 6,w 1,nb 6)	13	(lb 3,w 2,nb 4)	9
TOTAL	(for 4 wkts dec)	302	(for 8 wkts)	180

HAMPSHIRE	O	M	R	W	O	M	R	W	FALL OF WICKETS				
										WOR	HAM	WOR	HAM
Joseph	30	4	128	2	8	2	19	0	1st	167	9	40	20
Scott	7	0	38	0	1.4	0	8	0	2nd	331	26		27
Tremlett	23	4	61	3	6	2	22	0	3rd	378	120		34
Maru	29	5	92	0	3	0	13	1	4th	388	141		101
Udal	24	4	95	1					5th	403			120
Nicholas	4	0	13	0	5	0	27	0	6th	404			130
Smith					2	0	22	0	7th				167
									8th				179
WORCS	O	M	R	W	O	M	R	W	9th				
Newport	16	6	23	2	18	2	61	0	10th				
McEwan	12	1	40	0	11	1	38	3					
Lampitt	18	2	39	1	9	0	29	1					
Illingworth	32	6	99	1	21	8	44	3					
Tolley	4	0	15	0									
Hick	17	1	74	0	1.5	0	5	0					
D'Oliveira	1	0	6	0									

YORKSHIRE vs. ESSEX

at Middlesbrough on 11th, 13th August 1990
Toss : Yorkshire.   Umpires : B.Hassan and A.A.Jones
Essex won by an innings and 11 runs (Yorks 4 pts (Bt: 1, Bw: 3) Essex 24 pts (Bt: 4, Bw: 4))

ESSEX

Batsman	How out	Runs
N.Shahid	c Robinson b Jarvis	3
J.P.Stephenson	b Gough	62
P.J.Prichard	b Jarvis	1
M.E.Waugh	not out	207
N.Hussain	c Blakey b Pickles	6
M.A.Garnham +	c Robinson b Gough	35
D.R.Pringle *	c Byas b Pickles	9
N.A.Foster	c Robinson b Carrick	8
S.J.W.Andrew	c Robinson b Carrick	0
J.H.Childs	c Byas b Jarvis	11
P.M.Such	b Jarvis	2
Extras	(lb 5,w 1,nb 1)	7
TOTAL		351

YORKSHIRE

Batsman	How out	Runs	How out	Runs
M.D.Moxon *	c Stephenson b Foster	1	c Waugh b Pringle	27
A.A.Metcalfe	c Shahid b Pringle	60	c Garnham b Andrew	0
K.Sharp	b Such	42	c Pringle b Foster	16
P.E.Robinson	b Pringle	3	c Stephenson b Andrew	39
R.J.Blakey +	c Prichard b Pringle	5	c Garnham b Andrew	26
D.Byas	lbw b Foster	7	c Shahid b Childs	6
P.Carrick	b Such	19	c Shahid b Andrew	3
C.S.Pickles	c Hussain b Such	20	c Shahid b Such	19
P.J.Hartley	lbw b Foster	0	c Garnham b Andrew	5
P.W.Jarvis	not out	8	b Such	0
D.Gough	lbw b Foster	1	not out	0
Extras	(lb 14)	14	(b 8,lb 9,nb 2)	19
TOTAL		180		160

YORKSHIRE	O	M	R	W	O	M	R	W	FALL OF WICKETS				
										ESS	YOR	YOR	ESS
Jarvis	23.5	4	53	4					1st	20	10	2	
Hartley	20	2	71	0					2nd	22	101	30	
Pickles	20	5	68	2					3rd	145	104	57	
Gough	14	1	54	2					4th	160	119	109	
Carrick	22	6	88	2					5th	252	120	124	
Moxon	3	0	12	0					6th	279	143	126	
									7th	306	151	154	
ESSEX	O	M	R	W	O	M	R	W	8th	308	151	160	
Foster	16	3	63	4	6	0	14	1	9th	343	171	160	
Andrew	6	1	28	0	13.1	2	55	5	10th	351	180	160	
Pringle	11	6	15	3	6	1	18	1					
Childs	5	0	26	0	4	0	17	1					
Such	19	6	34	3	11	3	39	2					

NOTTINGHAMSHIRE vs. GLAMORGAN

at Worksop on 11th, 13th, 14th August 1990
Toss : Glamorgan.   Umpires : D.J.Constant and D.O.Oslear
Glamorgan won by 238 runs (Notts 7 pts (Bt: 4, Bw: 3) Glamorgan 22 pts (Bt: 4, Bw: 2))

GLAMORGAN

Batsman	How out	Runs	How out	Runs
A.R.Butcher *	c Evans b Saxelby	13	not out	121
H.Morris	c French b Afford	110	not out	102
P.A.Cottey	c Broad b Pick	5		
M.P.Maynard	b Afford	115		
I.V.A.Richards	c Pick b Saxelby	127		
A.Dale	c Johnson b Evans	7		
R.D.B.Croft	run out	1		
C.P.Metson +	c Cooper b Saxelby	29		
S.L.Watkin	lbw b Saxelby	0		
S.Bastien	not out	10		
M.Frost	lbw b Cooper	0		
Extras	(lb 6,nb 4)	10	(b 4,lb 6,w 1,nb 2)	13
TOTAL		427	(for 0 wkts dec)	236

NOTTINGHAMSHIRE

Batsman	How out	Runs	How out	Runs
R.A.Pick	b Bastien	11	(9) c Cottey b Bastien	2
M.Newell	c Metson b Bastien	10	c Cottey b Bastien	42
B.C.Broad	c Metson b Croft	98	(1) c Metson b Watkin	10
R.T.Robinson *	c Metson b Watkin	46	(3) c Maynard b Frost	8
P.Johnson	c Metson b Bastien	44	(4) c Dale b Frost	12
D.J.R.Martindale	not out	35	(5) c Metson b Bastien	1
K.P.Evans	not out	60	(6) lbw b Bastien	26
B.N.French +			(7) c Maynard b Croft	1
K.E.Cooper			(8) b Bastien	2
K.Saxelby			c Dale b Watkin	3
J.A.Afford			not out	1
Extras	(lb 3,w 3,nb 3)	9	(lb 2,w 1,nb 1)	4
TOTAL	(for 5 wkts dec)	313		112

NOTTS	O	M	R	W	O	M	R	W	FALL OF WICKETS				
										GLA	NOT	GLA	NOT
Pick	13	1	65	1	13	1	55	0	1st	33	19		18
Saxelby	23	4	92	4	12	1	47	0	2nd	57	39		28
Cooper	21.2	4	95	1	9	1	40	0	3rd	221	152		42
Evans	18	3	69	1	7	1	37	0	4th	274	216		55
Afford	29	4	100	2	16	4	47	0	5th	309	216		99
									6th	315			100
GLAMORGAN	O	M	R	W	O	M	R	W	7th	399			102
Watkin	19	2	79	1	10	1	45	2	8th	399			104
Bastien	20	5	71	3	10	2	31	5	9th	427			107
Frost	22	2	79	0	7	0	32	2	10th	427			112
Croft	22	5	65	1	3	1	2	1					
Dale	7	0	16	0									

GLOUCESTERSHIRE vs. KENT

at Bristol on 11th, 13th, 14th August
Toss : Kent.   Umpires : D.R.Shepherd and P.B.Wight
Match drawn (Gloucestershire 4 pts (Bt: 2, Bw: 2) Kent 6 pts (Bt: 4, Bw: 2))

KENT

Batsman	How out	Runs
S.G.Hinks	c Hodgson b Alleyne	53
M.R.Benson *	c Williams b Walsh	65
N.R.Taylor	c Alleyne b Walsh	22
G.R.Cowdrey	c Walsh b Alleyne	80
T.R.Ward	c Walsh b Curran	82
M.V.Fleming	c Athey b Curran	45
S.A.Marsh +	c Hodgson b Walsh	54
D.J.M.Kelleher	c Williams b Walsh	35
R.P.Davis	c sub b Curran	20
C.Penn	not out	23
M.M.Patel		
Extras	(b 1,lb 8,w 1,nb 9)	19
TOTAL	(for 9 wkts dec)	498

GLOUCESTERSHIRE

Batsman	How out	Runs	How out	Runs
G.D.Hodgson	c Marsh b Penn	2	c Benson b Davis	17
A.J.Wright *	b Davis	16	run out	9
P.W.Romaines	c Hinks b Penn	8	c Cowdrey b Davis	21
C.W.J.Athey	c Marsh b Fleming	83	c & b Penn	71
M.W.Alleyne	c Davis b Patel	47	(6) c Ward b Davis	40
K.M.Curran	not out	45	(7) c & b Davis	13
J.W.Lloyds	not out	0	(8) not out	6
C.A.Walsh			(5) b Davis	55
R.C.J.Williams +			not out	0
D.V.Lawrence			st Marsh b Davis	0
S.N.Barnes				
Extras	(b 2,lb 7,w 1,nb 10)	20	(b 7,lb 13,nb 4)	24
TOTAL	(for 5 wkts dec)	221	(for 8 wkts)	256

GLOUCS	O	M	R	W	O	M	R	W	FALL OF WICKETS				
										KEN	GLO	GLO	KEN
Walsh	24	2	117	4					1st	98	2	20	
Curran	22	4	97	3					2nd	145	32	53	
Lawrence	14	4	69	0					3rd	150	33	56	
Barnes	17	1	51	0					4th	293	127	134	
Lloyds	30	6	114	0					5th	350	221	214	
Alleyne	13	3	41	2					6th	362		237	
									7th	448		256	
KENT	O	M	R	W	O	M	R	W	8th	454		256	
Penn	20	5	44	2	13	0	59	1	9th	498			
Kelleher	20	7	35	0	9	1	18	0	10th				
Davis	19	6	59	1	22.5	1	111	6					
Patel	17	4	38	1	11	1	30	0					
Fleming	18	5	36	1	7	0	18	0					

BRITANNIC ASSURANCE CHAMPIONSHIP

NORTHANTS vs. LANCASHIRE

at Northampton on 11th, 13th, 14th August 1990
Toss : Northants.   Umpires : J.H.Harris and D.S.Thompsett
Match drawn (Northants 6 pts (Bt: 4, Bw: 2) Lancashire 5 pts (Bt: 4, Bw: 1))

NORTHANTS

A.Fordham	c Bramhall b Patterson	172	lbw b DeFreitas	24	
N.A.Felton	c DeFreitas b Hughes	66	c Hughes b DeFreitas	51	
W.Larkins *	b Hughes	56			
R.J.Bailey	not out	62	(3) st Bramhall b Hughes	30	
D.J.Capel	c DeFreitas b Hughes	19	(4) c Jesty b Hughes	9	
R.G.Williams	not out	11	(5) not out	10	
D.Ripley +			(6) c Speak b Fowler	34	
S.J.Brown			(7) not out	4	
W.W.Davis					
N.G.B.Cook					
M.A.Robinson					
Extras	(b 14,lb 14,nb 7)	35	(lb 2)	2	
TOTAL	(for 4 wkts dec)	421	(for 5 wkts dec)	164	

LANCASHIRE

G.D.Mendis	b Brown	50	c Capel b Davis	5	
G.Fowler	c Felton b Davis	30	c Williams b Davis	47	
G.D.Lloyd	st Ripley b Cook	59	c Ripley b Robinson	8	
T.E.Jesty	c Capel b Robinson	56	lbw b Cook	8	
N.J.Speak	c Cook b Williams	8	b Capel	0	
P.A.J.DeFreitas	not out	100	st Ripley b Cook	15	
I.D.Austin	run out	5	c Bailey b Davis	11	
D.P.Hughes *	not out	1	not out	1	
S.Bramhall +			not out	0	
P.J.Martin					
B.P.Patterson					
Extras	(b 4,lb 12,w 1,nb 10)	27	(lb 6,w 1,nb 8)	15	
TOTAL	(for 6 wkts dec)	333	(for 7 wkts)	110	

LANCASHIRE	O	M	R	W	O	M	R	W
Patterson	14	2	54	1	6	0	32	0
DeFreitas	15	3	59	0	11	3	23	2
Martin	17	3	64	0	5	0	15	0
Austin	24	5	73	0				
Hughes	30	1	143	3	13	4	45	2
Jesty					2	2	0	0
Fowler					2.1	0	33	1
Lloyd					2	0	14	0

NORTHANTS	O	M	R	W	O	M	R	W
Davis	25	2	85	1	14.4	2	28	3
Robinson	18.2	1	81	1	6	1	19	1
Cook	21	12	53	1	7	2	19	2
Capel	6	2	10	0	8	1	22	1
Brown	8	1	31	1				
Williams	19	7	57	1	9	4	16	0

FALL OF WICKETS				
	NOR	LAN	NOR	LAN
1st	179	79	47	10
2nd	294	84	94	36
3rd	325	180	109	58
4th	365	199	114	59
5th		294	155	84
6th		331		95
7th				108
8th				
9th				
10th				

MIDDLESEX vs. SUSSEX

at Lord's on 11th, 13th, 14th August 1990
Toss : Middlesex.   Umpires : B.J.Meyer and A.G.T.Whitehead
Match drawn (Middlesex 7 pts (Bt: 4, Bw: 3) Sussex 4 pts (Bt: 2, Bw: 2))

MIDDLESEX

D.L.Haynes	not out	255			
M.A.Roseberry	b Donelan	22	(1) lbw b Salisbury	37	
M.W.Gatting *	b Dodemaide	28			
M.R.Ramprakash	c Dodemaide b Salisbury	28	(2) c Wells C.M. b Donelan	5	
K.R.Brown	st Moores b Donelan	2			
P.R.Downton +	c & b Salisbury	3			
J.E.Emburey	c Moores b Salisbury	14			
P.N.Weekes	b Pigott	51	(3) lbw b Donelan	2	
N.F.Williams	lbw b Dodemaide	9	(4) not out	55	
P.C.R.Tufnell	not out	3	(5) not out	0	
N.G.Cowans					
Extras	(b 8,lb 16,nb 10)	34	(b 5,lb 2,nb 1)	8	
TOTAL	(for 8 wkts dec)	449	(for 3 wkts)	107	

SUSSEX

N.J.Lenham	c Downton b Williams	5	
J.W.Hall	c Roseberry b Emburey	49	
D.M.Smith	c Downton b Weekes	42	
A.P.Wells	lbw b Emburey	9	
M.P.Speight	lbw b Cowans	52	
C.M.Wells *	c Brown b Tufnell	1	
A.I.C.Dodemaide	c Brown b Tufnell	26	
P.Moores +	c Brown b Haynes	49	
A.C.S.Pigott	c Gatting b Tufnell	58	
I.D.K.Salisbury	not out	40	
B.T.P.Donelan	not out	8	
Extras	(b 18,lb 14,w 3,nb 13)	48	
TOTAL	(for 9 wkts dec)	387	

SUSSEX	O	M	R	W	O	M	R	W
Pigott	23	2	105	1				
Dodemaide	32	6	75	2				
Donelan	37	5	116	2	22	7	38	2
Salisbury	31	3	115	3	20	4	60	1
Wells C.M.	2	0	14	0	2	0	2	0

MIDDLESEX	O	M	R	W	O	M	R	W
Cowans	11	2	30	1				
Williams	20	4	69	1				
Tufnell	54	20	85	3				
Emburey	51	17	85	2				
Weekes	26	6	68	1				
Haynes	7	1	18	1				

FALL OF WICKETS				
	MID	SUS	MID	SUS
1st	99	9	17	
2nd	188	93	27	
3rd	251	113	103	
4th	270	126		
5th	279	129		
6th	331	196		
7th	427	203		
8th	444	300		
9th		363		
10th				

SURREY vs. LEICESTERSHIRE

at The Oval on 11th, 13th, 14th August 1990
Toss : Leicestershire.   Umpires : J.D.Bond and B.Leadbeater
Surrey won by an innings and 5 runs (Surrey 24 pts (Bt: 4, Bw: 4) Leics 4 pts (Bt: 2, Bw: 2))

LEICESTERSHIRE

T.J.Boon	b Waqar Younis	32	c Ward b Bicknell M.P.	56	
N.E.Briers *	c Greig b Bicknell M.P.	22	b Waqar Younis	16	
J.J.Whitaker	b Waqar Younis	20	b Feltham	23	
P.Willey	b Waqar Younis	1	lbw b Feltham	3	
L.Potter	not out	52	c Greig b Feltham	19	
J.D.R.Benson	c Kendrick b Waqar Younis	7	c Lynch b Bicknell M.P.	5	
P.A.Nixon +	c & b Medlycott	46	not out	17	
G.J.Parsons	run out	14	lbw b Feltham	7	
J.P.Agnew	b Bicknell M.P.	4	b Waqar Younis	3	
A.D.Mullally	c Ward b Bicknell M.P.	9	c & b Feltham	8	
D.J.Millns	b Bicknell M.P.	1	b Feltham	4	
Extras	(b 15,lb 12,w 2,nb 7)	36	(b 6,lb 2,w 1,nb 1)	10	
TOTAL		244		171	

SURREY

D.J.Bicknell	c Whitaker b Millns	111	
G.S.Clinton	c Nixon b Parsons	34	
A.J.Stewart	c Nixon b Mullally	3	
D.M.Ward +	c Benson b Parsons	33	
N.M.Kendrick	c Potter b Millns	9	
M.A.Lynch	c Nixon b Parsons	12	
I.A.Greig *	c & b Parsons	84	
M.A.Feltham	c Whitaker b Parsons	38	
K.T.Medlycott	not out	21	
M.P.Bicknell	c Whitaker b Parsons	23	
Waqar Younis	not out	10	
Extras	(b 6,lb 26,w 1,nb 9)	42	
TOTAL	(for 9 wkts dec)	420	

SURREY	O	M	R	W	O	M	R	W
Waqar Younis	23	2	72	4	17	3	41	2
Bicknell M.P.	22	3	42	4	22	3	69	2
Feltham	15	4	40	0	18.5	4	53	6
Medlycott	20	6	44	1				
Greig	2	0	16	0				
Kendrick	4	1	3	0				

LEICS	O	M	R	W	O	M	R	W
Agnew	30	2	126	0				
Mullally	9	3	14	1				
Millns	25	1	97	2				
Parsons	31	5	75	6				
Willey	18	4	60	0				
Potter	6	0	16	0				

FALL OF WICKETS				
	LEI	SUR	LEI	SUR
1st	55	14	53	
2nd	80	57	99	
3rd	84	97	104	
4th	89	178	107	
5th	99	194	118	
6th	192	274	138	
7th	212	355	146	
8th	225	362	155	
9th	237	400	164	
10th	244		171	

HEADLINES

11th - 14th August

● Essex moved into position to threaten the leaders, as Mark Waugh hit a career best 207* and Essex's bowlers dismantled Yorkshire twice in less than 100 overs

● Surrey also won by an innings, defeating Leicestershire at The Oval as Darren Bicknell made 111 and Mark Feltham returned career best bowling figures of 6 for 53

● Glamorgan's batsmen did much as they pleased against Notts, Viv Richards making his third 100 in succession, and Hugh Morris hitting 100s in both innings, as he and Alan Butcher gave further evidence of being one of the most prolific opening pairs with an unbroken stand of 236. Steve Bastien's 5 for 31 as Notts capitulated in just 30 overs was a career best

● After Desmond Haynes had improved his career best to 255*, it was left to the spinners to bowl Middlesex to victory over Sussex, but the visitors resisted for 169 overs in their first innings, as the leaders were again frustrated

● Worcestershire finished two wickets short of victory over Hampshire. Rupert Cox scored his maiden 100 in his second first-class match, and on the last day Linden Joseph stood firm to deny Worcester

● First-class debut: S.Bramhall (Lancashire)

NATWEST TROPHY SEMI-FINALS

LANCASHIRE vs. MIDDLESEX
at Old Trafford on 15th, 16th (no play), 17th August 1990
Toss : Lancashire.   Umpires: D.J.Constant and B.J.Meyer
Lancashire won by 5 wickets

MIDDLESEX

D.L.Haynes	not out	149
M.A.Roseberry	lbw b Allott	16
M.W.Gatting *	b Watkinson	53
M.R.Ramprakash	run out	45
K.R.Brown	c Hegg b Wasim Akram	1
P.R.Downton +	not out	4
J.E.Emburey		
N.F.Williams		
S.P.Hughes		
A.R.C.Fraser		
N.G.Cowans		
Extras	(b 6,lb 11,w 8,nb 3)	28
TOTAL	(60 overs)(for 4 wkts)	296

LANCASHIRE

G.D.Mendis	not out	121
G.Fowler	b Cowans	8
M.A.Atherton	b Hughes	34
N.H.Fairbrother	c Downton b Hughes	48
M.Watkinson	c Downton b Fraser	43
Wasim Akram	b Fraser	14
P.A.J.DeFreitas	not out	2
W.K.Hegg +		
I.D.Austin		
D.P.Hughes *		
P.J.W.Allott		
Extras	(b 1,lb 21,w 3,nb 4)	29
TOTAL	(55.5 overs)(for 5 wkts)	299

LANCASHIRE	O	M	R	W	FALL OF WICKETS		
						MID	LAN
Allott	12	3	40	1			
DeFreitas	12	0	52	0	1st	23	23
Wasim Akram	12	2	65	1	2nd	147	83
Watkinson	12	1	62	1	3rd	269	185
Austin	12	1	60	0	4th	271	269
					5th		293
MIDDLESEX	O	M	R	W	6th		
Cowans	12	1	40	1	7th		
Fraser	11.5	0	43	2	8th		
Williams	10	0	72	0	9th		
Hughes	12	0	68	2	10th		
Emburey	10	0	54	0			

Man of the match: G.D.Mendis

HEADLINES

NatWest Trophy
Semi-Finals

15th - 17th August

● Both semi-finals were rain-affected, and it was almost 8-30pm on Wednesday evening before the first finalist was known: after David Gower and Malcolm Marshall with a competition best 77 had looked to swing the match their way, Hampshire lost their last six wickets for 37 as Mark Robinson and Curtly Ambrose again proved the ideal end-of-innings bowling combination

● At one stage it looked as if the other match would be decided by a bowling competition, but the weather cleared just in time for the contest to be completed on the third afternoon. Desmond Haynes's 149*, his first NatWest 100, had seemed to put Middlesex in a strong posisiton, but Lancashire reached their target of 297 with four overs to spare, Gehan Mendis making an unbeaten 121, his third 100 in the competition

HAMPSHIRE vs. NORTHANTS
at Southampton on 15th August 1990
Toss : Hants. Umpires: K.J.Lyons and A.G.T.Whitehead
Northants won by 1 run

NORTHANTS

A.Fordham	c Ayling b Bakker	1
N.A.Felton	c Gower b Connor	31
W.Larkins	c Parks b Ayling	48
A.J.Lamb *	c Smith C.L. b Maru	58
D.J.Capel	c Nicholas b Maru	43
R.J.Bailey	c Parks b Connor	8
R.G.Williams	b Connor	44
D.Ripley +	c Maru b Marshall	7
C.E.L.Ambrose	s Parks b Ayling	22
N.G.B.Cook	not out	6
M.A.Robinson	b Connor	0
Extras	(lb 6,w 9,nb 1)	16
TOTAL	(60 overs)	284

HAMPSHIRE

V.P.Terry	c Robinson b Cook	24
C.L.Smith	c Felton b Robinson	0
R.A.Smith	c Ripley b Capel	20
D.I.Gower	c Capel b Williams	86
M.D.Marshall	c & b Cook	77
M.C.J.Nicholas *	c Lamb b Cook	29
J.R.Ayling	c Williams b Robinson	8
R.J.Parks +	c Felton b Ambrose	4
R.J.Maru	c Capel b Robinson	10
C.A.Connor	not out	7
P.J.Bakker	run out	2
Extras	(lb 12,w 4)	16
TOTAL	(60 overs)	283

HAMPSHIRE	O	M	R	W	FALL OF WICKETS		
						NOR	HAM
Marshall	12	3	37	1	1st	6	6
Bakker	12	2	41	1	2nd	70	37
Connor	12	1	73	4	3rd	111	55
Ayling	12	0	76	2	4th	177	196
Maru	12	0	51	2	5th	205	246
NORTHANTS	O	M	R	W	6th	205	253
Ambrose	12	4	29	1	7th	230	259
Robinson	12	1	62	3	8th	272	269
Cook	12	3	52	3	9th	284	280
Capel	12	1	67	1	10th	284	283
Williams	12	1	61	1			

Man of the match: M.D.Marshall

Gehan Mendis, the backbone of Lancashire's perfectly-paced reply to the daunting target set by Middlesex.

REFUGE ASSURANCE LEAGUE

DERBYSHIRE vs. MIDDLESEX
at Derby on 19th August 1990
Toss : Middlesex. Umpires : J.C.Balderstone and P.B.Wight
No result (Derbyshire 2 pts Middlesex 2 pts)

DERBYSHIRE

K.J.Barnett *	c Haynes b Williams	5
P.D.Bowler +	b Fraser	50
J.E.Morris	c Roseberry b Cowans	48
A.P.Kuiper	lbw b Emburey	18
C.J.Adams	run out	3
T.J.G.O'Gorman	not out	0
B.Roberts		
A.E.Warner		
D.E.Malcolm		
S.J.Base		
O.H.Mortensen		
Extras	(lb 3,nb 1)	4
TOTAL	(14 overs)(for 5 wkts)	128

MIDDLESEX

D.L.Haynes	not out	48
M.A.Roseberry	c Bowler b Warner	0
M.W.Gatting *	run out	7
M.R.Ramprakash	not out	26
K.R.Brown		
P.R.Downton +		
J.E.Emburey		
N.F.Williams		
S.P.Hughes		
A.R.C.Fraser		
N.G.Cowans		
Extras	(lb 1,w 2,nb 1)	4
TOTAL	(9.2 overs)(for 2 wkts)	85

MIDDLESEX	O	M	R	W	FALL OF WICKETS		
						DER	MID
Cowans	2	0	26	1			
Williams	3	0	27	1	1st	29	1
Hughes	3	0	18	0	2nd	100	10
Emburey	3	0	30	1	3rd	116	
Fraser	3	0	24	1	4th	128	
					5th	128	
DERBYSHIRE	O	M	R	W	6th		
Warner	3	0	20	1	7th		
Mortensen	3	0	22	0	8th		
Malcolm	2	0	17	0	9th		
Kuiper	1	0	15	0	10th		
Base	0.2	0	10	0			

NOTTINGHAMSHIRE vs. GLOUCS
at Trent Bridge on 19th August 1990
Toss : Nottinghamshire. Umpires : J.D.Bond and N.T.Plews
No result (Notts 2 pts Gloucs 2 pts)

GLOUCESTERSHIRE

C.W.J.Athey	lbw b Cooper	2
K.M.Curran	b Cooper	15
P.Bainbridge	c French b Mike	2
R.C.Russell +	c French b Mike	45
M.W.Alleyne	c Stephenson b Mike	19
C.A.Walsh	c Saxelby b Stephenson	23
A.J.Wright *	not out	21
P.W.Romaines	not out	15
G.D.Hodgson		
E.T.Milburn		
D.V.Lawrence		
Extras	(lb 6,w 2,nb 2)	10
TOTAL	(20 overs)(for 6 wkts)	152

NOTTINGHAMSHIRE

B.C.Broad	c Athey b Alleyne	22
R.T.Robinson *	c Hodgson b Lawrence	6
P.Johnson	not out	25
M.Saxelby	not out	24
M.Newell		
F.D.Stephenson		
K.P.Evans		
B.N.French +		
G.W.Mike		
E.E.Hemmings		
K.E.Cooper		
Extras	(b 1,lb 2,w 3)	6
TOTAL	(11.4 overs)(for 2 wkts)	83

NOTTS	O	M	R	W	FALL OF WICKETS		
						GLO	NOT
Mike	4	0	30	3			
Cooper	4	0	21	2	1st	6	18
Evans	4	0	27	0	2nd	11	37
Stephenson	4	0	28	1	3rd	45	
Hemmings	3	0	30	0	4th	79	
Saxelby	1	0	10	0	5th	109	
					6th	120	
GLOUCS	O	M	R	W	7th		
Lawrence	4	0	23	1	8th		
Curran	2	0	11	0	9th		
Alleyne	2	0	12	1	10th		
Walsh	2	0	15	0			
Milburn	1	0	15	0			
Bainbridge	0.4	0	4	0			

WORCESTERSHIRE vs. NORTHANTS
at Worcester on 19th August 1990
Toss : Northants. Umpires : D.J.Constant and B.Leadbeater
No result (Worcestershire 2 pts Northants 2 pts)

WORCESTERSHIRE

T.S.Curtis *	not out	83
G.J.Lord	c Ripley b Penberthy	78
G.A.Hick	c Penberthy b Cook	26
D.B.D'Oliveira	c Wild b Robinson	58
D.A.Leatherdale	b Robinson	0
M.J.Weston	not out	3
S.J.Rhodes +		
R.K.Illingworth		
P.J.Newport		
S.R.Lampitt		
S.M.McEwan		
Extras	(lb 11,w 3,nb 3)	17
TOTAL	(35 overs)(for 4 wkts)	265

NORTHANTS

A.Fordham	c McEwan b Weston	21
W.Larkins	c Curtis b Newport	1
A.J.Lamb *	c Leatherdale b Newport	10
D.J.Capel	not out	1
R.J.Bailey	not out	0
D.J.Wild		
A.L.Penberthy		
D.Ripley +		
W.W.Davis		
N.G.B.Cook		
M.A.Robinson		
Extras	(w 2)	2
TOTAL	(8.4 overs)(for 3 wkts)	35

NORTHANTS	O	M	R	W	FALL OF WICKETS		
						WOR	NOR
Davis	8	0	58	0			
Robinson	5	0	36	2	1st	116	7
Larkins	3	0	20	0	2nd	151	33
Capel	5	0	35	0	3rd	248	35
Cook	8	0	54	1	4th	251	
Penberthy	5	0	45	1	5th		
Wild	1	0	6	0	6th		
					7th		
WORCS	O	M	R	W	8th		
Newport	4.4	0	15	2	9th		
Weston	4	0	20	1	10th		

WARWICKSHIRE vs. LEICESTERSHIRE
at Edgbaston on 19th August 1990
Toss : Warwickshire. Umpires : J.W.Holder and K.E.Palmer
No result (Warwickshire 2 pts Leicestershire 2 pts)

LEICESTERSHIRE

T.J.Boon	b Small	5
N.E.Briers *	b Munton	2
B.Smith	st Piper b Booth	29
C.C.Lewis	lbw b Small	43
J.D.R.Benson	b Small	14
L.Potter	not out	7
M.I.Gidley	not out	2
P.A.Nixon +		
G.J.Parsons		
A.D.Mullally		
D.J.Millns		
Extras	(b 1,lb 10,w 8)	19
TOTAL	(28.1 overs)(for 5 wkts)	121

WARWICKSHIRE

A.J.Moles	
Asif Din	
T.M.Moody	
P.A.Smith	
T.A.Lloyd *	
S.J.Green	
N.M.K.Smith	
K.J.Piper +	
G.C.Small	
P.A.Booth	
T.A.Munton	
Extras	
TOTAL	

WARWICKS	O	M	R	W	FALL OF WICKETS		
						LEI	WAR
Small	8	0	20	3			
Munton	6.1	1	8	1	1st	5	
Moody	3	0	23	0	2nd	15	
Booth	5	0	33	1	3rd	81	
Smith P.A.	6	0	26	0	4th	109	
					5th	118	
LEICS	O	M	R	W	6th		
					7th		
					8th		
					9th		
					10th		

HEADLINES

19th August

● On a day that could have seen Derbyshire win the Sunday League for the first time, nothing was decided as heavy rain, returning with a vengeance, put paid to all six matches, two without a ball bowled

● Middlesex had looked set to beat Derbyshire at Derby with Haynes and Ramprakash going well and Nottinghamshire were well placed to beat Gloucestershire at Trent Bridge in the two matches that most affected the top of the table

● All was left to the last round of matches with Derbyshire, Lancashire and Middlesex all able to win the League and Notts competing with Hampshire for the remaining place in the Refuge Cup

ESSEX vs SURREY
at Chemsford on 19th August 1990
Match abandoned without a ball being bowled
(Essex 2pts Surrey 2pts)

KENT vs SUSSEX
at Canterbury on 19th August 1990
Match abandoned without a ball being bowled
(Kent 2pts Sussex 2pts)

TOUR MATCHES

BRITANNIC ASS. CHAMPIONSHIP

TCCB U25 XI vs. INDIA

at Edgbaston on 15th, 16th, 17th August 1990
Toss : TCCB U25 XI.   Umpires : M.J.Harris and D.O.Oslear
Match drawn

INDIA

W.V.Raman	lbw b Stephenson	61	(2) lbw b Munton	56
N.S.Sidhu	c Blakey b Lampitt	13	(1) not out	108
S.V.Manjrekar	c Stephenson b Medlycott	116		
D.B.Vengsarkar	c Hussain b Bicknell M.P.	54		
S.R.Tendulkar	c Lampitt b Bicknell M.P.	39	not out	30
R.J.Shastri *	lbw b Bicknell M.P.	4		
M.Prabhakar	not out	2	(4) st Blakey b Medlycott	23
N.R.Mongia +	not out	1	(3) b Illingworth	11
A.Wasson				
S.K.Sharma				
A.R.Kumble				
Extras	(lb 2,nb 1)	3	(b 3,lb 6,nb 1)	10
TOTAL	(for 6 wkts dec)	293	(for 3 wkts dec)	238

TCCB U25 XI

J.P.Stephenson *	c Mongia b Kumble	116	not out	41
N.Shahid	st Mongia b Shastri	39	lbw b Prabhakar	0
G.P.Thorpe	b Sharma	18	lbw b Sharma	5
N.Hussain	not out	37		
P.Johnson	b Wasson	3	(4) lbw b Prabhakar	1
R.J.Blakey +			(5) not out	40
K.T.Medlycott				
R.K.Illingworth				
S.R.Lampitt				
M.P.Bicknell				
T.A.Munton				
Extras	(b 8,lb 1,nb 10)	19	(b 7,lb 15,nb 1)	23
TOTAL	(for 4 wkts dec)	232	(for 3 wkts)	110

TCCB U25 XI	O	M	R	W	O	M	R	W
Munton	23	9	49	0	14	6	26	1
Bicknell M.P.	22	6	50	3	9	2	26	0
Lampitt	18	2	62	1	8	0	33	0
Medlycott	9	1	46	1	5	0	29	1
Stephenson	6	2	18	1	6	2	16	0
Illingworth	24	5	66	0	17	3	58	1
Shahid					5	0	41	0

INDIA	O	M	R	W	O	M	R	W
Prabhakar	5	0	13	0	7	3	13	2
Sharma	16	1	57	1	10	3	24	1
Wasson	19.3	1	74	1	14	6	18	0
Tendulkar	14	3	40	0	6	1	24	0
Shastri	5	3	11	1				
Kumble	19	8	28	1	5	1	9	0

FALL OF WICKETS

	IND	U25	IND	U25
1st	33	118	134	1
2nd	118	175	167	12
3rd	220	214	194	19
4th	278	232		
5th	287			
6th	290			
7th				
8th				
9th				
10th				

GLAMORGAN vs. INDIA

at Swansea on 18th, 19th (no play), 20th August 1990
Toss : India.   Umpires : A.A.Jones and K.J.Lyons
Match drawn

INDIA

N.S.Sidhu	c James b Dale	54	not out	76
W.V.Raman	b Dale	59	not out	20
S.V.Manjrekar	lbw b Anthony	4		
Kapil Dev	b Anthony	0		
M.Azharuddin *	c Maynard b Anthony	21		
S.R.Tendulkar	c Cottey b Croft	68		
K.S.More +	c Metson b Croft	8		
N.R.Mongia	b Dale	60		
S.K.Sharma	c Morris b Croft	9		
A.R.Kumble	not out	35		
A.Wasson				
Extras	(lb 8,w 3,nb 1)	12	(w 2)	2
TOTAL	(for 9 wkts dec)	330	(for 0 wkts dec)	98

GLAMORGAN

S.P.James	c More b Sharma	7	c More b Wasson	15
H.Morris	not out	23	c Sidhu b Wasson	73
P.A.Cottey	lbw b Kapil Dev	0	c More b Wasson	29
M.P.Maynard	not out	4	b Wasson	26
A.R.Butcher *			lbw b Wasson	12
A.Dale			c More b Kumble	0
R.D.B.Croft			not out	50
H.A.Anthony			c More b Wasson	0
C.P.Metson +			not out	50
S.J.Dennis				
S.Bastien				
Extras	(lb 1,nb 4)	5	(b 8,lb 2,nb 8)	18
TOTAL	(for 2 wkts dec)	39	(for 7 wkts)	273

GLAMORGAN	O	M	R	W	O	M	R	W
Anthony	25	3	95	3	1	0	2	0
Bastien	22	7	61	0				
Dennis	15	2	63	0				
Croft	17	3	82	3				
Dale	8.3	1	21	3	9	0	62	0
Maynard					9	1	34	0

INDIA	O	M	R	W	O	M	R	W
Kapil Dev	6	3	8	1	19	3	58	0
Sharma	5	1	23	1	9	2	48	0
Wasson	1	0	5	0	23	3	89	6
Kumble	1	0	2	0	21	8	51	1
Tendulkar					1	0	5	0
Raman					2	0	12	0

FALL OF WICKETS

	IND	GLA	IND	GLA
1st	115	14		63
2nd	126	31		116
3rd	126			132
4th	128			167
5th	168			168
6th	210			170
7th	227			170
8th	240			
9th	330			
10th				

LANCASHIRE vs. YORKSHIRE

at Old Trafford on 18th, 19th (no play), 20th, 21st August
Toss : Lancashire. Umpires : R.A.White and A.G.T.Whitehead
Match drawn (Lancashire 5 pts (Bt: 4, Bw: 1) Yorkshire 4 pts (Bt: 1, Bw: 3))

LANCASHIRE

G.D.Mendis	c Batty b Hartley	13	(3) not out	15
G.Fowler	c Batty b Hartley	7	not out	50
M.A.Atherton	c Byas b Carrick	108		
N.H.Fairbrother	c Moxon b Hartley	99		
M.Watkinson	c Robinson b Carrick	138		
Wasim Akram	c Hartley b Carrick	8	(1) c Blakey b Jarvis	6
P.A.J.DeFreitas	b Batty	4		
W.K.Hegg +	c Byas b Carrick	3		
I.D.Austin	not out	21		
D.P.Hughes *	c Byas b Hartley	16		
P.J.W.Allott	st Blakey b Carrick	2		
Extras	(b 10,lb 2,nb 2)	14	(w 1,nb 1)	2
TOTAL		433	(for 1 wkt dec)	73

YORKSHIRE

M.D.Moxon	not out	90	c Fowler b Atherton	50
A.A.Metcalfe	lbw b DeFreitas	2	c Allott b Watkinson	39
K.Sharp	retired hurt	5	(10) not out	9
P.E.Robinson	c Hughes b Watkinson	70	(3) c Hughes b Watkinson	9
R.J.Blakey +	c Allott b Watkinson	1	(4) c Hegg b Atherton	4
D.Byas	not out	2	(5) c Allott b Atherton	39
P.Carrick *			(6) lbw b Watkinson	57
C.S.Pickles			(7) c Hegg b Watkinson	16
P.J.Hartley			(8) lbw b Wasim Akram	0
P.W.Jarvis			(9) b Watkinson	11
J.D.Batty			not out	7
Extras	(b 8,lb 1,w 2,nb 9)	20	(b 10,lb 6,nb 9)	25
TOTAL	(for 3 wkts dec)	190	(for 9 wkts)	266

YORKSHIRE	O	M	R	W	O	M	R	W
Jarvis	20	3	73	0	3	2	2	1
Hartley	22	1	109	4	2.1	0	10	0
Pickles	12	0	57	0	5	1	17	0
Carrick	40	11	98	5				
Batty	22	1	84	1				
Metcalfe					5.4	0	44	0

LANCASHIRE	O	M	R	W	O	M	R	W
Wasim Akram	16	1	47	0	21	8	46	1
DeFreitas	12	1	44	1	5	0	30	0
Austin	4	2	5	0				
Allott	4	1	10	0				
Atherton	12	3	42	0	25	6	69	3
Watkinson	10	3	24	2	44	12	105	5
Hughes	8	5	9	0				

FALL OF WICKETS

	LAN	YOR	LAN	YOR
1st	18	3	11	77
2nd	29	171		107
3rd	164	177		109
4th	335			116
5th	349			178
6th	354			223
7th	365			224
8th	392			237
9th	422			258
10th	433			

HEADLINES

15th - 17th August

● The TCCB Under-25 XI's match against the Indians at Edgbaston proved a disappointing spectacle, except for contrasting 100s by Sanjay Manjrekar, Navjot Sidhu and the Under-25 XI's captain John Stephenson

18th - 20th August

● India's county programme ended with another draw, their match against Glamorgan at Swansea not recovering from the loss of the second day, although Atul Wasson was able to stake his claim for a Test place with six second innings wickets

18th -21st August

● Lancashire were denied victory over Yorkshire in the Roses Match at Old Trafford by the narrowest of margins, Kevin Sharp coming to the crease with a broken thumb to bat out time with number 11, Jeremy Batty. Mike Atherton had made his 7th 100 of the summer and Mike Watkinson a career best 138, before the pair combined to take eight second innings wickets

● Jimmy Cook moved on relentlessly, hitting his 8th 100 of the season and surpassing his 1989 run aggregate, as Somerset at last gained their second Championship win of the year at the expense of Hampshire at Taunton

BRITANNIC ASSURANCE CHAMPIONSHIP

SOMERSET vs. HAMPSHIRE

at Taunton on 18th, 19th, 20th, 21st August 1990
Toss : Hampshire.   Umpires : J.H.Harris and B.Hassan
Somerset won by 5 wickets (Somerset 22 pts (Bt: 4, Bw: 2) Hampshire 8 pts (Bt: 4, Bw: 4))

HAMPSHIRE

Batsman		1st			2nd
V.P.Terry	c Jones b Rose	96	c & b Harden		59
C.L.Smith	lbw b Mallender	1	c & b Harden		88
D.I.Gower	c Burns b Jones	14	c Harden b Lefebvre		29
R.A.Smith	c Burns b Mallender	58	not out		13
M.D.Marshall	lbw b Swallow	58			
M.C.J.Nicholas *	lbw b Jones	0	(5) not out		6
J.R.Ayling	not out	62			
R.J.Maru	c Lefebvre b Mallender	46			
R.J.Parks +	lbw b Mallender	1			
C.A.Connor	not out	29			
P.J.Bakker	b Mallender	20			
Extras	(lb 11,nb 5)	16	(lb 4,nb 2)		6
TOTAL	(for 9 wkts dec)	401	(for 3 wkts dec)		201

SOMERSET

Batsman		1st		2nd
S.J.Cook	c Parks b Maru	114	lbw b Marshall	77
P.M.Roebuck	c Connor b Bakker	0	c Parks b Nicholas	19
A.N.Hayhurst	c Parks b Connor	28	st Parks b Maru	47
C.J.Tavare *	c Parks b Maru	66	run out	64
R.J.Harden	lbw b Marshall	0	c Gower b Connor	36
N.D.Burns +	c & b Maru	37	(7) not out	8
G.D.Rose	c Smith C.L. b Marshall	13	(6) not out	33
R.P.Lefebvre	c Parks b Maru	37		
N.A.Mallender	b Marshall	17		
A.N.Jones	not out	8		
I.G.Swallow	not out	0		
Extras	(lb 11,nb 6)	17	(b 10,lb 8,w 1,nb 1)	20
TOTAL	(for 9 wkts dec)	301	(for 5 wkts)	304

SOMERSET	O	M	R	W	O	M	R	W
Jones	22	3	87	2	9	1	21	0
Mallender	27	3	102	5	8	1	23	0
Lefebvre	19	6	59	0	12.4	1	40	1
Rose	15	2	48	1	3	2	2	0
Hayhurst	12	2	40	0	6	0	38	0
Swallow	17	7	37	1				
Roebuck	4	0	17	0	8	0	34	0
Harden					8	0	39	2

HAMPSHIRE	O	M	R	W	O	M	R	W
Bakker	22	6	58	1	11	0	53	0
Marshall	16	3	43	3	11	2	34	1
Connor	17	2	75	1	8	0	45	1
Maru	37.3	5	103	4	24.2	2	123	1
Nicholas	6	2	11	0	2	0	7	1
Smith C.L.					1	0	2	0
Ayling					3	0	22	0

FALL OF WICKETS

	HAM	SOM	HAM	SOM
1st	4	1	135	84
2nd	26	65	182	147
3rd	129	179	182	155
4th	221	180		246
5th	222	181		272
6th	242	194		
7th	347	273		
8th	356	284		
9th	401	292		
10th				

WORCESTERSHIRE vs. NORTHANTS

at Worcester on 18th, 20th, 21st August 1990
Toss : Northants. Umpires : D.J.Constant and B.Leadbeater
Match drawn (Worcestershire 6 pts (Bt: 2, Bw: 4) Northants 6 pts (Bt: 2, Bw: 4))

NORTHANTS

Batsman		1st		2nd
A.Fordham	c Hick b Lampitt	81	c Rhodes b Newport	19
N.A.Felton	c Rhodes b Dilley	10	c Rhodes b McEwan	11
W.Larkins	c D'Oliveira b Newport	27	c Rhodes b Illingworth	26
R.J.Bailey	c McEwan b Lampitt	7	run out	66
D.J.Capel	st Rhodes b Illingworth	12	lbw b Dilley	0
A.J.Lamb *	c Illingworth b McEwan	63	c Rhodes b Illingworth	28
A.L.Penberthy	c Rhodes b Hick	1	c Lampitt b Hick	21
D.Ripley +	c Hick b Illingworth	14	not out	26
C.E.L.Ambrose	b Illingworth	12	b Illingworth	12
N.G.B.Cook	b Illingworth	2	not out	7
M.A.Robinson	not out	0		
Extras	(b 1,lb 5,w 1,nb 6)	13	(b 2,lb 12,nb 1)	15
TOTAL		242	(for 8 wkts dec)	231

WORCESTERSHIRE

Batsman		1st		2nd
T.S.Curtis *	lbw b Ambrose	48	lbw b Ambrose	12
G.J.Lord	c Ripley b Capel	17	lbw b Robinson	6
S.M.McEwan	b Cook	14		
G.A.Hick	c Ripley b Cook	34	(3) st Ripley b Cook	50
D.B.D'Oliveira	c Penberthy b Cook	0	(4) c & b Robinson	21
D.A.Leatherdale	c Capel b Cook	52	(5) c Felton b Cook	7
S.R.Lampitt	lbw b Ambrose	0	(6) c Lamb b Cook	16
S.J.Rhodes +	not out	44	(7) not out	28
R.K.Illingworth	lbw b Robinson	9	(8) lbw b Cook	0
P.J.Newport	c Larkins b Robinson	1	(9) not out	8
G.R.Dilley	b Cook	8		
Extras	(lb 2,nb 4)	6	(b 4,lb 2,nb 3)	9
TOTAL		233	(for 7 wkts)	157

WORCS	O	M	R	W	O	M	R	W
Dilley	16	3	36	1	10	0	48	1
Newport	17	2	67	1	6	1	11	1
McEwan	11	1	39	1	5	2	11	1
Lampitt	17	7	44	2	4	0	18	0
Illingworth	17.4	6	29	4	38	12	63	3
Hick	7	0	21	1	24	8	66	1

NORTHANTS	O	M	R	W	O	M	R	W
Ambrose	26	7	53	2	11	3	28	1
Robinson	22	3	63	2	13	4	40	2
Capel	4	0	13	1				
Cook	40.1	17	80	5	19.4	3	57	4
Bailey	8	1	22	0	7	2	26	0

FALL OF WICKETS

	NOR	WOR	NOR	WOR
1st	27	25	19	19
2nd	114	44	51	20
3rd	132	88	77	70
4th	132	92	78	85
5th	168	153	121	111
6th	182	153	184	132
7th	223	171	190	132
8th	233	196	221	
9th	241	198		
10th	242	233		

DERBYSHIRE vs. MIDDLESEX

at Derby on 18th, 20th, 21st August 1990
Toss : Derbyshire. Umpires : J.C.Balderstone and P.B.Wight
Derbyshire won by 171 runs (Derbyshire 22 pts (Bt: 2, Bw: 4) Middlesex 6 pts (Bt: 2, Bw: 4))

DERBYSHIRE

Batsman		1st		2nd
K.J.Barnett *	c Downton b Fraser	3	c Gatting b Emburey	7
P.D.Bowler	b Emburey	38	c Gatting b Emburey	56
J.E.Morris	b Emburey	67	c Roseberry b Tufnell	12
T.J.G.O'Gorman	c Brown b Emburey	55	c Brown b Fraser	20
A.P.Kuiper	b Fraser	0	c Downton b Emburey	30
B.Roberts	c Haynes b Williams	27	not out	48
K.M.Krikken +	c Brown b Emburey	6	c Roseberry b Emburey	0
G.Miller	lbw b Cowans	1	not out	32
M.Jean-Jacques	not out	17		
S.J.Base	lbw b Emburey	0		
O.H.Mortensen	c Brown b Fraser	1		
Extras	(b 10,lb 24,w 1,nb 2)	37	(lb 16,nb 9)	25
TOTAL		249	(for 6 wkts dec)	230

MIDDLESEX

Batsman		1st		2nd
M.A.Roseberry	c Bowler b Mortensen	7	(2) b Base	2
N.F.Williams	lbw b Base	5	(8) c Bowler b Miller	3
M.W.Gatting *	not out	119	(5) c Kuiper b Base	4
M.R.Ramprakash	lbw b Base	1	(3) lbw b Base	8
D.L.Haynes	b Mortensen	12	(1) c Kuiper b Mortensen	8
K.R.Brown	c Krikken b Mortensen	7	(4) c Kuiper b Base	12
P.R.Downton +	c & b Mortensen	4	(6) c Barnett b Base	3
J.E.Emburey	b Miller	14	(7) c Bowler b Jean-Jacques	12
A.R.C.Fraser	b Base	8	st Krikken b Miller	26
P.C.R.Tufnell	c O'Gorman b Miller	10	lbw b Miller	5
N.G.Cowans	c Jean-Jacques b Miller	0	not out	5
Extras	(b 10,lb 7,nb 5)	22	(b 8,lb 2,nb 1)	11
TOTAL		209		99

MIDDLESEX	O	M	R	W	O	M	R	W
Fraser	19.1	4	49	3	19	5	46	1
Williams	16	2	56	1	10	1	39	0
Cowans	12	3	40	1	4	0	14	0
Tufnell	16	6	38	0	16	3	29	1
Emburey	18	4	32	5	36	8	71	4
Ramprakash					2	0	15	0

DERBYSHIRE	O	M	R	W	O	M	R	W
Base	27	4	92	3	14	3	28	5
Mortensen	22	11	29	4	10	4	21	1
Miller	14.5	3	31	3	9.5	3	21	3
Jean-Jacques	15	2	40	0	5	0	19	1

FALL OF WICKETS

	DER	MID	DER	MID
1st	4	13	36	4
2nd	112	17	70	18
3rd	119	28	91	22
4th	126	79	131	28
5th	176	89	137	37
6th	203	97	143	38
7th	204	155		41
8th	236	166		88
9th	236	205		94
10th	249	209		99

WARWICKSHIRE vs. LEICESTERSHIRE

at Edgbaston on 18th, 20th, 21st August 1990
Toss : Leicestershire. Umpires : J.W.Holder and K.E.Palmer
Leicestershire won by 6 wickets (Warwickshire 5 pts (Bt: 1, Bw: 4) Leics 22 pts (Bt: 2, Bw: 4))

WARWICKSHIRE

Batsman		1st		2nd
A.J.Moles	c Nixon b Agnew	5	c Willey b Lewis	30
J.D.Ratcliffe	c Lewis b Agnew	15	lbw b Parsons	14
T.A.Lloyd *	c Lewis b Agnew	0	lbw b Agnew	4
T.M.Moody	c Willey b Parsons	26	c Willey b Agnew	117
P.A.Smith	b Millns	22	c Lewis b Agnew	2
D.A.Reeve	c Nixon b Millns	1	c Boon b Agnew	31
Asif Din	lbw b Parsons	0	c Briers b Agnew	1
K.J.Piper +	c Agnew b Parsons	36	b Lewis	11
G.C.Small	b Lewis	16	not out	10
P.A.Booth	c sub b Parsons	14	c Potter b Lewis	10
T.A.Munton	not out	0	b Lewis	0
Extras	(lb 12,w 2,nb 5)	19	(b 8,lb 4,nb 7)	19
TOTAL		154		249

LEICESTERSHIRE

Batsman		1st		2nd
T.J.Boon	c Moles b Reeve	40	c Lloyd b Munton	5
N.E.Briers *	lbw b Reeve	33	c sub b Reeve	55
J.J.Whitaker	b Moody	16	c Small b Munton	13
P.Willey	c Piper b Munton	46	not out	51
L.Potter	c Piper b Small	13	lbw b Reeve	3
C.C.Lewis	c Munton b Smith	38	not out	25
J.D.R.Benson	c Moles b Munton	1		
P.A.Nixon +	not out	25		
G.J.Parsons	b Reeve	1		
J.P.Agnew	c Moody b Reeve	0		
D.J.Millns	run out	4		
Extras	(b 5,lb 19,w 1)	25	(lb 9,w 1)	10
TOTAL		242	(for 4 wkts)	162

LEICESTERSHIRE	O	M	R	W	O	M	R	W
Agnew	18	5	51	3	21	4	75	5
Lewis	17	4	48	1	24.5	6	70	4
Parsons	10	2	21	4	16	3	53	1
Millns	10	1	22	2	11	2	39	0

WARWICKSHIRE	O	M	R	W	O	M	R	W
Small	20	8	34	1	9	2	36	0
Munton	22	5	74	2	11	2	21	2
Booth	5	1	7	0	5.2	0	34	0
Smith	10	1	25	1	2	0	11	0
Moody	12	2	36	1				
Reeve	20	7	42	4	14	1	51	2

FALL OF WICKETS

	WAR	LEI	WAR	LEI
1st	20	78	38	17
2nd	27	101	47	43
3rd	27	109	60	107
4th	72	156	71	121
5th	75	170	208	
6th	76	171	217	
7th	81	224	222	
8th	122	229	232	
9th	154	231	249	
10th	154	242	249	

BRITANNIC ASSURANCE CHAMPIONSHIP

SUSSEX vs. KENT

at Hove on 18th, 20th, 21st August 1990
Toss : Sussex.   Umpires : P.J.Eele and R.Julian
Match drawn (Sussex 5 pts (Bt: 3, Bw: 2) Kent 6 pts (Bt: 4, Bw: 2))

KENT

S.G.Hinks	b Dodemaide	7	b Dodemaide	4
M.R.Benson	retired hurt	115		
N.R.Taylor	c Pigott b Dodemaide	61	(2) not out	70
G.R.Cowdrey	b Dodemaide	29	lbw b Pigott	34
T.R.Ward	lbw b Donelan	64	c Moores b Pigott	12
M.V.Fleming	b Pigott	30	b Pigott	16
C.S.Cowdrey *	c Lenham b Donelan	20	b Pigott	0
S.A.Marsh +	not out	70		
R.P.Davis	c Speight b Pigott	29	(3) c Moores b Pigott	0
P.S.De Villiers	not out	15	(8) not out	19
T.Wren				
Extras	(b 3,lb 3,w 2,nb 1)	9	(b 5,lb 1)	6
TOTAL	(for 7 wkts dec)	449	(for 6 wkts dec)	161

SUSSEX

N.J.Lenham	b Fleming	86	c Cowdrey C.S. b Fleming	20
J.W.Hall	b Fleming	24	c sub b Davis	52
P.Moores +	run out	23	(9) not out	1
A.P.Wells	c Ward b Davis	78	c & b Davis	36
M.P.Speight	c Cowdrey C.S. b Fleming	14	lbw b Davis	1
C.M.Wells *	not out	41	not out	42
D.M.Smith	not out	6	(3) c Ward b Davis	71
A.I.C.Dodemaide			(7) c De Villiers b Davis	13
A.C.S.Pigott			(8) c Ward b Davis	10
B.T.P.Donelan				
R.A.Bunting				
Extras	(b 14,lb 4,w 6,nb 3)	27	(b 14,lb 5)	19
TOTAL	(for 5 wkts dec)	299	(for 7 wkts)	265

SUSSEX	O	M	R	W	O	M	R	W
Pigott	22	5	93	2	18	2	77	5
Dodemaide	31	4	123	3	12.4	2	43	1
Bunting	22	5	88	0	7	1	28	0
Wells C.M.	19	5	80	0				
Donelan	16	4	59	2	3	0	7	0

KENT	O	M	R	W	O	M	R	W
De Villiers	14	1	34	0	14	3	46	0
Wren	21	4	74	0	7	0	39	0
Fleming	27	10	65	3	14	3	38	1
Cowdrey C.S.	5	0	16	0				
Davis	31	11	89	1	31.4	10	97	6
Ward	2	0	3	0	5	0	26	0

FALL OF WICKETS

	KEN	SUS	KEN	SUS
1st	60	53	5	50
2nd	212	129	6	132
3rd	227	180	54	193
4th	311	202	72	198
5th	311	293	116	201
6th	365		116	221
7th	418			247
8th				
9th				
10th				

NOTTINGHAMSHIRE vs. GLOUCESTERSHIRE

at Trent Bridge on 18th, 20th, 21st August 1990
Toss : Gloucestershire.   Umpires : J.D.Bond and N.T.Plews
Match drawn (Nottinghamshire 7 pts (Bt: 3, Bw: 4) Gloucestershire 6 pts (Bt: 2, Bw: 4))

GLOUCESTERSHIRE

A.J.Wright *	lbw b Pick	2	(2) b Pick	0
G.D.Hodgson	b Stephenson	4	(1) c French b Stephenson	0
P.Bainbridge	b Stephenson	6	c French b Stephenson	29
C.W.J.Athey	lbw b Pick	37	c Newell b Pick	0
M.W.Alleyne	lbw b Pick	1	lbw b Pick	69
K.M.Curran	lbw b Stephenson	54	b Stephenson	7
R.C.Russell +	b Afford	79	not out	103
C.A.Walsh	lbw b Pick	29	(9) c Saxelby b Hemmings	18
M.C.J.Ball	c Robinson b Hemmings	14	(8) c Stephenson b Hemmings	1
D.V.Lawrence	st French b Afford	0	c Evans b Afford	18
S.N.Barnes	not out	0	b Pick	3
Extras	(lb 5,w 1,nb 7)	13	(b 2,nb 5)	7
TOTAL		239		255

NOTTINGHAMSHIRE

B.C.Broad	c Russell b Walsh	13	c Russell b Alleyne	35
M.Newell	c Alleyne b Lawrence	78	c Russell b Walsh	6
R.T.Robinson *	lbw b Lawrence	123	c Hodgson b Walsh	13
D.J.R.Martindale	lbw b Lawrence	0	not out	66
M.Saxelby	not out	11	c Walsh b Curran	13
K.P.Evans	lbw b Lawrence	0	c Russell b Curran	0
F.D.Stephenson	c Alleyne b Lawrence	0	c Bainbridge b Curran	0
B.N.French +	b Alleyne	5	lbw b Lawrence	4
E.E.Hemmings	b Alleyne	0	c Curran b Lawrence	0
R.A.Pick	c & b Alleyne	3	not out	4
J.A.Afford	b Walsh	0		
Extras	(b 4,lb 10,w 1,nb 11)	26	(b 1,lb 5,w 1,nb 7)	14
TOTAL		259	(for 8 wkts)	155

NOTTS	O	M	R	W	O	M	R	W
Stephenson	18	0	66	3	27	4	94	3
Pick	18	2	70	4	21.1	10	45	4
Evans	13	3	51	0	9	1	38	0
Afford	13.1	4	28	2	17	8	28	1
Hemmings	9	3	19	1	29	7	48	2

GLOUCS	O	M	R	W	O	M	R	W
Walsh	23.1	6	44	2	13	0	41	2
Curran	15	3	36	0	9	0	35	3
Lawrence	18	1	51	5	10.5	2	41	2
Barnes	13	5	39	0				
Alleyne	9	3	23	3	6	1	23	1
Athey	2	1	2	0				
Ball	11	1	32	0	2	0	9	0
Bainbridge	5	0	18	0				

FALL OF WICKETS

	GLO	NOT	GLO	NOT
1st	4	26	0	20
2nd	6	229	2	42
3rd	15	231	2	85
4th	16	234	61	109
5th	104	234	79	110
6th	117	234	121	111
7th	161	250	137	140
8th	222	250	168	147
9th	238	258	231	
10th	239	259	255	

HEADLINES

18th - 21st August

● Derbyshire became the first county in 1990 to be penalised 25 points by the TCCB for producing an unsatisfactory pitch at Derby. On the field the county had a successful time, defeating Middlesex by 171 runs, despite 119 not out from Mike Gatting and nine wickets for John Emburey.

● Essex took advantage of Middlesex's misfortune to move within striking distance of the top of the table by beating Surrey by 283 runs at Chelmsford. Neil Foster, relishing more favourable bowling conditions, returned match figures of 11 for 76 as Surrey offered little fight in either innings

● Warwicks dropped to third place with a disappointing performance against Leics, brightened only by another batting exhibition from Tom Moody. He completed 1,000 first-class runs for the season in his 12th innings and hit his seventh 100 in eight matches, unprecented achievements for a player in his first season of county cricket

● Six second innings wickets for Richard Davis, making 24 in three matches for the slow left-armer, could not bring Kent victory over Sussex at Hove, while the efforts of Richard Illingworth and Nick Cook went similarly unrewarded as Worcestershire drew with Northants

● David Lawrence's hat-trick changed the character of Gloucestershire's match agianst Notts at Trent Bridge: the home side had been 10 runs behind with nine wickets in hand, yet finished with a lead of just 20.

ESSEX vs. SURREY

at Chelmsford on 18th, 20th, 21st August 1990
Toss : Surrey.   Umpires : H.D.Bird and J.H.Hampshire
Essex won by 283 runs (Essex 22 pts (Bt: 2, Bw: 4) Surrey 4 pts (Bt: 0, Bw: 4))

ESSEX

G.A.Gooch *	c Greig b Waqar Younis	9	c Clinton b Robinson	53
J.P.Stephenson	c Greig b Waqar Younis	7	b Murphy	36
P.J.Prichard	c Medlycott b Murphy	27	c Ward b Greig	42
M.E.Waugh	c Ward b Waqar Younis	0	not out	79
N.Hussain	b Murphy	29	c Kendrick b Greig	8
N.Shahid	lbw b Murphy	27	(7) not out	55
M.A.Garnham +	c Thorpe b Murphy	32		
N.A.Foster	c Medlycott b Murphy	58	(6) c Ward b Greig	0
M.C.Ilott	lbw b Robinson	7		
J.H.Childs	run out	4		
S.J.W.Andrew	not out	9		
Extras	(b 12,lb 14,w 1)	27	(b 4,lb 2,w 2)	8
TOTAL		236	(for 5 wkts dec)	281

SURREY

G.S.Clinton	c Gooch b Ilott	10	c Garnham b Andrew	32
A.J.Stewart	lbw b Andrew	53	c Ilott b Foster	11
N.M.Kendrick	b Andrew	12	(9) c Hussain b Ilott	3
G.P.Thorpe	c Garnham b Andrew	0	(3) c Garnham b Foster	0
D.M.Ward +	c Shahid b Andrew	0	(4) c Shahid b Andrew	11
M.A.Lynch	b Foster	4	(5) b Childs	25
J.D.Robinson	hit wicket b Foster	0	(6) b Foster	18
I.A.Greig *	c Garnham b Foster	0	(7) c Gooch b Foster	4
K.T.Medlycott	c Hussain b Foster	20	(8) not out	11
Waqar Younis	not out	11	b Foster	1
A.J.Murphy	b Foster	1	c Waugh b Foster	0
Extras	(lb 2,nb 1)	3	(lb 4)	4
TOTAL		114		120

SURREY	O	M	R	W	O	M	R	W
Waqar Younis	18.3	4	51	3	11	2	64	0
Murphy	26.1	4	67	5	18	0	73	1
Robinson	21.3	5	49	1	15	4	39	1
Greig	4	0	16	0	15	0	60	3
Medlycott	3	0	27	0				
Kendrick					8	0	39	0

ESSEX	O	M	R	W	O	M	R	W
Foster	19.2	4	44	5	18	6	32	6
Ilott	17	5	41	1	14	2	40	1
Andrew	11	3	27	4	9	2	34	2
Childs					6	2	10	1

FALL OF WICKETS

	ESS	SUR	ESS	SUR
1st	9	13	80	27
2nd	28	47	98	27
3rd	28	57	168	58
4th	79	70	186	59
5th	82	78	186	99
6th	142	78		101
7th	156	78		112
8th	209	96		115
9th	218	110		120
10th	236	114		120

REFUGE ASSURANCE LEAGUE

GLAMORGAN vs. WORCESTERSHIRE
at Swansea on 26th August 1990
Toss : Glam. Umpires : R.Palmer and A.G.T.Whitehead
Worcestershire won by 34 runs (Glam 0 pts Worcs 4 pts)

WORCESTERSHIRE

T.S.Curtis	c Richards b Dale	95
G.J.Lord	lbw b Watkin	7
G.A.Hick	st Metson b Croft	31
D.B.D'Oliveira	b Richards	14
I.T.Botham	b Dale	4
P.A.Neale *	c Croft b Watkin	7
S.J.Rhodes +	not out	23
R.K.Illingworth	run out	1
P.J.Newport	st Metson b Dale	0
S.R.Lampitt	run out	6
S.M.McEwan		
Extras	(lb 15,w 11)	26
TOTAL	(40 overs)(for 9 wkts)	214

GLAMORGAN

M.P.Maynard	c & b Lampitt	36
H.Morris	c Illingworth b Newport	7
I.V.A.Richards	c & b Newport	3
A.R.Butcher *	c & b Newport	30
P.A.Cottey	st Rhodes b Illingworth	8
A.Dale	c D'Oliveira b Hick	34
R.D.B.Croft	c Hick b McEwan	13
C.P.Metson +	run out	10
S.L.Watkin	b Lampitt	0
S.J.Dennis	c Neale b Newport	14
M.Frost	not out	1
Extras	(lb 9,w 14,nb 1)	24
TOTAL	(37.2 overs)	180

GLAMORGAN	O	M	R	W	FALL OF WICKETS		
						WOR	GLA
Frost	6	0	32	0			
Watkin	7	1	33	2	1st	17	17
Dennis	8	0	42	0	2nd	97	23
Croft	8	0	39	1	3rd	126	85
Richards	3	0	18	1	4th	153	87
Dale	8	0	35	3	5th	172	107
					6th	188	137
WORCS	O	M	R	W	7th	206	162
McEwan	8	0	52	1	8th	207	162
Newport	6.2	1	19	3	9th	214	164
Lampitt	7	0	28	2	10th		180
Illingworth	8	1	19	2			
Hick	8	0	53	1			

NORTHANTS vs. GLOUCESTERSHIRE
at Northampton on 26th August 1990
Toss : Gloucestershire. Umpires : P.J.Eele and K.E.Palmer
Northants won by 2 runs (Northants 4 pts Gloucs 0 pts)

NORTHANTS

G.Cook	b Curran	16
W.Larkins *	c Alleyne b Milburn	109
A.Fordham	c Wright b Bainbridge	50
R.J.Bailey	c Milburn b Alleyne	20
D.J.Capel	c Barnes b Alleyne	16
N.A.Felton	b Walsh	24
D.J.Wild	b Walsh	15
W.W.Davis	c Barnes b Curran	9
W.M.Noon +	c & b Curran	0
J.G.Thomas	c & b Walsh	4
N.G.B.Cook	not out	0
Extras	(b 1,lb 5,w 4,nb 1)	11
TOTAL	(40 overs)	274

GLOUCESTERSHIRE

C.W.J.Athey	c & b Thomas	22
M.W.Alleyne	c Cook N.G.B. b Wild	38
P.Bainbridge	c Felton b Wild	2
K.M.Curran	c Capel b Thomas	92
A.J.Wright *	b Capel	50
P.W.Romaines	b Davis	31
C.A.Walsh	b Davis	14
G.D.Hodgson	not out	2
E.T.Milburn	not out	4
R.C.J.Williams +		
S.N.Barnes		
Extras	(lb 10,w 6,nb 1)	17
TOTAL	(40 overs)(for 7 wkts)	272

GLOUCS	O	M	R	W	FALL OF WICKETS		
						NOR	GLO
Barnes	6	0	22	0			
Walsh	8	0	36	3	1st	28	44
Curran	8	0	45	3	2nd	111	58
Milburn	5	0	54	1	3rd	200	105
Alleyne	7	0	49	2	4th	201	208
Bainbridge	6	0	62	1	5th	225	245
					6th	245	265
NORTHANTS	O	M	R	W	7th	268	266
Thomas	8	0	43	2	8th	268	
Davis	8	0	40	2	9th	273	
Capel	8	0	62	1	10th	274	
Wild	8	0	58	2			
Cook N.G.B.	8	0	59	0			

LEICESTERSHIRE vs. KENT
at Leicester on 26th August 1990
Toss : Leics. Umpires : B.Dudleston and D.O.Oslear
Leicestershire won by 6 wickets (Leics 4 pts Kent 0 pts)

KENT

S.G.Hinks	c & b Benson	60
N.R.Taylor	c Whitaker b Parsons	52
T.R.Ward	c Whitaker b Parsons	0
G.R.Cowdrey	c Benson b Millns	43
C.S.Cowdrey *	c Nixon b Millns	6
M.V.Fleming	b Benson	9
S.A.Marsh +	not out	18
V.J.Wells	not out	7
D.J.M.Kelleher		
R.P.Davis		
T.Wren		
Extras	(lb 5,w 9)	14
TOTAL	(39 overs)(for 6 wkts)	209

LEICESTERSHIRE

T.J.Boon	run out	97
N.E.Briers *	c Hinks b Wren	16
B.Smith	lbw b Davis	6
J.J.Whitaker	c & b Fleming	20
C.C.Lewis	not out	58
J.D.R.Benson	not out	1
W.K.M.Benjamin		
P.A.Nixon +		
G.J.Parsons		
M.I.Gidley		
D.J.Millns		
Extras	(lb 4,w 7,nb 1)	12
TOTAL	(38.5 overs)(for 4 wkts)	210

LEICS	O	M	R	W	FALL OF WICKETS		
						KEN	LEI
Benjamin	7	0	40	0			
Parsons	8	0	37	2	1st	110	42
Lewis	8	0	23	0	2nd	117	55
Millns	8	0	47	2	3rd	122	109
Gidley	3	0	24	0	4th	164	202
Benson	5	0	33	2	5th	175	
					6th	188	
KENT	O	M	R	W	7th		
Kelleher	7.5	0	50	0	8th		
Wren	6	0	31	1	9th		
Davis	8	1	29	1	10th		
Ward	8	0	44	0			
Fleming	8	0	47	1			
Wells	1	0	5	0			

SUSSEX vs. SOMERSET
at Hove on 26th August 1990
Toss : Sussex. Umpires : J.C.Balderstone and R.A.White
Somerset won by 60 runs (Sussex 0 pts Somerset 4 pts)

SOMERSET

S.J.Cook	c Pigott b Lenham	45
R.J.Bartlett	c Moores b Dodemaide	2
C.J.Tavare *	b Wells C.M.	12
R.J.Harden	c Moores b Wells C.M.	0
G.D.Rose	c Gould b Pigott	7
A.N.Hayhurst	not out	70
N.D.Burns +	c & b Dodemaide	58
R.P.Lefebvre	b Pigott	7
A.N.Jones	c Lenham b Dodemaide	2
H.R.J.Trump	b Dodemaide	0
J.C.Hallett	not out	3
Extras	(b 1,lb 1,w 14)	16
TOTAL	(40 overs)(for 9 wkts)	222

SUSSEX

N.J.Lenham	c Burns b Jones	19
I.J.Gould	b Jones	5
A.P.Wells	c Jones b Trump	31
M.P.Speight	c Burns b Hayhurst	21
C.M.Wells *	c Jones b Hayhurst	3
K.Greenfield	b Hayhurst	31
A.I.C.Dodemaide	not out	31
A.C.S.Pigott	c Hayhurst b Trump	14
P.Moores +	b Hayhurst	1
I.D.K.Salisbury	run out	7
B.T.P.Donelan	b Lefebvre	7
Extras	(b 1,lb 11,w 10,nb 2)	24
TOTAL	(35.4 overs)	162

SUSSEX	O	M	R	W	FALL OF WICKETS		
						SOM	SUS
Dodemaide	8	0	40	4			
Wells C.M.	7	1	28	2	1st	14	12
Pigott	8	0	39	2	2nd	38	37
Salisbury	6	0	32	0	3rd	38	79
Donelan	6	0	37	0	4th	61	85
Lenham	5	0	44	1	5th	99	91
					6th	182	98
SOMERSET	O	M	R	W	7th	193	120
Jones	7	0	31	2	8th	197	122
Rose	5	0	12	0	9th	198	145
Hallett	4	1	18	0	10th		162
Lefebvre	4.4	0	22	1			
Hayhurst	8	0	37	4			
Trump	7	0	30	2			

YORKSHIRE vs. MIDDLESEX
at Scarborough on 26th August 1990
Toss : Yorkshire. Umpires : J.W.Holder and D.S.Thompsett
Yorkshire won by 44 runs (Yorkshire 4 pts Middlesex 0 pts)

YORKSHIRE

M.D.Moxon *	run out	38
A.A.Metcalfe	c Carr b Cowans	84
R.J.Blakey +	c Ramprakash b Cowans	63
P.E.Robinson	c Weekes b Cowans	11
D.Byas	run out	22
C.Chapman	not out	36
P.J.Hartley	b Emburey	1
P.Carrick	run out	7
C.S.Pickles		
P.W.Jarvis		
A.Sidebottom		
Extras	(lb 6,w 3)	9
TOTAL	(40 overs)(for 7 wkts)	271

MIDDLESEX

D.L.Haynes	lbw b Carrick	60
M.A.Roseberry	lbw b Jarvis	9
M.R.Ramprakash	c Hartley b Carrick	34
K.R.Brown	c Robinson b Hartley	16
J.D.Carr	run out	9
J.E.Emburey *	c Metcalfe b Carrick	14
P.R.Downton +	c & b Pickles	28
P.N.Weekes	not out	29
N.G.Cowans	c Blakey b Hartley	0
S.P.Hughes	b Jarvis	14
N.R.Taylor	not out	5
Extras	(lb 8,w 1)	9
TOTAL	(40 overs)(for 9 wkts)	227

MIDDLESEX	O	M	R	W	FALL OF WICKETS		
						YOR	MID
Cowans	8	0	43	3			
Taylor	8	0	46	0	1st	60	19
Hughes	8	1	52	0	2nd	169	106
Emburey	8	0	57	1	3rd	192	123
Weekes	4	0	36	0	4th	204	135
Haynes	4	0	31	0	5th	249	137
					6th	264	151
YORKSHIRE	O	M	R	W	7th	271	190
Jarvis	8	0	41	2	8th		193
Sidebottom	8	0	33	0	9th		218
Hartley	8	0	51	2	10th		
Pickles	8	0	50	1			
Carrick	8	0	44	3			

HAMPSHIRE vs. SURREY
at Southampton on 26th August 1990
Toss : Hampshire. Umpires : J.D.Bond and A.A.Jones
Surrey won by 4 runs (Hampshire 0 pts Surrey 4 pts)

SURREY

A.J.Stewart +	c Nicholas b Connor	36
A.Brown	b Tremlett	24
G.P.Thorpe	lbw b Tremlett	26
D.M.Ward	not out	102
M.A.Lynch	b Maru	26
J.D.Robinson	c Middleton b Maru	7
I.A.Greig *	not out	16
K.T.Medlycott		
C.K.Bullen		
Waqar Younis		
A.J.Murphy		
Extras	(b 1,lb 3,w 4,nb 3)	11
TOTAL	(38 overs)(for 5 wkts)	248

HAMPSHIRE

V.P.Terry	run out	56
T.C.Middleton	run out	72
M.C.J.Nicholas *	b Waqar Younis	59
M.D.Marshall	lbw b Waqar Younis	0
C.L.Smith	c Stewart b Murphy	0
J.R.Ayling	run out	3
R.J.Parks +	b Waqar Younis	10
R.J.Maru	c Stewart b Murphy	1
T.M.Tremlett	c Brown b Greig	21
C.A.Connor	not out	4
P.J.Bakker	not out	2
Extras	(b 4,lb 8,w 4)	16
TOTAL	(38 overs)(for 9 wkts)	244

HAMPSHIRE	O	M	R	W	FALL OF WICKETS		
						SUR	HAM
Bakker	5	0	35	0			
Marshall	8	0	50	0	1st	44	100
Tremlett	8	0	33	2	2nd	69	192
Connor	7	0	45	1	3rd	103	192
Maru	5	0	31	2	4th	154	193
Ayling	5	0	50	0	5th	186	196
					6th		200
SURREY	O	M	R	W	7th		203
Murphy	8	0	41	2	8th		223
Robinson	5	0	22	0	9th		235
Greig	5	0	37	1	10th		
Medlycott	7	0	49	0			
Waqar Younis	8	0	40	3			
Bullen	5	0	43	0			

REFUGE ASSURANCE LEAGUE

DERBYSHIRE vs. ESSEX
at Derby on 26th August 1990
Toss : Essex. Umpires : D.J.Constant and R.Julian
Derbyshire won by 5 wickets (Derbyshire 4 pts Essex 0 pts)

ESSEX
B.R.Hardie *	b Warner	76
J.P.Stephenson	c Barnett b Mortensen	3
M.E.Waugh	c Adams b Kuiper	59
P.J.Prichard	c Mortensen b Kuiper	25
N.Hussain	not out	12
N.Shahid	not out	9
M.A.Garnham +		
M.C.Ilott		
J.H.Childs		
S.J.W.Andrew		
P.M.Such		
Extras	(b 1,lb 11,w 7)	19
TOTAL	(40 overs)(for 4 wkts)	203

DERBYSHIRE
K.J.Barnett *	c Garnham b Ilott	7
P.D.Bowler +	c Stephenson b Childs	43
B.Roberts	lbw b Waugh	45
A.P.Kuiper	c Prichard b Waugh	56
T.J.G.O'Gorman	c Such b Ilott	12
C.J.Adams	not out	27
S.C.Goldsmith	not out	5
A.E.Warner		
S.J.Base		
M.Jean-Jacques		
O.H.Mortensen		
Extras	(b 1,lb 6,w 5)	12
TOTAL	(39.3 overs)(for 5 wkts)	207

DERBYSHIRE	O	M	R	W
Mortensen	8	2	10	1
Warner	8	0	36	1
Base	8	0	33	0
Jean-Jacques	6	0	47	0
Goldsmith	4	0	25	0
Kuiper	6	0	40	2

ESSEX	O	M	R	W
Andrew	8	0	53	0
Ilott	7.3	0	41	2
Such	8	0	28	0
Childs	8	0	38	1
Waugh	8	0	40	2

FALL OF WICKETS	ESS	DER
1st	7	19
2nd	133	98
3rd	177	116
4th	185	168
5th		179
6th		
7th		
8th		
9th		
10th		

LANCASHIRE vs. WARWICKSHIRE
at Old Trafford on 26th August 1990
Toss : Warwickshire. Umpires : J.H.Harris and B.Hassan
Lancashire won by 49 runs (Lancs 4 pts Warwicks 0 pts)

LANCASHIRE
G.D.Mendis	lbw b Munton	9
G.Fowler	b Smith	69
G.D.Lloyd	c Asif Din b Twose	31
N.H.Fairbrother	c Asif Din b Twose	20
M.Watkinson	b Smith	22
Wasim Akram	b Reeve	31
P.A.J.DeFreitas	c Moody b Benjamin	32
W.K.Hegg +	not out	10
I.D.Austin	not out	2
D.P.Hughes *		
P.J.W.Allott		
Extras	(b 1,lb 7,w 6,nb 1)	15
TOTAL	(39 overs)(for 7 wkts)	241

WARWICKSHIRE
A.J.Moles	b DeFreitas	70
Asif Din	c Hegg b Allott	1
T.M.Moody	b Allott	17
T.A.Lloyd *	b Wasim Akram	16
D.A.Reeve	lbw b Watkinson	0
R.G.Twose	c Fowler b Watkinson	6
N.M.K.Smith	c Lloyd b Watkinson	10
K.J.Piper +	b Watkinson	30
J.E.Benjamin	c Austin b Watkinson	24
T.A.Munton	not out	4
G.C.Small	absent hurt	
Extras	(b 1,lb 8,w 4,nb 1)	14
TOTAL	(35.4 overs)	192

WARWICKS	O	M	R	W
Small	0.3	0	3	0
Moody	3.3	0	32	0
Munton	7	0	45	1
Benjamin	8	0	41	1
Reeve	6	0	31	1
Twose	6	0	38	2
Smith	8	2	43	2

LANCASHIRE	O	M	R	W
DeFreitas	8	0	34	1
Allott	8	0	51	2
Wasim Akram	6	0	21	1
Watkinson	7.4	0	46	5
Austin	6	0	31	0

FALL OF WICKETS	LAN	WAR
1st	17	3
2nd	100	45
3rd	138	78
4th	143	79
5th	172	99
6th	226	116
7th	231	136
8th		178
9th		192
10th		

REFUGE ASSURANCE LEAGUE

Final Table

		P	W	L	T	NR	Away wins	Pts	R/Rate
1	Derbyshire (5)	16	12	0	3	1	6	50	87.35
2	Lancashire (1)	16	11	0	3	2	7	48	100.18
3	Middlesex (9)	16	10	0	5	1	5	42	95.40
4	Notts (4)	16	10	0	5	1	4	42	89.31
5	Hampshire (6)	16	9	0	5	2	4	40	88.82
6	Yorkshire (11)	16	9	0	6	1	4	38	83.60
7	Surrey (7)	16	9	0	6	1	3	38	90.39
8	Somerset (10)	16	8	0	8	0	4	32	91.25
9	Gloucs (16)	16	7	0	7	2	2	32	87.80
10	Worcs (2)	16	7	0	8	1	4	30	84.96
11	Kent (12)	16	7	0	8	1	3	30	85.94
12	Essex (3)	16	6	0	9	1	3	26	90.56
13	Sussex (13)	16	5	0	9	2	2	24	85.90
14	Warwicks (15)	16	5	0	10	1	2	22	80.69
15	Glamorgan (17)	16	4	0	11	1	2	18	84.20
16	Leics (14)	16	4	0	11	1	1	18	76.59
17	Northants (8)	16	3	0	12	1	1	14	86.40

HEADLINES

26th August

- Derbyshire won the Sunday title for the first time when they beat Essex by five wickets with three balls to spare at Derby. Ole Mortensen, the meanest bowler in the league, gave Derbyshire the initiative by conceding only 10 runs in his eight overs, and Adrian Kuiper's quickfire 56 took them to the brink of victory

- Lancashire's emphatic victory over Warwickshire at Old Trafford was good enough only to secure second place. Graeme Fowler passed 50 for the 10th time in 15 innings to finish with an aggregate of 773 runs - a county record for the Sunday League - and Mike Watkinson returned his best Sunday figures

- Middlesex's challenge for the title came to a disappointing end at Scarborough where Yorkshire beat them by 44 runs after Ashley Metcalfe and Richard Blakey had put the home side on course for a massive total

- There was also disappointment for Hampshire who just missed out on the fourth place in the Refuge Cup after being beaten by four runs by Surrey at Southampton. David Ward made his first Sunday 100 in Surrey's total of 248 for 5, then Waqar Younis, the leading wicket-taker in the league with 31 wickets, inspired a Hampshire collapse from 192 for 1

- Elsewhere there was less at stake but record books again had to be adjusted. Jimmy Cook took his record aggregate for the season to 902 as Somerset beat Sussex at Hove by 60 runs, while Tim Curtis's 95 in Worcestershire's victory over Glamorgan at Swansea gave him a county record aggregate of 784, 31 runs ahead of Graeme Hick

- The bottom two teams in the table ended their seasons with rare victories, bottom placed Northamptonshire narrowly defeating Gloucestershire at Northampton, Wayne Larkins hitting his 9th Sunday 100, and Leicestershire beating Kent by six wickets at Leicester after a career best 97 from Tim Boon

BRITANNIC ASSURANCE CHAMPIONSHIP

SUSSEX vs. SOMERSET

at Hove on 23rd, 24th, 25th, 27th August 1990
Toss : Somerset. Umpires : J.C.Balderstone and R.A.White
Somerset won by 10 wickets (Sussex 3 pts (Bt: 1, Bw: 2) Somerset 23 pts (Bt: 3, Bw: 4))

SUSSEX

N.J.Lenham	c Burns b Lefebvre	45	c Trump b Hayhurst	123
J.W.Hall	c Townsend b Jones	1	c Townsend b Rose	2
K.Greenfield	c Burns b Mallender	5	c & b Hayhurst	11
A.P.Wells	lbw b Mallender	2	b Rose	14
M.P.Speight	c Hayhurst b Jones	2	c Burns b Jones	11
C.M.Wells *	c Burns b Rose	4	c Burns b Lefebvre	2
A.I.C.Dodemaide	not out	57	c & b Jones	112
P.Moores +	c Tavare b Lefebvre	8	c Tavare b Trump	38
A.C.S.Pigott	lbw b Rose	2	c Cook b Harden	23
I.D.K.Salisbury	c Burns b Lefebvre	3	not out	30
R.A.Bunting	c Burns b Hayhurst	14	c Tavare b Hayhurst	8
Extras	(lb 4,w 1,nb 5)	10	(lb 3,nb 5)	8
TOTAL		153		382

SOMERSET

S.J.Cook	c Moores b Pigott	13		
G.T.J.Townsend	c Moores b Dodemaide	0	not out	0
A.N.Hayhurst	c Moores b Dodemaide	11		
C.J.Tavare *	c Speight b Pigott	219		
R.J.Harden	c Moores b Pigott	59		
H.R.J.Trump	c Moores b Dodemaide	0		
N.D.Burns +	c Wells C.M. b Bunting	28	(1) not out	13
G.D.Rose	b Dodemaide	54		
R.P.Lefebvre	b Pigott	6		
N.A.Mallender	not out	87		
A.N.Jones	not out	24		
Extras	(b 8,lb 9,nb 7)	24		0
TOTAL	(for 9 wkts dec)	525	(for 0 wkts)	13

SOMERSET	O	M	R	W	O	M	R	W
Jones	11	2	47	2	34	5	117	2
Mallender	13	5	31	2				
Rose	11	4	22	2	26	5	95	2
Lefebvre	17	4	46	3	24	9	48	1
Hayhurst	3.4	2	3	1	23	6	58	3
Trump					23	9	49	1
Harden					4	0	12	1

SUSSEX	O	M	R	W	O	M	R	W
Pigott	37	6	119	4				
Dodemaide	36	5	117	4				
Bunting	33	8	77	1				
Wells C.M.	23	1	111	0				
Salisbury	29	9	80	0	1	0	5	0
Lenham	3	0	4	0				
Greenfield					0.3	0	8	0

FALL OF WICKETS

	SUS	SOM	SUS	SOM
1st	19	2	14	
2nd	43	20	69	
3rd	45	30	105	
4th	51	132	119	
5th	68	137	148	
6th	78	176	183	
7th	108	292	258	
8th	111	301	290	
9th	122	484	365	
10th	153		382	

HAMPSHIRE vs. SURREY

at Southampton on 23rd, 24th, 25th, 27th August 1990
Toss : Hampshire. Umpires : J.D.Bond and A.A.Jones
Surrey won by 9 wickets (Hampshire 2 pts (Bt: 1, Bw: 1) Surrey 23 pts (Bt: 3, Bw: 4))

HAMPSHIRE

T.C.Middleton	b Waqar Younis	25	b Feltham	33
C.L.Smith	b Waqar Younis	43	c Greig b Bicknell	111
M.C.J.Nicholas *	c Lynch b Bicknell	70	b Waqar Younis	19
V.P.Terry	c Waqar Younis b Bicknell	8	lbw b Bicknell	6
M.D.Marshall	lbw b Feltham	6	c Stewart b Medlycott	31
R.M.F.Cox	c Stewart b Feltham	0	lbw b Feltham	23
A.N Aymes +	lbw b Waqar Younis	6	lbw b Feltham	48
R.J.Maru	c Lynch b Waqar Younis	0	c Lynch b Waqar Younis	36
S.D.Udal	b Waqar Younis	not out	not out	28
C.A.Connor	b Waqar Younis	12	c Bicknell b Feltham	20
P.J.Bakker	not out	12	b Feltham	10
Extras	(b 6,w 2,nb 7)	15	(b 9,lb 5,w 3,nb 11)	28
TOTAL		197		393

SURREY

R.I.Alikhan	b Connor	72	lbw b Bakker	0
G.S.Clinton	c & b Maru	21		
A.J.Stewart +	c Nicholas b Maru	72	not out	27
D.M.Ward	c Nicholas b Connor	191		
M.A.Lynch	c Nicholas b Maru	13		
I.A.Greig *	c Terry b Bakker	11	(2) not out	45
M.A.Feltham	c Marshall b Udal	30		
K.T.Medlycott	run out	15		
M.P.Bicknell	c Udal b Connor	40		
N.M.Kendrick	c Middleton b Connor	7		
Waqar Younis	not out	13		
Extras	(b 1,lb 16,nb 15)	32	(b 2,lb 1)	3
TOTAL		517	(for 1 wkt)	75

SURREY	O	M	R	W	O	M	R	W
Waqar Younis	21	5	66	6	36	4	132	2
Bicknell	18	4	46	2	32	9	75	2
Feltham	17	1	64	2	30.5	2	109	5
Greig	8	2	15	0				
Medlycott					25	4	63	1

HAMPSHIRE	O	M	R	W	O	M	R	W
Bakker	25	8	65	1	3	1	18	1
Marshall	32	12	64	0				
Maru	54	13	129	3				
Connor	27.3	3	112	4	3	0	29	0
Udal	21	6	87	1	1	0	9	0
Nicholas	12	2	43	0	0.3	0	16	0

FALL OF WICKETS

	HAM	SUR	HAM	SUR
1st	72	42	106	0
2nd	77	175	156	
3rd	104	217	184	
4th	115	238	190	
5th	115	273	227	
6th	143	374	251	
7th	143	408	330	
8th	143	494	335	
9th	158	502	369	
10th	197	517	393	

LEICESTERSHIRE vs. KENT

at Leicester on 23rd, 24th, 25th, 27th August 1990
Toss : Kent. Umpires : B.Dudleston and D.O.Oslear
Leicestershire won by 2 wickets (Leicestershire 22 pts (Bt: 2, Bw: 4) Kent 3 pts (Bt: 1, Bw: 2))

KENT

S.G.Hinks	c Nixon b Benjamin	6	b Millns	163
T.R.Ward	c Parsons b Agnew	14	b Benjamin	29
V.J.Wells	c Nixon b Parsons	40	(4) c Boon b Parsons	28
G.R.Cowdrey	b Millns	16	(5) b Millns	135
M.V.Fleming	b Millns	0	(6) c Briers b Millns	14
C.S.Cowdrey *	c Willey b Parsons	5	(8) c Whitaker b Parsons	2
S.A.Marsh +	c Nixon b Parsons	5	(9) not out	31
R.P.Davis	c Hepworth b Benjamin	36	(3) c Nixon b Agnew	4
P.S.De Villiers	c Nixon b Millns	21	(10) not out	20
M.M.Patel	not out	3	(7) c Nixon b Parsons	5
A.P.Igglesden	b Benjamin	0		
Extras	(lb 1,w 1,nb 11)	13	(b 11,lb 12,w 9,nb 18)	50
TOTAL		169	(for 8 wkts dec)	481

LEICESTERSHIRE

T.J.Boon	c Marsh b Wells	66	c Marsh b Fleming	20
N.E.Briers *	b Wells	62	c Cowdrey G.R. b Patel	75
J.J.Whitaker	c Davis b Wells	0	b Patel	100
P.Willey	c Davis b De Villiers	14	c Ward b Davis	25
L.Potter	lbw b Wells	30	c Wells b Patel	27
P.N.Hepworth	lbw b Wells	43	(8) c sub b Davis	7
W.K.M.Benjamin	c De Villiers b Fleming	18	c Fleming b Patel	53
P.A.Nixon +	c Marsh b Igglesden	4	(9) not out	11
G.J.Parsons	c Hinks b Igglesden	20	(6) c sub b Patel	2
J.P.Agnew	b Fleming	6	not out	3
D.J.Millns	not out	0		
Extras	(b 4,lb 15,w 1,nb 4)	24	(b 13,lb 11)	24
TOTAL		304	(for 8 wkts)	347

LEICESTERSHIRE	O	M	R	W	O	M	R	W
Benjamin	14.3	2	52	3	27	4	70	1
Agnew	15	4	39	1	23	5	69	1
Millns	11	1	37	3	30	7	88	3
Parsons	12	3	40	3	27	8	104	3
Willey					19	5	84	0
Potter					15	4	43	0

KENT	O	M	R	W	O	M	R	W
De Villiers	24	9	57	1	7	0	31	0
Igglesden	30	7	84	2	2	0	11	0
Davis	19	7	47	0	27.3	4	120	2
Fleming	18	5	25	2	14	4	36	1
Patel	10	3	29	0	27	3	96	5
Wells	18	7	43	5	8	1	29	0
Cowdrey C.S.					1	1	0	0

FALL OF WICKETS

	KEN	LEI	KEN	LEI
1st	15	133	48	30
2nd	26	139	65	194
3rd	61	144	136	210
4th	62	177	394	250
5th	98	190	418	258
6th	104	229	420	291
7th	109	272	423	328
8th	156	287	440	338
9th	169	294		
10th	169	304		

YORKSHIRE vs. MIDDLESEX

at Headingley on 23rd, 24th, 25th, 27th August 1990
Toss : Middlesex. Umpires : J.W.Holder and D.S.Thompsett
Middlesex won by 64 runs (Yorkshire 5 pts (Bt: 2, Bw: 3) Middlesex 23 pts (Bt: 4, Bw: 3))

MIDDLESEX

D.L.Haynes	lbw b Pickles	131	b Batty	57
M.A.Roseberry	c Blakey b Gough	2	c Grayson b Gough	80
M.R.Ramprakash	c Blakey b Jarvis	29	c Robinson b Batty	29
K.R.Brown	c Byas b Jarvis	56	c Pickles b Batty	0
M.W.Gatting *	c Robinson b Carrick	91	(7) lbw b Gough	10
P.R.Downton +	b Pickles	12	(5) b Jarvis	1
J.E.Emburey	lbw b Gough	0	(6) c Metcalfe b Jarvis	51
S.P.Hughes	c Moxon b Jarvis	4	(9) not out	10
P.C.R.Tufnell	c Grayson b Gough	37	(8) c Robinson b Batty	5
C.W.Taylor	not out	0		
N.G.Cowans	c Metcalfe b Gough	0		
Extras	(b 1,lb 14)	15	(b 5,lb 2,w 1)	8
TOTAL		377	(for 8 wkts dec)	251

YORKSHIRE

M.D.Moxon *	c Downton b Tufnell	95	c Hughes b Cowans	7
A.A.Metcalfe	c Downton b Hughes	26	lbw b Cowans	26
P.Grayson	b Hughes	4	c sub b Cowans	18
P.E.Robinson	c Downton b Hughes	0	c Downton b Taylor	72
R.J.Blakey +	c & b Tufnell	14	c Emburey b Taylor	16
D.Byas	c Emburey b Hughes	36	lbw b Cowans	12
P.Carrick	c Emburey b Hughes	34	c Downton b Taylor	20
C.S.Pickles	c & b Cowans	37	c Emburey b Taylor	1
P.W.Jarvis	b Cowans	14	not out	43
D.Gough	lbw b Hughes	21	lbw b Cowans	9
J.D.Batty	not out	0	c Downton b Taylor	21
Extras	(b 1,lb 9,w 1,nb 6)	17	(b 10,lb 8,w 1,nb 2)	21
TOTAL		298		266

YORKSHIRE	O	M	R	W	O	M	R	W
Jarvis	23	4	74	3	16	3	51	2
Gough	17.5	2	68	4	19	6	43	2
Pickles	20	2	80	2	9	1	39	0
Moxon	2	0	23	0				
Byas	2	0	14	0				
Carrick	29	8	61	1	14	5	35	0
Batty	13	3	42	0	23	4	76	4

MIDDLESEX	O	M	R	W	O	M	R	W
Cowans	22	6	55	2	21	6	67	5
Hughes	28.2	5	101	5	23	2	66	0
Taylor	14	2	46	1	14.5	4	33	5
Emburey	19	6	43	0	12	2	32	0
Tufnell	26	9	41	2	21	5	50	0
Haynes	2	0	2	0				

FALL OF WICKETS

	MID	YOR	MID	YOR
1st	10	63	104	34
2nd	116	73	156	34
3rd	182	81	158	60
4th	270	108	159	97
5th	304	158	190	127
6th	305	206	208	172
7th	328	238	219	176
8th	373	266	251	192
9th	377	294		233
10th	377	298		266

BRITANNIC ASSURANCE CHAMPIONSHIP

HEADLINES

23rd - 27th August

● A programme of seven four-day matches produced a full house of positive results and more heavy scoring. Essex continued their relentless march up the Championship table, briefly taking over at the top, following their two-day demolition of a demoralised Derbyshire side. Mark Ilott returned a career best 5 for 34 in the first innings and Neil Foster match figures of 8 for 96 as Essex swept to their third successive victory

● Middlesex, having seen their lead evaporate over recent weeks, gained their first win in seven matches by beating Yorkshire by 66 runs at Headingley to remain a single point ahead of Essex. Desmond Haynes hit his 8th 100 of the summer as he became the third man to complete 2,000 first-class runs and, with Yorkshire having been left the whole of the last day to score 341 to win, Norman Cowans and newcomer Charles Taylor bowled Middlesex to victory

● Other rivals for the Championship continued to fall away. Although Warwickshire retained third position their catastrophic 323-run defeat at the hands of neighbours Worcestershire at Worcester signalled the end of their title aspirations. Tim Curtis's career best 197* helped the home side to a lead of 419 and Dilley, Newport and McEwan needed less than 30 overs to seal victory

● Hampshire's challenge faded as they were beaten by nine wickets by Surrey at Southampton, David Ward improving his career best to 191 as Surrey gained a first innings lead of 320 which gave them a vicelike grip on the match

● The number of double centuries made in the season still threatened to reach record proportions as Mark Alleyne made 256 for Gloucestershire against Northamptonshire at Northampton and Chris Tavare hit 219 for Somerset against Sussex at Hove. Both innings were career bests and both contributed to impressive victories for their counties. Even career best scores from Neil Lenham and Tony Dodemaide could not help bottom of the table Sussex

● The most closely contested match of the round came at Leicester where Leicestershire beat Kent by two wickets with three balls to spare. Kent's reserve wicket-keeper Vince Wells turned bowler with remarkable effect but could not prevent the home side taking a first innings lead of 135; a fourth wicket stand of 268 between Simon Hinks and Graham Cowdrey gave Kent the initiative but the pendulum swung once more as Leicestershire reached their target of 347 in the 75th over

● First-class debut: G.T.J.Townsend (Somerset)

DERBYSHIRE vs. ESSEX

at Derby on 23rd, 24th August 1990
Toss : Derbyshire.   Umpires : D.J.Constant and R.Julian
Essex won by an innings and 94 runs (Derbys 3 pts (Bt: 0, Bw: 3) Essex 24 pts (Bt: 4, Bw: 4))

DERBYSHIRE

K.J.Barnett *	lbw b Ilott	4	b Ilott	3
P.D.Bowler	c Waugh b Ilott	11	b Foster	5
T.J.G.O'Gorman	c Garnham b Foster	1	c Garnham b Foster	4
C.J.Adams	c Garnham b Foster	0	c Garnham b Andrew	41
B.Roberts	b Ilott	13	c & b Foster	7
S.C.Goldsmith	c Shahid b Foster	11	lbw b Andrew	32
K.M.Krikken +	b Ilott	2	c Hussain b Ilott	14
G.Miller	c Garnham b Foster	19	absent hurt	
I.R.Bishop	not out	39	(8) lbw b Andrew	17
A.E.Warner	c Garnham b Foster	4	(9) lbw b Andrew	0
M.Jean-Jacques	lbw b Ilott	0	(10) not out	0
Extras	(lb 6)	6	(lb 4)	4
TOTAL		110		127

ESSEX

N.Shahid	c Krikken b Warner	55
J.P.Stephenson	c Adams b Warner	11
P.J.Prichard	run out	103
M.E.Waugh	c Barnett b Jean-Jacques	61
M.C.Ilott	c Adams b Bishop	6
N.Hussain	c Adams b Goldsmith	28
M.A.Garnham +	c Roberts b Warner	8
D.R.Pringle *	b Goldsmith	0
N.A.Foster	c Adams b Bishop	25
J.H.Childs	c Krikken b Bishop	8
S.J.W.Andrew	not out	6
Extras	(lb 6,w 3,nb 11)	20
TOTAL		331

ESSEX	O	M	R	W	O	M	R	W
Foster	16	6	39	5	11	1	57	3
Ilott	18.4	8	34	5	10.4	3	34	2
Andrew	6	2	18	0	11	2	30	4
Pringle	3	0	13	0				
Childs					3	2	2	0

DERBYSHIRE	O	M	R	W	O	M	R	W
Bishop	23.5	7	57	3				
Warner	24	7	56	3				
Jean-Jacques	24	3	105	1				
Goldsmith	33	6	105	2				
Barnett	1	0	2	0				

FALL OF WICKETS	DER	ESS	DER	ESS
1st	5	59	8	
2nd	16	79	12	
3rd	16	205	12	
4th	17	234	22	
5th	41	274	84	
6th	41	284	99	
7th	47	284	125	
8th	91	294	125	
9th	101	316	127	
10th	110	331		

WORCESTERSHIRE vs. WARWICKSHIRE

at Worcester on 23rd, 24th, 25th, 27th August 1990
Toss : Worcestershire.   Umpires : J.H.Harris and B.Hassan
Worcestershire won by 323 runs (Worcs 23 pts (Bt: 3, Bw: 4) Warwicks 6 pts (Bt: 2, Bw: 4))

WORCESTERSHIRE

T.S.Curtis	c Lloyd b Small	27	not out	197
G.J.Lord	lbw b Small	7	c Piper b Munton	25
G.A.Hick	c Piper b Small	14	b Reeve	42
D.B.D'Oliveira	c Piper b Small	0	c Moles b Booth	30
P.A.Neale *	c Twose b Reeve	46	c Piper b Twose	17
S.R.Lampitt	c Piper b Small	0	c & b Munton	4
S.J.Rhodes +	b Reeve	96	not out	30
R.K.Illingworth	lbw b Munton	13		
P.J.Newport	c Piper b Munton	7		
G.R.Dilley	c Lloyd b Small	35		
S.M.McEwan	not out	12		
Extras	(lb 7,w 1)	8	(b 8,lb 20,w 2,nb 1)	31
TOTAL		265	(for 5 wkts dec)	376

WARWICKSHIRE

A.J.Moles	c Neale b Dilley	59	b Dilley	8
J.D.Ratcliffe	c Lampitt b Newport	29	lbw b Newport	4
T.A.Lloyd *	c Neale b Lampitt	12	lbw b Newport	2
T.M.Moody	c Rhodes b McEwan	21	c Rhodes b Dilley	6
R.G.Twose	b Newport	9	lbw b Dilley	0
D.A.Reeve	c D'Oliveira b Lampitt	27	b McEwan	25
N.M.K.Smith	c D'Oliveira b Newport	20	b Newport	20
K.J.Piper +	b Dilley	14	c Rhodes b Newport	0
G.C.Small	not out	5	c Illingworth b Newport	12
P.A.Booth	c Rhodes b Lampitt	2	c Rhodes b McEwan	5
T.A.Munton	c Curtis b Lampitt	1	not out	5
Extras	(b 1,lb 7,w 2,nb 13)	23	(lb 3,w 1,nb 5)	9
TOTAL		222		96

WARWICKS	O	M	R	W	O	M	R	W
Small	29	5	94	6	25	12	61	0
Munton	27	6	84	2	27	9	66	2
Reeve	23	3	60	2	25	8	85	1
Moody	3	0	11	0				
Booth	7	5	9	0	36	10	93	1
Smith					6	0	33	0
Twose					5	1	10	1

WORCS	O	M	R	W	O	M	R	W
Dilley	16	2	56	2	10	0	45	3
Newport	19	5	60	3	14.3	4	37	5
McEwan	14	2	49	1	5	2	11	2
Illingworth	1	0	2	0				
Lampitt	14	1	47	4				

FALL OF WICKETS	WOR	WAR	WOR	WAR
1st	35	66	78	14
2nd	40	101	155	16
3rd	40	123	204	16
4th	57	146	258	19
5th	57	150	273	45
6th	145	182		71
7th	169	209		71
8th	183	212		82
9th	217	214		88
10th	265	222		96

BRITANNIC ASS. CHAMPIONSHIP

TOUR MATCHES

NORTHANTS vs. GLOUCESTERSHIRE

at Northampton on 23rd, 24th, 25th, 27th August 1990
Toss : Gloucestershire. Umpires : P.J.Eele and K.E.Palmer
Gloucestershire won by 157 runs (Northants 5 pts (Bt: 4, Bw: 1) Gloucs 22 pts (Bt: 3, Bw: 3))

GLOUCESTERSHIRE

G.D.Hodgson	c Ripley b Ambrose	4	lbw b Ambrose		22
A.J.Wright *	c Felton b Capel	11	c Felton b Thomas		4
P.Bainbridge	c Ripley b Penberthy	19	c Felton b Capel		45
C.W.J.Athey	lbw b Capel	79	not out		88
M.W.Alleyne	c Cook b Penberthy	256	lbw b Ambrose		38
K.M.Curran	c Ripley b Williams	19	b Penberthy		19
J.W.Lloyds	b Cook	35	not out		16
R.C.J.Williams +	not out	35			
C.A.Walsh	c Penberthy b Cook	31			
D.V.Lawrence	c Bailey b Penberthy	3			
M.C.J.Ball	c & b Cook	4			
Extras	(b 2,lb 21,w 1,nb 1)	25	(b 5,lb 9)		14
TOTAL		521	(for 5 wkts dec)		246

NORTHANTS

A.Fordham	st Williams b Bainbridge	64	lbw b Lawrence		41
N.A.Felton	b Bainbridge	41	c Lloyds b Walsh		15
W.Larkins *	c Williams b Lawrence	36	b Walsh		1
R.J.Bailey	c Hodgson b Lawrence	105	c Wright b Walsh		4
D.J.Capel	b Lawrence	38	c Ball b Walsh		2
R.G.Williams	b Walsh	1	b Curran		15
A.L.Penberthy	c Hodgson b Alleyne	28	c Williams b Curran		18
D.Ripley +	lbw b Curran	34	not out		41
J.G.Thomas	b Curran	0	b Lloyds		5
C.E.L.Ambrose	lbw b Lawrence	10	st Williams b Lloyds		18
N.G.B.Cook	not out	0	c Wright b Lawrence		11
Extras	(b 11,lb 8,w 6,nb 20)	45	(b 8,lb 8,w 4,nb 17)		37
TOTAL		402			208

NORTHANTS	O	M	R	W	O	M	R	W		FALL OF WICKETS				
											GLO	NOR	GLO	NOR
Ambrose	27	5	77	1	16	7	35	2	1st		10	99	10	53
Thomas	19	6	58	0	13	2	59	1	2nd		33	133	54	57
Capel	28	5	90	2	8	2	16	1	3rd		47	174	75	63
Penberthy	20	1	83	3	11	1	51	1	4th		246	318	163	71
Cook	28	5	97	3	17	1	58	0	5th		297	320	220	71
Williams	33	5	73	1	5	0	13	0	6th		390	320		101
Bailey	3	0	20	0					7th		472	385		114
									8th		511	385		123
GLOUCS	O	M	R	W	O	M	R	W	9th		517	388		179
Walsh	18	3	63	1	19	3	101	4	10th		521	402		208
Lawrence	24.5	2	90	4	13.1	1	53	2						
Curran	22	2	68	2	7	1	17	2						
Ball	6	1	35	0										
Bainbridge	12	1	38	2										
Alleyne	11	4	36	1										
Lloyds	12	2	53	0	8	1	21	2						

GLAMORGAN vs. SRI LANKA

at Ebbw Vale on 22nd, 23rd, 24th August 1990
Toss : Glamorgan. Umpires : M.J.Harris and R.Palmer
Match drawn

GLAMORGAN

S.P.James	c Mahanama b Wijeguna'	47	c Mahanama b Labrooy		0
H.Morris *	c Tillekaratne b Labrooy	37	c Mahanama b Wijeguna'		126
P.A.Cottey	lbw b Wijegunawardene	0	c Attapatu b Ramanayake		0
M.P.Maynard	c Attapatu b Labrooy	20	b Labrooy		14
G.C.Holmes	c Jayasuriya b Labrooy	0	c Wijeguna' b Labrooy		92
A.Dale	b Wijetunga	36	c Kuruppu b Gurusinha		14
R.D.B.Croft	b Labrooy	20	c De Silva b Wijeguna'		32
M.L.Roberts +	lbw b Labrooy	25	c Mahanama b Wijetunga		22
H.A.Anthony	c Attapatu b Wijetunga	12	st Tillekaratne b Wijetunga		14
S.L.Watkin	lbw b Ramanayake	1	not out		2
M.Frost	not out	2			
Extras	(b 1,lb 6,w 1,nb 27)	35	(b 2,lb 10,w 3,nb 24)		39
TOTAL		235	(for 9 wkts dec)		355

SRI LANKA

R.S.Mahanama	lbw b Anthony	9	lbw b Frost		35
D.S.B.P.Kuruppu	lbw b Watkin	45	c Watkin b Dale		15
A.P.Gurusinha	c Roberts b Watkin	58	c Morris b Frost		23
P.A.De Silva *	b Croft	45	lbw b Holmes		2
H.P.Tillekaratne +	c Cottey b Dale	30	c Roberts b Frost		5
S.T.Jayasuriya	lbw b Watkin	24	c James b Croft		19
M.Attapatu	c Roberts b Dale	23	not out		71
G.F.Labrooy	c Roberts b Dale	7	c Maynard b Watkin		69
C.P.Ramanayake	not out	8	not out		3
K.I.W.Wijegunawardene					
P.Wijetunga					
Extras	(lb 5,w 1,nb 3)	9	(b 4,lb 2,w 1,nb 1)		8
TOTAL	(for 8 wkts dec)	258	(for 7 wkts)		250

SRI LANKA	O	M	R	W	O	M	R	W		FALL OF WICKETS			
											GLA	SRI	GLA	SRI
Labrooy	21	2	97	5	23	5	84	3	1st		53	21	0	34
Ramanayake	14	1	61	1	15	0	64	1	2nd		54	99	8	74
Wijegunawardene	13	2	30	2	15	1	79	2	3rd		86	152	33	81
Wijetunga	24	6	40	2	18.4	1	85	2	4th		90	186	224	81
Gurusinha					15	6	31	1	5th		154	207	260	87
GLAMORGAN	O	M	R	W	O	M	R	W	6th		165	225	287	109
Watkin	21	5	92	3	15	7	48	1	7th		190	238	327	221
Anthony	12	2	47	1	4	2	14	0	8th		208	258	336	
Frost	14	3	51	0	14	3	44	3	9th		214		355	
Croft	10	3	38	1	13	1	89	1	10th		235			
Dale	9.3	3	54	3	12	1	43	1						
Holmes					6	1	6	1						

NOTTINGHAMSHIRE vs. SRI LANKA

at Cleethorpes on 25th, 26th, 27th August 1990
Toss : Nottinghamshire. Umpires : B.Leadbeater and H.J.Rhodes
Match drawn

NOTTINGHAMSHIRE

P.Pollard	b Ramanayake	5	c Jayasuriya b Labrooy		5
M.Newell	c Tillekaratne b Gurusinha	112	c Attapatu b Labrooy		6
R.T.Robinson *	c Mahanama b Gurusinha	18	run out		36
P.Johnson	c Mahanama b Gurusinha	1	c Mahanama b Wick'singhe		54
D.J.R.Martindale	c Tillekaratne b Labrooy	26	c Mahanama b Ramanayake		13
K.P.Evans	c Jayasuriya b Wick'singhe	55	(7) run out		2
F.D.Stephenson	not out	27	(6) c Labrooy b Wick'singhe		65
C.W.Scott +	not out	13	b Wickremasinghe		31
K.E.Cooper			not out		10
R.A.Pick			b Labrooy		5
J.A.Afford			c sub b Labrooy		2
Extras	(b 9,lb 17,nb 20)	46	(b 1,lb 7,w 1,nb 13)		22
TOTAL	(for 6 wkts dec)	303			251

SRI LANKA

R.S.Mahanama	lbw b Stephenson	114	(1) lbw b Pick		44
C.Hathurasinghe	lbw b Cooper	84	(4) not out		17
A.P.Gurusinha	not out	37	(3) not out		14
P.A.De Silva *	c Pollard b Cooper	1	(2) lbw b Cooper		22
H.P.Tillekaratne +	c Evans b Pick	0			
S.T.Jayasuriya	c Johnson b Afford	15			
M.Attapatu	not out	9			
G.F.Labrooy					
C.P.Ramanayake					
P.Wijetunga					
P.Wickremasinghe					
Extras	(b 4,lb 10,nb 7)	21	(b 2,lb 8,nb 3)		13
TOTAL	(for 5 wkts dec)	281	(for 2 wkts)		110

SRI LANKA	O	M	R	W	O	M	R	W		FALL OF WICKETS			
											NOT	SRI	NOT	SRI
Labrooy	19.4	2	68	1	14.2	3	60	4	1st		13	210	13	69
Ramanayake	14	0	60	1	15	0	70	1	2nd		55	221	22	81
Wickremasinghe	24	9	63	1	26	3	95	3	3rd		60	223	101	
Gurusinha	15	2	38	3					4th		139	224	117	
Hathurasinghe	3	3	0	0					5th		259	250	129	
Wijetunga	9	1	29	0	1	0	13	0	6th		261		145	
De Silva	6	1	19	0	2	1	5	0	7th				232	
NOTTS	O	M	R	W	O	M	R	W	8th				234	
Pick	19	3	54	1	11	3	33	1	9th				239	
Cooper	25	10	67	2	11	2	31	1	10th				251	
Afford	22	5	74	1										
Evans	14	0	38	0	6	0	19	0						
Stephenson	12	3	34	1	6	1	17	0						
Newell	1	1	0	0										

HEADLINES

22nd - 27th August

● The fourth touring party to visit this country in 1990, a Sri Lankan side looking to gain experience, made a promising start with drawn matches against Glamorgan and Nottinghamshire. Graeme Labrooy impressed with eight wickets while, for Glamorgan, Hugh Morris made a county record 9th 100 of the season.

● Roshan Mahanama and Chandika Hathurasinghe shared an opening stand of 210 in another competent batting performance against Notts, but again the match was drawn

CORNHILL TEST MATCH

ENGLAND vs. INDIA

at The Oval on 23rd, 24th, 25th, 27th, 28th August 1990
Toss : India.   Umpires : N.T.Plews and D.R.Shepherd
Match drawn

INDIA

R.J.Shastri	c Lamb b Malcolm	187
N.S.Sidhu	c Russell b Fraser	12
S.V.Manjrekar	c Russell b Malcolm	22
D.B.Vengsarkar	c & b Atherton	33
M.Azharuddin *	c Russell b Williams	78
M.Prabhakar	lbw b Fraser	28
S.R.Tendulkar	c Lamb b Williams	21
Kapil Dev	st Russell b Hemmings	110
K.S.More +	not out	61
A.Wasson	b Hemmings	15
N.D.Hirwani	not out	2
Extras	(b 7,lb 8,w 6,nb 16)	37
TOTAL	(for 9 wkts dec)	606

ENGLAND

G.A.Gooch *	c Shastri b Hirwani	85	c Vengsarkar b Hirwani		88
M.A.Atherton	c More b Prabhakar	7	lbw b Kapil Dev		86
N.F.Williams	lbw b Prabhakar	38			
D.I.Gower	lbw b Wasson	8	(3) not out		157
J.E.Morris	c More b Wasson	7	(4) c More b Wasson		32
A.J.Lamb	b Kapil Dev	7	(5) c Shastri b Kapil Dev		52
R.A.Smith	c Manjrekar b Shastri	57	(6) not out		7
R.C.Russell +	run out	35			
E.E.Hemmings	c Vengsarkar b Prabhakar	51			
A.R.C.Fraser	c More b Prabhakar	0			
D.E.Malcolm	not out	15			
Extras	(b 8,lb 9,w 4,nb 9)	30	(b 16,lb 22,w 6,nb 11)		55
TOTAL		340	(for 4 wkts dec)		477

ENGLAND	O	M	R	W	O	M	R	W
Malcolm	35	7	110	2				
Fraser	42	17	112	2				
Williams	41	5	148	2				
Gooch	12	1	44	0				
Hemmings	36	3	117	2				
Atherton	7	0	60	1				

INDIA	O	M	R	W	O	M	R	W
Kapil Dev	25	7	70	1	24	5	66	2
Prabhakar	32.4	9	74	4	25	8	56	0
Wasson	19	3	79	2	18	2	94	1
Hirwani	35	12	71	1	59	18	137	1
Shastri	12	2	29	1	28	2	86	0

FALL OF WICKETS

	IND	ENG	IND	ENG
1st	16	18		176
2nd	61	92		251
3rd	150	111		334
4th	289	120		463
5th	335	139		
6th	368	231		
7th	478	233		
8th	552	295		
9th	576	299		
10th		340		

Man of the match: R.J.Shastri (India)

Ravi Shastri, whose marathon innings formed the basis for India's largest total against England.

HEADLINES

England vs India: Third Cornhill Test
23rd - 28th August

● After the first three days of the Oval Test, it looked as though the summer could end on a disappointing note for England, but, after they had been forced to follow on 266 runs behind, an innings of great character and skill from David Gower brought England to safety, won the series and banished doubts about his own future in Test cricket

● After winning the toss, it was India's turn to take advantage of a pefect wicket and a lacklustre bowling attack, as they made their highest total against England. Ravi Shastri batted almost 10 hours for his 10th Test 100 and his highest Test score and Kapil Dev weighed in with his 7th Test 100, his first in England

● Although Graham Gooch again top scored with 85 it was only Eddie Hemmings's second Test 50 and a last-wicket stand of 41 with Devon Malcolm who improved his Test best for the second innings in succession that took England to 340

● Thoughts of India levelling the series were first rendered unlikely by an opening partnership of 176 by Gooch and Mike Atherton, their fourth better than 150 in six Tests, and finally dispelled by David Gower's unbeaten 157, the 16th 100 of his Test career and his second against India

● Graham Gooch crowned his record-breaking summer by beating Sir Donald Bradman's aggregate of 974 Test runs in 1930 and becoming the first man to score 1,000 runs in Test matches in an English season. His batting master-class was finally ended by Narendra Hirwani with 1058 runs to his name, 752 in six innings against India, by a long margin a record in a three-match series

● England had come to the end of a summer which had seen them beat both New Zealand and India, remain unbeaten in a full Test summer for the first time since 1978, and take their record under Gooch's leadership in 1990 to played 8, won 3 drawn 5

● Test debut: N.F.Williams (England)

● Men of the series: G.A.Gooch (England); M.Azharuddin (India)

TOUR MATCHES

BRITANNIC ASS. CHAMPIONSHIP

WORLD XI vs. INDIA

at Scarborough on 29th, 30th, 31st August 1990
Toss : World XI.   Umpires : J.H.Hampshire and B.Leadbeater
Match drawn

WORLD XI

Mudassar Nazar	c Kapil Dev b Wasson	29	not out		107
C.G.Greenidge *	lbw b Sharma	23	b Sharma		0
R.B.Richardson	c Prabhakar b Kumble	65	c Raman b Sharma		42
M.J.Greatbatch	not out	168	not out		128
R.A.Harper	st Mongia b Raman	17			
P.R.Sleep	c Kumble b Kapil Dev	42			
D.L.Bairstow +					
E.A.Moseley					
C.Sharma					
M.R.Whitney					
C.Pringle					
Extras	(b 2,lb 18,nb 15)	35	(b 1,lb 15,nb 7)		23
TOTAL	(for 5 wkts dec)	379	(for 2 wkts dec)		300

INDIA

W.V.Raman	c Greenidge b Pringle	58	b Whitney		13
N.R.Mongia +	c Bairstow b Whitney	10	c Bairstow b Moseley		15
S.V.Manjrekar *	c Whitney b Sleep	59	(5) c Bairstow b Whitney		62
S.R.Tendulkar	c Pringle b Harper	23	c Pringle b Sleep		108
D.B.Vengsarkar	c Greatbatch b Whitney	3	(6) not out		25
M.Prabhakar	b Harper	15	(7) c Greatbatch b Harper		10
Kapil Dev	c Harper b Pringle	19	(3) c Richardson b Whitney		3
A.R.Kumble	lbw b Harper	2	not out		5
K.S.More	c Bairstow b Sleep	18			
S.K.Sharma	not out	34			
A.Wasson	b Harper	24			
Extras	(b 8,lb 8,w 4,nb 7)	27	(lb 6,nb 6)		12
TOTAL		292	(for 6 wkts)		253

INDIA	O	M	R	W	O	M	R	W
Sharma	20	3	91	1	9	0	53	2
Prabhakar	4	0	7	0	13	3	45	0
Wasson	8	1	42	1				
Tendulkar	12	1	70	0	7	0	32	0
Kumble	24	4	103	1	17	1	72	0
Raman	8	1	44	1				
Kapil Dev	0.4	0	2	1	5	0	28	0
More					8	0	54	0

WORLD XI	O	M	R	W	O	M	R	W
Moseley	9	2	22	0	12	1	36	1
Whitney	14	4	51	2	13	1	46	3
Pringle	12	0	49	2	7	1	36	0
Sharma	8	0	39	0	5	0	30	0
Harper	17.4	4	68	4	16	4	36	1
Sleep	7	0	47	2	12	1	63	1

FALL OF WICKETS

	WXI	IND	WXI	IND
1st	44	59	6	34
2nd	72	114	77	34
3rd	189	154		43
4th	252	168		198
5th	379	169		225
6th		199		243
7th		206		
8th		229		
9th		245		
10th		292		

WARWICKSHIRE vs. SRI LANKA

at Edgbaston on 29th, 30th, 31st August 1990
Toss : Warwickshire.   Umpires : M.J.Harris and R.Julian
Sri Lanka won by 8 wickets

WARWICKSHIRE

A.J.Moles	b Wijegunawardene	117	c Attapatu b Madurasinghe		38
J.D.Ratcliffe	c Attapatu b Ramanayake	5	c Tillekeratne b Wijeguna'		14
D.P.Ostler	c Wijeguna' b Madurasinghe	56	lbw b Ramanayake		3
S.J.Green	c Jayasuriya b Madurasinghe	44	c Kuruppu b Wijeguna'		0
R.G.Twose	not out	64	(6) c Attapatu b Madurasinghe		4
D.A.Reeve *	lbw b Madurasinghe	5	(5) lbw b Ramanayake		1
N.M.K.Smith	b Ramanayake	1	c De Silva b Hathurasinghe		43
K.J.Piper +	lbw b Ramanayake	19	b Madurasinghe		0
J.E.Benjamin	b Madurasinghe	2	(11) b Hathurasinghe		14
P.A.Booth	b Wijegunawardene	8	(9) lbw b Madurasinghe		1
A.A.Donald	not out	4	(10) not out		0
Extras	(lb 8,nb 16)	24	(b 4,lb 7,nb 4)		15
TOTAL	(for 9 wkts dec)	349			133

SRI LANKA

R.S.Mahanama	lbw b Benjamin	30			
C.Hathurasinghe	b Twose	19	(1) lbw b Donald		19
D.S.B.P.Kuruppu	c sub b Reeve	1	(2) c Piper b Booth		40
P.A.De Silva *	lbw b Reeve	67	(3) not out		54
H.P.Tillekaratne +	not out	109	(4) not out		29
S.T.Jayasuriya	not out	78			
M.Attapatu					
C.P.Ramanayake					
K.I.W.Wijegunawardene					
M.A.W.R.Madurasinghe					
F.S.Ahangama					
Extras	(b 4,lb 8,w 1,nb 10)	23	(b 5,lb 6,nb 4)		15
TOTAL	(for 4 wkts dec)	327	(for 2 wkts)		157

SRI LANKA	O	M	R	W	O	M	R	W
Ramanayake	27	4	96	3	22	5	53	2
Ahangama	1.3	0	4	0				
Wijeguna'	19.3	4	82	2	15	3	31	2
Hathurasinghe	6	2	14	0	3.1	3	2	2
Madurasinghe	40	6	120	4	17	6	35	4
De Silva	9	1	25	0				

WARWICKS	O	M	R	W	O	M	R	W
Donald	11.5	4	33	0	9	1	35	1
Benjamin	12	0	59	1	5	0	22	0
Reeve	14	3	46	2	6	1	29	0
Twose	13	4	40	1				
Booth	17	1	77	0	11.3	3	41	1
Smith	22	3	60	0	2	0	19	0

FALL OF WICKETS

	WAR	SRI	WAR	SRI
1st	10	42	23	59
2nd	142	44	30	107
3rd	209	58	33	
4th	269	164	46	
5th	281		57	
6th	293		83	
7th	321		83	
8th	324		101	
9th	345		132	
10th			133	

NORTHANTS vs. ESSEX

at Northampton on 29th, 30th, 31st August 1990
Toss : Essex.   Umpires : D.J.Constant and K.J.Lyons
Match drawn (Northants 7 pts (Bt: 4, Bw:3) Essex 5 pts (Bt: 4, Bw: 1))

ESSEX

G.A.Gooch *	c & b Williams	174	c Lamb b Bailey		126
J.P.Stephenson	b Penberthy	76	c Davis b Thomas		82
P.J.Prichard	c Fordham b Williams	22	not out		29
M.E.Waugh	b Davis	1	b Penberthy		16
N.Hussain	not out	30	b Penberthy		3
M.A.Garnham +	lbw b Davis	1	not out		23
D.R.Pringle	lbw b Williams	1			
N.A.Foster	c Fordham b Williams	50			
M.C.Ilott					
J.H.Childs					
P.M.Such					
Extras	(b 5,lb 12,w 1,nb 17)	35	(lb 14,w 1,nb 9)		24
TOTAL	(for 7 wkts dec)	390	(for 4 wkts dec)		303

NORTHANTS

A.Fordham	lbw b Foster	16
N.A.Felton	c Stephenson b Foster	0
D.Ripley +	c Garnham b Waugh	50
W.Larkins	c Waugh b Stephenson	207
R.J.Bailey *	lbw b Pringle	108
A.J.Lamb	c Prichard b Such	134
R.G.Williams	not out	21
A.L.Penberthy	not out	15
W.W.Davis		
J.G.Thomas		
M.A.Robinson		
Extras	(b 14,lb 21,nb 6)	41
TOTAL	(for 6 wkts dec)	592

NORTHANTS	O	M	R	W	O	M	R	W
Davis	24	1	76	2	5	0	37	0
Robinson	14	0	75	0	15	0	69	0
Thomas	13	2	60	0	14	3	49	1
Penberthy	20	4	59	1	14	1	67	2
Williams	26.4	8	99	4	4	1	8	0
Bailey	1	0	4	0	16	4	59	1
Felton					1	1	0	0

ESSEX	O	M	R	W	O	M	R	W
Foster	31	6	115	2				
Ilott	27	4	115	0				
Pringle	14	2	46	1				
Waugh	19	1	96	1				
Childs	14	4	46	0				
Such	15	1	57	1				
Stephenson	9	1	40	1				
Gooch	6	0	42	0				

FALL OF WICKETS

	ESS	NOR	ESS	NOR
1st	227	9	220	
2nd	300	45	231	
3rd	301	94	254	
4th	308	303	258	
5th	310	514		
6th	313	561		
7th	390			
8th				
9th				
10th				

HEADLINES

29th - 31st August

● India managed their 10th draw in 13 first-class matches on their tour, but the Scarborough crowd was given plenty of entertainment in their encounter with Michael Parkinson's World XI. Mark Greatbatch hit 100s in both innings and Mudassar Nazar also made a hundred for the World XI, while Sachin Tendulkar made his second 100 of the tour for the Indians, who finished well short of their target of 388

● By contrast, Sri Lanka gained their first first-class victory over an English county as they outplayed Warwickshire to win by eight wickets at Edgbaston. Hashan Tillekeratne and Stanley Jayasuriya shared a fifth wicket stand of 163 in the Sri Lankan first innings and Ranjith Madurasinghe claimed four wickets in each innings

BRITANNIC ASSURANCE CHAMPIONSHIP

HAMPSHIRE vs. KENT

at Bournemouth on 29th, 30th, 31st August 1990
Toss : Hampshire.   Umpires : J.H.Harris and B.Hassan
Match drawn (Hampshire 4 pts (Bt: 2, Bw: 2) Kent 6 pts (Bt: 4, Bw: 2))

HAMPSHIRE

Batsman	Dismissal	R	Dismissal	R
T.C.Middleton	lbw b Kelleher	4	c Taylor b Patel	104
C.L.Smith	c Davis b Merrick	32	c Marsh b Fleming	53
D.I.Gower	c Marsh b Wells	44	c Davis b Wells	3
R.A.Smith	c Patel b Davis	9	c sub b Davis	74
M.C.J.Nicholas *	c Fleming b Wells	1	not out	42
A.N Aymes +	c Davis b Merrick	70	not out	10
T.M.Tremlett	c Davis b Fleming	78		
R.J.Maru	c Cowdrey b Fleming	34		
L.A.Joseph	not out	2		
S.D.Udal				
P.J.Bakker				
Extras	(lb 4,w 1,nb 3)	8	(b 1,lb 9,nb 1)	11
TOTAL	(for 8 wkts dec)	282	(for 4 wkts dec)	297

KENT

Batsman	Dismissal	R	Dismissal	R
S.G.Hinks	c Smith C.L. b Bakker	0	run out	27
T.R.Ward	c Smith R.A. b Tremlett	175	c Smith C.L. b Joseph	8
V.J.Wells	c Middleton b Maru	58	lbw b Udal	9
G.R.Cowdrey	c & b Maru	47	c sub b Udal	41
S.A.Marsh +	c Bakker b Joseph	3	(7) b Bakker	34
M.V.Fleming	not out	45	b Udal	76
N.R.Taylor *			(5) lbw b Tremlett	0
D.J.M.Kelleher			c Nicholas b Bakker	9
R.P.Davis			lbw b Bakker	0
M.M.Patel			not out	0
T.A.Merrick			not out	0
Extras	(lb 3)	3	(b 1,lb 5,nb 1)	7
TOTAL	(for 5 wkts dec)	331	(for 9 wkts)	211

KENT	O	M	R	W	O	M	R	W	FALL OF WICKETS				
										HAM	KEN	HAM	KEN
Merrick	28	8	62	2	5.2	3	8	0	1st	14	0	137	18
Kelleher	16	4	54	1	6	2	14	0	2nd	71	131	156	49
Davis	14	4	31	1	30.5	2	127	1	3rd	80	215	192	55
Wells	13	3	29	2	8	4	8	1	4th	85	227	266	55
Fleming	30.5	9	75	2	6	0	18	1	5th	108	331		146
Patel	16	4	27	0	29.4	6	112	1	6th	210			173
Ward					1	1	0	0	7th	275			202
HAMPSHIRE	O	M	R	W	O	M	R	W	8th	282			210
Bakker	14	1	73	1	11	3	24	3	9th				211
Joseph	10	1	76	1	12	1	67	1	10th				
Tremlett	7.4	1	46	1	6	0	44	1					
Maru	18.3	6	48	2									
Udal	16	2	80	0	18	4	70	3					
Smith R.A.	0.3	0	5	0									

GLAMORGAN vs. DERBYSHIRE

at Cardiff on 29th, 30th, 31st August 1990
Toss : Derbyshire.   Umpires : A.A.Jones and R.Palmer
Match drawn (Glamorgan 8 pts (Bt: 4, Bw: 4) Derbyshire 4 pts (Bt: 1, Bw: 3))

GLAMORGAN

Batsman	Dismissal	R	Dismissal	R
A.R.Butcher *	b Base	4	not out	13
H.Morris	not out	160	c Mortensen b Morris	4
P.A.Cottey	c Adams b Malcolm	8	b Adams	3
M.P.Maynard	c Barnett b Warner	20	not out	11
I.V.A.Richards	c Roberts b Mortensen	0		
A.Dale	lbw b Mortensen	16		
R.D.B.Croft	c & b Barnett	31		
C.P.Metson +	c Bowler b Barnett	22		
S.L.Watkin	c Krikken b Warner	8		
S.Bastien	not out	9		
M.Frost				
Extras	(lb 10,w 3,nb 10)	23	(b 4,lb 1,w 1,nb 4)	10
TOTAL	(for 8 wkts dec)	301	(for 2 wkts)	41

DERBYSHIRE

Batsman	Dismissal	R
P.D.Bowler	b Croft	28
C.J.Adams	c Butcher b Watkin	14
J.E.Morris	b Croft	40
B.Roberts	lbw b Frost	5
S.J.Base	c Morris b Croft	0
A.P.Kuiper	b Frost	0
K.J.Barnett *	c Metson b Watkin	30
K.M.Krikken +	lbw b Frost	0
A.E.Warner	b Watkin	59
D.E.Malcolm	b Frost	2
O.H.Mortensen	not out	1
Extras	(b 4,lb 5)	9
TOTAL		188

DERBYSHIRE	O	M	R	W	O	M	R	W	FALL OF WICKETS				
										GLA	DER	GLA	DER
Malcolm	16	4	61	1					1st	6	23	8	
Base	18	3	73	1	2	0	14	0	2nd	40	81	30	
Mortensen	18	6	48	2					3rd	79	92		
Warner	16	2	53	2					4th	80	92		
Barnett	21.4	2	56	2					5th	123	92		
Morris					4	0	17	1	6th	206	92		
Adams					2	0	5	1	7th	262	94		
GLAMORGAN	O	M	R	W	O	M	R	W	8th	285	167		
Watkin	14.4	0	39	3					9th		170		
Bastien	7	0	41	0					10th		188		
Dale	2	0	9	0									
Frost	18	3	80	4									
Croft	10	4	10	3									

NOTTINGHAMSHIRE vs. WORCESTERSHIRE

at Trent Bridge on 29th, 30th, 31st August 1990
Toss : Nottinghamshire.   Umpires : H.D.Bird and J.D.Bond
Match drawn (Nottinghamshire 7 pts (Bt: 4, Bw: 3) Worcestershire 8 pts (Bt: 4, Bw: 4))

NOTTINGHAMSHIRE

Batsman	Dismissal	R	Dismissal	R
B.C.Broad	c Illingworth b Hick	156	c Hick b Newport	7
M.Newell	c Rhodes b Newport	1	run out	16
D.J.R.Martindale	c Newport b Lampitt	37	c Rhodes b Newport	14
P.Johnson	c Neale b Hick	98	c Neale b McEwan	13
R.T.Robinson *	b Lampitt	39	c Rhodes b Illingworth	45
K.P.Evans	c Neale b Illingworth	12	c Hick b Newport	0
F.D.Stephenson	b Newport	25	c Rhodes b Illingworth	30
B.N.French +	b Newport	3	c Hick b Illingworth	25
E.E.Hemmings	not out	12	not out	6
K.E.Cooper	b Newport	7	not out	1
R.A.Pick	not out	4		
Extras	(b 2,lb 3,nb 3)	8	(lb 1,w 2,nb 4)	7
TOTAL	(for 9 wkts dec)	402	(for 8 wkts dec)	164

WORCESTERSHIRE

Batsman	Dismissal	R	Dismissal	R
T.S.Curtis	b Evans	82	not out	84
G.J.Lord	c French b Pick	13	c Pick b Hemmings	12
S.M.McEwan	b Stephenson	6		
G.A.Hick	c French b Stephenson	4	(3) c Broad b Hemmings	18
D.A.Leatherdale	b Stephenson	2	(4) lbw b Cooper	10
P.A.Neale *	lbw b Cooper	74	(5) not out	5
S.R.Lampitt	lbw b Hemmings	40		
S.J.Rhodes +	not out	50		
R.K.Illingworth	not out	15		
P.J.Newport				
G.R.Dilley				
Extras	(lb 6,nb 9)	15	(b 1,lb 5,nb 1)	7
TOTAL	(for 7 wkts dec)	301	(for 3 wkts)	136

WORCS	O	M	R	W	O	M	R	W	FALL OF WICKETS				
										NOT	WOR	NOT	WOR
Dilley	12	3	47	0					1st	2	22	16	57
Newport	18.4	2	75	4	23	7	50	3	2nd	107	49	41	89
McEwan	14	1	76	0	13	4	41	1	3rd	290	53	55	119
Lampitt	22	2	90	2	10	1	38	0	4th	303	57	59	
Illingworth	22	5	79	1	18	9	34	3	5th	336	153	59	
Hick	8	0	30	2					6th	368	197	106	
NOTTS	O	M	R	W	O	M	R	W	7th	375	251	142	
Stephenson	21.2	3	72	3	12	1	51	0	8th	382		161	
Pick	18	2	72	1	3	0	21	0	9th	390			
Cooper	16	4	48	1	7	0	28	1	10th				
Hemmings	25	7	54	1	12	1	27	2					
Evans	17	2	49	1	1	0	3	0					

HEADLINES

29th - 31st August

● Although they could extract only five points from their drawn match with Northants, Essex moved four points ahead of Middlesex in the Championship table. Batsmen from both sides made the most of a pitch full of runs with Graham Gooch leading the way once more. He hit 100s in both innings to take his aggregate of runs in first-class cricket to 2614 and his tally of 100s to 12. Northants prevented any hope of an Essex victory by compiling their highest total as Wayne Larkins made the season's latest double century

● Hampshire, Lancashire, Leicestershire and Worcestershire could all have moved into third place behind Essex and Middlesex had they forced victory but remarkably Sussex were the only county to win yet remained rooted to the bottom of the table.

● Kent's Trevor Ward made a swashbuckling career best 175 against Hampshire at Bournemouth but the home side finished only one wicket short of victory, while heavy drizzle ruined first-class cricket's return to Blackpool where Lancs and Surrey barely had time to complete one innings

● Chris Broad made his 8th 100 of the season in Notts' draw with Worcestershire at Trent Bridge, while another left-handed opener, Hugh Morris, enjoying an even more prolific season, hit his 10th 100 of the summer, and a career best into the bargain, as Glamorgan took first innings advantage over Derbyshire at Cardiff

BRITANNIC ASSURANCE CHAMPIONSHIP

LANCASHIRE vs. SURREY

at Blackpool on 29th (no play), 30th, 31st August 1990
Toss : Lancashire. Umpires : B.J.Meyer and R.A.White
Match drawn (Lancashire 3 pts (Bt: 3, Bw: 0) Surrey 3 pts (Bt: 0, Bw: 3))

LANCASHIRE

G.D.Mendis	c Lynch b Bicknell M.P.	94
G.Fowler	lbw b Murphy	42
G.D.Lloyd	lbw b Medlycott	1
N.H.Fairbrother	c Stewart b Murphy	8
T.E.Jesty	b Waqar Younis	25
M.Watkinson	lbw b Waqar Younis	0
Wasim Akram	c Bicknell D.J. b Feltham	17
P.A.J.DeFreitas	b Bicknell M.P.	13
W.K.Hegg +	not out	34
I.D.Austin	not out	6
D.P.Hughes *		
Extras	(b 3,lb 6,w 2,nb 10)	21
TOTAL	(for 8 wkts dec)	261

SURREY

D.J.Bicknell	lbw b Wasim Akram	25
R.I.Alikhan	c Hegg b DeFreitas	9
A.J.Stewart +	not out	23
D.M.Ward	not out	16
M.A.Lynch		
I.A.Greig *		
M.A.Feltham		
K.T.Medlycott		
M.P.Bicknell		
Waqar Younis		
A.J.Murphy		
Extras	(b 1,lb 2,nb 6)	9
TOTAL	(for 2 wkts dec)	82

SURREY	O	M	R	W	O	M	R	W		FALL OF WICKETS			
											LAN	SUR	LAN	SUR
Waqar Younis	18	4	65	2					1st	97	40		
Bicknell M.P.	18	3	65	2					2nd	100	48		
Feltham	13	4	40	1					3rd	112			
Murphy	17	1	73	2					4th	170			
Medlycott	5	1	9	1					5th	170			
									6th	198			
LANCASHIRE	O	M	R	W	O	M	R	W	7th	217			
Wasim Akram	11	2	32	1					8th	218			
DeFreitas	8	4	31	1					9th				
Watkinson	6	3	13	0					10th				
Austin	4	2	3	0									

LEICESTERSHIRE vs. SUSSEX

at Leicester on 29th, 30th, 31st August 1990
Toss : Leicestershire. Umpires : M.J.Kitchen and A.G.T.Whitehead
Sussex won by 29 runs (Leicestershire 4 pts (Bt: 3, Bw: 1) Sussex 23 pts (Bt: 4, Bw: 3))

SUSSEX

N.J.Lenham	lbw b Parsons	58	c Whitticase b Parsons	40
J.W.Hall	lbw b Willey	34	c Whitticase b Lewis	17
K.Greenfield	c sub b Millns	38	(4) b Willey	20
A.P.Wells *	not out	109	(5) c Parsons b Millns	43
M.P.Speight	c Potter b Millns	45	(7) lbw b Millns	53
A.I.C.Dodemaide	not out	17	lbw b Lewis	0
I.D.K.Salisbury			(3) c Potter b Parsons	6
J.A.North			c Willey b Millns	0
P.Moores +			c Lewis b Millns	18
A.C.S.Pigott			not out	6
R.A.Bunting			c Lewis b Parsons	0
Extras	(lb 6,w 1,nb 6)	13	(lb 6,nb 1)	7
TOTAL	(for 4 wkts dec)	314		210

LEICESTERSHIRE

T.J.Boon	lbw b Pigott	6	run out	14
N.E.Briers *	c Dodemaide b Pigott	0	c Moores b Salisbury	78
J.J.Whitaker	c Bunting b Pigott	16	b Dodemaide	42
P.Willey	c Wells b North	112	c Lenham b Salisbury	35
L.Potter	b Pigott	51	c Greenfield b Salisbury	4
C.C.Lewis	st Moores b Salisbury	20	st Moores b Salisbury	54
P.N.Hepworth	c Moores b Pigott	17	run out	0
P.Whitticase +	not out	11	c Wells b Salisbury	4
G.J.Parsons	not out	1	b Pigott	1
J.P.Agnew			not out	2
D.J.Millns			b Pigott	1
Extras	(b 9,lb 5,w 2,nb 2)	18	(lb 6,nb 2)	8
TOTAL	(for 7 wkts dec)	252		243

LEICS	O	M	R	W	O	M	R	W		FALL OF WICKETS			
											SUS	LEI	SUS	LEI
Agnew	9	2	35	0					1st	90	1	49	34
Lewis	23	3	62	0	14	1	36	2	2nd	98	6	59	114
Millns	16	1	67	2	11	3	48	4	3rd	186	34	82	156
Parsons	17	5	53	1	20	2	90	3	4th	277	135	96	160
Willey	27	10	61	1	17	9	30	1	5th		174	97	183
Potter	8	1	30	0					6th		234	166	187
									7th		247	166	212
SUSSEX	O	M	R	W	O	M	R	W	8th			192	224
Pigott	17	5	52	5	10.1	2	41	2	9th			205	240
Dodemaide	20	4	30	0	18	1	64	1	10th			210	243
Bunting	15	7	21	0	5	0	27	0					
North	14	0	48	1	4	0	26	0					
Salisbury	33.4	9	87	1	17	1	79	5					

LEADING FIRST-CLASS AVERAGES
at 31st August 1990

BATTING AVERAGES Qualifying requirements : 6 completed innings

Name	M	I	NO	Runs	HS	Avge	100s	50s
G.A.Gooch	16	28	3	2614	333	104.56	12	7
T.M.Moody	9	15	2	1163	168	89.46	7	1
G.A.Hick	18	29	8	1820	252 *	86.66	5	13
S.J.Cook	22	37	7	2373	313 *	79.10	8	10
N.H.Fairbrother	19	29	7	1708	366	77.63	4	9
B.R.Hardie	11	16	7	686	125	76.22	2	4
M.E.Waugh	20	30	6	1823	207 *	75.95	7	8
M.A.Crawley	10	12	3	672	105 *	74.66	2	5
M.A.Atherton	18	29	3	1821	191	70.03	7	11
D.L.Haynes	20	35	4	2158	255 *	69.61	8	6
C.J.Tavare	22	28	4	1603	219	66.79	3	12
R.A.Smith	16	26	7	1266	181	66.63	5	7
D.M.Ward	21	29	7	1462	191	66.45	5	1
D.J.Bicknell	12	18	4	926	169	66.14	3	5
R.J.Bailey	21	35	8	1742	204 *	64.51	6	8
A.J.Lamb	15	25	4	1342	235	63.90	5	4
A.R.Butcher	20	35	5	1869	151 *	62.30	6	12
C.L.Smith	21	36	6	1860	148	62.00	4	12
I.V.A.Richards	18	28	5	1425	164 *	61.95	7	3
J.P.Stephenson	22	37	8	1749	202 *	60.31	4	11

BOWLING AVERAGES Qualifying requirements : 20 wickets taken

Name	O	M	R	W	Avge	Best	5wI	10wM
I.R.Bishop	335.4	77	912	50	18.24	6-71	2	-
M.D.Marshall	461	116	1165	59	19.74	7-47	2	1
O.H.Mortensen	281.5	81	702	32	21.93	4-22	-	-
Waqar Younis	389	66	1245	54	23.05	7-73	3	1
D.J.Millns	173.4	33	568	24	23.66	5-47	1	-
G.J.Parsons	265.5	74	784	33	23.75	6-75	2	-
M.C.Ilott	178.1	42	544	22	24.72	5-34	2	-
K.J.Barnett	251.3	47	661	25	26.44	4-28	-	-
C.A.Walsh	498.1	85	1680	63	26.66	8-58	3	1
M.P.Bicknell	636.5	148	1751	65	26.93	5-34	1	-
C.E.L.Ambrose	418	109	1139	42	27.11	5-49	3	-
A.R.C.Fraser	448.2	104	1145	42	27.26	6-30	3	-
D.A.Reeve	362.4	108	901	33	27.30	4-42	-	-
N.A.Foster	646	135	1994	72	27.69	6-32	4	1
J.E.Benjamin	388.3	68	1205	43	28.02	5-29	4	-
R.K.Illingworth	749	241	1808	64	28.25	5-59	1	-
D.J.Capel	234	51	711	25	28.44	5-74	1	-
M.A.Feltham	329	57	1081	37	29.21	6-53	2	-
D.R.Pringle	358.3	90	994	34	29.23	5-66	1	-
I.T.Botham	194.4	38	614	21	29.23	4-65	-	-

Britannic Assurance Championship Table
at 31st August 1990

		P	W	L	D	T	Bt	Bl	Pts
1	Essex (2)	19	8	1	10	0	64	46	238
2	Middlesex (3)	19	8	1	10	0	61	45	234
3	Warwicks (8)	19	6	7	6	0	45	58	199
4	Hampshire (6)	20	6	4	10	0	62	40	198
5	Leicestershire (13)	20	6	6	8	0	55	46	197
6	Lancashire (4)	20	5	3	12	0	61	49	190
7	Worcestershire (1)	19	5	1	13	0	58	50	188
8	Surrey (12)	19	4	3	12	0	47	58	177
9	Glamorgan (17)	19	5	3	11	0	57	38	175
10	Derbyshire (7)	20	6	6	8	0	52	48	171
11	Notts (11)	19	4	5	10	0	44	54	162
12	Somerset (14)	20	3	3	14	0	66	41	155
13	Yorkshire (16)	20	3	9	8	0	45	51	144
14	Kent (15)	20	3	6	11	0	61	33	142
	Northants (5)	20	2	9	9	0	56	54	142
16	Gloucestershire (9)	19	3	6	10	0	40	49	137
17	Sussex (10)	20	3	7	10	0	49	39	136

Surrey's total includes 8 points for batting second in a drawn match in which scores finished level. Derbyshire had 25 points deducted for an unsatisfactory pitch.

NATWEST TROPHY FINAL

TOUR MATCHES

LANCASHIRE vs. NORTHANTS

at Lord's on 1st September 1990
Toss : Lancashire. Umpires : J.W.Holder and D.R.Shepherd
Lancashire won by 7 wickets

NORTHANTS

A.Fordham	lbw b DeFreitas	5
N.A.Felton	c Allott b DeFreitas	4
W.Larkins	c Hegg b DeFreitas	7
A.J.Lamb *	lbw b DeFreitas	8
R.J.Bailey	c Hegg b DeFreitas	7
D.J.Capel	run out	36
R.G.Williams	b Watkinson	9
D.Ripley +	b Watkinson	13
C.E.L.Ambrose	run out	48
N.G.B.Cook	b Austin	9
M.A.Robinson	not out	3
Extras	(b 1,lb 10,w 9,nb 2)	22
TOTAL	(60 overs)	171

LANCASHIRE

G.D.Mendis	c Ripley b Capel	14
G.Fowler	c Cook b Robinson	7
M.A.Atherton	not out	38
N.H.Fairbrother	c Ambrose b Williams	81
M.Watkinson	not out	24
Wasim Akram		
P.A.J.DeFreitas		
W.K.Hegg +		
I.D.Austin		
D.P.Hughes *		
P.J.W.Allott		
Extras	(lb 4,w 2,nb 3)	9
TOTAL	(45.4 overs)(for 3 wkts)	173

LANCASHIRE	O	M	R	W	FALL OF WICKETS		
						NOR	LAN
Allott	12	3	29	0			
DeFreitas	12	5	26	5	1st	8	16
Wasim Akram	12	0	35	0	2nd	19	28
Watkinson	12	1	29	2	3rd	20	142
Austin	12	4	41	1	4th	38	
					5th	39	
NORTHANTS	O	M	R	W	6th	56	
Ambrose	10	1	23	0	7th	87	
Robinson	9	2	26	1	8th	126	
Cook	10.4	2	50	0	9th	166	
Capel	9	0	44	1	10th	171	
Williams	7	0	26	1			

Man of the match: P.A.J.DeFreitas

HEADLINES

NatWest Trophy Final

1st September

● Lancashire made history by becoming the first county to win both knockout competitions in the same season and also the first to win the 60-over version on five occasions, skipper David Hughes having played in all five winning sides

● Even in a summer that has seen almost uniformly heavy scoring, the final was effectively decided in the first hour's play. Hughes won the toss, asked Northants to bat and Phil DeFreitas captured the first five wickets for 19 runs in his 7-over opening spell. Northants were 39 for 5 and, although they managed to bat out their 60 overs, their total of 171 was never enough to test Lancashire. DeFreitas's final figures of 5 for 26 were his best in the competition and have been bettered only by Joel Garner in the 28 finals

● Neil Fairbrother put the result beyond doubt with 81 from 68 balls and Lancs secured victory by seven wickets with more than 14 overs to spare

SURREY vs. SRI LANKA

at The Oval on 2nd September 1990
Toss : Sri Lanka. Umpires : B.Hassan and R.Julian
Surrey won by 14 runs

SURREY

D.J.Bicknell	c & b De Silva	86
R.I.Alikhan	b Gurusinha	22
G.P.Thorpe *	c Attapatu b De Silva	63
J.D.Robinson	c Wickremasinghe b De Silva	33
A.Brown	c Wickremasinghe b De Silva	2
K.T.Medlycott	c Tillekaratne b Labrooy	20
C.K.Bullen	not out	1
N.F.Sargeant +		
N.M.Kendrick		
A.H.Gray		
A.J.Murphy		
Extras	(b 2,lb 10,w 14)	26
TOTAL	(55 overs)(for 6 wkts)	253

SRI LANKA

D.S.B.P.Kuruppu	c Murphy b Bullen	33
H.P.Tillekaratne +	c Bullen b Murphy	45
A.P.Gurusinha	lbw b Bullen	4
P.A.De Silva *	c Robinson b Kendrick	35
S.T.Jayasuriya	c Bicknell b Kendrick	32
R.S.Mahanama	hit wicket b Kendrick	24
M.Attapatu	b Gray	19
G.F.Labrooy	c Bullen b Murphy	28
P.Wickremasinghe	b Gray	12
R.Madurasinghe	not out	1
K.Wijegunawardene	c Medlycott b Murphy	1
Extras	(lb 3,w 2)	5
TOTAL	(53.5 overs)	239

SRI LANKA	O	M	R	W	FALL OF WICKETS		
						SUR	SRI
Labrooy	11	2	49	1			
Wickremasinghe	8	1	45	0	1st	70	64
Gurusinha	8	2	20	1	2nd	164	77
Madurasinghe	11	1	33	0	3rd	200	97
Wijegunawardene	9	1	39	0	4th	205	145
De Silva	8	0	55	4	5th	239	169
SURREY	O	M	R	W	6th	253	191
Gray	10	1	35	2	7th		207
Murphy	10.5	0	61	3	8th		237
Thorpe	3	1	15	0	9th		237
Robinson	5	0	25	0	10th		239
Bullen	11	1	37	2			
Medlycott	8	0	42	0			
Kendrick	6	0	21	3			

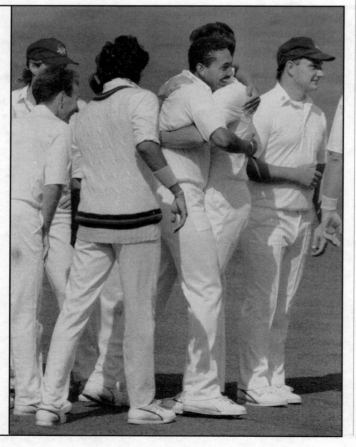

Lancashire's man of the match Phillip De Freitas receives congratulations on yet another success.

SOMERSET vs. SRI LANKA

at Taunton on 3rd September 1990
Toss : Sri Lanka. Umpires : A.A.Jones and P.B.Wight
Somerset won by 71 runs

SOMERSET

S.J.Cook	c Mahanama b Ramanayake	13
G.T.J.Townsend	run out	77
P.M.Roebuck	c & b Madurasinghe	95
G.D.Rose	c Wickremasinghe b Gurusinha	2
R.J.Harden	c Kuruppu b Ramanayake	25
N.D.Burns +	not out	29
C.J.Tavare *	not out	5
M.Lathwell		
P.Rendell		
A.Caddick		
A.N.Jones		
Extras	(lb 14,nb 2)	16
TOTAL	(48 overs)(for 5 wkts)	262

SRI LANKA

D.S.B.P.Kuruppu	lbw b Rose	1
H.P.Tillekaratne +	c Cook b Rose	23
A.P.Gurusinha	c Burns b Rose	1
P.A.De Silva *	c Burns b Rendell	33
S.T.Jayasuriya	c Rendell b Rose	6
R.S.Mahanama	c & b Rendell	11
M.Attapatu	not out	63
C.P.Ramanayake	lbw b Roebuck	12
P.Wickremasinghe	not out	24
K.I.W.Wijegunawardene		
M.A.W.R.Madurasinghe		
Extras	(lb 7,w 7,nb 3)	17
TOTAL	(48 overs)(for 7 wkts)	191

SRI LANKA	O	M	R	W	FALL OF WICKETS		
						SOM	SRI
Ramanayake	8	0	47	2			
Wickremasinghe	10	1	45	0	1st	23	4
Gurusinha	11	0	59	1	2nd	193	21
Wijegunawardene	9	0	50	0	3rd	198	31
Madurasinghe	10	0	47	1	4th	200	47
					5th	251	72
SOMERSET	O	M	R	W	6th		88
Jones	6	0	31	0	7th		119
Rose	6	1	16	4	8th		
Rendell	11	1	46	2	9th		
Caddick	6	1	19	0	10th		
Roebuck	11	0	30	1			
Lathwell	7	1	35	0			
Harden	1	0	7	0			

SEEBOARD TROPHY

SCARBOROUGH F'VAL

SUSSEX vs. KENT
at Hove on 2nd September 1990
Toss : Kent. Umpires : D.J.Constant and A.G.T.Whitehead
Kent won by 45 runs

KENT		
T.R.Ward	c Greenfield b Donelan	67
V.J.Wells	b Threlfall	18
J.I.Longley	c Moores b Dodemaide	3
G.R.Cowdrey	st Moores b Salisbury	43
N.R.Taylor *	c Smith b Lenham	30
M.V.Fleming	st Moores b Salisbury	6
S.A.Marsh +	st Moores b Donelan	52
D.J.M.Kelleher	c Greenfield b Donelan	2
M.A.Ealham	c Moores b Salisbury	4
M.N.Patel	c Salisbury b Dodemaide	1
T.Wren	not out	0
Extras	(b 1,lb 3,w 3)	7
TOTAL	(48.1 overs)	233

SUSSEX		
N.J.Lenham	b Fleming	47
D.M.Smith	lbw b Wren	14
K.Greenfield	c & b Taylor	34
A.P.Wells *	run out	5
I.J.Gould	c Longley b Ward	9
A.I.C.Dodemaide	c Marsh b Fleming	40
C.C.Remy	c Ealham b Fleming	16
P.Moores +	run out	2
I.D.K.Salisbury	c Marsh b Fleming	0
B.T.P.Donelan	c Wells b Wren	10
P.W.Threlfall	not out	0
Extras	(lb 6,w 3,nb 2)	11
TOTAL	(45.4 overs)	188

SUSSEX	O	M	R	W	FALL OF WICKETS		
						KEN	SUS
Dodemaide	9	2	20	2			
Threlfall	10	0	55	1	1st	20	51
Remy	4	0	32	0	2nd	29	75
Donelan	10	2	34	3	3rd	133	89
Salisbury	10	0	59	3	4th	133	113
Lenham	5.1	0	29	1	5th	143	133
					6th	220	162
KENT	O	M	R	W	7th	223	165
Wren	7	1	18	2	8th	229	167
Kelleher	2	0	19	0	9th	233	184
Patel	10	0	48	0	10th	233	188
Ward	10	0	23	1			
Fleming	7.4	0	30	4			
Ealham	3	0	14	0			
Taylor	6	0	30	1			

KENT vs. SURREY
at Hove on 4th September 1990
Toss : Kent. Umpires : D.J.Constant and A.G.T.Whitehead
Kent won by 35 runs

KENT		
T.R.Ward	b Robinson	41
V.J.Wells	run out	107
J.I.Longley	lbw b Waqar Younis	0
G.R.Cowdrey	b Murphy	78
N.R.Taylor *	b Greig	25
M.V.Fleming	not out	43
S.A.Marsh +	c Bicknell D.J. b Bicknell M.P.	2
D.J.M.Kelleher	not out	20
M.A.Ealham		
M.M.Patel		
T.Wren		
Extras	(b 4,lb 10,w 8)	22
TOTAL	(50 overs)(for 6 wkts)	338

SURREY		
D.J.Bicknell	c Marsh b Ealham	2
J.D.Robinson	b Ealham	98
G.P.Thorpe	c Marsh b Patel	78
A.J.Stewart +	c Wren b Ealham	52
D.M.Ward	b Wren	26
M.A.Lynch	b Ealham	0
I.A.Greig *	c Cowdrey b Ealham	4
C.K.Bullen	c Fleming b Ealham	6
M.P.Bicknell	b Ealham	2
Waqar Younis	not out	13
A.J.Murphy	c & b Ealham	2
Extras	(lb 3,w 14,nb 3)	20
TOTAL	(48.4 overs)	303

SURREY	O	M	R	W	FALL OF WICKETS		
						KEN	SUR
Bicknell M.P.	10	1	43	1	1st	78	18
Murphy	10	1	71	1	2nd	79	166
Waqar Younis	10	1	57	1	3rd	223	244
Robinson	10	1	54	1	4th	256	255
Bullen	4	0	49	0	5th	277	256
Greig	6	0	50	1	6th	286	266
					7th		281
KENT	O	M	R	W	8th		286
Wren	10	0	49	1	9th		301
Ealham	9.4	0	49	8	10th		303
Patel	8	0	50	1			
Ward	4	0	20	0			
Fleming	7	0	64	0			
Kelleher	10	0	68	0			

YORKSHIRE vs. WORLD XI
at Scarborough on 1st September 1990
Toss : World XI. Umpires : J.H.Hampshire and B.Leadbeater
World XI won by 7 runs

WORLD XI		
J.E.Morris	c & b Pickles	60
C.L.Hooper	c Hartley b Carrick	62
N.Hussain	c Blakey b Jarvis	30
M.E.Waugh	c Carrick b Jarvis	17
M.J.Greatbatch	lbw b Pickles	4
B.C.Lara	b Hartley	34
C.Sharma	c Moxon b Hartley	28
F.D.Stephenson	b Hartley	15
B.N.French +	not out	7
I.R.Bishop	not out	11
E.E.Hemmings *		
Extras	(lb 6,w 2,nb 2)	10
TOTAL	(50 overs)(for 8 wkts)	278

YORKSHIRE		
M.D.Moxon *	c Morris b Stephenson	19
A.A.Metcalfe	c French b Waugh	22
S.A.Kellett	b Hooper	57
P.E.Robinson	b Bishop	114
R.J.Blakey +	c Greatbatch b Hemmings	13
D.Byas	c French b Hemmings	1
P.Carrick	c Morris b Bishop	18
C.S.Pickles	not out	11
P.J.Hartley	b Stephenson	3
P.W.Jarvis	not out	0
J.D.Batty		
Extras	(b 1,lb 4,w 5,nb 3)	13
TOTAL	(50 overs)(for 8 wkts)	271

YORKSHIRE	O	M	R	W	FALL OF WICKETS		
						WXI	YOR
Jarvis	10	0	61	2			
Hartley	10	0	68	3	1st	121	26
Pickles	10	0	56	2	2nd	130	53
Batty	10	0	56	0	3rd	176	139
Carrick	10	0	31	1	4th	177	187
					5th	192	190
WORLD XI	O	M	R	W	6th	234	223
Bishop	10	1	56	2	7th	260	268
Stephenson	10	0	52	2	8th	261	271
Sharma	5	0	35	0	9th		
Waugh	5	0	27	1	10th		
Hemmings	10	0	45	2			
Hooper	10	1	51	1			

SURREY vs. WARWICKSHIRE
at Hove on 3rd September 1990
Toss : Surrey. Umpires : D.J.Constant and A.G.T.Whitehead
Surrey won by 4 wickets

WARWICKSHIRE		
Asif Din	c Bicknell D.J. b Greig	51
K.J.Piper +	lbw b Bullen	44
D.P.Ostler	c Lynch b Bullen	6
S.J.Green	b Waqar Younis	21
P.A.Smith	c Stewart b Waqar Younis	6
D.A.Reeve *	lbw b Waqar Younis	42
N.M.K.Smith	c Stewart b Bicknell M.P.	13
R.G.Twose	not out	8
A.A.Donald	not out	16
G.Smith		
T.A.Munton		
Extras	(b 2,lb 17,w 2)	21
TOTAL	(50 overs)(for 7 wkts)	228

SURREY		
D.J.Bicknell	c Twose b Reeve	33
G.S.Clinton	c Piper b Munton	8
G.P.Thorpe	c Twose b Reeve	30
A.J.Stewart +	c Smith N.M.K. b Reeve	36
D.M.Ward	c Piper b Smith G.	27
M.A.Lynch	not out	65
I.A.Greig *	run out	2
C.K.Bullen	not out	11
M.P.Bicknell		
Waqar Younis		
A.J.Murphy		
Extras	(lb 9,w 7,nb 2)	18
TOTAL	(49.1 overs)(for 6 wkts)	230

SURREY	O	M	R	W	FALL OF WICKETS		
						WAR	SUR
Bicknell M.P.	10	1	38	1			
Murphy	10	0	47	0	1st	86	24
Greig	6	0	26	1	2nd	104	68
Thorpe	4	0	21	0	3rd	133	104
Waqar Younis	10	2	31	3	4th	134	133
Bullen	10	0	46	2	5th	161	165
					6th	202	168
WARWICKS	O	M	R	W	7th	204	
Donald	10	3	24	1	8th		
Munton	10	0	64	1	9th		
Smith G.	9.1	2	38	1	10th		
Reeve	10	0	53	2			
Smith P.A.	10	0	42	0			

HEADLINES

1st - 6th September

● In the traditional quiet spell before the English season moves into its final stages competitive cricket could still be found at Scarborough and Hove

● Hampshire won the four-county knockout competition at Scarborough, as the Festival continued, while Mark Ealham's figures of 8 for 49 helped Kent beat Surrey in the final of the Seeboard Trophy at Hove in a contest that produced 641 runs

● Sri Lanka found Surrey and Somerset formidable opposition as the tourists lost the two one-day matches that formed part of their learning tour

HAMPSHIRE vs. WORCESTERSHIRE
at Scarborough on 2nd September 1990
Toss : WorcS. Umpires : B.Leadbeater and D.O.Oslear
Hampshire won by 81 runs

HAMPSHIRE		
V.P.Terry	st Rhodes b Illingworth	95
T.C.Middleton	b Botham	39
R.A.Smith	b Botham	6
M.C.J.Nicholas *	b Hick	6
R.M.F.Cox	c & b Hick	43
J.R.Ayling	c Botham b Illingworth	22
A.N Aymes +	not out	11
S.D.Udal	not out	0
T.M.Tremlett		
C.A.Connor		
P.J.Bakker		
Extras	(b 4,lb 17,w 6)	27
TOTAL	(50 overs)(for 6 wkts)	249

WORCESTERSHIRE		
T.S.Curtis	c Smith b Tremlett	16
G.J.Lord	b Bakker	1
D.A.Leatherdale	c Terry b Connor	5
I.T.Botham	b Connor	1
G.A.Hick	b Udal	20
P.A.Neale *	run out	1
M.J.Weston	lbw b Nicholas	19
S.J.Rhodes +	c Terry b Tremlett	22
R.K.Illingworth	b Nicholas	29
N.V.Radford	not out	39
S.M.McEwan	b Nicholas	0
Extras	(b 2,lb 9,w 4)	15
TOTAL	(45 overs)	168

WORCS	O	M	R	W	FALL OF WICKETS		
						HAM	WOR
McEwan	8	0	35	0			
Weston	6	1	18	0	1st	96	8
Radford	9	0	40	0	2nd	107	13
Illingworth	10	0	62	2	3rd	135	16
Botham	7	0	30	2	4th	208	45
Hick	10	0	43	2	5th	226	46
					6th	247	46
HAMPSHIRE	O	M	R	W	7th		82
Connor	6	2	14	2	8th		97
Bakker	7	0	21	1	9th		166
Tremlett	10	1	24	2	10th		168
Udal	9	0	42	1			
Ayling	6	0	28	0			
Nicholas	7	0	28	3			

SCARBOROUGH FESTIVAL

REFUGE ASS. CUP

YORKSHIRE vs. ESSEX
at Scarborough on 3rd September 1990
Toss : Essex. Umpires : B.Leadbeater and D.O.Oslear
Essex won by 82 runs

ESSEX

J.P.Stephenson *	st Bairstow b Carrick	57
N.Shahid	lbw b Jarvis	16
M.E.Waugh	b Jarvis	0
P.J.Prichard	c Hartley b Pickles	86
N.Hussain	c Byas b Pickles	31
M.A.Garnham +	c & b Pickles	37
A.G.J.Fraser	run out	0
T.D.Topley	not out	
M.C.Ilott	not out	6
S.J.W.Andrew		
P.M.Such		
Extras	(lb 3,w 8,nb 3)	14
TOTAL	(50 overs)(for 7 wkts)	247

YORKSHIRE

M.D.Moxon *	c Garnham b Andrew	4
S.A.Kellett	b Such	28
R.J.Blakey	c Garnham b Andrew	0
P.E.Robinson	c Prichard b Topley	26
D.Byas	c Waugh b Such	22
D.L.Bairstow +	b Stephenson	36
P.Carrick	b Stephenson	12
C.S.Pickles	b Waugh	1
P.J.Hartley	c Topley b Shahid	16
P.W.Jarvis	b Stephenson	3
J.D.Batty	not out	5
Extras	(lb 1,w 5,nb 6)	12
TOTAL	(47.2 overs)	165

YORKSHIRE	O	M	R	W	FALL OF WICKETS	ESS	YOR
Jarvis	10	1	48	2			
Hartley	10	0	52	0	1st	20	6
Pickles	9	0	40	3	2nd	20	6
Batty	9	0	40	0	3rd	163	50
Carrick	10	0	54	1	4th	178	73
Byas	2	0	10	0	5th	239	112
					6th	239	132
ESSEX	O	M	R	W	7th	241	135
Andrew	4	0	35	2	8th		141
Ilott	7	4	11	0	9th		147
Topley	6	0	15	1	10th		165
Such	10	0	32	2			
Fraser	4	0	16	0			
Stephenson	10	0	42	3			
Waugh	6	0	9	1			
Shahid	0.2	0	4	1			

ESSEX vs. HAMPSHIRE
at Scarborough on 4th September 1990
Toss : Essex. Umpires : B.Leadbeater and D.O.Oslear
Hampshire won by 5 wickets

ESSEX

J.P.Stephenson *	c Smith b Ayling	18
N.Shahid	c Middleton b Connor	10
M.E.Waugh	c Connor b Turner	30
P.J.Prichard	st Aymes b Udal	21
N.Hussain	c Nicholas b Tremlett	39
M.A.Garnham +	c Turner b Nicholas	4
A.G.J.Fraser	run out	0
T.D.Topley	b Turner	1
M.C.Ilott	b Nicholas	17
S.J.W.Andrew	b Nicholas	0
P.M.Such	not out	6
Extras	(b 2,lb 3,w 12,nb 2)	19
TOTAL	(49.5 overs)	165

HAMPSHIRE

M.C.J.Nicholas *	run out	57
T.C.Middleton	c sub b Fraser	53
R.M.F.Cox	b Stephenson	4
J.R.Ayling	c & b Fraser	25
R.A.Smith	not out	14
V.P.Terry	c Ilott b Topley	1
A.N.Aymes +	not out	1
T.M.Tremlett		
S.D.Udal		
C.A.Connor		
I.J.Turner		
Extras	(lb 3,w 7,nb 1)	11
TOTAL	(45.1 overs)(for 5 wkts)	166

HAMPSHIRE	O	M	R	W	FALL OF WICKETS	ESS	HAM
Connor	7	0	21	1			
Tremlett	7.5	2	16	1	1st	19	96
Udal	10	0	25	1	2nd	34	101
Ayling	7	0	26	1	3rd	72	140
Turner	8	0	44	2	4th	89	163
Nicholas	10	1	28	3	5th	106	164
					6th	109	
ESSEX	O	M	R	W	7th	118	
Topley	7	1	19	1	8th	144	
Ilott	7	1	20	0	9th	144	
Such	10	1	22	0	10th	165	
Andrew	5	0	29	0			
Shahid	2	0	6	0			
Stephenson	7	0	31	1			
Waugh	4	0	11	0			
Fraser	3	0	24	2			
Prichard	0.1	0	1	0			

YORKSHIRE vs. YORKSHIREMEN
at Scarborough on 6th September 1990
Toss : Yorks'men. Umpires : B.Leadbeater and D.O.Oslear
Yorkshire won by 8 wickets

YORKSHIREMEN

T.J.Boon	c Pickles b Jarvis	82
P.N.Hepworth	b Sidebottom	9
J.J.Whitaker	lbw b Hartley	10
J.D.Love	b Pickles	10
D.L.Bairstow *	b Hartley	25
S.J.Rhodes +	not out	66
M.Beardshall	not out	4
R.K.Illingworth		
P.A.Booth		
I.G.Swallow		
N.A.Mallender		
Extras	(b 2,lb 9,w 9,nb 3)	23
TOTAL	(50 overs)(for 5 wkts)	229

YORKSHIRE

A.A.Metcalfe *	c Love b Booth	65
D.Byas	c Rhodes b Love	59
R.J.Blakey +	not out	69
P.E.Robinson	not out	25
S.A.Kellett		
K.Sharp		
C.S.Pickles		
P.J.Hartley		
P.W.Jarvis		
A.Sidebottom		
J.D.Batty		
Extras	(b 1,lb 6,w 8,nb 2)	17
TOTAL	(37.5 overs)(for 2 wkts)	235

YORKSHIRE	O	M	R	W	FALL OF WICKETS	YMN	YOR
Jarvis	9	1	42	1			
Sidebottom	8	2	13	1	1st	24	96
Hartley	10	0	59	2	2nd	56	156
Pickles	10	1	48	1	3rd	81	
Batty	10	0	37	0	4th	153	
Byas	3	0	19	0	5th	187	
					6th		
YORKS'MEN	O	M	R	W	7th		
Beardshall	4.5	0	58	0	8th		
Mallender	6	0	26	0	9th		
Illingworth	9	0	53	0	10th		
Swallow	8	0	48	0			
Booth	7	0	24	1			
Love	3	0	19	1			

HEADLINES

Refuge Assurance Cup
Semi-Finals

5th September

● Middlesex gained some compensation for their NatWest Trophy semi-final defeat by beating Lancashire by 45 runs at Old Trafford to reach their first Refuge Cup final.

● Desmond Haynes and Michael Roseberry's opening stand of 153 laid the base for a Middlesex total of 272 for 6 which proved too many even for Lancashire who thus failed in their quest for a hat-trick of knockout titles

● Derbyshire reached the Refuge final for the first time in similar fashion, Adrian Kuiper building on an opening stand of 118 between Kim Barnett and Peter Bowler, and Nottinghamshire finished 22 short of victory, despite Tim Robinson's 96, the highest score made in the three years of the competition

---

DERBYSHIRE vs. NOTTINGHAMSHIRE
at Derby on 5th September 1990
Toss : Notts. Umpires : B.Dudleston and R.Palmer
Derbyshire won by 22 runs

DERBYSHIRE

K.J.Barnett *	c Johnson b Saxelby	83
P.D.Bowler +	c Evans b Cooper	59
J.E.Morris	c Robinson b Evans	0
A.P.Kuiper	c Mike b Stephenson	74
T.J.G.O'Gorman	not out	20
B.Roberts		
C.J.Adams		
A.E.Warner		
D.E.Malcolm		
S.J.Base		
O.H.Mortensen		
Extras	(lb 12,w 7)	19
TOTAL	(40 overs)(for 4 wkts)	255

NOTTINGHAMSHIRE

B.C.Broad	c Barnett b Mortensen	28
M.Newell	b Warner	10
P.Johnson	b Warner	2
R.T.Robinson *	c Warner b Malcolm	96
M.Saxelby	lbw b Base	9
F.D.Stephenson	run out	7
K.P.Evans	not out	55
G.W.Mike	run out	6
B.N.French +	b Kuiper	0
E.E.Hemmings	not out	6
K.E.Cooper		
Extras	(lb 5,w 6,nb 3)	14
TOTAL	(40 overs)(for 8 wkts)	233

NOTTS	O	M	R	W	FALL OF WICKETS	DER	NOT
Cooper	8	0	40	1			
Stephenson	8	1	49	1	1st	118	16
Evans	8	0	58	1	2nd	134	22
Mike	8	0	48	0	3rd	168	48
Hemmings	3	0	23	0	4th	255	69
Saxelby	5	0	25	1	5th		87
					6th		199
DERBYSHIRE	O	M	R	W	7th		207
Mortensen	8	0	27	1	8th		207
Warner	8	0	41	2	9th		
Malcolm	8	0	45	1	10th		
Base	8	0	65	1			
Kuiper	8	0	50	1			

Man of the match: R.T.Robinson

LANCASHIRE vs. MIDDLESEX
at Old Trafford on 5th September 1990
Toss : Lancashire. Umpires : H.D.Bird and A.G.T.Whitehead
Middlesex won by 45 runs

MIDDLESEX

D.L.Haynes	c Atherton b Hughes	72
M.A.Roseberry	c Allott b Hughes	86
M.R.Ramprakash	c Lloyd b Austin	22
K.R.Brown	not out	48
J.C.Pooley	c Hegg b DeFreitas	6
P.R.Downton +	b Watkinson	14
J.E.Emburey *	run out	0
N.F.Williams	not out	10
S.P.Hughes		
A.R.C.Fraser		
P.C.R.Tufnell		
Extras	(b 5,lb 6,w 3)	14
TOTAL	(40 overs)(for 6 wkts)	272

LANCASHIRE

G.Fowler	b Emburey	20
M.A.Atherton	run out	33
G.D.Lloyd	c Downton b Fraser	65
N.H.Fairbrother	c Brown b Hughes	56
M.Watkinson	c Hughes b Emburey	10
Wasim Akram	s Downton b Emburey	7
P.A.J.DeFreitas	c Hughes b Emburey	2
W.K.Hegg +	not out	19
I.D.Austin	not out	10
D.P.Hughes *		
P.J.W.Allott		
Extras	(b 2,lb 9,w 1,nb 3)	15
TOTAL	(40 overs)(for 7 wkts)	227

LANCASHIRE	O	M	R	W	FALL OF WICKETS	MID	LAN
Allott	4	0	33	0			
DeFreitas	8	0	71	1	1st	153	59
Wasim Akram	5	0	27	0	2nd	191	66
Watkinson	7	0	50	1	3rd	192	147
Austin	8	0	40	1	4th	216	167
Hughes	8	0	40	2	5th	245	186
					6th	246	190
MIDDLESEX	O	M	R	W	7th		227
Fraser	8	3	28	1	8th		
Williams	8	0	32	0	9th		
Tufnell	8	0	57	0	10th		
Emburey	8	1	39	4			
Hughes	8	0	60	1			

Man of the match: M.A.Roseberry

TOUR MATCH

BRITANNIC ASS. CHAMPIONSHIP

SUSSEX vs. SRI LANKA

at Hove on 5th, 6th, 7th September 1990
Toss : Sussex. Umpires : G.I.Burgess and J.H.Harris
Match drawn

SRI LANKA

D.S.B.P.Kuruppu +	b Threlfall	51	(4) lbw b Threlfall	4
C.Hathurasinghe	c Moores b Dodemaide	136	run out	31
A.P.Gurusinha	not out	3	c Moores b Threlfall	0
R.S.Mahanama	run out	8	(1) b Dodemaide	14
S.T.Jayasuriya	c Moores b Threlfall	32	(7) c Parker b Lenham	0
P.A.De Silva *	c Wells b Pigott	43	c Hall b Threlfall	5
M.Attapatu	not out	49	(5) not out	74
G.F.Labrooy	c Hall b Pigott	0	(9) b Dodemaide	22
R.Madurasinghe			(8) run out	11
P.Wickremasinghe			c Wells b Pigott	17
P.Wijetunga			not out	5
Extras	(b 2,lb 20,nb 3)	25	(lb 1,w 3,nb 1)	5
TOTAL	(for 6 wkts dec)	347	(for 9 wkts dec)	188

SUSSEX

N.J.Lenham	c Kuruppu b Labrooy	1	c Kuruppu b Labrooy	1
J.W.Hall	c Jayasuriya b Wijetunga	40	(7) c De Silva b Madurasinghe	0
D.M.Smith	lbw b Labrooy	0	(2) c Wijetunga b Gurusinha	29
A.P.Wells	c Kuruppu b Madurasinghe	96	c De Silva b Wickremasinghe	20
P.W.G.Parker *	not out	83	(3) b Wickremasinghe	21
M.P.Speight	not out	5	(5) c De Silva b Wijetunga	21
A.I.C.Dodemaide			(6) not out	33
P.Moores +			not out	14
A.C.S.Pigott				
I.D.K.Salisbury				
P.W.Threlfall				
Extras	(b 1,lb 7,nb 6)	14	(lb 1,nb 7)	8
TOTAL	(for 4 wkts dec)	239	(for 6 wkts)	147

SUSSEX	O	M	R	W	O	M	R	W		FALL OF WICKETS				
											SRI	SUS	SRI	SUS
Dodemaide	23	6	73	1	26	4	65	2	1st	99	11	20	7
Threlfall	14	3	44	2	16	5	45	3	2nd	164	11	21	49
Pigott	20.5	5	74	2	4	1	7	1	3rd	234	104	25	67
Lenham	14.1	4	31	0	11	3	29	1	4th	268	197	62	84
Salisbury	25	5	103	0	11	3	41	0	5th	340		85	101
									6th	341		94	102
SRI LANKA	O	M	R	W	O	M	R	W	7th			118	
Labrooy	12	0	38	2	9	0	40	1	8th			148	
Wickremasinghe	13	3	41	0	12	6	30	2	9th			182	
Wijetunga	7	0	40	1	9	4	15	1	10th				
Hathurasinghe	2	0	12	0									
Madurasinghe	16.5	1	92	1	9	1	17	1					
Gurusinha	3	0	8	0	7	0	36	1					
Jayasuriya					1	0	4	0					
Attapatu					1	0	4	0					

MIDDLESEX vs. NOTTINGHAMSHIRE

at Lord's on 7th, 8th, 9th, 10th September 1990
Toss : Middlesex. Umpires : D.J.Constant and A.G.T.Whitehead
Middlesex won by 10 wickets (Middlesex 24 pts (Bt: 4, Bw: 4) Notts 3 pts (Bt: 2, Bw: 1))

MIDDLESEX

D.L.Haynes	b Stephenson	29	not out	44
M.A.Roseberry	lbw b Pick	11	not out	20
M.W.Gatting *	c French b Stephenson	30		
M.R.Ramprakash	c Martindale b Hemmings	132		
K.R.Brown	not out	200		
P.R.Downton +	c Stephenson b Cooper	63		
J.E.Emburey	not out	22		
N.F.Williams				
A.R.C.Fraser				
P.C.R.Tufnell				
N.G.Cowans				
Extras	(b 5,lb 10,nb 8)	23		0
TOTAL	(for 5 wkts dec)	510	(for 0 wkts)	64

NOTTINGHAMSHIRE

B.C.Broad	b Tufnell	38	b Fraser	20
M.Newell	lbw b Williams	6	b Cowans	80
R.T.Robinson *	lbw b Cowans	57	run out	105
P.Johnson	c Williams b Tufnell	2	retired hurt	12
D.J.R.Martindale	c Brown b Tufnell	32	c Gatting b Fraser	11
F.D.Stephenson	c Downton b Cowans	7	c Downton b Cowans	20
B.N.French +	not out	40	c Downton b Cowans	1
E.E.Hemmings	c Tufnell b Williams	3	c Brown b Emburey	6
K.E.Cooper	lbw b Fraser	5	(10) b Cowans	21
R.A.Pick	b Williams	35	(9) lbw b Emburey	26
J.A.Afford	b Tufnell	3	not out	0
Extras	(lb 3,w 1,nb 3)	7	(b 9,lb 10,w 1,nb 13)	33
TOTAL		235		335

NOTTS	O	M	R	W	O	M	R	W		FALL OF WICKETS			
											MID	NOT NOT	MID
Stephenson	33	5	89	2					1st	38	8	32
Cooper	31	3	134	1	5	1	10	0	2nd	42	71	211
Pick	22	3	79	1					3rd	108	87	240
Afford	29	10	76	0	3	1	23	0	4th	296	130	273
Hemmings	29.3	2	117	1	7	0	31	0	5th	464	142	277
									6th		144	285
MIDDLESEX	O	M	R	W	O	M	R	W	7th		150	297
Fraser	23	5	63	1	34	9	84	2	8th		155	335
Williams	13	4	41	3					9th		220	335
Cowans	14	2	26	2	24	11	46	4	10th		235	
Emburey	25	7	33	0	43	14	85	2				
Tufnell	26.5	6	69	4	47	16	93	0				
Haynes					2	1	8	0				

HEADLINES

5th - 10th September

● Sri Lanka kept up their unbeaten record in first-class matches with a draw against Sussex. Hathurasinghe scored a century and Attapatu impressed with innings of 49* and 74* to keep Sussex on the defensive.

7th - 10th September

● Middlesex moved back to the top of the Championship table after beating Notts by 10 wickets at Lord's. Keith Brown hit a career best 200 not out as Middlesex reached 510 for 5 declared; Notts followed on 275 behind, and when a stand of 179 between Mike Newell and Tim Robinson threatened to deny Middlesex, Norman Cowans took four crucial wickets and ended Paul Johnson's season with a broken thumb

● Essex slipped 14 points behind Middlesex after again coming up against Northamptonshire's batsmen in record-breaking form at Chelmsford. When Essex were 170 for 3 in their first innings after bowling Northants out for 196 there was no sign of the traumas ahead for Graham Gooch's side. After losing their last seven wickets for 74 Essex gained a lead of only 48, then watched Northants bat them out of the match as they improved their record total for the second match in succession, Gooch's men the victims on both occasions. When Allan Lamb eventually declared at 636 for 6, Essex needed 589 to win and barely reached halfway

ESSEX vs. NORTHANTS

at Chelmsford on 7th, 8th, 9th, 10th September 1990
Toss : Essex. Umpires : B.J.Meyer and R.Palmer
Northants won by 276 runs (Essex 6 pts (Bt: 2, Bw: 4) Northants 21 pts (Bt: 1, Bw: 4))

NORTHANTS

A.Fordham	c Garnham b Andrew	23	c Foster b Ilott	159
N.A.Felton	c Waugh b Foster	25	b Foster	56
W.Larkins	c Prichard b Ilott	37	c Hussain b Foster	0
R.J.Bailey	c Garnham b Waugh	28	lbw b Foster	107
A.J.Lamb *	c & b Waugh	22	c sub b Childs	165
A.L.Penberthy	c Foster b Waugh	0	c Hussain b Andrew	83
R.G.Williams	lbw b Waugh	0	not out	12
D.Ripley +	c Shahid b Waugh	18		
C.E.L.Ambrose	lbw b Foster	9		
J.G.Thomas	c & b Foster	15		
M.A.Robinson	not out	0		
Extras	(lb 6,w 1,nb 12)	19	(b 10,lb 29,w 2,nb 13)	54
TOTAL		196	(for 6 wkts dec)	636

ESSEX

G.A.Gooch *	c Penberthy b Robinson	92	c Felton b Robinson	40
J.P.Stephenson	c Thomas b Ambrose	0	b Ambrose	76
P.J.Prichard	c Ripley b Ambrose	7	c Williams b Penberthy	5
N.Shahid	b Thomas	26	(7) c Thomas b Williams	43
M.E.Waugh	c Bailey b Ambrose	44	(4) c Lamb b Ambrose	36
N.Hussain	b Robinson	17	c Ripley b Thomas	24
M.A.Garnham +	c & b Ambrose	34	(8) c Penberthy b Robinson	10
N.A.Foster	c Larkins b Thomas	11	(9) b Robinson	12
M.C.Ilott	c Felton b Robinson	0	(5) c Thomas b Ambrose	0
J.H.Childs	c Williams b Thomas	4	not out	21
S.J.W.Andrew	not out	1	c Thomas b Williams	35
Extras	(lb 6,w 1,nb 1)	8	(lb 8,nb 2)	10
TOTAL		244		312

ESSEX	O	M	R	W	O	M	R	W		FALL OF WICKETS			
											NOR	ESS NOR	ESS
Foster	19.2	4	67	3	29	7	79	3				
Ilott	11	3	28	1	26	4	120	1	1st	42	3	157	83
Andrew	9	0	58	1	23	1	132	1	2nd	53	29	175	94
Waugh	12	3	37	5	24	4	87	0	3rd	117	81	286	134
Childs					37	5	119	1	4th	121	170	434	134
Stephenson					2	0	17	0	5th	122	170	584	173
Gooch					18	5	43	0	6th	122	192	636	199
									7th	151	221		221
NORTHANTS	O	M	R	W	O	M	R	W	8th	176	225		256
Ambrose	23.4	3	67	4	19	6	52	3	9th	196	238		263
Robinson	22	5	73	3	15	2	89	3	10th	196	244		312
Penberthy	9	1	34	0	6	0	27	1				
Thomas	13	0	64	3	11	0	72	1				
Williams					12.1	2	64	2				

BRITANNIC ASSURANCE CHAMPIONSHIP

YORKSHIRE vs. DERBYSHIRE

at Scarborough on 7th, 8th, 9th, 10th September 1990
Toss : Derbyshire.   Umpires : H.D.Bird and J.D.Bond
Yorkshire won by 4 wickets (Yorkshire 22 pts (Bt: 4, Bw: 2) Derbyshire 4 pts (Bt: 4, Bw: 0))

DERBYSHIRE

P.D.Bowler	c Blakey b Jarvis	4	(2) c Blakey b Jarvis	13
J.E.Morris	c & b Carrick	109	(1) c Byas b Hartley	36
T.J.G.O'Gorman	b Pickles	21	not out	82
C.J.Adams	c Metcalfe b Carrick	101	c Robinson b Hartley	17
B.Roberts	b Pickles	31	not out	44
K.J.Barnett *	c Robinson b Carrick	47		
K.M.Krikken +	c Pickles b Carrick	35		
I.R.Bishop	not out	103		
A.E.Warner	not out	10		
D.E.Malcolm				
G.Miller				
Extras	(lb 13,w 1)	14	(b 2,lb 5,nb 2)	9
TOTAL	(for 7 wkts dec)	475	(for 3 wkts dec)	201

YORKSHIRE

M.D.Moxon *	b Bishop	14	c Adams b Miller	94
A.A.Metcalfe	not out	150	lbw b Warner	32
S.A.Kellett	b Warner	22	b Warner	2
P.E.Robinson	not out	150	run out	14
R.J.Blakey +			not out	91
D.Byas			c Krikken b Malcolm	13
P.Carrick			b Bishop	31
C.S.Pickles			not out	4
P.J.Hartley				
P.W.Jarvis				
J.D.Batty				
Extras	(b 9,lb 18,w 7,nb 7)	41	(b 9,lb 7,nb 3)	19
TOTAL	(for 2 wkts dec)	377	(for 6 wkts)	300

YORKSHIRE	O	M	R	W	O	M	R	W		FALL OF WICKETS				
Jarvis	29	1	124	1	12	4	32	1			DER	YOR	DER	YOR
Hartley	23	2	109	0	15	6	58	2	1st	4	34	47	83
Pickles	20.4	4	72	2					2nd	95	84	61	109
Carrick	39	14	90	4	8	2	10	0	3rd	158		92	148
Batty	17	3	67	0	11	2	42	0	4th	229			178
Robinson					2.3	0	18	0	5th	323			225
Metcalfe					2	0	34	0	6th	326			295
									7th	411			
DERBYSHIRE	O	M	R	W	O	M	R	W	8th				
Bishop	15	3	50	1	16.5	1	61	1	9th				
Malcolm	15	1	56	0	16	1	83	1	10th				
Warner	14	3	43	1	16	0	64	2					
Miller	25	2	92	0	9	0	68	1					
Barnett	21	1	58	0	1	0	8	0					
Morris	9	0	44	0									
Adams	1.4	0	7	0									

WARWICKSHIRE vs. SOMERSET

at Edgbaston on 7th, 8th, 9th, 10th September 1990
Toss : Warwickshire.   Umpires : J.H.Hampshire and D.O.Oslear
Match drawn (Warwickshire 6 pts (Bt: 4, Bw: 2) Somerset 6 pts (Bt: 3, Bw: 3))

WARWICKSHIRE

A.J.Moles	c Rose b Jones	2	c Burns b Jones	44
J.D.Ratcliffe	lbw b Jones	6	lbw b Hayhurst	20
Asif Din	lbw b Hayhurst	55	c Tavare b Hayhurst	0
D.P.Ostler	lbw b Hayhurst	11	c Hayhurst b Lefebvre	1
P.A.Smith	c Harden b Hayhurst	4	lbw b Jones	75
D.A.Reeve *	run out	58	not out	81
K.J.Piper +	b Rose	111	c Townsend b Jones	0
G.C.Small	lbw b Lefebvre	7	b Lefebvre	5
P.A.Booth	c Swallow b Rose	60	c Rose b Jones	15
A.A.Donald	b Rose	7	b Lefebvre	0
T.A.Munton	not out	0	not out	29
Extras	(b 4,lb 9,w 4,nb 2)	19	(lb 6,w 4,nb 4)	14
TOTAL		340	(for 9 wkts dec)	290

SOMERSET

S.J.Cook	c Moles b Smith	52	c Moles b Munton	27
G.T.J.Townsend	c Piper b Munton	15	c Piper b Small	6
A.N.Hayhurst	c Ostler b Munton	57	not out	56
C.J.Tavare *	lbw b Donald	10	c Reeve b Munton	2
R.J.Harden	lbw b Munton	32		
N.D.Burns +	b Smith	88	(5) b Booth	28
G.D.Rose	c Ratcliffe b Munton	41	(6) not out	14
R.P.Lefebvre	b Smith	27		
I.G.Swallow	not out	14		
H.R.J.Trump	b Smith	2		
A.N.Jones	c Booth b Smith	8		
Extras	(b 7,lb 19,w 3,nb 2)	31	(b 4,lb 1)	5
TOTAL		377	(for 4 wkts)	138

SOMERSET	O	M	R	W	O	M	R	W		FALL OF WICKETS			
Jones	27	2	110	2	33	8	72	4		WAR	SOM	WAR	SOM
Rose	19.2	3	49	3	12	2	54	0	1st	10	57	43	12
Hayhurst	21	1	82	3	26	8	68	2	2nd	17	84	45	43
Lefebvre	21	6	44	1	26	7	48	3	3rd	56	102	52	57
Swallow	12	4	26	0	12	4	23	0	4th	60	176	75	114
Trump	9	3	16	0	2	2	19	0	5th	91	185	178	
									6th	203	278	178	
WARWICKSHIRE	O	M	R	W	O	M	R	W	7th	215	340	192	
Donald	27	5	91	1	10	2	36	0	8th	327	351	210	
Small	24	5	58	0	6	0	18	1	9th	335	359	215	
Munton	33	11	66	4	9	5	7	2	10th	340	377		
Smith	16.1	5	48	5	3.5	0	17	0					
Reeve	12	2	26	0									
Booth	23	4	57	0	8	0	37	1					
Asif Din	2	1	5	0	4	0	18	0					

GLOUCESTERSHIRE vs. WORCESTERSHIRE

at Bristol on 7th, 8th, 9th, 10th September 1990
Toss : Gloucestershire.   Umpires : D.R.Shepherd and P.B.Wight
Match drawn (Gloucestershire 5 pts (Bt: 4, Bw: 1) Worcestershire 5 pts (Bt: 4, Bw: 1))

GLOUCESTERSHIRE

G.D.Hodgson	c Rhodes b Illingworth	109	lbw b Newport	22
A.J.Wright *	b Newport	21	st Rhodes b Illingworth	72
P.Bainbridge	c Rhodes b Illingworth	129	(4) lbw b Illingworth	39
C.W.J.Athey	c Lord b Illingworth	18	(5) not out	34
M.W.Alleyne	c & b Radford	52	(6) c & b Illingworth	8
K.M.Curran	c Rhodes b Illingworth	18	(7) not out	35
R.C.Russell +	c Curtis b D'Oliveira	76		
J.W.Lloyds	not out	71		
C.A.Walsh	c Curtis b D'Oliveira	18		
D.V.Lawrence	not out	6	(3) lbw b Newport	0
D.A.Graveney				
Extras	(b 1,lb 22,nb 10)	33	(b 2,lb 3,nb 4)	9
TOTAL	(for 8 wkts dec)	551	(for 5 wkts dec)	219

WORCESTERSHIRE

T.S.Curtis	lbw b Graveney	96	lbw b Lawrence	8
G.J.Lord	b Lloyds	64	not out	70
G.A.Hick	c Alleyne b Bainbridge	110	c Wright b Graveney	38
D.B.D'Oliveira	c Alleyne b Graveney	5	b Graveney	0
P.A.Neale *	c Alleyne b Bainbridge	95	b Walsh	3
S.R.Lampitt	not out	45	not out	20
S.J.Rhodes +	not out	7		
R.K.Illingworth				
P.J.Newport				
N.V.Radford				
G.R.Dilley				
Extras	(b 7,lb 8,w 1,nb 12)	28	(lb 6,nb 3)	9
TOTAL	(for 5 wkts dec)	450	(for 4 wkts)	148

WORCS	O	M	R	W	O	M	R	W		FALL OF WICKETS			
Dilley	21	3	54	0	10	0	43	0		GLO	WOR	GLO	WOR
Radford	25	6	98	1	12	1	45	0	1st	52	114	67	23
Newport	29	7	80	1	10	3	19	2	2nd	234	219	72	88
Lampitt	25	2	103	0	4	0	16	0	3rd	284	245	115	88
Illingworth	46	12	121	4	27	7	91	3	4th	323	343	150	103
Hick	13	1	49	0					5th	365	431	164	
D'Oliveira	2.3	0	23	2					6th	381			
									7th	526			
GLOUCS	O	M	R	W	O	M	R	W	8th	544			
Walsh	28	8	83	0	10	2	24	1	9th				
Lawrence	15	0	55	0	7	0	30	1	10th				
Curran	15	8	25	0	8	1	21	0					
Graveney	53	15	96	2	19	3	58	2					
Lloyds	23	1	97	1	6	0	9	0					
Alleyne	4	1	26	0									
Bainbridge	16.4	4	39	2									
Athey	6	1	14	0									

KENT vs. SURREY

at Canterbury on 7th, 8th, 9th, 10th September 1990
Toss : Kent.   Umpires : M.J.Kitchen and D.S.Thompsett
Match drawn (Kent 4 pts (Bt: 4, Bw: 0) Surrey 6 pts (Bt: 4, Bw: 2))

KENT

S.G.Hinks	c Lynch b Robinson	16	c Gray b Robinson	19
T.R.Ward	c Kendrick b Murphy	55	c & b Gray	10
V.J.Wells	lbw b Gray	50	b Murphy	11
G.R.Cowdrey	b Gray	8	c Lynch b Murphy	9
N.R.Taylor *	c Robinson b Murphy	204	(6) c Stewart b Gray	142
M.V.Fleming	c Stewart b Greig	9	(7) b Murphy	80
S.A.Marsh +	c Kendrick b Murphy	17	(8) not out	25
D.J.M.Kelleher	c sub b Gray	44	(9) lbw b Gray	6
R.P.Davis	c Stewart b Murphy	5	(5) lbw b Robinson	46
M.M.Patel	c Lynch b Murphy	3	b Gray	0
T.Wren	not out	5	not out	1
Extras	(b 1,lb 5,w 1,nb 2)	9	(b 6,lb 17,nb 6)	29
TOTAL		425	(for 9 wkts)	378

SURREY

D.J.Bicknell	c & b Wells	186	
G.S.Clinton	c Marsh b Wren	57	
A.J.Stewart +	c Taylor b Wells	1	
D.M.Ward	c Kelleher b Wells	263	
M.A.Lynch	not out	73	
I.A.Greig *	c & b Wells	0	
J.D.Robinson	c Marsh b Fleming	16	
N.M.Kendrick	c Wells b Kelleher	0	
A.H.Gray	c Hinks b Kelleher	11	
M.P.Bicknell	b Kelleher	28	
A.J.Murphy	run out	1	
Extras	(b 2,lb 4,w 1,nb 5)	12	
TOTAL		648	

SURREY	O	M	R	W	O	M	R	W		FALL OF WICKETS			
Gray	35	7	80	3	32.4	9	83	4		KEN	SUR	KEN	SUR
Bicknell M.P.	3.3	1	12	0					1st	62	99	31	
Murphy	32.1	6	99	5	33	4	112	3	2nd	74	100	37	
Robinson	21	3	95	1	24	5	84	2	3rd	90	513	52	
Kendrick	12	1	73	0	7	1	19	0	4th	252	530	68	
Greig	14	0	60	1	10	0	57	0	5th	266	531	185	
									6th	293	566	339	
KENT	O	M	R	W	O	M	R	W	7th	385	571	345	
Kelleher	34.5	2	148	3					8th	392	607	358	
Wren	33	3	128	1					9th	402	646	358	
Davis	11	1	49	0					10th	425	648		
Wells	35	4	126	4									
Fleming	37	4	127	1									
Patel	24	4	64	0									

BRITANNIC ASS. CHAMPIONSHIP

TOUR MATCHES

GLAMORGAN vs. HAMPSHIRE

at Pontypridd on 7th, 8th, 9th September 1990
Toss : Glamorgan.   Umpires : R.Julian and K.E.Palmer
Hampshire won by 8 wickets (Glamorgan 6 pts (Bt: 2, Bw: 4) Hants 24 pts (Bt: 4, Bw: 4))

GLAMORGAN

A.R.Butcher *	b Udal	58	c Terry b Tremlett	33
H.Morris	lbw b Udal	29	lbw b Tremlett	45
P.A.Cottey	lbw b Maru	13	(5) c Aymes b Marshall	23
M.P.Maynard	c Maru b Marshall	50	c Terry b Marshall	27
A.Dale	c Smith R.A. b Maru	14	(6) c Aymes b Marshall	0
S.P.James	c Gower b Maru	1	(3) run out	2
R.D.B.Croft	not out	27	c Terry b Marshall	10
C.P.Metson +	b Marshall	0	c Smith R.A. b Marshall	15
S.L.Watkin	c Smith R.A. b Marshall	5	b Udal	3
S.Bastien	c Maru b Marshall	2	c Gower b Marshall	0
M.Frost	c Aymes b Marshall	0	not out	4
Extras	(b 6,lb 1,w 1,nb 3)	11	(b 1,lb 7,w 1,nb 1)	10
TOTAL		210		172

HAMPSHIRE

V.P.Terry	c Dale b Croft	36	b Frost	8
C.L.Smith	lbw b Frost	1	not out	25
D.I.Gower	c Metson b Watkin	17	c Cottey b Frost	23
R.A.Smith	b Watkin	42	not out	14
R.J.Maru	lbw b Bastien	5		
M.D.Marshall	c Croft b Frost	51		
M.C.J.Nicholas *	run out	5		
A.N Aymes +	not out	75		
T.M.Tremlett	c Maynard b Croft	23		
S.D.Udal	c Metson b Bastien	28		
P.J.Bakker	c James b Bastien	12		
Extras	(b 4,lb 11,nb 3)	18	(b 1,nb 1)	2
TOTAL		313	(for 2 wkts)	72

HAMPSHIRE	O	M	R	W	O	M	R	W	FALL OF WICKETS				
										GLA	HAM	GLA	HAM
Bakker	17	4	51	0	11	0	46	0	1st	63	15	77	11
Marshall	22.4	6	45	5	22.4	8	47	6	2nd	95	48	79	52
Tremlett	8	2	29	0	7	3	15	2	3rd	118	87	84	
Udal	19	5	56	2	17	7	34	1	4th	168	101	119	
Maru	15	8	22	3	8	4	22	0	5th	174	105	121	
									6th	174	158	150	
GLAMORGAN	O	M	R	W	O	M	R	W	7th	174	160	151	
Frost	19	3	59	2	6	1	25	2	8th	194	230	156	
Watkin	22	3	100	2	6	1	18	0	9th	200	295	157	
Bastien	23.4	5	70	3					10th	210	313	172	
Croft	26	8	69	2	5.2	1	28	0					

LANCASHIRE vs. SRI LANKA

at Old Trafford on 8th, 9th, 10th September 1990
Toss : Sri Lanka.   Umpires : J.C.Balderstone and R.A.White
Match drawn

SRI LANKA

R.S.Mahanama	c Bramhall b Yates	103	b Speak	93
C.Hathurasinghe	c Lloyd b Martin	15	run out	31
D.S.B.P.Kuruppu	c Fitton b Martin	2	not out	56
P.A.De Silva *	c Fairbrother b Yates	95	not out	14
H.P.Tillekaratne +	lbw b Folley	44		
M.Attapatu	c & b Yates	6		
S.T.Jayasuriya	c De Silva b Wijetunga	105		
P.Wickremasinghe	b Yates	0		
R.Madurasinghe	not out	28		
K.I.W.Wijegunawardene				
P.Wijetunga				
Extras	(b 3,lb 3,nb 2)	8	(lb 5)	5
TOTAL	(for 7 wkts dec)	406	(for 2 wkts dec)	199

LANCASHIRE

G.D.Lloyd	st Tillekaratne b Wijetunga	96	st Kuruppu b Madurasinghe	34
N.J.Speak	b Madurasinghe	43	c Tillekaratne b Madurasinghe	52
S.P.Titchard	lbw b Madurasinghe	11	c De Silva b Madurasinghe	1
N.H.Fairbrother *	c Mahanama b Wijetunga	6	c Fairbrother b Wijetunga	26
M.A.Crawley	c De Silva b Wijetunga	42	b De Silva	48
I.D.Austin	c Wijeguna' b Madurasinghe	3	(7) c Wijeguna' b De Silva	24
J.D.Fitton	c Hath'singhe b Mad'singhe	13	(6) c & b Wijetunga	6
G.Yates	c De Silva b Jayasuriya	42	not out	15
I.Folley	not out	47	run out	5
S.Bramhall +	c Tillekaratne b Wijetunga	0	not out	1
P.J.Martin	c De Silva b Madurasinghe	2		
Extras	(b 3,lb 4,nb 1)	8	(b 6,lb 8,nb 1)	15
TOTAL		313	(for 8 wkts)	227

LANCASHIRE	O	M	R	W	O	M	R	W	FALL OF WICKETS				
										SRI	LAN	SRI	LAN
Martin	23	2	84	2	12	4	34	0	1st	31	115	75	51
Austin	9.5	3	23	0					2nd	35	143	179	61
Crawley	8	1	9	0	6	2	16	0	3rd	203	155		113
Folley	35.1	4	126	1	7	0	25	0	4th	224	160		130
Fitton	19	4	64	0	7	1	18	0	5th	248	178		141
Yates	38	9	94	4	8	0	39	0	6th	274	204		191
Fairbrother					7	0	29	0	7th	277	221		207
Speak					5	0	26	1	8th		298		225
Lloyd					1	0	7	0	9th		303		
									10th		313		
SRI LANKA	O	M	R	W	O	M	R	W					
Wickremasinghe	3	0	11	0	1	0	11	0					
Wijegunawardene	3	1	16	0	1	0	5	0					
Wijetunga	38	6	133	4	23	6	83	2					
Madurasinghe	37.3	7	108	5	26	3	89	3					
De Silva	2	0	7	0	6	0	25	2					
Jayasuriya	5	0	14	1	1	1	0	0					
Attapatu	3	0	17	0									

HAMPSHIRE vs. SRI LANKA

at Southampton on 12th, 13th, 14th September 1990
Toss : Hampshire.   Umpires : K.E.Palmer and R.C.Tolchard
Match drawn

HAMPSHIRE

V.P.Terry	c Wijeguna' b Madurasinghe	120
T.C.Middleton	c Kuruppu b Ramanayake	22
M.C.J.Nicholas *	c Mahanama b Ramanayake	0
J.R.Ayling	c Wijeguna' b Madurasinghe	59
D.I.Gower	c & b Madurasinghe	0
R.M.F.Cox	b Wijegunawardene	34
A.N Aymes +	not out	62
R.J.Maru	c Tillekaratne b Hathurasinghe	6
S.D.Udal	c De Silva b Ramanayake	14
C.A.Connor	not out	29
P.J.Bakker		
Extras	(lb 5,w 2,nb 14)	21
TOTAL	(for 8 wkts dec)	367

SRI LANKA

R.S.Mahanama	c Aymes b Bakker	32	lbw b Udal	56
C.Hathurasinghe	c Maru b Connor	1	c Nicholas b Bakker	5
D.S.B.P.Kuruppu	lbw b Maru	24	c Gower b Maru	21
P.A.De Silva *	lbw b Bakker	2	not out	221
H.P.Tillekaratne +	st Aymes b Maru	10	b Maru	100
S.T.Jayasuriya	c Middleton b Maru	18	c Aymes b Udal	54
M.Attapatu	c Gower b Udal	9	st Aymes b Udal	0
G.F.Labrooy	c Connor b Udal	5	st Aymes b Udal	18
C.P.Ramanayake	not out	5	not out	9
R.Madurasinghe	c Cox b Maru	4		
K.Wijegunawardene	c Cox b Maru	0		
Extras	(lb 1,nb 7)	8	(b 5,lb 6,w 3,nb 8)	22
TOTAL		118	(for 7 wkts dec)	506

SRI LANKA	O	M	R	W	O	M	R	W	FALL OF WICKETS			
										HAM	SRI	SRI	HAM
Labrooy	12	1	53	0					1st	45	4	7	
Ramanayake	26	2	106	3					2nd	45	53	84	
Madurasinghe	30	4	99	3					3rd	151	55	94	
Wijeguna'	21	2	75	1					4th	151	76	357	
Hathurasinghe	7	2	29	1					5th	242	88	457	
									6th	260	103	459	
HAMPSHIRE	O	M	R	W	O	M	R	W	7th	290	108	491	
Bakker	13	1	36	2	17	0	87	1	8th	325	109		
Connor	10	2	32	1	16	2	63	0	9th		118		
Ayling	7	4	9	0	16	4	38	0	10th		118		
Maru	11.5	4	25	5	50	20	119	2					
Udal	7	2	15	2	40	9	139	4					
Nicholas					4	0	29	0					
Middleton					4	0	19	0					
Cox					1	0	7	0					

HEADLINES

7th-10th September

● Hampshire climbed above Warwickshire into third place after match figures of 11 for 92 from Malcolm Marshall had taken them to a three-day victory over Glamorgan at Pontypridd. Adrian Aymes also played his part, hitting a career best 75* to gain Hampshire a first innings lead of 103. Glamorgan's Hugh Morris, overlooked by the England selectors, became the fourth man to complete 2,000 runs for the season

● Yorkshire were the only other winners, their four-wicket victory over Derbyshire at Scarborough lifting fears of a bottom-place finish. Ian Bishop hit his first first-class 100

● Kent's match with Surrey was another rich in statistical incident: Neil Taylor, having made a career best 204 in the first innings, became the second batsman to score a double century and a century in the same match for Kent, after Arthur Fagg; Darren Bicknell and David Ward both made career bests as they shared a stand of 413, a record for Surrey's third wicket.

8th-14th September

● The Sri Lankans' tour ended on a high note as their captain, Aravinda De Silva, made an epic unbeaten 221, the 30th double-century of the summer, to save his side from defeat by Hampshire at Southampton in rousing style.

BRITANNIC ASSURANCE CHAMPIONSHIP

ESSEX vs. KENT

at Chelmsford on 12th, 13th, 14th, 15th September 1990
Toss : Essex. Umpires : J.C.Balderstone and A.G.T.Whitehead
Match drawn (Essex 6 pts (Bt: 4, Bw: 2) Kent 6 pts (Bt: 4, Bw: 2))

KENT

S.G.Hinks	c & b Childs	43	b Andrew		16
T.R.Ward	c Garnham b Foster	79	c Hussain b Ilott		7
V.J.Wells	c Waugh b Andrew	34	lbw b Ilott		46
G.R.Cowdrey	c Hussain b Childs	0	c Garnham b Waugh		33
N.R.Taylor *	c Garnham b Foster	56	c Garnham b Foster		86
M.V.Fleming	c Foster b Ilott	36	c Hussain b Childs		36
S.A.Marsh +	b Foster	70	b Foster		47
R.M.Ellison	not out	44	not out		68
D.J.M.Kelleher	c Garnham b Ilott	1	lbw b Foster		6
R.P.Davis	b Shahid b Ilott	0	b Foster		52
T.Wren	c Foster b Shahid	16	c sub b Foster		0
Extras	(b 5,lb 5,w 6,nb 14)	30	(b 7,lb 10,w 1,nb 9)		27
TOTAL		409			424

ESSEX

J.P.Stephenson	c Marsh b Ellison	11			
N.Shahid	b Ellison	20	(1) c Ellison b Kelleher		0
P.J.Prichard	c Marsh b Fleming	102			
M.E.Waugh	c Davis b Wren	169			
N.Hussain	c Marsh b Wren	45			
M.A.Garnham +	c Marsh b Kelleher	33			
N.A.Foster	b Fleming	14			
M.C.Ilott	not out	42	(2) not out		0
J.H.Childs	c Taylor b Ellison	26			
S.J.W.Andrew	c & b Ellison	11	(3) not out		8
G.A.Gooch *	absent hurt				
Extras	(lb 8,w 8,nb 19)	35	(w 1,nb 1)		2
TOTAL		508	(for 1 wkt)		10

ESSEX	O	M	R	W	O	M	R	W	FALL OF WICKETS				
										KEN	ESS	KEN	ESS
Foster	37	8	108	3	41.3	9	94	5	1st	115	26	8	0
Ilott	31	7	73	3	26	4	72	2	2nd	155	41	38	
Andrew	21	0	99	1	24	3	78	1	3rd	156	280	97	
Waugh	5	1	21	0	14	4	37	1	4th	187	357	129	
Childs	37	14	79	2	31	10	60	1	5th	253	375	221	
Stephenson	4	0	18	0	3	1	9	0	6th	271	398	251	
Shahid	2.3	1	1	1	17	5	43	0	7th	363	429	293	
Hussain					2	1	14	0	8th	366	495	309	
									9th	366	508	424	
KENT	**O**	**M**	**R**	**W**	**O**	**M**	**R**	**W**	10th	409		424	
Wren	28	1	135	2									
Ellison	24.4	2	76	4									
Fleming	25	1	87	2									
Wells	3	0	22	0									
Kelleher	12	1	68	1	1	0	10	1					
Davis	26	3	112	0									

LEICESTERSHIRE vs. NORTHANTS

at Leicester on 12th, 13th, 14th, 15th September 1990
Toss : Northants. Umpires : J.D.Bond and B.Leadbeater
Northants won by 171 runs (Leics 7 pts (Bt: 4, Bw: 3) Northants 22 pts (Bt: 4, Bw: 2))

NORTHANTS

A.Fordham	c Whitticase b Millns	85	c Potter b Millns		0
N.A.Felton	c Potter b Lewis	5	b Agnew		13
W.Larkins	b Millns	27	c Millns b Lewis		0
R.J.Bailey	lbw b Parsons	77	lbw b Agnew		33
A.J.Lamb *	c Whitticase b Millns	67	b Willey		67
A.L.Penberthy	c Whitticase b Millns	52	c Lewis b Parsons		10
R.G.Williams	b Millns	1	b Lewis		89
D.Ripley +	c Agnew b Lewis	6	not out		109
C.E.L.Ambrose	not out	55	c Whitticase b Lewis		0
N.G.B.Cook	b Millns	28	b Agnew		13
M.A.Robinson	lbw b Lewis	0	not out		1
Extras	(lb 6,w 1,nb 8)	15	(b 11,lb 9,w 1,nb 11)		32
TOTAL		351	(for 9 wkts dec)		367

LEICESTERSHIRE

T.J.Boon	c Larkins b Ambrose	13	c Ripley b Robinson		0
N.E.Briers *	c & b Bailey	176	c Fordham b Ambrose		0
J.J.Whitaker	c Robinson b Ambrose	28	c Ripley b Ambrose		92
P.Willey	c Bailey b Ambrose	0	c Larkins b Cook		30
L.Potter	b Ambrose	45	not out		31
C.C.Lewis	b Ambrose	1	c Cook b Ambrose		0
P.N.Hepworth	c Penberthy b Williams	49	lbw b Ambrose		0
P.Whitticase +	b Ambrose	11	b Ambrose		0
G.J.Parsons	c Bailey b Ambrose	8	run out		0
J.P.Agnew	c Cook b Penberthy	24	c Fordham b Williams		6
D.J.Millns	not out	1	absent hurt		
Extras	(b 8,lb 15,w 1,nb 2)	26	(b 6)		6
TOTAL		382			165

LEICS	O	M	R	W	O	M	R	W	FALL OF WICKETS				
										NOR	LEI	NOR	LEI
Agnew	26	5	96	0	26	4	69	3	1st	26	36	0	1
Lewis	33.3	8	83	3	30	6	84	3	2nd	102	115	2	3
Parsons	19	2	91	1	20	1	88	1	3rd	128	120	50	98
Millns	22	3	63	6	11	0	31	1	4th	128	213	66	150
Willey	6	0	12	0	20	4	56	1	5th	218	215	103	150
Potter					4	1	19	0	6th	230	316	172	158
									7th	263	341	288	158
NORTHANTS	**O**	**M**	**R**	**W**	**O**	**M**	**R**	**W**	8th	266	351	295	158
Ambrose	28	5	89	7	15	4	66	5	9th	350	380	363	165
Robinson	23	3	117	0	8	2	23	1	10th	351	382		
Penberthy	15.5	3	57	1	7	0	26	0					
Cook	37	18	56	0	8	2	37	1					
Williams	6	1	27	1	6	4	7	1					
Bailey	8	2	13	1									

GLOUCESTERSHIRE vs. SUSSEX

at Bristol on 12th, 13th, 14th September 1990
Toss : Gloucestershire. Umpires : P.J.Eele and K.J.Lyons
Gloucs won by an innings and 86 runs (Glos 24 pts (Bt: 4, Bw: 4) Sussex 4 pts (Bt: 1, Bw: 3))

SUSSEX

N.J.Lenham	b Curran	11	lbw b Walsh		33
D.M.Smith	c Lloyds b Graveney	52	c Curran b Lawrence		0
P.W.G.Parker *	c Graveney b Curran	0	c Wright b Graveney		8
A.P.Wells	c Wright b Curran	5	c & b Graveney		27
M.P.Speight	c & b Graveney	34	c Athey b Graveney		13
A.I.C.Dodemaide	c Curran b Walsh	17	c Curran b Lawrence		20
P.Moores	c Lloyds b Graveney	0	b Walsh		72
A.C.S.Pigott	c Russell b Graveney	1	lbw b Lawrence		0
I.D.K.Salisbury	b Walsh	0	c Alleyne b Graveney		15
B.T.P.Donelan	not out	37	b Graveney		15
R.A.Bunting	c Athey b Graveney	4	not out		0
Extras	(lb 10,nb 8)	18	(b 2,lb 5,nb 7)		14
TOTAL		179			202

GLOUCESTERSHIRE

G.D.Hodgson	c Salisbury b Pigott	1	
A.J.Wright *	c Salisbury b Pigott	3	
P.Bainbridge	c Moores b Bunting	97	
C.W.J.Athey	c Moores b Pigott	4	
M.W.Alleyne	c Donelan b Dodemaide	15	
D.V.Lawrence	lbw b Salisbury	13	
K.M.Curran	not out	144	
R.C.Russell +	c Moores b Donelan	31	
J.W.Lloyds	b Dodemaide	50	
C.A.Walsh	b Pigott	63	
D.A.Graveney	c Moores b Pigott	3	
Extras	(b 21,lb 17,w 1,nb 4)	43	
TOTAL		467	

GLOUCS	O	M	R	W	O	M	R	W	FALL OF WICKETS				
										SUS	GLO	SUS	GLO
Walsh	17	2	45	2	15	3	46	2	1st	22	4	7	
Lawrence	12	4	17	0	15	3	59	3	2nd	53	5	29	
Curran	15	6	24	3	11	5	20	0	3rd	103	19	55	
Bainbridge	6	1	7	0					4th	110	52	83	
Athey	4	1	15	0					5th	112	82	88	
Alleyne	5	1	16	0					6th	113	173	132	
Graveney	23.4	7	45	5	37.2	15	59	5	7th	113	244	136	
Lloyds					5	1	11	0	8th	140	331	150	
									9th	155	453	198	
SUSSEX	**O**	**M**	**R**	**W**	**O**	**M**	**R**	**W**	10th	179	467	202	
Dodemaide	28	6	83	2									
Pigott	37.3	7	87	5									
Bunting	22	4	67	1									
Salisbury	29	6	103	1									
Donelan	31	8	89	1									

NOTTINGHAMSHIRE vs. LANCASHIRE

at Trent Bridge on 12th, 13th, 14th, 15th September 1990
Toss : Nottinghamshire. Umpires : J.H.Hampshire and B.J.Meyer
Lancashire won by 10 wickets (Notts 5 pts (Bt: 2, Bw: 3) Lancashire 24 pts (Bt: 4, Bw: 4))

LANCASHIRE

G.D.Mendis	b Evans	85	not out		23
G.Fowler	c French b Cooper	1	not out		20
M.A.Atherton	c Randall b Stephenson	81			
N.H.Fairbrother *	lbw b Evans	0			
G.D.Lloyd	c Mike b Afford	31			
M.Watkinson	c Stephenson b Afford	4			
P.A.J.DeFreitas	c French b Evans	49			
W.K.Hegg +	c French b Afford	48			
G.Yates	c Cooper b Mike	106			
P.J.Martin	c French b Evans	21			
P.J.W.Allott	not out	55			
Extras	(lb 7,w 5,nb 6)	18	(lb 7,nb 1)		8
TOTAL		499	(for 0 wkts)		51

NOTTINGHAMSHIRE

B.C.Broad	c Mendis b Watkinson	42	c Martin b Yates		122
M.Newell	c Allott b Martin	0	c Atherton b DeFreitas		12
R.T.Robinson *	c Lloyd b Martin	8	lbw b Watkinson		23
D.W.Randall	lbw b Martin	0	c Fairbrother b Atherton		24
D.J.R.Martindale	c Fairbrother b DeFreitas	22	c Hegg b Atherton		6
K.P.Evans	c Fowler b Watkinson	49	b Yates		55
F.D.Stephenson	c Martin b Watkinson	24	c Watkinson b Atherton		51
B.N.French +	c Fowler b DeFreitas	16	c Fairbrother b Atherton		19
G.W.Mike	not out	18	c Hegg b Atherton		9
K.E.Cooper	c Mendis b DeFreitas	5	not out		9
J.A.Afford	c Atherton b Martin	5	c Martin b Atherton		0
Extras	(b 4,lb 9)	13	(b 9,lb 13,w 1,nb 2)		25
TOTAL		202			346

NOTTS	O	M	R	W	O	M	R	W	FALL OF WICKETS				
										LAN	NOT	NOT	LAN
Stephenson	29	3	131	1					1st	8	20	20	
Cooper	30	8	93	1					2nd	151	34	63	
Mike	17.2	3	80	1	4	0	24	0	3rd	151	34	147	
Evans	28	4	95	4	4	1	20	0	4th	194	65	161	
Afford	29	5	93	3					5th	211	97	247	
									6th	216	144	258	
LANCASHIRE	**O**	**M**	**R**	**W**	**O**	**M**	**R**	**W**	7th	299	165	323	
DeFreitas	25	7	63	3	14	5	33	1	8th	320	181	323	
Martin	20.3	4	68	4	10	3	30	0	9th	383	197	346	
Watkinson	16	3	34	3	17	1	73	1	10th	499	202	346	
Allott	14	8	18	0	15	7	41	0					
Yates	2	0	6	0	28	6	69	2					
Atherton					21.3	4	78	6					

BRITANNIC ASSURANCE CHAMPIONSHIP

SOMERSET vs. WORCESTERSHIRE

at Taunton on 12th, 13th, 14th, 15th September 1990
Toss : Worcestershire. Umpires : R.Julian and D.R.Shepherd (replaced by J.H.Harris)
Worcestershire won by 173 runs (Somerset 5 pts (Bt: 4, Bw: 1) Worcs 23 pts (Bt: 4, Bw: 3))

WORCESTERSHIRE

T.S.Curtis	c Tavare b Jones	156	c Swallow b Jones	10
G.J.Lord	c Tavare b Jones	6	lbw b Mallender	80
G.A.Hick	c Tavare b Mallender	154	lbw b Jones	81
D.B.D'Oliveira	b Jones	14	c Burns b Jones	60
P.A.Neale *	lbw b Mallender	40	lbw b Mallender	12
S.R.Lampitt	lbw b Mallender	16	c Burns b Jones	10
S.J.Rhodes +	c Harden b Mallender	6	not out	34
R.K.Illingworth	c Lefebvre b Jones	8	b Jones	3
P.J.Newport	not out	65	not out	7
N.V.Radford	c Lefebvre b Hayhurst	14		
S.M.McEwan	not out	30		
Extras	(lb 9,nb 2)	11	(b 12,lb 10,nb 2)	24
TOTAL	(for 9 wkts dec)	520	(for 7 wkts dec)	321

SOMERSET

A.N.Hayhurst	c Rhodes b Lampitt	50	c Hick b Newport	22
S.J.Cook	c Neale b Illingworth	143	c Hick b Radford	13
R.J.Bartlett	c D'Oliveira b Newport	73	c Rhodes b Radford	12
C.J.Tavare *	c Rhodes b Newport	18	b Radford	5
R.J.Harden	not out	51	c D'Oliveira b Radford	90
N.D.Burns +	b Newport	0	c Hick b Newport	0
G.D.Rose	b Lampitt	29	lbw b Lampitt	36
R.P.Lefebvre	c Hick b Lampitt	0	c D'Oliveira b McEwan	15
I.G.Swallow	run out		b Illingworth	0
N.A.Mallender	c Hick b Lampitt	15	c Hick b Lampitt	23
A.N.Jones	b Illingworth	41	not out	2
Extras	(b 1,lb 3,w 3,nb 11)	18	(lb 1,w 1,nb 6)	8
TOTAL		442		226

SOMERSET	O	M	R	W	O	M	R	W
Jones	35	6	154	4	21	2	76	5
Mallender	33	7	100	4	24	4	75	2
Rose	6	1	15	0	9	1	51	0
Lefebvre	30	9	67	0	4	2	3	0
Hayhurst	22	2	87	1	8	1	43	0
Swallow	24	5	88	0	9	0	51	0

WORCS	O	M	R	W	O	M	R	W
Newport	28	4	95	3	13	1	74	2
McEwan	26	1	116	0	8	0	39	1
Lampitt	24	3	97	4	10.5	1	43	2
Radford	18	6	75	0	13	2	55	4
Illingworth	22.5	5	55	2	8	3	10	1
Hick	1	1	0	0	2	0	4	0

FALL OF WICKETS	WOR	SOM	WOR	SOM
1st	43	132	28	23
2nd	307	252	166	50
3rd	331	295	198	52
4th	346	296	252	56
5th	386	296	268	57
6th	398	345	279	119
7th	411	345	284	172
8th	411	352		173
9th	432	372		212
10th		442		226

WARWICKSHIRE vs. GLAMORGAN

at Edgbaston on 12th, 13th, 14th, 15th September 1990
Toss : Glamorgan. Umpires : N.T.Plews and P.B.Wight
Warwicks won by 170 runs (Warwicks 24 pts (Bt: 4, Bw: 4) Glamorgan 5 pts (Bt: 3, Bw: 2))

WARWICKSHIRE

A.J.Moles	c Metson b Frost	0	c Dale b Croft	8
J.D.Ratcliffe	b Anthony	41	lbw b Frost	0
Asif Din	lbw b Watkin	40	(4) b Frost	34
T.A.Lloyd *	c Metson b Frost	78	(5) lbw b Watkin	39
P.A.Smith	c Dale b Watkin	117	(6) lbw b Watkin	0
D.A.Reeve	not out	68	(7) c Croft b Watkin	45
K.J.Piper +	c Metson b Anthony	8	(8) b Croft	65
G.C.Small	c Metson b Watkin	2	(9) c Maynard b Croft	4
P.A.Booth	c Metson b Watkin	0	(3) c Metson b Watkin	10
A.A.Donald	b Watkin	7	b Anthony	3
T.A.Munton	c Metson b Frost	23	not out	1
Extras	(lb 8,w 3,nb 10)	21	(b 1,lb 5)	6
TOTAL		405		215

GLAMORGAN

A.R.Butcher *	c Asif Din b Smith	71	c Ratcliffe b Munton	3
H.Morris	c Lloyd b Smith	73	lbw b Munton	20
S.P.James	lbw b Smith	0	lbw b Munton	0
M.P.Maynard	st Piper b Booth	8	lbw b Munton	79
P.A.Cottey	c Lloyd b Munton	52	c Moles b Booth	22
A.Dale	c Piper b Donald	5	c Piper b Munton	9
R.D.B.Croft	lbw b Donald	0	c Piper b Donald	12
H.A.Anthony	st Piper b Booth	9	c Piper b Booth	13
C.P.Metson +	c Piper b Munton	23	lbw b Donald	4
S.L.Watkin	b Munton	0	not out	15
M.Frost	not out	6	c Reeve b Donald	12
Extras	(b 6,lb 6,nb 1)	13	(b 6,lb 3,nb 1)	10
TOTAL		251		199

GLAMORGAN	O	M	R	W	O	M	R	W
Anthony	26	9	70	2	16	2	38	1
Frost	23.2	4	78	3	17	2	49	2
Watkin	36	9	100	5	19	4	48	4
Dale	14	1	64	0	4	1	10	0
Croft	28	3	85	0	35.1	13	64	3

WARWICKS	O	M	R	W	O	M	R	W
Small	10	4	44	0	9	3	14	0
Munton	13.3	1	44	5	18	3	64	5
Donald	14	4	51	2	10.4	2	33	3
Booth	25	11	44	2	18	8	48	2
Reeve	3	0	13	0				
Smith	13	4	43	3	9	3	31	0

FALL OF WICKETS	WAR	GLA	WAR	GLA
1st	1	141	1	13
2nd	78	146	13	13
3rd	94	151	26	27
4th	281	161	91	101
5th	296	168	91	124
6th	327	168	102	151
7th	342	169	191	154
8th	342	214	196	158
9th	350	214	207	170
10th	405	251	215	199

SURREY vs. MIDDLESEX

at The Oval on 12th, 13th, 14th, 15th September 1990
Toss : Surrey. Umpires : B.Dudleston and B.Hassan
Match drawn (Surrey 5 pts (Bt: 3, Bw: 2) Middlesex 6 pts (Bt: 4, Bw: 2))

SURREY

D.J.Bicknell	c Gatting b Fraser	41	b Hughes	114
R.I.Alikhan	c Haynes b Cowans	119	c Roseberry b Fraser	13
A.J.Stewart +	b Fraser	0	(5) c Emburey b Tufnell	47
D.M.Ward	c Haynes b Tufnell	75	(6) c Downton b Tufnell	6
M.A.Lynch	c Emburey b Fraser	17	(4) c Downton b Hughes	22
I.A.Greig *	c Ramprakash b Emburey	31	(7) lbw b Hughes	30
J.D.Robinson	c Haynes b Emburey	72	(3) c Ramprakash b Fraser	0
M.A.Feltham	c Emburey b Fraser	101	c Fraser b Ramprakash	58
K.T.Medlycott	c Downton b Fraser	5	b Emburey	44
N.M.Kendrick	not out	6	lbw b Downton	14
Waqar Younis			not out	4
Extras	(b 1,lb 3,nb 9)	13	(b 8,lb 10,w 1,nb 2)	21
TOTAL	(for 9 wkts dec)	480		373

MIDDLESEX

D.L.Haynes	b Waqar Younis	69		
M.A.Roseberry	c Greig b Waqar Younis	28	(4) not out	27
M.W.Gatting *	retired hurt	0		
M.R.Ramprakash	c Stewart b Waqar Younis	54	(3) not out	40
K.R.Brown	c Feltham b Kendrick	21		
P.R.Downton +	c Waqar Younis b Kendrick	48		
J.E.Emburey	c Kendrick b Feltham	66		
A.R.C.Fraser	b Feltham	92		
S.P.Hughes	c Medlycott b Feltham	15	(1) c Stewart b Alikhan	4
P.C.R.Tufnell	not out	23		
N.G.Cowans			(2) c Feltham b Lynch	31
Extras	(b 2,lb 6,w 1)	9		0
TOTAL	(for 8 wkts dec)	425	(for 2 wkts)	102

MIDDLESEX	O	M	R	W	O	M	R	W
Fraser	32.4	9	95	5	20	9	44	2
Cowans	24	6	76	1	15	5	49	0
Hughes	21	1	89	0	16	1	56	3
Emburey	45	10	96	2	23	5	49	1
Haynes	4	0	17	0	4	0	13	0
Tufnell	35	10	103	1	30	8	90	2
Ramprakash					10	4	17	1
Brown					5	2	31	0
Roseberry					4	3	2	0
Downton					1.1	0	4	1

SURREY	O	M	R	W	O	M	R	W
Waqar Younis	28	4	91	3				
Feltham	20.4	4	69	3				
Greig	11	1	41	0				
Robinson	17	2	59	0				
Medlycott	8	1	35	0				
Kendrick	30	8	122	2				
Alikhan					7	1	12	1
Bicknell					7	1	15	0
Lynch					5	0	43	1
Stewart					5	0	32	0

FALL OF WICKETS	SUR	MID	SUR	MID
1st	106	100	29	6
2nd	108	108	29	45
3rd	210	145	71	
4th	238	197	184	
5th	282	267	194	
6th	320	354	236	
7th	444	389	237	
8th	453	425	344	
9th	480		365	
10th			373	

HEADLINES

12th - 15th September

● Both Middlesex and Essex were frustrated by determined opposition as Middlesex remained 14 points ahead at the top of the table. Both teams were further disrupted by injuries to their captains and most influential players: Graham Gooch suffered a broken right thumb, while Mike Gatting suffered a badly bruised left elbow

● Victory over Kent could have taken Essex two points clear of Middlesex, but Essex were denied by a ninth-wicket partnership of 115 between Richard Ellison and Richard Davis; earlier Mark Waugh had completed 2,000 runs for the season

● A Middlesex win over Surrey could have brought the Championship pennant back to Lord's, but Ian Greig's side were giving nothing away to their neighbours and comfortably maintained their unbeaten record at The Oval. Rehan Alikhan and Mark Feltham both made maiden first-class 100s and Jonathan Robinson a career best 72 in Surrey's first-innings, but their lead was reduced to 55 by a hard-hitting 92, another career best, from Angus Fraser; Darren Bicknell ensured that there would be no dramatic Surrey second innings collapse and Ian Greig refused to risk a declaration: the Championship would be decided in the final round of matches

BRIT. ASS. C'SHIP	REFUGE ASSURANCE CUP FINAL

HEADLINES

12th-15th September

● All five remaining matches did produce positive results, with a string of counties still in contention for the minor placings. Warwckshire reclaimed third place with victory over Glamorgan at Edgbaston, as Paul Smith made his first 100 of the season and Tim Munton celebrated selection for the England A tour with eight wickets for 108. Consolation for Glamorgan was provided by Alan Butcher who passed 2,000 runs in a season for the first time.

● Lancashire remained in line for a top five finish with a 10-wicket victory over Nottinghamshire at Trent Bridge. Gary Yates, sharing a last-wicket partnership of 116 with Paul Allott, made a century on his Championship debut, and Michael Atherton improved his best bowling figures for the third time in the season. Chris Broad's 9th 100 of the summer, as he also completed 2,000 runs, was in vain.

● Worcestershire were still able to finish the season in third place following their hard-earned win over Somerset at Taunton, bowling the home side out twice in a match that produced over 1,500 runs. It was no surprise that Graeme Hick, who reached 2,000 runs for the third time in five seasons, and Jimmy Cook, who became the second man past the 2,500 mark, both made 100s, and Tim Curtis hit 156 as he and Hick added 264 for the second-wicket in the visitors' first innings.

● Both Kevin Curran and David Graveney were parting company with Gloucestershire at the end of the season, and both showed what the county would be missing in Gloucester's innings victory over Sussex at Bristol: Curran hit a career best 144* as well as taking three wickets, and Graveney returned match figures of 10 for 104, as Sussex remained favourites for the wooden spoon

● Northants were grateful to Curtly Ambrose for their decisive victory over Leicestershire: he produced match figures of 12 for 155, the best of the season, as six Leicester batsmen failed to score in their second innings

DERBYSHIRE vs. MIDDLESEX

at Edgbaston on 16th September 1990
Toss : Middlesex.   Umpires : D.J.Constant and M.J.Kitchen
Middlesex won by 5 wickets

DERBYSHIRE

K.J.Barnett *	b Weekes	42
P.D.Bowler +	b Hughes	11
J.E.Morris	c Weekes b Haynes	46
A.P.Kuiper	c Fraser b Weekes	9
T.J.G.O'Gorman	b Fraser	10
B.Roberts	b Hughes	21
C.J.Adams	run out	13
A.E.Warner	not out	28
S.J.Base	not out	1
D.E.Malcolm		
O.H.Mortensen		
Extras	(b 1,lb 9,w 5,nb 1)	16
TOTAL	(40 overs)(for 7 wkts)	197

MIDDLESEX

D.L.Haynes	b Malcolm	49
M.A.Roseberry	b Warner	17
M.W.Gatting *	b Malcolm	44
M.R.Ramprakash	c Bowler b Warner	1
K.R.Brown	c Barnett b Malcolm	40
P.R.Downton +	not out	34
J.E.Emburey	not out	5
P.N.Weekes		
A.R.C.Fraser		
S.P.Hughes		
N.G.Cowans		
Extras	(b 1,lb 5,w 4,nb 1)	11
TOTAL	(39.4 overs)(for 5 wkts)	201

MIDDLESEX	O	M	R	W		FALL OF WICKETS	
						DER	MID
Fraser	8	0	32	1			
Cowans	6	0	22	0	1st	32	23
Hughes	8	0	45	2	2nd	81	115
Emburey	7	0	37	0	3rd	113	120
Weekes	8	1	35	2	4th	116	120
Haynes	3	0	16	1	5th	145	191
					6th	151	
DERBYSHIRE	O	M	R	W	7th	196	
Warner	8	0	35	2	8th		
Mortensen	8	0	19	0	9th		
Malcolm	8	0	41	3	10th		
Base	8	0	53	0			
Kuiper	7.4	0	47	0			

Man of the match: P.R.Downton

HEADLINES

Refuge Assurance Cup Final

16th September

● Middlesex became the third winners of the Refuge Assurance Cup by beating Derbyshire by five wickets at Edgbaston in a final that only really came to life in the last 15 overs of the match, when three wickets from Devon Malcolm put the result into some doubt.
Middlesex had always looked in control as none of the Derbyshire big guns ever got going with the bat, and Desmond Haynes and the quickly recovered Mike Gatting took Middlesex to 115 for 1. After both had been bowled by Malcolm, Keith Brown and Paul Downton took Middlesex to within seven of their target, eventually achieved with two balls to spare

Paul Downton, who finished his benefit season with the Man of the match award in the Refuge Assurance Cup Final, but whose future career after is still in doubt after an eye injury earlier in the year.

BRITANNIC ASSURANCE CHAMPIONSHIP

SUSSEX vs. MIDDLESEX
at Hove on 18th, 19th, 20th September 1990
Toss : Middlesex. Umpires : K.E.Palmer and D.S.Thompsett
Middx won by an innings and 57 runs (Sx 3 pts (Bt: 1, Bw: 2) Middx 24 pts (Bt: 4, Bw: 4))

SUSSEX
N.J.Lenham	c Emburey b Williams	9	lbw b Fraser	5
D.M.Smith	c Downton b Cowans	32	lbw b Cowans	10
P.W.G.Parker *	c Brown b Hughes	24	b Cowans	16
A.P.Wells	b Gatting	6	c Downton b Fraser	50
M.P.Speight	c Downton b Hughes	33	b Fraser	12
A.I.C.Dodemaide	b Fraser	18	c Downton b Fraser	16
P.Moores +	c sub b Hughes	4	lbw b Hughes	10
J.A.North	lbw b Cowans	7	not out	19
A.C.S.Pigott	c Fraser b Gatting	4	c sub b Gatting	9
I.D.K.Salisbury	not out	18	b Hughes	0
R.A.Bunting	c Emburey b Hughes	11	lbw b Hughes	0
Extras	(b 10,lb 6,nb 5)	21	(b 8,lb 4,w 1,nb 7)	20
TOTAL		187		167

MIDDLESEX
D.L.Haynes	c Moores b Bunting	46
M.A.Roseberry	run out	83
M.W.Gatting *	c Parker b Lenham	51
M.R.Ramprakash	lbw b Bunting	13
K.R.Brown	not out	116
P.R.Downton +	lbw b North	5
J.E.Emburey	c Smith b Dodemaide	48
N.F.Williams	c Wells b Dodemaide	18
A.R.C.Fraser	b Salisbury	13
S.P.Hughes	lbw b Salisbury	0
N.G.Cowans	c Pigott b North	0
Extras	(b 1,lb 12,w 1,nb 4)	18
TOTAL		411

MIDDLESEX	O	M	R	W	O	M	R	W
Fraser	21	4	55	1	17	4	47	4
Williams	3	1	9	1				
Cowans	12	5	19	2	16	4	33	2
Hughes	17.1	4	34	4	16.5	3	55	3
Gatting	18	8	42	2	8	5	7	1
Emburey	10	5	12	0	3	0	13	0
Haynes	1	1	0	0				

SUSSEX	O	M	R	W	O	M	R	W
Dodemaide	28	2	128	2				
Pigott	24	4	92	0				
Bunting	17	4	49	2				
North	16.2	4	43	2				
Lenham	19	4	48	1				
Salisbury	11	2	38	2				

FALL OF WICKETS	SUS	MID	SUS	MID
1st	19	133	10	
2nd	42	135	17	
3rd	78	168	46	
4th	103	225	74	
5th	130	244	119	
6th	136	352	126	
7th	151	389	158	
8th	151	410	167	
9th	170	410	167	
10th	187	411	167	

SURREY vs. ESSEX
at The Oval on 18th, 19th, 20th, 21st September 1990
Toss : Essex. Umpires : A.A.Jones and P.B.Wight
Match drawn (Surrey 2 pts (Bt: 0, Bw: 2) Essex 7 pts (Bt: 3, Bw: 4))

ESSEX
J.P.Stephenson	c Lynch b Greig	51
N.Shahid	c Lynch b Greig	42
P.J.Prichard	c Stewart b Murphy	28
N.Hussain	run out	197
B.R.Hardie	c sub b Kendrick	42
M.A.Garnham +	c Lynch b Greig	5
J.J.B.Lewis	not out	116
N.A.Foster *	c Bicknell D.J. b Murphy	19
M.C.Ilott	c Waqar Younis b Kendrick	5
J.H.Childs	c Stewart b Bicknell M.P.	0
S.J.W.Andrew	c sub b Bicknell M.P.	18
Extras	(b 4,lb 11,nb 1)	16
TOTAL		539

SURREY
D.J.Bicknell	b Foster	0	c & b Foster	50
R.I.Alikhan	lbw b Foster	16	c Hardie b Shahid	138
D.M.Ward	c Shahid b Andrew	58	(4) b Stephenson	208
A.J.Stewart +	c Shahid b Foster	2	(3) c Garnham b Foster	51
M.A.Lynch	c Garnham b Ilott	12	b Shahid	16
I.A.Greig *	c Garnham b Foster	11	not out	57
J.D.Robinson	run out	7	b Shahid	0
M.P.Bicknell	c Hussain b Foster	13	not out	49
N.M.Kendrick	lbw b Ilott	1		
Waqar Younis	c Lewis b Foster	14		
A.J.Murphy	not out	0		
Extras	(lb 2,w 1,nb 3)	6	(b 9,lb 20,w 1,nb 14)	44
TOTAL		140	(for 6 wkts dec)	613

SURREY	O	M	R	W	O	M	R	W
Bicknell M.P.	30.5	8	64	2				
Waqar Younis	5	0	21	0				
Murphy	41	9	154	2				
Robinson	14	0	44	0				
Greig	42	6	150	3				
Kendrick	20	1	64	2				
Alikhan	5	0	22	0				
Bicknell D.J.	2	0	5	0				

ESSEX	O	M	R	W	O	M	R	W
Foster	17.3	2	72	6	29	10	88	2
Ilott	16	3	42	2	34	2	157	0
Andrew	9	4	24	1	18	4	65	0
Childs					21	3	51	0
Shahid					25	4	91	3
Stephenson					29	7	116	1
Hardie					1	0	16	0

FALL OF WICKETS	ESS	SUR	SUR	ESS
1st	96	0	80	
2nd	103	76	184	
3rd	133	78	423	
4th	262	80	455	
5th	275	96	511	
6th	469	112	514	
7th	496	113		
8th	515	120		
9th	519	135		
10th	539	140		

WORCESTERSHIRE vs. GLAMORGAN
at Worcester on 18th, 19th, 20th, 21st September 1990
Toss : Worcestershire. Umpires : P.J.Eele and R.Julian
Worcestershire won by 261 runs (Worcs 24 pts (Bt: 4, Bw: 4) Glamorgan 6 pts (Bt: 2, Bw: 4))

WORCESTERSHIRE
T.S.Curtis	lbw b Frost	16	c James b Watkin	60
G.J.Lord	c Maynard b Bastien	127	c Maynard b Croft	57
G.A.Hick	c Metson b Watkin	6	not out	138
D.B.D'Oliveira	c Metson b Bastien	22	b Bastien	12
P.A.Neale *	b Bastien	4	c Morris b Bastien	17
S.R.Lampitt	lbw b Bastien	34	c Metson b Watkin	18
S.J.Rhodes +	c Cottey b Bastien	0	c Maynard b Bastien	22
R.K.Illingworth	c Metson b Watkin	48	not out	7
N.V.Radford	lbw b Watkin	13		
G.R.Dilley	not out	45		
S.M.McEwan	b Bastien	11		
Extras	(b 4,lb 4,nb 1)	9	(lb 12)	12
TOTAL		335	(for 6 wkts dec)	343

GLAMORGAN
S.P.James	lbw b Dilley	7	c D'Oliveira b Dilley	0
H.Morris	c Rhodes b McEwan	71	b Dilley	50
P.A.Cottey	c Rhodes b Lampitt	19	c Curtis b Dilley	3
M.P.Maynard	b Radford	4	c Rhodes b McEwan	35
A.R.Butcher *	c Hick b McEwan	21	c Lord b Illingworth	61
A.Dale	lbw b McEwan	7	c Rhodes b McEwan	0
R.D.B.Croft	not out	26	c Neale b Lampitt	27
C.P.Metson +	c Rhodes b Lampitt	10	lbw b Lampitt	4
S.L.Watkin	c McEwan b Radford	19	b Dilley	4
S.Bastien	c Rhodes b Radford	0	c Lord b Dilley	12
M.Frost	lbw b Radford	0	not out	4
Extras	(b 5,lb 6,nb 7)	18	(lb 8,w 1,nb 6)	15
TOTAL		202		215

GLAMORGAN	O	M	R	W	O	M	R	W
Frost	23	2	71	1	12	3	44	0
Watkin	31	7	124	3	20	5	47	2
Bastien	24	8	75	6	17	0	76	3
Croft	20	5	41	0	28	3	110	1
Dale	10	5	16	0	11	1	54	0

WORCS	O	M	R	W	O	M	R	W
Dilley	13	1	35	1	14	1	72	5
Radford	20	4	58	4	11	1	31	0
McEwan	18	6	31	3	9	4	30	2
Lampitt	22	7	52	2	12	2	52	2
Illingworth	14	7	15	0	9	5	22	1

FALL OF WICKETS	WOR	GLA	WOR	GLA
1st	24	20	117	1
2nd	43	86	138	18
3rd	95	91	168	68
4th	107	123	198	102
5th	212	142	248	107
6th	212	145	314	152
7th	213	177		156
8th	239	198		191
9th	307	200		199
10th	335	202		215

LANCASHIRE vs. WARWICKSHIRE
at Old Trafford on 18th, 19th, 20th, 21st September 1990 (no play)
Toss : Lancashire. Umpires : D.J.Constant and B.Leadbeater
Match drawn (Lancashire 3 pts (Bt: 0, Bw: 3) Warwickshire 2 pts (Bt: 2, Bw: 0))

WARWICKSHIRE
A.J.Moles	c Fairbrother b Watkinson	9
J.D.Ratcliffe	c Hegg b Atherton	17
Asif Din	c DeFreitas b Watkinson	24
T.A.Lloyd *	c Atherton b Martin	35
P.A.Booth	c Lloyd b Yates	0
P.A.Smith	c Watkinson b Martin	1
D.A.Reeve	not out	121
K.J.Piper +	c Hegg b Watkinson	23
G.C.Small	c Hegg b Atherton	30
T.A.Munton	c Atherton b Watkinson	8
A.A.Donald	c & b Watkinson	8
Extras	(lb 4)	4
TOTAL		280

LANCASHIRE
G.D.Mendis	not out	22
M.A.Atherton	not out	22
J.P.Crawley		
N.H.Fairbrother *		
G.D.Lloyd		
M.Watkinson		
P.A.J.DeFreitas		
W.K.Hegg +		
G.Yates		
I.D.Austin		
P.J.Martin		
Extras	(lb 4)	4
TOTAL	(for 0 wkts)	48

LANCASHIRE	O	M	R	W	O	M	R	W
DeFreitas	4	0	6	0				
Martin	29	6	88	2				
Watkinson	24.3	6	65	5				
Austin	13	8	23	0				
Atherton	23	6	52	2				
Yates	21	6	42	1				

WARWICKS	O	M	R	W	O	M	R	W
Munton	3	0	16	0				
Donald	6	0	24	0				
Booth	3	1	4	0				

FALL OF WICKETS	WAR	LAN	WAR	LAN
1st	14			
2nd	50			
3rd	73			
4th	78			
5th	79			
6th	92			
7th	154			
8th	188			
9th	231			
10th	280			

BRITANNIC ASSURANCE CHAMPIONSHIP

HAMPSHIRE vs. GLOUCESTERSHIRE

at Southampton on 18th, 19th, 20th, 21st September 1990
Toss : Gloucestershire.   Umpires : J.H.Harris and R.Palmer
Hampshire won by 2 wickets (Hampshire 21 pts (Bt: 1, Bw: 4) Gloucs 7 pts (Bt: 3, Bw: 4))

GLOUCESTERSHIRE

G.D.Hodgson	c Aymes b Bakker	58	c & b Maru	76
A.J.Wright *	c Terry b Marshall	19	c Aymes b Maru	19
P.Bainbridge	c Aymes b Connor	16	c Nicholas b Maru	30
M.W.Alleyne	c Aymes b Bakker	18	(6) c Gower b Maru	33
K.M.Curran	c Bakker b Maru	78	(7) not out	101
R.C.Russell +	b Ayling	23	(8) c Smith R.A. b Connor	24
J.W.Lloyds	b Maru	0	(9) c Smith R.A. b Maru	24
E.T.Milburn	c Middleton b Maru	0	(10) not out	3
C.A.Walsh	c Terry b Ayling	20		
D.V.Lawrence	b Marshall	18	(4) lbw b Maru	0
D.A.Graveney	not out	1	(5) c Marshall b Ayling	20
Extras	(lb 5,nb 7)	12	(b 6,lb 6,nb 8)	20
TOTAL		263	(for 8 wkts dec)	350

HAMPSHIRE

V.P.Terry	c Alleyne b Curran	1	c Russell b Graveney	46
T.C.Middleton	c Russell b Curran	5	c Russell b Curran	82
D.I.Gower	c Lawrence b Curran	14	b Graveney	4
R.A.Smith	b Walsh	8	c Russell b Walsh	124
M.D.Marshall	c Russell b Lawrence	21	c Walsh b Graveney	46
M.C.J.Nicholas *	c Wright b Lawrence	4	not out	54
J.R.Ayling	b Walsh	28	c Wright b Graveney	10
A.N Aymes +	not out	44	c Russell b Graveney	2
R.J.Maru	c Lloyds b Curran	20	run out	42
C.A.Connor	b Walsh	2	not out	0
P.J.Bakker	c & b Curran	7		
Extras	(b 4,lb 3,nb 8)	15	(b 5,lb 16,nb 15)	36
TOTAL		169	(for 8 wkts)	446

HAMPSHIRE	O	M	R	W	O	M	R	W
Marshall	21	4	54	2	27	7	70	0
Bakker	21	8	51	2	18	4	61	0
Connor	17	4	56	1	24	5	55	1
Ayling	16	5	57	2	21	6	55	1
Maru	14	4	40	3	53.4	18	97	6

GLOUCS	O	M	R	W	O	M	R	W
Walsh	18	3	51	3	25	4	93	1
Lawrence	9	2	30	2	19	1	64	0
Curran	17.2	3	63	5	18	2	86	1
Milburn	4	1	10	0	3	0	24	0
Graveney	9	5	8	0	35	5	140	5
Bainbridge					4	0	18	0

FALL OF WICKETS				
	GLO	HAM	GLO	HAM
1st	35	3	39	80
2nd	62	24	93	89
3rd	114	33	93	244
4th	121	40	135	312
5th	172	51	172	339
6th	177	64	228	358
7th	177	128	278	362
8th	210	155	333	442
9th	239	158		
10th	263	169		

NOTTINGHAMSHIRE vs. YORKSHIRE

at Trent Bridge on 18th, 19th, 20th, 21st September 1990
Toss : Nottinghamshire.   Umpires : J.W.Holder and M.J.Kitchen
Yorkshire won by 4 wickets (Nottinghamshire 3 pts (Bt: 3, Bw: 0) Yorks 21 pts (Bt: 3, Bw: 2))

NOTTINGHAMSHIRE

B.C.Broad	lbw b Hartley	40	st Blakey b Grayson	43
M.Newell	b Hartley	38	not out	89
R.T.Robinson *	not out	220	not out	36
D.W.Randall	lbw b Hartley	10		
D.J.R.Martindale	c Byas b Pickles	11		
K.P.Evans	b Pickles	43		
F.D.Stephenson	c Byas b Jarvis	95		
B.N.French +	not out	2		
E.E.Hemmings				
K.E.Cooper				
J.A.Afford				
Extras	(b 3,lb 14,w 1,nb 5)	23	(b 3,lb 4)	7
TOTAL	(for 6 wkts dec)	482	(for 1 wkt dec)	175

YORKSHIRE

M.D.Moxon *	c French b Cooper	42	c Martindale b Stephenson	83
A.A.Metcalfe	not out	194	c & b Cooper	107
S.A.Kellett	c Evans b Hemmings	27	(6) c & b Cooper	20
P.E.Robinson	not out	62	(3) lbw b Cooper	5
R.J.Blakey +			(4) c Afford b Cooper	64
D.Byas			(5) lbw b Evans	8
P.Grayson			not out	6
C.S.Pickles			not out	23
C.White				
P.J.Hartley				
P.W.Jarvis				
Extras	(lb 6,nb 3)	9	(b 1,lb 7,nb 3)	11
TOTAL	(for 2 wkts dec)	334	(for 6 wkts)	327

YORKSHIRE	O	M	R	W	O	M	R	W
Jarvis	27	1	106	1	2	0	9	0
Hartley	35	7	95	3	6	0	23	0
Pickles	32	9	120	2	7	3	16	0
White	17	2	66	0	11	1	65	0
Grayson	28	6	78	0	13	4	55	1

NOTTS	O	M	R	W	O	M	R	W
Stephenson	0.2	0	4	0	5	0	30	1
Cooper	27.4	9	70	1	29.5	3	128	3
Evans	25.2	9	71	0	16	0	79	2
Hemmings	27	5	102	1	11	1	49	0
Afford	35	12	81	0	4	0	33	0

FALL OF WICKETS				
	NOT	YOR	NOT	YOR
1st	62	89	93	143
2nd	109	163		152
3rd	125			246
4th	175			260
5th	272			298
6th	469			299
7th				
8th				
9th				
10th				

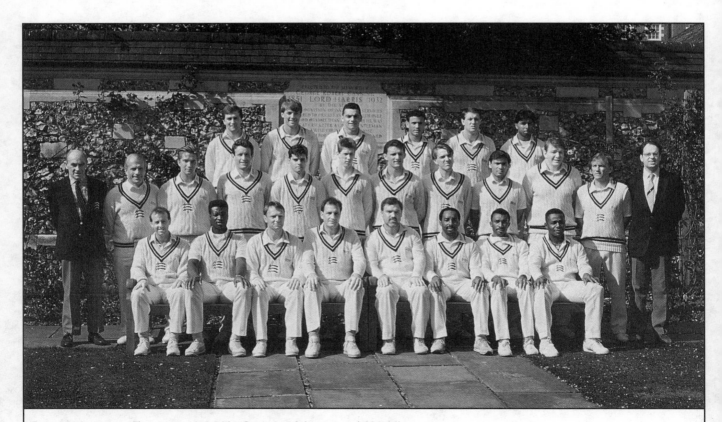

Britannic Assurance Champions 1990: Mike Gatting with his successful Middlesex team.

BRITANNIC ASSURANCE CHAMPIONSHIP

DERBYSHIRE vs. LEICESTERSHIRE

at Derby on 18th, 19th, 20th, 21st September 1990
Toss : Derbyshire.   Umpires : H.D.Bird and R.A.White
Match drawn (Derbyshire 6 pts (Bt: 2, Bw: 4) Leicestershire 6 pts (Bt: 2, Bw: 4))

LEICESTERSHIRE

T.J.Boon	c Barnett b Base	15	lbw b Base		7
N.E.Briers *	b Bishop	99	b Bishop		2
J.J.Whitaker	c Barnett b Base	65	c Barnett b Bishop		20
P.Willey	b Bishop	1	b Base		0
L.Potter	c Krikken b Bishop	2	lbw b Barnett		65
C.C.Lewis	lbw b Bishop	0	(7) c Adams b Base		54
P.N.Hepworth	not out	14	(6) not out		55
P.A.Nixon +	c Roberts b Bishop	17			
C.Hawkes	c Krikken b Mortensen	3	(8) not out		2
J.P.Agnew	c Krikken b Mortensen	6			
A.D.Mullally	lbw b Mortensen	0			
Extras	(b 5,lb 10,w 2,nb 8)	25	(b 1,lb 9,nb 1)		11
TOTAL		247	(for 6 wkts)		216

DERBYSHIRE

K.J.Barnett *	b Lewis	4
T.J.G.O'Gorman	c Hawkes b Mullally	100
K.M.Krikken +	b Mullally	1
B.Roberts	b Agnew	15
C.J.Adams	b Lewis	54
Z.A.Sadiq	b Lewis	0
S.C.Goldsmith	b Lewis	0
I.R.Bishop	c Nixon b Lewis	3
S.J.Base	b Lewis	2
D.G.Cork	c Briers b Mullally	7
O.H.Mortensen	not out	5
Extras	(lb 12,nb 5)	17
TOTAL		208

DERBYSHIRE	O	M	R	W	O	M	R	W
Bishop	26	8	62	5	14	3	39	2
Mortensen	22.3	8	40	3	12	2	43	0
Base	18	6	51	2	18	7	51	3
Cork	10	1	39	0	14	5	31	0
Goldsmith	14	2	40	0				
Adams					3	0	12	0
Barnett					20	6	30	1

LEICS	O	M	R	W	O	M	R	W
Lewis	24	4	58	6				
Mullally	20	7	56	3				
Agnew	10	1	42	1				
Hawkes	14	3	40	0				

FALL OF WICKETS

	LEI	DER	LEI	DER
1st	54	18	9	
2nd	187	19	9	
3rd	196	77	9	
4th	197	175	48	
5th	197	181	136	
6th	200	181	209	
7th	221	189		
8th	233	195		
9th	247	195		
10th	247	208		

BRITANNIC ASSURANCE CHAMPIONSHIP

Final Table

		P	W	L	D	T	Bt	Bl	Pts
1	Middlesex (3)	22	10	1	11	0	73	55	288
2	Essex (2)	22	8	2	12	0	73	56	257
3	Hampshire (6)	22	8	4	10	0	67	48	243
4	Worcestershire (1)	22	7	1	14	0	70	58	240
5	Warwickshire (8)	22	7	7	8	0	55	64	231
6	Lancashire (4)	22	6	3	13	0	65	56	217
7	Leicestershire (13)	22	6	7	9	0	61	53	210
8	Glamorgan (17)	22	5	6	11	0	64	48	192
9	Surrey (12)	22	4	3	15	0	54	64	190
10	Yorkshire (16)	22	5	9	8	0	52	55	187
11	Northants (5)	22	4	9	9	0	61	60	185
12	Derbyshire (7)	22	6	7	9	0	58	52	181
13	Notts (11)	22	4	8	10	0	51	58	173
	Gloucestershire (9)	22	4	7	11	0	51	58	173
15	Somerset (14)	22	3	4	15	0	73	45	166
16	Kent (15)	22	3	6	13	0	69	35	152
17	Sussex (10)	22	3	9	10	0	51	44	143

Surrey's total includes 8 points for a drawn match where scores finished level

Derbyshire were penalised 25 points by the TCCB for preparing an unsatisfactory pitch

HEADLINES

18th -21st September

● Middlesex won the County Championship for the fifth time in 15 years when they defeated Sussex at Hove. Simon Hughes produced his best figures of the summer as Sussex managed only 187 in their first innings, then Keith Brown, who contributed many important runs through the season, made his fifth 100 to bring the visitors a lead of 224. Sussex, now guaranteed bottom place in the table, did not hold up the champions elect for long

● Essex's Championship hopes were briefly kept alive at The Oval when they forced Surrey to follow on 399 runs behind, but after Middlesex's victory over Sussex had put the title beyond their reach, Essex had to suffer in the field for almost two full days as Surrey reached 613 for 6. Batting landmarks again played their part: a career best 197 from Nasser Hussain and a century on his first-class debut from Jonathan Lewis had taken Essex to 539, while in Surrey's second innings, Rehan Alikhan improved his career best and David Ward completed 2,000 runs as he made the 32nd double century of the summer, a record for an English season. With eight wickets in the match Neal Foster finished well ahead of the bowling field with 94

● The battle for third place was not decided until the last ball of the season had been delivered; Hampshire claimed third position by reaching 446 for 8, the second highest total ever made to win a Championship match, to beat Gloucestershire. Robin Smith's sixth 100 of the season put Hampshire on course, and an eighth-wicket stand of 80 between Mark Nicholas and Rajesh Maru took them to the brink of victory.

● Hampshire's remarkable finish denied Worcestershire third place despite their victory over Glamorgan. Graeme Hick took his first-class aggregate against the Welsh county in 1990 past 500 with his 8th 100 of the season, and a return to form and fitness by Graham Dilley and Neal Radford proved too much for the Glamorgan batsmen

● Warwickshire and Lancashire had began their match at Old Trafford with hopes of third place, but they were washed away by Manchester's weather. So Warwicks had to be content with fifth place, Lancashire sixth

● Victory over Derbyshire at Derby could have lifted Leicestershire into the top five, but a delayed start on the final day put paid to any hopes of a positive result

● Yorkshire finished the season with their second successive victory,defeating Notts by four wickets. Tim Robinson's 220* in Notts' first innings total of 482 for 6 was a career best but Ashley Metcalfe took the batting honours to set the seal on a run-drenched season: he hit 100s in both innings, becoming the 10th man to reach the 2,000 mark, and his second innings 107 was the 428th first-class 100 of the summer, beating the record of 414 posted in 1928

● First-class debuts: J.J.B.Lewis (Essex); C.Hawkes (Leicestershire)

STATISTICAL SUMMARY

INDIVIDUAL DOUBLE CENTURIES

366	N.H.Fairbrother	Lancashire v Surrey	The Oval
333	G.A.Gooch	England v India (1st Test)	Lord's
313*	S.J.Cook	Somerset v Glamorgan	Taunton
291	I.A.Greig	Surrey v Lancashire	The Oval
263	D.M.Ward	Surrey v Kent	Canterbury
256	M.W.Alleyne	Gloucs v Northants	N'hampton
255*	D.L.Haynes	Middlesex v Sussex	Lord's
252*	G.A.Hick	Worcs v Glamorgan	Aberg'enny
245	P.J.Prichard	Essex v Leicestershire	Chelmsford
235	A.J.Lamb	Northants v Yorkshire	Headingley
234	S.G.Hinks	Kent v Middlesex	Canterbury
227*	B.C.Broad	Notts v Kent	Tdge Wells
224*	A.J.Moles	Warwicks v Glamorgan	Swansea
221*	P.A.De Silva	Sri Lankans v Hampshire	Southampton
220*	D.L.Haynes	Middlesex v Essex	Ilford
220*	R.T.Robinson	Notts v Yorkshire	Trent Bridge
219	C.J.Tavare	Somerset v Sussex	Hove
218*	M.D.Moxon	Yorkshire v Sussex	Eastbourne
215	G.A.Gooch	Essex v Leicestershire	Chelmsford
210	P.D.Bowler	Derbyshire v Kent	Chesterfield
208	D.M.Ward	Surrey v Essex	The Oval
207*	M.E.Waugh	Essex v Yorkshire	Middlesboro'
207	W.Larkins	Northants v Essex	N'hampton
206*	A.Fordham	Northants v Yorkshire	Headingley
204*	R.J.Bailey	Northants v Sussex	N'hampton
204	N.R.Taylor	Kent v Surrey	Canterbury
204	M.E.Waugh	Essex v Gloucestershire	Ilford
203*	N.H.Fairbrother	Lancashire v Warwickshire	Coventry
202*	D.A.Reeve	Warwicks v Northants	N'hampton
202*	J.P.Stephenson	Essex v Somerset	Bath
201*	P.M.Roebuck	Somerset v Worcestershire	Worcester
200*	K.R.Brown	Middlesex v Notts	Lord's

HUNDREDS IN BOTH INNINGS OF THE SAME MATCH

C.W.J.Athey	108* & 122	Gloucs v Worcs	Bristol
G.A.Gooch	333 & 123	England v India	Lord's
G.A.Gooch	174 & 126	Essex v Northants	N'hampton
M.J.Greatbatch	168* & 128*	World XI v Indians	Scarboro'
D.L.Haynes	181 & 129	Middlesex v N.Z.	Lord's
G.A.Hick	252* & 108*	Worcs v Glamorgan	Aberg'enny
A.A.Metcalfe	194* & 107	Yorkshire v Notts	Trent Bridge
H.Morris	122 & 109	Glamorgan v Notts	Worksop
J.E.Morris	122 & 109	Derbyshire v Somerset	Taunton
M.R.Ramprakash	100* & 125	Middlesex v Kent	Canterbury
I.V.A.Richards	111 & 118*	Glamorgan v Essex	Southend
N.R.Taylor	204 & 142	Kent v Surrey	Canterbury

THREE HUNDREDS IN SUCCESSIVE INNINGS

K.J.Barnett	107	Derbyshire v Gloucs	Derby
	123	Derbyshire v Sussex	Hove
	109	Derbyshire v Lancs	Liverpool
G.A.Gooch	177	Essex v Lancashire	Colchester
	333 & 123	England v India	Lord's
M.R.Ramprakash	146*	Middlesex v Somerset	Uxbridge
	100* & 125	Middlesex v Kent	Canterbury
I.V.A.Richards	111 & 118*	Glamorgan v Essex	Southend
	127	Glamorgan v Notts	Worksop

MOST RUNS WITHOUT BEING DISMISSED

645	G.A.Hick
473	P.M.Roebuck
440	N.H.Fairbrother
431	A.J.Moles

HIGHEST PARTNERSHIPS

413	3rd	D.J.Bicknell & D.M.Ward	Surrey v Kent	Canterbury
403	2nd	G.A.Gooch & P.J.Prichard	Essex v Leics	Chelmsford
393	3rd	A.Fordham & A.J.Lamb	N'hants v Yorks	Headingley
366	4th	S.G.Hinks & N.R.Taylor	Kent v Middx	Canterbury
364	3rd	M.Atherton & N.Fairbrother	Lancs v Surrey	The Oval
321	1st	D.J.Bicknell & G.S.Clinton	Surrey v N'hants	The Oval
309	3rd	G.A.Gooch & A.J.Lamb	England v India	Lord's
306	1st	D.L.Haynes & M.Roseberry	Middx v Essex	Ilford

BEST INNINGS BOWLING FIGURES

9-113	G.D.Harrison	Ireland v Scotland	Edinburgh
8-58	C.A.Walsh	Gloucestershire v Northants	Cheltenham
7-47	M.D.Marshall	Hampshire v Derbyshire	Portsmouth
7-61	N.F.Williams	Middlesex v Kent	Lord's
7-73	Waqar Younis	Surrey v Warwickshire	The Oval
7-75	J.G.Thomas	Northants v Glamorgan	N'hampton
7-89	C.E.L.Ambrose	Northants v Leicestershire	Leicester
7-92	K.T.Medlycott	Surrey v Notts	Trent Bridge
7-120	J.G.Bracewell	New Zealand v Comb Univ	Fenner's
7-128	R.A.Pick	Notts v Leicestershire	Leicester

BEST MATCH BOWLING FIGURES

12-155	C.E.L.Ambrose	Northants v Leicestershire	Leicester
12-227	J.G.Bracewell	New Zealand v Comb Univ	Fenner's
11-76	N.A.Foster	Essex v Surrey	Chelmsford
11-99	C.A.Walsh	Gloucestershire v Northants	Cheltenham
11-128	Waqar Younis	Surrey v Warwickshire	The Oval
11-142	M.D.Marshall	Hampshire v Glamorgan	Pontypridd
10-82	M.Frost	Glamorgan v Gloucs	Bristol
10-104	D.A.Graveney	Gloucestershire v Sussex	Bristol
10-107	M.D.Marshall	Hampshire v Derbyshire	Portsmouth
10-119	C.C.Lewis	Leicestershire v Glamorgan	Cardiff
10-142	R.P.Davis	Kent v Leicestershire	Dartford
10-148	M.M.Patel	Kent v Leicestershire	Dartford
10-191	R.A.Pick	Notts v Leicestershire	Leicester

HAT-TRICKS

D.V.Lawrence	Gloucestershire v Notts	Trent Bridge
S.M.McEwan	Worcestershire v Leics	Leicester
P.A.Smith	Warwickshire v Sussex	Eastbourne

HIGHEST TOTALS

863	Lancashire v Surrey	The Oval
760-6 dec	Essex v Leicestershire	Chelmsford
707-9 dec	Surrey v Lancashire	The Oval
653-4 dec	England v India (1st Test)	Lord's
648	Surrey v Kent	Canterbury
636-6 dec	Northants v Essex	Chelmsford
613-6 dec	Surrey v Essex	The Oval
606-9 dec	India v England (3rd Test)	The Oval
600-8 dec	Hampshire v Sussex	S'hampton
592-6 dec	Northants v Essex	N'hampton
558-6 dec	Lancashire v Oxford U	The Parks
551-8 dec	Gloucestershire v Worcs	Bristol
539	Essex v Surrey	The Oval
535-2 dec	Somerset v Glamorgan	Cardiff
525-9 dec	Somerset v Sussex	Hove
521	Gloucs v Northants	N'hampton
520-9 dec	Worcestershire v Somerset	Taunton
520	Leicestershire v Essex	Chelmsford
519	England v India (2nd Test)	Old Trafford
517	Surrey v Hampshire	S'hampton
514-4 dec	Worcestershire v Glamorgan	Aberg'enny
514-5 dec	Derbyshire v Kent	Chesterfield
512-6 dec	Indians v Minor Counties	Trowbridge
510-5 dec	Middlesex v Notts	Lord's
508	Essex v Kent	Chelmsford
506-7 dec	Sri Lankans v Hampshire	S'hampton
500-5 dec	Somerset v Sussex	Taunton

LOWEST TOTALS

50	Northants v Derbyshire	N'hampton
72	Derbyshire v Gloucestershire	Derby
96	Warwickshire v Worcs	Worcester
99	Middlesex v Derbyshire	Derby

HIGHEST MATCH AGGREGATES

1650	Surrey v Lancashire	The Oval
1641	Glamorgan v Worcestershire	Aberg'enny
1614	England v India (2nd Test)	Old Trafford
1603	England v India (1st Test)	Lord's

THE
AVERAGES

CORNHILL TEST MATCHES

ENGLAND v NEW ZEALAND

ENGLAND

BATTING AVERAGES - Including fielding

Name	Matches	Inns	NO	Runs	HS	Avge	100s	50s	Ct	St
M.A.Atherton	3	5	0	357	151	71.40	1	3	3	-
G.A.Gooch	3	5	0	306	154	61.20	1	1	3	-
G.C.Small	3	4	2	84	44*	42.00	-	-	1	-
A.J.Lamb	3	5	1	129	84*	32.25	-	1	2	-
R.A.Smith	3	5	0	152	64	30.40	-	2	2	-
A.J.Stewart	3	5	0	147	54	29.40	-	1	5	-
P.A.J.DeFreitas	2	2	0	52	38	26.00	-	-	-	-
R.C.Russell	3	4	0	84	43	21.00	-	-	7	-
C.C.Lewis	1	2	0	33	32	16.50	-	-	-	-
N.H.Fairbrother	3	5	1	59	33*	14.75	-	-	1	-
E.E.Hemmings	3	4	1	33	20	11.00	-	-	-	-
D.E.Malcolm	3	4	2	4	4*	2.00	-	-	-	-

BOWLING AVERAGES

Name	Overs	Mdns	Runs	Wkts	Avge	Best	5wI	10wM
D.E.Malcolm	118.4	38	269	15	17.93	5-46	2	-
E.E.Hemmings	107.3	44	215	10	21.50	6-58	1	-
P.A.J.DeFreitas	59.4	9	175	6	29.16	5-53	1	-
C.C.Lewis	41	8	127	4	31.75	3-76	-	-
G.C.Small	104	27	290	5	58.00	2-49	-	-
M.A.Atherton	10	6	17	0	-	-	-	-
G.A.Gooch	13	7	25	0	-	-	-	-

NEW ZEALAND

BATTING AVERAGES - Including fielding

Name	Matches	Inns	NO	Runs	HS	Avge	100s	50s	Ct	St
T.J.Franklin	3	5	1	227	101	56.75	1	1	2	-
J.G.Wright	3	5	0	177	98	35.40	-	1	-	-
A.C.Parore	1	2	1	32	20	32.00	-	-	4	1
I.D.S.Smith	2	2	1	29	27	29.00	-	-	2	-
M.J.Greatbatch	3	4	0	115	47	28.75	-	-	-	-
A.H.Jones	3	5	0	143	49	28.60	-	-	1	-
R.J.Hadlee	3	4	0	107	86	26.75	-	1	2	-
M.W.Priest	1	1	0	26	26	26.00	-	-	-	-
M.D.Crowe	3	4	0	96	59	24.00	-	1	1	-
M.C.Snedden	3	4	2	36	21*	18.00	-	-	2	-
K.R.Rutherford	2	3	0	47	29	15.66	-	-	2	-
J.G.Bracewell	3	4	0	57	28	14.25	-	-	3	-
D.K.Morrison	3	5	2	9	6	3.00	-	-	1	-

BOWLING AVERAGES

Name	Overs	Mdns	Runs	Wkts	Avge	Best	5wI	10wM
R.J.Hadlee	133.5	24	384	16	24.00	5-53	1	-
M.W.Priest	12	4	26	1	26.00	1-26	-	-
J.G.Bracewell	148	41	400	12	33.33	4-38	-	-
A.H.Jones	13	3	42	1	42.00	1-40	-	-
M.C.Snedden	101	30	264	6	44.00	3-106	-	-
D.K.Morrison	85.4	15	351	7	50.14	4-64	-	-
K.R.Rutherford	3	0	18	0	-	-	-	-

ENGLAND v INDIA

ENGLAND

BATTING AVERAGES - Including fielding

Name	Matches	Inns	NO	Runs	HS	Avge	100s	50s	Ct	St
R.A.Smith	3	6	4	361	121*	180.50	2	2	1	-
G.A.Gooch	3	6	0	752	333	125.33	3	2	4	-
D.I.Gower	3	6	2	291	157*	72.75	1	-	-	-
M.A.Atherton	3	6	0	378	131	63.00	1	3	3	-
A.J.Lamb	3	6	0	364	139	60.66	2	1	2	-
N.F.Williams	1	1	0	38	38	38.00	-	-	-	-
E.E.Hemmings	3	2	0	70	51	35.00	-	1	-	-
R.C.Russell	3	3	1	59	35	29.50	-	-	11	1
D.E.Malcolm	3	2	1	28	15*	28.00	-	-	-	-
J.E.Morris	3	5	2	71	32	23.66	-	-	3	-
C.C.Lewis	2	1	0	3	3	3.00	-	-	4	-
A.R.C.Fraser	3	2	0	1	1	0.50	-	-	-	-

BOWLING AVERAGES

Name	Overs	Mdns	Runs	Wkts	Avge	Best	5wI	10wM
A.R.C.Fraser	159.1	41	460	16	28.75	5-104	2	-
E.E.Hemmings	137.2	26	454	11	41.27	3-75	-	-
C.C.Lewis	65	8	281	5	56.20	2-26	-	-
D.E.Malcolm	110	16	436	7	62.28	2-65	-	-
G.A.Gooch	18	4	70	1	70.00	1-26	-	-
N.F.Williams	41	5	148	2	74.00	2-148	-	-
M.A.Atherton	28	3	161	1	161.00	1-60	-	-

INDIA

BATTING AVERAGES - Including fielding

Name	Matches	Inns	NO	Runs	HS	Avge	100s	50s	Ct	St
M.Azharuddin	3	5	0	426	179	85.20	2	1	1	-
R.J.Shastri	3	5	0	336	187	67.20	2	-	2	-
S.R.Tendulkar	3	5	1	245	119*	61.25	1	1	3	-
Kapil Dev	3	5	1	220	110	55.00	1	1	-	-
S.V.Manjrekar	3	5	0	216	93	43.20	-	2	4	-
M.Prabhakar	3	5	1	132	67*	33.00	-	1	-	-
D.B.Vengsarkar	3	5	0	158	52	31.60	-	1	3	-
K.S.More	3	4	1	91	61*	30.33	-	1	8	-
S.K.Sharma	1	2	0	38	38	19.00	-	-	-	-
N.D.Hirwani	3	4	3	17	15*	17.00	-	-	-	-
A.Wasson	1	1	0	15	15	15.00	-	-	-	-
N.S.Sidhu	3	5	0	56	30	11.20	-	-	-	-
A.R.Kumble	1	1	0	2	2	2.00	-	-	-	-

BOWLING AVERAGES

Name	Overs	Mdns	Runs	Wkts	Avge	Best	5wI	10wM
A.R.Kumble	60	10	170	3	56.66	3-105	-	-
A.Wasson	37	5	173	3	57.66	2-79	-	-
Kapil Dev	128	23	445	7	63.57	2-66	-	-
N.D.Hirwani	212	41	586	9	65.11	4-174	-	-
S.K.Sharma	48	5	197	3	65.66	2-75	-	-
M.Prabhakar	155	28	554	8	69.25	4-74	-	-
R.J.Shastri	95.5	6	341	2	170.50	1-29	-	-

TEXACO TROPHY

ENGLAND v NEW ZEALAND

ENGLAND

BATTING AVERAGES - Including fielding

Name	Matches	Inns	NO	Runs	HS	Avge	100s	50s	Ct	St
G.A.Gooch	2	2	1	167	112 *	167.00	1	1	-	-
R.A.Smith	2	2	0	133	128	66.50	1	-	2	-
R.C.Russell	2	2	1	60	47 *	60.00	-	-	2	1
A.J.Stewart	2	2	0	61	33	30.50	-	-	1	-
A.J.Lamb	2	2	0	22	18	11.00	-	-	1	-
D.I.Gower	2	2	0	5	4	2.50	-	-	1	-
D.R.Pringle	1	1	1	30	30 *		-	-	-	-
P.A.J.DeFreitas	2	1	1	1	1 *		-	-	-	-
E.E.Hemmings	2	0	0	0	0		-	-	-	-
C.C.Lewis	2	0	0	0	0		-	-	-	-
D.E.Malcolm	1	0	0	0	0		-	-	-	-
G.C.Small	2	0	0	0	0		-	-	1	-

BOWLING AVERAGES

Name	Overs	Mdns	Runs	Wkts	Avge	Best	5wI
D.E.Malcolm	11	5	19	2	9.50	2-19	-
G.A.Gooch	4	0	23	2	11.50	2-23	-
C.C.Lewis	22	1	105	4	26.25	3-54	-
G.C.Small	22	1	102	2	51.00	1-43	-
P.A.J.DeFreitas	21.5	1	117	1	117.00	1-47	-
D.R.Pringle	7	0	45	0	-	-	-
E.E.Hemmings	22	2	85	0	-	-	-

NEW ZEALAND

BATTING AVERAGES - Including fielding

Name	Matches	Inns	NO	Runs	HS	Avge	100s	50s	Ct	St
M.J.Greatbatch	2	2	1	213	111	213.00	2	-	-	-
J.G.Wright	2	2	0	67	52	33.50	-	1	-	-
A.H.Jones	2	2	0	66	51	33.00	-	1	-	-
M.D.Crowe	2	2	0	53	46	26.50	-	-	2	-
R.J.Hadlee	2	2	1	21	12	21.00	-	-	-	-
M.W.Priest	2	2	0	26	24	13.00	-	-	-	-
C.Pringle	2	1	0	1	1	1.00	-	-	-	-
K.R.Rutherford	2	2	1	0	0 *	0.00	-	-	-	-
I.D.S.Smith	2	2	2	42	25 *		-	-	2	-
J.P.Millmow	2	0	0	0	0		-	-	1	-
D.K.Morrison	2	0	0	0	0		-	-	1	-

BOWLING AVERAGES

Name	Overs	Mdns	Runs	Wkts	Avge	Best	5wI
R.J.Hadlee	22	6	80	4	20.00	2-34	-
C.Pringle	20.3	2	98	3	32.66	2-45	-
M.W.Priest	22	2	93	1	93.00	1-34	-
D.K.Morrison	20	0	108	1	108.00	1-70	-
J.P.Millmow	20	1	112	0	-	-	-

ENGLAND v INDIA

ENGLAND

BATTING AVERAGES - Including fielding

Name	Matches	Inns	NO	Runs	HS	Avge	100s	50s	Ct	St
R.A.Smith	2	2	0	109	103	54.50	1	-	-	-
D.I.Gower	2	2	0	75	50	37.50	-	1	1	-
M.A.Atherton	2	2	0	66	59	33.00	-	1	2	-
R.C.Russell	2	2	0	64	50	32.00	-	1	-	1
A.J.Lamb	2	2	0	59	56	29.50	-	1	-	-
G.A.Gooch	2	2	0	52	45	26.00	-	-	-	-
C.C.Lewis	2	2	0	13	7	6.50	-	-	-	-
P.A.J.DeFreitas	2	2	0	12	11	6.00	-	-	-	-
D.E.Malcolm	1	1	0	4	4	4.00	-	-	-	-
G.C.Small	1	1	0	4	4	4.00	-	-	-	-
E.E.Hemmings	2	2	0	3	3	1.50	-	-	-	-
A.R.C.Fraser	2	2	2	4	4 *		-	-	-	-

BOWLING AVERAGES

Name	Overs	Mdns	Runs	Wkts	Avge	Best	5wI
C.C.Lewis	20	0	112	3	37.33	2-58	-
E.E.Hemmings	22	1	89	2	44.50	2-53	-
D.E.Malcolm	11	0	57	1	57.00	1-57	-
G.C.Small	10	0	73	1	73.00	1-73	-
A.R.C.Fraser	22	4	75	1	75.00	1-38	-
P.A.J.DeFreitas	21	1	99	1	99.00	1-40	-

INDIA

BATTING AVERAGES - Including fielding

Name	Matches	Inns	NO	Runs	HS	Avge	100s	50s	Ct	St
S.V.Manjrekar	2	2	0	141	82	70.50	-	2	1	-
R.J.Shastri	2	2	1	56	33	56.00	-	-	1	-
D.B.Vengsarkar	1	1	0	54	54	54.00	-	1	1	-
N.S.Sidhu	2	2	0	62	39	31.00	-	-	-	-
S.R.Tendulkar	2	2	0	50	31	25.00	-	-	-	-
W.V.Raman	1	1	0	0	0	0.00	-	-	-	-
M.Azharuddin	2	2	2	118	63 *		-	-	2	-
Kapil Dev	2	1	1	5	5 *		-	-	1	-
K.S.More	2	0	0	0	0		-	-	2	-
M.Prabhakar	2	0	0	0	0		-	-	1	-
S.K.Sharma	2	0	0	0	0		-	-	-	-
A.R.Kumble	2	0	0	0	0		-	-	-	-

BOWLING AVERAGES

Name	Overs	Mdns	Runs	Wkts	Avge	Best	5wI
M.Prabhakar	21.3	1	98	6	16.33	3-40	-
Kapil Dev	22	3	89	4	22.25	2-40	-
S.K.Sharma	21	1	107	3	35.66	2-57	-
A.R.Kumble	22	3	87	2	43.50	2-29	-
R.J.Shastri	22	0	92	2	46.00	1-40	-
S.R.Tendulkar	1	0	10	0	-	-	-

CORNHILL TEST MATCHES / TEXACO TROPHY

ENGLAND:
ALL TEST MATCHES

BATTING AVERAGES - Including fielding

Name	Matches	Inns	NO	Runs	HS	Avge	100s	50s	Ct	St
G.A.Gooch	6	11	0	1058	333	96.18	4	3	7	-
R.A.Smith	6	11	4	513	121 *	73.28	2	4	3	-
D.I.Gower	3	6	2	291	157 *	72.75	1	-	-	-
M.A.Atherton	6	11	0	735	151	66.81	2	6	6	-
A.J.Lamb	6	11	1	493	139	49.30	2	2	4	-
G.C.Small	3	4	2	84	44 *	42.00	-	-	1	-
N.F.Williams	1	1	0	38	38	38.00	-	-	-	-
A.J.Stewart	3	5	0	147	54	29.40	-	1	5	-
P.A.J.DeFreitas	2	2	0	52	38	26.00	-	-	-	-
R.C.Russell	6	7	1	143	43	23.83	-	-	18	1
J.E.Morris	3	5	2	71	32	23.66	-	-	3	-
E.E.Hemmings	6	6	1	103	51	20.60	-	1	-	-
N.H.Fairbrother	3	5	1	59	33 *	14.75	-	-	1	-
C.C.Lewis	3	3	0	36	32	12.00	-	-	4	-
D.E.Malcolm	6	6	3	32	15 *	10.66	-	-	-	-
A.R.C.Fraser	3	2	0	1	1	0.50	-	-	-	-

BOWLING AVERAGES

Name	Overs	Mdns	Runs	Wkts	Avge	Best	5wI	10wM
A.R.C.Fraser	159.1	41	460	16	28.75	5-104	2	-
P.A.J.DeFreitas	59.4	9	175	6	29.16	5-53	1	-
E.E.Hemmings	244.5	70	669	21	31.85	6-58	1	-
D.E.Malcolm	228.4	54	705	22	32.04	5-46	2	-
C.C.Lewis	106	16	408	9	45.33	3-76	-	-
G.C.Small	104	27	290	5	58.00	2-49	-	-
N.F.Williams	41	5	148	2	74.00	2-148	-	-
G.A.Gooch	31	11	95	1	95.00	1-26	-	-
M.A.Atherton	38	9	178	1	178.00	1-60	-	-

ENGLAND:
ALL ONE-DAY INTERNATIONALS

BATTING AVERAGES - Including fielding

Name	Matches	Inns	NO	Runs	HS	Avge	100s	50s	Ct	St
G.A.Gooch	4	4	1	219	112 *	73.00	1	1	-	-
R.A.Smith	4	4	0	242	128	60.50	2	-	2	-
R.C.Russell	4	4	1	124	50	41.33	-	1	2	2
M.A.Atherton	2	2	0	66	59	33.00	-	1	2	-
A.J.Stewart	2	2	0	61	33	30.50	-	-	1	-
A.J.Lamb	4	4	0	81	56	20.25	-	1	1	-
D.I.Gower	4	4	0	80	50	20.00	-	1	2	-
P.A.J.DeFreitas	4	3	0	13	11	6.50	-	-	-	-
C.C.Lewis	4	2	0	13	7	6.50	-	-	-	-
D.E.Malcolm	2	1	0	4	4	4.00	-	-	-	-
G.C.Small	3	1	0	4	4	4.00	-	-	1	-
E.E.Hemmings	4	2	0	3	3	1.50	-	-	-	-
D.R.Pringle	1	1	1	30	30 *		-	-	-	-
A.R.C.Fraser	2	2	2	4	4 *		-	-	-	-

BOWLING AVERAGES

Name	Overs	Mdns	Runs	Wkts	Avge	Best	5wI
G.A.Gooch	4	0	23	2	11.50	2-23	-
D.E.Malcolm	22	5	76	3	25.33	2-19	-
C.C.Lewis	42	1	217	7	31.00	3-54	-
G.C.Small	32	1	175	3	58.33	1-43	-
A.R.C.Fraser	22	4	75	1	75.00	1-38	-
E.E.Hemmings	44	3	174	2	87.00	2-53	-
P.A.J.DeFreitas	42.5	2	216	2	108.00	1-40	-
D.R.Pringle	7	0	45	0	-	-	-

TOURISTS – ALL FIRST-CLASS MATCHES

NEW ZEALAND

BATTING AVERAGES - Including fielding

Name	Matches	Inns	NO	Runs	HS	Avge	100s	50s	Ct	St
M.D.Crowe	9	13	3	537	123 *	53.70	1	5	5	-
A.H.Jones	10	16	3	692	121 *	53.23	1	5	3	-
J.G.Wright	9	15	2	653	121	50.23	1	5	2	-
K.R.Rutherford	8	13	5	376	68 *	47.00	-	1	7	-
T.J.Franklin	11	17	1	731	103	45.68	2	5	3	-
J.J.Crowe	8	15	4	493	132	44.81	1	2	6	-
M.W.Priest	9	11	3	345	72	43.12	-	3	6	-
M.J.Greatbatch	10	14	1	448	85	34.46	-	4	5	-
R.J.Hadlee	5	6	0	204	90	34.00	-	2	4	-
J.G.Bracewell	8	8	3	169	40 *	33.80	-	-	5	-
S.A.Thomson	5	5	4	32	20	32.00	-	-	5	-
A.C.Parore	7	6	1	131	43	26.20	-	-	14	1
I.D.S.Smith	6	4	1	65	34	21.66	-	-	5	-
M.C.Snedden	7	6	3	38	21 *	12.66	-	-	3	-
C.Pringle	4	1	0	6	6	6.00	-	-	2	-
D.K.Morrison	9	6	2	14	6	3.50	-	-	3	-
W.Watson	2	1	1	17	17 *	-	-	-	-	-
J.P.Millmow	5	1	1	2	2 *	-	-	-	2	-

BOWLING AVERAGES

Name	Overs	Mdns	Runs	Wkts	Avge	Best	5wI	10wM
R.J.Hadlee	201.5	39	586	24	24.41	5-27	2	-
M.C.Snedden	231.5	56	633	23	27.52	5-63	1	-
A.H.Jones	26	4	87	3	29.00	1-1	-	-
J.G.Bracewell	383.3	102	1120	34	32.94	7-120	2	1
J.P.Millmow	105	14	391	11	35.54	3-66	-	-
D.K.Morrison	234.4	36	889	21	42.33	4-64	-	-
C.Pringle	125	31	398	8	49.75	2-67	-	-
W.Watson	54	10	177	3	59.00	2-67	-	-
M.W.Priest	312.4	90	907	14	64.78	3-35	-	-
S.A.Thomson	106.2	18	435	5	87.00	2-84	-	-
M.D.Crowe	8	3	20	0	-	-	-	-
K.R.Rutherford	42	3	196	0	-	-	-	-

INDIA

BATTING AVERAGES - Including fielding

Name	Matches	Inns	NO	Runs	HS	Avge	100s	50s	Ct	St
M.Azharuddin	9	11	1	770	179	77.00	3	3	3	-
R.J.Shastri	9	11	1	644	187	64.40	4	1	6	-
S.R.Tendulkar	11	19	4	945	119 *	63.00	2	6	5	-
S.V.Manjrekar	11	17	3	814	158 *	58.14	2	6	6	-
D.B.Vengsarkar	10	14	4	576	83 *	57.60	-	6	4	-
W.V.Raman	8	15	2	623	127	47.92	1	7	6	-
N.S.Sidhu	9	17	3	639	142	45.64	2	4	1	-
N.R.Mongia	8	11	4	269	63 *	38.42	-	2	9	3
Kapil Dev	9	12	2	377	110	37.70	1	2	3	-
S.K.Sharma	9	7	3	132	38	33.00	-	-	2	-
K.S.More	9	11	2	295	95	32.77	-	2	17	1
M.Prabhakar	10	14	3	296	76	26.90	-	2	4	-
Venkatapathy Raju	6	6	2	105	40 *	26.25	-	-	-	-
A.Wasson	9	3	1	47	24	23.50	-	-	-	-
A.R.Kumble	7	5	2	63	35 *	21.00	-	-	1	-
N.D.Hirwani	9	5	3	17	15 *	8.50	-	-	3	-

BOWLING AVERAGES

Name	Overs	Mdns	Runs	Wkts	Avge	Best	5wI	10wM
N.D.Hirwani	399.2	59	1280	31	41.29	5-117	1	-
A.R.Kumble	212	40	660	14	47.14	6-49	1	-
A.Wasson	207.3	24	886	18	49.22	6-89	1	-
Kapil Dev	246.4	59	744	13	57.23	2-28	-	-
Venkatapathy Raju	182.3	41	528	9	58.66	4-73	-	-
M.Prabhakar	281	47	994	16	62.12	4-74	-	-
S.K.Sharma	227	36	873	13	67.15	2-53	-	-
W.V.Raman	15	2	72	1	72.00	1-44	-	-
R.J.Shastri	199.2	30	607	7	86.71	2-80	-	-
S.R.Tendulkar	79	12	268	3	89.33	3-79	-	-
K.S.More	8	0	54	0	-	-	-	-

ZIMBABWE

BATTING AVERAGES - Including fielding

Name	Matches	Inns	NO	Runs	HS	Avge	100s	50s	Ct	St
A.H.Shah	3	3	0	215	185	71.66	1	-	-	-
J.P.Brent	2	4	2	101	34 *	50.50	-	-	-	-
G.A.Briant	2	3	0	109	69	36.33	-	1	1	-
C.M.Robertson	3	6	1	168	125	33.60	1	-	1	-
G.W.Flower	2	4	1	97	65	32.33	-	1	4	-
A.J.Pycroft	3	5	1	120	55	30.00	-	1	2	-
I.P.Butchart	3	5	1	115	71	28.75	-	1	-	-
W.R.James	3	6	1	143	52	28.60	-	1	4	-
D.F.Dolphin	2	1	0	25	25	25.00	-	-	-	-
E.A.Brandes	2	3	1	40	22	20.00	-	-	1	-
K.J.Arnott	1	2	0	2	2	1.00	-	-	-	-
A.J.Traicos	2	1	0	1	1	1.00	-	-	5	-
E.Dube	2	1	0	1	1	1.00	-	-	-	-
K.G.Duers	2	1	1	11	11 *	-	-	-	-	-
M.P.Jarvis	1	1	1	1	1 *	-	-	-	-	-

BOWLING AVERAGES

Name	Overs	Mdns	Runs	Wkts	Avge	Best	5wI	10wM
E.A.Brandes	49.2	12	165	7	23.57	4-35	-	-
G.W.Flower	29.5	4	101	3	33.66	2-33	-	-
A.H.Shah	75	17	193	5	38.60	2-46	-	-
J.P.Brent	26	6	79	2	39.50	2-28	-	-
A.J.Traicos	84	22	186	4	46.50	3-43	-	-
M.P.Jarvis	30	7	101	2	50.50	2-61	-	-
K.G.Duers	74	17	266	5	53.20	2-63	-	-
I.P.Butchart	41	7	156	2	78.00	1-39	-	-
D.F.Dolphin	39	10	134	1	134.00	1-29	-	-
E.Dube	25	4	107	0	-	-	-	-

SRI LANKA

BATTING AVERAGES - Including fielding

Name	Matches	Inns	NO	Runs	HS	Avge	100s	50s	Ct	St
P.A.De Silva	6	12	4	563	221 *	70.37	1	3	10	-
M.Attapatu	6	8	4	241	74 *	60.25	-	2	7	-
H.P.Tillekaratne	5	9	2	349	109 *	49.85	2	-	7	2
R.S.Mahanama	6	10	0	494	114	49.40	2	2	10	-
S.T.Jayasuriya	6	9	2	345	105 *	49.28	1	2	5	-
A.P.Gurusinha	3	6	3	138	58	46.00	-	1	-	-
C.Hathurasinghe	5	10	0	385	136	38.50	1	1	1	-
D.S.B.P.Kuruppu	5	10	1	259	56 *	28.77	-	2	7	1
M.A.W.R.Madurasinghe	4	3	1	43	28 *	21.50	-	-	1	-
G.F.Labrooy	4	6	0	121	69	20.16	-	1	1	-
P.Wickremasinghe	3	2	0	17	17	8.50	-	-	-	-
K.I.W.Wijegunawardene	4	1	0	0	0	0.00	-	-	6	-
C.P.Ramanayake	4	4	4	25	9 *	-	-	-	-	-
P.Wijetunga	4	1	1	5	5 *	-	-	-	2	-
F.S.Ahangama	1	0	0	0	0	-	-	-	-	-

BOWLING AVERAGES

Name	Overs	Mdns	Runs	Wkts	Avge	Best	5wI	10wM
S.T.Jayasuriya	7	1	18	1	18.00	1-14	-	-
C.Hathurasinghe	21.1	8	58	3	19.33	2-3	-	-
A.P.Gurusinha	40	8	113	5	22.60	3-38	-	-
R.Madurasinghe	176.2	28	560	21	26.66	5-108	1	-
G.F.Labrooy	111	13	440	16	27.50	5-97	1	-
K.Wijegunawardene	87.3	13	318	9	35.33	2-30	-	-
P.Wijetunga	129.4	24	438	12	36.50	4-133	-	-
P.A.De Silva	25	3	81	2	40.50	2-25	-	-
P.Wickremasinghe	79	17	251	6	41.83	3-95	-	-
C.P.Ramanayake	133	12	510	12	42.50	3-96	-	-
F.S.Ahangama	1.3	0	4	0	-	-	-	-
M.Attapatu	4	0	21	0	-	-	-	-

BRITANNIC ASSURANCE CHAMPIONSHIP

DERBYSHIRE

BATTING AVERAGES - Including fielding

Name	Matches	Inns	NO	Runs	HS	Avge	100s	50s	Ct	St
J.E.Morris	16	26	4	1353	157*	61.50	6	6	8	-
K.J.Barnett	22	36	5	1572	141	50.71	5	8	14	-
P.D.Bowler	21	37	4	1408	210	42.66	3	7	15	-
T.J.G.O'Gorman	6	11	1	393	100	39.30	1	3	3	-
A.M.Brown	7	11	1	379	139*	37.90	1	1	6	-
B.Roberts	22	35	7	1038	124*	37.07	2	4	23	-
G.Miller	13	13	7	208	47*	34.66	-	-	4	-
I.R.Bishop	12	15	4	326	103*	29.63	1	-	2	-
C.J.Adams	21	32	3	800	101	27.58	1	5	22	-
S.J.Base	13	13	2	215	58	19.54	-	2	4	-
A.P.Kuiper	10	15	0	288	48	19.20	-	-	9	-
K.M.Krikken	21	28	2	426	77*	16.38	-	1	58	3
S.C.Goldsmith	11	16	1	216	34	14.40	-	-	7	-
M.Jean-Jacques	10	11	4	80	25	11.42	-	-	2	-
D.E.Malcolm	9	6	2	44	20*	11.00	-	-	-	-
O.H.Mortensen	11	11	9	20	5*	10.00	-	-	5	-
A.E.Warner	14	19	2	160	59	9.41	-	1	2	-
D.G.Cork	1	1	0	7	7	7.00	-	-	-	-
F.A.Griffith	1	1	0	1	1	1.00	-	-	-	-
Z.A.Sadiq	1	1	0	0	0	0.00	-	-	-	-

BOWLING AVERAGES

Name	Overs	Mdns	Runs	Wkts	Avge	Best	5wI	10wM
I.R.Bishop	395.3	89	1087	59	18.42	6-71	3	-
F.A.Griffith	11	2	20	1	20.00	1-20	-	-
O.H.Mortensen	301.2	88	764	32	23.87	4-22	-	-
D.E.Malcolm	277.4	44	947	30	31.56	4-63	-	-
C.J.Adams	8.1	0	36	1	36.00	1-5	-	-
A.P.Kuiper	108.3	25	325	9	36.11	4-69	-	-
K.J.Barnett	267.1	42	720	19	37.89	3-49	-	-
S.J.Base	414.3	68	1402	35	40.05	6-105	2	-
A.E.Warner	393.3	67	1330	33	40.30	3-56	-	-
G.Miller	427.2	94	1285	31	41.45	6-45	1	-
S.C.Goldsmith	112	19	347	7	49.57	2-105	-	-
M.Jean-Jacques	261.2	33	983	19	51.73	6-60	1	-
P.D.Bowler	8	0	56	1	56.00	1-48	-	-
J.E.Morris	20	0	123	1	123.00	1-17	-	-
B.Roberts	7	0	26	0	-	-	-	-
D.G.Cork	24	6	70	0	-	-	-	-

ESSEX

BATTING AVERAGES - Including fielding

Name	Matches	Inns	NO	Runs	HS	Avge	100s	50s	Ct	St
G.A.Gooch	11	18	2	1586	215	99.12	7	5	7	-
M.E.Waugh	21	32	6	2009	207*	77.26	8	7	18	-
B.R.Hardie	11	15	5	650	125	65.00	2	3	7	-
J.P.Stephenson	22	37	7	1525	202*	50.83	2	12	14	-
N.Shahid	18	27	7	964	125	48.20	1	6	22	-
P.J.Prichard	20	30	3	1276	245	47.25	4	4	8	-
N.Hussain	14	21	2	714	197	37.57	1	2	14	-
M.A.Garnham	22	26	7	589	84*	31.00	-	2	46	1
D.R.Pringle	15	13	2	318	84	28.90	-	1	7	-
N.A.Foster	22	22	2	530	101	26.50	1	2	13	-
P.M.Such	10	5	3	44	27	22.00	-	-	2	-
T.D.Topley	7	4	1	55	23	18.33	-	-	5	-
M.C.Ilott	8	10	2	123	42*	15.37	-	-	1	-
S.J.W.Andrew	16	15	7	119	35	14.87	-	-	1	-
A.C.Seymour	2	3	2	14	10*	14.00	-	-	-	-
J.H.Childs	21	16	5	123	26	11.18	-	-	7	-
A.W.Lilley	1	1	0	1	1	1.00	-	-	-	-
J.J.B.Lewis	1	1	1	116	116*	-	1	-	1	-

BOWLING AVERAGES

Name	Overs	Mdns	Runs	Wkts	Avge	Best	5wI	10wM
N.A.Foster	819.2	175	2502	94	26.61	6-32	6	1
D.R.Pringle	325.3	81	927	29	31.96	5-66	1	-
T.D.Topley	178	25	557	16	34.81	4-67	-	-
P.M.Such	252.3	58	682	18	37.88	3-34	-	-
M.C.Ilott	289.1	60	951	25	38.04	5-34	1	-
S.J.W.Andrew	449	67	1763	43	41.00	5-55	1	-
J.H.Childs	595.1	189	1435	25	57.40	4-56	-	-
N.Shahid	106.2	18	413	7	59.00	3-91	-	-
M.E.Waugh	183	33	731	12	60.91	5-37	1	-
J.P.Stephenson	96	22	383	3	127.66	1-16	-	-
A.W.Lilley	1	0	7	0	-	-	-	-
P.J.Prichard	1.4	0	11	0	-	-	-	-
B.R.Hardie	1	0	16	0	-	-	-	-
N.Hussain	4	1	29	0	-	-	-	-
G.A.Gooch	35	8	125	0	-	-	-	-

BRITANNIC ASSURANCE CHAMPIONSHIP

GLAMORGAN

BATTING AVERAGES - Including fielding

Name	Matches	Inns	NO	Runs	HS	Avge	100s	50s	Ct	St
I.V.A.Richards	18	28	5	1425	164 *	61.95	7	3	8	-
A.R.Butcher	21	39	5	2044	151 *	60.11	6	14	8	-
H.Morris	22	41	4	1914	160 *	51.73	8	9	12	-
M.P.Maynard	19	34	5	1306	125 *	45.03	2	10	13	-
R.D.B.Croft	14	23	10	570	91 *	43.84	-	3	2	-
N.G.Cowley	13	16	4	523	76	43.58	-	6	8	-
I.Smith	6	8	1	293	112 *	41.85	1	2	1	-
G.C.Holmes	7	10	3	260	125 *	37.14	1	-	1	-
P.A.Cottey	17	30	5	816	125	32.64	2	4	9	-
M.J.Cann	5	8	0	180	64	22.50	-	2	2	-
H.A.Anthony	2	3	0	52	39	17.33	-	-	-	-
A.Dale	7	11	0	179	92	16.27	-	1	6	-
C.P.Metson	22	26	4	302	34	13.72	-	-	58	-
M.L.Roberts	1	1	0	13	13	13.00	-	-	-	-
S.L.Watkin	22	22	7	170	25 *	11.33	-	-	5	-
S.Bastien	10	9	3	47	12	7.83	-	-	-	-
M.Frost	18	17	7	40	12	4.00	-	-	2	-
S.J.Dennis	12	8	1	23	6	3.28	-	-	3	-
S.P.James	3	6	0	10	7	1.66	-	-	2	-
S.R.Barwick	3	2	2	2	2 *	-	-	-	-	-

BOWLING AVERAGES

Name	Overs	Mdns	Runs	Wkts	Avge	Best	5wI	10wM
S.Bastien	274.5	47	1075	35	30.71	6-75	2	-
M.Frost	509.1	63	1919	56	34.26	5-40	2	1
S.L.Watkin	731.1	118	2489	61	40.80	5-100	1	-
H.A.Anthony	62	13	207	5	41.40	2-70	-	-
S.J.Dennis	283	53	957	20	47.85	5-76	1	-
R.D.B.Croft	357.1	76	1126	23	48.95	3-10	-	-
N.G.Cowley	296.3	58	851	11	77.36	3-84	-	-
S.R.Barwick	124.4	27	396	5	79.20	3-76	-	-
G.C.Holmes	21	3	85	1	85.00	1-44	-	-
I.V.A.Richards	137	26	426	5	85.20	2-27	-	-
P.A.Cottey	18	0	116	1	116.00	1-49	-	-
A.R.Butcher	25.3	2	153	1	153.00	1-16	-	-
I.Smith	33	3	157	1	157.00	1-43	-	-
M.J.Cann	35	3	162	1	162.00	1-39	-	-
H.Morris	6	0	62	0	-	-	-	-
M.P.Maynard	20	1	150	0	-	-	-	-
A.Dale	51	8	187	0	-	-	-	-

GLOUCESTERSHIRE

BATTING AVERAGES - Including fielding

Name	Matches	Inns	NO	Runs	HS	Avge	100s	50s	Ct	St
C.W.J.Athey	21	32	6	1384	131	53.23	3	8	18	-
K.M.Curran	22	32	8	1261	144 *	52.54	3	5	15	-
M.W.Alleyne	11	17	0	763	256	44.88	2	2	9	-
P.Bainbridge	18	25	2	1019	152	44.30	2	4	4	-
R.C.Russell	11	16	1	651	120	43.40	2	3	27	-
J.W.Lloyds	21	29	10	704	93	37.05	-	3	15	-
G.D.Hodgson	21	34	2	1059	109	33.09	1	9	10	-
P.W.Romaines	5	7	1	177	61	29.50	-	1	2	-
C.A.Walsh	19	19	3	464	63 *	29.00	-	3	6	-
I.P.Butcher	9	13	3	280	102	28.00	1	-	-	-
A.W.Stovold	2	4	0	104	74	26.00	-	1	-	-
A.J.Wright	22	36	3	809	112	24.51	1	4	21	-
R.C.J.Williams	7	7	3	82	44 *	20.50	-	-	22	4
G.A.Tedstone	4	3	0	42	23	14.00	-	-	3	-
D.A.Graveney	12	12	4	100	46 *	12.50	-	-	5	-
M.C.J.Ball	3	5	0	39	15	7.80	-	-	2	-
D.V.Lawrence	20	21	3	124	29	6.88	-	-	6	-
E.T.Milburn	1	2	1	3	3 *	3.00	-	-	-	-
S.N.Barnes	7	7	1	11	6	1.83	-	-	2	-
P.A.Owen	3	2	0	2	1	1.00	-	-	-	-
M.W.Bell	2	2	1	0	0 *	0.00	-	-	-	-
K.B.S.Jarvis	1	2	2	1	1 *	-	-	-	-	-

BOWLING AVERAGES

Name	Overs	Mdns	Runs	Wkts	Avge	Best	5wI	10wM
M.W.Alleyne	77	23	254	11	23.09	3-23	-	-
C.A.Walsh	583.1	98	1961	70	28.01	8-58	3	1
K.M.Curran	561.3	105	1839	60	30.65	5-63	1	-
D.V.Lawrence	418.3	45	1679	50	33.58	5-51	2	-
M.W.Bell	44	7	114	3	38.00	2-38	-	-
D.A.Graveney	462.4	126	1145	29	39.48	5-45	3	1
P.Bainbridge	137.4	24	426	9	47.33	3-23	-	-
S.N.Barnes	138	25	388	8	48.50	2-10	-	-
J.W.Lloyds	314.5	52	1175	24	48.95	4-11	-	-
C.W.J.Athey	36.5	9	104	2	52.00	2-13	-	-
P.A.Owen	57	7	239	4	59.75	2-37	-	-
K.B.S.Jarvis	12	1	61	1	61.00	1-61	-	-
G.A.Tedstone	2	1	1	0	-	-	-	-
A.J.Wright	0.5	0	7	0	-	-	-	-
E.T.Milburn	7	1	34	0	-	-	-	-
M.C.J.Ball	34	7	114	0	-	-	-	-

BRITANNIC ASSURANCE CHAMPIONSHIP

HAMPSHIRE

BATTING AVERAGES - Including fielding

Name	Matches	Inns	NO	Runs	HS	Avge	100s	50s	Ct	St
K.D.James	1	2	1	154	104*	154.00	1	1	-	-
L.A.Joseph	4	4	3	83	43*	83.00	-	-	1	-
T.M.Tremlett	8	5	3	143	78	71.50	-	1	1	-
R.A.Smith	11	18	4	897	181	64.07	4	3	7	-
A.N Aymes	4	7	3	255	75*	63.75	-	2	7	-
C.L.Smith	20	35	7	1678	132*	59.92	3	12	11	-
T.C.Middleton	16	28	3	1216	127	48.64	5	5	8	-
R.M.F.Cox	3	6	2	186	104*	46.50	1	-	1	-
M.D.Marshall	18	24	3	962	117	45.81	2	6	7	-
J.R.Ayling	7	9	2	288	62*	41.14	-	2	2	-
V.P.Terry	19	31	3	1084	165	38.71	3	4	21	-
D.I.Gower	14	21	1	684	145	34.20	1	2	14	-
R.J.Maru	22	18	2	513	59	32.06	-	3	25	-
M.C.J.Nicholas	20	30	8	670	78*	30.45	-	5	7	-
S.D.Udal	6	5	2	65	28*	21.66	-	-	2	-
R.J.Parks	18	19	9	203	36*	20.30	-	-	46	4
C.A.Connor	19	9	3	119	46	19.83	-	-	9	-
P.J.Bakker	14	9	4	95	20	19.00	-	-	3	-
R.J.Scott	6	10	2	144	71	18.00	-	1	4	-
J.R.Wood	2	2	0	28	17	14.00	-	-	1	-
I.J.Turner	4	2	1	1	1	1.00	-	-	2	-
K.J.Shine	6	0	0	0	0	-	-	-	1	-

BOWLING AVERAGES

Name	Overs	Mdns	Runs	Wkts	Avge	Best	5wI	10wM
M.D.Marshall	554.2	141	1381	72	19.18	7-47	4	2
C.L.Smith	22	8	76	3	25.33	3-35	-	-
R.J.Scott	36.4	5	165	5	33.00	2-5	-	-
P.J.Bakker	371.2	86	1195	33	36.21	5-101	1	-
C.A.Connor	462.1	77	1623	44	36.88	5-96	1	-
T.M.Tremlett	120.5	30	393	10	39.30	3-33	-	-
R.J.Maru	720.1	178	2087	53	39.37	6-97	1	-
K.J.Shine	129.4	17	501	12	41.75	4-52	-	-
J.R.Ayling	135.2	35	454	10	45.40	2-48	-	-
I.J.Turner	108.2	28	326	7	46.57	2-60	-	-
S.D.Udal	191.3	35	746	16	46.62	4-144	-	-
K.D.James	28	8	74	1	74.00	1-43	-	-
L.A.Joseph	82	12	406	5	81.20	2-128	-	-
M.C.J.Nicholas	54.2	7	209	2	104.50	1-7	-	-
R.A.Smith	0.3	0	5	0	-	-	-	-
T.C.Middleton	1	0	10	0	-	-	-	-
V.P.Terry	1	0	19	0	-	-	-	-

KENT

BATTING AVERAGES - Including fielding

Name	Matches	Inns	NO	Runs	HS	Avge	100s	50s	Ct	St
N.R.Taylor	20	35	4	1752	204	56.51	5	10	8	-
G.R.Cowdrey	20	36	5	1471	135	47.45	3	8	8	-
M.R.Benson	14	23	1	1029	159	46.77	5	3	5	-
M.V.Fleming	17	30	5	940	102	37.60	1	5	6	-
R.M.Ellison	13	18	6	444	81	37.00	-	3	5	-
S.G.Hinks	22	41	0	1484	234	36.19	4	5	8	-
C.S.Cowdrey	11	21	4	599	107*	35.23	2	2	9	-
S.A.Marsh	22	34	8	867	114*	33.34	1	5	46	4
T.R.Ward	15	28	1	863	175	31.96	2	5	14	-
V.J.Wells	8	15	0	352	58	23.46	-	2	8	-
P.S.De Villiers	12	15	3	264	37	22.00	-	-	6	-
R.P.Davis	22	32	3	504	59	17.37	-	2	24	-
C.Penn	6	6	2	66	23*	16.50	-	-	1	-
M.M.Patel	9	12	5	104	41*	14.85	-	-	2	-
A.P.Igglesden	13	17	9	105	24	13.12	-	-	5	-
M.A.Ealham	2	2	1	13	13*	13.00	-	-	-	-
D.J.M.Kelleher	5	8	0	101	44	12.62	-	-	2	-
T.A.Merrick	5	7	2	60	35	12.00	-	-	-	-
T.Wren	5	5	2	23	16	7.66	-	-	2	-
M.C.Dobson	1	2	0	6	6	3.00	-	-	-	-

BOWLING AVERAGES

Name	Overs	Mdns	Runs	Wkts	Avge	Best	5wI	10wM
S.A.Marsh	8.4	0	36	2	18.00	2-20	-	-
V.J.Wells	85	19	257	12	21.41	5-43	1	-
T.A.Merrick	146.2	31	376	13	28.92	4-66	-	-
S.G.Hinks	15	2	60	2	30.00	1-15	-	-
A.P.Igglesden	306	42	1093	30	36.43	4-79	-	-
P.S.De Villiers	304.5	58	992	25	39.68	6-70	1	-
M.A.Ealham	34.2	5	120	3	40.00	2-33	-	-
R.P.Davis	839.1	202	2648	65	40.73	6-59	4	1
M.M.Patel	297.5	72	836	20	41.80	6-57	2	1
C.S.Cowdrey	57	12	173	4	43.25	2-20	-	-
R.M.Ellison	260.5	45	869	19	45.73	4-76	-	-
M.R.Benson	8	2	46	1	46.00	1-14	-	-
M.V.Fleming	360.5	81	994	18	55.22	3-65	-	-
T.R.Ward	53	6	225	4	56.25	2-48	-	-
D.J.M.Kelleher	112.5	20	398	7	56.85	3-148	-	-
N.R.Taylor	21	5	57	1	57.00	1-19	-	-
C.Penn	158	33	535	9	59.44	3-45	-	-
T.Wren	122	14	489	6	81.50	2-78	-	-
M.C.Dobson	3.1	1	7	0	-	-	-	-
G.R.Cowdrey	3.3	0	32	0	-	-	-	-

BRITANNIC ASSURANCE CHAMPIONSHIP

LANCASHIRE

BATTING AVERAGES - Including fielding

Name	Matches	Inns	NO	Runs	HS	Avge	100s	50s	Ct	St
G.Yates	2	1	0	106	106	106.00	1	-	-	-
N.H.Fairbrother	17	24	6	1544	366	85.77	3	9	18	-
M.A.Atherton	12	18	4	1053	191	75.21	4	6	16	-
G.D.Mendis	21	35	6	1551	180	53.48	4	8	15	-
T.E.Jesty	17	24	6	785	98	43.61	-	7	6	-
W.K.Hegg	20	21	6	617	100*	41.13	1	2	47	2
P.A.J.DeFreitas	15	17	3	506	100*	36.14	1	2	5	-
M.Watkinson	18	22	2	706	138	35.30	1	4	8	-
I.D.Austin	11	12	5	238	58	34.00	-	1	-	-
G.Fowler	21	35	6	938	126	32.34	2	2	15	-
G.D.Lloyd	11	15	1	434	70	31.00	-	4	7	-
P.J.W.Allott	13	6	2	114	55*	28.50	-	1	9	-
D.P.Hughes	18	17	7	237	57	23.70	-	1	13	-
J.D.Fitton	14	11	5	114	25*	19.00	-	-	2	-
P.J.Martin	9	6	3	42	21	14.00	-	-	5	-
Wasim Akram	7	10	1	117	32	11.70	-	-	-	-
N.J.Speak	3	4	0	41	30	10.25	-	-	2	-
S.N.V.Waterton	1	1	0	3	3	3.00	-	-	4	-
B.P.Patterson	10	4	1	5	4*	1.66	-	-	2	-
J.P.Crawley	1	0	0	0	0	-	-	-	-	-
S.Bramhall	1	1	1	0	0*	-	-	-	1	1

BOWLING AVERAGES

Name	Overs	Mdns	Runs	Wkts	Avge	Best	5wI	10wM
M.A.Atherton	356.3	84	1111	42	26.45	6-78	3	-
T.E.Jesty	8	3	27	1	27.00	1-20	-	-
G.Fowler	4.1	2	33	1	33.00	1-33	-	-
M.Watkinson	503.2	120	1572	47	33.44	5-65	3	-
B.P.Patterson	281.4	45	1015	29	35.00	4-52	-	-
P.A.J.DeFreitas	408.5	96	1219	33	36.93	6-39	1	-
P.J.Martin	240.3	46	750	20	37.50	4-68	-	-
D.P.Hughes	280.4	61	918	24	38.25	4-25	-	-
G.Yates	51	12	117	3	39.00	2-69	-	-
Wasim Akram	191	43	594	15	39.60	3-76	-	-
P.J.W.Allott	266	77	730	18	40.55	4-23	-	-
I.D.Austin	208.1	64	536	10	53.60	3-42	-	-
J.D.Fitton	428.4	86	1365	14	97.50	3-69	-	-
G.D.Lloyd	2.1	0	22	0	-	-	-	-

LEICESTERSHIRE

BATTING AVERAGES - Including fielding

Name	Matches	Inns	NO	Runs	HS	Avge	100s	50s	Ct	St
N.E.Briers	22	43	3	1846	176	46.15	4	11	7	-
J.J.Whitaker	22	42	4	1575	116	41.44	3	7	12	-
C.C.Lewis	13	21	5	632	189*	39.50	1	2	11	-
T.J.Boon	22	43	4	1522	138	39.02	2	11	12	-
W.K.M.Benjamin	11	13	2	382	101*	34.72	1	3	3	-
L.Potter	22	36	5	1028	109*	33.16	1	7	22	-
P.N.Hepworth	4	8	2	185	55*	30.83	-	1	1	-
J.D.R.Benson	16	24	6	525	86	29.16	-	2	9	-
P.Willey	20	37	6	892	112	28.77	1	4	10	-
M.I.Gidley	4	5	1	113	73	28.25	-	1	2	-
P.A.Nixon	17	20	6	379	46	27.07	-	-	44	1
G.J.F.Ferris	5	6	0	104	35	17.33	-	-	-	-
J.P.Agnew	22	26	5	257	46*	12.23	-	-	5	-
G.J.Parsons	8	12	2	101	20	10.10	-	-	3	-
A.D.Mullally	18	18	6	113	29	9.41	-	-	3	-
P.Whitticase	5	7	2	39	11*	7.80	-	-	13	-
C.Hawkes	1	2	1	5	3	5.00	-	-	1	-
D.J.Millns	8	10	5	23	10*	4.60	-	-	3	-
B.Smith	1	1	1	15	15*	-	-	-	1	-
L.B.Taylor	1	0	0	0	0	-	-	-	-	-

BOWLING AVERAGES

Name	Overs	Mdns	Runs	Wkts	Avge	Best	5wI	10wM
D.J.Millns	164.1	20	568	25	22.72	6-63	1	-
G.J.Parsons	247.5	56	821	31	26.48	6-75	2	-
C.C.Lewis	411.2	80	1238	44	28.13	6-55	2	1
W.K.M.Benjamin	260.3	60	769	27	28.48	5-73	2	-
A.D.Mullally	464.2	116	1351	37	36.51	4-59	-	-
J.P.Agnew	612	108	2196	59	37.22	5-54	5	-
G.J.F.Ferris	101.2	16	404	9	44.88	4-44	-	-
P.Willey	377.4	101	1016	20	50.80	2-7	-	-
L.Potter	169	39	583	6	97.16	2-2	-	-
J.D.R.Benson	35.5	1	145	1	145.00	1-83	-	-
T.J.Boon	3.5	0	25	0	-	-	-	-
L.B.Taylor	9	1	34	0	-	-	-	-
C.Hawkes	14	3	40	0	-	-	-	-
M.I.Gidley	61	15	228	0	-	-	-	-

BRITANNIC ASSURANCE CHAMPIONSHIP

MIDDLESEX

BATTING AVERAGES - Including fielding

Name	Matches	Inns	NO	Runs	HS	Avge	100s	50s	Ct	St
D.L.Haynes	22	37	5	2036	255 *	63.62	6	7	14	-
M.W.Gatting	22	36	7	1685	170 *	58.10	4	9	19	-
K.R.Brown	22	33	7	1416	200 *	54.46	5	8	27	-
M.R.Ramprakash	22	38	8	1327	146 *	44.23	4	5	6	-
M.A.Roseberry	22	40	3	1497	135	40.45	3	10	21	-
J.E.Emburey	22	31	7	698	111 *	29.08	1	2	31	-
P.N.Weekes	2	2	0	53	51	26.50	-	1	1	-
P.R.Downton	15	23	1	530	63	24.09	-	3	40	2
A.R.C.Fraser	12	11	2	213	92	23.66	-	1	3	-
P.C.R.Tufnell	20	20	9	235	37	21.36	-	-	7	-
N.F.Williams	19	22	3	390	55 *	20.52	-	2	4	-
C.W.Taylor	2	2	1	13	13	13.00	-	-	-	-
S.P.Hughes	15	17	5	109	23 *	9.08	-	-	3	-
P.Farbrace	7	7	2	45	17 *	9.00	-	-	15	2
N.G.Cowans	16	16	6	81	31	8.10	-	-	3	-
N.R.Taylor	1	1	0	0	0	0.00	-	-	1	-
M.J.Thursfield	1	0	0	0	0	-	-	-	-	-

BOWLING AVERAGES

Name	Overs	Mdns	Runs	Wkts	Avge	Best	5wI	10wM
P.R.Downton	1.1	0	4	1	4.00	1-4	-	-
N.R.Taylor	14	5	44	3	14.66	3-44	-	-
M.W.Gatting	45	18	113	7	16.14	4-2	-	-
C.W.Taylor	47.5	7	139	6	23.16	5-33	1	-
A.R.C.Fraser	436.5	103	1073	41	26.17	6-30	2	-
N.F.Williams	469.1	88	1430	49	29.18	7-61	2	-
N.G.Cowans	415	115	1127	36	31.30	5-67	1	-
J.E.Emburey	902	254	1911	57	33.52	5-32	2	-
P.C.R.Tufnell	948.5	254	2389	65	36.75	6-79	2	-
S.P.Hughes	333	60	1121	28	40.03	5-101	1	-
M.J.Thursfield	17	4	45	1	45.00	1-24	-	-
D.L.Haynes	35	7	113	2	56.50	1-18	-	-
P.N.Weekes	54	8	183	3	61.00	2-115	-	-
M.R.Ramprakash	34	5	147	2	73.50	1-17	-	-
M.A.Roseberry	11	3	74	1	74.00	1-58	-	-
K.R.Brown	6	2	49	0	-	-	-	-

NORTHAMPTONSHIRE

BATTING AVERAGES - Including fielding

Name	Matches	Inns	NO	Runs	HS	Avge	100s	50s	Ct	St
A.J.Lamb	10	16	3	1040	235	80.00	4	3	5	-
R.J.Bailey	22	37	8	1965	204 *	67.75	7	9	16	-
A.Fordham	22	38	2	1653	206 *	45.91	4	8	22	-
N.A.Felton	20	35	2	1484	122	44.97	4	9	18	-
D.J.Capel	17	27	5	904	113	41.09	2	6	15	-
D.Ripley	20	27	6	634	109 *	30.19	1	2	28	6
W.Larkins	15	25	0	701	207	28.04	2	2	8	-
R.G.Williams	16	24	4	482	96	24.10	-	3	6	-
A.L.Penberthy	11	16	2	334	83	23.85	-	3	8	-
G.Cook	8	11	1	200	49	20.00	-	-	2	-
C.E.L.Ambrose	14	17	5	203	55 *	16.91	-	1	1	-
W.W.Davis	8	6	0	96	47	16.00	-	-	2	-
J.G.Thomas	11	11	2	131	48	14.55	-	-	7	-
N.G.B.Cook	17	17	7	133	30	13.30	-	-	9	-
J.W.Govan	2	3	0	38	17	12.66	-	-	-	-
D.J.Wild	1	2	0	17	17	8.50	-	-	-	-
S.J.Brown	3	2	1	6	4 *	6.00	-	-	-	-
W.M.Noon	2	2	0	4	2	2.00	-	-	4	1
A.R.Roberts	2	3	0	5	5	1.66	-	-	1	-
J.Hughes	4	7	0	4	2	0.57	-	-	-	-
M.A.Robinson	17	16	10	3	1 *	0.50	-	-	5	-

BOWLING AVERAGES

Name	Overs	Mdns	Runs	Wkts	Avge	Best	5wI	10wM
C.E.L.Ambrose	483.4	124	1353	58	23.32	7-89	5	1
D.J.Capel	234	51	711	25	28.44	5-74	1	-
N.G.B.Cook	507.1	159	1320	40	33.00	5-44	2	-
R.G.Williams	417.3	116	1165	31	37.58	4-94	-	-
A.Fordham	9	0	39	1	39.00	1-25	-	-
J.G.Thomas	288.2	49	1098	28	39.21	7-75	1	-
J.W.Govan	33	5	120	3	40.00	2-56	-	-
A.L.Penberthy	196	23	768	19	40.42	4-91	-	-
M.A.Robinson	520.1	98	1794	38	47.21	3-47	-	-
R.J.Bailey	168.2	29	604	11	54.90	3-82	-	-
S.J.Brown	52	7	221	4	55.25	1-31	-	-
W.W.Davis	216.5	25	747	12	62.25	3-28	-	-
A.R.Roberts	63	14	207	3	69.00	2-123	-	-
J.Hughes	66	12	293	3	97.66	2-57	-	-
N.A.Felton	19	1	113	1	113.00	1-48	-	-
D.J.Wild	12.5	4	42	0	-	-	-	-
W.Larkins	10	1	45	0	-	-	-	-

BRITANNIC ASSURANCE CHAMPIONSHIP

NOTTINGHAMSHIRE

BATTING AVERAGES - Including fielding

Name	Matches	Inns	NO	Runs	HS	Avge	100s	50s	Ct	St
B.C.Broad	22	43	2	2226	227*	54.29	9	3	7	-
K.P.Evans	12	22	8	638	100*	45.57	1	3	9	-
R.T.Robinson	22	43	5	1693	220*	44.55	4	8	12	-
P.Johnson	19	36	2	1294	165*	38.05	2	8	13	-
D.W.Randall	15	28	1	987	178	36.55	2	5	14	-
M.Newell	12	23	1	653	89*	29.68	-	5	4	-
D.J.R.Martindale	14	24	3	559	108*	26.61	1	2	5	-
F.D.Stephenson	19	33	6	715	121	26.48	1	3	5	-
P.Pollard	5	10	0	254	72	25.40	-	1	4	-
M.Saxelby	7	13	3	232	51	23.20	-	1	3	-
E.E.Hemmings	11	14	4	230	83	23.00	-	1	2	-
R.A.Pick	14	15	6	199	35	22.11	-	-	4	-
B.N.French	22	34	9	506	105*	20.24	1	-	46	11
G.W.Mike	3	5	1	45	18*	11.25	-	-	3	-
K.E.Cooper	20	25	5	217	35*	10.85	-	-	9	-
R.J.Evans	1	2	0	15	11	7.50	-	-	1	-
K.Saxelby	4	6	0	42	20	7.00	-	-	3	-
J.A.Afford	19	21	7	14	5	1.00	-	-	7	-
M.G.Field-Buss	1	2	0	0	0	0.00	-	-	-	-

BOWLING AVERAGES

Name	Overs	Mdns	Runs	Wkts	Avge	Best	5wI	10wM
R.A.Pick	443.5	70	1507	48	31.39	7-128	1	1
F.D.Stephenson	592.4	90	2047	53	38.62	6-84	2	-
E.E.Hemmings	443.3	127	1175	30	39.16	5-99	1	-
K.P.Evans	292	60	1085	27	40.18	4-57	-	-
K.E.Cooper	667.4	141	2105	51	41.27	5-56	3	-
K.Saxelby	89	19	309	7	44.14	4-92	-	-
J.A.Afford	627	186	1804	38	47.47	4-137	-	-
M.Saxelby	56.4	8	260	3	86.66	1-21	-	-
G.W.Mike	54.2	9	230	2	115.00	1-59	-	-
M.Newell	2.2	0	13	0	-	-	-	-
M.G.Field-Buss	10	2	43	0	-	-	-	-

SOMERSET

BATTING AVERAGES - Including fielding

Name	Matches	Inns	NO	Runs	HS	Avge	100s	50s	Ct	St
S.J.Cook	22	38	6	2432	313*	76.00	8	11	10	-
A.N.Hayhurst	21	33	7	1554	170	59.76	4	8	9	-
R.J.Harden	22	29	7	1257	104*	57.13	2	11	18	-
P.M.Roebuck	16	25	5	1085	201*	54.25	2	6	6	-
C.J.Tavare	22	30	4	1399	219	53.80	2	11	15	-
G.D.Rose	22	26	9	897	97*	52.76	-	7	14	-
J.J.E.Hardy	7	13	5	343	91	42.87	-	1	5	-
R.J.Bartlett	1	2	0	85	73	42.50	-	1	-	-
N.D.Burns	22	31	9	863	166	39.22	1	4	42	1
N.A.Mallender	19	10	3	177	87*	25.28	-	1	3	-
A.N.Jones	20	9	5	100	41	25.00	-	-	4	-
I.G.Swallow	21	17	7	187	32	18.70	-	-	11	-
R.P.Lefebvre	16	16	3	214	53	16.46	-	1	8	-
G.T.J.Townsend	2	4	1	21	15	7.00	-	-	3	-
H.R.J.Trump	7	5	1	11	4*	2.75	-	-	3	-
J.C.Hallett	2	1	0	0	0	0.00	-	-	-	-

BOWLING AVERAGES

Name	Overs	Mdns	Runs	Wkts	Avge	Best	5wI	10wM
S.J.Cook	8	0	42	2	21.00	2-25	-	-
N.A.Mallender	538.2	114	1555	51	30.49	5-46	2	-
J.C.Hallett	40.2	7	135	4	33.75	2-40	-	-
G.D.Rose	530.4	93	1807	51	35.43	5-52	1	-
A.N.Jones	539.4	81	1990	52	38.26	6-75	2	-
R.P.Lefebvre	493.1	132	1258	30	41.93	5-30	1	-
R.J.Harden	64	6	254	6	42.33	2-39	-	-
A.N.Hayhurst	291.2	46	974	17	57.29	3-58	-	-
H.R.J.Trump	164	41	520	9	57.77	3-58	-	-
P.M.Roebuck	160.3	37	460	7	65.71	2-34	-	-
I.G.Swallow	642.1	150	2042	31	65.87	3-88	-	-
N.D.Burns	0.3	0	8	0	-	-	-	-
C.J.Tavare	17.2	0	162	0	-	-	-	-

BRITANNIC ASSURANCE CHAMPIONSHIP

SURREY

BATTING AVERAGES - Including fielding

Name	Matches	Inns	NO	Runs	HS	Avge	100s	50s	Ct	St
D.M.Ward	22	31	7	1843	263	76.79	6	3	26	2
D.J.Bicknell	13	20	4	1199	186	74.93	5	5	2	-
I.A.Greig	22	26	5	1130	291	53.81	2	4	16	-
R.I.Alikhan	11	16	2	726	138	51.85	2	4	3	-
A.J.Stewart	12	21	6	709	100 *	47.26	1	7	17	-
G.S.Clinton	18	29	4	1092	146	43.68	1	6	5	-
M.A.Lynch	22	29	4	1049	104	41.96	1	7	29	-
M.P.Bicknell	19	15	7	309	50 *	38.62	-	1	8	-
M.A.Feltham	14	14	3	373	101	33.90	1	2	10	-
Waqar Younis	14	9	7	56	14	28.00	-	-	4	-
G.P.Thorpe	16	24	4	537	86	26.85	-	3	8	-
K.T.Medlycott	20	22	7	389	44	25.93	-	-	13	-
P.D.Atkins	1	2	1	23	23	23.00	-	-	-	-
J.D.Robinson	7	9	0	151	72	16.77	-	1	1	-
N.M.Kendrick	11	12	4	124	52 *	15.50	-	1	11	-
A.H.Gray	6	2	0	22	11	11.00	-	-	5	-
A.J.Murphy	12	6	3	6	4 *	2.00	-	-	1	-
N.F.Sargeant	2	1	0	1	1	1.00	-	-	5	-

BOWLING AVERAGES

Name	Overs	Mdns	Runs	Wkts	Avge	Best	5wI	10wM
Waqar Younis	422	70	1357	57	23.80	7-73	3	1
M.P.Bicknell	597.5	137	1653	60	27.55	5-34	1	-
M.A.Feltham	334.4	59	1082	39	27.74	6-53	2	-
A.H.Gray	212.4	43	556	16	34.75	4-83	-	-
K.T.Medlycott	617.5	134	2020	53	38.11	7-92	3	-
A.J.Murphy	404.2	76	1367	30	45.56	5-67	2	-
N.M.Kendrick	273	50	987	17	58.05	4-110	-	-
J.D.Robinson	118.3	21	393	6	65.50	2-84	-	-
I.A.Greig	199.1	19	805	12	67.08	3-60	-	-
R.I.Alikhan	20	1	83	1	83.00	1-12	-	-
M.A.Lynch	27	5	130	1	130.00	1-43	-	-
D.J.Bicknell	9	1	20	0	-	-	-	-
A.J.Stewart	5	0	32	0	-	-	-	-
G.P.Thorpe	9	1	69	0	-	-	-	-

SUSSEX

BATTING AVERAGES - Including fielding

Name	Matches	Inns	NO	Runs	HS	Avge	100s	50s	Ct	St
N.J.Lenham	19	35	1	1499	123	44.08	4	7	6	-
P.W.G.Parker	12	21	2	778	107	40.94	2	4	5	-
M.P.Speight	21	39	6	1349	131	40.87	2	11	13	-
A.P.Wells	21	39	6	1245	144 *	37.72	3	5	9	-
B.T.P.Donelan	9	13	6	211	53	30.14	-	1	3	-
C.M.Wells	19	31	4	812	107	30.07	1	4	3	-
J.W.Hall	17	31	1	888	125	29.60	1	5	3	-
A.I.C.Dodemaide	22	35	6	854	112	29.44	1	4	9	-
D.M.Smith	8	14	2	324	71	27.00	-	2	2	-
I.D.K.Salisbury	18	23	10	313	68	24.07	-	1	13	-
I.J.Gould	7	11	1	229	73	22.90	-	2	7	-
P.Moores	22	35	3	680	106 *	21.25	1	2	46	10
A.C.S.Pigott	20	29	5	451	64 *	18.79	-	4	10	-
K.Greenfield	2	4	0	74	38	18.50	-	-	1	-
A.M.Babington	2	2	0	28	20	14.00	-	-	2	-
A.R.Hansford	4	6	1	55	29	11.00	-	-	1	-
R.A.Bunting	13	13	5	85	24 *	10.62	-	-	2	-
J.A.North	3	5	1	41	19 *	10.25	-	-	1	-
R.Hanley	2	4	0	32	28	8.00	-	-	-	-
C.C.Remy	1	1	1	4	4 *	-	-	-	-	-

BOWLING AVERAGES

Name	Overs	Mdns	Runs	Wkts	Avge	Best	5wI	10wM
A.C.S.Pigott	516.1	88	1916	51	37.56	5-52	3	-
A.I.C.Dodemaide	681.1	112	2206	56	39.39	6-106	1	-
B.T.P.Donelan	258.4	50	853	19	44.89	3-79	-	-
I.D.K.Salisbury	535.1	103	1796	40	44.90	5-32	2	-
J.A.North	49.2	10	147	3	49.00	2-43	-	-
R.A.Bunting	298	54	1113	21	53.00	2-36	-	-
A.R.Hansford	123.5	21	425	7	60.71	3-91	-	-
C.M.Wells	366	67	1195	17	70.29	3-48	-	-
A.M.Babington	43	7	166	2	83.00	2-109	-	-
C.C.Remy	17	0	91	1	91.00	1-37	-	-
N.J.Lenham	60.5	10	223	2	111.50	1-48	-	-
A.P.Wells	29	4	144	1	144.00	1-88	-	-
K.Greenfield	0.3	0	8	0	-	-	-	-
P.Moores	2	1	8	0	-	-	-	-
I.J.Gould	5	0	18	0	-	-	-	-
P.W.G.Parker	8	0	59	0	-	-	-	-

BRITANNIC ASSURANCE CHAMPIONSHIP

WARWICKSHIRE

BATTING AVERAGES - Including fielding

Name	Matches	Inns	NO	Runs	HS	Avge	100s	50s	Ct	St
T.M.Moody	7	12	2	866	168	86.60	5	1	4	-
D.A.Reeve	22	34	11	1265	202 *	55.00	2	5	23	-
A.J.Moles	22	42	8	1669	224 *	49.08	3	10	12	-
G.W.Humpage	11	18	3	552	74	36.80	-	5	28	-
J.E.Benjamin	12	11	6	169	41	33.80	-	-	4	-
D.P.Ostler	9	15	2	432	71	33.23	-	4	9	-
P.A.Smith	12	20	4	520	117	32.50	1	3	1	-
N.M.K.Smith	7	9	2	214	83 *	30.57	-	1	2	-
G.Smith	1	1	0	30	30	30.00	-	-	1	-
J.D.Ratcliffe	14	27	3	689	81 *	28.70	-	3	7	-
Asif Din	21	37	3	874	70	25.70	-	5	10	-
K.J.Piper	14	18	1	432	111	25.41	1	1	39	4
A.I.Kallicharran	5	8	1	175	72	25.00	-	2	5	-
T.A.Lloyd	15	27	1	646	101	24.84	1	4	7	-
P.A.Booth	7	12	0	177	60	14.75	-	1	2	-
R.G.Twose	4	6	0	88	51	14.66	-	1	3	-
A.R.K.Pierson	11	9	5	57	16 *	14.25	-	-	1	-
G.C.Small	12	18	2	212	55	13.25	-	1	3	-
T.A.Munton	22	23	9	121	29 *	8.64	-	-	9	-
A.A.Donald	14	18	3	118	24 *	7.86	-	-	-	-

BOWLING AVERAGES

Name	Overs	Mdns	Runs	Wkts	Avge	Best	5wI	10wM
G.Smith	26.5	3	81	4	20.25	3-36	-	-
P.A.Smith	148.5	34	497	20	24.85	5-48	1	-
T.A.Munton	748.3	174	2086	75	27.81	5-33	2	-
D.A.Reeve	319.4	93	782	28	27.92	4-42	-	-
J.E.Benjamin	322.3	51	1036	34	30.47	5-71	3	-
G.C.Small	321.4	78	900	27	33.33	6-94	2	-
A.A.Donald	355.1	81	988	28	35.28	3-28	-	-
A.R.K.Pierson	302.4	55	965	25	38.60	5-101	1	-
P.A.Booth	214.2	70	495	12	41.25	4-55	-	-
T.M.Moody	38	7	145	3	48.33	1-7	-	-
R.G.Twose	26	2	101	2	50.50	1-10	-	-
T.A.Lloyd	9	1	58	1	58.00	1-58	-	-
A.J.Moles	22	2	133	2	66.50	2-56	-	-
N.M.K.Smith	109.5	20	350	5	70.00	2-76	-	-
Asif Din	133.2	24	569	6	94.83	1-5	-	-
G.W.Humpage	7	2	34	0	-	-	-	-

WORCESTERSHIRE

BATTING AVERAGES - Including fielding

Name	Matches	Inns	NO	Runs	HS	Avge	100s	50s	Ct	St
G.A.Hick	19	33	8	2273	252 *	90.92	8	13	24	-
T.S.Curtis	21	38	8	1650	197 *	55.00	4	6	13	-
G.J.Lord	12	23	2	983	190	46.81	3	5	4	-
P.A.Neale	19	29	9	934	122	46.70	2	3	12	-
S.J.Rhodes	21	24	10	653	96	46.64	-	5	59	8
G.R.Dilley	10	8	4	185	45 *	46.25	-	-	2	-
D.B.D'Oliveira	21	32	2	1179	155	39.30	2	7	33	-
I.T.Botham	12	17	1	576	113	36.00	1	4	7	-
R.K.Illingworth	20	19	6	452	117	34.76	1	2	7	-
P.J.Newport	19	15	5	318	96	31.80	-	2	5	-
P.Bent	6	10	0	315	79	31.50	-	2	-	-
D.A.Leatherdale	4	6	0	154	70	25.66	-	2	2	-
S.M.McEwan	13	10	3	163	54	23.28	-	1	4	-
N.V.Radford	10	6	1	104	43 *	20.80	-	-	4	-
S.R.Lampitt	21	22	5	286	45 *	16.82	-	-	10	-
C.M.Tolley	6	6	1	79	29	15.80	-	-	2	-
M.J.Weston	5	8	1	80	38 *	11.42	-	-	1	-
S.R.Bevins	1	1	1	6	6 *	-	-	-	3	-
R.D.Stemp	2	2	2	3	3 *	-	-	-	1	-

BOWLING AVERAGES

Name	Overs	Mdns	Runs	Wkts	Avge	Best	5wI	10wM
R.K.Illingworth	804.5	261	1946	71	27.40	5-59	1	-
S.M.McEwan	310	61	970	32	30.31	3-31	-	-
S.R.Lampitt	539.3	96	1794	57	31.47	5-34	2	-
P.J.Newport	563.2	104	1806	57	31.68	6-73	3	-
I.T.Botham	174.4	34	546	17	32.11	4-65	-	-
G.A.Hick	208.5	41	645	20	32.25	5-37	1	-
G.R.Dilley	224.2	30	818	24	34.08	5-62	2	-
D.B.D'Oliveira	11.3	1	80	2	40.00	2-23	-	-
C.M.Tolley	88	14	326	5	65.20	2-66	-	-
N.V.Radford	245	38	999	14	71.35	4-55	-	-
R.D.Stemp	45	14	123	1	123.00	1-32	-	-
M.J.Weston	7	1	23	0	-	-	-	-
T.S.Curtis	5.3	1	43	0	-	-	-	-

BRITANNIC ASSURANCE CHAMPIONSHIP

YORKSHIRE

BATTING AVERAGES - Including fielding

Name	Matches	Inns	NO	Runs	HS	Avge	100s	50s	Ct	St
A.A.Metcalfe	21	40	3	1854	194 *	50.10	6	6	10	-
K.Sharp	8	12	5	316	53 *	45.14	-	1	1	-
P.Grayson	4	7	4	135	44 *	45.00	-	-	2	-
P.E.Robinson	22	38	7	1389	150 *	44.80	1	12	18	-
M.D.Moxon	19	36	5	1353	218 *	43.64	2	6	13	-
S.A.Kellett	14	25	2	699	75 *	30.39	-	6	7	-
C.S.Pickles	15	21	7	424	57 *	30.28	-	2	6	-
D.L.Bairstow	5	6	0	179	61	29.83	-	1	9	-
R.J.Blakey	22	39	7	928	111	29.00	1	5	41	8
D.Byas	17	27	3	693	83	28.87	-	5	19	-
A.Sidebottom	2	4	0	104	38	26.00	-	-	1	-
P.Carrick	18	22	2	515	64	25.75	-	3	7	-
P.W.Jarvis	15	16	4	212	43 *	17.66	-	-	2	-
P.J.Hartley	16	14	1	215	75	16.53	-	1	7	-
C.White	8	9	1	106	38	13.25	-	-	3	-
C.Chapman	2	4	0	47	20	11.75	-	-	2	-
D.Gough	13	16	5	116	24	10.54	-	-	1	-
J.D.Batty	7	5	2	30	21	10.00	-	-	4	-
S.D.Fletcher	10	13	3	39	19	3.90	-	-	3	-
P.Berry	2	4	4	45	31 *	-	-	-	1	-
I.J.Houseman	2	1	1	0	0 *	-	-	-	-	-

BOWLING AVERAGES

Name	Overs	Mdns	Runs	Wkts	Avge	Best	5wI	10wM
P.E.Robinson	3.3	0	28	1	28.00	1-10	-	-
A.Sidebottom	44	9	121	4	30.25	3-54	-	-
P.Carrick	601	170	1570	46	34.13	5-49	3	-
S.D.Fletcher	268.5	58	936	27	34.66	5-94	1	-
P.J.Hartley	481.1	79	1754	48	36.54	6-57	2	-
P.W.Jarvis	405.2	68	1393	37	37.64	4-53	-	-
D.Gough	256.4	43	984	24	41.00	4-68	-	-
C.S.Pickles	296.1	59	1107	25	44.28	3-56	-	-
C.White	122	12	519	9	57.66	5-74	1	-
M.D.Moxon	57	9	175	3	58.33	1-10	-	-
J.D.Batty	195	29	722	12	60.16	4-76	-	-
D.Byas	69	14	253	3	84.33	3-55	-	-
P.Berry	44.3	4	172	2	86.00	1-48	-	-
P.Grayson	63	13	227	1	227.00	1-55	-	-
A.A.Metcalfe	9.1	0	88	0	-	-	-	-
I.J.Houseman	30	6	129	0	-	-	-	-

BRITANNIC ASSURANCE CHAMPIONSHIP

BATTING AVERAGES - Including fielding
Qualifying requirements : 6 completed innings

Name	Matches	Inns	NO	Runs	HS	Avge	100s	50s	Ct	St
G.A.Gooch	11	18	2	1586	215	99.12	7	5	7	-
G.A.Hick	19	33	8	2273	252 *	90.92	8	13	24	-
T.M.Moody	7	12	2	866	168	86.60	5	1	4	-
N.H.Fairbrother	17	24	6	1544	366	85.77	3	9	18	-
A.J.Lamb	10	16	3	1040	235	80.00	4	3	5	-
M.E.Waugh	21	32	6	2009	207 *	77.26	8	7	18	-
D.M.Ward	22	31	7	1843	263	76.79	6	3	26	2
S.J.Cook	22	38	6	2432	313 *	76.00	8	11	10	-
M.A.Atherton	12	18	4	1053	191	75.21	4	6	16	-
D.J.Bicknell	13	20	4	1199	186	74.93	5	5	2	-
R.J.Bailey	22	37	8	1965	204 *	67.75	7	9	16	-
B.R.Hardie	11	15	5	650	125	65.00	2	3	7	-
R.A.Smith	11	18	4	897	181	64.07	4	3	7	-
D.L.Haynes	22	37	5	2036	255 *	63.62	6	7	14	-
I.V.A.Richards	18	28	5	1425	164 *	61.95	7	3	8	-
J.E.Morris	16	26	4	1353	157 *	61.50	6	6	8	-
A.R.Butcher	21	39	5	2044	151 *	60.11	6	14	8	-
C.L.Smith	20	35	7	1678	132 *	59.92	3	12	11	-
A.N.Hayhurst	21	33	7	1554	170	59.76	4	8	9	-
M.W.Gatting	22	36	7	1685	170 *	58.10	4	9	19	-
R.J.Harden	22	29	7	1257	104 *	57.13	2	11	18	-
N.R.Taylor	20	35	4	1752	204	56.51	5	10	8	-
T.S.Curtis	21	38	8	1650	197 *	55.00	4	13	13	-
D.A.Reeve	22	34	11	1265	202 *	55.00	2	5	23	-
K.R.Brown	22	33	7	1416	200 *	54.46	5	8	27	-
B.C.Broad	22	43	2	2226	227 *	54.29	9	3	7	-
P.M.Roebuck	16	25	5	1085	201 *	54.25	2	6	6	-
I.A.Greig	22	26	5	1130	291	53.81	2	4	16	-
C.J.Tavare	22	30	4	1399	219	53.80	2	11	15	-
G.D.Mendis	21	35	6	1551	180	53.48	4	8	15	-
C.W.J.Athey	21	32	6	1384	131	53.23	3	8	18	-
G.D.Rose	22	26	9	897	97 *	52.76	-	7	14	-
K.M.Curran	22	32	8	1261	144 *	52.54	3	5	15	-
R.I.Alikhan	11	16	2	726	138	51.85	2	4	3	-
H.Morris	22	41	4	1914	160 *	51.73	8	9	12	-
J.P.Stephenson	22	37	7	1525	202 *	50.83	2	12	14	-
K.J.Barnett	22	36	5	1572	141	50.71	5	8	14	-
A.A.Metcalfe	21	40	3	1854	194 *	50.10	6	6	10	-
A.J.Moles	22	42	8	1669	224 *	49.08	3	10	12	-
T.C.Middleton	16	28	3	1216	127	48.64	5	5	8	-
N.Shahid	18	27	7	964	125	48.20	1	6	22	-
G.R.Cowdrey	20	36	5	1471	135	47.45	3	8	8	-
A.J.Stewart	12	21	6	709	100 *	47.26	1	7	17	-
P.J.Prichard	20	30	3	1276	245	47.25	4	4	8	-
G.J.Lord	12	23	2	983	190	46.81	3	5	4	-
M.R.Benson	14	23	1	1029	159	46.77	5	3	5	-
P.A.Neale	19	29	9	934	122	46.70	2	3	12	-
S.J.Rhodes	21	24	10	653	96	46.64	-	5	59	8
N.E.Briers	22	43	3	1846	176	46.15	4	11	7	-
A.Fordham	22	38	2	1653	206 *	45.91	4	8	22	-
M.D.Marshall	18	24	3	962	117	45.81	2	6	7	-
K.P.Evans	12	22	8	638	100 *	45.57	1	3	9	-
K.Sharp	8	12	5	316	53 *	45.14	-	1	1	-
M.P.Maynard	19	34	5	1306	125	45.03	2	10	13	-
N.A.Felton	20	35	2	1484	122	44.97	4	9	18	-
M.W.Alleyne	11	17	0	763	256	44.88	2	2	9	-
P.E.Robinson	22	38	7	1389	150 *	44.80	1	12	18	-
R.T.Robinson	22	43	5	1693	220 *	44.55	4	8	12	-
P.Bainbridge	18	25	2	1019	152	44.30	2	4	4	-
M.R.Ramprakash	22	38	8	1327	146 *	44.23	4	5	6	-
N.J.Lenham	19	35	1	1499	123	44.08	4	7	6	-
R.D.B.Croft	14	23	10	570	91 *	43.84	-	3	2	-
G.S.Clinton	18	29	4	1092	146	43.68	1	6	5	-
M.D.Moxon	19	36	5	1353	218 *	43.64	2	6	13	-
T.E.Jesty	17	24	6	785	98	43.61	-	7	6	-
N.G.Cowley	13	16	4	523	76	43.58	-	6	8	-
R.C.Russell	11	16	1	651	120	43.40	2	3	27	-
J.J.E.Hardy	7	13	5	343	91	42.87	-	1	5	-
P.D.Bowler	21	37	4	1408	210	42.66	3	7	15	-
M.A.Lynch	22	29	4	1049	104	41.96	1	7	29	-
I.Smith	6	8	1	293	112 *	41.85	1	2	1	-
J.J.Whitaker	22	42	4	1575	116	41.44	3	7	12	-

Name	Matches	Inns	NO	Runs	HS	Avge	100s	50s	Ct	St
J.R.Ayling	7	9	2	288	62 *	41.14	-	2	2	-
W.K.Hegg	20	21	6	617	100 *	41.13	1	2	47	2
D.J.Capel	17	27	5	904	113	41.09	2	6	15	-
P.W.G.Parker	12	21	2	778	107	40.94	2	4	5	-
M.P.Speight	21	39	6	1349	131	40.87	2	11	13	-
M.A.Roseberry	22	40	3	1497	135	40.45	3	10	21	-
C.C.Lewis	13	21	5	632	189 *	39.50	1	2	11	-
D.B.D'Oliveira	21	32	2	1179	155	39.30	2	7	33	-
T.J.G.O'Gorman	6	11	1	393	100	39.30	1	3	3	-
N.D.Burns	22	31	9	863	166	39.22	1	4	42	1
T.J.Boon	22	40	4	1522	138	39.02	2	11	12	-
V.P.Terry	19	31	3	1084	165	38.71	3	4	21	-
M.P.Bicknell	19	15	7	309	50 *	38.62	-	1	8	-
P.Johnson	19	36	2	1294	165 *	38.05	2	8	13	-
A.M.Brown	7	11	1	379	139 *	37.90	1	1	6	-
A.P.Wells	21	39	6	1245	144 *	37.72	3	5	9	-
M.V.Fleming	17	30	5	940	102	37.60	1	5	6	-
N.Hussain	14	21	2	714	197	37.57	1	2	14	-
G.C.Holmes	7	10	3	260	125 *	37.14	1	-	1	-
B.Roberts	22	35	7	1038	124 *	37.07	2	4	23	-
J.W.Lloyds	21	29	10	704	93	37.05	-	3	15	-
R.M.Ellison	13	18	4	444	81	37.00	-	3	5	-
G.W.Humpage	11	18	3	552	74	36.80	-	5	28	-
D.W.Randall	15	28	1	987	178	36.55	2	5	14	-
S.G.Hinks	22	41	0	1484	234	36.19	4	5	8	-
P.A.J.DeFreitas	15	17	3	506	100 *	36.14	1	2	5	-
I.T.Botham	12	17	1	576	113	36.00	1	4	7	-
M.Watkinson	18	22	2	706	138	35.30	1	4	8	-
C.S.Cowdrey	11	21	4	599	107 *	35.23	2	2	9	-
R.K.Illingworth	20	19	6	452	117	34.76	1	2	7	-
W.K.M.Benjamin	11	13	2	382	101 *	34.72	1	3	3	-
G.Miller	13	13	7	208	47 *	34.66	-	-	4	-
D.I.Gower	14	21	1	684	145	34.20	1	2	14	-
I.D.Austin	11	12	5	238	58	34.00	-	1	-	-
M.A.Feltham	14	14	3	373	101	33.90	1	1	10	-
S.A.Marsh	22	34	8	867	114 *	33.34	1	5	46	4
D.P.Ostler	9	15	2	432	71	33.23	-	4	9	-
L.Potter	22	36	5	1028	109 *	33.16	1	7	22	-
G.D.Hodgson	21	34	2	1059	109	33.09	1	9	10	-
P.A.Cottey	17	30	5	816	125	32.64	2	4	9	-
P.A.Smith	12	20	4	520	117	32.50	1	3	1	-
G.Fowler	21	35	6	938	126	32.34	2	2	15	-
R.J.Maru	22	18	2	513	59	32.06	-	3	25	-
T.R.Ward	15	28	1	863	175	31.96	2	5	14	-
P.J.Newport	19	15	5	318	96	31.80	-	2	5	-
P.Bent	6	10	0	315	79	31.50	-	2	-	-
M.A.Garnham	22	26	7	589	84 *	31.00	-	2	46	1
G.D.Lloyd	11	15	1	434	70	31.00	-	4	7	-
P.N.Hepworth	4	8	2	185	55 *	30.83	-	1	1	-
N.M.K.Smith	7	9	2	214	83 *	30.57	-	1	2	-
M.C.J.Nicholas	20	30	8	670	78 *	30.45	-	5	7	-
S.A.Kellett	14	25	2	699	75 *	30.39	-	6	17	-
C.S.Pickles	15	21	7	424	57 *	30.28	-	2	6	-
D.Ripley	20	27	6	634	109 *	30.19	1	2	28	6
B.T.P.Donelan	9	13	6	211	53	30.14	-	1	3	-
C.M.Wells	19	31	4	812	107	30.07	1	4	3	-
D.L.Bairstow	5	6	0	179	61	29.83	-	1	9	-
M.Newell	12	23	1	653	89 *	29.68	-	5	4	-
I.R.Bishop	12	15	4	326	103 *	29.63	1	-	2	-
J.W.Hall	17	31	1	888	125	29.60	1	5	3	-
P.W.Romaines	5	7	1	177	61	29.50	-	1	2	-
A.I.C.Dodemaide	22	35	6	854	112	29.44	1	4	9	-
J.D.R.Benson	16	24	6	525	86	29.16	-	2	9	-
J.E.Emburey	22	31	7	698	111 *	29.08	1	2	31	-
R.J.Blakey	22	39	7	928	111	29.00	1	5	41	8
C.A.Walsh	19	19	3	464	63 *	29.00	-	3	6	-
D.R.Pringle	15	13	2	318	84	28.90	-	1	7	-
D.Byas	17	27	3	693	83	28.87	-	5	19	-
P.Willey	20	37	6	892	112	28.77	1	4	10	-
J.D.Ratcliffe	14	27	3	689	81 *	28.70	-	3	7	-
W.Larkins	15	25	0	701	207	28.04	2	2	8	-
I.P.Butcher	9	13	3	280	102	28.00	1	-	-	-
C.J.Adams	21	32	3	800	101	27.58	1	5	22	-
P.A.Nixon	17	20	6	379	46	27.07	-	-	44	1
D.M.Smith	8	14	2	324	71	27.00	-	2	2	-

BRITANNIC ASSURANCE CHAMPIONSHIP

Name	Matches	Inns	NO	Runs	HS	Avge	100s	50s	Ct	St
G.P.Thorpe	16	24	4	537	86	26.85	-	3	8	-
D.J.R.Martindale	14	24	3	559	108*	26.61	1	2	5	-
N.A.Foster	22	22	2	530	101	26.50	1	2	13	-
F.D.Stephenson	19	33	6	715	121	26.48	1	3	5	-
K.T.Medlycott	20	22	7	389	44	25.93	-	-	13	-
P.Carrick	18	22	2	515	64	25.75	-	3	7	-
Asif Din	21	37	3	874	70	25.70	-	5	10	-
D.A.Leatherdale	4	6	0	154	70	25.66	-	2	2	-
K.J.Piper	14	18	1	432	111	25.41	1	1	39	4
P.Pollard	5	10	0	254	72	25.40	-	1	4	-
N.A.Mallender	19	10	3	177	87*	25.28	-	1	3	-
A.I.Kallicharran	5	8	1	175	72	25.00	-	2	5	-
T.A.Lloyd	15	27	1	646	101	24.84	1	4	7	-
A.J.Wright	22	36	3	809	112	24.51	1	4	21	-
R.G.Williams	16	24	4	482	96	24.10	-	3	6	-
P.R.Downton	15	23	1	530	63	24.09	-	3	40	2
I.D.K.Salisbury	18	23	10	313	68	24.07	-	1	13	-
A.L.Penberthy	11	16	2	334	83	23.85	-	3	8	-
D.P.Hughes	18	17	7	237	57	23.70	-	1	13	-
A.R.C.Fraser	12	11	2	213	92	23.66	-	1	3	-
V.J.Wells	8	15	0	352	58	23.46	-	2	8	-
S.M.McEwan	13	10	3	163	54	23.28	-	1	4	-
M.Saxelby	7	13	3	232	51	23.20	-	1	3	-
E.E.Hemmings	11	14	4	230	83	23.00	-	1	2	-
I.J.Gould	7	11	1	229	73	22.90	-	2	7	-
M.J.Cann	5	8	0	180	64	22.50	-	2	2	-
R.A.Pick	14	15	6	199	35	22.11	-	-	4	-
P.S.De Villiers	12	15	3	264	37	22.00	-	-	6	-
P.C.R.Tufnell	20	20	9	235	37	21.36	-	-	7	-
P.Moores	22	35	3	680	106*	21.25	1	2	46	10
N.F.Williams	19	22	3	390	55*	20.52	-	2	4	-
R.J.Parks	18	19	9	203	36*	20.30	-	-	46	4
B.N.French	22	34	9	506	105*	20.24	1	-	46	11
G.Cook	8	11	1	200	49	20.00	-	-	2	-
C.A.Connor	19	9	3	119	46	19.83	-	-	9	-
S.J.Base	13	13	2	215	58	19.54	-	2	4	-
A.P.Kuiper	10	15	0	288	48	19.20	-	-	9	-
J.D.Fitton	14	11	5	114	25*	19.00	-	-	2	-
A.C.S.Pigott	20	29	5	451	64*	18.79	-	4	10	-
I.G.Swallow	21	17	7	187	32	18.70	-	-	11	-
R.J.Scott	6	10	2	144	71	18.00	-	1	4	-
P.W.Jarvis	15	16	4	212	43*	17.66	-	-	2	-
R.P.Davis	22	32	3	504	59	17.37	-	2	24	-
G.J.F.Ferris	5	6	0	104	35	17.33	-	-	-	-
C.E.L.Ambrose	14	17	5	203	55*	16.91	-	1	1	-
S.R.Lampitt	21	22	5	286	45*	16.82	-	-	10	-
J.D.Robinson	7	9	0	151	72	16.77	-	1	1	-
P.J.Hartley	16	14	1	215	75	16.53	-	1	7	-
R.P.Lefebvre	16	16	3	214	53	16.46	-	1	8	-
K.M.Krikken	21	28	2	426	77*	16.38	-	1	58	3
A.Dale	7	11	0	179	92	16.27	-	1	6	-
W.W.Davis	8	6	0	96	47	16.00	-	-	2	-
N.M.Kendrick	11	12	4	124	52*	15.50	-	1	11	-
M.C.Ilott	8	10	2	123	42*	15.37	-	-	1	-
S.J.W.Andrew	16	15	7	119	35	14.87	-	-	1	-
M.M.Patel	9	12	5	104	41*	14.85	-	-	2	-
P.A.Booth	7	12	0	177	60	14.75	-	1	2	-
R.G.Twose	4	6	0	88	51	14.66	-	1	3	-
J.G.Thomas	11	11	2	131	48	14.55	-	-	7	-
S.C.Goldsmith	11	16	1	216	34	14.40	-	-	7	-
C.P.Metson	22	26	4	302	34	13.72	-	-	58	-
N.G.B.Cook	17	17	7	133	30	13.30	-	-	9	-
G.C.Small	12	18	2	212	55	13.25	-	1	3	-
C.White	8	9	1	106	38	13.25	-	-	3	-
A.P.Igglesden	13	17	9	105	24	13.12	-	-	5	-
D.J.M.Kelleher	5	8	0	101	44	12.62	-	-	2	-
D.A.Graveney	12	12	4	100	46*	12.50	-	-	5	-
J.P.Agnew	22	26	5	257	46*	12.23	-	-	5	-
Wasim Akram	7	10	0	117	32	11.70	-	-	-	-
M.Jean-Jacques	10	11	4	80	25	11.42	-	-	2	-
M.J.Weston	5	8	1	80	38*	11.42	-	-	1	-
S.L.Watkin	22	22	7	170	25*	11.33	-	-	5	-
J.H.Childs	21	16	5	123	26	11.18	-	-	7	-
K.E.Cooper	20	25	5	217	35*	10.85	-	-	9	-
R.A.Bunting	13	13	5	85	24*	10.62	-	-	2	-
D.Gough	13	16	5	116	24	10.54	-	-	1	-
G.J.Parsons	8	12	2	101	20	10.10	-	-	3	-
A.D.Mullally	18	18	6	113	29	9.41	-	-	3	-
A.E.Warner	14	19	2	160	59	9.41	-	1	2	-
S.P.Hughes	15	17	5	109	23*	9.08	-	-	3	-
T.A.Munton	22	23	9	121	29*	8.64	-	-	9	-
N.G.Cowans	16	16	6	81	31	8.10	-	-	3	-
A.A.Donald	14	18	3	118	24*	7.86	-	-	6	-
S.Bastien	10	9	3	47	12	7.83	-	-	2	-
K.Saxelby	4	6	0	42	20	7.00	-	-	3	-
D.V.Lawrence	20	21	3	124	29	6.88	-	-	6	-
M.Frost	18	17	7	40	12	4.00	-	-	2	-
S.D.Fletcher	10	13	3	39	19	3.90	-	-	3	-
S.J.Dennis	12	8	1	23	6	3.28	-	-	3	-
S.N.Barnes	7	7	1	11	6	1.83	-	-	2	-
S.P.James	3	6	0	10	7	1.66	-	-	2	-
J.A.Afford	19	21	7	14	5	1.00	-	-	7	-
J.Hughes	4	7	0	4	2	0.57	-	-	-	-
M.A.Robinson	17	16	10	3	1*	0.50	-	-	5	-

BRITANNIC ASSURANCE CHAMPIONSHIP

BOWLING AVERAGES
Qualifying requirements : 10 wickets taken

Name	Overs	Mdns	Runs	Wkts	Avge	Best	5wI	10wM
I.R.Bishop	395.3	89	1087	59	18.42	6-71	3	-
M.D.Marshall	554.2	141	1381	72	19.18	7-47	4	2
V.J.Wells	85	19	257	12	21.41	5-43	1	-
D.J.Millns	164.1	20	568	25	22.72	6-63	1	-
M.W.Alleyne	77	23	254	11	23.09	3-23	-	-
C.E.L.Ambrose	483.4	124	1353	58	23.32	7-89	5	1
Waqar Younis	422	70	1357	57	23.80	7-73	3	1
O.H.Mortensen	301.2	88	764	32	23.87	4-22	-	-
P.A.Smith	148.5	34	497	20	24.85	5-48	1	-
A.R.C.Fraser	436.5	103	1073	41	26.17	6-30	2	-
M.A.Atherton	356.3	84	1111	42	26.45	6-78	3	-
G.J.Parsons	247.5	56	821	31	26.48	6-75	2	-
N.A.Foster	819.2	175	2502	94	26.61	6-32	6	1
R.K.Illingworth	804.5	261	1946	71	27.40	5-59	1	-
M.P.Bicknell	597.5	137	1653	60	27.55	5-34	1	-
M.A.Feltham	334.4	59	1082	39	27.74	6-53	2	-
T.A.Munton	748.3	174	2086	75	27.81	5-33	2	-
D.A.Reeve	319.4	93	782	28	27.92	4-42	-	-
C.A.Walsh	583.1	98	1961	70	28.01	8-58	3	1
C.C.Lewis	411.2	80	1238	44	28.13	6-55	2	1
D.J.Capel	234	51	711	25	28.44	5-74	1	-
W.K.M.Benjamin	260.3	60	769	27	28.48	5-73	2	-
T.A.Merrick	146.2	31	376	13	28.92	4-66	-	-
N.F.Williams	469.1	88	1430	49	29.18	7-61	2	-
S.M.McEwan	310	61	970	32	30.31	3-31	-	-
J.E.Benjamin	322.3	51	1036	34	30.47	5-71	3	-
N.A.Mallender	538.2	114	1555	51	30.49	5-46	2	-
K.M.Curran	561.3	105	1839	60	30.65	5-63	1	-
S.Bastien	274.5	47	1075	35	30.71	6-75	2	-
N.G.Cowans	415	115	1127	36	31.30	5-67	1	-
R.A.Pick	443.5	70	1507	48	31.39	7-128	1	1
S.R.Lampitt	539.3	96	1794	57	31.47	5-34	2	-
D.E.Malcolm	277.4	44	947	30	31.56	4-63	-	-
P.J.Newport	563.2	104	1806	57	31.68	6-73	3	-
D.R.Pringle	325.3	81	927	29	31.96	5-66	1	-
I.T.Botham	174.4	34	546	17	32.11	4-65	-	-
G.A.Hick	208.5	41	645	20	32.25	5-37	1	-
N.G.B.Cook	507.1	159	1320	40	33.00	5-44	2	-
G.C.Small	321.4	78	900	27	33.33	6-94	2	-
M.Watkinson	503.2	120	1572	47	33.44	5-65	3	-
J.E.Emburey	902	254	1911	57	33.52	5-32	2	-
D.V.Lawrence	418.3	45	1679	50	33.58	5-51	2	-
G.R.Dilley	224.2	30	818	24	34.08	5-62	2	-
P.Carrick	601	170	1570	46	34.13	5-49	3	-
M.Frost	509.1	63	1919	56	34.26	5-40	2	1
S.D.Fletcher	268.5	58	936	27	34.66	5-94	1	-
A.H.Gray	212.4	43	556	16	34.75	4-83	-	-
T.D.Topley	178	25	557	16	34.81	4-67	-	-
B.P.Patterson	281.4	45	1015	29	35.00	4-52	-	-
A.A.Donald	355.1	81	988	28	35.28	3-28	-	-
G.D.Rose	530.4	93	1807	51	35.43	5-52	1	-
P.J.Bakker	371.2	86	1195	33	36.21	5-101	1	-
A.P.Igglesden	306	42	1093	30	36.43	4-79	-	-
A.D.Mullally	464.2	116	1351	37	36.51	4-59	-	-
P.J.Hartley	481.1	79	1754	48	36.54	6-57	2	-
P.C.R.Tufnell	948.5	254	2389	65	36.75	6-79	2	-
C.A.Connor	462.1	77	1623	44	36.88	5-96	1	-
P.A.J.DeFreitas	408.5	96	1219	33	36.93	6-39	1	-
J.P.Agnew	612	108	2196	59	37.22	5-54	5	-
P.J.Martin	240.3	46	750	20	37.50	4-68	-	-
A.C.S.Pigott	516.1	88	1916	51	37.56	5-52	3	-
R.G.Williams	417.3	116	1165	31	37.58	4-94	-	-
P.W.Jarvis	405.2	68	1393	37	37.64	4-53	-	-
P.M.Such	252.3	58	682	18	37.88	3-34	-	-
K.J.Barnett	267.1	42	720	19	37.89	3-49	-	-
M.C.Ilott	289.1	60	951	25	38.04	5-34	1	-
K.T.Medlycott	617.5	134	2020	53	38.11	7-92	3	-
D.P.Hughes	280.4	61	918	24	38.25	4-25	-	-
A.N.Jones	539.4	81	1990	52	38.26	6-75	2	-
A.R.K.Pierson	302.4	55	965	25	38.60	5-101	1	-
F.D.Stephenson	592.4	90	2047	53	38.62	6-84	2	-
E.E.Hemmings	443.3	127	1175	30	39.16	5-99	1	-
J.G.Thomas	288.2	49	1098	28	39.21	7-75	1	-
T.M.Tremlett	120.5	30	393	10	39.30	3-33	-	-
R.J.Maru	720.1	178	2087	53	39.37	6-97	1	-
A.I.C.Dodemaide	681.1	112	2206	56	39.39	6-106	1	-
D.A.Graveney	462.4	126	1145	29	39.48	5-45	3	1
Wasim Akram	191	43	594	15	39.60	3-76	-	-
P.S.De Villiers	304.5	58	992	25	39.68	6-70	1	-
S.P.Hughes	333	60	1121	28	40.03	5-101	1	-
S.J.Base	414.3	68	1402	35	40.05	6-105	2	-
K.P.Evans	292	60	1085	27	40.18	4-57	-	-
A.E.Warner	393.3	67	1330	33	40.30	3-56	-	-
A.L.Penberthy	196	23	768	19	40.42	4-91	-	-
P.J.W.Allott	266	77	730	18	40.55	4-23	-	-
R.P.Davis	839.1	202	2648	65	40.73	6-59	4	1
S.L.Watkin	731.1	118	2489	61	40.80	5-100	1	-
S.J.W.Andrew	449	67	1763	43	41.00	5-55	1	-
D.Gough	256.4	43	984	24	41.00	4-68	-	-
P.A.Booth	214.2	70	495	12	41.25	4-55	-	-
K.E.Cooper	667.4	141	2105	51	41.27	5-56	3	-
G.Miller	427.2	94	1285	31	41.45	6-45	1	-
K.J.Shine	129.4	17	501	12	41.75	4-52	-	-
M.M.Patel	297.5	72	836	20	41.80	6-57	2	1
R.P.Lefebvre	493.1	132	1258	30	41.93	5-30	1	-
C.S.Pickles	296.1	59	1107	25	44.28	3-56	-	-
B.T.P.Donelan	258.4	50	853	19	44.89	3-79	-	-
I.D.K.Salisbury	535.1	103	1796	40	44.90	5-32	2	-
J.R.Ayling	135.2	35	454	10	45.40	2-48	-	-
A.J.Murphy	404.2	76	1367	30	45.56	5-67	2	-
R.M.Ellison	260.5	45	869	19	45.73	4-76	-	-
S.D.Udal	191.3	35	746	16	46.62	4-144	-	-
M.A.Robinson	520.1	98	1794	38	47.21	3-47	-	-
J.A.Afford	627	186	1804	38	47.47	4-137	-	-
S.J.Dennis	283	53	957	20	47.85	5-76	1	-
R.D.B.Croft	357.1	76	1126	23	48.95	3-10	-	-
J.W.Lloyds	314.5	52	1175	24	48.95	4-11	-	-
P.Willey	377.4	101	1016	20	50.80	2-7	-	-
M.Jean-Jacques	261.2	33	983	19	51.73	6-60	1	-
R.A.Bunting	298	54	1113	21	53.00	2-36	-	-
I.D.Austin	208.1	64	536	10	53.60	3-42	-	-
R.J.Bailey	168.2	29	604	11	54.90	3-82	-	-
M.V.Fleming	360.5	81	994	18	55.22	3-65	-	-
A.N.Hayhurst	291.2	46	974	17	57.29	3-58	-	-
J.H.Childs	595.1	189	1435	25	57.40	4-56	-	-
N.M.Kendrick	273	50	987	17	58.05	4-110	-	-
J.D.Batty	195	29	722	12	60.16	4-76	-	-
M.E.Waugh	183	33	731	12	60.91	5-37	1	-
W.W.Davis	216.5	25	747	12	62.25	3-28	-	-
I.G.Swallow	642.1	150	2042	31	65.87	3-88	-	-
I.A.Greig	199.1	19	805	12	67.08	3-60	-	-
C.M.Wells	366	67	1195	17	70.29	3-48	-	-
N.V.Radford	245	38	999	14	71.35	4-55	-	-
N.G.Cowley	296.3	58	851	11	77.36	3-84	-	-
J.D.Fitton	428.4	86	1365	14	97.50	3-69	-	-

ALL FIRST-CLASS MATCHES

BATTING AVERAGES - Including fielding
Qualifying requirements : 6 completed innings

Name	Matches	Inns	NO	Runs	HS	Avge	100s	50s	Ct	St
G.A.Gooch	18	30	3	2746	333	101.70	12	8	15	-
G.A.Hick	21	35	9	2347	252*	90.26	8	14	26	-
T.M.Moody	9	15	2	1163	168	89.46	7	1	4	-
M.Azharuddin	9	11	1	770	179	77.00	3	3	3	-
D.M.Ward	24	34	7	2072	263	76.74	7	3	32	3
M.E.Waugh	22	33	6	2072	207*	76.74	8	8	18	-
S.J.Cook	24	41	7	2608	313*	76.70	9	11	11	-
B.R.Hardie	12	17	7	728	125	72.80	2	4	11	-
M.A.Atherton	20	31	4	1924	191	71.25	7	12	24	-
P.A.De Silva	6	12	4	563	221*	70.37	1	3	10	-
N.H.Fairbrother	22	32	7	1740	366	69.60	4	9	20	-
D.J.Bicknell	15	23	4	1317	186	69.31	5	6	2	-
M.A.Crawley	11	14	3	762	105*	69.27	2	5	9	-
D.L.Haynes	23	39	5	2346	255*	69.00	8	7	14	-
R.A.Smith	18	30	8	1454	181	66.09	6	7	11	-
R.J.Shastri	9	11	1	644	187	64.40	4	1	6	-
R.J.Bailey	23	39	8	1987	204*	64.09	7	9	16	-
A.J.Lamb	17	29	4	1596	235	63.84	6	5	9	-
S.R.Tendulkar	11	19	4	945	119*	63.00	2	6	5	-
I.V.A.Richards	18	28	5	1425	164*	61.95	7	3	8	-
N.R.Taylor	22	37	5	1979	204	61.84	7	10	9	-
C.L.Smith	22	38	7	1886	148	60.83	4	12	14	-
R.J.Harden	24	31	7	1460	104*	60.83	3	12	18	-
A.R.Butcher	23	41	5	2116	151*	58.77	6	15	8	-
C.J.Tavare	24	32	4	1638	219	58.50	3	12	16	-
S.V.Manjrekar	11	17	3	814	158*	58.14	2	6	6	-
A.N.Hayhurst	22	35	8	1559	170	57.74	4	8	9	-
D.B.Vengsarkar	10	14	4	576	83*	57.60	-	6	4	-
M.J.Greatbatch	11	16	3	744	168*	57.23	2	4	7	-
J.P.Stephenson	25	41	8	1887	202*	57.18	4	13	16	-
M.W.Gatting	23	37	7	1704	170*	56.80	4	9	20	-
T.S.Curtis	22	39	8	1731	197*	55.83	4	7	13	-
G.D.Rose	24	29	11	1000	97*	55.55	-	8	14	-
H.Morris	25	46	5	2276	160*	55.51	10	10	14	-
I.A.Greig	24	29	6	1259	291	54.73	2	5	16	-
D.A.Reeve	25	38	12	1412	202*	54.30	3	5	26	-
B.C.Broad	22	43	2	2226	227*	54.29	9	3	7	-
J.E.Morris	21	33	6	1459	157*	54.03	6	6	12	-
K.R.Brown	24	36	8	1505	200*	53.75	5	8	30	-
M.D.Crowe	9	13	3	537	123*	53.70	1	5	5	-
G.D.Mendis	21	35	6	1551	180	53.48	4	8	15	-
A.H.Jones	10	16	3	692	121*	53.23	1	5	5	-
C.W.J.Athey	23	35	7	1474	131	52.64	3	9	18	-
R.I.Alikhan	11	16	2	726	138	51.85	2	4	3	-
W.M.van der Merwe	8	9	3	310	84	51.66	-	3	6	-
A.A.Metcalfe	23	44	4	2047	194*	51.17	6	7	10	-
K.M.Curran	23	33	8	1267	144*	50.68	3	5	15	-
J.G.Wright	9	15	2	653	121	50.23	1	5	2	-
K.J.Barnett	24	39	6	1648	141	49.93	5	9	14	-
N.E.Briers	24	44	4	1996	176	49.90	5	11	7	-
H.P.Tillekaratne	5	9	2	349	109*	49.85	2	-	7	2
R.S.Mahanama	6	10	0	494	114	49.40	2	2	10	-
P.M.Roebuck	18	28	5	1134	201*	49.30	2	6	6	-
S.T.Jayasuriya	6	9	2	345	105*	49.28	1	2	5	-
M.R.Benson	16	25	1	1171	159	48.79	5	5	5	-
A.J.Moles	24	46	8	1854	224*	48.78	4	10	12	-
P.J.Prichard	22	32	3	1407	245	48.51	5	4	9	-
M.R.Ramprakash	24	42	10	1541	146*	48.15	5	6	6	-
M.D.Moxon	22	40	6	1633	218*	48.02	3	7	14	-
W.V.Raman	8	15	2	623	127	47.92	1	7	6	-
G.R.Cowdrey	22	39	6	1576	135	47.75	3	8	9	-
T.C.Middleton	18	29	3	1238	127	47.61	5	5	9	-
D.J.Capel	18	29	6	1092	123	47.47	3	7	16	-
K.R.Rutherford	8	13	5	376	68*	47.00	-	1	7	-
P.W.G.Parker	15	25	4	985	107	46.90	2	6	8	-
D.I.Gower	20	32	5	1263	157*	46.77	3	3	17	-
G.S.Clinton	20	32	4	1292	146	46.14	1	8	6	-
K.P.Evans	15	25	9	738	100*	46.12	1	4	13	-
J.R.Ayling	9	11	3	368	62*	46.00	-	3	2	-
M.D.Marshall	18	24	3	962	117	45.81	2	6	7	-
T.J.Franklin	11	17	1	731	103	45.68	2	5	3	-
N.S.Sidhu	9	17	3	639	142	45.64	2	4	1	-
G.J.Lord	13	24	2	1003	190	45.59	3	5	4	-
N.Shahid	19	29	7	1003	125	45.59	1	6	22	-
M.A.Lynch	24	32	5	1227	104	45.44	1	9	30	-
N.J.Speak	6	9	0	409	138	45.44	1	3	3	-
J.J.Whitaker	24	45	6	1767	124*	45.30	4	8	14	-
R.E.Morris	9	12	1	498	96	45.27	-	6	1	-
J.J.Crowe	8	15	4	493	132	44.81	1	2	6	-
R.D.B.Croft	16	26	11	672	91*	44.80	-	4	2	-
S.J.Rhodes	22	25	10	672	96	44.80	-	5	61	8
P.A.Neale	21	32	10	976	122	44.36	2	3	12	-
P.Bainbridge	20	28	3	1107	152	44.28	2	5	4	-
G.D.Lloyd	14	20	2	796	96	44.22	-	8	4	-
A.Fordham	24	42	2	1767	206*	44.17	4	9	22	-
M.P.Maynard	23	41	7	1501	125*	44.14	2	11	15	-
M.J.Kilborn	6	8	1	309	95	44.14	-	2	5	-
P.E.Robinson	23	39	7	1402	150*	43.81	1	12	20	-
R.T.Robinson	23	45	5	1747	220*	43.67	4	8	12	-
T.E.Jesty	17	24	6	785	98	43.61	-	7	6	-
A.P.Wells	24	44	7	1611	144*	43.54	4	7	12	-
M.W.Priest	9	11	3	345	72	43.12	-	3	6	-
A.J.Stewart	17	29	6	984	100*	42.78	1	9	24	-
G.C.Holmes	10	15	4	465	125*	42.27	1	2	2	-
W.K.Hegg	21	22	6	674	100*	42.12	1	3	49	2
P.D.Bowler	22	39	5	1428	210	42.00	3	7	17	-
V.P.Terry	22	35	3	1332	165	41.62	5	4	24	-
N.J.Lenham	22	41	1	1663	123	41.57	4	9	6	-
N.A.Felton	22	39	2	1538	122	41.56	4	9	19	-
A.M.Brown	8	12	2	413	139*	41.30	1	1	7	-
N.G.Cowley	14	17	4	536	76	41.23	-	6	9	-
I.Smith	7	10	2	328	112*	41.00	1	2	1	-
T.J.G.O'Gorman	7	12	1	448	100	40.72	1	4	4	-
C.S.Cowdrey	13	24	6	733	107*	40.72	3	2	9	-
M.W.Alleyne	13	21	0	854	256	40.66	2	3	11	-
M.P.Speight	23	41	7	1375	131	40.44	2	11	14	-
M.A.Roseberry	24	44	4	1593	135	39.82	3	11	23	-
K.Sharp	9	13	5	318	53*	39.75	-	1	1	-
N.D.Burns	24	34	10	951	166	39.62	1	5	42	1
R.M.Ellison	15	19	7	473	81	39.41	-	3	6	-
G.Miller	14	14	8	233	47*	38.83	-	-	7	-
P.A.J.DeFreitas	18	20	3	660	102	38.82	2	2	7	-
M.P.Bicknell	21	16	8	310	50*	38.75	-	1	8	-
C.Hathurasinghe	5	10	0	385	136	38.50	1	1	1	-
N.R.Mongia	8	11	4	269	63*	38.42	-	2	9	3
D.B.D'Oliveira	23	35	2	1263	155	38.27	2	7	33	-
J.W.Lloyds	24	34	12	839	93	38.13	-	4	16	-
P.Johnson	23	43	3	1518	165*	37.95	3	9	14	-
R.C.Russell	17	23	2	794	120	37.81	2	3	45	1
Kapil Dev	9	12	2	377	110	37.70	1	2	3	-
M.V.Fleming	19	32	6	980	102	37.69	1	5	6	-
N.Hussain	16	23	3	752	197	37.60	1	2	16	-
T.J.Boon	24	45	4	1539	138	37.53	2	11	13	-
S.G.Hinks	24	43	0	1588	234	36.93	4	6	8	-
G.D.Hodgson	24	40	4	1320	126	36.66	2	10	12	-
D.W.Randall	15	28	1	987	178	36.55	2	5	14	-
M.Watkinson	19	23	2	754	138	35.90	1	4	8	-
M.C.J.Nicholas	23	35	10	895	104	35.80	1	5	9	-
B.Roberts	24	38	7	1108	124*	35.74	2	4	23	-
P.J.Newport	21	18	6	424	98	35.33	-	3	6	-
I.T.Botham	13	18	1	595	113	35.00	1	4	7	-
G.W.Humpage	13	22	4	628	74	34.88	-	5	30	-
J.D.R.Benson	18	27	6	725	106	34.52	1	3	12	-
S.P.James	16	31	2	1000	131*	34.48	4	5	11	-
I.P.Butcher	12	19	4	513	102	34.20	1	2	4	-
C.S.Pickles	16	22	8	478	57*	34.14	-	3	6	-
D.R.Pringle	17	15	2	443	84	34.07	-	3	9	-
M.Newell	15	27	2	851	112	34.04	1	6	4	-
R.J.Hadlee	5	6	0	204	90	34.00	-	2	4	-
P.Willey	22	40	6	1150	177	33.82	2	5	10	-
S.A.Marsh	24	35	8	911	114*	33.74	1	5	49	5
W.K.M.Benjamin	12	15	2	437	101*	33.61	1	4	3	-
P.A.Cottey	20	35	5	1001	156	33.36	3	4	12	-
A.I.C.Dodemaide	24	38	8	1001	112	33.36	2	4	9	-
C.M.Wells	20	33	5	933	113*	33.32	2	4	5	-
R.K.Illingworth	23	22	6	532	117	33.25	1	3	7	-
C.C.Lewis	17	26	5	697	189*	33.19	1	2	15	-

ALL FIRST-CLASS MATCHES

Name	Matches	Inns	NO	Runs	HS	Avge	100s	50s	Ct	St
J.J.E.Hardy	9	16	5	361	91	32.81	-	1	6	-
P.W.Romaines	7	11	2	295	95	32.77	-	2	2	-
K.S.More	9	11	2	295	95	32.77	-	2	17	1
L.Potter	23	38	5	1080	109*	32.72	1	7	23	-
J.W.Hall	20	37	2	1140	125	32.57	2	5	6	-
P.A.Smith	12	20	4	520	117	32.50	1	3	1	-
G.Fowler	21	35	6	938	126	32.34	2	2	15	-
T.R.Ward	15	28	1	863	175	31.96	2	5	14	-
A.L.Penberthy	12	17	3	435	101*	31.07	1	3	8	-
C.J.Adams	23	34	4	932	111*	31.06	2	5	25	-
S.A.Kellett	16	28	3	774	75*	30.96	-	6	8	-
P.N.Hepworth	4	8	2	185	55*	30.83	-	1	1	-
N.M.K.Smith	10	14	2	370	83*	30.83	-	1	4	-
I.D.Austin	13	15	6	276	58	30.66	-	1	-	-
P.D.Lunn	8	10	4	184	44*	30.66	-	-	1	-
M.Saxelby	8	15	4	335	73	30.45	-	2	3	-
R.J.Blakey	25	43	9	1033	111	30.38	1	6	45	9
B.T.P.Donelan	11	13	6	211	53	30.14	-	1	4	-
D.J.R.Martindale	17	28	3	751	138	30.04	2	2	5	-
D.P.Ostler	11	19	2	510	71	30.00	-	5	9	-
D.L.Bairstow	6	6	0	179	61	29.83	-	1	13	-
D.Ripley	21	28	6	656	109*	29.81	1	2	28	6
M.A.Garnham	24	28	7	615	84*	29.28	-	2	49	2
M.A.Feltham	15	16	3	379	101	29.15	1	2	11	-
R.J.Maru	25	20	2	520	59	28.88	-	3	30	-
P.Bent	7	12	0	346	79	28.83	-	2	-	-
F.D.Stephenson	20	35	7	807	121	28.82	1	4	5	-
D.S.B.P.Kuruppu	5	10	1	259	56*	28.77	-	2	7	1
D.Byas	19	29	4	704	83	28.16	-	5	21	-
J.E.Emburey	23	32	7	702	111*	28.08	1	2	33	-
W.Larkins	15	25	0	701	207	28.04	2	3	8	-
J.D.Ratcliffe	16	31	3	780	81*	27.85	-	3	7	-
Asif Din	22	39	4	974	100*	27.82	1	5	10	-
I.R.Bishop	13	16	4	333	103*	27.75	1	-	2	-
G.P.Thorpe	18	28	6	608	86	27.63	-	3	9	-
P.A.Nixon	19	23	8	411	46	27.40	-	-	49	1
C.A.Walsh	20	20	3	464	63*	27.29	-	3	6	-
R.G.Williams	17	26	5	566	96	26.95	-	4	6	-
M.Prabhakar	10	14	3	296	76	26.90	-	2	4	-
J.E.Benjamin	15	14	7	188	41	26.85	-	-	4	-
R.G.Twose	6	10	1	241	64*	26.77	-	3	3	-
P.R.Downton	16	24	2	587	63	26.68	-	4	42	3
N.A.Foster	22	22	2	530	101	26.50	1	2	13	-
G.Cook	9	12	1	287	87	26.09	-	1	2	-
A.J.Wright	23	38	3	911	112	26.02	1	5	23	-
P.Carrick	18	22	2	515	64	25.75	-	3	7	-
D.A.Leatherdale	4	6	0	154	70	25.66	-	2	2	-
K.T.Medlycott	23	25	9	410	44	25.62	-	-	14	-
N.A.Mallender	20	10	3	177	87*	25.28	-	1	3	-
D.M.Smith	9	16	2	353	71	25.21	-	2	2	-
T.A.Lloyd	15	27	1	646	101	24.84	1	4	7	-
G.J.Turner	9	12	0	298	59	24.83	-	2	5	-
C.A.Connor	22	10	4	148	46	24.66	-	-	10	-
A.I.Kallicharran	7	10	1	221	72	24.55	-	2	5	-
I.D.K.Salisbury	20	23	10	313	68	24.07	-	1	13	-
A.P.Kuiper	12	17	0	407	68	23.94	-	2	10	-
D.P.Hughes	18	17	7	237	57	23.70	-	1	13	-
I.J.Gould	8	12	2	235	73	23.50	-	2	8	-
V.J.Wells	8	15	0	352	58	23.46	-	2	8	-
S.M.McEwan	15	12	5	164	54	23.42	-	1	5	-
K.J.Piper	16	21	1	461	111	23.05	1	1	40	4
M.J.Lowrey	10	18	2	363	72	22.68	-	2	1	-
E.E.Hemmings	17	20	5	333	83	22.20	-	2	2	-
R.Heap	10	19	2	376	63	22.11	-	2	3	-
P.S.De Villiers	12	15	3	264	37	22.00	-	-	6	-
P.C.R.Tufnell	23	22	9	283	37	21.76	-	-	8	-
P.Moores	25	36	4	694	106*	21.68	1	2	53	10
N.F.Williams	21	24	3	448	51	21.33	-	2	4	-
P.Pollard	7	13	0	277	72	21.30	-	1	5	-
P.Farbrace	8	8	2	124	79	20.66	-	1	17	2
M.J.Cann	6	10	0	206	64	20.60	-	2	2	-
R.A.Pick	17	16	6	204	35	20.40	-	-	6	-
B.N.French	22	34	9	506	105*	20.24	1	-	46	11
D.H.Shufflebotham	8	9	3	121	29	20.16	-	-	1	-
G.F.Labrooy	4	6	0	121	69	20.16	-	1	1	-
J.C.M.Atkinson	11	21	2	374	72	19.68	-	2	7	-
R.J.Parks	20	21	10	216	36*	19.63	-	-	49	4
S.J.Base	13	13	2	215	58	19.54	-	2	4	-
A.R.C.Fraser	15	13	2	214	92	19.45	-	1	3	-
R.J.Turner	9	16	0	302	38	18.87	-	-	8	4
A.C.S.Pigott	21	29	5	451	64*	18.79	-	4	10	-
S.R.Lampitt	23	24	5	356	45*	18.73	-	-	11	-
I.G.Swallow	23	17	7	187	32	18.70	-	-	12	-
K.M.Krikken	22	29	2	488	77*	18.07	-	2	60	3
R.J.Scott	6	10	2	144	71	18.00	-	1	4	-
G.B.A.Dyer	4	8	2	107	23	17.83	-	-	-	-
P.W.Jarvis	15	16	4	212	43*	17.66	-	-	2	-
J.D.Robinson	8	10	0	175	72	17.50	-	1	1	-
R.P.Davis	24	32	3	504	59	17.37	-	2	27	-
G.J.F.Ferris	6	6	0	104	35	17.33	-	-	1	-
P.A.Booth	10	16	2	240	60	17.14	-	2	3	-
N.V.Radford	12	8	1	118	43*	16.85	-	-	6	-
W.W.Davis	9	7	1	101	47	16.83	-	-	2	-
S.C.Goldsmith	12	17	1	267	51	16.68	-	1	9	-
J.D.Fitton	15	13	5	133	25*	16.62	-	-	3	-
R.P.Lefebvre	17	16	3	214	53	16.46	-	1	8	-
G.C.Small	15	22	4	296	55	16.44	-	1	4	-
A.Dale	9	14	0	229	92	16.35	-	1	6	-
C.P.Metson	23	27	5	352	50*	16.00	-	1	59	-
H.A.Anthony	6	8	0	127	39	15.87	-	-	-	-
C.E.L.Ambrose	18	18	5	203	55*	15.61	-	1	1	-
P.J.Hartley	17	15	1	218	75	15.57	-	1	8	-
N.M.Kendrick	13	12	4	124	52*	15.50	-	1	14	-
M.C.Ilott	9	10	2	123	42*	15.37	-	-	1	-
J.G.Thomas	12	13	3	152	48	15.20	-	-	9	-
M.M.Patel	9	12	5	104	41*	14.85	-	-	2	-
M.J.Morris	10	17	3	206	45	14.71	-	-	4	-
D.A.Hagan	9	12	0	175	47	14.58	-	-	2	-
C.White	10	11	2	127	38	14.11	-	-	4	-
M.Jean-Jacques	12	13	5	107	25	13.37	-	-	2	-
S.J.W.Andrew	18	16	7	119	35	13.22	-	-	1	-
A.P.Igglesden	14	17	9	105	24	13.12	-	-	5	-
N.G.B.Cook	19	19	8	143	30	13.00	-	-	10	-
N.G.Cowans	18	17	7	127	46*	12.70	-	-	3	-
D.J.M.Kelleher	5	8	0	101	44	12.62	-	-	2	-
Wasim Akram	8	11	0	135	32	12.27	-	-	-	-
J.P.Agnew	22	26	5	257	46*	12.23	-	-	5	-
D.A.Graveney	13	13	4	107	46*	11.88	-	-	7	-
K.E.Cooper	21	26	6	227	35*	11.35	-	-	9	-
P.S.Gerrans	9	9	0	102	39	11.33	-	-	4	-
G.J.Parsons	10	13	3	112	20	11.20	-	-	4	-
J.H.Childs	23	16	5	123	26	11.18	-	-	7	-
D.Gough	14	17	6	123	24	11.18	-	-	1	-
T.A.Merrick	7	8	2	66	35	11.00	-	-	1	-
S.L.Watkin	24	25	8	187	25*	11.00	-	-	6	-
R.A.Bunting	15	13	5	85	24*	10.62	-	-	1	-
M.J.Weston	6	10	1	90	38*	10.00	-	-	1	-
D.E.Malcolm	16	13	5	76	20*	9.50	-	-	4	-
A.D.Mullally	19	18	6	113	29	9.41	-	-	4	-
A.E.Warner	14	19	2	160	59	9.41	-	1	2	-
A.A.Donald	16	22	6	148	25*	9.25	-	-	2	-
S.P.Hughes	17	18	5	111	23*	8.53	-	-	3	-
T.A.Munton	25	24	9	125	29*	8.33	-	-	9	-
R.H.J.Jenkins	9	12	5	58	19*	8.28	-	-	1	-
R.A.Pyman	10	14	2	98	23*	8.16	-	-	2	-
S.Bastien	12	9	3	47	12	7.83	-	-	2	-
D.V.Lawrence	23	24	3	163	35	7.76	-	-	7	-
K.Saxelby	5	6	0	42	20	7.00	-	-	3	-
A.J.Buzza	10	12	3	49	21	5.44	-	-	3	-
M.Frost	20	18	8	42	12	4.20	-	-	2	-
S.D.Fletcher	11	13	3	39	19	3.90	-	-	3	-
S.N.Barnes	10	9	2	23	12*	3.28	-	-	3	-
S.J.Dennis	14	8	1	23	6	3.28	-	-	3	-
J.A.Afford	22	22	7	16	5	1.06	-	-	7	-
J.Hughes	4	7	0	4	2	0.57	-	-	-	-
M.A.Robinson	19	16	10	3	1*	0.50	-	-	5	-

ALL FIRST-CLASS MATCHES

BOWLING AVERAGES

Qualifying requirements : 10 wickets taken

Name	Overs	Mdns	Runs	Wkts	Avge	Best	5wI	10wM
I.R.Bishop	407.3	92	1124	59	19.05	6-71	3	-
M.D.Marshall	554.2	141	1381	72	19.18	7-47	4	2
D.J.Millns	206.4	36	662	31	21.35	6-63	2	-
V.J.Wells	85	19	257	12	21.41	5-43	1	-
O.H.Mortensen	316.2	91	785	35	22.42	4-22	-	-
C.E.L.Ambrose	503.4	127	1413	61	23.16	7-89	5	1
Waqar Younis	422	70	1357	57	23.80	7-73	3	1
R.J.Hadlee	201.5	39	586	24	24.41	5-27	2	-
M.W.Alleyne	112	29	391	16	24.43	3-23	-	-
P.A.Smith	148.5	34	497	20	24.85	5-48	1	-
N.A.Foster	819.2	175	2502	94	26.61	6-32	6	1
M.W.R.Madurasinghe	176.2	28	560	21	26.66	5-108	1	-
A.R.C.Fraser	596	144	1533	57	26.89	6-30	4	-
M.P.Bicknell	671.1	157	1827	67	27.26	5-34	1	-
G.F.Labrooy	111	13	440	16	27.50	5-97	1	-
G.J.Parsons	304.5	77	963	35	27.51	6-75	2	-
M.C.Snedden	231.5	56	633	23	27.52	5-63	1	-
J.E.Benjamin	388.3	68	1205	43	28.02	5-29	4	-
C.A.Walsh	611.1	107	2022	72	28.08	8-58	3	1
R.K.Illingworth	875.5	280	2122	75	28.29	5-59	1	-
D.J.Capel	234	51	711	25	28.44	5-74	1	-
D.A.Reeve	377.4	110	940	33	28.48	4-42	-	-
T.A.Merrick	184.3	45	488	17	28.70	4-66	-	-
M.A.Feltham	349.4	61	1150	40	28.75	6-53	2	-
T.A.Munton	827.1	199	2254	78	28.89	5-33	2	-
K.J.Barnett	293.3	54	757	26	29.11	4-28	-	-
D.R.Pringle	358.3	90	994	34	29.23	5-66	1	-
I.T.Botham	194.4	38	614	21	29.23	4-65	-	-
N.F.Williams	529.1	98	1618	54	29.96	7-61	2	-
C.C.Lewis	536.2	102	1697	56	30.30	6-55	2	1
S.Bastien	317.1	57	1187	39	30.43	6-75	2	-
K.M.Curran	598.3	111	1961	64	30.64	5-63	1	-
W.K.M.Benjamin	284.3	63	858	28	30.64	5-73	2	-
M.A.Atherton	433.3	103	1398	45	31.06	6-78	3	-
N.A.Mallender	554.2	116	1585	51	31.07	5-46	2	-
S.M.McEwan	375.2	75	1189	38	31.28	3-31	-	-
P.J.Newport	626.2	116	2001	63	31.76	6-54	4	-
N.G.Cowans	460	124	1247	39	31.97	5-67	1	-
J.E.Emburey	942.3	275	1957	61	32.08	5-32	2	-
G.A.Hick	208.5	41	645	20	32.25	5-37	1	-
T.D.Topley	223	33	713	22	32.40	4-67	-	-
D.E.Malcolm	518.2	99	1688	52	32.46	5-46	2	-
R.A.Pick	494.5	83	1657	51	32.49	7-128	1	1
S.R.Lampitt	565.3	98	1889	58	32.56	5-34	2	-
A.P.Kuiper	125.3	29	393	12	32.75	4-69	-	-
J.G.Bracewell	383.3	102	1120	34	32.94	7-120	2	1
M.C.Ilott	322.1	65	1036	31	33.41	5-34	2	-
M.Watkinson	508.2	122	1578	47	33.57	5-65	3	-
G.R.Dilley	224.2	30	818	24	34.08	5-62	1	-
N.G.B.Cook	527.1	167	1364	40	34.10	5-44	2	-
D.V.Lawrence	497.3	53	1979	58	34.12	5-51	2	-
P.Carrick	601	170	1570	46	34.13	5-49	3	-
P.J.Hartley	491	80	1781	52	34.25	6-57	2	-
M.Frost	557.1	74	2047	59	34.69	5-40	2	1
B.P.Patterson	281.4	45	1015	29	35.00	4-52	-	-
A.H.Gray	239.5	43	666	19	35.05	4-83	-	-
J.P.Millmow	105	14	391	11	35.54	3-66	-	-
P.C.R.Tufnell	1036.5	281	2635	74	35.60	6-79	4	-
S.D.Fletcher	292.5	60	1035	29	35.69	5-94	1	-
P.M.Such	272.4	67	715	20	35.75	3-34	-	-
A.P.Igglesden	326	47	1150	32	35.93	4-79	-	-
A.L.Penberthy	207.4	29	791	22	35.95	4-91	-	-
P.A.J.DeFreitas	489.3	109	1440	40	36.00	6-39	2	-
E.E.Hemmings	688.2	197	1844	51	36.15	6-58	2	-
K.P.Evans	356	78	1232	34	36.23	4-50	-	-
P.Wijetunga	129.4	24	438	12	36.50	4-133	-	-
R.J.Maru	851.1	219	2420	66	36.66	6-97	2	-
A.N.Jones	572.4	92	2055	56	36.69	6-75	2	-
G.D.Rose	571.4	99	1951	53	36.81	5-52	1	-
A.C.S.Pigott	541	94	1997	54	36.98	5-52	3	-
D.Gough	279.4	49	1037	28	37.03	4-68	-	-
G.C.Small	425.4	105	1190	32	37.18	6-94	1	-
J.P.Agnew	612	108	2196	59	37.22	5-54	5	-
G.Miller	461	114	1308	35	37.37	6-45	1	-
M.A.Crawley	224.5	38	750	20	37.50	6-92	1	-
A.A.Donald	391	89	1089	29	37.55	3-28	-	-
S.N.Barnes	207	45	602	16	37.62	4-51	-	-
P.W.Jarvis	405.2	68	1393	37	37.64	4-53	-	-
A.D.Mullally	487.2	117	1446	38	38.05	4-59	-	-
C.A.Connor	510.1	88	1789	47	38.06	5-96	1	-
D.P.Hughes	280.4	61	918	24	38.25	4-25	-	-
D.A.Graveney	485.4	137	1189	31	38.35	5-45	3	1
A.R.K.Pierson	302.4	55	965	25	38.60	5-101	1	-
H.A.Anthony	142.4	32	466	12	38.83	3-95	-	-
R.G.Williams	432.3	119	1204	31	38.83	4-94	-	-
F.D.Stephenson	610.4	94	2098	54	38.85	6-84	2	-
P.J.Bakker	436.2	90	1439	37	38.89	5-101	1	-
R.P.Davis	908.1	221	2844	73	38.95	6-40	5	1
S.P.Hughes	386.2	73	1287	33	39.00	5-101	1	-
K.T.Medlycott	748.5	170	2382	61	39.04	7-92	3	-
T.M.Tremlett	120.5	30	393	10	39.30	3-33	-	-
S.L.Watkin	796.1	137	2712	69	39.30	5-100	1	-
K.J.Shine	156.4	30	552	14	39.42	4-52	-	-
P.J.Martin	275.3	52	868	22	39.45	4-68	-	-
P.S.De Villiers	304.5	58	992	25	39.68	6-70	1	-
Wasim Akram	204	44	640	16	40.00	3-76	-	-
S.J.Base	414.3	68	1402	35	40.05	6-105	2	-
G.J.F.Ferris	138.2	29	482	12	40.16	4-44	-	-
A.I.C.Dodemaide	763.1	130	2457	61	40.27	6-106	1	-
A.E.Warner	393.3	67	1330	33	40.30	3-56	-	-
J.G.Thomas	305.2	51	1171	29	40.37	7-75	1	-
P.J.W.Allott	266	77	730	18	40.55	4-23	-	-
K.E.Cooper	703.4	153	2203	54	40.79	5-56	3	-
S.D.Udal	238.3	46	900	22	40.90	4-139	-	-
S.J.W.Andrew	503	75	1897	46	41.23	5-55	1	-
N.D.Hirwani	399.2	59	1280	31	41.29	5-117	1	-
R.P.Lefebvre	506.1	137	1281	31	41.32	5-30	1	-
C.S.Pickles	325.1	72	1163	28	41.53	3-56	-	-
M.M.Patel	297.5	72	836	20	41.80	6-57	2	1
D.K.Morrison	234.4	36	889	21	42.33	4-64	-	-
C.P.Ramanayake	133	12	510	12	42.50	3-96	-	-
M.Jean-Jacques	300	42	1106	25	44.24	6-60	1	-
A.J.Murphy	404.2	76	1367	30	45.56	5-67	2	-
J.A.Afford	688	209	1944	42	46.28	4-137	-	-
C.White	159	23	608	13	46.76	5-74	1	-
P.Bainbridge	162.4	30	515	11	46.81	3-23	-	-
A.R.Kumble	212	40	660	14	47.14	6-49	1	-
A.J.Buzza	287	47	1086	23	47.21	4-87	-	-
M.A.Robinson	559.1	105	1889	40	47.22	3-47	-	-
P.Willey	421.4	119	1091	23	47.43	2-7	-	-
R.D.B.Croft	397.1	83	1335	28	47.67	3-10	-	-
N.M.Kendrick	348	66	1194	25	47.76	4-110	-	-
M.J.Lowrey	151.2	33	483	10	48.30	2-13	-	-
C.Pringle	144	32	483	10	48.30	2-49	-	-
S.J.Dennis	322	61	1071	22	48.68	5-76	1	-
M.V.Fleming	394.5	94	1072	22	48.72	3-65	-	-
P.A.Booth	250.5	75	636	13	48.92	4-55	-	-
A.Wasson	207.3	24	886	18	49.22	6-89	1	-
I.D.K.Salisbury	601.1	113	2075	42	49.40	5-32	2	-
B.T.P.Donelan	304.4	56	1000	20	50.00	3-79	-	-
R.A.Bunting	360	61	1314	26	50.53	2-36	-	-
R.M.Ellison	308.5	51	963	19	50.68	4-76	-	-
J.R.Ayling	181.2	46	572	11	52.00	2-48	-	-
R.J.Bailey	168.2	29	604	11	54.90	3-82	-	-
I.D.Austin	245	76	662	12	55.16	3-42	-	-
J.W.Lloyds	382.5	60	1429	25	57.16	4-11	-	-
Kapil Dev	246.4	59	744	13	57.23	2-28	-	-
C.Penn	186	35	636	11	57.81	3-45	-	-
P.S.Gerrans	208	40	695	12	57.91	3-86	-	-
J.H.Childs	655.5	211	1590	27	58.88	4-56	-	-
J.D.Batty	195	29	722	12	60.16	4-76	-	-
M.Prabhakar	281	47	994	16	62.12	4-74	-	-
W.W.Davis	237.5	27	812	13	62.46	3-28	-	-
R.A.Pyman	308.4	81	938	15	62.53	2-29	-	-
Asif Din	159.1	30	635	10	63.50	3-17	-	-
R.H.J.Jenkins	281.4	41	959	15	63.93	5-100	1	-
A.N.Hayhurst	321.2	50	1087	17	63.94	3-58	-	-

ALL FIRST-CLASS MATCHES

Name	Overs	Mdns	Runs	Wkts	Avge	Best	5wI	10wM
I.G.Swallow	689.1	161	2174	34	63.94	3-88	-	-
M.E.Waugh	191	33	771	12	64.25	5-37	1	-
M.W.Priest	312.4	90	907	14	64.78	3-35	-	-
I.A.Greig	216.1	21	858	13	66.00	3-60	-	-
N.V.Radford	302	49	1195	18	66.38	4-55	-	-
S.K.Sharma	227	36	873	13	67.15	2-53	-	-
C.M.Wells	374	68	1237	17	72.76	3-48	-	-
N.G.Cowley	316.3	64	900	12	75.00	3-84	-	-
G.J.Turner	212.2	39	819	10	81.90	3-100	-	-
J.D.Fitton	454.4	91	1447	14	103.35	3-69	-	-

REFUGE ASSURANCE LEAGUE AND CUP

BATTING AVERAGES - Including fielding
Qualifying requirements : 4 completed innings

Name	Matches	Inns	NO	Runs	HS	Avge	100s	50s	Ct	St
G.A.Hick	13	13	3	751	114*	75.10	1	5	4	-
S.J.Cook	16	16	2	902	136*	64.42	3	6	7	-
M.Newell	10	8	3	312	109*	62.40	1	2	4	-
T.S.Curtis	15	15	2	784	124	60.30	1	7	4	-
M.R.Ramprakash	18	17	5	638	147*	53.16	1	3	6	-
G.Fowler	16	16	1	793	108	52.86	2	8	7	-
R.A.Smith	10	10	0	517	122	51.70	1	4	5	-
M.A.Atherton	10	10	1	462	111	51.33	1	4	5	-
D.L.Haynes	18	17	2	753	107*	50.20	1	6	7	-
Asif Din	15	14	3	545	113	49.54	1	3	5	-
G.D.Lloyd	16	14	2	577	100*	48.08	1	5	6	-
N.R.Taylor	13	13	0	614	95	47.23	-	6	5	-
R.T.Robinson	17	17	4	610	116	46.92	2	4	7	-
R.J.Blakey	15	15	2	609	100*	46.84	1	4	12	2
K.J.Barnett	18	18	0	824	127	45.77	2	6	7	-
M.D.Moxon	10	10	0	455	105	45.50	1	2	3	-
R.J.Harden	16	16	7	397	53	44.11	-	1	6	-
G.P.Thorpe	15	15	3	514	85	42.83	-	4	2	-
C.W.J.Athey	16	15	2	546	113	42.00	2	3	5	-
A.I.Kallicharran	6	6	1	210	76	42.00	-	2	-	-
D.J.Capel	15	15	2	543	121	41.76	2	1	5	-
P.Johnson	17	17	1	668	114	41.75	3	2	4	-
K.Sharp	7	7	2	207	71	41.40	-	1	4	-
C.C.Lewis	11	11	3	331	93*	41.37	-	2	4	-
N.J.Lenham	12	12	1	444	78	40.36	-	5	5	-
N.Hussain	7	7	3	161	66*	40.25	-	1	7	-
M.A.Roseberry	18	18	1	678	86	39.88	-	8	6	-
D.W.Randall	8	8	3	198	54*	39.60	-	1	2	-
M.W.Gatting	16	14	3	435	124*	39.54	1	2	6	-
K.M.Curran	16	15	3	465	92	38.75	-	4	1	-
G.A.Gooch	10	10	0	386	136	38.60	1	3	3	-
A.J.Moles	7	6	0	229	81	38.16	-	2	1	-
D.R.Pringle	11	11	3	305	63	38.12	-	2	4	-
I.V.A.Richards	14	14	1	490	77	37.69	-	4	8	-
A.P.Wells	13	13	2	413	98	37.54	-	3	1	-
P.A.Cottey	6	5	1	150	50*	37.50	-	1	2	-
S.G.Hinks	15	15	0	562	89	37.46	-	7	1	-
V.P.Terry	15	14	1	482	113*	37.07	1	5	11	-
K.R.Brown	18	15	4	406	68	36.90	-	3	5	-
A.J.Stewart	8	7	0	258	125	36.85	1	1	4	-
A.P.Kuiper	18	18	4	516	74	36.85	-	4	9	-
M.P.Maynard	14	14	1	479	100	36.84	1	2	6	-
M.E.Waugh	15	15	0	552	111	36.80	1	3	5	-
N.H.Fairbrother	13	13	1	441	86*	36.75	-	3	5	-
B.C.Broad	17	17	1	586	106*	36.62	1	4	4	-
J.R.Ayling	15	10	6	144	47*	36.00	-	-	-	-
P.D.Bowler	16	16	1	539	59	35.93	-	6	23	1
A.I.C.Dodemaide	14	14	6	280	31*	35.00	-	-	6	-
G.S.Clinton	5	4	0	139	45	34.75	-	-	1	-
B.Roberts	18	14	4	345	77*	34.50	-	2	5	-
A.Fordham	15	15	1	481	74	34.35	-	5	2	-
T.J.Boon	16	16	0	545	97	34.06	-	5	5	-
D.I.Gower	13	12	2	340	66*	34.00	-	3	5	-
J.E.Morris	15	15	0	508	134	33.86	1	3	3	-
C.L.Smith	10	9	2	237	89	33.85	-	1	2	-
G.D.Mendis	7	7	1	202	71	33.66	-	1	4	-
G.D.Rose	16	15	2	430	148	33.07	1	-	6	-
D.M.Ward	15	15	3	394	102*	32.83	1	2	13	1
B.R.Hardie	13	13	1	392	76	32.66	-	4	4	-
J.J.Whitaker	14	14	1	422	83	32.46	-	3	6	-
R.J.Scott	13	12	0	386	76	32.16	-	5	3	-
R.J.Bailey	16	16	1	477	71	31.80	-	4	3	-
G.R.Cowdrey	14	14	3	347	70*	31.54	-	1	3	-
I.A.Greig	15	14	7	217	43	31.00	-	-	3	-
J.P.Stephenson	14	12	1	341	109	31.00	1	2	5	-
M.A.Lynch	15	14	2	399	58	30.69	-	1	4	-
A.J.Wright	16	15	1	429	68	30.64	-	4	13	-
W.Larkins	11	11	0	334	109	30.36	2	1	1	-
M.P.Speight	13	13	1	353	77	29.41	-	2	4	-
T.M.Moody	15	14	1	382	64	29.38	-	4	5	-
M.Watkinson	14	13	6	203	33*	29.00	-	-	4	-
P.Willey	10	10	1	259	68*	28.77	-	2	6	-
T.R.Ward	11	11	0	311	80	28.27	-	2	1	-
N.E.Briers	16	16	1	424	90*	28.26	-	1	6	-
M.C.J.Nicholas	14	13	4	254	59	28.22	-	1	8	-
C.J.Tavare	16	16	1	421	86	28.06	-	4	7	-
P.J.Prichard	14	13	1	331	64	27.58	-	2	4	-
A.J.Lamb	9	9	0	248	70	27.55	-	1	2	-
A.A.Metcalfe	15	15	0	403	84	26.86	-	4	9	-
M.Saxelby	11	9	2	188	34	26.85	-	-	5	-
M.A.Feltham	14	13	2	293	61	26.63	-	2	3	-
N.A.Felton	10	10	1	239	64	26.55	-	1	4	-
A.R.Butcher	15	15	2	345	52	26.53	-	2	6	-
I.Smith	9	9	2	185	46	26.42	-	-	2	-
R.J.Bartlett	8	8	0	211	55	26.37	-	3	3	-
S.C.Goldsmith	12	9	5	104	50	26.00	-	1	2	-
P.W.G.Parker	10	9	0	233	72	25.88	-	1	4	-
D.J.Bicknell	5	5	0	128	75	25.60	-	1	-	-
M.W.Alleyne	16	13	5	203	39*	25.37	-	-	5	-
P.Bainbridge	14	11	2	228	59*	25.33	-	1	3	-
S.A.Marsh	15	12	3	227	38	25.22	-	-	10	-
P.W.Romaines	16	12	3	227	47	25.22	-	-	4	-
G.W.Humpage	10	9	3	151	40*	25.16	-	-	5	-
Wasim Akram	13	8	1	175	50	25.00	-	1	1	-
P.R.Downton	13	7	2	124	34*	24.80	-	-	5	5
A.C.S.Pigott	12	10	2	195	37	24.37	-	-	7	-
P.M.Roebuck	8	8	1	195	85	24.37	-	1	1	-
C.J.Adams	18	16	6	243	58*	24.30	-	1	8	-
D.P.Ostler	7	6	2	97	30	24.25	-	-	3	-
K.T.Medlycott	13	7	3	96	44*	24.00	-	-	4	-
I.J.Gould	11	11	0	260	68	23.63	-	3	2	-
D.Byas	15	13	4	212	35*	23.55	-	-	4	-
M.D.Marshall	16	14	3	259	46	23.54	-	-	1	-
I.T.Botham	12	12	1	257	45	23.36	-	-	3	-
R.O.Butcher	11	7	2	116	44*	23.20	-	-	4	-
C.S.Cowdrey	15	14	2	277	46	23.08	-	-	7	-
J.D.R.Benson	16	15	5	230	67	23.00	-	1	4	-
M.A.Garnham	15	11	4	161	40*	23.00	-	-	11	1
D.A.Reeve	14	13	2	252	41	22.90	-	-	5	-
T.A.Lloyd	13	10	2	173	63	21.62	-	1	1	-
R.C.Russell	10	9	0	191	62	21.22	-	1	6	2
J.E.Emburey	18	11	5	126	32	21.00	-	-	3	-
H.Morris	15	15	0	311	68	20.73	-	1	4	-
P.A.J.DeFreitas	13	8	2	124	35*	20.66	-	-	1	-
T.E.Jesty	8	7	1	124	25	20.66	-	-	1	-
D.B.D'Oliveira	15	14	1	266	58	20.46	-	2	3	-
P.J.Hartley	12	10	3	143	51	20.42	-	1	3	-
R.G.Williams	8	8	3	99	35	19.80	-	-	2	-
P.E.Robinson	15	14	1	257	58*	19.76	-	1	5	-
P.A.Neale	13	11	1	197	40	19.70	-	-	5	-
S.J.Rhodes	15	9	3	117	35*	19.50	-	-	14	3
A.N.Hayhurst	14	11	1	192	70*	19.20	-	1	4	-
M.V.Fleming	14	13	4	172	29*	19.11	-	-	3	-
C.P.Metson	14	10	5	95	30*	19.00	-	-	10	2
M.J.Weston	12	10	1	171	90	19.00	-	1	2	-
A.Dale	9	7	1	113	42	18.83	-	-	3	-
G.D.Hodgson	9	8	2	113	28	18.83	-	-	5	-
F.D.Stephenson	17	13	2	207	42	18.81	-	-	3	-
N.D.Burns	16	12	1	202	58	18.36	-	1	13	1
A.E.Warner	15	7	3	72	28*	18.00	-	-	3	-
S.A.Kellett	4	4	0	70	32	17.50	-	-	1	-
J.W.Lloyds	12	10	3	122	38*	17.42	-	-	5	-
N.M.K.Smith	12	8	1	122	38*	17.42	-	-	4	-
R.P.Lefebvre	12	7	2	86	28	17.20	-	-	4	-
T.J.G.O'Gorman	7	7	2	85	32	17.00	-	-	-	-
R.M.Ellison	8	8	3	83	43	16.60	-	-	2	-
R.G.Twose	12	9	2	113	40	16.14	-	-	1	-
B.N.French	17	9	3	96	34*	16.00	-	-	12	3
C.M.Wells	14	14	0	220	64	15.71	-	1	2	-
S.R.Lampitt	14	9	4	78	25*	15.60	-	-	7	-
P.Carrick	13	9	2	106	30	15.14	-	-	4	-
N.A.Foster	13	11	4	106	39*	15.14	-	-	4	-
P.A.Smith	9	7	0	102	33	14.57	-	-	3	-
D.J.Wild	13	12	2	142	48*	14.20	-	-	1	-
B.Smith	4	4	0	55	29	13.75	-	-	3	-
L.Potter	13	12	2	128	33	12.80	-	-	4	-
C.A.Walsh	15	7	1	76	23	12.66	-	-	3	-

REFUGE ASSURANCE LEAGUE AND CUP

Name	Matches	Inns	NO	Runs	HS	Avge	100s	50s	Ct	St
W.W.Davis	11	9	1	97	24	12.12	-	-	2	-
R.J.Parks	15	6	1	56	23*	11.20	-	-	10	2
D.Ripley	12	9	3	67	26	11.16	-	-	5	1
P.W.Jarvis	11	5	1	42	28*	10.50	-	-	3	-
A.W.Lilley	6	5	1	41	10	10.25	-	-	-	-
K.J.Piper	8	5	1	40	30	10.00	-	-	3	4
J.D.Robinson	4	4	0	40	16	10.00	-	-	1	-
P.Moores	14	11	4	67	17*	9.57	-	-	14	4
P.J.Newport	14	8	2	57	16*	9.50	-	-	3	-
R.K.Illingworth	11	5	1	35	16*	8.75	-	-	6	-
D.A.Leatherdale	11	9	1	70	35	8.75	-	-	6	-
G.W.Mike	8	4	0	33	13	8.25	-	-	2	-
W.M.Noon	4	4	0	33	21	8.25	-	-	2	-
C.C.Remy	6	5	1	33	12*	8.25	-	-	2	-
P.A.Nixon	14	8	3	39	10	7.80	-	-	15	1
K.E.Cooper	17	6	1	37	21	7.40	-	-	2	-
N.G.Cowley	9	7	2	37	17	7.40	-	-	2	-
R.J.Maru	16	6	2	29	12*	7.25	-	-	6	-
J.G.Thomas	9	7	2	35	19*	7.00	-	-	1	-
P.Pollard	4	4	0	27	13	6.75	-	-	1	-
S.J.Dennis	15	6	1	30	14	6.00	-	-	2	-
P.S.De Villiers	4	4	0	21	10	5.25	-	-	-	-
T.D.Topley	13	8	2	22	10	3.66	-	-	3	-
C.S.Pickles	9	5	1	7	6	1.75	-	-	5	-
J.P.Agnew	12	5	0	8	5	1.60	-	-	-	-

BOWLING AVERAGES

Qualifying requirements : 5 wickets taken

Name	Overs	Mdns	Runs	Wkts	Avge	Best	5wI
Waqar Younis	82.2	1	396	31	12.77	5-26	1
T.M.Tremlett	45	2	167	12	13.91	3-22	-
P.W.Jarvis	80.5	4	317	19	16.68	5-18	1
M.P.Bicknell	76.2	3	316	18	17.55	4-14	-
D.V.Lawrence	45	1	223	12	18.58	5-18	1
J.E.Emburey	129.1	12	664	34	19.52	4-26	-
A.C.S.Pigott	95	3	509	25	20.36	4-42	-
E.E.Hemmings	81	3	377	18	20.94	5-33	1
T.A.Merrick	74.3	3	319	15	21.26	4-24	-
M.D.Moxon	24.5	0	128	6	21.33	3-29	-
P.Carrick	97	5	443	20	22.15	3-28	-
R.K.Illingworth	80	3	311	14	22.21	3-19	-
P.J.Hartley	83.5	4	405	18	22.50	5-38	1
C.A.Walsh	103.5	6	410	18	22.77	3-28	-
D.Byas	36	0	183	8	22.87	3-26	-
D.R.Pringle	78	4	438	19	23.05	4-27	-
I.T.Botham	67	1	346	15	23.06	4-25	-
Wasim Akram	88.1	0	447	19	23.52	4-19	-
F.D.Stephenson	123	11	577	24	24.04	4-28	-
P.J.Newport	102	8	385	16	24.06	3-19	-
C.C.Lewis	76.3	2	362	15	24.13	4-34	-
D.J.Wild	44.4	0	243	10	24.30	3-8	-
N.A.Foster	96.3	3	467	19	24.57	4-21	-
R.P.Davis	84	1	395	16	24.68	4-25	-
A.I.C.Dodemaide	109	7	484	19	25.47	4-40	-
C.S.Cowdrey	52	0	306	12	25.50	4-57	-
M.Watkinson	99	0	562	22	25.54	5-46	1
S.R.Lampitt	89	3	491	19	25.84	5-67	1
J.D.R.Benson	24	1	158	6	26.33	2-33	-
T.A.Munton	111.5	13	424	16	26.50	5-23	1
A.R.C.Fraser	71	7	292	11	26.54	4-28	-
P.A.J.DeFreitas	102.3	2	531	20	26.55	4-22	-
N.J.Lenham	33	0	219	8	27.37	2-54	-
S.J.Base	104	3	549	20	27.45	4-28	-
D.E.Malcolm	92	2	467	17	27.47	4-21	-
S.L.Watkin	88.3	5	470	17	27.64	5-23	1
P.J.Bakker	65	6	363	13	27.92	3-31	-
R.J.Scott	30.4	0	171	6	28.50	2-8	-
K.T.Medlycott	93	1	485	17	28.52	3-20	-
G.W.Mike	55	1	347	12	28.91	3-30	-
M.W.Alleyne	107.5	2	589	20	29.45	3-25	-
M.V.Fleming	104	2	502	17	29.52	3-30	-
A.P.Kuiper	93.4	1	598	20	29.90	3-50	-
J.R.Ayling	91	3	450	15	30.00	4-37	-
A.Dale	43	0	241	8	30.12	3-35	-

Name	Overs	Mdns	Runs	Wkts	Avge	Best	5wI
S.N.Barnes	41	1	211	7	30.14	3-39	-
A.N.Hayhurst	86	1	453	15	30.20	4-37	-
N.F.Williams	112	4	574	19	30.21	4-49	-
A.J.Murphy	59	1	303	10	30.30	2-15	-
J.E.Benjamin	79	4	334	11	30.36	2-29	-
C.A.Connor	86.1	5	426	14	30.42	4-11	-
R.G.Twose	45.4	3	245	8	30.62	2-11	-
I.V.A.Richards	69.5	1	431	14	30.78	3-37	-
D.J.Millns	29	2	187	6	31.16	2-47	-
J.G.Thomas	59	3	313	10	31.30	3-21	-
A.R.Clarke	59.3	0	315	10	31.50	2-23	-
M.Frost	92.4	3	505	16	31.56	4-30	-
A.N.Jones	50	1	254	8	31.75	2-25	-
N.G.Cowley	54	3	286	9	31.77	2-17	-
P.A.Smith	29	1	162	5	32.40	3-34	-
M.D.Marshall	104	5	458	14	32.71	2-33	-
S.P.Hughes	67.5	3	393	12	32.75	4-19	-
R.J.Maru	70.5	0	394	12	32.83	3-38	-
A.Sidebottom	69	7	230	7	32.85	2-18	-
I.D.K.Salisbury	52	2	296	9	32.88	3-36	-
W.K.M.Benjamin	57	5	264	8	33.00	3-36	-
C.White	24.1	0	165	5	33.00	2-49	-
N.A.Mallender	100.5	4	436	13	33.53	4-32	-
S.M.McEwan	75.4	0	437	13	33.61	3-38	-
A.E.Warner	101	0	538	16	33.62	3-18	-
J.P.Agnew	88.1	10	370	11	33.63	2-35	-
P.Willey	58	0	303	9	33.66	2-12	-
M.C.Ilott	70	3	304	9	33.77	2-24	-
G.D.Rose	113.3	1	610	18	33.88	3-33	-
D.A.Reeve	83.1	5	412	12	34.33	4-36	-
N.G.Cowans	87	6	456	13	35.07	3-43	-
J.C.Hallett	45.3	2	246	7	35.14	3-41	-
M.E.Waugh	52	1	317	9	35.22	3-37	-
A.D.Mullally	97.1	3	431	12	35.91	2-20	-
M.Jean-Jacques	30	0	180	5	36.00	3-47	-
N.M.K.Smith	67.3	3	399	11	36.27	3-36	-
S.R.Barwick	32.1	3	182	5	36.40	2-30	-
O.H.Mortensen	118	9	364	10	36.40	3-16	-
M.A.Feltham	76	2	369	10	36.90	2-23	-
K.M.Curran	113	2	518	14	37.00	3-45	-
G.A.Hick	33.5	1	222	6	37.00	3-47	-
P.Bainbridge	74.1	0	410	11	37.27	2-7	-
T.D.Topley	93.5	2	488	13	37.53	2-22	-
M.I.Gidley	31.1	0	188	5	37.60	3-45	-
S.D.Fletcher	78.1	2	416	11	37.81	4-63	-
M.A.Atherton	29	0	190	5	38.00	3-33	-
I.D.Austin	108.1	2	622	16	38.87	3-33	-
A.P.Igglesden	52.5	2	236	6	39.33	4-24	-
R.M.Ellison	52	0	239	6	39.83	2-45	-
A.R.Hansford	36	1	240	6	40.00	2-48	-
L.B.Taylor	46	2	244	6	40.66	3-34	-
C.Penn	39.3	2	208	5	41.60	2-30	-
K.Saxelby	53.5	0	378	9	42.00	2-44	-
P.J.W.Allott	105	5	466	11	42.36	3-28	-
R.P.Lefebvre	82.5	0	468	11	42.54	4-35	-
K.P.Evans	87.4	1	514	12	42.83	4-30	-
M.Saxelby	40	0	259	6	43.16	2-48	-
J.A.Afford	55	2	305	7	43.57	2-39	-
C.S.Pickles	57	0	305	7	43.57	4-36	-
N.G.B.Cook	93	4	533	12	44.41	3-36	-
S.J.Brown	39	0	226	5	45.20	3-26	-
M.J.Weston	62	0	279	6	46.50	2-33	-
M.A.Robinson	88.3	7	528	11	48.00	2-23	-
M.W.Gatting	53	1	304	6	50.66	2-29	-
T.M.Moody	55.3	2	315	6	52.50	2-42	-
D.J.Capel	72.5	3	383	7	54.71	2-34	-
C.M.Wells	106.5	6	384	7	54.85	2-28	-
K.E.Cooper	126	8	571	10	57.10	2-21	-
G.C.Small	62.3	3	290	5	58.00	3-20	-
I.G.Swallow	69	2	365	6	60.83	2-44	-
C.K.Bullen	101	2	492	8	61.50	3-13	-
W.W.Davis	77.5	5	393	6	65.50	2-32	-
G.Miller	72	2	397	6	66.16	2-22	-
J.H.Childs	86	6	412	6	68.66	2-38	-
S.J.Dennis	99.4	1	527	6	87.83	1-14	-

NATWEST TROPHY

BATTING AVERAGES - Including fielding

Qualifying requirements : 1 completed innings

Name	Matches	Inns	NO	Runs	HS	Avge	100s	50s	Ct	St
G.A.Gooch	2	2	0	247	144	247.00	2	-	2	-
A.A.Metcalfe	3	3	2	175	127*	175.00	1	-	1	-
J.E.Morris	2	2	1	168	94*	168.00	-	2	-	-
M.D.Moxon	3	3	2	164	107*	164.00	1	1	1	-
D.L.Haynes	4	4	2	274	149*	137.00	1	2	1	-
G.D.Mendis	5	5	2	327	121*	109.00	1	2	-	-
M.W.Gatting	4	4	2	205	79*	102.50	-	3	2	-
I.V.A.Richards	3	3	1	201	118	100.50	1	1	-	-
N.J.Lenham	2	2	1	88	47	88.00	-	-	-	-
A.R.Butcher	3	3	1	175	104*	87.50	1	-	2	-
P.W.G.Parker	2	2	1	87	83	87.00	-	1	-	-
D.B.D'Oliveira	3	3	2	86	51*	86.00	-	1	-	-
A.P.Wells	2	1	0	85	85	85.00	-	1	-	-
J.W.Lloyds	3	3	2	79	73*	79.00	-	1	-	-
N.H.Fairbrother	5	5	1	304	86	76.00	-	3	1	-
P.Bainbridge	2	2	1	69	56*	69.00	-	1	1	-
H.Morris	3	3	0	200	116	66.66	1	-	1	-
P.A.C.Bail	1	1	0	66	66	66.00	-	1	-	-
G.A.Hick	3	3	1	129	78*	64.50	-	1	-	-
B.C.Broad	2	2	0	128	115	64.00	1	-	-	-
G.D.Rose	2	2	0	126	110	63.00	1	-	1	-
Asif Din	2	2	0	124	66	62.00	-	2	1	-
K.R.Brown	4	3	1	120	103*	60.00	1	-	1	-
G.D.Reynolds	1	1	0	60	60	60.00	-	1	-	-
M.A.Lynch	2	1	0	59	59	59.00	-	1	1	-
D.J.Capel	5	4	0	233	101	58.25	1	1	3	-
P.J.Prichard	2	2	1	58	37*	58.00	-	-	-	-
J.Graham-Brown	1	1	0	58	58	58.00	-	-	-	-
D.W.Randall	1	1	0	56	56	56.00	-	1	-	-
C.W.J.Athey	3	3	1	111	81*	55.50	-	1	-	-
M.S.A.McEvoy	1	1	0	55	55	55.00	-	1	-	-
T.M.Moody	2	2	0	109	58	54.50	-	2	2	-
M.Watkinson	5	4	1	162	90	54.00	-	1	1	-
N.Priestley	1	1	0	54	54	54.00	-	1	-	1
O.Henry	1	1	0	53	53	53.00	-	1	-	-
T.S.Curtis	3	3	0	158	112	52.66	1	-	1	-
P.J.Hartley	3	1	0	52	52	52.00	-	1	-	-
N.M.K.Smith	1	1	0	52	52	52.00	-	1	-	-
J.W.Edrich	1	1	0	52	52	52.00	-	1	-	-
A.Fordham	5	5	0	255	130	51.00	1	1	2	-
M.R.Ramprakash	4	3	0	152	104	50.66	1	-	1	-
M.J.Weston	3	3	0	152	98	50.66	-	1	2	-
A.J.Lamb	5	5	1	195	68*	48.75	-	3	2	-
A.N.Hayhurst	2	2	0	97	51	48.50	-	1	-	-
A.J.Stewart	2	1	0	48	48	48.00	-	-	1	-
C.L.Smith	4	4	0	188	106	47.00	1	1	2	-
T.R.Ward	1	1	0	47	47	47.00	-	-	-	-
M.E.Waugh	2	1	0	47	47	47.00	-	-	1	-
A.J.Wright	3	3	0	141	92	47.00	-	1	2	-
J.Abrahams	1	1	0	47	47	47.00	-	-	-	-
S.G.Lynch	1	1	0	46	46	46.00	-	-	1	-
R.T.Robinson	2	2	0	91	61	45.50	-	1	1	-
R.J.Parks	4	3	2	45	27*	45.00	-	-	5	1
B.Roberts	2	2	1	45	31	45.00	-	-	1	-
G.D.Hodgson	3	3	0	133	52	44.33	-	1	-	-
J.P.Stephenson	2	1	0	44	44	44.00	-	-	-	-
S.J.Cook	2	2	0	87	45	43.50	-	-	1	-
A.J.Moles	2	2	0	87	60	43.50	-	1	2	-
P.A.Neale	3	1	0	43	43	43.00	-	-	2	-
G.K.Brown	1	1	0	42	42	42.00	-	-	-	-
G.S.Clinton	2	2	0	83	50	41.50	-	1	-	-
A.I.Kallicharran	1	1	0	41	41	41.00	-	-	-	-
M.Saxelby	1	1	0	41	41	41.00	-	-	1	-
D.I.Gower	4	4	0	159	86	39.75	-	1	4	-
M.A.Atherton	5	5	1	156	55	39.00	-	1	4	-
D.M.Smith	1	1	0	39	39	39.00	-	-	-	-
K.T.Medlycott	2	1	0	38	38	38.00	-	-	-	-
N.G.Cowley	3	2	1	37	32*	37.00	-	-	-	-
A.P.Kuiper	2	2	0	74	49	37.00	-	-	-	-
A.B.Russell	1	1	0	37	37	37.00	-	-	-	-
G.D.Lloyd	1	1	1	36	36	36.00	-	-	-	-
D.A.Reeve	2	2	1	36	36*	36.00	-	-	-	-
G.E.Loveday	1	1	0	36	36	36.00	-	-	-	-
D.Shaw	1	1	0	36	36	36.00	-	-	-	-
M.C.J.Nicholas	4	4	1	107	50	35.66	-	1	3	-
R.A.Smith	4	4	0	141	59	35.25	-	1	2	-
A.Needham	1	1	0	35	35	35.00	-	-	-	-
V.P.Terry	4	4	0	137	76	34.25	-	1	1	-
D.R.Pringle	2	1	0	33	33	33.00	-	-	1	-
W.Larkins	4	4	0	128	52	32.00	-	1	1	-
C.C.Lewis	1	1	0	32	32	32.00	-	-	1	-
G.S.Calway	1	1	0	32	32	32.00	-	-	1	-
A.J.Dutton	1	1	0	32	32	32.00	-	-	-	-
P.M.Roebuck	2	2	0	63	43	31.50	-	-	1	-
B.R.Hardie	1	1	0	31	31	31.00	-	-	1	-
P.Johnson	2	2	0	62	48	31.00	-	-	1	-
G.P.Thorpe	2	2	1	31	16	31.00	-	-	1	-
N.C.J.Gandon	1	1	0	31	31	31.00	-	-	-	-
R.J.Bailey	5	5	1	123	72*	30.75	-	1	-	-
K.J.Barnett	2	2	0	60	59	30.00	-	1	-	-
M.L.Simmons	1	1	0	30	30	30.00	-	-	-	-
N.A.Felton	5	5	0	149	70	29.80	-	1	2	-
P.A.Cottey	2	2	1	29	27	29.00	-	-	1	-
S.G.Hinks	2	2	0	58	43	29.00	-	-	-	-
M.A.Roseberry	4	4	0	115	48	28.75	-	-	1	-
P.R.Oliver	1	1	0	28	28	28.00	-	-	-	-
B.G.Evans	1	1	0	27	27	27.00	-	-	1	-
R.D.B.Croft	1	1	0	26	26	26.00	-	-	-	-
I.J.Gould	1	1	0	26	26	26.00	-	-	-	-
N.J.Archer	1	1	0	26	26	26.00	-	-	-	-
P.Burn	1	1	0	26	26	26.00	-	-	1	-
G.C.Ford	1	1	0	26	26	26.00	-	-	-	-
J.B.R.Jones	1	1	0	26	26	26.00	-	-	-	-
R.G.Swan	1	1	0	26	26	26.00	-	-	-	-
C.Stone	1	1	0	25	25	25.00	-	-	-	-
R.P.Merriman	1	1	0	25	25	25.00	-	-	-	-
R.J.Finney	1	1	0	25	25	25.00	-	-	-	-
G.Fowler	4	4	0	98	52	24.50	-	1	-	-
M.D.Marshall	4	4	0	96	77	24.00	-	1	-	-
J.J.Whitaker	1	1	0	24	24	24.00	-	-	-	-
R.A.Evans	1	1	0	24	24	24.00	-	-	1	-
C.E.L.Ambrose	5	3	0	70	48	23.33	-	-	3	-
G.P.Savin	1	1	0	23	23	23.00	-	-	-	-
R.G.Williams	5	4	1	68	44	22.66	-	-	3	-
G.W.Humpage	2	2	0	45	43	22.50	-	-	-	1
I.Smith	1	1	0	22	22	22.00	-	-	1	-
S.J.S.Warke	1	1	0	22	22	22.00	-	-	-	-
R.J.Blakey	3	1	0	21	21	21.00	-	-	7	1
B.N.French	2	2	0	42	35	21.00	-	-	5	-
S.C.Goldsmith	2	1	0	21	21	21.00	-	-	-	-
D.J.M.Kelleher	1	1	0	21	21	21.00	-	-	-	-
N.R.C.Maclaurin	1	1	0	21	21	21.00	-	-	-	-
C.A.Connor	4	2	1	20	13	20.00	-	-	1	-
G.R.Cowdrey	2	2	0	40	37	20.00	-	-	-	-
P.W.Romaines	1	1	0	20	20	20.00	-	-	-	-
M.R.Davies	1	1	0	20	20	20.00	-	-	-	-
J.Foster	1	1	0	20	20	20.00	-	-	-	-
S.G.Plumb	1	1	0	20	20	20.00	-	-	-	-
M.Newell	2	2	0	39	35	19.50	-	-	1	-
T.J.Boon	1	1	0	19	19	19.00	-	-	-	-
R.J.Maru	4	3	1	38	22	19.00	-	-	2	-
L.Potter	1	1	0	19	19	19.00	-	-	-	-
S.Burrow	1	1	0	19	19	19.00	-	-	-	-
D.Cartledge	1	1	0	19	19	19.00	-	-	1	-
B.M.W.Patterson	1	1	0	19	19	19.00	-	-	-	-
J.R.Ayling	4	4	1	54	29	18.00	-	-	1	-
D.R.Turner	1	1	0	18	18	18.00	-	-	-	-
D.P.Simpkins	1	1	0	18	18	18.00	-	-	-	-
D.M.Stamp	1	1	0	18	18	18.00	-	-	-	-
P.Farbrace	2	1	0	17	17	17.00	-	-	4	-
N.P.G.Wright	1	1	0	17	17	17.00	-	-	-	-
F.D.Stephenson	2	2	0	33	29	16.50	-	-	-	-
K.N.Foyle	1	1	0	16	16	16.00	-	-	-	-
N.A.Riddell	1	1	0	16	16	16.00	-	-	-	-
P.B.Wormald	1	1	0	16	16	16.00	-	-	-	-
C.G.Greenidge	1	1	0	15	15	15.00	-	-	-	-
T.A.Lloyd	1	1	0	15	15	15.00	-	-	-	-

NATWEST TROPHY

Name	Matches	Inns	NO	Runs	HS	Avge	100s	50s	Ct	St
T.S.Smith	1	1	0	15	15	15.00	-	-	1	-
S.Smith	1	1	0	15	15	15.00	-	-	-	-
P.Carrick	3	1	0	14	14	14.00	-	-	-	-
Wasim Akram	5	3	1	28	14	14.00	-	-	2	-
A.W.Bee	1	1	0	14	14	14.00	-	-	-	-
J.Glendenen	1	1	0	14	14	14.00	-	-	-	-
P.V.Simmons	1	1	0	14	14	14.00	-	-	-	-
N.R.Taylor	2	2	1	13	13*	13.00	-	-	1	-
A.R.Harwood	1	1	0	13	13	13.00	-	-	2	-
T.A.Lester	1	1	0	13	13	13.00	-	-	-	-
G.T.Hedley	1	1	0	13	13	13.00	-	-	-	-
D.J.Bicknell	1	1	0	12	12	12.00	-	-	-	-
R.P.Davis	2	1	0	12	12	12.00	-	-	1	-
R.J.Harden	2	1	0	12	12	12.00	-	-	-	-
P.A.Nixon	1	1	0	12	12	12.00	-	-	1	-
R.C.Russell	3	1	0	12	12	12.00	-	-	3	1
P.A.Brown	1	1	0	12	12	12.00	-	-	-	-
J.R.Hall	1	1	0	12	12	12.00	-	-	1	-
M.G.Lickley	1	1	0	12	12	12.00	-	-	-	-
P.S.De Villiers	2	2	0	24	14	12.00	-	-	-	-
A.J.Pugh	1	1	0	12	12	12.00	-	-	2	-
R.O.Butcher	2	2	0	23	22	11.50	-	-	1	-
J.D.R.Benson	1	1	0	11	11	11.00	-	-	-	-
M.P.Maynard	3	3	0	33	24	11.00	-	-	-	-
D.M.Ward	2	1	0	11	11	11.00	-	-	4	-
S.M.Clements	1	1	0	11	11	11.00	-	-	-	-
W.G.Merry	1	1	0	11	11	11.00	-	-	-	-
S.Williams	1	1	0	11	11	11.00	-	-	-	-
J.P.Addison	1	1	0	10	10	10.00	-	-	-	-
B.S.Jackson	1	1	0	10	10	10.00	-	-	1	-
R.N.R.Vartan	1	1	0	10	10	10.00	-	-	1	-
C.P.Metson	3	1	0	9	9	9.00	-	-	2	-
J.C.M.Lewis	1	1	0	9	9	9.00	-	-	-	-
R.Kingshott	1	1	0	9	9	9.00	-	-	-	-
P.D.Bowler	2	2	0	16	14	8.00	-	-	3	-
N.E.Briers	1	1	0	8	8	8.00	-	-	1	-
N.G.B.Cook	5	3	1	16	9	8.00	-	-	4	-
S.J.Dean	1	1	0	8	8	8.00	-	-	-	-
D.Ripley	5	4	1	23	13	7.66	-	-	2	-
W.K.M.Benjamin	1	1	0	7	7	7.00	-	-	-	-
M.R.Benson	1	1	0	7	7	7.00	-	-	-	-
A.Dale	2	2	1	7	4*	7.00	-	-	-	-
M.V.Fleming	1	1	0	7	7	7.00	-	-	-	-
R.K.Illingworth	3	1	0	7	7	7.00	-	-	1	-
P.E.Robinson	3	1	0	7	7	7.00	-	-	2	-
C.A.Walsh	3	1	0	7	7	7.00	-	-	-	-
N.French	1	1	0	7	7	7.00	-	-	-	-
J.Hartley	1	1	0	7	7	7.00	-	-	1	-
P.M.Jobson	1	1	0	7	7	7.00	-	-	1	-
N.R.Taylor	1	1	0	7	7	7.00	-	-	-	-
J.Thompson	1	1	0	7	7	7.00	-	-	-	-
P.W.Jarvis	1	1	0	6	6	6.00	-	-	-	-
G.R.Black	1	1	0	6	6	6.00	-	-	1	-
D.A.Hale	1	1	0	6	6	6.00	-	-	-	-
N.Shardlow	1	1	0	6	6	6.00	-	-	-	-
C.S.Cowdrey	2	2	0	11	6	5.50	-	-	1	-
P.J.Bakker	4	2	1	5	3*	5.00	-	-	-	-
K.E.Cooper	2	2	0	10	10	5.00	-	-	-	-
M.A.Feltham	1	1	0	5	5	5.00	-	-	-	-
C.Gladwin	1	1	0	5	5	5.00	-	-	-	-
T.Butler	1	1	0	5	5	5.00	-	-	-	-
D.Marshall	1	1	0	5	5	5.00	-	-	-	-
W.Morton	1	1	0	5	5	5.00	-	-	-	-
J.P.Taylor	1	1	0	5	5	5.00	-	-	-	-
D.R.Thomas	1	1	0	5	5	5.00	-	-	-	-
R.Lamba	1	1	0	5	5	5.00	-	-	1	-
T.J.Barry	1	1	0	5	5	5.00	-	-	-	-
R.Bates	1	1	0	5	5	5.00	-	-	-	-
M.P.Rea	1	1	0	5	5	5.00	-	-	-	-
D.Byas	3	1	0	4	4	4.00	-	-	4	-
G.C.Small	2	2	0	8	8	4.00	-	-	-	-
M.P.Speight	2	1	0	4	4	4.00	-	-	2	-
J.F.Sykes	1	1	0	4	4	4.00	-	-	-	-
A.D.Brown	1	1	0	4	4	4.00	-	-	-	-
J.H.Edwards	1	1	0	4	4	4.00	-	-	-	-
P.J.Garner	1	1	0	4	4	4.00	-	-	1	-
R.C.Turpin	1	1	0	4	4	4.00	-	-	-	-
D.P.Ostler	1	1	0	4	4	4.00	-	-	-	-
N.G.Hames	1	1	0	4	4	4.00	-	-	-	-
P.A.J.DeFreitas	5	2	1	3	2*	3.00	-	-	-	-
M.A.Robinson	5	3	2	3	3*	3.00	-	-	2	-
G.D.Harrison	1	1	0	3	3	3.00	-	-	-	-
A.Mildenhall	1	1	0	3	3	3.00	-	-	-	-
A.N.Nelson	1	1	0	3	3	3.00	-	-	-	-
I.D.Graham	1	1	0	3	3	3.00	-	-	-	-
S.N.Warman	1	1	0	3	3	3.00	-	-	-	-
S.J.Rhodes	3	1	0	2	2	2.00	-	-	3	-
K.A.Arnold	1	1	0	2	2	2.00	-	-	-	-
A.R.Fothergill	1	1	0	2	2	2.00	-	-	-	-
R.S.Yeabsley	1	1	0	2	2	2.00	-	-	-	-
T.Parton	1	1	0	2	2	2.00	-	-	1	-
D.E.Mattocks	1	1	0	2	2	2.00	-	-	-	-
E.E.Hemmings	2	2	0	3	3	1.50	-	-	1	-
K.M.Curran	3	3	0	4	2	1.33	-	-	-	-
A.I.C.Dodemaide	2	1	0	1	1	1.00	-	-	-	-
J.D.Love	1	1	0	1	1	1.00	-	-	-	-
A.C.S.Pigott	2	1	0	1	1	1.00	-	-	1	-
C.C.Remy	1	1	0	1	1	1.00	-	-	-	-
T.J.A.Scriven	1	1	0	1	1	1.00	-	-	-	-
A.Sidebottom	3	1	0	1	1	1.00	-	-	2	-
R.G.Twose	1	1	0	1	1	1.00	-	-	1	-
D.A.Lewis	1	1	0	1	1	1.00	-	-	-	-
I.L.Philip	1	1	0	1	1	1.00	-	-	-	-
I.L.Pont	1	1	0	1	1	1.00	-	-	-	-
M.C.Woodman	1	1	0	1	1	1.00	-	-	1	-
I.Fletcher	1	1	0	1	1	1.00	-	-	-	-
S.B.Dixon	1	1	0	1	1	1.00	-	-	-	-
A.R.Dunlop	1	1	0	1	1	1.00	-	-	-	-
C.J.Adams	2	1	0	0	0	0.00	-	-	1	-
S.N.Barnes	2	1	0	0	0	0.00	-	-	1	-
A.R.Clarke	2	1	0	0	0	0.00	-	-	1	-
K.P.Evans	1	1	0	0	0	0.00	-	-	1	-
N.A.Foster	2	1	0	0	0	0.00	-	-	-	-
S.A.Kellett	3	1	0	0	0	0.00	-	-	-	-
D.V.Lawrence	2	1	0	0	0	0.00	-	-	-	-
D.E.Malcolm	2	1	0	0	0	0.00	-	-	-	-
S.A.Marsh	1	1	0	0	0	0.00	-	-	1	-
G.Miller	2	1	0	0	0	0.00	-	-	1	-
P.Moores	2	1	0	0	0	0.00	-	-	2	1
O.H.Mortensen	2	1	0	0	0	0.00	-	-	-	-
P.G.Newman	1	1	0	0	0	0.00	-	-	-	-
P.J.Newport	2	1	0	0	0	0.00	-	-	-	-
N.V.Radford	1	1	0	0	0	0.00	-	-	-	-
M.D.Bailey	1	1	0	0	0	0.00	-	-	-	-
P.G.Duthie	1	1	0	0	0	0.00	-	-	-	-
N.A.Folland	1	1	0	0	0	0.00	-	-	-	-
R.C.Green	1	1	0	0	0	0.00	-	-	-	-
S.Greensword	1	1	0	0	0	0.00	-	-	-	-
P.B.Jackson	1	1	0	0	0	0.00	-	-	-	-
K.G.Rice	1	1	0	0	0	0.00	-	-	-	-
S.N.V.Waterton	1	1	0	0	0	0.00	-	-	-	1
B.H.White	1	1	0	0	0	0.00	-	-	-	-
C.L.Parfitt	1	1	0	0	0	0.00	-	-	-	-
J.W.Hall	1	1	0	0	0	0.00	-	-	-	-
R.I.Dawson	1	1	0	0	0	0.00	-	-	-	-
J.K.Tierney	1	1	0	0	0	0.00	-	-	-	-
G.A.R.Harris	1	1	0	0	0	0.00	-	-	-	-
I.Young	1	1	0	0	0	0.00	-	-	-	-
M.J.Peck	1	1	0	0	0	0.00	-	-	-	-
A.K.Golding	1	1	0	0	0	0.00	-	-	1	-
P.V.Lewis	1	1	0	0	0	0.00	-	-	-	-
J.Weaver	1	1	0	0	0	0.00	-	-	2	-
D.Page	1	1	0	0	0	0.00	-	-	-	-
B.S.Percy	1	1	0	0	0	0.00	-	-	2	-
D.B.Storer	1	1	0	0	0	0.00	-	-	-	-
J.R.Airey	1	1	0	0	0	0.00	-	-	-	-
F.L.Q.Handley	1	1	0	0	0	0.00	-	-	-	-
M.S.Taylor	1	1	0	0	0	0.00	-	-	-	-
A.Johnston	1	1	0	0	0	0.00	-	-	-	-

NATWEST TROPHY

BOWLING AVERAGES

Qualifying requirements : 1 wicket taken

Name	Overs	Mdns	Runs	Wkts	Avge	Best	5wI
M.V.Fleming	3	1	4	2	2.00	2-4	-
D.J.M.Kelleher	9	3	16	3	5.33	3-16	-
C.M.Wells	9	6	6	1	6.00	1-6	-
R.P.Lefebvre	21.3	6	61	9	6.77	7-15	1
N.J.Lenham	9	0	25	3	8.33	2-12	-
D.B.D'Oliveira	5	0	17	2	8.50	2-17	-
M.D.Moxon	7	2	19	2	9.50	2-19	-
P.Carrick	36	9	68	7	9.71	3-8	-
A.I.C.Dodemaide	23	8	79	8	9.87	6-9	1
C.A.Walsh	31	4	106	10	10.60	6-21	1
Asif Din	11	2	54	5	10.80	5-40	1
P.C.R.Tufnell	12	2	22	2	11.00	2-22	-
R.J.Bailey	12	2	49	4	12.25	3-47	-
Waqar Younis	24	5	62	5	12.40	3-23	-
O.H.Mortensen	23	6	51	4	12.75	3-29	-
G.R.Cowdrey	2.3	0	13	1	13.00	1-13	-
P.J.Hartley	32.5	3	136	10	13.60	5-46	1
M.M.Patel	12	6	29	2	14.50	2-29	-
A.K.Golding	12	4	29	2	14.50	2-29	-
M.A.Atherton	18	1	59	4	14.75	2-15	-
N.A.Foster	24	8	61	4	15.25	3-26	-
R.A.Evans	12	1	46	3	15.33	3-46	-
P.A.J.DeFreitas	50	12	156	10	15.60	5-26	1
S.R.Lampitt	35.4	2	128	8	16.00	5-22	1
J.F.Sykes	6	0	16	1	16.00	1-16	-
R.P.Merriman	3	0	32	2	16.00	2-32	-
K.E.Cooper	20	3	65	4	16.25	3-16	-
T.J.Barry	12	2	49	3	16.33	3-49	-
N.A.Mallender	16	5	33	2	16.50	2-4	-
D.Gough	19	3	67	4	16.75	2-22	-
A.E.Warner	24	2	84	5	16.80	4-39	-
S.J.W.Andrew	12	2	34	2	17.00	2-34	-
D.J.Hartley	9.3	1	35	2	17.50	2-35	-
R.M.Ellison	12	6	18	1	18.00	1-18	-
Wasim Akram	50.1	3	182	10	18.20	4-34	-
M.D.Marshall	44	6	131	7	18.71	4-17	-
M.W.Alleyne	29	4	114	6	19.00	5-30	1
P.J.Newport	22	0	100	5	20.00	4-46	-
I.Smith	4	0	20	1	20.00	1-20	-
D.Surridge	12	0	61	3	20.33	3-61	-
S.L.Watkin	35	5	102	5	20.40	3-18	-
J.G.Thomas	10	2	21	1	21.00	1-21	-
J.P.Agnew	12	1	44	2	22.00	2-44	-
C.Stone	12	2	44	2	22.00	2-44	-
M.A.Robinson	56	5	206	9	22.88	3-33	-
D.Byas	3	0	23	1	23.00	1-23	-
P.J.W.Allott	34	10	93	4	23.25	3-24	-
D.A.Graveney	18.5	0	47	2	23.50	2-26	-
A.P.Igglesden	14	1	47	2	23.50	2-13	-
D.R.Pringle	23.3	3	94	4	23.50	2-30	-
B.K.Shantry	10	1	47	2	23.50	2-47	-
E.E.Hemmings	19.3	4	95	4	23.75	3-42	-
J.P.Stephenson	4	0	24	1	24.00	1-24	-
P.B.Wormwald	5.1	1	24	1	24.00	1-24	-
A.R.C.Fraser	47.5	3	171	7	24.42	4-44	-
A.Needham	12	0	50	2	25.00	2-50	-
I.T.Botham	31.1	2	151	6	25.16	3-44	-
T.A.Munton	18	1	77	3	25.66	3-46	-
F.D.Stephenson	17	3	52	2	26.00	2-40	-
G.R.Black	11	2	52	2	26.00	2-52	-
J.Hartley	8	1	26	1	26.00	1-26	-
N.G.Cowans	45	8	158	6	26.33	2-25	-
K.P.Evans	12	3	53	2	26.50	2-53	-
I.J.Curtis	12	0	53	2	26.50	2-53	-
A.W.Bee	10	4	27	1	27.00	1-27	-
A.N.Nelson	5	0	27	1	27.00	1-27	-
A.D.Mullally	12	0	55	2	27.50	2-55	-
J.R.Ayling	45	5	197	7	28.14	3-30	-
D.E.Malcolm	24	4	85	3	28.33	3-54	-
I.V.A.Richards	26	0	114	4	28.50	2-43	-
R.A.Pick	21	3	86	3	28.66	3-22	-
C.A.Connor	42	4	203	7	29.00	4-73	-
I.D.Austin	53	5	205	7	29.28	3-36	-
A.R.Clarke	22	7	59	2	29.50	2-53	-
N.G.B.Cook	58.4	12	209	7	29.85	3-52	-
R.P.Davis	21	3	60	2	30.00	1-27	-
P.G.Newman	10	0	30	1	30.00	1-30	-
B.S.Percy	6	0	30	1	30.00	1-30	-
M.Watkinson	46	3	181	6	30.16	3-14	-
W.G.Merry	11	0	62	2	31.00	2-62	-
D.Marshall	12	0	63	2	31.50	2-63	-
J.H.Jones	9	2	32	1	32.00	1-32	-
A.Mildenhall	8	2	32	1	32.00	1-32	-
C.E.L.Ambrose	54.1	11	136	4	34.00	1-15	-
W.K.M.Benjamin	12	4	34	1	34.00	1-34	-
S.P.Hughes	12	0	68	2	34.00	2-68	-
R.G.Williams	51	5	244	7	34.85	3-86	-
C.C.Lewis	12	1	35	1	35.00	1-35	-
G.T.Hedley	12	1	35	1	35.00	1-35	-
R.J.Maru	45	1	211	6	35.16	3-46	-
D.C.Blank	12	0	74	2	37.00	2-74	-
R.I.Dawson	4	0	37	1	37.00	1-37	-
A.Sidebottom	34	8	76	2	38.00	1-20	-
M.G.Stear	9	0	39	1	39.00	1-39	-
M.P.Bicknell	24	3	79	2	39.50	1-16	-
M.Frost	31	5	123	3	41.00	3-50	-
T.M.Moody	10.1	0	41	1	41.00	1-7	-
A.Dale	9	1	42	1	42.00	1-14	-
S.Burrow	12	1	42	1	42.00	1-42	-
S.C.Goldsmith	10.2	0	43	1	43.00	1-20	-
J.E.Emburey	46	7	174	4	43.50	3-27	-
M.C.Ilott	9	0	45	1	45.00	1-45	-
A.P.Kuiper	16	1	45	1	45.00	1-20	-
R.K.Illingworth	36	9	92	2	46.00	2-44	-
A.J.Murphy	12	1	46	1	46.00	1-46	-
J.W.Lloyds	6	0	50	1	50.00	1-6	-
M.C.Woodman	12	3	50	1	50.00	1-50	-
M.W.Gatting	8	0	51	1	51.00	1-31	-
G.D.Rose	14	1	51	1	51.00	1-40	-
K.M.Curran	32	7	104	2	52.00	2-30	-
N.A.Folland	3	0	52	1	52.00	1-52	-
I.L.Pont	12	0	52	1	52.00	1-52	-
S.G.Lynch	7	0	52	1	52.00	1-52	-
P.Willey	12	2	54	1	54.00	1-54	-
S.D.Fletcher	24	1	109	2	54.50	2-53	-
P.J.Bakker	43	6	164	3	54.66	1-41	-
P.S.De Villiers	16	4	57	1	57.00	1-29	-
D.L.Haynes	20	3	59	1	59.00	1-41	-
J.R.Airey	10	0	60	1	60.00	1-60	-
M.A.Feltham	11.4	0	65	1	65.00	1-65	-
N.G.Cowley	32	3	135	2	67.50	2-71	-
A.C.S.Pigott	19	2	70	1	70.00	1-14	-
T.J.A.Scriven	12	0	73	1	73.00	1-73	-
D.V.Lawrence	14	0	77	1	77.00	1-62	-
A.N.Jones	16	1	84	1	84.00	1-20	-
G.Miller	22	1	87	1	87.00	1-56	-
C.K.Bullen	24	1	88	1	88.00	1-42	-
K.T.Medlycott	24	1	91	1	91.00	1-64	-
S.N.Barnes	18	1	93	1	93.00	1-64	-
D.J.Capel	39	1	205	2	102.50	1-44	-
J.H.Childs	24	1	104	1	104.00	1-44	-

BENSON & HEDGES CUP

BATTING AVERAGES - Including fielding

Qualifying requirements : 1 completed innings

Name	Matches	Inns	NO	Runs	HS	Avge	100s	50s	Ct	St
R.A.Smith	3	3	2	185	132	185.00	1	-	-	-
R.T.Robinson	6	6	4	355	106*	177.50	1	3	1	-
D.R.Pringle	4	3	2	151	77*	151.00	-	2	-	-
M.R.Benson	3	2	0	203	118	101.50	1	1	-	-
C.L.Smith	4	3	1	201	154*	100.50	1	-	2	-
G.A.Gooch	4	4	1	285	102	95.00	1	2	1	-
A.P.Kuiper	4	4	2	185	106*	92.50	1	-	1	-
I.D.Austin	7	5	4	88	61*	88.00	-	1	-	-
P.E.Robinson	4	4	2	173	73*	86.50	-	2	-	-
N.A.Folland	4	4	2	172	78*	86.00	-	2	1	-
A.J.Stewart	5	5	1	334	84*	83.50	-	4	1	-
I.T.Botham	5	4	1	235	138*	78.33	1	2	-	-
C.M.Wells	4	4	1	229	101	76.33	1	1	-	-
C.W.J.Athey	4	3	1	152	83*	76.00	-	1	2	-
O.Henry	3	3	1	134	62*	67.00	-	1	2	-
P.D.Bowler	4	4	0	263	109	65.75	1	2	3	1
D.L.Haynes	5	5	0	326	131	65.20	1	2	4	-
J.J.E.Hardy	2	2	0	128	109	64.00	1	-	2	-
T.R.Ward	4	4	1	191	94	63.66	-	2	2	-
D.R.Thomas	2	2	1	63	49*	63.00	-	-	-	-
M.J.Weston	4	4	1	179	99*	59.66	-	1	1	-
W.Larkins	3	3	0	177	111	59.00	1	-	3	-
J.W.Lloyds	3	2	1	59	53*	59.00	-	1	-	-
N.H.Fairbrother	7	7	2	290	95*	58.00	-	3	3	-
M.A.Atherton	7	7	2	288	74	57.60	-	3	2	-
C.S.Cowdrey	4	4	1	172	67*	57.33	-	2	-	-
N.E.Briers	3	3	1	110	93*	55.00	-	1	-	-
S.J.Cook	6	6	0	329	177	54.83	1	1	3	-
A.J.Moles	2	2	0	109	57	54.50	-	2	-	-
F.D.Stephenson	6	6	3	162	98*	54.00	-	1	-	-
M.J.Roberts	4	4	0	216	121	54.00	1	1	1	-
D.J.Bicknell	4	4	0	215	119	53.75	1	1	-	-
R.J.Blakey	4	4	0	212	79	53.00	-	3	2	-
P.Whitticase	3	2	1	52	45	52.00	-	-	4	-
P.Johnson	6	6	1	258	104*	51.60	1	2	3	-
A.C.S.Pigott	3	2	1	50	38*	50.00	-	-	-	-
T.S.Curtis	7	7	1	299	97	49.83	-	3	1	-
S.C.Goldsmith	3	2	1	49	45*	49.00	-	-	-	-
N.V.Radford	6	4	2	98	40	49.00	-	-	5	-
R.J.Turner	4	4	3	49	25*	49.00	-	-	2	1
P.Willey	1	1	0	49	49	49.00	-	-	-	-
D.M.Ward	5	5	2	145	46*	48.33	-	-	4	2
A.R.Fothergill	3	2	1	48	45*	48.00	-	-	5	-
R.J.Bailey	4	4	1	140	92*	46.66	-	1	1	-
C.J.Tavare	6	6	1	233	93	46.60	-	1	2	-
M.P.Maynard	5	5	0	230	84	46.00	-	2	-	-
V.P.Terry	4	4	0	180	134	45.00	1	-	3	-
P.W.Jarvis	4	2	1	44	42	44.00	-	-	1	-
P.J.Prichard	4	4	0	175	107	43.75	1	-	-	-
G.S.Clinton	5	5	0	217	77	43.40	-	2	2	-
P.Moores	4	3	0	130	76	43.33	-	1	1	1
C.M.Tolley	4	4	0	171	77	42.75	-	2	1	-
T.J.Boon	3	3	0	127	84	42.33	-	1	-	-
I.L.Philip	4	4	0	169	95	42.25	-	1	1	-
S.P.James	4	4	0	168	63	42.00	-	2	2	-
N.M.K.Smith	3	2	1	41	30*	41.00	-	-	1	-
A.J.Wright	4	3	0	122	97	40.66	-	1	-	-
H.Morris	5	5	0	203	106	40.60	1	1	6	-
M.P.Speight	4	4	0	160	71	40.00	-	1	1	-
N.R.Taylor	4	3	0	117	90	39.00	-	1	-	-
M.A.Garnham	4	3	2	38	21*	38.00	-	-	5	1
J.E.Morris	4	4	0	152	123	38.00	1	-	1	-
R.C.Russell	4	3	1	76	46*	38.00	-	-	4	-
A.P.Wells	4	4	0	150	74	37.50	-	2	-	-
A.R.Butcher	5	5	0	185	95	37.00	-	2	2	-
R.G.Swan	4	4	0	148	53	37.00	-	1	-	-
D.Byas	2	1	0	36	36	36.00	-	-	-	-
M.W.Gatting	4	4	0	142	66	35.50	-	2	-	-
M.P.Bicknell	5	2	1	35	27*	35.00	-	-	5	-
R.P.Lefebvre	6	3	1	70	37	35.00	-	-	-	-
C.E.L.Ambrose	4	3	2	34	12	34.00	-	-	3	-
P.R.Downton	5	5	2	102	40	34.00	-	-	9	-
A.J.Lamb	1	1	0	34	34	34.00	-	-	-	-
P.W.G.Parker	4	4	1	101	85*	33.66	-	1	1	-
G.A.Hick	6	6	1	165	64	33.00	-	2	6	-
J.J.Whitaker	3	3	0	99	46	33.00	-	-	1	-
G.D.Rose	6	6	1	163	64	32.60	-	1	-	-
P.Bainbridge	4	3	1	65	55	32.50	-	1	2	-
P.M.Roebuck	5	4	0	129	91	32.25	-	1	3	-
M.W.Alleyne	4	3	1	64	30	32.00	-	-	3	-
A.I.C.Dodemaide	4	1	0	32	32	32.00	-	-	1	-
S.A.Kellett	3	3	0	96	45	32.00	-	-	-	-
K.J.Barnett	4	4	0	124	94	31.00	-	1	2	-
Asif Din	4	4	0	123	50	30.75	-	1	1	-
T.A.Lloyd	3	3	0	90	72	30.00	-	1	3	-
T.M.Moody	3	3	0	90	41	30.00	-	-	-	-
M.E.Waugh	4	4	1	90	62	30.00	-	1	2	-
A.N.Hayhurst	6	5	1	119	76	29.75	-	1	-	-
C.G.Greenidge	4	4	0	117	50	29.25	-	1	1	-
P.A.J.DeFreitas	7	6	1	145	75*	29.00	-	1	-	-
M.Watkinson	7	7	1	174	50	29.00	-	1	-	-
R.J.Harden	6	6	2	115	53*	28.75	-	1	2	-
A.A.Metcalfe	4	4	0	113	38	28.25	-	-	2	-
K.R.Brown	5	5	0	141	56	28.20	-	1	1	-
S.G.Plumb	4	3	0	84	63	28.00	-	1	1	-
M.D.Marshall	3	2	0	55	31	27.50	-	-	-	-
B.Roberts	4	3	1	55	46	27.50	-	-	1	-
N.F.Williams	5	4	2	55	28	27.50	-	-	-	-
B.C.Broad	6	6	0	163	49	27.16	-	-	1	-
C.K.Bullen	3	2	1	27	17*	27.00	-	-	2	-
R.J.Scott	2	2	0	54	47	27.00	-	-	-	-
C.J.Adams	4	4	0	80	44	26.66	-	-	2	-
G.Fowler	7	7	0	185	96	26.42	-	1	2	-
P.A.Neale	6	6	1	129	50	25.80	-	1	4	-
A.Fordham	3	3	0	76	67	25.33	-	1	-	-
D.I.Gower	3	3	1	50	44*	25.00	-	-	1	-
G.K.Brown	4	4	0	98	46	24.50	-	-	2	-
C.C.Lewis	3	3	1	48	23	24.00	-	-	3	-
K.M.Curran	4	3	0	69	55	23.00	-	1	1	-
M.A.Crawley	4	4	0	90	46	22.50	-	-	-	-
B.N.French	6	4	1	67	25	22.33	-	-	5	2
G.P.Thorpe	5	5	1	89	50*	22.25	-	1	-	-
J.D.R.Benson	2	2	0	44	43	22.00	-	-	-	-
G.C.Holmes	5	5	0	109	62	21.80	-	1	3	-
R.K.Illingworth	5	4	1	63	36*	21.00	-	-	-	-
D.B.D'Oliveira	7	6	1	104	57	20.80	-	1	6	-
I.V.A.Richards	5	5	0	104	28	20.80	-	-	2	-
G.D.Mendis	7	7	0	145	40	20.71	-	-	2	-
N.J.Lenham	3	3	0	62	37	20.66	-	-	-	-
I.J.Gould	4	4	2	41	16*	20.50	-	-	1	-
D.A.Reeve	4	4	1	61	29*	20.33	-	-	1	-
B.R.Hardie	4	4	0	81	34	20.25	-	-	1	-
J.E.Benjamin	2	1	0	20	20	20.00	-	-	1	-
N.D.Burns	6	4	1	60	21	20.00	-	-	4	1
C.P.Metson	5	5	1	78	23	19.50	-	-	3	-
A.I.Kallicharran	4	4	0	77	32	19.25	-	-	1	-
P.J.Newport	7	4	1	57	28	19.00	-	-	3	-
Wasim Akram	3	3	1	38	28	19.00	-	-	-	-
D.R.Brown	3	3	0	57	24	19.00	-	-	1	-
B.M.W.Patterson	4	4	0	76	42	19.00	-	-	1	-
M.A.Roseberry	4	4	0	73	38	18.25	-	-	1	-
P.A.Booth	2	2	1	18	13*	18.00	-	-	1	-
C.White	3	2	1	18	17*	18.00	-	-	-	-
G.W.Humpage	4	4	1	52	30*	17.33	-	-	8	-
S.R.Lampitt	6	4	1	52	41	17.33	-	-	4	-
R.G.Williams	1	1	0	17	17	17.00	-	-	-	-
N.A.Felton	1	1	0	16	16	16.00	-	-	-	-
D.W.Randall	6	6	0	95	39	15.83	-	-	1	-
M.R.Ramprakash	5	5	0	78	44	15.60	-	-	1	-
S.J.Base	4	2	1	15	15*	15.00	-	-	-	-
D.J.Capel	3	3	0	45	33	15.00	-	-	1	-
A.Dale	4	4	0	60	40	15.00	-	-	-	-
A.W.Lilley	3	2	0	30	23	15.00	-	-	-	-
T.A.Merrick	3	2	1	15	14	15.00	-	-	1	-
J.D.Moir	4	3	2	15	7*	15.00	-	-	-	-
D.Ripley	4	4	1	44	27	14.66	-	-	2	-
J.R.Ayling	2	1	0	14	14	14.00	-	-	-	-

BENSON & HEDGES CUP

Name	Matches	Inns	NO	Runs	HS		Avge	100s	50s	Ct	St
S.R.Barwick	4	2	1	14	13	*	14.00	-	-	-	-
J.W.Govan	3	3	0	42	30		14.00	-	-	-	-
W.M.van der Merwe	4	4	0	55	27		13.75	-	-	1	-
S.Greensword	4	3	0	41	28		13.66	-	-	-	-
A.C.Storie	2	2	0	27	19		13.50	-	-	-	-
G.Cook	3	3	0	40	28		13.33	-	-	1	-
G.J.Lord	2	2	0	26	26		13.00	-	-	-	-
M.Newell	1	1	0	13	13		13.00	-	-	-	-
P.A.Smith	1	1	0	13	13		13.00	-	-	-	-
N.V.Knight	2	2	0	25	16		12.50	-	-	-	-
R.O.Butcher	5	5	0	62	23		12.40	-	-	3	-
R.M.Ellison	1	1	0	12	12		12.00	-	-	1	-
S.P.Hughes	4	2	0	24	22		12.00	-	-	-	-
N.A.Mallender	4	3	2	12	6	*	12.00	-	-	3	-
S.A.Marsh	4	3	0	35	17		11.66	-	-	3	-
J.G.Thomas	4	3	0	35	32		11.66	-	-	1	-
N.G.Cowans	4	3	1	23	12		11.50	-	-	-	-
E.E.Hemmings	5	3	1	23	12	*	11.50	-	-	2	-
A.E.Warner	3	2	0	23	16		11.50	-	-	1	-
I.A.Greig	5	4	1	34	15		11.33	-	-	2	-
M.A.Ealham	4	3	1	22	17	*	11.00	-	-	1	-
A.Sidebottom	4	2	1	11	9	*	11.00	-	-	2	-
S.Sharp	2	2	1	11	11	*	11.00	-	-	1	-
D.L.Bairstow	2	2	1	10	9		10.00	-	-	1	-
A.L.Penberthy	1	1	0	10	10		10.00	-	-	-	-
R.G.Twose	3	2	0	19	17		9.50	-	-	-	-
G.C.Small	4	3	0	28	22		9.33	-	-	1	-
R.J.Maru	4	1	0	9	9		9.00	-	-	1	-
T.A.Lester	3	2	0	18	14		9.00	-	-	-	-
J.C.M.Atkinson	4	4	0	35	16		8.75	-	-	-	-
I.G.Swallow	6	3	0	26	18		8.66	-	-	2	-
N.A.Foster	4	1	0	8	8		8.00	-	-	-	-
M.D.Moxon	3	3	0	24	11		8.00	-	-	-	-
T.J.G.O'Gorman	1	1	0	8	8		8.00	-	-	-	-
I.Smith	4	4	0	32	21		8.00	-	-	1	-
J.E.Emburey	5	5	2	23	12		7.66	-	-	4	-
T.M.Orrell	2	2	0	15	15		7.50	-	-	1	-
N.G.Cowley	5	5	0	35	19		7.00	-	-	1	-
J.I.Longley	4	4	0	28	14		7.00	-	-	-	-
S.L.Watkin	4	4	2	14	6		7.00	-	-	-	-
D.Cowan	4	3	1	14	7		7.00	-	-	-	-
M.J.Smith	1	1	0	7	7		7.00	-	-	-	-
M.A.Lynch	5	5	0	33	24		6.60	-	-	5	-
G.R.Cowdrey	3	2	0	12	12		6.00	-	-	3	-
S.N.V.Waterton	1	1	0	6	6		6.00	-	-	1	-
A.J.Mack	4	1	0	6	6		6.00	-	-	-	-
P.Carrick	3	2	0	11	8		5.50	-	-	-	-
A.N.Jones	5	3	1	11	7		5.50	-	-	-	-
L.Potter	3	3	0	16	10		5.33	-	-	2	-
D.E.Malcolm	3	2	1	5	5		5.00	-	-	-	-
P.Pollard	3	3	0	15	5		5.00	-	-	1	-
A.Walker	1	1	0	5	5		5.00	-	-	-	-
D.J.Wild	3	3	0	15	15		5.00	-	-	-	-
S.J.Rhodes	5	3	0	14	8		4.66	-	-	6	-
A.W.Stovold	4	3	0	14	8		4.66	-	-	-	-
A.B.Russell	2	2	0	9	9		4.50	-	-	-	-
M.A.Feltham	2	1	0	4	4		4.00	-	-	-	-
M.Frost	4	2	1	4	3		4.00	-	-	-	-
J.P.Stephenson	4	3	1	8	4	*	4.00	-	-	1	-
Waqar Younis	1	1	0	4	4		4.00	-	-	-	-
C.A.Connor	4	1	0	3	3		3.00	-	-	-	-
M.V.Fleming	3	2	0	6	6		3.00	-	-	-	-
D.M.Smith	1	1	0	3	3		3.00	-	-	1	-
N.R.Taylor	4	1	0	3	3		3.00	-	-	1	-
S.J.Dennis	3	3	1	5	2	*	2.50	-	-	-	-
W.K.M.Benjamin	1	1	0	2	2		2.00	-	-	-	-
J.Boiling	4	1	0	2	2		2.00	-	-	3	-
P.A.Cottey	1	1	0	2	2		2.00	-	-	-	-
K.D.James	2	2	0	4	2		2.00	-	-	-	-
I.D.K.Salisbury	2	1	0	2	2		2.00	-	-	-	-
S.G.Hinks	4	4	0	7	3		1.75	-	-	3	-
G.D.Hodgson	1	1	0	1	1		1.00	-	-	-	-
K.T.Medlycott	4	1	0	1	1		1.00	-	-	1	-
T.A.Munton	4	2	1	1	1	*	1.00	-	-	1	-
M.A.Robinson	4	3	2	1	1		1.00	-	-	-	-
C.A.Walsh	3	1	0	1	1		1.00	-	-	-	-
P.J.Hartley	2	2	0	1	1		0.50	-	-	-	-
D.J.R.Martindale	1	1	0	0	0		0.00	-	-	-	-
M.Saxelby	1	1	0	0	0		0.00	-	-	-	-
K.J.Shine	4	1	0	0	0		0.00	-	-	-	-
A.W.Bee	3	2	0	0	0		0.00	-	-	1	-
P.S.De Villiers	1	1	0	0	0		0.00	-	-	1	-

BOWLING AVERAGES

Qualifying requirements : 1 wicket taken

Name	Overs	Mdns	Runs	Wkts	Avge	Best	5wI
M.C.J.Nicholas	1	0	2	1	2.00	1-2	-
C.E.L.Ambrose	44	9	100	9	11.11	3-19	-
G.C.Small	44	4	123	11	11.18	4-22	-
J.P.Stephenson	20	0	80	7	11.42	3-22	-
C.S.Cowdrey	22	2	100	8	12.50	3-29	-
S.C.Goldsmith	10	0	38	3	12.66	3-38	-
W.K.M.Benjamin	9	3	29	2	14.50	2-29	-
A.E.Warner	33	2	126	8	15.75	3-31	-
M.Frost	39.2	8	146	9	16.22	4-57	-
Wasim Akram	31	0	98	6	16.33	3-29	-
M.A.Atherton	14	1	52	3	17.33	3-32	-
M.A.Ealham	30	1	141	8	17.62	4-57	-
N.F.Williams	54	7	201	11	18.27	3-37	-
J.R.Hemstock	10	1	37	2	18.50	2-37	-
P.S.De Villiers	10	0	37	2	18.50	2-37	-
G.R.Dilley	50.5	4	211	11	19.18	4-48	-
A.J.Mack	41	5	154	8	19.25	2-22	-
K.Saxelby	11	3	39	2	19.50	2-39	-
C.Penn	10.5	1	40	2	20.00	2-40	-
K.M.Curran	32	2	141	7	20.14	3-29	-
J.D.Robinson	11	0	41	2	20.50	2-41	-
J.R.Ayling	10	0	63	3	21.00	2-22	-
P.J.Bakker	10	3	21	1	21.00	1-21	-
P.J.Hartley	20	3	63	3	21.00	3-34	-
M.J.Weston	6	1	21	1	21.00	1-21	-
M.Watkinson	62.4	3	261	12	21.75	4-58	-
N.V.Radford	56.3	9	218	10	21.80	4-26	-
P.A.J.DeFreitas	65	5	242	11	22.00	3-36	-
I.D.Austin	65	11	244	11	22.18	4-25	-
P.J.Newport	62	8	206	9	22.88	4-25	-
E.T.Milburn	5	1	23	1	23.00	1-23	-
N.R.Taylor	41	5	165	7	23.57	3-52	-
J.E.Benjamin	22	6	72	3	24.00	2-32	-
G.D.Rose	55	6	240	10	24.00	4-37	-
S.R.Barwick	41	3	193	8	24.12	4-67	-
N.A.Foster	43	6	145	6	24.16	3-18	-
B.P.Patterson	31.1	9	73	3	24.33	1-6	-
C.L.Parfitt	44	6	122	5	24.40	4-16	-
A.N.Jones	46.5	3	223	9	24.77	4-41	-
M.E.Waugh	6	0	25	1	25.00	1-25	-
S.J.Base	40	4	176	7	25.14	3-33	-
N.J.Lenham	9	0	51	2	25.50	1-3	-
W.M.van der Merwe	42.4	7	179	7	25.57	2-34	-
J.P.Agnew	28	4	103	4	25.75	3-20	-
L.B.Taylor	29.4	1	131	5	26.20	3-65	-
M.P.Bicknell	51.5	9	237	9	26.33	2-27	-
S.M.McEwan	11	0	53	2	26.50	2-53	-
C.A.Connor	34	1	162	6	27.00	3-40	-
Waqar Younis	11	0	55	2	27.50	2-55	-
F.D.Stephenson	66	4	249	9	27.66	3-33	-
J.E.Emburey	51.2	3	198	7	28.28	2-27	-
K.E.Cooper	64.2	11	199	7	28.42	3-25	-
J.H.Childs	38	3	144	5	28.80	3-37	-
A.N.Hayhurst	42	0	176	6	29.33	2-23	-
I.T.Botham	50	7	209	7	29.85	2-29	-
D.J.Capel	28	1	91	3	30.33	2-29	-
G.C.Holmes	19	0	92	3	30.66	2-27	-
C.White	9	0	31	1	31.00	1-31	-
S.P.Hughes	43.5	0	187	6	31.16	3-37	-
G.A.Hick	30	0	125	4	31.25	3-36	-
P.J.W.Allott	67	12	190	6	31.66	2-23	-
S.D.Fletcher	41.5	4	162	5	32.40	2-23	-
D.E.Malcolm	30	2	131	4	32.75	3-55	-

BENSON & HEDGES CUP

Name	Overs	Mdns	Runs	Wkts	Avge	Best	5wI
N.A.Mallender	35	6	102	3	34.00	2-32	-
L.Potter	11	1	34	1	34.00	1-26	-
J.G.Thomas	39	0	204	6	34.00	4-45	-
A.J.Murphy	29	5	138	4	34.50	2-36	-
K.D.James	16	3	70	2	35.00	1-34	-
P.M.Roebuck	14	0	70	2	35.00	2-13	-
R.A.Pick	63.4	2	284	8	35.50	3-50	-
T.A.Munton	39	3	143	4	35.75	2-28	-
P.A.Booth	15	1	72	2	36.00	2-39	-
D.V.Lawrence	11	3	36	1	36.00	1-36	-
R.A.Evans	10	1	36	1	36.00	1-36	-
A.C.S.Pigott	31	5	109	3	36.33	2-33	-
D.R.Pringle	38.4	4	148	4	37.00	2-28	-
C.A.Walsh	23	2	74	2	37.00	2-32	-
P.W.Jarvis	43	3	186	5	37.20	2-29	-
R.J.Maru	27	2	149	4	37.25	3-46	-
A.D.Mullally	21	5	75	2	37.50	1-28	-
M.A.Crawley	44	7	113	3	37.66	1-18	-
M.W.Alleyne	24.5	1	151	4	37.75	4-42	-
T.A.Merrick	19.4	2	76	2	38.00	2-30	-
A.I.C.Dodemaide	44	4	193	5	38.60	2-36	-
S.Greensword	34	2	155	4	38.75	3-38	-
M.W.Gatting	33	1	158	4	39.50	3-65	-
K.T.Medlycott	44	0	198	5	39.60	3-48	-
C.K.Bullen	33	4	120	3	40.00	2-35	-
I.V.A.Richards	51	1	200	5	40.00	3-38	-
R.P.Davis	30	1	121	3	40.33	2-40	-
M.V.Fleming	15	2	41	1	41.00	1-27	-
S.R.Lampitt	55	4	250	6	41.66	2-43	-
K.J.Shine	32.2	1	167	4	41.75	4-68	-
A.A.Donald	11	1	42	1	42.00	1-42	-
D.Cowan	39.2	1	212	5	42.40	3-36	-
N.G.Cowans	44	5	171	4	42.75	2-22	-
N.G.Cowley	53	2	173	4	43.25	1-23	-
D.A.Reeve	41	4	175	4	43.75	2-27	-
M.A.Robinson	38.4	1	176	4	44.00	2-47	-
J.D.Moir	44	7	179	4	44.75	2-51	-
G.P.Thorpe	7	0	45	1	45.00	1-30	-
E.E.Hemmings	54	8	182	4	45.50	2-33	-
R.P.Lefebvre	58.2	4	230	5	46.00	2-39	-
D.R.Brown	30.3	2	140	3	46.66	3-50	-
S.J.Dennis	25	3	95	2	47.50	1-37	-
J.A.Afford	66	9	240	5	48.00	2-47	-
J.A.North	8	0	48	1	48.00	1-48	-
D.Byas	13	1	50	1	50.00	1-13	-
I.G.Swallow	45.5	3	207	4	51.75	2-32	-
A.Sidebottom	40.1	7	156	3	52.00	1-35	-
D.R.Thomas	16	3	53	1	53.00	1-24	-
P.Bainbridge	24	3	108	2	54.00	2-31	-
D.L.Haynes	12	0	57	1	57.00	1-23	-
I.A.Greig	36.2	0	176	3	58.66	2-35	-
C.C.Lewis	31	4	119	2	59.50	2-42	-
G.A.Gooch	28	3	122	2	61.00	1-27	-
N.M.K.Smith	15	0	63	1	63.00	1-43	-
O.H.Mortensen	40	9	131	2	65.50	1-43	-
M.Smith	40	2	205	3	68.33	2-46	-
J.C.Hallett	11	0	70	1	70.00	1-52	-
P.Carrick	22	1	71	1	71.00	1-31	-
P.C.R.Tufnell	18	0	78	1	78.00	1-42	-
A.P.Kuiper	37.4	0	235	3	78.33	3-71	-
S.L.Watkin	44	7	163	2	81.50	1-32	-
J.W.Govan	23	4	85	1	85.00	1-55	-
K.B.S.Jarvis	17	1	87	1	87.00	1-30	-
G.Miller	22	0	88	1	88.00	1-46	-
R.K.Illingworth	46	1	182	2	91.00	1-42	-
R.C.Green	40.1	2	183	2	91.50	1-49	-
I.D.K.Salisbury	17	0	92	1	92.00	1-60	-
A.Dale	21	2	93	1	93.00	1-21	-
D.A.Graveney	22	1	95	1	95.00	1-40	-
T.D.Topley	31	2	101	1	101.00	1-16	-
A.R.Clarke	22	1	123	1	123.00	1-53	-
A.R.Hansford	44	0	265	2	132.50	2-55	-
A.W.Bee	24	1	146	1	146.00	1-67	-
J.Boiling	33	1	152	1	152.00	1-37	-
C.M.Wells	42	4	190	1	190.00	1-45	-

ALL ONE-DAY MATCHES

BATTING AVERAGES - Including fielding
Qualifying requirements : 6 completed innings

Name	Matches	Inns	NO	Runs	HS	Avge	100s	50s	Ct	St
G.A.Gooch	22	22	3	1304	144	68.63	6	7	6	-
R.T.Robinson	25	25	8	1056	116	62.11	3	8	9	-
D.L.Haynes	27	26	4	1353	149 *	61.50	3	10	12	-
S.J.Cook	27	27	3	1440	177	60.00	4	8	12	-
M.D.Crowe	8	8	2	358	106 *	59.66	1	1	5	-
G.A.Hick	23	23	5	1065	114 *	59.16	1	8	11	-
R.A.Smith	23	23	3	1105	132	55.25	4	5	11	-
T.S.Curtis	26	26	3	1257	124	54.65	2	10	6	-
M.J.Greatbatch	9	8	1	378	111	54.00	2	2	1	-
A.J.Moles	13	12	1	578	102 *	52.54	1	6	3	-
D.R.Pringle	18	16	6	519	77 *	51.90	-	4	5	-
N.H.Fairbrother	25	25	4	1035	145	49.28	1	9	9	-
M.R.Benson	7	6	0	293	118	48.83	1	2	2	-
M.A.Atherton	24	24	4	972	111	48.60	1	9	13	-
C.L.Smith	18	16	3	626	154 *	48.15	2	2	6	-
C.W.J.Athey	23	21	4	809	113	47.58	2	5	7	-
A.J.Stewart	20	18	1	809	125	47.58	1	6	9	-
G.D.Lloyd	17	15	2	613	100 *	47.15	1	5	6	-
K.Sharp	11	9	3	278	71	46.33	-	1	6	-
M.W.Gatting	24	22	5	782	124 *	46.00	1	7	9	-
C.J.Tavare	25	25	5	920	162 *	46.00	1	6	9	-
M.Newell	13	11	3	364	109 *	45.50	1	2	5	-
R.J.Blakey	27	25	3	999	100 *	45.40	1	9	22	3
J.E.Morris	25	25	2	1017	134	44.21	2	6	6	-
K.J.Barnett	27	26	0	1133	127	43.57	3	8	11	-
A.P.Kuiper	24	24	6	775	106 *	43.05	1	4	10	-
P.Johnson	25	25	2	988	114	42.95	4	4	8	-
Asif Din	24	23	3	853	113	42.65	1	7	9	-
M.D.Moxon	20	20	2	765	107 *	42.50	2	4	7	-
G.D.Mendis	19	19	3	674	121 *	42.12	1	3	6	-
N.R.Taylor	21	20	1	799	95	42.05	-	7	7	-
M.R.Ramprakash	28	26	5	874	147 *	41.61	2	3	7	-
K.R.Brown	28	24	6	746	103 *	41.44	1	5	7	-
G.Fowler	27	27	1	1076	108	41.38	2	10	4	-
D.J.Capel	23	22	2	821	121	41.05	3	2	8	-
C.K.Bullen	24	14	8	244	93 *	40.66	-	1	12	-
B.C.Broad	27	27	2	1016	115	40.64	2	6	5	-
A.I.C.Dodemaide	24	19	6	520	131	40.00	1	-	8	-
P.D.Bowler	23	23	1	877	109	39.86	1	9	29	2
I.V.A.Richards	22	22	2	795	118	39.75	1	5	10	-
T.R.Ward	18	18	1	657	94	38.64	-	5	3	-
I.T.Botham	21	19	4	579	138 *	38.60	1	1	6	-
N.J.Lenham	20	20	2	694	78	38.55	-	6	5	-
G.P.Thorpe	26	26	5	805	85	38.33	-	7	3	-
A.A.Metcalfe	26	26	2	918	127 *	38.25	1	7	13	-
V.P.Terry	26	25	1	899	134	37.45	2	7	17	-
T.J.Boon	22	22	0	813	97	36.95	-	7	5	-
A.Fordham	23	23	1	812	130	36.90	1	7	4	-
G.S.Clinton	14	13	0	479	77	36.84	-	3	3	-
D.J.Bicknell	13	13	0	476	119	36.61	1	3	6	-
R.J.Harden	25	24	9	549	53 *	36.60	-	2	8	-
N.Hussain	13	12	4	289	66 *	36.12	-	1	9	-
W.Larkins	18	18	0	639	111	35.50	3	2	5	-
P.J.Prichard	23	22	3	674	107	35.47	1	3	8	-
A.P.Wells	22	21	2	674	98	35.47	-	6	3	-
M.P.Maynard	22	22	1	742	100	35.33	1	5	5	-
A.R.Butcher	23	23	3	705	104 *	35.25	1	4	10	-
P.Willey	13	13	2	384	72 *	34.90	-	3	8	-
M.A.Roseberry	26	26	1	866	86	34.64	-	8	6	-
D.I.Gower	25	24	3	726	97	34.57	-	6	12	-
G.D.Rose	25	24	3	721	148	34.33	2	1	7	-
C.C.Lewis	20	18	4	475	93 *	33.92	-	3	9	-
D.M.Ward	25	24	5	643	102 *	33.84	1	2	23	3
M.Watkinson	26	24	8	539	90	33.68	-	2	5	-
R.J.Bailey	25	25	3	740	92 *	33.63	-	6	4	-
T.M.Moody	24	22	1	706	67	33.61	-	7	11	-
A.J.Wright	24	22	1	700	97	33.33	-	6	16	-
P.E.Robinson	27	24	5	629	114	33.10	1	3	9	-
A.I.Kallicharran	11	11	1	328	76	32.80	-	2	-	-
P.W.G.Parker	19	18	2	521	90	32.56	-	4	6	-
M.J.Weston	20	18	2	521	99 *	32.56	-	3	5	-
G.C.Holmes	10	10	2	259	62	32.37	-	3	5	-
B.Roberts	25	20	6	453	77 *	32.35	-	2	8	-
J.P.Stephenson	25	20	2	580	109	32.22	2	3	7	-
P.M.Roebuck	16	15	0	482	95	32.13	-	3	4	-
M.E.Waugh	25	24	1	736	111	32.00	1	6	7	-
P.Bainbridge	21	17	5	381	59 *	31.75	-	3	7	-
R.J.Scott	15	14	0	440	76	31.42	-	5	3	-
M.P.Speight	22	21	1	623	77	31.15	-	4	7	-
H.Morris	23	23	0	714	116	31.04	2	3	10	-
I.L.Philip	6	6	0	184	95	30.66	-	1	1	-
G.R.Cowdrey	21	20	3	520	78	30.58	-	2	7	-
A.J.Lamb	20	20	1	578	70	30.42	-	5	5	-
M.C.J.Nicholas	22	19	5	424	59	30.28	-	3	13	-
P.A.Cottey	9	8	2	181	50 *	30.16	-	1	3	-
K.M.Curran	23	21	3	538	92	29.88	-	5	2	-
S.G.Hinks	21	21	0	627	89	29.85	-	7	4	-
J.J.Whitaker	20	20	1	564	83	29.68	-	3	7	-
B.R.Hardie	18	18	1	504	76	29.64	-	4	6	-
D.W.Randall	15	15	3	349	56	29.08	-	2	3	-
N.E.Briers	21	21	2	549	93 *	28.89	-	2	7	-
J.W.Lloyds	18	15	6	260	73 *	28.88	-	2	5	-
J.D.Robinson	7	7	1	173	98	28.83	-	1	3	-
P.R.Downton	20	13	5	230	40	28.75	-	-	16	5
N.V.Radford	15	10	4	169	40	28.16	-	-	6	-
M.A.Lynch	24	23	3	556	65 *	27.80	-	3	7	-
M.W.Alleyne	23	17	7	276	39 *	27.60	-	-	8	-
C.G.Greenidge	8	7	0	193	50	27.57	-	1	2	-
C.S.Cowdrey	21	20	3	460	67 *	27.05	-	2	8	-
N.A.Felton	16	16	1	404	70	26.93	-	2	6	-
R.C.Russell	21	17	2	403	62	26.86	-	2	15	5
R.J.Bartlett	8	8	0	211	55	26.37	-	3	3	-
J.R.Ayling	23	17	7	259	47 *	25.90	-	-	1	-
A.N.Hayhurst	22	18	2	408	76	25.50	-	3	4	-
M.Saxelby	13	11	2	229	41	25.44	-	-	6	-
S.C.Goldsmith	18	13	6	177	50	25.28	-	1	2	-
S.A.Kellett	13	10	0	251	57	25.10	-	1	1	-
C.M.Wells	20	19	1	451	101	25.05	1	2	2	-
G.D.Hodgson	13	12	2	247	52	24.70	-	1	5	-
P.W.Romaines	17	13	3	247	47	24.70	-	-	4	-
A.C.S.Pigott	17	13	3	246	38 *	24.60	-	-	8	-
D.Byas	25	19	5	338	59	24.14	-	1	11	-
M.D.Marshall	23	20	3	410	77	24.11	-	1	1	-
D.B.D'Oliveira	25	23	4	456	58	24.00	-	4	9	-
M.A.Garnham	24	18	7	255	40 *	23.18	-	-	21	2
T.A.Lloyd	17	14	2	278	72	23.16	-	2	4	-
F.D.Stephenson	28	23	5	417	98 *	23.16	-	1	3	-
N.M.K.Smith	19	13	2	251	52	22.81	-	1	7	-
I.A.Greig	24	21	8	296	43	22.76	-	-	5	-
N.D.Burns	25	18	4	316	58	22.57	-	1	21	2
D.A.Reeve	23	22	2	406	42	22.55	-	-	10	-
I.J.Gould	18	18	3	337	68	22.46	-	3	3	-
M.A.Feltham	18	16	2	312	61	22.28	-	2	3	-
R.P.Lefebvre	20	10	3	156	37	22.28	-	-	4	-
Wasim Akram	21	14	3	241	50	21.90	-	1	3	-
P.A.Neale	23	19	2	370	50	21.76	-	1	11	-
J.D.R.Benson	20	19	5	304	67	21.71	-	1	4	-
C.J.Adams	25	22	7	323	58 *	21.53	-	1	11	-
G.J.Lord	6	6	0	129	78	21.50	-	1	-	-
R.J.Parks	24	11	5	127	27 *	21.16	-	-	22	5
S.A.Marsh	22	18	3	316	52	21.06	-	1	18	-
T.E.Jesty	8	7	1	124	25	20.66	-	-	1	-
D.L.Bairstow	12	11	4	144	36	20.57	-	-	5	2
R.G.Williams	14	13	4	184	44	20.44	-	-	5	-
P.A.J.DeFreitas	29	19	5	285	75 *	20.35	-	1	1	-
R.M.Ellison	10	10	4	122	43	20.33	-	-	4	-
B.N.French	28	17	5	242	35	20.16	-	-	24	5
S.J.Rhodes	25	15	4	221	66 *	20.09	-	1	24	4
G.W.Humpage	18	17	4	261	43	20.07	-	-	13	1
I.Smith	14	14	2	239	46	19.91	-	-	4	-
P.Moores	23	18	4	278	76	19.85	-	1	19	9
K.T.Medlycott	21	11	3	156	44 *	19.50	-	-	8	-
J.E.Emburey	27	18	9	168	32	18.66	-	-	9	-
C.P.Metson	22	16	6	182	30 *	18.20	-	-	15	2
M.V.Fleming	20	18	5	234	43 *	18.00	-	-	4	-
P.J.Hartley	20	15	3	215	52	17.91	-	2	5	-
D.P.Ostler	9	8	2	107	30	17.83	-	-	3	-

ALL ONE-DAY MATCHES

Name	Matches	Inns	NO	Runs	HS	Avge	100s	50s	Ct	St
I.G.Swallow	23	11	5	103	31	17.16	-	-	4	-
R.O.Butcher	18	14	2	201	44 *	16.75	-	-	8	-
S.R.Lampitt	23	14	6	133	41	16.62	-	-	13	-
A.Dale	15	13	2	180	42	16.36	-	-	3	-
R.G.Twose	19	15	4	179	40	16.27	-	-	6	-
A.E.Warner	20	10	4	96	28 *	16.00	-	-	4	-
B.M.W.Patterson	6	6	0	95	42	15.83	-	-	1	-
T.J.G.O'Gorman	8	8	2	93	32	15.50	-	-	-	-
R.K.Illingworth	21	11	2	134	36 *	14.88	-	-	7	-
M.A.Ealham	16	8	2	85	29 *	14.16	-	-	12	-
P.Carrick	23	15	3	168	30	14.00	-	-	6	-
P.W.Jarvis	21	10	3	95	42	13.57	-	-	5	-
L.Potter	18	17	3	190	33	13.57	-	-	8	-
P.A.Smith	11	9	0	121	33	13.44	-	-	-	-
N.A.Foster	20	14	5	118	39 *	13.11	-	-	4	-
W.W.Davis	11	9	1	97	24	12.12	-	-	2	-
D.J.Wild	16	15	2	157	48 *	12.07	-	-	1	-
E.E.Hemmings	26	14	4	120	32 *	12.00	-	-	6	-
A.W.Lilley	10	8	1	83	23	11.85	-	-	-	-
P.J.Newport	23	13	9	114	28	11.40	-	-	6	-
D.Ripley	21	17	5	134	27	11.16	-	-	9	1
R.J.Maru	24	10	3	76	22	10.85	-	-	9	-
C.A.Walsh	21	9	1	84	23	10.50	-	-	3	-
N.G.Cowley	17	14	3	109	32 *	9.90	-	-	3	-
K.E.Cooper	25	10	3	66	21	9.42	-	-	5	-
J.G.Thomas	14	10	2	70	32	8.75	-	-	3	-
N.G.Cowans	22	8	2	51	27	8.50	-	-	2	-
P.A.Nixon	16	9	3	51	12	8.50	-	-	17	1
D.A.Leatherdale	15	10	1	75	35	8.33	-	-	6	-
C.C.Remy	10	9	2	53	16	7.57	-	-	2	-
P.S.De Villiers	7	7	0	45	14	6.42	-	-	1	-
G.C.Small	19	9	1	49	22	6.12	-	-	3	-
P.Pollard	7	7	0	42	13	6.00	-	-	2	-
W.K.M.Benjamin	13	8	2	31	11	5.16	-	-	2	-
J.I.Longley	6	6	0	31	14	5.16	-	-	1	-
S.J.Dennis	21	9	2	35	14	5.00	-	-	3	-
T.D.Topley	22	11	4	33	10 *	4.71	-	-	7	-
I.D.K.Salisbury	17	9	3	28	14 *	4.66	-	-	6	-
D.E.Malcolm	20	8	2	18	9	3.00	-	-	1	-

BOWLING AVERAGES
Qualifying requirements : 10 wickets taken

Name	Overs	Mdns	Runs	Wkts	Avge	Best	5wI
Waqar Younis	137.2	9	601	42	14.31	5-26	1
T.M.Tremlett	73.5	5	257	17	15.11	3-22	-
J.P.Stephenson	62	0	317	18	17.61	3-22	-
G.R.Dilley	50.5	4	211	11	19.18	4-48	-
C.A.Walsh	157.5	12	590	30	19.66	6-21	1
Kapil Dev	53	9	219	11	19.90	3-76	-
C.E.L.Ambrose	105.1	21	267	13	20.53	3-19	-
P.Carrick	197	17	747	36	20.75	3-8	-
Wasim Akram	169.2	3	727	35	20.77	4-19	-
C.S.Cowdrey	79	2	435	20	21.75	4-57	-
P.J.Hartley	166.4	10	783	36	21.75	5-38	2
N.A.Foster	171.4	19	692	31	22.32	4-21	-
M.P.Bicknell	181.1	17	761	34	22.38	4-14	-
J.E.Emburey	226.3	22	1036	45	23.02	4-26	-
P.J.Newport	186	16	691	30	23.03	4-25	-
T.A.Merrick	94.1	5	395	17	23.23	4-24	-
N.J.Lenham	68.1	2	353	15	23.53	2-12	-
A.C.S.Pigott	145	10	688	29	23.72	4-42	-
D.V.Lawrence	70	4	336	14	24.00	5-18	1
I.T.Botham	155.1	10	736	30	24.53	4-25	-
A.I.C.Dodemaide	202	23	875	35	25.00	6-9	1
M.A.Atherton	61	2	301	12	25.08	3-32	-
M.Watkinson	207.4	6	1004	40	25.10	5-46	1
S.J.W.Andrew	51	5	255	10	25.50	4-36	-
P.W.Jarvis	186.5	15	794	31	25.61	5-18	1
A.E.Warner	158	4	748	29	25.79	4-39	-
M.A.Ealham	95.4	2	491	19	25.84	8-49	1
F.D.Stephenson	231.4	21	988	38	26.00	4-28	-
S.R.Lampitt	179.4	9	869	33	26.33	5-22	2
P.A.J.DeFreitas	260.2	21	1145	43	26.62	5-26	1
M.V.Fleming	136.4	5	641	24	26.70	4-30	-
D.R.Pringle	147.1	11	725	27	26.85	4-27	-
A.D.Mullally	141.1	11	599	22	27.22	6-38	1
R.P.Davis	135	5	576	21	27.42	4-25	-
S.J.Base	155	7	770	28	27.50	4-28	-
C.A.Connor	175.1	12	826	30	27.53	4-11	-
D.J.Wild	52.4	2	276	10	27.60	3-8	-
M.Frost	163	16	774	28	27.64	4-25	-
G.D.Rose	188.3	9	917	33	27.78	4-16	-
D.E.Malcolm	168	13	759	27	28.11	4-21	-
A.R.C.Fraser	140.5	14	538	19	28.31	4-28	-
M.W.Alleyne	161.4	7	854	30	28.46	5-30	1
S.R.Barwick	73.1	6	375	13	28.84	4-67	-
G.W.Mike	55	1	347	12	28.91	3-30	-
J.R.Ayling	159	8	764	26	29.38	4-37	-
T.A.Munton	218.5	19	864	29	29.79	5-23	1
J.P.Agnew	139.1	16	538	18	29.88	3-20	-
R.P.Lefebvre	162.4	10	759	25	30.36	7-15	1
A.N.Hayhurst	130	1	643	21	30.61	4-37	-
S.L.Watkin	167.3	17	735	24	30.62	5-23	1
C.S.Pickles	108	4	526	17	30.94	4-36	-
E.E.Hemmings	225.3	19	976	31	31.48	5-33	1
I.D.Austin	226.1	18	1071	34	31.50	4-25	-
C.C.Lewis	172.3	9	790	25	31.60	4-34	-
P.J.Bakker	125	15	569	18	31.61	3-31	-
J.G.Thomas	108	5	538	17	31.64	4-45	-
I.V.A.Richards	146.5	2	745	23	32.39	3-37	-
S.P.Hughes	123.4	3	648	20	32.40	4-19	-
W.K.M.Benjamin	105	15	425	13	32.69	3-36	-
N.G.Cowans	191	20	851	26	32.73	3-43	-
A.N.Jones	118.5	5	592	18	32.88	4-41	-
N.F.Williams	207	14	994	30	33.13	4-49	-
N.A.Mallender	157.5	15	597	18	33.16	4-32	-
K.M.Curran	177	11	763	23	33.17	3-29	-
O.H.Mortensen	192	25	577	17	33.94	3-16	-
M.D.Marshall	173	12	714	21	34.00	4-17	-
G.C.Small	153.3	9	646	19	34.00	4-22	-
L.B.Taylor	75.4	3	375	11	34.09	3-34	-
I.D.K.Salisbury	114.3	8	582	17	34.23	4-25	-
R.J.Maru	142.5	3	754	22	34.27	3-38	-
J.E.Benjamin	137	16	515	15	34.33	2-29	-
A.J.Murphy	139.5	8	689	20	34.45	3-61	-

ALL ONE-DAY MATCHES

Name	Overs	Mdns	Runs	Wkts	Avge	Best	5wI
R.A.Pick	108.4	5	483	14	34.50	3-22	-
D.Byas	70	1	347	10	34.70	3-26	-
R.K.Illingworth	181	13	700	20	35.00	3-19	-
P.J.W.Allott	206	27	749	21	35.66	3-24	-
K.T.Medlycott	180	2	856	24	35.66	3-20	-
M.E.Waugh	83	2	428	12	35.66	3-37	-
S.M.McEwan	97.4	0	540	15	36.00	3-38	-
A.Sidebottom	151.1	24	475	13	36.53	2-18	-
A.P.Kuiper	147.2	2	878	24	36.58	3-50	-
N.V.Radford	110.3	9	478	13	36.76	4-26	-
A.Dale	73	3	376	10	37.60	3-35	-
P.Willey	92	5	414	11	37.63	2-12	-
K.Saxelby	64.5	3	417	11	37.90	2-39	-
M.A.Robinson	183.1	13	910	24	37.91	3-33	-
A.R.Clarke	103.3	8	497	13	38.23	2-23	-
D.A.Reeve	154.1	11	702	18	39.00	4-36	-
N.G.Cowley	139	8	594	15	39.60	2-17	-
K.E.Cooper	210.2	22	835	21	39.76	3-16	-
N.M.K.Smith	111.3	5	601	15	40.06	3-36	-
N.R.Taylor	85.5	5	401	10	40.10	3-52	-
P.Bainbridge	126.2	5	604	15	40.26	2-7	-
K.P.Evans	99.4	4	567	14	40.50	4-30	-
N.G.B.Cook	162.4	17	787	19	41.42	3-36	-
S.D.Fletcher	154	7	746	18	41.44	4-63	-
M.A.Feltham	99.4	2	502	12	41.83	2-23	-
M.C.Ilott	102	9	419	10	41.90	2-24	-
G.A.Hick	105.5	3	508	12	42.33	3-36	-
M.W.Gatting	94	2	513	11	46.63	3-65	-
T.D.Topley	160.5	5	750	16	46.87	2-22	-
R.G.Williams	98	5	517	11	47.00	3-86	-
J.A.Afford	132	17	571	12	47.58	2-39	-
G.Miller	127	3	618	12	51.50	4-46	-
T.M.Moody	116.4	7	623	12	51.91	3-49	-
C.K.Bullen	194	9	856	16	53.50	3-13	-
J.H.Childs	159	11	697	13	53.61	3-37	-
D.J.Capel	139.5	5	679	12	56.58	2-29	-
I.G.Swallow	135.5	5	689	10	68.90	2-32	-

PLAYER
RECORDS

EDITOR'S NOTE

The records that follow refer to all players who have appeared in any of the matches featured in the preceding pages. Under each player there is a sub-section for each of the competitions in which he appeared and also categories of Other First-Class and Other One-Day for those matches outside the major competitions. Where players have represented more than one team every attempt has been made to make it clear whom they were representing in each match listed. In the case of all those playing in Cornhill Test Matches, the Texaco Trophy or the Britannic Assurance Championship their country and/or county are listed against the player's name. All others listed are credited with the teams for which they played most regularly – naturally there are several who played for Oxford or Cambridge University and also represented Combined Universities in the Benson & Hedges Cup or against the New Zealand tourists. Similarly there are those who appeared for Minor Counties as well as for their individual minor county in the NatWest Trophy. Sub-headings within the match listings have been introduced where it was felt appropriate to indicate the team represented and in a number of cases a further sub-head has been used to indicate that the listing has reverted to the original team.

PLAYER RECORDS A

J. ABRAHAMS - *Shropshire*

Opposition	Venue	Date	Batting	Fielding	Bowling
NATWEST TROPHY					
Derbyshire	Chesterfield	June 27	47		0-31

BATTING AVERAGES - Including fielding

	Matches	Inns	NO	Runs	HS	Avge	100s	50s	Ct	St
NatWest Trophy	1	1	0	47	47	47.00	-	-	-	-
ALL ONE-DAY	1	1	0	47	47	47.00	-	-	-	-

BOWLING AVERAGES

	Overs	Mdns	Runs	Wkts	Avge	Best	5wI	10wM
NatWest Trophy	6	0	31	0	-	-	-	
ALL ONE-DAY	6	0	31	0	-	-	-	

C.J. ADAMS - *Derbyshire*

Opposition	Venue	Date	Batting	Fielding	Bowling
BRITANNIC ASSURANCE					
Notts	Trent Bridge	April 26	3 & 11 *	1Ct	
Northants	Northampton	May 3	24	2Ct	
Lancashire	Derby	May 15	9 & 36		
Somerset	Taunton	May 19	58 & 23	1Ct	
Yorkshire	Chesterfield	May 23	12 & 10	1Ct	
Notts	Derby	May 26	14 & 4 *	2Ct	
Surrey	The Oval	June 6	3		
Warwickshire	Derby	June 16	6 *		
Leicestershire	Leicester	June 20	5	1Ct	0-12
Gloucs	Derby	June 30	7 & 48		
Sussex	Hove	July 4	91	1Ct	
Lancashire	Liverpool	July 7		1Ct	
Essex	Colchester	July 18	33 & 7		
Hampshire	Portsmouth	July 21	4 & 1	1Ct	
Worcestershire	Derby	July 25	32 & 63	2Ct	
Kent	Chesterfield	Aug 4	52	1Ct	
Northants	Chesterfield	Aug 8	5 & 12	1Ct	
Essex	Derby	Aug 23	0 & 41	4Ct	
Glamorgan	Cardiff	Aug 29	14	1Ct	1-5
Yorkshire	Scarborough	Sept 7	101 & 17	1Ct	0-7
Leicestershire	Derby	Sept 18	54	1Ct	0-12
REFUGE ASSURANCE					
Sussex	Hove	April 22	30 *		
Worcestershire	Derby	April 29	26	3Ct	
Northants	Northampton	May 6	5	2Ct	
Yorkshire	Headingley	May 13	7		
Somerset	Taunton	May 20	0 *		
Notts	Derby	June 10	0		
Warwickshire	Derby	June 17	58 *		
Surrey	The Oval	June 24	19		
Gloucs	Derby	July 1	2 *		
Lancashire	Old Trafford	July 8	14	1Ct	
Leicestershire	Knypersley	July 15	9	1Ct	
Hampshire	Portsmouth	July 22	21		
Glamorgan	Swansea	July 29	9 *		
Kent	Chesterfield	Aug 5	8		
Middlesex	Derby	Aug 19	3		
Essex	Derby	Aug 26	27 *	1Ct	
Notts	Derby	Sept 5			
Middlesex	Edgbaston	Sept 16	13		
NATWEST TROPHY					
Shropshire	Chesterfield	June 27			
Lancashire	Derby	July 11	0	1Ct	
BENSON & HEDGES CUP					
Sussex	Derby	April 24	2 *	1Ct	
Somerset	Taunton	May 1	8		
Min Counties	Wellington	May 10	44		
Middlesex	Derby	May 12	26	1Ct	
OTHER FIRST-CLASS					
Cambridge U	Fenner's	April 18	111 *	2Ct	
New Zealand	Derby	June 2	21	1Ct	1-20
OTHER ONE-DAY					
India	Chesterfield	July 16	0		

BATTING AVERAGES - Including fielding

	Matches	Inns	NO	Runs	HS	Avge	100s	50s	Ct	St
Britannic Assurance	21	32	3	800	101	27.58	1	5	22	-
Refuge Assurance	18	16	6	243	58 *	24.30	-	1	8	-
NatWest Trophy	2	1	0	0	0	0.00	-	-	1	-
Benson & Hedges Cup	4	4	1	80	44	26.66	-	-	2	-
Other First-Class	2	2	1	132	111 *	132.00	1	-	3	-
Other One-Day	1	1	0	0	0	0.00	-	-	-	-
ALL FIRST-CLASS	23	34	4	932	111 *	31.06	2	5	25	-
ALL ONE-DAY	25	22	7	323	58 *	21.53	-	1	11	-

BOWLING AVERAGES

	Overs	Mdns	Runs	Wkts	Avge	Best	5wI	10wM
Britannic Assurance	8.1	0	36	1	36.00	1-5		
Refuge Assurance								
NatWest Trophy								
Benson & Hedges Cup								
Other First-Class	6	1	20	1	20.00	1-20	-	-
Other One-Day								
ALL FIRST-CLASS	14.1	1	56	2	28.00	1-5	-	-
ALL ONE-DAY								

J.P. ADDISON - *Staffordshire*

Opposition	Venue	Date	Batting	Fielding	Bowling
NATWEST TROPHY					
Northants	Northampton	June 27	10		

BATTING AVERAGES - Including fielding

	Matches	Inns	NO	Runs	HS	Avge	100s	50s	Ct	St
NatWest Trophy	1	1	0	10	10	10.00	-	-	-	-
ALL ONE-DAY	1	1	0	10	10	10.00	-	-	-	-

BOWLING AVERAGES

Did not bowl

J.A. AFFORD - *Nottinghamshire*

Opposition	Venue	Date	Batting	Fielding	Bowling
BRITANNIC ASSURANCE					
Derbyshire	Trent Bridge	April 26	2		2-39 & 2-21
Leicestershire	Leicester	May 15	1 *	1Ct	1-28 & 0-27
Northants	Trent Bridge	May 23	0 *		3-90 & 0-74
Derbyshire	Derby	May 26	0		0-21 & 1-13
Kent	Tunbridge We	June 2		1Ct	3-30 & 0-21
Surrey	Trent Bridge	June 20	0 * & 0		1-84
Leicestershire	Trent Bridge	June 30	0 *	1Ct	1-23 & 1-62
Yorkshire	Scarborough	July 4			1-87
Sussex	Trent Bridge	July 7	0		0-72 & 2-47
Hampshire	Portsmouth	July 18	0 * & 1	1Ct	1-58 & 1-38
Lancashire	Southport	July 25	0 & 0		4-137 & 2-58
Middlesex	Trent Bridge	July 28			0-11 & 1-75
Essex	Southend	Aug 4	1 & 0		0-59 & 0-18
Somerset	Weston	Aug 8	0	2Ct	3-102
Glamorgan	Worksop	Aug 11	1 *		2-100 & 0-47
Gloucs	Trent Bridge	Aug 18	0		2-28 & 1-28
Middlesex	Lord's	Sept 7	3 & 0 *		0-76 & 0-23
Lancashire	Trent Bridge	Sept 12	5 & 0		3-93
Yorkshire	Trent Bridge	Sept 18		1Ct	0-81 & 0-33
REFUGE ASSURANCE					
Middlesex	Lord's	May 13		1Ct	1-41
Surrey	Trent Bridge	May 20		2Ct	1-24
Derbyshire	Derby	June 10			0-26
Kent	Canterbury	June 17	0 *		0-12
Somerset	Bath	June 24			0-25
Sussex	Trent Bridge	July 8			1-40
Hampshire	Southampton	July 15			1-74

A PLAYER RECORDS

Northants	Trent Bridge	July 29			1-24
Glamorgan	Trent Bridge	Aug 12		1Ct	2-39

NATWEST TROPHY

Bucks	Marlow	June 27	2*		0-26

BENSON & HEDGES CUP

Essex	Chelmsford	April 24			1-63
Leicestershire	Trent Bridge	May 1			1-37
Scotland	Glasgow	May 8			0-31
Northants	Trent Bridge	May 12			1-19
Essex	Chelmsford	May 30			2-47
Worcestershire	Trent Bridge	June 13			0-43

OTHER FIRST-CLASS

Oxford Univ	The Parks	June 6			0-9
Cambridge U	Fenner's	June 16			2-13 & 1-44
Sri Lanka	Cleethorpes	Aug 25	2		1-74

BATTING AVERAGES - Including fielding

	Matches	Inns	NO	Runs	HS	Avge	100s	50s	Ct	St
Britannic Assurance	19	21	7	14	5	1.00	-	-	7	-
Refuge Assurance	9	1	1	0	0*	-	-	-	4	-
NatWest Trophy	1	1	1	2	2*	-	-	-	-	-
Benson & Hedges Cup	6	0	0	0	0	-	-	-	-	-
Other First-Class	3	1	0	2	2	2.00	-	-	-	-
ALL FIRST-CLASS	22	22	7	16	5	1.06	-	-	7	-
ALL ONE-DAY	16	2	2	2	2*	-	-	-	4	-

BOWLING AVERAGES

	Overs	Mdns	Runs	Wkts	Avge	Best	5wI	10wM
Britannic Assurance	627	186	1804	38	47.47	4-137	-	-
Refuge Assurance	55	2	305	7	43.57	2-39	-	
NatWest Trophy	11	6	26	0				
Benson & Hedges Cup	66	9	240	5	48.00	2-47	-	
Other First-Class	61	23	140	4	35.00	2-13	-	
ALL FIRST-CLASS	688	209	1944	42	46.28	4-137	-	-
ALL ONE-DAY	132	17	571	12	47.58	2-39	-	

J.P. AGNEW - *Leicestershire*

Opposition	Venue	Date	Batting	Fielding	Bowling

BRITANNIC ASSURANCE

Glamorgan	Cardiff	April 26	0	1Ct	0-12 & 2-92
Essex	Chelmsford	May 3	37		0-170
Notts	Leicester	May 15	36 & 4		5-85
Lancashire	Old Trafford	May 19	6	1Ct	0-76 & 2-43
Somerset	Leicester	May 26	36		0-84 & 1-18
Hampshire	Leicester	June 2	0		2-115
Northants	Northampton	June 6	8		0-23
Middlesex	Leicester	June 16	0		1-60 & 0-62
Derbyshire	Leicester	June 20		1Ct	0-25 & 3-33
Gloucs	Gloucester	June 23	46*		5-70
Notts	Trent Bridge	June 30	8*		2-97
Glamorgan	Hinckley	July 7			5-89 & 0-8
Essex	Leicester	July 25	5		4-73 & 3-106
Yorkshire	Sheffield	July 28	4*		5-54 & 3-54
Worcestershire	Leicester	Aug 4	0 & 1		2-73
Kent	Dartford	Aug 8	0 & 12		0-44 & 0-28
Surrey	The Oval	Aug 11	4 & 3		0-126
Warwickshire	Edgbaston	Aug 18	0	1Ct	3-51 & 5-75
Kent	Leicester	Aug 23	6 & 3*		1-39 & 1-69
Sussex	Leicester	Aug 29	2*		0-35
Northants	Leicester	Sept 12	24 & 6	1Ct	0-96 & 3-69
Derbyshire	Derby	Sept 18	6		1-42

REFUGE ASSURANCE

Northants	Leicester	April 22	1		0-25
Glamorgan	Cardiff	April 29	1		1-20
Essex	Leicester	May 6			2-39
Lancashire	Old Trafford	May 20			1-39
Somerset	Leicester	May 27			1-20
Hampshire	Leicester	June 3	5		1-35
Sussex	Leicester	June 10			1-25
Middlesex	Leicester	June 17			2-35
Gloucs	Gloucester	June 24			1-22
Notts	Trent Bridge	July 1	1		0-25
Derbyshire	Knypersley	July 15	0		1-52
Yorkshire	Sheffield	July 29			0-33

NATWEST TROPHY

Hampshire	Leicester	June 27			2-44

BENSON & HEDGES CUP

Northants	Leicester	April 24			0-49
Notts	Trent Bridge	May 1	1*		1-34
Scotland	Leicester	May 12			3-20

OTHER ONE-DAY

New Zealand	Leicester	June 14			1-21

BATTING AVERAGES - Including fielding

	Matches	Inns	NO	Runs	HS	Avge	100s	50s	Ct	St
Britannic Assurance	22	26	5	257	46*	12.23	-	-	5	-
Refuge Assurance	12	5	0	8	5	1.60	-	-	-	-
NatWest Trophy	1	0	0	0	0	-	-	-	-	-
Benson & Hedges Cup	3	1	1	1	1*	-	-	-	-	-
Other One-Day	1	0	0	0	0	-	-	-	-	-
ALL FIRST-CLASS	22	26	5	257	46*	12.23	-	-	5	-
ALL ONE-DAY	17	6	1	9	5	1.80	-	-	-	-

BOWLING AVERAGES

	Overs	Mdns	Runs	Wkts	Avge	Best	5wI	10wM
Britannic Assurance	612	108	2196	59	37.22	5-54	5	-
Refuge Assurance	88.1	10	370	11	33.63	2-35	-	
NatWest Trophy	12	1	44	2	22.00	2-44	-	
Benson & Hedges Cup	28	4	103	4	25.75	3-20	-	
Other One-Day	11	1	21	1	21.00	1-21	-	
ALL FIRST-CLASS	612	108	2196	59	37.22	5-54	5	-
ALL ONE-DAY	139.1	16	538	18	29.88	3-20	-	

F.S. AHANGAMA - *Sri Lanka*

Opposition	Venue	Date	Batting	Fielding	Bowling

OTHER FIRST-CLASS

Warwickshire	Edgbaston	Aug 29			0-4

BATTING AVERAGES - Including fielding

	Matches	Inns	NO	Runs	HS	Avge	100s	50s	Ct	St
Other First-Class	1	0	0	0	0	-	-	-	-	-
ALL FIRST-CLASS	1	0	0	0	0	-	-	-	-	-

BOWLING AVERAGES

	Overs	Mdns	Runs	Wkts	Avge	Best	5wI	10wM
Other First-Class	1.3	0	4	0	-	-	-	-
ALL FIRST-CLASS	1.3	0	4	0	-	-	-	-

J.R. AIREY - *Lincolnshire*

Opposition	Venue	Date	Batting	Fielding	Bowling

NATWEST TROPHY

Gloucs	Gloucester	June 27	0		1-60

BATTING AVERAGES - Including fielding

	Matches	Inns	NO	Runs	HS	Avge	100s	50s	Ct	St
NatWest Trophy	1	1	0	0	0	0.00	-	-	-	-
ALL ONE-DAY	1	1	0	0	0	0.00	-	-	-	-

BOWLING AVERAGES

	Overs	Mdns	Runs	Wkts	Avge	Best	5wI	10wM
NatWest Trophy	10	0	60	1	60.00	1-60	-	
ALL ONE-DAY	10	0	60	1	60.00	1-60	-	

PLEYER RECORDS

R.I. ALIKHAN - *Surrey*

Opposition	Venue	Date	Batting			Fielding	Bowling
BRITANNIC ASSURANCE							
Lancashire	The Oval	May 3	55				
Middlesex	Lord's	May 23	20	&	0 *	2Ct	0-2
Derbyshire	The Oval	June 6	39	&	82 *		0-1 & 0-29
Yorkshire	Harrogate	June 9	31				
Worcestershire	The Oval	June 16	23	&	21		0-17
Notts	Trent Bridge	June 20	88			1Ct	
Glamorgan	Cardiff	June 30					
Hampshire	Southampton	Aug 23	72	&	0		
Lancashire	Blackpool	Aug 29	9				
Middlesex	The Oval	Sept 12	119	&	13		1-12
Essex	The Oval	Sept 18	16	&	138		0-22

OTHER ONE-DAY

Sri Lanka	The Oval	Sept 2	22				

BATTING AVERAGES - Including fielding

	Matches	Inns	NO	Runs	HS	Avge	100s	50s	Ct	St
Britannic Assurance	11	16	2	726	138	51.85	2	4	3	-
Other One-Day	1	1	0	22	22	22.00	-	-	-	-
ALL FIRST-CLASS	11	16	2	726	138	51.85	2	4	3	-
ALL ONE-DAY	1	1	0	22	22	22.00	-	-	-	-

BOWLING AVERAGES

	Overs	Mdns	Runs	Wkts	Avge	Best	5wI	10wM
Britannic Assurance	20	1	83	1	83.00	1-12	-	-
Other One-Day								
ALL FIRST-CLASS	20	1	83	1	83.00	1-12	-	-
ALL ONE-DAY								

M.W. ALLEYNE - *Gloucestershire*

Opposition	Venue	Date	Batting			Fielding	Bowling
BRITANNIC ASSURANCE							
Glamorgan	Bristol	May 15	0	&	6		3-47 & 0-9
Hampshire	Gloucester	June 20					
Glamorgan	Swansea	July 4					0-14
Surrey	Cheltenham	July 28	118	&	15		0-15
Warwickshire	Bristol	Aug 8	34	&	13		1-4
Kent	Bristol	Aug 11	47	&	40	1Ct	2-41
Notts	Trent Bridge	Aug 18	1	&	69	3Ct	3-23 & 1-23
Northants	Northampton	Aug 23	256	&	38		1-36
Worcestershire	Bristol	Sept 7	52	&	8	3Ct	0-26
Sussex	Bristol	Sept 12	15			1Ct	0-16
Hampshire	Southampton	Sept 18	18	&	33	1Ct	

REFUGE ASSURANCE

Glamorgan	Bristol	April 22	11			2-45
Hampshire	Southampton	May 6				0-41
Essex	Chelmsford	May 13				3-25
Warwickshire	Moreton-in-M	May 20	13 *	1Ct		3-40
Middlesex	Lord's	May 27	1			1-35
Somerset	Bristol	June 3				1-26
Lancashire	Old Trafford	June 10	18			2-42
Leicestershire	Gloucester	June 24	14			1-36
Derbyshire	Derby	July 1	7			0-32
Worcestershire	Worcester	July 8	8 *			1-51
Sussex	Swindon	July 15	20	1Ct		0-49
Yorkshire	Cheltenham	July 22	14 *			1-38
Surrey	Cheltenham	July 29	1 *			1-35
Kent	Bristol	Aug 12	39 *	2Ct		1-33
Notts	Trent Bridge	Aug 19	19			1-12
Northants	Northampton	Aug 26	38	1Ct		2-49

NATWEST TROPHY

Lincolnshire	Gloucester	June 27				5-30
Kent	Bristol	July 11				1-33
Lancashire	Old Trafford	Aug 1	9 *			0-51

BENSON & HEDGES CUP

Worcestershire	Bristol	April 24	23 *	1Ct		0-59

Glamorgan	Cardiff	May 1	30				4-42
Kent	Canterbury	May 10					0-22
Warwickshire	Bristol	May 12	11			2Ct	0-28

OTHER FIRST-CLASS

Zimbabwe	Bristol	May 19	37	&	54	1Ct	1-42
India	Bristol	Aug 4	0	&	0	1Ct	3-41 & 1-54

BATTING AVERAGES - Including fielding

	Matches	Inns	NO	Runs	HS	Avge	100s	50s	Ct	St
Britannic Assurance	11	17	0	763	256	44.88	2	2	9	-
Refuge Assurance	16	13	5	203	39 *	25.37	-	-	5	-
NatWest Trophy	3	1	1	9	9 *	-	-	-	-	-
Benson & Hedges Cup	4	3	1	64	30	32.00	-	-	3	-
Other First-Class	2	4	0	91	54	22.75	-	1	2	-
ALL FIRST-CLASS	13	21	0	854	256	40.66	2	3	11	-
ALL ONE-DAY	23	17	7	276	39 *	27.60	-	-	8	-

BOWLING AVERAGES

	Overs	Mdns	Runs	Wkts	Avge	Best	5wI	10wM
Britannic Assurance	77	23	254	11	23.09	3-23	-	-
Refuge Assurance	107.5	2	589	20	29.45	3-25	-	-
NatWest Trophy	29	4	114	6	19.00	5-30	1	
Benson & Hedges Cup	24.5	1	151	4	37.75	4-42	-	-
Other First-Class	35	6	137	5	27.40	3-41	-	-
ALL FIRST-CLASS	112	29	391	16	24.43	3-23	-	-
ALL ONE-DAY	161.4	7	854	30	28.46	5-30	1	

P.J.W. ALLOTT - *Lancashire*

Opposition	Venue	Date	Batting	Fielding	Bowling
BRITANNIC ASSURANCE					
Derbyshire	Derby	May 15		1Ct	1-40 & 0-26
Glamorgan	Colwyn Bay	May 26		2Ct	4-23 & 0-54
Sussex	Horsham	June 2	42	1Ct	2-30 & 0-10
Gloucs	Old Trafford	June 9		1Ct	0-39
Middlesex	Old Trafford	June 20			0-32
Hampshire	Old Trafford	June 23			0-26 & 0-10
Kent	Maidstone	June 30	0	1Ct	2-55 & 1-16
Derbyshire	Liverpool	July 7			
Warwickshire	Coventry	July 18			1-45 & 0-31
Essex	Colchester	July 21	10 *		1-76 & 0-59
Notts	Southport	July 25	5		4-37 & 2-52
Yorkshire	Old Trafford	Aug 18	2	2Ct	0-10
Notts	Trent Bridge	Sept 12	55 *	1Ct	0-18 & 0-41

REFUGE ASSURANCE

Middlesex	Old Trafford	April 22			0-20
Notts	Trent Bridge	April 29			2-29
Surrey	The Oval	May 6		1Ct	0-40
Leicestershire	Old Trafford	May 20		1Ct	0-46
Glamorgan	Colwyn Bay	May 27			0-28
Gloucs	Old Trafford	June 10			0-46
Hampshire	Old Trafford	June 24			
Kent	Maidstone	July 1			3-28
Derbyshire	Old Trafford	July 8	12	2Ct	1-34
Worcestershire	Old Trafford	July 15			0-31
Essex	Colchester	July 22			1-40
Yorkshire	Scarborough	Aug 5			2-21
Northants	Northampton	Aug 12		2Ct	0-19
Warwickshire	Old Trafford	Aug 26			2-51
Middlesex	Old Trafford	Sept 5		1Ct	0-33

NATWEST TROPHY

Durham	Old Trafford	June 27			3-24
Middlesex	Old Trafford	Aug 15			1-40
Northants	Lord's	Sept 1		1Ct	0-29

BENSON & HEDGES CUP

Surrey	Old Trafford	April 24			0-35
Combined U	Fenner's	May 1		1Ct	2-23
Hampshire	Old Trafford	May 8			0-29
Yorkshire	Headingley	May 10		1Ct	1-22
Surrey	Old Trafford	May 30		1Ct	2-25
Somerset	Old Trafford	June 13		1Ct	0-34
Worcestershire	Lord's	July 14			1-22

A PLImport...

A — PLAYER RECORDS

BATTING AVERAGES - Including fielding

	Matches	Inns	NO	Runs	HS	Avge	100s	50s	Ct	St
Britannic Assurance	13	6	2	114	55 *	28.50	-	1	9	-
Refuge Assurance	15	1	1	12	12	12.00	-	-	7	-
NatWest Trophy	3	0	0	0	0	-	-	-	1	-
Benson & Hedges Cup	7	0	0	0	0	-	-	-	4	-
ALL FIRST-CLASS	13	6	2	114	55 *	28.50	-	1	9	-
ALL ONE-DAY	25	1	0	12	12	12.00	-	-	12	-

BOWLING AVERAGES

	Overs	Mdns	Runs	Wkts	Avge	Best	5wI	10wM
Britannic Assurance	266	77	730	18	40.55	4-23	-	-
Refuge Assurance	105	5	466	11	42.36	3-28	-	
NatWest Trophy	34	10	93	4	23.25	3-24	-	
Benson & Hedges Cup	67	12	190	6	31.66	2-23	-	
ALL FIRST-CLASS	266	77	730	18	40.55	4-23	-	-
ALL ONE-DAY	206	27	749	21	35.66	3-24	-	

S.A. ALMAER - *Oxford University*

Opposition	Venue	Date	Batting	Fielding	Bowling
OTHER FIRST-CLASS					
Somerset	The Parks	April 18	4		2Ct

BATTING AVERAGES - Including fielding

	Matches	Inns	NO	Runs	HS	Avge	100s	50s	Ct	St
Other First-Class	1	1	0	4	4	4.00	-	-	2	-
ALL FIRST-CLASS	1	1	0	4	4	4.00	-	-	2	-

BOWLING AVERAGES
Did not bowl

C.E.L. AMBROSE - *Northamptonshire*

Opposition	Venue	Date	Batting	Fielding	Bowling
BRITANNIC ASSURANCE					
Yorkshire	Headingley	April 26			5-49 & 1-70
Warwickshire	Northampton	May 15	11 * & 16		1-80
Warwickshire	Edgbaston	June 2	23 *		5-53 & 3-55
Leicestershire	Northampton	June 6			3-54
Glamorgan	Northampton	June 9			0-65 & 0-58
Middlesex	Luton	June 23	6 & 3		2-53 & 2-38
Yorkshire	Northampton	July 7		14	1-42
Kent	Northampton	July 18	0 *		5-59 & 1-47
Gloucs	Cheltenham	July 25	8 & 6		2-53
Derbyshire	Chesterfield	Aug 8		0 *	2-90 & 0-20
Worcestershire	Worcester	Aug 18	12 & 12		2-53 & 1-28
Gloucs	Northampton	Aug 23	10 & 18		1-77 & 2-35
Essex	Chelmsford	Sept 7	9	1Ct	4-67 & 3-52
Leicestershire	Leicester	Sept 12	55 * & 0		7-89 & 5-66
REFUGE ASSURANCE					
Warwickshire	Edgbaston	April 29			0-31
NATWEST TROPHY					
Staffordshire	Northampton	June 27			1-15
Notts	Northampton	July 11		2Ct	1-30
Worcestershire	Northampton	Aug 1	0		1-39
Hampshire	Southampton	Aug 15	22		1-29
Lancashire	Lord's	Sept 1	48	1Ct	0-23
BENSON & HEDGES CUP					
Leicestershire	Leicester	April 24			3-19
Essex	Northampton	May 8	12		1-35
Scotland	Northampton	May 10	11 *		3-26
Notts	Trent Bridge	May 12	11 *	3Ct	2-20
OTHER FIRST-CLASS					
New Zealand	Northampton	June 16	0		3-60

BATTING AVERAGES - Including fielding

	Matches	Inns	NO	Runs	HS	Avge	100s	50s	Ct	St
Britannic Assurance	14	17	5	203	55 *	16.91	-	1	1	-
Refuge Assurance	1	0	0	0	0	-	-	-	-	-
NatWest Trophy	5	3	0	70	48	23.33	-	-	3	-
Benson & Hedges Cup	4	3	2	34	12	34.00	-	-	3	-
Other First-Class	1	1	0	0	0	0.00	-	-	-	-
ALL FIRST-CLASS	15	18	5	203	55 *	15.61	-	1	1	-
ALL ONE-DAY	10	6	2	104	48	26.00	-	-	6	-

BOWLING AVERAGES

	Overs	Mdns	Runs	Wkts	Avge	Best	5wI	10wM
Britannic Assurance	483.4	124	1353	58	23.32	7-89	5	1
Refuge Assurance	7	1	31	0	-	-	-	-
NatWest Trophy	54.1	11	136	4	34.00	1-15	-	-
Benson & Hedges Cup	44	9	100	9	11.11	3-19	-	-
Other First-Class	20	3	60	3	20.00	3-60	-	-
ALL FIRST-CLASS	503.4	127	1413	61	23.16	7-89	5	1
ALL ONE-DAY	105.1	21	267	13	20.53	3-19	-	-

S.J.W. ANDREW - *Essex*

Opposition	Venue	Date	Batting	Fielding	Bowling
BRITANNIC ASSURANCE					
Middlesex	Lord's	April 26			3-93 & 1-79
Leicestershire	Chelmsford	May 3			0-72 & 0-31
Hampshire	Southampton	May 23	0		0-50 & 1-42
Middlesex	Ilford	June 2	15		0-61
Warwickshire	Edgbaston	June 9			0-44
Derbyshire	Colchester	July 18	1		4-60 & 2-49
Lancashire	Colchester	July 21	0		1-81 & 0-51
Leicestershire	Leicester	July 25	3 *		2-62 & 2-39
Sussex	Chelmsford	July 28	0 *	1Ct	2-108 & 1-60
Glamorgan	Southend	Aug 8	12 *		2-66 & 2-67
Yorkshire	Middlesbr'gh	Aug 11	0		0-28 & 5-55
Surrey	Chelmsford	Aug 18	9 *		4-27 & 2-34
Derbyshire	Derby	Aug 23	6 *		0-18 & 4-30
Northants	Chelmsford	Sept 7	1 * & 35		1-58 & 1-132
Kent	Chelmsford	Sept 12	11 & 8 *		1-99 & 1-78
Surrey	The Oval	Sept 18	18		1-24 & 0-65
REFUGE ASSURANCE					
Glamorgan	Ilford	June 3			0-38
Yorkshire	Middlesbr'gh	Aug 12		5	2-30
Derbyshire	Derby	Aug 26			0-53
NATWEST TROPHY					
Scotland	Chelmsford	June 27			2-34
OTHER FIRST-CLASS					
Cambridge U	Fenner's	May 16			2-39 & 1-34
New Zealand	Chelmsford	June 30	0		0-45 & 0-16
OTHER ONE-DAY					
Zimbabwe	Chelmsford	May 14			4-36
Yorkshire	Scarborough	Sept 3			2-35
Hampshire	Scarborough	Sept 4		0	0-29

BATTING AVERAGES - Including fielding

	Matches	Inns	NO	Runs	HS	Avge	100s	50s	Ct	St
Britannic Assurance	16	15	7	119	35	14.87	-	-	1	-
Refuge Assurance	3	1	0	5	5	5.00	-	-	-	-
NatWest Trophy	1	0	0	0	0	-	-	-	-	-
Other First-Class	2	1	0	0	0	0.00	-	-	-	-
Other One-Day	3	1	0	0	0	0.00	-	-	-	-
ALL FIRST-CLASS	18	16	7	119	35	13.22	-	-	1	-
ALL ONE-DAY	7	2	0	5	5	2.50	-	-	-	-

BOWLING AVERAGES

	Overs	Mdns	Runs	Wkts	Avge	Best	5wI	10wM
Britannic Assurance	449	67	1763	43	41.00	5-55	1	-
Refuge Assurance	19	2	121	2	60.50	2-30	-	-
NatWest Trophy	12	2	34	2	17.00	2-34	-	-
Other First-Class	54	8	134	3	44.66	2-39	-	-
Other One-Day	20	1	100	6	16.66	4-36	-	-
ALL FIRST-CLASS	503	75	1897	46	41.23	5-55	1	-
ALL ONE-DAY	51	5	255	10	25.50	4-36	-	-

PLAYER RECORDS

H.A. ANTHONY - *Glamorgan*

Opposition	Venue	Date	Batting		Fielding	Bowling
BRITANNIC ASSURANCE						
Lancashire	Colwyn Bay	May 26	39			2-99
Warwickshire	Edgbaston	Sept 12	0 &	13		2-70 & 1-38
OTHER FIRST-CLASS						
Oxford U	The Parks	April 14	19			2-72
Oxford U	The Parks	June 2	30			1-29
India	Swansea	Aug 18		0		3-95 & 0-2
Sri Lanka	Ebbw Vale	Aug 22	12 &	14		1-47 & 0-14

BATTING AVERAGES - Including fielding

	Matches	Inns	NO	Runs	HS	Avge	100s	50s	Ct	St
Britannic Assurance	2	3	0	52	39	17.33	-	-	-	-
Other First-Class	4	5	0	75	30	15.00	-	-	-	-
ALL FIRST-CLASS	6	8	0	127	39	15.87	-	-	-	-

BOWLING AVERAGES

	Overs	Mdns	Runs	Wkts	Avge	Best	5wI	10wM
Britannic Assurance	62	13	207	5	41.40	2-70	-	-
Other First-Class	80.4	19	259	7	37.00	3-95	-	-
ALL FIRST-CLASS	142.4	32	466	12	38.83	3-95	-	-

N.J. ARCHER - *Staffordshire*

Opposition	Venue	Date	Batting	Fielding	Bowling
NATWEST TROPHY					
Northants	Northampton	June 27	26		

BATTING AVERAGES - Including fielding

	Matches	Inns	NO	Runs	HS	Avge	100s	50s	Ct	St
NatWest Trophy	1	1	0	26	26	26.00	-	-	-	-
ALL ONE-DAY	1	1	0	26	26	26.00	-	-	-	-

BOWLING AVERAGES
Did not bowl

K.A. ARNOLD - *Oxfordshire & Minor Counties*

Opposition	Venue	Date	Batting	Fielding	Bowling
NATWEST TROPHY					
Kent	Oxford	June 27	2		0-48
OTHER FIRST-CLASS					
For Minor Counties					
India	Trowbridge	July 11		2Ct	1-113

BATTING AVERAGES - Including fielding

	Matches	Inns	NO	Runs	HS	Avge	100s	50s	Ct	St
NatWest Trophy	1	1	0	2	2	2.00	-	-	-	-
Other First-Class	1	0	0	0	0	-	-	-	2	-
ALL FIRST-CLASS	1	0	0	0	0	-	-	-	2	-
ALL ONE-DAY	1	1	0	2	2	2.00	-	-	-	-

BOWLING AVERAGES

	Overs	Mdns	Runs	Wkts	Avge	Best	5wI	10wM
NatWest Trophy	12	3	48	0			-	-
Other First-Class	28	6	113	1	113.00	1-113	-	-
ALL FIRST-CLASS	28	6	113	1	113.00	1-113	-	-
ALL ONE-DAY	12	3	48	0			-	-

K.J. ARNOTT - *Zimbabwe*

Opposition	Venue	Date	Batting		Fielding	Bowling
OTHER FIRST-CLASS						
Lancashire	Old Trafford	May 23	0 &	2		
OTHER ONE-DAY						
Sussex	Hove	May 13	11			
Essex	Chelmsford	May 14	6		1Ct	

BATTING AVERAGES - Including fielding

	Matches	Inns	NO	Runs	HS	Avge	100s	50s	Ct	St
Other First-Class	1	2	0	2	2	1.00	-	-	-	-
Other One-Day	2	2	0	17	11	8.50	-	-	1	-
ALL FIRST-CLASS	1	2	0	2	2	1.00	-	-	-	-
ALL ONE-DAY	2	2	0	17	11	8.50	-	-	1	-

BOWLING AVERAGES
Did not bowl

J. ARSCOTT - *Cambridge University*

Opposition	Venue	Date	Batting		Fielding	Bowling
OTHER FIRST-CLASS						
Essex	Fenner's	May 16	9 &	10		
Gloucs	Fenner's	May 23	13 &	43 *	0Ct,2St	

BATTING AVERAGES - Including fielding

	Matches	Inns	NO	Runs	HS	Avge	100s	50s	Ct	St
Other First-Class	2	4	1	75	43 *	25.00	-	-	-	2
ALL FIRST-CLASS	2	4	1	75	43 *	25.00	-	-	-	2

BOWLING AVERAGES
Did not bowl

ASIF DIN - *Warwickshire*

Opposition	Venue	Date	Batting		Fielding	Bowling
BRITANNIC ASSURANCE						
Yorkshire	Edgbaston	May 3	0 &	23	2Ct	0-6
Northants	Northampton	May 15	3		1Ct	0-5 & 1-13
Notts	Edgbaston	May 19	41 &	61	1Ct	0-9 & 0-15
Worcestershire	Edgbaston	May 26	70 &	1		
Northants	Edgbaston	June 2	5 &	9	1Ct	
Middlesex	Lord's	June 6	49 &	44		
Essex	Edgbaston	June 9	42			
Derbyshire	Derby	June 16	17 * &	30		0-85
Yorkshire	Sheffield	June 20	0 &	0		1-5
Kent	Edgbaston	June 23	19 &	14		1-18 & 0-14
Somerset	Taunton	July 4	45 &	4		0-41
Surrey	The Oval	July 7	22 &	4		0-6
Lancashire	Coventry	July 18	45 &	1		0-11 & 1-37
Glamorgan	Swansea	July 25	47 &	6		0-50 & 1-39
Hampshire	Edgbaston	July 28			2Ct	0-67 & 1-62
Sussex	Eastbourne	Aug 4	57 * &	0 *	2Ct	0-17 & 0-29
Gloucs	Bristol	Aug 8	0 &	65		0-17
Leicestershire	Edgbaston	Aug 18	0 &	1		
Somerset	Edgbaston	Sept 7	55 &	0		0-5 & 0-18
Glamorgan	Edgbaston	Sept 12	40 &	34	1Ct	
Lancashire	Old Trafford	Sept 18	24			
REFUGE ASSURANCE						
Northants	Edgbaston	April 29	23			
Yorkshire	Edgbaston	May 6	40			
Gloucs	Moreton-in-M	May 20	59			
Worcestershire	Worcester	May 27	86 *			
Middlesex	Lord's	June 3	17		1Ct	
Essex	Edgbaston	June 10	4			0-17
Derbyshire	Derby	June 17	11		1Ct	
Kent	Edgbaston	June 24	19 *			
Glamorgan	Edgbaston	July 15	46			

A   PLAYER RECORDS

Notts	Edgbaston	July 22	43		
Hampshire	Edgbaston	July 29	77 *		
Sussex	Eastbourne	Aug 5	6	1Ct	
Somerset	Weston	Aug 12	113		
Leicestershire	Edgbaston	Aug 19			
Lancashire	Old Trafford	Aug 26	1	2Ct	

NATWEST TROPHY

Hertfordshire	St Albans	June 27	66	1Ct	5-40
Yorkshire	Headingley	July 11	58		0-14

BENSON & HEDGES CUP

Glamorgan	Edgbaston	April 24	50	1Ct	
Kent	Canterbury	May 8	9		
Worcestershire	Edgbaston	May 10	37		
Gloucs	Bristol	May 12	27		

OTHER FIRST-CLASS

Cambridge U	Fenner's	April 26	0 & 100 *		3-17 & 1-49

OTHER ONE-DAY

Surrey	Harrogate	June 13	0	2Ct	
Yorkshire	Harrogate	June 15	10		2-58
Surrey	Hove	Sept 3	51		

BATTING AVERAGES - Including fielding

	Matches	Inns	NO	Runs	HS	Avge	100s	50s	Ct	St
Britannic Assurance	21	37	3	874	70	25.70	-	5	10	-
Refuge Assurance	15	14	3	545	113	49.54	1	3	5	-
NatWest Trophy	2	2	0	124	66	62.00	-	2	1	-
Benson & Hedges Cup	4	4	0	123	50	30.75	-	1	1	-
Other First-Class	1	2	1	100	100 *	100.00	1	-	-	-
Other One-Day	3	3	0	61	51	20.33	-	1	2	-
ALL FIRST-CLASS	22	39	4	974	100 *	27.82	1	5	10	-
ALL ONE-DAY	24	23	3	853	113	42.65	1	7	9	-

BOWLING AVERAGES

	Overs	Mdns	Runs	Wkts	Avge	Best	5wI	10wM
Britannic Assurance	133.2	24	569	6	94.83	1-5	-	-
Refuge Assurance	2	0	17	0			-	
NatWest Trophy	11	2	54	5	10.80	5-40	1	
Benson & Hedges Cup								
Other First-Class	25.5	6	66	4	16.50	3-17	-	
Other One-Day	10	0	58	2	29.00	2-58		
ALL FIRST-CLASS	159.1	30	635	10	63.50	3-17	-	-
ALL ONE-DAY	23	1	129	7	18.42	5-40	1	

M.A. ATHERTON - *Lancashire & England*

Opposition	Venue	Date	Batting	Fielding	Bowling
CORNHILL TEST MATCHES					
New Zealand	Trent Bridge	June 7	151		
New Zealand	Lord's	June 21	0 & 54		0-0
New Zealand	Edgbaston	July 5	82 & 70	3Ct	0-17
India	Lord's	July 26	8 & 72	1Ct	0-11
India	Old Trafford	Aug 9	131 & 74	1Ct	0-68 & 0-22
India	The Oval	Aug 23	7 & 86	1Ct	1-60
TEXACO TROPHY					
India	Headingley	July 18	7	1Ct	
India	Trent Bridge	July 20	59	1Ct	
BRITANNIC ASSURANCE					
Worcestershire	Old Trafford	April 26	50		0-32 & 0-36
Surrey	The Oval	May 3	191	1Ct	0-75 & 1-25
Derbyshire	Derby	May 15	93 & 51		5-95 & 2-82
Leicestershire	Old Trafford	May 19	10 * & 3	2Ct	4-89 & 0-55
Glamorgan	Colwyn Bay	May 26	15		0-11 & 0-19
Sussex	Horsham	June 2	76 & 0 *	2Ct	2-47 & 0-4
Kent	Maidstone	June 30	101 & 44	1Ct	0-1 & 4-23
Essex	Colchester	July 21	11 & 108 *	2Ct	3-73 & 3-106
Yorkshire	Headingley	Aug 4	64 & 25	3Ct	5-26 & 2-71
Yorkshire	Old Trafford	Aug 18	108		0-42 & 3-69
Notts	Trent Bridge	Sept 12	81	2Ct	6-78
Warwickshire	Old Trafford	Sept 18	22 *	2Ct	2-52
REFUGE ASSURANCE					
Middlesex	Old Trafford	April 22	63		0-24
Notts	Trent Bridge	April 29	5	1Ct	3-33

Surrey	The Oval	May 6	76 *	1Ct	
Leicestershire	Old Trafford	May 20	33	1Ct	0-40
Glamorgan	Colwyn Bay	May 27	74		0-66
Kent	Maidstone	July 1	13		
Worcestershire	Old Trafford	July 15	1	1Ct	
Essex	Colchester	July 22	111		
Yorkshire	Scarborough	Aug 5	53		2-27
Middlesex	Old Trafford	Sept 5	33	1Ct	

NATWEST TROPHY

Durham	Old Trafford	June 27	4		1-7
Derbyshire	Derby	July 11	55	1Ct	1-37
Gloucs	Old Trafford	Aug 1	25	3Ct	2-15
Middlesex	Old Trafford	Aug 15	34		
Northants	Lord's	Sept 1	38 *		

BENSON & HEDGES CUP

Surrey	Old Trafford	April 24	44	1Ct	3-32
Combined U	Fenner's	May 1	69 *		
Hampshire	Old Trafford	May 8	2		
Yorkshire	Headingley	May 10	3		
Surrey	Old Trafford	May 30	74	1Ct	0-20
Somerset	Old Trafford	June 13	56 *		
Worcestershire	Lord's	July 14	40		

OTHER FIRST-CLASS

For MCC

Worcestershire	Lord's	April 17	19	1Ct	

For Lancashire

Oxford U	The Parks	June 16	117	1Ct	1-99 & 1-10

BATTING AVERAGES - Including fielding

	Matches	Inns	NO	Runs	HS	Avge	100s	50s	Ct	St
Cornhill Test Matches	6	11	0	735	151	66.81	2	6	6	-
Texaco Trophy	2	2	0	66	59	33.00	-	1	2	-
Britannic Assurance	12	18	4	1053	191	75.21	4	6	16	-
Refuge Assurance	10	10	1	462	111	51.33	1	4	5	-
NatWest Trophy	5	5	1	156	55	39.00	-	1	4	-
Benson & Hedges Cup	7	7	2	288	74	57.60	-	3	2	-
Other First-Class	2	2	0	136	117	68.00	1	-	2	-
ALL FIRST-CLASS	20	31	4	1924	191	71.25	7	12	24	-
ALL ONE-DAY	24	24	4	972	111	48.60	1	9	13	-

BOWLING AVERAGES

	Overs	Mdns	Runs	Wkts	Avge	Best	5wI	10wM
Cornhill Test Matches	38	9	178	1	178.00	1-60	-	-
Texaco Trophy								
Britannic Assurance	356.3	84	1111	42	26.45	6-78	3	-
Refuge Assurance	29	0	190	5	38.00	3-33	-	
NatWest Trophy	18	1	59	4	14.75	2-15	-	
Benson & Hedges Cup	14	1	52	3	17.33	3-32	-	
Other First-Class	39	10	109	2	54.50	1-10	-	
ALL FIRST-CLASS	433.3	103	1398	45	31.06	6-78	3	-
ALL ONE-DAY	61	2	301	12	25.08	3-32	-	

C.W.J. ATHEY - *Gloucestershire*

Opposition	Venue	Date	Batting	Fielding	Bowling
BRITANNIC ASSURANCE					
Somerset	Taunton	April 26	68 & 39	2Ct	
Glamorgan	Bristol	May 15	8 & 0	4Ct	0-4
Middlesex	Lord's	May 26	31 & 69		2-13
Somerset	Bristol	June 2	37	3Ct	0-9 & 0-2
Essex	Ilford	June 6	9		0-25
Lancashire	Old Trafford	June 9	33		
Sussex	Hove	June 16	131		
Hampshire	Gloucester	June 20	14 *		
Leicestershire	Gloucester	June 23	5	1Ct	
Derbyshire	Derby	June 30	12 & 21	2Ct	
Glamorgan	Swansea	July 4	35 *		
Worcestershire	Worcester	July 7	15 & 32	1Ct	
Yorkshire	Cheltenham	July 21	68		0-13
Northants	Cheltenham	July 25	27		0-7
Surrey	Cheltenham	July 28	0 & 86 *		
Warwickshire	Bristol	Aug 8	108 * & 122	2Ct	
Kent	Bristol	Aug 11	83 & 71	1Ct	
Notts	Trent Bridge	Aug 18	37 & 0		0-2
Northants	Northampton	Aug 23	79 & 88 *		
Worcestershire	Bristol	Sept 7	18 & 34 *		0-14

PLEAYER RECORDS A

Sussex	Bristol	Sept 12	4	2Ct	0-15

REFUGE ASSURANCE

Glamorgan	Bristol	April 22	15	1Ct	
Hampshire	Southampton	May 6			
Essex	Chelmsford	May 13	101*		
Warwickshire	Moreton-in-M	May 20	4	1Ct	
Middlesex	Lord's	May 27	29		
Somerset	Bristol	June 3	53*		
Lancashire	Old Trafford	June 10	6		
Leicestershire	Gloucester	June 24	15		
Derbyshire	Derby	July 1	17		
Worcestershire	Worcester	July 8	63		
Sussex	Swindon	July 15	23		
Yorkshire	Cheltenham	July 22	80		
Surrey	Cheltenham	July 29	113		
Kent	Bristol	Aug 12	3	2Ct	
Notts	Trent Bridge	Aug 19	2	1Ct	
Northants	Northampton	Aug 26	22		

NATWEST TROPHY

Lincolnshire	Gloucester	June 27	81*		
Kent	Bristol	July 11	22		
Lancashire	Old Trafford	Aug 1	8		0-14

BENSON & HEDGES CUP

Worcestershire	Bristol	April 24	49	1Ct	
Glamorgan	Cardiff	May 1	20	1Ct	
Kent	Canterbury	May 10			
Warwickshire	Bristol	May 12	83*		

OTHER FIRST-CLASS

Zimbabwe	Bristol	May 19	8* & 2		
India	Bristol	Aug 4	80		0-2 & 0-39

BATTING AVERAGES - Including fielding

	Matches	Inns	NO	Runs	HS	Avge	100s	50s	Ct	St
Britannic Assurance	21	32	6	1384	131	53.23	3	8	18	-
Refuge Assurance	16	15	2	546	113	42.00	2	3	5	-
NatWest Trophy	3	3	1	111	81*	55.50	-	1	-	-
Benson & Hedges Cup	4	3	1	152	83*	76.00	-	1	2	-
Other First-Class	2	3	1	90	80	45.00	-	1	-	-
ALL FIRST-CLASS	23	35	7	1474	131	52.64	3	9	18	-
ALL ONE-DAY	23	21	4	809	113	47.58	2	5	7	-

BOWLING AVERAGES

	Overs	Mdns	Runs	Wkts	Avge	Best	5wI	10wM
Britannic Assurance	36.5	9	104	2	52.00	2-13	-	-
Refuge Assurance								
NatWest Trophy	3	0	14	0	-	-		
Benson & Hedges Cup								
Other First-Class	14	1	41	0	-	-		
ALL FIRST-CLASS	50.5	10	145	2	72.50	2-13	-	-
ALL ONE-DAY	3	0	14	0	-	-		

P.D. ATKINS - *Surrey*

Opposition	Venue	Date	Batting	Fielding	Bowling

BRITANNIC ASSURANCE

Middlesex	Lord's	May 23	23 & 0*	

BATTING AVERAGES - Including fielding

	Matches	Inns	NO	Runs	HS	Avge	100s	50s	Ct	St
Britannic Assurance	1	2	1	23	23	23.00	-	-	-	-
ALL FIRST-CLASS	1	2	1	23	23	23.00	-	-	-	-

BOWLING AVERAGES
Did not bowl

J.C.M.ATKINSON-*Cambridge U & Somerset*

Opposition	Venue	Date	Batting	Fielding	Bowling

REFUGE ASSURANCE
For Somerset

Surrey	Weston	Aug 5	8	

BENSON & HEDGES CUP
For Combined Universities

Lancashire	Fenner's	May 1	10	
Yorkshire	Headingley	May 8	16	
Surrey	The Parks	May 10	9	
Hampshire	Southampton	May 12	0	

OTHER FIRST-CLASS
For Cambridge University

Northants	Fenner's	April 14	2 & 47*		
Derbyshire	Fenner's	April 18	36 & 23	1Ct	1-27
Warwickshire	Fenner's	April 26	41 & 17	1Ct	0-40
Middlesex	Fenner's	May 3	6 & 17		
Essex	Fenner's	May 16	51 & 0		0-23
Gloucs	Fenner's	May 23	72 & 34	2Ct	0-9
Notts	Fenner's	June 16	0 & 5	2Ct	0-2
Kent	Fenner's	June 20	0* & 0		

For Combined Universities

New Zealand	Fenner's	June 27	10 & 4	1Ct	

For Cambridge University

Sussex	Hove	June 30	2 & 0		
Oxford Univ	Lord's	July 4	7		

BATTING AVERAGES - Including fielding

	Matches	Inns	NO	Runs	HS	Avge	100s	50s	Ct	St
Refuge Assurance	1	1	0	8	8	8.00	-	-	-	-
Benson & Hedges Cup	4	4	0	35	16	8.75	-	-	-	-
Other First-Class	11	21	2	374	72	19.68	-	2	7	-
ALL FIRST-CLASS	11	21	2	374	72	19.68	-	2	7	-
ALL ONE-DAY	5	5	0	43	16	8.60	-	-	-	-

BOWLING AVERAGES

	Overs	Mdns	Runs	Wkts	Avge	Best	5wI	10wM
Refuge Assurance								
Benson & Hedges Cup								
Other First-Class	23	3	101	1	101.00	1-27	-	-
ALL FIRST-CLASS	23	3	101	1	101.00	1-27	-	-
ALL ONE-DAY								

M. ATTAPATU - *Sri Lanka*

Opposition	Venue	Date	Batting	Fielding	Bowling

OTHER FIRST-CLASS

Glamorgan	Ebbw Vale	Aug 22	23 & 71*	3Ct	
Notts	Cleethorpes	Aug 25	9*	1Ct	
Warwickshire	Edgbaston	Aug 29		3Ct	
Sussex	Hove	Sept 5	49* & 74*		0-4
Lancashire	Old Trafford	Sept 8	6		0-17
Hampshire	Southampton	Sept 12	9 & 0		

OTHER ONE-DAY

Surrey	The Oval	Sept 2	19	1Ct	
Somerset	Taunton	Sept 3	63*		

BATTING AVERAGES - Including fielding

	Matches	Inns	NO	Runs	HS	Avge	100s	50s	Ct	St
Other First-Class	6	8	4	241	74*	60.25	-	2	7	-
Other One-Day	2	2	1	82	63*	82.00	-	1	1	-
ALL FIRST-CLASS	6	8	4	241	74*	60.25	-	2	7	-
ALL ONE-DAY	2	2	1	82	63*	82.00	-	1	1	-

BOWLING AVERAGES

	Overs	Mdns	Runs	Wkts	Avge	Best	5wI	10wM
Other First-Class	4	0	21	0	-	-		
Other One-Day								
ALL FIRST-CLASS	4	0	21	0	-	-		
ALL ONE-DAY								

PLAYER RECORDS

I.D. AUSTIN - *Lancashire*

Opposition	Venue	Date	Batting	Fielding	Bowling
BRITANNIC ASSURANCE					
Gloucs	Old Trafford	June 9	26 *		3-42
Middlesex	Old Trafford	June 20	45 *		0-58
Hampshire	Old Trafford	June 23			0-18 & 0-28
Derbyshire	Liverpool	July 7	29 & 27 *		0-33 & 1-18
Warwickshire	Coventry	July 18	9		0-48 & 0-19
Somerset	Old Trafford	July 28	1		2-44 & 2-19
Worcestershire	Kid'minster	Aug 8	0 & 58		2-105
Northants	Northampton	Aug 11	5 & 11		0-73
Yorkshire	Old Trafford	Aug 18	21 *		0-5
Surrey	Blackpool	Aug 29	6 *		0-3
Warwickshire	Old Trafford	Sept 18			0-23
REFUGE ASSURANCE					
Middlesex	Old Trafford	April 22	8 *		0-45
Notts	Trent Bridge	April 29			1-38
Surrey	The Oval	May 6			0-56
Leicestershire	Old Trafford	May 20	2		3-33
Glamorgan	Colwyn Bay	May 27	10 *	2Ct	2-51
Gloucs	Old Trafford	June 10	1 *		0-57
Hampshire	Old Trafford	June 24			
Kent	Maidstone	July 1			1-27
Derbyshire	Old Trafford	July 8	3		0-53
Worcestershire	Old Trafford	July 15			2-26
Essex	Colchester	July 22	10		1-67
Somerset	Old Trafford	July 29			3-34
Yorkshire	Scarborough	Aug 5			2-21
Northants	Northampton	Aug 12			0-43
Warwickshire	Old Trafford	Aug 26	2 *	1Ct	0-31
Middlesex	Old Trafford	Sept 5	0 *		1-40
NATWEST TROPHY					
Durham	Old Trafford	June 27			3-36
Derbyshire	Derby	July 11	13 *		2-46
Gloucs	Old Trafford	Aug 1			1-22
Middlesex	Old Trafford	Aug 15			0-60
Northants	Lord's	Sept 1			1-41
BENSON & HEDGES CUP					
Surrey	Old Trafford	April 24	1 *		4-25
Combined U	Fenner's	May 1	61 *		1-42
Hampshire	Old Trafford	May 8	9 *		0-26
Yorkshire	Headingley	May 10	0 *		1-14
Surrey	Old Trafford	May 30			1-45
Somerset	Old Trafford	June 13			2-48
Worcestershire	Lord's	July 14	17		2-44
OTHER FIRST-CLASS					
Zimbabwe	Old Trafford	May 23	11 *		2-93 & 0-10
Sri Lanka	Old Trafford	Sept 8	3 & 24		0-23

BATTING AVERAGES - Including fielding

	Matches	Inns	NO	Runs	HS	Avge	100s	50s	Ct	St
Britannic Assurance	11	12	5	238	58	34.00	-	1	-	-
Refuge Assurance	16	8	5	36	10 *	12.00	-	-	3	-
NatWest Trophy	5	1	1	13	13 *	-	-	-	-	-
Benson & Hedges Cup	7	5	4	88	61 *	88.00	-	1	-	-
Other First-Class	2	3	1	38	24	19.00	-	-	-	-
ALL FIRST-CLASS	13	15	6	276	58	30.66	-	1	-	-
ALL ONE-DAY	28	14	10	137	61 *	34.25	-	1	3	-

BOWLING AVERAGES

	Overs	Mdns	Runs	Wkts	Avge	Best	5wI	10wM
Britannic Assurance	208.1	64	536	10	53.60	3-42	-	-
Refuge Assurance	108.1	2	622	16	38.87	3-33	-	
NatWest Trophy	53	5	205	7	29.28	3-36	-	
Benson & Hedges Cup	65	11	244	11	22.18	4-25	-	
Other First-Class	36.5	12	126	2	63.00	2-93	-	-
ALL FIRST-CLASS	245	76	662	12	55.16	3-42	-	-
ALL ONE-DAY	226.1	18	1071	34	31.50	4-25	-	-

J.R. AYLING - *Hampshire*

Opposition	Venue	Date	Batting	Fielding	Bowling
BRITANNIC ASSURANCE					
Notts	Portsmouth	July 18	61		0-12 & 1-14
Derbyshire	Portsmouth	July 21	31 & 5		1-61 & 1-23
Sussex	Arundel	July 25	28 * & 22	1Ct	1-36 & 1-36
Northants	Bournemouth	Aug 4		1Ct	0-15 & 2-48
Middlesex	Bournemouth	Aug 8	41		0-63 & 0-12
Somerset	Taunton	Aug 18	62 *		0-22
Gloucs	Southampton	Sept 18	28 & 10		2-57 & 1-55
REFUGE ASSURANCE					
Gloucs	Southampton	May 6	2 *		
Somerset	Taunton	May 13			0-38
Yorkshire	Headingley	May 27	13		1-16
Leicestershire	Leicester	June 3	23 *		2-28
Middlesex	Basingstoke	June 10	9		1-27
Glamorgan	Bournemouth	June 17	5 *		1-39
Lancashire	Old Trafford	June 24			
Sussex	Hove	July 1	17 *		1-52
Essex	Southampton	July 8			2-40
Notts	Southampton	July 15			4-37
Derbyshire	Portsmouth	July 22	0 *		1-9
Warwickshire	Edgbaston	July 29	25		1-27
Northants	Bournemouth	Aug 5			0-44
Worcestershire	Worcester	Aug 12	47 *		1-43
Surrey	Southampton	Aug 26	3		0-50
NATWEST TROPHY					
Leicestershire	Leicester	June 27	29		2-34
Essex	Chelmsford	July 11	10 *		0-57
Yorkshire	Southampton	Aug 1	7		3-30
Northants	Southampton	Aug 15	8	1Ct	2-76
BENSON & HEDGES CUP					
Yorkshire	Southampton	April 24	14		1-41
Lancashire	Old Trafford	May 8			2-22
OTHER FIRST-CLASS					
India	Southampton	July 4	21 *		1-45 & 0-26
Sri Lanka	Southampton	Sept 12	59		0-9 & 0-38
OTHER ONE-DAY					
Worcestershire	Scarborough	Sept 2	22		0-28
Essex	Scarborough	Sept 4	25		1-26

BATTING AVERAGES - Including fielding

	Matches	Inns	NO	Runs	HS	Avge	100s	50s	Ct	St
Britannic Assurance	7	9	2	288	62 *	41.14	-	2	2	-
Refuge Assurance	15	10	6	144	47 *	36.00	-	-	-	-
NatWest Trophy	4	4	1	54	29	18.00	-	-	1	-
Benson & Hedges Cup	2	1	0	14	14	14.00	-	-	-	-
Other First-Class	2	2	1	80	59	80.00	-	1	-	-
Other One-Day	2	2	0	47	25	23.50	-	-	-	-
ALL FIRST-CLASS	9	11	3	368	62 *	46.00	-	3	2	-
ALL ONE-DAY	23	17	7	259	47 *	25.90	-	-	1	-

BOWLING AVERAGES

	Overs	Mdns	Runs	Wkts	Avge	Best	5wI	10wM
Britannic Assurance	135.2	35	454	10	45.40	2-48	-	
Refuge Assurance	91	3	450	15	30.00	4-37	-	
NatWest Trophy	45	5	197	7	28.14	3-30	-	
Benson & Hedges Cup	10	0	63	3	21.00	2-22	-	
Other First-Class	46	11	118	1	118.00	1-45	-	-
Other One-Day	13	0	54	1	54.00	1-26	-	
ALL FIRST-CLASS	181.2	46	572	11	52.00	2-48	-	-
ALL ONE-DAY	159	8	764	26	29.38	4-37	-	

PLER RECORDS
PLAYER RECORDS

A

A.N. AYMES - *Hampshire*

Opposition	Venue	Date	Batting	Fielding	Bowling

BRITANNIC ASSURANCE

Surrey	Southampton	Aug 23	6 & 48		
Kent	Bournemouth	Aug 29	70 & 10*		
Glamorgan	Pontypridd	Sept 7	75*	3Ct	
Gloucs	Southampton	Sept 18	44*& 2	4Ct	

REFUGE ASSURANCE

| Yorkshire | Headingley | May 27 | 15* | | |

OTHER FIRST-CLASS

| Sri Lanka | Southampton | Sept 12 | 62* | 2Ct,3St | |

OTHER ONE-DAY

| Worcestershire | Scarborough | Sept 2 | 11* | | |
| Essex | Scarborough | Sept 4 | 1* | 0Ct,1St | |

BATTING AVERAGES - Including fielding

	Matches	Inns	NO	Runs	HS	Avge	100s	50s	Ct	St
Britannic Assurance	4	7	3	255	75*	63.75	-	2	7	-
Refuge Assurance	1	1	1	15	15*	-	-	-	-	-
Other First-Class	1	1	1	62	62*	-	-	1	2	3
Other One-Day	2	2	2	12	11*	-	-	-	-	1
ALL FIRST-CLASS	5	8	4	317	75*	79.25	-	3	9	3
ALL ONE-DAY	3	3	3	27	15*	-	-	-	-	1

BOWLING AVERAGES
Did not bowl

M. AZHARUDDIN - *India*

Opposition	Venue	Date	Batting	Fielding	Bowling

CORNHILL TEST MATCHES

England	Lord's	July 26	121 & 37	1Ct	
England	Old Trafford	Aug 9	179 & 11		
England	The Oval	Aug 23	78		

TEXACO TROPHY

| England | Headingley | July 18 | 55* | | |
| England | Trent Bridge | July 20 | 63* | 2Ct | |

OTHER FIRST-CLASS

Yorkshire	Headingley	June 30	75*		
Hampshire	Southampton	July 4	74		
Min Counties	Trowbridge	July 11	105	1Ct	
Leicestershire	Leicester	July 21	46		
Gloucs	Bristol	Aug 4	23	1Ct	
Glamorgan	Swansea	Aug 18	21		

OTHER ONE-DAY

League CC	Sunderland	June 28	20		
Scotland	Glasgow	July 14			
Derbyshire	Chesterfield	July 16	7	1Ct	

BATTING AVERAGES - Including fielding

	Matches	Inns	NO	Runs	HS	Avge	100s	50s	Ct	St
Cornhill Test Matches	3	5	0	426	179	85.20	2	1	1	-
Texaco Trophy	2	2	2	118	63*	-	-	2	2	-
Other First-Class	6	6	1	344	105	68.80	1	2	2	-
Other One-Day	3	2	0	27	20	13.50	-	-	1	-
ALL FIRST-CLASS	9	11	1	770	179	77.00	3	3	3	-
ALL ONE-DAY	5	4	2	145	63*	72.50	-	2	3	-

BOWLING AVERAGES
Did not bowl

B — PLAYER RECORDS

A.M. BABINGTON - *Sussex*

Opposition	Venue	Date	Batting	Fielding	Bowling
BRITANNIC ASSURANCE					
Glamorgan	Hove	May 19	20		0-57
Somerset	Taunton	May 23	8	2Ct	2-109
REFUGE ASSURANCE					
Glamorgan	Hove	May 20			0-21
OTHER FIRST-CLASS					
New Zealand	Hove	May 26			1-36 & 0-54
OTHER ONE-DAY					
Zimbabwe	Hove	May 13			1-20

BATTING AVERAGES - Including fielding

	Matches	Inns	NO	Runs	HS	Avge	100s	50s	Ct	St
Britannic Assurance	2	2	0	28	20	14.00	-	-	2	-
Refuge Assurance	1	0	0	0	0	-	-	-	-	-
Other First-Class	1	0	0	0	0	-	-	-	-	-
Other One-Day	1	0	0	0	0	-	-	-	-	-
ALL FIRST-CLASS	3	2	0	28	20	14.00	-	-	2	-
ALL ONE-DAY	2	0	0	0	0	-	-	-	-	-

BOWLING AVERAGES

	Overs	Mdns	Runs	Wkts	Avge	Best	5wI	10wM
Britannic Assurance	43	7	166	2	83.00	2-109	-	-
Refuge Assurance	4	0	21	0	-	-	-	-
Other First-Class	20	0	90	1	90.00	1-36	-	-
Other One-Day	9	2	20	1	20.00	1-20	-	-
ALL FIRST-CLASS	63	7	256	3	85.33	2-109	-	-
ALL ONE-DAY	13	2	41	1	41.00	1-20	-	-

P.A.C. BAIL - *Wiltshire*

Opposition	Venue	Date	Batting	Fielding	Bowling
NATWEST TROPHY					
Surrey	Trowbridge	June 27	66		

BATTING AVERAGES - Including fielding

	Matches	Inns	NO	Runs	HS	Avge	100s	50s	Ct	St
NatWest Trophy	1	1	0	66	66	66.00	-	1	-	-
ALL ONE-DAY	1	1	0	66	66	66.00	-	1	-	-

BOWLING AVERAGES
Did not bowl

M.D. BAILEY - *Suffolk*

Opposition	Venue	Date	Batting	Fielding	Bowling
NATWEST TROPHY					
Worcestershire	Bury St Ed's	June 27	0		0-18

BATTING AVERAGES - Including fielding

	Matches	Inns	NO	Runs	HS	Avge	100s	50s	Ct	St
NatWest Trophy	1	1	0	0	0	0.00	-	-	-	-
ALL ONE-DAY	1	1	0	0	0	0.00	-	-	-	-

BOWLING AVERAGES

	Overs	Mdns	Runs	Wkts	Avge	Best	5wI	10wM
NatWest Trophy	6	0	18	0	-	-	-	-
ALL ONE-DAY	6	0	18	0	-	-	-	-

R.J. BAILEY - *Northamptonshire*

Opposition	Venue	Date	Batting	Fielding	Bowling
BRITANNIC ASSURANCE					
Yorkshire	Headingley	April 26	16		
Derbyshire	Northampton	May 3	30 & 8		0-12
Warwickshire	Northampton	May 15	0 & 31		0-15
Notts	Trent Bridge	May 23	65 & 54 *		
Warwickshire	Edgbaston	June 2	40		
Leicestershire	Northampton	June 6			
Glamorgan	Northampton	June 9	38 & 47 *	2Ct	
Middlesex	Luton	June 23	73 & 87		
Somerset	Taunton	June 30	80 * & 101	2Ct	0-37
Surrey	The Oval	July 4	33		0-34
Yorkshire	Northampton	July 7	0 & 6	2Ct	2-81
Kent	Northampton	July 18	138 *	1Ct	1-5 & 1-71
Sussex	Northampton	July 21	24 * & 204 *	2Ct	0-22 & 3-82
Gloucs	Cheltenham	July 25	36 & 3		1-36
Hampshire	Bournemouth	Aug 4	5 & 6		0-21
Derbyshire	Chesterfield	Aug 8	79 & 134 *	1Ct	1-44
Lancashire	Northampton	Aug 11	62 * & 30	1Ct	
Worcestershire	Worcester	Aug 18	7 & 66		0-22 & 0-26
Gloucs	Northampton	Aug 23	105 & 4	1Ct	0-20
Essex	Northampton	Aug 29	108		0-4 & 1-59
Essex	Chelmsford	Sept 7	28 & 107	1Ct	
Leicestershire	Leicester	Sept 12	77 & 33	3Ct	1-13
REFUGE ASSURANCE					
Leicestershire	Leicester	April 22	70	1Ct	
Warwickshire	Edgbaston	April 29	58		
Derbyshire	Northampton	May 6	29		
Kent	Northampton	May 27	11		
Surrey	The Oval	June 3	20		
Glamorgan	Northampton	June 10	71		
Middlesex	Northampton	June 24	60		
Somerset	Taunton	July 1	6		
Yorkshire	Tring	July 8	18		
Essex	Chelmsford	July 15	26		1-31
Sussex	Well'borough	July 22	4	1Ct	
Notts	Trent Bridge	July 29	4		
Hampshire	Bournemouth	Aug 5	33	1Ct	
Lancashire	Northampton	Aug 12	47		0-20
Worcestershire	Worcester	Aug 19	0 *		
Gloucs	Northampton	Aug 26	20		
NATWEST TROPHY					
Staffordshire	Northampton	June 27	72 *		1-2
Notts	Northampton	July 11	7		3-47
Worcestershire	Northampton	Aug 1	29		
Hampshire	Southampton	Aug 15	8		
Lancashire	Lord's	Sept 1	7		
BENSON & HEDGES CUP					
Leicestershire	Leicester	April 24	92 *		
Essex	Northampton	May 8	29		
Scotland	Northampton	May 10	1		
Notts	Trent Bridge	May 12	18	1Ct	
OTHER FIRST-CLASS					
New Zealand	Northampton	June 16	0 & 22		

BATTING AVERAGES - Including fielding

	Matches	Inns	NO	Runs	HS	Avge	100s	50s	Ct	St
Britannic Assurance	22	37	8	1965	204 *	67.75	7	9	16	-
Refuge Assurance	16	16	1	477	71	31.80	-	4	3	-
NatWest Trophy	5	5	1	123	72 *	30.75	-	1	-	-
Benson & Hedges Cup	4	4	1	140	92 *	46.66	-	1	1	-
Other First-Class	1	2	0	22	22	11.00	-	-	-	-
ALL FIRST-CLASS	23	39	8	1987	204 *	64.09	7	9	16	-
ALL ONE-DAY	25	25	3	740	92 *	33.63	-	6	4	-

BOWLING AVERAGES

	Overs	Mdns	Runs	Wkts	Avge	Best	5wI	10wM
Britannic Assurance	168.2	29	604	11	54.90	3-82	-	-
Refuge Assurance	8	0	51	1	51.00	1-31	-	-
NatWest Trophy	12	2	49	4	12.25	3-47	-	-
Benson & Hedges Cup								
Other First-Class								
ALL FIRST-CLASS	168.2	29	604	11	54.90	3-82	-	-
ALL ONE-DAY	20	2	100	5	20.00	3-47	-	-

PLAYER RECORDS

P. BAINBRIDGE - *Gloucestershire*

Opposition	Venue	Date	Batting	Fielding	Bowling
BRITANNIC ASSURANCE					
Glamorgan	Bristol	May 15	35 & 1	1Ct	1-36 & 0-12
Middlesex	Lord's	May 26	2 & 22	2Ct	0-9
Somerset	Bristol	June 2	29		
Essex	Ilford	June 6	64		1-65 & 0-11
Lancashire	Old Trafford	June 9	72		0-32
Sussex	Hove	June 16	3		0-6
Leicestershire	Gloucester	June 23		74	0-16
Derbyshire	Derby	June 30	6 & 40		
Glamorgan	Swansea	July 4			0-17
Worcestershire	Worcester	July 7	31 *& 7		0-42 & 3-23
Yorkshire	Cheltenham	July 21	152		0-37
Northants	Cheltenham	July 25	34		
Surrey	Cheltenham	July 28	37 *		
Notts	Trent Bridge	Aug 18	6 & 29	1Ct	0-18
Northants	Northampton	Aug 23	19 & 45		2-38
Worcestershire	Bristol	Sept 7	129 & 39		2-39
Sussex	Bristol	Sept 12	97		0-7
Hampshire	Southampton	Sept 18	16 & 30		0-18
REFUGE ASSURANCE					
Hampshire	Southampton	May 6			2-52
Essex	Chelmsford	May 13			2-46
Warwickshire	Moreton-in-M	May 20	41 *	1Ct	1-24
Middlesex	Lord's	May 27	18		0-40
Somerset	Bristol	June 3		1Ct	2-7
Lancashire	Old Trafford	June 10	39	1Ct	0-39
Leicestershire	Gloucester	June 24	20		1-21
Derbyshire	Derby	July 1	21		0-27
Worcestershire	Worcester	July 8	15		0-25
Sussex	Swindon	July 15	0		1-52
Yorkshire	Cheltenham	July 22	11		
Kent	Bristol	Aug 12	59 *		1-11
Notts	Trent Bridge	Aug 19	2		0-4
Northants	Northampton	Aug 26	2		1-62
NATWEST TROPHY					
Lincolnshire	Gloucester	June 27	13		0-15
Kent	Bristol	July 11	56 *	1Ct	0-38
BENSON & HEDGES CUP					
Worcestershire	Bristol	April 24	0 *		0-37
Glamorgan	Cardiff	May 1	55		0-19
Kent	Canterbury	May 10		1Ct	0-21
Warwickshire	Bristol	May 12	10	1Ct	2-31
OTHER FIRST-CLASS					
Zimbabwe	Bristol	May 19	4 *& 23		0-29
Cambridge U	Fenner's	May 23	61		1-33 & 1-27
OTHER ONE-DAY					
For MCC					
New Zealand	Lord's	May 7	19 *	1Ct	2-33

BATTING AVERAGES - Including fielding

	Matches	Inns	NO	Runs	HS	Avge	100s	50s	Ct	St
Britannic Assurance	18	25	2	1019	152	44.30	2	4	4	-
Refuge Assurance	14	11	2	228	59 *	25.33	-	1	3	-
NatWest Trophy	2	2	1	69	56 *	69.00	-	1	1	-
Benson & Hedges Cup	4	3	1	65	55	32.50	-	1	2	-
Other First-Class	2	3	1	88	61	44.00	-	1	-	-
Other One-Day	1	1	1	19	19 *	-	-	-	1	-
ALL FIRST-CLASS	20	28	3	1107	152	44.28	2	5	4	-
ALL ONE-DAY	21	17	5	381	59 *	31.75	-	3	7	-

BOWLING AVERAGES

	Overs	Mdns	Runs	Wkts	Avge	Best	5wI	10wM
Britannic Assurance	137.4	24	426	9	47.33	3-23	-	-
Refuge Assurance	74.1	0	410	11	37.27	2-7	-	-
NatWest Trophy	17.1	1	53	0	-	-	-	-
Benson & Hedges Cup	24	3	108	2	54.00	2-31	-	-
Other First-Class	25	6	89	2	44.50	1-27	-	-
Other One-Day	11	1	33	2	16.50	2-33	-	-
ALL FIRST-CLASS	162.4	30	515	11	46.81	3-23	-	-
ALL ONE-DAY	126.2	5	604	15	40.26	2-7	-	-

D.L. BAIRSTOW - *Yorkshire*

Opposition	Venue	Date	Batting	Fielding	Bowling
BRITANNIC ASSURANCE					
Derbyshire	Chesterfield	May 23	19 & 21	1Ct	
Hampshire	Headingley	May 26	37 & 9	2Ct	
Worcestershire	Worcester	June 2	61	3Ct	
Kent	Tunbridge We	June 6		2Ct	
Surrey	Harrogate	June 9	32	1Ct	
REFUGE ASSURANCE					
Derbyshire	Headingley	May 13	1 *	2Ct	
Kent	Canterbury	May 20	10		
Hampshire	Headingley	May 27	21		
Worcestershire	Worcester	June 3	5 *		
Surrey	Hull	June 10	21 *		
Sussex	Hove	June 17	14	0Ct,1St	
BENSON & HEDGES CUP					
Lancashire	Headingley	May 10	9		
Surrey	The Oval	May 12	1 *	1Ct	
OTHER FIRST-CLASS					
For World XI					
India	Scarborough	Aug 29		4Ct	
OTHER ONE-DAY					
Sussex	Harrogate	June 14		1Ct	
Warwickshire	Harrogate	June 15	1	1Ct	
Essex	Scarborough	Sept 3	36	0Ct,1St	
For Yorkshiremen					
Yorkshire	Scarborough	Sept 6	25		

BATTING AVERAGES - Including fielding

	Matches	Inns	NO	Runs	HS	Avge	100s	50s	Ct	St
Britannic Assurance	5	6	0	179	61	29.83	-	1	9	-
Refuge Assurance	6	6	3	72	21 *	24.00	-	-	2	1
Benson & Hedges Cup	2	2	1	10	9	10.00	-	-	1	-
Other First-Class	1	0	0	0	0	-	-	-	4	-
Other One-Day	4	3	0	62	36	20.66	-	-	2	1
ALL FIRST-CLASS	6	6	0	179	61	29.83	-	1	13	-
ALL ONE-DAY	12	11	4	144	36	20.57	-	-	5	2

BOWLING AVERAGES
Did not bowl

P.J. BAKKER - *Hampshire*

Opposition	Venue	Date	Batting	Fielding	Bowling
BRITANNIC ASSURANCE					
Sussex	Southampton	May 15			4-51 & 1-21
Leicestershire	Leicester	June 2			4-51 & 1-46
Somerset	Basingstoke	June 6			0-24 & 0-35
Glamorgan	Southampton	June 16			1-14 & 0-54
Notts	Portsmouth	July 18	1 *		1-28 & 1-57
Derbyshire	Portsmouth	July 21	16 *& 10		1-45 & 0-24
Warwickshire	Edgbaston	July 28			0-44 & 0-17
Northants	Bournemouth	Aug 4		1Ct	0-26 & 3-38
Middlesex	Bournemouth	Aug 8	7 *		5-101 & 2-19
Somerset	Taunton	Aug 18	20		1-58 & 0-53
Surrey	Southampton	Aug 23	12 *& 10		1-65 & 1-18
Kent	Bournemouth	Aug 29		1Ct	1-73 & 3-24
Glamorgan	Pontypridd	Sept 7	12		0-51 & 0-64
Gloucs	Southampton	Sept 18	7	1Ct	2-51 & 0-61
REFUGE ASSURANCE					
Somerset	Taunton	May 13			2-42
Middlesex	Basingstoke	June 10	0 *		0-23
Glamorgan	Bournemouth	June 17			3-33
Sussex	Hove	July 1	9		1-48
Essex	Southampton	July 8			1-30
Notts	Southampton	July 15			0-52
Derbyshire	Portsmouth	July 22			3-31
Warwickshire	Edgbaston	July 29			2-33
Northants	Bournemouth	Aug 5			1-36
Surrey	Southampton	Aug 26	2 *		0-35

B PLAYER RECORDS

NATWEST TROPHY

Leicestershire	Leicester	June 27			1-51
Essex	Chelmsford	July 11			1-60
Yorkshire	Southampton	Aug 1	3 *		0-12
Northants	Southampton	Aug 15	2		1-41

BENSON & HEDGES CUP

Combined U	Southampton	May 12		1-21

OTHER FIRST-CLASS

India	Southampton	July 4		1-84 & 0-37
Sri Lanka	Southampton	Sept 12		2-36 & 1-87

OTHER ONE-DAY

Worcestershire	Scarborough	Sept 2		1-21

BATTING AVERAGES - Including fielding

	Matches	Inns	NO	Runs	HS	Avge	100s	50s	Ct	St
Britannic Assurance	14	9	4	95	20	19.00	-	-	3	-
Refuge Assurance	10	3	2	11	9	11.00	-	-	-	-
NatWest Trophy	4	2	1	5	3 *	5.00	-	-	-	-
Benson & Hedges Cup	1	0	0	0	0	-	-	-	-	-
Other First-Class	2	0	0	0	0	-	-	-	-	-
Other One-Day	1	0	0	0	0	-	-	-	-	-
ALL FIRST-CLASS	16	9	4	95	20	19.00	-	-	3	-
ALL ONE-DAY	16	5	3	16	9	8.00	-	-	-	-

BOWLING AVERAGES

	Overs	Mdns	Runs	Wkts	Avge	Best	5wI	10wM
Britannic Assurance	371.2	86	1195	33	36.21	5-101	1	-
Refuge Assurance	65	6	363	13	27.92	3-31	-	
NatWest Trophy	43	6	164	3	54.66	1-41	-	
Benson & Hedges Cup	10	3	21	1	21.00	1-21	-	
Other First-Class	65	4	244	4	61.00	2-36	-	-
Other One-Day	7	0	21	1	21.00	1-21	-	
ALL FIRST-CLASS	436.2	90	1439	37	38.89	5-101	1	-
ALL ONE-DAY	125	15	569	18	31.61	3-31	-	

M.C.J. BALL - Gloucestershire

Opposition	Venue	Date	Batting			Fielding	Bowling
BRITANNIC ASSURANCE							
Glamorgan	Bristol	May 15	5	&	15	1Ct	0-34 & 0-4
Notts	Trent Bridge	Aug 18	14	&	1		0-32 & 0-9
Northants	Northampton	Aug 23	4			1Ct	0-35
REFUGE ASSURANCE							
Hampshire	Southampton	May 6				2Ct	0-31
Essex	Chelmsford	May 13					0-18
Warwickshire	Moreton-in-M	May 20					1-17
Middlesex	Lord's	May 27	1				0-20
BENSON & HEDGES CUP							
Kent	Canterbury	May 10					0-28
Warwickshire	Bristol	May 12					0-40
OTHER FIRST-CLASS							
Cambridge U	Fenner's	May 23				2Ct	1-50 & 2-37

BATTING AVERAGES - Including fielding

	Matches	Inns	NO	Runs	HS	Avge	100s	50s	Ct	St
Britannic Assurance	3	5	0	39	15	7.80	-	-	2	-
Refuge Assurance	4	1	0	1	1	1.00	-	-	2	-
Benson & Hedges Cup	2	0	0	0	0	-	-	-	-	-
Other First-Class	1	0	0	0	0	-	-	-	2	-
ALL FIRST-CLASS	4	5	0	39	15	7.80	-	-	4	-
ALL ONE-DAY	6	1	0	1	1	1.00	-	-	2	-

BOWLING AVERAGES

	Overs	Mdns	Runs	Wkts	Avge	Best	5wI	10wM
Britannic Assurance	34	7	114	0			-	
Refuge Assurance	16	0	86	1	86.00	1-17	-	
Benson & Hedges Cup	10	0	68	0			-	
Other First-Class	28	8	87	3	29.00	2-37	-	
ALL FIRST-CLASS	62	15	201	3	67.00	2-37	-	
ALL ONE-DAY	26	0	154	1	154.00	1-17	-	

A.S. BARNARD - Shropshire

Opposition	Venue	Date	Batting	Fielding	Bowling
NATWEST TROPHY					
Derbyshire	Chesterfield	June 27			0-19

BATTING AVERAGES - Including fielding

	Matches	Inns	NO	Runs	HS	Avge	100s	50s	Ct	St
NatWest Trophy	1	0	0	0	0	-	-	-	-	-
ALL ONE-DAY	1	0	0	0	0	-	-	-	-	-

BOWLING AVERAGES

	Overs	Mdns	Runs	Wkts	Avge	Best	5wI	10wM
NatWest Trophy	6	1	19	0	-	-	-	-
ALL ONE-DAY	6	1	19	0	-	-	-	-

S.N. BARNES - Gloucestershire

Opposition	Venue	Date	Batting			Fielding	Bowling
BRITANNIC ASSURANCE							
Derbyshire	Derby	June 30	6			1Ct	2-10 & 2-75
Glamorgan	Swansea	July 4					1-47
Worcestershire	Worcester	July 7	0	&	0	1Ct	2-74 & 0-6
Surrey	Cheltenham	July 28	2				1-19 & 0-29
Warwickshire	Bristol	Aug 8	0				0-38
Kent	Bristol	Aug 11					0-51
Notts	Trent Bridge	Aug 18	0 *	&	3		0-39
REFUGE ASSURANCE							
Somerset	Bristol	June 3					0-26
Sussex	Swindon	July 15	0 *				2-46
Yorkshire	Cheltenham	July 22					0-53
Surrey	Cheltenham	July 29				1Ct	3-39
Kent	Bristol	Aug 12					2-25
Northants	Northampton	Aug 26				2Ct	0-22
NATWEST TROPHY							
Kent	Bristol	July 11					0-29
Lancashire	Old Trafford	Aug 1	0			1Ct	1-64
OTHER FIRST-CLASS							
Zimbabwe	Bristol	May 19	0				0-80
Cambridge U	Fenner's	May 23					4-65 & 4-51
India	Bristol	Aug 4	12 *			1Ct	0-18

BATTING AVERAGES - Including fielding

	Matches	Inns	NO	Runs	HS	Avge	100s	50s	Ct	St
Britannic Assurance	7	7	1	11	6	1.83	-	-	2	-
Refuge Assurance	6	1	1	0	0 *	-	-	-	3	-
NatWest Trophy	2	1	0	0	0	0.00	-	-	1	-
Other First-Class	3	2	1	12	12 *	12.00	-	-	1	-
ALL FIRST-CLASS	10	9	2	23	12 *	3.28	-	-	3	-
ALL ONE-DAY	8	2	1	0	0 *	0.00	-	-	4	-

BOWLING AVERAGES

	Overs	Mdns	Runs	Wkts	Avge	Best	5wI	10wM
Britannic Assurance	138	25	388	8	48.50	2-10	-	-
Refuge Assurance	41	1	211	7	30.14	3-39	-	
NatWest Trophy	18	1	93	1	93.00	1-64	-	
Other First-Class	69	20	214	8	26.75	4-51	-	
ALL FIRST-CLASS	207	45	602	16	37.62	4-51	-	
ALL ONE-DAY	59	2	304	8	38.00	3-39	-	

K.J. BARNETT - Derbyshire

Opposition	Venue	Date	Batting	Fielding	Bowling
BRITANNIC ASSURANCE					
Notts	Trent Bridge	April 26	73	1Ct	1-7 & 3-49
Northants	Northampton	May 3	58	1Ct	0-1

PLAYER RECORDS — B

Lancashire	Derby	May 15	69 & 33			3-81 & 0-28
Somerset	Taunton	May 19	94			0-83 & 1-14
Yorkshire	Chesterfield	May 23	38 & 141			1-37 & 0-12
Notts	Derby	May 26	29 & 46 *			1-28
Surrey	The Oval	June 6	1 & 51 *			
Warwickshire	Derby	June 16	131			0-5 & 1-39
Leicestershire	Leicester	June 20	31 * & 0			0-25
Gloucs	Derby	June 30	7 & 107			2-19
Sussex	Hove	July 4	123			
Lancashire	Liverpool	July 7	109 & 90 *			0-9
Essex	Colchester	July 18	38 & 0			2-12
Hampshire	Portsmouth	July 21	13 & 63	3Ct		0-19
Worcestershire	Derby	July 25	9 & 23	1Ct		1-61
Kent	Chesterfield	Aug 4	64 & 10 *			0-2 & 0-3
Northants	Chesterfield	Aug 8	20 & 3	1Ct		0-32
Middlesex	Derby	Aug 18	3 & 7	1Ct		
Essex	Derby	Aug 23	4 & 3	1Ct		0-2
Glamorgan	Cardiff	Aug 29	30	2Ct		2-56
Yorkshire	Scarborough	Sept 7	47			0-58 & 0-8
Leicestershire	Derby	Sept 18	4	3Ct		1-30

REFUGE ASSURANCE

Sussex	Hove	April 22	60			0-22
Worcestershire	Derby	April 29	66			
Northants	Northampton	May 6	23	1Ct		
Yorkshire	Headingley	May 13	29			1-12
Somerset	Taunton	May 20	100	1Ct		1-55
Notts	Derby	June 10	63			0-34
Warwickshire	Derby	June 17	19			
Surrey	The Oval	June 24	0			
Gloucs	Derby	July 1	57			
Lancashire	Old Trafford	July 8	85	1Ct		
Leicestershire	Knypersley	July 15	39			1-9
Hampshire	Portsmouth	July 22	5			
Glamorgan	Swansea	July 29	14	1Ct		
Kent	Chesterfield	Aug 5	127			
Middlesex	Derby	Aug 19	5			
Essex	Derby	Aug 26	7	1Ct		
Notts	Derby	Sept 5	83	1Ct		
Middlesex	Edgbaston	Sept 16	42	1Ct		

NATWEST TROPHY

Shropshire	Chesterfield	June 27	1			
Lancashire	Derby	July 11	59			

BENSON & HEDGES CUP

Sussex	Derby	April 24	94			
Somerset	Taunton	May 1	0			0-9
Min Counties	Wellington	May 10	8	1Ct		
Middlesex	Derby	May 12	22	1Ct		

OTHER FIRST-CLASS

Cambridge U	Fenner's	April 18	62			3-9 & 4-28
New Zealand	Derby	June 2	14 * & 0			

OTHER ONE-DAY

India	Chesterfield	July 16	115	2Ct		
For England XI						
Rest of World	Jesmond	Aug 2				1-58
Rest of World	Jesmond	Aug 3	10			0-10

BATTING AVERAGES - Including fielding

	Matches	Inns	NO	Runs	HS	Avge	100s	50s	Ct	St
Britannic Assurance	22	36	5	1572	141	50.71	5	8	14	-
Refuge Assurance	18	18	0	824	127	45.77	2	6	7	-
NatWest Trophy	2	2	0	60	59	30.00	-	1	-	-
Benson & Hedges Cup	4	4	0	124	94	31.00	-	1	2	-
Other First-Class	2	3	1	76	62	38.00	-	1	-	-
Other One-Day	3	2	0	125	115	62.50	1	-	2	-
ALL FIRST-CLASS	24	39	6	1648	141	49.93	5	9	14	-
ALL ONE-DAY	27	26	0	1133	127	43.57	3	8	11	-

BOWLING AVERAGES

	Overs	Mdns	Runs	Wkts	Avge	Best	5wI	10wM
Britannic Assurance	267.1	42	720	19	37.89	3-49	-	-
Refuge Assurance	25	0	132	3	44.00	1-9	-	-
NatWest Trophy								
Benson & Hedges Cup	1	0	9	0				
Other First-Class	26.2	12	37	7	5.28	4-28	-	-
Other One-Day	11	0	68	1	68.00	1-58	-	-
ALL FIRST-CLASS	293.3	54	757	26	29.11	4-28	-	-
ALL ONE-DAY	37	0	209	4	52.25	1-9	-	-

T.J. BARRY - *Buckinghamshire*

Opposition	Venue	Date	Batting	Fielding	Bowling
NATWEST TROPHY					
Notts	Marlow	June 27	5		3-49

BATTING AVERAGES - Including fielding

	Matches	Inns	NO	Runs	HS	Avge	100s	50s	Ct	St
NatWest Trophy	1	1	0	5	5	5.00	-	-	-	-
ALL ONE-DAY	1	1	0	5	5	5.00	-	-	-	-

BOWLING AVERAGES

	Overs	Mdns	Runs	Wkts	Avge	Best	5wI	10wM
NatWest Trophy	12	2	49	3	16.33	3-49	-	
ALL ONE-DAY	12	2	49	3	16.33	3-49	-	

R.J. BARTLETT - *Somerset*

Opposition	Venue	Date	Batting	Fielding	Bowling
BRITANNIC ASSURANCE					
Worcestershire	Taunton	Sept 12	73 & 12		
REFUGE ASSURANCE					
Worcestershire	Taunton	April 22	2		
Essex	Bath	June 17	16	1Ct	
Notts	Bath	June 24	50	1Ct	
Middlesex	Lord's	July 8	54	1Ct	
Yorkshire	Scarborough	July 15	21		
Glamorgan	Neath	July 22	11		
Lancashire	Old Trafford	July 29	55		
Sussex	Hove	Aug 26	2		

BATTING AVERAGES - Including fielding

	Matches	Inns	NO	Runs	HS	Avge	100s	50s	Ct	St
Britannic Assurance	1	2	0	85	73	42.50	-	1	-	-
Refuge Assurance	8	8	0	211	55	26.37	-	3	3	-
ALL FIRST-CLASS	1	2	0	85	73	42.50	-	1	-	-
ALL ONE-DAY	8	8	0	211	55	26.37	-	3	3	-

BOWLING AVERAGES
Did not bowl

S.R. BARWICK - *Glamorgan*

Opposition	Venue	Date	Batting	Fielding	Bowling
BRITANNIC ASSURANCE					
Somerset	Cardiff	May 3			0-107 & 1-56
Kent	Swansea	May 23	0 *		0-72 & 0-18
Northants	Northampton	June 9	2 *		3-76 & 1-67
REFUGE ASSURANCE					
Gloucs	Bristol	April 22			1-24
Leicestershire	Cardiff	April 29	0 *	1Ct	2-30
Sussex	Hove	May 20			0-40
Lancashire	Colwyn Bay	May 27			1-54
Essex	Ilford	June 3			1-34
BENSON & HEDGES CUP					
Warwickshire	Edgbaston	April 24			2-44
Gloucs	Cardiff	May 1	1		1-37
Worcestershire	Worcester	May 8			4-67
Worcestershire	Worcester	May 30	13 *		1-45
OTHER FIRST-CLASS					
Oxford U	The Parks	April 14			1-16
Oxford U	The Parks	June 2			3-29

BATTING AVERAGES - Including fielding

	Matches	Inns	NO	Runs	HS	Avge	100s	50s	Ct	St
Britannic Assurance	3	2	2	2	2 *	-	-	-	-	-

B   PLAYER RECORDS

Refuge Assurance	5	1	1	0	0*	-	-	-	1	-
Benson & Hedges Cup	4	2	1	14	13*	14.00	-	-	-	-
Other First-Class	2	0	0	0	0	-	-	-	-	-
ALL FIRST-CLASS	5	2	2	2	2*	-	-	-	-	-
ALL ONE-DAY	9	3	2	14	13*	14.00	-	-	1	-

BOWLING AVERAGES

	Overs	Mdns	Runs	Wkts	Avge	Best	5wI	10wM
Britannic Assurance	124.4	27	396	5	79.20	3-76	-	-
Refuge Assurance	32.1	3	182	5	36.40	2-30	-	
Benson & Hedges Cup	41	3	193	8	24.12	4-67	-	
Other First-Class	34	16	45	4	11.25	3-29	-	-
ALL FIRST-CLASS	158.4	43	441	9	49.00	3-29	-	-
ALL ONE-DAY	73.1	6	375	13	28.84	4-67	-	

S.J. BASE - *Derbyshire*

Opposition	Venue	Date	Batting	Fielding	Bowling
BRITANNIC ASSURANCE					
Notts	Trent Bridge	April 26	34		1-89 & 1-56
Lancashire	Derby	May 15	54 & 16*		0-67 & 0-30
Yorkshire	Chesterfield	May 23	58 & 7	1Ct	2-72 & 0-29
Surrey	The Oval	June 6	0		0-38 & 0-33
Warwickshire	Derby	June 16		1Ct	2-88
Sussex	Hove	July 4			1-65
Lancashire	Liverpool	July 7			2-79 & 2-79
Essex	Colchester	July 18	26 & 4	1Ct	0-90 & 0-29
Worcestershire	Derby	July 25	14 & 0*		6-105
Kent	Chesterfield	Aug 4		1Ct	3-85 & 1-59
Middlesex	Derby	Aug 18	0		3-92 & 5-28
Glamorgan	Cardiff	Aug 29	0		1-73 & 0-14
Leicestershire	Derby	Sept 18	2		2-51 & 3-51
REFUGE ASSURANCE					
Sussex	Hove	April 22			4-28
Worcestershire	Derby	April 29			4-32
Northants	Northampton	May 6			0-40
Yorkshire	Headingley	May 13	0		2-33
Notts	Derby	June 10			1-52
Warwickshire	Derby	June 17	0*		2-32
Gloucs	Derby	July 1			1-25
Lancashire	Old Trafford	July 8		1Ct	3-49
Leicestershire	Knypersley	July 15			1-20
Hampshire	Portsmouth	July 22	2		0-37
Glamorgan	Swansea	July 29		1Ct	1-40
Middlesex	Derby	Aug 19			0-10
Essex	Derby	Aug 26			0-33
Notts	Derby	Sept 5			1-65
Middlesex	Edgbaston	Sept 16	1*		0-53
BENSON & HEDGES CUP					
Sussex	Derby	April 24			1-46
Somerset	Taunton	May 1	15*		1-54
Min Counties	Wellington	May 10	0		3-33
Middlesex	Derby	May 12			2-43
OTHER ONE-DAY					
India	Chesterfield	July 16			1-45

BATTING AVERAGES - Including fielding

	Matches	Inns	NO	Runs	HS	Avge	100s	50s	Ct	St
Britannic Assurance	13	13	2	215	58	19.54	-	2	4	-
Refuge Assurance	15	4	2	3	2	1.50	-	-	2	-
Benson & Hedges Cup	4	2	1	15	15*	15.00	-	-	-	-
Other One-Day	1	0	0	0	0	-	-	-	-	-
ALL FIRST-CLASS	13	13	2	215	58	19.54	-	2	4	-
ALL ONE-DAY	20	6	3	18	15*	6.00	-	-	2	-

BOWLING AVERAGES

	Overs	Mdns	Runs	Wkts	Avge	Best	5wI	10wM
Britannic Assurance	414.3	68	1402	35	40.05	6-105	2	-
Refuge Assurance	104	3	549	20	27.45	4-28	-	
Benson & Hedges Cup	40	4	176	7	25.14	3-33	-	
Other One-Day	11	0	45	1	45.00	1-45	-	
ALL FIRST-CLASS	414.3	68	1402	35	40.05	6-105	2	-
ALL ONE-DAY	155	7	770	28	27.50	4-28	-	

S. BASTIEN - *Glamorgan*

Opposition	Venue	Date	Batting	Fielding	Bowling
BRITANNIC ASSURANCE					
Somerset	Bath	June 20			1-64
Yorkshire	Cardiff	June 23			2-49 & 1-67
Worcestershire	Abergavenny	July 21			1-90 & 0-61
Warwickshire	Swansea	July 25			0-81 & 2-11
Middlesex	Lord's	Aug 4	11 & 0		2-81 & 2-72
Essex	Southend	Aug 8	3*		2-60 & 2-75
Notts	Worksop	Aug 11	10*		3-71 & 5-31
Derbyshire	Cardiff	Aug 29	9*		0-41
Hampshire	Pontypridd	Sept 7	2 & 0		3-70
Worcestershire	Worcester	Sept 18	0 & 12		6-75 & 3-76
REFUGE ASSURANCE					
Derbyshire	Swansea	July 29			1-21
OTHER FIRST-CLASS					
Oxford U	The Parks	June 2			4-51
India	Swansea	Aug 18			0-61

BATTING AVERAGES - Including fielding

	Matches	Inns	NO	Runs	HS	Avge	100s	50s	Ct	St
Britannic Assurance	10	9	3	47	12	7.83	-	-	-	-
Refuge Assurance	1	0	0	0	0	-	-	-	-	-
Other First-Class	2	0	0	0	0	-	-	-	-	-
ALL FIRST-CLASS	12	9	3	47	12	7.83	-	-	-	-
ALL ONE-DAY	1	0	0	0	0	-	-	-	-	-

BOWLING AVERAGES

	Overs	Mdns	Runs	Wkts	Avge	Best	5wI	10wM
Britannic Assurance	274.5	47	1075	35	30.71	6-75	2	-
Refuge Assurance	4	0	21	1	21.00	1-21	-	
Other First-Class	42.2	10	112	4	28.00	4-51	-	-
ALL FIRST-CLASS	317.1	57	1187	39	30.43	6-75	2	-
ALL ONE-DAY	4	0	21	1	21.00	1-21	-	

R. BATES - *Lincolnshire*

Opposition	Venue	Date	Batting	Fielding	Bowling
NATWEST TROPHY					
Gloucs	Gloucester	June 27	5		

BATTING AVERAGES - Including fielding

	Matches	Inns	NO	Runs	HS	Avge	100s	50s	Ct	St
NatWest Trophy	1	1	0	5	5	5.00	-	-	-	-
ALL ONE-DAY	1	1	0	5	5	5.00	-	-	-	-

BOWLING AVERAGES
Did not bowl

J.D. BATTY - *Yorkshire*

Opposition	Venue	Date	Batting	Fielding	Bowling
BRITANNIC ASSURANCE					
Gloucs	Cheltenham	July 21			4-137
Somerset	Scarborough	July 25		1Ct	1-83 & 0-41
Leicestershire	Sheffield	July 28	2 & 0	1Ct	2-124
Sussex	Eastbourne	Aug 8			0-26
Lancashire	Old Trafford	Aug 18	7*	2Ct	1-84
Middlesex	Headingley	Aug 23	0* & 21		0-42 & 4-76
Derbyshire	Scarborough	Sept 7			0-67 & 0-42
OTHER ONE-DAY					
World XI	Scarborough	Sept 1			0-56
Essex	Scarborough	Sept 3	5*		0-40
Yorkshiremen	Scarborough	Sept 6			0-37

PLAYER RECORDS

BATTING AVERAGES - Including fielding

	Matches	Inns	NO	Runs	HS	Avge	100s	50s	Ct	St
Britannic Assurance	7	5	2	30	21	10.00	-	-	4	-
Other One-Day	3	1	1	5	5*		-	-	-	-
ALL FIRST-CLASS	7	5	2	30	21	10.00	-	-	4	-
ALL ONE-DAY	3	1	1	5	5*		-	-	-	-

BOWLING AVERAGES

	Overs	Mdns	Runs	Wkts	Avge	Best	5wI	10wM
Britannic Assurance	195	29	722	12	60.16	4-76	-	-
Other One-Day	29	0	133	0	-	-	-	-
ALL FIRST-CLASS	195	29	722	12	60.16	4-76	-	-
ALL ONE-DAY	29	0	133	0	-	-	-	-

M. BEARDSHALL - *Yorkshiremen*

Opposition	Venue	Date	Batting	Fielding	Bowling
OTHER ONE-DAY					
Yorkshire	Scarborough	Sept 6	4*		0-58

BATTING AVERAGES - Including fielding

	Matches	Inns	NO	Runs	HS	Avge	100s	50s	Ct	St
Other One-Day	1	1	1	4	4*	-	-	-	-	-
ALL ONE-DAY	1	1	1	4	4*	-	-	-	-	-

BOWLING AVERAGES

	Overs	Mdns	Runs	Wkts	Avge	Best	5wI	10wM
Other One-Day	4.5	0	58	0	-	-	-	-
ALL ONE-DAY	4.5	0	58	0	-	-	-	-

A.W. BEE - *Scotland*

Opposition	Venue	Date	Batting	Fielding	Bowling
NATWEST TROPHY					
Essex	Chelmsford	June 27	14		1-27
BENSON & HEDGES CUP					
Essex	Glasgow	May 1	0		1-67
Northants	Northampton	May 10	0	1Ct	0-58
Leicestershire	Leicester	May 12			0-21
OTHER FIRST-CLASS					
Ireland	Edinburgh	Aug 11	29*		0-53 & 0-20
OTHER ONE-DAY					
India	Glasgow	July 14	2*		2-35

BATTING AVERAGES - Including fielding

	Matches	Inns	NO	Runs	HS	Avge	100s	50s	Ct	St
NatWest Trophy	1	1	0	14	14	14.00	-	-	-	-
Benson & Hedges Cup	3	2	0	0	0	0.00	-	-	1	-
Other First-Class	1	1	1	29	29*	-	-	-	-	-
Other One-Day	1	1	1	2	2*	-	-	-	-	-
ALL FIRST-CLASS	1	1	1	29	29*	-	-	-	-	-
ALL ONE-DAY	5	4	1	16	14	5.33	-	-	1	-

BOWLING AVERAGES

	Overs	Mdns	Runs	Wkts	Avge	Best	5wI	10wM
NatWest Trophy	10	4	27	1	27.00	1-27	-	-
Benson & Hedges Cup	24	1	146	1	146.00	1-67	-	-
Other First-Class	28	11	73	0	-	-	-	-
Other One-Day	11	1	35	2	17.50	2-35	-	-
ALL FIRST-CLASS	28	11	73	0	-	-	-	-
ALL ONE-DAY	45	6	208	4	52.00	2-35	-	-

M.W. BELL - *Gloucestershire*

Opposition	Venue	Date	Batting	Fielding	Bowling
BRITANNIC ASSURANCE					
Glamorgan	Swansea	July 4			1-76
Worcestershire	Worcester	July 7	0 & 0*		2-38
REFUGE ASSURANCE					
Yorkshire	Cheltenham	July 22			0-38

BATTING AVERAGES - Including fielding

	Matches	Inns	NO	Runs	HS	Avge	100s	50s	Ct	St
Britannic Assurance	2	2	1	0	0*	0.00	-	-	-	-
Refuge Assurance	1	0	0	0	0	-	-	-	-	-
ALL FIRST-CLASS	2	2	1	0	0*	0.00	-	-	-	-
ALL ONE-DAY	1	0	0	0	0	-	-	-	-	-

BOWLING AVERAGES

	Overs	Mdns	Runs	Wkts	Avge	Best	5wI	10wM
Britannic Assurance	44	7	114	3	38.00	2-38	-	-
Refuge Assurance	4	0	38	0	-	-	-	-
ALL FIRST-CLASS	44	7	114	3	38.00	2-38	-	-
ALL ONE-DAY	4	0	38	0	-	-	-	-

J.E. BENJAMIN - *Warwickshire*

Opposition	Venue	Date	Batting	Fielding	Bowling
BRITANNIC ASSURANCE					
Northants	Northampton	May 15	14		0-16 & 0-23
Notts	Edgbaston	May 19	14 & 1	1Ct	0-41 & 2-55
Worcestershire	Edgbaston	May 26	12* & 12*		1-52 & 0-6
Middlesex	Lord's	June 6		1Ct	5-71 & 0-30
Essex	Edgbaston	June 9			2-79
Yorkshire	Sheffield	June 20	1	1Ct	1-37 & 5-83
Kent	Edgbaston	June 23	3* & 15*		3-31 & 1-34
Somerset	Taunton	July 4			4-86 & 0-31
Surrey	The Oval	July 7	28* & 41	1Ct	1-37 & 5-72
Lancashire	Coventry	July 18	28*		3-97 & 1-42
Glamorgan	Swansea	July 25			0-45 & 0-24
Hampshire	Edgbaston	July 28			0-37 & 0-7
REFUGE ASSURANCE					
Gloucs	Moreton-in-M	May 20	1		1-21
Worcestershire	Worcester	May 27			0-27
Middlesex	Lord's	June 3			1-31
Essex	Edgbaston	June 10	10*		1-18
Kent	Edgbaston	June 24	14*		2-29
Surrey	The Oval	July 8	8*		1-38
Glamorgan	Edgbaston	July 15	5		1-34
Notts	Edgbaston	July 22	3*		1-20
Hampshire	Edgbaston	July 29			1-29
Somerset	Weston	Aug 12		1Ct	1-46
Lancashire	Old Trafford	Aug 26	24		1-41
NATWEST TROPHY					
Hertfordshire	St Albans	June 27	1*	1Ct	0-9
Yorkshire	Headingley	July 11	2*		0-40
BENSON & HEDGES CUP					
Worcestershire	Edgbaston	May 10	20	1Ct	1-40
Gloucs	Bristol	May 12			2-32
OTHER FIRST-CLASS					
Cambridge U	Fenner's	April 26			5-29 & 0-12
New Zealand	Edgbaston	May 30	3*		3-45 & 0-2
Sri Lanka	Edgbaston	Aug 29	2 & 14		1-59 & 0-22
OTHER ONE-DAY					
Surrey	Harrogate	June 13	7*	1Ct	1-25
Yorkshire	Harrogate	June 15			0-35

BATTING AVERAGES - Including fielding

	Matches	Inns	NO	Runs	HS	Avge	100s	50s	Ct	St
Britannic Assurance	12	11	6	169	41	33.80	-	-	4	-
Refuge Assurance	11	7	4	65	24	21.66	-	-	1	-
NatWest Trophy	2	2	2	3	2*	-	-	-	1	-

B — PLAYER RECORDS

Benson & Hedges Cup	2	1	0	20	20	20.00	-	-	1	-
Other First-Class	3	3	1	19	14	9.50	-	-	-	-
Other One-Day	2	1	1	7	7*	-	-	-	1	-
ALL FIRST-CLASS	15	14	7	188	41	26.85	-	-	4	-
ALL ONE-DAY	17	11	7	95	24	23.75	-	-	4	-

BOWLING AVERAGES

	Overs	Mdns	Runs	Wkts	Avge	Best	5wI	10wM
Britannic Assurance	322.3	51	1036	34	30.47	5-71	3	-
Refuge Assurance	79	4	334	11	30.36	2-29	-	
NatWest Trophy	14	2	49	0			-	
Benson & Hedges Cup	22	6	72	3	24.00	2-32	-	
Other First-Class	66	17	169	9	18.77	5-29	1	-
Other One-Day	22	4	60	1	60.00	1-25	-	
ALL FIRST-CLASS	388.3	68	1205	43	28.02	5-29	4	-
ALL ONE-DAY	137	16	515	15	34.33	2-29	-	

W.K.M. BENJAMIN - *Leicestershire*

Opposition	Venue	Date	Batting	Fielding	Bowling
BRITANNIC ASSURANCE					
Lancashire	Old Trafford	May 19	65		
Northants	Northampton	June 6	33	1Ct	0-33
Middlesex	Leicester	June 16		1	5-73
Derbyshire	Leicester	June 20	101 *		0-17 & 3-35
Gloucs	Gloucester	June 23	16	1Ct	2-44
Notts	Trent Bridge	June 30	0		5-109 & 0-12
Glamorgan	Hinckley	July 7			1-59 & 1-17
Essex	Leicester	July 25	54 & 9 *	1Ct	4-51 & 0-48
Yorkshire	Sheffield	July 28	16		2-78 & 0-40
Worcestershire	Leicester	Aug 4	10 & 6		0-31
Kent	Leicester	Aug 23	18 & 53		3-52 & 1-70
REFUGE ASSURANCE					
Glamorgan	Cardiff	April 29	5		2-26
Lancashire	Old Trafford	May 20			0-23
Sussex	Leicester	June 10			1-13
Middlesex	Leicester	June 17	2 *		0-59
Gloucs	Gloucester	June 24			3-36
Derbyshire	Knypersley	July 15	11	1Ct	2-32
Yorkshire	Sheffield	July 29	3		0-35
Kent	Leicester	Aug 26			0-40
NATWEST TROPHY					
Hampshire	Leicester	June 27	7		1-34
BENSON & HEDGES CUP					
Notts	Trent Bridge	May 1	2		2-29
OTHER FIRST-CLASS					
India	Leicester	July 21	55 & 0		1-81 & 0-8
OTHER ONE-DAY					
New Zealand	Leicester	June 14	0 *		1-27
For Rest of World					
England XI	Jesmond	Aug 2	1		0-50
England XI	Jesmond	Aug 3		1Ct	1-21

BATTING AVERAGES - Including fielding

	Matches	Inns	NO	Runs	HS	Avge	100s	50s	Ct	St
Britannic Assurance	11	13	2	382	101 *	34.72	1	3	3	-
Refuge Assurance	8	4	1	21	11	7.00	-	-	1	-
NatWest Trophy	1	1	0	7	7	7.00	-	-	-	-
Benson & Hedges Cup	1	1	0	2	2	2.00	-	-	-	-
Other First-Class	1	2	0	55	55	27.50	-	1	-	-
Other One-Day	3	2	1	1	1	1.00	-	-	1	-
ALL FIRST-CLASS	12	15	2	437	101 *	33.61	1	4	3	-
ALL ONE-DAY	13	8	2	31	11	5.16	-	-	2	-

BOWLING AVERAGES

	Overs	Mdns	Runs	Wkts	Avge	Best	5wI	10wM
Britannic Assurance	260.3	60	769	27	28.48	5-73	2	-
Refuge Assurance	57	5	264	8	33.00	3-36	-	
NatWest Trophy	12	4	34	1	34.00	1-34	-	
Benson & Hedges Cup	9	3	29	2	14.50	2-29	-	
Other First-Class	24	3	89	1	89.00	1-81	-	
Other One-Day	27	3	98	2	49.00	1-21	-	

ALL FIRST-CLASS	284.3	63	858	28	30.64	5-73	2	-
ALL ONE-DAY	105	15	425	13	32.69	3-36	-	

J.D.R. BENSON - *Leicestershire*

Opposition	Venue	Date	Batting	Fielding	Bowling
BRITANNIC ASSURANCE					
Glamorgan	Cardiff	April 26	9	1Ct	
Essex	Chelmsford	May 3	8 & 10 *		0-11
Somerset	Leicester	May 26	29 * & 13	1Ct	0-7
Hampshire	Leicester	June 2	11 & 29 *		
Northants	Northampton	June 6	86		
Middlesex	Leicester	June 16		45 1Ct	
Derbyshire	Leicester	June 20	9		
Gloucs	Gloucester	June 23	45		
Notts	Trent Bridge	June 30	11 & 62	2Ct	0-43
Glamorgan	Hinckley	July 7	35 *		0-1 & 1-83
Essex	Leicester	July 25	12 & 34 *		
Yorkshire	Sheffield	July 28	0	2Ct	
Worcestershire	Leicester	Aug 4	28 * & 2		
Kent	Dartford	Aug 8	9 & 25	1Ct	
Surrey	The Oval	Aug 11	7 & 5	1Ct	
Warwickshire	Edgbaston	Aug 18	1		
REFUGE ASSURANCE					
Northants	Leicester	April 22	8		
Glamorgan	Cardiff	April 29	3		
Essex	Leicester	May 6	12		1-13
Lancashire	Old Trafford	May 20	21		1-16
Somerset	Leicester	May 27	17 *		
Hampshire	Leicester	June 3	7		1-16
Sussex	Leicester	June 10		1Ct	
Middlesex	Leicester	June 17	36 *		
Gloucs	Gloucester	June 24	8 *		
Notts	Trent Bridge	July 1	2		
Derbyshire	Knypersley	July 15	1		
Yorkshire	Sheffield	July 29	18 *		
Worcestershire	Leicester	Aug 5	15		0-26
Surrey	The Oval	Aug 12	67	1Ct	1-54
Warwickshire	Edgbaston	Aug 19	14		
Kent	Leicester	Aug 26	1 *	2Ct	2-33
NATWEST TROPHY					
Hampshire	Leicester	June 27	11		
BENSON & HEDGES CUP					
Northants	Leicester	April 24	1		
Notts	Trent Bridge	May 1	43		
OTHER FIRST-CLASS					
Oxford U	The Parks	May 23	94	2Ct	0-12
India	Leicester	July 21	0 & 106	1Ct	
OTHER ONE-DAY					
New Zealand	Leicester	June 14	19		

BATTING AVERAGES - Including fielding

	Matches	Inns	NO	Runs	HS	Avge	100s	50s	Ct	St
Britannic Assurance	16	24	6	525	86	29.16	-	2	9	-
Refuge Assurance	16	15	5	230	67	23.00	-	1	4	-
NatWest Trophy	1	1	0	11	11	11.00	-	-	-	-
Benson & Hedges Cup	2	2	0	44	43	22.00	-	-	-	-
Other First-Class	2	3	0	200	106	66.66	1	1	3	-
Other One-Day	1	1	0	19	19	19.00	-	-	-	-
ALL FIRST-CLASS	18	27	6	725	106	34.52	1	3	12	-
ALL ONE-DAY	20	19	5	304	67	21.71	-	1	4	-

BOWLING AVERAGES

	Overs	Mdns	Runs	Wkts	Avge	Best	5wI	10wM
Britannic Assurance	35.5	1	145	1	145.00	1-83	-	-
Refuge Assurance	24	1	158	6	26.33	2-33	-	
NatWest Trophy								
Benson & Hedges Cup								
Other First-Class	4	2	12	0				
Other One-Day								
ALL FIRST-CLASS	39.5	3	157	1	157.00	1-83	-	-
ALL ONE-DAY	24	1	158	6	26.33	2-33	-	

PLASTER RECORDS

B

M.R. BENSON - *Kent*

Opposition	Venue	Date	Batting			Fielding	Bowling
BRITANNIC ASSURANCE							
Sussex	Folkestone	May 3	109	&	13	1Ct	
Middlesex	Lord's	May 15	0	&	24		
Glamorgan	Swansea	May 23	17	&	96		0-28
Notts	Tunbridge We	June 2	34	&	1	1Ct	
Yorkshire	Tunbridge We	June 6	57				1-14
Somerset	Canterbury	June 9	0	&	116	1Ct	0-4
Essex	Maidstone	June 4	159				
Northants	Northampton	July 18	10				
Middlesex	Canterbury	July 25	45	&	10		
Worcestershire	Canterbury	July 28	10	&	8	1Ct	
Derbyshire	Chesterfield	Aug 4	0	&	15		
Leicestershire	Dartford	Aug 8	107	&	18		
Gloucs	Bristol	Aug 11	65			1Ct	
Sussex	Hove	Aug 18	115 *				
REFUGE ASSURANCE							
Somerset	Canterbury	June 10	55			2Ct	
Worcestershire	Canterbury	July 29	24				
Derbyshire	Chesterfield	Aug 5	4				
NATWEST TROPHY							
Gloucs	Bristol	July 11	7				
BENSON & HEDGES CUP							
Warwickshire	Canterbury	May 8	85				
Gloucs	Canterbury	May 10					
Glamorgan	Swansea	May 12	118				
OTHER FIRST-CLASS							
For MCC							
Worcestershire	Lord's	April 17	52				
For Kent							
India	Canterbury	July 7	90				

BATTING AVERAGES - Including fielding

	Matches	Inns	NO	Runs	HS	Avge	100s	50s	Ct	St
Britannic Assurance	14	23	1	1029	159	46.77	5	3	5	-
Refuge Assurance	3	3	0	83	55	27.66	-	1	2	-
NatWest Trophy	1	1	0	7	7	7.00	-	-	-	-
Benson & Hedges Cup	3	2	0	203	118	101.50	1	1	-	-
Other First-Class	2	2	0	142	90	71.00	-	2	-	-
ALL FIRST-CLASS	16	25	1	1171	159	48.79	5	5	5	-
ALL ONE-DAY	7	6	0	293	118	48.83	1	2	2	-

BOWLING AVERAGES

	Overs	Mdns	Runs	Wkts	Avge	Best	5wI	10wM
Britannic Assurance	8	2	46	1	46.00	1-14	-	-
Refuge Assurance								
NatWest Trophy								
Benson & Hedges Cup								
Other First-Class								
ALL FIRST-CLASS	8	2	46	1	46.00	1-14	-	-
ALL ONE-DAY								

P. BENT - *Worcestershire*

Opposition	Venue	Date	Batting			Fielding	Bowling
BRITANNIC ASSURANCE							
Yorkshire	Worcester	June 2	39				
Sussex	Worcester	June 20			5		
Middlesex	Lord's	June 30	7	&	13		
Gloucs	Worcester	July 7	44	&	22		
Somerset	Worcester	July 18	1	&	36		
Glamorgan	Abergavenny	July 21	69	&	79		
OTHER FIRST-CLASS							
New Zealand	Worcester	May 12	22	&	9		

BATTING AVERAGES - Including fielding

	Matches	Inns	NO	Runs	HS	Avge	100s	50s	Ct	St
Britannic Assurance	6	10	0	315	79	31.50	-	2	-	-
Other First-Class	1	2	0	31	22	15.50	-	-	-	-

| ALL FIRST-CLASS | 7 | 12 | 0 | 346 | 79 | 28.83 | - | 2 | - | - |

BOWLING AVERAGES
Did not bowl

P. BERRY - *Yorkshire*

Opposition	Venue	Date	Batting			Fielding	Bowling
BRITANNIC ASSURANCE							
Northants	Headingley	April 26	4 * &		31 *		1-101
Derbyshire	Chesterfield	May 23	6 * &		4 *	1Ct	1-48 & 0-23
BENSON & HEDGES CUP							
Hampshire	Southampton	April 24					0-28

BATTING AVERAGES - Including fielding

	Matches	Inns	NO	Runs	HS	Avge	100s	50s	Ct	St
Britannic Assurance	2	4	4	45	31 *	-	-	-	1	-
Benson & Hedges Cup	1	0	0	0	0	-	-	-	-	-
ALL FIRST-CLASS	2	4	4	45	31 *	-	-	-	1	-
ALL ONE-DAY	1	0	0	0	0	-	-	-	-	-

BOWLING AVERAGES

	Overs	Mdns	Runs	Wkts	Avge	Best	5wI	10wM
Britannic Assurance	44.3	4	172	2	86.00	1-48	-	-
Benson & Hedges Cup	5	0	28	0	-	-	-	-
ALL FIRST-CLASS	44.3	4	172	2	86.00	1-48	-	-
ALL ONE-DAY	5	0	28	0	-	-	-	-

S.R. BEVINS - *Worcestershire*

Opposition	Venue	Date	Batting			Fielding	Bowling
BRITANNIC ASSURANCE							
Notts	Worcester	May 3	6 *			3Ct	
REFUGE ASSURANCE							
Notts	Worcester	May 6				3Ct,1St	
BENSON & HEDGES CUP							
Glamorgan	Worcester	May 8	0 *				
Warwickshire	Edgbaston	May 10				2Ct,1St	
OTHER FIRST-CLASS							
New Zealand	Worcester	May 12	10	&	1	3Ct	

BATTING AVERAGES - Including fielding

	Matches	Inns	NO	Runs	HS	Avge	100s	50s	Ct	St
Britannic Assurance	1	1	1	6	6 *	-	-	-	3	-
Refuge Assurance	1	0	0	0	0	-	-	-	3	1
Benson & Hedges Cup	2	1	1	0	0 *	-	-	-	2	1
Other First-Class	1	2	0	11	10	5.50	-	-	3	-
ALL FIRST-CLASS	2	3	1	17	10	8.50	-	-	6	-
ALL ONE-DAY	3	1	1	0	0 *	-	-	-	5	2

BOWLING AVERAGES
Did not bowl

D.J. BICKNELL - *Surrey*

Opposition	Venue	Date	Batting			Fielding	Bowling
BRITANNIC ASSURANCE							
Sussex	Hove	April 26	65	&	2		
Hampshire	The Oval	May 19	41 *				
Glamorgan	Cardiff	June 30	59 *				
Northants	The Oval	July 4	169				
Warwickshire	The Oval	July 7	1	&	9		
Sussex	Guildford	July 18	143	&	6		
Kent	Guildford	July 21	4	&	9 *		

B — PLAYER RECORDS

Gloucs	Cheltenham	July 28	83 * &	81				
Leicestershire	The Oval	Aug 11	111					
Lancashire	Blackpool	Aug 29	25			1Ct		
Kent	Canterbury	Sept 7	186					
Middlesex	The Oval	Sept 12	41 &	114			0-15	
Essex	The Oval	Sept 18	0 &	50	1Ct		0-5	

REFUGE ASSURANCE

Sussex	Hove	April 29	21
Glamorgan	Cardiff	July 1	6
Warwickshire	The Oval	July 8	0
Middlesex	The Oval	July 15	75
Kent	The Oval	July 22	26

NATWEST TROPHY

Middlesex	Uxbridge	July 11	12

BENSON & HEDGES CUP

Lancashire	Old Trafford	April 24	9
Hampshire	The Oval	May 1	119
Combined U	The Parks	May 10	32
Yorkshire	The Oval	May 12	55

OTHER FIRST-CLASS

Oxford U	The Parks	May 16	33 & 63
India	The Oval	Aug 1	22

OTHER ONE-DAY

Sri Lanka	The Oval	Sept 2	86	1Ct
Warwickshire	Hove	Sept 3	33	1Ct
Kent	Hove	Sept 4	2	1Ct

BATTING AVERAGES - Including fielding

	Matches	Inns	NO	Runs	HS	Avge	100s	50s	Ct	St
Britannic Assurance	13	20	4	1199	186	74.93	5	5	2	-
Refuge Assurance	5	5	0	128	75	25.60	-	1	-	-
NatWest Trophy	1	1	0	12	12	12.00	-	-	-	-
Benson & Hedges Cup	4	4	0	215	119	53.75	1	1	-	-
Other First-Class	2	3	0	118	63	39.33	-	1	-	-
Other One-Day	3	3	0	121	86	40.33	-	1	3	-
ALL FIRST-CLASS	15	23	4	1317	186	69.31	5	6	2	-
ALL ONE-DAY	13	13	0	476	119	36.61	1	3	3	-

BOWLING AVERAGES

	Overs	Mdns	Runs	Wkts	Avge	Best	5wI	10wM
Britannic Assurance	9	1	20	0	-	-	-	-
Refuge Assurance								
NatWest Trophy								
Benson & Hedges Cup								
Other First-Class								
Other One-Day								
ALL FIRST-CLASS	9	1	20	0	-	-	-	-
ALL ONE-DAY								

M.P. BICKNELL - *Surrey*

Opposition	Venue	Date	Batting	Fielding	Bowling

BRITANNIC ASSURANCE

Opposition	Venue	Date	Batting	Fielding	Bowling
Sussex	Hove	April 26	50 *		0-71 & 0-59
Lancashire	The Oval	May 3	42		1-175
Hampshire	The Oval	May 19			0-43 & 3-39
Middlesex	Lord's	May 23	26 *	1Ct	1-72 & 3-25
Derbyshire	The Oval	June 6			0-64
Yorkshire	Harrogate	June 9	0	2Ct	3-40
Worcestershire	The Oval	June 16	15 *	1Ct	4-70 & 0-15
Notts	Trent Bridge	June 20			5-34 & 3-46
Glamorgan	Cardiff	June 30	0 *		4-87 & 2-36
Northants	The Oval	July 4			4-58
Warwickshire	The Oval	July 7	6 *	1Ct	3-56 & 1-32
Sussex	Guildford	July 18	8	1Ct	0-32 & 0-52
Gloucs	Cheltenham	July 28	7	1Ct	4-63 & 1-17
Somerset	Weston	Aug 4	2 *		4-79 & 0-15
Leicestershire	The Oval	Aug 11	23		4-42 & 2-69
Hampshire	Southampton	Aug 23	40	1Ct	2-46 & 2-75
Lancashire	Blackpool	Aug 29			2-65
Kent	Canterbury	Sept 7	28		0-12
Essex	The Oval	Sept 18	13 & 49 *		2-64

REFUGE ASSURANCE

Sussex	Hove	April 29	4 *		0-33
Lancashire	The Oval	May 6		1Ct	2-48
Notts	Trent Bridge	May 20	11 *		2-23
Northants	The Oval	June 3		2Ct	1-21
Yorkshire	Hull	June 10		1Ct	1-20
Worcestershire	The Oval	June 17			1-19
Glamorgan	Cardiff	July 1			0-16
Warwickshire	The Oval	July 8	0		1-34
Middlesex	The Oval	July 15		1Ct	4-14
Gloucs	Cheltenham	July 29	4 *		0-24
Somerset	Weston	Aug 5			2-38
Leicestershire	The Oval	Aug 12		1Ct	4-26

NATWEST TROPHY

Wiltshire	Trowbridge	June 27			1-16
Middlesex	Uxbridge	July 11	4 *	1Ct	1-63

BENSON & HEDGES CUP

Lancashire	Old Trafford	April 24	27 *	2Ct	2-48
Hampshire	The Oval	May 1		1Ct	2-48
Combined U	The Parks	May 10		1Ct	2-27
Yorkshire	The Oval	May 12			2-53
Lancashire	Old Trafford	May 30	8	1Ct	1-61

OTHER FIRST-CLASS

Oxford U	The Parks	May 16	1 *		4-80 & 0-18
For TCCB U25 XI					
India	Edgbaston	Aug 15			3-50 & 0-26

OTHER ONE-DAY

Warwickshire	Harrogate	June 13	10		3-48
Warwickshire	Hove	Sept 3			1-38
Kent	Hove	Sept 4	2		1-43

BATTING AVERAGES - Including fielding

	Matches	Inns	NO	Runs	HS	Avge	100s	50s	Ct	St
Britannic Assurance	19	15	7	309	50 *	38.62	-	1	8	-
Refuge Assurance	12	4	3	19	11 *	19.00	-	-	6	-
NatWest Trophy	2	1	1	4	4 *		-	-	1	-
Benson & Hedges Cup	5	2	1	35	27 *	35.00	-	-	5	-
Other First-Class	2	1	1	1	1 *		-	-	-	-
Other One-Day	3	2	0	12	10	6.00	-	-	-	-
ALL FIRST-CLASS	21	16	8	310	50 *	38.75	-	1	8	-
ALL ONE-DAY	22	9	5	70	27 *	17.50	-	-	12	-

BOWLING AVERAGES

	Overs	Mdns	Runs	Wkts	Avge	Best	5wI	10wM
Britannic Assurance	597.5	137	1653	60	27.55	5-34	1	-
Refuge Assurance	76.2	3	316	18	17.55	4-14	-	-
NatWest Trophy	24	3	79	2	39.50	1-16	-	-
Benson & Hedges Cup	51.5	9	237	9	26.33	2-27	-	-
Other First-Class	73.2	20	174	7	24.85	4-80	-	-
Other One-Day	29	2	129	5	25.80	3-48	-	-
ALL FIRST-CLASS	671.1	157	1827	67	27.26	5-34	1	-
ALL ONE-DAY	181.1	17	761	34	22.38	4-14	-	-

I.R. BISHOP - *Derbyshire*

Opposition	Venue	Date	Batting	Fielding	Bowling

BRITANNIC ASSURANCE

Opposition	Venue	Date	Batting	Fielding	Bowling
Northants	Northampton	May 3	19	1Ct	1-48 & 4-25
Yorkshire	Chesterfield	May 23	0		4-62 & 3-42
Notts	Derby	May 26	8		3-60 & 2-57
Gloucs	Derby	June 30	10		4-38 & 2-44
Sussex	Hove	July 4	0 *	1Ct	5-90
Essex	Colchester	July 18	26 & 9		3-41 & 1-21
Hampshire	Portsmouth	July 21	27 * & 31		3-72 & 2-32
Kent	Chesterfield	Aug 4			6-71 & 1-45
Northants	Chesterfield	Aug 8	34 & 0		1-27 & 2-43
Essex	Derby	Aug 23	39 * & 17		3-57
Yorkshire	Scarborough	Sept 7	103 *		1-50 & 1-61
Leicestershire	Derby	Sept 18	3		5-62 & 2-39

OTHER FIRST-CLASS

New Zealand	Derby	June 2		7	0-37

PLAINER RECORDS

PLAYER RECORDS

B

OTHER ONE-DAY

India	Chesterfield	July 16		1-44

For Rest of World

England XI	Jesmond	Aug 2	1 *	0-40
England XI	Jesmond	Aug 3		0-7

For World XI

Yorkshire	Scarborough	Sept 1	11 *	2-56

BATTING AVERAGES - Including fielding

	Matches	Inns	NO	Runs	HS	Avge	100s	50s	Ct	St
Britannic Assurance	12	15	4	326	103 *	29.63	1	-	2	-
Other First-Class	1	1	0	7	7	7.00	-	-	-	-
Other One-Day	4	2	2	12	11 *	-	-	-	-	-
ALL FIRST-CLASS	13	16	4	333	103 *	27.75	1	-	2	-
ALL ONE-DAY	4	2	2	12	11 *	-	-	-	-	-

BOWLING AVERAGES

	Overs	Mdns	Runs	Wkts	Avge	Best	5wI	10wM
Britannic Assurance	395.3	89	1087	59	18.42	6-71	3	-
Other First-Class	12	3	37	0	-	-	-	-
Other One-Day	36	4	147	3	49.00	2-56	-	
ALL FIRST-CLASS	407.3	92	1124	59	19.05	6-71	3	-
ALL ONE-DAY	36	4	147	3	49.00	2-56	-	

G.R. BLACK - *Buckinghamshire*

Opposition	Venue	Date	Batting	Fielding	Bowling

NATWEST TROPHY

Notts	Marlow	June 27	6	1Ct	2-52

BATTING AVERAGES - Including fielding

	Matches	Inns	NO	Runs	HS	Avge	100s	50s	Ct	St
NatWest Trophy	1	1	0	6	6	6.00	-	-	1	-
ALL ONE-DAY	1	1	0	6	6	6.00	-	-	1	-

BOWLING AVERAGES

	Overs	Mdns	Runs	Wkts	Avge	Best	5wI	10wM
NatWest Trophy	11	2	52	2	26.00	2-52		
ALL ONE-DAY	11	2	52	2	26.00	2-52	-	

R.J. BLAKEY - *Yorkshire*

Opposition	Venue	Date	Batting	Fielding	Bowling

BRITANNIC ASSURANCE

Northants	Headingley	April 26	25	&	0	
Warwickshire	Edgbaston	May 3	6	&	24	3Ct
Derbyshire	Chesterfield	May 23	9	&	25	3Ct
Hampshire	Headingley	May 26	17	&	20	1Ct
Worcestershire	Worcester	June 2	0	&	8	1Ct
Kent	Tunbridge We	June 6	9 *	&	1 *	
Surrey	Harrogate	June 9	1	&	2 *	2Ct
Warwickshire	Sheffield	June 20	1	&	8	3Ct
Glamorgan	Cardiff	June 23			71 *	2Ct
Notts	Scarborough	July 4	46 *			
Northants	Northampton	July 7	17	&	57	2Ct,1St
Middlesex	Uxbridge	July 18	0	&	42	1Ct,2St
Gloucs	Cheltenham	July 21	9	&	94	2Ct
Somerset	Scarborough	July 25	29	&	111	3Ct
Leicestershire	Sheffield	July 28	36	&	12	1Ct
Lancashire	Headingley	Aug 4	22	&	3	2Ct,3St
Sussex	Eastbourne	Aug 8	2 *			9Ct
Essex	Middlesbr'gh	Aug 11	5	&	26	1Ct
Lancashire	Old Trafford	Aug 18	1	&	4	1Ct,1St
Middlesex	Headingley	Aug 23	14	&	16	2Ct
Derbyshire	Scarborough	Sept 7			91 *	2Ct
Notts	Trent Bridge	Sept 18			64	0Ct,1St

REFUGE ASSURANCE

Notts	Trent Bridge	April 22	30		3Ct
Warwickshire	Edgbaston	May 6	9		

Derbyshire	Headingley	May 13	1	1Ct
Kent	Canterbury	May 20	9	
Hampshire	Headingley	May 27	22	1Ct
Worcestershire	Worcester	June 3	79	1Ct
Surrey	Hull	June 10	38	
Sussex	Hove	June 17	23	1Ct
Northants	Tring	July 8	42	0Ct,1St
Somerset	Scarborough	July 15	52	1Ct
Gloucs	Cheltenham	July 22	100 *	1Ct
Leicestershire	Sheffield	July 29	30 *	1Ct,1St
Lancashire	Scarborough	Aug 5	35	
Essex	Middlesbr'gh	Aug 12	76	1Ct
Middlesex	Scarborough	Aug 26	63	1Ct

NATWEST TROPHY

Norfolk	Headingley	June 27		2Ct
Warwickshire	Headingley	July 11		2Ct
Hampshire	Southampton	Aug 1	21	3Ct,1St

BENSON & HEDGES CUP

Hampshire	Southampton	April 24	66	
Combined U	Headingley	May 8	65	2Ct
Lancashire	Headingley	May 10	2	
Surrey	The Oval	May 12	79	

OTHER FIRST-CLASS

Zimbabwe	Headingley	May 16	5 &	58 *	1Ct
India	Headingley	June 30		2	2Ct

For TCCB U25 XI

India	Edgbaston	Aug 15	40 *	1Ct,1St

OTHER ONE-DAY

Sussex	Harrogate	June 14	21	
Warwickshire	Harrogate	June 15	54	
World XI	Scarborough	Sept 1	13	1Ct
Essex	Scarborough	Sept 3	0	
Yorkshiremen	Scarborough	Sept 6	69 *	

BATTING AVERAGES - Including fielding

	Matches	Inns	NO	Runs	HS	Avge	100s	50s	Ct	St
Britannic Assurance	22	39	7	928	111	29.00	1	5	41	8
Refuge Assurance	15	15	2	609	100 *	46.84	1	4	12	2
NatWest Trophy	3	1	0	21	21	21.00	-	-	7	1
Benson & Hedges Cup	4	4	0	212	79	53.00	-	3	2	-
Other First-Class	3	4	2	105	58 *	52.50	-	1	4	1
Other One-Day	5	5	1	157	69 *	39.25	-	2	1	-
ALL FIRST-CLASS	25	43	9	1033	111	30.38	1	6	45	9
ALL ONE-DAY	27	25	3	999	100 *	45.40	1	9	22	3

BOWLING AVERAGES

Did not bowl

D.C. BLANK - *Staffordshire*

Opposition	Venue	Date	Batting	Fielding	Bowling

NATWEST TROPHY

Northants	Northampton	June 27	1 *		2-74

BATTING AVERAGES - Including fielding

	Matches	Inns	NO	Runs	HS	Avge	100s	50s	Ct	St
NatWest Trophy	1	1	1	1	1 *	-	-	-	-	-
ALL ONE-DAY	1	1	1	1	1 *	-	-	-	-	-

BOWLING AVERAGES

	Overs	Mdns	Runs	Wkts	Avge	Best	5wI	10wM
NatWest Trophy	12	0	74	2	37.00	2-74		
ALL ONE-DAY	12	0	74	2	37.00	2-74	-	

B PLAYER RECORDS

J. BOILING - *Combined Universities*

Opposition	Venue	Date	Batting	Fielding	Bowling
BENSON & HEDGES CUP					
Lancashire	Fenner's	May 1		1Ct	1-37
Yorkshire	Headingley	May 8		2Ct	0-11
Surrey	The Parks	May 10			0-33
Hampshire	Southampton	May 12	2		0-71
OTHER ONE-DAY					
For Duchess of Norfolk's XI					
New Zealand	Arundel	May 6			1-57

BATTING AVERAGES - Including fielding

	Matches	Inns	NO	Runs	HS	Avge	100s	50s	Ct	St
Benson & Hedges Cup	4	1	0	2	2	2.00	-	-	3	-
Other One-Day	1	0	0	0	0	-	-	-	-	-
ALL ONE-DAY	5	1	0	2	2	2.00	-	-	3	-

BOWLING AVERAGES

	Overs	Mdns	Runs	Wkts	Avge	Best	5wI	10wM
Benson & Hedges Cup	33	1	152	1	152.00	1-37	-	
Other One-Day	9	0	57	1	57.00	1-57	-	
ALL ONE-DAY	42	1	209	2	104.50	1-37	-	

T.J. BOON - Leicestershire

Opposition	Venue	Date	Batting	Fielding	Bowling
BRITANNIC ASSURANCE					
Glamorgan	Cardiff	April 26	72 & 61 *	2Ct	
Essex	Chelmsford	May 3	90 & 89		
Notts	Leicester	May 15	1 & 27	2Ct	
Lancashire	Old Trafford	May 19	84 & 30	1Ct	
Somerset	Leicester	May 26	128 & 10		
Hampshire	Leicester	June 2	6 & 1	1Ct	
Northants	Northampton	June 6	4 & 18 *		
Middlesex	Leicester	June 16	10 & 51		
Derbyshire	Leicester	June 20	8 & 5 *		
Gloucs	Gloucester	June 23	138		
Notts	Trent Bridge	June 30	40 & 8		0-5
Glamorgan	Hinckley	July 7	51 & 75 *		0-20
Essex	Leicester	July 25	13 & 20	1Ct	
Yorkshire	Sheffield	July 28	76 & 11		
Worcestershire	Leicester	Aug 4	42 & 40	1Ct	
Kent	Dartford	Aug 8	18 & 21	2Ct	
Surrey	The Oval	Aug 11	32 & 56		
Warwickshire	Edgbaston	Aug 18	40 & 5	1Ct	
Kent	Leicester	Aug 23	66 & 20	1Ct	
Sussex	Leicester	Aug 29	6 & 14		
Northants	Leicester	Sept 12	13 & 0		
Derbyshire	Derby	Sept 18	15 & 7		
REFUGE ASSURANCE					
Northants	Leicester	April 22	9		
Glamorgan	Cardiff	April 29	2	1Ct	
Essex	Leicester	May 6	56	2Ct	
Lancashire	Old Trafford	May 20	46	1Ct	
Somerset	Leicester	May 27	18		
Hampshire	Leicester	June 3	6		
Sussex	Leicester	June 10	29		
Middlesex	Leicester	June 17	84		
Gloucs	Gloucester	June 24	15		
Notts	Trent Bridge	July 1	13		
Derbyshire	Knypersley	July 15	2		
Yorkshire	Sheffield	July 29	88		
Worcestershire	Leicester	Aug 5	16		
Surrey	The Oval	Aug 12	59	1Ct	
Warwickshire	Edgbaston	Aug 19	5		
Kent	Leicester	Aug 26	97		
NATWEST TROPHY					
Hampshire	Leicester	June 27	19		
BENSON & HEDGES CUP					
Northants	Leicester	April 24	84		
Notts	Trent Bridge	May 1	4		
Scotland	Leicester	May 12	39		
OTHER FIRST-CLASS					
Oxford U	The Parks	May 23		1Ct	0-14
India	Leicester	July 21	1 & 16		
OTHER ONE-DAY					
New Zealand	Leicester	June 14	40		
For Yorkshiremen					
Yorkshire	Scarborough	Sept 6	82		

BATTING AVERAGES - Including fielding

	Matches	Inns	NO	Runs	HS	Avge	100s	50s	Ct	St
Britannic Assurance	22	43	4	1522	138	39.02	2	11	12	-
Refuge Assurance	16	16	0	545	97	34.06	-	5	5	-
NatWest Trophy	1	1	0	19	19	19.00	-	-	-	-
Benson & Hedges Cup	3	3	0	127	84	42.33	-	1	-	-
Other First-Class	2	2	0	17	16	8.50	-	-	1	-
Other One-Day	2	2	0	122	82	61.00	-	1	-	-
ALL FIRST-CLASS	24	45	4	1539	138	37.53	2	11	13	-
ALL ONE-DAY	22	22	0	813	97	36.95	-	7	5	-

BOWLING AVERAGES

	Overs	Mdns	Runs	Wkts	Avge	Best	5wI	10wM
Britannic Assurance	3.5	0	25	0	-	-	-	-
Refuge Assurance								
NatWest Trophy								
Benson & Hedges Cup								
Other First-Class	3	0	14	0	-	-	-	-
Other One-Day								
ALL FIRST-CLASS	6.5	0	39	0	-	-	-	-
ALL ONE-DAY								

P.A. BOOTH - *Warwickshire*

Opposition	Venue	Date	Batting	Fielding	Bowling
BRITANNIC ASSURANCE					
Yorkshire	Edgbaston	May 3	15	1Ct	0-4 & 4-55
Worcestershire	Edgbaston	May 26	3 & 43		1-67 & 1-36
Leicestershire	Edgbaston	Aug 18	14 & 10		0-7 & 0-34
Worcestershire	Worcester	Aug 23	2 & 5		0-9 & 1-93
Somerset	Edgbaston	Sept 7	60 & 15	1Ct	0-57 & 1-37
Glamorgan	Edgbaston	Sept 12	0 & 10		2-44 & 2-48
Lancashire	Old Trafford	Sept 18	0		0-4
REFUGE ASSURANCE					
Yorkshire	Edgbaston	May 6			1-46
Leicestershire	Edgbaston	Aug 19			1-33
BENSON & HEDGES CUP					
Glamorgan	Edgbaston	April 24	13 *	1Ct	2-39
Kent	Canterbury	May 8	5		0-33
OTHER FIRST-CLASS					
Cambridge U	Fenner's	April 26	3 *	1Ct	0-23
New Zealand	Edgbaston	May 30	51 *		
Sri Lanka	Edgbaston	Aug 29	8 & 1		0-77 & 1-41
OTHER ONE-DAY					
For Yorkshiremen					
Yorkshire	Scarborough	Sept 6			1-24

BATTING AVERAGES - Including fielding

	Matches	Inns	NO	Runs	HS	Avge	100s	50s	Ct	St
Britannic Assurance	7	12	0	177	60	14.75	-	1	2	-
Refuge Assurance	2	0	0	0	0	-	-	-	-	-
Benson & Hedges Cup	2	2	1	18	13 *	18.00	-	-	1	-
Other First-Class	3	4	2	63	51 *	31.50	-	1	1	-
Other One-Day	1	0	0	0	0	-	-	-	-	-
ALL FIRST-CLASS	10	16	2	240	60	17.14	-	2	3	-
ALL ONE-DAY	5	2	1	18	13 *	18.00	-	-	1	-

BOWLING AVERAGES

	Overs	Mdns	Runs	Wkts	Avge	Best	5wI	10wM
Britannic Assurance	214.2	70	495	12	41.25	4-55	-	-
Refuge Assurance	13	0	79	2	39.50	1-33	-	
Benson & Hedges Cup	15	1	72	2	36.00	2-39	-	
Other First-Class	36.3	5	141	1	141.00	1-41	-	-

PLANNER RECORDS

PLAYER RECORDS — B

Other One-Day	7	0	24	1	24.00	1-24	-
ALL FIRST-CLASS	250.5	75	636	13	48.92	4-55	-
ALL ONE-DAY	35	1	175	5	35.00	2-39	-

D. BORTHWICK - *League C.C. XI*

Opposition	Venue	Date	Batting	Fielding	Bowling
OTHER ONE-DAY					
India	Sunderland	June 28	1	1Ct	

BATTING AVERAGES - Including fielding

	Matches	Inns	NO	Runs	HS	Avge	100s	50s	Ct	St
Other One-Day	1	1	0	1	1	1.00	-	-	1	-
ALL ONE-DAY	1	1	0	1	1	1.00	-	-	1	-

BOWLING AVERAGES
Did not bowl

I.T. BOTHAM - *Worcestershire*

Opposition	Venue	Date	Batting			Fielding	Bowling
BRITANNIC ASSURANCE							
Lancashire	Old Trafford	April 26	17	&	50 *	1Ct	0-24
Essex	Worcester	May 19	53	&	5		1-58
Warwickshire	Edgbaston	May 26	48				2-46
Yorkshire	Worcester	June 2	86			1Ct	4-65
Surrey	The Oval	June 16	113			1Ct	0-24
Sussex	Worcester	June 20			50		2-32
Middlesex	Lord's	June 30	4	&	0	1Ct	2-71
Gloucs	Worcester	July 7	2	&	16	2Ct	1-20
Glamorgan	Abergavenny	July 21	29				2-55 & 1-40
Derbyshire	Derby	July 25	27			1Ct	0-12 & 0-26
Kent	Canterbury	July 28	4	&	46		1-44 & 1-29
Leicestershire	Leicester	Aug 4	26				
REFUGE ASSURANCE							
Somerset	Taunton	April 22	24				2-39
Derbyshire	Derby	April 29	15				0-27
Essex	Worcester	May 20	5				4-25
Warwickshire	Worcester	May 27	29			1Ct	0-43
Yorkshire	Worcester	June 3	12				0-4
Surrey	The Oval	June 17	27				0-32
Sussex	Worcester	June 24	19			1Ct	3-40
Middlesex	Lord's	July 1	35				1-42
Gloucs	Worcester	July 8	41 *				2-40
Kent	Canterbury	July 29	45			1Ct	3-54
Leicestershire	Leicester	Aug 5	1				
Glamorgan	Swansea	Aug 26	4				
NATWEST TROPHY							
Suffolk	Bury St Ed's	June 27					3-44
Somerset	Taunton	July 11	0 *				2-65
Northants	Northampton	Aug 1	86 *				1-42
BENSON & HEDGES CUP							
Gloucs	Bristol	April 24	138 *			1Ct	1-69
Kent	Worcester	May 1	37				0-19
Glamorgan	Worcester	May 30	22				2-29
Notts	Trent Bridge	June 13					2-43
Lancashire	Lord's	July 14	38			1Ct	2-49
OTHER FIRST-CLASS							
MCC	Lord's	April 17	19				4-68
OTHER ONE-DAY							
Hampshire	Scarborough	Sept 2	1			1Ct	2-30

BATTING AVERAGES - Including fielding

	Matches	Inns	NO	Runs	HS	Avge	100s	50s	Ct	St
Britannic Assurance	12	17	1	576	113	36.00	1	4	7	-
Refuge Assurance	12	12	1	257	45	23.36	-	-	3	-
NatWest Trophy	3	2	2	86	86 *		-	1	-	-
Benson & Hedges Cup	5	4	1	235	138 *	78.33	1	-	2	-
Other First-Class	1	1	0	19	19	19.00	-	-	-	-

Other One-Day	1	1	0	1	1	1.00	-	-	1	-
ALL FIRST-CLASS	13	18	1	595	113	35.00	1	4	7	-
ALL ONE-DAY	21	19	4	579	138 *	38.60	1	1	6	-

BOWLING AVERAGES

	Overs	Mdns	Runs	Wkts	Avge	Best	5wI	10wM
Britannic Assurance	174.4	34	546	17	32.11	4-65	-	-
Refuge Assurance	67	1	346	15	23.06	4-25	-	
NatWest Trophy	31.1	2	151	6	25.16	3-44	-	
Benson & Hedges Cup	50	7	209	7	29.85	2-29	-	
Other First-Class	20	4	68	4	17.00	4-68	-	-
Other One-Day	7	0	30	2	15.00	2-30	-	
ALL FIRST-CLASS	194.4	38	614	21	29.23	4-65	-	-
ALL ONE-DAY	155.1	10	736	30	24.53	4-25	-	

P.D. BOWLER - *Derbyshire*

Opposition	Venue	Date	Batting			Fielding	Bowling
BRITANNIC ASSURANCE							
Notts	Trent Bridge	April 26	20	&	11	4Ct	
Northants	Northampton	May 3	24				
Lancashire	Derby	May 15	24	&	54		
Somerset	Taunton	May 19	6	&	25		
Yorkshire	Chesterfield	May 23	29			3Ct	
Notts	Derby	May 26	8	&	23		
Surrey	The Oval	June 6	75	&	85 *	1Ct	
Warwickshire	Derby	June 16	120			1Ct	1-48
Leicestershire	Leicester	June 20	36 * &		0		0-8
Gloucs	Derby	June 30	5	&	23		
Sussex	Hove	July 4	50				
Lancashire	Liverpool	July 7	115 * &		30		
Essex	Colchester	July 18	33	&	4		
Hampshire	Portsmouth	July 21	58	&	56		
Worcestershire	Derby	July 25	36	&	18		
Kent	Chesterfield	Aug 4	210	&	13 *	2Ct	
Northants	Chesterfield	Aug 8	22	&	40		
Middlesex	Derby	Aug 18	38	&	56	3Ct	
Essex	Derby	Aug 23	11	&	5		
Glamorgan	Cardiff	Aug 29	28			1Ct	
Yorkshire	Scarborough	Sept 7	4	&	13		
REFUGE ASSURANCE							
Sussex	Hove	April 22	51			4Ct	
Worcestershire	Derby	April 29	40			2Ct	
Northants	Northampton	May 6	30			2Ct	
Yorkshire	Headingley	May 13	5				
Notts	Derby	June 10	45			2Ct	
Warwickshire	Derby	June 17	0			3Ct	
Surrey	The Oval	June 24	50			1Ct	
Gloucs	Derby	July 1	5			1Ct	
Lancashire	Old Trafford	July 8	40			2Ct	
Leicestershire	Knypersley	July 15	4			2Ct	
Glamorgan	Swansea	July 29	52 *			2Ct,1St	
Kent	Chesterfield	Aug 5	54				
Middlesex	Derby	Aug 19	50			1Ct	
Essex	Derby	Aug 26	43				
Notts	Derby	Sept 5	59				
Middlesex	Edgbaston	Sept 16	11			1Ct	
NATWEST TROPHY							
Shropshire	Chesterfield	June 27	14			2Ct	
Lancashire	Derby	July 11	2			1Ct	
BENSON & HEDGES CUP							
Sussex	Derby	April 24	61			1Ct	
Somerset	Taunton	May 1	109			0Ct,1St	
Min Counties	Wellington	May 10	16			1Ct	
Middlesex	Derby	May 12	77			1Ct	
OTHER FIRST-CLASS							
New Zealand	Derby	June 2	11 * &		9	2Ct	0-25
OTHER ONE-DAY							
India	Chesterfield	July 16	59				

BATTING AVERAGES - Including fielding

	Matches	Inns	NO	Runs	HS	Avge	100s	50s	Ct	St
Britannic Assurance	21	37	4	1408	210	42.66	3	7	15	-
Refuge Assurance	16	16	1	539	59	35.93	-	6	23	1

B   PLAYER RECORDS

NatWest Trophy	2	2	0	16	14	8.00	-	- 3	-
Benson & Hedges Cup	4	4	0	263	109	65.75	1	2 3	1
Other First-Class	1	2	1	20	11 *	20.00	-	- 2	-
Other One-Day	1	1	0	59	59	59.00	-	1	-
ALL FIRST-CLASS	22	39	5	1428	210	42.00	3	7 17	-
ALL ONE-DAY	23	23	1	877	109	39.86	1	9 29	2

BOWLING AVERAGES

	Overs	Mdns	Runs	Wkts	Avge	Best	5wI	10wM
Britannic Assurance	8	0	56	1	56.00	1-48	-	-
Refuge Assurance								
NatWest Trophy								
Benson & Hedges Cup								
Other First-Class	3	0	25	0	-	-	-	-
Other One-Day								
ALL FIRST-CLASS	11	0	81	1	81.00	1-48	-	-
ALL ONE-DAY								

J.G. BRACEWELL - *New Zealand*

Opposition	Venue	Date	Batting	Fielding	Bowling
CORNHILL TEST MATCHES					
England	Trent Bridge	June 7	28		2-75
England	Lord's	June 21	4	3Ct	2-72 & 2-85
England	Edgbaston	July 5	25 & 0		2-130 & 4-38
OTHER FIRST-CLASS					
Sussex	Hove	May 26			0-99 & 0-138
Warwickshire	Edgbaston	May 30	31 *	1Ct	1-27 & 4-66
Derbyshire	Derby	June 2	40 * & 3 *		2-58
Northants	Northampton	June 16			2-78 & 1-27
Combined U	Fenner's	June 27	38	1Ct	5-107 & 7-120
OTHER ONE-DAY					
D of Norfolk	Arundel	May 6			0-57

BATTING AVERAGES - Including fielding

	Matches	Inns	NO	Runs	HS	Avge	100s	50s	Ct	St
Cornhill Test Matches	3	4	0	57	28	14.25	-	-	3	-
Other First-Class	5	4	3	112	40 *	112.00	-	-	2	-
Other One-Day	1	0	0	0	0	-	-	-	-	-
ALL FIRST-CLASS	8	8	3	169	40 *	33.80	-	-	5	-
ALL ONE-DAY	1	0	0	0	0	-	-	-	-	-

BOWLING AVERAGES

	Overs	Mdns	Runs	Wkts	Avge	Best	5wI	10wM
Cornhill Test Matches	148	41	400	12	33.33	4-38	-	-
Other First-Class	235.3	61	720	22	32.72	7-120	2	1
Other One-Day	9	0	57	0	-	-	-	-
ALL FIRST-CLASS	383.3	102	1120	34	32.94	7-120	2	1
ALL ONE-DAY	9	0	57	0	-	-	-	-

S. BRAMHALL - *Lancashire*

Opposition	Venue	Date	Batting	Fielding	Bowling
BRITANNIC ASSURANCE					
Northants	Northampton	Aug 11		0 * 1Ct,1St	
OTHER FIRST-CLASS					
Sri Lanka	Old Trafford	Sept 8	0 & 1 * 0Ct,1St		

BATTING AVERAGES - Including fielding

	Matches	Inns	NO	Runs	HS	Avge	100s	50s	Ct	St
Britannic Assurance	1	1	0	0	0 *	-	-	-	1	1
Other First-Class	1	2	1	1	1 *	1.00	-	-	-	1
ALL FIRST-CLASS	2	3	2	1	1 *	1.00	-	-	1	2

BOWLING AVERAGES
Did not bowl

E.A. BRANDES - *Zimbabwe*

Opposition	Venue	Date	Batting	Fielding	Bowling
OTHER FIRST-CLASS					
Yorkshire	Headingley	May 16	22	1Ct	3-75 & 0-23
Gloucs	Bristol	May 19	10 & 8 *		0-32 & 4-35
OTHER ONE-DAY					
Sussex	Hove	May 13	23		2-39
Essex	Chelmsford	May 14	7		1-58

BATTING AVERAGES - Including fielding

	Matches	Inns	NO	Runs	HS	Avge	100s	50s	Ct	St
Other First-Class	2	3	1	40	22	20.00	-	-	1	-
Other One-Day	2	2	0	30	23	15.00	-	-	-	-
ALL FIRST-CLASS	2	3	1	40	22	20.00	-	-	1	-
ALL ONE-DAY	2	2	0	30	23	15.00	-	-	-	-

BOWLING AVERAGES

	Overs	Mdns	Runs	Wkts	Avge	Best	5wI	10wM
Other First-Class	49.2	12	165	7	23.57	4-35	-	-
Other One-Day	22	2	97	3	32.33	2-39	-	
ALL FIRST-CLASS	49.2	12	165	7	23.57	4-35	-	-
ALL ONE-DAY	22	2	97	3	32.33	2-39	-	

J.P. BRENT - *Zimbabwe*

Opposition	Venue	Date	Batting	Fielding	Bowling
OTHER FIRST-CLASS					
Yorkshire	Headingley	May 16	17 & 34 *		0-29 & 0-9
Gloucs	Bristol	May 19	23 & 27 *		2-28 & 0-13
OTHER ONE-DAY					
Essex	Chelmsford	May 14	32		0-34

BATTING AVERAGES - Including fielding

	Matches	Inns	NO	Runs	HS	Avge	100s	50s	Ct	St
Other First-Class	2	4	2	101	34 *	50.50	-	-	-	-
Other One-Day	1	1	0	32	32	32.00	-	-	-	-
ALL FIRST-CLASS	2	4	2	101	34 *	50.50	-	-	-	-
ALL ONE-DAY	1	1	0	32	32	32.00	-	-	-	-

BOWLING AVERAGES

	Overs	Mdns	Runs	Wkts	Avge	Best	5wI	10wM
Other First-Class	26	6	79	2	39.50	2-28	-	-
Other One-Day	6	0	34	0	-	-	-	
ALL FIRST-CLASS	26	6	79	2	39.50	2-28	-	-
ALL ONE-DAY	6	0	34	0	-	-	-	

G.A. BRIANT - Zimbabwe

Opposition	Venue	Date	Batting	Fielding	Bowling
OTHER FIRST-CLASS					
Yorkshire	Headingley	May 16	5 & 35		
Gloucs	Bristol	May 19	69	1Ct	
OTHER ONE-DAY					
Sussex	Hove	May 13	7	1Ct	
Essex	Chelmsford	May 14	17	1Ct	

BATTING AVERAGES - Including fielding

	Matches	Inns	NO	Runs	HS	Avge	100s	50s	Ct	St
Other First-Class	2	3	0	109	69	36.33	-	1	1	-
Other One-Day	2	2	0	24	17	12.00	-	-	2	-
ALL FIRST-CLASS	2	3	0	109	69	36.33	-	1	1	-
ALL ONE-DAY	2	2	0	24	17	12.00	-	-	2	-

PLANNING PLAYER RECORDS | B

BOWLING AVERAGES
Did not bowl

N.E. BRIERS - *Leicestershire*

Opposition	Venue	Date	Batting			Fielding	Bowling
BRITANNIC ASSURANCE							
Glamorgan	Cardiff	April 26	21	&	10	1Ct	
Essex	Chelmsford	May 3	65	&	104	1Ct	
Notts	Leicester	May 15	157 *	&	22		
Lancashire	Old Trafford	May 19	0	&	81 *	1Ct	
Somerset	Leicester	May 26	39	&	5		
Hampshire	Leicester	June 2	0	&	29		
Northants	Northampton	June 6	6	&	5		
Middlesex	Leicester	June 16	23	&	34		
Derbyshire	Leicester	June 20	29	&	14 *		
Gloucs	Gloucester	June 23	67				
Notts	Trent Bridge	June 30	30	&	8		
Glamorgan	Hinckley	July 7	80	&	22		
Essex	Leicester	July 25	92	&	1		
Yorkshire	Sheffield	July 28	45	&	21	1Ct	
Worcestershire	Leicester	Aug 4	111	&	17		
Kent	Dartford	Aug 8	55	&	35		
Surrey	The Oval	Aug 11	22	&	16		
Warwickshire	Edgbaston	Aug 18	33	&	55	1Ct	
Kent	Leicester	Aug 23	62	&	75	1Ct	
Sussex	Leicester	Aug 29	0	&	78		
Northants	Leicester	Sept 12	176	&	0		
Derbyshire	Derby	Sept 18	99	&	2	1Ct	
REFUGE ASSURANCE							
Northants	Leicester	April 22	10				
Glamorgan	Cardiff	April 29	37			1Ct	
Essex	Leicester	May 6	5			1Ct	
Lancashire	Old Trafford	May 20	26				
Somerset	Leicester	May 27	6			1Ct	
Hampshire	Leicester	June 3	9			1Ct	
Sussex	Leicester	June 10	31			1Ct	
Middlesex	Leicester	June 17	46				
Gloucs	Gloucester	June 24	90 *			1Ct	
Notts	Trent Bridge	July 1	33				
Derbyshire	Knypersley	July 15	29				
Yorkshire	Sheffield	July 29	37				
Worcestershire	Leicester	Aug 5	42				
Surrey	The Oval	Aug 12	5				
Warwickshire	Edgbaston	Aug 19	2				
Kent	Leicester	Aug 26	16				
NATWEST TROPHY							
Hampshire	Leicester	June 27	8			1Ct	
BENSON & HEDGES CUP							
Northants	Leicester	April 24	7				
Notts	Trent Bridge	May 1	10				
Scotland	Leicester	May 12	93 *				
OTHER FIRST-CLASS							
Oxford U	The Parks	May 23					
India	Leicester	July 21	150 *				
OTHER ONE-DAY							
New Zealand	Leicester	June 14	7				

BATTING AVERAGES - Including fielding
	Matches	Inns	NO	Runs	HS	Avge	100s	50s	Ct	St
Britannic Assurance	22	43	3	1846	176	46.15	4	11	7	-
Refuge Assurance	16	16	1	424	90 *	28.26	-	1	6	-
NatWest Trophy	1	1	0	8	8	8.00	-	-	1	-
Benson & Hedges Cup	3	3	1	110	93 *	55.00	-	1	-	-
Other First-Class	2	1	1	150	150 *		-	1	-	-
Other One-Day	1	1	0	7	7	7.00	-	-	-	-
ALL FIRST-CLASS	24	44	4	1996	176	49.90	5	11	7	-
ALL ONE-DAY	21	21	2	549	93 *	28.89	-	2	7	-

BOWLING AVERAGES
Did not bowl

B.C. BROAD - *Nottinghamshire*

Opposition	Venue	Date	Batting			Fielding	Bowling
BRITANNIC ASSURANCE							
Derbyshire	Trent Bridge	April 26	180	&	5	1Ct	
Worcestershire	Worcester	May 3	2	&	16		
Leicestershire	Leicester	May 15	3	&	23		
Warwickshire	Edgbaston	May 19	119	&	30		
Northants	Trent Bridge	May 23	49	&	0		
Derbyshire	Derby	May 26	45	&	50		
Kent	Tunbridge We	June 2	227 *	&	1	1Ct	
Surrey	Trent Bridge	June 20	30	&	30		
Leicestershire	Trent Bridge	June 30	40	&	112 *	1Ct	
Yorkshire	Scarborough	July 4			126		
Sussex	Trent Bridge	July 7	12	&	34	1Ct	
Hampshire	Portsmouth	July 18	8	&	13		
Lancashire	Southport	July 25	122	&	46	1Ct	
Middlesex	Trent Bridge	July 28	140	&	25		
Essex	Southend	Aug 4	19	&	84		
Somerset	Weston	Aug 8	4	&	7		
Glamorgan	Worksop	Aug 11	98	&	10	1Ct	
Gloucs	Trent Bridge	Aug 18	13	&	35		
Worcestershire	Trent Bridge	Aug 29	156	&	7	1Ct	
Middlesex	Lord's	Sept 7	38	&	20		
Lancashire	Trent Bridge	Sept 12	42	&	122		
Yorkshire	Trent Bridge	Sept 18	40	&	43		
REFUGE ASSURANCE							
Yorkshire	Trent Bridge	April 22	4				
Lancashire	Trent Bridge	April 29	13			1Ct	
Worcestershire	Worcester	May 6	0				
Middlesex	Lord's	May 13	72				
Surrey	Trent Bridge	May 20	106 *			1Ct	
Derbyshire	Derby	June 10	11				
Kent	Canterbury	June 17	8			2Ct	
Somerset	Bath	June 24	18				
Leicestershire	Trent Bridge	July 1	57				
Sussex	Trent Bridge	July 8	61				
Hampshire	Southampton	July 15	86				
Warwickshire	Edgbaston	July 22	1				
Northants	Trent Bridge	July 29	38				
Essex	Southend	Aug 5	35				
Glamorgan	Trent Bridge	Aug 12	26				
Gloucs	Trent Bridge	Aug 19	22				
Derbyshire	Derby	Sept 5	28				
NATWEST TROPHY							
Bucks	Marlow	June 27	115				
Northants	Northampton	July 11	13				
BENSON & HEDGES CUP							
Essex	Chelmsford	April 24	22				
Leicestershire	Trent Bridge	May 1	49			1Ct	
Scotland	Glasgow	May 8	14				
Northants	Trent Bridge	May 12	8				
Essex	Chelmsford	May 30	38				
Worcestershire	Trent Bridge	June 13	32				
OTHER ONE-DAY							
For England XI							
Rest of World	Jesmond	Aug 2	84 *				
Rest of World	Jesmond	Aug 3	55				

BATTING AVERAGES - Including fielding
	Matches	Inns	NO	Runs	HS	Avge	100s	50s	Ct	St
Britannic Assurance	22	43	2	2226	227 *	54.29	9	3	7	-
Refuge Assurance	17	17	1	586	106 *	36.62	1	4	4	-
NatWest Trophy	2	2	0	128	115	64.00	1	-	-	-
Benson & Hedges Cup	6	6	0	163	49	27.16	-	-	1	-
Other One-Day	2	2	1	139	84 *	139.00	-	2	-	-
ALL FIRST-CLASS	22	43	2	2226	227 *	54.29	9	3	7	-
ALL ONE-DAY	27	27	2	1016	115	40.64	2	6	5	-

BOWLING AVERAGES
Did not bowl

B   PLAYER RECORDS

A. BROWN - *Surrey*

Opposition	Venue	Date	Batting	Fielding	Bowling
REFUGE ASSURANCE					
Middlesex	The Oval	July 15	2		
Somerset	Weston	Aug 5	32	2Ct	
Leicestershire	The Oval	Aug 12	56	1Ct	
Hampshire	Southampton	Aug 26	24	1Ct	
OTHER ONE-DAY					
Sri Lanka	The Oval	Sept 2	2		

BATTING AVERAGES - Including fielding

	Matches	Inns	NO	Runs	HS	Avge	100s	50s	Ct	St
Refuge Assurance	4	4	0	114	56	28.50	-	1	4	-
Other One-Day	1	1	0	2	2	2.00	-	-	-	-
ALL ONE-DAY	5	5	0	116	56	23.20	-	1	4	-

BOWLING AVERAGES
Did not bowl

A.D. BROWN - *Suffolk*

Opposition	Venue	Date	Batting	Fielding	Bowling
NATWEST TROPHY					
Worcestershire	Bury St Ed's	June 27	4		

BATTING AVERAGES - Including fielding

	Matches	Inns	NO	Runs	HS	Avge	100s	50s	Ct	St
NatWest Trophy	1	1	0	4	4	4.00	-	-	-	-
ALL ONE-DAY	1	1	0	4	4	4.00	-	-	-	-

BOWLING AVERAGES
Did not bowl

A.M. BROWN - *Derbyshire*

Opposition	Venue	Date	Batting			Fielding	Bowling
BRITANNIC ASSURANCE							
Notts	Trent Bridge	April 26	54	&	20	2Ct	
Northants	Northampton	May 3	44				
Essex	Colchester	July 18	3	&	0	1Ct	
Hampshire	Portsmouth	July 21	24	&	15	1Ct	
Worcestershire	Derby	July 25	32	&	42	1Ct	
Kent	Chesterfield	Aug 4	6			1Ct	
Northants	Chesterfield	Aug 8	139 *				
OTHER FIRST-CLASS							
Cambridge U	Fenner's	April 18	34 *			1Ct	

BATTING AVERAGES - Including fielding

	Matches	Inns	NO	Runs	HS	Avge	100s	50s	Ct	St
Britannic Assurance	7	11	1	379	139 *	37.90	1	1	6	-
Other First-Class	1	1	1	34	34 *	-	-	-	1	-
ALL FIRST-CLASS	8	12	2	413	139 *	41.30	1	1	7	-

BOWLING AVERAGES
Did not bowl

D.R. BROWN - *Scotland*

Opposition	Venue	Date	Batting	Fielding	Bowling
BENSON & HEDGES CUP					
Notts	Glasgow	May 8	24	1Ct	0-43
Northants	Northampton	May 10	16		3-50

| Leicestershire | Leicester | May 12 | 17 | | 0-47 |

BATTING AVERAGES - Including fielding

	Matches	Inns	NO	Runs	HS	Avge	100s	50s	Ct	St
Benson & Hedges Cup	3	3	0	57	24	19.00	-	-	1	-
ALL ONE-DAY	3	3	0	57	24	19.00	-	-	1	-

BOWLING AVERAGES

	Overs	Mdns	Runs	Wkts	Avge	Best	5wI	10wM
Benson & Hedges Cup	30.3	2	140	3	46.66	3-50	-	
ALL ONE-DAY	30.3	2	140	3	46.66	3-50	-	

G.K. BROWN - *Durham & Minor Counties*

Opposition	Venue	Date	Batting			Fielding	Bowling
NATWEST TROPHY							
Lancashire	Old Trafford	June 27	42				
BENSON & HEDGES CUP							
For Minor Counties							
Middlesex	Lord's	April 24	32			1Ct	
Sussex	Marlow	May 1	46			1Ct	
Somerset	Taunton	May 8	4				
Derbyshire	Wellington	May 10	16				
OTHER FIRST-CLASS							
For Minor Counties							
India	Trowbridge	July 11	103	&	89 *		1-39

BATTING AVERAGES - Including fielding

	Matches	Inns	NO	Runs	HS	Avge	100s	50s	Ct	St
NatWest Trophy	1	1	0	42	42	42.00	-	-	-	-
Benson & Hedges Cup	4	4	0	98	46	24.50	-	-	2	-
Other First-Class	1	2	1	192	103	192.00	1	1	-	-
ALL FIRST-CLASS	1	2	1	192	103	192.00	1	1	-	-
ALL ONE-DAY	5	5	0	140	46	28.00	-	-	2	-

BOWLING AVERAGES

	Overs	Mdns	Runs	Wkts	Avge	Best	5wI	10wM
NatWest Trophy								
Benson & Hedges Cup								
Other First-Class	9	1	39	1	39.00	1-39	-	-
ALL FIRST-CLASS	9	1	39	1	39.00	1-39	-	-
ALL ONE-DAY								

K.R. BROWN - *Middlesex*

Opposition	Venue	Date	Batting			Fielding	Bowling
BRITANNIC ASSURANCE							
Essex	Lord's	April 26	141	&	12		
Kent	Lord's	May 15	58				
Surrey	Lord's	May 23	16	&	56		
Gloucs	Lord's	May 26	5	&	60		0-18
Essex	Ilford	June 2				3Ct	
Warwickshire	Lord's	June 6	15	&	41 *		
Leicestershire	Leicester	June 16	0			2Ct	
Lancashire	Old Trafford	June 20			21 *		
Northants	Luton	June 23	69			2Ct	
Worcestershire	Lord's	June 30	52				
Yorkshire	Uxbridge	July 18	109 *	&	12 *	4Ct	
Somerset	Uxbridge	July 21	46	&	9	1Ct	
Kent	Canterbury	July 25	57 *	&	5	1Ct	
Notts	Trent Bridge	July 28	4	&	55	1Ct	
Glamorgan	Lord's	Aug 4	120	&	4	2Ct	
Hampshire	Bournemouth	Aug 8	23	&	12	1Ct	
Sussex	Lord's	Aug 11	2			3Ct	
Derbyshire	Derby	Aug 18	7	&	12	4Ct	
Yorkshire	Headingley	Aug 23	56	&	0		
Notts	Lord's	Sept 7	200 *			2Ct	
Surrey	The Oval	Sept 12	21				0-31
Sussex	Hove	Sept 18	116 *			1Ct	

PLAYER RECORDS

REFUGE ASSURANCE

Lancashire	Old Trafford	April 22	2 *	1Ct	
Essex	Lord's	April 29	50	1Ct	
Kent	Folkestone	May 6	20		
Notts	Lord's	May 13	56		
Gloucs	Lord's	May 27	39 *		
Warwickshire	Lord's	June 3			
Hampshire	Basingstoke	June 10	13 *	1Ct	
Leicestershire	Leicester	June 17	8		
Northants	Northampton	June 24			
Worcestershire	Lord's	July 1	14		0-4
Somerset	Lord's	July 8	15		
Surrey	The Oval	July 15	12	1Ct	0-16
Glamorgan	Lord's	Aug 5	5		
Sussex	Lord's	Aug 12	68		
Derbyshire	Derby	Aug 19			
Yorkshire	Scarborough	Aug 26	16		
Lancashire	Old Trafford	Sept 5	48 *	1Ct	
Derbyshire	Edgbaston	Sept 16	40		

NATWEST TROPHY

Berkshire	Lord's	June 27	16		
Surrey	Uxbridge	July 11	103 *	1Ct	
Glamorgan	Lord's	Aug 1			
Lancashire	Old Trafford	Aug 15	1		

BENSON & HEDGES CUP

Min Counties	Lord's	April 24	56	
Sussex	Hove	May 8	12	
Somerset	Lord's	May 10	31	1Ct
Derbyshire	Derby	May 12	34	
Somerset	Taunton	May 30	8	

OTHER FIRST-CLASS

Cambridge U	Fenner's	May 3	42	3Ct	1-16
New Zealand	Lord's	May 19	23 & 24 *		

OTHER ONE-DAY

For MCC

New Zealand	Lord's	May 7	79 *

BATTING AVERAGES - Including fielding

	Matches	Inns	NO	Runs	HS	Avge	100s	50s	Ct	St
Britannic Assurance	22	33	7	1416	200 *	54.46	5	8	27	-
Refuge Assurance	18	15	4	406	68	36.90	-	3	5	-
NatWest Trophy	4	3	1	120	103 *	60.00	1	-	1	-
Benson & Hedges Cup	5	5	0	141	56	28.20	-	1	1	-
Other First-Class	2	3	1	89	42	44.50	-	-	3	-
Other One-Day	1	1	1	79	79 *	-	-	-	1	-
ALL FIRST-CLASS	24	36	8	1505	200 *	53.75	5	8	30	-
ALL ONE-DAY	28	24	6	746	103 *	41.44	1	5	7	-

BOWLING AVERAGES

	Overs	Mdns	Runs	Wkts	Avge	Best	5wI	10wM
Britannic Assurance	6	2	49	0	-	-	-	-
Refuge Assurance	3	0	20	0	-	-	-	-
NatWest Trophy								
Benson & Hedges Cup								
Other First-Class	10	2	16	1	16.00	1-16	-	-
Other One-Day								
ALL FIRST-CLASS	16	4	65	1	65.00	1-16	-	-
ALL ONE-DAY	3	0	20	0	-	-	-	-

P.A. BROWN - *Devon*

Opposition	Venue	Date	Batting	Fielding	Bowling

NATWEST TROPHY

Somerset	Torquay	June 27	12

BATTING AVERAGES - Including fielding

	Matches	Inns	NO	Runs	HS	Avge	100s	50s	Ct	St
NatWest Trophy	1	1	0	12	12	12.00	-	-	-	-
ALL ONE-DAY	1	1	0	12	12	12.00	-	-	-	-

BOWLING AVERAGES

Did not bowl

S.J. BROWN - *Northamptonshire*

Opposition	Venue	Date	Batting	Fielding	Bowling
BRITANNIC ASSURANCE					
Kent	Northampton	July 18	2		1-81 & 0-22
Sussex	Northampton	July 21			1-46 & 1-41
Lancashire	Northampton	Aug 11		4 *	1-31
REFUGE ASSURANCE					
Leicestershire	Leicester	April 22			3-26
Somerset	Taunton	July 1	0		0-55
Essex	Chelmsford	July 15			0-39
Sussex	Well'borough	July 22	3 *		0-48
Hampshire	Bournemouth	Aug 5			2-37
Lancashire	Northampton	Aug 12			0-21
OTHER FIRST-CLASS					
Cambridge U	Fenner's	April 14		2Ct	1-18 & 1-11

BATTING AVERAGES - Including fielding

	Matches	Inns	NO	Runs	HS	Avge	100s	50s	Ct	St
Britannic Assurance	3	2	1	6	4 *	6.00	-	-	-	-
Refuge Assurance	6	2	1	3	3 *	3.00	-	-	-	-
Other First-Class	1	0	0	0	0	-	-	-	2	-
ALL FIRST-CLASS	4	2	1	6	4 *	6.00	-	-	2	-
ALL ONE-DAY	6	2	1	3	3 *	3.00	-	-	-	-

BOWLING AVERAGES

	Overs	Mdns	Runs	Wkts	Avge	Best	5wI	10wM
Britannic Assurance	52	7	221	4	55.25	1-31	-	-
Refuge Assurance	39	0	226	5	45.20	3-26	-	-
Other First-Class	21	10	29	2	14.50	1-11	-	-
ALL FIRST-CLASS	73	17	250	6	41.66	1-11	-	-
ALL ONE-DAY	39	0	226	5	45.20	3-26	-	-

C.K. BULLEN - *Surrey*

Opposition	Venue	Date	Batting	Fielding	Bowling
REFUGE ASSURANCE					
Sussex	Hove	April 29	3		1-40
Lancashire	The Oval	May 6			0-46
Notts	Trent Bridge	May 20	23 *		0-36
Northants	The Oval	June 3	1 *	2Ct	3-13
Yorkshire	Hull	June 10			0-21
Worcestershire	The Oval	June 17			0-29
Derbyshire	The Oval	June 24		1Ct	0-38
Glamorgan	Cardiff	July 1			1-28
Warwickshire	The Oval	July 8	0		0-22
Middlesex	The Oval	July 15		1Ct	0-38
Kent	The Oval	July 22		1Ct	1-25
Gloucs	Cheltenham	July 29	25		1-41
Somerset	Weston	Aug 5			0-37
Leicestershire	The Oval	Aug 12	12 *	3Ct	1-35
Hampshire	Southampton	Aug 26			0-43
NATWEST TROPHY					
Wiltshire	Trowbridge	June 27	93 *		1-42
Middlesex	Uxbridge	July 11	20 *		0-46
BENSON & HEDGES CUP					
Lancashire	Old Trafford	April 24	17 *	1Ct	2-35
Combined U	The Parks	May 10			1-48
Lancashire	Old Trafford	May 30	10	1Ct	0-37
OTHER ONE-DAY					
Warwickshire	Harrogate	June 13	22		0-24
Sri Lanka	The Oval	Sept 2	1 *	2Ct	2-37
Warwickshire	Hove	Sept 3	11 *		2-46
Kent	Hove	Sept 4	6		0-49

BATTING AVERAGES - Including fielding

	Matches	Inns	NO	Runs	HS	Avge	100s	50s	Ct	St
Refuge Assurance	15	6	3	64	25	21.33	-	-	8	-
NatWest Trophy	2	2	2	113	93 *	-	-	1	-	-
Benson & Hedges Cup	3	2	1	27	17 *	27.00	-	-	2	-

PLAYER RECORDS

Other One-Day	4	4	2	40	22	20.00	-	-	2	-
ALL ONE-DAY	24	14	8	244	93*	40.66	-	1	12	-

BOWLING AVERAGES

	Overs	Mdns	Runs	Wkts	Avge	Best	5wI	10wM
Refuge Assurance	101	2	492	8	61.50	3-13	-	
NatWest Trophy	24	1	88	1	88.00	1-42	-	
Benson & Hedges Cup	33	4	120	3	40.00	2-35	-	
Other One-Day	36	2	156	4	39.00	2-37	-	
ALL ONE-DAY	194	9	856	16	53.50	3-13	-	

R.A. BUNTING - *Sussex*

Opposition	Venue	Date	Batting	Fielding	Bowling
BRITANNIC ASSURANCE					
Lancashire	Horsham	June 2	10* & 0		1-61 & 1-20
Gloucs	Hove	June 16		1Ct	2-91 & 0-21
Worcestershire	Worcester	June 20			2-40
Derbyshire	Hove	July 4	24*		1-100
Notts	Trent Bridge	July 7			2-42 & 0-46
Northants	Northampton	July 21			1-79 & 1-68
Essex	Chelmsford	July 28	11*		2-53 & 2-36
Warwickshire	Eastbourne	Aug 4	1* & 2		2-89 & 0-10
Kent	Hove	Aug 18			0-88 & 0-28
Somerset	Hove	Aug 23	14 & 8		1-77
Leicestershire	Leicester	Aug 29	0	1Ct	0-21 & 0-27
Gloucs	Bristol	Sept 12	4 & 0*		1-67
Middlesex	Hove	Sept 18	11 & 0		2-49
REFUGE ASSURANCE					
Essex	Chelmsford	July 29			0-12
OTHER FIRST-CLASS					
New Zealand	Hove	May 26			1-42 & 1-45
Cambridge U	Hove	June 30			2-60 & 1-54
OTHER ONE-DAY					
Zimbabwe	Hove	May 13	6	1Ct	0-30
Yorkshire	Harrogate	June 14	5*		0-28

BATTING AVERAGES - Including fielding

	Matches	Inns	NO	Runs	HS	Avge	100s	50s	Ct	St
Britannic Assurance	13	13	5	85	24*	10.62	-	-	2	-
Refuge Assurance	1	0	0	0	0	-	-	-	-	-
Other First-Class	2	0	0	0	0	-	-	-	-	-
Other One-Day	2	2	1	11	6	11.00	-	-	1	-
ALL FIRST-CLASS	15	13	5	85	24*	10.62	-	-	2	-
ALL ONE-DAY	3	2	1	11	6	11.00	-	-	1	-

BOWLING AVERAGES

	Overs	Mdns	Runs	Wkts	Avge	Best	5wI	10wM
Britannic Assurance	298	54	1113	21	53.00	2-36	-	-
Refuge Assurance	1	0	12	0	-	-		-
Other First-Class	62	7	201	5	40.20	2-60	-	-
Other One-Day	17.3	2	58	0	-	-		-
ALL FIRST-CLASS	360	61	1314	26	50.53	2-36	-	-
ALL ONE-DAY	18.3	2	70	0	-	-		

P. BURN - *Durham*

Opposition	Venue	Date	Batting	Fielding	Bowling
NATWEST TROPHY					
Lancashire	Old Trafford	June 27	26	1Ct	
OTHER FIRST-CLASS					
For Minor Counties					
India	Trowbridge	July 11	0 & 47*		

BATTING AVERAGES - Including fielding

	Matches	Inns	NO	Runs	HS	Avge	100s	50s	Ct	St
NatWest Trophy	1	1	0	26	26	26.00	-	-	1	-
Other First-Class	1	2	1	47	47*	47.00	-	-	-	-
ALL FIRST-CLASS	1	2	1	47	47*	47.00	-	-	-	-
ALL ONE-DAY	1	1	0	26	26	26.00	-	-	1	-

BOWLING AVERAGES
Did not bowl

N.D. BURNS - *Somerset*

Opposition	Venue	Date	Batting	Fielding	Bowling
BRITANNIC ASSURANCE					
Gloucs	Taunton	April 26	166	3Ct,1St	
Glamorgan	Cardiff	May 3	28	2Ct	
Derbyshire	Taunton	May 19	10	2Ct	0-8
Sussex	Taunton	May 23	14*	2Ct	
Leicestershire	Leicester	May 26	2*	1Ct	
Gloucs	Bristol	June 2	16 & 38	2Ct	
Hampshire	Basingstoke	June 6		1Ct	
Kent	Canterbury	June 9	31 & 40	3Ct	
Essex	Bath	June 16		2Ct	
Glamorgan	Bath	June 20	71*		
Northants	Taunton	June 30	0 & 7	1Ct	
Warwickshire	Taunton	July 4	0 & 3*	1Ct	
Worcestershire	Worcester	July 18	27*		
Middlesex	Uxbridge	July 21	37* & 4*	2Ct	
Yorkshire	Scarborough	July 25	33 & 72	2Ct	
Lancashire	Old Trafford	July 28	7 & 10	2Ct	
Surrey	Weston	Aug 4	25	1Ct	
Notts	Weston	Aug 8	56	3Ct	
Hampshire	Taunton	Aug 18	1 & 8*	2Ct	
Sussex	Hove	Aug 23	28 & 13*	7Ct	
Warwickshire	Edgbaston	Sept 7	88 & 28	1Ct	
Worcestershire	Taunton	Sept 12	0 & 0	2Ct	
REFUGE ASSURANCE					
Worcestershire	Taunton	April 22	19	0Ct,1St	
Hampshire	Taunton	May 13	13*		
Derbyshire	Taunton	May 20	30		
Leicestershire	Leicester	May 27	3	1Ct	
Gloucs	Bristol	June 3	20		
Kent	Canterbury	June 10	14		
Essex	Bath	June 17	0		
Notts	Bath	June 24	10	3Ct	
Northants	Taunton	July 1		4Ct	
Middlesex	Lord's	July 8			
Yorkshire	Scarborough	July 15	1	1Ct	
Glamorgan	Neath	July 22			
Lancashire	Old Trafford	July 29	8	1Ct	
Surrey	Weston	Aug 5	26	1Ct	
Warwickshire	Weston	Aug 12			
Sussex	Hove	Aug 26	58	2Ct	
NATWEST TROPHY					
Devon	Torquay	June 27		1Ct	
Worcestershire	Taunton	July 11	25*	1Ct	
BENSON & HEDGES CUP					
Derbyshire	Taunton	May 1			
Min Counties	Taunton	May 8		1Ct,1St	
Middlesex	Lord's	May 10	21	1Ct	
Sussex	Hove	May 12	6*	1Ct	
Middlesex	Taunton	May 30	12		
Lancashire	Old Trafford	June 13	21	1Ct	
OTHER FIRST-CLASS					
Oxford U	The Parks	April 18	28*		
New Zealand	Taunton	May 16	1 & 59		
OTHER ONE-DAY					
Sri Lanka	Taunton	Sept 3	29*	2Ct	

BATTING AVERAGES - Including fielding

	Matches	Inns	NO	Runs	HS	Avge	100s	50s	Ct	St
Britannic Assurance	22	31	9	863	166	39.22	1	4	42	1
Refuge Assurance	16	12	1	202	58	18.36	-	1	13	1
NatWest Trophy	2	1	1	25	25*	-	-	-	2	-
Benson & Hedges Cup	6	4	1	60	21	20.00	-	-	4	1
Other First-Class	2	3	1	88	59	44.00	-	1	1	-
Other One-Day	1	1	1	29	29*	-	-	-	2	-
ALL FIRST-CLASS	24	34	10	951	166	39.62	1	5	42	1
ALL ONE-DAY	25	18	4	316	58	22.57	-	1	21	2

PLACER RECORDS — B

BOWLING AVERAGES

	Overs	Mdns	Runs	Wkts	Avge	Best	5wI	10wM
Britannic Assurance	0.3	0	8	0	-	-	-	-
Refuge Assurance								
NatWest Trophy								
Benson & Hedges Cup								
Other First-Class								
Other One-Day								
ALL FIRST-CLASS	0.3	0	8	0	-	-	-	-
ALL ONE-DAY								

S. BURROW - *Buckinghamshire*

Opposition	Venue	Date	Batting	Fielding	Bowling
NATWEST TROPHY					
Notts	Marlow	June 27	19		1-42

BATTING AVERAGES - Including fielding

	Matches	Inns	NO	Runs	HS	Avge	100s	50s	Ct	St
NatWest Trophy	1	1	0	19	19	19.00	-	-	-	-
ALL ONE-DAY	1	1	0	19	19	19.00	-	-	-	-

BOWLING AVERAGES

	Overs	Mdns	Runs	Wkts	Avge	Best	5wI	10wM
NatWest Trophy	12	1	42	1	42.00	1-42	-	
ALL ONE-DAY	12	1	42	1	42.00	1-42	-	

I.P. BUTCHART - *Zimbabwe*

Opposition	Venue	Date	Batting	Fielding	Bowling
OTHER FIRST-CLASS					
Yorkshire	Headingley	May 16	18 & 15 *		0-19 & 1-39
Gloucs	Bristol	May 19	6 & 5		0-23
Lancashire	Old Trafford	May 23	71		1-48 & 0-27
OTHER ONE-DAY					
Sussex	Hove	May 13	24	1Ct	0-30

BATTING AVERAGES - Including fielding

	Matches	Inns	NO	Runs	HS	Avge	100s	50s	Ct	St
Other First-Class	3	5	1	115	71	28.75	-	1	-	-
Other One-Day	1	1	0	24	24	24.00	-	-	1	-
ALL FIRST-CLASS	3	5	1	115	71	28.75	-	1	-	-
ALL ONE-DAY	1	1	0	24	24	24.00	-	-	1	-

BOWLING AVERAGES

	Overs	Mdns	Runs	Wkts	Avge	Best	5wI	10wM
Other First-Class	41	7	156	2	78.00	1-39	-	-
Other One-Day	5	0	30	0	-	-	-	-
ALL FIRST-CLASS	41	7	156	2	78.00	1-39	-	-
ALL ONE-DAY	5	0	30	0	-	-	-	-

A.R. BUTCHER - *Glamorgan*

Opposition	Venue	Date	Batting	Fielding	Bowling
BRITANNIC ASSURANCE					
Leicestershire	Cardiff	April 26	10 & 4		
Gloucs	Bristol	May 15	83 & 53		
Sussex	Hove	May 19	139		1-16
Kent	Swansea	May 23	151 *& 50		0-17
Lancashire	Colwyn Bay	May 26	46 & 66 *	1Ct	0-17
Northants	Northampton	June 9	43 & 36		
Hampshire	Southampton	June 16	7 & 51		0-17
Somerset	Bath	June 20	83 *	1Ct	0-45
Yorkshire	Cardiff	June 23	50 & 17	1Ct	
Surrey	Cardiff	June 30	67 & 21	1Ct	

Gloucs	Swansea	July 4	19		
Leicestershire	Hinckley	July 7	115 & 30	1Ct	
Worcestershire	Abergavenny	July 21	79 & 130		0-28
Warwickshire	Swansea	July 25	33 & 116		
Middlesex	Lord's	Aug 4	34 & 54	1Ct	0-13
Essex	Southend	Aug 8	0 & 59		
Notts	Worksop	Aug 11	13 & 121 *		
Derbyshire	Cardiff	Aug 29	4 & 13 *	1Ct	
Hampshire	Pontypridd	Sept 7	58 & 33		
Warwickshire	Edgbaston	Sept 12	71 & 3		
Worcestershire	Worcester	Sept 18	21 & 61		
REFUGE ASSURANCE					
Gloucs	Bristol	April 22	8	1Ct	
Leicestershire	Cardiff	April 29	17		
Kent	Llanelli	May 13	38		
Sussex	Hove	May 20	6	2Ct	
Lancashire	Colwyn Bay	May 27	38	1Ct	
Essex	Ilford	June 3	1	1Ct	
Northants	Northampton	June 10	40		
Hampshire	Bournemouth	June 17	52		
Surrey	Cardiff	July 1	0 *	1Ct	
Warwickshire	Edgbaston	July 15	6 *		
Somerset	Neath	July 22	18		
Derbyshire	Swansea	July 29	28		
Middlesex	Lord's	Aug 5	52		1-20
Notts	Trent Bridge	Aug 12	11		
Worcestershire	Swansea	Aug 26	30		
NATWEST TROPHY					
Dorset	Swansea	June 27	41	1Ct	
Sussex	Cardiff	July 11	30	1Ct	
Middlesex	Lord's	Aug 1	104 *		
BENSON & HEDGES CUP					
Warwickshire	Edgbaston	April 24	11	1Ct	
Gloucs	Cardiff	May 1	95		
Worcestershire	Worcester	May 8	57	1Ct	
Kent	Swansea	May 12	6		
Worcestershire	Worcester	May 30	16		
OTHER FIRST-CLASS					
Oxford U	The Parks	April 14	60		
India	Swansea	Aug 18	12		

BATTING AVERAGES - Including fielding

	Matches	Inns	NO	Runs	HS	Avge	100s	50s	Ct	St
Britannic Assurance	21	39	5	2044	151 *	60.11	6	14	8	-
Refuge Assurance	15	15	2	345	52	26.53	-	2	6	-
NatWest Trophy	3	3	1	175	104 *	87.50	1	-	2	-
Benson & Hedges Cup	5	5	0	185	95	37.00	-	2	2	-
Other First-Class	2	2	0	72	60	36.00	-	1	-	-
ALL FIRST-CLASS	23	41	5	2116	151 *	58.77	6	15	8	-
ALL ONE-DAY	23	23	3	705	104 *	35.25	1	4	10	-

BOWLING AVERAGES

	Overs	Mdns	Runs	Wkts	Avge	Best	5wI	10wM
Britannic Assurance	25.3	2	153	1	153.00	1-16	-	-
Refuge Assurance	4	0	20	1	20.00	1-20	-	-
NatWest Trophy								
Benson & Hedges Cup								
Other First-Class								
ALL FIRST-CLASS	25.3	2	153	1	153.00	1-16	-	-
ALL ONE-DAY	4	0	20	1	20.00	1-20	-	-

I.P. BUTCHER - *Gloucestershire*

Opposition	Venue	Date	Batting	Fielding	Bowling
BRITANNIC ASSURANCE					
Middlesex	Lord's	May 26	102 & 31		
Somerset	Bristol	June 2	41		
Essex	Ilford	June 6	5		
Sussex	Hove	June 16	42 & 3 *		
Hampshire	Gloucester	June 20	4		
Leicestershire	Gloucester	June 23	0		
Derbyshire	Derby	June 30	0 & 0 *		
Glamorgan	Swansea	July 4	25 *		
Worcestershire	Worcester	July 7	27 & 0		

B	PLAYER RECORDS

REFUGE ASSURANCE

Lancashire	Old Trafford	June 10	13

OTHER FIRST-CLASS

Zimbabwe	Bristol	May 19	78	&	26 *	
Cambridge U	Fenner's	May 23	79	&	8	3Ct
India	Bristol	Aug 4	41	&	1	1Ct

BATTING AVERAGES - Including fielding

	Matches	Inns	NO	Runs	HS	Avge	100s	50s	Ct	St
Britannic Assurance	9	13	3	280	102	28.00	1	-	-	-
Refuge Assurance	1	1	0	13	13	13.00	-	-	-	-
Other First-Class	3	6	1	233	79	46.60	-	2	4	-
ALL FIRST-CLASS	12	19	4	513	102	34.20	1	2	4	-
ALL ONE-DAY	1	1	0	13	13	13.00	-	-	-	-

BOWLING AVERAGES
Did not bowl

R.O. BUTCHER - *Middlesex*

Opposition	Venue	Date	Batting	Fielding	Bowling
REFUGE ASSURANCE					
Essex	Lord's	April 29	44 *	1Ct	
Kent	Folkestone	May 6	27 *		
Notts	Lord's	May 13	7		
Gloucs	Lord's	May 27			
Warwickshire	Lord's	June 3			
Hampshire	Basingstoke	June 10		1Ct	
Leicestershire	Leicester	June 17	22	1Ct	
Northants	Northampton	June 24		1Ct	
Worcestershire	Lord's	July 1	1		
Somerset	Lord's	July 8	12		
Surrey	The Oval	July 15	3		
NATWEST TROPHY					
Berkshire	Lord's	June 27	22	1Ct	
Surrey	Uxbridge	July 11	1		
BENSON & HEDGES CUP					
Min Counties	Lord's	April 24	23		
Sussex	Hove	May 8	5	1Ct	
Somerset	Lord's	May 10	3	2Ct	
Derbyshire	Derby	May 12	9		
Somerset	Taunton	May 30	22		
OTHER FIRST-CLASS					
Cambridge U	Fenner's	May 3	29 * & 32	2Ct	0-2
New Zealand	Lord's	May 19	0 & 22 *	1Ct	

BATTING AVERAGES - Including fielding

	Matches	Inns	NO	Runs	HS	Avge	100s	50s	Ct	St
Refuge Assurance	11	7	2	116	44 *	23.20	-	-	4	-
NatWest Trophy	2	2	0	23	22	11.50	-	-	1	-
Benson & Hedges Cup	5	5	0	62	23	12.40	-	-	3	-
Other First-Class	2	4	2	83	32	41.50	-	-	3	-
ALL FIRST-CLASS	2	4	2	83	32	41.50	-	-	3	-
ALL ONE-DAY	18	14	2	201	44 *	16.75	-	-	8	-

BOWLING AVERAGES

	Overs	Mdns	Runs	Wkts	Avge	Best	5wI	10wM
Refuge Assurance								
NatWest Trophy								
Benson & Hedges Cup								
Other First-Class	2	0	2	0	-	-	-	-
ALL FIRST-CLASS	2	0	2	0	-	-	-	-
ALL ONE-DAY								

T. BUTLER - *Buckinghamshire*

Opposition	Venue	Date	Batting	Fielding	Bowling
NATWEST TROPHY					
Notts	Marlow	June 27	5		

BATTING AVERAGES - Including fielding

	Matches	Inns	NO	Runs	HS	Avge	100s	50s	Ct	St
NatWest Trophy	1	1	0	5	5	5.00	-	-	-	-
ALL ONE-DAY	1	1	0	5	5	5.00	-	-	-	-

BOWLING AVERAGES
Did not bowl

A.J. BUZZA - *Cambridge University*

Opposition	Venue	Date	Batting	Fielding	Bowling
OTHER FIRST-CLASS					
Derbyshire	Fenner's	April 18	0 & 9 *		2-117 & 1-27
Warwickshire	Fenner's	April 26	1		4-108 & 0-4
Middlesex	Fenner's	May 3	0	1Ct	2-55 & 2-25
Essex	Fenner's	May 16	21 & 0	1Ct	0-90 & 0-17
Gloucs	Fenner's	May 23	6 & 1		1-97 & 2-91
Notts	Fenner's	June 16	0		0-54 & 0-50
Kent	Fenner's	June 20		1 *	1-106
For Combined Universities					
New Zealand	Fenner's	June 27	0 *	1Ct	1-44 & 4-87
For Cambridge University					
Sussex	Hove	June 30	10		0-65 & 1-34
Oxford U	Lord's	July 4			2-15

BATTING AVERAGES - Including fielding

	Matches	Inns	NO	Runs	HS	Avge	100s	50s	Ct	St
Other First-Class	10	12	3	49	21	5.44	-	-	3	-
ALL FIRST-CLASS	10	12	3	49	21	5.44	-	-	3	-

BOWLING AVERAGES

	Overs	Mdns	Runs	Wkts	Avge	Best	5wI	10wM
Other First-Class	287	47	1086	23	47.21	4-87	-	-
ALL FIRST-CLASS	287	47	1086	23	47.21	4-87	-	-

D. BYAS - *Yorkshire*

Opposition	Venue	Date	Batting	Fielding	Bowling
BRITANNIC ASSURANCE					
Northants	Headingley	April 26	0 & 0	1Ct	0-23
Derbyshire	Chesterfield	May 23	67 & 6	4Ct	0-28 & 3-55
Hampshire	Headingley	May 26	29 & 0		0-13
Glamorgan	Cardiff	June 23	79		0-23
Notts	Scarborough	July 4			0-15
Northants	Northampton	July 7	28 & 35		0-19
Middlesex	Uxbridge	July 18	83 & 17		
Gloucs	Cheltenham	July 21	63 * & 0 *	1Ct	0-14
Somerset	Scarborough	July 25	36 & 32	2Ct	0-15 & 0-14
Leicestershire	Sheffield	July 28	5 & 81	1Ct	0-20
Lancashire	Headingley	Aug 4	0 & 9		
Sussex	Eastbourne	Aug 8		1Ct	
Essex	Middlesbr'gh	Aug 11	7 & 6	2Ct	
Lancashire	Old Trafford	Aug 18	2 * & 39	3Ct	
Middlesex	Headingley	Aug 23	36 & 12	1Ct	0-14
Derbyshire	Scarborough	Sept 7		13	1Ct
Notts	Trent Bridge	Sept 18		8	2Ct
REFUGE ASSURANCE					
Notts	Trent Bridge	April 22	7		0-23
Warwickshire	Edgbaston	May 6	7		1-27
Derbyshire	Headingley	May 13	30 *	1Ct	2-33
Kent	Canterbury	May 20	25		0-19
Hampshire	Headingley	May 27	2	1Ct	3-26

PLAYER RECORDS

Worcestershire	Worcester	June 3	14		
Surrey	Hull	June 10	2		1-22
Sussex	Hove	June 17	26	1Ct	0-16
Northants	Tring	July 8	18 *		1-17
Somerset	Scarborough	July 15	6 *		
Gloucs	Cheltenham	July 22			
Leicestershire	Sheffield	July 29			
Lancashire	Scarborough	Aug 5	35 *		
Essex	Middlesbr'gh	Aug 12	18	1Ct	
Middlesex	Scarborough	Aug 26	22		

NATWEST TROPHY

Norfolk	Headingley	June 27		1Ct	
Warwickshire	Headingley	July 11		1Ct	1-23
Hampshire	Southampton	Aug 1	4	2Ct	

BENSON & HEDGES CUP

Hampshire	Southampton	April 24			1-13
Surrey	The Oval	May 12	36		0-37

OTHER FIRST-CLASS

Zimbabwe	Headingley	May 16	3	1Ct	1-40 & 0-20
India	Headingley	June 30	8 *	1Ct	0-29 & 0-16

OTHER ONE-DAY

Sussex	Harrogate	June 14		2Ct	0-7
Warwickshire	Harrogate	June 15	4 *		0-55
World XI	Scarborough	Sept 1	1		
Essex	Scarborough	Sept 3	22	1Ct	0-10
Yorkshiremen	Scarborough	Sept 6	59		0-19

BATTING AVERAGES - Including fielding

	Matches	Inns	NO	Runs	HS	Avge	100s	50s	Ct	St
Britannic Assurance	17	27	3	693	83	28.87	-	5	19	-
Refuge Assurance	15	13	4	212	35 *	23.55	-	-	4	-
NatWest Trophy	3	1	0	4	4	4.00	-	-	4	-
Benson & Hedges Cup	2	1	0	36	36	36.00	-	-		-
Other First-Class	2	2	1	11	8 *	11.00	-	-	2	-
Other One-Day	5	4	1	86	59	28.66	-	1	3	-
ALL FIRST-CLASS	19	29	4	704	83	28.16	-	5	21	-
ALL ONE-DAY	25	19	5	338	59	24.14	-	1	11	-

BOWLING AVERAGES

	Overs	Mdns	Runs	Wkts	Avge	Best	5wI	10wM
Britannic Assurance	69	14	253	3	84.33	3-55	-	
Refuge Assurance	36	0	183	8	22.87	3-26	-	
NatWest Trophy	3	0	23	1	23.00	1-23		
Benson & Hedges Cup	13	1	50	1	50.00	1-13	-	
Other First-Class	27	5	105	1	105.00	1-40	-	-
Other One-Day	18	0	91	0	-	-	-	
ALL FIRST-CLASS	96	19	358	4	89.50	3-55	-	-
ALL ONE-DAY	70	1	347	10	34.70	3-26	-	

A.B. BYRAM - *Shropshire*

Opposition	Venue	Date	Batting	Fielding	Bowling

NATWEST TROPHY

Derbyshire	Chesterfield	June 27	20 *		0-35

BATTING AVERAGES - Including fielding

	Matches	Inns	NO	Runs	HS	Avge	100s	50s	Ct	St
NatWest Trophy	1	1	1	20	20 *	-	-	-	-	-
ALL ONE-DAY	1	1	1	20	20 *	-	-	-	-	-

BOWLING AVERAGES

	Overs	Mdns	Runs	Wkts	Avge	Best	5wI	10wM
NatWest Trophy	6	0	35	0	-	-	-	
ALL ONE-DAY	6	0	35	0	-	-	-	

PLAYER RECORDS

A. CADDICK - *Somerset*

Opposition	Venue	Date	Batting	Fielding	Bowling
OTHER ONE-DAY					
Sri Lanka	Taunton	Sept 3			0-19

BATTING AVERAGES - Including fielding

	Matches	Inns	NO	Runs	HS	Avge	100s	50s	Ct	St
Other One-Day	1	0	0	0	0	-	-	-	-	-
ALL ONE-DAY	1	0	0	0	0	-	-	-	-	-

BOWLING AVERAGES

	Overs	Mdns	Runs	Wkts	Avge	Best	5wI	10wM
Other One-Day	6	1	19	0	-	-	-	-
ALL ONE-DAY	6	1	19	0	-	-	-	-

P.J. CALEY - *Suffolk*

Opposition	Venue	Date	Batting	Fielding	Bowling
NATWEST TROPHY					
Worcestershire	Bury St Ed's	June 27	39*		0-49

BATTING AVERAGES - Including fielding

	Matches	Inns	NO	Runs	HS	Avge	100s	50s	Ct	St
NatWest Trophy	1	1	1	39	39*	-	-	-	-	-
ALL ONE-DAY	1	1	1	39	39*	-	-	-	-	-

BOWLING AVERAGES

	Overs	Mdns	Runs	Wkts	Avge	Best	5wI	10wM
NatWest Trophy	9	0	49	0	-	-	-	-
ALL ONE-DAY	9	0	49	0	-	-	-	-

G.S. CALWAY - *Dorset*

Opposition	Venue	Date	Batting	Fielding	Bowling
NATWEST TROPHY					
Glamorgan	Swansea	June 27	32	1Ct	0-29

BATTING AVERAGES - Including fielding

	Matches	Inns	NO	Runs	HS	Avge	100s	50s	Ct	St
NatWest Trophy	1	1	0	32	32	32.00	-	-	1	-
ALL ONE-DAY	1	1	0	32	32	32.00	-	-	1	-

BOWLING AVERAGES

	Overs	Mdns	Runs	Wkts	Avge	Best	5wI	10wM
NatWest Trophy	4	0	29	0	-	-	-	-
ALL ONE-DAY	4	0	29	0	-	-	-	-

M.J. CANN - *Glamorgan*

Opposition	Venue	Date	Batting	Fielding	Bowling
BRITANNIC ASSURANCE					
Leicestershire	Cardiff	April 26	11 & 17		
Somerset	Cardiff	May 3	64 & 54		0-22 & 0-44
Sussex	Hove	May 19	13	1Ct	1-39
Kent	Swansea	May 23	10	1Ct	0-1 & 0-56
Lancashire	Colwyn Bay	May 26	4 & 7		
OTHER FIRST-CLASS					
Oxford U	The Parks	June 2	19 & 7		

BATTING AVERAGES - Including fielding

	Matches	Inns	NO	Runs	HS	Avge	100s	50s	Ct	St
Britannic Assurance	5	8	0	180	64	22.50	-	2	2	-
Other First-Class	1	2	0	26	19	13.00	-	-	-	-
ALL FIRST-CLASS	6	10	0	206	64	20.60	-	2	2	-

BOWLING AVERAGES

	Overs	Mdns	Runs	Wkts	Avge	Best	5wI	10wM
Britannic Assurance	35	3	162	1	162.00	1-39	-	-
Other First-Class								
ALL FIRST-CLASS	35	3	162	1	162.00	1-39	-	-

D.J. CAPEL - *Northamptonshire*

Opposition	Venue	Date	Batting	Fielding	Bowling
BRITANNIC ASSURANCE					
Yorkshire	Headingley	April 26	21*		2-40 & 3-72
Derbyshire	Northampton	May 3	11 & 2	1Ct	4-83
Notts	Trent Bridge	May 23	4		1-45 & 0-60
Warwickshire	Edgbaston	June 2	89	1Ct	5-74 & 0-21
Leicestershire	Northampton	June 6		4Ct	2-49 & 2-4
Glamorgan	Northampton	June 9	113 & 64*	1Ct	0-20 & 1-17
Middlesex	Luton	June 23	12 & 15		0-21
Somerset	Taunton	June 30	13* & 21*		
Surrey	The Oval	July 4	19		
Yorkshire	Northampton	July 7	64 & 83	1Ct	0-24 & 0-17
Kent	Northampton	July 18	85	2Ct	
Sussex	Northampton	July 21	12 & 29		0-13
Gloucs	Cheltenham	July 25	10 & 4	1Ct	
Derbyshire	Chesterfield	Aug 8	103* & 50	1Ct	
Lancashire	Northampton	Aug 11	19 & 9	2Ct	0-10 & 1-22
Worcestershire	Worcester	Aug 18	12 & 0	1Ct	1-13
Gloucs	Northampton	Aug 23	38 & 2		2-90 & 1-16
REFUGE ASSURANCE					
Leicestershire	Leicester	April 22	47*	1Ct	1-18
Warwickshire	Edgbaston	April 29	20		1-35
Derbyshire	Northampton	May 6	39		1-46
Kent	Northampton	May 27	38	1Ct	1-40
Surrey	The Oval	June 3	0	1Ct	0-22
Glamorgan	Northampton	June 10	121		0-34
Middlesex	Northampton	June 24	46		0-31
Somerset	Taunton	July 1	11		
Yorkshire	Tring	July 8	25		0-26
Essex	Chelmsford	July 15	56		
Sussex	Well'borough	July 22	115		
Notts	Trent Bridge	July 29	4	1Ct	2-34
Lancashire	Northampton	Aug 12	4		
Worcestershire	Worcester	Aug 19	1*		0-35
Gloucs	Northampton	Aug 26	16	1Ct	1-62
NATWEST TROPHY					
Staffordshire	Northampton	June 27		1Ct	
Notts	Northampton	July 11	101		0-43
Worcestershire	Northampton	Aug 1	53		0-51
Hampshire	Southampton	Aug 15	43	2Ct	1-67
Lancashire	Lord's	Sept 1	36		1-44
BENSON & HEDGES CUP					
Leicestershire	Leicester	April 24	33		1-38
Essex	Northampton	May 8	12		0-24
Scotland	Northampton	May 10	0		2-29
OTHER FIRST-CLASS					
New Zealand	Northampton	June 16	123 & 65*	1Ct	

BATTING AVERAGES - Including fielding

	Matches	Inns	NO	Runs	HS	Avge	100s	50s	Ct	St
Britannic Assurance	17	27	5	904	113	41.09	2	6	15	-
Refuge Assurance	15	15	2	543	121	41.76	2	1	5	-
NatWest Trophy	5	4	0	233	101	58.25	1	1	3	-
Benson & Hedges Cup	3	3	0	45	33	15.00	-	-	-	-
Other First-Class	1	2	1	188	123	188.00	1	1	1	-
ALL FIRST-CLASS	18	29	6	1092	123	47.47	3	7	16	-
ALL ONE-DAY	23	22	2	821	121	41.05	3	2	8	-

PLACE PLAYER RECORDS

PLAYER RECORDS

C

BOWLING AVERAGES

	Overs	Mdns	Runs	Wkts	Avge	Best	5wI	10wM
Britannic Assurance	234	51	711	25	28.44	5-74	1	-
Refuge Assurance	72.5	3	383	7	54.71	2-34	-	-
NatWest Trophy	39	1	205	2	102.50	1-44	-	-
Benson & Hedges Cup	28	1	91	3	30.33	2-29	-	-
Other First-Class								
ALL FIRST-CLASS	234	51	711	25	28.44	5-74	1	-
ALL ONE-DAY	139.5	5	679	12	56.58	2-29	-	-

J.D. CARR - *Middlesex*

Opposition	Venue	Date	Batting	Fielding	Bowling
REFUGE ASSURANCE					
Lancashire	Old Trafford	April 22			0-20
Yorkshire	Scarborough	Aug 26	9	1Ct	

BATTING AVERAGES - Including fielding

	Matches	Inns	NO	Runs	HS	Avge	100s	50s	Ct	St
Refuge Assurance	2	1	0	9	9	9.00	-	-	1	-
ALL ONE-DAY	2	1	0	9	9	9.00	-	-	1	-

BOWLING AVERAGES

	Overs	Mdns	Runs	Wkts	Avge	Best	5wI	10wM
Refuge Assurance	3.4	0	20	0				
ALL ONE-DAY	3.4	0	20	0				

P. CARRICK - *Yorkshire*

Opposition	Venue	Date	Batting	Fielding	Bowling
BRITANNIC ASSURANCE					
Northants	Headingley	April 26	37 & 23		0-89
Warwickshire	Edgbaston	May 3	7 & 14		1-31 & 2-35
Hampshire	Headingley	May 26	23 & 32		1-46
Worcestershire	Worcester	June 2	2		2-70
Kent	Tunbridge We	June 6			0-40
Surrey	Harrogate	June 9	64		0-65
Warwickshire	Sheffield	June 20	1 * & 3	1Ct	0-29
Glamorgan	Cardiff	June 23			1-67
Notts	Scarborough	July 4			2-69
Northants	Northampton	July 7	27	3Ct	2-91 & 4-98
Middlesex	Uxbridge	July 18	52 & 10	1Ct	5-99 & 1-22
Gloucs	Cheltenham	July 21	17		0-144
Lancashire	Headingley	Aug 4	34 * & 5		4-107
Sussex	Eastbourne	Aug 8		1Ct	5-49 & 4-37
Essex	Middlesbr'gh	Aug 11	19 & 3		2-88
Lancashire	Old Trafford	Aug 18	57		5-98
Middlesex	Headingley	Aug 23	34 & 20		1-61 & 0-35
Derbyshire	Scarborough	Sept 7	31	1Ct	4-90 & 0-10
REFUGE ASSURANCE					
Notts	Trent Bridge	April 22	1		1-27
Warwickshire	Edgbaston	May 6	22		1-39
Hampshire	Headingley	May 27	14		1-39
Worcestershire	Worcester	June 3	0 *	1Ct	1-34
Surrey	Hull	June 10	7		0-22
Sussex	Hove	June 17	24 *	1Ct	3-28
Northants	Tring	July 8		1Ct	2-22
Somerset	Scarborough	July 15		1Ct	1-18
Gloucs	Cheltenham	July 22			2-47
Leicestershire	Sheffield	July 29		1Ct	2-29
Lancashire	Scarborough	Aug 5	1		0-48
Essex	Middlesbr'gh	Aug 12	30		3-46
Middlesex	Scarborough	Aug 26	7		3-44
NATWEST TROPHY					
Norfolk	Headingley	June 27			3-8
Warwickshire	Headingley	July 11			3-26
Hampshire	Southampton	Aug 1	14		1-34
BENSON & HEDGES CUP					
Hampshire	Southampton	April 24			1-31
Combined U	Headingley	May 8	8		0-40
Lancashire	Headingley	May 10	3		
OTHER ONE-DAY					
Sussex	Harrogate	June 14			3-39
Warwickshire	Harrogate	June 15	7 *		3-41
World XI	Scarborough	Sept 1	18	1Ct	1-31
Essex	Scarborough	Sept 3	12		1-54

BATTING AVERAGES - Including fielding

	Matches	Inns	NO	Runs	HS	Avge	100s	50s	Ct	St
Britannic Assurance	18	22	2	515	64	25.75	-	3	7	-
Refuge Assurance	13	9	2	106	30	15.14	-	-	5	-
NatWest Trophy	3	1	0	14	14	14.00	-	-	-	-
Benson & Hedges Cup	3	2	0	11	8	5.50	-	-	-	-
Other One-Day	4	3	1	37	18	18.50	-	-	1	-
ALL FIRST-CLASS	18	22	2	515	64	25.75	-	3	7	-
ALL ONE-DAY	23	15	3	168	30	14.00	-	-	6	-

BOWLING AVERAGES

	Overs	Mdns	Runs	Wkts	Avge	Best	5wI	10wM
Britannic Assurance	601	170	1570	46	34.13	5-49	3	-
Refuge Assurance	97	5	443	20	22.15	3-28	-	-
NatWest Trophy	36	9	68	7	9.71	3-8	-	-
Benson & Hedges Cup	22	1	71	1	71.00	1-31	-	-
Other One-Day	42	2	165	8	20.62	3-39	-	-
ALL FIRST-CLASS	601	170	1570	46	34.13	5-49	3	-
ALL ONE-DAY	197	17	747	36	20.75	3-8	-	-

D. CARTLEDGE - *Staffordshire*

Opposition	Venue	Date	Batting	Fielding	Bowling
NATWEST TROPHY					
Northants	Northampton	June 27	19	1Ct	0-23

BATTING AVERAGES - Including fielding

	Matches	Inns	NO	Runs	HS	Avge	100s	50s	Ct	St
NatWest Trophy	1	1	0	19	19	19.00	-	-	1	-
ALL ONE-DAY	1	1	0	19	19	19.00	-	-	1	-

BOWLING AVERAGES

	Overs	Mdns	Runs	Wkts	Avge	Best	5wI	10wM
NatWest Trophy	4	0	23	0				
ALL ONE-DAY	4	0	23	0				

C. CHAPMAN - *Yorkshire*

Opposition	Venue	Date	Batting	Fielding	Bowling
BRITANNIC ASSURANCE					
Northants	Northampton	July 7	5 & 17		
Middlesex	Uxbridge	July 18	20 & 5	2Ct	
REFUGE ASSURANCE					
Northants	Tring	July 8		1Ct	
Middlesex	Scarborough	Aug 26	36 *		

BATTING AVERAGES - Including fielding

	Matches	Inns	NO	Runs	HS	Avge	100s	50s	Ct	St
Britannic Assurance	2	4	0	47	20	11.75	-	-	2	-
Refuge Assurance	2	1	1	36	36 *		-	-	1	-
ALL FIRST-CLASS	2	4	0	47	20	11.75	-	-	2	-
ALL ONE-DAY	2	1	1	36	36 *		-	-	1	-

BOWLING AVERAGES
Did not bowl

C		PLAYER RECORDS

S. CHAUHAN - *Oxford University*

Opposition	Venue	Date	Batting	Fielding	Bowling
OTHER FIRST-CLASS					
Leicestershire	The Parks	May 23	25		1-58
Glamorgan	The Parks	June 2	4		
Notts	The Parks	June 6			

BATTING AVERAGES - Including fielding

	Matches	Inns	NO	Runs	HS	Avge	100s	50s	Ct	St
Other First-Class	3	2	0	29	25	14.50	-	-	-	-
ALL FIRST-CLASS	3	2	0	29	25	14.50	-	-	-	-

BOWLING AVERAGES

	Overs	Mdns	Runs	Wkts	Avge	Best	5wI	10wM
Other First-Class	15	1	58	1	58.00	1-58	-	-
ALL FIRST-CLASS	15	1	58	1	58.00	1-58	-	-

J.H. CHILDS - *Essex*

Opposition	Venue	Date	Batting	Fielding	Bowling
BRITANNIC ASSURANCE					
Leicestershire	Chelmsford	May 3			0-88 & 1-93
Worcestershire	Worcester	May 19			0-9
Hampshire	Southampton	May 23	0		0-49 & 2-24
Middlesex	Ilford	June 2	10 *		0-58
Gloucs	Ilford	June 6			1-48
Warwickshire	Edgbaston	June 9			0-66
Somerset	Bath	June 16		1Ct	0-21
Kent	Maidstone	June 4			0-41
Derbyshire	Colchester	July 18	2		1-57 & 1-7
Lancashire	Colchester	July 21	13 *		1-63 & 1-45
Leicestershire	Leicester	July 25	13		0-31
Sussex	Chelmsford	July 28	0	1Ct	3-51 & 4-56
Notts	Southend	Aug 4	2	2Ct	0-10 & 4-104
Glamorgan	Southend	Aug 8	8 * &	1 * 2Ct	0-69 & 0-35
Yorkshire	Middlesbr'gh	Aug 11	11		0-26 & 1-17
Surrey	Chelmsford	Aug 18	4		1-10
Derbyshire	Derby	Aug 23	8		0-2
Northants	Northampton	Aug 29			0-46
Northants	Chelmsford	Sept 7	4 &	21 *	1-119
Kent	Chelmsford	Sept 12	26	1Ct	2-79 & 1-60
Surrey	The Oval	Sept 18	0		0-51
REFUGE ASSURANCE					
Kent	Chelmsford	April 22	2		2-38
Middlesex	Lord's	April 29	3 *		0-24
Leicestershire	Leicester	May 6			0-29
Gloucs	Chelmsford	May 13			0-35
Worcestershire	Worcester	May 20	5 *		0-14
Warwickshire	Edgbaston	June 10			1-19
Somerset	Bath	June 17			1-14
Hampshire	Southampton	July 8		1Ct	0-36
Northants	Chelmsford	July 15			0-38
Lancashire	Colchester	July 22			0-37
Sussex	Chelmsford	July 29	4 *		1-47
Notts	Southend	Aug 5	1 *		0-43
Derbyshire	Derby	Aug 26			1-38
NATWEST TROPHY					
Scotland	Chelmsford	June 27			1-44
Hampshire	Chelmsford	July 11			0-60
BENSON & HEDGES CUP					
Notts	Chelmsford	April 24		1Ct	0-42
Scotland	Glasgow	May 1		1Ct	3-37
Northants	Northampton	May 8			1-25
Notts	Chelmsford	May 30			1-40
OTHER FIRST-CLASS					
Cambridge U	Fenner's	May 16			1-39 & 0-18
New Zealand	Chelmsford	June 30			1-76 & 0-22
OTHER ONE-DAY					
Zimbabwe	Chelmsford	May 14			1-37

BATTING AVERAGES - Including fielding

	Matches	Inns	NO	Runs	HS	Avge	100s	50s	Ct	St
Britannic Assurance	21	16	5	123	26	11.18	-	-	7	-
Refuge Assurance	13	5	4	15	5 *	15.00	-	-	1	-
NatWest Trophy	2	0	0	0	0		-	-	-	-
Benson & Hedges Cup	4	0	0	0	0		-	-	2	-
Other First-Class	2	0	0	0	0		-	-	-	-
Other One-Day	1	0	0	0	0		-	-	-	-
ALL FIRST-CLASS	23	16	5	123	26	11.18	-	-	7	-
ALL ONE-DAY	20	5	4	15	5 *	15.00	-	-	3	-

BOWLING AVERAGES

	Overs	Mdns	Runs	Wkts	Avge	Best	5wI	10wM
Britannic Assurance	595.1	189	1435	25	57.40	4-56	-	-
Refuge Assurance	86	6	412	6	68.66	2-38	-	
NatWest Trophy	24	1	104	1	104.00	1-44	-	
Benson & Hedges Cup	38	3	144	5	28.80	3-37	-	
Other First-Class	60.4	22	155	2	77.50	1-39	-	-
Other One-Day	11	1	37	1	37.00	1-37	-	
ALL FIRST-CLASS	655.5	211	1590	27	58.88	4-56	-	-
ALL ONE-DAY	159	11	697	13	53.61	3-37	-	

A.R. CLARKE - *Sussex*

Opposition	Venue	Date	Batting	Fielding	Bowling
REFUGE ASSURANCE					
Surrey	Hove	April 29	0 *		2-23
Glamorgan	Hove	May 20			1-47
Leicestershire	Leicester	June 10			0-40
Worcestershire	Worcester	June 24	1 *		1-42
Hampshire	Hove	July 1		1Ct	1-26
Notts	Trent Bridge	July 8	0 *		1-37
Gloucs	Swindon	July 15	0		2-58
Warwickshire	Eastbourne	Aug 5	4 *		2-42
NATWEST TROPHY					
Ireland	Downpatrick	June 27		1Ct	0-6
Glamorgan	Cardiff	July 11	0		2-53
BENSON & HEDGES CUP					
Min Counties	Marlow	May 1			1-53
Middlesex	Hove	May 8			0-70

BATTING AVERAGES - Including fielding

	Matches	Inns	NO	Runs	HS	Avge	100s	50s	Ct	St
Refuge Assurance	8	5	4	5	4 *	5.00	-	-	1	-
NatWest Trophy	2	1	0	0	0	0.00	-	-	1	-
Benson & Hedges Cup	2	0	0	0	0		-	-	-	-
ALL ONE-DAY	12	6	4	5	4 *	2.50	-	-	2	-

BOWLING AVERAGES

	Overs	Mdns	Runs	Wkts	Avge	Best	5wI	10wM
Refuge Assurance	59.3	0	315	10	31.50	2-23	-	
NatWest Trophy	22	7	59	2	29.50	2-53	-	
Benson & Hedges Cup	22	1	123	1	123.00	1-53	-	
ALL ONE-DAY	103.3	8	497	13	38.23	2-23	-	

M.W. CLEAL - *Somerset*

Opposition	Venue	Date	Batting	Fielding	Bowling
REFUGE ASSURANCE					
Hampshire	Taunton	May 13			1-41
Derbyshire	Taunton	May 20	13 *		0-27
Leicestershire	Leicester	May 27	8 *		1-27
Gloucs	Bristol	June 3	0		1-14
Kent	Canterbury	June 10	0		0-9
Notts	Bath	June 24	12 *	1Ct	0-17

BATTING AVERAGES - Including fielding

	Matches	Inns	NO	Runs	HS	Avge	100s	50s	Ct	St
Refuge Assurance	6	5	3	33	13 *	16.50	-	-	1	-

PLAYER RECORDS

C

	Overs	Mdns	Runs	Wkts	Avge	Best	5wI	10wM
ALL ONE-DAY	6	5	3	33	13*	16.50	-	-	1	-

BOWLING AVERAGES

	Overs	Mdns	Runs	Wkts	Avge	Best	5wI	10wM
Refuge Assurance	23	0	135	3	45.00	1-14	-
ALL ONE-DAY	23	0	135	3	45.00	1-14	-

S.M. CLEMENTS - *Suffolk*

Opposition	Venue	Date	Batting	Fielding	Bowling
NATWEST TROPHY					
Worcestershire	Bury St Ed's	June 27	11		

BATTING AVERAGES - Including fielding

	Matches	Inns	NO	Runs	HS	Avge	100s	50s	Ct	St
NatWest Trophy	1	1	0	11	11	11.00	-	-	-	-
ALL ONE-DAY	1	1	0	11	11	11.00	-	-	-	-

BOWLING AVERAGES
Did not bowl

G.S. CLINTON - *Surrey*

Opposition	Venue	Date	Batting		Fielding	Bowling
BRITANNIC ASSURANCE						
Sussex	Hove	April 26	43 &	98		
Lancashire	The Oval	May 3	8 &	15		
Hampshire	The Oval	May 19	73 &	37 *		
Derbyshire	The Oval	June 6		70 *	1Ct	
Yorkshire	Harrogate	June 9		5		
Worcestershire	The Oval	June 16	33 * &	80		
Notts	Trent Bridge	June 20	1			
Glamorgan	Cardiff	June 30	41 &	22	1Ct	
Northants	The Oval	July 4	146			
Warwickshire	The Oval	July 7	18 &	33		1Ct
Sussex	Guildford	July 18	1 &	93		
Kent	Guildford	July 21	38 &	8	* 1Ct	
Gloucs	Cheltenham	July 28	38 &	13		
Somerset	Weston	Aug 4	8 &	16		
Leicestershire	The Oval	Aug 11	34			
Essex	Chelmsford	Aug 18	10 &	32	1Ct	
Hampshire	Southampton	Aug 23	21			
Kent	Canterbury	Sept 7	57			
REFUGE ASSURANCE						
Lancashire	The Oval	May 6	26		1Ct	
Notts	Trent Bridge	May 20	40			
Yorkshire	Hull	June 10	28			
Derbyshire	The Oval	June 24	45			
Glamorgan	Cardiff	July 1				
NATWEST TROPHY						
Wiltshire	Trowbridge	June 27	50			
Middlesex	Uxbridge	July 11	33			
BENSON & HEDGES CUP						
Lancashire	Old Trafford	April 24	40			
Hampshire	The Oval	May 1	9			
Combined U	The Parks	May 10	61		1Ct	
Yorkshire	The Oval	May 12	30		1Ct	
Lancashire	Old Trafford	May 30	77			
OTHER FIRST-CLASS						
Oxford U	The Parks	May 16	29		1Ct	
India	The Oval	Aug 1	97 &	74		
OTHER ONE-DAY						
Warwickshire	Harrogate	June 13	32			
Warwickshire	Hove	Sept 3	8			

BATTING AVERAGES - Including fielding

	Matches	Inns	NO	Runs	HS	Avge	100s	50s	Ct	St
Britannic Assurance	18	29	4	1092	146	43.68	1	6	5	-

				Refuge Assurance	5	4	0	139	45	34.75	-	-	1	-

	Matches	Inns	NO	Runs	HS	Avge	100s	50s	Ct	St
Refuge Assurance	5	4	0	139	45	34.75	-	-	1	-
NatWest Trophy	2	2	0	83	50	41.50	-	1	-	-
Benson & Hedges Cup	5	5	0	217	77	43.40	-	2	2	-
Other First-Class	2	3	0	200	97	66.66	-	2	1	-
Other One-Day	2	2	0	40	32	20.00	-	-	-	-
ALL FIRST-CLASS	20	32	4	1292	146	46.14	1	8	6	-
ALL ONE-DAY	14	13	0	479	77	36.84	-	3	3	-

BOWLING AVERAGES
Did not bowl

M.F. COHEN - *Ireland*

Opposition	Venue	Date	Batting	Fielding	Bowling
OTHER FIRST-CLASS					
Scotland	Edinburgh	Aug 11	60 & 15		
OTHER ONE-DAY					
New Zealand	Downpatrick	May 9	8		
New Zealand	Belfast	May 10	2		

BATTING AVERAGES - Including fielding

	Matches	Inns	NO	Runs	HS	Avge	100s	50s	Ct	St
Other First-Class	1	2	0	75	60	37.50	-	1	-	-
Other One-Day	2	2	0	10	8	5.00	-	-	-	-
ALL FIRST-CLASS	1	2	0	75	60	37.50	-	1	-	-
ALL ONE-DAY	2	2	0	10	8	5.00	-	-	-	-

BOWLING AVERAGES
Did not bowl

C.A. CONNOR - *Hampshire*

Opposition	Venue	Date	Batting		Fielding	Bowling
BRITANNIC ASSURANCE						
Kent	Canterbury	April 26			1Ct	2-38 & 3-44
Sussex	Southampton	May 15				1-52 & 2-80
Surrey	The Oval	May 19				2-84 & 0-13
Essex	Southampton	May 23			1Ct	1-95 & 1-71
Yorkshire	Headingley	May 26			1Ct	2-79 & 5-96
Leicestershire	Leicester	June 2			2Ct	1-46 & 1-54
Somerset	Basingstoke	June 6				0-23 & 1-20
Glamorgan	Southampton	June 16			1Ct	2-86
Gloucs	Gloucester	June 20			1Ct	1-17
Lancashire	Old Trafford	June 23				0-1 & 0-12
Notts	Portsmouth	July 18	2 *			2-29 & 1-41
Derbyshire	Portsmouth	July 21	46 &	6		1-58 & 2-49
Sussex	Arundel	July 25				0-20 & 1-23
Warwickshire	Edgbaston	July 28				2-23 & 0-39
Northants	Bournemouth	Aug 4			1Ct	2-21 & 0-22
Middlesex	Bournemouth	Aug 8	2			0-15
Somerset	Taunton	Aug 18	29 *		1Ct	1-75 & 1-45
Surrey	Southampton	Aug 23	12 &	20		4-112 & 0-29
Gloucs	Southampton	Sept 18	2 &	0 *		1-56 & 1-55
REFUGE ASSURANCE						
Kent	Canterbury	April 29			2Ct	1-49
Gloucs	Southampton	May 6				
Somerset	Taunton	May 13				0-48
Yorkshire	Headingley	May 27				3-31
Leicestershire	Leicester	June 3				2-35
Middlesex	Basingstoke	June 10	3			1-18
Glamorgan	Bournemouth	June 17				0-26
Lancashire	Old Trafford	June 24				
Sussex	Hove	July 1	4		1Ct	0-18
Notts	Southampton	July 15				1-49
Derbyshire	Portsmouth	July 22				4-11
Warwickshire	Edgbaston	July 29				0-45
Northants	Bournemouth	Aug 5				1-51
Surrey	Southampton	Aug 26	4 *			1-45
NATWEST TROPHY						
Leicestershire	Leicester	June 27				0-49
Essex	Chelmsford	July 11				2-71

Yorkshire	Southampton	Aug 1	13	1Ct	1-10
Northants	Southampton	Aug 15	7 *		4-73

BENSON & HEDGES CUP

Yorkshire	Southampton	April 24			1-25
Surrey	The Oval	May 1	3		0-71
Lancashire	Old Trafford	May 8			2-26
Combined U	Southampton	May 12			3-40

OTHER FIRST-CLASS

Oxford U	The Parks	May 3			
India	Southampton	July 4			1-43 & 1-28
Sri Lanka	Southampton	Sept 12	29 *	1Ct	1-32 & 0-63

OTHER ONE-DAY

Worcestershire	Scarborough	Sept 2			2-14
Essex	Scarborough	Sept 4		1Ct	1-21

BATTING AVERAGES - Including fielding

	Matches	Inns	NO	Runs	HS	Avge	100s	50s	Ct	St
Britannic Assurance	19	9	3	119	46	19.83	-	-	9	-
Refuge Assurance	14	3	1	11	4 *	5.50	-	-	3	-
NatWest Trophy	4	2	1	20	13	20.00	-	-	1	-
Benson & Hedges Cup	4	1	0	3	3	3.00	-	-	-	-
Other First-Class	3	1	1	29	29 *	-	-	-	1	-
Other One-Day	2	0	0	0	0	-	-	-	1	-
ALL FIRST-CLASS	22	10	4	148	46	24.66	-	-	10	-
ALL ONE-DAY	24	6	2	34	13	8.50	-	-	5	-

BOWLING AVERAGES

	Overs	Mdns	Runs	Wkts	Avge	Best	5wI	10wM
Britannic Assurance	462.1	77	1623	44	36.88	5-96	1	-
Refuge Assurance	86.1	5	426	14	30.42	4-11	-	
NatWest Trophy	42	4	203	7	29.00	4-73	-	
Benson & Hedges Cup	34	1	162	6	27.00	3-40	-	
Other First-Class	48	11	166	3	55.33	1-28	-	
Other One-Day	13	2	35	3	11.66	2-14	-	
ALL FIRST-CLASS	510.1	88	1789	47	38.06	5-96	1	-
ALL ONE-DAY	175.1	12	826	30	27.53	4-11	-	

G. COOK - *Northamptonshire*

Opposition	Venue	Date	Batting	Fielding	Bowling

BRITANNIC ASSURANCE

Yorkshire	Headingley	April 26			
Derbyshire	Northampton	May 3	44 & 3		
Warwickshire	Northampton	May 15	33 & 13		
Notts	Trent Bridge	May 23	49		
Warwickshire	Edgbaston	June 2	34		
Leicestershire	Northampton	June 6	8 *		
Glamorgan	Northampton	June 9	7 & 0		
Middlesex	Luton	June 23	8 & 1	2Ct	

REFUGE ASSURANCE

Gloucs	Northampton	Aug 26	16		

BENSON & HEDGES CUP

Leicestershire	Leicester	April 24	6	1Ct	
Essex	Northampton	May 8	28		
Scotland	Northampton	May 10	6		

OTHER FIRST-CLASS

Cambridge U	Fenner's	April 14	87		

BATTING AVERAGES - Including fielding

	Matches	Inns	NO	Runs	HS	Avge	100s	50s	Ct	St
Britannic Assurance	8	11	1	200	49	20.00	-	-	2	-
Refuge Assurance	1	1	0	16	16	16.00	-	-	-	-
Benson & Hedges Cup	3	3	0	40	28	13.33	-	-	1	-
Other First-Class	1	1	0	87	87	87.00	-	1	-	-
ALL FIRST-CLASS	9	12	1	287	87	26.09	-	1	2	-
ALL ONE-DAY	4	4	0	56	28	14.00	-	-	1	-

BOWLING AVERAGES
Did not bowl

N.G.B. COOK - *Northamptonshire*

Opposition	Venue	Date	Batting	Fielding	Bowling

BRITANNIC ASSURANCE

Yorkshire	Headingley	April 26			0-8 & 0-8
Derbyshire	Northampton	May 3	9 *		
Warwickshire	Edgbaston	June 2			0-0
Leicestershire	Northampton	June 6		1Ct	0-17 & 0-11
Glamorgan	Northampton	June 9			2-17 & 0-108
Middlesex	Luton	June 23	18 & 0	1Ct	4-79 & 0-31
Somerset	Taunton	June 30			1-69 & 2-63
Surrey	The Oval	July 4	0		0-34
Yorkshire	Northampton	July 7	30 & 1 *		5-44 & 1-25
Kent	Northampton	July 18	1		1-33 & 2-59
Sussex	Northampton	July 21		1Ct	4-89 & 0-21
Hampshire	Bournemouth	Aug 4	2 * & 7 *		0-73
Derbyshire	Chesterfield	Aug 8	0 * & 4	1Ct	0-55 & 2-19
Lancashire	Northampton	Aug 11		1Ct	1-53 & 2-19
Worcestershire	Worcester	Aug 18	2 & 7 *		5-80 & 4-57
Gloucs	Northampton	Aug 23	0 * & 11	2Ct	3-97 & 0-58
Leicestershire	Leicester	Sept 12	28 & 13	2Ct	0-56 & 1-37

REFUGE ASSURANCE

Leicestershire	Leicester	April 22			2-31
Warwickshire	Edgbaston	April 29			1-40
Surrey	The Oval	June 3	7 *	1Ct	0-11
Glamorgan	Northampton	June 10		1Ct	2-40
Middlesex	Northampton	June 24	1		0-13
Somerset	Taunton	July 1	5		0-42
Yorkshire	Tring	July 8	1		0-60
Essex	Chelmsford	July 15			1-42
Sussex	Well'borough	July 22	0 *	1Ct	3-36
Notts	Trent Bridge	July 29			0-21
Hampshire	Bournemouth	Aug 5		1Ct	2-42
Lancashire	Northampton	Aug 12		1Ct	0-42
Worcestershire	Worcester	Aug 19			1-54
Gloucs	Northampton	Aug 26	0 *	1Ct	0-59

NATWEST TROPHY

Staffordshire	Northampton	June 27			1-31
Notts	Northampton	July 11		1Ct	1-42
Worcestershire	Northampton	Aug 1	1	1Ct	2-34
Hampshire	Southampton	Aug 15	6 *	1Ct	3-52
Lancashire	Lord's	Sept 1	9	1Ct	0-50

BENSON & HEDGES CUP

Leicestershire	Leicester	April 24		1Ct	0-45

OTHER FIRST-CLASS

Cambridge U	Fenner's	April 14	0 *	1Ct	0-2 & 0-0
New Zealand	Northampton	June 16	10		0-42

BATTING AVERAGES - Including fielding

	Matches	Inns	NO	Runs	HS	Avge	100s	50s	Ct	St
Britannic Assurance	17	17	7	133	30	13.30	-	-	9	-
Refuge Assurance	14	6	3	14	7 *	4.66	-	-	6	-
NatWest Trophy	5	3	1	16	9	8.00	-	-	4	-
Benson & Hedges Cup	1	0	0	0	0		-	-	1	-
Other First-Class	2	2	1	10	10	10.00	-	-	1	-
ALL FIRST-CLASS	19	19	8	143	30	13.00	-	-	10	-
ALL ONE-DAY	20	9	4	30	9	6.00	-	-	11	-

BOWLING AVERAGES

	Overs	Mdns	Runs	Wkts	Avge	Best	5wI	10wM
Britannic Assurance	507.1	159	1320	40	33.00	5-44	2	-
Refuge Assurance	93	4	533	12	44.41	3-36	-	
NatWest Trophy	58.4	12	209	7	29.85	3-52	-	
Benson & Hedges Cup	11	1	45	0		-	-	
Other First-Class	20	8	44	0		-	-	
ALL FIRST-CLASS	527.1	167	1364	40	34.10	5-44	2	-
ALL ONE-DAY	162.4	17	787	19	41.42	3-36	-	

PLAYER RECORDS

S.J. COOK - *Somerset*

Opposition	Venue	Date	Batting			Fielding	Bowling
BRITANNIC ASSURANCE							
Gloucs	Taunton	April 26	16	&	62 *		
Glamorgan	Cardiff	May 3	313 *			2Ct	
Derbyshire	Taunton	May 19	1	&	5		2-25
Sussex	Taunton	May 23	197				0-12
Leicestershire	Leicester	May 26	42	&	8	1Ct	
Gloucs	Bristol	June 2	40	&	81	1Ct	
Hampshire	Basingstoke	June 6	59 *	&	29		
Kent	Canterbury	June 9	36			1Ct	
Essex	Bath	June 16	32	&	19 *		
Glamorgan	Bath	June 20	61				
Northants	Taunton	June 30	65	&	112 *		
Warwickshire	Taunton	July 4	35	&	137		
Worcestershire	Worcester	July 18	6	&	39		
Middlesex	Uxbridge	July 21	152	&	85	1Ct	
Yorkshire	Scarborough	July 25	21	&	53	1Ct	
Lancashire	Old Trafford	July 28	49	&	64	1Ct	
Surrey	Weston	Aug 4	52	&	116 *		
Notts	Weston	Aug 8	6			1Ct	0-5
Hampshire	Taunton	Aug 18	114	&	77		
Sussex	Hove	Aug 23	13			1Ct	
Warwickshire	Edgbaston	Sept 7	52	&	27		
Worcestershire	Taunton	Sept 12	143	&	13		
REFUGE ASSURANCE							
Worcestershire	Taunton	April 22	18			1Ct	
Hampshire	Taunton	May 13	132				
Derbyshire	Taunton	May 20	53				
Leicestershire	Leicester	May 27	60			1Ct	
Gloucs	Bristol	June 3	10				
Kent	Canterbury	June 10	50			3Ct	
Essex	Bath	June 17	23				
Notts	Bath	June 24	3				
Northants	Taunton	July 1	88				
Middlesex	Lord's	July 8	58				
Yorkshire	Scarborough	July 15	52				
Glamorgan	Neath	July 22	136 *				
Lancashire	Old Trafford	July 29	41				
Surrey	Weston	Aug 5	21				
Warwickshire	Weston	Aug 12	112 *			2Ct	
Sussex	Hove	Aug 26	45				
NATWEST TROPHY							
Devon	Torquay	June 27	42				
Worcestershire	Taunton	July 11	45			1Ct	
BENSON & HEDGES CUP							
Derbyshire	Taunton	May 1	66			1Ct	
Min Counties	Taunton	May 8	27			1Ct	
Middlesex	Lord's	May 10	6				
Sussex	Hove	May 12	177			1Ct	
Middlesex	Taunton	May 30	4				
Lancashire	Old Trafford	June 13	49				
OTHER FIRST-CLASS							
Oxford U	The Parks	April 18	28			1Ct	
New Zealand	Taunton	May 16	31	&	117 *		
OTHER ONE-DAY							
For Rest of World							
England XI	Jesmond	Aug 2	39				
England XI	Jesmond	Aug 3	70 *				
For Somerset							
Sri Lanka	Taunton	Sept 3	13			1Ct	

BATTING AVERAGES - Including fielding

	Matches	Inns	NO	Runs	HS	Avge	100s	50s	Ct	St
Britannic Assurance	22	38	6	2432	313 *	76.00	8	11	10	-
Refuge Assurance	16	16	2	902	136 *	64.42	3	6	7	-
NatWest Trophy	2	2	0	87	45	43.50	-	-	1	-
Benson & Hedges Cup	6	6	0	329	177	54.83	1	1	3	-
Other First-Class	2	3	1	176	117 *	88.00	1	-	1	-
Other One-Day	3	3	1	122	70 *	61.00	-	1	1	-
ALL FIRST-CLASS	24	41	7	2608	313 *	76.70	9	11	11	-
ALL ONE-DAY	27	27	3	1440	177	60.00	4	8	12	-

BOWLING AVERAGES

	Overs	Mdns	Runs	Wkts	Avge	Best	5wI	10wM
Britannic Assurance	8	0	42	2	21.00	2-25		

Refuge Assurance
NatWest Trophy
Benson & Hedges Cup
Other First-Class
Other One-Day

ALL FIRST-CLASS	8	0	42	2	21.00	2-25	- -
ALL ONE-DAY							

K.E. COOPER - *Nottinghamshire*

Opposition	Venue	Date	Batting			Fielding	Bowling
BRITANNIC ASSURANCE							
Derbyshire	Trent Bridge	April 26	12			1Ct	3-75 & 0-17
Worcestershire	Worcester	May 3	1	&	1		1-113
Warwickshire	Edgbaston	May 19					3-72 & 1-43
Northants	Trent Bridge	May 23	4				2-65 & 0-59
Derbyshire	Derby	May 26	16	&	35 *	1Ct	5-72 & 2-36
Kent	Tunbridge We	June 2					2-40 & 0-57
Surrey	Trent Bridge	June 20	7	&	1		0-52
Leicestershire	Trent Bridge	June 30	29			2Ct	2-47 & 5-56
Yorkshire	Scarborough	July 4					0-69
Sussex	Trent Bridge	July 7	0				2-79 & 0-37
Hampshire	Portsmouth	July 18	6	&	7	1Ct	2-49 & 1-15
Lancashire	Southport	July 25	0	&	24		1-94 & 0-11
Middlesex	Trent Bridge	July 28	3 *			1Ct	5-108 & 1-41
Essex	Southend	Aug 4	10 *	&	4		1-76 & 0-19
Somerset	Weston	Aug 8	7				3-57
Glamorgan	Worksop	Aug 11				1Ct	1-95 & 0-40
Worcestershire	Trent Bridge	Aug 29	7	&	1 *		1-48 & 1-28
Middlesex	Lord's	Sept 7	5	&	21		1-134 & 0-10
Lancashire	Trent Bridge	Sept 12	5	&	9 *	1Ct	1-93
Yorkshire	Trent Bridge	Sept 18				1Ct	1-70 & 3-128
REFUGE ASSURANCE							
Yorkshire	Trent Bridge	April 22					0-24
Lancashire	Trent Bridge	April 29	21				0-32
Worcestershire	Worcester	May 6	4				1-32
Middlesex	Lord's	May 13					0-40
Surrey	Trent Bridge	May 20					0-19
Derbyshire	Derby	June 10	1 *				0-29
Kent	Canterbury	June 17	1				0-33
Somerset	Bath	June 24	9			1Ct	1-32
Leicestershire	Trent Bridge	July 1				1Ct	0-21
Sussex	Trent Bridge	July 8					1-18
Hampshire	Southampton	July 15	1				1-44
Warwickshire	Edgbaston	July 22					0-50
Northants	Trent Bridge	July 29					1-62
Essex	Southend	Aug 5					1-49
Glamorgan	Trent Bridge	Aug 12					1-25
Gloucs	Trent Bridge	Aug 19					2-21
Derbyshire	Derby	Sept 5					1-40
NATWEST TROPHY							
Bucks	Marlow	June 27	10				3-16
Northants	Northampton	July 11	0				1-49
BENSON & HEDGES CUP							
Essex	Chelmsford	April 24					1-37
Leicestershire	Trent Bridge	May 1				2Ct	3-25
Scotland	Glasgow	May 8	11 *			1Ct	0-33
Northants	Trent Bridge	May 12	8 *				2-41
Essex	Chelmsford	May 30					1-34
Worcestershire	Trent Bridge	June 13					0-29
OTHER FIRST-CLASS							
Sri Lanka	Cleethorpes	Aug 25	10 *				2-67 & 1-31

BATTING AVERAGES - Including fielding

	Matches	Inns	NO	Runs	HS	Avge	100s	50s	Ct	St
Britannic Assurance	20	25	5	217	35 *	10.85	-	-	9	-
Refuge Assurance	17	6	1	37	21	7.40	-	-	2	-
NatWest Trophy	2	2	0	10	10	5.00	-	-	-	-
Benson & Hedges Cup	6	2	2	19	11 *	-	-	-	3	-
Other First-Class	1	1	1	10	10 *	-	-	-	-	-
ALL FIRST-CLASS	21	26	6	227	35 *	11.35	-	-	9	-
ALL ONE-DAY	25	10	3	66	21	9.42	-	-	5	-

C   PLAYER RECORDS

BOWLING AVERAGES

	Overs	Mdns	Runs	Wkts	Avge	Best	5wI	10wM
Britannic Assurance	667.4	141	2105	51	41.27	5-56	3	-
Refuge Assurance	126	8	571	10	57.10	2-21	-	-
NatWest Trophy	20	3	65	4	16.25	3-16	-	-
Benson & Hedges Cup	64.2	11	199	7	28.42	3-25	-	-
Other First-Class	36	12	98	3	32.66	2-67	-	-
ALL FIRST-CLASS	703.4	153	2203	54	40.79	5-56	3	-
ALL ONE-DAY	210.2	22	835	21	39.76	3-16	-	-

D.G. CORK - *Derbyshire*

Opposition	Venue	Date	Batting	Fielding	Bowling
BRITANNIC ASSURANCE					
Leicestershire	Derby	Sept 18	7		0-39 & 0-31
OTHER FIRST-CLASS					
New Zealand	Derby	June 2	2 *		1-49 & 1-4

BATTING AVERAGES - Including fielding

	Matches	Inns	NO	Runs	HS	Avge	100s	50s	Ct	St
Britannic Assurance	1	1	0	7	7	7.00	-	-	-	-
Other First-Class	1	1	1	2	2*	-	-	-	-	-
ALL FIRST-CLASS	2	2	1	9	7	9.00	-	-	-	-

BOWLING AVERAGES

	Overs	Mdns	Runs	Wkts	Avge	Best	5wI	10wM
Britannic Assurance	24	6	70	0	-	-	-	-
Other First-Class	15	2	53	2	26.50	1-4	-	-
ALL FIRST-CLASS	39	8	123	2	61.50	1-4	-	-

P.A. COTTEY - *Glamorgan*

Opposition	Venue	Date	Batting			Fielding	Bowling
BRITANNIC ASSURANCE							
Sussex	Hove	May 19	43 *			1Ct	0-44
Kent	Swansea	May 23	21				0-23
Lancashire	Colwyn Bay	May 26	8	&	13		
Northants	Northampton	June 9	11	&	2		
Yorkshire	Cardiff	June 23	18	&	36 *	1Ct	
Surrey	Cardiff	June 30	19	&	35 *		
Gloucs	Swansea	July 4	12				
Leicestershire	Hinckley	July 7	3	&	125	1Ct	
Worcestershire	Abergavenny	July 21	100 *	&	1		
Warwickshire	Swansea	July 25	50	&	2		1-49
Middlesex	Lord's	Aug 4	0	&	33		
Essex	Southend	Aug 8	51	&	85 *	2Ct	
Notts	Worksop	Aug 11	5			2Ct	
Derbyshire	Cardiff	Aug 29	8	&	3		
Hampshire	Pontypridd	Sept 7	13	&	23	1Ct	
Warwickshire	Edgbaston	Sept 12	52	&	22		
Worcestershire	Worcester	Sept 18	19	&	3	1Ct	
REFUGE ASSURANCE							
Sussex	Hove	May 20	36				
Northants	Northampton	June 10	28				
Surrey	Cardiff	July 1				1Ct	
Middlesex	Lord's	Aug 5	28			1Ct	
Notts	Trent Bridge	Aug 12	50 *				
Worcestershire	Swansea	Aug 26	8				
NATWEST TROPHY							
Dorset	Swansea	June 27	2 *			1Ct	
Sussex	Cardiff	July 11	27				
BENSON & HEDGES CUP							
Warwickshire	Edgbaston	April 24	2				
OTHER FIRST-CLASS							
Oxford U	The Parks	June 2	156			1Ct	
India	Swansea	Aug 18	0	&	29	1Ct	
Sri Lanka	Ebbw Vale	Aug 22	0	&	0	1Ct	

BATTING AVERAGES - Including fielding

	Matches	Inns	NO	Runs	HS	Avge	100s	50s	Ct	St
Britannic Assurance	17	30	5	816	125	32.64	2	4	9	-
Refuge Assurance	6	5	1	150	50 *	37.50	-	1	2	-
NatWest Trophy	2	2	1	29	27	29.00	-	-	1	-
Benson & Hedges Cup	1	1	0	2	2	2.00	-	-	-	-
Other First-Class	3	5	0	185	156	37.00	1	-	3	-
ALL FIRST-CLASS	20	35	5	1001	156	33.36	3	4	12	-
ALL ONE-DAY	9	8	2	181	50 *	30.16	-	1	3	-

BOWLING AVERAGES

	Overs	Mdns	Runs	Wkts	Avge	Best	5wI	10wM
Britannic Assurance	18	0	116	1	116.00	1-49	-	-
Refuge Assurance								
NatWest Trophy								
Benson & Hedges Cup								
Other First-Class								
ALL FIRST-CLASS	18	0	116	1	116.00	1-49	-	-
ALL ONE-DAY								

D. COWAN - *Scotland*

Opposition	Venue	Date	Batting	Fielding	Bowling
BENSON & HEDGES CUP					
Essex	Glasgow	May 1	7		0-80
Notts	Glasgow	May 8			1-51
Northants	Northampton	May 10	4 *		3-36
Leicestershire	Leicester	May 12	3		1-45
OTHER ONE-DAY					
India	Glasgow	July 14	1 *		0-48

BATTING AVERAGES - Including fielding

	Matches	Inns	NO	Runs	HS	Avge	100s	50s	Ct	St
Benson & Hedges Cup	4	3	1	14	7	7.00	-	-	-	-
Other One-Day	1	1	1	1	1*	-	-	-	-	-
ALL ONE-DAY	5	4	2	15	7	7.50	-	-	-	-

BOWLING AVERAGES

	Overs	Mdns	Runs	Wkts	Avge	Best	5wI	10wM
Benson & Hedges Cup	39.2	1	212	5	42.40	3-36	-	-
Other One-Day	9.3	0	48	0	-	-	-	-
ALL ONE-DAY	48.5	1	260	5	52.00	3-36	-	-

N.G. COWANS - *Middlesex*

Opposition	Venue	Date	Batting			Fielding	Bowling
BRITANNIC ASSURANCE							
Essex	Lord's	April 26	2				0-43 & 0-32
Kent	Lord's	May 15	0 *				2-41 & 0-39
Surrey	Lord's	May 23	6	&	5		0-36
Gloucs	Lord's	May 26					0-36 & 1-24
Worcestershire	Lord's	June 30	1				3-23 & 1-36
Yorkshire	Uxbridge	July 18	2				0-21 & 0-7
Kent	Canterbury	July 25			2 *		0-57 & 3-20
Notts	Trent Bridge	July 28	11 *	&	0	1Ct	3-80 & 1-70
Glamorgan	Lord's	Aug 4			12 *	1Ct	2-50 & 0-8
Hampshire	Bournemouth	Aug 8			4 *		0-49
Sussex	Lord's	Aug 11					1-30
Derbyshire	Derby	Aug 18	0	&	5 *		1-40 & 0-14
Yorkshire	Headingley	Aug 23	0			1Ct	2-55 & 5-67
Notts	Lord's	Sept 7					2-26 & 4-46
Surrey	The Oval	Sept 12			31		1-76 & 0-49
Sussex	Hove	Sept 18	0				2-19 & 2-33
REFUGE ASSURANCE							
Essex	Lord's	April 29					2-40
Kent	Folkestone	May 6					1-29
Notts	Lord's	May 13	27				1-52
Gloucs	Lord's	May 27					2-27
Worcestershire	Lord's	July 1					2-43
Somerset	Lord's	July 8			0 *		0-59

PLAYER RECORDS

C

Surrey	The Oval	July 15	0		1-46
Glamorgan	Lord's	Aug 5			0-46
Sussex	Lord's	Aug 12			0-23
Derbyshire	Derby	Aug 19			1-26
Yorkshire	Scarborough	Aug 26	0		3-43
Derbyshire	Edgbaston	Sept 16			0-22

NATWEST TROPHY

Berkshire	Lord's	June 27			2-25
Surrey	Uxbridge	July 11		1Ct	2-45
Glamorgan	Lord's	Aug 1		1Ct	1-48
Lancashire	Old Trafford	Aug 15			1-40

BENSON & HEDGES CUP

Sussex	Hove	May 8			0-66
Somerset	Lord's	May 10	10 *		2-35
Derbyshire	Derby	May 12	12		0-48
Somerset	Taunton	May 30	1		2-22

OTHER FIRST-CLASS

For MCC					
Worcestershire	Lord's	April 17	46 *		1-39
For Middlesex					
New Zealand	Lord's	May 19			1-56 & 1-25

OTHER ONE-DAY

For England XI					
Rest of World	Jesmond	Aug 2			3-44
Rest of World	Jesmond	Aug 3	1		0-22

BATTING AVERAGES - Including fielding

	Matches	Inns	NO	Runs	HS	Avge	100s	50s	Ct	St
Britannic Assurance	16	16	6	81	31	8.10	-	-	3	-
Refuge Assurance	12	4	1	27	27	9.00	-	-	-	-
NatWest Trophy	4	0	0	0	0	-	-	-	2	-
Benson & Hedges Cup	4	3	1	23	12	11.50	-	-	-	-
Other First-Class	2	1	1	46	46 *	-	-	-	-	-
Other One-Day	2	1	0	1	1	1.00	-	-	-	-
ALL FIRST-CLASS	18	17	7	127	46 *	12.70	-	-	3	-
ALL ONE-DAY	22	8	2	51	27	8.50	-	-	2	-

BOWLING AVERAGES

	Overs	Mdns	Runs	Wkts	Avge	Best	5wI	10wM
Britannic Assurance	415	115	1127	36	31.30	5-67	1	-
Refuge Assurance	87	6	456	13	35.07	3-43	-	
NatWest Trophy	45	8	158	6	26.33	2-25	-	
Benson & Hedges Cup	44	5	171	4	42.75	2-22	-	
Other First-Class	45	9	120	3	40.00	1-25	-	-
Other One-Day	15	1	66	3	22.00	3-44	-	
ALL FIRST-CLASS	460	124	1247	39	31.97	5-67	1	-
ALL ONE-DAY	191	20	851	26	32.73	3-43	-	

C.S. COWDREY - *Kent*

Opposition	Venue	Date	Batting	Fielding	Bowling

BRITANNIC ASSURANCE

Hampshire	Canterbury	April 26	79 & 107	1Ct	0-13 & 0-14
Sussex	Folkestone	May 3	24 & 0 *	1Ct	
Middlesex	Lord's	May 15	47 & 44		1-41 & 0-2
Somerset	Canterbury	June 9	0 & 14		0-9
Warwickshire	Edgbaston	June 23	56 * & 0	2Ct	1-5
Lancashire	Maidstone	June 30	6 & 28	1Ct	2-20 & 0-10
Essex	Maidstone	June 4	3 *	1Ct	0-4
Northants	Northampton	July 18	0 & 107 *	1Ct	0-39
Surrey	Guildford	July 21	20 & 27		
Sussex	Hove	Aug 18	20 & 0	2Ct	0-16
Leicestershire	Leicester	Aug 23	15 & 2		0-0

REFUGE ASSURANCE

Essex	Chelmsford	April 22	11		0-9
Hampshire	Canterbury	April 29	18	2Ct	
Middlesex	Folkestone	May 6	20		0-24
Glamorgan	Llanelli	May 13	3		1-36
Yorkshire	Canterbury	May 20	18	1Ct	0-12
Northants	Northampton	May 27	45 *	2Ct	4-57
Somerset	Canterbury	June 10	26 *	1Ct	2-20
Notts	Canterbury	June 17	13		1-15
Warwickshire	Edgbaston	June 24	46		3-19
Lancashire	Maidstone	July 1	33		1-35
Surrey	The Oval	July 22	7		
Worcestershire	Canterbury	July 29	4		0-9
Derbyshire	Chesterfield	Aug 5		1Ct	0-50
Gloucs	Bristol	Aug 12	27		0-20
Leicestershire	Leicester	Aug 26	6		

NATWEST TROPHY

Oxfordshire	Oxford	June 27	6	1Ct	
Gloucs	Bristol	July 11	5		0-29

BENSON & HEDGES CUP

Worcestershire	Worcester	May 1	6		2-19
Warwickshire	Canterbury	May 8	64		3-29
Gloucs	Canterbury	May 10	67 *		
Glamorgan	Swansea	May 12	35		3-52

OTHER FIRST-CLASS

Cambridge U	Fenner's	June 20	102 *		
India	Canterbury	July 7	20 * & 12		0-19

BATTING AVERAGES - Including fielding

	Matches	Inns	NO	Runs	HS	Avge	100s	50s	Ct	St
Britannic Assurance	11	21	4	599	107 *	35.23	2	2	9	-
Refuge Assurance	15	14	2	277	46	23.08	-	-	7	-
NatWest Trophy	2	2	0	11	6	5.50	-	-	1	-
Benson & Hedges Cup	4	4	1	172	67 *	57.33	-	2	-	-
Other First-Class	2	3	2	134	102 *	134.00	1	-	-	-
ALL FIRST-CLASS	13	24	6	733	107 *	40.72	3	2	9	-
ALL ONE-DAY	21	20	3	460	67 *	27.05	-	2	8	-

BOWLING AVERAGES

	Overs	Mdns	Runs	Wkts	Avge	Best	5wI	10wM
Britannic Assurance	57	12	173	4	43.25	2-20	-	-
Refuge Assurance	52	0	306	12	25.50	4-57	-	
NatWest Trophy	5	0	29	0	-	-	-	
Benson & Hedges Cup	22	2	100	8	12.50	3-29	-	
Other First-Class	4	0	19	0	-	-	-	-
ALL FIRST-CLASS	61	12	192	4	48.00	2-20	-	-
ALL ONE-DAY	79	2	435	20	21.75	4-57	-	

G.R. COWDREY - *Kent*

Opposition	Venue	Date	Batting	Fielding	Bowling

BRITANNIC ASSURANCE

Hampshire	Canterbury	April 26	87 & 30		
Glamorgan	Swansea	May 23	68 * & 80 *	1Ct	
Notts	Tunbridge We	June 2	27 & 51		
Yorkshire	Tunbridge We	June 6	67		0-19
Somerset	Canterbury	June 9	42 & 10		
Warwickshire	Edgbaston	June 23	20 & 22 *	1Ct	0-13
Lancashire	Maidstone	June 30	40 & 14	1Ct	
Essex	Maidstone	June 4	116		
Northants	Northampton	July 18	0 & 4		
Surrey	Guildford	July 21	71 & 119 *		
Middlesex	Canterbury	July 25	22		
Worcestershire	Canterbury	July 28	57 & 9		
Derbyshire	Chesterfield	Aug 4	6 & 21	1Ct	
Leicestershire	Dartford	Aug 8	39 & 17 *	1Ct	
Gloucs	Bristol	Aug 11	80	1Ct	
Sussex	Hove	Aug 18	29 & 34		
Leicestershire	Leicester	Aug 23	16 & 135	1Ct	
Hampshire	Bournemouth	Aug 29	47 & 41	1Ct	
Surrey	Canterbury	Sept 7	8 & 9		
Essex	Chelmsford	Sept 12	0 & 33		

REFUGE ASSURANCE

Essex	Chelmsford	April 22	6		
Hampshire	Canterbury	April 29	22		
Middlesex	Folkestone	May 6	28	1Ct	
Glamorgan	Llanelli	May 13	5	1Ct	
Yorkshire	Canterbury	May 20	31 *		
Northants	Northampton	May 27	70 *		
Somerset	Canterbury	June 10	6		
Notts	Canterbury	June 17	46	1Ct	
Warwickshire	Edgbaston	June 24	16		
Lancashire	Maidstone	July 1	0		
Surrey	The Oval	July 22	14		
Derbyshire	Chesterfield	Aug 5	36 *		
Gloucs	Bristol	Aug 12	24		

C   PLAYER RECORDS

Leicestershire	Leicester	Aug 26	43		

NATWEST TROPHY

Oxfordshire	Oxford	June 27	3		
Gloucs	Bristol	July 11	37		1-13

BENSON & HEDGES CUP

Worcestershire	Worcester	May 1	0	1Ct	
Gloucs	Canterbury	May 10			
Glamorgan	Swansea	May 12	12	2Ct	0-23

OTHER FIRST-CLASS

Cambridge U	Fenner's	June 20	34	1Ct	
India	Canterbury	July 7	44 & 27 *		0-0 & 0-12

OTHER ONE-DAY

Sussex	Hove	Sept 2	43		
Surrey	Hove	Sept 4	78	1Ct	

BATTING AVERAGES - Including fielding

	Matches	Inns	NO	Runs	HS	Avge	100s	50s	Ct	St
Britannic Assurance	20	36	5	1471	135	47.45	3	8	8	-
Refuge Assurance	14	14	3	347	70 *	31.54	-	1	3	-
NatWest Trophy	2	2	0	40	37	20.00	-	-	-	-
Benson & Hedges Cup	3	2	0	12	12	6.00	-	-	3	-
Other First-Class	2	3	1	105	44	52.50	-	-	1	-
Other One-Day	2	2	0	121	78	60.50	-	1	1	-
ALL FIRST-CLASS	22	39	6	1576	135	47.75	3	8	9	-
ALL ONE-DAY	21	20	3	520	78	30.58	-	2	7	-

BOWLING AVERAGES

	Overs	Mdns	Runs	Wkts	Avge	Best	5wI	10wM
Britannic Assurance	3.3	0	32	0	-	-	-	-
Refuge Assurance								
NatWest Trophy	2.3	0	13	1	13.00	1-13	-	
Benson & Hedges Cup	5	0	23	0	-	-	-	
Other First-Class	3	1	12	0	-	-	-	
Other One-Day								
ALL FIRST-CLASS	6.3	1	44	0	-	-	-	
ALL ONE-DAY	7.3	0	36	1	36.00	1-13	-	

▬▬▬▬▬▬
N.G. COWLEY - *Glamorgan*

Opposition	Venue	Date	Batting	Fielding	Bowling

BRITANNIC ASSURANCE

Opposition	Venue	Date	Batting	Fielding	Bowling
Somerset	Cardiff	May 3	43 & 8 *		0-88
Gloucs	Bristol	May 15	51 * & 61		1-25 & 1-14
Sussex	Hove	May 19		2Ct	1-18 & 0-28
Kent	Swansea	May 23	76		0-75 & 1-67
Lancashire	Colwyn Bay	May 26	4	1Ct	3-84
Northants	Northampton	June 9	0		0-65 & 0-14
Hampshire	Southampton	June 16	58	1Ct	1-47
Somerset	Bath	June 20			0-4
Gloucs	Swansea	July 4	44		0-6
Leicestershire	Hinckley	July 7	13	2Ct	0-46 & 1-19
Worcestershire	Abergavenny	July 21	2 * & 63	1Ct	1-101 & 0-1
Warwickshire	Swansea	July 25	30 & 10		1-111 & 0-9
Middlesex	Lord's	Aug 4	52 * & 8	1Ct	0-29

REFUGE ASSURANCE

Opposition	Venue	Date	Batting	Fielding	Bowling
Gloucs	Bristol	April 22	17		2-36
Leicestershire	Cardiff	April 29	0		2-26
Kent	Llanelli	May 13	0 *		1-27
Sussex	Hove	May 20			0-15
Lancashire	Colwyn Bay	May 27	1	1Ct	0-35
Northants	Northampton	June 10	2 *	1Ct	0-43
Hampshire	Bournemouth	June 17	7		1-43
Warwickshire	Edgbaston	July 15			2-17
Somerset	Neath	July 22	10		1-44

NATWEST TROPHY

Opposition	Venue	Date	Batting	Fielding	Bowling
Dorset	Swansea	June 27			0-31
Sussex	Cardiff	July 11	32 *		2-71
Middlesex	Lord's	Aug 1	5		0-33

BENSON & HEDGES CUP

Opposition	Venue	Date	Batting	Fielding	Bowling
Warwickshire	Edgbaston	April 24	19		1-23
Gloucs	Cardiff	May 1	1		1-40
Worcestershire	Worcester	May 8	11		1-33

Kent	Swansea	May 12	4	1Ct	1-55
Worcestershire	Worcester	May 30	0		0-22

OTHER FIRST-CLASS

Oxford U	The Parks	April 14	13	1Ct	1-49

BATTING AVERAGES - Including fielding

	Matches	Inns	NO	Runs	HS	Avge	100s	50s	Ct	St
Britannic Assurance	13	16	4	523	76	43.58	-	6	8	-
Refuge Assurance	9	7	2	37	17	7.40	-	-	2	-
NatWest Trophy	3	2	1	37	32 *	37.00	-	-	-	-
Benson & Hedges Cup	5	5	0	35	19	7.00	-	-	1	-
Other First-Class	1	1	0	13	13	13.00	-	-	1	-
ALL FIRST-CLASS	14	17	4	536	76	41.23	-	6	9	-
ALL ONE-DAY	17	14	3	109	32 *	9.90	-	-	3	-

BOWLING AVERAGES

	Overs	Mdns	Runs	Wkts	Avge	Best	5wI	10wM
Britannic Assurance	296.3	58	851	11	77.36	3-84	-	-
Refuge Assurance	54	3	286	9	31.77	2-17	-	
NatWest Trophy	32	3	135	2	67.50	2-71	-	
Benson & Hedges Cup	53	2	173	4	43.25	1-23	-	
Other First-Class	20	6	49	1	49.00	1-49	-	-
ALL FIRST-CLASS	316.3	64	900	12	75.00	3-84	-	-
ALL ONE-DAY	139	8	594	15	39.60	2-17	-	

▬▬▬▬▬▬
R.M.F. COX - *Hampshire*

Opposition	Venue	Date	Batting	Fielding	Bowling

BRITANNIC ASSURANCE

Opposition	Venue	Date	Batting	Fielding	Bowling
Sussex	Arundel	July 25	9 & 35 *	1Ct	
Worcestershire	Worcester	Aug 11	104 * & 15		
Surrey	Southampton	Aug 23	0 & 23		

REFUGE ASSURANCE

Opposition	Venue	Date	Batting	Fielding	Bowling
Worcestershire	Worcester	Aug 12	2 *		

OTHER FIRST-CLASS

Opposition	Venue	Date	Batting	Fielding	Bowling
Sri Lanka	Southampton	Sept 12	34	2Ct	0-1

OTHER ONE-DAY

Opposition	Venue	Date	Batting	Fielding	Bowling
Worcestershire	Scarborough	Sept 2	43		
Essex	Scarborough	Sept 4	4		

BATTING AVERAGES - Including fielding

	Matches	Inns	NO	Runs	HS	Avge	100s	50s	Ct	St
Britannic Assurance	3	6	2	186	104 *	46.50	1	-	1	-
Refuge Assurance	1	1	1	2	2 *	-	-	-	-	-
Other First-Class	1	1	0	34	34	34.00	-	-	2	-
Other One-Day	2	2	0	47	43	23.50	-	-	-	-
ALL FIRST-CLASS	4	7	2	220	104 *	44.00	1	-	3	-
ALL ONE-DAY	3	3	1	49	43	24.50	-	-	-	-

BOWLING AVERAGES

	Overs	Mdns	Runs	Wkts	Avge	Best	5wI	10wM
Britannic Assurance								
Refuge Assurance								
Other First-Class	1	0	1	0	-	-	-	-
Other One-Day								
ALL FIRST-CLASS	1	0	1	0	-	-	-	-
ALL ONE-DAY								

▬▬▬▬▬▬
J.P. CRAWLEY - *Lancashire*

Opposition	Venue	Date	Batting	Fielding	Bowling

BRITANNIC ASSURANCE

Opposition	Venue	Date	Batting	Fielding	Bowling
Warwickshire	Old Trafford	Sept 18			

OTHER FIRST-CLASS

Opposition	Venue	Date	Batting	Fielding	Bowling
Zimbabwe	Old Trafford	May 23	1 & 76 *	1Ct	
Oxford U	The Parks	June 16	26		

PLAYER RECORDS

C

BATTING AVERAGES - Including fielding

	Matches	Inns	NO	Runs	HS	Avge	100s	50s	Ct	St
Britannic Assurance	1	0	0	0	0	-	-	-	-	-
Other First-Class	2	3	1	103	76 *	51.50	-	1	1	-
ALL FIRST-CLASS	3	3	1	103	76 *	51.50	-	1	1	-

BOWLING AVERAGES
Did not bowl

M.A. CRAWLEY - *Oxford University & Lancashire*

Opposition	Venue	Date	Batting	Fielding	Bowling
BENSON & HEDGES CUP					
For Combined Universities					
Lancashire	Fenner's	May 1	46		1-18
Yorkshire	Headingley	May 8	9		1-21
Surrey	The Parks	May 10	9		1-34
Hampshire	Southampton	May 12	26		0-40
OTHER FIRST-CLASS					
For Oxford University					
Glamorgan	The Parks	April 14	103 *	2Ct	6-92
Somerset	The Parks	April 18	33	2Ct	0-63
Hampshire	The Parks	May 3	9	1Ct	1-100 & 0-16
Surrey	The Parks	May 16	60 & 47	3Ct	1-29 & 2-83
Leicestershire	The Parks	May 23	50 & 105 *		1-50
Glamorgan	The Parks	June 2	67		1-94
Notts	The Parks	June 6			1-36
Lancashire	The Parks	June 16	91 *		1-64
For Combined Universities					
New Zealand	Fenner's	June 27	47 & 5	1Ct	1-30 & 2-22
For Oxford University					
Cambridge U	Lord's	July 4	55		3-46
For Lancashire					
Sri Lanka	Old Trafford	Sept 8	42 & 48		0-9 & 0-16

BATTING AVERAGES - Including fielding

	Matches	Inns	NO	Runs	HS	Avge	100s	50s	Ct	St
Benson & Hedges Cup	4	4	0	90	46	22.50	-	-	-	-
Other First-Class	11	14	3	762	105 *	69.27	2	5	9	-
ALL FIRST-CLASS	11	14	3	762	105 *	69.27	2	5	9	-
ALL ONE-DAY	4	4	0	90	46	22.50	-	-	-	-

BOWLING AVERAGES

	Overs	Mdns	Runs	Wkts	Avge	Best	5wI	10wM
Benson & Hedges Cup	44	7	113	3	37.66	1-18	-	-
Other First-Class	224.5	38	750	20	37.50	6-92	1	-
ALL FIRST-CLASS	224.5	38	750	20	37.50	6-92	1	-
ALL ONE-DAY	44	7	113	3	37.66	1-18	-	-

R.D.B. CROFT - *Glamorgan*

Opposition	Venue	Date	Batting	Fielding	Bowling
BRITANNIC ASSURANCE					
Leicestershire	Cardiff	April 26	5 & 27 *		1-42 & 0-3
Somerset	Bath	June 20	17 *		0-12
Surrey	Cardiff	June 30	35 & 20 *		0-46 & 3-46
Gloucs	Swansea	July 4	68		0-23
Leicestershire	Hinckley	July 7	25 * & 0 *		1-46 & 1-33
Worcestershire	Abergavenny	July 21	28 & 91 *		1-71 & 0-61
Warwickshire	Swansea	July 25	74 * & 12 *		1-54 & 0-12
Middlesex	Lord's	Aug 4	15 & 13		3-100 & 1-16
Essex	Southend	Aug 8	6		0-63 & 0-24
Notts	Worksop	Aug 11	1		1-65 & 1-2
Derbyshire	Cardiff	Aug 29	31		3-10
Hampshire	Pontypridd	Sept 7	27 * & 10	1Ct	2-69 & 0-28
Warwickshire	Edgbaston	Sept 12	0 & 12	1Ct	0-85 & 3-64
Worcestershire	Worcester	Sept 18	26 * & 27		0-41 & 1-110

REFUGE ASSURANCE

Middlesex	Lord's	Aug 5	6		0-52
Notts	Trent Bridge	Aug 12	31		0-40
Worcestershire	Swansea	Aug 26	13	1Ct	1-39

NATWEST TROPHY

Middlesex	Lord's	Aug 1	26		0-44

OTHER FIRST-CLASS

India	Swansea	Aug 18	50 *		3-82
Sri Lanka	Ebbw Vale	Aug 22	20 & 32		1-38 & 1-89

BATTING AVERAGES - Including fielding

	Matches	Inns	NO	Runs	HS	Avge	100s	50s	Ct	St
Britannic Assurance	14	23	10	570	91 *	43.84	-	3	2	-
Refuge Assurance	3	3	0	50	31	16.66	-	-	1	-
NatWest Trophy	1	1	0	26	26	26.00	-	-	-	-
Other First-Class	2	3	1	102	50 *	51.00	-	1	-	-
ALL FIRST-CLASS	16	26	11	672	91 *	44.80	-	4	2	-
ALL ONE-DAY	4	4	0	76	31	19.00	-	-	1	-

BOWLING AVERAGES

	Overs	Mdns	Runs	Wkts	Avge	Best	5wI	10wM
Britannic Assurance	357.1	76	1126	23	48.95	3-10	-	-
Refuge Assurance	24	0	131	1	131.00	1-39	-	-
NatWest Trophy	10	0	44	0				
Other First-Class	40	7	209	5	41.80	3-82	-	-
ALL FIRST-CLASS	397.1	83	1335	28	47.67	3-10	-	-
ALL ONE-DAY	34	0	175	1	175.00	1-39	-	-

J.J. CROWE - *New Zealand*

Opposition	Venue	Date	Batting	Fielding	Bowling
OTHER FIRST-CLASS					
Worcestershire	Worcester	May 12	13	1Ct	
Somerset	Taunton	May 16	0 & 30	1Ct	
Middlesex	Lord's	May 19	14 & 20		
Sussex	Hove	May 26	48 & 81 *		
Warwickshire	Edgbaston	May 30	9 * & 10 *	1Ct	
Derbyshire	Derby	June 2	1 & 47	1Ct	
Combined U	Fenner's	June 27	132 & 64	2Ct	
Essex	Chelmsford	June 30	9 * & 15		
OTHER ONE-DAY					
D of Norfolk	Arundel	May 6	43		
MCC	Lord's	May 7	1		
Ireland	Belfast	May 10	19	1Ct	
Leicestershire	Leicester	June 14	7	1Ct	

BATTING AVERAGES - Including fielding

	Matches	Inns	NO	Runs	HS	Avge	100s	50s	Ct	St
Other First-Class	8	15	4	493	132	44.81	1	2	6	-
Other One-Day	4	4	0	70	43	17.50	-	-	2	-
ALL FIRST-CLASS	8	15	4	493	132	44.81	1	2	6	-
ALL ONE-DAY	4	4	0	70	43	17.50	-	-	2	-

BOWLING AVERAGES
Did not bowl

M.D. CROWE - *New Zealand*

Opposition	Venue	Date	Batting	Fielding	Bowling
CORNHILL TEST MATCHES					
England	Trent Bridge	June 7	59	1Ct	
England	Lord's	June 21	1		
England	Edgbaston	July 5	11 & 25		
TEXACO TROPHY					
England	Headingley	May 23	46	2Ct	
England	The Oval	May 25	7		

C PLAYER RECORDS

OTHER FIRST-CLASS

Somerset	Taunton	May 16	55*&	64		0-16
Middlesex	Lord's	May 19	13 &	13*		
Sussex	Hove	May 26	65 &	24		0-4
Warwickshire	Edgbaston	May 30	52			
Derbyshire	Derby	June 2	32		2Ct	
Essex	Chelmsford	June 30	123*		2Ct	

OTHER ONE-DAY

D of Norfolk	Arundel	May 6	89*	1Ct	
MCC	Lord's	May 7	26	1Ct	
Ireland	Downpatrick	May 9	48		
Leicestershire	Leicester	June 14	20	1Ct	0-6
For Rest of World					
England XI	Jesmond	Aug 2	16		
England XI	Jesmond	Aug 3	106*		0-26

BATTING AVERAGES - Including fielding

	Matches	Inns	NO	Runs	HS	Avge	100s	50s	Ct	St
Cornhill Test Matches	3	4	0	96	59	24.00	-	1	1	-
Texaco Trophy	2	2	0	53	46	26.50	-	-	2	-
Other First-Class	6	9	3	441	123*	73.50	1	4	4	-
Other One-Day	6	6	2	305	106*	76.25	1	1	3	-
ALL FIRST-CLASS	9	13	3	537	123*	53.70	1	5	5	-
ALL ONE-DAY	8	8	2	358	106*	59.66	1	1	5	-

BOWLING AVERAGES

	Overs	Mdns	Runs	Wkts	Avge	Best	5wI	10wM
Cornhill Test Matches								
Texaco Trophy								
Other First-Class	8	3	20	0	-	-	-	-
Other One-Day	6.4	0	32	0	-	-	-	-
ALL FIRST-CLASS	8	3	20	0	-	-	-	-
ALL ONE-DAY	6.4	0	32	0	-	-	-	-

K.M. CURRAN - *Gloucestershire*

Opposition	Venue	Date	Batting		Fielding	Bowling

BRITANNIC ASSURANCE

Somerset	Taunton	April 26	41 &	13		2-91 & 0-8
Glamorgan	Bristol	May 15	47 &	44	1Ct	1-39 & 0-35
Middlesex	Lord's	May 26	9*&	53*	1Ct	4-64
Somerset	Bristol	June 2	103*			2-41 & 0-14
Essex	Ilford	June 6	39		1Ct	1-93
Lancashire	Old Trafford	June 9	48			1-68
Sussex	Hove	June 16	15			0-33 & 3-64
Hampshire	Gloucester	June 20				
Leicestershire	Gloucester	June 23	0			4-100
Derbyshire	Derby	June 30	24 &	3	1Ct	0-3 & 1-75
Glamorgan	Swansea	July 4			1Ct	4-92
Worcestershire	Worcester	July 7	7 &	19		3-76 & 1-37
Yorkshire	Cheltenham	July 21	8		1Ct	2-84 & 0-30
Northants	Cheltenham	July 25	86			4-37 & 1-58
Surrey	Cheltenham	July 28	46 &	25	1Ct	0-26 & 2-59
Warwickshire	Bristol	Aug 8	15 &	83*	3Ct	3-50 & 2-70
Kent	Bristol	Aug 11	45*&	13		3-97
Notts	Trent Bridge	Aug 18	54 &	7	1Ct	0-36 & 3-35
Northants	Northampton	Aug 23	19 &	19		2-68 & 2-17
Worcestershire	Bristol	Sept 7	18 &	35*		0-25 & 0-21
Sussex	Bristol	Sept 12	144*		3Ct	3-24 & 0-20
Hampshire	Southampton	Sept 18	78 &	101*	1Ct	5-63 & 1-86

REFUGE ASSURANCE

Glamorgan	Bristol	April 22	37		1-22
Hampshire	Southampton	May 6			0-41
Essex	Chelmsford	May 13	5*		0-43
Warwickshire	Moreton-in-M	May 20	75		1-22
Middlesex	Lord's	May 27	13		0-37
Somerset	Bristol	June 3	29*		1-22
Lancashire	Old Trafford	June 10	7		0-52
Leicestershire	Gloucester	June 24	14		2-38
Derbyshire	Derby	July 1	4		1-20
Worcestershire	Worcester	July 8	56		0-39
Sussex	Swindon	July 15	52		2-21
Yorkshire	Cheltenham	July 22	31*		1-31
Surrey	Cheltenham	July 29	23		1-50
Kent	Bristol	Aug 12	12		1-24
Notts	Trent Bridge	Aug 19	15		0-11
Northants	Northampton	Aug 26	92	1Ct	3-45

NATWEST TROPHY

Lincolnshire	Gloucester	June 27	2	0-11
Kent	Bristol	July 11	1	2-30
Lancashire	Old Trafford	Aug 1	1	0-63

BENSON & HEDGES CUP

Worcestershire	Bristol	April 24	55	1Ct	3-53
Glamorgan	Cardiff	May 1	14		3-29
Kent	Canterbury	May 10			0-23
Warwickshire	Bristol	May 12	0		1-36

OTHER FIRST-CLASS

Zimbabwe	Bristol	May 19	6	3-80 & 1-42

BATTING AVERAGES - Including fielding

	Matches	Inns	NO	Runs	HS	Avge	100s	50s	Ct	St
Britannic Assurance	22	32	8	1261	144*	52.54	3	5	15	-
Refuge Assurance	16	15	3	465	92	38.75	-	4	1	-
NatWest Trophy	3	3	0	4	2	1.33	-	-	-	-
Benson & Hedges Cup	4	3	0	69	55	23.00	-	1	1	-
Other First-Class	1	1	0	6	6	6.00	-	-	-	-
ALL FIRST-CLASS	23	33	8	1267	144*	50.68	3	5	15	-
ALL ONE-DAY	23	21	3	538	92	29.88	-	5	2	-

BOWLING AVERAGES

	Overs	Mdns	Runs	Wkts	Avge	Best	5wI	10wM
Britannic Assurance	561.3	105	1839	60	30.65	5-63	1	-
Refuge Assurance	113	2	518	14	37.00	3-45	-	-
NatWest Trophy	32	7	104	2	52.00	2-30	-	-
Benson & Hedges Cup	32	2	141	7	20.14	3-29	-	-
Other First-Class	37	6	122	4	30.50	3-80	-	-
ALL FIRST-CLASS	598.3	111	1961	64	30.64	5-63	1	-
ALL ONE-DAY	177	11	763	23	33.17	3-29	-	-

D.M. CURTIS - *Oxford University*

Opposition	Venue	Date	Batting		Fielding	Bowling

OTHER FIRST-CLASS

Leicestershire	The Parks	May 23	0 &	19		0-8
Glamorgan	The Parks	June 2	43			
Notts	The Parks	June 6				
Cambridge U	Lord's	July 4	27			

BATTING AVERAGES - Including fielding

	Matches	Inns	NO	Runs	HS	Avge	100s	50s	Ct	St
Other First-Class	4	4	0	89	43	22.25	-	-	-	-
ALL FIRST-CLASS	4	4	0	89	43	22.25	-	-	-	-

BOWLING AVERAGES

	Overs	Mdns	Runs	Wkts	Avge	Best	5wI	10wM
Other First-Class	1	0	8	0	-	-	-	-
ALL FIRST-CLASS	1	0	8	0	-	-	-	-

I.J. CURTIS - *Oxfordshire*

Opposition	Venue	Date	Batting	Fielding	Bowling

NATWEST TROPHY

Kent	Oxford	June 27	0*		2-53

BATTING AVERAGES - Including fielding

	Matches	Inns	NO	Runs	HS	Avge	100s	50s	Ct	St
NatWest Trophy	1	1	1	0	0*	-	-	-	-	-
ALL ONE-DAY	1	1	1	0	0*	-	-	-	-	-

BOWLING AVERAGES

	Overs	Mdns	Runs	Wkts	Avge	Best	5wI	10wM
NatWest Trophy	12	0	53	2	26.50	2-53	-	
ALL ONE-DAY	12	0	53	2	26.50	2-53	-	

PLAYER RECORDS

C

T.S. CURTIS - *Worcestershire*

Opposition	Venue	Date	Batting			Fielding	Bowling
BRITANNIC ASSURANCE							
Lancashire	Old Trafford	April 26	7	&	37		0-5
Notts	Worcester	May 3	46			2Ct	
Essex	Worcester	May 19	48	&	2	1Ct	0-8
Warwickshire	Edgbaston	May 26	34	&	47 *	1Ct	
Yorkshire	Worcester	June 2	13				
Surrey	The Oval	June 16	0	&	31 *	1Ct	
Sussex	Worcester	June 20	27				
Middlesex	Lord's	June 30	30	&	0	1Ct	
Gloucs	Worcester	July 7	4	&	21	2Ct	
Somerset	Worcester	July 18	6	&	24		
Glamorgan	Abergavenny	July 21	23	&	111 *		0-30
Derbyshire	Derby	July 25	17				
Leicestershire	Leicester	Aug 4	151 * &		6	1Ct	
Lancashire	Kid'minster	Aug 8	56	&	4 *		
Hampshire	Worcester	Aug 11	71	&	38 *		
Northants	Worcester	Aug 18	48	&	12		
Warwickshire	Worcester	Aug 23	27	&	197 *	1Ct	
Notts	Trent Bridge	Aug 29	82	&	84 *		
Gloucs	Bristol	Sept 7	96	&	8	2Ct	
Somerset	Taunton	Sept 12	156	&	10		
Glamorgan	Worcester	Sept 18	16	&	60	1Ct	
REFUGE ASSURANCE							
Somerset	Taunton	April 22	124				
Derbyshire	Derby	April 29	7				
Notts	Worcester	May 6	73				
Essex	Worcester	May 20	34				
Warwickshire	Worcester	May 27	61				
Yorkshire	Worcester	June 3	76				
Surrey	The Oval	June 17	0				
Sussex	Worcester	June 24	58				
Middlesex	Lord's	July 1	16				
Gloucs	Worcester	July 8	93 *			1Ct	
Lancashire	Old Trafford	July 15	32			1Ct	
Leicestershire	Leicester	Aug 5	19			1Ct	
Hampshire	Worcester	Aug 12	13				
Northants	Worcester	Aug 19	83 *			1Ct	
Glamorgan	Swansea	Aug 26	95				
NATWEST TROPHY							
Suffolk	Bury St Ed's	June 27	16				
Somerset	Taunton	July 11	112				
Northants	Northampton	Aug 1	30			1Ct	
BENSON & HEDGES CUP							
Gloucs	Bristol	April 24	2				
Kent	Worcester	May 1	11				
Glamorgan	Worcester	May 8	36				
Warwickshire	Edgbaston	May 10	97				
Glamorgan	Worcester	May 30	76 *			1Ct	
Notts	Trent Bridge	June 13	61				
Lancashire	Lord's	July 14	16				
OTHER FIRST-CLASS							
MCC	Lord's	April 17	81				
OTHER ONE-DAY							
Hampshire	Scarborough	Sept 2	16				

BATTING AVERAGES - Including fielding

	Matches	Inns	NO	Runs	HS	Avge	100s	50s	Ct	St
Britannic Assurance	21	38	8	1650	197 *	55.00	4	6	13	-
Refuge Assurance	15	15	2	784	124	60.30	1	7	4	-
NatWest Trophy	3	3	0	158	112	52.66	1	-	1	-
Benson & Hedges Cup	7	7	1	299	97	49.83	-	3	1	-
Other First-Class	1	1	0	81	81	81.00	-	1	-	-
Other One-Day	1	1	0	16	16	16.00	-	-	-	-
ALL FIRST-CLASS	22	39	8	1731	197 *	55.83	4	7	13	-
ALL ONE-DAY	26	26	3	1257	124	54.65	2	10	6	-

BOWLING AVERAGES

	Overs	Mdns	Runs	Wkts	Avge	Best	5wI	10wM
Britannic Assurance	5.3	1	43	0	-	-	-	-
Refuge Assurance								
NatWest Trophy								
Benson & Hedges Cup								
Other First-Class								
Other One-Day								

	Overs	Mdns	Runs	Wkts	Avge	Best	5wI	10wM
ALL FIRST-CLASS	5.3	1	43	0	-	-	-	-
ALL ONE-DAY								

D — PLAYER RECORDS

A. DALE - *Glamorgan & Combined Univ*

Opposition	Venue	Date	Batting			Fielding	Bowling
BRITANNIC ASSURANCE							
Surrey	Cardiff	June 30	25	&	4	1Ct	
Essex	Southend	Aug 8	92				0-18
Notts	Worksop	Aug 11	7			2Ct	0-16
Derbyshire	Cardiff	Aug 29	16				0-9
Hampshire	Pontypridd	Sept 7	14	&	0	1Ct	
Warwickshire	Edgbaston	Sept 12	5	&	9	2Ct	0-64 & 0-10
Worcestershire	Worcester	Sept 18	7	&	0		0-16 & 0-54
REFUGE ASSURANCE							
Gloucs	Bristol	April 22	42			1Ct	1-41
Leicestershire	Cardiff	April 29	3				1-22
Surrey	Cardiff	July 1					0-16
Warwickshire	Edgbaston	July 15				1Ct	1-29
Somerset	Neath	July 22	14			1Ct	1-28
Derbyshire	Swansea	July 29	13*				0-17
Middlesex	Lord's	Aug 5	0				1-38
Notts	Trent Bridge	Aug 12	7				0-15
Worcestershire	Swansea	Aug 26	34				3-35
NATWEST TROPHY							
Dorset	Swansea	June 27	4*				0-28
Middlesex	Lord's	Aug 1	3				1-14
BENSON & HEDGES CUP							
For Combined Universities							
Lancashire	Fenner's	May 1	2				1-21
Yorkshire	Headingley	May 8	16				0-38
Surrey	The Parks	May 10	40				0-13
Hampshire	Southampton	May 12	2				0-21
OTHER FIRST-CLASS							
India	Swansea	Aug 18			0		3-21 & 0-62
Sri Lanka	Ebbw Vale	Aug 22	36	&	14		3-25 & 1-43

BATTING AVERAGES - Including fielding

	Matches	Inns	NO	Runs	HS	Avge	100s	50s	Ct	St
Britannic Assurance	7	11	0	179	92	16.27	-	1	6	-
Refuge Assurance	9	7	1	113	42	18.83	-	-	3	-
NatWest Trophy	2	2	1	7	4*	7.00	-	-	-	-
Benson & Hedges Cup	4	4	0	60	40	15.00	-	-	-	-
Other First-Class	2	3	0	50	36	16.66	-	-	-	-
ALL FIRST-CLASS	9	14	0	229	92	16.35	-	1	6	-
ALL ONE-DAY	15	13	2	180	42	16.36	-	-	3	-

BOWLING AVERAGES

	Overs	Mdns	Runs	Wkts	Avge	Best	5wI	10wM
Britannic Assurance	51	8	187	0	-	-	-	-
Refuge Assurance	43	0	241	8	30.12	3-35	-	
NatWest Trophy	9	1	42	1	42.00	1-14	-	
Benson & Hedges Cup	21	2	93	1	93.00	1-21	-	
Other First-Class	39	5	151	7	21.57	3-21	-	-
ALL FIRST-CLASS	90	13	338	7	48.28	3-21	-	-
ALL ONE-DAY	73	3	376	10	37.60	3-35	-	

H. DAVIES - *Oxford University*

Opposition	Venue	Date	Batting			Fielding	Bowling
OTHER FIRST-CLASS							
Hampshire	The Parks	May 3	24				3-93
Surrey	The Parks	May 16	2	&	1*		0-25
Leicestershire	The Parks	May 23	9*				0-112
Notts	The Parks	June 6					0-31

BATTING AVERAGES - Including fielding

	Matches	Inns	NO	Runs	HS	Avge	100s	50s	Ct	St
Other First-Class	4	4	2	36	24	18.00	-	-	-	-
ALL FIRST-CLASS	4	4	2	36	24	18.00	-	-	-	-

BOWLING AVERAGES

	Overs	Mdns	Runs	Wkts	Avge	Best	5wI	10wM
Other First-Class	54	6	261	3	87.00	3-93	-	-
ALL FIRST-CLASS	54	6	261	3	87.00	3-93	-	-

M. DAVIES - *Glamorgan*

Opposition	Venue	Date	Batting	Fielding	Bowling
OTHER FIRST-CLASS					
Oxford U	The Parks	June 2	5*	1Ct	0-16

BATTING AVERAGES - Including fielding

	Matches	Inns	NO	Runs	HS	Avge	100s	50s	Ct	St
Other First-Class	1	1	1	5	5*	-	-	-	1	-
ALL FIRST-CLASS	1	1	1	5	5*	-	-	-	1	-

BOWLING AVERAGES

	Overs	Mdns	Runs	Wkts	Avge	Best	5wI	10wM
Other First-Class	8	1	16	0	-	-	-	-
ALL FIRST-CLASS	8	1	16	0	-	-	-	-

M.R. DAVIES - *Shropshire*

Opposition	Venue	Date	Batting	Fielding	Bowling
NATWEST TROPHY					
Derbyshire	Chesterfield	June 27	20		

BATTING AVERAGES - Including fielding

	Matches	Inns	NO	Runs	HS	Avge	100s	50s	Ct	St
NatWest Trophy	1	1	0	20	20	20.00	-	-	-	-
ALL ONE-DAY	1	1	0	20	20	20.00	-	-	-	-

BOWLING AVERAGES
Did not bowl

R.P. DAVIS - *Kent*

Opposition	Venue	Date	Batting			Fielding	Bowling
BRITANNIC ASSURANCE							
Hampshire	Canterbury	April 26			1	1Ct	1-96 & 0-63
Sussex	Folkestone	May 3	3			1Ct	2-75 & 6-59
Middlesex	Lord's	May 15	6*	&	0	1Ct	1-25 & 0-23
Glamorgan	Swansea	May 23			12	2Ct	0-74 & 4-97
Notts	Tunbridge We	June 2	9	&	13	1Ct	3-155
Yorkshire	Tunbridge We	June 6				1Ct	
Somerset	Canterbury	June 9	0	&	8*	1Ct	2-50 & 0-18
Warwickshire	Edgbaston	June 23	5			2Ct	2-70 & 3-61
Lancashire	Maidstone	June 30	59	&	19	1Ct	4-49 & 4-54
Essex	Maidstone	June 4					2-76
Northants	Northampton	July 18	43	&	41		0-109
Surrey	Guildford	July 21	0	&	4		0-89 & 0-9
Middlesex	Canterbury	July 25			12		1-104 & 0-56
Worcestershire	Canterbury	July 28	8	&	2*	1Ct	0-54 & 1-46
Derbyshire	Chesterfield	Aug 4	41	&	26	1Ct	1-152
Leicestershire	Dartford	Aug 8	0			1Ct	6-63 & 4-79
Gloucs	Bristol	Aug 11	20			2Ct	1-59 & 6-111
Sussex	Hove	Aug 18	29	&	0	1Ct	1-89 & 6-97
Leicestershire	Leicester	Aug 23	36	&	4	2Ct	0-47 & 2-120
Hampshire	Bournemouth	Aug 29			0	4Ct	1-31 & 1-127
Surrey	Canterbury	Sept 7	5	&	46		0-49
Essex	Chelmsford	Sept 12	0	&	52	1Ct	0-112
REFUGE ASSURANCE							
Hampshire	Canterbury	April 29					4-25
Middlesex	Folkestone	May 6					1-29
Glamorgan	Llanelli	May 13					0-27
Yorkshire	Canterbury	May 20				1Ct	2-30
Northants	Northampton	May 27				1Ct	0-29
Somerset	Canterbury	June 10					0-17
Notts	Canterbury	June 17			0*	1Ct	2-25
Warwickshire	Edgbaston	June 24			2*	2Ct	2-11

PLANER RECORDS

Lancashire	Maidstone	July 1	14		0-33
Surrey	The Oval	July 22	0		1-30
Worcestershire	Canterbury	July 29			2-30
Derbyshire	Chesterfield	Aug 5			1-64
Gloucs	Bristol	Aug 12	0*		0-16
Leicestershire	Leicester	Aug 26			1-29

NATWEST TROPHY

Oxfordshire	Oxford	June 27			1-27
Gloucs	Bristol	July 11	12	1Ct	1-33

BENSON & HEDGES CUP

Worcestershire	Worcester	May 1	0*		1-36
Warwickshire	Canterbury	May 8			2-40
Glamorgan	Swansea	May 12		1Ct	0-45

OTHER FIRST-CLASS

Cambridge U	Fenner's	June 20		1Ct	6-40
India	Canterbury	July 7		2Ct	1-66 & 1-90

BATTING AVERAGES - Including fielding

	Matches	Inns	NO	Runs	HS	Avge	100s	50s	Ct	St
Britannic Assurance	22	32	3	504	59	17.37	-	2	24	-
Refuge Assurance	14	5	3	16	14	8.00	-	-	5	-
NatWest Trophy	2	1	0	12	12	12.00	-	-	1	-
Benson & Hedges Cup	3	1	1	0	0*	-	-	-	1	-
Other First-Class	2	0	0	0		-	-	-	3	-
ALL FIRST-CLASS	24	32	3	504	59	17.37	-	2	27	-
ALL ONE-DAY	19	7	4	28	14	9.33	-	-	7	-

BOWLING AVERAGES

	Overs	Mdns	Runs	Wkts	Avge	Best	5wI	10wM
Britannic Assurance	839.1	202	2648	65	40.73	6-59	4	1
Refuge Assurance	84	1	395	16	24.68	4-25	-	
NatWest Trophy	21	3	60	2	30.00	1-27	-	
Benson & Hedges Cup	30	1	121	3	40.33	2-40	-	
Other First-Class	69	19	196	8	24.50	6-40	1	-
ALL FIRST-CLASS	908.1	221	2844	73	38.95	6-40	5	1
ALL ONE-DAY	135	5	576	21	27.42	4-25	-	

W.W. DAVIS - *Northamptonshire*

Opposition	Venue	Date	Batting	Fielding	Bowling
BRITANNIC ASSURANCE					
Derbyshire	Northampton	May 3	23 & 0		1-85
Notts	Trent Bridge	May 23	4		1-50 & 1-63
Somerset	Taunton	June 30		1Ct	0-45 & 1-72
Surrey	The Oval	July 4	9		0-70
Sussex	Northampton	July 21			2-75
Hampshire	Bournemouth	Aug 4	13 & 47		0-61
Lancashire	Northampton	Aug 11			1-85 & 3-28
Essex	Northampton	Aug 29		1Ct	2-76 & 0-37
REFUGE ASSURANCE					
Derbyshire	Northampton	May 6	4*		0-42
Kent	Northampton	May 27	19		0-49
Surrey	The Oval	June 3	9	1Ct	0-13
Glamorgan	Northampton	June 10			1-39
Middlesex	Northampton	June 24	7		0-19
Somerset	Taunton	July 1	3		0-25
Yorkshire	Tring	July 8	20		1-38
Essex	Chelmsford	July 15	2		0-38
Sussex	Well'borough	July 22	24	1Ct	2-32
Worcestershire	Worcester	Aug 19			0-58
Gloucs	Northampton	Aug 26	9		2-40
OTHER FIRST-CLASS					
New Zealand	Northampton	June 16	5*		1-65

BATTING AVERAGES - Including fielding

	Matches	Inns	NO	Runs	HS	Avge	100s	50s	Ct	St
Britannic Assurance	8	6	0	96	47	16.00	-	-	2	-
Refuge Assurance	11	9	1	97	24	12.12	-	-	2	-
Other First-Class	1	1	1	5	5*	-	-	-	-	-
ALL FIRST-CLASS	9	7	1	101	47	16.83	-	-	2	-
ALL ONE-DAY	11	9	1	97	24	12.12	-	-	2	-

BOWLING AVERAGES

	Overs	Mdns	Runs	Wkts	Avge	Best	5wI	10wM
Britannic Assurance	216.5	25	747	12	62.25	3-28	-	-
Refuge Assurance	77.5	5	393	6	65.50	2-32	-	-
Other First-Class	21	2	65	1	65.00	1-65	-	-
ALL FIRST-CLASS	237.5	27	812	13	62.46	3-28	-	-
ALL ONE-DAY	77.5	5	393	6	65.50	2-32	-	-

R.I. DAWSON - *Devon*

Opposition	Venue	Date	Batting	Fielding	Bowling
NATWEST TROPHY					
Somerset	Torquay	June 27	0		1-37

BATTING AVERAGES - Including fielding

	Matches	Inns	NO	Runs	HS	Avge	100s	50s	Ct	St
NatWest Trophy	1	1	0	0	0	0.00	-	-	-	-
ALL ONE-DAY	1	1	0	0	0	0.00	-	-	-	-

BOWLING AVERAGES

	Overs	Mdns	Runs	Wkts	Avge	Best	5wI	10wM
NatWest Trophy	4	0	37	1	37.00	1-37	-	
ALL ONE-DAY	4	0	37	1	37.00	1-37	-	

A. DAY - *League C.C. XI*

Opposition	Venue	Date	Batting	Fielding	Bowling
OTHER ONE-DAY					
India	Sunderland	June 28	1		2-71

BATTING AVERAGES - Including fielding

	Matches	Inns	NO	Runs	HS	Avge	100s	50s	Ct	St
Other One-Day	1	1	0	1	1	1.00	-	-	-	-
ALL ONE-DAY	1	1	0	1	1	1.00	-	-	-	-

BOWLING AVERAGES

	Overs	Mdns	Runs	Wkts	Avge	Best	5wI	10wM
Other One-Day	11	1	71	2	35.50	2-71	-	
ALL ONE-DAY	11	1	71	2	35.50	2-71	-	

S.J. DEAN - *Staffordshire*

Opposition	Venue	Date	Batting	Fielding	Bowling
NATWEST TROPHY					
Northants	Northampton	June 27	8		

BATTING AVERAGES - Including fielding

	Matches	Inns	NO	Runs	HS	Avge	100s	50s	Ct	St
NatWest Trophy	1	1	0	8	8	8.00	-	-	-	-
ALL ONE-DAY	1	1	0	8	8	8.00	-	-	-	-

BOWLING AVERAGES
Did not bowl

D   PLADER RECORDS

P.A.J. DEFREITAS - *Lancashire & England*

Opposition	Venue	Date	Batting	Fielding	Bowling
CORNHILL TEST MATCHES					
New Zealand	Trent Bridge	June 7	14		5-53 & 1-0
New Zealand	Lord's	June 21	38		0-122
TEXACO TROPHY					
New Zealand	Headingley	May 23	1*		0-70
New Zealand	The Oval	May 25			1-47
India	Headingley	July 18	11		1-40
India	Trent Bridge	July 20	1		0-59
BRITANNIC ASSURANCE					
Worcestershire	Old Trafford	April 26		1Ct	2-62 & 0-51
Surrey	The Oval	May 3	31		1-99 & 0-10
Derbyshire	Derby	May 15	79		1-70 & 1-36
Leicestershire	Old Trafford	May 19	19*		1-78 & 0-23
Glamorgan	Colwyn Bay	May 26	21		3-53 & 2-61
Sussex	Horsham	June 2	26		0-27 & 6-39
Kent	Maidstone	June 30	6 & 7*	1Ct	2-43 & 2-55
Derbyshire	Liverpool	July 7	16 & 11		0-44 & 2-35
Essex	Colchester	July 21	41		2-68 & 0-69
Yorkshire	Headingley	Aug 4	66 & 2		0-7
Northants	Northampton	Aug 11	100* & 15	2Ct	0-59 & 2-23
Yorkshire	Old Trafford	Aug 18	4		1-44 & 0-30
Surrey	Blackpool	Aug 29	13		1-31
Notts	Trent Bridge	Sept 12	49		3-63 & 1-33
Warwickshire	Old Trafford	Sept 18		1Ct	0-6
REFUGE ASSURANCE					
Middlesex	Old Trafford	April 22	6		0-35
Notts	Trent Bridge	April 29	7*		3-36
Surrey	The Oval	May 6			3-48
Leicestershire	Old Trafford	May 20	7		2-40
Glamorgan	Colwyn Bay	May 27	35*		1-42
Kent	Maidstone	July 1			2-48
Derbyshire	Old Trafford	July 8	17		2-53
Worcestershire	Old Trafford	July 15		1Ct	0-28
Essex	Colchester	July 22	18		1-38
Somerset	Old Trafford	July 29			0-36
Northants	Northampton	Aug 12			4-22
Warwickshire	Old Trafford	Aug 26	32		1-34
Middlesex	Old Trafford	Sept 5	2		1-71
NATWEST TROPHY					
Durham	Old Trafford	June 27			1-22
Derbyshire	Derby	July 11	1		3-34
Gloucs	Old Trafford	Aug 1			1-22
Middlesex	Old Trafford	Aug 15	2*		0-52
Northants	Lord's	Sept 1			5-26
BENSON & HEDGES CUP					
Surrey	Old Trafford	April 24	20		0-33
Combined U	Fenner's	May 1	12		1-38
Hampshire	Old Trafford	May 8	75*		1-14
Yorkshire	Headingley	May 10	10		3-36
Surrey	Old Trafford	May 30	0		3-40
Somerset	Old Trafford	June 13			1-51
Worcestershire	Lord's	July 14	28		2-30
OTHER FIRST-CLASS					
Oxford U	The Parks	June 16	102	2Ct	1-39 & 0-7

BATTING AVERAGES - Including fielding

	Matches	Inns	NO	Runs	HS	Avge	100s	50s	Ct	St
Cornhill Test Matches	2	2	0	52	38	26.00	-	-	-	-
Texaco Trophy	4	3	1	13	11	6.50	-	-	-	-
Britannic Assurance	15	17	3	506	100*	36.14	1	2	5	-
Refuge Assurance	13	8	1	124	35*	20.66	-	-	1	-
NatWest Trophy	5	2	1	3	2*	3.00	-	-	-	-
Benson & Hedges Cup	7	6	1	145	75*	29.00	-	1	-	-
Other First-Class	1	1	0	102	102	102.00	1	-	2	-
ALL FIRST-CLASS	18	20	3	660	102	38.82	2	2	7	-
ALL ONE-DAY	29	19	5	285	75*	20.35	-	1	1	-

BOWLING AVERAGES

	Overs	Mdns	Runs	Wkts	Avge	Best	5wI	10wM
Cornhill Test Matches	59.4	9	175	6	29.16	5-53	1	-
Texaco Trophy	42.5	2	216	2	108.00	1-40	-	-
Britannic Assurance	408.5	96	1219	33	36.93	6-39	1	-
Refuge Assurance	102.3	2	531	20	26.55	4-22	-	-
NatWest Trophy	50	12	156	10	15.60	5-26	1	-
Benson & Hedges Cup	65	5	242	11	22.00	3-36	-	-
Other First-Class	21	4	46	1	46.00	1-39	-	-
ALL FIRST-CLASS	489.3	109	1440	40	36.00	6-39	2	-
ALL ONE-DAY	260.2	21	1145	43	26.62	5-26	1	

S.J. DENNIS - *Glamorgan*

Opposition	Venue	Date	Batting	Fielding	Bowling
BRITANNIC ASSURANCE					
Leicestershire	Cardiff	April 26	3 & 2	1Ct	5-76 & 0-16
Somerset	Cardiff	May 3			1-125 & 1-16
Gloucs	Bristol	May 15	6 & 0		2-46 & 1-35
Sussex	Hove	May 19			1-36 & 3-83
Kent	Swansea	May 23	6		0-39 & 2-53
Hampshire	Southampton	June 16			1-83
Somerset	Bath	June 20			0-20
Yorkshire	Cardiff	June 23		1Ct	1-34 & 1-58
Surrey	Cardiff	June 30	2		0-11 & 0-5
Gloucs	Swansea	July 4	4*		1-23
Leicestershire	Hinckley	July 7	0		0-79 & 0-28
Warwickshire	Swansea	July 25		1Ct	0-91
REFUGE ASSURANCE					
Gloucs	Bristol	April 22			1-35
Leicestershire	Cardiff	April 29	7		0-13
Kent	Llanelli	May 13		1Ct	0-28
Sussex	Hove	May 20			1-25
Lancashire	Colwyn Bay	May 27			1-38
Essex	Ilford	June 3	3		0-23
Northants	Northampton	June 10			1-63
Hampshire	Bournemouth	June 17	1*	1Ct	0-43
Surrey	Cardiff	July 1			1-14
Warwickshire	Edgbaston	July 15			0-24
Somerset	Neath	July 22	5		0-67
Derbyshire	Swansea	July 29			0-26
Middlesex	Lord's	Aug 5	0		1-54
Notts	Trent Bridge	Aug 12			0-32
Worcestershire	Swansea	Aug 26	14		0-42
NATWEST TROPHY					
Dorset	Swansea	June 27		1Ct	0-28
Sussex	Cardiff	July 11			0-44
Middlesex	Lord's	Aug 1			0-27
BENSON & HEDGES CUP					
Warwickshire	Edgbaston	April 24	2		0-20
Gloucs	Cardiff	May 1	2*		1-38
Kent	Swansea	May 12	1		1-37
OTHER FIRST-CLASS					
Oxford U	The Parks	April 14			2-51
India	Swansea	Aug 18			0-63

BATTING AVERAGES - Including fielding

	Matches	Inns	NO	Runs	HS	Avge	100s	50s	Ct	St
Britannic Assurance	12	8	1	23	6	3.28	-	-	3	-
Refuge Assurance	15	6	1	30	14	6.00	-	-	2	-
NatWest Trophy	3	0	0	0	0	-	-	-	1	-
Benson & Hedges Cup	3	3	1	5	2*	2.50	-	-	-	-
Other First-Class	2	0	0	0	0	-	-	-	-	-
ALL FIRST-CLASS	14	8	1	23	6	3.28	-	-	3	-
ALL ONE-DAY	21	9	2	35	14	5.00	-	-	3	-

BOWLING AVERAGES

	Overs	Mdns	Runs	Wkts	Avge	Best	5wI	10wM
Britannic Assurance	283	53	957	20	47.85	5-76	1	-
Refuge Assurance	99.4	1	527	6	87.83	1-14	-	-
NatWest Trophy	19	0	99	0	-	-	-	-
Benson & Hedges Cup	25	3	95	2	47.50	1-37	-	-
Other First-Class	39	8	114	2	57.00	2-51	-	-
ALL FIRST-CLASS	322	61	1071	22	48.68	5-76	1	-
ALL ONE-DAY	143.4	4	721	8	90.12	1-14	-	-

PLAYER RECORDS

J. DERRICK - *Glamorgan*

Opposition	Venue	Date	Batting	Fielding	Bowling
REFUGE ASSURANCE					
Lancashire	Colwyn Bay	May 27			0-26
Hampshire	Bournemouth	June 17	19		
Surrey	Cardiff	July 1			0-12
OTHER FIRST-CLASS					
Oxford U	The Parks	June 2	28 *		0-58

BATTING AVERAGES - Including fielding

	Matches	Inns	NO	Runs	HS	Avge	100s	50s	Ct	St
Refuge Assurance	3	1	0	19	19	19.00	-	-	-	-
Other First-Class	1	1	1	28	28*	-	-	-	-	-
ALL FIRST-CLASS	1	1	1	28	28*	-	-	-	-	-
ALL ONE-DAY	3	1	0	19	19	19.00	-	-	-	-

BOWLING AVERAGES

	Overs	Mdns	Runs	Wkts	Avge	Best	5wI	10wM
Refuge Assurance	4	0	38	0	-	-	-	-
Other First-Class	9	2	58	0	-	-	-	-
ALL FIRST-CLASS	9	2	58	0	-	-	-	-
ALL ONE-DAY	4	0	38	0	-	-	-	-

P.A. DE SILVA - *Sri Lanka*

Opposition	Venue	Date	Batting	Fielding	Bowling
OTHER FIRST-CLASS					
Glamorgan	Ebbw Vale	Aug 22	45 & 2	1Ct	
Notts	Cleethorpes	Aug 25	1 & 14 *		0-19 & 0-5
Warwickshire	Edgbaston	Aug 29	67 & 54 *	1Ct	0-25
Sussex	Hove	Sept 5	43 & 5	3Ct	
Lancashire	Old Trafford	Sept 8	95 & 14 *	4Ct	0-7 & 2-25
Hampshire	Southampton	Sept 12	2 & 221 *	1Ct	
OTHER ONE-DAY					
Surrey	The Oval	Sept 2	35	1Ct	4-55
Somerset	Taunton	Sept 3	33		

BATTING AVERAGES - Including fielding

	Matches	Inns	NO	Runs	HS	Avge	100s	50s	Ct	St
Other First-Class	6	12	4	563	221*	70.37	1	3	10	-
Other One-Day	2	2	0	68	35	34.00	-	-	1	-
ALL FIRST-CLASS	6	12	4	563	221*	70.37	1	3	10	-
ALL ONE-DAY	2	2	0	68	35	34.00	-	-	1	-

BOWLING AVERAGES

	Overs	Mdns	Runs	Wkts	Avge	Best	5wI	10wM
Other First-Class	25	3	81	2	40.50	2-25	-	-
Other One-Day	8	0	55	4	13.75	4-55	-	-
ALL FIRST-CLASS	25	3	81	2	40.50	2-25	-	-
ALL ONE-DAY	8	0	55	4	13.75	4-55	-	-

P.S. DE VILLIERS - *Kent*

Opposition	Venue	Date	Batting	Fielding	Bowling
BRITANNIC ASSURANCE					
Sussex	Folkestone	May 3	37	1Ct	1-84 & 2-37
Glamorgan	Swansea	May 23			0-39 & 4-69
Yorkshire	Tunbridge We	June 6			1-10
Somerset	Canterbury	June 9	15 & 0		0-51 & 0-7
Lancashire	Maidstone	June 30	0 & 33	2Ct	2-73 & 2-58
Essex	Maidstone	June 4			2-84
Northants	Northampton	July 18	0		2-78
Surrey	Guildford	July 21	32 & 28		1-57
Middlesex	Canterbury	July 25	9		0-32 & 6-70

Opposition	Venue	Date	Batting	Fielding	Bowling
Derbyshire	Chesterfield	Aug 4	5 & 30	1Ct	1-75
Sussex	Hove	Aug 18	15 * & 19 *	1Ct	0-34 & 0-46
Leicestershire	Leicester	Aug 23	21 & 20 *	1Ct	1-57 & 0-31
REFUGE ASSURANCE					
Warwickshire	Edgbaston	June 24	10		1-17
Lancashire	Maidstone	July 1	1		1-53
Surrey	The Oval	July 22	6		1-26
Gloucs	Bristol	Aug 12	4		0-25
NATWEST TROPHY					
Oxfordshire	Oxford	June 27	10		0-28
Gloucs	Bristol	July 11	14		1-29
BENSON & HEDGES CUP					
Glamorgan	Swansea	May 12	0	1Ct	2-37

BATTING AVERAGES - Including fielding

	Matches	Inns	NO	Runs	HS	Avge	100s	50s	Ct	St
Britannic Assurance	12	15	3	264	37	22.00	-	-	6	-
Refuge Assurance	4	4	0	21	10	5.25	-	-	-	-
NatWest Trophy	2	2	0	24	14	12.00	-	-	-	-
Benson & Hedges Cup	1	1	0	0	0	0.00	-	-	1	-
ALL FIRST-CLASS	12	15	3	264	37	22.00	-	-	6	-
ALL ONE-DAY	7	7	0	45	14	6.42	-	-	1	-

BOWLING AVERAGES

	Overs	Mdns	Runs	Wkts	Avge	Best	5wI	10wM
Britannic Assurance	304.5	58	992	25	39.68	6-70	1	-
Refuge Assurance	28	4	121	3	40.33	1-17	-	-
NatWest Trophy	16	4	57	1	57.00	1-29	-	-
Benson & Hedges Cup	10	0	37	2	18.50	2-37	-	-
ALL FIRST-CLASS	304.5	58	992	25	39.68	6-70	1	-
ALL ONE-DAY	54	8	215	6	35.83	2-37	-	-

G.R. DILLEY - *Worcestershire*

Opposition	Venue	Date	Batting	Fielding	Bowling
BRITANNIC ASSURANCE					
Lancashire	Old Trafford	April 26			0-80 & 0-9
Notts	Worcester	May 3	8	1Ct	1-13 & 5-62
Essex	Worcester	May 19	0 * & 40		0-76 & 0-33
Warwickshire	Edgbaston	May 26	32 *	1Ct	1-34 & 0-33
Gloucs	Worcester	July 7	17 *		1-26 & 3-16
Northants	Worcester	Aug 18	8		1-36 & 1-48
Warwickshire	Worcester	Aug 23	35		2-56 & 3-45
Notts	Trent Bridge	Aug 29			0-47
Gloucs	Bristol	Sept 7			0-54 & 0-43
Glamorgan	Worcester	Sept 18	45 *		1-35 & 5-72
BENSON & HEDGES CUP					
Gloucs	Bristol	April 24			3-43
Kent	Worcester	May 1			4-48
Glamorgan	Worcester	May 8	5 *		2-45
Warwickshire	Edgbaston	May 10			1-36
Glamorgan	Worcester	May 30			1-39

BATTING AVERAGES - Including fielding

	Matches	Inns	NO	Runs	HS	Avge	100s	50s	Ct	St
Britannic Assurance	10	8	4	185	45*	46.25	-	-	2	-
Benson & Hedges Cup	5	1	1	5	5*		-	-	-	-
ALL FIRST-CLASS	10	8	4	185	45*	46.25	-	-	2	-
ALL ONE-DAY	5	1	1	5	5*		-	-	-	-

BOWLING AVERAGES

	Overs	Mdns	Runs	Wkts	Avge	Best	5wI	10wM
Britannic Assurance	224.2	30	818	24	34.08	5-62	2	-
Benson & Hedges Cup	50.5	4	211	11	19.18	4-48	-	-
ALL FIRST-CLASS	224.2	30	818	24	34.08	5-62	2	-
ALL ONE-DAY	50.5	4	211	11	19.18	4-48	-	-

D — PLAYER RECORDS

S.B. DIXON - *Norfolk*

Opposition	Venue	Date	Batting	Fielding	Bowling

NATWEST TROPHY

Opposition	Venue	Date	Batting	Fielding	Bowling
Yorkshire	Headingley	June 27	1		

BATTING AVERAGES - Including fielding

	Matches	Inns	NO	Runs	HS	Avge	100s	50s	Ct	St
NatWest Trophy	1	1	0	1	1	1.00	-	-	-	-
ALL ONE-DAY	1	1	0	1	1	1.00	-	-	-	-

BOWLING AVERAGES
Did not bowl

M.C. DOBSON - *Kent*

Opposition	Venue	Date	Batting	Fielding	Bowling
BRITANNIC ASSURANCE					
Lancashire	Maidstone	June 30	0 & 6		0-7

BATTING AVERAGES - Including fielding

	Matches	Inns	NO	Runs	HS	Avge	100s	50s	Ct	St
Britannic Assurance	1	2	0	6	6	3.00	-	-	-	-
ALL FIRST-CLASS	1	2	0	6	6	3.00	-	-	-	-

BOWLING AVERAGES

	Overs	Mdns	Runs	Wkts	Avge	Best	5wI	10wM
Britannic Assurance	3.1	1	7	0	-	-	-	-
ALL FIRST-CLASS	3.1	1	7	0	-	-	-	-

A.I.C. DODEMAIDE - *Sussex*

Opposition	Venue	Date	Batting	Fielding	Bowling
BRITANNIC ASSURANCE					
Surrey	Hove	April 26			1-96 & 1-38
Kent	Folkestone	May 3	9 & 13	1Ct	4-105 & 4-29
Hampshire	Southampton	May 15	10 & 37 *		2-161
Glamorgan	Hove	May 19	3 & 45		1-81
Somerset	Taunton	May 23	0 & 20		1-115
Lancashire	Horsham	June 2	70 & 14	1Ct	6-106
Gloucs	Hove	June 16	11	1Ct	3-95 & 0-6
Worcestershire	Worcester	June 20			0-32
Derbyshire	Hove	July 4	33		0-81
Notts	Trent Bridge	July 7	72 & 7		3-44 & 1-39
Surrey	Guildford	July 18	11	1Ct	4-84 & 1-23
Northants	Northampton	July 21	26 & 14		1-55 & 1-26
Hampshire	Arundel	July 25	2 & 2 *	2Ct	1-31 & 0-23
Essex	Chelmsford	July 28	79 * & 35 *	1Ct	1-41 & 0-46
Warwickshire	Eastbourne	Aug 4	4 & 1		3-84 & 2-45
Yorkshire	Eastbourne	Aug 8	40 & 0		0-57
Middlesex	Lord's	Aug 11	26	1Ct	2-75
Kent	Hove	Aug 18	13		3-123 & 1-43
Somerset	Hove	Aug 23	57 * & 112		4-117
Leicestershire	Leicester	Aug 29	17 * & 0	1Ct	0-30 & 1-64
Gloucs	Bristol	Sept 12	17 & 20		2-83
Middlesex	Hove	Sept 18	18 & 16		2-128
REFUGE ASSURANCE					
Derbyshire	Hove	April 22	24 *		0-38
Surrey	Hove	April 29	17		0-43
Glamorgan	Hove	May 20	25 *	1Ct	0-32
Leicestershire	Leicester	June 10	26		1-20
Yorkshire	Hove	June 17	20	1Ct	1-32
Worcestershire	Worcester	June 24	24	1Ct	3-27
Hampshire	Hove	July 1	1 *		3-50
Notts	Trent Bridge	July 8	22		0-46
Gloucs	Swindon	July 15	23	1Ct	2-22
Northants	Well'borough	July 22	19		1-38
Essex	Chelmsford	July 29	26 *	1Ct	1-51
Warwickshire	Eastbourne	Aug 5	3		2-21
Middlesex	Lord's	Aug 12	19 *		1-24
Somerset	Hove	Aug 26	31 *	1Ct	4-40
NATWEST TROPHY					
Ireland	Downpatrick	June 27			6-9
Glamorgan	Cardiff	July 11	1		2-70
BENSON & HEDGES CUP					
Derbyshire	Derby	April 24			1-37
Min Counties	Marlow	May 1		1Ct	0-52
Middlesex	Hove	May 8			2-36
Somerset	Hove	May 12	32		2-68
OTHER FIRST-CLASS					
New Zealand	Hove	May 26	4 & 110 *		1-56 & 1-57
Sri Lanka	Hove	Sept 5	33 *		1-73 & 2-65
OTHER ONE-DAY					
For Duchess of Norfolk's XI					
New Zealand	Arundel	May 6	131		
For Rest of World					
England XI	Jesmond	Aug 2	36		0-67
England XI	Jesmond	Aug 3		1Ct	1-32
For Sussex					
Kent	Hove	Sept 2	40		2-20

BATTING AVERAGES - Including fielding

	Matches	Inns	NO	Runs	HS	Avge	100s	50s	Ct	St
Britannic Assurance	22	35	6	854	112	29.44	1	4	9	-
Refuge Assurance	14	14	6	280	31 *	35.00	-	-	6	-
NatWest Trophy	2	1	0	1	1	1.00	-	-	-	-
Benson & Hedges Cup	4	1	0	32	32	32.00	-	-	1	-
Other First-Class	2	3	2	147	110 *	147.00	1	-	-	-
Other One-Day	4	3	0	207	131	69.00	1	-	1	-
ALL FIRST-CLASS	24	38	8	1001	112	33.36	2	4	9	-
ALL ONE-DAY	24	19	6	520	131	40.00	1	-	8	-

BOWLING AVERAGES

	Overs	Mdns	Runs	Wkts	Avge	Best	5wI	10wM
Britannic Assurance	681.1	112	2206	56	39.39	6-106	1	-
Refuge Assurance	109	7	484	19	25.47	4-40	-	-
NatWest Trophy	23	8	79	8	9.87	6-9	1	-
Benson & Hedges Cup	44	4	193	5	38.60	2-36	-	-
Other First-Class	82	18	251	5	50.20	2-65	-	-
Other One-Day	26	4	119	3	39.66	2-20	-	-
ALL FIRST-CLASS	763.1	130	2457	61	40.27	6-106	1	-
ALL ONE-DAY	202	23	875	35	25.00	6-9	1	-

M. DOIDGE - *Yorkshire*

Opposition	Venue	Date	Batting	Fielding	Bowling
OTHER FIRST-CLASS					
India	Headingley	June 30			0-54 & 0-52

BATTING AVERAGES - Including fielding

	Matches	Inns	NO	Runs	HS	Avge	100s	50s	Ct	St
Other First-Class	1	0	0	0	0	-	-	-	-	-
ALL FIRST-CLASS	1	0	0	0	0	-	-	-	-	-

BOWLING AVERAGES

	Overs	Mdns	Runs	Wkts	Avge	Best	5wI	10wM
Other First-Class	24	5	106	0	-	-	-	-
ALL FIRST-CLASS	24	5	106	0	-	-	-	-

D.B. D'OLIVEIRA - *Worcestershire*

Opposition	Venue	Date	Batting	Fielding	Bowling
BRITANNIC ASSURANCE					
Lancashire	Old Trafford	April 26	155		0-12
Notts	Worcester	May 3	9		
Essex	Worcester	May 19	32 & 25	1Ct	
Warwickshire	Edgbaston	May 26	29	2Ct	

PLAYER RECORDS

Yorkshire	Worcester	June 2	41				4Ct	
Surrey	The Oval	June 16	0				1Ct	
Sussex	Worcester	June 20			79			
Middlesex	Lord's	June 30	13	&	87 *		1Ct	
Gloucs	Worcester	July 7	69	&	26		4Ct	
Somerset	Worcester	July 18	55	&	24			
Glamorgan	Abergavenny	July 21	121				2Ct	0-39
Derbyshire	Derby	July 25	87					
Kent	Canterbury	July 28	21	&	4		2Ct	
Leicestershire	Leicester	Aug 4	5	&	44 *		3Ct	
Lancashire	Kid'minster	Aug 8	59				3Ct	
Hampshire	Worcester	Aug 11	30				3Ct	0-6
Northants	Worcester	Aug 18	0	&	21		1Ct	
Warwickshire	Worcester	Aug 23	0	&	30		2Ct	
Gloucs	Bristol	Sept 7	5	&	0			2-23
Somerset	Taunton	Sept 12	14	&	60		3Ct	
Glamorgan	Worcester	Sept 18	22	&	12		1Ct	

REFUGE ASSURANCE

Somerset	Taunton	April 22	0 *	
Derbyshire	Derby	April 29	10	
Notts	Worcester	May 6	6	
Essex	Worcester	May 20	41	
Warwickshire	Worcester	May 27	3	
Yorkshire	Worcester	June 3	1	1Ct
Surrey	The Oval	June 17	53	
Sussex	Worcester	June 24	16	
Middlesex	Lord's	July 1	2	
Gloucs	Worcester	July 8		
Lancashire	Old Trafford	July 15	3	
Kent	Canterbury	July 29	35	1Ct
Leicestershire	Leicester	Aug 5	24	
Northants	Worcester	Aug 19	58	
Glamorgan	Swansea	Aug 26	14	1Ct

NATWEST TROPHY

Suffolk	Bury St Ed's	June 27	33 *		2-17
Somerset	Taunton	July 11	51 *		
Northants	Northampton	Aug 1	2		

BENSON & HEDGES CUP

Gloucs	Bristol	April 24	2	1Ct
Kent	Worcester	May 1	7	1Ct
Glamorgan	Worcester	May 8	57	1Ct
Warwickshire	Edgbaston	May 10	3	
Glamorgan	Worcester	May 30	12 *	2Ct
Notts	Trent Bridge	June 13		1Ct
Lancashire	Lord's	July 14	23	

OTHER FIRST-CLASS

MCC	Lord's	April 17	12		
New Zealand	Worcester	May 12	48	&	24

BATTING AVERAGES - Including fielding

	Matches	Inns	NO	Runs	HS	Avge	100s	50s	Ct	St
Britannic Assurance	21	32	2	1179	155	39.30	2	7	33	-
Refuge Assurance	15	14	1	266	58	20.46	-	2	3	-
NatWest Trophy	3	3	2	86	51 *	86.00	-	1	-	-
Benson & Hedges Cup	7	6	1	104	57	20.80	-	1	6	-
Other First-Class	2	3	0	84	48	28.00	-	-	-	-
ALL FIRST-CLASS	23	35	2	1263	155	38.27	2	7	33	-
ALL ONE-DAY	25	23	4	456	58	24.00	-	4	9	-

BOWLING AVERAGES

	Overs	Mdns	Runs	Wkts	Avge	Best	5wI	10wM
Britannic Assurance	11.3	1	80	2	40.00	2-23	-	-
Refuge Assurance								
NatWest Trophy	5	0	17	2	8.50	2-17	-	
Benson & Hedges Cup								
Other First-Class								
ALL FIRST-CLASS	11.3	1	80	2	40.00	2-23	-	-
ALL ONE-DAY	5	0	17	2	8.50	2-17	-	

D.F. DOLPHIN - *Zimbabwe*

Opposition	Venue	Date	Batting	Fielding	Bowling

OTHER FIRST-CLASS

Gloucs	Bristol	May 19			0-58 & 1-29
Lancashire	Old Trafford	May 23	25		0-28 & 0-19

BATTING AVERAGES - Including fielding

	Matches	Inns	NO	Runs	HS	Avge	100s	50s	Ct	St
Other First-Class	2	1	0	25	25	25.00	-	-	-	-
ALL FIRST-CLASS	2	1	0	25	25	25.00	-	-	-	-

BOWLING AVERAGES

	Overs	Mdns	Runs	Wkts	Avge	Best	5wI	10wM
Other First-Class	39	10	134	1	134.00	1-29	-	-
ALL FIRST-CLASS	39	10	134	1	134.00	1-29	-	-

A.A. DONALD - *Warwickshire*

Opposition	Venue	Date	Batting			Fielding	Bowling

BRITANNIC ASSURANCE

Yorkshire	Edgbaston	May 3	16				2-56 & 1-41
Northants	Northampton	May 15	24				1-51 & 1-45
Notts	Edgbaston	May 19	24 *	&	9 *		1-38 & 0-5
Worcestershire	Edgbaston	May 26	10 *	&	0		2-54 & 0-10
Northants	Edgbaston	June 2	0	&	1		1-56
Middlesex	Lord's	June 6					3-60 & 1-26
Essex	Edgbaston	June 9					1-53
Yorkshire	Sheffield	June 20	4				1-30 & 1-65
Kent	Edgbaston	June 23	0	&	1		1-19 & 3-28
Somerset	Taunton	July 4					1-58 & 0-27
Surrey	The Oval	July 7	0	&	3		1-31
Somerset	Edgbaston	Sept 7	7	&	1		1-91 & 0-36
Glamorgan	Edgbaston	Sept 12	7	&	3		2-51 & 3-33
Lancashire	Old Trafford	Sept 18	8				0-24

BENSON & HEDGES CUP

Glamorgan	Edgbaston	April 24			1-42

OTHER FIRST-CLASS

New Zealand	Edgbaston	May 30	25 *	&	1		0-24 & 0-9
Sri Lanka	Edgbaston	Aug 29	4 *	&	0 *		0-33 & 1-35

OTHER ONE-DAY

Surrey	Harrogate	June 13	0		1Ct	1-41
Yorkshire	Harrogate	June 15				1-53
Surrey	Hove	Sept 3	16 *			1-24

BATTING AVERAGES - Including fielding

	Matches	Inns	NO	Runs	HS	Avge	100s	50s	Ct	St
Britannic Assurance	14	18	3	118	24 *	7.86	-	-	-	-
Benson & Hedges Cup	1	0	0	0	0	-	-	-	-	-
Other First-Class	2	4	3	30	25 *	30.00	-	-	-	-
Other One-Day	3	2	1	16	16 *	16.00	-	-	1	-
ALL FIRST-CLASS	16	22	6	148	25 *	9.25	-	-	-	-
ALL ONE-DAY	4	2	1	16	16 *	16.00	-	-	1	-

BOWLING AVERAGES

	Overs	Mdns	Runs	Wkts	Avge	Best	5wI	10wM
Britannic Assurance	355.1	81	988	28	35.28	3-28	-	-
Benson & Hedges Cup	11	1	42	1	42.00	1-42		
Other First-Class	35.5	8	101	1	101.00	1-35		
Other One-Day	32	3	118	3	39.33	1-24		
ALL FIRST-CLASS	391	89	1089	29	37.55	3-28	-	-
ALL ONE-DAY	43	4	160	4	40.00	1-24		

B.T.P. DONELAN - *Sussex*

Opposition	Venue	Date	Batting			Fielding	Bowling

BRITANNIC ASSURANCE

Lancashire	Horsham	June 2	8	&	0	1Ct	0-27 & 0-1
Surrey	Guildford	July 18	11 *				0-42 & 1-70
Hampshire	Arundel	July 25	11 *			1Ct	0-44 & 3-79
Essex	Chelmsford	July 28	31	&	12 *		0-33 & 3-86
Warwickshire	Eastbourne	Aug 4	6	&	53		1-46 & 2-19
Yorkshire	Eastbourne	Aug 8	9	&	10 *		2-97
Middlesex	Lord's	Aug 11	8 *				2-116 & 2-38
Kent	Hove	Aug 18					2-59 & 0-7

D | PLAYER RECORDS

Gloucs	Bristol	Sept 12	37 * & 15	1Ct	1-89

REFUGE ASSURANCE

Essex	Chelmsford	July 29			1-43
Middlesex	Lord's	Aug 12			1-23
Somerset	Hove	Aug 26	4		0-37

OTHER FIRST-CLASS

New Zealand	Hove	May 26		1Ct	1-15 & 0-62
Cambridge U	Hove	June 30			0-26 & 0-44

OTHER ONE-DAY

Yorkshire	Harrogate	June 14	4		0-25
Kent	Hove	Sept 2	10		3-34

BATTING AVERAGES - Including fielding

	Matches	Inns	NO	Runs	HS	Avge	100s	50s	Ct	St
Britannic Assurance	9	13	6	211	53	30.14	-	1	3	-
Refuge Assurance	3	1	0	4	4	4.00	-	-	-	-
Other First-Class	2	0	0	0	0	-	-	-	1	-
Other One-Day	2	2	0	14	10	7.00	-	-	-	-
ALL FIRST-CLASS	11	13	6	211	53	30.14	-	1	4	-
ALL ONE-DAY	5	3	0	18	10	6.00	-	-	-	-

BOWLING AVERAGES

	Overs	Mdns	Runs	Wkts	Avge	Best	5wI	10wM
Britannic Assurance	258.4	50	853	19	44.89	3-79	-	-
Refuge Assurance	22	2	103	2	51.50	1-23	-	
Other First-Class	46	6	147	1	147.00	1-15	-	
Other One-Day	21	4	59	3	19.66	3-34	-	
ALL FIRST-CLASS	304.4	56	1000	20	50.00	3-79	-	-
ALL ONE-DAY	43	6	162	5	32.40	3-34	-	-

K. DONOHUE - *Devon*

Opposition	Venue	Date	Batting	Fielding	Bowling

NATWEST TROPHY

Somerset	Torquay	June 27	18 *		0-101

BATTING AVERAGES - Including fielding

	Matches	Inns	NO	Runs	HS	Avge	100s	50s	Ct	St
NatWest Trophy	1	1	1	18	18 *	-	-	-	-	-
ALL ONE-DAY	1	1	1	18	18 *	-	-	-	-	-

BOWLING AVERAGES

	Overs	Mdns	Runs	Wkts	Avge	Best	5wI	10wM
NatWest Trophy	12	2	101	0	-	-	-	
ALL ONE-DAY	12	2	101	0	-	-	-	-

P.R. DOWNTON - *Middlesex*

Opposition	Venue	Date	Batting	Fielding	Bowling

BRITANNIC ASSURANCE

Essex	Lord's	April 26	47 & 42 *	4Ct	
Kent	Lord's	May 15	19	3Ct	
Surrey	Lord's	May 23	3 & 55	2Ct	
Gloucs	Lord's	May 26	63 & 25	0Ct,2St	
Essex	Ilford	June 2		5Ct	
Warwickshire	Lord's	June 6	4 & 11		
Notts	Trent Bridge	July 28	16 & 20	3Ct	
Glamorgan	Lord's	Aug 4	4 & 6	3Ct	
Hampshire	Bournemouth	Aug 8	38 & 38		
Sussex	Lord's	Aug 11	3	2Ct	
Derbyshire	Derby	Aug 18	4 & 3	2Ct	
Yorkshire	Headingley	Aug 23	12 & 1	6Ct	
Notts	Lord's	Sept 7	63	3Ct	
Surrey	The Oval	Sept 12	48	3Ct	1-4
Sussex	Hove	Sept 18	5	4Ct	

REFUGE ASSURANCE

Lancashire	Old Trafford	April 22	

Essex	Lord's	April 29	6	2Ct,1St	
Kent	Folkestone	May 6	9 *	0Ct,2St	
Notts	Lord's	May 13	10		
Gloucs	Lord's	May 27		1Ct	
Warwickshire	Lord's	June 3			
Hampshire	Basingstoke	June 10		1Ct	
Glamorgan	Lord's	Aug 5		0Ct,1St	
Sussex	Lord's	Aug 12	23		
Derbyshire	Derby	Aug 19			
Yorkshire	Scarborough	Aug 26	28		
Lancashire	Old Trafford	Sept 5	14	1Ct,1St	
Derbyshire	Edgbaston	Sept 16	34 *		

NATWEST TROPHY

Glamorgan	Lord's	Aug 1			
Lancashire	Old Trafford	Aug 15	4 *	2Ct	

BENSON & HEDGES CUP

Min Counties	Lord's	April 24	17 *	1Ct	
Sussex	Hove	May 8	15 *	1Ct	
Somerset	Lord's	May 10	15	2Ct	
Derbyshire	Derby	May 12	40	2Ct	
Somerset	Taunton	May 30	15	3Ct	

OTHER FIRST-CLASS

New Zealand	Lord's	May 19	57 *	2Ct,1St	

BATTING AVERAGES - Including fielding

	Matches	Inns	NO	Runs	HS	Avge	100s	50s	Ct	St
Britannic Assurance	15	23	1	530	63	24.09	-	3	40	1
Refuge Assurance	13	7	2	124	34 *	24.80	-	-	5	5
NatWest Trophy	2	1	1	4	4 *	-	-	-	2	-
Benson & Hedges Cup	5	5	2	102	40	34.00	-	-	9	-
Other First-Class	1	1	1	57	57 *	-	-	1	2	1
ALL FIRST-CLASS	16	24	2	587	63	26.68	-	4	42	3
ALL ONE-DAY	20	13	5	230	40	28.75	-	-	16	5

BOWLING AVERAGES

	Overs	Mdns	Runs	Wkts	Avge	Best	5wI	10wM
Britannic Assurance	1.1	0	4	1	4.00	1-4	-	-
Refuge Assurance								
NatWest Trophy								
Benson & Hedges Cup								
Other First-Class								
ALL FIRST-CLASS	1.1	0	4	1	4.00	1-4	-	-
ALL ONE-DAY								

E. DUBE - *Zimbabwe*

Opposition	Venue	Date	Batting	Fielding	Bowling

OTHER FIRST-CLASS

Yorkshire	Headingley	May 16	1		0-19 & 0-22
Lancashire	Old Trafford	May 23			0-48 & 0-18

OTHER ONE-DAY

Sussex	Hove	May 13	0 *		0-43

BATTING AVERAGES - Including fielding

	Matches	Inns	NO	Runs	HS	Avge	100s	50s	Ct	St
Other First-Class	2	1	0	1	1	1.00	-	-	-	-
Other One-Day	1	1	1	0	0 *	-	-	-	-	-
ALL FIRST-CLASS	2	1	0	1	1	1.00	-	-	-	-
ALL ONE-DAY	1	1	1	0	0 *	-	-	-	-	-

BOWLING AVERAGES

	Overs	Mdns	Runs	Wkts	Avge	Best	5wI	10wM
Other First-Class	25	4	107	0	-	-	-	-
Other One-Day	8	0	43	0	-	-	-	-
ALL FIRST-CLASS	25	4	107	0	-	-	-	-
ALL ONE-DAY	8	0	43	0	-	-	-	-

PLAINER RECORDS

D

K.G. DUERS - *Zimbabwe*

Opposition	Venue	Date	Batting	Fielding	Bowling
OTHER FIRST-CLASS					
Yorkshire	Headingley	May 16	11 *		2-63 & 0-48
Lancashire	Old Trafford	May 23			2-96 & 1-59
OTHER ONE-DAY					
Essex	Chelmsford	May 14		1	2-52

BATTING AVERAGES - Including fielding

	Matches	Inns	NO	Runs	HS	Avge	100s	50s	Ct	St
Other First-Class	2	1	1	11	11 *	-	-	-	-	-
Other One-Day	1	1	0	1	1	1.00	-	-	-	-
ALL FIRST-CLASS	2	1	1	11	11 *	-	-	-	-	-
ALL ONE-DAY	1	1	0	1	1	1.00	-	-	-	-

BOWLING AVERAGES

	Overs	Mdns	Runs	Wkts	Avge	Best	5wI	10wM
Other First-Class	74	17	266	5	53.20	2-63	-	-
Other One-Day	11	0	52	2	26.00	2-52	-	
ALL FIRST-CLASS	74	17	266	5	53.20	2-63	-	-
ALL ONE-DAY	11	0	52	2	26.00	2-52	-	

A.R. DUNLOP - *Ireland*

Opposition	Venue	Date	Batting	Fielding	Bowling
NATWEST TROPHY					
Sussex	Downpatrick	June 27	1		
OTHER FIRST-CLASS					
Scotland	Edinburgh	Aug 11	56	1Ct	0-37

BATTING AVERAGES - Including fielding

	Matches	Inns	NO	Runs	HS	Avge	100s	50s	Ct	St
NatWest Trophy	1	1	0	1	1	1.00	-	-	-	-
Other First-Class	1	1	0	56	56	56.00	-	1	1	-
ALL FIRST-CLASS	1	1	0	56	56	56.00	-	1	1	-
ALL ONE-DAY	1	1	0	1	1	1.00	-	-	-	-

BOWLING AVERAGES

	Overs	Mdns	Runs	Wkts	Avge	Best	5wI	10wM
NatWest Trophy								
Other First-Class	10	0	37	0	-	-	-	-
ALL FIRST-CLASS	10	0	37	0	-	-	-	-
ALL ONE-DAY								

P.G. DUTHIE - *Scotland*

Opposition	Venue	Date	Batting	Fielding	Bowling
NATWEST TROPHY					
Essex	Chelmsford	June 27	0		0-37

BATTING AVERAGES - Including fielding

	Matches	Inns	NO	Runs	HS	Avge	100s	50s	Ct	St
NatWest Trophy	1	1	0	0	0	0.00	-	-	-	-
ALL ONE-DAY	1	1	0	0	0	0.00	-	-	-	-

BOWLING AVERAGES

	Overs	Mdns	Runs	Wkts	Avge	Best	5wI	10wM
NatWest Trophy	8	0	37	0	-	-	-	-
ALL ONE-DAY	8	0	37	0	-	-	-	-

A.J. DUTTON - *Staffordshire*

Opposition	Venue	Date	Batting	Fielding	Bowling
NATWEST TROPHY					
Northants	Northampton	June 27	32		0-52

BATTING AVERAGES - Including fielding

	Matches	Inns	NO	Runs	HS	Avge	100s	50s	Ct	St
NatWest Trophy	1	1	0	32	32	32.00	-	-	-	-
ALL ONE-DAY	1	1	0	32	32	32.00	-	-	-	-

BOWLING AVERAGES

	Overs	Mdns	Runs	Wkts	Avge	Best	5wI	10wM
NatWest Trophy	12	1	52	0	-	-	-	
ALL ONE-DAY	12	1	52	0	-	-	-	

G.B.A. DYER - *Cambridge University*

Opposition	Venue	Date	Batting	Fielding	Bowling
OTHER FIRST-CLASS					
Warwickshire	Fenner's	April 26	19 & 20 *		
Middlesex	Fenner's	May 3	23 & 9 *		
Essex	Fenner's	May 16	17 & 14		
Gloucs	Fenner's	May 23	1 & 4		

BATTING AVERAGES - Including fielding

	Matches	Inns	NO	Runs	HS	Avge	100s	50s	Ct	St
Other First-Class	4	8	2	107	23	17.83	-	-	-	-
ALL FIRST-CLASS	4	8	2	107	23	17.83	-	-	-	-

BOWLING AVERAGES
Did not bowl

R.J. DYER - *Staffordshire*

Opposition	Venue	Date	Batting	Fielding	Bowling
NATWEST TROPHY					
Northants	Northampton	June 27			0-49

BATTING AVERAGES - Including fielding

	Matches	Inns	NO	Runs	HS	Avge	100s	50s	Ct	St
NatWest Trophy	1	0	0	0	0	-	-	-	-	-
ALL ONE-DAY	1	0	0	0	0	-	-	-	-	-

BOWLING AVERAGES

	Overs	Mdns	Runs	Wkts	Avge	Best	5wI	10wM
NatWest Trophy	8	0	49	0	-	-	-	-
ALL ONE-DAY	8	0	49	0	-	-	-	-

E PLAYER RECORDS

M.A. EALHAM - Kent

Opposition	Venue	Date	Batting	Fielding	Bowling
BRITANNIC ASSURANCE					
Middlesex	Lord's	May 15	0 & 13*		1-39 & 2-33
Glamorgan	Swansea	May 23			0-48
REFUGE ASSURANCE					
Essex	Chelmsford	April 22		2Ct	0-29
Hampshire	Canterbury	April 29			0-35
Middlesex	Folkestone	May 6		1Ct	1-47
Glamorgan	Llanelli	May 13	29*	1Ct	0-37
Yorkshire	Canterbury	May 20			2-25
Northants	Northampton	May 27		1Ct	0-33
Somerset	Canterbury	June 10			0-42
Notts	Canterbury	June 17	2	1Ct	0-18
Warwickshire	Edgbaston	June 24	25	2Ct	
Lancashire	Maidstone	July 1	3	1Ct	0-21
BENSON & HEDGES CUP					
Worcestershire	Worcester	May 1	5		4-57
Warwickshire	Canterbury	May 8	0	1Ct	2-37
Gloucs	Canterbury	May 10			2-47
Glamorgan	Swansea	May 12	17*		
OTHER ONE-DAY					
Sussex	Hove	Sept 2	4	1Ct	0-14
Surrey	Hove	Sept 4		1Ct	8-49

BATTING AVERAGES - Including fielding

	Matches	Inns	NO	Runs	HS	Avge	100s	50s	Ct	St
Britannic Assurance	2	2	1	13	13*	13.00	-	-	-	-
Refuge Assurance	10	4	1	59	29*	19.66	-	-	9	-
Benson & Hedges Cup	4	3	1	22	17*	11.00	-	-	1	-
Other One-Day	2	1	0	4	4	4.00	-	-	2	-
ALL FIRST-CLASS	2	2	1	13	13*	13.00	-	-	-	-
ALL ONE-DAY	16	8	2	85	29*	14.16	-	-	12	-

BOWLING AVERAGES

	Overs	Mdns	Runs	Wkts	Avge	Best	5wI	10wM
Britannic Assurance	34.2	5	120	3	40.00	2-33	-	-
Refuge Assurance	53	1	287	3	95.66	2-25	-	-
Benson & Hedges Cup	30	1	141	8	17.62	4-57	-	-
Other One-Day	12.4	0	63	8	7.87	8-49	1	
ALL FIRST-CLASS	34.2	5	120	3	40.00	2-33	-	-
ALL ONE-DAY	95.4	2	491	19	25.84	8-49	1	

J.W. EDRICH - Suffolk

Opposition	Venue	Date	Batting	Fielding	Bowling
NATWEST TROPHY					
Worcestershire	Bury St Ed's	June 27	52		

BATTING AVERAGES - Including fielding

	Matches	Inns	NO	Runs	HS	Avge	100s	50s	Ct	St
NatWest Trophy	1	1	0	52	52	52.00	-	1	-	-
ALL ONE-DAY	1	1	0	52	52	52.00	-	1	-	-

BOWLING AVERAGES
Did not bowl

J.H. EDWARDS - Devon

Opposition	Venue	Date	Batting	Fielding	Bowling
NATWEST TROPHY					
Somerset	Torquay	June 27	4		

BATTING AVERAGES - Including fielding

	Matches	Inns	NO	Runs	HS	Avge	100s	50s	Ct	St
NatWest Trophy	1	1	0	4	4	4.00	-	-	-	-
ALL ONE-DAY	1	1	0	4	4	4.00	-	-	-	-

BOWLING AVERAGES
Did not bowl

M.T. ELLIS - Norfolk

Opposition	Venue	Date	Batting	Fielding	Bowling
NATWEST TROPHY					
Yorkshire	Headingley	June 27	0*		0-12

BATTING AVERAGES - Including fielding

	Matches	Inns	NO	Runs	HS	Avge	100s	50s	Ct	St
NatWest Trophy	1	1	1	0	0*	-	-	-	-	-
ALL ONE-DAY	1	1	1	0	0*	-	-	-	-	-

BOWLING AVERAGES

	Overs	Mdns	Runs	Wkts	Avge	Best	5wI	10wM
NatWest Trophy	2.2	0	12	0	-	-	-	-
ALL ONE-DAY	2.2	0	12	0	-	-	-	-

R.M. ELLISON - Kent

Opposition	Venue	Date	Batting	Fielding	Bowling
BRITANNIC ASSURANCE					
Hampshire	Canterbury	April 26	0	1Ct	0-43 & 0-12
Sussex	Folkestone	May 3	81		3-70 & 0-10
Yorkshire	Tunbridge We	June 6			
Somerset	Canterbury	June 9	31* & 6*	1Ct	0-101 & 0-38
Warwickshire	Edgbaston	June 23	6 & 8*		2-36 & 0-23
Lancashire	Maidstone	June 30	41 & 12*		0-38 & 1-41
Essex	Maidstone	June 4			0-46
Northants	Northampton	July 18	24	1Ct	3-85
Surrey	Guildford	July 21	10 & 0		2-44
Middlesex	Canterbury	July 25	9		1-37 & 0-45
Worcestershire	Canterbury	July 28	0 & 1		2-65 & 1-33
Derbyshire	Chesterfield	Aug 4	41 & 62		0-26
Essex	Chelmsford	Sept 12	44* & 68*	2Ct	4-76
REFUGE ASSURANCE					
Essex	Chelmsford	April 22	0	1Ct	2-45
Hampshire	Canterbury	April 29	3*		1-23
Middlesex	Folkestone	May 6	11*		1-32
Notts	Canterbury	June 17	9	1Ct	0-18
Warwickshire	Edgbaston	June 24	8		0-27
Lancashire	Maidstone	July 1	43		0-24
Surrey	The Oval	July 22	0		1-33
Worcestershire	Canterbury	July 29	9*		1-37
NATWEST TROPHY					
Gloucs	Bristol	July 11	27*	1Ct	1-18
BENSON & HEDGES CUP					
Worcestershire	Worcester	May 1	12	1Ct	0-14
OTHER FIRST-CLASS					
Cambridge U	Fenner's	June 20			0-20 & 0-24
India	Canterbury	July 7	29*	1Ct	0-27 & 0-23

BATTING AVERAGES - Including fielding

	Matches	Inns	NO	Runs	HS	Avge	100s	50s	Ct	St
Britannic Assurance	13	18	6	444	81	37.00	-	3	5	-
Refuge Assurance	8	8	3	83	43	16.60	-	-	2	-
NatWest Trophy	1	1	1	27	27*	-	-	-	1	-
Benson & Hedges Cup	1	1	0	12	12	12.00	-	-	1	-
Other First-Class	2	1	1	29	29*	-	-	-	1	-
ALL FIRST-CLASS	15	19	7	473	81	39.41	-	3	6	-
ALL ONE-DAY	10	10	4	122	43	20.33	-	-	4	-

BOWLING AVERAGES

	Overs	Mdns	Runs	Wkts	Avge	Best	5wI	10wM
Britannic Assurance	260.5	45	869	19	45.73	4-76	-	-
Refuge Assurance	52	0	239	6	39.83	2-45	-	

PLANER RECORDS

NatWest Trophy	12	6	18	1	18.00	1-18	-
Benson & Hedges Cup	6	2	14	0	-	-	-
Other First-Class	48	6	94	0	-	-	-
ALL FIRST-CLASS	308.5	51	963	19	50.68	4-76	-
ALL ONE-DAY	70	8	271	7	38.71	2-45	-

J.E. EMBUREY - *Middlesex*

Opposition	Venue	Date	Batting			Fielding	Bowling
BRITANNIC ASSURANCE							
Essex	Lord's	April 26	41	&	21 *	1Ct	0-53 & 0-23
Kent	Lord's	May 15	3			4Ct	0-7 & 0-16
Surrey	Lord's	May 23	10	&	17		1-58
Gloucs	Lord's	May 26	38 *	&	30 *	2Ct	1-63 & 4-69
Essex	Ilford	June 2					5-61 & 0-80
Warwickshire	Lord's	June 6	18	&	5 *	2Ct	1-48
Leicestershire	Leicester	June 16	16				0-2 & 4-57
Lancashire	Old Trafford	June 20			6	2Ct	1-35
Northants	Luton	June 23	13				4-55 & 3-80
Worcestershire	Lord's	June 30	9			4Ct	2-27 & 0-52
Yorkshire	Uxbridge	July 18	45			3Ct	4-51 & 3-62
Somerset	Uxbridge	July 21	1 *	&	11	1Ct	0-57 & 1-52
Kent	Canterbury	July 25			0	1Ct	0-93 & 3-3
Notts	Trent Bridge	July 28	0	&	10	1Ct	3-61 & 0-16
Glamorgan	Lord's	Aug 4	23	&	7		1-88 & 0-28
Hampshire	Bournemouth	Aug 8	111 *	&	36	1Ct	0-63
Sussex	Lord's	Aug 11	14				2-85
Derbyshire	Derby	Aug 18	14	&	12		5-32 & 4-71
Yorkshire	Headingley	Aug 23	0	&	51	4Ct	0-43 & 0-32
Notts	Lord's	Sept 7	22 *				0-33 & 2-85
Surrey	The Oval	Sept 12	66			3Ct	2-96 & 1-49
Sussex	Hove	Sept 18	48			2Ct	0-12 & 0-13
REFUGE ASSURANCE							
Lancashire	Old Trafford	April 22				1Ct	1-35
Essex	Lord's	April 29	10 *			1Ct	3-49
Kent	Folkestone	May 6					2-36
Notts	Lord's	May 13	4			1Ct	0-53
Gloucs	Lord's	May 27					2-30
Warwickshire	Lord's	June 3					2-21
Hampshire	Basingstoke	June 10					2-19
Leicestershire	Leicester	June 17	5 *				1-52
Northants	Northampton	June 24					4-26
Worcestershire	Lord's	July 1	8 *				4-39
Somerset	Lord's	July 8	32				1-40
Surrey	The Oval	July 15	15				2-39
Glamorgan	Lord's	Aug 5	6 *				4-32
Sussex	Lord's	Aug 12	27			1Ct	0-30
Derbyshire	Derby	Aug 19					1-30
Yorkshire	Scarborough	Aug 26	14				1-57
Lancashire	Old Trafford	Sept 5	0				4-39
Derbyshire	Edgbaston	Sept 16	5 *				0-37
NATWEST TROPHY							
Berkshire	Lord's	June 27	4 *				1-17
Surrey	Uxbridge	July 11	15 *				0-76
Glamorgan	Lord's	Aug 1				1Ct	3-27
Lancashire	Old Trafford	Aug 15					0-54
BENSON & HEDGES CUP							
Min Counties	Lord's	April 24	0			1Ct	2-27
Sussex	Hove	May 8	4 *			1Ct	1-57
Somerset	Lord's	May 10	12			1Ct	1-37
Derbyshire	Derby	May 12	1				1-41
Somerset	Taunton	May 30	6 *			1Ct	2-36
OTHER FIRST-CLASS							
Cambridge U	Fenner's	May 3			4	2Ct	4-33 & 0-13

BATTING AVERAGES - Including fielding

	Matches	Inns	NO	Runs	HS	Avge	100s	50s	Ct	St
Britannic Assurance	22	31	7	698	111 *	29.08	1	2	31	-
Refuge Assurance	18	11	5	126	32	21.00	-	-	4	-
NatWest Trophy	4	2	2	19	15 *	-	-	-	1	-
Benson & Hedges Cup	5	5	2	23	12	7.66	-	-	4	-
Other First-Class	1	1	0	4	4	4.00	-	-	2	-
ALL FIRST-CLASS	23	32	7	702	111 *	28.08	1	2	33	-
ALL ONE-DAY	27	18	9	168	32	18.66	-	-	9	-

BOWLING AVERAGES

	Overs	Mdns	Runs	Wkts	Avge	Best	5wI	10wM
Britannic Assurance	902	254	1911	57	33.52	5-32	2	-
Refuge Assurance	129.1	12	664	34	19.52	4-26	-	-
NatWest Trophy	46	7	174	4	43.50	3-27	-	-
Benson & Hedges Cup	51.2	3	198	7	28.28	2-27	-	-
Other First-Class	40.3	21	46	4	11.50	4-33	-	-
ALL FIRST-CLASS	942.3	275	1957	61	32.08	5-32	2	-
ALL ONE-DAY	226.3	22	1036	45	23.02	4-26	-	-

B.G. EVANS - *Hertfordshire*

Opposition	Venue	Date	Batting	Fielding	Bowling
NATWEST TROPHY					
Warwickshire	St Albans	June 27	27	1Ct	

BATTING AVERAGES - Including fielding

	Matches	Inns	NO	Runs	HS	Avge	100s	50s	Ct	St
NatWest Trophy	1	1	0	27	27	27.00	-	-	1	-
ALL ONE-DAY	1	1	0	27	27	27.00	-	-	1	-

BOWLING AVERAGES
Did not bowl

K.P. EVANS - *Nottinghamshire*

Opposition	Venue	Date	Batting			Fielding	Bowling
BRITANNIC ASSURANCE							
Yorkshire	Scarborough	July 4			12 *		2-73
Sussex	Trent Bridge	July 7	29	&	21 *	1Ct	3-69 & 0-47
Hampshire	Portsmouth	July 18	8	&	7	2Ct	3-76
Lancashire	Southport	July 25	48 *	&	34 *	2Ct	4-57 & 0-15
Middlesex	Trent Bridge	July 28	28 *	&	24 *		3-54 & 1-72
Essex	Southend	Aug 4	51	&	31		2-53
Somerset	Weston	Aug 8	0	&	100 *		1-57
Glamorgan	Worksop	Aug 11	60 *	&	26	1Ct	1-69 & 0-37
Gloucs	Trent Bridge	Aug 18	0	&	0	1Ct	0-51 & 0-38
Worcestershire	Trent Bridge	Aug 29	12	&	0		1-49 & 0-3
Lancashire	Trent Bridge	Sept 12	49	&	55		4-95 & 0-20
Yorkshire	Trent Bridge	Sept 18	43			2Ct	0-71 & 2-79
REFUGE ASSURANCE							
Lancashire	Trent Bridge	April 29	0				1-42
Derbyshire	Derby	June 10				1Ct	1-39
Kent	Canterbury	June 17	30			1Ct	0-34
Somerset	Bath	June 24	18 *				1-40
Leicestershire	Trent Bridge	July 1					4-30
Sussex	Trent Bridge	July 8	7 *				0-46
Warwickshire	Edgbaston	July 22	1				1-57
Northants	Trent Bridge	July 29	28 *				1-42
Essex	Southend	Aug 5					2-52
Glamorgan	Trent Bridge	Aug 12				1Ct	0-47
Gloucs	Trent Bridge	Aug 19					0-27
Derbyshire	Derby	Sept 5	55 *			1Ct	1-58
NATWEST TROPHY							
Northants	Northampton	July 11	0			1Ct	2-53
OTHER FIRST-CLASS							
Oxford U	The Parks	June 6	43 *				1-13
Cambridge U	Fenner's	June 16				3Ct	4-50 & 2-27
Sri Lanka	Cleethorpes	Aug 25	55	&	2	1Ct	0-38 & 0-19

BATTING AVERAGES - Including fielding

	Matches	Inns	NO	Runs	HS	Avge	100s	50s	Ct	St
Britannic Assurance	12	22	8	638	100 *	45.57	1	3	9	-
Refuge Assurance	12	7	4	139	55 *	46.33	-	1	4	-
NatWest Trophy	1	1	0	0	0	0.00	-	-	1	-
Other First-Class	3	3	1	100	55	50.00	-	1	4	-
ALL FIRST-CLASS	15	25	9	738	100 *	46.12	1	4	13	-
ALL ONE-DAY	13	8	4	139	55 *	34.75	-	1	5	-

E — PLAYER RECORDS

BOWLING AVERAGES

	Overs	Mdns	Runs	Wkts	Avge	Best	5wI	10wM
Britannic Assurance	292	60	1085	27	40.18	4-57	-	-
Refuge Assurance	87.4	1	514	12	42.83	4-30	-	
NatWest Trophy	12	3	53	2	26.50	2-53	-	
Other First-Class	64	18	147	7	21.00	4-50	-	-
ALL FIRST-CLASS	356	78	1232	34	36.23	4-50	-	-
ALL ONE-DAY	99.4	4	567	14	40.50	4-30	-	

R.A. EVANS - *Oxfordshire & Minor Counties*

Opposition	Venue	Date	Batting	Fielding	Bowling
NATWEST TROPHY					
Kent	Oxford	June 27	24	1Ct	3-46
BENSON & HEDGES CUP					
For Minor Counties					
Middlesex	Lord's	April 24	5 *		1-36
OTHER FIRST-CLASS					
For Minor Counties					
India	Trowbridge	July 11	4 *		2-147

BATTING AVERAGES - Including fielding

	Matches	Inns	NO	Runs	HS	Avge	100s	50s	Ct	St
NatWest Trophy	1	1	0	24	24	24.00	-	-	1	-
Benson & Hedges Cup	1	1	1	5	5 *	-	-	-	-	-
Other First-Class	1	1	1	4	4 *	-	-	-	-	-
ALL FIRST-CLASS	1	1	1	4	4 *	-	-	-	-	-
ALL ONE-DAY	2	2	1	29	24	29.00	-	-	1	-

BOWLING AVERAGES

	Overs	Mdns	Runs	Wkts	Avge	Best	5wI	10wM
NatWest Trophy	12	1	46	3	15.33	3-46	-	
Benson & Hedges Cup	10	1	36	1	36.00	1-36	-	
Other First-Class	28	1	147	2	73.50	2-147	-	-
ALL FIRST-CLASS	28	1	147	2	73.50	2-147	-	-
ALL ONE-DAY	22	2	82	4	20.50	3-46	-	

R.J. EVANS - *Nottinghamshire*

Opposition	Venue	Date	Batting	Fielding	Bowling
BRITANNIC ASSURANCE					
Worcestershire	Worcester	May 3	11 & 4	1Ct	
OTHER FIRST-CLASS					
Oxford U	The Parks	June 6	1		
Cambridge U	Fenner's	June 16	21 * & 0 *		0-24

BATTING AVERAGES - Including fielding

	Matches	Inns	NO	Runs	HS	Avge	100s	50s	Ct	St
Britannic Assurance	1	2	0	15	11	7.50	-	-	1	-
Other First-Class	2	3	2	22	21 *	22.00	-	-	-	-
ALL FIRST-CLASS	3	5	2	37	21 *	12.33	-	-	1	-

BOWLING AVERAGES

	Overs	Mdns	Runs	Wkts	Avge	Best	5wI	10wM
Britannic Assurance								
Other First-Class	6	1	24	0	-	-	-	-
ALL FIRST-CLASS	6	1	24	0	-	-	-	-

PLASER RECORDS — F

PLAYER RECORDS

N.H. FAIRBROTHER - *Lancs & England*

Opposition	Venue	Date	Batting			Fielding	Bowling
CORNHILL TEST MATCHES							
New Zealand	Trent Bridge	June 7	19				
New Zealand	Lord's	June 21	2	&	33 *	1Ct	
New Zealand	Edgbaston	July 5	2	&	3		
BRITANNIC ASSURANCE							
Worcestershire	Old Trafford	April 26	74 *			1Ct	
Surrey	The Oval	May 3	366				
Derbyshire	Derby	May 15	63	&	65 *	2Ct	
Leicestershire	Old Trafford	May 19			46	1Ct	
Glamorgan	Colwyn Bay	May 26	60			1Ct	
Sussex	Horsham	June 2	22	&	10 *	3Ct	
Kent	Maidstone	June 30	6	&	47		
Warwickshire	Coventry	July 18	203 *	&	50		
Essex	Colchester	July 21	24	&	109 *		
Notts	Southport	July 25	93	&	10	1Ct	
Somerset	Old Trafford	July 28	91			2Ct	
Yorkshire	Headingley	Aug 4	5	&	7	1Ct	
Worcestershire	Kid'minster	Aug 8	22	&	64 *	1Ct	
Yorkshire	Old Trafford	Aug 18	99				
Surrey	Blackpool	Aug 29	8				
Notts	Trent Bridge	Sept 12	0			3Ct	
Warwickshire	Old Trafford	Sept 18				1Ct	
REFUGE ASSURANCE							
Middlesex	Old Trafford	April 22	1				
Notts	Trent Bridge	April 29	19			1Ct	
Surrey	The Oval	May 6	51			1Ct	
Leicestershire	Old Trafford	May 20	27				
Glamorgan	Colwyn Bay	May 27	27			1Ct	
Kent	Maidstone	July 1	45			1Ct	
Worcestershire	Old Trafford	July 15	36				
Essex	Colchester	July 22	23				
Somerset	Old Trafford	July 29	47				
Yorkshire	Scarborough	Aug 5	3			1Ct	
Northants	Northampton	Aug 12	86 *				
Warwickshire	Old Trafford	Aug 26	20				
Middlesex	Old Trafford	Sept 5	56				
NATWEST TROPHY							
Durham	Old Trafford	June 27	50 *				
Derbyshire	Derby	July 11	39			1Ct	
Gloucs	Old Trafford	Aug 1	86				
Middlesex	Old Trafford	Aug 15	48				
Northants	Lord's	Sept 1	81				
BENSON & HEDGES CUP							
Surrey	Old Trafford	April 24	95 *				
Combined U	Fenner's	May 1	25			1Ct	
Hampshire	Old Trafford	May 8	8			1Ct	
Yorkshire	Headingley	May 10	12				
Surrey	Old Trafford	May 30	61 *			1Ct	
Somerset	Old Trafford	June 13	78				
Worcestershire	Lord's	July 14	11				
OTHER FIRST-CLASS							
Oxford U	The Parks	June 16	105				
Sri Lanka	Old Trafford	Sept 8	6	&	26	1Ct	0-29

BATTING AVERAGES - Including fielding

	Matches	Inns	NO	Runs	HS	Avge	100s	50s	Ct	St
Cornhill Test Matches	3	5	1	59	33 *	14.75	-	-	1	-
Britannic Assurance	17	24	6	1544	366	85.77	3	9	18	-
Refuge Assurance	13	13	1	441	86 *	36.75	-	3	5	-
NatWest Trophy	5	5	1	304	86	76.00	-	3	1	-
Benson & Hedges Cup	7	7	2	290	95 *	58.00	-	3	3	-
Other First-Class	2	3	0	137	105	45.66	1	-	1	-
ALL FIRST-CLASS	22	32	7	1740	366	69.60	4	9	20	-
ALL ONE-DAY	25	25	4	1035	95 *	49.28	-	9	9	-

BOWLING AVERAGES

	Overs	Mdns	Runs	Wkts	Avge	Best	5wI	10wM
Cornhill Test Matches								
Britannic Assurance								
Refuge Assurance								
NatWest Trophy								
Benson & Hedges Cup								
Other First-Class	7	0	29	0	-	-	-	-

ALL FIRST-CLASS	7	0	29	0	-	-	-	-
ALL ONE-DAY								

P. FARBRACE - *Middlesex*

Opposition	Venue	Date	Batting	Fielding	Bowling
BRITANNIC ASSURANCE					
Leicestershire	Leicester	June 16	5	3Ct	
Lancashire	Old Trafford	June 20		17 *	
Northants	Luton	June 23	0	2Ct,1St	
Worcestershire	Lord's	June 30	14	1Ct,1St	
Yorkshire	Uxbridge	July 18	2	4Ct	
Somerset	Uxbridge	July 21	4 *	2Ct	
Kent	Canterbury	July 25	3	3Ct	
REFUGE ASSURANCE					
Leicestershire	Leicester	June 17		1Ct,1St	
Northants	Northampton	June 24		0Ct,2St	
Worcestershire	Lord's	July 1	3	1Ct,1St	
Somerset	Lord's	July 8	0		
Surrey	The Oval	July 15	2		
NATWEST TROPHY					
Berkshire	Lord's	June 27	17	1Ct	
Surrey	Uxbridge	July 11		3Ct	
OTHER FIRST-CLASS					
Cambridge U	Fenner's	May 3	79	2Ct	

BATTING AVERAGES - Including fielding

	Matches	Inns	NO	Runs	HS	Avge	100s	50s	Ct	St
Britannic Assurance	7	7	4	45	17 *	9.00	-	-	15	2
Refuge Assurance	5	3	0	5	3	1.66	-	-	2	4
NatWest Trophy	2	1	0	17	17	17.00	-	-	4	-
Other First-Class	1	1	0	79	79	79.00	-	1	2	-
ALL FIRST-CLASS	8	8	2	124	79	20.66	-	1	17	2
ALL ONE-DAY	7	4	0	22	17	5.50	-	-	6	4

BOWLING AVERAGES
Did not bowl

M.A. FELTHAM - *Surrey*

Opposition	Venue	Date	Batting			Fielding	Bowling
BRITANNIC ASSURANCE							
Hampshire	The Oval	May 19			3 *	1Ct	1-51 & 0-31
Derbyshire	The Oval	June 6				1Ct	2-40
Yorkshire	Harrogate	June 9			21		2-45 & 0-21
Glamorgan	Cardiff	June 30			30 *		2-60 & 2-32
Northants	The Oval	July 4					0-42
Warwickshire	The Oval	July 7			22 *		0-15 & 4-59
Sussex	Guildford	July 18	0			1Ct	1-44 & 1-36
Kent	Guildford	July 21	55			1Ct	4-86 & 1-32
Gloucs	Cheltenham	July 28	14	&	1	3Ct	2-73 & 0-17
Somerset	Weston	Aug 4	0	&	0		0-23
Leicestershire	The Oval	Aug 11	38			1Ct	0-40 & 6-53
Hampshire	Southampton	Aug 23	30				2-64 & 5-109
Lancashire	Blackpool	Aug 29					1-40
Middlesex	The Oval	Sept 12	101	&	58	2Ct	3-69
REFUGE ASSURANCE							
Sussex	Hove	April 29			7 *		1-30
Lancashire	The Oval	May 6					0-28
Notts	Trent Bridge	May 20	14				0-34
Northants	The Oval	June 3			1 *	2Ct	2-23
Yorkshire	Hull	June 10	16				1-10
Worcestershire	The Oval	June 17	56				0-19
Derbyshire	The Oval	June 24	42				0-15
Glamorgan	Cardiff	July 1	12				0-25
Warwickshire	The Oval	July 8	61			1Ct	2-23
Middlesex	The Oval	July 15	4				0-23
Kent	The Oval	July 22	9				1-26
Gloucs	Cheltenham	July 29	47				0-44
Somerset	Weston	Aug 5	24				2-40
Leicestershire	The Oval	Aug 12	0				1-29

F PLAYER RECORDS

NATWEST TROPHY

Middlesex	Uxbridge	July 11	5		1-65

BENSON & HEDGES CUP

Lancashire	Old Trafford	April 24	4		0-28
Hampshire	The Oval	May 1			0-24

OTHER FIRST-CLASS

India	The Oval	Aug 1	1 & 5	1Ct	1-48 & 0-20

OTHER ONE-DAY

Warwickshire	Harrogate	June 13	10		1-16

BATTING AVERAGES - Including fielding

	Matches	Inns	NO	Runs	HS	Avge	100s	50s	Ct	St
Britannic Assurance	14	14	3	373	101	33.90	1	2	10	-
Refuge Assurance	14	13	2	293	61	26.63	-	2	3	-
NatWest Trophy	1	1	0	5	5	5.00	-	-	-	-
Benson & Hedges Cup	2	1	0	4	4	4.00	-	-	-	-
Other First-Class	1	2	0	6	5	3.00	-	-	1	-
Other One-Day	1	1	0	10	10	10.00	-	-	-	-
ALL FIRST-CLASS	15	16	3	379	101	29.15	1	2	11	-
ALL ONE-DAY	18	16	2	312	61	22.28	-	2	3	-

BOWLING AVERAGES

	Overs	Mdns	Runs	Wkts	Avge	Best	5wI	10wM
Britannic Assurance	334.4	59	1082	39	27.74	6-53	2	-
Refuge Assurance	76	2	369	10	36.90	2-23	-	
NatWest Trophy	11.4	0	65	1	65.00	1-65	-	
Benson & Hedges Cup	9	0	52	0			-	
Other First-Class	15	2	68	1	68.00	1-48	-	
Other One-Day	3	0	16	1	16.00	1-16	-	
ALL FIRST-CLASS	349.4	61	1150	40	28.75	6-53	2	-
ALL ONE-DAY	99.4	2	502	12	41.83	2-23	-	

N.A. FELTON - Northamptonshire

Opposition	Venue	Date	Batting	Fielding	Bowling

BRITANNIC ASSURANCE

Warwickshire	Northampton	May 15	8 & 75	2Ct	
Notts	Trent Bridge	May 23	11 & 119 *		
Warwickshire	Edgbaston	June 2	8		
Leicestershire	Northampton	June 6	22		
Glamorgan	Northampton	June 9	122 & 44		
Middlesex	Luton	June 23	19 & 11	1Ct	
Somerset	Taunton	June 30	101 & 7	1Ct	
Surrey	The Oval	July 4	2		
Yorkshire	Northampton	July 7	66 & 106	3Ct	0-65
Kent	Northampton	July 18	90	2Ct	
Sussex	Northampton	July 21	78 & 42	1Ct	
Gloucs	Cheltenham	July 25	6 & 82 *		
Hampshire	Bournemouth	Aug 4	26 & 99		
Derbyshire	Chesterfield	Aug 8	5 & 42	1Ct	1-48
Lancashire	Northampton	Aug 11	66 & 51	1Ct	
Worcestershire	Worcester	Aug 18	10 & 11	1Ct	
Gloucs	Northampton	Aug 23	41 & 15	3Ct	
Essex	Northampton	Aug 29	0		0-0
Essex	Chelmsford	Sept 7	25 & 56	2Ct	
Leicestershire	Leicester	Sept 12	5 & 13		

REFUGE ASSURANCE

Derbyshire	Northampton	May 6	19		
Kent	Northampton	May 27	64	1Ct	
Surrey	The Oval	June 3	10		
Glamorgan	Northampton	June 10	21		
Middlesex	Northampton	June 24	10		
Somerset	Taunton	July 1	41	1Ct	
Yorkshire	Tring	July 8	9		
Notts	Trent Bridge	July 29	33 *		
Lancashire	Northampton	Aug 12	8	1Ct	
Gloucs	Northampton	Aug 26	24	1Ct	

NATWEST TROPHY

Staffordshire	Northampton	June 27	70		
Notts	Northampton	July 11	32		
Worcestershire	Northampton	Aug 1	12		
Hampshire	Southampton	Aug 15	31	2Ct	
Lancashire	Lord's	Sept 1	4		

BENSON & HEDGES CUP

Notts	Trent Bridge	May 12	16	

OTHER FIRST-CLASS

Cambridge U	Fenner's	April 14	26 & 3	1Ct	
New Zealand	Northampton	June 16	3 & 22		

BATTING AVERAGES - Including fielding

	Matches	Inns	NO	Runs	HS	Avge	100s	50s	Ct	St
Britannic Assurance	20	35	2	1484	122	44.97	4	9	18	-
Refuge Assurance	10	10	1	239	64	26.55	-	1	4	-
NatWest Trophy	5	5	0	149	70	29.80	-	1	2	-
Benson & Hedges Cup	1	1	0	16	16	16.00	-	-	-	-
Other First-Class	2	4	0	54	26	13.50	-	-	1	-
ALL FIRST-CLASS	22	39	2	1538	122	41.56	4	9	19	-
ALL ONE-DAY	16	16	1	404	70	26.93	-	2	6	-

BOWLING AVERAGES

	Overs	Mdns	Runs	Wkts	Avge	Best	5wI	10wM
Britannic Assurance	19	1	113	1	113.00	1-48	-	-
Refuge Assurance								
NatWest Trophy								
Benson & Hedges Cup								
Other First-Class								
ALL FIRST-CLASS	19	1	113	1	113.00	1-48	-	-
ALL ONE-DAY								

G.J.F. FERRIS - Leicestershire

Opposition	Venue	Date	Batting	Fielding	Bowling

BRITANNIC ASSURANCE

Glamorgan	Cardiff	April 26	24		4-44 & 2-57
Essex	Chelmsford	May 3	11		0-100
Notts	Leicester	May 15	35 & 0		2-37 & 0-19
Somerset	Leicester	May 26	33		0-55 & 0-15
Hampshire	Leicester	June 2	1		1-77

REFUGE ASSURANCE

Somerset	Leicester	May 27			2-28
Hampshire	Leicester	June 3	6		0-27

OTHER FIRST-CLASS

Oxford U	The Parks	May 23		1Ct	1-45 & 2-33

BATTING AVERAGES - Including fielding

	Matches	Inns	NO	Runs	HS	Avge	100s	50s	Ct	St
Britannic Assurance	5	6	0	104	35	17.33	-	-	-	-
Refuge Assurance	2	1	0	6	6	6.00	-	-	-	-
Other First-Class	1	0	0	0		-	-	-	1	-
ALL FIRST-CLASS	6	6	0	104	35	17.33	-	-	1	-
ALL ONE-DAY	2	1	0	6	6	6.00	-	-	-	-

BOWLING AVERAGES

	Overs	Mdns	Runs	Wkts	Avge	Best	5wI	10wM
Britannic Assurance	101.2	16	404	9	44.88	4-44	-	-
Refuge Assurance	13	1	55	2	27.50	2-28	-	
Other First-Class	37	13	78	3	26.00	2-33	-	
ALL FIRST-CLASS	138.2	29	482	12	40.16	4-44	-	-
ALL ONE-DAY	13	1	55	2	27.50	2-28	-	

M.G. FIELD-BUSS - Nottinghamshire

Opposition	Venue	Date	Batting	Fielding	Bowling

BRITANNIC ASSURANCE

Surrey	Trent Bridge	June 20	0 & 0		0-43

OTHER FIRST-CLASS

Oxford U	The Parks	June 6			0-5
Cambridge U	Fenner's	June 16			3-14 & 0-37

PLASIER RECORDS F

PLAYER RECORDS

BATTING AVERAGES - Including fielding

	Matches	Inns	NO	Runs	HS	Avge	100s	50s	Ct	St
Britannic Assurance	1	2	0	0	0	0.00	-	-	-	-
Other First-Class	2	0	0	0	0		-	-	-	-
ALL FIRST-CLASS	3	2	0	0	0	0.00	-	-	-	-

BOWLING AVERAGES

	Overs	Mdns	Runs	Wkts	Avge	Best	5wI	10wM
Britannic Assurance	10	2	43	0			-	-
Other First-Class	38.5	14	56	3	18.66	3-14	-	-
ALL FIRST-CLASS	48.5	16	99	3	33.00	3-14	-	-

R.J. FINNEY - *Norfolk*

Opposition	Venue	Date	Batting	Fielding	Bowling
NATWEST TROPHY					
Yorkshire	Headingley	June 27	25		

BATTING AVERAGES - Including fielding

	Matches	Inns	NO	Runs	HS	Avge	100s	50s	Ct	St
NatWest Trophy	1	1	0	25	25	25.00	-	-	-	-
ALL ONE-DAY	1	1	0	25	25	25.00	-	-	-	-

BOWLING AVERAGES
Did not bowl

J.D. FITTON - *Lancashire*

Opposition	Venue	Date	Batting	Fielding	Bowling
BRITANNIC ASSURANCE					
Worcestershire	Old Trafford	April 26			0-79 & 0-70
Surrey	The Oval	May 3	3		3-185 & 0-42
Derbyshire	Derby	May 15		1Ct	2-82 & 3-69
Leicestershire	Old Trafford	May 19		0 *	1-54 & 0-54
Glamorgan	Colwyn Bay	May 26	25 *		0-17 & 0-25
Sussex	Horsham	June 2	25		1-56
Gloucs	Old Trafford	June 9			1-111
Middlesex	Old Trafford	June 20	13 *		0-35
Hampshire	Old Trafford	June 23			0-75 & 0-34
Kent	Maidstone	June 30	0		
Derbyshire	Liverpool	July 7	6 * & 4		0-66 & 0-43
Warwickshire	Coventry	July 18	10		1-48 & 0-44
Notts	Southport	July 25	3	1Ct	2-61 & 0-33
Somerset	Old Trafford	July 28	25 *		0-17 & 0-65
REFUGE ASSURANCE					
Gloucs	Old Trafford	June 10			1-53
Hampshire	Old Trafford	June 24			
OTHER FIRST-CLASS					
Sri Lanka	Old Trafford	Sept 8	13 & 6	1Ct	0-64 & 0-18

BATTING AVERAGES - Including fielding

	Matches	Inns	NO	Runs	HS	Avge	100s	50s	Ct	St
Britannic Assurance	14	11	5	114	25 *	19.00	-	-	2	-
Refuge Assurance	2	0	0	0	0		-	-	-	-
Other First-Class	1	2	0	19	13	9.50	-	-	1	-
ALL FIRST-CLASS	15	13	5	133	25 *	16.62	-	-	3	-
ALL ONE-DAY	2	0	0	0	0		-	-	-	-

BOWLING AVERAGES

	Overs	Mdns	Runs	Wkts	Avge	Best	5wI	10wM
Britannic Assurance	428.4	86	1365	14	97.50	3-69	-	-
Refuge Assurance	8	0	53	1	53.00	1-53	-	-
Other First-Class	26	5	82	0			-	-
ALL FIRST-CLASS	454.4	91	1447	14	103.35	3-69	-	-
ALL ONE-DAY	8	0	53	1	53.00	1-53	-	-

S.M. FITZGERALD - *Dorset*

Opposition	Venue	Date	Batting	Fielding	Bowling
NATWEST TROPHY					
Glamorgan	Swansea	June 27	2 *	0Ct,2St	

BATTING AVERAGES - Including fielding

	Matches	Inns	NO	Runs	HS	Avge	100s	50s	Ct	St
NatWest Trophy	1	1	1	2	2 *	-	-	-	-	2
ALL ONE-DAY	1	1	1	2	2 *	-	-	-	-	2

BOWLING AVERAGES
Did not bowl

M.V. FLEMING - *Kent*

Opposition	Venue	Date	Batting	Fielding	Bowling
BRITANNIC ASSURANCE					
Hampshire	Canterbury	April 26	6 * & 20		1-50 & 1-23
Sussex	Folkestone	May 3	53 & 39	1Ct	0-20 & 0-21
Middlesex	Lord's	May 15	69 & 12		0-49 & 0-23
Glamorgan	Swansea	May 23	10 * & 45 *	1Ct	0-48 & 0-20
Notts	Tunbridge We	June 2	1 & 102	1Ct	0-78
Yorkshire	Tunbridge We	June 6	18		
Somerset	Canterbury	June 9	37 & 6		0-5
Warwickshire	Edgbaston	June 23	3 & 0		0-22 & 1-21
Essex	Maidstone	June 4	0 *		1-23
Worcestershire	Canterbury	July 28	59 & 42		0-46
Leicestershire	Dartford	Aug 8	31	1Ct	0-20
Gloucs	Bristol	Aug 11	45		1-36 & 0-18
Sussex	Hove	Aug 18	30 & 16		3-65 & 1-38
Leicestershire	Leicester	Aug 23	0 & 14	1Ct	2-25 & 1-36
Hampshire	Bournemouth	Aug 29	45 * & 76	1Ct	2-75 & 1-18
Surrey	Canterbury	Sept 7	9 & 80		1-127
Essex	Chelmsford	Sept 12	36 & 36		2-87
REFUGE ASSURANCE					
Essex	Chelmsford	April 22	24 *		1-43
Hampshire	Canterbury	April 29	29 *	2Ct	2-39
Glamorgan	Llanelli	May 13	18		3-30
Yorkshire	Canterbury	May 20	13		1-47
Northants	Northampton	May 27			1-25
Somerset	Canterbury	June 10	11 *		1-27
Notts	Canterbury	June 17	21		1-21
Warwickshire	Edgbaston	June 24	2		0-39
Lancashire	Maidstone	July 1	8		1-51
Surrey	The Oval	July 22	4		1-21
Worcestershire	Canterbury	July 29	8		1-32
Derbyshire	Chesterfield	Aug 5	15 *		1-60
Gloucs	Bristol	Aug 12	10		2-20
Leicestershire	Leicester	Aug 26	9	1Ct	1-47
NATWEST TROPHY					
Oxfordshire	Oxford	June 27	7		2-4
BENSON & HEDGES CUP					
Worcestershire	Worcester	May 1	6		1-27
Warwickshire	Canterbury	May 8	0		0-14
Gloucs	Canterbury	May 10			
OTHER FIRST-CLASS					
Cambridge U	Fenner's	June 20	19 *		1-13 & 0-14
India	Canterbury	July 7	21		1-23 & 2-28
OTHER ONE-DAY					
Sussex	Hove	Sept 2	6 .		4-30
Surrey	Hove	Sept 4	43 *	1Ct	0-64

BATTING AVERAGES - Including fielding

	Matches	Inns	NO	Runs	HS	Avge	100s	50s	Ct	St
Britannic Assurance	17	30	5	940	102	37.60	1	5	6	-
Refuge Assurance	14	13	4	172	29 *	19.11	-	-	3	-
NatWest Trophy	1	1	0	7	7	7.00	-	-	-	-
Benson & Hedges Cup	3	2	0	6	6	3.00	-	-	-	-
Other First-Class	2	2	1	40	21	40.00	-	-	-	-
Other One-Day	2	2	1	49	43 *	49.00	-	-	1	-

F — PLAYER RECORDS

ALL FIRST-CLASS	19	32	6	980	102	37.69	1	5	6	-
ALL ONE-DAY	20	18	5	234	43*	18.00	-	-	4	-

BOWLING AVERAGES

	Overs	Mdns	Runs	Wkts	Avge	Best	5wI	10wM
Britannic Assurance	360.5	81	994	18	55.22	3-65	-	-
Refuge Assurance	104	2	502	17	29.52	3-30	-	
NatWest Trophy	3	1	4	2	2.00	2-4	-	
Benson & Hedges Cup	15	2	41	1	41.00	1-27	-	
Other First-Class	34	13	78	4	19.50	2-28	-	
Other One-Day	14.4	0	94	4	23.50	4-30	-	
ALL FIRST-CLASS	394.5	94	1072	22	48.72	3-65	-	-
ALL ONE-DAY	136.4	5	641	24	26.70	4-30	-	

I. FLETCHER - *Hertfordshire*

Opposition	Venue	Date	Batting	Fielding	Bowling
NATWEST TROPHY					
Warwickshire	St Albans	June 27	1		

BATTING AVERAGES - Including fielding

	Matches	Inns	NO	Runs	HS	Avge	100s	50s	Ct	St
NatWest Trophy	1	1	0	1	1	1.00	-	-	-	-
ALL ONE-DAY	1	1	0	1	1	1.00	-	-	-	-

BOWLING AVERAGES
Did not bowl

S.D. FLETCHER - *Yorkshire*

Opposition	Venue	Date	Batting		Fielding	Bowling
BRITANNIC ASSURANCE						
Northants	Headingley	April 26	1 &	19		0-109
Warwickshire	Edgbaston	May 3	11* &	0		4-47 & 0-18
Derbyshire	Chesterfield	May 23	2 &	0		3-57 & 1-100
Hampshire	Headingley	May 26	6			1-57 & 1-66
Worcestershire	Worcester	June 2	0*			2-31
Northants	Northampton	July 7	0		2Ct	2-44 & 5-94
Middlesex	Uxbridge	July 18	0* &	0		1-29 & 0-10
Gloucs	Cheltenham	July 21				2-98
Somerset	Scarborough	July 25				1-47 & 1-12
Lancashire	Headingley	Aug 4	0 &	0	1Ct	0-55 & 3-62
REFUGE ASSURANCE						
Notts	Trent Bridge	April 22				0-31
Warwickshire	Edgbaston	May 6			1Ct	0-27
Derbyshire	Headingley	May 13				1-37
Kent	Canterbury	May 20	1*			2-32
Hampshire	Headingley	May 27	6			1-34
Worcestershire	Worcester	June 3				1-42
Northants	Tring	July 8			1Ct	0-34
Somerset	Scarborough	July 15				2-40
Gloucs	Cheltenham	July 22				0-36
Leicestershire	Sheffield	July 29				0-40
Lancashire	Scarborough	Aug 5	2		1Ct	4-63
NATWEST TROPHY						
Warwickshire	Headingley	July 11				0-56
Hampshire	Southampton	Aug 1	6*			2-53
BENSON & HEDGES CUP						
Hampshire	Southampton	April 24				2-42
Combined U	Headingley	May 8				0-44
Lancashire	Headingley	May 10	15*			2-23
Surrey	The Oval	May 12				1-53
OTHER FIRST-CLASS						
India	Headingley	June 30				2-82 & 0-17
OTHER ONE-DAY						
Warwickshire	Harrogate	June 15				0-59

BATTING AVERAGES - Including fielding

	Matches	Inns	NO	Runs	HS	Avge	100s	50s	Ct	St
Britannic Assurance	10	13	3	39	19	3.90	-	-	3	-
Refuge Assurance	11	3	1	9	6	4.50	-	-	3	-
NatWest Trophy	2	1	1	6	6*	-	-	-	-	-
Benson & Hedges Cup	4	1	1	15	15*	-	-	-	-	-
Other First-Class	1	0	0	0	0	-	-	-	-	-
Other One-Day	1	0	0	0	0	-	-	-	-	-
ALL FIRST-CLASS	11	13	3	39	19	3.90	-	-	3	-
ALL ONE-DAY	18	5	3	30	15*	15.00	-	-	3	-

BOWLING AVERAGES

	Overs	Mdns	Runs	Wkts	Avge	Best	5wI	10wM
Britannic Assurance	268.5	58	936	27	34.66	5-94	1	-
Refuge Assurance	78.1	2	416	11	37.81	4-63	-	
NatWest Trophy	24	1	109	2	54.50	2-53	-	
Benson & Hedges Cup	41.5	4	162	5	32.40	2-23	-	
Other First-Class	24	2	99	2	49.50	2-82	-	
Other One-Day	10	0	59	0			-	
ALL FIRST-CLASS	292.5	60	1035	29	35.69	5-94	1	-
ALL ONE-DAY	154	7	746	18	41.44	4-63	-	

G.W. FLOWER - *Zimbabwe*

Opposition	Venue	Date	Batting		Fielding	Bowling
OTHER FIRST-CLASS						
Yorkshire	Headingley	May 16	0 &	12	2Ct	2-33
Lancashire	Old Trafford	May 23	65 &	20*	2Ct	1-68

BATTING AVERAGES - Including fielding

	Matches	Inns	NO	Runs	HS	Avge	100s	50s	Ct	St
Other First-Class	2	4	1	97	65	32.33	-	1	4	-
ALL FIRST-CLASS	2	4	1	97	65	32.33	-	1	4	-

BOWLING AVERAGES

	Overs	Mdns	Runs	Wkts	Avge	Best	5wI	10wM
Other First-Class	29.5	4	101	3	33.66	2-33	-	-
ALL FIRST-CLASS	29.5	4	101	3	33.66	2-33	-	-

N.A. FOLLAND - *Devon & Minor Counties*

Opposition	Venue	Date	Batting		Fielding	Bowling
NATWEST TROPHY						
Somerset	Torquay	June 27	0			1-52
BENSON & HEDGES CUP						
For Minor Counties						
Middlesex	Lord's	April 24	53*			
Sussex	Marlow	May 1	78*			
Somerset	Taunton	May 8	16			
Derbyshire	Wellington	May 10	25		1Ct	
OTHER FIRST-CLASS						
For Minor Counties						
India	Trowbridge	July 11	26 &	82		

BATTING AVERAGES - Including fielding

	Matches	Inns	NO	Runs	HS	Avge	100s	50s	Ct	St
NatWest Trophy	1	1	0	0	0	0.00	-	-	-	-
Benson & Hedges Cup	4	4	2	172	78*	86.00	-	2	1	-
Other First-Class	1	2	0	108	82	54.00	-	1	-	-
ALL FIRST-CLASS	1	2	0	108	82	54.00	-	1	-	-
ALL ONE-DAY	5	5	2	172	78*	57.33	-	2	1	-

BOWLING AVERAGES

	Overs	Mdns	Runs	Wkts	Avge	Best	5wI	10wM
NatWest Trophy	3	0	52	1	52.00	1-52	-	
Benson & Hedges Cup								
Other First-Class								
ALL ONE-DAY	3	0	52	1	52.00	1-52	-	

PLEYER RECORDS

PLAYER RECORDS F

I. FOLLEY - *Lancashire*

Opposition	Venue	Date	Batting	Fielding	Bowling
OTHER FIRST-CLASS					
Zimbabwe	Old Trafford	May 23			1-78 & 1-30
Oxford U	The Parks	June 16			1-120 & 2-18
Sri Lanka	Old Trafford	Sept 8	47 * & 5		1-126 & 0-25

BATTING AVERAGES - Including fielding

	Matches	Inns	NO	Runs	HS	Avge	100s	50s	Ct	St
Other First-Class	3	2	1	52	47 *	52.00	-	-	-	-
ALL FIRST-CLASS	3	2	1	52	47 *	52.00	-	-	-	-

BOWLING AVERAGES

	Overs	Mdns	Runs	Wkts	Avge	Best	5wI	10wM
Other First-Class	114.1	18	397	6	66.16	2-18	-	-
ALL FIRST-CLASS	114.1	18	397	6	66.16	2-18	-	-

G.C. FORD - *Oxfordshire*

Opposition	Venue	Date	Batting	Fielding	Bowling
NATWEST TROPHY					
Kent	Oxford	June 27	26		

BATTING AVERAGES - Including fielding

	Matches	Inns	NO	Runs	HS	Avge	100s	50s	Ct	St
NatWest Trophy	1	1	0	26	26	26.00	-	-	-	-
ALL ONE-DAY	1	1	0	26	26	26.00	-	-	-	-

BOWLING AVERAGES
Did not bowl

A. FORDHAM - *Northamptonshire*

Opposition	Venue	Date	Batting	Fielding	Bowling
BRITANNIC ASSURANCE					
Yorkshire	Headingley	April 26	206 *	3Ct	
Derbyshire	Northampton	May 3	10 & 32	1Ct	
Warwickshire	Northampton	May 15	37 & 18		
Notts	Trent Bridge	May 23	21 & 74	1Ct	
Warwickshire	Edgbaston	June 2	33	3Ct	
Leicestershire	Northampton	June 6	59 *		
Glamorgan	Northampton	June 9	27 & 45	1Ct	
Middlesex	Luton	June 23	4 & 7	1Ct	
Somerset	Taunton	June 30	6 & 128	1Ct	
Surrey	The Oval	July 4	3		
Yorkshire	Northampton	July 7	12 & 59	2Ct	1-25
Kent	Northampton	July 18	2	2Ct	0-14
Sussex	Northampton	July 21	9 & 26	1Ct	
Gloucs	Cheltenham	July 25	13 & 1	1Ct	
Hampshire	Bournemouth	Aug 4	58 & 1		
Derbyshire	Chesterfield	Aug 8	74 & 4	1Ct	
Lancashire	Northampton	Aug 11	172 & 24		
Worcestershire	Worcester	Aug 18	81 & 19		
Gloucs	Northampton	Aug 23	64 & 41		
Essex	Northampton	Aug 29	16	2Ct	
Essex	Chelmsford	Sept 7	23 & 159		
Leicestershire	Leicester	Sept 12	85 & 0	2Ct	
REFUGE ASSURANCE					
Warwickshire	Edgbaston	April 29	29 *		
Derbyshire	Northampton	May 6	0		
Kent	Northampton	May 27	28		
Surrey	The Oval	June 3	7	1Ct	
Glamorgan	Northampton	June 10	0		
Middlesex	Northampton	June 24	4		
Somerset	Taunton	July 1	53		
Yorkshire	Tring	July 8	28		
Essex	Chelmsford	July 15	74	1Ct	
Sussex	Well'borough	July 22	21		

Opposition	Venue	Date	Batting	Fielding	Bowling
Notts	Trent Bridge	July 29	59		
Hampshire	Bournemouth	Aug 5	63		
Lancashire	Northampton	Aug 12	44		
Worcestershire	Worcester	Aug 19	21		
Gloucs	Northampton	Aug 26	50		
NATWEST TROPHY					
Staffordshire	Northampton	June 27	130		0-3
Notts	Northampton	July 11	23	1Ct	
Worcestershire	Northampton	Aug 1	96	1Ct	
Hampshire	Southampton	Aug 15	1		
Lancashire	Lord's	Sept 1	5		
BENSON & HEDGES CUP					
Essex	Northampton	May 8	9		
Scotland	Northampton	May 10	0		
Notts	Trent Bridge	May 12	67		
OTHER FIRST-CLASS					
Cambridge U	Fenner's	April 14	17 & 54		0-4
New Zealand	Northampton	June 16	20 & 23		

BATTING AVERAGES - Including fielding

	Matches	Inns	NO	Runs	HS	Avge	100s	50s	Ct	St
Britannic Assurance	22	38	2	1653	206 *	45.91	4	8	22	-
Refuge Assurance	15	15	1	481	74	34.35	-	5	2	-
NatWest Trophy	5	5	0	255	130	51.00	1	1	2	-
Benson & Hedges Cup	3	3	0	76	67	25.33	-	1	-	-
Other First-Class	2	4	0	114	54	28.50	-	1	-	-
ALL FIRST-CLASS	24	42	2	1767	206 *	44.17	4	9	22	-
ALL ONE-DAY	23	23	1	812	130	36.90	1	7	4	-

BOWLING AVERAGES

	Overs	Mdns	Runs	Wkts	Avge	Best	5wI	10wM
Britannic Assurance	9	0	39	1	39.00	1-25	-	-
Refuge Assurance								
NatWest Trophy	2	1	3	0				
Benson & Hedges Cup								
Other First-Class	1	0	4	0				
ALL FIRST-CLASS	10	0	43	1	43.00	1-25	-	-
ALL ONE-DAY	2	1	3	0				

J. FOSTER - *Shropshire*

Opposition	Venue	Date	Batting	Fielding	Bowling
NATWEST TROPHY					
Derbyshire	Chesterfield	June 27	20		

BATTING AVERAGES - Including fielding

	Matches	Inns	NO	Runs	HS	Avge	100s	50s	Ct	St
NatWest Trophy	1	1	0	20	20	20.00	-	-	-	-
ALL ONE-DAY	1	1	0	20	20	20.00	-	-	-	-

BOWLING AVERAGES
Did not bowl

N.A. FOSTER - *Essex*

Opposition	Venue	Date	Batting	Fielding	Bowling
BRITANNIC ASSURANCE					
Middlesex	Lord's	April 26		1Ct	1-86 & 2-39
Leicestershire	Chelmsford	May 3	101		3-102 & 0-30
Worcestershire	Worcester	May 19		1Ct	3-70 & 4-64
Hampshire	Southampton	May 23	40		1-43 & 1-33
Middlesex	Ilford	June 2	0 & 13		1-60
Gloucs	Ilford	June 6			4-104
Warwickshire	Edgbaston	June 9			0-68
Somerset	Bath	June 16			1-56 & 0-25
Kent	Maidstone	June 4			0-107
Derbyshire	Colchester	July 18	32		3-75 & 6-49
Lancashire	Colchester	July 21	4	1Ct	1-98 & 1-30
Leicestershire	Leicester	July 25	23 & 32 *	1Ct	1-70 & 3-47
Sussex	Chelmsford	July 28	2 * & 30		1-102 & 0-23

Notts	Southend	Aug 4	22			4-73 & 2-59
Glamorgan	Southend	Aug 8	18 & 16		2Ct	3-71 & 0-46
Yorkshire	Middlesbr'gh	Aug 11	8			4-63 & 1-14
Surrey	Chelmsford	Aug 18	58 & 0			5-44 & 6-32
Derbyshire	Derby	Aug 23	25		1Ct	5-39 & 3-57
Northants	Northampton	Aug 29	50			2-115
Northants	Chelmsford	Sept 7	11 & 12		3Ct	3-67 & 3-79
Kent	Chelmsford	Sept 12	14		2Ct	3-108 & 5-94
Surrey	The Oval	Sept 18	19		1Ct	6-72 & 2-88

REFUGE ASSURANCE

Kent	Chelmsford	April 22	6		4-21
Middlesex	Lord's	April 29	19	1Ct	0-51
Leicestershire	Leicester	May 6	8		1-37
Gloucs	Chelmsford	May 13	11 *	1Ct	2-22
Worcestershire	Worcester	May 20	0		1-38
Glamorgan	Ilford	June 3	0 *		1-33
Warwickshire	Edgbaston	June 10			2-35
Somerset	Bath	June 17	39 *		2-16
Hampshire	Southampton	July 8	4		2-43
Northants	Chelmsford	July 15			1-36
Lancashire	Colchester	July 22	4 *		2-42
Sussex	Chelmsford	July 29	5	1Ct	0-43
Notts	Southend	Aug 5	10	1Ct	1-50

NATWEST TROPHY

Scotland	Chelmsford	June 27			3-26
Hampshire	Chelmsford	July 11	0		1-35

BENSON & HEDGES CUP

Notts	Chelmsford	April 24			1-46
Scotland	Glasgow	May 1			2-44
Northants	Northampton	May 8			3-18
Notts	Chelmsford	May 30	8		0-37

OTHER ONE-DAY

Zimbabwe	Chelmsford	May 14	4 *		2-19

BATTING AVERAGES - Including fielding

	Matches	Inns	NO	Runs	HS	Avge	100s	50s	Ct	St
Britannic Assurance	22	22	2	530	101	26.50	1	2	13	-
Refuge Assurance	13	11	4	106	39 *	15.14	-	-	4	-
NatWest Trophy	2	1	0	0	0	0.00	-	-	-	-
Benson & Hedges Cup	4	1	0	8	8	8.00	-	-	-	-
Other One-Day	1	1	1	4	4 *	-	-	-	-	-
ALL FIRST-CLASS	22	22	2	530	101	26.50	1	2	13	-
ALL ONE-DAY	20	14	5	118	39 *	13.11	-	-	4	-

BOWLING AVERAGES

	Overs	Mdns	Runs	Wkts	Avge	Best	5wI	10wM
Britannic Assurance	819.2	175	2502	94	26.61	6-32	6	1
Refuge Assurance	96.3	3	467	19	24.57	4-21	-	
NatWest Trophy	24	8	61	4	15.25	3-26	-	
Benson & Hedges Cup	43	6	145	6	24.16	3-18	-	
Other One-Day	8.1	2	19	2	9.50	2-19	-	
ALL FIRST-CLASS	819.2	175	2502	94	26.61	6-32	6	1
ALL ONE-DAY	171.4	19	692	31	22.32	4-21	-	

A.R. FOTHERGILL - *Durham & M. Counties*

Opposition	Venue	Date	Batting	Fielding	Bowling

NATWEST TROPHY

Lancashire	Old Trafford	June 27	2		

BENSON & HEDGES CUP

For Minor Counties

Sussex	Marlow	May 1		1Ct	
Somerset	Taunton	May 8	45 *	2Ct	
Derbyshire	Wellington	May 10	3	2Ct	

OTHER FIRST-CLASS

For Minor Counties

India	Trowbridge	July 11	3		

BATTING AVERAGES - Including fielding

	Matches	Inns	NO	Runs	HS	Avge	100s	50s	Ct	St
NatWest Trophy	1	1	0	2	2	2.00	-	-	-	-
Benson & Hedges Cup	3	2	1	48	45 *	48.00	-	-	5	-
Other First-Class	1	1	0	3	3	3.00	-	-	-	-

ALL FIRST-CLASS	1	1	0	3	3	3.00	-	-	-	-
ALL ONE-DAY	4	3	1	50	45 *	25.00	-	-	5	-

BOWLING AVERAGES
Did not bowl

G. FOWLER - *Lancashire*

Opposition	Venue	Date	Batting	Fielding	Bowling

BRITANNIC ASSURANCE

Worcestershire	Old Trafford	April 26	16 & 35 *		
Surrey	The Oval	May 3	20	1Ct	
Derbyshire	Derby	May 15	25 & 23	1Ct	
Leicestershire	Old Trafford	May 19	115 * & 22		
Glamorgan	Colwyn Bay	May 26	22		
Sussex	Horsham	June 2	54 *		
Gloucs	Old Trafford	June 9	126		
Middlesex	Old Trafford	June 20	24		
Hampshire	Old Trafford	June 23	15 * & 17	1Ct	
Kent	Maidstone	June 30	3 & 13	3Ct	
Derbyshire	Liverpool	July 7	19 & 31		
Warwickshire	Coventry	July 18	0 & 30		
Essex	Colchester	July 21	12 & 9		
Notts	Southport	July 25	18 & 6		
Somerset	Old Trafford	July 28	10	1Ct	0-0
Yorkshire	Headingley	Aug 4	43 & 6	4Ct	
Worcestershire	Kid'minster	Aug 8	9 & 18		
Northants	Northampton	Aug 11	30 & 47		1-33
Yorkshire	Old Trafford	Aug 18	7 & 50 *	2Ct	
Surrey	Blackpool	Aug 29	42		
Notts	Trent Bridge	Sept 12	1 & 20 *	2Ct	

REFUGE ASSURANCE

Middlesex	Old Trafford	April 22	101		
Notts	Trent Bridge	April 29	52	2Ct	
Surrey	The Oval	May 6	84		
Leicestershire	Old Trafford	May 20	108		
Glamorgan	Colwyn Bay	May 27	2		
Gloucs	Old Trafford	June 10	6	1Ct	
Hampshire	Old Trafford	June 24	1 *		
Kent	Maidstone	July 1	59	1Ct	
Derbyshire	Old Trafford	July 8	57		
Worcestershire	Old Trafford	July 15	33	1Ct	
Essex	Colchester	July 22	5		
Somerset	Old Trafford	July 29	60	1Ct	
Yorkshire	Scarborough	Aug 5	55		
Northants	Northampton	Aug 12	81		
Warwickshire	Old Trafford	Aug 26	69	1Ct	
Middlesex	Old Trafford	Sept 5	20		

NATWEST TROPHY

Durham	Old Trafford	June 27	31		
Gloucs	Old Trafford	Aug 1	52		
Middlesex	Old Trafford	Aug 15	8		
Northants	Lord's	Sept 1	7		

BENSON & HEDGES CUP

Surrey	Old Trafford	April 24	9		
Combined U	Fenner's	May 1	18		
Hampshire	Old Trafford	May 8	1		
Yorkshire	Headingley	May 10	36	1Ct	
Surrey	Old Trafford	May 30	96	1Ct	
Somerset	Old Trafford	June 13	14		
Worcestershire	Lord's	July 14	11		

BATTING AVERAGES - Including fielding

	Matches	Inns	NO	Runs	HS	Avge	100s	50s	Ct	St
Britannic Assurance	21	35	6	938	126	32.34	2	2	15	-
Refuge Assurance	16	16	1	793	108	52.86	2	8	7	-
NatWest Trophy	4	4	0	98	52	24.50	-	1	-	-
Benson & Hedges Cup	7	7	0	185	96	26.42	-	1	2	-
ALL FIRST-CLASS	21	35	6	938	126	32.34	2	2	15	-
ALL ONE-DAY	27	27	1	1076	108	41.38	2	10	9	-

BOWLING AVERAGES

	Overs	Mdns	Runs	Wkts	Avge	Best	5wI	10wM
Britannic Assurance	4.1	2	33	1	33.00	1-33	-	-
Refuge Assurance								
NatWest Trophy								
Benson & Hedges Cup								

PLAYER RECORDS

ALL FIRST-CLASS	4.1	2	33	1	33.00	1-33 — —
ALL ONE-DAY						

K.N. FOYLE - *Wiltshire*

Opposition	Venue	Date	Batting	Fielding	Bowling
NATWEST TROPHY					
Surrey	Trowbridge	June 27	16		

BATTING AVERAGES - Including fielding

	Matches	Inns	NO	Runs	HS	Avge	100s	50s	Ct	St
NatWest Trophy	1	1	0	16	16	16.00	-	-	-	-
ALL ONE-DAY	1	1	0	16	16	16.00	-	-	-	-

BOWLING AVERAGES
Did not bowl

T.J. FRANKLIN - *New Zealand*

Opposition	Venue	Date	Batting	Fielding	Bowling
CORNHILL TEST MATCHES					
England	Trent Bridge	June 7	33 & 22 *	1Ct	
England	Lord's	June 21	101	1Ct	
England	Edgbaston	July 5	66 & 5		
OTHER FIRST-CLASS					
Worcestershire	Worcester	May 12	28 & 50		
Somerset	Taunton	May 16	103 & 30		
Sussex	Hove	May 26	0 & 78		
Warwickshire	Edgbaston	May 30	2	1Ct	
Derbyshire	Derby	June 2	19 & 9		
Northants	Northampton	June 16	92		
Combined U	Fenner's	June 27	19		
Essex	Chelmsford	June 30	74		
OTHER ONE-DAY					
D of Norfolk	Arundel	May 6	82		
MCC	Lord's	May 7	29		
Ireland	Downpatrick	May 9	26	1Ct	

BATTING AVERAGES - Including fielding

	Matches	Inns	NO	Runs	HS	Avge	100s	50s	Ct	St
Cornhill Test Matches	3	5	1	227	101	56.75	1	1	2	-
Other First-Class	8	12	0	504	103	42.00	1	4	1	-
Other One-Day	3	3	0	137	82	45.66	-	1	1	-
ALL FIRST-CLASS	11	17	1	731	103	45.68	2	5	3	-
ALL ONE-DAY	3	3	0	137	82	45.66	-	1	1	-

BOWLING AVERAGES
Did not bowl

A.G.J. FRASER - *Essex*

Opposition	Venue	Date	Batting	Fielding	Bowling
OTHER ONE-DAY					
Yorkshire	Scarborough	Sept 3	0		0-16
Hampshire	Scarborough	Sept 4	0	1Ct	2-24

BATTING AVERAGES - Including fielding

	Matches	Inns	NO	Runs	HS	Avge	100s	50s	Ct	St
Other One-Day	2	2	0	0	0	0.00	-	-	1	-
ALL ONE-DAY	2	2	0	0	0	0.00	-	-	1	-

BOWLING AVERAGES

	Overs	Mdns	Runs	Wkts	Avge	Best	5wI	10wM
Other One-Day	7	0	40	2	20.00	2-24		
ALL ONE-DAY	7	0	40	2	20.00	2-24		

A.R.C. FRASER - *Middlesex & England*

Opposition	Venue	Date	Batting	Fielding	Bowling
CORNHILL TEST MATCHES					
India	Lord's	July 26			5-104 & 3-39
India	Old Trafford	Aug 9	1		5-124 & 1-81
India	The Oval	Aug 23	0		2-112
TEXACO TROPHY					
India	Headingley	July 18	4 *		0-37
India	Trent Bridge	July 20	0 *		1-38
BRITANNIC ASSURANCE					
Kent	Lord's	May 15	0		0-30 & 3-79
Warwickshire	Lord's	June 6	7		0-18 & 0-23
Leicestershire	Leicester	June 16	12		1-34 & 2-45
Lancashire	Old Trafford	June 20			1-52
Northants	Luton	June 23	1 *	1Ct	0-22 & 2-11
Worcestershire	Lord's	June 30	27		2-40 & 3-53
Somerset	Uxbridge	July 21			1-66 & 1-11
Glamorgan	Lord's	Aug 4	4 * & 23		0-76 & 6-30
Derbyshire	Derby	Aug 18	8 & 26		3-49 & 1-46
Notts	Lord's	Sept 7			1-63 & 2-84
Surrey	The Oval	Sept 12	92	1Ct	5-95 & 2-44
Sussex	Hove	Sept 18	13	1Ct	1-55 & 4-47
REFUGE ASSURANCE					
Hampshire	Basingstoke	June 10			2-26
Leicestershire	Leicester	June 17			1-34
Northants	Northampton	June 24			1-16
Worcestershire	Lord's	July 1			0-15
Somerset	Lord's	July 8	6		0-49
Surrey	The Oval	July 15	4 *		0-40
Glamorgan	Lord's	Aug 5			4-28
Derbyshire	Derby	Aug 19			1-24
Lancashire	Old Trafford	Sept 5			1-28
Derbyshire	Edgbaston	Sept 16		1Ct	1-32
NATWEST TROPHY					
Berkshire	Lord's	June 27			1-37
Surrey	Uxbridge	July 11			4-44
Glamorgan	Lord's	Aug 1			0-47
Lancashire	Old Trafford	Aug 15			2-43

BATTING AVERAGES - Including fielding

	Matches	Inns	NO	Runs	HS	Avge	100s	50s	Ct	St
Cornhill Test Matches	3	2	0	1	1	0.50	-	-	-	-
Texaco Trophy	2	2	2	4	4 *	-	-	-	-	-
Britannic Assurance	12	11	2	213	92	23.66	-	1	3	-
Refuge Assurance	10	2	1	10	6	10.00	-	-	1	-
NatWest Trophy	4	0	0	0	0	-	-	-	-	-
ALL FIRST-CLASS	15	13	2	214	92	19.45	-	1	3	-
ALL ONE-DAY	16	4	3	14	6	14.00	-	-	1	-

BOWLING AVERAGES

	Overs	Mdns	Runs	Wkts	Avge	Best	5wI	10wM
Cornhill Test Matches	159.1	41	460	16	28.75	5-104	2	-
Texaco Trophy	22	4	75	1	75.00	1-38		
Britannic Assurance	436.5	103	1073	41	26.17	6-30	2	-
Refuge Assurance	71	7	292	11	26.54	4-28	-	
NatWest Trophy	47.5	3	171	7	24.42	4-44	-	
ALL FIRST-CLASS	596	144	1533	57	26.89	6-30	4	-
ALL ONE-DAY	140.5	14	538	19	28.31	4-28	-	

B.N. FRENCH - *Nottinghamshire*

Opposition	Venue	Date	Batting	Fielding	Bowling
BRITANNIC ASSURANCE					
Derbyshire	Trent Bridge	April 26	25 & 1 *	1Ct,2St	
Worcestershire	Worcester	May 3	10 & 0	1Ct,1St	
Leicestershire	Leicester	May 15	37	2Ct,1St	
Warwickshire	Edgbaston	May 19	1 * & 25 *	3Ct,1St	
Northants	Trent Bridge	May 23	33	2Ct,1St	
Derbyshire	Derby	May 26	9 & 105 *	4Ct	
Kent	Tunbridge We	June 2	0	6Ct	
Surrey	Trent Bridge	June 20	0 & 14 *		

F   PLAYER RECORDS

Leicestershire	Trent Bridge	June 30	27		3Ct,1St
Yorkshire	Scarborough	July 4			
Sussex	Trent Bridge	July 7	5 & 17 *		4Ct
Hampshire	Portsmouth	July 18	0 & 21		1Ct
Lancashire	Southport	July 25	6 & 1		1Ct,2St
Middlesex	Trent Bridge	July 28	4		2Ct
Essex	Southend	Aug 4	25 & 0		4Ct
Somerset	Weston	Aug 8	24 *		1Ct,1St
Glamorgan	Worksop	Aug 11	1		1Ct
Gloucs	Trent Bridge	Aug 18	5 & 4		2Ct,1St
Worcestershire	Trent Bridge	Aug 29	3 & 25		2Ct
Middlesex	Lord's	Sept 7	40 * & 1		1Ct
Lancashire	Trent Bridge	Sept 12	16 & 19		4Ct
Yorkshire	Trent Bridge	Sept 18	2 *		1Ct

REFUGE ASSURANCE

Yorkshire	Trent Bridge	April 22	15 *		2Ct
Lancashire	Trent Bridge	April 29	11		1Ct
Worcestershire	Worcester	May 6	9		1Ct
Middlesex	Lord's	May 13			0Ct,2St
Surrey	Trent Bridge	May 20			
Derbyshire	Derby	June 10	17 *		2Ct
Kent	Canterbury	June 17	0		
Somerset	Bath	June 24	1		
Leicestershire	Trent Bridge	July 1			1Ct
Sussex	Trent Bridge	July 8			1Ct
Hampshire	Southampton	July 15	9		
Warwickshire	Edgbaston	July 22	34 *		0Ct,1St
Northants	Trent Bridge	July 29			
Essex	Southend	Aug 5			1Ct
Glamorgan	Trent Bridge	Aug 12			1Ct
Gloucs	Trent Bridge	Aug 19			2Ct
Derbyshire	Derby	Sept 5	0		

NATWEST TROPHY

Bucks	Marlow	June 27	7		2Ct
Northants	Northampton	July 11	35		3Ct

BENSON & HEDGES CUP

Essex	Chelmsford	April 24			
Leicestershire	Trent Bridge	May 1	14 *		2Ct
Scotland	Glasgow	May 8	25		
Northants	Trent Bridge	May 12	24		2Ct,1St
Essex	Chelmsford	May 30			1Ct,1St
Worcestershire	Trent Bridge	June 13	4		

OTHER ONE-DAY

For England XI

Rest of World	Jesmond	Aug 2			
Rest of World	Jesmond	Aug 3	30		

For World XI

Yorkshire	Scarborough	Sept 1	7 *		2Ct

BATTING AVERAGES - Including fielding

	Matches	Inns	NO	Runs	HS	Avge	100s	50s	Ct	St
Britannic Assurance	22	34	9	506	105 *	20.24	1	-	46	11
Refuge Assurance	17	9	3	96	34 *	16.00	-	-	12	3
NatWest Trophy	2	2	0	42	35	21.00	-	-	5	-
Benson & Hedges Cup	6	4	1	67	25	22.33	-	-	5	2
Other One-Day	3	2	1	37	30	37.00	-	-	2	-
ALL FIRST-CLASS	22	34	9	506	105 *	20.24	1	-	46	11
ALL ONE-DAY	28	17	5	242	35	20.16	-	-	24	5

BOWLING AVERAGES
Did not bowl

N. FRENCH - *Lincolnshire*

Opposition	Venue	Date	Batting	Fielding	Bowling

NATWEST TROPHY

Gloucs	Gloucester	June 27	7		0-42

BATTING AVERAGES - Including fielding

	Matches	Inns	NO	Runs	HS	Avge	100s	50s	Ct	St
NatWest Trophy	1	1	0	7	7	7.00	-	-	-	-
ALL ONE-DAY	1	1	0	7	7	7.00	-	-	-	-

BOWLING AVERAGES

	Overs	Mdns	Runs	Wkts	Avge	Best	5wI	10wM
NatWest Trophy	12	1	42	0	-	-	-	-
ALL ONE-DAY	12	1	42	0	-	-	-	-

M. FROST - *Glamorgan*

Opposition	Venue	Date	Batting	Fielding	Bowling

BRITANNIC ASSURANCE

Leicestershire	Cardiff	April 26	1 & 0		4-117 & 0-26
Gloucs	Bristol	May 15	1 & 4 *		5-42 & 5-40
Sussex	Hove	May 19		1Ct	4-62 & 0-96
Lancashire	Colwyn Bay	May 26	0		0-81
Northants	Northampton	June 9	4		4-82 & 3-58
Hampshire	Southampton	June 16			1-107
Yorkshire	Cardiff	June 23			0-23 & 2-64
Surrey	Cardiff	June 30	0		0-48 & 2-33
Gloucs	Swansea	July 4			0-31
Leicestershire	Hinckley	July 7	0 *	1Ct	2-56 & 0-31
Worcestershire	Abergavenny	July 21			0-109 & 0-38
Middlesex	Lord's	Aug 4	4 * & 0 *		2-110 & 3-24
Essex	Southend	Aug 8			2-73 & 1-51
Notts	Worksop	Aug 11	0		0-79 & 2-32
Derbyshire	Cardiff	Aug 29			4-80
Hampshire	Pontypridd	Sept 7	0 & 4 *		2-59 & 2-49
Warwickshire	Edgbaston	Sept 12	6 * & 12		3-78 & 2-49
Worcestershire	Worcester	Sept 18	0 & 4 *		1-71 & 0-44

REFUGE ASSURANCE

Leicestershire	Cardiff	April 29			3-30
Kent	Llanelli	May 13			2-45
Sussex	Hove	May 20			0-51
Lancashire	Colwyn Bay	May 27			2-39
Essex	Ilford	June 3			1-26
Northants	Northampton	June 10			4-30
Hampshire	Bournemouth	June 17			2-49
Surrey	Cardiff	July 1			2-22
Warwickshire	Edgbaston	July 15			0-21
Somerset	Neath	July 22	2 *		0-46
Derbyshire	Swansea	July 29			0-26
Middlesex	Lord's	Aug 5	6	1Ct	0-40
Notts	Trent Bridge	Aug 12			0-48
Worcestershire	Swansea	Aug 26	1 *		0-32

NATWEST TROPHY

Dorset	Swansea	June 27			3-50
Sussex	Cardiff	July 11			0-34
Middlesex	Lord's	Aug 1			0-39

BENSON & HEDGES CUP

Gloucs	Cardiff	May 1			2-14
Worcestershire	Worcester	May 8			4-25
Kent	Swansea	May 12	1 *		3-56
Worcestershire	Worcester	May 30	3		0-51

OTHER FIRST-CLASS

Oxford U	The Parks	April 14			0-33
Sri Lanka	Ebbw Vale	Aug 22	2 *		0-51 & 3-44

BATTING AVERAGES - Including fielding

	Matches	Inns	NO	Runs	HS	Avge	100s	50s	Ct	St
Britannic Assurance	18	17	7	40	12	4.00	-	-	2	-
Refuge Assurance	14	3	2	9	6	9.00	-	-	1	-
NatWest Trophy	3	0	0	0	0		-	-	-	-
Benson & Hedges Cup	4	2	1	4	3	4.00	-	-	-	-
Other First-Class	2	1	1	2	2 *	-	-	-	-	-
ALL FIRST-CLASS	20	18	8	42	12	4.20	-	-	2	-
ALL ONE-DAY	21	5	3	13	6	6.50	-	-	1	-

BOWLING AVERAGES

	Overs	Mdns	Runs	Wkts	Avge	Best	5wI	10wM
Britannic Assurance	509.1	63	1919	56	34.26	5-40	2	1
Refuge Assurance	92.4	3	505	16	31.56	4-30	-	
NatWest Trophy	31	5	123	3	41.00	3-50	-	
Benson & Hedges Cup	39.2	8	146	9	16.22	4-25	-	
Other First-Class	48	11	128	3	42.66	3-44	-	
ALL FIRST-CLASS	557.1	74	2047	59	34.69	5-40	2	1
ALL ONE-DAY	163	16	774	28	27.64	4-25	-	

PLASER RECORDS

J. GALLIAN - *Lancashire*

Opposition	Venue	Date	Batting	Fielding	Bowling
OTHER FIRST-CLASS					
Oxford U	The Parks	June 16	17 *		1-50 & 0-15

BATTING AVERAGES - Including fielding
	Matches	Inns	NO	Runs	HS	Avge	100s	50s	Ct	St
Other First-Class	1	1	1	17	17 *	-	-	-	-	-
ALL FIRST-CLASS	1	1	1	17	17 *	-	-	-	-	-

BOWLING AVERAGES
	Overs	Mdns	Runs	Wkts	Avge	Best	5wI	10wM
Other First-Class	21	8	65	1	65.00	1-50	-	-
ALL FIRST-CLASS	21	8	65	1	65.00	1-50	-	-

N.C.J. GANDON - *Lincolnshire*

Opposition	Venue	Date	Batting	Fielding	Bowling
NATWEST TROPHY					
Gloucs	Gloucester	June 27	31		

BATTING AVERAGES - Including fielding
	Matches	Inns	NO	Runs	HS	Avge	100s	50s	Ct	St
NatWest Trophy	1	1	0	31	31	31.00	-	-	-	-
ALL ONE-DAY	1	1	0	31	31	31.00	-	-	-	-

BOWLING AVERAGES
Did not bowl

P.J. GARNER - *Oxfordshire*

Opposition	Venue	Date	Batting	Fielding	Bowling
NATWEST TROPHY					
Kent	Oxford	June 27	4	1Ct	

BATTING AVERAGES - Including fielding
	Matches	Inns	NO	Runs	HS	Avge	100s	50s	Ct	St
NatWest Trophy	1	1	0	4	4	4.00	-	-	1	-
ALL ONE-DAY	1	1	0	4	4	4.00	-	-	1	-

BOWLING AVERAGES
Did not bowl

M.A. GARNHAM - *Essex*

Opposition	Venue	Date	Batting	Fielding	Bowling
BRITANNIC ASSURANCE					
Middlesex	Lord's	April 26	36 *	3Ct	
Leicestershire	Chelmsford	May 3	0	2Ct	
Worcestershire	Worcester	May 19		1Ct	
Hampshire	Southampton	May 23	62 *	1Ct,1St	
Middlesex	Ilford	June 2	36		
Gloucs	Ilford	June 6	20 *	2Ct	
Warwickshire	Edgbaston	June 9	26 *		
Somerset	Bath	June 16	10		
Kent	Maidstone	June 4	17 *		
Derbyshire	Colchester	July 18	16	3Ct	
Lancashire	Colchester	July 21	17	2Ct	
Leicestershire	Leicester	July 25	8 & 7	1Ct	
Sussex	Chelmsford	July 28	8 & 20	3Ct	
Notts	Southend	Aug 4	22	2Ct	
Glamorgan	Southend	Aug 8	84 * & 19	2Ct	
Yorkshire	Middlesbr'gh	Aug 11	35	3Ct	
Surrey	Chelmsford	Aug 18	32	4Ct	
Derbyshire	Derby	Aug 23	8	6Ct	
Northants	Northampton	Aug 29	1 & 23 *	1Ct	
Northants	Chelmsford	Sept 7	34 & 10	2Ct	
Kent	Chelmsford	Sept 12	33	5Ct	
Surrey	The Oval	Sept 18	5	3Ct	
REFUGE ASSURANCE					
Kent	Chelmsford	April 22	10	2Ct	
Middlesex	Lord's	April 29	26	3Ct	
Leicestershire	Leicester	May 6	4	1Ct	
Gloucs	Chelmsford	May 13	24 *		
Worcestershire	Worcester	May 20	5	1Ct	
Glamorgan	Ilford	June 3			
Warwickshire	Edgbaston	June 10		0Ct,1St	
Somerset	Bath	June 17	12 *		
Hampshire	Southampton	July 8	40 *		
Northants	Chelmsford	July 15	29 *	1Ct	
Lancashire	Colchester	July 22		1Ct	
Sussex	Chelmsford	July 29	6		
Notts	Southend	Aug 5	5		
Yorkshire	Middlesbr'gh	Aug 12	0	1Ct	
Derbyshire	Derby	Aug 26		1Ct	
NATWEST TROPHY					
Scotland	Chelmsford	June 27		1Ct	
Hampshire	Chelmsford	July 11	1 *		
BENSON & HEDGES CUP					
Notts	Chelmsford	April 24	12 *	2Ct	
Scotland	Glasgow	May 1	5	1Ct	
Northants	Northampton	May 8		1Ct	
Notts	Chelmsford	May 30	21 *	1Ct,1St	
OTHER FIRST-CLASS					
Cambridge U	Fenner's	May 16	26	2Ct	
New Zealand	Chelmsford	June 30	0	1Ct,1St	
OTHER ONE-DAY					
Zimbabwe	Chelmsford	May 14	14	2Ct	
Yorkshire	Scarborough	Sept 3	37	2Ct	
Hampshire	Scarborough	Sept 4	4		

BATTING AVERAGES - Including fielding
	Matches	Inns	NO	Runs	HS	Avge	100s	50s	Ct	St
Britannic Assurance	22	26	7	589	84 *	31.00	-	2	46	1
Refuge Assurance	15	11	4	161	40 *	23.00	-	-	11	1
NatWest Trophy	2	1	1	1	1 *	-	-	-	1	-
Benson & Hedges Cup	4	3	2	38	21 *	38.00	-	-	5	1
Other First-Class	2	2	0	26	26	13.00	-	-	3	1
Other One-Day	3	3	0	55	37	18.33	-	-	4	-
ALL FIRST-CLASS	24	28	7	615	84 *	29.28	-	2	49	2
ALL ONE-DAY	24	18	7	255	40 *	23.18	-	-	21	2

BOWLING AVERAGES
Did not bowl

M.W. GATTING - *Middlesex*

Opposition	Venue	Date	Batting	Fielding	Bowling
BRITANNIC ASSURANCE					
Essex	Lord's	April 26	41 & 32 *		
Kent	Lord's	May 15	58 & 87 *	1Ct	4-2
Surrey	Lord's	May 23	20 & 13	1Ct	0-6
Gloucs	Lord's	May 26	16 & 4	1Ct	0-13
Essex	Ilford	June 2	34	1Ct	
Warwickshire	Lord's	June 6	23	1Ct	0-43
Leicestershire	Leicester	June 16	4 & 41 *	1Ct	
Lancashire	Old Trafford	June 20	95		
Northants	Luton	June 23	62 & 0	2Ct	
Worcestershire	Lord's	June 30	26		
Yorkshire	Uxbridge	July 18	86 & 28	2Ct	
Somerset	Uxbridge	July 21	170 * & 36		
Kent	Canterbury	July 25	52 & 101		
Notts	Trent Bridge	July 28	6 & 169 *		
Glamorgan	Lord's	Aug 4	89 & 21	3Ct	
Hampshire	Bournemouth	Aug 8	3 & 35	1Ct	
Sussex	Lord's	Aug 11	28	1Ct	
Derbyshire	Derby	Aug 18	119 * & 4	2Ct	
Yorkshire	Headingley	Aug 23	91 & 10		

G PLAYER RECORDS

Notts	Lord's	Sept 7	30	1Ct	
Surrey	The Oval	Sept 12	0 *	1Ct	
Sussex	Hove	Sept 18	51		2-42 & 1-7

REFUGE ASSURANCE

Lancashire	Old Trafford	April 22			0-38
Essex	Lord's	April 29	7		1-41
Kent	Folkestone	May 6			0-52
Notts	Lord's	May 13	0		2-48
Gloucs	Lord's	May 27	5	1Ct	0-13
Warwickshire	Lord's	June 3	6 *		0-20
Hampshire	Basingstoke	June 10	27	1Ct	0-18
Leicestershire	Leicester	June 17	124 *	1Ct	1-34
Northants	Northampton	June 24	76 *		2-29
Worcestershire	Lord's	July 1	9		0-11
Somerset	Lord's	July 8	24	1Ct	
Surrey	The Oval	July 15	2	1Ct	
Glamorgan	Lord's	Aug 5	99		
Sussex	Lord's	Aug 12	5	1Ct	
Derbyshire	Derby	Aug 19	7		
Derbyshire	Edgbaston	Sept 16	44		

NATWEST TROPHY

Berkshire	Lord's	June 27	79 *		1-31
Surrey	Uxbridge	July 11	3		0-20
Glamorgan	Lord's	Aug 1	70 *	2Ct	
Lancashire	Old Trafford	Aug 15	53		

BENSON & HEDGES CUP

Sussex	Hove	May 8	54		1-41
Somerset	Lord's	May 10	66		3-65
Derbyshire	Derby	May 12	6		0-24
Somerset	Taunton	May 30	16	1Ct	0-28

OTHER FIRST-CLASS

Cambridge U	Fenner's	May 3	19	1Ct	0-19 & 0-6

BATTING AVERAGES - Including fielding

	Matches	Inns	NO	Runs	HS	Avge	100s	50s	Ct	St
Britannic Assurance	22	36	7	1685	170 *	58.10	4	9	19	-
Refuge Assurance	16	14	3	435	124 *	39.54	1	2	6	-
NatWest Trophy	4	4	2	205	79 *	102.50	-	3	2	-
Benson & Hedges Cup	4	4	0	142	66	35.50	-	2	1	-
Other First-Class	1	1	0	19	19	19.00	-	-	1	-
ALL FIRST-CLASS	23	37	7	1704	170 *	56.80	4	9	20	-
ALL ONE-DAY	24	22	5	782	124 *	46.00	1	7	9	-

BOWLING AVERAGES

	Overs	Mdns	Runs	Wkts	Avge	Best	5wI	10wM
Britannic Assurance	45	18	113	7	16.14	4-2	-	-
Refuge Assurance	53	1	304	6	50.66	2-29	-	-
NatWest Trophy	8	0	51	1	51.00	1-31	-	-
Benson & Hedges Cup	33	1	158	4	39.50	3-65	-	-
Other First-Class	11	3	25	0	-	-	-	-
ALL FIRST-CLASS	56	21	138	7	19.71	4-2	-	-
ALL ONE-DAY	94	2	513	11	46.63	3-65	-	-

P.S. GERRANS - Oxford University

Opposition	Venue	Date	Batting	Fielding	Bowling

OTHER FIRST-CLASS

Opposition	Venue	Date	Batting	Fielding	Bowling
Glamorgan	The Parks	April 14	0	1Ct	0-80
Somerset	The Parks	April 18			2-56
Surrey	The Parks	May 16	0		1-50 & 3-86
Leicestershire	The Parks	May 23	0 & 22		0-73
Glamorgan	The Parks	June 2	18	2Ct	2-94 & 0-4
Notts	The Parks	June 6			1-58
Lancashire	The Parks	June 16	39		0-80
For Combined Universities					
New Zealand	Fenner's	June 27	0 & 7	1Ct	2-59 & 1-18
For Oxford University					
Cambridge U	Lord's	July 4	16		0-37

BATTING AVERAGES - Including fielding

	Matches	Inns	NO	Runs	HS	Avge	100s	50s	Ct	St
Other First-Class	9	9	0	102	39	11.33	-	-	4	-
ALL FIRST-CLASS	9	9	0	102	39	11.33	-	-	4	-

BOWLING AVERAGES

	Overs	Mdns	Runs	Wkts	Avge	Best	5wI	10wM
Other First-Class	208	40	695	12	57.91	3-86	-	-
ALL FIRST-CLASS	208	40	695	12	57.91	3-86	-	-

M.I. GIDLEY - Leicestershire

Opposition	Venue	Date	Batting	Fielding	Bowling

BRITANNIC ASSURANCE

Opposition	Venue	Date	Batting	Fielding	Bowling
Glamorgan	Cardiff	April 26	73	2Ct	0-1 & 0-31
Essex	Chelmsford	May 3	9		0-121
Notts	Leicester	May 15	8 & 21 *		0-23 & 0-9
Lancashire	Old Trafford	May 19	2		0-43

REFUGE ASSURANCE

Opposition	Venue	Date	Batting	Fielding	Bowling
Northants	Leicester	April 22	10		1-28
Essex	Leicester	May 6	6 *		1-51
Worcestershire	Leicester	Aug 5	14 *		0-40
Surrey	The Oval	Aug 12	5 *		3-45
Warwickshire	Edgbaston	Aug 19	2 *		
Kent	Leicester	Aug 26			0-24

BENSON & HEDGES CUP

Opposition	Venue	Date	Batting	Fielding	Bowling
Notts	Trent Bridge	May 1	20 *		0-16
Scotland	Leicester	May 12			0-23

OTHER FIRST-CLASS

Opposition	Venue	Date	Batting	Fielding	Bowling
Oxford U	The Parks	May 23			0-27 & 1-54

BATTING AVERAGES - Including fielding

	Matches	Inns	NO	Runs	HS	Avge	100s	50s	Ct	St
Britannic Assurance	4	5	1	113	73	28.25	-	1	2	-
Refuge Assurance	6	5	4	37	14 *	37.00	-	-	-	-
Benson & Hedges Cup	2	1	1	20	20 *	-	-	-	-	-
Other First-Class	1	0	0	0	0	-	-	-	-	-
ALL FIRST-CLASS	5	5	1	113	73	28.25	-	1	2	-
ALL ONE-DAY	8	6	5	57	20 *	57.00	-	-	-	-

BOWLING AVERAGES

	Overs	Mdns	Runs	Wkts	Avge	Best	5wI	10wM
Britannic Assurance	61	15	228	0	-	-	-	-
Refuge Assurance	31.1	0	188	5	37.60	3-45	-	-
Benson & Hedges Cup	12	1	39	0	-	-	-	-
Other First-Class	33	12	81	1	81.00	1-54	-	-
ALL FIRST-CLASS	94	27	309	1	309.00	1-54	-	-
ALL ONE-DAY	43.1	1	227	5	45.40	3-45	-	-

C. GLADWIN - Suffolk

Opposition	Venue	Date	Batting	Fielding	Bowling

NATWEST TROPHY

Opposition	Venue	Date	Batting	Fielding	Bowling
Worcestershire	Bury St Ed's	June 27	5		0-6

BATTING AVERAGES - Including fielding

	Matches	Inns	NO	Runs	HS	Avge	100s	50s	Ct	St
NatWest Trophy	1	1	0	5	5	5.00	-	-	-	-
ALL ONE-DAY	1	1	0	5	5	5.00	-	-	-	-

BOWLING AVERAGES

	Overs	Mdns	Runs	Wkts	Avge	Best	5wI	10wM
NatWest Trophy	1	0	6	0	-	-	-	-
ALL ONE-DAY	1	0	6	0	-	-	-	-

PLAYER RECORDS

G

J. GLENDENEN - *Durham*

Opposition	Venue	Date	Batting	Fielding	Bowling
NATWEST TROPHY					
Lancashire	Old Trafford	June 27	14		

BATTING AVERAGES - Including fielding

	Matches	Inns	NO	Runs	HS	Avge	100s	50s	Ct	St
NatWest Trophy	1	1	0	14	14	14.00	-	-	-	-
ALL ONE-DAY	1	1	0	14	14	14.00	-	-	-	-

BOWLING AVERAGES
Did not bowl

A.K. GOLDING - *Suffolk*

Opposition	Venue	Date	Batting	Fielding	Bowling
NATWEST TROPHY					
Worcestershire	Bury St Ed's	June 27	0	1Ct	2-29

BATTING AVERAGES - Including fielding

	Matches	Inns	NO	Runs	HS	Avge	100s	50s	Ct	St
NatWest Trophy	1	1	0	0	0	0.00	-	-	1	-
ALL ONE-DAY	1	1	0	0	0	0.00	-	-	1	-

BOWLING AVERAGES

	Overs	Mdns	Runs	Wkts	Avge	Best	5wI	10wM
NatWest Trophy	12	4	29	2	14.50	2-29	-	
ALL ONE-DAY	12	4	29	2	14.50	2-29	-	

D.J. GOLDSMITH - *Buckinghamshire*

Opposition	Venue	Date	Batting	Fielding	Bowling
NATWEST TROPHY					
Notts	Marlow	June 27	0*		

BATTING AVERAGES - Including fielding

	Matches	Inns	NO	Runs	HS	Avge	100s	50s	Ct	St
NatWest Trophy	1	1	1	0	0*	-	-	-	-	-
ALL ONE-DAY	1	1	1	0	0*	-	-	-	-	-

BOWLING AVERAGES
Did not bowl

S.C. GOLDSMITH - *Derbyshire*

Opposition	Venue	Date	Batting			Fielding	Bowling
BRITANNIC ASSURANCE							
Northants	Northampton	May 3	34				1-21
Lancashire	Derby	May 15	24	&	4		0-39
Yorkshire	Chesterfield	May 23	0	&	8	3Ct	1-21
Notts	Derby	May 26	30				
Leicestershire	Leicester	June 20				8	1-24
Gloucs	Derby	June 30	5	&	7*		
Sussex	Hove	July 4	11			1Ct	1-40
Lancashire	Liverpool	July 7			7	3Ct	0-24 & 0-8
Essex	Colchester	July 18	11	&	24		1-25
Essex	Derby	Aug 23	11	&	32		2-105
Leicestershire	Derby	Sept 18	0				0-40
REFUGE ASSURANCE							
Northants	Northampton	May 6	13				
Yorkshire	Headingley	May 13	7				0-10
Somerset	Taunton	May 20				1Ct	
Notts	Derby	June 10	0*				
Warwickshire	Derby	June 17	50				
Surrey	The Oval	June 24	14*				
Gloucs	Derby	July 1				1Ct	
Lancashire	Old Trafford	July 8	7*				
Leicestershire	Knypersley	July 15	4*				0-14
Hampshire	Portsmouth	July 22	4				0-42
Glamorgan	Swansea	July 29					0-6
Essex	Derby	Aug 26	5*				0-25
NATWEST TROPHY							
Shropshire	Chesterfield	June 27					0-23
Lancashire	Derby	July 11	21				1-20
BENSON & HEDGES CUP							
Somerset	Taunton	May 1	4				
Min Counties	Wellington	May 10	45*				3-38
Middlesex	Derby	May 12					
OTHER FIRST-CLASS							
Cambridge U	Fenner's	April 18	51			2Ct	0-15 & 0-21
OTHER ONE-DAY							
India	Chesterfield	July 16	3				0-71

BATTING AVERAGES - Including fielding

	Matches	Inns	NO	Runs	HS	Avge	100s	50s	Ct	St
Britannic Assurance	11	16	1	216	34	14.40	-	-	7	-
Refuge Assurance	12	9	5	104	50	26.00	-	1	2	-
NatWest Trophy	2	1	0	21	21	21.00	-	-	-	-
Benson & Hedges Cup	3	2	1	49	45*	49.00	-	-	-	-
Other First-Class	1	1	0	51	51	51.00	-	1	2	-
Other One-Day	1	1	0	3	3	3.00	-	-	-	-
ALL FIRST-CLASS	12	17	1	267	51	16.68	-	1	9	-
ALL ONE-DAY	18	13	6	177	50	25.28	-	1	2	-

BOWLING AVERAGES

	Overs	Mdns	Runs	Wkts	Avge	Best	5wI	10wM
Britannic Assurance	112	19	347	7	49.57	2-105	-	-
Refuge Assurance	15	0	97	0			-	-
NatWest Trophy	10.2	0	43	1	43.00	1-20	-	-
Benson & Hedges Cup	10	0	38	3	12.66	3-38	-	-
Other First-Class	16	3	36	0			-	-
Other One-Day	10.4	0	71	0			-	-
ALL FIRST-CLASS	128	22	383	7	54.71	2-105	-	-
ALL ONE-DAY	46	0	249	4	62.25	3-38	-	-

G.A. GOOCH - *Essex & England*

Opposition	Venue	Date	Batting			Fielding	Bowling
CORNHILL TEST MATCHES							
New Zealand	Trent Bridge	June 7	0			2Ct	
New Zealand	Lord's	June 21	85	&	37		0-25
New Zealand	Edgbaston	July 5	154	&	30	1Ct	
India	Lord's	July 26	333	&	123	2Ct	1-26
India	Old Trafford	Aug 9	116	&	7	2Ct	
India	The Oval	Aug 23	85	&	88		0-44
TEXACO TROPHY							
New Zealand	Headingley	May 23	55				2-23
New Zealand	The Oval	May 25	112*				
India	Headingley	July 18	45				
India	Trent Bridge	July 20	7				
BRITANNIC ASSURANCE							
Middlesex	Lord's	April 26	137	&	39		0-0
Leicestershire	Chelmsford	May 3	215				
Worcestershire	Worcester	May 19	121	&	42*	3Ct	
Middlesex	Ilford	June 2	0	&	120		0-36
Somerset	Bath	June 16	72				
Lancashire	Colchester	July 21	17	&	177	1Ct	
Notts	Southend	Aug 4	87	&	65*	1Ct	0-4
Surrey	Chelmsford	Aug 18	9	&	53	2Ct	
Northants	Northampton	Aug 29	174	&	126		0-42
Northants	Chelmsford	Sept 7	92	&	40		0-43
Kent	Chelmsford	Sept 12					
REFUGE ASSURANCE							
Kent	Chelmsford	April 22	3				0-28

G PLAYER RECORDS

Middlesex	Lord's	April 29	3		0-44
Leicestershire	Leicester	May 6	65		1-66
Gloucs	Chelmsford	May 13	56		
Worcestershire	Worcester	May 20	30		0-35
Glamorgan	Ilford	June 3	58	1Ct	
Somerset	Bath	June 17	34	1Ct	
Northants	Chelmsford	July 15	0	1Ct	
Lancashire	Colchester	July 22	1		0-24
Notts	Southend	Aug 5	136		1-34

NATWEST TROPHY
Scotland	Chelmsford	June 27	103 *		
Hampshire	Chelmsford	July 11	144	2Ct	

BENSON & HEDGES CUP
Notts	Chelmsford	April 24	102		0-51
Scotland	Glasgow	May 1	2		1-44
Northants	Northampton	May 8	94 *	1Ct	
Notts	Chelmsford	May 30	87		1-27

OTHER FIRST-CLASS
New Zealand	Chelmsford	June 30	102 *	1Ct	

OTHER ONE-DAY
Zimbabwe	Chelmsford	May 14	105		0-17
For England XI					
Rest of World	Jesmond	Aug 2	62		

BATTING AVERAGES - Including fielding
	Matches	Inns	NO	Runs	HS	Avge	100s	50s	Ct	St
Cornhill Test Matches	6	11	0	1058	333	96.18	4	5	7	-
Texaco Trophy	4	4	1	219	112 *	73.00	1	1	-	-
Britannic Assurance	11	18	2	1586	215	99.12	7	5	7	-
Refuge Assurance	10	10	0	386	136	38.60	1	3	3	-
NatWest Trophy	2	2	1	247	144	247.00	2	-	2	-
Benson & Hedges Cup	4	4	1	285	102	95.00	1	2	1	-
Other First-Class	1	1	1	102	102 *	-	1	-	1	-
Other One-Day	2	2	0	167	105	83.50	1	1	-	-
ALL FIRST-CLASS	18	30	3	2746	333	101.70	12	8	15	-
ALL ONE-DAY	22	22	3	1304	144	68.63	6	7	6	-

BOWLING AVERAGES
	Overs	Mdns	Runs	Wkts	Avge	Best	5wI	10wM
Cornhill Test Matches	31	11	95	1	95.00	1-26	-	-
Texaco Trophy	4	0	23	2	11.50	2-23	-	-
Britannic Assurance	35	8	125	0				
Refuge Assurance	37	0	231	2	115.50	1-34	-	-
NatWest Trophy								
Benson & Hedges Cup	28	3	122	2	61.00	1-27	-	-
Other First-Class								
Other One-Day	7	1	17	0				
ALL FIRST-CLASS	66	19	220	1	220.00	1-26	-	-
ALL ONE-DAY	76	4	393	6	65.50	2-23	-	-

D. GOUGH - *Yorkshire*

Opposition	Venue	Date	Batting	Fielding	Bowling
BRITANNIC ASSURANCE					
Warwickshire	Edgbaston	May 3	4 & 3 *		0-53
Hampshire	Headingley	May 26	7 * & 8	1Ct	1-67 & 3-61
Kent	Tunbridge We	June 6			0-94
Surrey	Harrogate	June 9	1 *		0-24
Warwickshire	Sheffield	June 20			3-36 & 0-34
Glamorgan	Cardiff	June 23			2-72 & 0-44
Notts	Scarborough	July 4			0-46
Middlesex	Uxbridge	July 18	11 & 2		1-40
Somerset	Scarborough	July 25	7 *		3-77 & 2-47
Leicestershire	Sheffield	July 28	24 & 2		0-53 & 0-34
Lancashire	Headingley	Aug 4	3 & 13		1-37
Essex	Middlesbr'gh	Aug 11	1 & 0 *		2-54
Middlesex	Headingley	Aug 23	21 & 9		4-68 & 2-43
REFUGE ASSURANCE					
Notts	Trent Bridge	April 22			1-29
Warwickshire	Edgbaston	May 6			0-20
Derbyshire	Headingley	May 13			0-26
Kent	Canterbury	May 20	4	2Ct	1-54
Hampshire	Headingley	May 27	17 *		0-17

NATWEST TROPHY
Norfolk	Headingley	June 27			2-22
Warwickshire	Headingley	July 11		1Ct	2-45

BENSON & HEDGES CUP
Surrey	The Oval	May 12			0-27

OTHER FIRST-CLASS
Zimbabwe	Headingley	May 16	7 *		1-21 & 3-32

BATTING AVERAGES - Including fielding
	Matches	Inns	NO	Runs	HS	Avge	100s	50s	Ct	St
Britannic Assurance	13	16	5	116	24	10.54	-	-	1	-
Refuge Assurance	5	2	1	21	17 *	21.00	-	-	2	-
NatWest Trophy	2	0	0	0	0		-	-	1	-
Benson & Hedges Cup	1	0	0	0	0		-	-	-	-
Other First-Class	1	1	1	7	7 *	-	-	-	-	-
ALL FIRST-CLASS	14	17	6	123	24	11.18	-	-	1	-
ALL ONE-DAY	8	2	1	21	17 *	21.00	-	-	3	-

BOWLING AVERAGES
	Overs	Mdns	Runs	Wkts	Avge	Best	5wI	10wM
Britannic Assurance	256.4	43	984	24	41.00	4-68	-	-
Refuge Assurance	26	0	146	2	73.00	1-29	-	
NatWest Trophy	19	3	67	4	16.75	2-22	-	
Benson & Hedges Cup	6	0	27	0				
Other First-Class	23	6	53	4	13.25	3-32	-	-
ALL FIRST-CLASS	279.4	49	1037	28	37.03	4-68	-	-
ALL ONE-DAY	51	3	240	6	40.00	2-22	-	

I.J. GOULD - *Sussex*

Opposition	Venue	Date	Batting	Fielding	Bowling
BRITANNIC ASSURANCE					
Surrey	Hove	April 26	62 *	1Ct	0-10
Kent	Folkestone	May 3	0 & 33		0-8
Hampshire	Southampton	May 15	6 & 1	2Ct	
Glamorgan	Hove	May 19	9 & 11		
Somerset	Taunton	May 23	30	1Ct	
Notts	Trent Bridge	July 7	4	2Ct	
Essex	Chelmsford	July 28	73 & 0	1Ct	
REFUGE ASSURANCE					
Derbyshire	Hove	April 22	0		
Surrey	Hove	April 29	9		
Glamorgan	Hove	May 20	41		
Leicestershire	Leicester	June 10	8		
Yorkshire	Hove	June 17	0		
Worcestershire	Worcester	June 24	12		
Hampshire	Hove	July 1	68		
Notts	Trent Bridge	July 8	6		
Northants	Well'borough	July 22	55	1Ct	
Essex	Chelmsford	July 29	56		
Somerset	Hove	Aug 26	5	1Ct	
NATWEST TROPHY					
Ireland	Downpatrick	June 27	26		
BENSON & HEDGES CUP					
Derbyshire	Derby	April 24	7		
Min Counties	Marlow	May 1	16 *		0-16
Middlesex	Hove	May 8	12 *	1Ct	
Somerset	Hove	May 12	6		
OTHER FIRST-CLASS					
New Zealand	Hove	May 26	6 *	1Ct	0-1
OTHER ONE-DAY					
For Duchess of Norfolk's XI					
New Zealand	Arundel	May 6	1 *		
For Sussex					
Kent	Hove	Sept 2	9		

BATTING AVERAGES - Including fielding
	Matches	Inns	NO	Runs	HS	Avge	100s	50s	Ct	St
Britannic Assurance	7	11	1	229	73	22.90	-	2	7	-
Refuge Assurance	11	11	0	260	68	23.63	-	3	2	-
NatWest Trophy	1	1	0	26	26	26.00	-	-	-	-
Benson & Hedges Cup	4	4	2	41	16 *	20.50	-	-	1	-

PLAYER RECORDS

Other First-Class	1	1	1	6	6 *	-	-	-	1	-
Other One-Day	2	2	1	10	9	10.00	-	-	-	-
ALL FIRST-CLASS	8	12	2	235	73	23.50	-	2	8	-
ALL ONE-DAY	18	18	3	337	68	22.46	-	3	3	-

BOWLING AVERAGES

	Overs	Mdns	Runs	Wkts	Avge	Best	5wI	10wM
Britannic Assurance	5	0	18	0	-	-	-	-
Refuge Assurance								
NatWest Trophy								
Benson & Hedges Cup	3	0	16	0	-	-	-	-
Other First-Class	0.4	0	1	0	-	-	-	-
Other One-Day								
ALL FIRST-CLASS	5.4	0	19	0	-	-	-	-
ALL ONE-DAY	3	0	16	0	-	-	-	-

▮ J.W. GOVAN - *Northamptonshire*

Opposition	Venue	Date	Batting	Fielding	Bowling
BRITANNIC ASSURANCE					
Derbyshire	Northampton	May 3	17 & 4		1-19
Notts	Trent Bridge	May 23	17		2-56 & 0-45
REFUGE ASSURANCE					
Derbyshire	Northampton	May 6	5	1Ct	1-27
Kent	Northampton	May 27	9 *		0-28
Hampshire	Bournemouth	Aug 5			0-23
BENSON & HEDGES CUP					
Essex	Northampton	May 8	11		0-3
Scotland	Northampton	May 10	30		1-55
Notts	Trent Bridge	May 12	1		0-27
OTHER FIRST-CLASS					
Cambridge U	Fenner's	April 14	3		2-12 & 0-10

BATTING AVERAGES - Including fielding

	Matches	Inns	NO	Runs	HS	Avge	100s	50s	Ct	St
Britannic Assurance	2	3	0	38	17	12.66	-	-	-	-
Refuge Assurance	3	2	1	14	9 *	14.00	-	-	1	-
Benson & Hedges Cup	3	3	0	42	30	14.00	-	-	-	-
Other First-Class	1	1	0	3	3	3.00	-	-	-	-
ALL FIRST-CLASS	3	4	0	41	17	10.25	-	-	-	-
ALL ONE-DAY	6	5	1	56	30	14.00	-	-	1	-

BOWLING AVERAGES

	Overs	Mdns	Runs	Wkts	Avge	Best	5wI	10wM
Britannic Assurance	33	5	120	3	40.00	2-56	-	-
Refuge Assurance	15	0	78	1	78.00	1-27	-	-
Benson & Hedges Cup	23	4	85	1	85.00	1-55	-	-
Other First-Class	14	9	22	2	11.00	2-12	-	-
ALL FIRST-CLASS	47	14	142	5	28.40	2-12	-	-
ALL ONE-DAY	38	4	163	2	81.50	1-27	-	-

▮ D.I. GOWER - *Hampshire & England*

Opposition	Venue	Date	Batting	Fielding	Bowling
CORNHILL TEST MATCHES					
India	Lord's	July 26	40 & 32 *		
India	Old Trafford	Aug 9	38 & 16		
India	The Oval	Aug 23	8 & 157 *		
TEXACO TROPHY					
New Zealand	Headingley	May 23	1	1Ct	
New Zealand	The Oval	May 25	4		
India	Headingley	July 18	50	1Ct	
India	Trent Bridge	July 20	25		
BRITANNIC ASSURANCE					
Sussex	Southampton	May 15	145	2Ct	
Surrey	The Oval	May 19	4 & 69	2Ct	
Yorkshire	Headingley	May 26	64 & 33	3Ct	

Leicestershire	Leicester	June 2	25	
Somerset	Basingstoke	June 6	1 & 26	
Glamorgan	Southampton	June 16	41	1Ct
Gloucs	Gloucester	June 20		
Lancashire	Old Trafford	June 23	49	
Derbyshire	Portsmouth	July 21	48 & 3	
Northants	Bournemouth	Aug 4	28 *	2Ct
Somerset	Taunton	Aug 18	14 & 29	1Ct
Kent	Bournemouth	Aug 29	44 & 3	
Glamorgan	Pontypridd	Sept 7	17 & 23	2Ct
Gloucs	Southampton	Sept 18	14 & 4	1Ct

REFUGE ASSURANCE				
Kent	Canterbury	April 29	32	
Gloucs	Southampton	May 6	0	
Somerset	Taunton	May 13	12	
Yorkshire	Headingley	May 27	12	1Ct
Leicestershire	Leicester	June 3	53	
Middlesex	Basingstoke	June 10	23	
Glamorgan	Bournemouth	June 17	1	
Lancashire	Old Trafford	June 24		
Sussex	Hove	July 1	10	
Essex	Southampton	July 8	66	4Ct
Notts	Southampton	July 15	66 *	
Derbyshire	Portsmouth	July 22	47 *	
Northants	Bournemouth	Aug 5	18	

NATWEST TROPHY				
Leicestershire	Leicester	June 27	28	1Ct
Essex	Chelmsford	July 11	19	2Ct
Yorkshire	Southampton	Aug 1	26	
Northants	Southampton	Aug 15	86	1Ct

BENSON & HEDGES CUP				
Surrey	The Oval	May 1	6	1Ct
Lancashire	Old Trafford	May 8	44 *	
Combined U	Southampton	May 12	0	

OTHER FIRST-CLASS				
Oxford U	The Parks	May 3	72 & 46	1Ct
India	Southampton	July 4	44 * & 126 *	
Sri Lanka	Southampton	Sept 12	0	2Ct

OTHER ONE-DAY				
For MCC				
New Zealand	Lord's	May 7	97	

BATTING AVERAGES - Including fielding

	Matches	Inns	NO	Runs	HS	Avge	100s	50s	Ct	St
Cornhill Test Matches	3	6	2	291	157 *	72.75	1	-	-	-
Texaco Trophy	4	4	0	80	50	20.00	-	1	2	-
Britannic Assurance	14	21	1	684	145	34.20	1	2	14	-
Refuge Assurance	13	12	2	340	66 *	34.00	-	3	5	-
NatWest Trophy	4	4	0	159	86	39.75	-	1	4	-
Benson & Hedges Cup	3	3	1	50	44 *	25.00	-	-	1	-
Other First-Class	3	5	2	288	126 *	96.00	1	1	3	-
Other One-Day	1	1	0	97	97	97.00	-	1	-	-
ALL FIRST-CLASS	20	32	5	1263	157 *	46.77	3	3	17	-
ALL ONE-DAY	25	24	5	726	97	34.57	-	6	12	-

BOWLING AVERAGES
Did not bowl

▮ I.D. GRAHAM - *Suffolk*

Opposition	Venue	Date	Batting	Fielding	Bowling
NATWEST TROPHY					
Worcestershire	Bury St Ed's	June 27	3		0-37

BATTING AVERAGES - Including fielding

	Matches	Inns	NO	Runs	HS	Avge	100s	50s	Ct	St
NatWest Trophy	1	1	0	3	3	3.00	-	-	-	-
ALL ONE-DAY	1	1	0	3	3	3.00	-	-	-	-

BOWLING AVERAGES
Did not bowl

G PLAYER RECORDS

J. GRAHAM-BROWN - *Dorset*

Opposition	Venue	Date	Batting	Fielding	Bowling
NATWEST TROPHY					
Glamorgan	Swansea	June 27	58		0-3

BATTING AVERAGES - Including fielding

	Matches	Inns	NO	Runs	HS	Avge	100s	50s	Ct	St
NatWest Trophy	1	1	0	58	58	58.00	-	1	-	-
ALL ONE-DAY	1	1	0	58	58	58.00	-	1	-	-

BOWLING AVERAGES

	Overs	Mdns	Runs	Wkts	Avge	Best	5wI	10wM
NatWest Trophy	1	0	3	0	-	-	-	-
ALL ONE-DAY	1	0	3	0	-	-	-	-

R. GRANT - *Staffordshire*

Opposition	Venue	Date	Batting	Fielding	Bowling
NATWEST TROPHY					
Northants	Northampton	June 27			0-56

BATTING AVERAGES - Including fielding

	Matches	Inns	NO	Runs	HS	Avge	100s	50s	Ct	St
NatWest Trophy	1	0	0	0	0	-	-	-	-	-
ALL ONE-DAY	1	0	0	0	0	-	-	-	-	-

BOWLING AVERAGES

	Overs	Mdns	Runs	Wkts	Avge	Best	5wI	10wM
NatWest Trophy	12	2	56	0	-	-	-	-
ALL ONE-DAY	12	2	56	0	-	-	-	-

D.A. GRAVENEY - *Gloucestershire*

Opposition	Venue	Date	Batting		Fielding	Bowling
BRITANNIC ASSURANCE						
Somerset	Taunton	April 26	2 &	5	1Ct	0-62 & 0-12
Middlesex	Lord's	May 26		3		2-89 & 0-61
Somerset	Bristol	June 2				4-53 & 0-38
Essex	Ilford	June 6	0 *			1-101
Lancashire	Old Trafford	June 9	19 *			1-39
Sussex	Hove	June 16	0			0-9 & 0-48
Hampshire	Gloucester	June 20				
Leicestershire	Gloucester	June 23		46 *	1Ct	0-96
Worcestershire	Worcester	July 7	1 &	0		1-64 & 1-67
Worcestershire	Bristol	Sept 7				2-96 & 2-58
Sussex	Bristol	Sept 12	3		3Ct	5-45 & 5-59
Hampshire	Southampton	Sept 18	1 * &	20		0-8 & 5-140
REFUGE ASSURANCE						
Glamorgan	Bristol	April 22				1-20
Worcestershire	Worcester	July 8				0-42
NATWEST TROPHY						
Lincolnshire	Gloucester	June 27			1Ct	2-26
Kent	Bristol	July 11			1Ct	0-21
BENSON & HEDGES CUP						
Worcestershire	Bristol	April 24				1-40
Glamorgan	Cardiff	May 1	12 *		1Ct	0-55
OTHER FIRST-CLASS						
Zimbabwe	Bristol	May 19	7		2Ct	2-44

BATTING AVERAGES - Including fielding

	Matches	Inns	NO	Runs	HS	Avge	100s	50s	Ct	St
Britannic Assurance	12	12	4	100	46 *	12.50	-	-	5	-

Refuge Assurance	2	0	0	0	0	-	-	-	-	-
NatWest Trophy	2	0	0	0	0	-	-	-	2	-
Benson & Hedges Cup	2	1	1	12	12 *	-	-	-	1	-
Other First-Class	1	1	0	7	7	7.00	-	-	2	-
ALL FIRST-CLASS	13	13	4	107	46 *	11.88	-	-	7	-
ALL ONE-DAY	6	1	1	12	12 *	-	-	-	3	-

BOWLING AVERAGES

	Overs	Mdns	Runs	Wkts	Avge	Best	5wI	10wM
Britannic Assurance	462.4	126	1145	29	39.48	5-45	3	1
Refuge Assurance	16	1	62	1	62.00	1-20	-	
NatWest Trophy	18.5	0	47	2	23.50	2-26	-	
Benson & Hedges Cup	22	1	95	1	95.00	1-40	-	
Other First-Class	23	11	44	2	22.00	2-44	-	
ALL FIRST-CLASS	485.4	137	1189	31	38.35	5-45	3	1
ALL ONE-DAY	56.5	2	204	4	51.00	2-26	-	

A.H. GRAY - *Surrey*

Opposition	Venue	Date	Batting	Fielding	Bowling
BRITANNIC ASSURANCE					
Sussex	Hove	April 26	11		1-58
Middlesex	Lord's	May 23			2-68
Worcestershire	The Oval	June 16		1Ct	1-41 & 0-8
Glamorgan	Cardiff	June 30		1Ct	0-42 & 1-29
Kent	Guildford	July 21		1Ct	2-54 & 2-93
Kent	Canterbury	Sept 7	11	2Ct	3-80 & 4-83
BENSON & HEDGES CUP					
Lancashire	Old Trafford	April 24			0-52
Combined U	The Parks	May 10			0-20
OTHER FIRST-CLASS					
India	The Oval	Aug 1		2Ct	3-69 & 0-41
OTHER ONE-DAY					
Warwickshire	Harrogate	June 13	9 *		2-55
Sri Lanka	The Oval	Sept 2			2-35

BATTING AVERAGES - Including fielding

	Matches	Inns	NO	Runs	HS	Avge	100s	50s	Ct	St
Britannic Assurance	6	2	0	22	11	11.00	-	-	5	-
Benson & Hedges Cup	2	0	0	0	0	-	-	-	-	-
Other First-Class	1	0	0	0	0	-	-	-	2	-
Other One-Day	2	1	1	9	9 *	-	-	-	-	-
ALL FIRST-CLASS	7	2	0	22	11	11.00	-	-	7	-
ALL ONE-DAY	4	1	1	9	9 *	-	-	-	-	-

BOWLING AVERAGES

	Overs	Mdns	Runs	Wkts	Avge	Best	5wI	10wM
Britannic Assurance	212.4	43	556	16	34.75	4-83	-	-
Benson & Hedges Cup	21	2	72	0	-	-	-	-
Other First-Class	27.1	0	110	3	36.66	3-69	-	-
Other One-Day	21	2	90	4	22.50	2-35	-	-
ALL FIRST-CLASS	239.5	43	666	19	35.05	4-83	-	-
ALL ONE-DAY	42	4	162	4	40.50	2-35	-	-

P. GRAYSON - *Yorkshire*

Opposition	Venue	Date	Batting		Fielding	Bowling
BRITANNIC ASSURANCE						
Somerset	Scarborough	July 25	44 * &	16 *		0-66 & 0-23
Leicestershire	Sheffield	July 28	36 * &	11		0-5
Middlesex	Headingley	Aug 23	4 &	18	2Ct	
Notts	Trent Bridge	Sept 18		6 *		0-78 & 1-55
OTHER FIRST-CLASS						
Zimbabwe	Headingley	May 16	10			0-8 & 0-35

PLAINER RECORDS

PLAYER RECORDS

G

BATTING AVERAGES - Including fielding

	Matches	Inns	NO	Runs	HS	Avge	100s	50s	Ct	St
Britannic Assurance	4	7	4	135	44 *	45.00	-	-	2	-
Other First-Class	1	1	0	10	10	10.00	-	-	-	-
ALL FIRST-CLASS	5	8	4	145	44 *	36.25	-	-	2	-

BOWLING AVERAGES

	Overs	Mdns	Runs	Wkts	Avge	Best	5wI	10wM
Britannic Assurance	63	13	227	1	227.00	1-55	-	-
Other First-Class	17	6	43	0	-	-	-	-
ALL FIRST-CLASS	80	19	270	1	270.00	1-55	-	-

M.J. GREATBATCH - *New Zealand*

Opposition	Venue	Date	Batting	Fielding	Bowling
CORNHILL TEST MATCHES					
England	Trent Bridge	June 7	1		
England	Lord's	June 21	47		
England	Edgbaston	July 5	45 & 22		
TEXACO TROPHY					
England	Headingley	May 23	102 *		
England	The Oval	May 25	111		
OTHER FIRST-CLASS					
Worcestershire	Worcester	May 12	1 & 19	2Ct	
Somerset	Taunton	May 16	85		
Middlesex	Lord's	May 19	34 & 52		
Sussex	Hove	May 26	26 & 51 *	1Ct	
Derbyshire	Derby	June 2	3	1Ct	
Northants	Northampton	June 16	0		
Combined U	Fenner's	June 27	62	1Ct	
For World XI					
India	Scarborough	Aug 29	168 * & 128 *	2Ct	
OTHER ONE-DAY					
D of Norfolk	Arundel	May 6	20		
MCC	Lord's	May 7	52		
Ireland	Belfast	May 10	32		0-3
Leicestershire	Leicester	June 14	0		
For Rest of World					
England XI	Jesmond	Aug 2	57		
England XI	Jesmond	Aug 3			0-9
For World XI					
Yorkshire	Scarborough	Sept 1	4	1Ct	

BATTING AVERAGES - Including fielding

	Matches	Inns	NO	Runs	HS	Avge	100s	50s	Ct	St
Cornhill Test Matches	3	4	0	115	47	28.75	-	-	-	-
Texaco Trophy	2	2	1	213	111	213.00	2	-	-	-
Other First-Class	8	12	3	629	168 *	69.88	2	4	7	-
Other One-Day	7	6	0	165	57	27.50	-	2	1	-
ALL FIRST-CLASS	11	16	3	744	168 *	57.23	2	4	7	-
ALL ONE-DAY	9	8	1	378	111	54.00	2	2	1	-

BOWLING AVERAGES

	Overs	Mdns	Runs	Wkts	Avge	Best	5wI	10wM
Cornhill Test Matches								
Texaco Trophy								
Other First-Class								
Other One-Day	5	0	12	0	-	-	-	-
ALL FIRST-CLASS								
ALL ONE-DAY	5	0	12	0	-	-	-	-

R.C. GREEN - *Suffolk & Minor Counties*

Opposition	Venue	Date	Batting	Fielding	Bowling
NATWEST TROPHY					
Worcestershire	Bury St Ed's	June 27	0		0-38

BENSON & HEDGES CUP

Middlesex	Lord's	April 24			1-49
Sussex	Marlow	May 1			1-51
Somerset	Taunton	May 8			0-57
Derbyshire	Wellington	May 10	5 *		0-26

BATTING AVERAGES - Including fielding

	Matches	Inns	NO	Runs	HS	Avge	100s	50s	Ct	St
NatWest Trophy	1	1	0	0	0	0.00	-	-	-	-
Benson & Hedges Cup	4	1	1	5	5 *	-	-	-	-	-
ALL ONE-DAY	5	2	1	5	5 *	5.00	-	-	-	-

BOWLING AVERAGES

	Overs	Mdns	Runs	Wkts	Avge	Best	5wI	10wM
NatWest Trophy	11	1	38	0	-	-	-	-
Benson & Hedges Cup	40.1	2	183	2	91.50	1-49	-	-
ALL ONE-DAY	51.1	3	221	2	110.50	1-49	-	-

S.J. GREEN - *Warwickshire*

Opposition	Venue	Date	Batting	Fielding	Bowling
REFUGE ASSURANCE					
Somerset	Weston	Aug 12	25		
Leicestershire	Edgbaston	Aug 19			
OTHER FIRST-CLASS					
Sri Lanka	Edgbaston	Aug 29	44 & 0		
OTHER ONE-DAY					
Surrey	Hove	Sept 3	21		

BATTING AVERAGES - Including fielding

	Matches	Inns	NO	Runs	HS	Avge	100s	50s	Ct	St
Refuge Assurance	2	1	0	25	25	25.00	-	-	-	-
Other First-Class	1	2	0	44	44	22.00	-	-	-	-
Other One-Day	1	1	0	21	21	21.00	-	-	-	-
ALL FIRST-CLASS	1	2	0	44	44	22.00	-	-	-	-
ALL ONE-DAY	3	2	0	46	25	23.00	-	-	-	-

BOWLING AVERAGES
Did not bowl

K. GREENFIELD - *Sussex*

Opposition	Venue	Date	Batting	Fielding	Bowling
BRITANNIC ASSURANCE					
Somerset	Hove	Aug 23	5 & 11		0-8
Leicestershire	Leicester	Aug 29	38 & 20	1Ct	
REFUGE ASSURANCE					
Somerset	Hove	Aug 26	2		
OTHER FIRST-CLASS					
Cambridge U	Hove	June 30	102 * & 54 *		
OTHER ONE-DAY					
Zimbabwe	Hove	May 13	10		
Yorkshire	Harrogate	June 14	10		
Kent	Hove	Sept 2	34	2Ct	

BATTING AVERAGES - Including fielding

	Matches	Inns	NO	Runs	HS	Avge	100s	50s	Ct	St
Britannic Assurance	2	4	0	74	38	18.50	-	-	1	-
Refuge Assurance	1	1	0	2	2	2.00	-	-	-	-
Other First-Class	1	2	2	156	102 *	-	1	1	-	-
Other One-Day	3	3	0	54	34	18.00	-	-	2	-
ALL FIRST-CLASS	3	6	2	230	102 *	57.50	1	1	1	-
ALL ONE-DAY	4	4	0	56	34	14.00	-	-	2	-

G   PLAYER RECORDS

BOWLING AVERAGES

	Overs	Mdns	Runs	Wkts	Avge	Best	5wI	10wM
Britannic Assurance	0.3	0	8	0	-	-	-	-
Refuge Assurance								
Other First-Class								
Other One-Day								
ALL FIRST-CLASS	0.3	0	8	0	-	-	-	-
ALL ONE-DAY								

C.G. GREENIDGE - *Scotland*

Opposition	Venue	Date	Batting	Fielding	Bowling
NATWEST TROPHY					
Essex	Chelmsford	June 27	15		
BENSON & HEDGES CUP					
Essex	Glasgow	May 1	50		
Notts	Glasgow	May 8	1	1Ct	
Northants	Northampton	May 10	32		
Leicestershire	Leicester	May 12	34		
OTHER FIRST-CLASS					
For World XI					
India	Scarborough	Aug 29	23 & 0	1Ct	
OTHER ONE-DAY					
For Scotland					
India	Glasgow	July 14	34	1Ct	
For Rest of World					
England XI	Jesmond	Aug 2	27		
England XI	Jesmond	Aug 3			2-0

BATTING AVERAGES - Including fielding

	Matches	Inns	NO	Runs	HS	Avge	100s	50s	Ct	St
NatWest Trophy	1	1	0	15	15	15.00	-	-	-	-
Benson & Hedges Cup	4	4	0	117	50	29.25	-	1	1	-
Other First-Class	1	2	0	23	23	11.50	-	-	1	-
Other One-Day	3	2	0	61	34	30.50	-	-	1	-
ALL FIRST-CLASS	1	2	0	23	23	11.50	-	-	1	-
ALL ONE-DAY	8	7	0	193	50	27.57	-	1	2	-

BOWLING AVERAGES

	Overs	Mdns	Runs	Wkts	Avge	Best	5wI	10wM
NatWest Trophy								
Benson & Hedges Cup								
Other First-Class								
Other One-Day	0.2	0	0	2	0.00	2-0	-	
ALL FIRST-CLASS								
ALL ONE-DAY	0.2	0	0	2	0.00	2-0	-	

S. GREENSWORD - *Durham & M. Counties*

Opposition	Venue	Date	Batting	Fielding	Bowling
NATWEST TROPHY					
Lancashire	Old Trafford	June 27	0		0-23
BENSON & HEDGES CUP					
For Minor Counties					
Middlesex	Lord's	April 24	3		0-30
Sussex	Marlow	May 1			1-53
Somerset	Taunton	May 8	10		0-34
Derbyshire	Wellington	May 10	28		3-38
OTHER FIRST-CLASS					
For Minor Counties					
India	Trowbridge	July 11	1	1Ct	0-52

BATTING AVERAGES - Including fielding

	Matches	Inns	NO	Runs	HS	Avge	100s	50s	Ct	St
NatWest Trophy	1	1	0	0	0	0.00	-	-	-	-
Benson & Hedges Cup	4	3	0	41	28	13.66	-	-	-	-

Other First-Class	1	1	0	1	1	1.00	-	-	1	-
ALL FIRST-CLASS	1	1	0	1	1	1.00	-	-	1	-
ALL ONE-DAY	5	4	0	41	28	10.25	-	-	-	-

BOWLING AVERAGES

	Overs	Mdns	Runs	Wkts	Avge	Best	5wI	10wM
NatWest Trophy	6	1	23	0	-	-	-	-
Benson & Hedges Cup	34	2	155	4	38.75	3-38	-	
Other First-Class	19	6	52	0	-	-	-	-
ALL FIRST-CLASS	19	6	52	0	-	-	-	-
ALL ONE-DAY	40	3	178	4	44.50	3-38	-	

I.A. GREIG - *Surrey*

Opposition	Venue	Date	Batting	Fielding	Bowling
BRITANNIC ASSURANCE					
Sussex	Hove	April 26	9		0-19 & 0-45
Lancashire	The Oval	May 3	291	2Ct	2-73
Hampshire	The Oval	May 19	34 & 4		1-40
Middlesex	Lord's	May 23	44	2Ct	0-5 & 0-8
Derbyshire	The Oval	June 6		2Ct	0-36
Yorkshire	Harrogate	June 9	72		
Worcestershire	The Oval	June 16	6		0-17
Notts	Trent Bridge	June 20			0-9
Glamorgan	Cardiff	June 30	25		0-14
Northants	The Oval	July 4		1Ct	
Warwickshire	The Oval	July 7	30 * & 34		
Sussex	Guildford	July 18	37	1Ct	
Kent	Guildford	July 21	89 *	1Ct	0-36
Gloucs	Cheltenham	July 28	1 & 34	1Ct	0-6 & 2-77
Somerset	Weston	Aug 4	123 * & 24		0-55 & 0-0
Leicestershire	The Oval	Aug 11	84	2Ct	0-16
Essex	Chelmsford	Aug 18	0 & 4	2Ct	0-16 & 3-60
Hampshire	Southampton	Aug 23	11 & 45 *	1Ct	0-15
Lancashire	Blackpool	Aug 29			
Kent	Canterbury	Sept 7	0		1-60 & 0-57
Middlesex	The Oval	Sept 12	31 & 30	1Ct	0-41
Essex	The Oval	Sept 18	11 & 57 *		3-150
REFUGE ASSURANCE					
Sussex	Hove	April 29	2		
Lancashire	The Oval	May 6	21 *		
Notts	Trent Bridge	May 20	12		
Northants	The Oval	June 3	19	1Ct	
Yorkshire	Hull	June 10	2 *		
Worcestershire	The Oval	June 17			
Derbyshire	The Oval	June 24	8 *		
Glamorgan	Cardiff	July 1	23		
Warwickshire	The Oval	July 8	43	1Ct	
Middlesex	The Oval	July 15	4 *	1Ct	0-16
Kent	The Oval	July 22	0 *		0-22
Gloucs	Cheltenham	July 29	14		
Somerset	Weston	Aug 5	27 *		
Leicestershire	The Oval	Aug 12	26		
Hampshire	Southampton	Aug 26	16 *		1-37
NATWEST TROPHY					
Wiltshire	Trowbridge	June 27			
BENSON & HEDGES CUP					
Lancashire	Old Trafford	April 24	1		0-45
Hampshire	The Oval	May 1	9 *	2Ct	2-35
Combined U	The Parks	May 10			1-51
Yorkshire	The Oval	May 12	15		0-45
Lancashire	Old Trafford	May 30	9		
OTHER FIRST-CLASS					
Oxford U	The Parks	May 16	17		1-38 & 0-15
India	The Oval	Aug 1	36 & 76 *		
OTHER ONE-DAY					
Warwickshire	Harrogate	June 13	39		
Warwickshire	Hove	Sept 3	2		1-26
Kent	Hove	Sept 4	4		1-50

BATTING AVERAGES - Including fielding

	Matches	Inns	NO	Runs	HS	Avge	100s	50s	Ct	St
Britannic Assurance	22	26	5	1130	291	53.81	2	4	16	-

PLHYER RECORDS

Refuge Assurance	15	14	7	217	43	31.00	-	-	3	-
NatWest Trophy	1	0	0	0	0	-	-	-	-	-
Benson & Hedges Cup	5	4	1	34	15	11.33	-	-	2	-
Other First-Class	2	3	1	129	76 *	64.50	-	1	-	-
Other One-Day	3	3	0	45	39	15.00	-	-	-	-
ALL FIRST-CLASS	24	29	6	1259	291	54.73	2	5	16	-
ALL ONE-DAY	24	21	8	296	43	22.76	-	-	5	-

BOWLING AVERAGES

	Overs	Mdns	Runs	Wkts	Avge	Best	5wI	10wM
Britannic Assurance	199.1	19	805	12	67.08	3-60	-	-
Refuge Assurance	12	0	75	1	75.00	1-37	-	
NatWest Trophy								
Benson & Hedges Cup	36.2	0	176	3	58.66	2-35	-	
Other First-Class	17	2	53	1	53.00	1-38	-	-
Other One-Day	12	0	76	2	38.00	1-26	-	
ALL FIRST-CLASS	216.1	21	858	13	66.00	3-60	-	-
ALL ONE-DAY	60.2	0	327	6	54.50	2-35	-	

F.A. GRIFFITH - *Derbyshire*

Opposition	Venue	Date	Batting	Fielding	Bowling
BRITANNIC ASSURANCE					
Northants	Northampton	May 3	1		1-20

BATTING AVERAGES - Including fielding

	Matches	Inns	NO	Runs	HS	Avge	100s	50s	Ct	St
Britannic Assurance	1	1	0	1	1	1.00	-	-	-	-
ALL FIRST-CLASS	1	1	0	1	1	1.00	-	-	-	-

BOWLING AVERAGES

	Overs	Mdns	Runs	Wkts	Avge	Best	5wI	10wM
Britannic Assurance	11	2	20	1	20.00	1-20	-	-
ALL FIRST-CLASS	11	2	20	1	20.00	1-20	-	-

A.P. GURUSINHA - *Sri Lanka*

Opposition	Venue	Date	Batting		Fielding	Bowling
OTHER FIRST-CLASS						
Glamorgan	Ebbw Vale	Aug 22	58 &	23		1-31
Notts	Cleethorpes	Aug 25	37 * &	17 *		3-38
Sussex	Hove	Sept 5	3 * &	0		0-8 & 1-36
OTHER ONE-DAY						
Surrey	The Oval	Sept 2	4			1-20
Somerset	Taunton	Sept 3	1			1-59

BATTING AVERAGES - Including fielding

	Matches	Inns	NO	Runs	HS	Avge	100s	50s	Ct	St
Other First-Class	3	6	3	138	58	46.00	-	1	-	-
Other One-Day	2	2	0	5	4	2.50	-	-	-	-
ALL FIRST-CLASS	3	6	3	138	58	46.00	-	1	-	-
ALL ONE-DAY	2	2	0	5	4	2.50	-	-	-	-

BOWLING AVERAGES

	Overs	Mdns	Runs	Wkts	Avge	Best	5wI	10wM
Other First-Class	40	8	113	5	22.60	3-38	-	-

H — PLAYER RECORDS

R.J.HADLEE - New Zealand

Opposition	Venue	Date	Batting	Fielding	Bowling
CORNHILL TEST MATCHES					
England	Trent Bridge	June 7	0		4-89
England	Lord's	June 21	86		3-113 & 1-32
England	Edgbaston	July 5	8 & 13	2Ct	3-97 & 5-53
TEXACO TROPHY					
England	Headingley	May 23	12		2-46
England	The Oval	May 25	9*		2-34
OTHER FIRST-CLASS					
Worcestershire	Worcester	May 12	90		5-27 & 2-72
Middlesex	Lord's	May 19		7 2Ct	1-78 & 0-25
OTHER ONE-DAY					
Ireland	Downpatrick	May 9		1Ct	3-25
Ireland	Belfast	May 10	20	2Ct	2-13

BATTING AVERAGES - Including fielding

	Matches	Inns	NO	Runs	HS	Avge	100s	50s	Ct	St
Cornhill Test Matches	3	4	0	107	86	26.75	-	1	2	-
Texaco Trophy	2	2	1	21	12	21.00	-	-	-	-
Other First-Class	2	2	0	97	90	48.50	-	1	2	-
Other One-Day	2	1	0	20	20	20.00	-	-	3	-
ALL FIRST-CLASS	5	6	0	204	90	34.00	-	2	4	-
ALL ONE-DAY	4	3	1	41	20	20.50	-	-	3	-

BOWLING AVERAGES

	Overs	Mdns	Runs	Wkts	Avge	Best	5wI	10wM
Cornhill Test Matches	133.5	24	384	16	24.00	5-53	1	-
Texaco Trophy	22	6	80	4	20.00	2-34	-	
Other First-Class	68	15	202	8	25.25	5-27	1	-
Other One-Day	17	3	38	5	7.60	3-25	-	
ALL FIRST-CLASS	201.5	39	586	24	24.41	5-27	2	-
ALL ONE-DAY	39	9	118	9	13.11	3-25	-	

D.A. HAGAN - Oxford University

Opposition	Venue	Date	Batting	Fielding	Bowling
OTHER FIRST-CLASS					
Glamorgan	The Parks	April 14	47		
Somerset	The Parks	April 18	7		
Hampshire	The Parks	May 3	14		
Surrey	The Parks	May 16	17 & 12		
Leicestershire	The Parks	May 23	0 & 6		
Glamorgan	The Parks	June 2	43		
Notts	The Parks	June 6	15		
Lancashire	The Parks	June 16	1 & 5	1Ct	
Cambridge U	Lord's	July 4	8	1Ct	

BATTING AVERAGES - Including fielding

	Matches	Inns	NO	Runs	HS	Avge	100s	50s	Ct	St
Other First-Class	9	12	0	175	47	14.58	-	-	2	-
ALL FIRST-CLASS	9	12	0	175	47	14.58	-	-	2	-

BOWLING AVERAGES
Did not bowl

D.J. HAGGO - Scotland

Opposition	Venue	Date	Batting	Fielding	Bowling
BENSON & HEDGES CUP					
Essex	Glasgow	May 1	18*		
Notts	Glasgow	May 8	2*		
OTHER FIRST-CLASS					
Ireland	Edinburgh	Aug 11	34	0Ct,2St	

OTHER ONE-DAY

India	Glasgow	July 14	6	1Ct	

BATTING AVERAGES - Including fielding

	Matches	Inns	NO	Runs	HS	Avge	100s	50s	Ct	St
Benson & Hedges Cup	2	2	2	20	18*	-	-	-	-	-
Other First-Class	1	1	0	34	34	34.00	-	-	-	2
Other One-Day	1	1	0	6	6	6.00	-	-	1	-
ALL FIRST-CLASS	1	1	0	34	34	34.00	-	-	-	2
ALL ONE-DAY	3	3	2	26	18*	26.00	-	-	1	-

BOWLING AVERAGES
Did not bowl

D.A. HALE - Oxfordshire

Opposition	Venue	Date	Batting	Fielding	Bowling
NATWEST TROPHY					
Kent	Oxford	June 27	6		0-15

BATTING AVERAGES - Including fielding

	Matches	Inns	NO	Runs	HS	Avge	100s	50s	Ct	St
NatWest Trophy	1	1	0	6	6	6.00	-	-	-	-
ALL ONE-DAY	1	1	0	6	6	6.00	-	-	-	-

BOWLING AVERAGES

	Overs	Mdns	Runs	Wkts	Avge	Best	5wI	10wM
NatWest Trophy	4	0	15	0	-	-	-	-
ALL ONE-DAY	4	0	15	0	-	-	-	-

J.R. HALL - Dorset

Opposition	Venue	Date	Batting	Fielding	Bowling
NATWEST TROPHY					
Glamorgan	Swansea	June 27	12	1Ct	0-26

BATTING AVERAGES - Including fielding

	Matches	Inns	NO	Runs	HS	Avge	100s	50s	Ct	St
NatWest Trophy	1	1	0	12	12	12.00	-	-	1	-
ALL ONE-DAY	1	1	0	12	12	12.00	-	-	1	-

BOWLING AVERAGES

	Overs	Mdns	Runs	Wkts	Avge	Best	5wI	10wM
NatWest Trophy	6	2	26	0	-	-	-	-
ALL ONE-DAY	6	2	26	0	-	-	-	-

J.W. HALL - Sussex

Opposition	Venue	Date	Batting	Fielding	Bowling
BRITANNIC ASSURANCE					
Glamorgan	Hove	May 19	8 & 7		
Somerset	Taunton	May 23	6 & 1		
Lancashire	Horsham	June 2	24 & 15		
Gloucs	Hove	June 16	19 & 17		
Worcestershire	Worcester	June 20	72		
Derbyshire	Hove	July 4	6	1Ct	
Notts	Trent Bridge	July 7	125 & 59*		
Surrey	Guildford	July 18	16 & 21		
Northants	Northampton	July 21	42 & 7		
Hampshire	Arundel	July 25	4 & 36	1Ct	
Essex	Chelmsford	July 28	62 & 50		
Warwickshire	Eastbourne	Aug 4	30 & 12	1Ct	
Yorkshire	Eastbourne	Aug 8	32 & 38		

PLARYER RECORDS

Middlesex	Lord's	Aug 11	49	
Kent	Hove	Aug 18	24 & 52	
Somerset	Hove	Aug 23	1 & 2	
Leicestershire	Leicester	Aug 29	34 & 17	

NATWEST TROPHY

Glamorgan	Cardiff	July 11	0

OTHER FIRST-CLASS

New Zealand	Hove	May 26	120 * & 40	
Cambridge U	Hove	June 30	3 & 49	1Ct
Sri Lanka	Hove	Sept 5	40 & 0	2Ct

OTHER ONE-DAY

Zimbabwe	Hove	May 13	53

BATTING AVERAGES - Including fielding

	Matches	Inns	NO	Runs	HS	Avge	100s	50s	Ct	St
Britannic Assurance	17	31	1	888	125	29.60	1	5	3	-
NatWest Trophy	1	1	0	0	0	0.00	-	-	-	-
Other First-Class	3	6	1	252	120 *	50.40	1	-	3	-
Other One-Day	1	1	0	53	53	53.00	-	1	-	-
ALL FIRST-CLASS	20	37	2	1140	125	32.57	2	5	6	-
ALL ONE-DAY	2	2	0	53	53	26.50	-	1	-	-

BOWLING AVERAGES
Did not bowl

J.C. HALLETT - *Somerset*

Opposition	Venue	Date	Batting	Fielding	Bowling
BRITANNIC ASSURANCE					
Gloucs	Bristol	June 2	0		1-63
Kent	Canterbury	June 9			2-40 & 1-32
REFUGE ASSURANCE					
Gloucs	Bristol	June 3	4 *		0-28
Notts	Bath	June 24			2-39
Northants	Taunton	July 1			0-27
Middlesex	Lord's	July 8			0-23
Yorkshire	Scarborough	July 15	0 *		1-23
Glamorgan	Neath	July 22			3-41
Lancashire	Old Trafford	July 29			1-31
Warwickshire	Weston	Aug 12			0-16
Sussex	Hove	Aug 26	3 *		0-18
BENSON & HEDGES CUP					
Derbyshire	Taunton	May 1			1-52
Min Counties	Taunton	May 8			0-18
OTHER FIRST-CLASS					
New Zealand	Taunton	May 16			0-52 & 2-51

BATTING AVERAGES - Including fielding

	Matches	Inns	NO	Runs	HS	Avge	100s	50s	Ct	St
Britannic Assurance	2	1	0	0	0	0.00	-	-	-	-
Refuge Assurance	9	3	3	7	4 *	-	-	-	-	-
Benson & Hedges Cup	2	0	0	0	0	-	-	-	-	-
Other First-Class	1	0	0	0	0	-	-	-	-	-
ALL FIRST-CLASS	3	1	0	0	0	0.00	-	-	-	-
ALL ONE-DAY	11	3	3	7	4 *	-	-	-	-	-

BOWLING AVERAGES

	Overs	Mdns	Runs	Wkts	Avge	Best	5wI	10wM
Britannic Assurance	40.2	7	135	4	33.75	2-40	-	-
Refuge Assurance	45.3	2	246	7	35.14	3-41	-	
Benson & Hedges Cup	11	0	70	1	70.00	1-52	-	
Other First-Class	25.3	2	103	2	51.50	2-51	-	-
ALL FIRST-CLASS	65.5	9	238	6	39.66	2-40	-	-
ALL ONE-DAY	56.3	2	316	8	39.50	3-41	-	

N.G. HAMES - *Buckinghamshire*

Opposition	Venue	Date	Batting	Fielding	Bowling
NATWEST TROPHY					
Notts	Marlow	June 27	4		

BATTING AVERAGES - Including fielding

	Matches	Inns	NO	Runs	HS	Avge	100s	50s	Ct	St
NatWest Trophy	1	1	0	4	4	4.00	-	-	-	-
ALL ONE-DAY	1	1	0	4	4	4.00	-	-	-	-

BOWLING AVERAGES
Did not bowl

F.L.Q. HANDLEY - *Norfolk*

Opposition	Venue	Date	Batting	Fielding	Bowling
NATWEST TROPHY					
Yorkshire	Headingley	June 27	0		

BATTING AVERAGES - Including fielding

	Matches	Inns	NO	Runs	HS	Avge	100s	50s	Ct	St
NatWest Trophy	1	1	0	0	0	0.00	-	-	-	-
ALL ONE-DAY	1	1	0	0	0	0.00	-	-	-	-

BOWLING AVERAGES
Did not bowl

R. HANLEY - *Sussex*

Opposition	Venue	Date	Batting	Fielding	Bowling
BRITANNIC ASSURANCE					
Warwickshire	Eastbourne	Aug 4	2 & 28		
Yorkshire	Eastbourne	Aug 8	2 & 0		
REFUGE ASSURANCE					
Warwickshire	Eastbourne	Aug 5	11		
Middlesex	Lord's	Aug 12		1Ct	

BATTING AVERAGES - Including fielding

	Matches	Inns	NO	Runs	HS	Avge	100s	50s	Ct	St
Britannic Assurance	2	4	0	32	28	8.00	-	-	-	-
Refuge Assurance	2	1	0	11	11	11.00	-	-	1	-
ALL FIRST-CLASS	2	4	0	32	28	8.00	-	-	-	-
ALL ONE-DAY	2	1	0	11	11	11.00	-	-	1	-

BOWLING AVERAGES
Did not bowl

A.R. HANSFORD - *Sussex*

Opposition	Venue	Date	Batting	Fielding	Bowling
BRITANNIC ASSURANCE					
Surrey	Hove	April 26			1-84 & 1-41
Kent	Folkestone	May 3	19 & 2		3-91 & 0-31
Hampshire	Southampton	May 15	3 *& 29		2-102
Yorkshire	Eastbourne	Aug 8	2 & 0	1Ct	0-76
REFUGE ASSURANCE					
Derbyshire	Hove	April 22	5 *		0-35
Surrey	Hove	April 29			2-48
Essex	Chelmsford	July 29			2-62
Warwickshire	Eastbourne	Aug 5	2	1Ct	1-49
Middlesex	Lord's	Aug 12			1-46

BENSON & HEDGES CUP

Opposition	Venue	Date	Batting	Bowling
Derbyshire	Derby	April 24		0-58
Min Counties	Marlow	May 1		0-70
Middlesex	Hove	May 8		2-55
Somerset	Hove	May 12	2 *	0-82

OTHER ONE-DAY
For Duchess of Norfolk's XI

Opposition	Venue	Date	Fielding	Bowling
New Zealand	Arundel	May 6	1Ct	1-58

BATTING AVERAGES - Including fielding

	Matches	Inns	NO	Runs	HS	Avge	100s	50s	Ct	St
Britannic Assurance	4	6	1	55	29	11.00	-	-	1	-
Refuge Assurance	5	2	1	7	5 *	7.00	-	-	1	-
Benson & Hedges Cup	4	1	1	2	2 *	-	-	-	-	-
Other One-Day	1	0	0	0	0	-	-	-	1	-
ALL FIRST-CLASS	4	6	1	55	29	11.00	-	-	1	-
ALL ONE-DAY	10	3	2	9	5 *	9.00	-	-	2	-

BOWLING AVERAGES

	Overs	Mdns	Runs	Wkts	Avge	Best	5wI	10wM
Britannic Assurance	123.5	21	425	7	60.71	3-91	-	-
Refuge Assurance	36	1	240	6	40.00	2-48	-	
Benson & Hedges Cup	44	0	265	2	132.50	2-55	-	
Other One-Day	9	0	58	1	58.00	1-58	-	
ALL FIRST-CLASS	123.5	21	425	7	60.71	3-91	-	-
ALL ONE-DAY	89	1	563	9	62.55	2-48	-	

R.J. HARDEN - *Somerset*

Opposition	Venue	Date	Batting	Fielding	Bowling

BRITANNIC ASSURANCE

Opposition	Venue	Date	Batting		Fielding	Bowling
Gloucs	Taunton	April 26	46		1Ct	
Glamorgan	Cardiff	May 3		64	1Ct	0-21
Derbyshire	Taunton	May 19	69 * &	42	1Ct	1-60
Sussex	Taunton	May 23	51		1Ct	0-43
Leicestershire	Leicester	May 26	44		3Ct	
Gloucs	Bristol	June 2	81		1Ct	
Hampshire	Basingstoke	June 6				
Kent	Canterbury	June 9	52 * &	50 *		
Essex	Bath	June 16				2-54
Glamorgan	Bath	June 20			2Ct	0-12
Northants	Taunton	June 30	23 &	28		
Warwickshire	Taunton	July 4	9		1Ct	
Worcestershire	Worcester	July 18	0 * &	29		
Middlesex	Uxbridge	July 21	17 &	38	1Ct	
Yorkshire	Scarborough	July 25	101 &	24		
Lancashire	Old Trafford	July 28	60 &	2		
Surrey	Weston	Aug 4	104 * &	55 *	1Ct	
Notts	Weston	Aug 8	0			0-13
Hampshire	Taunton	Aug 18	0 &	36	3Ct	2-39
Sussex	Hove	Aug 23	59			1-12
Warwickshire	Edgbaston	Sept 7	32		1Ct	
Worcestershire	Taunton	Sept 12	51 * &	90	1Ct	

REFUGE ASSURANCE

Opposition	Venue	Date	Batting	Fielding
Worcestershire	Taunton	April 22	35	
Hampshire	Taunton	May 13	13 *	
Derbyshire	Taunton	May 20	30	1Ct
Leicestershire	Leicester	May 27	31 *	
Gloucs	Bristol	June 3	3	
Kent	Canterbury	June 10	21 *	
Essex	Bath	June 17	13	
Notts	Bath	June 24	2	
Northants	Taunton	July 1	22 *	
Middlesex	Lord's	July 8	41 *	2Ct
Yorkshire	Scarborough	July 15	28	2Ct
Glamorgan	Neath	July 22	32 *	1Ct
Lancashire	Old Trafford	July 29	32	
Surrey	Weston	Aug 5	53	
Warwickshire	Weston	Aug 12	41 *	
Sussex	Hove	Aug 26	0	

NATWEST TROPHY

Opposition	Venue	Date	Batting
Devon	Torquay	June 27	
Worcestershire	Taunton	July 11	12

BENSON & HEDGES CUP

Opposition	Venue	Date	Batting	Fielding
Derbyshire	Taunton	May 1	3 *	1Ct

Opposition	Venue	Date	Batting	Fielding	Bowling
Min Counties	Taunton	May 8	53 *		
Middlesex	Lord's	May 10	5		
Sussex	Hove	May 12	15		
Middlesex	Taunton	May 30	23		
Lancashire	Old Trafford	June 13	16	1Ct	

OTHER FIRST-CLASS

Opposition	Venue	Date	Batting	Bowling
Oxford U	The Parks	April 18	99	
New Zealand	Taunton	May 16	104	0-22

OTHER ONE-DAY

Opposition	Venue	Date	Batting	Bowling
Sri Lanka	Taunton	Sept 3	25	0-7

BATTING AVERAGES - Including fielding

	Matches	Inns	NO	Runs	HS	Avge	100s	50s	Ct	St
Britannic Assurance	22	29	7	1257	104 *	57.13	2	11	18	-
Refuge Assurance	16	16	7	397	53	44.11	-	1	6	-
NatWest Trophy	2	1	0	12	12	12.00	-	-	-	-
Benson & Hedges Cup	6	6	2	115	53 *	28.75	-	1	2	-
Other First-Class	2	2	0	203	104	101.50	1	1	-	-
Other One-Day	1	1	0	25	25	25.00	-	-	-	-
ALL FIRST-CLASS	24	31	7	1460	104 *	60.83	3	12	18	-
ALL ONE-DAY	25	24	9	549	53 *	36.60	-	2	8	-

BOWLING AVERAGES

	Overs	Mdns	Runs	Wkts	Avge	Best	5wI	10wM
Britannic Assurance	64	6	254	6	42.33	2-39	-	-
Refuge Assurance								
NatWest Trophy								
Benson & Hedges Cup								
Other First-Class	3	0	22	0	-	-	-	-
Other One-Day	1	0	7	0	-	-	-	-
ALL FIRST-CLASS	67	6	276	6	46.00	2-39	-	-
ALL ONE-DAY	1	0	7	0	-	-	-	-

B.R. HARDIE - *Essex*

Opposition	Venue	Date	Batting	Fielding	Bowling

BRITANNIC ASSURANCE

Opposition	Venue	Date	Batting		Fielding	Bowling
Middlesex	Lord's	April 26	21 &	0 *		
Leicestershire	Chelmsford	May 3	74 *			
Worcestershire	Worcester	May 19	59		2Ct	
Hampshire	Southampton	May 23	125 &	31		
Middlesex	Ilford	June 2	74			
Gloucs	Ilford	June 6	110 * &	13		
Warwickshire	Edgbaston	June 9	2			
Somerset	Bath	June 16	22 *			
Kent	Maidstone	June 4		12	1Ct	
Derbyshire	Colchester	July 18	24 &	41 *	3Ct	
Surrey	The Oval	Sept 18	42		1Ct	0-16

REFUGE ASSURANCE

Opposition	Venue	Date	Batting	Fielding
Kent	Chelmsford	April 22	56	
Middlesex	Lord's	April 29	16	
Leicestershire	Leicester	May 6	2	
Gloucs	Chelmsford	May 13	42	
Worcestershire	Worcester	May 20	54	1Ct
Glamorgan	Ilford	June 3	30	
Warwickshire	Edgbaston	June 10	54	
Somerset	Bath	June 17	7	1Ct
Hampshire	Southampton	July 8	4	1Ct
Lancashire	Colchester	July 22	2 *	1Ct
Sussex	Chelmsford	July 29	44	
Yorkshire	Middlesbr'gh	Aug 12	5	
Derbyshire	Derby	Aug 26	76	

NATWEST TROPHY

Opposition	Venue	Date	Batting	Fielding
Scotland	Chelmsford	June 27	31	1Ct

BENSON & HEDGES CUP

Opposition	Venue	Date	Batting	Fielding
Notts	Chelmsford	April 24	20	
Scotland	Glasgow	May 1	34	
Northants	Northampton	May 8	27	
Notts	Chelmsford	May 30	0	1Ct

OTHER FIRST-CLASS

Opposition	Venue	Date	Batting		Fielding
Cambridge U	Fenner's	May 16	22 * &	56 *	4Ct

PLER RECORDS   **H**

BATTING AVERAGES - Including fielding

	Matches	Inns	NO	Runs	HS	Avge	100s	50s	Ct	St
Britannic Assurance	11	15	5	650	125	65.00	2	3	7	-
Refuge Assurance	13	13	1	392	76	32.66	-	4	4	-
NatWest Trophy	1	1	0	31	31	31.00	-	-	1	-
Benson & Hedges Cup	4	4	0	81	34	20.25	-	-	1	-
Other First-Class	1	2	2	78	56*	-	-	1	4	-
ALL FIRST-CLASS	12	17	7	728	125	72.80	2	4	11	-
ALL ONE-DAY	18	18	1	504	76	29.64	-	4	6	-

BOWLING AVERAGES

	Overs	Mdns	Runs	Wkts	Avge	Best	5wI	10wM
Britannic Assurance	1	0	16	0	-	-	-	-
Refuge Assurance								
NatWest Trophy								
Benson & Hedges Cup								
Other First-Class								
ALL FIRST-CLASS	1	0	16	0	-	-	-	-
ALL ONE-DAY								

J.J.E. HARDY - *Somerset*

Opposition	Venue	Date	Batting			Fielding	Bowling
BRITANNIC ASSURANCE							
Gloucs	Taunton	April 26	4	&	30*	1Ct	
Glamorgan	Cardiff	May 3	7	&	0	1Ct	
Derbyshire	Taunton	May 19	4	&	91		
Hampshire	Basingstoke	June 6	30*	&	23*		
Kent	Canterbury	June 9	42	&	47*	2Ct	
Essex	Bath	June 16	42	&	13*	1Ct	
Glamorgan	Bath	June 20	10				
BENSON & HEDGES CUP							
Derbyshire	Taunton	May 1	109			2Ct	
Lancashire	Old Trafford	June 13	19				
OTHER FIRST-CLASS							
Oxford U	The Parks	April 18	0				
New Zealand	Taunton	May 16	13	&	5	1Ct	

BATTING AVERAGES - Including fielding

	Matches	Inns	NO	Runs	HS	Avge	100s	50s	Ct	St
Britannic Assurance	7	13	5	343	91	42.87	-	1	5	-
Benson & Hedges Cup	2	2	0	128	109	64.00	1	-	2	-
Other First-Class	2	3	0	18	13	6.00	-	-	1	-
ALL FIRST-CLASS	9	16	5	361	91	32.81	-	1	6	-
ALL ONE-DAY	2	2	0	128	109	64.00	1	-	2	-

BOWLING AVERAGES
Did not bowl

R.A. HARPER - *World XI*

Opposition	Venue	Date	Batting	Fielding	Bowling
OTHER FIRST-CLASS					
India	Scarborough	Aug 29	17	1Ct	4-68 & 1-36

BATTING AVERAGES - Including fielding

	Matches	Inns	NO	Runs	HS	Avge	100s	50s	Ct	St
Other First-Class	1	1	0	17	17	17.00	-	-	1	-
ALL FIRST-CLASS	1	1	0	17	17	17.00	-	-	1	-

BOWLING AVERAGES

	Overs	Mdns	Runs	Wkts	Avge	Best	5wI	10wM
Other First-Class	33.4	8	104	5	20.80	4-68	-	-
ALL FIRST-CLASS	33.4	8	104	5	20.80	4-68	-	-

G.A.R. HARRIS - *Hertfordshire*

Opposition	Venue	Date	Batting	Fielding	Bowling
NATWEST TROPHY					
Warwickshire	St Albans	June 27	0		0-67

BATTING AVERAGES - Including fielding

	Matches	Inns	NO	Runs	HS	Avge	100s	50s	Ct	St
NatWest Trophy	1	1	0	0	0	0.00	-	-	-	-
ALL ONE-DAY	1	1	0	0	0	0.00	-	-	-	-

BOWLING AVERAGES

	Overs	Mdns	Runs	Wkts	Avge	Best	5wI	10wM
NatWest Trophy	12	0	67	0	-	-	-	-
ALL ONE-DAY	12	0	67	0	-	-	-	-

G.D. HARRISON - *Ireland*

Opposition	Venue	Date	Batting	Fielding	Bowling
NATWEST TROPHY					
Sussex	Downpatrick	June 27	3		0-9
OTHER FIRST-CLASS					
Scotland	Edinburgh	Aug 11	1		9-113
OTHER ONE-DAY					
New Zealand	Downpatrick	May 9	6		0-42
New Zealand	Belfast	May 10	17		2-25

BATTING AVERAGES - Including fielding

	Matches	Inns	NO	Runs	HS	Avge	100s	50s	Ct	St
NatWest Trophy	1	1	0	3	3	3.00	-	-	-	-
Other First-Class	1	1	0	1	1	1.00	-	-	-	-
Other One-Day	2	2	0	23	17	11.50	-	-	-	-
ALL FIRST-CLASS	1	1	0	1	1	1.00	-	-	-	-
ALL ONE-DAY	3	3	0	26	17	8.66	-	-	-	-

BOWLING AVERAGES

	Overs	Mdns	Runs	Wkts	Avge	Best	5wI	10wM
NatWest Trophy	3.1	0	9	0	-	-	-	-
Other First-Class	43.2	11	113	9	12.55	9-113	1	-
Other One-Day	21	5	67	2	33.50	2-25	-	-
ALL FIRST-CLASS	43.2	11	113	9	12.55	9-113	1	-
ALL ONE-DAY	24.1	5	76	2	38.00	2-25	-	-

D.J. HARTLEY - *Berkshire*

Opposition	Venue	Date	Batting	Fielding	Bowling
NATWEST TROPHY					
Middlesex	Lord's	June 27			2-35

BATTING AVERAGES - Including fielding

	Matches	Inns	NO	Runs	HS	Avge	100s	50s	Ct	St
NatWest Trophy	1	0	0	0	0	-	-	-	-	-
ALL ONE-DAY	1	0	0	0	0	-	-	-	-	-

BOWLING AVERAGES

	Overs	Mdns	Runs	Wkts	Avge	Best	5wI	10wM
NatWest Trophy	9.3	1	35	2	17.50	2-35	-	-
ALL ONE-DAY	9.3	1	35	2	17.50	2-35	-	-

H — PLAYER RECORDS

J. HARTLEY - *Oxfordshire*

Opposition	Venue	Date	Batting	Fielding	Bowling
NATWEST TROPHY					
Kent	Oxford	June 27	7	1Ct	1-26

BATTING AVERAGES - Including fielding

	Matches	Inns	NO	Runs	HS	Avge	100s	50s	Ct	St
NatWest Trophy	1	1	0	7	7	7.00	-	-	1	-
ALL ONE-DAY	1	1	0	7	7	7.00	-	-	1	-

BOWLING AVERAGES

	Overs	Mdns	Runs	Wkts	Avge	Best	5wI	10wM
NatWest Trophy	8	1	26	1	26.00	1-26	-	
ALL ONE-DAY	8	1	26	1	26.00	1-26	-	

P.J. HARTLEY - *Yorkshire*

Opposition	Venue	Date	Batting	Fielding	Bowling
BRITANNIC ASSURANCE					
Derbyshire	Chesterfield	May 23	75 & 11	1Ct	3-80 & 2-74
Hampshire	Headingley	May 26	3 & 5		2-68 & 1-52
Worcestershire	Worcester	June 2	36	1Ct	2-92
Kent	Tunbridge We	June 6			3-105
Warwickshire	Sheffield	June 20	13		6-57 & 0-21
Glamorgan	Cardiff	June 23		1Ct	3-51 & 1-35
Notts	Scarborough	July 4			1-75
Northants	Northampton	July 7	40	1Ct	2-56 & 0-66
Middlesex	Uxbridge	July 18	11 & 9 *	1Ct	2-76 & 1-24
Gloucs	Cheltenham	July 21			3-111
Leicestershire	Sheffield	July 28	0 & 7		5-106 & 1-20
Sussex	Eastbourne	Aug 8		1Ct	0-50 & 1-60
Essex	Middlesbr'gh	Aug 11	0 & 5		0-71
Lancashire	Old Trafford	Aug 18	0	1Ct	4-109 & 0-10
Derbyshire	Scarborough	Sept 7			0-109 & 2-58
Notts	Trent Bridge	Sept 18			3-95 & 0-23
REFUGE ASSURANCE					
Warwickshire	Edgbaston	May 6	3 *		0-16
Hampshire	Headingley	May 27	14		2-24
Worcestershire	Worcester	June 3	7	1Ct	5-38
Surrey	Hull	June 10	8		1-22
Sussex	Hove	June 17	5 *		1-26
Northants	Tring	July 8	51	1Ct	3-37
Somerset	Scarborough	July 15	27		1-42
Gloucs	Cheltenham	July 22			0-36
Leicestershire	Sheffield	July 29			2-42
Lancashire	Scarborough	Aug 5	18		0-44
Essex	Middlesbr'gh	Aug 12	9 *		1-27
Middlesex	Scarborough	Aug 26	1	1Ct	2-51
NATWEST TROPHY					
Norfolk	Headingley	June 27			3-28
Warwickshire	Headingley	July 11			2-62
Hampshire	Southampton	Aug 1	52		5-46
BENSON & HEDGES CUP					
Combined U	Headingley	May 8	0		3-34
Lancashire	Headingley	May 10	1		0-29
OTHER FIRST-CLASS					
Zimbabwe	Headingley	May 16	3	1Ct	4-27
OTHER ONE-DAY					
World XI	Scarborough	Sept 1	3	1Ct	3-68
Essex	Scarborough	Sept 3	16	1Ct	0-52
Yorkshiremen	Scarborough	Sept 6			2-59

BATTING AVERAGES - Including fielding

	Matches	Inns	NO	Runs	HS	Avge	100s	50s	Ct	St
Britannic Assurance	16	14	1	215	75	16.53	-	1	7	-
Refuge Assurance	12	10	3	143	51	20.42	-	1	3	-
NatWest Trophy	3	1	0	52	52	52.00	-	1	-	-
Benson & Hedges Cup	2	2	0	1	1	0.50	-	-	-	-
Other First-Class	1	1	0	3	3	3.00	-	-	1	-
Other One-Day	3	2	0	19	16	9.50	-	-	2	-
ALL FIRST-CLASS	17	15	1	218	75	15.57	-	1	8	-
ALL ONE-DAY	20	15	3	215	52	17.91	-	2	5	-

BOWLING AVERAGES

	Overs	Mdns	Runs	Wkts	Avge	Best	5wI	10wM
Britannic Assurance	481.1	79	1754	48	36.54	6-57	2	-
Refuge Assurance	83.5	4	405	18	22.50	5-38	1	
NatWest Trophy	32.5	3	136	10	13.60	5-46	1	
Benson & Hedges Cup	20	3	63	3	21.00	3-34	-	
Other First-Class	9.5	1	27	4	6.75	4-27	-	
Other One-Day	30	0	179	5	35.80	3-68	-	
ALL FIRST-CLASS	491	80	1781	52	34.25	6-57	2	-
ALL ONE-DAY	166.4	10	783	36	21.75	5-38	2	

A.R. HARWOOD - *Buckinghamshire*

Opposition	Venue	Date	Batting	Fielding	Bowling
NATWEST TROPHY					
Notts	Marlow	June 27	13	2Ct	

BATTING AVERAGES - Including fielding

	Matches	Inns	NO	Runs	HS	Avge	100s	50s	Ct	St
NatWest Trophy	1	1	0	13	13	13.00	-	-	2	-
ALL ONE-DAY	1	1	0	13	13	13.00	-	-	2	-

BOWLING AVERAGES
Did not bowl

C. HATHURASINGHE - *Sri Lanka*

Opposition	Venue	Date	Batting	Fielding	Bowling
OTHER FIRST-CLASS					
Notts	Cleethorpes	Aug 25	84 & 44		0-0
Warwickshire	Edgbaston	Aug 29	19 & 19		0-14 & 2-3
Sussex	Hove	Sept 5	136 & 31		0-12
Lancashire	Old Trafford	Sept 8	15 & 31	1Ct	
Hampshire	Southampton	Sept 12	1 & 5		1-29

BATTING AVERAGES - Including fielding

	Matches	Inns	NO	Runs	HS	Avge	100s	50s	Ct	St
Other First-Class	5	10	0	385	136	38.50	1	1	1	-
ALL FIRST-CLASS	5	10	0	385	136	38.50	1	1	1	-

BOWLING AVERAGES

	Overs	Mdns	Runs	Wkts	Avge	Best	5wI	10wM
Other First-Class	21.1	8	58	3	19.33	2-3	-	-
ALL FIRST-CLASS	21.1	8	58	3	19.33	2-3	-	-

C. HAWKES - *Leicestershire*

Opposition	Venue	Date	Batting	Fielding	Bowling
BRITANNIC ASSURANCE					
Derbyshire	Derby	Sept 18	3 & 2 *	1Ct	0-40

BATTING AVERAGES - Including fielding

	Matches	Inns	NO	Runs	HS	Avge	100s	50s	Ct	St
Britannic Assurance	1	2	1	5	3	5.00	-	-	1	-
ALL FIRST-CLASS	1	2	1	5	3	5.00	-	-	1	-

BOWLING AVERAGES

	Overs	Mdns	Runs	Wkts	Avge	Best	5wI	10wM
Britannic Assurance	14	3	40	0	-	-	-	-
ALL FIRST-CLASS	14	3	40	0	-	-	-	-

PLAYER RECORDS

A.N. HAYHURST - *Somerset*

Opposition	Venue	Date	Batting		Fielding	Bowling
BRITANNIC ASSURANCE						
Glamorgan	Cardiff	May 3	110 *			0-37 & 1-39
Derbyshire	Taunton	May 19	90 &	0	2Ct	0-42
Sussex	Taunton	May 23	170			0-22
Leicestershire	Leicester	May 26	34 &	22 *		1-35 & 0-10
Gloucs	Bristol	June 2	15 &	17 *		0-18
Hampshire	Basingstoke	June 6		31 *		1-12 & 0-18
Kent	Canterbury	June 9	55 &	9		1-36 & 0-48
Essex	Bath	June 16	65 *		2Ct	0-39 & 0-11
Glamorgan	Bath	June 20	48			
Northants	Taunton	June 30	81 &	28 *		0-12 & 0-13
Warwickshire	Taunton	July 4	6 &	3		
Worcestershire	Worcester	July 18	119 &	16		0-29
Middlesex	Uxbridge	July 21	15			
Yorkshire	Scarborough	July 25	170 &	24	1Ct	2-19
Lancashire	Old Trafford	July 28	6 &	30		0-6
Surrey	Weston	Aug 4	40			0-11 & 1-59
Notts	Weston	Aug 8	79		1Ct	0-24 & 0-15
Hampshire	Taunton	Aug 18	28 &	47		0-40 & 0-38
Sussex	Hove	Aug 23	11		2Ct	1-3 & 3-58
Warwickshire	Edgbaston	Sept 7	57 &	56 *	1Ct	3-82 & 2-68
Worcestershire	Taunton	Sept 12	50 &	22		1-87 & 0-43
REFUGE ASSURANCE						
Hampshire	Taunton	May 13	38		1Ct	0-35
Derbyshire	Taunton	May 20	13			0-47
Leicestershire	Leicester	May 27	1			0-33
Gloucs	Bristol	June 3	4			1-13
Kent	Canterbury	June 10	3			0-34
Essex	Bath	June 17	20			1-41
Notts	Bath	June 24	8			2-21
Northants	Taunton	July 1				1-42
Middlesex	Lord's	July 8				2-30
Yorkshire	Scarborough	July 15	16			1-43
Glamorgan	Neath	July 22				2-24
Lancashire	Old Trafford	July 29	17		1Ct	0-23
Surrey	Weston	Aug 5	2		1Ct	1-30
Sussex	Hove	Aug 26	70 *		1Ct	4-37
NATWEST TROPHY						
Devon	Torquay	June 27	51			
Worcestershire	Taunton	July 11	46			0-14
BENSON & HEDGES CUP						
Derbyshire	Taunton	May 1				2-23
Min Counties	Taunton	May 8	76			1-36
Middlesex	Lord's	May 10	20			2-43
Sussex	Hove	May 12	5 *			1-42
Middlesex	Taunton	May 30	17			0-16
Lancashire	Old Trafford	June 13	1			0-16
OTHER FIRST-CLASS						
New Zealand	Taunton	May 16	3 * &	2		0-55 & 0-58

BATTING AVERAGES - Including fielding

	Matches	Inns	NO	Runs	HS	Avge	100s	50s	Ct	St
Britannic Assurance	21	33	7	1554	170	59.76	4	8	9	-
Refuge Assurance	14	11	1	192	70 *	19.20	-	1	4	-
NatWest Trophy	2	2	0	97	51	48.50	-	1	-	-
Benson & Hedges Cup	6	5	1	119	76	29.75	-	1	-	-
Other First-Class	1	2	1	5	3 *	5.00	-	-	-	-
ALL FIRST-CLASS	22	35	8	1559	170	57.74	4	8	9	-
ALL ONE-DAY	22	18	2	408	76	25.50	-	3	4	-

BOWLING AVERAGES

	Overs	Mdns	Runs	Wkts	Avge	Best	5wI	10wM
Britannic Assurance	291.2	46	974	17	57.29	3-58	-	-
Refuge Assurance	86	1	453	15	30.20	4-37	-	
NatWest Trophy	2	0	14	0	-	-	-	
Benson & Hedges Cup	42	0	176	6	29.33	2-23	-	
Other First-Class	30	4	113	0	-	-	-	
ALL FIRST-CLASS	321.2	50	1087	17	63.94	3-58	-	-
ALL ONE-DAY	130	1	643	21	30.61	4-37	-	-

D.L. HAYNES - Middlesex

Opposition	Venue	Date	Batting		Fielding	Bowling
BRITANNIC ASSURANCE						
Essex	Lord's	April 26	24 &	116		
Kent	Lord's	May 15	36 &	25	2Ct	
Surrey	Lord's	May 23	33 &	0		0-4 & 0-0
Gloucs	Lord's	May 26	24 &	49		
Essex	Ilford	June 2	220 *		1Ct	
Warwickshire	Lord's	June 6	67 &	0		
Leicestershire	Leicester	June 16	85 &	68 *		
Lancashire	Old Trafford	June 20		49	1Ct	
Northants	Luton	June 23	9 &	69 *		
Worcestershire	Lord's	June 30	40		1Ct	
Yorkshire	Uxbridge	July 18	18 &	26	1Ct	0-4
Somerset	Uxbridge	July 21	41 &	108	1Ct	
Kent	Canterbury	July 25	9 &	0	1Ct	1-47
Notts	Trent Bridge	July 28	21 &	0	1Ct	
Glamorgan	Lord's	Aug 4	173		1Ct	
Hampshire	Bournemouth	Aug 8	75 &	0		
Sussex	Lord's	Aug 11	255 *			1-18
Derbyshire	Derby	Aug 18	12 &	8	1Ct	
Yorkshire	Headingley	Aug 23	131 &	57		0-2
Notts	Lord's	Sept 7	29 &	44 *		0-8
Surrey	The Oval	Sept 12	69		3Ct	0-17 & 0-13
Sussex	Hove	Sept 18	46			0-0
REFUGE ASSURANCE						
Lancashire	Old Trafford	April 22	107 *			0-34
Essex	Lord's	April 29	31			
Kent	Folkestone	May 6	67			0-12
Notts	Lord's	May 13	10			1-17
Gloucs	Lord's	May 27	50			
Warwickshire	Lord's	June 3	50		1Ct	0-8
Hampshire	Basingstoke	June 10	19		1Ct	0-21
Leicestershire	Leicester	June 17	49			1-29
Northants	Northampton	June 24			1Ct	
Worcestershire	Lord's	July 1	11		1Ct	0-21
Somerset	Lord's	July 8	82			0-41
Surrey	The Oval	July 15	4		1Ct	1-39
Glamorgan	Lord's	Aug 5	37		1Ct	0-12
Sussex	Lord's	Aug 12	7			
Derbyshire	Derby	Aug 19	48 *		1Ct	
Yorkshire	Scarborough	Aug 26	60			0-31
Lancashire	Old Trafford	Sept 5	72			
Derbyshire	Edgbaston	Sept 16	49			1-16
NATWEST TROPHY						
Berkshire	Lord's	June 27	50		1Ct	0-18
Surrey	Uxbridge	July 11	0			1-41
Glamorgan	Lord's	Aug 1	75 *			
Lancashire	Old Trafford	Aug 15	149 *			
BENSON & HEDGES CUP						
Min Counties	Lord's	April 24	80		1Ct	0-19
Sussex	Hove	May 8	131			1-23
Somerset	Lord's	May 10	28		1Ct	
Derbyshire	Derby	May 12	64		1Ct	
Somerset	Taunton	May 30	23		1Ct	0-15
OTHER FIRST-CLASS						
New Zealand	Lord's	May 19	181 &	129		

BATTING AVERAGES - Including fielding

	Matches	Inns	NO	Runs	HS	Avge	100s	50s	Ct	St
Britannic Assurance	22	37	5	2036	255 *	63.62	6	7	14	-
Refuge Assurance	18	17	2	753	107 *	50.20	1	6	7	-
NatWest Trophy	4	4	2	274	149 *	137.00	1	2	1	-
Benson & Hedges Cup	5	5	0	326	131	65.20	1	2	4	-
Other First-Class	1	2	0	310	181	155.00	2	-	-	-
ALL FIRST-CLASS	23	39	5	2346	255 *	69.00	8	7	14	-
ALL ONE-DAY	27	26	4	1353	149 *	61.50	3	10	12	-

BOWLING AVERAGES

	Overs	Mdns	Runs	Wkts	Avge	Best	5wI	10wM
Britannic Assurance	35	7	113	2	56.50	1-18	-	-
Refuge Assurance	50.2	1	281	4	70.25	1-16	-	-
NatWest Trophy	20	3	59	1	59.00	1-41	-	-
Benson & Hedges Cup	12	0	57	1	57.00	1-23	-	-
Other First-Class								

H   PLAYER RECORDS

ALL FIRST-CLASS	35	7	113	2	56.50 1-18 - -
ALL ONE-DAY	82.2	4	397	6	66.16 1-16 -

R. HEAP - *Cambridge University*

Opposition	Venue	Date	Batting	Fielding	Bowling
OTHER FIRST-CLASS					
Northants	Fenner's	April 14	18 & 37		
Derbyshire	Fenner's	April 18	4 & 0	1Ct	
Warwickshire	Fenner's	April 26	0 & 17		
Middlesex	Fenner's	May 3	15 & 23		
Essex	Fenner's	May 16	50 & 2	1Ct	
Gloucs	Fenner's	May 23	11 & 0		
Notts	Fenner's	June 16	4 & 31		
Kent	Fenner's	June 20	27 * & 17		
Sussex	Hove	June 30	63 & 20 *	1Ct	
Oxford U	Lord's	July 4	37		

BATTING AVERAGES - Including fielding

	Matches	Inns	NO	Runs	HS	Avge	100s	50s	Ct	St
Other First-Class	10	19	2	376	63	22.11	-	2	3	-
ALL FIRST-CLASS	10	19	2	376	63	22.11	-	2	3	-

BOWLING AVERAGES
Did not bowl

N. HEATON - *League C.C. XI*

Opposition	Venue	Date	Batting	Fielding	Bowling
OTHER ONE-DAY					
India	Sunderland	June 28	41		

BATTING AVERAGES - Including fielding

	Matches	Inns	NO	Runs	HS	Avge	100s	50s	Ct	St
Other One-Day	1	1	0	41	41	41.00	-	-	-	-
ALL ONE-DAY	1	1	0	41	41	41.00	-	-	-	-

BOWLING AVERAGES
Did not bowl

G.T. HEDLEY - *Berkshire*

Opposition	Venue	Date	Batting	Fielding	Bowling
NATWEST TROPHY					
Middlesex	Lord's	June 27	13		1-35

BATTING AVERAGES - Including fielding

	Matches	Inns	NO	Runs	HS	Avge	100s	50s	Ct	St
NatWest Trophy	1	1	0	13	13	13.00	-	-	-	-
ALL ONE-DAY	1	1	0	13	13	13.00	-	-	-	-

BOWLING AVERAGES

	Overs	Mdns	Runs	Wkts	Avge	Best	5wI	10wM
NatWest Trophy	12	1	35	1	35.00	1-35	-	
ALL ONE-DAY	12	1	35	1	35.00	1-35	-	

W.K. HEGG - *Lancashire*

Opposition	Venue	Date	Batting	Fielding	Bowling
BRITANNIC ASSURANCE					
Worcestershire	Old Trafford	April 26		3Ct	
Surrey	The Oval	May 3	45	1Ct,1St	
Derbyshire	Derby	May 15		2Ct	
Leicestershire	Old Trafford	May 19	1	3Ct,1St	
Glamorgan	Colwyn Bay	May 26	82 *	4Ct	
Sussex	Horsham	June 2	10	4Ct	
Gloucs	Old Trafford	June 9	0	2Ct	
Middlesex	Old Trafford	June 20	14	3Ct	
Hampshire	Old Trafford	June 23		1Ct	
Kent	Maidstone	June 30	20 * & 0	3Ct	
Derbyshire	Liverpool	July 7	83 & 34	2Ct	
Warwickshire	Coventry	July 18	9 & 20 *	2Ct	
Essex	Colchester	July 21	100 *	3Ct	
Somerset	Old Trafford	July 28	33	4Ct	
Yorkshire	Headingley	Aug 4	29 & 0 *	2Ct	
Worcestershire	Kid'minster	Aug 8	47 & 5		
Yorkshire	Old Trafford	Aug 18	3	2Ct	
Surrey	Blackpool	Aug 29	34 *	1Ct	
Notts	Trent Bridge	Sept 12	48	2Ct	
Warwickshire	Old Trafford	Sept 18		3Ct	
REFUGE ASSURANCE					
Middlesex	Old Trafford	April 22			
Notts	Trent Bridge	April 29		0Ct,1St	
Leicestershire	Old Trafford	May 20	0	1Ct	
Glamorgan	Colwyn Bay	May 27			
Gloucs	Old Trafford	June 10	2 *	2Ct,1St	
Kent	Maidstone	July 1		1Ct	
Derbyshire	Old Trafford	July 8	10		
Worcestershire	Old Trafford	July 15		1Ct	
Essex	Colchester	July 22	24 *		
Somerset	Old Trafford	July 29			
Yorkshire	Scarborough	Aug 5	1 *	1Ct	
Northants	Northampton	Aug 12			
Warwickshire	Old Trafford	Aug 26	10 *	1Ct	
Middlesex	Old Trafford	Sept 5	19 *	1Ct	
NATWEST TROPHY					
Durham	Old Trafford	June 27		1Ct	
Derbyshire	Derby	July 11	13 *	1Ct	
Gloucs	Old Trafford	Aug 1		3Ct	
Middlesex	Old Trafford	Aug 15		1Ct	
Northants	Lord's	Sept 1		2Ct	
BENSON & HEDGES CUP					
Surrey	Old Trafford	April 24		4Ct,1St	
Combined U	Fenner's	May 1		1Ct	
Hampshire	Old Trafford	May 8			
Yorkshire	Headingley	May 10		2Ct	
Surrey	Old Trafford	May 30	10 *		
Somerset	Old Trafford	June 13		3Ct	
Worcestershire	Lord's	July 14	31 *	3Ct	
OTHER FIRST-CLASS					
For MCC					
Worcestershire	Lord's	April 17	57	2Ct	

BATTING AVERAGES - Including fielding

	Matches	Inns	NO	Runs	HS	Avge	100s	50s	Ct	St
Britannic Assurance	20	21	6	617	100 *	41.13	1	2	47	2
Refuge Assurance	14	7	5	66	24 *	33.00	-	-	8	2
NatWest Trophy	5	1	1	13	13 *	-	-	-	8	-
Benson & Hedges Cup	7	2	2	41	31 *	-	-	-	13	1
Other First-Class	1	1	0	57	57	57.00	-	1	2	-
ALL FIRST-CLASS	21	22	6	674	100 *	42.12	1	3	49	2
ALL ONE-DAY	26	10	8	120	31 *	60.00	-	-	29	3

BOWLING AVERAGES
Did not bowl

E.E. HEMMINGS - *Notts & England*

Opposition	Venue	Date	Batting	Fielding	Bowling
CORNHILL TEST MATCHES					
New Zealand	Trent Bridge	June 7	13 *		1-47 & 0-0
New Zealand	Lord's	June 21	0		2-67
New Zealand	Edgbaston	July 5	20 & 0		6-58 & 1-43
India	Lord's	July 26			2-109 & 2-79
India	Old Trafford	Aug 9	19		2-74 & 3-75
India	The Oval	Aug 23	51		2-117

PLAYER RECORDS H

TEXACO TROPHY

New Zealand	Headingley	May 23				0-51
New Zealand	The Oval	May 25				0-34
India	Headingley	July 18	3			0-36
India	Trent Bridge	July 20	0			2-53

BRITANNIC ASSURANCE

Derbyshire	Trent Bridge	April 26	15				3-64 & 1-22
Worcestershire	Worcester	May 3	24 &	4 *			3-117
Leicestershire	Leicester	May 15	83			1Ct	1-58 & 2-3
Warwickshire	Edgbaston	May 19		16 *			2-46 & 3-108
Kent	Tunbridge We	June 2				1Ct	0-52 & 1-15
Leicestershire	Trent Bridge	June 30	17				1-52 & 0-60
Essex	Southend	Aug 4	32 &	12			5-99 & 0-32
Gloucs	Trent Bridge	Aug 18	0 &	0			1-19 & 2-48
Worcestershire	Trent Bridge	Aug 29	12 *&	6 *			1-54 & 2-27
Middlesex	Lord's	Sept 7	3 &	6			1-117 & 0-31
Yorkshire	Trent Bridge	Sept 18					1-102 & 0-49

REFUGE ASSURANCE

Yorkshire	Trent Bridge	April 22				2-28
Lancashire	Trent Bridge	April 29	12			2-18
Worcestershire	Worcester	May 6	24			0-41
Middlesex	Lord's	May 13			1Ct	5-33
Surrey	Trent Bridge	May 20			1Ct	4-48
Kent	Canterbury	June 17	15		1Ct	1-17
Leicestershire	Trent Bridge	July 1				0-33
Hampshire	Southampton	July 15	32 *			0-36
Warwickshire	Edgbaston	July 22	2 *			2-34
Essex	Southend	Aug 5				2-36
Gloucs	Trent Bridge	Aug 19				0-30
Derbyshire	Derby	Sept 5	6 *			0-23

NATWEST TROPHY

Bucks	Marlow	June 27	3		1Ct	3-42
Northants	Northampton	July 11	0			1-53

BENSON & HEDGES CUP

Essex	Chelmsford	April 24			1Ct	1-49
Leicestershire	Trent Bridge	May 1	5			0-10
Northants	Trent Bridge	May 12	6			1-30
Essex	Chelmsford	May 30			1Ct	2-33
Worcestershire	Trent Bridge	June 13	12 *			0-60

OTHER ONE-DAY

For England XI

Rest of World	Jesmond	Aug 2				1-50
Rest of World	Jesmond	Aug 3	0			0-53

For World XI

Yorkshire	Scarborough	Sept 1				2-45

BATTING AVERAGES - Including fielding

	Matches	Inns	NO	Runs	HS	Avge	100s	50s	Ct	St
Cornhill Test Matches	6	6	1	103	51	20.60	-	1	-	-
Texaco Trophy	4	2	0	3	3	1.50	-	-	-	-
Britannic Assurance	11	14	4	230	83	23.00	-	1	2	-
Refuge Assurance	12	6	3	91	32 *	30.33	-	-	3	-
NatWest Trophy	2	2	0	3	3	1.50	-	-	1	-
Benson & Hedges Cup	5	3	1	23	12 *	11.50	-	-	2	-
Other One-Day	3	1	0	0	0	0.00	-	-	-	-
ALL FIRST-CLASS	17	20	5	333	83	22.20	-	2	2	-
ALL ONE-DAY	26	14	4	120	32 *	12.00	-	-	6	-

BOWLING AVERAGES

	Overs	Mdns	Runs	Wkts	Avge	Best	5wI	10wM
Cornhill Test Matches	244.5	70	669	21	31.85	6-58	1	-
Texaco Trophy	44	3	174	2	87.00	2-53	-	
Britannic Assurance	443.3	127	1175	30	39.16	5-99	1	-
Refuge Assurance	81	3	377	18	20.94	5-33	1	
NatWest Trophy	19.3	4	95	4	23.75	3-42	-	
Benson & Hedges Cup	54	8	182	4	45.50	2-33	-	
Other One-Day	27	1	148	3	49.33	2-45	-	
ALL FIRST-CLASS	688.2	197	1844	51	36.15	6-58	2	-
ALL ONE-DAY	225.3	19	976	31	31.48	5-33	1	

J.R. HEMSTOCK - *Middlesex*

Opposition	Venue	Date	Batting	Fielding	Bowling
REFUGE ASSURANCE					
Lancashire	Old Trafford	April 22			0-43
BENSON & HEDGES CUP					
Min Counties	Lord's	April 24			2-37

BATTING AVERAGES - Including fielding

	Matches	Inns	NO	Runs	HS	Avge	100s	50s	Ct	St
Refuge Assurance	1	0	0	0	0	-	-	-	-	-
Benson & Hedges Cup	1	0	0	0	0	-	-	-	-	-
ALL ONE-DAY	2	0	0	0	0	-	-	-	-	-

BOWLING AVERAGES

	Overs	Mdns	Runs	Wkts	Avge	Best	5wI	10wM
Refuge Assurance	8	0	43	0	-	-	-	-
Benson & Hedges Cup	10	1	37	2	18.50	2-37	-	
ALL ONE-DAY	18	1	80	2	40.00	2-37	-	

I.M. HENDERSON - *Oxford University*

Opposition	Venue	Date	Batting	Fielding	Bowling
OTHER FIRST-CLASS					
Glamorgan	The Parks	April 14			0-36 & 0-8
Somerset	The Parks	April 18		1Ct	2-92
Surrey	The Parks	May 16	44		0-24 & 0-23
Glamorgan	The Parks	June 2	1 *		3-102 & 1-17
Lancashire	The Parks	June 16	1 *	1Ct	0-146
Cambridge U	Lord's	July 4	0 *		0-21

BATTING AVERAGES - Including fielding

	Matches	Inns	NO	Runs	HS	Avge	100s	50s	Ct	St
Other First-Class	6	4	3	46	44	46.00	-	-	2	-
ALL FIRST-CLASS	6	4	3	46	44	46.00	-	-	2	-

BOWLING AVERAGES

	Overs	Mdns	Runs	Wkts	Avge	Best	5wI	10wM
Other First-Class	105.2	9	469	6	78.16	3-102	-	-
ALL FIRST-CLASS	105.2	9	469	6	78.16	3-102	-	-

O. HENRY - *Scotland*

Opposition	Venue	Date	Batting	Fielding	Bowling
NATWEST TROPHY					
Essex	Chelmsford	June 27	53		0-21
BENSON & HEDGES CUP					
Essex	Glasgow	May 1	24	1Ct	0-54
Notts	Glasgow	May 8	62 *		0-5
Leicestershire	Leicester	May 12	48	1Ct	0-29
OTHER FIRST-CLASS					
Ireland	Edinburgh	Aug 11	23		2-54 & 0-52
OTHER ONE-DAY					
India	Glasgow	July 14	74		1-50

BATTING AVERAGES - Including fielding

	Matches	Inns	NO	Runs	HS	Avge	100s	50s	Ct	St
NatWest Trophy	1	1	0	53	53	53.00	-	1	-	-
Benson & Hedges Cup	3	3	1	134	62 *	67.00	-	1	2	-
Other First-Class	1	1	0	23	23	23.00	-	-	-	-
Other One-Day	1	1	0	74	74	74.00	-	1	-	-
ALL FIRST-CLASS	1	1	0	23	23	23.00	-	-	-	-
ALL ONE-DAY	5	5	1	261	74	65.25	-	3	2	-

H PLAYER RECORDS

BOWLING AVERAGES

	Overs	Mdns	Runs	Wkts	Avge	Best	5wI	10wM
NatWest Trophy	3	0	21	0	-	-	-	
Benson & Hedges Cup	22	2	88	0	-	-	-	
Other First-Class	33.4	3	106	2	53.00	2-54	-	-
Other One-Day	11	0	50	1	50.00	1-50	-	
ALL FIRST-CLASS	33.4	3	106	2	53.00	2-54	-	-
ALL ONE-DAY	36	2	159	1	159.00	1-50	-	

P.N. HEPWORTH - *Leicestershire*

Opposition	Venue	Date	Batting	Fielding	Bowling
BRITANNIC ASSURANCE					
Kent	Leicester	Aug 23	43 & 7	1Ct	
Sussex	Leicester	Aug 29	17 & 0		
Northants	Leicester	Sept 12	49 & 0		
Derbyshire	Derby	Sept 18	14 * & 55 *		
OTHER ONE-DAY					
For Yorkshiremen					
Yorkshire	Scarborough	Sept 6	9		

BATTING AVERAGES - Including fielding

	Matches	Inns	NO	Runs	HS	Avge	100s	50s	Ct	St
Britannic Assurance	4	8	2	185	55 *	30.83	-	1	1	-
Other One-Day	1	1	0	9	9	9.00	-	-	-	-
ALL FIRST-CLASS	4	8	2	185	55 *	30.83	-	1	1	-
ALL ONE-DAY	1	1	0	9	9	9.00	-	-	-	-

BOWLING AVERAGES
Did not bowl

S. HERZBERG - *Worcestershire*

Opposition	Venue	Date	Batting	Fielding	Bowling
REFUGE ASSURANCE					
Gloucs	Worcester	July 8			0-28

BATTING AVERAGES - Including fielding

	Matches	Inns	NO	Runs	HS	Avge	100s	50s	Ct	St
Refuge Assurance	1	0	0	0	0	-	-	-	-	-
ALL ONE-DAY	1	0	0	0	0	-	-	-	-	-

BOWLING AVERAGES

	Overs	Mdns	Runs	Wkts	Avge	Best	5wI	10wM
Refuge Assurance	5	0	28	0	-	-	-	
ALL ONE-DAY	5	0	28	0	-	-	-	

G.A. HICK - *Worcestershire*

Opposition	Venue	Date	Batting	Fielding	Bowling
BRITANNIC ASSURANCE					
Lancashire	Old Trafford	April 26	23 & 106 *		0-6 & 0-11
Notts	Worcester	May 3	97	1Ct	0-32
Surrey	The Oval	June 16	59		3-20
Sussex	Worcester	June 20	28	1Ct	0-37
Middlesex	Lord's	June 30	0 & 80	1Ct	0-28
Gloucs	Worcester	July 7	0 & 79		5-37 & 4-43
Somerset	Worcester	July 18	171 * & 69 *		0-12
Glamorgan	Abergavenny	July 21	252 * & 100 *	1Ct	0-0 & 0-61
Derbyshire	Derby	July 25	53	2Ct	0-39 & 2-45
Kent	Canterbury	July 28	66 & 22	2Ct	0-6
Leicestershire	Leicester	Aug 4	102 & 88 *	2Ct	
Lancashire	Kid'minster	Aug 8	67	1Ct	2-19
Hampshire	Worcester	Aug 11	72 & 50 *	1Ct	0-74 & 0-5
Northants	Worcester	Aug 18	34 & 50	2Ct	1-21 & 1-66
Warwickshire	Worcester	Aug 23	14 & 42		
Notts	Trent Bridge	Aug 29	4 & 18	3Ct	2-30
Gloucs	Bristol	Sept 7	110 & 38		0-49
Somerset	Taunton	Sept 12	154 & 81	6Ct	0-0 & 0-4
Glamorgan	Worcester	Sept 18	6 & 138 *	1Ct	
REFUGE ASSURANCE					
Somerset	Taunton	April 22	78 *		
Derbyshire	Derby	April 29	46		0-22
Notts	Worcester	May 6	114 *	2Ct	
Surrey	The Oval	June 17	16	1Ct	2-29
Sussex	Worcester	June 24	75		
Middlesex	Lord's	July 1	45		0-31
Gloucs	Worcester	July 8	67		0-23
Lancashire	Old Trafford	July 15	42		0-17
Kent	Canterbury	July 29	25		
Leicestershire	Leicester	Aug 5	98 *		
Hampshire	Worcester	Aug 12	88		3-47
Northants	Worcester	Aug 19	26		
Glamorgan	Swansea	Aug 26	31	1Ct	1-53
NATWEST TROPHY					
Suffolk	Bury St Ed's	June 27	78 *		0-30
Somerset	Taunton	July 11	2		0-49
Northants	Northampton	Aug 1	49		0-39
BENSON & HEDGES CUP					
Gloucs	Bristol	April 24	2	1Ct	0-25
Kent	Worcester	May 1	41	4Ct	
Glamorgan	Worcester	May 8	0		1-36
Warwickshire	Edgbaston	May 10	64		3-36
Notts	Trent Bridge	June 13	57 *	1Ct	0-12
Lancashire	Lord's	July 14	1		0-16
OTHER FIRST-CLASS					
MCC	Lord's	April 17	72	2Ct	
New Zealand	Worcester	May 12	2 *		
OTHER ONE-DAY					
Hampshire	Scarborough	Sept 2	20	1Ct	2-43

BATTING AVERAGES - Including fielding

	Matches	Inns	NO	Runs	HS	Avge	100s	50s	Ct	St
Britannic Assurance	19	33	8	2273	252 *	90.92	8	13	24	-
Refuge Assurance	13	13	3	751	114 *	75.10	1	5	4	-
NatWest Trophy	3	3	1	129	78 *	64.50	-	1	-	-
Benson & Hedges Cup	6	6	1	165	64	33.00	-	2	6	-
Other First-Class	2	2	1	74	72	74.00	-	1	2	-
Other One-Day	1	1	0	20	20	20.00	-	-	1	-
ALL FIRST-CLASS	21	35	9	2347	252 *	90.26	8	14	26	-
ALL ONE-DAY	23	23	5	1065	114 *	59.16	1	8	11	-

BOWLING AVERAGES

	Overs	Mdns	Runs	Wkts	Avge	Best	5wI	10wM
Britannic Assurance	208.5	41	645	20	32.25	5-37	1	-
Refuge Assurance	33.5	1	222	6	37.00	3-47	-	
NatWest Trophy	32	2	118	0	-	-	-	
Benson & Hedges Cup	30	0	125	4	31.25	3-36	-	
Other First-Class								
Other One-Day	10	0	43	2	21.50	2-43	-	
ALL FIRST-CLASS	208.5	41	645	20	32.25	5-37	1	-
ALL ONE-DAY	105.5	3	508	12	42.33	3-36	-	

S.G. HINKS - *Kent*

Opposition	Venue	Date	Batting	Fielding	Bowling
BRITANNIC ASSURANCE					
Hampshire	Canterbury	April 26	31 & 82	1Ct	1-16
Sussex	Folkestone	May 3	48 & 4		
Middlesex	Lord's	May 15	16 & 5		
Glamorgan	Swansea	May 23	107 & 4		
Notts	Tunbridge We	June 2	6 & 14		
Yorkshire	Tunbridge We	June 6	6		
Somerset	Canterbury	June 9	30 & 55	1Ct	1-15
Warwickshire	Edgbaston	June 23	66 & 15		
Lancashire	Maidstone	June 30	29 & 49		
Essex	Maidstone	June 4	1	1Ct	
Northants	Northampton	July 18	5 & 83		
Surrey	Guildford	July 21	120 & 1		
Middlesex	Canterbury	July 25	234 & 2	1Ct	

PLAYER RECORDS

Worcestershire	Canterbury	July 28	32	&	25		
Derbyshire	Chesterfield	Aug 4	0	&	9		0-29
Leicestershire	Dartford	Aug 8	14	&	37	1Ct	
Gloucs	Bristol	Aug 11	53			1Ct	
Sussex	Hove	Aug 18	7	&	4		
Leicestershire	Leicester	Aug 23	6	&	163	1Ct	
Hampshire	Bournemouth	Aug 29	0	&	27		
Surrey	Canterbury	Sept 7	16	&	19	1Ct	
Essex	Chelmsford	Sept 12	43	&	16		

REFUGE ASSURANCE

Essex	Chelmsford	April 22	50	
Hampshire	Canterbury	April 29	1	
Middlesex	Folkestone	May 6	86	
Glamorgan	Llanelli	May 13	74	
Yorkshire	Canterbury	May 20	89	
Northants	Northampton	May 27	11	
Somerset	Canterbury	June 10	1	
Notts	Canterbury	June 17	12	
Warwickshire	Edgbaston	June 24	6	
Lancashire	Maidstone	July 1	17	
Surrey	The Oval	July 22	41	
Worcestershire	Canterbury	July 29	51	
Derbyshire	Chesterfield	Aug 5	50	
Gloucs	Bristol	Aug 12	13	
Leicestershire	Leicester	Aug 26	60	1Ct

NATWEST TROPHY

Oxfordshire	Oxford	June 27	43	
Gloucs	Bristol	July 11	15	0-23

BENSON & HEDGES CUP

Worcestershire	Worcester	May 1	1	1Ct
Warwickshire	Canterbury	May 8	2	1Ct
Gloucs	Canterbury	May 10	3	
Glamorgan	Swansea	May 12	1	1Ct

OTHER FIRST-CLASS

Cambridge U	Fenner's	June 20	42
India	Canterbury	July 7	62

BATTING AVERAGES - Including fielding

	Matches	Inns	NO	Runs	HS	Avge	100s	50s	Ct	St
Britannic Assurance	22	41	0	1484	234	36.19	4	5	8	-
Refuge Assurance	15	15	0	562	89	37.46	-	7	1	-
NatWest Trophy	2	2	0	58	43	29.00	-	-	-	-
Benson & Hedges Cup	4	4	0	7	3	1.75	-	-	3	-
Other First-Class	2	2	0	104	62	52.00	-	1	-	-
ALL FIRST-CLASS	24	43	0	1588	234	36.93	4	6	8	-
ALL ONE-DAY	21	21	0	627	89	29.85	-	7	4	-

BOWLING AVERAGES

	Overs	Mdns	Runs	Wkts	Avge	Best	5wI	10wM
Britannic Assurance	15	2	60	2	30.00	1-15	-	-
Refuge Assurance								
NatWest Trophy	3	0	23	0	-	-	-	-
Benson & Hedges Cup								
Other First-Class								
ALL FIRST-CLASS	15	2	60	2	30.00	1-15	-	-
ALL ONE-DAY	3	0	23	0	-	-	-	-

N.D. HIRWANI - *India*

Opposition	Venue	Date	Batting	Fielding	Bowling

CORNHILL TEST MATCHES

England	Lord's	July 26	0 &	0 *		1-102 & 1-50
England	Old Trafford	Aug 9	15 *			4-174 & 1-52
England	The Oval	Aug 23	2 *			1-71 & 1-137

OTHER FIRST-CLASS

Yorkshire	Headingley	June 30			2-45
Hampshire	Southampton	July 4			1-25 & 0-39
Kent	Canterbury	July 7		1Ct	1-41 & 2-48
Leicestershire	Leicester	July 21		1Ct	2-79 & 2-103
Surrey	The Oval	Aug 1			3-122 & 4-71
Gloucs	Bristol	Aug 4	0	1Ct	5-117 & 0-4

BATTING AVERAGES - Including fielding

	Matches	Inns	NO	Runs	HS	Avge	100s	50s	Ct	St
Cornhill Test Matches	3	4	3	17	15 *	17.00	-	-	-	-
Other First-Class	6	1	0	0	0	0.00	-	-	3	-
ALL FIRST-CLASS	9	5	3	17	15 *	8.50	-	-	3	-

BOWLING AVERAGES

	Overs	Mdns	Runs	Wkts	Avge	Best	5wI	10wM
Cornhill Test Matches	212	41	586	9	65.11	4-174	-	-
Other First-Class	187.2	18	694	22	31.54	5-117	1	-
ALL FIRST-CLASS	399.2	59	1280	31	41.29	5-117	1	-

G.D. HODGSON - *Gloucestershire*

Opposition	Venue	Date	Batting			Fielding	Bowling

BRITANNIC ASSURANCE

Somerset	Taunton	April 26	8	&	25		
Middlesex	Lord's	May 26	65	&	25		
Somerset	Bristol	June 2	24				
Essex	Ilford	June 6	27				
Lancashire	Old Trafford	June 9	72			1Ct	
Sussex	Hove	June 16	0	&	33		
Hampshire	Gloucester	June 20	22 *				
Leicestershire	Gloucester	June 23	23 *	&	4		
Derbyshire	Derby	June 30	13	&	52		
Glamorgan	Swansea	July 4	23				
Worcestershire	Worcester	July 7	77	&	22		
Yorkshire	Cheltenham	July 21	65				
Northants	Cheltenham	July 25	50			1Ct	
Surrey	Cheltenham	July 28	54	&	44	2Ct	
Warwickshire	Bristol	Aug 8	8	&	8	1Ct	
Kent	Bristol	Aug 11	2	&	17	2Ct	
Notts	Trent Bridge	Aug 18	4	&	0	1Ct	
Northants	Northampton	Aug 23	4	&	22	2Ct	
Worcestershire	Bristol	Sept 7	109	&	22		
Sussex	Bristol	Sept 12	1				
Hampshire	Southampton	Sept 18	58	&	76		

REFUGE ASSURANCE

Glamorgan	Bristol	April 22	28	
Leicestershire	Gloucester	June 24	12	1Ct
Derbyshire	Derby	July 1	5 *	2Ct
Worcestershire	Worcester	July 8	10	
Sussex	Swindon	July 15	1	
Surrey	Cheltenham	July 29	28	1Ct
Kent	Bristol	Aug 12	27	
Notts	Trent Bridge	Aug 19		1Ct
Northants	Northampton	Aug 26	2 *	

NATWEST TROPHY

Lincolnshire	Gloucester	June 27	42
Kent	Bristol	July 11	39
Lancashire	Old Trafford	Aug 1	52

BENSON & HEDGES CUP

Worcestershire	Bristol	April 24	1

OTHER FIRST-CLASS

Zimbabwe	Bristol	May 19	126	&	6	
Cambridge U	Fenner's	May 23	51	&	39 *	1Ct
India	Bristol	Aug 4	16	&	23 *	1Ct

BATTING AVERAGES - Including fielding

	Matches	Inns	NO	Runs	HS	Avge	100s	50s	Ct	St
Britannic Assurance	21	34	2	1059	109	33.09	1	9	10	-
Refuge Assurance	9	8	2	113	28	18.83	-	-	5	-
NatWest Trophy	3	3	0	133	52	44.33	-	1	-	-
Benson & Hedges Cup	1	1	0	1	1	1.00	-	-	-	-
Other First-Class	3	6	2	261	126	65.25	1	1	2	-
ALL FIRST-CLASS	24	40	4	1320	126	36.66	2	10	12	-
ALL ONE-DAY	13	12	2	247	52	24.70	-	1	5	-

BOWLING AVERAGES

Did not bowl

H	**PLAYER RECORDS**

M. HOLLAND - *Wiltshire*

Opposition	Venue	Date	Batting	Fielding	Bowling
NATWEST TROPHY					
Surrey	Trowbridge	June 27	0 *		0-10

BATTING AVERAGES - Including fielding

	Matches	Inns	NO	Runs	HS	Avge	100s	50s	Ct	St
NatWest Trophy	1	1	1	0	0*	-	-	-	-	-
ALL ONE-DAY	1	1	1	0	0*	-	-	-	-	-

BOWLING AVERAGES

	Overs	Mdns	Runs	Wkts	Avge	Best	5wI	10wM
NatWest Trophy	5	2	10	0	-	-	-	-
ALL ONE-DAY	5	2	10	0	-	-	-	-

B. HOLMES - *League C.C. XI*

Opposition	Venue	Date	Batting	Fielding	Bowling
OTHER ONE-DAY					
India	Sunderland	June 28	0 *		1-22

BATTING AVERAGES - Including fielding

	Matches	Inns	NO	Runs	HS	Avge	100s	50s	Ct	St
Other One-Day	1	1	1	0	0*	-	-	-	-	-
ALL ONE-DAY	1	1	1	0	0*	-	-	-	-	-

BOWLING AVERAGES

	Overs	Mdns	Runs	Wkts	Avge	Best	5wI	10wM
Other One-Day	11	3	22	1	22.00	1-22	-	
ALL ONE-DAY	11	3	22	1	22.00	1-22	-	

G.C. HOLMES - *Glamorgan*

Opposition	Venue	Date	Batting	Fielding	Bowling
BRITANNIC ASSURANCE					
Leicestershire	Cardiff	April 26	14 & 11	1Ct	0-14
Somerset	Cardiff	May 3	125 * & 44		1-44
Gloucs	Bristol	May 15	12		
Northants	Northampton	June 9	9 & 0 *		
Hampshire	Southampton	June 16	14		
Somerset	Bath	June 20	1		0-27
Yorkshire	Cardiff	June 23	30 *		
REFUGE ASSURANCE					
Gloucs	Bristol	April 22	8	1Ct	
Kent	Llanelli	May 13	57	1Ct	1-32
Essex	Ilford	June 3	14 *		
Northants	Northampton	June 10	50 *		0-18
Derbyshire	Swansea	July 29	21		
BENSON & HEDGES CUP					
Warwickshire	Edgbaston	April 24	11	1Ct	0-28
Gloucs	Cardiff	May 1	9	1Ct	2-27
Worcestershire	Worcester	May 8	8	1Ct	
Kent	Swansea	May 12	62		1-30
Worcestershire	Worcester	May 30	19		0-7
OTHER FIRST-CLASS					
Oxford U	The Parks	April 14	62	1Ct	1-33
Oxford U	The Parks	June 2	39 & 12 *		1-8
Sri Lanka	Ebbw Vale	Aug 22	0 & 92		1-6

BATTING AVERAGES - Including fielding

	Matches	Inns	NO	Runs	HS	Avge	100s	50s	Ct	St
Britannic Assurance	7	10	3	260	125 *	37.14	1	-	1	-
Refuge Assurance	5	5	2	150	57	50.00	-	2	2	-
Benson & Hedges Cup	5	5	0	109	62	21.80	-	1	3	-
Other First-Class	3	5	1	205	92	51.25	-	2	1	-
ALL FIRST-CLASS	10	15	4	465	125 *	42.27	1	2	2	-
ALL ONE-DAY	10	10	2	259	62	32.37	-	3	5	-

BOWLING AVERAGES

	Overs	Mdns	Runs	Wkts	Avge	Best	5wI	10wM
Britannic Assurance	21	3	85	1	85.00	1-44	-	-
Refuge Assurance	7	0	50	1	50.00	1-32	-	-
Benson & Hedges Cup	19	0	92	3	30.66	2-27	-	-
Other First-Class	21	7	47	3	15.66	1-6	-	-
ALL FIRST-CLASS	42	10	132	4	33.00	1-6	-	-
ALL ONE-DAY	26	0	142	4	35.50	2-27	-	-

A.M. HOOPER - *Cambridge University*

Opposition	Venue	Date	Batting	Fielding	Bowling
OTHER FIRST-CLASS					
Northants	Fenner's	April 14	0	1Ct	
Derbyshire	Fenner's	April 18	0 & 5		

BATTING AVERAGES - Including fielding

	Matches	Inns	NO	Runs	HS	Avge	100s	50s	Ct	St
Other First-Class	2	3	0	5	5	1.66	-	-	1	-
ALL FIRST-CLASS	2	3	0	5	5	1.66	-	-	1	-

BOWLING AVERAGES
Did not bowl

C.L. HOOPER - *World XI*

Opposition	Venue	Date	Batting	Fielding	Bowling
OTHER ONE-DAY					
Yorkshire	Scarborough	Sept 1	62		1-51

BATTING AVERAGES - Including fielding

	Matches	Inns	NO	Runs	HS	Avge	100s	50s	Ct	St
Other One-Day	1	1	0	62	62	62.00	-	1	-	-
ALL ONE-DAY	1	1	0	62	62	62.00	-	1	-	-

BOWLING AVERAGES

	Overs	Mdns	Runs	Wkts	Avge	Best	5wI	10wM
Other One-Day	10	1	51	1	51.00	1-51	-	
ALL ONE-DAY	10	1	51	1	51.00	1-51	-	

I.J. HOUSEMAN - *Yorkshire*

Opposition	Venue	Date	Batting	Fielding	Bowling
BRITANNIC ASSURANCE					
Notts	Scarborough	July 4			0-40
Northants	Northampton	July 7	0 *		0-53 & 0-36
OTHER FIRST-CLASS					
India	Headingley	June 30			0-43 & 2-26

BATTING AVERAGES - Including fielding

	Matches	Inns	NO	Runs	HS	Avge	100s	50s	Ct	St
Britannic Assurance	2	1	1	0	0*	-	-	-	-	-
Other First-Class	1	0	0	0	0					
ALL FIRST-CLASS	3	1	1	0	0*	-	-	-	-	-

BOWLING AVERAGES

	Overs	Mdns	Runs	Wkts	Avge	Best	5wI	10wM
Britannic Assurance	30	6	129	0	-	-	-	-
Other First-Class	20	3	69	2	34.50	2-26	-	-
ALL FIRST-CLASS	50	9	198	2	99.00	2-26	-	-

PLAYER RECORDS

D.P. HUGHES - *Lancashire*

Opposition	Venue	Date	Batting	Fielding	Bowling
BRITANNIC ASSURANCE					
Worcestershire	Old Trafford	April 26			2-22
Surrey	The Oval	May 3	8 *	1Ct	2-105
Derbyshire	Derby	May 15			4-25
Leicestershire	Old Trafford	May 19	6		0-46
Glamorgan	Colwyn Bay	May 26	33	1Ct	
Sussex	Horsham	June 2	0	4Ct	
Gloucs	Old Trafford	June 9		1Ct	1-43
Middlesex	Old Trafford	June 20			0-24
Kent	Maidstone	June 30	1 & 0 *		
Derbyshire	Liverpool	July 7	25 * & 36 *		1-45 & 0-15
Warwickshire	Coventry	July 18	29 *	1Ct	0-73 & 2-54
Essex	Colchester	July 21	57		2-43 & 0-43
Notts	Southport	July 25	7	1Ct	1-12 & 1-30
Yorkshire	Headingley	Aug 4	14	1Ct	0-6
Worcestershire	Kid'minster	Aug 8	2 & 1		3-135
Northants	Northampton	Aug 11	1 * & 1 *	1Ct	3-143 & 2-45
Yorkshire	Old Trafford	Aug 18	16	2Ct	0-9
Surrey	Blackpool	Aug 29			
REFUGE ASSURANCE					
Middlesex	Old Trafford	April 22			0-20
Notts	Trent Bridge	April 29			
Surrey	The Oval	May 6			
Leicestershire	Old Trafford	May 20	0 *	1Ct	
Glamorgan	Colwyn Bay	May 27			1-4
Gloucs	Old Trafford	June 10			
Hampshire	Old Trafford	June 24			
Kent	Maidstone	July 1		1Ct	
Derbyshire	Old Trafford	July 8	21 *		
Worcestershire	Old Trafford	July 15		1Ct	
Essex	Colchester	July 22	8 *	1Ct	
Yorkshire	Scarborough	Aug 5		1Ct	
Northants	Northampton	Aug 12			0-49
Warwickshire	Old Trafford	Aug 26			
Middlesex	Old Trafford	Sept 5			2-40
NATWEST TROPHY					
Durham	Old Trafford	June 27			
Derbyshire	Derby	July 11			0-19
Gloucs	Old Trafford	Aug 1			
Middlesex	Old Trafford	Aug 15			
Northants	Lord's	Sept 1			
BENSON & HEDGES CUP					
Surrey	Old Trafford	April 24			
Combined U	Fenner's	May 1		1Ct	
Hampshire	Old Trafford	May 8			
Yorkshire	Headingley	May 10			
Surrey	Old Trafford	May 30			
Somerset	Old Trafford	June 13		2Ct	
Worcestershire	Lord's	July 14	1 *		

BATTING AVERAGES - Including fielding

	Matches	Inns	NO	Runs	HS	Avge	100s	50s	Ct	St
Britannic Assurance	18	17	7	237	57	23.70	-	1	13	-
Refuge Assurance	15	3	3	29	21 *	-	-	-	5	-
NatWest Trophy	5	0	0	0	0	-	-	-	-	-
Benson & Hedges Cup	7	1	1	1	1 *	-	-	-	3	-
ALL FIRST-CLASS	18	17	7	237	57	23.70	-	1	13	-
ALL ONE-DAY	27	4	4	30	21 *	-	-	-	8	-

BOWLING AVERAGES

	Overs	Mdns	Runs	Wkts	Avge	Best	5wI	10wM
Britannic Assurance	280.4	61	918	24	38.25	4-25	-	
Refuge Assurance	18	0	113	3	37.66	2-40	-	
NatWest Trophy	3	0	19	0				
Benson & Hedges Cup								
ALL FIRST-CLASS	280.4	61	918	24	38.25	4-25	-	-
ALL ONE-DAY	21	0	132	3	44.00	2-40	-	-

J. HUGHES - *Northamptonshire*

Opposition	Venue	Date	Batting	Fielding	Bowling
BRITANNIC ASSURANCE					
Surrey	The Oval	July 4	1		0-84
Gloucs	Cheltenham	July 25	1 & 0		0-69
Hampshire	Bournemouth	Aug 4	0 & 2		0-47
Derbyshire	Chesterfield	Aug 8	0 & 0		2-57 & 1-36
REFUGE ASSURANCE					
Notts	Trent Bridge	July 29	1 *		0-16

BATTING AVERAGES - Including fielding

	Matches	Inns	NO	Runs	HS	Avge	100s	50s	Ct	St
Britannic Assurance	4	7	0	4	2	0.57	-	-	-	-
Refuge Assurance	1	1	1	1	1 *	-	-	-	-	-
ALL FIRST-CLASS	4	7	0	4	2	0.57	-	-	-	-
ALL ONE-DAY	1	1	1	1	1 *	-	-	-	-	-

BOWLING AVERAGES

	Overs	Mdns	Runs	Wkts	Avge	Best	5wI	10wM
Britannic Assurance	66	12	293	3	97.66	2-57	-	-
Refuge Assurance	4	0	16	0				
ALL FIRST-CLASS	66	12	293	3	97.66	2-57	-	-
ALL ONE-DAY	4	0	16	0				-

S.P. HUGHES - *Middlesex*

Opposition	Venue	Date	Batting	Fielding	Bowling
BRITANNIC ASSURANCE					
Essex	Lord's	April 26	14 *		1-60 & 0-29
Kent	Lord's	May 15	4		1-50 & 1-43
Surrey	Lord's	May 23	0 & 23 *		3-57
Gloucs	Lord's	May 26	12 *	1Ct	0-37 & 1-16
Essex	Ilford	June 2			2-43 & 0-58
Warwickshire	Lord's	June 6	2		1-48 & 0-20
Leicestershire	Leicester	June 16	4		1-5 & 0-23
Lancashire	Old Trafford	June 20			0-32
Northants	Luton	June 23	1		
Yorkshire	Uxbridge	July 18	4		1-38 & 0-9
Kent	Canterbury	July 25	6 *		1-87 & 0-14
Hampshire	Bournemouth	Aug 8	6 & 0	1Ct	0-51
Yorkshire	Headingley	Aug 23	4 & 10 *	1Ct	5-101 & 0-66
Surrey	The Oval	Sept 12	15 & 4		0-89 & 3-56
Sussex	Hove	Sept 18	0		4-34 & 3-55
REFUGE ASSURANCE					
Essex	Lord's	April 29			1-37
Gloucs	Lord's	May 27			1-43
Warwickshire	Lord's	June 3			1-32
Hampshire	Basingstoke	June 10		1Ct	4-19
Leicestershire	Leicester	June 17			1-52
Northants	Northampton	June 24		1Ct	1-35
Derbyshire	Derby	Aug 19			0-18
Yorkshire	Scarborough	Aug 26	14		0-52
Lancashire	Old Trafford	Sept 5		2Ct	1-60
Derbyshire	Edgbaston	Sept 16			2-45
NATWEST TROPHY					
Lancashire	Old Trafford	Aug 15			2-68
BENSON & HEDGES CUP					
Sussex	Hove	May 8			1-47
Somerset	Lord's	May 10			1-39
Derbyshire	Derby	May 12	22		1-64
Somerset	Taunton	May 30	2		3-37
OTHER FIRST-CLASS					
Cambridge U	Fenner's	May 3	2		2-30 & 0-11
New Zealand	Lord's	May 19			3-87 & 0-38

BATTING AVERAGES - Including fielding

	Matches	Inns	NO	Runs	HS	Avge	100s	50s	Ct	St
Britannic Assurance	15	17	5	109	23 *	9.08	-	-	3	-
Refuge Assurance	10	1	0	14	14	14.00	-	-	4	-
NatWest Trophy	1	0	0	0	0	-	-	-	-	-

H PLAYER RECORDS

Benson & Hedges Cup	4	2	0	24	22	12.00	-	-	-
Other First-Class	2	1	0	2	2	2.00	-	-	-
ALL FIRST-CLASS	17	18	5	111	23*	8.53	-	-	3 -
ALL ONE-DAY	15	3	0	38	22	12.66	-	-	4 -

BOWLING AVERAGES

	Overs	Mdns	Runs	Wkts	Avge	Best	5wI	10wM
Britannic Assurance	333	60	1121	28	40.03	5-101	1	-
Refuge Assurance	67.5	3	393	12	32.75	4-19	-	
NatWest Trophy	12	0	68	2	34.00	2-68	-	
Benson & Hedges Cup	43.5	0	187	6	31.16	3-37	-	
Other First-Class	53.2	13	166	5	33.20	3-87	-	-
ALL FIRST-CLASS	386.2	73	1287	33	39.00	5-101	1	-
ALL ONE-DAY	123.4	3	648	20	32.40	4-19	-	

G.W. HUMPAGE - *Warwickshire*

Opposition	Venue	Date	Batting			Fielding	Bowling
BRITANNIC ASSURANCE							
Yorkshire	Edgbaston	May 3	52	&	19*	5Ct	
Northants	Northampton	May 15	13			5Ct	
Notts	Edgbaston	May 19	74	&	62	2Ct	
Worcestershire	Edgbaston	May 26	9	&	12	4Ct	
Northants	Edgbaston	June 2	13	&	42	2Ct	
Middlesex	Lord's	June 6	73			2Ct	
Essex	Edgbaston	June 9			43	2Ct	
Derbyshire	Derby	June 16			34		
Yorkshire	Sheffield	June 20	23	&	12	2Ct	
Somerset	Taunton	July 4	67*	&	0*	2Ct	0-3
Surrey	The Oval	July 7	0	&	4	2Ct	0-31
REFUGE ASSURANCE							
Northants	Edgbaston	April 29	22*				
Yorkshire	Edgbaston	May 6	16*				
Gloucs	Moreton-in-M	May 20	11			2Ct	
Worcestershire	Worcester	May 27	40*			1Ct	
Middlesex	Lord's	June 3	13				
Essex	Edgbaston	June 10	5				
Derbyshire	Derby	June 17	0				
Surrey	The Oval	July 8	33			1Ct	
Glamorgan	Edgbaston	July 15	11				
Somerset	Weston	Aug 12				1Ct	
NATWEST TROPHY							
Hertfordshire	St Albans	June 27	43			0Ct,1St	
Yorkshire	Headingley	July 11	2				
BENSON & HEDGES CUP							
Glamorgan	Edgbaston	April 24	15			2Ct	
Kent	Canterbury	May 8	1			2Ct	
Worcestershire	Edgbaston	May 10	6				
Gloucs	Bristol	May 12	30*			4Ct	
OTHER FIRST-CLASS							
Cambridge U	Fenner's	April 26	17	&	4*	2Ct	
New Zealand	Edgbaston	May 30	9	&	46		0-1
OTHER ONE-DAY							
Surrey	Harrogate	June 13	2				
Yorkshire	Harrogate	June 15	11				

BATTING AVERAGES - Including fielding

	Matches	Inns	NO	Runs	HS	Avge	100s	50s	Ct	St
Britannic Assurance	11	18	3	552	74	36.80	-	5	28	-
Refuge Assurance	10	9	3	151	40*	25.16	-	-	5	-
NatWest Trophy	2	2	0	45	43	22.50	-	-	-	1
Benson & Hedges Cup	4	4	1	52	30*	17.33	-	-	8	-
Other First-Class	2	4	1	76	46	25.33	-	-	2	-
Other One-Day	2	2	0	13	11	6.50	-	-	-	-
ALL FIRST-CLASS	13	22	4	628	74	34.88	-	5	30	-
ALL ONE-DAY	18	17	4	261	43	20.07	-	-	13	1

BOWLING AVERAGES

	Overs	Mdns	Runs	Wkts	Avge	Best	5wI	10wM
Britannic Assurance	7	2	34	0	-	-	-	-
Refuge Assurance								
NatWest Trophy								
Benson & Hedges Cup								

Other First-Class	2	1	1	0					
Other One-Day									
ALL FIRST-CLASS	9	3	35	0					
ALL ONE-DAY									

M. HUMPHRIES - *Staffordshire*

Opposition	Venue	Date	Batting	Fielding	Bowling
NATWEST TROPHY					
Northants	Northampton	June 27	5*	1Ct	

BATTING AVERAGES - Including fielding

	Matches	Inns	NO	Runs	HS	Avge	100s	50s	Ct	St
NatWest Trophy	1	1	1	5	5*	-	-	-	1	-
ALL ONE-DAY	1	1	1	5	5*	-	-	-	1	-

BOWLING AVERAGES
Did not bowl

N. HUSSAIN - *Essex*

Opposition	Venue	Date	Batting			Fielding	Bowling
BRITANNIC ASSURANCE							
Kent	Maidstone	June 4			41		
Derbyshire	Colchester	July 18	60			1Ct	
Lancashire	Colchester	July 21	40	&	9*		0-15
Leicestershire	Leicester	July 25	9	&	0	2Ct	
Sussex	Chelmsford	July 28	21	&	21		
Notts	Southend	Aug 4	64				
Glamorgan	Southend	Aug 8	33	&	29	1Ct	
Yorkshire	Middlesbr'gh	Aug 11	6			1Ct	
Surrey	Chelmsford	Aug 18	29	&	8	2Ct	
Derbyshire	Derby	Aug 23	28			1Ct	
Northants	Northampton	Aug 29	30*	&	3		
Northants	Chelmsford	Sept 7	17	&	24	2Ct	
Kent	Chelmsford	Sept 12	45			3Ct	0-14
Surrey	The Oval	Sept 18	197			1Ct	
REFUGE ASSURANCE							
Hampshire	Southampton	July 8	12				
Northants	Chelmsford	July 15	22			1Ct	
Lancashire	Colchester	July 22	12			1Ct	
Sussex	Chelmsford	July 29	32*			1Ct	
Notts	Southend	Aug 5	5			1Ct	
Yorkshire	Middlesbr'gh	Aug 12	66*			3Ct	
Derbyshire	Derby	Aug 26	12*				
NATWEST TROPHY							
Hampshire	Chelmsford	July 11	2*				
OTHER FIRST-CLASS							
New Zealand	Chelmsford	June 30	1			1Ct	0-28 & 0-5
For TCCB U25 XI							
India	Edgbaston	Aug 15	37*			1Ct	
OTHER ONE-DAY							
For England XI							
Rest of World	Jesmond	Aug 2				2Ct	
Rest of World	Jesmond	Aug 3	26				0-12
For World XI							
Yorkshire	Scarborough	Sept 1	30				
For Essex							
Yorkshire	Scarborough	Sept 3	31				
Hampshire	Scarborough	Sept 4	39				

BATTING AVERAGES - Including fielding

	Matches	Inns	NO	Runs	HS	Avge	100s	50s	Ct	St
Britannic Assurance	14	21	2	714	197	37.57	1	2	14	-
Refuge Assurance	7	7	3	161	66*	40.25	-	1	7	-
NatWest Trophy	1	1	1	2	2*	-	-	-	-	-
Other First-Class	2	2	1	38	37*	38.00	-	-	2	-
Other One-Day	5	4	0	126	39	31.50	-	-	2	-

PLAYER RECORDS

H

ALL FIRST-CLASS	16	23	3	752	197	37.60	1	2	16	-
ALL ONE-DAY	13	12	4	289	66 *	36.12	-	1	9	-

BOWLING AVERAGES

	Overs	Mdns	Runs	Wkts	Avge	Best	5wI	10wM
Britannic Assurance	4	1	29	0	-	-	-	-
Refuge Assurance								
NatWest Trophy								
Other First-Class	8	1	33	0	-	-	-	-
Other One-Day	0.3	0	12	0	-	-	-	
ALL FIRST-CLASS	12	2	62	0	-	-	-	-
ALL ONE-DAY	0.3	0	12	0	-	-	-	

G. HUTCHINSON - *Cambridge University*

Opposition	Venue	Date	Batting	Fielding	Bowling
OTHER FIRST-CLASS					
Notts	Fenner's	June 16	29		
Kent	Fenner's	June 20	2		

BATTING AVERAGES - Including fielding

	Matches	Inns	NO	Runs	HS	Avge	100s	50s	Ct	St
Other First-Class	2	2	0	31	29	15.50	-	-	-	-
ALL FIRST-CLASS	2	2	0	31	29	15.50	-	-	-	-

BOWLING AVERAGES
Did not bowl

I.J.F. HUTCHINSON -*Duchess of Norfolk's XI*

Opposition	Venue	Date	Batting	Fielding	Bowling
OTHER ONE-DAY					
New Zealand	Arundel	May 6	19		

BATTING AVERAGES - Including fielding

	Matches	Inns	NO	Runs	HS	Avge	100s	50s	Ct	St
Other One-Day	1	1	0	19	19	19.00	-	-	-	-
ALL ONE-DAY	1	1	0	19	19	19.00	-	-	-	-

BOWLING AVERAGES
Did not bowl

I PLAYER RECORDS

A.P. IGGLESDEN - *Kent*

Opposition	Venue	Date	Batting		Fielding	Bowling
BRITANNIC ASSURANCE						
Sussex	Folkestone	May 3	2*			4-86 & 1-44
Notts	Tunbridge We	June 2	0 &	1*		2-62 & 0-4
Yorkshire	Tunbridge We	June 6				0-11
Somerset	Canterbury	June 9	19*			2-85 & 1-42
Warwickshire	Edgbaston	June 23	5		2Ct	4-79 & 0-23
Lancashire	Maidstone	June 30	16* &	0		1-29
Northants	Northampton	July 18	24			2-41
Surrey	Guildford	July 21	15* &	6		4-88
Middlesex	Canterbury	July 25		1	2Ct	1-53 & 2-93
Worcestershire	Canterbury	July 28	13* &	0*	1Ct	3-97 & 0-23
Derbyshire	Chesterfield	Aug 4	1* &	2		1-113
Leicestershire	Dartford	Aug 8	0*			0-19 & 0-6
Leicestershire	Leicester	Aug 23	0			2-84 & 0-11
REFUGE ASSURANCE						
Somerset	Canterbury	June 10				1-27
Notts	Canterbury	June 17	0			4-24
Warwickshire	Edgbaston	June 24	1		1Ct	0-37
Lancashire	Maidstone	July 1	0*			0-39
Surrey	The Oval	July 22	3*		1Ct	0-29
Worcestershire	Canterbury	July 29				0-26
Derbyshire	Chesterfield	Aug 5				1-54
NATWEST TROPHY						
Oxfordshire	Oxford	June 27	12*			2-13
Gloucs	Bristol	July 11	2*			0-34
BENSON & HEDGES CUP						
Warwickshire	Canterbury	May 8	0*			0-31
OTHER FIRST-CLASS						
Cambridge U	Fenner's	June 20				1-12 & 1-45
OTHER ONE-DAY						
For England XI						
Rest of World	Jesmond	Aug 2				0-44
Rest of World	Jesmond	Aug 3	11*			0-26

BATTING AVERAGES - Including fielding

	Matches	Inns	NO	Runs	HS	Avge	100s	50s	Ct	St
Britannic Assurance	13	17	9	105	24	13.12	-	-	5	-
Refuge Assurance	7	4	2	4	3*	2.00	-	-	2	-
NatWest Trophy	2	2	2	14	12*	-	-	-	-	-
Benson & Hedges Cup	1	1	1	0	0*	-	-	-	-	-
Other First-Class	1	0	0	0	0	-	-	-	-	-
Other One-Day	2	1	1	11	11*	-	-	-	-	-
ALL FIRST-CLASS	14	17	9	105	24	13.12	-	-	5	-
ALL ONE-DAY	12	8	6	29	12*	14.50	-	-	2	-

BOWLING AVERAGES

	Overs	Mdns	Runs	Wkts	Avge	Best	5wI	10wM
Britannic Assurance	306	42	1093	30	36.43	4-79	-	-
Refuge Assurance	52.5	2	236	6	39.33	4-24	-	-
NatWest Trophy	14	1	47	2	23.50	2-13	-	-
Benson & Hedges Cup	5	0	31	0	-	-	-	-
Other First-Class	20	5	57	2	28.50	1-12	-	-
Other One-Day	13	1	70	0	-	-	-	-
ALL FIRST-CLASS	326	47	1150	32	35.93	4-79	-	-
ALL ONE-DAY	84.5	4	384	8	48.00	4-24	-	-

R.K. ILLINGWORTH - *Worcestershire*

Opposition	Venue	Date	Batting		Fielding	Bowling
BRITANNIC ASSURANCE						
Lancashire	Old Trafford	April 26	35*			4-46 & 0-5
Notts	Worcester	May 3	117			0-0 & 0-47
Essex	Worcester	May 19	89 &	9		0-45
Warwickshire	Edgbaston	May 26			1Ct	2-66 & 3-67
Sussex	Worcester	June 20		0*		1-82
Middlesex	Lord's	June 30	0			3-65
Gloucs	Worcester	July 7	50		1Ct	3-75 & 3-47
Somerset	Worcester	July 18				0-72 & 0-28
Glamorgan	Abergavenny	July 21			1Ct	1-80 & 2-124
Derbyshire	Derby	July 25	6			5-59 & 3-52
Kent	Canterbury	July 28	15			0-19 & 3-20
Leicestershire	Leicester	Aug 4				4-85 & 3-98
Lancashire	Kid'minster	Aug 8	19*			3-8 & 2-92
Hampshire	Worcester	Aug 11	9*			1-99 & 3-44
Northants	Worcester	Aug 18	9 &	0	1Ct	4-29 & 3-63
Warwickshire	Worcester	Aug 23	13		1Ct	0-2
Notts	Trent Bridge	Aug 29	15*		1Ct	1-79 & 3-34
Gloucs	Bristol	Sept 7			1Ct	4-121 & 3-91
Somerset	Taunton	Sept 12	8 &	3		2-55 & 1-10
Glamorgan	Worcester	Sept 18	48 &	7*		0-15 & 1-22
REFUGE ASSURANCE						
Somerset	Taunton	April 22			1Ct	2-46
Derbyshire	Derby	April 29	8			3-41
Notts	Worcester	May 6	3		1Ct	1-26
Essex	Worcester	May 20				1-41
Sussex	Worcester	June 24			1Ct	1-35
Middlesex	Lord's	July 1	16*			0-28
Kent	Canterbury	July 29				3-19
Leicestershire	Leicester	Aug 5				1-32
Hampshire	Worcester	Aug 12	7		1Ct	0-24
Northants	Worcester	Aug 19				
Glamorgan	Swansea	Aug 26	1		2Ct	2-19
NATWEST TROPHY						
Suffolk	Bury St Ed's	June 27			1Ct	0-26
Somerset	Taunton	July 11				0-22
Northants	Northampton	Aug 1	7			2-44
BENSON & HEDGES CUP						
Gloucs	Bristol	April 24	5			1-43
Kent	Worcester	May 1	36*			0-23
Glamorgan	Worcester	May 8	6			0-33
Warwickshire	Edgbaston	May 10				1-42
Lancashire	Lord's	July 14	16			0-41
OTHER FIRST-CLASS						
MCC	Lord's	April 17	6			0-4
New Zealand	Worcester	May 12	0 &	74		0-13 & 3-35
For TCCB U25 XI						
India	Edgbaston	Aug 15				0-66 & 1-58
OTHER ONE-DAY						
Hampshire	Scarborough	Sept 2	29			2-62
For Yorkshiremen						
Yorkshire	Scarborough	Sept 6				0-53

BATTING AVERAGES - Including fielding

	Matches	Inns	NO	Runs	HS	Avge	100s	50s	Ct	St
Britannic Assurance	20	19	6	452	117	34.76	1	2	7	-
Refuge Assurance	11	5	1	35	16*	8.75	-	-	6	-
NatWest Trophy	3	1	0	7	7	7.00	-	-	1	-
Benson & Hedges Cup	5	4	1	63	36*	21.00	-	-	-	-
Other First-Class	3	3	0	80	74	26.66	-	1	-	-
Other One-Day	2	1	0	29	29	29.00	-	-	-	-
ALL FIRST-CLASS	23	22	6	532	117	33.25	1	3	7	-
ALL ONE-DAY	21	11	2	134	36*	14.88	-	-	7	-

BOWLING AVERAGES

	Overs	Mdns	Runs	Wkts	Avge	Best	5wI	10wM
Britannic Assurance	804.5	261	1946	71	27.40	5-59	1	-
Refuge Assurance	80	3	311	14	22.21	3-19	-	-
NatWest Trophy	36	9	92	2	46.00	2-44	-	-
Benson & Hedges Cup	46	1	182	2	91.00	1-42	-	-
Other First-Class	71	19	176	4	44.00	3-35	-	-
Other One-Day	19	0	115	2	57.50	2-62	-	-
ALL FIRST-CLASS	875.5	280	2122	75	28.29	5-59	1	-
ALL ONE-DAY	181	13	700	20	35.00	3-19	-	-

M.C. ILOTT - *Essex*

Opposition	Venue	Date	Batting		Fielding	Bowling
BRITANNIC ASSURANCE						
Notts	Southend	Aug 4	37			2-63 & 3-48
Glamorgan	Southend	Aug 8	9 &	17		2-62 & 0-22
Surrey	Chelmsford	Aug 18	7		1Ct	1-41 & 1-40
Derbyshire	Derby	Aug 23	6			5-34 & 2-34

PLANER RECORDS I

Northants	Northampton	Aug 29			0-115
Northants	Chelmsford	Sept 7	0 & 0		1-28 & 1-120
Kent	Chelmsford	Sept 12	42 * & 0 *		3-73 & 2-72
Surrey	The Oval	Sept 18	5		2-42 & 0-157

REFUGE ASSURANCE

Leicestershire	Leicester	May 6			2-41
Gloucs	Chelmsford	May 13			0-34
Worcestershire	Worcester	May 20			0-28
Hampshire	Southampton	July 8	1 *		0-34
Northants	Chelmsford	July 15		1Ct	1-17
Lancashire	Colchester	July 22			2-44
Notts	Southend	Aug 5	3		0-41
Yorkshire	Middlesbr'gh	Aug 12	6		2-24
Derbyshire	Derby	Aug 26			2-41

NATWEST TROPHY

Hampshire	Chelmsford	July 11			1-45

BENSON & HEDGES CUP

Northants	Northampton	May 8			0-39

OTHER FIRST-CLASS

Cambridge U	Fenner's	May 16			1-42 & 5-43

OTHER ONE-DAY

Yorkshire	Scarborough	Sept 3	6 *		0-11
Hampshire	Scarborough	Sept 4	17	1Ct	0-20

BATTING AVERAGES - Including fielding

	Matches	Inns	NO	Runs	HS	Avge	100s	50s	Ct	St
Britannic Assurance	8	10	2	123	42 *	15.37	-	-	1	-
Refuge Assurance	9	3	1	10	6	5.00	-	-	1	-
NatWest Trophy	1	0	0	0	0	-	-	-	-	-
Benson & Hedges Cup	1	0	0	0	0	-	-	-	-	-
Other First-Class	1	0	0	0	0	-	-	-	-	-
Other One-Day	2	2	1	23	17	23.00	-	-	1	-
ALL FIRST-CLASS	9	10	2	123	42 *	15.37	-	-	1	-
ALL ONE-DAY	13	5	2	33	17	11.00	-	-	2	-

BOWLING AVERAGES

	Overs	Mdns	Runs	Wkts	Avge	Best	5wI	10wM
Britannic Assurance	289.1	60	951	25	38.04	5-34	1	-
Refuge Assurance	70	3	304	9	33.77	2-24	-	
NatWest Trophy	9	0	45	1	45.00	1-45	-	
Benson & Hedges Cup	9	1	39	0		-	-	
Other First-Class	33	5	85	6	14.16	5-43	1	-
Other One-Day	14	5	31	0		-	-	
ALL FIRST-CLASS	322.1	65	1036	31	33.41	5-34	2	-
ALL ONE-DAY	102	9	419	10	41.90	2-24	-	-

▬ M. INGHAM - *League C.C. XI*

Opposition	Venue	Date	Batting	Fielding	Bowling
OTHER ONE-DAY					
India	Sunderland	June 28	26	1Ct	

BATTING AVERAGES - Including fielding

	Matches	Inns	NO	Runs	HS	Avge	100s	50s	Ct	St
Other One-Day	1	1	0	26	26	26.00	-	-	1	-
ALL ONE-DAY	1	1	0	26	26	26.00	-	-	1	-

BOWLING AVERAGES
Did not bowl

▬ R. IRANI - *Lancashire*

Opposition	Venue	Date	Batting	Fielding	Bowling
OTHER FIRST-CLASS					
Zimbabwe	Old Trafford	May 23			1-61 & 1-12

BATTING AVERAGES - Including fielding

	Matches	Inns	NO	Runs	HS	Avge	100s	50s	Ct	St
Other First-Class	1	0	0	0	0		-	-	-	-
ALL FIRST-CLASS	1	0	0	0	0		-	-	-	-

BOWLING AVERAGES

	Overs	Mdns	Runs	Wkts	Avge	Best	5wI	10wM
Other First-Class	22	7	73	2	36.50	1-12	-	-
ALL FIRST-CLASS	22	7	73	2	36.50	1-12	-	-

J · PLAYER RECORDS

B.S. JACKSON - *Berkshire*

Opposition	Venue	Date	Batting	Fielding	Bowling
NATWEST TROPHY					
Middlesex	Lord's	June 27	10	1Ct	0-46

BATTING AVERAGES - Including fielding

	Matches	Inns	NO	Runs	HS	Avge	100s	50s	Ct	St
NatWest Trophy	1	1	0	10	10	10.00	-	-	1	-
ALL ONE-DAY	1	1	0	10	10	10.00	-	-	1	-

BOWLING AVERAGES

	Overs	Mdns	Runs	Wkts	Avge	Best	5wI	10wM
NatWest Trophy	10	1	46	0	-	-	-	-
ALL ONE-DAY	10	1	46	0	-	-	-	-

P.B. JACKSON - *Ireland*

Opposition	Venue	Date	Batting	Fielding	Bowling
NATWEST TROPHY					
Sussex	Downpatrick	June 27	0		
OTHER FIRST-CLASS					
Scotland	Edinburgh	Aug 11	59	0Ct,1St	
OTHER ONE-DAY					
New Zealand	Downpatrick	May 9	6	1Ct	
New Zealand	Belfast	May 10	17	0Ct,1St	

BATTING AVERAGES - Including fielding

	Matches	Inns	NO	Runs	HS	Avge	100s	50s	Ct	St
NatWest Trophy	1	1	0	0	0	0.00	-	-	-	-
Other First-Class	1	1	0	59	59	59.00	-	1	-	1
Other One-Day	2	2	0	23	17	11.50	-	-	1	1
ALL FIRST-CLASS	1	1	0	59	59	59.00	-	1	-	1
ALL ONE-DAY	3	3	0	23	17	7.66	-	-	1	1

BOWLING AVERAGES
Did not bowl

K.D. JAMES - *Hampshire*

Opposition	Venue	Date	Batting	Fielding	Bowling
BRITANNIC ASSURANCE					
Kent	Canterbury	April 26	50 & 104 *		0-31 & 1-43
REFUGE ASSURANCE					
Kent	Canterbury	April 29	4		1-33
BENSON & HEDGES CUP					
Yorkshire	Southampton	April 24	2		1-34
Surrey	The Oval	May 1	2		1-36

BATTING AVERAGES - Including fielding

	Matches	Inns	NO	Runs	HS	Avge	100s	50s	Ct	St
Britannic Assurance	1	2	1	154	104 *	154.00	1	1	-	-
Refuge Assurance	1	1	0	4	4	4.00	-	-	-	-
Benson & Hedges Cup	2	2	0	4	2	2.00	-	-	-	-
ALL FIRST-CLASS	1	2	1	154	104 *	154.00	1	1	-	-
ALL ONE-DAY	3	3	0	8	4	2.66	-	-	-	-

BOWLING AVERAGES

	Overs	Mdns	Runs	Wkts	Avge	Best	5wI	10wM
Britannic Assurance	28	8	74	1	74.00	1-43	-	-
Refuge Assurance	8	0	33	1	33.00	1-33	-	
Benson & Hedges Cup	16	3	70	2	35.00	1-34	-	
ALL FIRST-CLASS	28	8	74	1	74.00	1-43	-	-
ALL ONE-DAY	24	3	103	3	34.33	1-33	-	

S.P. JAMES - *Cambridge Univ & Glamorgan*

Opposition	Venue	Date	Batting	Fielding	Bowling
BRITANNIC ASSURANCE					
Hampshire	Pontypridd	Sept 7	1 & 2	1Ct	
Warwickshire	Edgbaston	Sept 12	0 & 0		
Worcestershire	Worcester	Sept 18	7 & 0	1Ct	
BENSON & HEDGES CUP					
For Combined Universities					
Lancashire	Fenner's	May 1	0	1Ct	
Yorkshire	Headingley	May 8	63	1Ct	
Surrey	The Parks	May 10	59		
Hampshire	Southampton	May 12	46		
OTHER FIRST-CLASS					
For Cambridge University					
Northants	Fenner's	April 14	39 & 6	2Ct	
Derbyshire	Fenner's	April 18	21 & 7		
Warwickshire	Fenner's	April 26	19 & 8	1Ct	
Middlesex	Fenner's	May 3	54 & 46	1Ct	
Essex	Fenner's	May 16	5 & 12	1Ct	
Gloucs	Fenner's	May 23	116 & 6		
Notts	Fenner's	June 16	1 & 104 *		
Kent	Fenner's	June 20	3 & 57		
For Combined Universities					
New Zealand	Fenner's	June 27	67 & 131 *		
For Cambridge University					
Sussex	Hove	June 30	61 & 102		
Oxford U	Lord's	July 4	56	2Ct	
For Glamorgan					
India	Swansea	Aug 18	7 & 15	2Ct	
Sri Lanka	Ebbw Vale	Aug 22	47 & 0		

BATTING AVERAGES - Including fielding

	Matches	Inns	NO	Runs	HS	Avge	100s	50s	Ct	St
Britannic Assurance	3	6	0	10	7	1.66	-	-	2	-
Benson & Hedges Cup	4	4	0	168	63	42.00	-	2	2	-
Other First-Class	13	25	2	990	131 *	43.04	4	5	9	-
ALL FIRST-CLASS	16	31	2	1000	131 *	34.48	4	5	11	-
ALL ONE-DAY	4	4	0	168	63	42.00	-	2	2	-

BOWLING AVERAGES
Did not bowl

W.R. JAMES - *Zimbabwe*

Opposition	Venue	Date	Batting	Fielding	Bowling
OTHER FIRST-CLASS					
Yorkshire	Headingley	May 16	16 & 0	2Ct	
Gloucs	Bristol	May 19	36 & 23	1Ct	
Lancashire	Old Trafford	May 23	16 * & 52	1Ct	
OTHER ONE-DAY					
Essex	Chelmsford	May 14	27		

BATTING AVERAGES - Including fielding

	Matches	Inns	NO	Runs	HS	Avge	100s	50s	Ct	St
Other First-Class	3	6	1	143	52	28.60	-	1	4	-
Other One-Day	1	1	0	27	27	27.00	-	-	-	-
ALL FIRST-CLASS	3	6	1	143	52	28.60	-	1	4	-
ALL ONE-DAY	1	1	0	27	27	27.00	-	-	-	-

BOWLING AVERAGES
Did not bowl

K.B.S. JARVIS - *Gloucestershire*

Opposition	Venue	Date	Batting	Fielding	Bowling
BRITANNIC ASSURANCE					
Somerset	Taunton	April 26	0 * & 1 *		1-61

PLAYER RECORDS

J

REFUGE ASSURANCE
Glamorgan	Bristol	April 22	0-45
Essex	Chelmsford	May 13	0-30

BENSON & HEDGES CUP
Glamorgan	Cardiff	May 1	0-32
Kent	Canterbury	May 10	1-30
Warwickshire	Bristol	May 12	0-25

OTHER FIRST-CLASS
Cambridge U	Fenner's	May 23	0-50 & 2-31

OTHER ONE-DAY
For MCC
New Zealand	Lord's	May 7	2-49

BATTING AVERAGES - Including fielding
	Matches	Inns	NO	Runs	HS	Avge	100s	50s	Ct	St
Britannic Assurance	1	2	2	1	1*	-	-	-	-	-
Refuge Assurance	2	0	0	0	0	-	-	-	-	-
Benson & Hedges Cup	3	0	0	0	0	-	-	-	-	-
Other First-Class	1	0	0	0	0	-	-	-	-	-
Other One-Day	1	0	0	0	0	-	-	-	-	-
ALL FIRST-CLASS	2	2	2	1	1*	-	-	-	-	-
ALL ONE-DAY	6	0	0	0	0	-	-	-	-	-

BOWLING AVERAGES
	Overs	Mdns	Runs	Wkts	Avge	Best	5wI	10wM
Britannic Assurance	12	1	61	1	61.00	1-61	-	-
Refuge Assurance	14	1	75	0		-	-	
Benson & Hedges Cup	17	1	87	1	87.00	1-30	-	-
Other First-Class	22	2	81	2	40.50	2-31	-	-
Other One-Day	11	1	49	2	24.50	2-49	-	
ALL FIRST-CLASS	34	3	142	3	47.33	2-31	-	-
ALL ONE-DAY	42	3	211	3	70.33	2-49	-	

M.P. JARVIS - *Zimbabwe*

Opposition	Venue	Date	Batting	Fielding	Bowling

OTHER FIRST-CLASS
Gloucs	Bristol	May 19	1*		0-40 & 2-61

OTHER ONE-DAY
Sussex	Hove	May 13	4		2-30
Essex	Chelmsford	May 14	5		2-44

BATTING AVERAGES - Including fielding
	Matches	Inns	NO	Runs	HS	Avge	100s	50s	Ct	St
Other First-Class	1	1	1	1	1*	-	-	-	-	-
Other One-Day	2	2	0	9	5	4.50	-	-	-	-
ALL FIRST-CLASS	1	1	1	1	1*	-	-	-	-	-
ALL ONE-DAY	2	2	0	9	5	4.50	-	-	-	-

BOWLING AVERAGES
	Overs	Mdns	Runs	Wkts	Avge	Best	5wI	10wM
Other First-Class	30	7	101	2	50.50	2-61	-	-
Other One-Day	19	5	74	4	18.50	2-30	-	
ALL FIRST-CLASS	30	7	101	2	50.50	2-61	-	-
ALL ONE-DAY	19	5	74	4	18.50	2-30	-	

P.W. JARVIS - *Yorkshire*

Opposition	Venue	Date	Batting	Fielding	Bowling

BRITANNIC ASSURANCE
Northants	Headingley	April 26	29 & 0		1-90	
Warwickshire	Edgbaston	May 3	0 & 6		2-52 & 0-22	
Derbyshire	Chesterfield	May 23	15 & 8		2-88 & 0-59	
Worcestershire	Worcester	June 2	17	1Ct	3-59	
Kent	Tunbridge We	June 6			1-16	
Surrey	Harrogate	June 9	7	1Ct	1-60	
Warwickshire	Sheffield	June 20	7*		0-52 & 2-43	
Glamorgan	Cardiff	June 23			0-83	
Lancashire	Headingley	Aug 4	27 & 20*		3-91 & 3-59	
Sussex	Eastbourne	Aug 8			3-56 & 3-39	
Essex	Middlesbr'gh	Aug 11	8* & 0		4-53	
Lancashire	Old Trafford	Aug 18	11		0-73 & 1-2	
Middlesex	Headingley	Aug 23	14 & 43*		3-74 & 2-51	
Derbyshire	Scarborough	Sept 7			1-124 & 1-32	
Notts	Trent Bridge	Sept 18			1-106 & 0-9	

REFUGE ASSURANCE
Notts	Trent Bridge	April 22	28*		2-26
Warwickshire	Edgbaston	May 6			0-21
Derbyshire	Headingley	May 13			5-18
Kent	Canterbury	May 20	1		0-37
Worcestershire	Worcester	June 3		3Ct	2-26
Surrey	Hull	June 10	3		1-19
Sussex	Hove	June 17			2-19
Leicestershire	Sheffield	July 29			2-25
Lancashire	Scarborough	Aug 5	3		0-69
Essex	Middlesbr'gh	Aug 12	7		3-16
Middlesex	Scarborough	Aug 26			2-41

NATWEST TROPHY
Hampshire	Southampton	Aug 1	6		0-58

BENSON & HEDGES CUP
Hampshire	Southampton	April 24			0-48
Combined U	Headingley	May 8	2*		2-29
Lancashire	Headingley	May 10	42	1Ct	1-51
Surrey	The Oval	May 12			2-58

OTHER ONE-DAY
Sussex	Harrogate	June 14		1Ct	2-29
Warwickshire	Harrogate	June 15			0-53
World XI	Scarborough	Sept 1	0*		2-61
Essex	Scarborough	Sept 3	3		2-48
Yorkshiremen	Scarborough	Sept 6			1-42

BATTING AVERAGES - Including fielding
	Matches	Inns	NO	Runs	HS	Avge	100s	50s	Ct	St
Britannic Assurance	15	16	4	212	43*	17.66	-	-	2	-
Refuge Assurance	11	5	1	42	28*	10.50	-	-	3	-
NatWest Trophy	1	1	0	6	6	6.00	-	-	-	-
Benson & Hedges Cup	4	2	1	44	42	44.00	-	-	1	-
Other One-Day	5	2	1	3	3	3.00	-	-	1	-
ALL FIRST-CLASS	15	16	4	212	43*	17.66	-	-	2	-
ALL ONE-DAY	21	10	3	95	42	13.57	-	-	5	-

BOWLING AVERAGES
	Overs	Mdns	Runs	Wkts	Avge	Best	5wI	10wM
Britannic Assurance	405.2	68	1393	37	37.64	4-53	-	-
Refuge Assurance	80.5	4	317	19	16.68	5-18	1	
NatWest Trophy	12	1	58	0		-		
Benson & Hedges Cup	43	3	186	5	37.20	2-29		
Other One-Day	51	7	233	7	33.28	2-29		
ALL FIRST-CLASS	405.2	68	1393	37	37.64	4-53	-	-
ALL ONE-DAY	186.5	15	794	31	25.61	5-18	1	

S.T. JAYASURIYA - *Sri Lanka*

Opposition	Venue	Date	Batting	Fielding	Bowling

OTHER FIRST-CLASS
Glamorgan	Ebbw Vale	Aug 22	24 & 19	1Ct	
Notts	Cleethorpes	Aug 25	15	2Ct	
Warwickshire	Edgbaston	Aug 29	78*	1Ct	
Sussex	Hove	Sept 5	32 & 0	1Ct	0-4
Lancashire	Old Trafford	Sept 8	105*		1-14 & 0-0
Hampshire	Southampton	Sept 12	18 & 54		

OTHER ONE-DAY
Surrey	The Oval	Sept 2	32		
Somerset	Taunton	Sept 3	6		

BATTING AVERAGES - Including fielding
	Matches	Inns	NO	Runs	HS	Avge	100s	50s	Ct	St
Other First-Class	6	9	2	345	105*	49.28	1	2	5	-
Other One-Day	2	2	0	38	32	19.00	-	-	-	-
ALL FIRST-CLASS	6	9	2	345	105*	49.28	1	2	5	-
ALL ONE-DAY	2	2	0	38	32	19.00	-	-	-	-

J | PLAYER RECORDS

BOWLING AVERAGES

	Overs	Mdns	Runs	Wkts	Avge	Best	5wI	10wM
Other First-Class	7	1	18	1	18.00	1-14	-	-
Other One-Day								
ALL FIRST-CLASS	7	1	18	1	18.00	1-14	-	-
ALL ONE-DAY								

M. JEAN-JACQUES - *Derbyshire*

Opposition	Venue	Date	Batting	Fielding	Bowling
BRITANNIC ASSURANCE					
Northants	Northampton	May 3	4		1-39
Lancashire	Derby	May 15	18 & 2	1Ct	1-112 & 2-55
Surrey	The Oval	June 6	25		0-47 & 0-49
Leicestershire	Leicester	June 20		4	1-93
Gloucs	Derby	June 30	7 & 3 *		2-26
Sussex	Hove	July 4	0 *		1-60
Lancashire	Liverpool	July 7			1-104 & 2-90
Kent	Chesterfield	Aug 4			0-84 & 6-60
Middlesex	Derby	Aug 18	17 *	1Ct	0-40 & 1-19
Essex	Derby	Aug 23	0 & 0 *		1-105
REFUGE ASSURANCE					
Notts	Derby	June 10			3-47
Surrey	The Oval	June 24			2-51
Glamorgan	Swansea	July 29			0-35
Essex	Derby	Aug 26			0-47
OTHER FIRST-CLASS					
Cambridge U	Fenner's	April 18	13 *		2-31 & 1-23
New Zealand	Derby	June 2	14		2-67 & 1-2

BATTING AVERAGES - Including fielding

	Matches	Inns	NO	Runs	HS	Avge	100s	50s	Ct	St
Britannic Assurance	10	11	4	80	25	11.42	-	-	2	-
Refuge Assurance	4	0	0	0	0	-	-	-	-	-
Other First-Class	2	2	1	27	14	27.00	-	-	-	-
ALL FIRST-CLASS	12	13	5	107	25	13.37	-	-	2	-
ALL ONE-DAY	4	0	0	0	0	-	-	-	-	-

BOWLING AVERAGES

	Overs	Mdns	Runs	Wkts	Avge	Best	5wI	10wM
Britannic Assurance	261.2	33	983	19	51.73	6-60	1	-
Refuge Assurance	30	0	180	5	36.00	3-47	-	-
Other First-Class	38.4	9	123	6	20.50	2-31	-	-
ALL FIRST-CLASS	300	42	1106	25	44.24	6-60	1	-
ALL ONE-DAY	30	0	180	5	36.00	3-47	-	-

R.H.J. JENKINS - *Cambridge University*

Opposition	Venue	Date	Batting	Fielding	Bowling
OTHER FIRST-CLASS					
Northants	Fenner's	April 14	0		0-59 & 1-52
Derbyshire	Fenner's	April 18	0 * & 1		0-47 & 0-37
Middlesex	Fenner's	May 3	0 *		1-96 & 5-100
Essex	Fenner's	May 16	6 & 11		2-68 & 0-48
Gloucs	Fenner's	May 23	3 * & 1		0-61 & 1-68
Notts	Fenner's	June 16	12		2-51 & 0-49
Kent	Fenner's	June 20		1	0-43
Sussex	Hove	June 30	19 * & 4 *		1-94 & 0-18
Oxford U	Lord's	July 4		1Ct	2-68

BATTING AVERAGES - Including fielding

	Matches	Inns	NO	Runs	HS	Avge	100s	50s	Ct	St
Other First-Class	9	12	5	58	19 *	8.28	-	-	1	-
ALL FIRST-CLASS	9	12	5	58	19 *	8.28	-	-	1	-

BOWLING AVERAGES

	Overs	Mdns	Runs	Wkts	Avge	Best	5wI	10wM
Other First-Class	281.4	41	959	15	63.93	5-100	1	-
ALL FIRST-CLASS	281.4	41	959	15	63.93	5-100	1	-

T.E. JESTY - *Lancashire*

Opposition	Venue	Date	Batting	Fielding	Bowling
BRITANNIC ASSURANCE					
Worcestershire	Old Trafford	April 26	54		1-20
Surrey	The Oval	May 3	18 *	1Ct	
Derbyshire	Derby	May 15	55 * & 15 *	1Ct	
Leicestershire	Old Trafford	May 19	0		
Glamorgan	Colwyn Bay	May 26	30		
Gloucs	Old Trafford	June 9		84 *	
Middlesex	Old Trafford	June 20	5		
Hampshire	Old Trafford	June 23		26 *	1Ct
Kent	Maidstone	June 30	98 & 4		
Derbyshire	Liverpool	July 7	27 & 4		
Warwickshire	Coventry	July 18	17 & 6		0-7
Essex	Colchester	July 21	66		
Notts	Southport	July 25	38 & 30 *		
Somerset	Old Trafford	July 28	30		1Ct
Worcestershire	Kid'minster	Aug 8	35 & 54		
Northants	Northampton	Aug 11	56 & 8	1Ct	0-0
Surrey	Blackpool	Aug 29	25		
REFUGE ASSURANCE					
Middlesex	Old Trafford	April 22	10		0-16
Notts	Trent Bridge	April 29	15	1Ct	1-9
Leicestershire	Old Trafford	May 20	19		
Glamorgan	Colwyn Bay	May 27	25		
Gloucs	Old Trafford	June 10	22		
Hampshire	Old Trafford	June 24			
Derbyshire	Old Trafford	July 8	20		
Somerset	Old Trafford	July 29	13 *		

BATTING AVERAGES - Including fielding

	Matches	Inns	NO	Runs	HS	Avge	100s	50s	Ct	St
Britannic Assurance	17	24	6	785	98	43.61	-	7	6	-
Refuge Assurance	8	7	1	124	25	20.66	-	-	1	-
ALL FIRST-CLASS	17	24	6	785	98	43.61	-	7	6	-
ALL ONE-DAY	8	7	1	124	25	20.66	-	-	1	-

BOWLING AVERAGES

	Overs	Mdns	Runs	Wkts	Avge	Best	5wI	10wM
Britannic Assurance	8	3	27	1	27.00	1-20	-	-
Refuge Assurance	4	0	25	1	25.00	1-9	-	-
ALL FIRST-CLASS	8	3	27	1	27.00	1-20	-	-
ALL ONE-DAY	4	0	25	1	25.00	1-9	-	-

P.M. JOBSON - *Oxfordshire*

Opposition	Venue	Date	Batting	Fielding	Bowling
NATWEST TROPHY					
Kent	Oxford	June 27	7	1Ct	

BATTING AVERAGES - Including fielding

	Matches	Inns	NO	Runs	HS	Avge	100s	50s	Ct	St
NatWest Trophy	1	1	0	7	7	7.00	-	-	1	-
ALL ONE-DAY	1	1	0	7	7	7.00	-	-	1	-

BOWLING AVERAGES
Did not bowl

P. JOHNSON - *Nottinghamshire*

Opposition	Venue	Date	Batting	Fielding	Bowling
BRITANNIC ASSURANCE					
Derbyshire	Trent Bridge	April 26	45 & 54	2Ct	
Worcestershire	Worcester	May 3	3 & 83		
Leicestershire	Leicester	May 15	4 & 11		
Warwickshire	Edgbaston	May 19	2 & 73		
Northants	Trent Bridge	May 23	27 & 165 *	1Ct	
Derbyshire	Derby	May 26	20 & 2		

PLAYER RECORDS

J

Kent	Tunbridge We	June 2	25	&	3	1Ct
Surrey	Trent Bridge	June 20	10	&	78	
Leicestershire	Trent Bridge	June 30	4			1Ct
Yorkshire	Scarborough	July 4			149	
Sussex	Trent Bridge	July 7	68	&	14	1Ct
Hampshire	Portsmouth	July 18	34	&	8	
Lancashire	Southport	July 25	4	&	82	2Ct
Middlesex	Trent Bridge	July 28	30	&	5	2Ct
Essex	Southend	Aug 4	34	&	60	1Ct
Somerset	Weston	Aug 8	4	&	12	1Ct
Glamorgan	Worksop	Aug 11	44	&	12	1Ct
Worcestershire	Trent Bridge	Aug 29	98	&	13	
Middlesex	Lord's	Sept 7	2	&	12 *	

REFUGE ASSURANCE

Yorkshire	Trent Bridge	April 22	39
Lancashire	Trent Bridge	April 29	15
Worcestershire	Worcester	May 6	58
Middlesex	Lord's	May 13	100
Surrey	Trent Bridge	May 20	63
Derbyshire	Derby	June 10	0
Kent	Canterbury	June 17	3
Somerset	Bath	June 24	1
Leicestershire	Trent Bridge	July 1	35
Sussex	Trent Bridge	July 8	104	1Ct
Hampshire	Southampton	July 15	9
Warwickshire	Edgbaston	July 22	114
Northants	Trent Bridge	July 29	29
Essex	Southend	Aug 5	48	2Ct
Glamorgan	Trent Bridge	Aug 12	23
Gloucs	Trent Bridge	Aug 19	25 *
Derbyshire	Derby	Sept 5	2	1Ct

NATWEST TROPHY

Bucks	Marlow	June 27	14	1Ct
Northants	Northampton	July 11	48	

BENSON & HEDGES CUP

Essex	Chelmsford	April 24	104 *	1Ct
Leicestershire	Trent Bridge	May 1	39	1Ct
Scotland	Glasgow	May 8	52	
Northants	Trent Bridge	May 12	9	1Ct
Essex	Chelmsford	May 30	50	
Worcestershire	Trent Bridge	June 13	4	

OTHER FIRST-CLASS
For Notts

Oxford U	The Parks	June 6	112 *			
Cambridge U	Fenner's	June 16	4	&	49	0-1
For TCCB U25 XI						
India	Edgbaston	Aug 15	3	&	1	
For Notts						
Sri Lanka	Cleethorpes	Aug 25	1	&	54	1Ct

BATTING AVERAGES - Including fielding

	Matches	Inns	NO	Runs	HS	Avge	100s	50s	Ct	St
Britannic Assurance	19	36	2	1294	165 *	38.05	2	8	13	-
Refuge Assurance	17	17	1	668	114	41.75	3	2	4	-
NatWest Trophy	2	2	0	62	48	31.00	-	-	1	-
Benson & Hedges Cup	6	6	1	258	104 *	51.60	1	2	3	-
Other First-Class	4	7	1	224	112 *	37.33	1	1	1	-
ALL FIRST-CLASS	23	43	3	1518	165 *	37.95	3	9	14	-
ALL ONE-DAY	25	25	2	988	114	42.95	4	4	8	-

BOWLING AVERAGES

	Overs	Mdns	Runs	Wkts	Avge	Best	5wI	10wM
Britannic Assurance								
Refuge Assurance								
NatWest Trophy								
Benson & Hedges Cup								
Other First-Class	1	0	1	0	-	-	-	-
ALL FIRST-CLASS	1	0	1	0	-	-	-	-
ALL ONE-DAY								

S.W. JOHNSON - *Cambridge University*

Opposition	Venue	Date	Batting	Fielding	Bowling

OTHER FIRST-CLASS

Northants	Fenner's	April 14	0	1Ct	2-86 & 0-17

Warwickshire	Fenner's	April 26	14 *		1-43 & 0-41
Essex	Fenner's	May 16	10 * &	2 *	0-59 & 0-23
Gloucs	Fenner's	May 23	1		0-44 & 0-25
Sussex	Hove	June 30	8 *		0-48 & 0-18
Oxford U	Lord's	July 4		1Ct	0-48

BATTING AVERAGES - Including fielding

	Matches	Inns	NO	Runs	HS	Avge	100s	50s	Ct	St
Other First-Class	6	6	4	35	14 *	17.50	-	-	2	-
ALL FIRST-CLASS	6	6	4	35	14 *	17.50	-	-	2	-

BOWLING AVERAGES

	Overs	Mdns	Runs	Wkts	Avge	Best	5wI	10wM
Other First-Class	113	14	452	3	150.66	2-86	-	-
ALL FIRST-CLASS	113	14	452	3	150.66	2-86	-	-

A. JOHNSTON - *Ireland*

Opposition	Venue	Date	Batting	Fielding	Bowling

NATWEST TROPHY

Sussex	Downpatrick	June 27	0		0-21

BATTING AVERAGES - Including fielding

	Matches	Inns	NO	Runs	HS	Avge	100s	50s	Ct	St
NatWest Trophy	1	1	0	0	0	0.00	-	-	-	-
ALL ONE-DAY	1	1	0	0	0	0.00	-	-	-	-

BOWLING AVERAGES

	Overs	Mdns	Runs	Wkts	Avge	Best	5wI	10wM
NatWest Trophy	4	0	21	0	-	-	-	-
ALL ONE-DAY	4	0	21	0	-	-	-	-

A.H. JONES - *New Zealand*

Opposition	Venue	Date	Batting	Fielding	Bowling

CORNHILL TEST MATCHES

England	Trent Bridge	June 7	39	&	13		
England	Lord's	June 21	49				1-40
England	Edgbaston	July 5	2	&	40	1Ct	0-2

TEXACO TROPHY

England	Headingley	May 23	51
England	The Oval	May 25	15

OTHER FIRST-CLASS

Worcestershire	Worcester	May 12	1	&	9			
Somerset	Taunton	May 16	57 * &	53			0-8 & 0-8
Middlesex	Lord's	May 19	41	&	70	1Ct	1-28
Warwickshire	Edgbaston	May 30	82			1Ct	
Derbyshire	Derby	June 2	121 *				
Northants	Northampton	June 16	46				
Essex	Chelmsford	June 30	3	&	66 *		1-1

OTHER ONE-DAY

MCC	Lord's	May 7	49	0-33
Ireland	Downpatrick	May 9		
Ireland	Belfast	May 10	32	0-27

BATTING AVERAGES - Including fielding

	Matches	Inns	NO	Runs	HS	Avge	100s	50s	Ct	St
Cornhill Test Matches	3	5	0	143	49	28.60	-	-	1	-
Texaco Trophy	2	2	0	66	51	33.00	-	1	-	-
Other First-Class	7	11	3	549	121 *	68.62	1	5	2	-
Other One-Day	3	2	0	81	49	40.50	-	-	-	-
ALL FIRST-CLASS	10	16	3	692	121 *	53.23	1	5	3	-
ALL ONE-DAY	5	4	0	147	51	36.75	-	1	-	-

BOWLING AVERAGES

	Overs	Mdns	Runs	Wkts	Avge	Best	5wI	10wM
Cornhill Test Matches	13	3	42	1	42.00	1-40	-	-
Texaco Trophy								

J PLAYER RECORDS

Other First-Class	13	1	45	2	22.50	1-1	-	-
Other One-Day	13	1	60	0	-	-	-	-
ALL FIRST-CLASS	26	4	87	3	29.00	1-1	-	-
ALL ONE-DAY	13	1	60	0	-	-	-	-

■ A.N. JONES - *Somerset*

Opposition	Venue	Date	Batting		Fielding	Bowling
BRITANNIC ASSURANCE						
Gloucs	Taunton	April 26	9			0-68 & 6-75
Glamorgan	Cardiff	May 3			1Ct	2-80 & 0-24
Derbyshire	Taunton	May 19		8*		3-85 & 0-26
Sussex	Taunton	May 23				2-71 & 1-11
Leicestershire	Leicester	May 26				0-34 & 1-26
Gloucs	Bristol	June 2	0*			1-96
Hampshire	Basingstoke	June 6				1-56
Kent	Canterbury	June 9				1-24
Essex	Bath	June 16				0-59
Glamorgan	Bath	June 20				1-15
Northants	Taunton	June 30				1-48 & 1-63
Warwickshire	Taunton	July 4	0			2-38 & 0-19
Worcestershire	Worcester	July 18				1-17 & 0-25
Middlesex	Uxbridge	July 21				0-47 & 1-69
Yorkshire	Scarborough	July 25			1Ct	1-78 & 1-54
Surrey	Weston	Aug 4				2-62 & 2-36
Hampshire	Taunton	Aug 18	8*		1Ct	2-87 & 0-21
Sussex	Hove	Aug 23	24*		1Ct	2-47 & 2-117
Warwickshire	Edgbaston	Sept 7	8			2-110 & 4-72
Worcestershire	Taunton	Sept 12	41 &	2*		4-154 & 5-76
REFUGE ASSURANCE						
Worcestershire	Taunton	April 22	10			0-40
Hampshire	Taunton	May 13				1-40
Derbyshire	Taunton	May 20				1-38
Kent	Canterbury	June 10				2-25
Essex	Bath	June 17	0			1-47
Surrey	Weston	Aug 5				1-33
Sussex	Hove	Aug 26	2		2Ct	2-31
NATWEST TROPHY						
Devon	Torquay	June 27				1-20
Worcestershire	Taunton	July 11				0-64
BENSON & HEDGES CUP						
Min Counties	Taunton	May 8				1-63
Middlesex	Lord's	May 10	7			1-49
Sussex	Hove	May 12				2-22
Middlesex	Taunton	May 30	3			4-41
Lancashire	Old Trafford	June 13	1*			1-48
OTHER FIRST-CLASS						
Oxford U	The Parks	April 18				2-17
New Zealand	Taunton	May 16			2Ct	1-20 & 1-28
OTHER ONE-DAY						
Sri Lanka	Taunton	Sept 3				0-31

BATTING AVERAGES - Including fielding

	Matches	Inns	NO	Runs	HS	Avge	100s	50s	Ct	St
Britannic Assurance	20	9	5	100	41	25.00	-	-	4	-
Refuge Assurance	7	3	0	12	10	4.00	-	-	2	-
NatWest Trophy	2	0	0	0	0	-	-	-	-	-
Benson & Hedges Cup	5	3	1	11	7	5.50	-	-	-	-
Other First-Class	2	0	0	0	0	-	-	-	2	-
Other One-Day	1	0	0	0	0	-	-	-	-	-
ALL FIRST-CLASS	22	9	5	100	41	25.00	-	-	6	-
ALL ONE-DAY	15	6	1	23	10	4.60	-	-	2	-

BOWLING AVERAGES

	Overs	Mdns	Runs	Wkts	Avge	Best	5wI	10wM
Britannic Assurance	539.4	81	1990	52	38.26	6-75	2	-
Refuge Assurance	50	1	254	8	31.75	2-25	-	-
NatWest Trophy	16	1	84	1	84.00	1-20	-	-
Benson & Hedges Cup	46.5	3	223	9	24.77	4-41	-	-
Other First-Class	33	11	65	4	16.25	2-17	-	-
Other One-Day	6	0	31	0	-	-	-	-
ALL FIRST-CLASS	572.4	92	2055	56	36.69	6-75	2	-
ALL ONE-DAY	118.5	5	592	18	32.88	4-41	-	-

■ J.B.R. JONES - *Shropshire*

Opposition	Venue	Date	Batting	Fielding	Bowling
NATWEST TROPHY					
Derbyshire	Chesterfield	June 27	26		

BATTING AVERAGES - Including fielding

	Matches	Inns	NO	Runs	HS	Avge	100s	50s	Ct	St
NatWest Trophy	1	1	0	26	26	26.00	-	-	-	-
ALL ONE-DAY	1	1	0	26	26	26.00	-	-	-	-

BOWLING AVERAGES
Did not bowl

■ J.H. JONES - *Berkshire*

Opposition	Venue	Date	Batting	Fielding	Bowling
NATWEST TROPHY					
Middlesex	Lord's	June 27			1-32

BATTING AVERAGES - Including fielding

	Matches	Inns	NO	Runs	HS	Avge	100s	50s	Ct	St
NatWest Trophy	1	0	0	0	0	-	-	-	-	-
ALL ONE-DAY	1	0	0	0	0	-	-	-	-	-

BOWLING AVERAGES

	Overs	Mdns	Runs	Wkts	Avge	Best	5wI	10wM
NatWest Trophy	9	2	32	1	32.00	1-32	-	-
ALL ONE-DAY	9	2	32	1	32.00	1-32	-	-

■ L.A. JOSEPH - *Hampshire*

Opposition	Venue	Date	Batting		Fielding	Bowling
BRITANNIC ASSURANCE						
Kent	Canterbury	April 26	25*			1-76
Somerset	Basingstoke	June 6	13			0-40
Worcestershire	Worcester	Aug 11		43*	1Ct	2-128 & 0-19
Kent	Bournemouth	Aug 29	2*			1-76 & 1-67
BENSON & HEDGES CUP						
Combined U	Southampton	May 12				0-38
OTHER FIRST-CLASS						
Oxford U	The Parks	May 3	69*			0-28
India	Southampton	July 4				2-28

BATTING AVERAGES - Including fielding

	Matches	Inns	NO	Runs	HS	Avge	100s	50s	Ct	St
Britannic Assurance	4	4	3	83	43*	83.00	-	-	1	-
Benson & Hedges Cup	1	0	0	0	0	-	-	-	-	-
Other First-Class	2	1	1	69	69*	-	-	-	1	-
ALL FIRST-CLASS	6	5	4	152	69*	152.00	-	1	1	-
ALL ONE-DAY	1	0	0	0	0	-	-	-	-	-

BOWLING AVERAGES

	Overs	Mdns	Runs	Wkts	Avge	Best	5wI	10wM
Britannic Assurance	82	12	406	5	81.20	2-128	-	-
Benson & Hedges Cup	11	1	38	0	-	-	-	-
Other First-Class	20	4	56	2	28.00	2-28	-	-
ALL FIRST-CLASS	102	16	462	7	66.00	2-28	-	-
ALL ONE-DAY	11	1	38	0	-	-	-	-

PLAYER RECORDS

K

A.I. KALLICHARRAN - *Warwickshire*

Opposition	Venue	Date	Batting	Fielding	Bowling
BRITANNIC ASSURANCE					
Yorkshire	Edgbaston	May 3	2 & 11 *	1Ct	
Northants	Northampton	May 15	72	3Ct	
Notts	Edgbaston	May 19	20 & 58		
Northants	Edgbaston	June 2	2 & 0	1Ct	
Middlesex	Lord's	June 6	10		
REFUGE ASSURANCE					
Northants	Edgbaston	April 29	76		
Yorkshire	Edgbaston	May 6	65		
Gloucs	Moreton-in-M	May 20	0		
Worcestershire	Worcester	May 27	5		
Middlesex	Lord's	June 3	41 *		
Kent	Edgbaston	June 24	23		
NATWEST TROPHY					
Hertfordshire	St Albans	June 27	41		
BENSON & HEDGES CUP					
Glamorgan	Edgbaston	April 24	13		
Kent	Canterbury	May 8	11		
Worcestershire	Edgbaston	May 10	32		
Gloucs	Bristol	May 12	21		
OTHER FIRST-CLASS					
Cambridge U	Fenner's	April 26	43		
New Zealand	Edgbaston	May 30	3		

BATTING AVERAGES - Including fielding

	Matches	Inns	NO	Runs	HS	Avge	100s	50s	Ct	St
Britannic Assurance	5	8	1	175	72	25.00	-	2	5	-
Refuge Assurance	6	6	1	210	76	42.00	-	2	-	-
NatWest Trophy	1	1	0	41	41	41.00	-	-	-	-
Benson & Hedges Cup	4	4	0	77	32	19.25	-	-	-	-
Other First-Class	2	2	0	46	43	23.00	-	-	-	-
ALL FIRST-CLASS	7	10	1	221	72	24.55	-	2	5	-
ALL ONE-DAY	11	11	1	328	76	32.80	-	2	-	-

BOWLING AVERAGES
Did not bowl

KAPIL DEV - *India*

Opposition	Venue	Date	Batting	Fielding	Bowling
CORNHILL TEST MATCHES					
England	Lord's	July 26	77 * & 7		1-120 & 0-53
England	Old Trafford	Aug 9	0 & 26		1-67 & 2-69
England	The Oval	Aug 23	110		1-70 & 2-66
TEXACO TROPHY					
England	Headingley	July 18		1Ct	2-49
England	Trent Bridge	July 20	5 *		2-40
OTHER FIRST-CLASS					
Yorkshire	Headingley	June 30		1Ct	0-13 & 1-37
Kent	Canterbury	July 7	17 & 59 *		0-58 & 0-20
Min Counties	Trowbridge	July 11	47		1-27 & 0-20
Gloucs	Bristol	Aug 4	12	1Ct	2-28
Glamorgan	Swansea	Aug 18	0		1-8 & 0-58
World XI	Scarborough	Aug 29	19 & 3	1Ct	1-2 & 0-28
OTHER ONE-DAY					
League CC	Sunderland	June 28	0	1Ct	2-29
Scotland	Glasgow	July 14	11 *	1Ct	2-25
Derbyshire	Chesterfield	July 16	1		3-76

BATTING AVERAGES - Including fielding

	Matches	Inns	NO	Runs	HS	Avge	100s	50s	Ct	St
Cornhill Test Matches	3	5	1	220	110	55.00	1	1	-	-
Texaco Trophy	2	1	1	5	5 *	-	-	-	1	-
Other First-Class	6	7	1	157	59 *	26.16	-	1	3	-
Other One-Day	3	3	1	12	11 *	6.00	-	-	2	-

ALL FIRST-CLASS	9	12	2	377	110	37.70	1	2	3	-
ALL ONE-DAY	5	4	2	17	11 *	8.50	-	-	3	-

BOWLING AVERAGES

	Overs	Mdns	Runs	Wkts	Avge	Best	5wI	10wM
Cornhill Test Matches	128	23	445	7	63.57	2-66	-	-
Texaco Trophy	22	3	89	4	22.25	2-40	-	-
Other First-Class	118.4	36	299	6	49.83	2-28	-	-
Other One-Day	31	6	130	7	18.57	3-76	-	-
ALL FIRST-CLASS	246.4	59	744	13	57.23	2-28	-	-
ALL ONE-DAY	53	9	219	11	19.90	3-76	-	-

D.J.M. KELLEHER - *Kent*

Opposition	Venue	Date	Batting	Fielding	Bowling
BRITANNIC ASSURANCE					
Lancashire	Maidstone	June 30	0 & 0	1Ct	1-30 & 0-21
Gloucs	Bristol	Aug 11	35		0-35 & 0-18
Hampshire	Bournemouth	Aug 29	9		1-54 & 0-14
Surrey	Canterbury	Sept 7	44 & 6	1Ct	3-148
Essex	Chelmsford	Sept 12	1 & 6		1-68 & 1-10
REFUGE ASSURANCE					
Gloucs	Bristol	Aug 12	2	1Ct	1-20
Leicestershire	Leicester	Aug 26			0-50
NATWEST TROPHY					
Oxfordshire	Oxford	June 27	21		3-16
OTHER ONE-DAY					
Sussex	Hove	Sept 2	2		0-19
Surrey	Hove	Sept 4	20 *		0-68

BATTING AVERAGES - Including fielding

	Matches	Inns	NO	Runs	HS	Avge	100s	50s	Ct	St
Britannic Assurance	5	8	0	101	44	12.62	-	-	2	-
Refuge Assurance	2	1	0	2	2	2.00	-	-	1	-
NatWest Trophy	1	1	0	21	21	21.00	-	-	-	-
Other One-Day	2	2	1	22	20 *	22.00	-	-	-	-
ALL FIRST-CLASS	5	8	0	101	44	12.62	-	-	2	-
ALL ONE-DAY	5	4	1	45	21	15.00	-	-	1	-

BOWLING AVERAGES

	Overs	Mdns	Runs	Wkts	Avge	Best	5wI	10wM
Britannic Assurance	112.5	20	398	7	56.85	3-148	-	-
Refuge Assurance	15.5	2	70	1	70.00	1-20	-	-
NatWest Trophy	9	3	16	3	5.33	3-16	-	-
Other One-Day	12	0	87	0	-	-	-	-
ALL FIRST-CLASS	112.5	20	398	7	56.85	3-148	-	-
ALL ONE-DAY	36.5	5	173	4	43.25	3-16	-	-

S.A. KELLETT - *Yorkshire*

Opposition	Venue	Date	Batting	Fielding	Bowling
BRITANNIC ASSURANCE					
Northants	Headingley	April 26	0 & 63		
Warwickshire	Edgbaston	May 3	31 & 31		
Derbyshire	Chesterfield	May 23	22 & 55		
Hampshire	Headingley	May 26	56 & 26	1Ct	
Worcestershire	Worcester	June 2	0 & 4 *		
Kent	Tunbridge We	June 6		2Ct	
Surrey	Harrogate	June 9	24		
Warwickshire	Sheffield	June 20	18 & 75 *		
Glamorgan	Cardiff	June 23	2 & 8	2Ct	
Somerset	Scarborough	July 25	15 & 57		
Leicestershire	Sheffield	July 28	47 & 54	1Ct	
Lancashire	Headingley	Aug 4	25 & 15	1Ct	
Derbyshire	Scarborough	Sept 7	22 & 2		
Notts	Trent Bridge	Sept 18	27 & 20		
REFUGE ASSURANCE					
Warwickshire	Edgbaston	May 6	21		
Derbyshire	Headingley	May 13	32	1Ct	

K	PLACER	PLAYER RECORDS

PLAYER RECORDS

Hampshire	Headingley	May 27	7
Northants	Tring	July 8	10

NATWEST TROPHY

Norfolk	Headingley	June 27	
Warwickshire	Headingley	July 11	
Hampshire	Southampton	Aug 1	0

BENSON & HEDGES CUP

Combined U	Headingley	May 8	29
Lancashire	Headingley	May 10	22
Surrey	The Oval	May 12	45

OTHER FIRST-CLASS

Zimbabwe	Headingley	May 16	0 & 39	1Ct
India	Headingley	June 30	36 *	

OTHER ONE-DAY

World XI	Scarborough	Sept 1	57
Essex	Scarborough	Sept 3	28
For Yorkshire			
Yorkshiremen	Scarborough	Sept 6	

BATTING AVERAGES - Including fielding

	Matches	Inns	NO	Runs	HS	Avge	100s	50s	Ct	St
Britannic Assurance	14	25	2	699	75 *	30.39	-	6	7	-
Refuge Assurance	4	4	0	70	32	17.50	-	-	1	-
NatWest Trophy	3	1	0	0	0	0.00	-	-	-	-
Benson & Hedges Cup	3	3	0	96	45	32.00	-	-	-	-
Other First-Class	2	3	1	75	39	37.50	-	-	1	-
Other One-Day	3	2	0	85	57	42.50	-	1	-	-
ALL FIRST-CLASS	16	28	3	774	75 *	30.96	-	6	8	-
ALL ONE-DAY	13	10	0	251	57	25.10	-	1	1	-

BOWLING AVERAGES
Did not bowl

N.M. KENDRICK - *Surrey*

Opposition	Venue	Date	Batting	Fielding	Bowling
BRITANNIC ASSURANCE					
Lancashire	The Oval	May 3	18 *	1Ct	1-192
Middlesex	Lord's	May 23	52 *	2Ct	1-12 & 2-25
Sussex	Guildford	July 18	2	2Ct	0-23 & 0-43
Kent	Guildford	July 21		1Ct	4-110 & 2-102
Somerset	Weston	Aug 4	0 *		1-87 & 2-73
Leicestershire	The Oval	Aug 11	9	1Ct	0-3
Essex	Chelmsford	Aug 18	12 & 3	1Ct	0-39
Hampshire	Southampton	Aug 23	7		
Kent	Canterbury	Sept 7	0	2Ct	0-73 & 0-19
Middlesex	The Oval	Sept 12	6 * & 14	1Ct	2-122
Essex	The Oval	Sept 18	1		2-64
REFUGE ASSURANCE					
Warwickshire	The Oval	July 8	2 *		0-20
OTHER FIRST-CLASS					
Oxford U	The Parks	May 16			1-20 & 3-79
India	The Oval	Aug 1		3Ct	2-58 & 2-50
OTHER ONE-DAY					
Sri Lanka	The Oval	Sept 2			3-21

BATTING AVERAGES - Including fielding

	Matches	Inns	NO	Runs	HS	Avge	100s	50s	Ct	St
Britannic Assurance	11	12	4	124	52 *	15.50	-	1	11	-
Refuge Assurance	1	1	1	2	2 *	-	-	-	-	-
Other First-Class	2	0	0	0	0	-	-	-	3	-
Other One-Day	1	0	0	0	0	-	-	-	-	-
ALL FIRST-CLASS	13	12	4	124	52 *	15.50	-	1	14	-
ALL ONE-DAY	2	1	1	2	2 *	-	-	-	-	-

BOWLING AVERAGES

	Overs	Mdns	Runs	Wkts	Avge	Best	5wI	10wM
Britannic Assurance	273	50	987	17	58.05	4-110	-	-
Refuge Assurance	3	0	20	0	-	-	-	-
Other First-Class	75	16	207	8	25.87	3-79	-	-
Other One-Day	6	0	21	3	7.00	3-21	-	-

ALL FIRST-CLASS	348	66	1194	25	47.76	4-110	-	-
ALL ONE-DAY	9	0	41	3	13.66	3-21	-

M.J. KILBORN - *Oxford University*

Opposition	Venue	Date	Batting	Fielding	Bowling
OTHER FIRST-CLASS					
Glamorgan	The Parks	April 14	83		
Somerset	The Parks	April 18	37		
Hampshire	The Parks	May 3	17	2Ct	
Surrey	The Parks	May 16	11 & 36 *	1Ct	
Lancashire	The Parks	June 16	95	1Ct	
For Combined Universities					
New Zealand	Fenner's	June 27	27 & 3	1Ct	

BATTING AVERAGES - Including fielding

	Matches	Inns	NO	Runs	HS	Avge	100s	50s	Ct	St
Other First-Class	6	8	1	309	95	44.14	-	2	5	-
ALL FIRST-CLASS	6	8	1	309	95	44.14	-	2	5	-

BOWLING AVERAGES
Did not bowl

R. KINGSHOTT - *Norfolk*

Opposition	Venue	Date	Batting	Fielding	Bowling
NATWEST TROPHY					
Yorkshire	Headingley	June 27	9		0-24

BATTING AVERAGES - Including fielding

	Matches	Inns	NO	Runs	HS	Avge	100s	50s	Ct	St
NatWest Trophy	1	1	0	9	9	9.00	-	-	-	-
ALL ONE-DAY	1	1	0	9	9	9.00	-	-	-	-

BOWLING AVERAGES

	Overs	Mdns	Runs	Wkts	Avge	Best	5wI	10wM
NatWest Trophy	6	2	24	0	-	-	-	-
ALL ONE-DAY	6	2	24	0	-	-	-	-

N.V. KNIGHT - *Combined Universities*

Opposition	Venue	Date	Batting	Fielding	Bowling
BENSON & HEDGES CUP					
Lancashire	Fenner's	May 1	9		
Hampshire	Southampton	May 12	16		

BATTING AVERAGES - Including fielding

	Matches	Inns	NO	Runs	HS	Avge	100s	50s	Ct	St
Benson & Hedges Cup	2	2	0	25	16	12.50	-	-	-	-
ALL ONE-DAY	2	2	0	25	16	12.50	-	-	-	-

BOWLING AVERAGES
Did not bowl

K.M. KRIKKEN - *Derbyshire*

Opposition	Venue	Date	Batting	Fielding	Bowling
BRITANNIC ASSURANCE					
Northants	Northampton	May 3	0	2Ct	
Lancashire	Derby	May 15	11 & 26	0Ct,1St	
Somerset	Taunton	May 19	24 & 77 *	2Ct,1St	
Yorkshire	Chesterfield	May 23	0	3Ct	

PLAYER RECORDS

Notts	Derby	May 26	31		5Ct
Surrey	The Oval	June 6	35		
Warwickshire	Derby	June 16			2Ct
Leicestershire	Leicester	June 20		30	1Ct
Gloucs	Derby	June 30	9 & 1		5Ct
Sussex	Hove	July 4	12		1Ct
Lancashire	Liverpool	July 7			3Ct
Essex	Colchester	July 18	4 & 43		6Ct
Hampshire	Portsmouth	July 21	0 & 0		8Ct
Worcestershire	Derby	July 25	4 & 13		3Ct
Kent	Chesterfield	Aug 4	27 *		7Ct
Northants	Chesterfield	Aug 8	0 & 24		2Ct
Middlesex	Derby	Aug 18	3 & 0		1Ct,1St
Essex	Derby	Aug 23	2 & 14		2Ct
Glamorgan	Cardiff	Aug 29	0		1Ct
Yorkshire	Scarborough	Sept 7	35		1Ct
Leicestershire	Derby	Sept 18	1		3Ct

REFUGE ASSURANCE

Yorkshire	Headingley	May 13	14		2Ct
Somerset	Taunton	May 20			
Hampshire	Portsmouth	July 22	0		

OTHER FIRST-CLASS

New Zealand	Derby	June 2	62		2Ct

OTHER ONE-DAY

India	Chesterfield	July 16	0 *		0Ct,1St

BATTING AVERAGES - Including fielding

	Matches	Inns	NO	Runs	HS	Avge	100s	50s	Ct	St
Britannic Assurance	21	28	2	426	77 *	16.38	-	1	58	3
Refuge Assurance	3	2	0	14	14	7.00	-	-	2	-
Other First-Class	1	1	0	62	62	62.00	-	1	2	-
Other One-Day	1	1	1	0	0 *	-	-	-	-	1
ALL FIRST-CLASS	22	29	2	488	77 *	18.07	-	2	60	3
ALL ONE-DAY	4	3	1	14	14	7.00	-	-	2	1

BOWLING AVERAGES
Did not bowl

A.P. KUIPER - *Derbyshire*

Opposition	Venue	Date	Batting	Fielding	Bowling
BRITANNIC ASSURANCE					
Notts	Trent Bridge	April 26	25 & 10		1-60 & 0-20
Lancashire	Derby	May 15	48 & 13	1Ct	
Somerset	Taunton	May 19	5 & 19	3Ct	1-46
Surrey	The Oval	June 6	37		0-15 & 0-13
Warwickshire	Derby	June 16	11		0-18
Leicestershire	Leicester	June 20		3	
Lancashire	Liverpool	July 7		8 2Ct	3-42 & 4-69
Worcestershire	Derby	July 25	38 & 41		0-42
Middlesex	Derby	Aug 18	0 & 30	3Ct	
Glamorgan	Cardiff	Aug 29	0		
REFUGE ASSURANCE					
Sussex	Hove	April 22	53 *	1Ct	2-30
Worcestershire	Derby	April 29	17		1-23
Northants	Northampton	May 6	62 *	1Ct	1-46
Yorkshire	Headingley	May 13	5		
Somerset	Taunton	May 20	21 *		1-48
Notts	Derby	June 10	46	3Ct	
Warwickshire	Derby	June 17	37		2-53
Surrey	The Oval	June 24	34	1Ct	2-32
Gloucs	Derby	July 1	0	1Ct	1-35
Lancashire	Old Trafford	July 8	7	1Ct	3-50
Leicestershire	Knypersley	July 15	42		
Hampshire	Portsmouth	July 22	1	1Ct	0-28
Glamorgan	Swansea	July 29	12		2-27
Kent	Chesterfield	Aug 5	22 *		2-74
Middlesex	Derby	Aug 19	18		0-15
Essex	Derby	Aug 26	56		2-40
Notts	Derby	Sept 5	74		1-50
Middlesex	Edgbaston	Sept 16	9		0-47
NATWEST TROPHY					
Shropshire	Chesterfield	June 27	49		1-20
Lancashire	Derby	July 11	25		0-25

BENSON & HEDGES CUP

Sussex	Derby	April 24	41 *		0-64
Somerset	Taunton	May 1	22		0-80
Min Counties	Wellington	May 10	16	1Ct	0-20
Middlesex	Derby	May 12	106 *		3-71

OTHER FIRST-CLASS

Cambridge U	Fenner's	April 18	51		1-16
New Zealand	Derby	June 2	68	1Ct	2-52

BATTING AVERAGES - Including fielding

	Matches	Inns	NO	Runs	HS	Avge	100s	50s	Ct	St
Britannic Assurance	10	15	0	288	48	19.20	-	-	9	-
Refuge Assurance	18	18	4	516	74	36.85	-	4	9	-
NatWest Trophy	2	2	0	74	49	37.00	-	-	-	-
Benson & Hedges Cup	4	4	2	185	106 *	92.50	1	-	1	-
Other First-Class	2	2	0	119	68	59.50	-	2	1	-
ALL FIRST-CLASS	12	17	0	407	68	23.94	-	2	10	-
ALL ONE-DAY	24	24	6	775	106 *	43.05	1	4	10	-

BOWLING AVERAGES

	Overs	Mdns	Runs	Wkts	Avge	Best	5wI	10wM
Britannic Assurance	108.3	25	325	9	36.11	4-69	-	-
Refuge Assurance	93.4	1	598	20	29.90	3-50	-	
NatWest Trophy	16	1	45	1	45.00	1-20	-	
Benson & Hedges Cup	37.4	0	235	3	78.33	3-71	-	
Other First-Class	17	4	68	3	22.66	2-52	-	
ALL FIRST-CLASS	125.3	29	393	12	32.75	4-69	-	-
ALL ONE-DAY	147.2	2	878	24	36.58	3-50	-	

A.R. KUMBLE - *India*

Opposition	Venue	Date	Batting	Fielding	Bowling
CORNHILL TEST MATCHES					
England	Old Trafford	Aug 9	2		3-105 & 0-65
TEXACO TROPHY					
England	Headingley	July 18			2-29
England	Trent Bridge	July 20			0-58
OTHER FIRST-CLASS					
Hampshire	Southampton	July 4			0-9 & 0-23
Min Counties	Trowbridge	July 11			6-49 & 0-54
Surrey	The Oval	Aug 1	19		2-75 & 0-15
TCCB U25 XI	Edgbaston	Aug 15			1-28 & 0-9
Glamorgan	Swansea	Aug 18	35 *		0-2 & 1-51
World XI	Scarborough	Aug 29	2 & 5 *	1Ct	1-103 & 0-72
OTHER ONE-DAY					
League CC	Sunderland	June 28	2 *		2-32
Scotland	Glasgow	July 14			0-57
Derbyshire	Chesterfield	July 16			0-26

BATTING AVERAGES - Including fielding

	Matches	Inns	NO	Runs	HS	Avge	100s	50s	Ct	St
Cornhill Test Matches	1	1	0	2	2	2.00	-	-	-	-
Texaco Trophy	2	0	0	0	0	-	-	-	-	-
Other First-Class	6	4	2	61	35 *	30.50	-	-	1	-
Other One-Day	3	1	1	2	2 *	-	-	-	-	-
ALL FIRST-CLASS	7	5	2	63	35 *	21.00	-	-	1	-
ALL ONE-DAY	5	1	1	2	2 *	-	-	-	-	-

BOWLING AVERAGES

	Overs	Mdns	Runs	Wkts	Avge	Best	5wI	10wM
Cornhill Test Matches	60	10	170	3	56.66	3-105	-	-
Texaco Trophy	22	3	87	2	43.50	2-29	-	-
Other First-Class	152	30	490	11	44.54	6-49	1	-
Other One-Day	32	5	115	2	57.50	2-32	-	
ALL FIRST-CLASS	212	40	660	14	47.14	6-49	1	-
ALL ONE-DAY	54	8	202	4	50.50	2-29	-	

K	PLANER RECORDS

PLAYER RECORDS

D.S.B.P. KURUPPU - *Sri Lanka*

Opposition	Venue	Date	Batting			Fielding	Bowling
OTHER FIRST-CLASS							
Glamorgan	Ebbw Vale	Aug 22	45	&	15	1Ct	
Warwickshire	Edgbaston	Aug 29	1	&	40	1Ct	
Sussex	Hove	Sept 5	51	&	4	3Ct	
Lancashire	Old Trafford	Sept 8	2	&	56 *	1Ct,1St	
Hampshire	Southampton	Sept 12	24	&	21	1Ct	
OTHER ONE-DAY							
Surrey	The Oval	Sept 2	33				
Somerset	Taunton	Sept 3	1			1Ct	

BATTING AVERAGES - Including fielding

	Matches	Inns	NO	Runs	HS	Avge	100s	50s	Ct	St
Other First-Class	5	10	1	259	56 *	28.77	-	2	7	1
Other One-Day	2	2	0	34	33	17.00	-	-	1	-
ALL FIRST-CLASS	5	10	1	259	56 *	28.77	-	2	7	1
ALL ONE-DAY	2	2	0	34	33	17.00	-	-	1	-

BOWLING AVERAGES
Did not bowl

PLAYER RECORDS

G.F. LABROOY - *Sri Lanka*

Opposition	Venue	Date	Batting			Fielding	Bowling
OTHER FIRST-CLASS							
Glamorgan	Ebbw Vale	Aug 22	7	&	69		5-97 & 3-84
Notts	Cleethorpes	Aug 25				1Ct	1-68 & 4-60
Sussex	Hove	Sept 5	0	&	22		2-38 & 1-40
Hampshire	Southampton	Sept 12	5	&	18		0-53
OTHER ONE-DAY							
Surrey	The Oval	Sept 2	28				1-49

BATTING AVERAGES - Including fielding

	Matches	Inns	NO	Runs	HS	Avge	100s	50s	Ct	St
Other First-Class	4	6	0	121	69	20.16	-	1	1	-
Other One-Day	1	1	0	28	28	28.00	-	-	-	-
ALL FIRST-CLASS	4	6	0	121	69	20.16	-	1	1	-
ALL ONE-DAY	1	1	0	28	28	28.00	-	-	-	-

BOWLING AVERAGES

	Overs	Mdns	Runs	Wkts	Avge	Best	5wI	10wM
Other First-Class	111	13	440	16	27.50	5-97	1	-
Other One-Day	11	2	49	1	49.00	1-49	-	
ALL FIRST-CLASS	111	13	440	16	27.50	5-97	1	-
ALL ONE-DAY	11	2	49	1	49.00	1-49	-	

D.R. LAING - *Nottinghamshire*

Opposition	Venue	Date	Batting	Fielding	Bowling
OTHER FIRST-CLASS					
Oxford U	The Parks	June 6	2		0-21

BATTING AVERAGES - Including fielding

	Matches	Inns	NO	Runs	HS	Avge	100s	50s	Ct	St
Other First-Class	1	1	0	2	2	2.00	-	-	-	-
ALL FIRST-CLASS	1	1	0	2	2	2.00	-	-	-	-

BOWLING AVERAGES

	Overs	Mdns	Runs	Wkts	Avge	Best	5wI	10wM
Other First-Class	5	1	21	0	-	-	-	-
ALL FIRST-CLASS	5	1	21	0	-	-	-	-

A.J. LAMB - *Northamptonshire & England*

Opposition	Venue	Date	Batting			Fielding	Bowling
CORNHILL TEST MATCHES							
New Zealand	Trent Bridge	June 7	0				
New Zealand	Lord's	June 21	39	&	84 *		
New Zealand	Edgbaston	July 5	2	&	4	2Ct	
India	Lord's	July 26	139	&	19		
India	Old Trafford	Aug 9	38	&	109		
India	The Oval	Aug 23	7	&	52	2Ct	
TEXACO TROPHY							
New Zealand	Headingley	May 23	18			1Ct	
New Zealand	The Oval	May 25	4				
India	Headingley	July 18	56				
India	Trent Bridge	July 20	3				
BRITANNIC ASSURANCE							
Yorkshire	Headingley	April 26	235			1Ct	
Derbyshire	Northampton	May 3	14 *				
Warwickshire	Edgbaston	June 2	48				
Somerset	Taunton	June 30	40	&	64 *		
Sussex	Northampton	July 21	135 *	&	1	1Ct	
Hampshire	Bournemouth	Aug 4	9	&	15		
Worcestershire	Worcester	Aug 18	63	&	28	1Ct	
Essex	Northampton	Aug 29	134			1Ct	
Essex	Chelmsford	Sept 7	22	&	165	1Ct	
Leicestershire	Leicester	Sept 12	0	&	67		
REFUGE ASSURANCE							
Leicestershire	Leicester	April 22	4			2Ct	
Warwickshire	Edgbaston	April 29	70				
Kent	Northampton	May 27	27				
Surrey	The Oval	June 3	0				
Somerset	Taunton	July 1	41				
Essex	Chelmsford	July 15	34				
Sussex	Well'borough	July 22	17				
Hampshire	Bournemouth	Aug 5	45				
Worcestershire	Worcester	Aug 19	10				
NATWEST TROPHY							
Staffordshire	Northampton	June 27	68 *			1Ct	
Notts	Northampton	July 11	61				
Worcestershire	Northampton	Aug 1	0				
Hampshire	Southampton	Aug 15	58			1Ct	
Lancashire	Lord's	Sept 1	8				
BENSON & HEDGES CUP							
Leicestershire	Leicester	April 24	34				
OTHER FIRST-CLASS							
New Zealand	Northampton	June 16	21	&	42		
OTHER ONE-DAY							
For England XI							
Rest of World	Jesmond	Aug 3	20				

BATTING AVERAGES - Including fielding

	Matches	Inns	NO	Runs	HS	Avge	100s	50s	Ct	St
Cornhill Test Matches	6	11	1	493	139	49.30	2	2	4	-
Texaco Trophy	4	4	0	81	56	20.25	-	1	1	-
Britannic Assurance	10	16	3	1040	235	80.00	4	3	5	-
Refuge Assurance	9	9	0	248	70	27.55	-	1	2	-
NatWest Trophy	5	5	1	195	68 *	48.75	-	3	2	-
Benson & Hedges Cup	1	1	0	34	34	34.00	-	-	-	-
Other First-Class	1	2	0	63	42	31.50	-	-	-	-
Other One-Day	1	1	0	20	20	20.00	-	-	-	-
ALL FIRST-CLASS	17	29	4	1596	235	63.84	6	5	9	-
ALL ONE-DAY	20	20	1	578	70	30.42	-	5	5	-

BOWLING AVERAGES
Did not bowl

R. LAMBA - *Ireland*

Opposition	Venue	Date	Batting	Fielding	Bowling
NATWEST TROPHY					
Sussex	Downpatrick	June 27	5	1Ct	
OTHER ONE-DAY					
New Zealand	Downpatrick	May 9	52		0-27
New Zealand	Belfast	May 10	5	1Ct	1-40

BATTING AVERAGES - Including fielding

	Matches	Inns	NO	Runs	HS	Avge	100s	50s	Ct	St
NatWest Trophy	1	1	0	5	5	5.00	-	-	1	-
Other One-Day	2	2	0	57	52	28.50	-	1	1	-
ALL ONE-DAY	3	3	0	62	52	20.66	-	1	2	-

BOWLING AVERAGES

	Overs	Mdns	Runs	Wkts	Avge	Best	5wI	10wM
NatWest Trophy								
Other One-Day	16	2	67	1	67.00	1-40	-	
ALL ONE-DAY	16	2	67	1	67.00	1-40	-	

L   PLAYER RECORDS

C.B. LAMBERT - *League C.C. XI*

Opposition	Venue	Date	Batting	Fielding	Bowling
OTHER ONE-DAY					
India	Sunderland	June 28	22	1Ct	

BATTING AVERAGES - Including fielding

	Matches	Inns	NO	Runs	HS	Avge	100s	50s	Ct	St
Other One-Day	1	1	0	22	22	22.00	-	-	1	-
ALL ONE-DAY	1	1	0	22	22	22.00	-	-	1	-

BOWLING AVERAGES
Did not bowl

D. LAMPITT - *League C.C. XI*

Opposition	Venue	Date	Batting	Fielding	Bowling
OTHER ONE-DAY					
India	Sunderland	June 28	15		

BATTING AVERAGES - Including fielding

	Matches	Inns	NO	Runs	HS	Avge	100s	50s	Ct	St
Other One-Day	1	1	0	15	15	15.00	-	-	-	-
ALL ONE-DAY	1	1	0	15	15	15.00	-	-	-	-

BOWLING AVERAGES
Did not bowl

S.R. LAMPITT - *Worcestershire*

Opposition	Venue	Date	Batting	Fielding	Bowling
BRITANNIC ASSURANCE					
Notts	Worcester	May 3	1	2Ct	3-40 & 1-60
Essex	Worcester	May 19	0 & 1		0-55
Warwickshire	Edgbaston	May 26	0		3-44 & 3-39
Yorkshire	Worcester	June 2	10		5-54 & 0-34
Surrey	The Oval	June 16	21 *	2Ct	0-20 & 1-40
Sussex	Worcester	June 20		3	0-55
Middlesex	Lord's	June 30	5		3-119
Gloucs	Worcester	July 7	20 *		0-38
Somerset	Worcester	July 18			0-70 & 3-46
Glamorgan	Abergavenny	July 21		2Ct	1-40 & 0-14
Derbyshire	Derby	July 25	16 *		5-34 & 1-52
Kent	Canterbury	July 28			0-42 & 0-45
Leicestershire	Leicester	Aug 4		6	2-43 & 2-68
Lancashire	Kid'minster	Aug 8		1Ct	1-16 & 3-58
Hampshire	Worcester	Aug 11		1Ct	1-39 & 1-29
Northants	Worcester	Aug 18	0 & 16	1Ct	2-44 & 0-18
Warwickshire	Worcester	Aug 23	0 & 4	1Ct	4-47
Notts	Trent Bridge	Aug 29	40		2-90 & 0-38
Gloucs	Bristol	Sept 7	45 * & 20 *		0-103 & 0-16
Somerset	Taunton	Sept 12	16 & 10		4-97 & 2-43
Glamorgan	Worcester	Sept 18	34 & 18		2-52 & 2-52
REFUGE ASSURANCE					
Notts	Worcester	May 6	4 *		2-22
Essex	Worcester	May 20			0-33
Warwickshire	Worcester	May 27	16 *		1-33
Yorkshire	Worcester	June 3	8		1-53
Surrey	The Oval	June 17	11		0-15
Sussex	Worcester	June 24	0 *		2-24
Middlesex	Lord's	July 1	25 *	2Ct	5-67
Gloucs	Worcester	July 8			2-56
Lancashire	Old Trafford	July 15	0		1-34
Kent	Canterbury	July 29		1Ct	1-38
Leicestershire	Leicester	Aug 5		2Ct	1-38
Hampshire	Worcester	Aug 12	8	1Ct	1-50
Northants	Worcester	Aug 19			
Glamorgan	Swansea	Aug 26	6	1Ct	2-28

NATWEST TROPHY

Opposition	Venue	Date	Batting	Fielding	Bowling
Suffolk	Bury St Ed's	June 27		1Ct	5-22
Somerset	Taunton	July 11		1Ct	2-48
Northants	Northampton	Aug 1		3 *	1-58

BENSON & HEDGES CUP

Kent	Worcester	May 1	6		1-47
Glamorgan	Worcester	May 8	41	1Ct	1-43
Warwickshire	Edgbaston	May 10	1 *	1Ct	1-35
Glamorgan	Worcester	May 30		1Ct	0-35
Notts	Trent Bridge	June 13		1Ct	1-47
Lancashire	Lord's	July 14	4		2-43

OTHER FIRST-CLASS

New Zealand	Worcester	May 12	40 & 30		
For TCCB U25 XI					
India	Edgbaston	Aug 15		1Ct	1-62 & 0-33

BATTING AVERAGES - Including fielding

	Matches	Inns	NO	Runs	HS	Avge	100s	50s	Ct	St
Britannic Assurance	21	22	5	286	45 *	16.82	-	-	10	-
Refuge Assurance	14	9	4	78	25 *	15.60	-	-	7	-
NatWest Trophy	3	1	1	3	3 *	-	-	-	2	-
Benson & Hedges Cup	6	4	1	52	41	17.33	-	-	4	-
Other First-Class	2	2	0	70	40	35.00	-	-	1	-
ALL FIRST-CLASS	23	24	5	356	45 *	18.73	-	-	11	-
ALL ONE-DAY	23	14	6	133	41	16.62	-	-	13	-

BOWLING AVERAGES

	Overs	Mdns	Runs	Wkts	Avge	Best	5wI	10wM
Britannic Assurance	539.3	96	1794	57	31.47	5-34	2	-
Refuge Assurance	89	3	491	19	25.84	5-67	1	
NatWest Trophy	35.4	2	128	8	16.00	5-22	1	
Benson & Hedges Cup	55	4	250	6	41.66	2-43	-	
Other First-Class	26	2	95	1	95.00	1-62	-	-
ALL FIRST-CLASS	565.3	98	1889	58	32.56	5-34	2	-
ALL ONE-DAY	179.4	9	869	33	26.33	5-22	2	

B.C. LARA - *World XI*

Opposition	Venue	Date	Batting	Fielding	Bowling
OTHER ONE-DAY					
Yorkshire	Scarborough	Sept 1	34		

BATTING AVERAGES - Including fielding

	Matches	Inns	NO	Runs	HS	Avge	100s	50s	Ct	St
Other One-Day	1	1	0	34	34	34.00	-	-	-	-
ALL ONE-DAY	1	1	0	34	34	34.00	-	-	-	-

BOWLING AVERAGES
Did not bowl

W. LARKINS - *Northamptonshire*

Opposition	Venue	Date	Batting	Fielding	Bowling
BRITANNIC ASSURANCE					
Yorkshire	Headingley	April 26	0		
Derbyshire	Northampton	May 3	1 & 0	1Ct	
Surrey	The Oval	July 4	107		
Yorkshire	Northampton	July 7	15 & 4		
Kent	Northampton	July 18	12	1Ct	
Sussex	Northampton	July 21	61 & 11		0-21
Gloucs	Cheltenham	July 25	16 & 30	1Ct	
Hampshire	Bournemouth	Aug 4	5 & 1		
Derbyshire	Chesterfield	Aug 8	16 & 5	1Ct	0-24
Lancashire	Northampton	Aug 11	56		
Worcestershire	Worcester	Aug 18	27 & 26	1Ct	
Gloucs	Northampton	Aug 23	36 & 1		
Essex	Northampton	Aug 29	207		
Essex	Chelmsford	Sept 7	37 & 0	1Ct	
Leicestershire	Leicester	Sept 12	27 & 0	2Ct	

PLAYER RECORDS L

Opposition	Venue	Date	Batting	Fielding	Bowling
REFUGE ASSURANCE					
Leicestershire	Leicester	April 22	17		
Warwickshire	Edgbaston	April 29	0		
Derbyshire	Northampton	May 6	13		
Yorkshire	Tring	July 8	12		
Essex	Chelmsford	July 15	6		
Sussex	Well'borough	July 22	7	1Ct	
Notts	Trent Bridge	July 29	58		2-34
Hampshire	Bournemouth	Aug 5	7		0-26
Lancashire	Northampton	Aug 12	104		
Worcestershire	Worcester	Aug 19	1		0-20
Gloucs	Northampton	Aug 26	109		
NATWEST TROPHY					
Notts	Northampton	July 11	21		
Worcestershire	Northampton	Aug 1	52	1Ct	
Hampshire	Southampton	Aug 15	48		
Lancashire	Lord's	Sept 1	7		
BENSON & HEDGES CUP					
Leicestershire	Leicester	April 24	46		
Essex	Northampton	May 8	20	2Ct	
Scotland	Northampton	May 10	111	1Ct	

BATTING AVERAGES - Including fielding

	Matches	Inns	NO	Runs	HS	Avge	100s	50s	Ct	St
Britannic Assurance	15	25	0	701	207	28.04	2	2	8	-
Refuge Assurance	11	11	0	334	109	30.36	2	1	1	-
NatWest Trophy	4	4	0	128	52	32.00	-	1	1	-
Benson & Hedges Cup	3	3	0	177	111	59.00	1	-	3	-
ALL FIRST-CLASS	15	25	0	701	207	28.04	2	2	8	-
ALL ONE-DAY	18	18	0	639	111	35.50	3	2	5	-

BOWLING AVERAGES

	Overs	Mdns	Runs	Wkts	Avge	Best	5wI	10wM
Britannic Assurance	10	1	45	0	-	-	-	
Refuge Assurance	13	0	80	2	40.00	2-34	-	
NatWest Trophy								
Benson & Hedges Cup								
ALL FIRST-CLASS	10	1	45	0	-	-	-	
ALL ONE-DAY	13	0	80	2	40.00	2-34	-	

M. LATHWELL - *Somerset*

Opposition	Venue	Date	Batting	Fielding	Bowling
OTHER ONE-DAY					
Sri Lanka	Taunton	Sept 3			0-35

BATTING AVERAGES - Including fielding

	Matches	Inns	NO	Runs	HS	Avge	100s	50s	Ct	St
Other One-Day	1	0	0	0	0	-	-	-	-	-
ALL ONE-DAY	1	0	0	0	0	-	-	-	-	-

BOWLING AVERAGES

	Overs	Mdns	Runs	Wkts	Avge	Best	5wI	10wM
Other One-Day	7	1	35	0	-	-	-	
ALL ONE-DAY	7	1	35	0	-	-	-	

D.V. LAWRENCE - *Gloucestershire*

Opposition	Venue	Date	Batting	Fielding	Bowling
BRITANNIC ASSURANCE					
Somerset	Taunton	April 26	3 & 9		1-77 & 0-21
Glamorgan	Bristol	May 15	1 & 1*	1Ct	0-65 & 2-40
Middlesex	Lord's	May 26	0		0-46 & 1-13
Somerset	Bristol	June 2		1Ct	2-65 & 1-41
Essex	Ilford	June 6		1Ct	1-57 & 0-17
Lancashire	Old Trafford	June 9			3-86
Sussex	Hove	June 16	0*	1Ct	1-30 & 0-56
Hampshire	Gloucester	June 20			
Leicestershire	Gloucester	June 23	29		1-84
Derbyshire	Derby	June 30	8		4-27 & 0-20
Yorkshire	Cheltenham	July 21	6	1Ct	2-94 & 1-34
Northants	Cheltenham	July 25	0		3-52 & 0-20
Surrey	Cheltenham	July 28	2		0-28 & 5-54
Warwickshire	Bristol	Aug 8	7		1-56 & 2-37
Kent	Bristol	Aug 11	0		0-69
Notts	Trent Bridge	Aug 18	0 & 18		5-51 & 2-41
Northants	Northampton	Aug 23	3		4-90 & 2-53
Worcestershire	Bristol	Sept 7	6* & 0		0-55 & 1-30
Sussex	Bristol	Sept 12	13		0-17 & 3-59
Hampshire	Southampton	Sept 18	18 & 0	1Ct	2-30 & 0-64
REFUGE ASSURANCE					
Glamorgan	Bristol	April 22			3-40
Middlesex	Lord's	May 27	1		1-39
Somerset	Bristol	June 3			5-18
Lancashire	Old Trafford	June 10		2Ct	1-38
Leicestershire	Gloucester	June 24	1*		1-47
Derbyshire	Derby	July 1		1Ct	0-18
Notts	Trent Bridge	Aug 19			1-23
NATWEST TROPHY					
Lincolnshire	Gloucester	June 27			0-15
Lancashire	Old Trafford	Aug 1	0		1-62
BENSON & HEDGES CUP					
Worcestershire	Bristol	April 24		2Ct	1-36
OTHER FIRST-CLASS					
For MCC					
Worcestershire	Lord's	April 17	4		2-105
For Gloucs					
Zimbabwe	Bristol	May 19	0		3-45 & 1-43
India	Bristol	Aug 4	35	1Ct	2-65 & 0-42

BATTING AVERAGES - Including fielding

	Matches	Inns	NO	Runs	HS	Avge	100s	50s	Ct	St
Britannic Assurance	20	21	3	124	29	6.88	-	-	6	-
Refuge Assurance	7	2	1	2	1*	2.00	-	-	3	-
NatWest Trophy	2	1	0	0	0	0.00	-	-	-	-
Benson & Hedges Cup	1	0	0	0	0	-	-	-	2	-
Other First-Class	3	3	0	39	35	13.00	-	-	1	-
ALL FIRST-CLASS	23	24	3	163	35	7.76	-	-	7	-
ALL ONE-DAY	10	3	1	2	1*	1.00	-	-	5	-

BOWLING AVERAGES

	Overs	Mdns	Runs	Wkts	Avge	Best	5wI	10wM
Britannic Assurance	418.3	45	1679	50	33.58	5-51	2	-
Refuge Assurance	45	1	223	12	18.58	5-18	1	
NatWest Trophy	14	0	77	1	77.00	1-62	-	
Benson & Hedges Cup	11	3	36	1	36.00	1-36	-	
Other First-Class	79	8	300	8	37.50	3-45	-	-
ALL FIRST-CLASS	497.3	53	1979	58	34.12	5-51	2	-
ALL ONE-DAY	70	4	336	14	24.00	5-18	1	

D.A. LEATHERDALE - *Worcestershire*

Opposition	Venue	Date	Batting	Fielding	Bowling
BRITANNIC ASSURANCE					
Lancashire	Kid'minster	Aug 8	70	1Ct	
Hampshire	Worcester	Aug 11	13	1Ct	
Northants	Worcester	Aug 18	52 & 7		
Notts	Trent Bridge	Aug 29	2 & 10		
REFUGE ASSURANCE					
Derbyshire	Derby	April 29	2	1Ct	
Notts	Worcester	May 6		1Ct	
Warwickshire	Worcester	May 27	3		
Yorkshire	Worcester	June 3	35		
Sussex	Worcester	June 24	6		
Middlesex	Lord's	July 1	0		0-40
Gloucs	Worcester	July 8		3Ct	0-12
Lancashire	Old Trafford	July 15	4		0-6
Kent	Canterbury	July 29	20*		
Hampshire	Worcester	Aug 12	0		
Northants	Worcester	Aug 19	0	1Ct	
NATWEST TROPHY					
Suffolk	Bury St Ed's	June 27			

L

PLAYER RECORDS

BENSON & HEDGES CUP

Glamorgan	Worcester	May 30
Notts	Trent Bridge	June 13

OTHER ONE-DAY

Hampshire	Scarborough	Sept 2	5

BATTING AVERAGES - Including fielding

	Matches	Inns	NO	Runs	HS	Avge	100s	50s	Ct	St
Britannic Assurance	4	6	0	154	70	25.66	-	2	2	-
Refuge Assurance	11	9	1	70	35	8.75	-	-	6	-
NatWest Trophy	1	0	0	0	0	-	-	-	-	-
Benson & Hedges Cup	2	0	0	0	0	-	-	-	-	-
Other One-Day	1	1	0	5	5	5.00	-	-	-	-
ALL FIRST-CLASS	4	6	0	154	70	25.66	-	2	2	-
ALL ONE-DAY	15	10	1	75	35	8.33	-	-	6	-

BOWLING AVERAGES

	Overs	Mdns	Runs	Wkts	Avge	Best	5wI	10wM
Britannic Assurance								
Refuge Assurance	9	0	58	0	-	-	-	
NatWest Trophy								
Benson & Hedges Cup								
Other One-Day								
ALL FIRST-CLASS								
ALL ONE-DAY	9	0	58	0	-	-	-	

R.P. LEFEBVRE - Somerset

Opposition	Venue	Date	Batting	Fielding	Bowling
BRITANNIC ASSURANCE					
Gloucs	Taunton	April 26	3	2Ct	5-30 & 0-66
Glamorgan	Cardiff	May 3			0-45 & 3-52
Derbyshire	Taunton	May 19	13		2-67 & 0-5
Sussex	Taunton	May 23			1-38 & 1-33
Leicestershire	Leicester	May 26			2-61 & 0-26
Northants	Taunton	June 30	0 * & 53		0-49 & 1-41
Warwickshire	Taunton	July 4	22		1-31
Worcestershire	Worcester	July 18		1Ct	0-49 & 1-33
Yorkshire	Scarborough	July 25	3 * & 25 *	1Ct	0-40 & 0-52
Lancashire	Old Trafford	July 28	0 & 2		0-22
Surrey	Weston	Aug 4	8	1Ct	1-47 & 1-72
Notts	Weston	Aug 8	0		1-20 & 1-24
Hampshire	Taunton	Aug 18	37	1Ct	0-59 & 1-40
Sussex	Hove	Aug 23	6		3-46 & 1-48
Warwickshire	Edgbaston	Sept 7	27		1-44 & 3-48
Worcestershire	Taunton	Sept 12	0 & 15	2Ct	0-67 & 0-3
REFUGE ASSURANCE					
Worcestershire	Taunton	April 22	11		0-54
Hampshire	Taunton	May 13			1-50
Derbyshire	Taunton	May 20	16 *		1-44
Leicestershire	Leicester	May 27	0	1Ct	0-42
Northants	Taunton	July 1		1Ct	4-35
Middlesex	Lord's	July 8		1Ct	1-37
Yorkshire	Scarborough	July 15	28		1-35
Glamorgan	Neath	July 22		1Ct	1-26
Lancashire	Old Trafford	July 29	14 *		0-44
Surrey	Weston	Aug 5	10		0-19
Warwickshire	Weston	Aug 12			1-60
Sussex	Hove	Aug 26	7		1-22
NATWEST TROPHY					
Devon	Torquay	June 27			7-15
Worcestershire	Taunton	July 11			2-46
BENSON & HEDGES CUP					
Derbyshire	Taunton	May 1			1-55
Min Counties	Taunton	May 8			1-44
Middlesex	Lord's	May 10	37		0-46
Sussex	Hove	May 12			2-39
Middlesex	Taunton	May 30	8		1-15
Lancashire	Old Trafford	June 13	25 *		0-31
OTHER FIRST-CLASS					
Oxford U	The Parks	April 18			1-23

BATTING AVERAGES - Including fielding

	Matches	Inns	NO	Runs	HS	Avge	100s	50s	Ct	St
Britannic Assurance	16	16	3	214	53	16.46	-	1	8	-
Refuge Assurance	12	7	2	86	28	17.20	-	-	4	-
NatWest Trophy	2	0	0	0	0	-	-	-	-	-
Benson & Hedges Cup	6	3	1	70	37	35.00	-	-	-	-
Other First-Class	1	0	0	0	0	-	-	-	-	-
ALL FIRST-CLASS	17	16	3	214	53	16.46	-	1	8	-
ALL ONE-DAY	20	10	3	156	37	22.28	-	-	4	-

BOWLING AVERAGES

	Overs	Mdns	Runs	Wkts	Avge	Best	5wI	10wM
Britannic Assurance	493.1	132	1258	30	41.93	5-30	1	-
Refuge Assurance	82.5	0	468	11	42.54	4-35	-	
NatWest Trophy	21.3	6	61	9	6.77	7-15	1	
Benson & Hedges Cup	58.2	4	230	5	46.00	2-39	-	
Other First-Class	13	5	23	1	23.00	1-23	-	-
ALL FIRST-CLASS	506.1	137	1281	31	41.32	5-30	1	-
ALL ONE-DAY	162.4	10	759	25	30.36	7-15	1	

N.J. LENHAM - Sussex

Opposition	Venue	Date	Batting		Fielding	Bowling
BRITANNIC ASSURANCE						
Surrey	Hove	April 26	85 &	44	2Ct	0-16
Kent	Folkestone	May 3	63 &	18		
Hampshire	Southampton	May 15	0 &	121		0-9
Glamorgan	Hove	May 19	34 &	18		0-18
Somerset	Taunton	May 23	51 &	108		0-17
Lancashire	Horsham	June 2	8 &	24		
Gloucs	Hove	June 16	37 &	84		
Worcestershire	Worcester	June 20	66			
Derbyshire	Hove	July 4		12	1Ct	
Notts	Trent Bridge	July 7	0 &	27		
Surrey	Guildford	July 18	46 &	109 *		0-9
Northants	Northampton	July 21	41 &	38	1Ct	0-24 & 1-78
Hampshire	Arundel	July 25	15 &	15		
Middlesex	Lord's	Aug 11	5			
Kent	Hove	Aug 18	86 &	20	1Ct	
Somerset	Hove	Aug 23	45 &	123		0-4
Leicestershire	Leicester	Aug 29	58 &	40	1Ct	
Gloucs	Bristol	Sept 12	11 &	33		
Middlesex	Hove	Sept 18	9 &	5		1-48
REFUGE ASSURANCE						
Derbyshire	Hove	April 22	0			
Surrey	Hove	April 29	12			
Glamorgan	Hove	May 20	62			
Leicestershire	Leicester	June 10	32		1Ct	
Yorkshire	Hove	June 17	16			1-21
Worcestershire	Worcester	June 24	3 *			1-5
Hampshire	Hove	July 1	72		3Ct	
Notts	Trent Bridge	July 8	60			1-36
Gloucs	Swindon	July 15	65			2-54
Northants	Well'borough	July 22	25			2-59
Middlesex	Lord's	Aug 12	78			
Somerset	Hove	Aug 26	19		1Ct	1-44
NATWEST TROPHY						
Ireland	Downpatrick	June 27	41 *			2-12
Glamorgan	Cardiff	July 11	47			1-13
BENSON & HEDGES CUP						
Derbyshire	Derby	April 24	22			1-32
Min Counties	Marlow	May 1	37			1-3
Middlesex	Hove	May 8	3			0-16
OTHER FIRST-CLASS						
New Zealand	Hove	May 26	64 &	6		
Cambridge U	Hove	June 30	70 &	22		2-26
Sri Lanka	Hove	Sept 5	1 &	1		0-31 & 1-29
OTHER ONE-DAY						
Zimbabwe	Hove	May 13	1			0-13
Yorkshire	Harrogate	June 14	52			1-16
Kent	Hove	Sept 2	47			1-29

PLAGE RECORDS

PLAYER RECORDS

L

BATTING AVERAGES - Including fielding

	Matches	Inns	NO	Runs	HS	Avge	100s	50s	Ct	St
Britannic Assurance	19	35	1	1499	123	44.08	4	7	6	-
Refuge Assurance	12	12	1	444	78	40.36	-	5	5	-
NatWest Trophy	2	2	1	88	47	88.00	-	-	-	-
Benson & Hedges Cup	3	3	0	62	37	20.66	-	-	-	-
Other First-Class	3	6	0	164	70	27.33	-	2	-	-
Other One-Day	3	3	0	100	52	33.33	-	1	-	-
ALL FIRST-CLASS	22	41	1	1663	123	41.57	4	9	6	-
ALL ONE-DAY	20	20	2	694	78	38.55	-	6	5	-

BOWLING AVERAGES

	Overs	Mdns	Runs	Wkts	Avge	Best	5wI	10wM
Britannic Assurance	60.5	10	223	2	111.50	1-48	-	-
Refuge Assurance	33	0	219	8	27.37	2-54	-	
NatWest Trophy	9	0	25	3	8.33	2-12	-	
Benson & Hedges Cup	9	0	51	2	25.50	1-3	-	
Other First-Class	32.1	8	86	3	28.66	2-26	-	-
Other One-Day	17.1	2	58	2	29.00	1-16	-	
ALL FIRST-CLASS	93	18	309	5	61.80	2-26	-	-
ALL ONE-DAY	68.1	2	353	15	23.53	2-12	-	

T.A. LESTER - *Oxfordshire & Min Counties*

Opposition	Venue	Date	Batting	Fielding	Bowling
NATWEST TROPHY					
Kent	Oxford	June 27	13		
BENSON & HEDGES CUP					
Middlesex	Lord's	April 24	4		
Sussex	Marlow	May 1			
Somerset	Taunton	May 8	14		
OTHER FIRST-CLASS					
For Minor Counties					
India	Trowbridge	July 11	4		

BATTING AVERAGES - Including fielding

	Matches	Inns	NO	Runs	HS	Avge	100s	50s	Ct	St
NatWest Trophy	1	1	0	13	13	13.00	-	-	-	-
Benson & Hedges Cup	3	2	0	18	14	9.00	-	-	-	-
Other First-Class	1	1	0	4	4	4.00	-	-	-	-
ALL FIRST-CLASS	1	1	0	4	4	4.00	-	-	-	-
ALL ONE-DAY	4	3	0	31	14	10.33	-	-	-	-

BOWLING AVERAGES
Did not bowl

J.K. LEVER - *Duchess of Norfolk's XI & MCC*

Opposition	Venue	Date	Batting	Fielding	Bowling
OTHER ONE-DAY					
For D of Norfolk					
New Zealand	Arundel	May 6			1-48
For MCC					
New Zealand	Lord's	May 7		1Ct	1-45

BATTING AVERAGES - Including fielding

	Matches	Inns	NO	Runs	HS	Avge	100s	50s	Ct	St
Other One-Day	2	0	0	0	0	-	-	-	1	-
ALL ONE-DAY	2	0	0	0	0	-	-	-	1	-

BOWLING AVERAGES

	Overs	Mdns	Runs	Wkts	Avge	Best	5wI	10wM
Other One-Day	20	2	93	2	46.50	1-45	-	
ALL ONE-DAY	20	2	93	2	46.50	1-45	-	

C.C. LEWIS - *Leicestershire & England*

Opposition	Venue	Date	Batting	Fielding	Bowling
CORNHILL TEST MATCHES					
New Zealand	Edgbaston	July 5	32 & 1		1-51 & 3-76
India	Lord's	July 26		2Ct	1-108 & 2-26
India	Old Trafford	Aug 9	3	2Ct	1-61 & 1-86
TEXACO TROPHY					
New Zealand	Headingley	May 23			3-54
New Zealand	The Oval	May 25			1-51
India	Headingley	July 18	6		2-58
India	Trent Bridge	July 20	7		1-54
BRITANNIC ASSURANCE					
Glamorgan	Cardiff	April 26	39		6-55 & 4-64
Essex	Chelmsford	May 3	189 *	1Ct	3-115
Notts	Leicester	May 15	1 & 2		2-92 & 0-34
Lancashire	Old Trafford	May 19	32	1Ct	0-21 & 2-20
Hampshire	Leicester	June 2	36 * & 40 *		1-56
Middlesex	Leicester	June 16	21	2Ct	3-98 & 1-11
Gloucs	Gloucester	June 23	6		1-73
Notts	Trent Bridge	June 30	28 * & 3	1Ct	0-23 & 0-28
Worcestershire	Leicester	Aug 4	27 & 16		0-76 & 2-31
Warwickshire	Edgbaston	Aug 18	38 & 25 *	3Ct	1-48 & 4-70
Sussex	Leicester	Aug 29	20 & 54	2Ct	0-62 & 2-36
Northants	Leicester	Sept 12	1 & 0	1Ct	3-83 & 3-84
Derbyshire	Derby	Sept 18	0 & 54		6-58
REFUGE ASSURANCE					
Northants	Leicester	April 22	9	1Ct	3-18
Essex	Leicester	May 6	93 *		1-42
Lancashire	Old Trafford	May 20	10		4-34
Sussex	Leicester	June 10	25 *	1Ct	3-36
Middlesex	Leicester	June 17	14	1Ct	1-64
Gloucs	Gloucester	June 24	30		1-41
Notts	Trent Bridge	July 1	36		0-27
Derbyshire	Knypersley	July 15	0		1-43
Worcestershire	Leicester	Aug 5	13	1Ct	1-34
Warwickshire	Edgbaston	Aug 19	43		
Kent	Leicester	Aug 26	58 *		0-23
NATWEST TROPHY					
Hampshire	Leicester	June 27	32	1Ct	1-35
BENSON & HEDGES CUP					
Northants	Leicester	April 24	5	1Ct	2-42
Notts	Trent Bridge	May 1	23	1Ct	0-28
Scotland	Leicester	May 12	20 *	1Ct	0-49
OTHER FIRST-CLASS					
India	Leicester	July 21	1 & 28		1-28 & 2-23
OTHER ONE-DAY					
New Zealand	Leicester	June 14	51	1Ct	0-57

BATTING AVERAGES - Including fielding

	Matches	Inns	NO	Runs	HS	Avge	100s	50s	Ct	St
Cornhill Test Matches	3	3	0	36	32	12.00	-	-	4	-
Texaco Trophy	4	2	0	13	7	6.50	-	-	-	-
Britannic Assurance	13	21	5	632	189 *	39.50	1	2	11	-
Refuge Assurance	11	11	3	331	93 *	41.37	-	2	4	-
NatWest Trophy	1	1	0	32	32	32.00	-	-	1	-
Benson & Hedges Cup	3	3	1	48	23	24.00	-	-	3	-
Other First-Class	1	2	0	29	28	14.50	-	-	-	-
Other One-Day	1	1	0	51	51	51.00	-	1	1	-
ALL FIRST-CLASS	17	26	5	697	189 *	33.19	1	2	15	-
ALL ONE-DAY	20	18	4	475	93 *	33.92	-	3	9	-

BOWLING AVERAGES

	Overs	Mdns	Runs	Wkts	Avge	Best	5wI	10wM
Cornhill Test Matches	106	16	408	9	45.33	3-76	-	-
Texaco Trophy	42	1	217	7	31.00	3-54	-	
Britannic Assurance	411.2	80	1238	44	28.13	6-55	2	1
Refuge Assurance	76.3	2	362	15	24.13	4-34	-	
NatWest Trophy	12	1	35	1	35.00	1-35	-	
Benson & Hedges Cup	31	4	119	2	59.50	2-42	-	
Other First-Class	19	6	51	3	17.00	2-23	-	-
Other One-Day	11	1	57	0				
ALL FIRST-CLASS	536.2	102	1697	56	30.30	6-55	2	1
ALL ONE-DAY	172.3	9	790	25	31.60	4-34	-	

L   PLAYER RECORDS

D.A. LEWIS - *Ireland*

Opposition	Venue	Date	Batting	Fielding	Bowling
NATWEST TROPHY					
Sussex	Downpatrick	June 27	1		
OTHER FIRST-CLASS					
Scotland	Edinburgh	Aug 11	6		0-55
OTHER ONE-DAY					
New Zealand	Downpatrick	May 9	19		0-9
New Zealand	Belfast	May 10	18		

BATTING AVERAGES - Including fielding

	Matches	Inns	NO	Runs	HS	Avge	100s	50s	Ct	St
NatWest Trophy	1	1	0	1	1	1.00	-	-	-	-
Other First-Class	1	1	0	6	6	6.00	-	-	-	-
Other One-Day	2	2	0	37	19	18.50	-	-	-	-
ALL FIRST-CLASS	1	1	0	6	6	6.00	-	-	-	-
ALL ONE-DAY	3	3	0	38	19	12.66	-	-	-	-

BOWLING AVERAGES

	Overs	Mdns	Runs	Wkts	Avge	Best	5wI	10wM
NatWest Trophy								
Other First-Class	11	0	55	0	-	-	-	-
Other One-Day	1	0	9	0	-	-	-	-
ALL FIRST-CLASS	11	0	55	0	-	-	-	-
ALL ONE-DAY	1	0	9	0	-	-	-	-

J.C.M. LEWIS - *Norfolk*

Opposition	Venue	Date	Batting	Fielding	Bowling
NATWEST TROPHY					
Yorkshire	Headingley	June 27	9		0-37

BATTING AVERAGES - Including fielding

	Matches	Inns	NO	Runs	HS	Avge	100s	50s	Ct	St
NatWest Trophy	1	1	0	9	9	9.00	-	-	-	-
ALL ONE-DAY	1	1	0	9	9	9.00	-	-	-	-

BOWLING AVERAGES

	Overs	Mdns	Runs	Wkts	Avge	Best	5wI	10wM
NatWest Trophy	8	2	37	0	-	-	-	-
ALL ONE-DAY	8	2	37	0	-	-	-	-

J.J.B. LEWIS - *Essex*

Opposition	Venue	Date	Batting	Fielding	Bowling
BRITANNIC ASSURANCE					
Surrey	The Oval	Sept 18	116 *	1Ct	

BATTING AVERAGES - Including fielding

	Matches	Inns	NO	Runs	HS	Avge	100s	50s	Ct	St
Britannic Assurance	1	1	1	116	116 *	-	1	-	1	-
ALL FIRST-CLASS	1	1	1	116	116 *	-	1	-	1	-

BOWLING AVERAGES
Did not bowl

P.V. LEWIS - *Dorset*

Opposition	Venue	Date	Batting	Fielding	Bowling
NATWEST TROPHY					
Glamorgan	Swansea	June 27	0		

BATTING AVERAGES - Including fielding

	Matches	Inns	NO	Runs	HS	Avge	100s	50s	Ct	St
NatWest Trophy	1	1	0	0	0	0.00	-	-	-	-
ALL ONE-DAY	1	1	0	0	0	0.00	-	-	-	-

BOWLING AVERAGES
Did not bowl

M.G. LICKLEY - *Berkshire*

Opposition	Venue	Date	Batting	Fielding	Bowling
NATWEST TROPHY					
Middlesex	Lord's	June 27	12		0-13

BATTING AVERAGES - Including fielding

	Matches	Inns	NO	Runs	HS	Avge	100s	50s	Ct	St
NatWest Trophy	1	1	0	12	12	12.00	-	-	-	-
ALL ONE-DAY	1	1	0	12	12	12.00	-	-	-	-

BOWLING AVERAGES

	Overs	Mdns	Runs	Wkts	Avge	Best	5wI	10wM
NatWest Trophy	1	0	13	0	-	-	-	-
ALL ONE-DAY	1	0	13	0	-	-	-	-

A.W. LILLEY - *Essex*

Opposition	Venue	Date	Batting	Fielding	Bowling
BRITANNIC ASSURANCE					
Warwickshire	Edgbaston	June 9	1		0-7
REFUGE ASSURANCE					
Kent	Chelmsford	April 22	10		
Middlesex	Lord's	April 29	10		
Leicestershire	Leicester	May 6	2		
Glamorgan	Ilford	June 3			
Warwickshire	Edgbaston	June 10	9 *		
Somerset	Bath	June 17	10		
BENSON & HEDGES CUP					
Notts	Chelmsford	April 24	7		
Scotland	Glasgow	May 1			0-7
Notts	Chelmsford	May 30	23		
OTHER ONE-DAY					
Zimbabwe	Chelmsford	May 14	12		

BATTING AVERAGES - Including fielding

	Matches	Inns	NO	Runs	HS	Avge	100s	50s	Ct	St
Britannic Assurance	1	1	0	1	1	1.00	-	-	-	-
Refuge Assurance	6	5	1	41	10	10.25	-	-	-	-
Benson & Hedges Cup	3	2	0	30	23	15.00	-	-	-	-
Other One-Day	1	1	0	12	12	12.00	-	-	-	-
ALL FIRST-CLASS	1	1	0	1	1	1.00	-	-	-	-
ALL ONE-DAY	10	8	1	83	23	11.85	-	-	-	-

BOWLING AVERAGES

	Overs	Mdns	Runs	Wkts	Avge	Best	5wI	10wM
Britannic Assurance	1	0	7	0	-	-	-	-
Refuge Assurance								
Benson & Hedges Cup	2	0	7	0	-	-	-	-
Other One-Day								

PLEER RECORDS

PLAYER RECORDS

ALL FIRST-CLASS	1	0	7	0	- - - -
ALL ONE-DAY	2	0	7	0	- - - -

N.J. LLONG - *Kent*

Opposition	Venue	Date	Batting	Fielding	Bowling
OTHER FIRST-CLASS					
Cambridge U	Fenner's	June 20		1Ct	0-24

BATTING AVERAGES - Including fielding

	Matches	Inns	NO	Runs	HS	Avge	100s	50s	Ct	St
Other First-Class	1	0	0	0	0	-	-	-	1	-
ALL FIRST-CLASS	1	0	0	0	0	-	-	-	1	-

BOWLING AVERAGES

	Overs	Mdns	Runs	Wkts	Avge	Best	5wI	10wM
Other First-Class	7	1	24	0	-	-	-	-
ALL FIRST-CLASS	7	1	24	0	-	-	-	-

G.D. LLOYD - *Lancashire*

Opposition	Venue	Date	Batting	Fielding	Bowling
BRITANNIC ASSURANCE					
Middlesex	Old Trafford	June 20	21		
Hampshire	Old Trafford	June 23	6		
Derbyshire	Liverpool	July 7	62 & 26	1Ct	
Notts	Southport	July 25	39 & 59*		
Somerset	Old Trafford	July 28	0	3Ct	
Yorkshire	Headingley	Aug 4	36 & 70		
Worcestershire	Kid'minster	Aug 8	2 & 14	1Ct	0-8
Northants	Northampton	Aug 11	59 & 8		0-14
Surrey	Blackpool	Aug 29	1		
Notts	Trent Bridge	Sept 12	31	1Ct	
Warwickshire	Old Trafford	Sept 18		1Ct	
REFUGE ASSURANCE					
Middlesex	Old Trafford	April 22	7		
Notts	Trent Bridge	April 29	47		
Surrey	The Oval	May 6			
Leicestershire	Old Trafford	May 20	10		
Glamorgan	Colwyn Bay	May 27	3		
Gloucs	Old Trafford	June 10	85		
Hampshire	Old Trafford	June 24			
Kent	Maidstone	July 1	100*		
Derbyshire	Old Trafford	July 8	1	1Ct	
Worcestershire	Old Trafford	July 15	65*		
Essex	Colchester	July 22	30		
Somerset	Old Trafford	July 29	57	1Ct	
Yorkshire	Scarborough	Aug 5	76		
Northants	Northampton	Aug 12	0	2Ct	
Warwickshire	Old Trafford	Aug 26	31	1Ct	
Middlesex	Old Trafford	Sept 5	65	1Ct	
NATWEST TROPHY					
Derbyshire	Derby	July 11	36		
OTHER FIRST-CLASS					
Zimbabwe	Old Trafford	May 23	78 & 76	1Ct	
Oxford U	The Parks	June 16	78*		
Sri Lanka	Old Trafford	Sept 8	96 & 34	1Ct	0-7

BATTING AVERAGES - Including fielding

	Matches	Inns	NO	Runs	HS	Avge	100s	50s	Ct	St
Britannic Assurance	11	15	1	434	70	31.00	-	4	7	-
Refuge Assurance	16	14	2	577	100*	48.08	1	5	6	-
NatWest Trophy	1	1	0	36	36	36.00	-	-	-	-
Other First-Class	3	5	1	362	96	90.50	-	4	2	-
ALL FIRST-CLASS	14	20	2	796	96	44.22	-	8	9	-
ALL ONE-DAY	17	15	2	613	100*	47.15	1	5	6	-

BOWLING AVERAGES

	Overs	Mdns	Runs	Wkts	Avge	Best	5wI	10wM
Britannic Assurance	2.1	0	22	0	-	-	-	-

Refuge Assurance							
NatWest Trophy							
Other First-Class	1	0	7	0	-	-	- -
ALL FIRST-CLASS	3.1	0	29	0			
ALL ONE-DAY							

T.A. LLOYD - *Warwickshire*

Opposition	Venue	Date	Batting	Fielding	Bowling
BRITANNIC ASSURANCE					
Yorkshire	Edgbaston	May 3	31 & 30		
Northants	Northampton	May 15	21		
Notts	Edgbaston	May 19	4 & 10		
Worcestershire	Edgbaston	May 26	9 & 9		
Northants	Edgbaston	June 2	65 & 10	1Ct	
Middlesex	Lord's	June 6	70*		
Lancashire	Coventry	July 18	1 & 8		
Glamorgan	Swansea	July 25	101 & 0		
Hampshire	Edgbaston	July 28	1 & 61		
Sussex	Eastbourne	Aug 4	1 & 28		
Gloucs	Bristol	Aug 8	11 & 5	1Ct	1-58
Leicestershire	Edgbaston	Aug 18	0 & 4	1Ct	
Worcestershire	Worcester	Aug 23	12 & 2	2Ct	
Glamorgan	Edgbaston	Sept 12	78 & 39	2Ct	
Lancashire	Old Trafford	Sept 18	35		
REFUGE ASSURANCE					
Northants	Edgbaston	April 29			
Yorkshire	Edgbaston	May 6			
Gloucs	Moreton-in-M	May 20	13		
Worcestershire	Worcester	May 27	0		
Middlesex	Lord's	June 3	0*		
Surrey	The Oval	July 8	5		
Glamorgan	Edgbaston	July 15	12		
Notts	Edgbaston	July 22	63		
Hampshire	Edgbaston	July 29	4	1Ct	
Sussex	Eastbourne	Aug 5	48		
Somerset	Weston	Aug 12	12*		
Leicestershire	Edgbaston	Aug 19			
Lancashire	Old Trafford	Aug 26	16		
NATWEST TROPHY					
Yorkshire	Headingley	July 11	15		
BENSON & HEDGES CUP					
Glamorgan	Edgbaston	April 24	10	2Ct	
Kent	Canterbury	May 8	72		
Worcestershire	Edgbaston	May 10	8	1Ct	

BATTING AVERAGES - Including fielding

	Matches	Inns	NO	Runs	HS	Avge	100s	50s	Ct	St
Britannic Assurance	15	27	1	646	101	24.84	1	4	7	-
Refuge Assurance	13	10	2	173	63	21.62	-	1	1	-
NatWest Trophy	1	1	0	15	15	15.00	-	-	-	-
Benson & Hedges Cup	3	3	0	90	72	30.00	-	1	3	-
ALL FIRST-CLASS	15	27	1	646	101	24.84	1	4	7	-
ALL ONE-DAY	17	14	2	278	72	23.16	-	2	4	-

BOWLING AVERAGES

	Overs	Mdns	Runs	Wkts	Avge	Best	5wI	10wM
Britannic Assurance	9	1	58	1	58.00	1-58	-	-
Refuge Assurance								
NatWest Trophy								
Benson & Hedges Cup								
ALL FIRST-CLASS	9	1	58	1	58.00	1-58	-	-
ALL ONE-DAY								

J.W. LLOYDS - *Gloucestershire*

Opposition	Venue	Date	Batting	Fielding	Bowling
BRITANNIC ASSURANCE					
Somerset	Taunton	April 26	0 & 93	1Ct	0-17 & 0-22
Glamorgan	Bristol	May 15	9 & 14		1-9

L — PLAYER RECORDS

Opposition	Venue	Date	Batting		Fielding	Bowling
Middlesex	Lord's	May 26	10*&	19		1-19 & 2-109
Somerset	Bristol	June 2	3		1Ct	
Essex	Ilford	June 6	29*			0-35 & 0-4
Lancashire	Old Trafford	June 9	0		1Ct	0-7
Sussex	Hove	June 16	43		1Ct	1-70
Hampshire	Gloucester	June 20				
Leicestershire	Gloucester	June 23	26		1Ct	2-21
Derbyshire	Derby	June 30	28*&	25*	1Ct	1-74
Glamorgan	Swansea	July 4				1-76
Worcestershire	Worcester	July 7	28 &	40		0-13 & 0-37
Yorkshire	Cheltenham	July 21	38		1Ct	0-73 & 2-61
Northants	Cheltenham	July 25	34		1Ct	0-16
Surrey	Cheltenham	July 28	23 &	8*	1Ct	3-65 & 1-80
Warwickshire	Bristol	Aug 8	14 &	18*	2Ct	2-51 & 4-11
Kent	Bristol	Aug 11	0*&	6*		0-114
Northants	Northampton	Aug 23	35 &	16*	1Ct	0-53 & 2-21
Worcestershire	Bristol	Sept 7	71*			1-97 & 0-9
Sussex	Bristol	Sept 12	50		2Ct	0-11
Hampshire	Southampton	Sept 18	0 &	24	1Ct	

REFUGE ASSURANCE

Opposition	Venue	Date	Batting	Fielding	Bowling
Hampshire	Southampton	May 6		2Ct	
Essex	Chelmsford	May 13	10		
Warwickshire	Moreton-in-M	May 20	0		
Middlesex	Lord's	May 27	36*		
Somerset	Bristol	June 3		1Ct	
Lancashire	Old Trafford	June 10	0		
Leicestershire	Gloucester	June 24	10	2Ct	
Derbyshire	Derby	July 1	21		2-13
Worcestershire	Worcester	July 8	2		0-28
Sussex	Swindon	July 15	38*		
Yorkshire	Cheltenham	July 22	0		0-47
Surrey	Cheltenham	July 29	5*		

NATWEST TROPHY

Opposition	Venue	Date	Batting	Fielding	Bowling
Lincolnshire	Gloucester	June 27	73*		1-6
Kent	Bristol	July 11	4*		
Lancashire	Old Trafford	Aug 1	2		0-44

BENSON & HEDGES CUP

Opposition	Venue	Date	Batting	Fielding	Bowling
Glamorgan	Cardiff	May 1	6		
Kent	Canterbury	May 10			
Warwickshire	Bristol	May 12	53*		

OTHER FIRST-CLASS

Opposition	Venue	Date	Batting		Fielding	Bowling
Zimbabwe	Bristol	May 19	31			0-26
Cambridge U	Fenner's	May 23	73*&	2*	1Ct	0-44 & 0-24
India	Bristol	Aug 4	8 &	21		0-24 & 1-136

BATTING AVERAGES - Including fielding

	Matches	Inns	NO	Runs	HS	Avge	100s	50s	Ct	St
Britannic Assurance	21	29	10	704	93	37.05	-	3	15	-
Refuge Assurance	12	10	3	122	38*	17.42	-	-	5	-
NatWest Trophy	3	3	2	79	73*	79.00	-	1	-	-
Benson & Hedges Cup	3	2	1	59	53*	59.00	-	1	-	-
Other First-Class	3	5	2	135	73*	45.00	-	1	1	-
ALL FIRST-CLASS	24	34	12	839	93	38.13	-	4	16	-
ALL ONE-DAY	18	15	6	260	73*	28.88	-	2	5	-

BOWLING AVERAGES

	Overs	Mdns	Runs	Wkts	Avge	Best	5wI	10wM
Britannic Assurance	314.5	52	1175	24	48.95	4-11	-	-
Refuge Assurance	12.3	0	88	2	44.00	2-13	-	
NatWest Trophy	6	0	50	1	50.00	1-6	-	
Benson & Hedges Cup								
Other First-Class	68	8	254	1	254.00	1-136	-	-
ALL FIRST-CLASS	382.5	60	1429	25	57.16	4-11	-	-
ALL ONE-DAY	18.3	0	138	3	46.00	2-13	-	

J.I. LONGLEY - Combined Univ & Kent

Opposition	Venue	Date	Batting	Fielding	Bowling

BENSON & HEDGES CUP
For Combined Universities

Opposition	Venue	Date	Batting	Fielding	Bowling
Lancashire	Fenner's	May 1	4		
Yorkshire	Headingley	May 8	14		
Surrey	The Parks	May 10	9		
Hampshire	Southampton	May 12	1		

OTHER ONE-DAY
For Kent

Opposition	Venue	Date	Batting	Fielding	Bowling
Sussex	Hove	Sept 2	3	1Ct	
Surrey	Hove	Sept 4	0		

BATTING AVERAGES - Including fielding

	Matches	Inns	NO	Runs	HS	Avge	100s	50s	Ct	St
Benson & Hedges Cup	4	4	0	28	14	7.00	-	-	-	-
Other One-Day	2	2	0	3	3	1.50	-	-	1	-
ALL ONE-DAY	6	6	0	31	14	5.16	-	-	1	-

BOWLING AVERAGES
Did not bowl

G.J. LORD - Worcestershire

Opposition	Venue	Date	Batting		Fielding	Bowling

BRITANNIC ASSURANCE

Opposition	Venue	Date	Batting		Fielding	Bowling
Lancashire	Old Trafford	April 26	9 &	19		
Notts	Worcester	May 3	12			
Kent	Canterbury	July 28	14 &	81		
Leicestershire	Leicester	Aug 4	19 &	35		
Lancashire	Kid'minster	Aug 8	101 &	0*	1Ct	
Hampshire	Worcester	Aug 11	190 &	19		
Northants	Worcester	Aug 18	17 &	6		
Warwickshire	Worcester	Aug 23	7 &	25		
Notts	Trent Bridge	Aug 29	13 &	12		
Gloucs	Bristol	Sept 7	64 &	70*	1Ct	
Somerset	Taunton	Sept 12	6 &	80		
Glamorgan	Worcester	Sept 18	127 &	57	2Ct	

REFUGE ASSURANCE

Opposition	Venue	Date	Batting	Fielding	Bowling
Hampshire	Worcester	Aug 12	17		
Northants	Worcester	Aug 19	78		
Glamorgan	Swansea	Aug 26	7		

BENSON & HEDGES CUP

Opposition	Venue	Date	Batting	Fielding	Bowling
Gloucs	Bristol	April 24	26		
Glamorgan	Worcester	May 8	0		

OTHER FIRST-CLASS

Opposition	Venue	Date	Batting	Fielding	Bowling
MCC	Lord's	April 17	20		

OTHER ONE-DAY

Opposition	Venue	Date	Batting	Fielding	Bowling
Hampshire	Scarborough	Sept 2	1		

BATTING AVERAGES - Including fielding

	Matches	Inns	NO	Runs	HS	Avge	100s	50s	Ct	St
Britannic Assurance	12	23	2	983	190	46.81	3	5	4	-
Refuge Assurance	3	3	0	102	78	34.00	-	1	-	-
Benson & Hedges Cup	2	2	0	26	26	13.00	-	-	-	-
Other First-Class	1	1	0	20	20	20.00	-	-	-	-
Other One-Day	1	1	0	1	1	1.00	-	-	-	-
ALL FIRST-CLASS	13	24	2	1003	190	45.59	3	5	4	-
ALL ONE-DAY	6	6	0	129	78	21.50	-	1	-	-

BOWLING AVERAGES
Did not bowl

J.D. LOVE - Lincolnshire

Opposition	Venue	Date	Batting	Fielding	Bowling

NATWEST TROPHY

Opposition	Venue	Date	Batting	Fielding	Bowling
Gloucs	Gloucester	June 27	1		0-11

OTHER ONE-DAY
For Yorkshiremen

Opposition	Venue	Date	Batting	Fielding	Bowling
Yorkshire	Scarborough	Sept 6	10	1Ct	1-19

BATTING AVERAGES - Including fielding

	Matches	Inns	NO	Runs	HS	Avge	100s	50s	Ct	St
NatWest Trophy	1	1	0	1	1	1.00	-	-	-	-
Other One-Day	1	1	0	10	10	10.00	-	-	1	-

PLACE

| ALL ONE-DAY | 2 | 2 | 0 | 11 | 10 | 5.50 | - | - | 1 | - |

BOWLING AVERAGES

	Overs	Mdns	Runs	Wkts	Avge	Best	5wI	10wM
NatWest Trophy	2	0	11	0	-	-	-	
Other One-Day	3	0	19	1	19.00	1-19	-	
ALL ONE-DAY	5	0	30	1	30.00	1-19	-	

G.E. LOVEDAY - Berkshire

Opposition	Venue	Date	Batting	Fielding	Bowling
NATWEST TROPHY					
Middlesex	Lord's	June 27	36		

BATTING AVERAGES - Including fielding

	Matches	Inns	NO	Runs	HS	Avge	100s	50s	Ct	St
NatWest Trophy	1	1	0	36	36	36.00	-	-	-	-
ALL ONE-DAY	1	1	0	36	36	36.00	-	-	-	-

BOWLING AVERAGES
Did not bowl

M.J. LOWREY - Cambridge University

Opposition	Venue	Date	Batting			Fielding	Bowling
OTHER FIRST-CLASS							
Northants	Fenner's	April 14	8	&	23 *		1-58 & 2-13
Derbyshire	Fenner's	April 18	4	&	1	1Ct	0-32
Warwickshire	Fenner's	April 26	1	&	24		0-18
Middlesex	Fenner's	May 3	6	&	12		0-58 & 0-29
Essex	Fenner's	May 16	6	&	69		1-26 & 0-22
Gloucs	Fenner's	May 23	20	&	45		2-59 & 0-6
Notts	Fenner's	June 16	19	&	25		1-55 & 1-5
Kent	Fenner's	June 20			4		2-72
Sussex	Hove	June 30	6	&	72		0-30
Oxford U	Lord's	July 4			18 *		

BATTING AVERAGES - Including fielding

	Matches	Inns	NO	Runs	HS	Avge	100s	50s	Ct	St
Other First-Class	10	18	2	363	72	22.68	-	2	1	-
ALL FIRST-CLASS	10	18	2	363	72	22.68	-	2	1	-

BOWLING AVERAGES

	Overs	Mdns	Runs	Wkts	Avge	Best	5wI	10wM
Other First-Class	151.2	33	483	10	48.30	2-13	-	-
ALL FIRST-CLASS	151.2	33	483	10	48.30	2-13	-	-

P.D. LUNN - Oxford University

Opposition	Venue	Date	Batting			Fielding	Bowling
OTHER FIRST-CLASS							
Glamorgan	The Parks	April 14	5			1Ct	
Somerset	The Parks	April 18	19 *				
Hampshire	The Parks	May 3	16				1-49
Surrey	The Parks	May 16	44 *	&	20		
Glamorgan	The Parks	June 2	11				
Notts	The Parks	June 6	22 *				
Lancashire	The Parks	June 16	3	&	9 *		1-34
Cambridge U	Lord's	July 4	35				0-9

BATTING AVERAGES - Including fielding

	Matches	Inns	NO	Runs	HS	Avge	100s	50s	Ct	St
Other First-Class	8	10	4	184	44 *	30.66	-	-	1	-
ALL FIRST-CLASS	8	10	4	184	44 *	30.66	-	-	1	-

BOWLING AVERAGES

	Overs	Mdns	Runs	Wkts	Avge	Best	5wI	10wM
Other First-Class	23	4	92	2	46.00	1-34	-	-
ALL FIRST-CLASS	23	4	92	2	46.00	1-34	-	-

M.A. LYNCH - Surrey

Opposition	Venue	Date	Batting			Fielding	Bowling
BRITANNIC ASSURANCE							
Sussex	Hove	April 26	70	&	46	2Ct	0-4 & 0-27
Lancashire	The Oval	May 3	95	&	6 *		0-17
Hampshire	The Oval	May 19	11	&	2		0-12
Middlesex	Lord's	May 23	46			1Ct	
Derbyshire	The Oval	June 6					0-27
Yorkshire	Harrogate	June 9			11	3Ct	
Worcestershire	The Oval	June 16			21	2Ct	
Notts	Trent Bridge	June 20	18 *				
Glamorgan	Cardiff	June 30			7	1Ct	
Northants	The Oval	July 4					
Warwickshire	The Oval	July 7	92	&	46	3Ct	
Sussex	Guildford	July 18	52	&	1 *		
Kent	Guildford	July 21	20			4Ct	0-0
Gloucs	Cheltenham	July 28	33	&	77	1Ct	
Somerset	Weston	Aug 4	97	&	104	1Ct	
Leicestershire	The Oval	Aug 11	12			1Ct	
Essex	Chelmsford	Aug 18	4	&	25		
Hampshire	Southampton	Aug 23	13			3Ct	
Lancashire	Blackpool	Aug 29				1Ct	
Kent	Canterbury	Sept 7	73 *			3Ct	
Middlesex	The Oval	Sept 12	17	&	22		1-43
Essex	The Oval	Sept 18	12	&	16	3Ct	
REFUGE ASSURANCE							
Sussex	Hove	April 29	9				2-2
Lancashire	The Oval	May 6	58				0-40
Notts	Trent Bridge	May 20	20				0-9
Northants	The Oval	June 3	37				
Yorkshire	Hull	June 10	8				
Worcestershire	The Oval	June 17	21 *				
Derbyshire	The Oval	June 24	48				
Glamorgan	Cardiff	July 1	38				
Warwickshire	The Oval	July 8	25				
Middlesex	The Oval	July 15	25				
Kent	The Oval	July 22	26				
Gloucs	Cheltenham	July 29	3				
Somerset	Weston	Aug 5	32 *				
Leicestershire	The Oval	Aug 12	23				
Hampshire	Southampton	Aug 26	26				
NATWEST TROPHY							
Wiltshire	Trowbridge	June 27				1Ct	
Middlesex	Uxbridge	July 11	59				
BENSON & HEDGES CUP							
Lancashire	Old Trafford	April 24	0			1Ct	
Hampshire	The Oval	May 1	8				0-52
Combined U	The Parks	May 10	1			1Ct	
Yorkshire	The Oval	May 12	0				0-14
Lancashire	Old Trafford	May 30	24			3Ct	
OTHER FIRST-CLASS							
Oxford U	The Parks	May 16	81 *			1Ct	
India	The Oval	Aug 1	94	&	3		
OTHER ONE-DAY							
Warwickshire	Hove	Sept 3	65 *			1Ct	
Kent	Hove	Sept 4	0				

BATTING AVERAGES - Including fielding

	Matches	Inns	NO	Runs	HS	Avge	100s	50s	Ct	St
Britannic Assurance	22	29	4	1049	104	41.96	1	7	29	-
Refuge Assurance	15	15	2	399	58	30.69	-	1	-	-
NatWest Trophy	2	1	0	59	59	59.00	-	1	1	-
Benson & Hedges Cup	5	5	0	33	24	6.60	-	-	5	-
Other First-Class	2	3	1	178	94	89.00	-	2	1	-
Other One-Day	2	2	1	65	65 *	65.00	-	1	1	-
ALL FIRST-CLASS	24	32	5	1227	104	45.44	1	9	30	-
ALL ONE-DAY	24	23	3	556	65 *	27.80	-	3	7	-

L	PLAYER RECORDS

BOWLING AVERAGES

	Overs	Mdns	Runs	Wkts	Avge	Best	5wI	10wM
Britannic Assurance	27	5	130	1	130.00	1-43	-	-
Refuge Assurance	7	0	51	2	25.50	2-2	-	
NatWest Trophy								
Benson & Hedges Cup	12	0	66	0	-	-	-	
Other First-Class								
Other One-Day								
ALL FIRST-CLASS	27	5	130	1	130.00	1-43	-	-
ALL ONE-DAY	19	0	117	2	58.50	2-2	-	

S.G. LYNCH - *Buckinghamshire*

Opposition	Venue	Date	Batting	Fielding	Bowling
NATWEST TROPHY					
Notts	Marlow	June 27	46	1Ct	1-52

BATTING AVERAGES - Including fielding

	Matches	Inns	NO	Runs	HS	Avge	100s	50s	Ct	St
NatWest Trophy	1	1	0	46	46	46.00	-	-	1	-
ALL ONE-DAY	1	1	0	46	46	46.00	-	-	1	-

BOWLING AVERAGES

	Overs	Mdns	Runs	Wkts	Avge	Best	5wI	10wM
NatWest Trophy	7	0	52	1	52.00	1-52	-	
ALL ONE-DAY	7	0	52	1	52.00	1-52	-	

PLAYER RECORDS

A.J. MACK - *Minor Counties*

Opposition	Venue	Date	Batting	Fielding	Bowling
BENSON & HEDGES CUP					
Middlesex	Lord's	April 24			2-47
Sussex	Marlow	May 1			2-36
Somerset	Taunton	May 8			2-22
Derbyshire	Wellington	May 10	6		2-49

BATTING AVERAGES - Including fielding

	Matches	Inns	NO	Runs	HS	Avge	100s	50s	Ct	St
Benson & Hedges Cup	4	1	0	6	6	6.00	-	-	-	-
ALL ONE-DAY	4	1	0	6	6	6.00	-	-	-	-

BOWLING AVERAGES

	Overs	Mdns	Runs	Wkts	Avge	Best	5wI	10wM
Benson & Hedges Cup	41	5	154	8	19.25	2-22	-	
ALL ONE-DAY	41	5	154	8	19.25	2-22	-	

N.R.C. MACLAURIN - *Hertfordshire*

Opposition	Venue	Date	Batting	Fielding	Bowling
NATWEST TROPHY					
Warwickshire	St Albans	June 27	21	1Ct	

BATTING AVERAGES - Including fielding

	Matches	Inns	NO	Runs	HS	Avge	100s	50s	Ct	St
NatWest Trophy	1	1	0	21	21	21.00	-	-	1	-
ALL ONE-DAY	1	1	0	21	21	21.00	-	-	1	-

BOWLING AVERAGES
Did not bowl

M.A.W.R. MADURASINGHE - *Sri Lanka*

Opposition	Venue	Date	Batting	Fielding	Bowling
OTHER FIRST-CLASS					
Warwickshire	Edgbaston	Aug 29			4-120 & 4-35
Sussex	Hove	Sept 5	11		1-92 & 1-17
Lancashire	Old Trafford	Sept 8	28 *		5-108 & 3-89
Hampshire	Southampton	Sept 12	4	1Ct	3-99
OTHER ONE-DAY					
Surrey	The Oval	Sept 2	1 *		0-33
Somerset	Taunton	Sept 3		1Ct	1-47

BATTING AVERAGES - Including fielding

	Matches	Inns	NO	Runs	HS	Avge	100s	50s	Ct	St
Other First-Class	4	3	1	43	28 *	21.50	-	-	1	-
Other One-Day	2	1	1	1	1 *	-	-	-	1	-
ALL FIRST-CLASS	4	3	1	43	28 *	21.50	-	-	1	-
ALL ONE-DAY	2	1	1	1	1 *	-	-	-	1	-

BOWLING AVERAGES

	Overs	Mdns	Runs	Wkts	Avge	Best	5wI	10wM
Other First-Class	176.2	28	560	21	26.66	5-108	1	-
Other One-Day	21	1	80	1	80.00	1-47	-	
ALL FIRST-CLASS	176.2	28	560	21	26.66	5-108	1	-
ALL ONE-DAY	21	1	80	1	80.00	1-47	-	

R.S. MAHANAMA - *Sri Lanka*

Opposition	Venue	Date	Batting		Fielding	Bowling
OTHER FIRST-CLASS						
Glamorgan	Ebbw Vale	Aug 22	9 &	35	4Ct	
Notts	Cleethorpes	Aug 25	114		4Ct	
Warwickshire	Edgbaston	Aug 29	30			
Sussex	Hove	Sept 5	8 &	14		
Lancashire	Old Trafford	Sept 8	103 &	93	1Ct	
Hampshire	Southampton	Sept 12	32 &	56	1Ct	
OTHER ONE-DAY						
Surrey	The Oval	Sept 2	24			
Somerset	Taunton	Sept 3	11		1Ct	

BATTING AVERAGES - Including fielding

	Matches	Inns	NO	Runs	HS	Avge	100s	50s	Ct	St
Other First-Class	6	10	0	494	114	49.40	2	2	10	-
Other One-Day	2	2	0	35	24	17.50	-	-	1	-
ALL FIRST-CLASS	6	10	0	494	114	49.40	2	2	10	-
ALL ONE-DAY	2	2	0	35	24	17.50	-	-	1	-

BOWLING AVERAGES
Did not bowl

B.J.M. MAHER - *Derbyshire*

Opposition	Venue	Date	Batting	Fielding	Bowling
OTHER FIRST-CLASS					
Cambridge U	Fenner's	April 18			

BATTING AVERAGES - Including fielding

	Matches	Inns	NO	Runs	HS	Avge	100s	50s	Ct	St
Other First-Class	1	0	0	0	0	-	-	-	-	-
ALL FIRST-CLASS	1	0	0	0	0	-	-	-	-	-

BOWLING AVERAGES
Did not bowl

M. MAHMOOD - *Scotland*

Opposition	Venue	Date	Batting	Fielding	Bowling
OTHER FIRST-CLASS					
Ireland	Edinburgh	Aug 11	3	1Ct	3-63 & 1-40

BATTING AVERAGES - Including fielding

	Matches	Inns	NO	Runs	HS	Avge	100s	50s	Ct	St
Other First-Class	1		1 03	3	3.00		-	-	1	-
ALL FIRST-CLASS	1		1 03	3	3.00		-	-	1	-

BOWLING AVERAGES

	Overs	Mdns	Runs	Wkts	Avge	Best	5wI	10wM
Other First-Class	31	9	103	4	25.75	3-63	-	-
ALL FIRST-CLASS	31	9	103	4	25.75	3-63	-	-

D.E. MALCOLM - *Derbyshire & England*

Opposition	Venue	Date	Batting	Fielding	Bowling
CORNHILL TEST MATCHES					
New Zealand	Trent Bridge	June 7	4 *		2-48 & 0-22
New Zealand	Lord's	June 21	0 *		5-94
New Zealand	Edgbaston	July 5	0 & 0		3-59 & 5-46

M PLAYER RECORDS

India	Lord's	July 26			1-106 & 2-65
India	Old Trafford	Aug 9	13		1-96 & 1-59
India	The Oval	Aug 23	15*		2-110

TEXACO TROPHY

New Zealand	The Oval	May 25			2-19
India	Headingley	July 18	4		1-57

BRITANNIC ASSURANCE

Northants	Northampton	May 3	20*		3-60 & 3-25
Somerset	Taunton	May 19	10		0-20 & 4-88
Notts	Derby	May 26	12		3-46 & 2-106
Warwickshire	Derby	June 16			4-63
Gloucs	Derby	June 30	0*		2-46 & 0-49
Hampshire	Portsmouth	July 21	0		2-90 & 2-39
Kent	Chesterfield	Aug 4			1-58 & 2-57
Glamorgan	Cardiff	Aug 29	2		1-61
Yorkshire	Scarborough	Sept 7			0-56 & 1-83

REFUGE ASSURANCE

Sussex	Hove	April 22			1-47
Worcestershire	Derby	April 29	0*		0-32
Northants	Northampton	May 6			3-34
Yorkshire	Headingley	May 13	0		0-28
Somerset	Taunton	May 20			2-48
Warwickshire	Derby	June 17	0		1-33
Gloucs	Derby	July 1			0-16
Leicestershire	Knypersley	July 15			4-21
Hampshire	Portsmouth	July 22	9	1Ct	2-50
Kent	Chesterfield	Aug 5			0-55
Middlesex	Derby	Aug 19			0-17
Notts	Derby	Sept 5			1-45
Middlesex	Edgbaston	Sept 16			3-41

NATWEST TROPHY

Shropshire	Chesterfield	June 27			0-31
Lancashire	Derby	July 11	0		3-54

BENSON & HEDGES CUP

Somerset	Taunton	May 1	0*		0-54
Min Counties	Wellington	May 10	5		1-22
Middlesex	Derby	May 12			3-55

OTHER FIRST-CLASS

New Zealand	Derby	June 2	0		0-36

BATTING AVERAGES - Including fielding

	Matches	Inns	NO	Runs	HS	Avge	100s	50s	Ct	St
Cornhill Test Matches	6	6	3	32	15*	10.66	-	-	-	-
Texaco Trophy	2	1	0	4	4	4.00	-	-	-	-
Britannic Assurance	9	6	2	44	20*	11.00	-	-	-	-
Refuge Assurance	13	4	1	9	9	3.00	-	-	1	-
NatWest Trophy	2	1	0	0	0	0.00	-	-	-	-
Benson & Hedges Cup	3	2	1	5	5	5.00	-	-	-	-
Other First-Class	1	1	0	0	0	0.00	-	-	-	-
ALL FIRST-CLASS	16	13	5	76	20*	9.50	-	-	-	-
ALL ONE-DAY	20	8	2	18	9	3.00	-	-	1	-

BOWLING AVERAGES

	Overs	Mdns	Runs	Wkts	Avge	Best	5wI	10wM
Cornhill Test Matches	228.4	54	705	22	32.04	5-46	2	-
Texaco Trophy	22	5	76	3	25.33	2-19	-	
Britannic Assurance	277.4	44	947	30	31.56	4-63	-	-
Refuge Assurance	92	2	467	17	27.47	4-21	-	
NatWest Trophy	24	4	85	3	28.33	3-54	-	
Benson & Hedges Cup	30	2	131	4	32.75	3-55	-	
Other First-Class	12	1	36	0	-	-	-	
ALL FIRST-CLASS	518.2	99	1688	52	32.46	5-46	2	-
ALL ONE-DAY	168	13	759	27	28.11	4-21	-	

N.A. MALLENDER - *Somerset*

Opposition	Venue	Date	Batting	Fielding	Bowling

BRITANNIC ASSURANCE

Opposition	Venue	Date	Batting	Fielding	Bowling
Gloucs	Taunton	April 26	0		4-46 & 0-55
Sussex	Taunton	May 23			1-21 & 1-24
Leicestershire	Leicester	May 26			0-51 & 2-62
Gloucs	Bristol	June 2	8		1-69
Hampshire	Basingstoke	June 6		1Ct	1-50 & 0-9
Kent	Canterbury	June 9			1-32 & 1-34
Essex	Bath	June 16			2-74
Glamorgan	Bath	June 20			1-27
Northants	Taunton	June 30		1Ct	1-70 & 0-33
Warwickshire	Taunton	July 4	0		0-24 & 2-4
Worcestershire	Worcester	July 18			1-35 & 1-13
Middlesex	Uxbridge	July 21			2-46 & 4-60
Yorkshire	Scarborough	July 25			1-42 & 1-69
Lancashire	Old Trafford	July 28	3* & 7		2-63
Surrey	Weston	Aug 4			0-49 & 0-47
Notts	Weston	Aug 8	17*	1Ct	5-46 & 3-69
Hampshire	Taunton	Aug 18	17		5-102 & 0-23
Sussex	Hove	Aug 23	87*		2-31
Worcestershire	Taunton	Sept 12	15 & 23		4-100 & 2-75

REFUGE ASSURANCE

Worcestershire	Taunton	April 22			0-26
Leicestershire	Leicester	May 27			0-28
Gloucs	Bristol	June 3	24		0-25
Kent	Canterbury	June 10			1-29
Essex	Bath	June 17	7*		2-30
Notts	Bath	June 24			1-34
Northants	Taunton	July 1		1Ct	1-24
Middlesex	Lord's	July 8			4-32
Yorkshire	Scarborough	July 15	3		1-51
Glamorgan	Neath	July 22			1-19
Lancashire	Old Trafford	July 29			1-37
Surrey	Weston	Aug 5	10*		0-44
Warwickshire	Weston	Aug 12			1-57

NATWEST TROPHY

Devon	Torquay	June 27			2-4
Worcestershire	Taunton	July 11			0-29

BENSON & HEDGES CUP

Middlesex	Lord's	May 10	3*	1Ct	2-32
Sussex	Hove	May 12		2Ct	0-14
Middlesex	Taunton	May 30	6*		1-25
Lancashire	Old Trafford	June 13	3		0-31

OTHER FIRST-CLASS

Oxford U	The Parks	April 18			0-30

OTHER ONE-DAY

For Yorkshiremen

Yorkshire	Scarborough	Sept 6			0-26

BATTING AVERAGES - Including fielding

	Matches	Inns	NO	Runs	HS	Avge	100s	50s	Ct	St
Britannic Assurance	19	10	3	177	87*	25.28	-	1	3	-
Refuge Assurance	13	4	0	44	24	22.00	-	-	1	-
NatWest Trophy	2	0	0	0	0		-	-	-	-
Benson & Hedges Cup	4	3	2	12	6*	12.00	-	-	3	-
Other First-Class	1	0	0	0	0		-	-	-	-
Other One-Day	1	0	0	0	0		-	-	-	-
ALL FIRST-CLASS	20	10	3	177	87*	25.28	-	1	3	-
ALL ONE-DAY	20	7	4	56	24	18.66	-	-	4	-

BOWLING AVERAGES

	Overs	Mdns	Runs	Wkts	Avge	Best	5wI	10wM
Britannic Assurance	538.2	114	1555	51	30.49	5-46	2	
Refuge Assurance	100.5	4	436	13	33.53	4-32	-	
NatWest Trophy	16	5	33	2	16.50	2-4	-	
Benson & Hedges Cup	35	6	102	3	34.00	2-32	-	
Other First-Class	16	2	30	0	-	-	-	
Other One-Day	6	0	26	0	-	-	-	
ALL FIRST-CLASS	554.2	116	1585	51	31.07	5-46	2	
ALL ONE-DAY	157.5	15	597	18	33.16	4-32	-	

S.J. MALONE - *Wiltshire*

Opposition	Venue	Date	Batting	Fielding	Bowling

NATWEST TROPHY

Opposition	Venue	Date	Batting	Fielding	Bowling
Surrey	Trowbridge	June 27	5*		0-54

BATTING AVERAGES - Including fielding

	Matches	Inns	NO	Runs	HS	Avge	100s	50s	Ct	St
NatWest Trophy	1	1	1	5	5*		-	-	-	-

PLAYER RECORDS

M

ALL ONE-DAY	1	1	1	5	5*	-	-	-	-	-

BOWLING AVERAGES

	Overs	Mdns	Runs	Wkts	Avge	Best	5wI	10wM
NatWest Trophy	9.1	0	54	0	-	-	-	
ALL ONE-DAY	9.1	0	54	0	-	-	-	

S.V. MANJREKAR - *India*

Opposition	Venue	Date	Batting	Fielding	Bowling

CORNHILL TEST MATCHES

Opposition	Venue	Date	Batting		Fielding	Bowling
England	Lord's	July 26	18 & 33		2Ct	
England	Old Trafford	Aug 9	93 & 50		1Ct	
England	The Oval	Aug 23	22		1Ct	

TEXACO TROPHY

England	Headingley	July 18	82		1Ct	
England	Trent Bridge	July 20	59			

OTHER FIRST-CLASS

Yorkshire	Headingley	June 30	158*			
Kent	Canterbury	July 7	20 & 9			
Min Counties	Trowbridge	July 11	40			
Leicestershire	Leicester	July 21	66 & 3*		1Ct	
Surrey	The Oval	Aug 1	9 & 52*		1Ct	
TCCB U25 XI	Edgbaston	Aug 15	116			
Glamorgan	Swansea	Aug 18	4			
World XI	Scarborough	Aug 29	59 & 62			

OTHER ONE-DAY

Scotland	Glasgow	July 14	31		2Ct	

BATTING AVERAGES - Including fielding

	Matches	Inns	NO	Runs	HS	Avge	100s	50s	Ct	St
Cornhill Test Matches	3	5	0	216	93	43.20	-	2	4	-
Texaco Trophy	2	2	0	141	82	70.50	-	2	1	-
Other First-Class	8	12	3	598	158*	66.44	2	4	2	-
Other One-Day	1	1	0	31	31	31.00	-	-	2	-
ALL FIRST-CLASS	11	17	3	814	158*	58.14	2	6	6	-
ALL ONE-DAY	3	3	0	172	82	57.33	-	2	3	-

BOWLING AVERAGES

Did not bowl

V.J. MARKS - *Duchess of Norfolk's XI*

Opposition	Venue	Date	Batting	Fielding	Bowling

OTHER ONE-DAY

New Zealand	Arundel	May 6			0-63

BATTING AVERAGES - Including fielding

	Matches	Inns	NO	Runs	HS	Avge	100s	50s	Ct	St
Other One-Day	1	0	0	0	0	0				
ALL ONE-DAY	1	0	0	0	0	0				

BOWLING AVERAGES

	Overs	Mdns	Runs	Wkts	Avge	Best	5wI	10wM
Other One-Day	10	0	63	0	-	-	-	
ALL ONE-DAY	10	0	63	0	-	-	-	

S.A. MARSH - *Kent*

Opposition	Venue	Date	Batting	Fielding	Bowling

BRITANNIC ASSURANCE

Hampshire	Canterbury	April 26	61* & 4		
Sussex	Folkestone	May 3	10 & 4*	4Ct	
Middlesex	Lord's	May 15	15 & 38	3Ct,1St	
Glamorgan	Swansea	May 23			
Notts	Tunbridge We	June 2	114* & 4	3Ct	
Yorkshire	Tunbridge We	June 6	41*	1Ct	
Somerset	Canterbury	June 9	5 & 8	1Ct	
Warwickshire	Edgbaston	June 23	5	3Ct	2-20
Lancashire	Maidstone	June 30	11 & 8	3Ct,1St	
Essex	Maidstone	June 4		2Ct	
Northants	Northampton	July 18	29 & 25*	2Ct	
Surrey	Guildford	July 21	7 & 11	2Ct	
Middlesex	Canterbury	July 25	61	2Ct	
Worcestershire	Canterbury	July 28	0 & 8	3Ct	
Derbyshire	Chesterfield	Aug 4	38 & 4		0-16
Leicestershire	Dartford	Aug 8	0	4Ct,1St	
Gloucs	Bristol	Aug 11	54	2Ct,1St	
Sussex	Hove	Aug 18	70*		
Leicestershire	Leicester	Aug 23	5 & 31*	3Ct	
Hampshire	Bournemouth	Aug 29	3 & 34	2Ct	
Surrey	Canterbury	Sept 7	17 & 25*	2Ct	
Essex	Chelmsford	Sept 12	70 & 47	4Ct	

REFUGE ASSURANCE

Essex	Chelmsford	April 22	27*		
Hampshire	Canterbury	April 29	15	1Ct	
Middlesex	Folkestone	May 6	18	1Ct	
Glamorgan	Llanelli	May 13	14	1Ct	
Yorkshire	Canterbury	May 20	2*	2Ct	
Northants	Northampton	May 27		1Ct	
Somerset	Canterbury	June 10			
Notts	Canterbury	June 17	20	2Ct	
Warwickshire	Edgbaston	June 24	9		
Lancashire	Maidstone	July 1	38	1Ct	
Surrey	The Oval	July 22	35		
Worcestershire	Canterbury	July 29	7	1Ct	
Derbyshire	Chesterfield	Aug 5			
Gloucs	Bristol	Aug 12	24		
Leicestershire	Leicester	Aug 26	18*		

NATWEST TROPHY

Gloucs	Bristol	July 11	0	1Ct	

BENSON & HEDGES CUP

Worcestershire	Worcester	May 1	17	2Ct	
Warwickshire	Canterbury	May 8	9	1Ct	
Gloucs	Canterbury	May 10			
Glamorgan	Swansea	May 12	9		

OTHER FIRST-CLASS

Cambridge U	Fenner's	June 20		2Ct	
India	Canterbury	July 7	44	1Ct,1St	

OTHER ONE-DAY

Sussex	Hove	Sept 2	52	2Ct	
Surrey	Hove	Sept 4	2	2Ct	

BATTING AVERAGES - Including fielding

	Matches	Inns	NO	Runs	HS	Avge	100s	50s	Ct	St
Britannic Assurance	22	34	8	867	114*	33.34	1	5	46	4
Refuge Assurance	15	12	3	227	38	25.22	-	-	10	-
NatWest Trophy	1	1	0	0	0	0.00	-	-	1	-
Benson & Hedges Cup	4	3	0	35	17	11.66	-	-	3	-
Other First-Class	2	1	0	44	44	44.00	-	-	3	1
Other One-Day	2	2	0	54	52	27.00	-	1	4	-
ALL FIRST-CLASS	24	35	8	911	114*	33.74	1	5	49	5
ALL ONE-DAY	22	18	3	316	52	21.06	-	1	18	-

BOWLING AVERAGES

	Overs	Mdns	Runs	Wkts	Avge	Best	5wI	10wM
Britannic Assurance	8.4	0	36	2	18.00	2-20	-	-
Refuge Assurance								
NatWest Trophy								
Benson & Hedges Cup								
Other First-Class								
Other One-Day								
ALL FIRST-CLASS	8.4	0	36	2	18.00	2-20	-	-
ALL ONE-DAY								

M   PLAYER RECORDS

D. MARSHALL - *Lincolnshire*

Opposition	Venue	Date	Batting	Fielding	Bowling
NATWEST TROPHY					
Gloucs	Gloucester	June 27	5		2-63

BATTING AVERAGES - Including fielding

	Matches	Inns	NO	Runs	HS	Avge	100s	50s	Ct	St
NatWest Trophy	1	1	0	5	5	5.00	-	-	-	-
ALL ONE-DAY	1	1	0	5	5	5.00	-	-	-	-

BOWLING AVERAGES

	Overs	Mdns	Runs	Wkts	Avge	Best	5wI	10wM
NatWest Trophy	12	0	63	2	31.50	2-63	-	
ALL ONE-DAY	12	0	63	2	31.50	2-63	-	

M.D. MARSHALL - *Hampshire*

Opposition	Venue	Date	Batting	Fielding	Bowling
BRITANNIC ASSURANCE					
Sussex	Southampton	May 15	85	2Ct	2-26 & 0-66
Surrey	The Oval	May 19	47 * & 51 *		3-65 & 0-14
Essex	Southampton	May 23	9		1-49 & 2-18
Yorkshire	Headingley	May 26	117 & 28		1-44 & 3-51
Leicestershire	Leicester	June 2	112	1Ct	2-44 & 3-44
Glamorgan	Southampton	June 16	4		0-9 & 2-63
Gloucs	Gloucester	June 20			1-20
Lancashire	Old Trafford	June 23	86		0-28 & 2-42
Notts	Portsmouth	July 18	5 & 23 *	1Ct	4-30 & 5-64
Derbyshire	Portsmouth	July 21	32 & 60	1Ct	3-60 & 7-47
Sussex	Arundel	July 25	11 & 34		3-35 & 0-18
Warwickshire	Edgbaston	July 28	26 & 10		0-17 & 0-27
Northants	Bournemouth	Aug 4			4-37 & 3-24
Middlesex	Bournemouth	Aug 8	9		2-54 & 2-28
Somerset	Taunton	Aug 18	58		3-43 & 1-34
Surrey	Southampton	Aug 23	6 & 31	1Ct	0-64
Glamorgan	Pontypridd	Sept 7	51		5-45 & 6-47
Gloucs	Southampton	Sept 18	21 & 46	1Ct	2-54 & 0-70
REFUGE ASSURANCE					
Kent	Canterbury	April 29	3		0-41
Gloucs	Southampton	May 6	6 *		
Somerset	Taunton	May 13			2-53
Yorkshire	Headingley	May 27	10		1-32
Leicestershire	Leicester	June 3	44		1-23
Middlesex	Basingstoke	June 10	46		0-19
Glamorgan	Bournemouth	June 17	1		0-23
Lancashire	Old Trafford	June 24			0-3
Sussex	Hove	July 1	19		1-50
Essex	Southampton	July 8	43 *		2-33
Notts	Southampton	July 15	7		2-36
Derbyshire	Portsmouth	July 22	1		1-4
Warwickshire	Edgbaston	July 29	24		2-36
Northants	Bournemouth	Aug 5	17 *	1Ct	1-33
Worcestershire	Worcester	Aug 12	38		1-22
Surrey	Southampton	Aug 26	0		0-50
NATWEST TROPHY					
Leicestershire	Leicester	June 27	6		0-32
Essex	Chelmsford	July 11	9		2-45
Yorkshire	Southampton	Aug 1	4		4-17
Northants	Southampton	Aug 15	77		1-37
BENSON & HEDGES CUP					
Yorkshire	Southampton	April 24	24		0-28
Surrey	The Oval	May 1	31		0-52
Lancashire	Old Trafford	May 8			0-45

BATTING AVERAGES - Including fielding

	Matches	Inns	NO	Runs	HS	Avge	100s	50s	Ct	St
Britannic Assurance	18	24	3	962	117	45.81	2	6	7	-
Refuge Assurance	16	14	3	259	46	23.54	-	-	1	-
NatWest Trophy	4	4	0	96	77	24.00	-	1	-	-
Benson & Hedges Cup	3	2	0	55	31	27.50	-	-	-	-
ALL FIRST-CLASS	18	24	3	962	117	45.81	2	6	7	-
ALL ONE-DAY	23	20	3	410	77	24.11	-	1	1	-

BOWLING AVERAGES

	Overs	Mdns	Runs	Wkts	Avge	Best	5wI	10wM
Britannic Assurance	554.2	141	1381	72	19.18	7-47	4	2
Refuge Assurance	104	5	458	14	32.71	2-33	-	
NatWest Trophy	44	6	131	7	18.71	4-17	-	
Benson & Hedges Cup	25	1	125	0	-	-	-	
ALL FIRST-CLASS	554.2	141	1381	72	19.18	7-47	4	2
ALL ONE-DAY	173	12	714	21	34.00	4-17	-	

P.J. MARTIN - *Lancashire*

Opposition	Venue	Date	Batting	Fielding	Bowling
BRITANNIC ASSURANCE					
Derbyshire	Derby	May 15			1-10
Leicestershire	Old Trafford	May 19			0-45 & 0-17
Notts	Southport	July 25	1 *	1Ct	3-57 & 3-110
Somerset	Old Trafford	July 28	9		2-55 & 1-50
Yorkshire	Headingley	Aug 4	10 *		1-54 & 3-48
Worcestershire	Kid'minster	Aug 8	1 * & 0	1Ct	0-39
Northants	Northampton	Aug 11			0-64 & 0-15
Notts	Trent Bridge	Sept 12	21	3Ct	4-68 & 0-30
Warwickshire	Old Trafford	Sept 18			2-88
REFUGE ASSURANCE					
Somerset	Old Trafford	July 29		1Ct	0-38
Yorkshire	Scarborough	Aug 5		1Ct	0-41
NATWEST TROPHY					
Derbyshire	Derby	July 11			0-28
Gloucs	Old Trafford	Aug 1			0-25
OTHER FIRST-CLASS					
Sri Lanka	Old Trafford	Sept 8	2		2-84 & 0-34

BATTING AVERAGES - Including fielding

	Matches	Inns	NO	Runs	HS	Avge	100s	50s	Ct	St
Britannic Assurance	9	6	3	42	21	14.00	-	-	5	-
Refuge Assurance	2	0	0	0	0	-	-	-	2	-
NatWest Trophy	2	0	0	0	0	-	-	-	-	-
Other First-Class	1	1	0	2	2	2.00	-	-	-	-
ALL FIRST-CLASS	10	7	3	44	21	11.00	-	-	5	-
ALL ONE-DAY	4	0	0	0	0	-	-	-	2	-

BOWLING AVERAGES

	Overs	Mdns	Runs	Wkts	Avge	Best	5wI	10wM
Britannic Assurance	240.3	46	750	20	37.50	4-68	-	-
Refuge Assurance	14	0	79	0	-	-	-	
NatWest Trophy	8	0	53	0	-	-	-	
Other First-Class	35	6	118	2	59.00	2-84	-	
ALL FIRST-CLASS	275.3	52	868	22	39.45	4-68	-	-
ALL ONE-DAY	22	0	132	0	-	-	-	

D.J.R. MARTINDALE - *Nottinghamshire*

Opposition	Venue	Date	Batting	Fielding	Bowling
BRITANNIC ASSURANCE					
Leicestershire	Leicester	May 15	9 & 43		
Warwickshire	Edgbaston	May 19	73 & 10		
Northants	Trent Bridge	May 23	0 & 108 *		
Derbyshire	Derby	May 26	12 & 2		
Kent	Tunbridge We	June 2	23	3Ct	
Surrey	Trent Bridge	June 20	0 & 33		
Leicestershire	Trent Bridge	June 30	7		
Yorkshire	Scarborough	July 4	4		
Glamorgan	Worksop	Aug 11	35 * & 1		
Gloucs	Trent Bridge	Aug 18	0 & 66 *		
Worcestershire	Trent Bridge	Aug 29	37 & 14		
Middlesex	Lord's	Sept 7	32 & 11	1Ct	
Lancashire	Trent Bridge	Sept 12	22 & 6		
Yorkshire	Trent Bridge	Sept 18	11	1Ct	

PLAYER RECORDS

BENSON & HEDGES CUP
Worcestershire Trent Bridge June 13   0

OTHER FIRST-CLASS
Oxford U   The Parks   June 6   15
Cambridge U   Fenner's   June 16   138
Sri Lanka   Cleethorpes   Aug 25   26 & 13

BATTING AVERAGES - Including fielding

	Matches	Inns	NO	Runs	HS	Avge	100s	50s	Ct	St
Britannic Assurance	14	24	3	559	108*	26.61	1	2	5	-
Benson & Hedges Cup	1	1	0	0	0	0.00	-	-	-	-
Other First-Class	3	4	0	192	138	48.00	1	-	-	-
ALL FIRST-CLASS	17	28	3	751	138	30.04	2	2	5	-
ALL ONE-DAY	1	1	0	0	0	0.00	-	-	-	-

BOWLING AVERAGES
Did not bowl

R.J. MARU - *Hampshire*

Opposition	Venue	Date	Batting	Fielding	Bowling
BRITANNIC ASSURANCE					
Kent	Canterbury	April 26		1Ct	0-64 & 1-87
Sussex	Southampton	May 15	54*	1Ct	1-10 & 3-49
Surrey	The Oval	May 19		3Ct	0-86 & 2-47
Essex	Southampton	May 23		2Ct	0-45 & 4-47
Yorkshire	Headingley	May 26	25	3Ct	0-43
Leicestershire	Leicester	June 2	59		0-26
Somerset	Basingstoke	June 6	17*		0-2
Glamorgan	Southampton	June 16	9	2Ct	2-68
Gloucs	Gloucester	June 20			0-0
Lancashire	Old Trafford	June 23			2-22
Notts	Portsmouth	July 18	19	2Ct	2-5 & 2-87
Derbyshire	Portsmouth	July 21	44 & 0		0-70 & 0-33
Sussex	Arundel	July 25		1Ct	0-105 & 1-51
Warwickshire	Edgbaston	July 28	53		1-67 & 2-90
Northants	Bournemouth	Aug 4		1Ct	4-37 & 2-64
Middlesex	Bournemouth	Aug 8	43	2Ct	0-153 & 1-40
Worcestershire	Worcester	Aug 11		7	1Ct	0-92 & 1-13
Somerset	Taunton	Aug 18	46	1Ct	4-103 & 1-123
Surrey	Southampton	Aug 23	0 & 36	1Ct	3-129
Kent	Bournemouth	Aug 29	34	1Ct	2-48
Glamorgan	Pontypridd	Sept 7	5	2Ct	3-22 & 0-22
Gloucs	Southampton	Sept 18	20 & 42	1Ct	3-40 & 6-97
REFUGE ASSURANCE					
Kent	Canterbury	April 29	12*		1-29
Gloucs	Southampton	May 6			
Somerset	Taunton	May 13		1Ct	1-38
Yorkshire	Headingley	May 27		2Ct	
Leicestershire	Leicester	June 3		2Ct	0-14
Middlesex	Basingstoke	June 10	9	1Ct	1-40
Glamorgan	Bournemouth	June 17	4*		3-38
Lancashire	Old Trafford	June 24			
Sussex	Hove	July 1	2		1-39
Essex	Southampton	July 8			1-41
Notts	Southampton	July 15			1-38
Derbyshire	Portsmouth	July 22			
Warwickshire	Edgbaston	July 29	1		0-12
Northants	Bournemouth	Aug 5			1-28
Worcestershire	Worcester	Aug 12			0-46
Surrey	Southampton	Aug 26	1		2-31
NATWEST TROPHY					
Leicestershire	Leicester	June 27	6*		3-46
Essex	Chelmsford	July 11			0-66
Yorkshire	Southampton	Aug 1	22	1Ct	1-48
Northants	Southampton	Aug 15	10	1Ct	2-51
BENSON & HEDGES CUP					
Yorkshire	Southampton	April 24			0-23
Surrey	The Oval	May 1	9		0-40
Lancashire	Old Trafford	May 8			1-40
Combined U	Southampton	May 12		1Ct	3-46
OTHER FIRST-CLASS					
Oxford U	The Parks	May 3	1	2Ct	4-89
India	Southampton	July 4		2Ct	2-69 & 0-31
Sri Lanka	Southampton	Sept 12	6	1Ct	5-25 & 2-119

BATTING AVERAGES - Including fielding

	Matches	Inns	NO	Runs	HS	Avge	100s	50s	Ct	St
Britannic Assurance	22	18	2	513	59	32.06	-	3	25	-
Refuge Assurance	16	6	2	29	12*	7.25	-	-	6	-
NatWest Trophy	4	3	1	38	22	19.00	-	-	2	-
Benson & Hedges Cup	4	1	0	9	9	9.00	-	-	1	-
Other First-Class	3	2	0	7	6	3.50	-	-	5	-
ALL FIRST-CLASS	25	20	2	520	59	28.88	-	3	30	-
ALL ONE-DAY	24	10	3	76	22	10.85	-	-	9	-

BOWLING AVERAGES

	Overs	Mdns	Runs	Wkts	Avge	Best	5wI	10wM
Britannic Assurance	720.1	178	2087	53	39.37	6-97	1	-
Refuge Assurance	70.5	0	394	12	32.83	3-38	-	
NatWest Trophy	45	1	211	6	35.16	3-46	-	
Benson & Hedges Cup	27	2	149	4	37.25	3-46	-	
Other First-Class	131	41	333	13	25.61	5-25	1	-
ALL FIRST-CLASS	851.1	219	2420	66	36.66	6-97	2	-
ALL ONE-DAY	142.5	3	754	22	34.27	3-38	-	

D.E. MATTOCKS - *Norfolk*

Opposition	Venue	Date	Batting	Fielding	Bowling
NATWEST TROPHY					
Yorkshire	Headingley	June 27	2		

BATTING AVERAGES - Including fielding

	Matches	Inns	NO	Runs	HS	Avge	100s	50s	Ct	St
NatWest Trophy	1	1	0	2	2	2.00	-	-	-	-
ALL ONE-DAY	1	1	0	2	2	2.00	-	-	-	-

BOWLING AVERAGES
Did not bowl

M.P. MAYNARD - *Glamorgan*

Opposition	Venue	Date	Batting	Fielding	Bowling
BRITANNIC ASSURANCE					
Leicestershire	Cardiff	April 26	6 & 92	2Ct	
Somerset	Cardiff	May 3	19 & 64		0-11
Gloucs	Bristol	May 15	55*		
Northants	Northampton	June 9	74 & 125*		
Hampshire	Southampton	June 16	20* & 1	1Ct	0-22
Somerset	Bath	June 20	33		0-28
Yorkshire	Cardiff	June 23	54 & 26*		
Surrey	Cardiff	June 30	22 & 5		
Gloucs	Swansea	July 4	63		
Leicestershire	Hinckley	July 7	59 & 47		
Worcestershire	Abergavenny	July 21	15 & 1	1Ct	
Warwickshire	Swansea	July 25	27 & 56	1Ct	0-89
Middlesex	Lord's	Aug 4	27 & 20	1Ct	
Essex	Southend	Aug 8	46 & 0		
Notts	Worksop	Aug 11	115	2Ct	
Derbyshire	Cardiff	Aug 29	20 & 11*		
Hampshire	Pontypridd	Sept 7	50 & 27	1Ct	
Warwickshire	Edgbaston	Sept 12	8 & 79	1Ct	
Worcestershire	Worcester	Sept 18	4 & 35	3Ct	
REFUGE ASSURANCE					
Gloucs	Bristol	April 22	11	2Ct	
Leicestershire	Cardiff	April 29	22		
Kent	Llanelli	May 13	20		
Lancashire	Colwyn Bay	May 27	100	1Ct	
Essex	Ilford	June 3	75		
Northants	Northampton	June 10	13		
Hampshire	Bournemouth	June 17	34	1Ct	
Surrey	Cardiff	July 1	11		
Warwickshire	Edgbaston	July 15	61*		
Somerset	Neath	July 22	0	1Ct	0-23
Derbyshire	Swansea	July 29	30		
Middlesex	Lord's	Aug 5	59		
Notts	Trent Bridge	Aug 12	7		
Worcestershire	Swansea	Aug 26	36		

M PLAYER RECORDS

NATWEST TROPHY

Dorset	Swansea	June 27	8
Sussex	Cardiff	July 11	24
Middlesex	Lord's	Aug 1	1

BENSON & HEDGES CUP

Warwickshire	Edgbaston	April 24	77
Gloucs	Cardiff	May 1	33
Worcestershire	Worcester	May 8	36
Kent	Swansea	May 12	84
Worcestershire	Worcester	May 30	0

OTHER FIRST-CLASS

Oxford U	The Parks	April 14	40	&	32 *		
Oxford U	The Parks	June 2	59				
India	Swansea	Aug 18	4 *	&	26	1Ct	0-34
Sri Lanka	Ebbw Vale	Aug 22	20	&	14	1Ct	

BATTING AVERAGES - Including fielding

	Matches	Inns	NO	Runs	HS	Avge	100s	50s	Ct	St
Britannic Assurance	19	34	5	1306	125 *	45.03	2	10	13	-
Refuge Assurance	14	14	1	479	100	36.84	1	3	5	-
NatWest Trophy	3	3	0	33	24	11.00	-	-	-	-
Benson & Hedges Cup	5	5	0	230	84	46.00	-	2	-	-
Other First-Class	4	7	2	195	59	39.00	-	1	2	-
ALL FIRST-CLASS	23	41	7	1501	125 *	44.14	2	11	15	-
ALL ONE-DAY	22	22	1	742	100	35.33	1	5	5	-

BOWLING AVERAGES

	Overs	Mdns	Runs	Wkts	Avge	Best	5wI	10wM
Britannic Assurance	20	1	150	0	-	-	-	-
Refuge Assurance	1	0	23	0	-	-	-	-
NatWest Trophy								
Benson & Hedges Cup								
Other First-Class	9	1	34	0	-	-	-	-
ALL FIRST-CLASS	29	2	184	0	-	-	-	-
ALL ONE-DAY	1	0	23	0	-	-	-	-

P. McCRUM - Ireland

Opposition	Venue	Date	Batting	Fielding	Bowling

NATWEST TROPHY

Sussex	Downpatrick	June 27	4 *		0-16

OTHER FIRST-CLASS

Scotland	Edinburgh	Aug 11	0		0-28

OTHER ONE-DAY

New Zealand	Downpatrick	May 9	1 *		1-26
New Zealand	Belfast	May 10	9 *		1-42

BATTING AVERAGES - Including fielding

	Matches	Inns	NO	Runs	HS	Avge	100s	50s	Ct	St
NatWest Trophy	1	1	1	4	4 *	-	-	-	-	-
Other First-Class	1	1	0	0	0	0.00	-	-	-	-
Other One-Day	2	2	2	10	9 *	-	-	-	-	-
ALL FIRST-CLASS	1	1	0	0	0	0.00	-	-	-	-
ALL ONE-DAY	3	3	3	14	9 *	-	-	-	-	-

BOWLING AVERAGES

	Overs	Mdns	Runs	Wkts	Avge	Best	5wI	10wM
NatWest Trophy	3	0	16	0	-	-	-	-
Other First-Class	12	3	28	0	-	-	-	-
Other One-Day	17.3	2	68	2	34.00	1-26	-	-
ALL FIRST-CLASS	12	3	28	0	-	-	-	-
ALL ONE-DAY	20.3	2	84	2	42.00	1-26	-	-

M.S.A. McEVOY - Suffolk

Opposition	Venue	Date	Batting	Fielding	Bowling

NATWEST TROPHY

Worcestershire	Bury St Ed's	June 27	55	

BATTING AVERAGES - Including fielding

	Matches	Inns	NO	Runs	HS	Avge	100s	50s	Ct	St
NatWest Trophy	1	1	0	55	55	55.00	-	1	-	-
ALL ONE-DAY	1	1	0	55	55	55.00	-	1	-	-

BOWLING AVERAGES
Did not bowl

S.M. McEWAN - Worcestershire

Opposition	Venue	Date	Batting		Fielding	Bowling

BRITANNIC ASSURANCE

Notts	Worcester	May 3	0		1Ct	2-26 & 3-57
Yorkshire	Worcester	June 2	54		1Ct	0-47 & 1-35
Surrey	The Oval	June 16	2			0-26 & 2-40
Sussex	Worcester	June 20				0-12
Middlesex	Lord's	June 30	27 *	& 7		2-51
Leicestershire	Leicester	Aug 4				3-62 & 1-37
Lancashire	Kid'minster	Aug 8				1-31 & 2-25
Hampshire	Worcester	Aug 11				0-40 & 3-38
Northants	Worcester	Aug 18	14		1Ct	1-39 & 1-11
Warwickshire	Worcester	Aug 23	12 *			1-49 & 2-11
Notts	Trent Bridge	Aug 29	6			0-76 & 1-41
Somerset	Taunton	Sept 12	30 *			0-116 & 1-39
Glamorgan	Worcester	Sept 18	11		1Ct	3-31 & 2-30

REFUGE ASSURANCE

Somerset	Taunton	April 22			1-49
Derbyshire	Derby	April 29	5		0-42
Notts	Worcester	May 6			2-32
Essex	Worcester	May 20		1Ct	
Warwickshire	Worcester	May 27			1-39
Yorkshire	Worcester	June 3	18 *		3-44
Surrey	The Oval	June 17	0		0-15
Sussex	Worcester	June 24			1-55
Middlesex	Lord's	July 1			0-33
Lancashire	Old Trafford	July 15			0-23
Leicestershire	Leicester	Aug 5			3-38
Hampshire	Worcester	Aug 12	3 *	1Ct	1-15
Northants	Worcester	Aug 19		1Ct	
Glamorgan	Swansea	Aug 26			1-52

NATWEST TROPHY

Suffolk	Bury St Ed's	June 27			0-15

BENSON & HEDGES CUP

Notts	Trent Bridge	June 13			2-53

OTHER FIRST-CLASS

MCC	Lord's	April 17			1Ct	2-101
New Zealand	Worcester	May 12	1 * &	0 *		3-49 & 1-69

OTHER ONE-DAY

Hampshire	Scarborough	Sept 2	0		0-35

BATTING AVERAGES - Including fielding

	Matches	Inns	NO	Runs	HS	Avge	100s	50s	Ct	St
Britannic Assurance	13	10	3	163	54	23.28	-	1	4	-
Refuge Assurance	14	4	2	26	18 *	13.00	-	-	3	-
NatWest Trophy	1	0	0	0	0		-	-	-	-
Benson & Hedges Cup	1	0	0	0	0		-	-	-	-
Other First-Class	2	2	2	1	1 *		-	-	1	-
Other One-Day	1	1	0	0	0	0.00	-	-	-	-
ALL FIRST-CLASS	15	12	5	164	54	23.42	-	1	5	-
ALL ONE-DAY	17	5	2	26	18 *	8.66	-	-	3	-

BOWLING AVERAGES

	Overs	Mdns	Runs	Wkts	Avge	Best	5wI	10wM
Britannic Assurance	310	61	970	32	30.31	3-31	-	-
Refuge Assurance	75.4	0	437	13	33.61	3-38	-	
NatWest Trophy	3	0	15	0		-	-	
Benson & Hedges Cup	11	0	53	2	26.50	2-53	-	
Other First-Class	65.2	14	219	6	36.50	3-49	-	
Other One-Day	8	0	35	0		-	-	
ALL FIRST-CLASS	375.2	75	1189	38	31.28	3-31	-	-
ALL ONE-DAY	97.4	0	540	15	36.00	3-38	-	-

PLAYER RECORDS

J. McGRADY - *Oxford University*

Opposition	Venue	Date	Batting	Fielding	Bowling
OTHER FIRST-CLASS					
Glamorgan	The Parks	April 14			
Somerset	The Parks	April 18			
Hampshire	The Parks	May 3	14	0Ct,1St	
Surrey	The Parks	May 16			
Leicestershire	The Parks	May 23	1		
Lancashire	The Parks	June 16		0Ct,1St	

BATTING AVERAGES - Including fielding

	Matches	Inns	NO	Runs	HS	Avge	100s	50s	Ct	St
Other First-Class	6	2	0	15	14	7.50	-	-	-	2
ALL FIRST-CLASS	6	2	0	15	14	7.50	-	-	-	2

BOWLING AVERAGES
Did not bowl

P.D. McKEOWN - *Lincolnshire*

Opposition	Venue	Date	Batting	Fielding	Bowling
NATWEST TROPHY					
Gloucs	Gloucester	June 27	3 *	1Ct	0-84

BATTING AVERAGES - Including fielding

	Matches	Inns	NO	Runs	HS	Avge	100s	50s	Ct	St
NatWest Trophy	1	1	1	3	3*	-	-	-	1	-
ALL ONE-DAY	1	1	1	3	3*	-	-	-	1	-

BOWLING AVERAGES

	Overs	Mdns	Runs	Wkts	Avge	Best	5wI	10wM
NatWest Trophy	12	1	84	0	-	-	-	-
ALL ONE-DAY	12	1	84	0	-	-	-	-

C.T. McKNIGHT - *Scotland*

Opposition	Venue	Date	Batting	Fielding	Bowling
OTHER FIRST-CLASS					
Ireland	Edinburgh	Aug 11	0		3-48 & 0-24
OTHER ONE-DAY					
India	Glasgow	July 14		1Ct	0-29

BATTING AVERAGES - Including fielding

	Matches	Inns	NO	Runs	HS	Avge	100s	50s	Ct	St
Other First-Class	1	1	0	0	0	0.00	-	-	-	-
Other One-Day	1	0	0	0	0	-	-	-	1	-
ALL FIRST-CLASS	1	1	0	0	0	0.00	-	-	-	-
ALL ONE-DAY	1	0	0	0	0	-	-	-	1	-

BOWLING AVERAGES

	Overs	Mdns	Runs	Wkts	Avge	Best	5wI	10wM
Other First-Class	23	5	72	3	24.00	3-48	-	-
Other One-Day	11	2	29	0	-	-	-	-
ALL FIRST-CLASS	23	5	72	3	24.00	3-48	-	-
ALL ONE-DAY	11	2	29	0	-	-	-	-

K.I. McLEOD - *League C.C. XI*

Opposition	Venue	Date	Batting	Fielding	Bowling
OTHER ONE-DAY					
India	Sunderland	June 28	46 *		1-44

BATTING AVERAGES - Including fielding

	Matches	Inns	NO	Runs	HS	Avge	100s	50s	Ct	St
Other One-Day	1	1	1	46	46 *	-	-	-	-	-
ALL ONE-DAY	1	1	1	46	46 *	-	-	-	-	-

BOWLING AVERAGES

	Overs	Mdns	Runs	Wkts	Avge	Best	5wI	10wM
Other One-Day	11	1	44	1	44.00	1-44	-	
ALL ONE-DAY	11	1	44	1	44.00	1-44	-	

K.T. MEDLYCOTT - *Surrey*

Opposition	Venue	Date	Batting	Fielding	Bowling
BRITANNIC ASSURANCE					
Sussex	Hove	April 26	29		0-67 & 2-101
Lancashire	The Oval	May 3	33		1-177
Hampshire	The Oval	May 19	30 * & 8	2Ct	0-47 & 1-84
Middlesex	Lord's	May 23	0	2Ct	4-91 & 4-65
Derbyshire	The Oval	June 6	6		4-14 & 0-21
Yorkshire	Harrogate	June 9		6	2-53 & 1-5
Worcestershire	The Oval	June 16		16 *	4-92 & 0-19
Notts	Trent Bridge	June 20		1Ct	7-92
Glamorgan	Cardiff	June 30		4 1Ct	4-77 & 0-19
Northants	The Oval	July 4			0-54
Warwickshire	The Oval	July 7	4 * & 23	1Ct	0-10 & 1-36
Sussex	Guildford	July 18	16	1Ct	5-121 & 2-61
Kent	Guildford	July 21	28		0-59 & 5-99
Gloucs	Cheltenham	July 28	14 * & 18 *	1Ct	2-82 & 1-97
Somerset	Weston	Aug 4	38		0-100 & 0-99
Leicestershire	The Oval	Aug 11	21 *	1Ct	1-44
Essex	Chelmsford	Aug 18	20 & 11 *	2Ct	0-27
Hampshire	Southampton	Aug 23	15		1-63
Lancashire	Blackpool	Aug 29			1-9
Middlesex	The Oval	Sept 12	5 & 44	1Ct	0-35
REFUGE ASSURANCE					
Sussex	Hove	April 29	17		0-30
Lancashire	The Oval	May 6		1Ct	1-39
Notts	Trent Bridge	May 20	2		0-35
Yorkshire	Hull	June 10			3-20
Worcestershire	The Oval	June 17		1Ct	2-33
Derbyshire	The Oval	June 24	4 *		1-37
Warwickshire	The Oval	July 8	27		3-43
Middlesex	The Oval	July 15	0 *		2-39
Kent	The Oval	July 22			2-40
Gloucs	Cheltenham	July 29	2	2Ct	3-47
Somerset	Weston	Aug 5			0-34
Leicestershire	The Oval	Aug 12	44 *		0-39
Hampshire	Southampton	Aug 26			0-49
NATWEST TROPHY					
Wiltshire	Trowbridge	June 27			0-27
Middlesex	Uxbridge	July 11	38		1-64
BENSON & HEDGES CUP					
Hampshire	The Oval	May 1			2-44
Combined U	The Parks	May 10			3-48
Yorkshire	The Oval	May 12		1Ct	0-53
Lancashire	Old Trafford	May 30	1		0-53
OTHER FIRST-CLASS					
Oxford U	The Parks	May 16		4	0-61 & 3-69
India	The Oval	Aug 1	2 * & 15 *	1Ct	3-102 & 0-55
For TCCB U25 XI					
India	Edgbaston	Aug 15			1-46 & 1-29
OTHER ONE-DAY					
Warwickshire	Harrogate	June 13	1	2Ct	1-40
Sri Lanka	The Oval	Sept 2	20	1Ct	0-42

BATTING AVERAGES - Including fielding

	Matches	Inns	NO	Runs	HS	Avge	100s	50s	Ct	St
Britannic Assurance	20	22	7	389	44	25.93	-	-	13	-
Refuge Assurance	13	7	3	96	44 *	24.00	-	-	4	-
NatWest Trophy	2	1	0	38	38	38.00	-	-	-	-
Benson & Hedges Cup	4	1	0	1	1	1.00	-	-	1	-
Other First-Class	3	3	2	21	15 *	21.00	-	-	1	-
Other One-Day	2	2	0	21	20	10.50	-	-	3	-

M — PLAYER RECORDS

ALL FIRST-CLASS	23	25	9	410	44		25.62	-	-	14	-
ALL ONE-DAY	21	11	3	156	44 *	19.50		-	-	8	-

BOWLING AVERAGES

	Overs	Mdns	Runs	Wkts	Avge	Best	5wI	10wM
Britannic Assurance	617.5	134	2020	53	38.11	7-92	3	
Refuge Assurance	93	1	485	17	28.52	3-20	-	
NatWest Trophy	24	1	91	1	91.00	1-64	-	
Benson & Hedges Cup	44	0	198	5	39.60	3-48	-	
Other First-Class	131	36	362	8	45.25	3-69	-	-
Other One-Day	19	0	82	1	82.00	1-40	-	
ALL FIRST-CLASS	748.5	170	2382	61	39.04	7-92	3	-
ALL ONE-DAY	180	2	856	24	35.66	3-20	-	

G.D. MENDIS - *Lancashire*

Opposition	Venue	Date	Batting			Fielding	Bowling
BRITANNIC ASSURANCE							
Worcestershire	Old Trafford	April 26	80	&	35 *		
Surrey	The Oval	May 3	102				
Derbyshire	Derby	May 15	90	&	4	2Ct	
Leicestershire	Old Trafford	May 19	113	&	82	1Ct	
Glamorgan	Colwyn Bay	May 26	90			1Ct	
Sussex	Horsham	June 2	9	&	11	2Ct	
Gloucs	Old Trafford	June 9	23				
Middlesex	Old Trafford	June 20	114			1Ct	
Hampshire	Old Trafford	June 23	37 *	&	23		
Derbyshire	Liverpool	July 7	7	&	25		
Warwickshire	Coventry	July 18	5	&	20 *	2Ct	
Essex	Colchester	July 21	9	&	20	1Ct	
Notts	Southport	July 25	180	&	21	2Ct	
Somerset	Old Trafford	July 28	29			1Ct	
Yorkshire	Headingley	Aug 4	54	&	10		
Worcestershire	Kid'minster	Aug 8	15	&	36		
Northants	Northampton	Aug 11	50	&	5		
Yorkshire	Old Trafford	Aug 18	13	&	15 *		
Surrey	Blackpool	Aug 29	94				
Notts	Trent Bridge	Sept 12	85	&	23 *	2Ct	
Warwickshire	Old Trafford	Sept 18	22 *				
REFUGE ASSURANCE							
Surrey	The Oval	May 6	45			1Ct	
Gloucs	Old Trafford	June 10	32			1Ct	
Hampshire	Old Trafford	June 24	1 *				
Derbyshire	Old Trafford	July 8	71				
Somerset	Old Trafford	July 29	7			1Ct	
Northants	Northampton	Aug 12	37			1Ct	
Warwickshire	Old Trafford	Aug 26	9				
NATWEST TROPHY							
Durham	Old Trafford	June 27	62 *				
Derbyshire	Derby	July 11	42				
Gloucs	Old Trafford	Aug 1	88				
Middlesex	Old Trafford	Aug 15	121 *				
Northants	Lord's	Sept 1	14				
BENSON & HEDGES CUP							
Surrey	Old Trafford	April 24	40				
Combined U	Fenner's	May 1	6			1Ct	
Hampshire	Old Trafford	May 8	9				
Yorkshire	Headingley	May 10	25				
Surrey	Old Trafford	May 30	9			1Ct	
Somerset	Old Trafford	June 13	37				
Worcestershire	Lord's	July 14	19				

BATTING AVERAGES - Including fielding

	Matches	Inns	NO	Runs	HS	Avge	100s	50s	Ct	St
Britannic Assurance	21	35	6	1551	180	53.48	4	8	15	-
Refuge Assurance	7	7	1	202	71	33.66	-	1	4	-
NatWest Trophy	5	5	2	327	121 *	109.00	1	2	-	-
Benson & Hedges Cup	7	7	0	145	40	20.71	-	-	2	-
ALL FIRST-CLASS	21	35	6	1551	180	53.48	4	8	15	-
ALL ONE-DAY	19	19	3	674	121 *	42.12	1	3	6	-

BOWLING AVERAGES
Did not bowl

T.A. MERRICK - *Kent*

Opposition	Venue	Date	Batting		Fielding	Bowling
BRITANNIC ASSURANCE						
Hampshire	Canterbury	April 26	0			1-83 & 1-24
Middlesex	Lord's	May 15	10 &	0		4-66 & 0-44
Notts	Tunbridge We	June 2	35 &	15		1-60 & 3-10
Warwickshire	Edgbaston	June 23	0 *			1-19
Hampshire	Bournemouth	Aug 29			0 *	2-62 & 0-8
REFUGE ASSURANCE						
Essex	Chelmsford	April 22				4-24
Hampshire	Canterbury	April 29				1-32
Middlesex	Folkestone	May 6		1 *		0-39
Glamorgan	Llanelli	May 13		8	1Ct	0-32
Yorkshire	Canterbury	May 20				3-22
Northants	Northampton	May 27				3-37
Somerset	Canterbury	June 10				2-26
Notts	Canterbury	June 17		12 *		1-26
Worcestershire	Canterbury	July 29		11	2Ct	1-38
Derbyshire	Chesterfield	Aug 5				0-43
BENSON & HEDGES CUP						
Worcestershire	Worcester	May 1		14		0-46
Warwickshire	Canterbury	May 8		1 *	1Ct	2-30
Gloucs	Canterbury	May 10				
OTHER FIRST-CLASS						
Cambridge U	Fenner's	June 20			1Ct	0-7 & 3-13
India	Canterbury	July 7		6		1-75 & 0-17

BATTING AVERAGES - Including fielding

	Matches	Inns	NO	Runs	HS	Avge	100s	50s	Ct	St
Britannic Assurance	5	7	2	60	35	12.00	-	-	1	-
Refuge Assurance	10	4	2	32	12 *	16.00	-	-	3	-
Benson & Hedges Cup	3	2	1	15	14	15.00	-	-	1	-
Other First-Class	2	1	0	6	6	6.00	-	-	1	-
ALL FIRST-CLASS	7	8	2	66	35	11.00	-	-	1	-
ALL ONE-DAY	13	6	3	47	14	15.66	-	-	4	-

BOWLING AVERAGES

	Overs	Mdns	Runs	Wkts	Avge	Best	5wI	10wM
Britannic Assurance	146.2	31	376	13	28.92	4-66	-	-
Refuge Assurance	74.3	3	319	15	21.26	4-24	-	
Benson & Hedges Cup	19.4	2	76	2	38.00	2-30	-	
Other First-Class	38.1	14	112	4	28.00	3-13	-	-
ALL FIRST-CLASS	184.3	45	488	17	28.70	4-66	-	-
ALL ONE-DAY	94.1	5	395	17	23.23	4-24	-	

R.P. MERRIMAN - *Dorset*

Opposition	Venue	Date	Batting	Fielding	Bowling
NATWEST TROPHY					
Glamorgan	Swansea	June 27	25		2-32

BATTING AVERAGES - Including fielding

	Matches	Inns	NO	Runs	HS	Avge	100s	50s	Ct	St
NatWest Trophy	1	1	0	25	25	25.00	-	-	-	-
ALL ONE-DAY	1	1	0	25	25	25.00	-	-	-	-

BOWLING AVERAGES

	Overs	Mdns	Runs	Wkts	Avge	Best	5wI	10wM
NatWest Trophy	3	0	32	2	16.00	2-32	-	
ALL ONE-DAY	3	0	32	2	16.00	2-32	-	

PLAYER RECORDS
M

W.G. MERRY - *Hertfordshire*

Opposition	Venue	Date	Batting	Fielding	Bowling
NATWEST TROPHY					
Warwickshire	St Albans	June 27	11		2-62

BATTING AVERAGES - Including fielding

	Matches	Inns	NO	Runs	HS	Avge	100s	50s	Ct	St
NatWest Trophy	1	1	0	11	11	11.00	-	-	-	-
ALL ONE-DAY	1	1	0	11	11	11.00	-	-	-	-

BOWLING AVERAGES

	Overs	Mdns	Runs	Wkts	Avge	Best	5wI	10wM
NatWest Trophy	11	0	62	2	31.00	2-62	-	
ALL ONE-DAY	11	0	62	2	31.00	2-62	-	

A.A. METCALFE - *Yorkshire*

Opposition	Venue	Date	Batting			Fielding	Bowling
BRITANNIC ASSURANCE							
Northants	Headingley	April 26	38	&	45		
Warwickshire	Edgbaston	May 3	33	&	24		
Derbyshire	Chesterfield	May 23	32	&	5	1Ct	
Hampshire	Headingley	May 26	22	&	35		
Worcestershire	Worcester	June 2	20	&	56 *		
Kent	Tunbridge We	June 6	0	&	14	1Ct	
Surrey	Harrogate	June 9	6	&	1		
Warwickshire	Sheffield	June 20	53	&	45		
Glamorgan	Cardiff	June 23	5	&	37		
Notts	Scarborough	July 4	75				
Northants	Northampton	July 7	48	&	79	2Ct	
Gloucs	Cheltenham	July 21	162	&	26		
Somerset	Scarborough	July 25	102	&	23	1Ct	0-10
Leicestershire	Sheffield	July 28	1	&	1		
Lancashire	Headingley	Aug 4	31	&	146	1Ct	
Sussex	Eastbourne	Aug 8	53			1Ct	
Essex	Middlesbr'gh	Aug 11	60	&	0		
Lancashire	Old Trafford	Aug 18	2	&	39		0-44
Middlesex	Headingley	Aug 23	26	&	26	2Ct	
Derbyshire	Scarborough	Sept 7	150 *	&	32	1Ct	0-34
Notts	Trent Bridge	Sept 18	194 *	&	107		
REFUGE ASSURANCE							
Notts	Trent Bridge	April 22	11				
Warwickshire	Edgbaston	May 6	56				
Derbyshire	Headingley	May 13	41				
Kent	Canterbury	May 20	32				
Hampshire	Headingley	May 27	0				
Worcestershire	Worcester	June 3	0			2Ct	
Surrey	Hull	June 10	16			2Ct	
Sussex	Hove	June 17	16				
Northants	Tring	July 8	55				
Somerset	Scarborough	July 15	14				
Gloucs	Cheltenham	July 22	0			1Ct	
Leicestershire	Sheffield	July 29	71			1Ct	
Lancashire	Scarborough	Aug 5	6				
Essex	Middlesbr'gh	Aug 12	1			2Ct	
Middlesex	Scarborough	Aug 26	84			1Ct	
NATWEST TROPHY							
Norfolk	Headingley	June 27	46 *				
Warwickshire	Headingley	July 11	127 *			1Ct	
Hampshire	Southampton	Aug 1	2				
BENSON & HEDGES CUP							
Hampshire	Southampton	April 24	36			2Ct	
Combined U	Headingley	May 8	11				
Lancashire	Headingley	May 10	28				
Surrey	The Oval	May 12	38				
OTHER FIRST-CLASS							
Zimbabwe	Headingley	May 16	49	&	30		
India	Headingley	June 30	40 *	&	74		
OTHER ONE-DAY							
Sussex	Harrogate	June 14	64				

Warwickshire	Harrogate	June 15	76	1Ct	
World XI	Scarborough	Sept 1	22		
Yorkshiremen	Scarborough	Sept 6	65		

BATTING AVERAGES - Including fielding

	Matches	Inns	NO	Runs	HS	Avge	100s	50s	Ct	St
Britannic Assurance	21	40	3	1854	194 *	50.10	6	6	10	-
Refuge Assurance	15	15	0	403	84	26.86	-	4	9	-
NatWest Trophy	3	3	2	175	127 *	175.00	1	-	1	-
Benson & Hedges Cup	4	4	0	113	38	28.25	-	-	2	-
Other First-Class	2	4	1	193	74	64.33	-	1	-	-
Other One-Day	4	4	0	227	76	56.75	-	3	1	-
ALL FIRST-CLASS	23	44	4	2047	194 *	51.17	6	7	10	-
ALL ONE-DAY	26	26	2	918	127 *	38.25	1	7	13	-

BOWLING AVERAGES

	Overs	Mdns	Runs	Wkts	Avge	Best	5wI	10wM
Britannic Assurance	9.1	0	88	0	-	-	-	-
Refuge Assurance								
NatWest Trophy								
Benson & Hedges Cup								
Other First-Class								
Other One-Day								
ALL FIRST-CLASS	9.1	0	88	0	-	-	-	-
ALL ONE-DAY								

C.P. METSON - *Glamorgan*

Opposition	Venue	Date	Batting			Fielding	Bowling
BRITANNIC ASSURANCE							
Leicestershire	Cardiff	April 26	8	&	5	2Ct	
Somerset	Cardiff	May 3			4 *		
Gloucs	Bristol	May 15	0	&	4	7Ct	
Sussex	Hove	May 19				3Ct	
Kent	Swansea	May 23			21		
Lancashire	Colwyn Bay	May 26	34			1Ct	
Northants	Northampton	June 9	0			5Ct	
Hampshire	Southampton	June 16			14 *	6Ct	
Somerset	Bath	June 20				1Ct	
Yorkshire	Cardiff	June 23	14			1Ct	
Surrey	Cardiff	June 30	21			1Ct	
Gloucs	Swansea	July 4	30				
Leicestershire	Hinckley	July 7	2				
Worcestershire	Abergavenny	July 21			12 *	1Ct	
Warwickshire	Swansea	July 25	7			1Ct	
Middlesex	Lord's	Aug 4	4	&	0	5Ct	
Essex	Southend	Aug 8	15 *			4Ct	
Notts	Worksop	Aug 11	29			6Ct	
Derbyshire	Cardiff	Aug 29	22			1Ct	
Hampshire	Pontypridd	Sept 7	0	&	15	2Ct	
Warwickshire	Edgbaston	Sept 12	23	&	4	7Ct	
Worcestershire	Worcester	Sept 18	10	&	4	4Ct	
REFUGE ASSURANCE							
Gloucs	Bristol	April 22	0 *				
Leicestershire	Cardiff	April 29	11				
Kent	Llanelli	May 13				2Ct	
Lancashire	Colwyn Bay	May 27	5 *			2Ct	
Essex	Ilford	June 3	1				
Northants	Northampton	June 10				2Ct	
Hampshire	Bournemouth	June 17	30 *			1Ct	
Surrey	Cardiff	July 1					
Warwickshire	Edgbaston	July 15				1Ct	
Somerset	Neath	July 22	10				
Derbyshire	Swansea	July 29	9			1Ct	
Middlesex	Lord's	Aug 5	2 *				
Notts	Trent Bridge	Aug 12	17 *			1Ct	
Worcestershire	Swansea	Aug 26	10			0Ct,2St	
NATWEST TROPHY							
Dorset	Swansea	June 27				2Ct	
Sussex	Cardiff	July 11					
Middlesex	Lord's	Aug 1	9				
BENSON & HEDGES CUP							
Warwickshire	Edgbaston	April 24	20				
Gloucs	Cardiff	May 1	14				
Worcestershire	Worcester	May 8	14 *			2Ct	
Kent	Swansea	May 12	23			1Ct	

M PLAYER RECORDS

Worcestershire Worcester	May 30	7	

OTHER FIRST-CLASS

India	Swansea	Aug 18	50 *	1Ct

BATTING AVERAGES - Including fielding

	Matches	Inns	NO	Runs	HS	Avge	100s	50s	Ct	St
Britannic Assurance	22	26	4	302	34	13.72	-	-	58	-
Refuge Assurance	14	10	5	95	30 *	19.00	-	-	10	2
NatWest Trophy	3	1	0	9	9	9.00	-	-	2	-
Benson & Hedges Cup	5	5	1	78	23	19.50	-	-	3	-
Other First-Class	1	1	1	50	50 *	-	-	1	1	-
ALL FIRST-CLASS	23	27	5	352	50 *	16.00	-	1	59	-
ALL ONE-DAY	22	16	6	182	30 *	18.20	-	-	15	2

BOWLING AVERAGES

Did not bowl

T.C. MIDDLETON - Hampshire

Opposition	Venue	Date	Batting			Fielding	Bowling

BRITANNIC ASSURANCE

Kent	Canterbury	April 26	127	&	23	2Ct	
Surrey	The Oval	May 19	1	&	20		
Essex	Southampton	May 23	104 *	&	11		
Somerset	Basingstoke	June 6	90	&	1		0-10
Gloucs	Gloucester	June 20					
Lancashire	Old Trafford	June 23	20	&	34 *	1Ct	
Notts	Portsmouth	July 18	37	&	5		
Derbyshire	Portsmouth	July 21	6	&	59		
Sussex	Arundel	July 25	50	&	28		
Warwickshire	Edgbaston	July 28	10	&	64	1Ct	
Northants	Bournemouth	Aug 4	123				
Middlesex	Bournemouth	Aug 8	31				
Worcestershire	Worcester	Aug 11	117 *	&	2	1Ct	
Surrey	Southampton	Aug 23	25	&	33	1Ct	
Kent	Bournemouth	Aug 29	4	&	104	1Ct	
Gloucs	Southampton	Sept 18	5	&	82	1Ct	

REFUGE ASSURANCE

Essex	Southampton	July 8			
Surrey	Southampton	Aug 26	72	1Ct	

OTHER FIRST-CLASS

India	Southampton	July 4			
Sri Lanka	Southampton	Sept 12	22	1Ct	0-19

OTHER ONE-DAY

Worcestershire	Scarborough	Sept 2	39	
Essex	Scarborough	Sept 4	53	1Ct

BATTING AVERAGES - Including fielding

	Matches	Inns	NO	Runs	HS	Avge	100s	50s	Ct	St
Britannic Assurance	16	28	3	1216	127	48.64	5	5	8	-
Refuge Assurance	2	1	0	72	72	72.00	-	1	1	-
Other First-Class	2	1	0	22	22	22.00	-	-	1	-
Other One-Day	2	2	0	92	53	46.00	-	1	1	-
ALL FIRST-CLASS	18	29	3	1238	127	47.61	5	5	9	-
ALL ONE-DAY	4	3	0	164	72	54.66	-	2	2	-

BOWLING AVERAGES

	Overs	Mdns	Runs	Wkts	Avge	Best	5wI	10wM
Britannic Assurance	1	0	10	0	-	-	-	-
Refuge Assurance								
Other First-Class	4	0	19	0	-	-	-	-
Other One-Day								
ALL FIRST-CLASS	5	0	29	0	-	-	-	-
ALL ONE-DAY								

G.W. MIKE - Nottinghamshire

Opposition	Venue	Date	Batting		Fielding	Bowling

BRITANNIC ASSURANCE

Derbyshire	Derby	May 26	11	& 7	1Ct	1-59 & 0-9
Middlesex	Trent Bridge	July 28	9		1Ct	0-12 & 0-46
Lancashire	Trent Bridge	Sept 12	18 *	& 0	1Ct	1-80 & 0-24

REFUGE ASSURANCE

Sussex	Trent Bridge	July 8	13		3-42
Hampshire	Southampton	July 15	10		0-26
Warwickshire	Edgbaston	July 22	4		1-54
Northants	Trent Bridge	July 29			2-41
Essex	Southend	Aug 5		1Ct	1-68
Glamorgan	Trent Bridge	Aug 12			2-38
Gloucs	Trent Bridge	Aug 19			3-30
Derbyshire	Derby	Sept 5	6	1Ct	0-48

OTHER FIRST-CLASS

Oxford U	The Parks	June 6		1Ct	0-33

BATTING AVERAGES - Including fielding

	Matches	Inns	NO	Runs	HS	Avge	100s	50s	Ct	St
Britannic Assurance	3	5	1	45	18 *	11.25	-	-	3	-
Refuge Assurance	8	4	0	33	13	8.25	-	-	2	-
Other First-Class	1	0	0	0	0	-	-	-	1	-
ALL FIRST-CLASS	4	5	1	45	18 *	11.25	-	-	4	-
ALL ONE-DAY	8	4	0	33	13	8.25	-	-	2	-

BOWLING AVERAGES

	Overs	Mdns	Runs	Wkts	Avge	Best	5wI	10wM
Britannic Assurance	54.2	9	230	2	115.00	1-59		
Refuge Assurance	55	1	347	12	28.91	3-30	-	
Other First-Class	6	1	33	0	-	-	-	-
ALL FIRST-CLASS	60.2	10	263	2	131.50	1-59	-	-
ALL ONE-DAY	55	1	347	12	28.91	3-30	-	

E.T. MILBURN - Gloucestershire

Opposition	Venue	Date	Batting		Fielding	Bowling

BRITANNIC ASSURANCE

Hampshire	Southampton	Sept 18	0	& 3 *		0-10 & 0-24

REFUGE ASSURANCE

Glamorgan	Bristol	April 22	5 *		0-11
Hampshire	Southampton	May 6			0-25
Surrey	Cheltenham	July 29			2-34
Kent	Bristol	Aug 12			0-24
Notts	Trent Bridge	Aug 19			0-15
Northants	Northampton	Aug 26	4 *	1Ct	1-54

BENSON & HEDGES CUP

Worcestershire	Bristol	April 24			1-23

OTHER FIRST-CLASS

India	Bristol	Aug 4	35	& 11 *		3-43 & 0-73

BATTING AVERAGES - Including fielding

	Matches	Inns	NO	Runs	HS	Avge	100s	50s	Ct	St
Britannic Assurance	1	2	1	3	3 *	3.00	-	-	-	-
Refuge Assurance	6	2	2	9	5 *	-	-	-	1	-
Benson & Hedges Cup	1	0	0	0	0	-	-	-	-	-
Other First-Class	1	2	1	46	35	46.00	-	-	-	-
ALL FIRST-CLASS	2	4	2	49	35	24.50	-	-	-	-
ALL ONE-DAY	7	2	2	9	5 *	-	-	-	1	-

BOWLING AVERAGES

	Overs	Mdns	Runs	Wkts	Avge	Best	5wI	10wM
Britannic Assurance	7	1	34	0	-	-	-	-
Refuge Assurance	24	0	163	3	54.33	2-34	-	-
Benson & Hedges Cup	5	1	23	1	23.00	1-23	-	-
Other First-Class	25.3	3	116	3	38.66	3-43	-	-
ALL FIRST-CLASS	32.3	4	150	3	50.00	3-43	-	-
ALL ONE-DAY	29	1	186	4	46.50	2-34	-	

PLATER RECORDS

PLAYER RECORDS | M

A. MILDENHALL - *Wiltshire*

Opposition	Venue	Date	Batting	Fielding	Bowling
NATWEST TROPHY					
Surrey	Trowbridge	June 27	3		1-32

BATTING AVERAGES - Including fielding

	Matches	Inns	NO	Runs	HS	Avge	100s	50s	Ct	St
NatWest Trophy	1	1	0	3	3	3.00	-	-	-	-
ALL ONE-DAY	1	1	0	3	3	3.00	-	-	-	-

BOWLING AVERAGES

	Overs	Mdns	Runs	Wkts	Avge	Best	5wI	10wM
NatWest Trophy	8	2	32	1	32.00	1-32	-	
ALL ONE-DAY	8	2	32	1	32.00	1-32	-	

G. MILLER - *Derbyshire*

Opposition	Venue	Date	Batting	Fielding	Bowling
BRITANNIC ASSURANCE					
Notts	Trent Bridge	April 26	10	1Ct	1-84 & 1-60
Lancashire	Derby	May 15	3 * & 1		1-111 & 0-45
Somerset	Taunton	May 19			1-69 & 3-57
Yorkshire	Chesterfield	May 23	47 *		0-38 & 6-45
Surrey	The Oval	June 6	10 *		1-13 & 0-30
Warwickshire	Derby	June 16		1Ct	0-11 & 0-71
Leicestershire	Leicester	June 20	1	1Ct	2-98
Lancashire	Liverpool	July 7			2-32 & 0-26
Essex	Colchester	July 18	24 * & 18 *		3-113
Northants	Chesterfield	Aug 8	36 & 6 *	1Ct	1-108 & 2-62
Middlesex	Derby	Aug 18	1 & 32 *		3-31 & 3-21
Essex	Derby	Aug 23	19		
Yorkshire	Scarborough	Sept 7			0-92 & 1-68
REFUGE ASSURANCE					
Sussex	Hove	April 22			0-38
Worcestershire	Derby	April 29	14 *		2-22
Somerset	Taunton	May 20			1-37
Notts	Derby	June 10			0-34
Warwickshire	Derby	June 17			0-38
Surrey	The Oval	June 24	2	1Ct	1-39
Gloucs	Derby	July 1			0-26
Lancashire	Old Trafford	July 8			1-50
Hampshire	Portsmouth	July 22			0-54
Kent	Chesterfield	Aug 5			1-59
NATWEST TROPHY					
Shropshire	Chesterfield	June 27			0-31
Lancashire	Derby	July 11	0	1Ct	1-56
BENSON & HEDGES CUP					
Sussex	Derby	April 24		1Ct	0-42
Somerset	Taunton	May 1			1-46
OTHER FIRST-CLASS					
Cambridge U	Fenner's	April 18	25 *	3Ct	1-9 & 3-14
OTHER ONE-DAY					
India	Chesterfield	July 16			4-46

BATTING AVERAGES - Including fielding

	Matches	Inns	NO	Runs	HS	Avge	100s	50s	Ct	St
Britannic Assurance	13	13	7	208	47 *	34.66	-	-	4	-
Refuge Assurance	10	2	1	16	14 *	16.00	-	-	1	-
NatWest Trophy	2	1	0	0	0	0.00	-	-	1	-
Benson & Hedges Cup	2	0	0	0	0	-	-	-	1	-
Other First-Class	1	1	1	25	25 *	-	-	-	3	-
Other One-Day	1	0	0	0	0	-	-	-	-	-
ALL FIRST-CLASS	14	14	8	233	47 *	38.83	-	-	7	-
ALL ONE-DAY	15	3	1	16	14 *	8.00	-	-	3	-

BOWLING AVERAGES

	Overs	Mdns	Runs	Wkts	Avge	Best	5wI	10wM
Britannic Assurance	427.2	94	1285	31	41.45	6-45	1	-
Refuge Assurance	72	2	397	6	66.16	2-22	-	

NatWest Trophy	22	1	87	1	87.00	1-56	-	
Benson & Hedges Cup	22	0	88	1	88.00	1-46	-	
Other First-Class	33.4	20	23	4	5.75	3-14	-	-
Other One-Day	11	0	46	4	11.50	4-46	-	
ALL FIRST-CLASS	461	114	1308	35	37.37	6-45	1	-
ALL ONE-DAY	127	3	618	12	51.50	4-46	-	

J.P. MILLMOW - *New Zealand*

Opposition	Venue	Date	Batting	Fielding	Bowling
TEXACO TROPHY					
England	Headingley	May 23		1Ct	0-65
England	The Oval	May 25			0-47
OTHER FIRST-CLASS					
Worcestershire	Worcester	May 12	2 *		2-59 & 3-66
Somerset	Taunton	May 16		1Ct	0-55 & 1-35
Warwickshire	Edgbaston	May 30			1-64 & 2-47
Derbyshire	Derby	June 2			0-13 & 1-36
Northants	Northampton	June 16		1Ct	1-16
OTHER ONE-DAY					
D of Norfolk	Arundel	May 6			2-55
MCC	Lord's	May 7			1-43
Ireland	Downpatrick	May 9			3-28
Leicestershire	Leicester	June 14	2 *		1-28

BATTING AVERAGES - Including fielding

	Matches	Inns	NO	Runs	HS	Avge	100s	50s	Ct	St
Texaco Trophy	2	0	0	0	0	-	-	-	1	-
Other First-Class	5	1	1	2	2 *	-	-	-	2	-
Other One-Day	4	1	1	2	2 *	-	-	-	-	-
ALL FIRST-CLASS	5	1	1	2	2 *	-	-	-	2	-
ALL ONE-DAY	6	1	1	2	2 *	-	-	-	1	-

BOWLING AVERAGES

	Overs	Mdns	Runs	Wkts	Avge	Best	5wI	10wM
Texaco Trophy	20	1	112	0	-	-	-	
Other First-Class	105	14	391	11	35.54	3-66	-	-
Other One-Day	42	7	154	7	22.00	3-28	-	
ALL FIRST-CLASS	105	14	391	11	35.54	3-66	-	-
ALL ONE-DAY	62	8	266	7	38.00	3-28	-	

D.J. MILLNS - *Leicestershire*

Opposition	Venue	Date	Batting	Fielding	Bowling
BRITANNIC ASSURANCE					
Somerset	Leicester	May 26		1 *	2-57
Northants	Northampton	June 6	1		0-19
Kent	Dartford	Aug 8	0 * & 10 *	2Ct	
Surrey	The Oval	Aug 11	1 & 4		2-97
Warwickshire	Edgbaston	Aug 18	4		2-22 & 0-39
Kent	Leicester	Aug 23	0 *		3-37 & 3-88
Sussex	Leicester	Aug 29		1	2-67 & 4-48
Northants	Leicester	Sept 12	1 *	1Ct	6-63 & 1-31
REFUGE ASSURANCE					
Somerset	Leicester	May 27			2-71
Worcestershire	Leicester	Aug 5			1-22
Surrey	The Oval	Aug 12	0	2Ct	1-47
Warwickshire	Edgbaston	Aug 19			
Kent	Leicester	Aug 26			2-47
OTHER FIRST-CLASS					
Oxford U	The Parks	May 23			5-47 & 1-47

BATTING AVERAGES - Including fielding

	Matches	Inns	NO	Runs	HS	Avge	100s	50s	Ct	St
Britannic Assurance	8	10	5	23	10 *	4.60	-	-	3	-
Refuge Assurance	5	1	0	0	0	0.00	-	-	2	-
Other First-Class	1	0	0	0	0					
ALL FIRST-CLASS	9	10	5	23	10 *	4.60	-	-	3	-

M   PLAYER RECORDS

ALL ONE-DAY	5	1	0	0	0.00	-	-	2	-

BOWLING AVERAGES

	Overs	Mdns	Runs	Wkts	Avge	Best	5wI	10wM
Britannic Assurance	164.1	20	568	25	22.72	6-63	1	-
Refuge Assurance	29	2	187	6	31.16	2-47	-	
Other First-Class	42.3	16	94	6	15.66	5-47	1	-
ALL FIRST-CLASS	206.4	36	662	31	21.35	6-63	2	-
ALL ONE-DAY	29	2	187	6	31.16	2-47	-	

J.D. MOIR - Scotland

Opposition	Venue	Date	Batting	Fielding	Bowling
NATWEST TROPHY					
Essex	Chelmsford	June 27	4 *		0-34
BENSON & HEDGES CUP					
Essex	Glasgow	May 1	5		0-50
Notts	Glasgow	May 8			1-43
Northants	Northampton	May 10	3 *		2-51
Leicestershire	Leicester	May 12	7 *		1-35
OTHER FIRST-CLASS					
Ireland	Edinburgh	Aug 11	12	1Ct	1-76
OTHER ONE-DAY					
India	Glasgow	July 14			0-34

BATTING AVERAGES - Including fielding

	Matches	Inns	NO	Runs	HS	Avge	100s	50s	Ct	St
NatWest Trophy	1	1	1	4	4 *	-	-	-	-	-
Benson & Hedges Cup	4	3	2	15	7 *	15.00	-	-	-	-
Other First-Class	1	1	0	12	12	12.00	-	-	1	-
Other One-Day	1	0	0	0	0	-	-	-	-	-
ALL FIRST-CLASS	1	1	0	12	12	12.00	-	-	1	-
ALL ONE-DAY	6	4	3	19	7 *	19.00	-	-	-	-

BOWLING AVERAGES

	Overs	Mdns	Runs	Wkts	Avge	Best	5wI	10wM
NatWest Trophy	10	3	34	0	-	-	-	
Benson & Hedges Cup	44	7	179	4	44.75	2-51	-	
Other First-Class	26.3	8	76	1	76.00	1-76	-	-
Other One-Day	9	1	34	0	-	-	-	
ALL FIRST-CLASS	26.3	8	76	1	76.00	1-76	-	-
ALL ONE-DAY	63	11	247	4	61.75	2-51	-	

A.J. MOLES - Warwickshire

Opposition	Venue	Date	Batting	Fielding	Bowling
BRITANNIC ASSURANCE					
Yorkshire	Edgbaston	May 3	6 & 32	2Ct	
Northants	Northampton	May 15	13	2Ct	
Notts	Edgbaston	May 19	13 & 35	1Ct	
Worcestershire	Edgbaston	May 26	76 & 56		
Northants	Edgbaston	June 2	40 & 13		
Middlesex	Lord's	June 6	128 * & 65 *		
Essex	Edgbaston	June 9	14 * & 97		
Derbyshire	Derby	June 16	70 * & 4		0-19
Yorkshire	Sheffield	June 20	21 & 60 *	1Ct	
Kent	Edgbaston	June 23	12 & 11		
Somerset	Taunton	July 4	14 & 6		2-56
Surrey	The Oval	July 7	16 & 1		
Lancashire	Coventry	July 18	31 & 100 *		
Glamorgan	Swansea	July 25	224 * & 83 *		
Hampshire	Edgbaston	July 28	24 & 36		0-6
Sussex	Eastbourne	Aug 4	58 & 39		
Gloucs	Bristol	Aug 8	94 & 12		0-52
Leicestershire	Edgbaston	Aug 18	5 & 30	2Ct	
Worcestershire	Worcester	Aug 23	59 & 8	1Ct	
Somerset	Edgbaston	Sept 7	2 & 44	2Ct	
Glamorgan	Edgbaston	Sept 12	0 & 8	1Ct	
Lancashire	Old Trafford	Sept 18	9		

REFUGE ASSURANCE				
Derbyshire	Derby	June 17	81	1Ct
Kent	Edgbaston	June 24	24	
Hampshire	Edgbaston	July 29	14	
Sussex	Eastbourne	Aug 5	3	
Somerset	Weston	Aug 12	37	
Leicestershire	Edgbaston	Aug 19		
Lancashire	Old Trafford	Aug 26	70	
NATWEST TROPHY				
Hertfordshire	St Albans	June 27	60	2Ct
Yorkshire	Headingley	July 11	27	
BENSON & HEDGES CUP				
Glamorgan	Edgbaston	April 24	52	
Gloucs	Bristol	May 12	57	
OTHER FIRST-CLASS				
Cambridge U	Fenner's	April 26	1 & 29	
Sri Lanka	Edgbastpn	Aug 29	117 & 38	
OTHER ONE-DAY				
Surrey	Harrogate	June 13	51	
Yorkshire	Harrogate	June 15	102 *	

BATTING AVERAGES - Including fielding

	Matches	Inns	NO	Runs	HS	Avge	100s	50s	Ct	St
Britannic Assurance	22	42	8	1669	224 *	49.08	3	10	12	-
Refuge Assurance	7	6	0	229	81	38.16	-	2	1	-
NatWest Trophy	2	2	0	87	60	43.50	-	1	2	-
Benson & Hedges Cup	2	2	0	109	57	54.50	-	2	-	-
Other First-Class	2	4	0	185	117	46.25	1	-	-	-
Other One-Day	2	2	1	153	102 *	153.00	1	1	-	-
ALL FIRST-CLASS	24	46	8	1854	224 *	48.78	4	10	12	-
ALL ONE-DAY	13	12	1	578	102 *	52.54	1	6	3	-

BOWLING AVERAGES

	Overs	Mdns	Runs	Wkts	Avge	Best	5wI	10wM
Britannic Assurance	22	2	133	2	66.50	2-56	-	-
Refuge Assurance								
NatWest Trophy								
Benson & Hedges Cup								
Other First-Class								
Other One-Day								
ALL FIRST-CLASS	22	2	133	2	66.50	2-56	-	-
ALL ONE-DAY								

N.R. MONGIA - India

Opposition	Venue	Date	Batting	Fielding	Bowling
OTHER FIRST-CLASS					
Hampshire	Southampton	July 4	14 *		
Min Counties	Trowbridge	July 11	43 *	2Ct,1St	
Leicestershire	Leicester	July 21	63 *	1Ct	
Surrey	The Oval	Aug 1	10 & 41	2Ct	
Gloucs	Bristol	Aug 4	1	3Ct	
TCCB U25 XI	Edgbaston	Aug 15	1 * & 11	1Ct,1St	
Glamorgan	Swansea	Aug 18	60		
World XI	Scarborough	Aug 29	10 & 15	0Ct,1St	

BATTING AVERAGES - Including fielding

	Matches	Inns	NO	Runs	HS	Avge	100s	50s	Ct	St
Other First-Class	8	11	4	269	63 *	38.42	-	2	9	3
ALL FIRST-CLASS	8	11	4	269	63 *	38.42	-	2	9	3

BOWLING AVERAGES
Did not bowl

T.M. MOODY - Warwickshire

Opposition	Venue	Date	Batting	Fielding	Bowling
BRITANNIC ASSURANCE					
Derbyshire	Derby	June 16	168		1-43

PLAYER RECORDS

M

BRITANNIC ASSURANCE (continued)

Lancashire	Coventry	July 18	30 & 96		0-25
Glamorgan	Swansea	July 25	40 & 103*	2Ct	
Hampshire	Edgbaston	July 28	48 & 101*	1Ct	0-23
Sussex	Eastbourne	Aug 4	110		1-7
Leicestershire	Edgbaston	Aug 18	26 & 117	1Ct	1-36
Worcestershire	Worcester	Aug 23	21 & 6		0-11

REFUGE ASSURANCE
Northants	Edgbaston	April 29	56		2-42
Yorkshire	Edgbaston	May 6	51*		1-38
Gloucs	Moreton-in-M	May 20	1		0-33
Worcestershire	Worcester	May 27	29		
Middlesex	Lord's	June 3	17		
Essex	Edgbaston	June 10	54		0-18
Derbyshire	Derby	June 17	45		1-38
Kent	Edgbaston	June 24	29	1Ct	1-27
Surrey	The Oval	July 8	3	1Ct	0-27
Glamorgan	Edgbaston	July 15	4	1Ct	0-6
Notts	Edgbaston	July 22	7	1Ct	
Hampshire	Edgbaston	July 29	5		
Sussex	Eastbourne	Aug 5	64		1-31
Leicestershire	Edgbaston	Aug 19			0-23
Lancashire	Old Trafford	Aug 26	17	1Ct	0-32

NATWEST TROPHY
Hertfordshire	St Albans	June 27	58	2Ct	1-7
Yorkshire	Headingley	July 11	51		0-34

BENSON & HEDGES CUP
Kent	Canterbury	May 8	33		0-50
Worcestershire	Edgbaston	May 10	41		0-29
Gloucs	Bristol	May 12	16		0-73

OTHER FIRST-CLASS
Cambridge U	Fenner's	April 26	147		0-33 & 0-6
New Zealand	Edgbaston	May 30	44 & 106		0-28

OTHER ONE-DAY
Surrey	Harrogate	June 13	31	1Ct	3-49
Yorkshire	Harrogate	June 15	67	2Ct	0-15
For Rest of World					
England XI	Jesmond	Aug 2	27		0-28
England XI	Jesmond	Aug 3		1Ct	2-23

BATTING AVERAGES - Including fielding
	Matches	Inns	NO	Runs	HS	Avge	100s	50s	Ct	St
Britannic Assurance	7	12	2	866	168	86.60	5	1	4	-
Refuge Assurance	15	14	1	382	64	29.38	-	4	5	-
NatWest Trophy	2	2	0	109	58	54.50	-	2	2	-
Benson & Hedges Cup	3	3	0	90	41	30.00	-	-	-	-
Other First-Class	2	3	0	297	147	99.00	2	-	-	-
Other One-Day	4	3	0	125	67	41.66	-	1	4	-
ALL FIRST-CLASS	9	15	2	1163	168	89.46	7	1	4	-
ALL ONE-DAY	24	22	1	706	67	33.61	-	7	11	-

BOWLING AVERAGES
	Overs	Mdns	Runs	Wkts	Avge	Best	5wI	10wM
Britannic Assurance	38	7	145	3	48.33	1-7	-	-
Refuge Assurance	55.3	2	315	6	52.50	2-42	-	-
NatWest Trophy	10.1	0	41	1	41.00	1-7	-	-
Benson & Hedges Cup	25	1	152	0	-	-	-	-
Other First-Class	21	8	67	0	-	-	-	-
Other One-Day	26	4	115	5	23.00	3-49	-	-
ALL FIRST-CLASS	59	15	212	3	70.66	1-7	-	-
ALL ONE-DAY	116.4	7	623	12	51.91	3-49		-

P. MOORES - *Sussex*

Opposition	Venue	Date	Batting	Fielding	Bowling

BRITANNIC ASSURANCE
Surrey	Hove	April 26	1 & 30		
Kent	Folkestone	May 3	0 & 46	4Ct	0-8
Hampshire	Southampton	May 15	7 & 5	2Ct,1St	
Glamorgan	Hove	May 19	3 & 106*	3Ct	
Somerset	Taunton	May 23	1	1Ct	
Lancashire	Horsham	June 2	28 & 2	3Ct	
Gloucs	Hove	June 16	6	2Ct,1St	
Worcestershire	Worcester	June 20		1Ct,2St	
Derbyshire	Hove	July 4	13	2Ct,1St	

BRITANNIC ASSURANCE (continued)

Notts	Trent Bridge	July 7	22 & 7*	3Ct	
Surrey	Guildford	July 18	24		
Northants	Northampton	July 21	10 & 8	1Ct	
Hampshire	Arundel	July 25	61	2Ct,2St	
Essex	Chelmsford	July 28	27 & 28	2Ct	
Warwickshire	Eastbourne	Aug 4	10 & 0	4Ct	
Yorkshire	Eastbourne	Aug 8	10 & 2	1Ct	
Middlesex	Lord's	Aug 11	49	1Ct,1St	
Kent	Hove	Aug 18	23 & 1*	2Ct	
Somerset	Hove	Aug 23	8 & 38	5Ct	
Leicestershire	Leicester	Aug 29	18	2Ct,2St	
Gloucs	Bristol	Sept 12	0 & 72	4Ct	
Middlesex	Hove	Sept 18	4 & 10	1Ct	

REFUGE ASSURANCE
Derbyshire	Hove	April 22	0	1Ct	
Surrey	Hove	April 29	0	2Ct	
Glamorgan	Hove	May 20			
Leicestershire	Leicester	June 10	17*	1Ct	
Yorkshire	Hove	June 17	8	3Ct	
Worcestershire	Worcester	June 24	13		
Hampshire	Hove	July 1		1Ct,1St	
Notts	Trent Bridge	July 8	10	1Ct	
Gloucs	Swindon	July 15	4*	1Ct,2St	
Northants	Well'borough	July 22	6*		
Essex	Chelmsford	July 29	2*	1Ct	
Warwickshire	Eastbourne	Aug 5	6	1Ct,1St	
Middlesex	Lord's	Aug 12			
Somerset	Hove	Aug 26	1	2Ct	

NATWEST TROPHY
Ireland	Downpatrick	June 27		2Ct	
Glamorgan	Cardiff	July 11	0	0Ct,1St	

BENSON & HEDGES CUP
Derbyshire	Derby	April 24		0Ct,1St	
Min Counties	Marlow	May 1	41		
Middlesex	Hove	May 8	76	1Ct	
Somerset	Hove	May 12	13		

OTHER FIRST-CLASS
New Zealand	Hove	May 26		1Ct	
Cambridge U	Hove	June 30		3Ct	
Sri Lanka	Hove	Sept 5	14*	3Ct	

OTHER ONE-DAY
Zimbabwe	Hove	May 13	39		
Yorkshire	Harrogate	June 14	40		
Kent	Hove	Sept 2	2	2Ct,3St	

BATTING AVERAGES - Including fielding
	Matches	Inns	NO	Runs	HS	Avge	100s	50s	Ct	St
Britannic Assurance	22	35	3	680	106*	21.25	1	2	46	10
Refuge Assurance	14	11	4	67	17*	9.57	-	-	14	4
NatWest Trophy	2	1	0	0	0	0.00	-	-	2	1
Benson & Hedges Cup	4	3	0	130	76	43.33	-	1	1	1
Other First-Class	3	1	1	14	14*	-	-	-	7	-
Other One-Day	3	3	0	81	40	27.00	-	-	2	3
ALL FIRST-CLASS	25	36	4	694	106*	21.68	1	2	53	10
ALL ONE-DAY	23	18	4	278	76	19.85	-	1	19	9

BOWLING AVERAGES
	Overs	Mdns	Runs	Wkts	Avge	Best	5wI	10wM
Britannic Assurance	2	1	8	0	-	-	-	-
Refuge Assurance								
NatWest Trophy								
Benson & Hedges Cup								
Other First-Class								
Other One-Day								
ALL FIRST-CLASS	2	1	8	0	-	-	-	-
ALL ONE-DAY								

K.S. MORE - *India*

Opposition	Venue	Date	Batting	Fielding	Bowling

CORNHILL TEST MATCHES
England	Lord's	July 26	8 & 16		
England	Old Trafford	Aug 9	6	4Ct	
England	The Oval	Aug 23	61*	4Ct	

M — PLAYER RECORDS

TEXACO TROPHY

England	Headingley	July 18		1Ct
England	Trent Bridge	July 20		1Ct

OTHER FIRST-CLASS

Yorkshire	Headingley	June 30					
Kent	Canterbury	July 7	32	&	27	1Ct	
Surrey	The Oval	Aug 1	12	&	12 *	0Ct,1St	
Gloucs	Bristol	Aug 4	95			3Ct	
Glamorgan	Swansea	Aug 18	8			5Ct	
World XI	Scarborough	Aug 29	18				0-54

OTHER ONE-DAY

League CC	Sunderland	June 28	51	2Ct,1St
Scotland	Glasgow	July 14		
Derbyshire	Chesterfield	July 16	6	

BATTING AVERAGES - Including fielding

	Matches	Inns	NO	Runs	HS	Avge	100s	50s	Ct	St
Cornhill Test Matches	3	4	1	91	61 *	30.33	-	1	8	-
Texaco Trophy	2	0	0	0	0	-	-	-	2	-
Other First-Class	6	7	1	204	95	34.00	-	1	9	1
Other One-Day	3	2	0	57	51	28.50	-	1	2	1
ALL FIRST-CLASS	9	11	2	295	95	32.77	-	2	17	1
ALL ONE-DAY	5	2	0	57	51	28.50	-	1	4	1

BOWLING AVERAGES

	Overs	Mdns	Runs	Wkts	Avge	Best	5wI	10wM
Cornhill Test Matches								
Texaco Trophy								
Other First-Class	8	0	54	0	-	-	-	-
Other One-Day								
ALL FIRST-CLASS	8	0	54	0	-	-	-	-
ALL ONE-DAY								

H. MORRIS - *Glamorgan*

Opposition	Venue	Date	Batting			Fielding	Bowling

BRITANNIC ASSURANCE

Opposition	Venue	Date				Fielding	Bowling
Leicestershire	Cardiff	April 26	33	&	32		
Somerset	Cardiff	May 3	52	&	19		
Gloucs	Bristol	May 15	7	&	1		
Sussex	Hove	May 19	73			2Ct	0-21
Kent	Swansea	May 23	100 *	&	29	2Ct	
Lancashire	Colwyn Bay	May 26	3	&	1		
Northants	Northampton	June 9	80	&	24		
Hampshire	Southampton	June 16	38 *	&	44		
Somerset	Bath	June 20			2		0-41
Yorkshire	Cardiff	June 23	102	&	28	1Ct	
Surrey	Cardiff	June 30	62	&	8	1Ct	
Gloucs	Swansea	July 4	21				
Leicestershire	Hinckley	July 7	53	&	0		
Worcestershire	Abergavenny	July 21	57	&	119	1Ct	
Warwickshire	Swansea	July 25	106	&	15		
Middlesex	Lord's	Aug 4	100	&	4	2Ct	
Essex	Southend	Aug 8	9	&	28	1Ct	
Notts	Worksop	Aug 11	110	&	102 *		
Derbyshire	Cardiff	Aug 29	160 *	&	4	1Ct	
Hampshire	Pontypridd	Sept 7	29	&	45		
Warwickshire	Edgbaston	Sept 12	73	&	20		
Worcestershire	Worcester	Sept 18	71	&	50	1Ct	

REFUGE ASSURANCE

Gloucs	Bristol	April 22	46	
Leicestershire	Cardiff	April 29	13	2Ct
Kent	Llanelli	May 13	0	
Sussex	Hove	May 20	68	
Lancashire	Colwyn Bay	May 27	6	
Essex	Ilford	June 3	18	
Northants	Northampton	June 10	40	2Ct
Hampshire	Bournemouth	June 17	7	
Surrey	Cardiff	July 1	48	
Warwickshire	Edgbaston	July 15	19	
Somerset	Neath	July 22	3	
Derbyshire	Swansea	July 29	16	
Middlesex	Lord's	Aug 5	11	
Notts	Trent Bridge	Aug 12	9	
Worcestershire	Swansea	Aug 26	7	

NATWEST TROPHY

Dorset	Swansea	June 27	116
Sussex	Cardiff	July 11	58
Middlesex	Lord's	Aug 1	26

BENSON & HEDGES CUP

Warwickshire	Edgbaston	April 24	1	
Gloucs	Cardiff	May 1	23	
Worcestershire	Worcester	May 8	57	2Ct
Kent	Swansea	May 12	16	4Ct
Worcestershire	Worcester	May 30	106	

OTHER FIRST-CLASS

Oxford U	The Parks	April 14	103				
India	Swansea	Aug 18	23 *	&	73	1Ct	
Sri Lanka	Ebbw Vale	Aug 22	37	&	126	1Ct	

BATTING AVERAGES - Including fielding

	Matches	Inns	NO	Runs	HS	Avge	100s	50s	Ct	St
Britannic Assurance	22	41	4	1914	160 *	51.73	8	9	12	-
Refuge Assurance	15	15	0	311	68	20.73	-	1	4	-
NatWest Trophy	3	3	0	200	116	66.66	1	1	-	-
Benson & Hedges Cup	5	5	0	203	106	40.60	1	1	6	-
Other First-Class	3	5	1	362	126	90.50	2	1	2	-
ALL FIRST-CLASS	25	46	5	2276	160 *	55.51	10	10	14	-
ALL ONE-DAY	23	23	0	714	116	31.04	2	3	10	-

BOWLING AVERAGES

	Overs	Mdns	Runs	Wkts	Avge	Best	5wI	10wM
Britannic Assurance	6	0	62	0	-	-	-	-
Refuge Assurance								
NatWest Trophy								
Benson & Hedges Cup								
Other First-Class								
ALL FIRST-CLASS	6	0	62	0	-	-	-	-
ALL ONE-DAY								

J.E. MORRIS - *Derbyshire & England*

Opposition	Venue	Date	Batting			Fielding	Bowling

CORNHILL TEST MATCHES

						Fielding	
India	Lord's	July 26	4 *			3Ct	
India	Old Trafford	Aug 9	13	&	15 *		
India	The Oval	Aug 23	7	&	32		

BRITANNIC ASSURANCE

						Fielding	Bowling
Notts	Trent Bridge	April 26	66	&	16 *		
Lancashire	Derby	May 15	27	&	52		
Somerset	Taunton	May 19	122	&	109		
Yorkshire	Chesterfield	May 23	60	&	5		
Notts	Derby	May 26	103	&	7		
Surrey	The Oval	June 6	25				
Warwickshire	Derby	June 16	103 *				0-52
Leicestershire	Leicester	June 20		63 *			
Gloucs	Derby	June 30	9	&	66	3Ct	0-10
Sussex	Hove	July 4	21			2Ct	
Lancashire	Liverpool	July 7	14	&	22		
Hampshire	Portsmouth	July 21	157 *	&	10	2Ct	
Kent	Chesterfield	Aug 4	32			1Ct	
Middlesex	Derby	Aug 18	67	&	12		
Glamorgan	Cardiff	Aug 29	40				1-17
Yorkshire	Scarborough	Sept 7	109	&	36		0-44

REFUGE ASSURANCE

Sussex	Hove	April 22	5	
Worcestershire	Derby	April 29	3	1Ct
Northants	Northampton	May 6	12	
Somerset	Taunton	May 20	134	
Notts	Derby	June 10	32	
Warwickshire	Derby	June 17	4	
Surrey	The Oval	June 24	45	
Gloucs	Derby	July 1	57	
Lancashire	Old Trafford	July 8	55	
Leicestershire	Knypersley	July 15	21	1Ct
Hampshire	Portsmouth	July 22	1	
Kent	Chesterfield	Aug 5	45	1Ct
Middlesex	Derby	Aug 19	48	
Notts	Derby	Sept 5	0	

PLASYER RECORDS

Middlesex	Edgbaston	Sept 16	46

NATWEST TROPHY

Shropshire	Chesterfield	June 27	94*
Lancashire	Derby	July 11	74

BENSON & HEDGES CUP

Sussex	Derby	April 24	23	
Somerset	Taunton	May 1	123	1Ct
Min Counties	Wellington	May 10	6	
Middlesex	Derby	May 12	0	

OTHER FIRST-CLASS

For MCC

Worcestershire	Lord's	April 17	15		

For Derbyshire

New Zealand	Derby	June 2	20	1Ct	0-47

OTHER ONE-DAY

For Derbyshire

India	Chesterfield	July 16	37	

For England XI

Rest of World	Jesmond	Aug 2	87*	
Rest of World	Jesmond	Aug 3	5	

For World XI

Yorkshire	Scarborough	Sept 1	60	2Ct

BATTING AVERAGES - Including fielding

	Matches	Inns	NO	Runs	HS	Avge	100s	50s	Ct	St
Cornhill Test Matches	3	5	2	71	32	23.66	-	-	3	-
Britannic Assurance	16	26	4	1353	157*	61.50	6	6	8	-
Refuge Assurance	15	15	0	508	134	33.86	1	2	3	-
NatWest Trophy	2	2	1	168	94*	168.00	-	2	-	-
Benson & Hedges Cup	4	4	0	152	123	38.00	1	-	1	-
Other First-Class	2	2	0	35	20	17.50	-	-	1	-
Other One-Day	4	4	1	189	87*	63.00	-	2	2	-
ALL FIRST-CLASS	21	33	6	1459	157*	54.03	6	6	12	-
ALL ONE-DAY	25	25	2	1017	134	44.21	2	6	6	-

BOWLING AVERAGES

	Overs	Mdns	Runs	Wkts	Avge	Best	5wI	10wM
Cornhill Test Matches								
Britannic Assurance	20	0	123	1	123.00	1-17	-	-
Refuge Assurance								
NatWest Trophy								
Benson & Hedges Cup								
Other First-Class	7	0	47	0	-	-	-	-
Other One-Day								
ALL FIRST-CLASS	27	0	170	1	170.00	1-17	-	-
ALL ONE-DAY								

M.J. MORRIS - Cambridge University

Opposition	Venue	Date	Batting		Fielding	Bowling
OTHER FIRST-CLASS						
Northants	Fenner's	April 14	5		1Ct	
Derbyshire	Fenner's	April 18	2 &	45		
Warwickshire	Fenner's	April 26	0 &	19		
Middlesex	Fenner's	May 3	9 &	32*	1Ct	
Essex	Fenner's	May 16	2 &	1	1Ct	
Gloucs	Fenner's	May 23	18 &	17	1Ct	
Notts	Fenner's	June 16	4 &	0*		
Kent	Fenner's	June 20	24			
Sussex	Hove	June 30	12 &	7		
Oxford U	Lord's	July 4	9*			

BATTING AVERAGES - Including fielding

	Matches	Inns	NO	Runs	HS	Avge	100s	50s	Ct	St
Other First-Class	10	17	3	206	45	14.71	-	-	4	-
ALL FIRST-CLASS	10	17	3	206	45	14.71	-	-	4	-

BOWLING AVERAGES
Did not bowl

R.E. MORRIS - Oxford University

Opposition	Venue	Date	Batting		Fielding	Bowling
OTHER FIRST-CLASS						
Glamorgan	The Parks	April 14	16			
Hampshire	The Parks	May 3	61			
Surrey	The Parks	May 16	96 &	31		
Leicestershire	The Parks	May 23	0 &	11		
Glamorgan	The Parks	June 2	0			
Notts	The Parks	June 6	73*		1Ct	
Lancashire	The Parks	June 16	61			
For Combined U						
New Zealand	Fenner's	June 27	75 &	53		
For Oxford U						
Cambridge U	Lord's	July 4	21			

BATTING AVERAGES - Including fielding

	Matches	Inns	NO	Runs	HS	Avge	100s	50s	Ct	St
Other First-Class	9	12	1	498	96	45.27	-	6	1	-
ALL FIRST-CLASS	9	12	1	498	96	45.27	-	6	1	-

BOWLING AVERAGES
Did not bowl

D.K. MORRISON - New Zealand

Opposition	Venue	Date	Batting		Fielding	Bowling
CORNHILL TEST MATCHES						
England	Trent Bridge	June 7	0 &	0*		1-96
England	Lord's	June 21	2*		1Ct	4-64 & 0-81
England	Edgbaston	July 5	1 &	6		2-81 & 0-29
TEXACO TROPHY						
England	Headingley	May 23				1-70
England	The Oval	May 25			1Ct	0-38
OTHER FIRST-CLASS						
Worcestershire	Worcester	May 12	5		2Ct	2-46 & 3-60
Middlesex	Lord's	May 19				0-100 & 1-67
Sussex	Hove	May 26				2-35
Derbyshire	Derby	June 2				0-16 & 2-40
Northants	Northampton	June 16				3-68 & 1-49
Essex	Chelmsford	June 30				0-57
OTHER ONE-DAY						
MCC	Lord's	May 7				0-33
Ireland	Belfast	May 10				0-20
Leicestershire	Leicester	June 14	2			1-27

BATTING AVERAGES - Including fielding

	Matches	Inns	NO	Runs	HS	Avge	100s	50s	Ct	St
Cornhill Test Matches	3	5	2	9	6	3.00	-	-	1	-
Texaco Trophy	2	0	0	0	0	-	-	-	1	-
Other First-Class	6	1	0	5	5	5.00	-	-	2	-
Other One-Day	3	1	0	2	2	2.00	-	-	-	-
ALL FIRST-CLASS	9	6	2	14	6	3.50	-	-	3	-
ALL ONE-DAY	5	1	0	2	2	2.00	-	-	1	-

BOWLING AVERAGES

	Overs	Mdns	Runs	Wkts	Avge	Best	5wI	10wM
Cornhill Test Matches	85.4	15	351	7	50.14	4-64	-	-
Texaco Trophy	20	0	108	1	108.00	1-70		
Other First-Class	149	21	538	14	38.42	3-60		
Other One-Day	24	3	80	1	80.00	1-27		
ALL FIRST-CLASS	234.4	36	889	21	42.33	4-64	-	-
ALL ONE-DAY	44	3	188	2	94.00	1-27		

M — PLAYER RECORDS

O.H. MORTENSEN - *Derbyshire*

Opposition	Venue	Date	Batting	Fielding	Bowling
BRITANNIC ASSURANCE					
Notts	Trent Bridge	April 26	5 *		4-67 & 1-14
Somerset	Taunton	May 19	2 * &	2 * 2Ct	0-17 & 1-25
Notts	Derby	May 26	0 *	1Ct	1-36 & 2-73
Gloucs	Derby	June 30	4		4-22 & 0-52
Sussex	Hove	July 4			2-77
Hampshire	Portsmouth	July 21		0 *	2-64 & 3-47
Worcestershire	Derby	July 25	0 *		0-4
Northants	Chesterfield	Aug 8	0 *		2-43 & 0-42
Middlesex	Derby	Aug 18	1	1Ct	4-29 & 1-21
Glamorgan	Cardiff	Aug 29	1 *	1Ct	2-48
Leicestershire	Derby	Sept 18	5 *		3-40 & 0-43
REFUGE ASSURANCE					
Sussex	Hove	April 22		1Ct	1-23
Worcestershire	Derby	April 29			2-15
Northants	Northampton	May 6			0-19
Yorkshire	Headingley	May 13	0 *		0-26
Somerset	Taunton	May 20			0-42
Surrey	The Oval	June 24			0-27
Gloucs	Derby	July 1			3-16
Lancashire	Old Trafford	July 8			0-25
Leicestershire	Knypersley	July 15			0-18
Hampshire	Portsmouth	July 22	2 *		1-35
Glamorgan	Swansea	July 29			1-17
Kent	Chesterfield	Aug 5			0-23
Middlesex	Derby	Aug 19			0-22
Essex	Derby	Aug 26		1Ct	1-10
Notts	Derby	Sept 5			1-27
Middlesex	Edgbaston	Sept 16			0-19
NATWEST TROPHY					
Shropshire	Chesterfield	June 27			3-29
Lancashire	Derby	July 11	0		1-22
BENSON & HEDGES CUP					
Sussex	Derby	April 24		1Ct	1-43
Somerset	Taunton	May 1			1-55
Min Counties	Wellington	May 10	2 *		0-15
Middlesex	Derby	May 12		1Ct	0-18
OTHER FIRST-CLASS					
Cambridge U	Fenner's	April 18			3-21
OTHER ONE-DAY					
India	Chesterfield	July 16			1-31

BATTING AVERAGES - Including fielding

	Matches	Inns	NO	Runs	HS	Avge	100s	50s	Ct	St
Britannic Assurance	11	11	9	20	5 *	10.00	-	-	5	-
Refuge Assurance	16	2	2	2	2 *	-	-	-	2	-
NatWest Trophy	2	1	0	0	0	0.00	-	-	-	-
Benson & Hedges Cup	4	1	1	2	2 *	-	-	-	2	-
Other First-Class	1	0	0	0	0	-	-	-	-	-
Other One-Day	1	0	0	0	0	-	-	-	-	-
ALL FIRST-CLASS	12	11	9	20	5 *	10.00	-	-	5	-
ALL ONE-DAY	23	4	3	4	2 *	4.00	-	-	4	-

BOWLING AVERAGES

	Overs	Mdns	Runs	Wkts	Avge	Best	5wI	10wM
Britannic Assurance	301.2	88	764	32	23.87	4-22	-	-
Refuge Assurance	118	9	364	10	36.40	3-16	-	
NatWest Trophy	23	6	51	4	12.75	3-29	-	
Benson & Hedges Cup	40	9	131	2	65.50	1-43	-	
Other First-Class	15	3	21	3	7.00	3-21	-	-
Other One-Day	11	1	31	1	31.00	1-31	-	
ALL FIRST-CLASS	316.2	91	785	35	22.42	4-22	-	-
ALL ONE-DAY	192	25	577	17	33.94	3-16	-	

W. MORTON - *Scotland*

Opposition	Venue	Date	Batting	Fielding	Bowling
NATWEST TROPHY					
Essex	Chelmsford	June 27	5		0-35

BATTING AVERAGES - Including fielding

	Matches	Inns	NO	Runs	HS	Avge	100s	50s	Ct	St
NatWest Trophy	1	1	0	5	5	5.00	-	-	-	-
ALL ONE-DAY	1	1	0	5	5	5.00	-	-	-	-

BOWLING AVERAGES

	Overs	Mdns	Runs	Wkts	Avge	Best	5wI	10wM
NatWest Trophy	2	0	35	0	-	-	-	-
ALL ONE-DAY	2	0	35	0	-	-	-	-

E.A. MOSELEY - *World XI*

Opposition	Venue	Date	Batting	Fielding	Bowling
OTHER FIRST-CLASS					
India	Scarborough	Aug 29			0-22 & 1-36

BATTING AVERAGES - Including fielding

	Matches	Inns	NO	Runs	HS	Avge	100s	50s	Ct	St
Other First-Class	1	0	0	0	0	-	-	-	-	-
ALL FIRST-CLASS	1	0	0	0	0	-	-	-	-	-

BOWLING AVERAGES

	Overs	Mdns	Runs	Wkts	Avge	Best	5wI	10wM
Other First-Class	21	3	58	1	58.00	1-36	-	-
ALL FIRST-CLASS	21	3	58	1	58.00	1-36	-	-

M.D. MOXON - *Yorkshire*

Opposition	Venue	Date	Batting	Fielding	Bowling
BRITANNIC ASSURANCE					
Warwickshire	Edgbaston	May 3	12 & 0	1Ct	
Derbyshire	Chesterfield	May 23	45 & 15	2Ct	
Worcestershire	Worcester	June 2	23 & 28		
Kent	Tunbridge We	June 6	24 * & 6 *		1-29
Surrey	Harrogate	June 9	10 & 23 *		
Warwickshire	Sheffield	June 20	3 & 46	2Ct	1-16
Glamorgan	Cardiff	June 23	27 & 10		0-36 & 1-10
Notts	Scarborough	July 4	123		
Middlesex	Uxbridge	July 18	12 & 23	1Ct	
Gloucs	Cheltenham	July 21	66 & 18	1Ct	
Somerset	Scarborough	July 25	23 & 4	1Ct	0-24 & 0-6
Leicestershire	Sheffield	July 28	21 & 17	1Ct	0-12 & 0-7
Lancashire	Headingley	Aug 4	14 & 39	2Ct	
Sussex	Eastbourne	Aug 8	218 *		
Essex	Middlesbr'gh	Aug 11	1 & 27		0-12
Lancashire	Old Trafford	Aug 18	90 * & 50	1Ct	
Middlesex	Headingley	Aug 23	95 & 7	1Ct	0-23
Derbyshire	Scarborough	Sept 7	14 & 94		
Notts	Trent Bridge	Sept 18	42 & 83		
REFUGE ASSURANCE					
Notts	Trent Bridge	April 22	37		
Kent	Canterbury	May 20	43		
Surrey	Hull	June 10	9		0-15
Sussex	Hove	June 17	39	1Ct	3-29
Somerset	Scarborough	July 15	105	1Ct	
Gloucs	Cheltenham	July 22	68	1Ct	3-52
Leicestershire	Sheffield	July 29	73		0-32
Lancashire	Scarborough	Aug 5	31		
Essex	Middlesbr'gh	Aug 12	12		
Middlesex	Scarborough	Aug 26	38		

PLAYER RECORDS

M

Left column

NATWEST TROPHY
Norfolk	Headingley	June 27	56 *		2-19
Warwickshire	Headingley	July 11	107 *		
Hampshire	Southampton	Aug 1	1	1Ct	

BENSON & HEDGES CUP
Hampshire	Southampton	April 24	11
Combined U	Headingley	May 8	4
Lancashire	Headingley	May 10	9

OTHER FIRST-CLASS
For MCC
Worcestershire	Lord's	April 17	12	
For Yorkshire
Zimbabwe	Headingley	May 16	130	1Ct
India	Headingley	June 30	45 * & 93	

OTHER ONE-DAY
Sussex	Harrogate	June 14	22	1Ct	1-26
Warwickshire	Harrogate	June 15	77	1Ct	0-3
World XI	Scarborough	Sept 1	19	1Ct	
Essex	Scarborough	Sept 3	4		

BATTING AVERAGES - Including fielding
	Matches	Inns	NO	Runs	HS	Avge	100s	50s	Ct	St
Britannic Assurance	19	36	5	1353	218 *	43.64	2	6	13	-
Refuge Assurance	10	10	0	455	105	45.50	1	2	3	-
NatWest Trophy	3	3	2	164	107 *	164.00	1	1	1	-
Benson & Hedges Cup	3	3	0	24	11	8.00	-	-	-	-
Other First-Class	3	4	1	280	130	93.33	1	1	1	-
Other One-Day	4	4	0	122	77	30.50	-	1	3	-
ALL FIRST-CLASS	22	40	6	1633	218 *	48.02	3	7	14	-
ALL ONE-DAY	20	20	2	765	107 *	42.50	2	4	7	-

BOWLING AVERAGES
	Overs	Mdns	Runs	Wkts	Avge	Best	5wI	10wM
Britannic Assurance	57	9	175	3	58.33	1-10	-	
Refuge Assurance	24.5	0	128	6	21.33	3-29	-	
NatWest Trophy	7	2	19	2	9.50	2-19	-	
Benson & Hedges Cup								
Other First-Class								
Other One-Day	12	4	29	1	29.00	1-26	-	
ALL FIRST-CLASS	57	9	175	3	58.33	1-10	-	
ALL ONE-DAY	43.5	6	176	9	19.55	3-29	-	

MUDASSAR NAZAR - *World XI*

Opposition	Venue	Date	Batting	Fielding	Bowling

OTHER FIRST-CLASS
India	Scarborough	Aug 29	29 & 107 *		

BATTING AVERAGES - Including fielding
	Matches	Inns	NO	Runs	HS	Avge	100s	50s	Ct	St
Other First-Class	1	2	1	136	107 *	136.00	1	-	-	-
ALL FIRST-CLASS	1	2	1	136	107 *	136.00	1	-	-	-

BOWLING AVERAGES
Did not bowl

A.D. MULLALLY - *Leicestershire*

Opposition	Venue	Date	Batting	Fielding	Bowling

BRITANNIC ASSURANCE
Glamorgan	Cardiff	April 26	16 *		0-10 & 1-67
Essex	Chelmsford	May 3	3		2-124
Notts	Leicester	May 15	0 & 0	1Ct	1-65 & 3-27
Lancashire	Old Trafford	May 19	2	1Ct	0-60 & 0-61
Somerset	Leicester	May 26	12 *		2-57 & 0-9
Hampshire	Leicester	June 2	29		3-68
Northants	Northampton	June 6	1 *		1-17
Middlesex	Leicester	June 16	0 *		1-34
Derbyshire	Leicester	June 20			0-10 & 2-28
Gloucs	Gloucester	June 23			2-37

Right column

Notts	Trent Bridge	June 30	2 *		2-43 & 0-17
Glamorgan	Hinckley	July 7		1Ct	0-84 & 0-26
Essex	Leicester	July 25	0		0-37 & 4-131
Yorkshire	Sheffield	July 28			2-45 & 4-59
Worcestershire	Leicester	Aug 4	0 & 3 *		0-56 & 1-78
Kent	Dartford	Aug 8	7 & 21		2-31
Surrey	The Oval	Aug 11	9 & 8		1-14
Derbyshire	Derby	Sept 18	0		3-56

REFUGE ASSURANCE
Northants	Leicester	April 22	0 *		0-33
Glamorgan	Cardiff	April 29	2		1-41
Essex	Leicester	May 6			2-32
Somerset	Leicester	May 27			0-36
Hampshire	Leicester	June 3	10 *	1Ct	2-27
Sussex	Leicester	June 10			1-28
Middlesex	Leicester	June 17			0-36
Gloucs	Gloucester	June 24			2-20
Notts	Trent Bridge	July 1	4		1-25
Derbyshire	Knypersley	July 15	5 *		1-37
Yorkshire	Sheffield	July 29			0-24
Worcestershire	Leicester	Aug 5			1-35
Surrey	The Oval	Aug 12	5	1Ct	1-57
Warwickshire	Edgbaston	Aug 19			

NATWEST TROPHY
Hampshire	Leicester	June 27			2-55

BENSON & HEDGES CUP
Northants	Leicester	April 24			1-47
Scotland	Leicester	May 12			1-28

OTHER FIRST-CLASS
India	Leicester	July 21		1Ct	1-78 & 0-17

OTHER ONE-DAY
New Zealand	Leicester	June 14			6-38

BATTING AVERAGES - Including fielding
	Matches	Inns	NO	Runs	HS	Avge	100s	50s	Ct	St
Britannic Assurance	18	18	6	113	29	9.41	-	-	3	-
Refuge Assurance	14	6	3	26	10 *	8.66	-	-	2	-
NatWest Trophy	1	0	0	0	0		-	-	-	-
Benson & Hedges Cup	2	0	0	0	0		-	-	-	-
Other First-Class	1	0	0	0	0		-	-	1	-
Other One-Day	1	0	0	0	0		-	-	-	-
ALL FIRST-CLASS	19	18	6	113	29	9.41	-	-	4	-
ALL ONE-DAY	18	6	3	26	10 *	8.66	-	-	2	-

BOWLING AVERAGES
	Overs	Mdns	Runs	Wkts	Avge	Best	5wI	10wM
Britannic Assurance	464.2	116	1351	37	36.51	4-59	-	
Refuge Assurance	97.1	3	431	12	35.91	2-20	-	
NatWest Trophy	12	0	55	2	27.50	2-55	-	
Benson & Hedges Cup	21	5	75	2	37.50	1-28	-	
Other First-Class	23	1	95	1	95.00	1-78	-	
Other One-Day	11	3	38	6	6.33	6-38	1	
ALL FIRST-CLASS	487.2	117	1446	38	38.05	4-59	-	
ALL ONE-DAY	141.1	11	599	22	27.22	6-38	1	

T.A. MUNTON - *Warwickshire*

Opposition	Venue	Date	Batting	Fielding	Bowling

BRITANNIC ASSURANCE
Yorkshire	Edgbaston	May 3	0		2-41 & 1-21
Northants	Northampton	May 15	1 *		5-33 & 4-44
Notts	Edgbaston	May 19	13 & 0	1Ct	2-85 & 2-57
Worcestershire	Edgbaston	May 26			4-45 & 0-12
Northants	Edgbaston	June 2	0 & 10 *		3-92
Middlesex	Lord's	June 6			0-36 & 2-21
Essex	Edgbaston	June 9		1Ct	2-72
Derbyshire	Derby	June 16	0 *		2-105
Yorkshire	Sheffield	June 20	1 *	1Ct	2-34 & 1-63
Kent	Edgbaston	June 23	4	1Ct	1-46 & 0-6
Somerset	Taunton	July 4			0-65 & 0-35
Surrey	The Oval	July 7	6 & 3		2-85 & 3-107
Lancashire	Coventry	July 18			3-75 & 0-30
Glamorgan	Swansea	July 25	14	2Ct	2-65 & 0-77
Hampshire	Edgbaston	July 28			1-50 & 0-24

M — PLAYER RECORDS

			Batting	Fielding	Bowling
Sussex	Eastbourne	Aug 4		1Ct	3-46 & 3-63
Gloucs	Bristol	Aug 8	2 & 0		2-69 & 1-40
Leicestershire	Edgbaston	Aug 18	0*& 0		2-74 & 2-21
Worcestershire	Worcester	Aug 23	1 & 5*	1Ct	2-84 & 2-66
Somerset	Edgbaston	Sept 7	0*& 29*		4-66 & 2-7
Glamorgan	Edgbaston	Sept 12	23 & 1*		3-44 & 5-64
Lancashire	Old Trafford	Sept 18	8		0-16

REFUGE ASSURANCE

			Batting	Fielding	Bowling
Northants	Edgbaston	April 29			1-22
Yorkshire	Edgbaston	May 6		1Ct	0-23
Gloucs	Moreton-in-M	May 20	3		5-23
Worcestershire	Worcester	May 27		1Ct	0-36
Middlesex	Lord's	June 3			0-19
Essex	Edgbaston	June 10	2*		0-23
Derbyshire	Derby	June 17		1Ct	0-25
Kent	Edgbaston	June 24			1-9
Surrey	The Oval	July 8	6*		1-25
Glamorgan	Edgbaston	July 15	2*		0-14
Notts	Edgbaston	July 22		1Ct	2-45
Hampshire	Edgbaston	July 29		1Ct	1-29
Sussex	Eastbourne	Aug 5			3-36
Somerset	Weston	Aug 12			0-42
Leicestershire	Edgbaston	Aug 19			1-8
Lancashire	Old Trafford	Aug 26	4*		1-45

NATWEST TROPHY

			Batting	Fielding	Bowling
Hertfordshire	St Albans	June 27			3-46
Yorkshire	Headingley	July 11	1*		0-31

BENSON & HEDGES CUP

			Batting	Fielding	Bowling
Glamorgan	Edgbaston	April 24			2-28
Kent	Canterbury	May 8	1*	1Ct	1-39
Worcestershire	Edgbaston	May 10	0		0-35
Gloucs	Bristol	May 12			1-41

OTHER FIRST-CLASS

			Batting	Fielding	Bowling
Cambridge U	Fenner's	April 26			0-17 & 2-40
New Zealand	Edgbaston	May 30	4		0-33 & 0-3
For TCCB U25 XI					
India	Edgbaston	Aug 15			0-49 & 1-26

OTHER ONE-DAY

For Warwickshire

			Batting	Fielding	Bowling
Surrey	Harrogate	June 13			1-36
Yorkshire	Harrogate	June 15			0-49
For England XI					
Rest of World	Jesmond	Aug 2		2Ct	4-38
Rest of World	Jesmond	Aug 3	0		0-33
For Warwickshire					
Surrey	Hove	Sept 3			1-64

BATTING AVERAGES - Including fielding

	Matches	Inns	NO	Runs	HS	Avge	100s	50s	Ct	St
Britannic Assurance	22	23	9	121	29*	8.64	-	-	9	-
Refuge Assurance	16	5	4	17	6*	17.00	-	-	5	-
NatWest Trophy	2	1	1	1	1*	-	-	-	-	-
Benson & Hedges Cup	4	2	1	1	1*	1.00	-	-	1	-
Other First-Class	3	1	0	4	4	4.00	-	-	-	-
Other One-Day	5	1	0	0	0	0.00	-	-	2	-
ALL FIRST-CLASS	25	24	9	125	29*	8.33	-	-	9	-
ALL ONE-DAY	27	9	6	19	6*	6.33	-	-	8	-

BOWLING AVERAGES

	Overs	Mdns	Runs	Wkts	Avge	Best	5wI	10wM
Britannic Assurance	748.3	174	2086	75	27.81	5-33	2	-
Refuge Assurance	111.5	13	424	16	26.50	5-23	1	
NatWest Trophy	18	1	77	3	25.66	3-46	-	
Benson & Hedges Cup	39	3	143	4	35.75	2-28	-	
Other First-Class	78.4	25	168	3	56.00	2-40	-	-
Other One-Day	50	2	220	6	36.66	4-38	-	
ALL FIRST-CLASS	827.1	199	2254	78	28.89	5-33	2	-
ALL ONE-DAY	218.5	19	864	29	29.79	5-23	1	

			Batting	Fielding	Bowling
Lancashire	The Oval	May 3			2-160
Hampshire	The Oval	May 19			1-65 & 1-65
Middlesex	Lord's	May 23		1Ct	2-50 & 1-75
Derbyshire	The Oval	June 6			0-59 & 0-7
Yorkshire	Harrogate	June 9	0*		0-45
Worcestershire	The Oval	June 16			0-64 & 0-12
Notts	Trent Bridge	June 20			1-9 & 0-34
Essex	Chelmsford	Aug 18	1 & 0		5-67 & 1-73
Lancashire	Blackpool	Aug 29			2-73
Kent	Canterbury	Sept 7	1		5-99 & 3-112
Essex	The Oval	Sept 18	0*		2-154

REFUGE ASSURANCE

			Batting	Fielding	Bowling
Sussex	Hove	April 29			1-41
Lancashire	The Oval	May 6			0-63
Notts	Trent Bridge	May 20			0-41
Northants	The Oval	June 3			2-15
Yorkshire	Hull	June 10			2-29
Worcestershire	The Oval	June 17			2-38
Derbyshire	The Oval	June 24			1-26
Glamorgan	Cardiff	July 1			0-9
Hampshire	Southampton	Aug 26			2-41

NATWEST TROPHY

			Batting	Fielding	Bowling
Wiltshire	Trowbridge	June 27			1-46

BENSON & HEDGES CUP

			Batting	Fielding	Bowling
Hampshire	The Oval	May 1			2-36
Yorkshire	The Oval	May 12			0-41
Lancashire	Old Trafford	May 30	0*		2-61

OTHER ONE-DAY

			Batting	Fielding	Bowling
Warwickshire	Harrogate	June 13	6*	1Ct	1-23
Sri Lanka	The Oval	Sept 2		1Ct	3-61
Warwickshire	Hove	Sept 3			0-47
Kent	Hove	Sept 4	2		1-71

BATTING AVERAGES - Including fielding

	Matches	Inns	NO	Runs	HS	Avge	100s	50s	Ct	St
Britannic Assurance	12	6	3	6	4*	2.00	-	-	1	-
Refuge Assurance	9	0	0	0	0	-	-	-	-	-
NatWest Trophy	1	0	0	0	0	-	-	-	-	-
Benson & Hedges Cup	3	1	1	0	0*	-	-	-	-	-
Other One-Day	4	2	1	8	6*	8.00	-	-	2	-
ALL FIRST-CLASS	12	6	3	6	4*	2.00	-	-	1	-
ALL ONE-DAY	17	3	2	8	6*	8.00	-	-	2	-

BOWLING AVERAGES

	Overs	Mdns	Runs	Wkts	Avge	Best	5wI	10wM
Britannic Assurance	404.2	76	1367	30	45.56	5-67	2	-
Refuge Assurance	59	1	303	10	30.30	2-15	-	
NatWest Trophy	12	1	46	1	46.00	1-46	-	
Benson & Hedges Cup	29	5	138	4	34.50	2-36	-	
Other One-Day	39.5	1	202	5	40.40	3-61	-	
ALL FIRST-CLASS	404.2	76	1367	30	45.56	5-67	2	-
ALL ONE-DAY	139.5	8	689	20	34.45	3-61	-	

A.J. MURPHY - *Surrey*

Opposition	Venue	Date	Batting	Fielding	Bowling
BRITANNIC ASSURANCE					
Sussex	Hove	April 26	4*		2-68 & 2-76

PLAYER RECORDS

P.A. NEALE - *Worcestershire*

Opposition	Venue	Date	Batting				Fielding	Bowling
BRITANNIC ASSURANCE								
Lancashire	Old Trafford	April 26	10					
Notts	Worcester	May 3	122					
Essex	Worcester	May 19	9	&	4			
Warwickshire	Edgbaston	May 26	29	&	39 *			
Yorkshire	Worcester	June 2	1					
Surrey	The Oval	June 16	36					
Sussex	Worcester	June 20			8			
Middlesex	Lord's	June 30	16	&	41 *			
Gloucs	Worcester	July 7	14	&	3 *			
Somerset	Worcester	July 18	49 *	&	22 *		1Ct	
Glamorgan	Abergavenny	July 21					1Ct	
Derbyshire	Derby	July 25	65				2Ct	
Kent	Canterbury	July 28	119 *	&	14 *			
Leicestershire	Leicester	Aug 4	20 *				1Ct	
Warwickshire	Worcester	Aug 23	46	&	17		2Ct	
Notts	Trent Bridge	Aug 29	74	&	5 *		3Ct	
Gloucs	Bristol	Sept 7	95	&	3			
Somerset	Taunton	Sept 12	40	&	12		1Ct	
Glamorgan	Worcester	Sept 18	4	&	17		1Ct	
REFUGE ASSURANCE								
Somerset	Taunton	April 22						
Derbyshire	Derby	April 29	40					
Notts	Worcester	May 6	11					
Essex	Worcester	May 20	1				1Ct	
Warwickshire	Worcester	May 27	23					
Yorkshire	Worcester	June 3	18					
Surrey	The Oval	June 17	3					
Sussex	Worcester	June 24	8				1Ct	
Middlesex	Lord's	July 1	13				1Ct	
Gloucs	Worcester	July 8						
Kent	Canterbury	July 29	39					
Leicestershire	Leicester	Aug 5	34 *				1Ct	
Glamorgan	Swansea	Aug 26	7				1Ct	
NATWEST TROPHY								
Suffolk	Bury St Ed's	June 27					1Ct	
Somerset	Taunton	July 11					1Ct	
Northants	Northampton	Aug 1	43					
BENSON & HEDGES CUP								
Gloucs	Bristol	April 24	30				1Ct	
Kent	Worcester	May 1	13					
Glamorgan	Worcester	May 8	31					
Warwickshire	Edgbaston	May 10	5 *				1Ct	
Glamorgan	Worcester	May 30	50					
Lancashire	Lord's	July 14	0				2Ct	
OTHER FIRST-CLASS								
MCC	Lord's	April 17	22 *					
New Zealand	Worcester	May 12	5	&	15			
OTHER ONE-DAY								
Hampshire	Scarborough	Sept 2	1					

BATTING AVERAGES - Including fielding

	Matches	Inns	NO	Runs	HS	Avge	100s	50s	Ct	St
Britannic Assurance	19	29	9	934	122	46.70	2	3	12	-
Refuge Assurance	13	11	1	197	40	19.70	-	-	5	-
NatWest Trophy	3	1	0	43	43	43.00	-	-	2	-
Benson & Hedges Cup	6	6	1	129	50	25.80	-	1	4	-
Other First-Class	2	3	1	42	22 *	21.00	-	-	-	-
Other One-Day	1	1	0	1	1	1.00	-	-	-	-
ALL FIRST-CLASS	21	32	10	976	122	44.36	2	3	12	-
ALL ONE-DAY	23	19	2	370	50	21.76	-	1	11	-

BOWLING AVERAGES
Did not bowl

A. NEEDHAM - *Hertfordshire*

Opposition	Venue	Date	Batting	Fielding	Bowling
NATWEST TROPHY					
Warwickshire	St Albans	June 27	35		2-50

BATTING AVERAGES - Including fielding

	Matches	Inns	NO	Runs	HS	Avge	100s	50s	Ct	St
NatWest Trophy	1	1	0	35	35	35.00	-	-	-	-
ALL ONE-DAY	1	1	0	35	35	35.00	-	-	-	-

BOWLING AVERAGES

	Overs	Mdns	Runs	Wkts	Avge	Best	5wI	10wM
NatWest Trophy	12	0	50	2	25.00	2-50	-	-
ALL ONE-DAY	12	0	50	2	25.00	2-50	-	-

A.N. NELSON - *Ireland*

Opposition	Venue	Date	Batting	Fielding	Bowling
NATWEST TROPHY					
Sussex	Downpatrick	June 27	3		1-27
OTHER FIRST-CLASS					
Scotland	Edinburgh	Aug 11	23 *		1-74

BATTING AVERAGES - Including fielding

	Matches	Inns	NO	Runs	HS	Avge	100s	50s	Ct	St
NatWest Trophy	1	1	0	3	3	3.00	-	-	-	-
Other First-Class	1	1	1	23	23 *	-	-	-	-	-
ALL FIRST-CLASS	1	1	1	23	23 *	-	-	-	-	-
ALL ONE-DAY	1	1	0	3	3	3.00	-	-	-	-

BOWLING AVERAGES

	Overs	Mdns	Runs	Wkts	Avge	Best	5wI	10wM
NatWest Trophy	5	0	27	1	27.00	1-27	-	-
Other First-Class	33	8	74	1	74.00	1-74	-	-
ALL FIRST-CLASS	33	8	74	1	74.00	1-74	-	-
ALL ONE-DAY	5	0	27	1	27.00	1-27	-	-

N. NELSON - *Ireland*

Opposition	Venue	Date	Batting	Fielding	Bowling
OTHER FIRST-CLASS					
Scotland	Edinburgh	Aug 11	0	1Ct	0-51

BATTING AVERAGES - Including fielding

	Matches	Inns	NO	Runs	HS	Avge	100s	50s	Ct	St
Other First-Class	1	1	0	0	0	0.00	-	-	1	-
ALL FIRST-CLASS	1	1	0	0	0	0.00	-	-	1	-

BOWLING AVERAGES

	Overs	Mdns	Runs	Wkts	Avge	Best	5wI	10wM
Other First-Class	15	0	51	0		-	-	-
ALL FIRST-CLASS	15	0	51	0		-	-	-

M. NEWELL - *Nottinghamshire*

Opposition	Venue	Date	Batting				Fielding	Bowling
BRITANNIC ASSURANCE								
Worcestershire	Worcester	May 3	6	&	30		1Ct	0-1
Leicestershire	Trent Bridge	June 30	7	&	26			
Yorkshire	Scarborough	July 4			0			0-12

N   PLAYER RECORDS

Sussex	Trent Bridge	July 7	8 &	85	1Ct	
Hampshire	Portsmouth	July 18	13 &	34	1Ct	
Somerset	Weston	Aug 8	59 &	7		
Glamorgan	Worksop	Aug 11	10 &	42		
Gloucs	Trent Bridge	Aug 18	78 &	6	1Ct	
Worcestershire	Trent Bridge	Aug 29	1 &	16		
Middlesex	Lord's	Sept 7	6 &	80		
Lancashire	Trent Bridge	Sept 12	0 &	12		
Yorkshire	Trent Bridge	Sept 18	38 &	89 *		

REFUGE ASSURANCE

Somerset	Bath	June 24	85	
Leicestershire	Trent Bridge	July 1	60 *	
Sussex	Trent Bridge	July 8	15	
Hampshire	Southampton	July 15	11 *	1Ct
Warwickshire	Edgbaston	July 22	6	
Northants	Trent Bridge	July 29	16	1Ct
Essex	Southend	Aug 5	109 *	2Ct
Glamorgan	Trent Bridge	Aug 12		
Gloucs	Trent Bridge	Aug 19		
Derbyshire	Derby	Sept 5	10	

NATWEST TROPHY

Bucks	Marlow	June 27	35	1Ct
Northants	Northampton	July 11	4	

BENSON & HEDGES CUP

Leicestershire	Trent Bridge	May 1	13	

OTHER FIRST-CLASS

Oxford U	The Parks	June 6	20 *		
Cambridge U	Fenner's	June 16	60		1-22
Sri Lanka	Cleethorpes	Aug 25	112 &	6	0-0

BATTING AVERAGES - Including fielding

	Matches	Inns	NO	Runs	HS	Avge	100s	50s	Ct	St
Britannic Assurance	12	23	1	653	89 *	29.68	-	5	4	-
Refuge Assurance	10	8	3	312	109 *	62.40	1	2	4	-
NatWest Trophy	2	2	0	39	35	19.50	-	-	1	-
Benson & Hedges Cup	1	1	0	13	13	13.00	-	-	-	-
Other First-Class	3	4	1	198	112	66.00	1	1	-	-
ALL FIRST-CLASS	15	27	2	851	112	34.04	1	6	4	-
ALL ONE-DAY	13	11	3	364	109 *	45.50	1	2	5	-

BOWLING AVERAGES

	Overs	Mdns	Runs	Wkts	Avge	Best	5wI	10wM
Britannic Assurance	2.2	0	13	0	-	-	-	-
Refuge Assurance								
NatWest Trophy								
Benson & Hedges Cup								
Other First-Class	6	3	22	1	22.00	1-22	-	-
ALL FIRST-CLASS	8.2	3	35	1	35.00	1-22	-	-
ALL ONE-DAY								

P.G. NEWMAN - *Durham*

Opposition	Venue	Date	Batting	Fielding	Bowling

NATWEST TROPHY

Lancashire	Old Trafford	June 27	0		1-30

BATTING AVERAGES - Including fielding

	Matches	Inns	NO	Runs	HS	Avge	100s	50s	Ct	St
NatWest Trophy	1	1	0	0	0	0.00	-	-	-	-
ALL ONE-DAY	1	1	0	0	0	0.00	-	-	-	-

BOWLING AVERAGES

	Overs	Mdns	Runs	Wkts	Avge	Best	5wI	10wM
NatWest Trophy	10	0	30	1	30.00	1-30	-	
ALL ONE-DAY	10	0	30	1	30.00	1-30	-	

P.J. NEWPORT - *Worcestershire*

Opposition	Venue	Date	Batting	Fielding	Bowling

BRITANNIC ASSURANCE

Lancashire	Old Trafford	April 26	5 *			0-61 & 0-14
Notts	Worcester	May 3	35		1Ct	4-44 & 0-42
Essex	Worcester	May 19	18 &	96		1-88 & 0-7
Warwickshire	Edgbaston	May 26	9			0-38 & 1-26
Yorkshire	Worcester	June 2	17			1-55
Surrey	The Oval	June 16	41			0-6 & 1-35
Sussex	Worcester	June 20		2		0-64
Somerset	Worcester	July 18			1Ct	1-70 & 0-46
Glamorgan	Abergavenny	July 21				0-72 & 3-87
Derbyshire	Derby	July 25	2			0-23 & 2-29
Kent	Canterbury	July 28	5 *			6-73 & 2-27
Leicestershire	Leicester	Aug 4			2Ct	1-84 & 2-56
Lancashire	Kid'minster	Aug 8				5-59 & 0-48
Hampshire	Worcester	Aug 11				2-23 & 0-61
Northants	Worcester	Aug 18	1 &	8 *		1-67 & 1-11
Warwickshire	Worcester	Aug 23	7			3-60 & 5-37
Notts	Trent Bridge	Aug 29			1Ct	4-75 & 3-50
Gloucs	Bristol	Sept 7				1-80 & 2-19
Somerset	Taunton	Sept 12	65 * &	7 *		3-95 & 2-74

REFUGE ASSURANCE

Somerset	Taunton	April 22				2-17
Derbyshire	Derby	April 29	12 *			1-30
Notts	Worcester	May 6				3-37
Essex	Worcester	May 20			1Ct	0-33
Warwickshire	Worcester	May 27	8			0-20
Yorkshire	Worcester	June 3	8			1-32
Surrey	The Oval	June 17	3			1-31
Sussex	Worcester	June 24	3			1-33
Lancashire	Old Trafford	July 15	16 *			0-31
Kent	Canterbury	July 29				1-18
Leicestershire	Leicester	Aug 5				1-36
Hampshire	Worcester	Aug 12	7		1Ct	0-33
Northants	Worcester	Aug 19				2-15
Glamorgan	Swansea	Aug 26	0		1Ct	3-19

NATWEST TROPHY

Somerset	Taunton	July 11				1-54
Northants	Northampton	Aug 1	0			4-46

BENSON & HEDGES CUP

Gloucs	Bristol	April 24	22 *		1Ct	0-23
Kent	Worcester	May 1	28			4-25
Glamorgan	Worcester	May 8	4		1Ct	1-28
Warwickshire	Edgbaston	May 10				0-21
Glamorgan	Worcester	May 30			1Ct	2-34
Notts	Trent Bridge	June 13				0-28
Lancashire	Lord's	July 14	3			2-47

OTHER FIRST-CLASS

MCC	Lord's	April 17	1 *		1Ct	0-85
New Zealand	Worcester	May 12	7 &	98		6-54 & 0-56

BATTING AVERAGES - Including fielding

	Matches	Inns	NO	Runs	HS	Avge	100s	50s	Ct	St
Britannic Assurance	19	15	5	318	96	31.80	-	2	5	-
Refuge Assurance	14	8	2	57	16 *	9.50	-	-	3	-
NatWest Trophy	2	1	0	0	0	0.00	-	-	-	-
Benson & Hedges Cup	7	4	1	57	28	19.00	-	-	3	-
Other First-Class	2	3	1	106	98	53.00	-	1	1	-
ALL FIRST-CLASS	21	18	6	424	98	35.33	-	3	6	-
ALL ONE-DAY	23	13	3	114	28	11.40	-	-	6	-

BOWLING AVERAGES

	Overs	Mdns	Runs	Wkts	Avge	Best	5wI	10wM
Britannic Assurance	563.2	104	1806	57	31.68	6-73	3	-
Refuge Assurance	102	8	385	16	24.06	3-19	-	
NatWest Trophy	22	0	100	5	20.00	4-46	-	
Benson & Hedges Cup	62	8	206	9	22.88	4-25	-	
Other First-Class	63	12	195	6	32.50	6-54	1	
ALL FIRST-CLASS	626.2	116	2001	63	31.76	6-54	4	
ALL ONE-DAY	186	16	691	30	23.03	4-25	-	

PLACE RECORDS

N

M.C.J. NICHOLAS - *Hampshire*

Opposition	Venue	Date	Batting			Fielding	Bowling
BRITANNIC ASSURANCE							
Sussex	Southampton	May 15	12			1Ct	
Essex	Southampton	May 23			32 *		
Yorkshire	Headingley	May 26	0	&	15		1-14
Leicestershire	Leicester	June 2	13				
Somerset	Basingstoke	June 6	23 *	&	23		
Glamorgan	Southampton	June 16	30				0-27
Gloucs	Gloucester	June 20					
Lancashire	Old Trafford	June 23	58 *				0-11
Notts	Portsmouth	July 18	70	&	9		
Derbyshire	Portsmouth	July 21	7	&	15	1Ct	
Sussex	Arundel	July 25	0	&	1		
Warwickshire	Edgbaston	July 28	16	&	78 *		0-24
Northants	Bournemouth	Aug 4	19 *				
Middlesex	Bournemouth	Aug 8	7				0-8 & 0-8
Worcestershire	Worcester	Aug 11	6	&	35		0-13 & 0-27
Somerset	Taunton	Aug 18	0	&	6 *		0-11 & 1-7
Surrey	Southampton	Aug 23	70	&	19	3Ct	0-43 & 0-16
Kent	Bournemouth	Aug 29	1	&	42 *	1Ct	
Glamorgan	Pontypridd	Sept 7	5				
Gloucs	Southampton	Sept 18	4	&	54 *	1Ct	
REFUGE ASSURANCE							
Gloucs	Southampton	May 6	15				
Somerset	Taunton	May 13	33 *				0-22
Yorkshire	Headingley	May 27	8			2Ct	
Leicestershire	Leicester	June 3	28 *				
Middlesex	Basingstoke	June 10	1				
Glamorgan	Bournemouth	June 17	16			2Ct	0-3
Lancashire	Old Trafford	June 24					
Sussex	Hove	July 1	27			1Ct	1-23
Notts	Southampton	July 15	46 *			1Ct	
Derbyshire	Portsmouth	July 22	4			1Ct	
Warwickshire	Edgbaston	July 29	0				
Northants	Bournemouth	Aug 5	0 *				
Worcestershire	Worcester	Aug 12	17				
Surrey	Southampton	Aug 26	59			1Ct	
NATWEST TROPHY							
Leicestershire	Leicester	June 27	19			1Ct	
Essex	Chelmsford	July 11	9 *			1Ct	
Yorkshire	Southampton	Aug 1	50				
Northants	Southampton	Aug 15	29			1Ct	
BENSON & HEDGES CUP							
Lancashire	Old Trafford	May 8				1Ct	
Combined U	Southampton	May 12					1-2
OTHER FIRST-CLASS							
Oxford U	The Parks	May 3	37 *	&	47	1Ct	0-21
India	Southampton	July 4	37 *	&	104		0-17
Sri Lanka	Southampton	Sept 12	0			1Ct	0-29
OTHER ONE-DAY							
Worcestershire	Scarborough	Sept 2	6				3-28
Essex	Scarborough	Sept 4	57			1Ct	3-28

BATTING AVERAGES - Including fielding

	Matches	Inns	NO	Runs	HS	Avge	100s	50s	Ct	St
Britannic Assurance	20	30	8	670	78 *	30.45	-	5	7	-
Refuge Assurance	14	13	4	254	59	28.22	-	1	8	-
NatWest Trophy	4	4	1	107	50	35.66	-	1	3	-
Benson & Hedges Cup	2	0	0	0	0	-	-	-	1	-
Other First-Class	3	5	2	225	104	75.00	1	-	2	-
Other One-Day	2	2	0	63	57	31.50	-	1	1	-
ALL FIRST-CLASS	23	35	10	895	104	35.80	1	5	9	-
ALL ONE-DAY	22	19	5	424	59	30.28	-	3	13	-

BOWLING AVERAGES

	Overs	Mdns	Runs	Wkts	Avge	Best	5wI	10wM
Britannic Assurance	54.2	7	209	2	104.50	1-7	-	-
Refuge Assurance	6	0	48	1	48.00	1-23	-	
NatWest Trophy								
Benson & Hedges Cup	1	0	2	1	2.00	1-2	-	
Other First-Class	15	2	67	0				
Other One-Day	17	1	56	6	9.33	3-28	-	
ALL FIRST-CLASS	69.2	9	276	2	138.00	1-7	-	-
ALL ONE-DAY	24	1	106	8	13.25	3-28	-	-

P.A. NIXON - *Leicestershire*

Opposition	Venue	Date	Batting			Fielding	Bowling
BRITANNIC ASSURANCE							
Lancashire	Old Trafford	May 19	33 *				
Somerset	Leicester	May 26			33	2Ct	
Hampshire	Leicester	June 2	0			1Ct	
Northants	Northampton	June 6	27				
Middlesex	Leicester	June 16			22	1Ct	
Derbyshire	Leicester	June 20	20 *			3Ct	
Gloucs	Gloucester	June 23	24 *			2Ct	
Notts	Trent Bridge	June 30			0	4Ct	
Glamorgan	Hinckley	July 7				6Ct,1St	
Essex	Leicester	July 25	11			5Ct	
Yorkshire	Sheffield	July 28	33			8Ct	
Worcestershire	Leicester	Aug 4	5	&	3		
Kent	Dartford	Aug 8	17	&	14		
Surrey	The Oval	Aug 11	46	&	17 *	3Ct	
Warwickshire	Edgbaston	Aug 18	25 *			2Ct	
Kent	Leicester	Aug 23	21	&	11 *	6Ct	
Derbyshire	Derby	Sept 18	17			1Ct	
REFUGE ASSURANCE							
Essex	Leicester	May 6				1Ct,1St	
Lancashire	Old Trafford	May 20	1 *			1Ct	
Somerset	Leicester	May 27	9 *				
Hampshire	Leicester	June 3	10			2Ct	
Sussex	Leicester	June 10				2Ct	
Middlesex	Leicester	June 17				1Ct	
Gloucs	Gloucester	June 24				2Ct	
Notts	Trent Bridge	July 1	6			1Ct	
Derbyshire	Knypersley	July 15	4			3Ct	
Yorkshire	Sheffield	July 29	8 *				
Worcestershire	Leicester	Aug 5	0				
Surrey	The Oval	Aug 12	1			1Ct	
Warwickshire	Edgbaston	Aug 19					
Kent	Leicester	Aug 26				1Ct	
NATWEST TROPHY							
Hampshire	Leicester	June 27	12			1Ct	
OTHER FIRST-CLASS							
Oxford U	The Parks	May 23	16 *			2Ct	
India	Leicester	July 21	3 *	&	13	3Ct	
OTHER ONE-DAY							
New Zealand	Leicester	June 14				1Ct	

BATTING AVERAGES - Including fielding

	Matches	Inns	NO	Runs	HS	Avge	100s	50s	Ct	St
Britannic Assurance	17	20	6	379	46	27.07	-	-	44	1
Refuge Assurance	14	8	3	39	10	7.80	-	-	15	1
NatWest Trophy	1	1	0	12	12	12.00	-	-	1	-
Other First-Class	2	3	2	32	16 *	32.00	-	-	5	-
Other One-Day	1	0	0	0	0	-	-	-	1	-
ALL FIRST-CLASS	19	23	8	411	46	27.40	-	-	49	1
ALL ONE-DAY	16	9	3	51	12	8.50	-	-	17	1

BOWLING AVERAGES
Did not bowl

W.M. NOON - *Northamptonshire*

Opposition	Venue	Date	Batting			Fielding	Bowling
BRITANNIC ASSURANCE							
Leicestershire	Northampton	June 6				3Ct	
Glamorgan	Northampton	June 9	2	&	2	1Ct,1St	
REFUGE ASSURANCE							
Derbyshire	Northampton	May 6	1				
Surrey	The Oval	June 3	21			1Ct	
Glamorgan	Northampton	June 10	11			1Ct	
Gloucs	Northampton	Aug 26	0				
OTHER FIRST-CLASS							
New Zealand	Northampton	June 16	2			1Ct	

BATTING AVERAGES - Including fielding

	Matches	Inns	NO	Runs	HS	Avge	100s	50s	Ct	St
Britannic Assurance	2	2	0	4	2	2.00	-	-	4	1
Refuge Assurance	4	4	0	33	21	8.25	-	-	2	-
Other First-Class	1	1	0	2	2	2.00	-	-	1	-
ALL FIRST-CLASS	3	3	0	6	2	2.00	-	-	5	1
ALL ONE-DAY	4	4	0	33	21	8.25	-	-	2	-

BOWLING AVERAGES
Did not bowl

J.A. NORTH - Sussex

Opposition	Venue	Date	Batting		Fielding	Bowling

BRITANNIC ASSURANCE

Kent	Folkestone	May 3	9 &	6	1Ct	0-30
Leicestershire	Leicester	Aug 29	0			1-48 & 0-26
Middlesex	Hove	Sept 18	7 &	19 *		2-43

REFUGE ASSURANCE

Gloucs	Swindon	July 15	1	1Ct	
Northants	Well'borough	July 22	15 *		2-45

BENSON & HEDGES CUP

Middlesex	Hove	May 8		1-48

OTHER FIRST-CLASS

Cambridge U	Hove	June 30	1-46 & 2-43

OTHER ONE-DAY

Yorkshire	Harrogate	June 14	6	0-17

BATTING AVERAGES - Including fielding

	Matches	Inns	NO	Runs	HS	Avge	100s	50s	Ct	St
Britannic Assurance	3	5	1	41	19 *	10.25	-	-	1	-
Refuge Assurance	2	2	1	16	15 *	16.00	-	-	1	-
Benson & Hedges Cup	1	0	0	0	0		-	-	-	-
Other First-Class	1	0	0	0	0	-				
Other One-Day	1	1	0	6	6	6.00	-	-	-	-
ALL FIRST-CLASS	4	5	1	41	19 *	10.25	-	-	1	-
ALL ONE-DAY	4	3	1	22	15 *	11.00	-	-	1	-

BOWLING AVERAGES

	Overs	Mdns	Runs	Wkts	Avge	Best	5wI	10wM
Britannic Assurance	49.2	10	147	3	49.00	2-43	-	-
Refuge Assurance	8	0	45	2	22.50	2-45	-	
Benson & Hedges Cup	8	0	48	1	48.00	1-48	-	
Other First-Class	33.5	7	89	3	29.66	2-43	-	-
Other One-Day	4	0	17	0	-	-	-	
ALL FIRST-CLASS	83.1	17	236	6	39.33	2-43	-	-
ALL ONE-DAY	20	0	110	3	36.66	2-45	-	

M.A.F. NULTY - Ireland

Opposition	Venue	Date	Batting	Fielding	Bowling

OTHER ONE-DAY

New Zealand	Downpatrick	May 9	1
New Zealand	Belfast	May 10	6

BATTING AVERAGES - Including fielding

	Matches	Inns	NO	Runs	HS	Avge	100s	50s	Ct	St
Other One-Day	2	2	0	7	6	3.50	-	-	-	-
ALL ONE-DAY	2	2	0	7	6	3.50	-	-	-	-

BOWLING AVERAGES
Did not bowl

PLAYER RECORDS

O

T.J.G. O'GORMAN - *Derbyshire*

Opposition	Venue	Date	Batting			Fielding	Bowling
BRITANNIC ASSURANCE							
Worcestershire	Derby	July 25	0	&	9		
Northants	Chesterfield	Aug 8	19	&	82	2Ct	
Middlesex	Derby	Aug 18	55	&	20	1Ct	
Essex	Derby	Aug 23	1	&	4		
Yorkshire	Scarborough	Sept 7	21	&	82 *		
Leicestershire	Derby	Sept 18	100				
REFUGE ASSURANCE							
Sussex	Hove	April 22	0				
Glamorgan	Swansea	July 29	32				
Kent	Chesterfield	Aug 5	11				
Middlesex	Derby	Aug 19	0 *				
Essex	Derby	Aug 26	12				
Notts	Derby	Sept 5	20 *				
Middlesex	Edgbaston	Sept 16	10				
BENSON & HEDGES CUP							
Sussex	Derby	April 24	8				
OTHER FIRST-CLASS							
Cambridge U	Fenner's	April 18	55			1Ct	

BATTING AVERAGES - Including fielding

	Matches	Inns	NO	Runs	HS	Avge	100s	50s	Ct	St
Britannic Assurance	6	11	1	393	100	39.30	1	3	3	-
Refuge Assurance	7	7	2	85	32	17.00	-	-	-	-
Benson & Hedges Cup	1	1	0	8	8	8.00	-	-	-	-
Other First-Class	1	1	0	55	55	55.00	-	1	1	-
ALL FIRST-CLASS	7	12	1	448	100	40.72	1	4	4	-
ALL ONE-DAY	8	8	2	93	32	15.50	-	-	-	-

BOWLING AVERAGES
Did not bowl

P.R. OLIVER - *Staffordshire*

Opposition	Venue	Date	Batting	Fielding	Bowling
NATWEST TROPHY					
Northants	Northampton	June 27	28		

BATTING AVERAGES - Including fielding

	Matches	Inns	NO	Runs	HS	Avge	100s	50s	Ct	St
NatWest Trophy	1	1	0	28	28	28.00	-	-	-	-
ALL ONE-DAY	1	1	0	28	28	28.00	-	-	-	-

BOWLING AVERAGES
Did not bowl

P. O'REILLY - *Ireland*

Opposition	Venue	Date	Batting	Fielding	Bowling
OTHER ONE-DAY					
New Zealand	Downpatrick	May 9	1 *	1Ct	0-22
New Zealand	Belfast	May 10	2 *		2-56

BATTING AVERAGES - Including fielding

	Matches	Inns	NO	Runs	HS	Avge	100s	50s	Ct	St
Other One-Day	2	2	2	3	2*	-	-	-	1	-
ALL ONE-DAY	2	2	2	3	2*	-	-	-	1	-

BOWLING AVERAGES

	Overs	Mdns	Runs	Wkts	Avge	Best	5wI	10wM
Other One-Day	14	0	78	2	39.00	2-56	-	
ALL ONE-DAY	14	0	78	2	39.00	2-56	-	

T.M. ORRELL - *Combined Universities*

Opposition	Venue	Date	Batting	Fielding	Bowling
BENSON & HEDGES CUP					
Yorkshire	Headingley	May 8	15	1Ct	
Surrey	The Parks	May 10	0		

BATTING AVERAGES - Including fielding

	Matches	Inns	NO	Runs	HS	Avge	100s	50s	Ct	St
Benson & Hedges Cup	2	2	0	15	15	7.50	-	-	1	-
ALL ONE-DAY	2	2	0	15	15	7.50	-	-	1	-

BOWLING AVERAGES
Did not bowl

D.P. OSTLER - *Warwickshire*

Opposition	Venue	Date	Batting			Fielding	Bowling
BRITANNIC ASSURANCE							
Worcestershire	Edgbaston	May 26	26	&	14		
Derbyshire	Derby	June 16	42 *				
Yorkshire	Sheffield	June 20	61				
Kent	Edgbaston	June 23	71	&	8		
Somerset	Taunton	July 4	11 *			1Ct	
Surrey	The Oval	July 7	30	&	59	1Ct	
Lancashire	Coventry	July 18	3	&	18	3Ct	
Gloucs	Bristol	Aug 8	54	&	23	3Ct	
Somerset	Edgbaston	Sept 7	11	&	1	1Ct	
REFUGE ASSURANCE							
Gloucs	Moreton-in-M	May 20	24 *				
Worcestershire	Worcester	May 27				1Ct	
Essex	Edgbaston	June 10	18				
Derbyshire	Derby	June 17	7 *			2Ct	
Kent	Edgbaston	June 24	3				
Surrey	The Oval	July 8	30				
Glamorgan	Edgbaston	July 15	15				
NATWEST TROPHY							
Yorkshire	Headingley	July 11	4				
OTHER FIRST-CLASS							
New Zealand	Edgbaston	May 30	19	&	0		
Sri Lanka	Edgbaston	Aug 29	56	&	3		
OTHER ONE-DAY							
Surrey	Hove	Sept 3	6				

BATTING AVERAGES - Including fielding

	Matches	Inns	NO	Runs	HS	Avge	100s	50s	Ct	St
Britannic Assurance	9	15	2	432	71	33.23	-	4	9	-
Refuge Assurance	7	6	2	97	30	24.25	-	-	3	-
NatWest Trophy	1	1	0	4	4	4.00	-	-	-	-
Other First-Class	2	4	0	78	56	19.50	-	1	-	-
Other One-Day	1	1	0	6	6	6.00	-	-	-	-
ALL FIRST-CLASS	11	19	2	510	71	30.00	-	5	9	-
ALL ONE-DAY	9	8	2	107	30	17.83	-	-	3	-

BOWLING AVERAGES
Did not bowl

P.A. OWEN - *Gloucestershire*

Opposition	Venue	Date	Batting	Fielding	Bowling
BRITANNIC ASSURANCE					
Yorkshire	Cheltenham	July 21	1		0-72 & 0-47
Northants	Cheltenham	July 25			0-12 & 1-13
Surrey	Cheltenham	July 28	1		2-37 & 1-58

O PLAYER RECORDS

BATTING AVERAGES - Including fielding

	Matches	Inns	NO	Runs	HS	Avge	100s	50s	Ct	St
Britannic Assurance	3	2	0	2	1	1.00	-	-	-	-
ALL FIRST-CLASS	3	2	0	2	1	1.00	-	-	-	-

BOWLING AVERAGES

	Overs	Mdns	Runs	Wkts	Avge	Best	5wI	10wM
Britannic Assurance	57	7	239	4	59.75	2-37	-	-
ALL FIRST-CLASS	57	7	239	4	59.75	2-37	-	-

P. OXLEY - *Berkshire*

Opposition	Venue	Date	Batting	Fielding	Bowling
NATWEST TROPHY					
Middlesex	Lord's	June 27	33*		

BATTING AVERAGES - Including fielding

	Matches	Inns	NO	Runs	HS	Avge	100s	50s	Ct	St
NatWest Trophy	1	1	1	33	33*	-	-	-	-	-
ALL ONE-DAY	1	1	1	33	33*	-	-	-	-	-

BOWLING AVERAGES
Did not bowl

PLEYER RECORDS

PLAYER RECORDS

P

D. PAGE - *Shropshire*

Opposition	Venue	Date	Batting	Fielding	Bowling
NATWEST TROPHY					
Derbyshire	Chesterfield	June 27	0		0-24

BATTING AVERAGES - Including fielding

	Matches	Inns	NO	Runs	HS	Avge	100s	50s	Ct	St
NatWest Trophy	1	1	0	0	0	0.00	-	-	-	-
ALL ONE-DAY	1	1	0	0	0	0.00	-	-	-	-

BOWLING AVERAGES

	Overs	Mdns	Runs	Wkts	Avge	Best	5wI	10wM
NatWest Trophy	5	0	24	0	-	-	-	-
ALL ONE-DAY	5	0	24	0	-	-	-	-

C.L. PARFITT - *Scotland*

Opposition	Venue	Date	Batting	Fielding	Bowling
NATWEST TROPHY					
Essex	Chelmsford	June 27	0		0-29
BENSON & HEDGES CUP					
Essex	Glasgow	May 1	1 *		1-41
Notts	Glasgow	May 8			4-16
Northants	Northampton	May 10		1Ct	0-26
Leicestershire	Leicester	May 12			0-39

BATTING AVERAGES - Including fielding

	Matches	Inns	NO	Runs	HS	Avge	100s	50s	Ct	St
NatWest Trophy	1	1	0	0	0	0.00	-	-	-	-
Benson & Hedges Cup	4	1	1	1	1 *	-	-	-	1	-
ALL ONE-DAY	5	2	1	1	1 *	1.00	-	-	1	-

BOWLING AVERAGES

	Overs	Mdns	Runs	Wkts	Avge	Best	5wI	10wM
NatWest Trophy	9.4	3	29	0	-	-	-	
Benson & Hedges Cup	44	6	122	5	24.40	4-16	-	
ALL ONE-DAY	53.4	9	151	5	30.20	4-16	-	

P.W.G. PARKER - *Sussex*

Opposition	Venue	Date	Batting			Fielding	Bowling
BRITANNIC ASSURANCE							
Surrey	Hove	April 26	100	&	42	1Ct	
Kent	Folkestone	May 3	107	&	19		
Glamorgan	Hove	May 19	57 *				
Gloucs	Hove	June 16	48 *	&	53		
Worcestershire	Worcester	June 20	14			1Ct	
Derbyshire	Hove	July 4			35		
Surrey	Guildford	July 18	11	&	64	2Ct	
Northants	Northampton	July 21	90	&	38		0-59
Hampshire	Arundel	July 25	0	&	18		
Essex	Chelmsford	July 28	20	&	14		
Gloucs	Bristol	Sept 12	0	&	8		
Middlesex	Hove	Sept 18	24	&	16	1Ct	
REFUGE ASSURANCE							
Derbyshire	Hove	April 22	0				
Surrey	Hove	April 29	28				
Glamorgan	Hove	May 20					
Leicestershire	Leicester	June 10	2				
Yorkshire	Hove	June 17	36			1Ct	
Worcestershire	Worcester	June 24	42				
Hampshire	Hove	July 1	12				
Gloucs	Swindon	July 15	7			1Ct	
Northants	Well'borough	July 22	34			1Ct	
Essex	Chelmsford	July 29	72			1Ct	

NATWEST TROPHY

Opposition	Venue	Date	Batting	Fielding	Bowling
Ireland	Downpatrick	June 27	4 *		
Glamorgan	Cardiff	July 11	83		

BENSON & HEDGES CUP

Opposition	Venue	Date	Batting	Fielding	Bowling
Derbyshire	Derby	April 24	8		
Min Counties	Marlow	May 1	85 *		
Middlesex	Hove	May 8	7	1Ct	
Somerset	Hove	May 12	1		

OTHER FIRST-CLASS

For MCC

Opposition	Venue	Date	Batting			Fielding	Bowling
Worcestershire	Lord's	April 17	93			1Ct	
For Sussex							
Cambridge U	Hove	June 30	10 *			1Ct	
Sri Lanka	Hove	Sept 5	83 *	&	21	1Ct	

OTHER ONE-DAY

For D of Norfolk

Opposition	Venue	Date	Batting	Fielding	Bowling
New Zealand	Arundel	May 6	90		0-1
For Sussex					
Zimbabwe	Hove	May 13	10		
Yorkshire	Harrogate	June 14	0	1Ct	0-4

BATTING AVERAGES - Including fielding

	Matches	Inns	NO	Runs	HS	Avge	100s	50s	Ct	St
Britannic Assurance	12	21	2	778	107	40.94	2	4	5	-
Refuge Assurance	10	9	0	233	72	25.88	-	1	4	-
NatWest Trophy	2	2	1	87	83	87.00	-	1	-	-
Benson & Hedges Cup	4	4	1	101	85 *	33.66	-	1	1	-
Other First-Class	3	4	2	207	93	103.50	-	2	3	-
Other One-Day	3	3	0	100	90	33.33	-	1	1	-
ALL FIRST-CLASS	15	25	4	985	107	46.90	2	6	8	-
ALL ONE-DAY	19	18	2	521	90	32.56	-	4	6	-

BOWLING AVERAGES

	Overs	Mdns	Runs	Wkts	Avge	Best	5wI	10wM
Britannic Assurance	8	0	59	0	-	-	-	-
Refuge Assurance								
NatWest Trophy								
Benson & Hedges Cup								
Other First-Class								
Other One-Day	1.2	0	5	0	-	-	-	-
ALL FIRST-CLASS	8	0	59	0	-	-	-	-
ALL ONE-DAY	1.2	0	5	0	-	-	-	-

R.J. PARKS - *Hampshire*

Opposition	Venue	Date	Batting			Fielding	Bowling
BRITANNIC ASSURANCE							
Kent	Canterbury	April 26	19 *			1Ct,1St	
Sussex	Southampton	May 15	36			4Ct	
Surrey	The Oval	May 19			5 *	2Ct	
Essex	Southampton	May 23	3 *			5Ct	
Yorkshire	Headingley	May 26	36 *	&	1 *	1Ct	
Leicestershire	Leicester	June 2	2			1Ct	
Somerset	Basingstoke	June 6	11	&	15 *	1Ct	
Glamorgan	Southampton	June 16	0			1Ct	
Gloucs	Gloucester	June 20					
Lancashire	Old Trafford	June 23	14 *			1Ct	
Notts	Portsmouth	July 18	0			4Ct	
Derbyshire	Portsmouth	July 21	0	&	8 *	7Ct	
Sussex	Arundel	July 25			15 *		
Warwickshire	Edgbaston	July 28	33			0Ct,1St	
Northants	Bournemouth	Aug 4				6Ct	
Middlesex	Bournemouth	Aug 8	4			5Ct,1St	
Worcestershire	Worcester	Aug 11			0	2Ct	
Somerset	Taunton	Aug 18	1			5Ct,1St	
REFUGE ASSURANCE							
Kent	Canterbury	April 29	4			0Ct,2St	
Gloucs	Southampton	May 6					
Somerset	Taunton	May 13				1Ct	
Leicestershire	Leicester	June 3				1Ct	
Middlesex	Basingstoke	June 10	11				
Glamorgan	Bournemouth	June 17					
Lancashire	Old Trafford	June 24					
Sussex	Hove	July 1	4				
Essex	Southampton	July 8				2Ct	

P PLAYER RECORDS

Notts	Southampton	July 15			1Ct
Derbyshire	Portsmouth	July 22			3Ct
Warwickshire	Edgbaston	July 29	23 *		2Ct
Northants	Bournemouth	Aug 5			
Worcestershire	Worcester	Aug 12	4		
Surrey	Southampton	Aug 26	10		

NATWEST TROPHY

Leicestershire	Leicester	June 27	14 *		1Ct
Essex	Chelmsford	July 11			1Ct
Yorkshire	Southampton	Aug 1	27 *		1Ct
Northants	Southampton	Aug 15	4		2Ct,1St

BENSON & HEDGES CUP

Yorkshire	Southampton	April 24	6 *		2Ct
Surrey	The Oval	May 1	20 *		2Ct
Lancashire	Old Trafford	May 8			1Ct,1St
Combined U	Southampton	May 12			1Ct

OTHER FIRST-CLASS

Oxford U	The Parks	May 3	5 * & 8		1Ct
India	Southampton	July 4			2Ct

OTHER ONE-DAY
For MCC

New Zealand	Lord's	May 7			1Ct,1St

BATTING AVERAGES - Including fielding

	Matches	Inns	NO	Runs	HS	Avge	100s	50s	Ct	St
Britannic Assurance	18	19	9	203	36 *	20.30	-	-	46	4
Refuge Assurance	15	6	1	56	23 *	11.20	-	-	10	2
NatWest Trophy	4	3	2	45	27 *	45.00	-	-	5	1
Benson & Hedges Cup	4	2	2	26	20 *	-	-	-	6	1
Other First-Class	2	2	1	13	8	13.00	-	-	3	-
Other One-Day	1	0	0	0	0	-	-	-	1	1
ALL FIRST-CLASS	20	21	10	216	36 *	19.63	-	-	49	4
ALL ONE-DAY	24	11	5	127	27 *	21.16	-	-	22	5

BOWLING AVERAGES
Did not bowl

A.C. PARORE - *New Zealand*

Opposition	Venue	Date	Batting	Fielding	Bowling

CORNHILL TEST MATCHES

England	Edgbaston	July 5	12 * & 20	4Ct,1St	

OTHER FIRST-CLASS

Somerset	Taunton	May 16	43	4Ct	
Sussex	Hove	May 26		2Ct	
Derbyshire	Derby	June 2	37		
Northants	Northampton	June 16		1Ct	
Combined U	Fenner's	June 27	15	3Ct	
Essex	Chelmsford	June 30	4		

OTHER ONE-DAY

D of Norfolk	Arundel	May 6			
MCC	Lord's	May 7	6	2Ct	
Ireland	Belfast	May 10	4 *	0Ct,1St	
Leicestershire	Leicester	June 14	19 *	1Ct	
For Rest of World					
England XI	Jesmond	Aug 2	5		
England XI	Jesmond	Aug 3		2Ct	

BATTING AVERAGES - Including fielding

	Matches	Inns	NO	Runs	HS	Avge	100s	50s	Ct	St
Cornhill Test Matches	1	2	1	32	20	32.00	-	-	4	1
Other First-Class	6	4	0	99	43	24.75	-	-	10	-
Other One-Day	6	4	2	34	19 *	17.00	-	-	5	1
ALL FIRST-CLASS	7	6	1	131	43	26.20	-	-	14	1
ALL ONE-DAY	6	4	2	34	19 *	17.00	-	-	5	1

BOWLING AVERAGES
Did not bowl

G.J. PARSONS - *Leicestershire*

Opposition	Venue	Date	Batting	Fielding	Bowling

BRITANNIC ASSURANCE

Essex	Leicester	July 25	19 *		1-22 & 0-54
Yorkshire	Sheffield	July 28			0-20 & 1-61
Kent	Dartford	Aug 8	15 & 13		5-31 & 1-18
Surrey	The Oval	Aug 11	14 & 7	1Ct	6-75
Warwickshire	Edgbaston	Aug 18	1		4-21 & 1-53
Kent	Leicester	Aug 23	20 & 2	1Ct	3-40 & 3-104
Sussex	Leicester	Aug 29	1 * & 1	1Ct	1-53 & 3-90
Northants	Leicester	Sept 12	8 & 0		1-91 & 1-88

REFUGE ASSURANCE

Glamorgan	Cardiff	April 29	12		0-53
Notts	Trent Bridge	July 1	11 *		0-24
Yorkshire	Sheffield	July 29			1-36
Worcestershire	Leicester	Aug 5	19 *		0-27
Surrey	The Oval	Aug 12	18		1-70
Warwickshire	Edgbaston	Aug 19			
Kent	Leicester	Aug 26			2-37

BENSON & HEDGES CUP

Scotland	Leicester	May 12			0-26

OTHER FIRST-CLASS

Oxford U	The Parks	May 23		1Ct	3-34 & 0-35
India	Leicester	July 21	11 *		1-73 & 0-0

BATTING AVERAGES - Including fielding

	Matches	Inns	NO	Runs	HS	Avge	100s	50s	Ct	St
Britannic Assurance	8	12	2	101	20	10.10	-	-	3	-
Refuge Assurance	7	4	2	60	19 *	30.00	-	-		
Benson & Hedges Cup	1	0	0	0	0		-	-		
Other First-Class	2	1	1	11	11 *	-	-	-	1	-
ALL FIRST-CLASS	10	13	3	112	20	11.20	-	-	4	-
ALL ONE-DAY	8	4	2	60	19 *	30.00	-	-	-	-

BOWLING AVERAGES

	Overs	Mdns	Runs	Wkts	Avge	Best	5wI	10wM
Britannic Assurance	247.5	56	821	31	26.48	6-75	2	-
Refuge Assurance	40	1	247	4	61.75	2-37	-	-
Benson & Hedges Cup	4	1	26	0	-	-	-	-
Other First-Class	57	21	142	4	35.50	3-34	-	-
ALL FIRST-CLASS	304.5	77	963	35	27.51	6-75	2	-
ALL ONE-DAY	44	2	273	4	68.25	2-37	-	-

T. PARTON - *Shropshire*

Opposition	Venue	Date	Batting	Fielding	Bowling

NATWEST TROPHY

Derbyshire	Chesterfield	June 27	2	1Ct	

BATTING AVERAGES - Including fielding

	Matches	Inns	NO	Runs	HS	Avge	100s	50s	Ct	St
NatWest Trophy	1	1	0	2	2	2.00	-	-	1	-
ALL ONE-DAY	1	1	0	2	2	2.00	-	-	1	-

BOWLING AVERAGES
Did not bowl

A.S. PATEL - *Durham*

Opposition	Venue	Date	Batting	Fielding	Bowling

NATWEST TROPHY

Lancashire	Old Trafford	June 27	31 *		0-12

BATTING AVERAGES - Including fielding

	Matches	Inns	NO	Runs	HS	Avge	100s	50s	Ct	St
NatWest Trophy	1	1	1	31	31 *					

PLAYER RECORDS

ALL ONE-DAY	1	1	1	31	31 *	-	-	-	-	-

BOWLING AVERAGES

	Overs	Mdns	Runs	Wkts	Avge	Best	5wI	10wM
NatWest Trophy	2	0	12	0	-	-	-	-
ALL ONE-DAY	2	0	12	0	-	-	-	-

M.M. PATEL - *Kent*

Opposition	Venue	Date	Batting	Fielding	Bowling
BRITANNIC ASSURANCE					
Northants	Northampton	July 18	41 *		1-81
Surrey	Guildford	July 21	2 & 0	1Ct	0-54 & 0-6
Middlesex	Canterbury	July 25	1 *		0-54
Derbyshire	Chesterfield	Aug 4	7 & 25 *		2-97
Leicestershire	Dartford	Aug 8	17		4-91 & 6-57
Gloucs	Bristol	Aug 11			1-38 & 0-30
Leicestershire	Leicester	Aug 23	3 * & 5		0-29 & 5-96
Hampshire	Bournemouth	Aug 29	0 *	1Ct	0-27 & 1-112
Surrey	Canterbury	Sept 7	3 & 0		0-64
NATWEST TROPHY					
Oxfordshire	Oxford	June 27			2-29
OTHER ONE-DAY					
Sussex	Hove	Sept 2	1		0-48
Surrey	Hove	Sept 4			1-50

BATTING AVERAGES - Including fielding

	Matches	Inns	NO	Runs	HS	Avge	100s	50s	Ct	St
Britannic Assurance	9	12	5	104	41 *	14.85	-	-	2	-
NatWest Trophy	1	0	0	0	0	-	-	-	-	-
Other One-Day	2	1	0	1	1	1.00	-	-	-	-
ALL FIRST-CLASS	9	12	5	104	41 *	14.85	-	-	2	-
ALL ONE-DAY	3	1	0	1	1	1.00	-	-	-	-

BOWLING AVERAGES

	Overs	Mdns	Runs	Wkts	Avge	Best	5wI	10wM
Britannic Assurance	297.5	72	836	20	41.80	6-57	2	1
NatWest Trophy	12	6	29	2	14.50	2-29	-	
Other One-Day	18	0	98	1	98.00	1-50	-	
ALL FIRST-CLASS	297.5	72	836	20	41.80	6-57	2	1
ALL ONE-DAY	30	6	127	3	42.33	2-29	-	

G.A. PATERSON - *Zimbabwe*

Opposition	Venue	Date	Batting	Fielding	Bowling
OTHER ONE-DAY					
Sussex	Hove	May 13	18		

BATTING AVERAGES - Including fielding

	Matches	Inns	NO	Runs	HS	Avge	100s	50s	Ct	St
Other One-Day	1	1	0	18	18	18.00	-	-	-	-
ALL ONE-DAY	1	1	0	18	18	18.00	-	-	-	-

BOWLING AVERAGES
Did not bowl

B.M.W. PATTERSON - *Scotland*

Opposition	Venue	Date	Batting	Fielding	Bowling
NATWEST TROPHY					
Essex	Chelmsford	June 27	19		
BENSON & HEDGES CUP					
Essex	Glasgow	May 1	42		
Notts	Glasgow	May 8	22		

Northants	Northampton	May 10		8	1Ct	
Leicestershire	Leicester	May 12		4		

OTHER FIRST-CLASS

Ireland	Edinburgh	Aug 11	60		3Ct	

OTHER ONE-DAY

India	Glasgow	July 14		0		

BATTING AVERAGES - Including fielding

	Matches	Inns	NO	Runs	HS	Avge	100s	50s	Ct	St
NatWest Trophy	1	1	0	19	19	19.00	-	-	-	-
Benson & Hedges Cup	4	4	0	76	42	19.00	-	-	1	-
Other First-Class	1	1	0	60	60	60.00	-	1	3	-
Other One-Day	1	1	0	0	0	0.00	-	-	-	-
ALL FIRST-CLASS	1	1	0	60	60	60.00	-	1	3	-
ALL ONE-DAY	6	6	0	95	42	15.83	-	-	1	-

BOWLING AVERAGES
Did not bowl

B.P. PATTERSON - *Lancashire*

Opposition	Venue	Date	Batting	Fielding	Bowling
BRITANNIC ASSURANCE					
Worcestershire	Old Trafford	April 26			2-55 & 1-27
Surrey	The Oval	May 3	0	1Ct	2-108
Leicestershire	Old Trafford	May 19			3-68 & 0-27
Glamorgan	Colwyn Bay	May 26			3-88 & 1-41
Sussex	Horsham	June 2	0		2-37 & 4-52
Gloucs	Old Trafford	June 9			2-43
Middlesex	Old Trafford	June 20			1-74
Somerset	Old Trafford	July 28	1		3-76 & 1-68
Yorkshire	Headingley	Aug 4	4 *	1Ct	2-77 & 1-88
Northants	Northampton	Aug 11			1-54 & 0-32
REFUGE ASSURANCE					
Surrey	The Oval	May 6			0-55
BENSON & HEDGES CUP					
Surrey	Old Trafford	April 24			1-6
Combined U	Fenner's	May 1			1-24
Hampshire	Old Trafford	May 8			0-10
Yorkshire	Headingley	May 10			1-33

BATTING AVERAGES - Including fielding

	Matches	Inns	NO	Runs	HS	Avge	100s	50s	Ct	St
Britannic Assurance	10	4	1	5	4 *	1.66	-	-	2	-
Refuge Assurance	1	0	0	0	0	-	-	-	-	-
Benson & Hedges Cup	4	0	0	0	0	-	-	-	-	-
ALL FIRST-CLASS	10	4	1	5	4 *	1.66	-	-	2	-
ALL ONE-DAY	5	0	0	0	0	-	-	-	-	-

BOWLING AVERAGES

	Overs	Mdns	Runs	Wkts	Avge	Best	5wI	10wM
Britannic Assurance	281.4	45	1015	29	35.00	4-52	-	-
Refuge Assurance	8	0	55	0	-	-	-	-
Benson & Hedges Cup	31.1	9	73	3	24.33	1-6	-	
ALL FIRST-CLASS	281.4	45	1015	29	35.00	4-52	-	-
ALL ONE-DAY	39.1	9	128	3	42.66	1-6	-	

T.J.T. PATTERSON - *Ireland*

Opposition	Venue	Date	Batting	Fielding	Bowling
OTHER FIRST-CLASS					
Scotland	Edinburgh	Aug 11	84	1Ct	
OTHER ONE-DAY					
New Zealand	Downpatrick	May 9	9		
New Zealand	Belfast	May 10	23	1Ct	

P | PLAYER RECORDS

BATTING AVERAGES - Including fielding

	Matches	Inns	NO	Runs	HS	Avge	100s	50s	Ct	St
Other First-Class	1	1	0	84	84	84.00	-	1	1	-
Other One-Day	2	2	0	32	23	16.00	-	-	1	-
ALL FIRST-CLASS	1	1	0	84	84	84.00	-	1	1	-
ALL ONE-DAY	2	2	0	32	23	16.00	-	-	1	-

BOWLING AVERAGES
Did not bowl

M.J. PECK - *Suffolk*

Opposition	Venue	Date	Batting	Fielding	Bowling
NATWEST TROPHY					
Worcestershire	Bury St Ed's	June 27	0		

BATTING AVERAGES - Including fielding

	Matches	Inns	NO	Runs	HS	Avge	100s	50s	Ct	St
NatWest Trophy	1	1	0	0	0	0.00	-	-	-	-
ALL ONE-DAY	1	1	0	0	0	0.00	-	-	-	-

BOWLING AVERAGES
Did not bowl

A.L. PENBERTHY - *Northamptonshire*

Opposition	Venue	Date	Batting		Fielding	Bowling
BRITANNIC ASSURANCE						
Warwickshire	Northampton	May 15	0 &	12	1Ct	4-91
Notts	Trent Bridge	May 23	67 *		2Ct	3-28 & 0-57
Warwickshire	Edgbaston	June 2	17			0-27 & 0-6
Leicestershire	Northampton	June 6				3-61
Glamorgan	Northampton	June 9	1			0-33
Yorkshire	Northampton	July 7	8 &	1		0-32 & 0-29
Worcestershire	Worcester	Aug 18	1 &	21	1Ct	
Gloucs	Northampton	Aug 23	28 &	18	1Ct	3-83 & 1-51
Essex	Northampton	Aug 29	15 *			1-59 & 2-67
Essex	Chelmsford	Sept 7	0 &	83	2Ct	0-34 & 1-27
Leicestershire	Leicester	Sept 12	52 &	10	1Ct	1-57 & 0-26
REFUGE ASSURANCE						
Leicestershire	Leicester	April 22	0 *			0-20
Kent	Northampton	May 27	6		1Ct	1-40
Surrey	The Oval	June 3	4		1Ct	0-19
Worcestershire	Worcester	Aug 19			1Ct	1-45
BENSON & HEDGES CUP						
Notts	Trent Bridge	May 12	10			
OTHER FIRST-CLASS						
Cambridge U	Fenner's	April 14	101 *			3-11 & 0-12

BATTING AVERAGES - Including fielding

	Matches	Inns	NO	Runs	HS	Avge	100s	50s	Ct	St
Britannic Assurance	11	16	2	334	83	23.85	-	3	8	-
Refuge Assurance	4	3	1	10	6	5.00	-	-	3	-
Benson & Hedges Cup	1	1	0	10	10	10.00	-	-	-	-
Other First-Class	1	1	1	101	101 *	-	1	-	-	-
ALL FIRST-CLASS	12	17	3	435	101 *	31.07	1	3	8	-
ALL ONE-DAY	5	4	1	20	10	6.66	-	-	3	-

BOWLING AVERAGES

	Overs	Mdns	Runs	Wkts	Avge	Best	5wI	10wM
Britannic Assurance	196	23	768	19	40.42	4-91	-	-
Refuge Assurance	15	0	124	2	62.00	1-40	-	
Benson & Hedges Cup								
Other First-Class	11.4	6	23	3	7.66	3-11	-	
ALL FIRST-CLASS	207.4	29	791	22	35.95	4-91	-	-
ALL ONE-DAY	15	0	124	2	62.00	1-40	-	

C. PENN - *Kent*

Opposition	Venue	Date	Batting		Fielding	Bowling
BRITANNIC ASSURANCE						
Hampshire	Canterbury	April 26	0 *			3-79 & 0-6
Middlesex	Lord's	May 15	3 &	0		3-45 & 0-46
Glamorgan	Swansea	May 23				0-44 & 0-39
Notts	Tunbridge We	June 2	23 &	17		0-105
Essex	Maidstone	June 4				0-68
Gloucs	Bristol	Aug 11	23 *		1Ct	2-44 & 1-59
REFUGE ASSURANCE						
Essex	Chelmsford	April 22				2-30
Middlesex	Folkestone	May 6				0-22
Glamorgan	Llanelli	May 13	20 *			1-51
Yorkshire	Canterbury	May 20				1-28
Northants	Northampton	May 27			1Ct	1-33
Gloucs	Bristol	Aug 12	0			0-44
BENSON & HEDGES CUP						
Gloucs	Canterbury	May 10				
Glamorgan	Swansea	May 12	8 *			2-40
OTHER FIRST-CLASS						
India	Canterbury	July 7			1Ct	2-40 & 0-61

BATTING AVERAGES - Including fielding

	Matches	Inns	NO	Runs	HS	Avge	100s	50s	Ct	St
Britannic Assurance	6	6	2	66	23 *	16.50	-	-	1	-
Refuge Assurance	6	2	1	20	20 *	20.00	-	-	1	-
Benson & Hedges Cup	2	1	1	8	8 *	-	-	-	-	-
Other First-Class	1	0	0	0	0	-	-	-	1	-
ALL FIRST-CLASS	7	6	2	66	23 *	16.50	-	-	2	-
ALL ONE-DAY	8	3	2	28	20 *	28.00	-	-	1	-

BOWLING AVERAGES

	Overs	Mdns	Runs	Wkts	Avge	Best	5wI	10wM
Britannic Assurance	158	33	535	9	59.44	3-45	-	-
Refuge Assurance	39.3	2	208	5	41.60	2-30	-	
Benson & Hedges Cup	10.5	1	40	2	20.00	2-40	-	
Other First-Class	28	2	101	2	50.50	2-40	-	
ALL FIRST-CLASS	186	35	636	11	57.81	3-45	-	-
ALL ONE-DAY	50.2	3	248	7	35.42	2-30	-	

T.L. PENNEY - *Warwickshire*

Opposition	Venue	Date	Batting	Fielding	Bowling
OTHER ONE-DAY					
Surrey	Harrogate	June 13	36		
Yorkshire	Harrogate	June 15	64 *		

BATTING AVERAGES - Including fielding

	Matches	Inns	NO	Runs	HS	Avge	100s	50s	Ct	St
Other One-Day	2	2	1	100	64 *	100.00	-	1	-	-
ALL ONE-DAY	2	2	1	100	64 *	100.00	-	1	-	-

BOWLING AVERAGES
Did not bowl

B.S. PERCY - *Buckinghamshire*

Opposition	Venue	Date	Batting	Fielding	Bowling
NATWEST TROPHY					
Notts	Marlow	June 27	0	2Ct	1-30

BATTING AVERAGES - Including fielding

	Matches	Inns	NO	Runs	HS	Avge	100s	50s	Ct	St
NatWest Trophy	1	1	0	0	0	0.00	-	-	2	-
ALL ONE-DAY	1	1	0	0	0	0.00	-	-	2	-

PLAINER RECORDS

PLAYER RECORDS

BOWLING AVERAGES

	Overs	Mdns	Runs	Wkts	Avge	Best	5wI	10wM
NatWest Trophy	6	0	30	1	30.00	1-30	-	
ALL ONE-DAY	6	0	30	1	30.00	1-30	-	

I.L. PHILIP - *Scotland*

Opposition	Venue	Date	Batting	Fielding	Bowling
NATWEST TROPHY					
Essex	Chelmsford	June 27	1		
BENSON & HEDGES CUP					
Essex	Glasgow	May 1	29		
Notts	Glasgow	May 8	16		
Northants	Northampton	May 10	95		
Leicestershire	Leicester	May 12	29	1Ct	
OTHER FIRST-CLASS					
Ireland	Edinburgh	Aug 11	100		
OTHER ONE-DAY					
India	Glasgow	July 14	14		

BATTING AVERAGES - Including fielding

	Matches	Inns	NO	Runs	HS	Avge	100s	50s	Ct	St
NatWest Trophy	1	1	0	1	1	1.00	-	-	-	-
Benson & Hedges Cup	4	4	0	169	95	42.25	-	1	1	-
Other First-Class	1	1	0	100	100	100.00	1	-	-	-
Other One-Day	1	1	0	14	14	14.00	-	-	-	-
ALL FIRST-CLASS	1	1	0	100	100	100.00	1	-	-	-
ALL ONE-DAY	6	6	0	184	95	30.66	-	1	1	-

BOWLING AVERAGES
Did not bowl

R.A. PICK - *Nottinghamshire*

Opposition	Venue	Date	Batting	Fielding	Bowling
BRITANNIC ASSURANCE					
Derbyshire	Trent Bridge	April 26	14 *		2-81
Worcestershire	Worcester	May 3	27 * & 0		4-119
Leicestershire	Leicester	May 15	22		7-128 & 3-56
Warwickshire	Edgbaston	May 19			2-46 & 1-56
Northants	Trent Bridge	May 23	3		3-64 & 1-40
Derbyshire	Derby	May 26	1 *		2-97 & 1-38
Kent	Tunbridge We	June 2			3-57 & 3-91
Leicestershire	Trent Bridge	June 30	34		0-52 & 0-12
Yorkshire	Scarborough	July 4		1Ct	0-74
Sussex	Trent Bridge	July 7	13 *	1Ct	3-49 & 2-40
Glamorgan	Worksop	Aug 11	11 & 2	1Ct	1-65 & 0-55
Gloucs	Trent Bridge	Aug 18	3 & 4 *		4-70 & 4-45
Worcestershire	Trent Bridge	Aug 29	4 *	1Ct	1-72 & 0-21
Middlesex	Lord's	Sept 7	35 & 26		1-79
REFUGE ASSURANCE					
Yorkshire	Trent Bridge	April 22			1-23
Lancashire	Trent Bridge	April 29	0 *		1-43
Worcestershire	Worcester	May 6	12		1-47
NATWEST TROPHY					
Bucks	Marlow	June 27	4 *		3-22
Northants	Northampton	July 11	5 *		0-64
BENSON & HEDGES CUP					
Essex	Chelmsford	April 24			1-37
Leicestershire	Trent Bridge	May 1			3-50
Scotland	Glasgow	May 8		1Ct	1-45
Northants	Trent Bridge	May 12			2-47
Essex	Chelmsford	May 30			1-60
Worcestershire	Trent Bridge	June 13			0-45
OTHER FIRST-CLASS					
Oxford U	The Parks	June 6			0-20
Cambridge U	Fenner's	June 16		2Ct	1-31 & 0-12

| | | | | | Sri Lanka | Cleethorpes | Aug 25 | | 5 | | 1-54 & 1-33 |

BATTING AVERAGES - Including fielding

	Matches	Inns	NO	Runs	HS	Avge	100s	50s	Ct	St
Britannic Assurance	14	15	6	199	35	22.11	-	-	4	-
Refuge Assurance	3	2	1	12	12	12.00	-	-	-	-
NatWest Trophy	2	2	2	9	5 *	-	-	-	-	-
Benson & Hedges Cup	6	0	0	0	0	-	-	-	1	-
Other First-Class	3	1	0	5	5	5.00	-	-	2	-
ALL FIRST-CLASS	17	16	6	204	35	20.40	-	-	6	-
ALL ONE-DAY	11	4	3	21	12	21.00	-	-	1	-

BOWLING AVERAGES

	Overs	Mdns	Runs	Wkts	Avge	Best	5wI	10wM
Britannic Assurance	443.5	70	1507	48	31.39	7-128	1	1
Refuge Assurance	24	0	113	3	37.66	1-23	-	
NatWest Trophy	21	3	86	3	28.66	3-22	-	
Benson & Hedges Cup	63.4	2	284	8	35.50	3-50	-	
Other First-Class	51	13	150	3	50.00	1-31	-	-
ALL FIRST-CLASS	494.5	83	1657	51	32.49	7-128	1	1
ALL ONE-DAY	108.4	5	483	14	34.50	3-22	-	

C.S. PICKLES - *Yorkshire*

Opposition	Venue	Date	Batting	Fielding	Bowling
BRITANNIC ASSURANCE					
Hampshire	Headingley	May 26	13 * & 57 *		2-64 & 0-25
Worcestershire	Worcester	June 2	30		1-30
Surrey	Harrogate	June 9	0	1Ct	2-45
Warwickshire	Sheffield	June 20	1		0-33 & 0-34
Middlesex	Uxbridge	July 18	17 & 18	1Ct	1-30
Gloucs	Cheltenham	July 21	28 *		0-45
Somerset	Scarborough	July 25	9 * & 1	1Ct	2-82 & 3-56
Leicestershire	Sheffield	July 28	14 & 56 *		0-65 & 1-9
Lancashire	Headingley	Aug 4	21 & 39	1Ct	1-69
Sussex	Eastbourne	Aug 8			2-28 & 2-23
Essex	Middlesbr'gh	Aug 11	20 & 19		2-68
Lancashire	Old Trafford	Aug 18	16		0-57 & 0-17
Middlesex	Headingley	Aug 23	37 & 1	1Ct	2-80 & 0-39
Derbyshire	Scarborough	Sept 7	4 *	1Ct	2-72
Notts	Trent Bridge	Sept 18	23 *		2-120 & 0-16
REFUGE ASSURANCE					
Kent	Canterbury	May 20	0		0-42
Hampshire	Headingley	May 27	6		0-30
Worcestershire	Worcester	June 3	0		1-43
Sussex	Hove	June 17		1Ct	0-24
Somerset	Scarborough	July 15	1 *	1Ct	4-36
Gloucs	Cheltenham	July 22			0-21
Leicestershire	Sheffield	July 29			0-21
Essex	Middlesbr'gh	Aug 12	0	2Ct	1-38
Middlesex	Scarborough	Aug 26		1Ct	1-50
OTHER FIRST-CLASS					
Zimbabwe	Headingley	May 16	54 *		2-29 & 1-27
OTHER ONE-DAY					
Sussex	Harrogate	June 14			2-26
Warwickshire	Harrogate	June 15			2-51
World XI	Scarborough	Sept 1	11 *	1Ct	2-56
Essex	Scarborough	Sept 3	1	1Ct	3-40
Yorkshiremen	Scarborough	Sept 6		1Ct	1-48

BATTING AVERAGES - Including fielding

	Matches	Inns	NO	Runs	HS	Avge	100s	50s	Ct	St
Britannic Assurance	15	21	7	424	57 *	30.28	-	2	6	-
Refuge Assurance	9	5	1	7	6	1.75	-	-	5	-
Other First-Class	1	1	1	54	54 *	-	-	1	-	-
Other One-Day	5	2	1	12	11 *	12.00	-	-	3	-
ALL FIRST-CLASS	16	22	8	478	57 *	34.14	-	3	6	-
ALL ONE-DAY	14	7	2	19	11 *	3.80	-	-	8	-

BOWLING AVERAGES

	Overs	Mdns	Runs	Wkts	Avge	Best	5wI	10wM
Britannic Assurance	296.1	59	1107	25	44.28	3-56	-	
Refuge Assurance	57	0	305	7	43.57	4-36		
Other First-Class	29	13	56	3	18.66	2-29		
Other One-Day	51	4	221	10	22.10	3-40		

P PLAYER RECORDS

ALL FIRST-CLASS	325.1	72	1163	28	41.53	3-56	-	-
ALL ONE-DAY	108	4	526	17	30.94	4-36	-	-

A.R.K. PIERSON - *Warwickshire*

Opposition	Venue	Date	Batting	Fielding	Bowling
BRITANNIC ASSURANCE					
Northants	Edgbaston	June 2	5 * & 9 *		1-49
Essex	Edgbaston	June 9			0-86
Derbyshire	Derby	June 16			0-84
Kent	Edgbaston	June 23	2 & 6		2-68 & 1-19
Somerset	Taunton	July 4			2-11 & 0-23
Surrey	The Oval	July 7	0 & 10 *		0-39
Lancashire	Coventry	July 18		1Ct	0-70 & 3-56
Glamorgan	Swansea	July 25			5-101 & 2-78
Hampshire	Edgbaston	July 28			3-73 & 2-66
Sussex	Eastbourne	Aug 4	9		0-8 & 2-65
Gloucs	Bristol	Aug 8	16 * & 0 *		2-69
REFUGE ASSURANCE					
Derbyshire	Derby	June 17		1Ct	2-24
Kent	Edgbaston	June 24			1-18
Glamorgan	Edgbaston	July 15	1	1Ct	1-38
Notts	Edgbaston	July 22			0-27
NATWEST TROPHY					
Hertfordshire	St Albans	June 27			0-49

BATTING AVERAGES - Including fielding

	Matches	Inns	NO	Runs	HS	Avge	100s	50s	Ct	St
Britannic Assurance	11	9	5	57	16 *	14.25	-	-	1	-
Refuge Assurance	4	1	0	1	1	1.00	-	-	2	-
NatWest Trophy	1	0	0	0	0	-	-	-	-	-
ALL FIRST-CLASS	11	9	5	57	16 *	14.25	-	-	1	-
ALL ONE-DAY	5	1	0	1	1	1.00	-	-	2	-

BOWLING AVERAGES

	Overs	Mdns	Runs	Wkts	Avge	Best	5wI	10wM
Britannic Assurance	302.4	55	965	25	38.60	5-101	1	-
Refuge Assurance	23	3	107	4	26.75	2-24	-	
NatWest Trophy	12	1	49	0	-	-	-	
ALL FIRST-CLASS	302.4	55	965	25	38.60	5-101	1	-
ALL ONE-DAY	35	4	156	4	39.00	2-24	-	

A.C.S. PIGOTT - *Sussex*

Opposition	Venue	Date	Batting	Fielding	Bowling
BRITANNIC ASSURANCE					
Surrey	Hove	April 26			2-77 & 0-17
Hampshire	Southampton	May 15	50 & 3		0-87
Glamorgan	Hove	May 19	8 & 54		1-86
Somerset	Taunton	May 23	2	1Ct	1-117
Lancashire	Horsham	June 2	14 & 6	2Ct	1-60
Worcestershire	Worcester	June 20		1Ct	1-68
Derbyshire	Hove	July 4		12	4-69
Notts	Trent Bridge	July 7	3	1Ct	3-47 & 0-18
Surrey	Guildford	July 18	33	1Ct	2-68 & 0-26
Northants	Northampton	July 21	5 * & 17 *		2-83 & 1-28
Hampshire	Arundel	July 25	64 * & 5		1-43 & 1-12
Essex	Chelmsford	July 28	0 & 1	1Ct	1-67 & 3-79
Warwickshire	Eastbourne	Aug 4	32 & 0	1Ct	3-101 & 0-21
Yorkshire	Eastbourne	Aug 8	29 * & 0		0-76
Middlesex	Lord's	Aug 11	58		1-105
Kent	Hove	Aug 18		10	1Ct	2-93 & 5-77
Somerset	Hove	Aug 23	2 & 23		4-119
Leicestershire	Leicester	Aug 29		6 *	5-52 & 2-41
Gloucs	Bristol	Sept 12	1 & 0		5-87
Middlesex	Hove	Sept 18	4 & 9	1Ct	0-92
REFUGE ASSURANCE					
Derbyshire	Hove	April 22	11		2-60
Glamorgan	Hove	May 20	24 *	2Ct	0-32

K.J. PIPER - *Warwickshire*

Opposition	Venue	Date	Batting	Fielding	Bowling
Yorkshire	Hove	June 17	19		2-35
Worcestershire	Worcester	June 24	4	3Ct	1-43
Hampshire	Hove	July 1			4-42
Notts	Trent Bridge	July 8	17		3-55
Gloucs	Swindon	July 15	10		3-35
Northants	Well'borough	July 22	37		3-60
Essex	Chelmsford	July 29	30		2-42
Warwickshire	Eastbourne	Aug 5	29 *		2-46
Middlesex	Lord's	Aug 12		1Ct	1-20
Somerset	Hove	Aug 26	14	1Ct	2-39
NATWEST TROPHY					
Ireland	Downpatrick	June 27			1-14
Glamorgan	Cardiff	July 11	1	1Ct	0-56
BENSON & HEDGES CUP					
Derbyshire	Derby	April 24	38 *		1-38
Min Counties	Marlow	May 1			0-38
Somerset	Hove	May 12	12		2-33
OTHER FIRST-CLASS					
Sri Lanka	Hove	Sept 5			2-74 & 1-7

BATTING AVERAGES - Including fielding

	Matches	Inns	NO	Runs	HS	Avge	100s	50s	Ct	St
Britannic Assurance	20	29	5	451	64 *	18.79	-	4	10	-
Refuge Assurance	12	10	2	195	37	24.37	-	-	7	-
NatWest Trophy	2	1	0	1	1	1.00	-	-	1	-
Benson & Hedges Cup	3	2	1	50	38 *	50.00	-	-	-	-
Other First-Class	1	0	0	0	0	-	-	-	-	-
ALL FIRST-CLASS	21	29	5	451	64 *	18.79	-	4	10	-
ALL ONE-DAY	17	13	3	246	38 *	24.60	-	-	8	-

BOWLING AVERAGES

	Overs	Mdns	Runs	Wkts	Avge	Best	5wI	10wM
Britannic Assurance	516.1	88	1916	51	37.56	5-52	3	-
Refuge Assurance	95	3	509	25	20.36	4-42	-	
NatWest Trophy	19	2	70	1	70.00	1-14	-	
Benson & Hedges Cup	31	5	109	3	36.33	2-33	-	
Other First-Class	24.5	6	81	3	27.00	2-74	-	
ALL FIRST-CLASS	541	94	1997	54	36.98	5-52	3	-
ALL ONE-DAY	145	10	688	29	23.72	4-42	-	

K.J. PIPER - *Warwickshire*

Opposition	Venue	Date	Batting	Fielding	Bowling
BRITANNIC ASSURANCE					
Yorkshire	Sheffield	June 20	49	3Ct	
Kent	Edgbaston	June 23	9 & 10		
Somerset	Taunton	July 4		5Ct,1St	
Surrey	The Oval	July 7	28 & 14	4Ct	
Lancashire	Coventry	July 18	40 *	2Ct	
Glamorgan	Swansea	July 25		3Ct,1St	
Hampshire	Edgbaston	July 28			
Sussex	Eastbourne	Aug 4	5	4Ct	
Gloucs	Bristol	Aug 8	0 & 9	3Ct	
Leicestershire	Edgbaston	Aug 18	36 & 11	2Ct	
Worcestershire	Worcester	Aug 23	14 & 0	6Ct	
Somerset	Edgbaston	Sept 7	111 & 0	2Ct	
Glamorgan	Edgbaston	Sept 12	8 & 65	5Ct,2St	
Lancashire	Old Trafford	Sept 18	23		
REFUGE ASSURANCE					
Kent	Edgbaston	June 24	4	0Ct,1St	
Surrey	The Oval	July 8	2	1Ct	
Glamorgan	Edgbaston	July 15	1		
Notts	Edgbaston	July 22		1Ct	
Hampshire	Edgbaston	July 29		0Ct,2St	
Sussex	Eastbourne	Aug 5	3 *	1Ct	
Leicestershire	Edgbaston	Aug 19		0Ct,1St	
Lancashire	Old Trafford	Aug 26	30		
OTHER FIRST-CLASS					
Cambridge U	Fenner's	April 26	10		
Sri Lanka	Edgbaston	Aug 29	19 & 0	1Ct	
OTHER ONE-DAY					
Surrey	Hove	Sept 3	44	2Ct	

PLALYER RECORDS

BATTING AVERAGES - Including fielding

	Matches	Inns	NO	Runs	HS	Avge	100s	50s	Ct	St
Britannic Assurance	14	18	1	432	111	25.41	1	1	39	4
Refuge Assurance	8	5	1	40	30	10.00	-	-	3	4
Other First-Class	2	3	0	29	19	9.66	-	-	1	-
Other One-Day	1	1	0	44	44	44.00	-	-	2	-
ALL FIRST-CLASS	16	21	1	461	111	23.05	1	1	40	4
ALL ONE-DAY	9	6	1	84	44	16.80	-	-	5	4

BOWLING AVERAGES
Did not bowl

S.G. PLUMB - *Minor Counties & Norfolk*

Opposition	Venue	Date	Batting	Fielding	Bowling
NATWEST TROPHY					
Yorkshire	Headingley	June 27	20		
BENSON & HEDGES CUP					
Middlesex	Lord's	April 24	5		
Sussex	Marlow	May 1			0-54
Somerset	Taunton	May 8	63		0-43
Derbyshire	Wellington	May 10	16	1Ct	0-23

BATTING AVERAGES - Including fielding

	Matches	Inns	NO	Runs	HS	Avge	100s	50s	Ct	St
NatWest Trophy	1	1	0	20	20	20.00	-	-	-	-
Benson & Hedges Cup	4	3	0	84	63	28.00	-	1	1	-
ALL ONE-DAY	5	4	0	104	63	26.00	-	1	1	-

BOWLING AVERAGES

	Overs	Mdns	Runs	Wkts	Avge	Best	5wI	10wM
NatWest Trophy								
Benson & Hedges Cup	23	0	120	0	-	-	-	-
ALL ONE-DAY	23	0	120	0	-	-	-	-

G.A. POINTER - *Cambridge University*

Opposition	Venue	Date	Batting	Fielding	Bowling
OTHER FIRST-CLASS					
Derbyshire	Fenner's	April 18	7 & 9		0-35 & 0-32

BATTING AVERAGES - Including fielding

	Matches	Inns	NO	Runs	HS	Avge	100s	50s	Ct	St
Other First-Class	1	2	0	16	9	8.00	-	-	-	-
ALL FIRST-CLASS	1	2	0	16	9	8.00	-	-	-	-

BOWLING AVERAGES

	Overs	Mdns	Runs	Wkts	Avge	Best	5wI	10wM
Other First-Class	17	3	67	0	-	-	-	-
ALL FIRST-CLASS	17	3	67	0	-	-	-	-

P. POLLARD - *Nottinghamshire*

Opposition	Venue	Date	Batting	Fielding	Bowling
BRITANNIC ASSURANCE					
Derbyshire	Trent Bridge	April 26	40 & 27	1Ct	
Hampshire	Portsmouth	July 18	21 & 21	1Ct	
Lancashire	Southport	July 25	0 & 27		
Middlesex	Trent Bridge	July 28	24 & 72	2Ct	
Essex	Southend	Aug 4	12 & 10		

REFUGE ASSURANCE

Yorkshire	Trent Bridge	April 22	3	
Lancashire	Trent Bridge	April 29	8	
Worcestershire	Worcester	May 6	13	
Warwickshire	Edgbaston	July 22	3	1Ct

BENSON & HEDGES CUP

Essex	Chelmsford	April 24	5	
Scotland	Glasgow	May 8	5	
Northants	Trent Bridge	May 12	5	1Ct

OTHER FIRST-CLASS

Cambridge U	Fenner's	June 16	13	
Sri Lanka	Cleethorpes	Aug 25	5 & 5	1Ct

BATTING AVERAGES - Including fielding

	Matches	Inns	NO	Runs	HS	Avge	100s	50s	Ct	St
Britannic Assurance	5	10	0	254	72	25.40	-	1	4	-
Refuge Assurance	4	4	0	27	13	6.75	-	-	1	-
Benson & Hedges Cup	3	3	0	15	5	5.00	-	-	1	-
Other First-Class	2	3	0	23	13	7.66	-	-	1	-
ALL FIRST-CLASS	7	13	0	277	72	21.30	-	1	5	-
ALL ONE-DAY	7	7	0	42	13	6.00	-	-	2	-

BOWLING AVERAGES
Did not bowl

I.L. PONT - *Lincolnshire*

Opposition	Venue	Date	Batting	Fielding	Bowling
NATWEST TROPHY					
Gloucs	Gloucester	June 27	1		1-52

BATTING AVERAGES - Including fielding

	Matches	Inns	NO	Runs	HS	Avge	100s	50s	Ct	St
NatWest Trophy	1	1	0	1	1	1.00	-	-	-	-
ALL ONE-DAY	1	1	0	1	1	1.00	-	-	-	-

BOWLING AVERAGES

	Overs	Mdns	Runs	Wkts	Avge	Best	5wI	10wM
NatWest Trophy	12	0	52	1	52.00	1-52	-	
ALL ONE-DAY	12	0	52	1	52.00	1-52	-	

N.R. POOK - *Glamorgan*

Opposition	Venue	Date	Batting	Fielding	Bowling
OTHER FIRST-CLASS					
Oxford U	The Parks	June 2	0 & 0*		0-19

BATTING AVERAGES - Including fielding

	Matches	Inns	NO	Runs	HS	Avge	100s	50s	Ct	St
Other First-Class	1	2	1	0	0*	0.00	-	-	-	-
ALL FIRST-CLASS	1	2	1	0	0*	0.00	-	-	-	-

BOWLING AVERAGES

	Overs	Mdns	Runs	Wkts	Avge	Best	5wI	10wM
Other First-Class	8	1	19	0	-	-	-	-
ALL FIRST-CLASS	8	1	19	0	-	-	-	-

J.C. POOLEY - *Middlesex*

Opposition	Venue	Date	Batting	Fielding	Bowling
REFUGE ASSURANCE					
Lancashire	Old Trafford	Sept 5	6		

P — PLAYER RECORDS

OTHER FIRST-CLASS
| Cambridge U Fenner's | May 3 | 8 & 13 | 1Ct | 0-11 |

BATTING AVERAGES - Including fielding
	Matches	Inns	NO	Runs	HS	Avge	100s	50s	Ct	St
Refuge Assurance	1	1	0	6	6	6.00	-	-	-	-
Other First-Class	1	2	0	21	13	10.50	-	-	1	-
ALL FIRST-CLASS	1	2	0	21	13	10.50	-	-	1	-
ALL ONE-DAY	1	1	0	6	6	6.00	-	-	-	-

BOWLING AVERAGES
	Overs	Mdns	Runs	Wkts	Avge	Best	5wI	10wM
Refuge Assurance								
Other First-Class	2	0	11	0	-	-	-	-
ALL FIRST-CLASS	2	0	11	0	-	-	-	-
ALL ONE-DAY								

M.W. POOLEY - *Gloucestershire*

Opposition	Venue	Date	Batting	Fielding	Bowling
REFUGE ASSURANCE					
Warwickshire	Moreton-in-M	May 20			2-29
OTHER FIRST-CLASS					
Cambridge U	Fenner's	May 23			2-51 & 0-16

BATTING AVERAGES - Including fielding
	Matches	Inns	NO	Runs	HS	Avge	100s	50s	Ct	St
Refuge Assurance	1	0	0	0	0		-	-	-	-
Other First-Class	1	0	0	0	0		-	-	-	-
ALL FIRST-CLASS	1	0	0	0	0		-	-	-	-
ALL ONE-DAY	1	0	0	0	0		-	-	-	-

BOWLING AVERAGES
	Overs	Mdns	Runs	Wkts	Avge	Best	5wI	10wM
Refuge Assurance	7	0	29	2	14.50	2-29	-	
Other First-Class	16	1	67	2	33.50	2-51	-	-
ALL FIRST-CLASS	16	1	67	2	33.50	2-51	-	-
ALL ONE-DAY	7	0	29	2	14.50	2-29	-	

L. POTTER - *Leicestershire*

Opposition	Venue	Date	Batting	Fielding	Bowling
BRITANNIC ASSURANCE					
Glamorgan	Cardiff	April 26	50	1Ct	0-21
Essex	Chelmsford	May 3	62 & 16 *		0-91
Notts	Leicester	May 15	24 & 50		
Lancashire	Old Trafford	May 19	55		1-8
Somerset	Leicester	May 26	41 * & 2	1Ct	0-16 & 0-5
Hampshire	Leicester	June 2	43 & 0	1Ct	
Northants	Northampton	June 6	14		
Middlesex	Leicester	June 16	7	2Ct	0-2 & 0-42
Derbyshire	Leicester	June 20	16	2Ct	
Gloucs	Gloucester	June 23	11	2Ct	0-49
Notts	Trent Bridge	June 30	0 & 48		1-78
Glamorgan	Hinckley	July 7	13	4Ct	2-2 & 0-48
Essex	Leicester	July 25	48 & 23	1Ct	
Yorkshire	Sheffield	July 28	109 *	1Ct	0-5
Worcestershire	Leicester	Aug 4	20 & 27	1Ct	0-12 & 0-22
Kent	Dartford	Aug 8	7 & 0		1-45 & 1-29
Surrey	The Oval	Aug 11	52 * & 19	1Ct	0-16
Warwickshire	Edgbaston	Aug 18	13 & 3	1Ct	
Kent	Leicester	Aug 23	30 & 27		0-43
Sussex	Leicester	Aug 29	51 & 4	2Ct	0-30
Northants	Leicester	Sept 12	45 & 31 *	2Ct	0-19
Derbyshire	Derby	Sept 18	2 & 65		
REFUGE ASSURANCE					
Glamorgan	Cardiff	April 29	6	1Ct	
Essex	Leicester	May 6	4	2Ct	
Lancashire	Old Trafford	May 20	32 *		

Somerset	Leicester	May 27	1		
Hampshire	Leicester	June 3	23		
Sussex	Leicester	June 10		1Ct	
Middlesex	Leicester	June 17	8		
Gloucs	Gloucester	June 24	2		
Derbyshire	Knypersley	July 15	6		
Yorkshire	Sheffield	July 29	0		1-51
Worcestershire	Leicester	Aug 5	33		
Surrey	The Oval	Aug 12	6		
Warwickshire	Edgbaston	Aug 19	7 *		

NATWEST TROPHY
| Hampshire | Leicester | June 27 | 19 | | |

BENSON & HEDGES CUP
Northants	Leicester	April 24	6		0-8
Notts	Trent Bridge	May 1	0		1-26
Scotland	Leicester	May 12	10	2Ct	

OTHER FIRST-CLASS
| India | Leicester | July 21 | 22 & 30 | 1Ct | 1-40 |

OTHER ONE-DAY
| New Zealand | Leicester | June 14 | 27 * | 2Ct | |

BATTING AVERAGES - Including fielding
	Matches	Inns	NO	Runs	HS	Avge	100s	50s	Ct	St
Britannic Assurance	22	36	5	1028	109 *	33.16	1	7	22	-
Refuge Assurance	13	12	2	128	33	12.80	-	-	4	-
NatWest Trophy	1	1	0	19	19	19.00	-	-	-	-
Benson & Hedges Cup	3	3	0	16	10	5.33	-	-	2	-
Other First-Class	1	2	0	52	30	26.00	-	-	1	-
Other One-Day	1	1	1	27	27 *		-	-	2	-
ALL FIRST-CLASS	23	38	5	1080	109 *	32.72	1	7	23	-
ALL ONE-DAY	18	17	3	190	33	13.57	-	-	8	-

BOWLING AVERAGES
	Overs	Mdns	Runs	Wkts	Avge	Best	5wI	10wM
Britannic Assurance	169	39	583	6	97.16	2-2	-	-
Refuge Assurance	7	0	51	1	51.00	1-51	-	
NatWest Trophy								
Benson & Hedges Cup	11	1	34	1	34.00	1-26	-	
Other First-Class	12	1	40	1	40.00	1-40	-	
Other One-Day								
ALL FIRST-CLASS	181	40	623	7	89.00	2-2	-	-
ALL ONE-DAY	18	1	85	2	42.50	1-26	-	

M. PRABHAKAR - *India*

Opposition	Venue	Date	Batting	Fielding	Bowling
CORNHILL TEST MATCHES					
England	Lord's	July 26	25 & 8		1-187 & 1-45
England	Old Trafford	Aug 9	4 & 67 *		1-112 & 1-80
England	The Oval	Aug 23	28		4-74 & 0-56
TEXACO TROPHY					
England	Headingley	July 18		1Ct	3-40
England	Trent Bridge	July 20			3-58
OTHER FIRST-CLASS					
Yorkshire	Headingley	June 30			0-38 & 0-48
Hampshire	Southampton	July 4	76		1-20 & 2-102
Kent	Canterbury	July 7			0-34
Leicestershire	Leicester	July 21	2 & 13	2Ct	0-35 & 0-6
Gloucs	Bristol	Aug 4	12 & 11 *	1Ct	1-53 & 2-26
TCCB U25 XI	Edgbaston	Aug 15	2 * & 23		0-13 & 2-13
World XI	Scarborough	Aug 29	15 & 10	1Ct	0-7 & 0-45
OTHER ONE-DAY					
Scotland	Glasgow	July 14			0-43
Derbyshire	Chesterfield	July 16	31		0-29

BATTING AVERAGES - Including fielding
	Matches	Inns	NO	Runs	HS	Avge	100s	50s	Ct	St
Cornhill Test Matches	3	5	1	132	67 *	33.00	-	1	-	-
Texaco Trophy	2	0	0	0	0		-	-	1	-
Other First-Class	7	9	2	164	76	23.42	-	1	4	-
Other One-Day	2	1	0	31	31	31.00	-	-	-	-

PLATER RECORDS

ALL FIRST-CLASS	10	14	3	296	76	26.90	-	2	4	-
ALL ONE-DAY	4	1	0	31	31	31.00	-	-	1	-

BOWLING AVERAGES

	Overs	Mdns	Runs	Wkts	Avge	Best	5wI	10wM
Cornhill Test Matches	155	28	554	8	69.25	4-74	-	-
Texaco Trophy	21.3	1	98	6	16.33	3-40	-	
Other First-Class	126	19	440	8	55.00	2-13	-	-
Other One-Day	21	4	72	0				
ALL FIRST-CLASS	281	47	994	16	62.12	4-74	-	-
ALL ONE-DAY	42.3	5	170	6	28.33	3-40	-	

P.J. PRICHARD - *Essex*

Opposition	Venue	Date	Batting			Fielding	Bowling
BRITANNIC ASSURANCE							
Middlesex	Lord's	April 26	10	&	49 *		
Leicestershire	Chelmsford	May 3	245			1Ct	
Worcestershire	Worcester	May 19	45				
Hampshire	Southampton	May 23	23	&	4		
Middlesex	Ilford	June 2	7	&	56 *	1Ct	
Gloucs	Ilford	June 6	45				
Warwickshire	Edgbaston	June 9	29				0-2
Somerset	Bath	June 16	115	&	4		
Kent	Maidstone	June 4			55		
Leicestershire	Leicester	July 25	2	&	0		
Sussex	Chelmsford	July 28	11	&	22	1Ct	
Notts	Southend	Aug 4	60			2Ct	
Glamorgan	Southend	Aug 8	34	&	94		0-9
Yorkshire	Middlesbr'gh	Aug 11	1			1Ct	
Surrey	Chelmsford	Aug 18	27	&	42		
Derbyshire	Derby	Aug 23	103				
Northants	Northampton	Aug 29	22	&	29 *	1Ct	
Northants	Chelmsford	Sept 7	7	&	5	1Ct	
Kent	Chelmsford	Sept 12	102				
Surrey	The Oval	Sept 18	28				
REFUGE ASSURANCE							
Kent	Chelmsford	April 22	18				
Middlesex	Lord's	April 29	35				
Leicestershire	Leicester	May 6	8				
Gloucs	Chelmsford	May 13	21			1Ct	
Worcestershire	Worcester	May 20	47			1Ct	
Glamorgan	Ilford	June 3	23 *				
Warwickshire	Edgbaston	June 10	8				
Somerset	Bath	June 17	64				
Hampshire	Southampton	July 8	12				
Northants	Chelmsford	July 15				1Ct	
Sussex	Chelmsford	July 29	64				
Notts	Southend	Aug 5	4				
Yorkshire	Middlesbr'gh	Aug 12	2				
Derbyshire	Derby	Aug 26	25			1Ct	
NATWEST TROPHY							
Scotland	Chelmsford	June 27	37 *				
Hampshire	Chelmsford	July 11	21				
BENSON & HEDGES CUP							
Notts	Chelmsford	April 24	17				
Scotland	Glasgow	May 1	107				
Northants	Northampton	May 8	26			1Ct	
Notts	Chelmsford	May 30	25				
OTHER FIRST-CLASS							
Cambridge U	Fenner's	May 16	116			1Ct	
New Zealand	Chelmsford	June 30	15				
OTHER ONE-DAY							
Zimbabwe	Chelmsford	May 14	3 *			2Ct	
Yorkshire	Scarborough	Sept 3	86			1Ct	
Hampshire	Scarborough	Sept 4	21				0-1

BATTING AVERAGES - Including fielding

	Matches	Inns	NO	Runs	HS	Avge	100s	50s	Ct	St
Britannic Assurance	20	30	3	1276	245	47.25	4	4	8	-
Refuge Assurance	14	13	1	331	64	27.58	-	2	4	-
NatWest Trophy	2	2	1	58	37 *	58.00	-	-	-	-
Benson & Hedges Cup	4	4	0	175	107	43.75	1	-	1	-
Other First-Class	2	2	0	131	116	65.50	1	-	1	-
Other One-Day	3	3	1	110	86	55.00	-	1	3	-

ALL FIRST-CLASS	22	32	3	1407	245	48.51	5	4	9	-
ALL ONE-DAY	23	22	3	674	107	35.47	1	3	8	-

BOWLING AVERAGES

	Overs	Mdns	Runs	Wkts	Avge	Best	5wI	10wM
Britannic Assurance	1.4	0	11	0				
Refuge Assurance								
NatWest Trophy								
Benson & Hedges Cup								
Other First-Class								
Other One-Day	0.1	0	1	0				
ALL FIRST-CLASS	1.4	0	11	0			-	-
ALL ONE-DAY	0.1	0	1	0			-	-

M.W. PRIEST - *New Zealand*

Opposition	Venue	Date	Batting			Fielding	Bowling
CORNHILL TEST MATCHES							
England	Trent Bridge	June 7	26				1-26
TEXACO TROPHY							
England	Headingley	May 23	2				0-59
England	The Oval	May 25	24				1-34
OTHER FIRST-CLASS							
Worcestershire	Worcester	May 12	13	&	16 *	2Ct	0-2 & 1-40
Somerset	Taunton	May 16					1-79 & 1-80
Middlesex	Lord's	May 19	51 *	&	19	1Ct	0-77 & 0-73
Sussex	Hove	May 26	72				0-42 & 0-66
Derbyshire	Derby	June 2	20	&	10		1-46
Northants	Northampton	June 16	32			1Ct	3-35 & 0-14
Combined U	Fenner's	June 27	55 *	&	31		3-93 & 0-79
Essex	Chelmsford	June 30				2Ct	3-155
OTHER ONE-DAY							
D of Norfolk	Arundel	May 6				1Ct	1-42
MCC	Lord's	May 7	28				0-40
Ireland	Downpatrick	May 9					0-31
Ireland	Belfast	May 10	18 *				1-39
Leicestershire	Leicester	June 14	1				1-26

BATTING AVERAGES - Including fielding

	Matches	Inns	NO	Runs	HS	Avge	100s	50s	Ct	St
Cornhill Test Matches	1	1	0	26	26	26.00	-	-	-	-
Texaco Trophy	2	2	0	26	24	13.00	-	-	-	-
Other First-Class	8	10	3	319	72	45.57	-	3	6	-
Other One-Day	5	3	1	47	28	23.50	-	-	1	-
ALL FIRST-CLASS	9	11	3	345	72	43.12	-	3	6	-
ALL ONE-DAY	7	5	1	73	28	18.25	-	-	1	-

BOWLING AVERAGES

	Overs	Mdns	Runs	Wkts	Avge	Best	5wI	10wM
Cornhill Test Matches	12	4	26	1	26.00	1-26	-	-
Texaco Trophy	22	2	93	1	93.00	1-34	-	
Other First-Class	300.4	86	881	13	67.76	3-35	-	-
Other One-Day	53	6	178	3	59.33	1-26	-	
ALL FIRST-CLASS	312.4	90	907	14	64.78	3-35	-	-
ALL ONE-DAY	75	8	271	4	67.75	1-26	-	

N. PRIESTLEY - *Lincolnshire*

Opposition	Venue	Date	Batting	Fielding	Bowling
NATWEST TROPHY					
Gloucs	Gloucester	June 27	54	0Ct,1St	

BATTING AVERAGES - Including fielding

	Matches	Inns	NO	Runs	HS	Avge	100s	50s	Ct	St
NatWest Trophy	1	1	0	54	54	54.00	-	1	-	1
ALL ONE-DAY	1	1	0	54	54	54.00	-	1	-	1

BOWLING AVERAGES
Did not bowl

P — PLAYER RECORDS

C. PRINGLE - *New Zealand*

Opposition	Venue	Date	Batting	Fielding	Bowling
TEXACO TROPHY					
England	Headingley	May 23			2-45
England	The Oval	May 25		1	1-53
OTHER FIRST-CLASS					
Sussex	Hove	May 26			1-66 & 1-61
Warwickshire	Edgbaston	May 30		2Ct	1-57 & 2-67
Combined U	Fenner's	June 27		6	1-28 & 0-16
Essex	Chelmsford	June 30			2-103
For World XI					
India	Scarborough	Aug 29		2Ct	2-49 & 0-36

BATTING AVERAGES - Including fielding

	Matches	Inns	NO	Runs	HS	Avge	100s	50s	Ct	St
Texaco Trophy	2	1	0	1	1	1.00	-	-	-	-
Other First-Class	5	1	0	6	6	6.00	-	-	4	-
ALL FIRST-CLASS	5	1	0	6	6	6.00	-	-	4	-
ALL ONE-DAY	2	1	0	1	1	1.00	-	-	-	-

BOWLING AVERAGES

	Overs	Mdns	Runs	Wkts	Avge	Best	5wI	10wM
Texaco Trophy	20.3	2	98	3	32.66	2-45	-	-
Other First-Class	144	32	483	10	48.30	2-49	-	-
ALL FIRST-CLASS	144	32	483	10	48.30	2-49	-	-
ALL ONE-DAY	20.3	2	98	3	32.66	2-45	-	-

D.R. PRINGLE - *Essex & England*

Opposition	Venue	Date	Batting	Fielding	Bowling
TEXACO TROPHY					
New Zealand	Headingley	May 23	30 *		0-45
BRITANNIC ASSURANCE					
Middlesex	Lord's	April 26			1-79 & 0-12
Worcestershire	Worcester	May 19		1Ct	3-67 & 5-66
Middlesex	Ilford	June 2	8		1-66
Gloucs	Ilford	June 6			0-52
Warwickshire	Edgbaston	June 9			2-72
Somerset	Bath	June 16			0-28 & 0-7
Kent	Maidstone	June 4		40 *	3-54
Derbyshire	Colchester	July 18	30		0-31 & 0-31
Lancashire	Colchester	July 21	45 & 6 *	1Ct	4-47 & 0-38
Leicestershire	Leicester	July 25	20 & 84	1Ct	3-51 & 0-19
Sussex	Chelmsford	July 28	21 & 39	2Ct	0-29 & 1-12
Notts	Southend	Aug 4	15	1Ct	1-74
Yorkshire	Middlesbr'gh	Aug 11	9	1Ct	3-15 & 1-18
Derbyshire	Derby	Aug 23	0		0-13
Northants	Northampton	Aug 29	1		1-46
REFUGE ASSURANCE					
Kent	Chelmsford	April 22	15	1Ct	0-43
Middlesex	Lord's	April 29	18		4-27
Gloucs	Chelmsford	May 13	21		1-49
Worcestershire	Worcester	May 20	48 *		2-48
Glamorgan	Ilford	June 3	9	1Ct	2-18
Warwickshire	Edgbaston	June 10	17 *		3-29
Somerset	Bath	June 17	37		1-23
Hampshire	Southampton	July 8	63		0-42
Northants	Chelmsford	July 15	61 *	1Ct	2-59
Lancashire	Colchester	July 22	1	1Ct	3-47
Sussex	Chelmsford	July 29	15		1-53
NATWEST TROPHY					
Scotland	Chelmsford	June 27		1Ct	2-30
Hampshire	Chelmsford	July 11	33		2-64
BENSON & HEDGES CUP					
Notts	Chelmsford	April 24	55 *		1-57
Scotland	Glasgow	May 1	77 *		1-28
Northants	Northampton	May 8			2-28
Notts	Chelmsford	May 30	19		0-35

OTHER FIRST-CLASS

Opposition	Venue	Date	Batting	Fielding	Bowling
Cambridge U	Fenner's	May 16	58	2Ct	3-16 & 1-11
New Zealand	Chelmsford	June 30	67		0-25 & 1-15

BATTING AVERAGES - Including fielding

	Matches	Inns	NO	Runs	HS	Avge	100s	50s	Ct	St
Texaco Trophy	1	1	0	30	30 *	-	-	-	-	-
Britannic Assurance	15	13	2	318	84	28.90	-	1	7	-
Refuge Assurance	11	11	3	305	63	38.12	-	2	4	-
NatWest Trophy	2	1	0	33	33	33.00	-	-	1	-
Benson & Hedges Cup	4	3	2	151	77 *	151.00	-	2	-	-
Other First-Class	2	2	0	125	67	62.50	-	2	2	-
ALL FIRST-CLASS	17	15	2	443	84	34.07	-	3	9	-
ALL ONE-DAY	18	16	6	519	77 *	51.90	-	4	5	-

BOWLING AVERAGES

	Overs	Mdns	Runs	Wkts	Avge	Best	5wI	10wM
Texaco Trophy	7	0	45	0	-	-	-	-
Britannic Assurance	325.3	81	927	29	31.96	5-66	1	-
Refuge Assurance	78	4	438	19	23.05	4-27	-	-
NatWest Trophy	23.3	3	94	4	23.50	2-30	-	-
Benson & Hedges Cup	38.4	4	148	4	37.00	2-28	-	-
Other First-Class	33	9	67	5	13.40	3-16	-	-
ALL FIRST-CLASS	358.3	90	994	34	29.23	5-66	1	-
ALL ONE-DAY	147.1	11	725	27	26.85	4-27	-	-

N.J. PRINGLE - *Somerset*

Opposition	Venue	Date	Batting	Fielding	Bowling
REFUGE ASSURANCE					
Northants	Taunton	July 1	1		
Warwickshire	Weston	Aug 12		1Ct	

BATTING AVERAGES - Including fielding

	Matches	Inns	NO	Runs	HS	Avge	100s	50s	Ct	St
Refuge Assurance	2	1	0	1	1	1.00	-	-	1	-
ALL ONE-DAY	2	1	0	1	1	1.00	-	-	1	-

BOWLING AVERAGES
Did not bowl

A.J. PUGH - *Devon*

Opposition	Venue	Date	Batting	Fielding	Bowling
NATWEST TROPHY					
Somerset	Torquay	June 27	12	2Ct	

BATTING AVERAGES - Including fielding

	Matches	Inns	NO	Runs	HS	Avge	100s	50s	Ct	St
NatWest Trophy	1	1	0	12	12	12.00	-	-	2	-
ALL ONE-DAY	1	1	0	12	12	12.00	-	-	2	-

BOWLING AVERAGES
Did not bowl

A.J. PYCROFT - *Zimbabwe*

Opposition	Venue	Date	Batting	Fielding	Bowling
OTHER FIRST-CLASS					
Yorkshire	Headingley	May 16	18 & 23	2Ct	
Gloucs	Bristol	May 19	9 & 15 *		
Lancashire	Old Trafford	May 23	55		

PLAYER RECORDS

OTHER ONE-DAY

Sussex	Hove	May 13	10
Essex	Chelmsford	May 14	62

BATTING AVERAGES - Including fielding

	Matches	Inns	NO	Runs	HS	Avge	100s	50s	Ct	St
Other First-Class	3	5	1	120	55	30.00	-	1	2	-
Other One-Day	2	2	0	72	62	36.00	-	1	-	-
ALL FIRST-CLASS	3	5	1	120	55	30.00	-	1	2	-
ALL ONE-DAY	2	2	0	72	62	36.00	-	1	-	-

BOWLING AVERAGES
Did not bowl

R.A. PYMAN - *Cambridge University*

Opposition	Venue	Date	Batting			Fielding	Bowling

OTHER FIRST-CLASS

Northants	Fenner's	April 14	4				2-62 & 2-29
Derbyshire	Fenner's	April 18	5	&	2		2-94 & 0-2
Warwickshire	Fenner's	April 26	21	&	23*		1-109 & 0-43
Middlesex	Fenner's	May 3	10			1Ct	1-54 & 0-31
Essex	Fenner's	May 16	0	&	10		2-46 & 2-36
Notts	Fenner's	June 16	11				1-72 & 0-50
Kent	Fenner's	June 20			0	1Ct	0-60

For Combined U

New Zealand	Fenner's	June 27	4	&	0*		0-56 & 0-12

For Cambridge U

Sussex	Hove	June 30	0	&	8		1-60 & 1-59
Oxford U	Lord's	July 4					0-63

BATTING AVERAGES - Including fielding

	Matches	Inns	NO	Runs	HS	Avge	100s	50s	Ct	St
Other First-Class	10	14	2	98	23*	8.16	-	-	2	-
ALL FIRST-CLASS	10	14	2	98	23*	8.16	-	-	2	-

BOWLING AVERAGES

	Overs	Mdns	Runs	Wkts	Avge	Best	5wI	10wM

R	**PLAYER RECORDS**

N.V. RADFORD - *Worcestershire*

Opposition	Venue	Date	Batting	Fielding	Bowling
BRITANNIC ASSURANCE					
Lancashire	Old Trafford	April 26			0-66 & 0-15
Essex	Worcester	May 19	10 & 10		1-95
Warwickshire	Edgbaston	May 26	43 *	1Ct	0-49 & 1-32
Somerset	Worcester	July 18			0-78 & 0-49
Glamorgan	Abergavenny	July 21			1-79 & 0-67
Derbyshire	Derby	July 25	14	1Ct	0-23 & 0-10
Kent	Canterbury	July 28		1Ct	1-33 & 1-41
Gloucs	Bristol	Sept 7		1Ct	1-98 & 0-45
Somerset	Taunton	Sept 12	14		0-75 & 4-55
Glamorgan	Worcester	Sept 18	13		4-58 & 0-31
REFUGE ASSURANCE					
Somerset	Taunton	April 22			0-20
Derbyshire	Derby	April 29	0		1-26
Notts	Worcester	May 6			1-30
Essex	Worcester	May 20	26 *		0-39
Warwickshire	Worcester	May 27	4		1-34
Lancashire	Old Trafford	July 15	2		0-24
Kent	Canterbury	July 29		1Ct	0-24
NATWEST TROPHY					
Northants	Northampton	Aug 1	0		0-23
BENSON & HEDGES CUP					
Gloucs	Bristol	April 24			1-45
Kent	Worcester	May 1	1 *	1Ct	0-13
Glamorgan	Worcester	May 8	40	2Ct	2-52
Warwickshire	Edgbaston	May 10	31	1Ct	3-41
Glamorgan	Worcester	May 30			4-26
Lancashire	Lord's	July 14	26 *	1Ct	0-41
OTHER FIRST-CLASS					
MCC	Lord's	April 17			4-116
New Zealand	Worcester	May 12	13 & 1	2Ct	0-33 & 0-47
OTHER ONE-DAY					
Hampshire	Scarborough	Sept 2	39 *		0-40

BATTING AVERAGES - Including fielding

	Matches	Inns	NO	Runs	HS	Avge	100s	50s	Ct	St
Britannic Assurance	10	6	1	104	43 *	20.80	-	-	4	-
Refuge Assurance	7	4	1	32	26 *	10.66	-	-	1	-
NatWest Trophy	1	1	0	0	0	0.00	-	-	-	-
Benson & Hedges Cup	6	4	2	98	40	49.00	-	-	5	-
Other First-Class	2	2	0	14	13	7.00	-	-	2	-
Other One-Day	1	1	1	39	39 *	-	-	-	-	-
ALL FIRST-CLASS	12	8	1	118	43 *	16.85	-	-	6	-
ALL ONE-DAY	15	10	4	169	40	28.16	-	-	6	-

BOWLING AVERAGES

	Overs	Mdns	Runs	Wkts	Avge	Best	5wI	10wM
Britannic Assurance	245	38	999	14	71.35	4-55	-	-
Refuge Assurance	41	0	197	3	65.66	1-26	-	
NatWest Trophy	4	0	23	0	-	-	-	
Benson & Hedges Cup	56.3	9	218	10	21.80	4-26	-	
Other First-Class	57	11	196	4	49.00	4-116	-	-
Other One-Day	9	0	40	0	-	-	-	
ALL FIRST-CLASS	302	49	1195	18	66.38	4-55	-	-
ALL ONE-DAY	110.3	9	478	13	36.76	4-26	-	-

W.V. RAMAN - *India*

Opposition	Venue	Date	Batting	Fielding	Bowling
TEXACO TROPHY					
England	Headingley	July 18	0		
OTHER FIRST-CLASS					
Yorkshire	Headingley	June 30	12 & 0		0-8
Hampshire	Southampton	July 4	26 & 22	2Ct	
Min Counties	Trowbridge	July 11	55	1Ct	
Surrey	The Oval	Aug 1	127 & 58	2Ct	
Gloucs	Bristol	Aug 4	0 & 56 *		0-7 & 0-1
TCCB U25 XI	Edgbaston	Aug 15	61 & 56		

Glamorgan	Swansea	Aug 18	59 & 20 *		0-12
World XI	Scarborough	Aug 29	58 & 13	1Ct	1-44
OTHER ONE-DAY					
League CC	Sunderland	June 28	0		
Scotland	Glasgow	July 14	89	1Ct	
Derbyshire	Chesterfield	July 16	17		

BATTING AVERAGES - Including fielding

	Matches	Inns	NO	Runs	HS	Avge	100s	50s	Ct	St
Texaco Trophy	1	1	0	0	0	0.00	-	-	-	-
Other First-Class	8	15	2	623	127	47.92	1	7	6	-
Other One-Day	3	3	0	106	89	35.33	-	1	1	-
ALL FIRST-CLASS	8	15	2	623	127	47.92	1	7	6	-
ALL ONE-DAY	4	4	0	106	89	26.50	-	1	1	-

BOWLING AVERAGES

	Overs	Mdns	Runs	Wkts	Avge	Best	5wI	10wM
Texaco Trophy								
Other First-Class	15	2	72	1	72.00	1-44	-	-
Other One-Day								
ALL FIRST-CLASS	15	2	72	1	72.00	1-44	-	-
ALL ONE-DAY								

C.P. RAMANAYAKE - *Sri Lanka*

Opposition	Venue	Date	Batting	Fielding	Bowling
OTHER FIRST-CLASS					
Glamorgan	Ebbw Vale	Aug 22	8 * & 3 *		1-61 & 1-64
Notts	Cleethorpes	Aug 25			1-60 & 1-70
Warwickshire	Edgbaston	Aug 29			3-96 & 2-53
Hampshire	Southampton	Sept 12	5 * & 9 *		3-106
OTHER ONE-DAY					
Somerset	Taunton	Sept 3	12		2-47

BATTING AVERAGES - Including fielding

	Matches	Inns	NO	Runs	HS	Avge	100s	50s	Ct	St
Other First-Class	4	4	4	25	9 *	-	-	-	-	-
Other One-Day	1	1	0	12	12	12.00	-	-	-	-
ALL FIRST-CLASS	4	4	4	25	9 *	-	-	-	-	-
ALL ONE-DAY	1	1	0	12	12	12.00	-	-	-	-

BOWLING AVERAGES

	Overs	Mdns	Runs	Wkts	Avge	Best	5wI	10wM
Other First-Class	133	12	510	12	42.50	3-96	-	-
Other One-Day	8	0	47	2	23.50	2-47	-	
ALL FIRST-CLASS	133	12	510	12	42.50	3-96	-	-
ALL ONE-DAY	8	0	47	2	23.50	2-47	-	

M.R. RAMPRAKASH - *Middlesex*

Opposition	Venue	Date	Batting	Fielding	Bowling
BRITANNIC ASSURANCE					
Essex	Lord's	April 26	12 & 1		0-8
Kent	Lord's	May 15	9 & 36 *	2Ct	
Surrey	Lord's	May 23	30 & 10		
Gloucs	Lord's	May 26	64 & 0	1Ct	
Essex	Ilford	June 2	30 *		
Warwickshire	Lord's	June 6	0 & 38		0-28
Leicestershire	Leicester	June 16	87 *		
Lancashire	Old Trafford	June 20	8		0-17
Northants	Luton	June 23	26 & 0 *		0-2
Worcestershire	Lord's	June 30	69		
Yorkshire	Uxbridge	July 18	9 & 15 *		
Somerset	Uxbridge	July 21	2 & 146 *		1-19
Kent	Canterbury	July 25	100 * & 125		0-41
Notts	Trent Bridge	July 28	46 & 52		
Glamorgan	Lord's	Aug 4	8 & 18		
Hampshire	Bournemouth	Aug 8	47 & 0	1Ct	
Sussex	Lord's	Aug 11	28 & 5		
Derbyshire	Derby	Aug 18	1 & 8		0-15
Yorkshire	Headingley	Aug 23	29 & 29		
Notts	Lord's	Sept 7	132		

PLADER RECORDS

Surrey	The Oval	Sept 12	54 & 40 *		2Ct	1-17
Sussex	Hove	Sept 18	13			

REFUGE ASSURANCE

Lancashire	Old Trafford	April 22	22		0-7
Essex	Lord's	April 29	40		
Kent	Folkestone	May 6	32		
Notts	Lord's	May 13	17	1Ct	
Gloucs	Lord's	May 27	88 *		
Warwickshire	Lord's	June 3		1Ct	
Hampshire	Basingstoke	June 10	52 *		
Leicestershire	Leicester	June 17	22		
Northants	Northampton	June 24	8 *	2Ct	
Worcestershire	Lord's	July 1	147 *		0-9
Somerset	Lord's	July 8	9		
Surrey	The Oval	July 15	60		
Glamorgan	Lord's	Aug 5	47	1Ct	1-5
Sussex	Lord's	Aug 12	11		
Derbyshire	Derby	Aug 19	26 *		
Yorkshire	Scarborough	Aug 26	34	1Ct	
Lancashire	Old Trafford	Sept 5	22		
Derbyshire	Edgbaston	Sept 16	1		

NATWEST TROPHY

Berkshire	Lord's	June 27	3	
Surrey	Uxbridge	July 11	104	
Glamorgan	Lord's	Aug 1		0-14
Lancashire	Old Trafford	Aug 15	45	

BENSON & HEDGES CUP

Min Counties	Lord's	April 24	2	
Sussex	Hove	May 8	44	1Ct
Somerset	Lord's	May 10	4	
Derbyshire	Derby	May 12	7	
Somerset	Taunton	May 30	21	

OTHER FIRST-CLASS

Cambridge U	Fenner's	May 3	118 * & 13 *	0-17
New Zealand	Lord's	May 19	21 & 62	

OTHER ONE-DAY
For MCC

New Zealand	Lord's	May 7	6

BATTING AVERAGES - Including fielding

	Matches	Inns	NO	Runs	HS	Avge	100s	50s	Ct	St
Britannic Assurance	22	38	8	1327	146 *	44.23	4	5	6	-
Refuge Assurance	18	17	5	638	147 *	53.16	1	3	6	-
NatWest Trophy	4	3	0	152	104	50.66	1	-	-	-
Benson & Hedges Cup	5	5	0	78	44	15.60	-	-	1	-
Other First-Class	2	4	2	214	118 *	107.00	1	1	-	-
Other One-Day	1	1	0	6	6	6.00	-	-	-	-
ALL FIRST-CLASS	24	42	10	1541	146 *	48.15	5	6	6	-
ALL ONE-DAY	28	26	5	874	147 *	41.61	2	3	7	-

BOWLING AVERAGES

	Overs	Mdns	Runs	Wkts	Avge	Best	5wI	10wM
Britannic Assurance	34	5	147	2	73.50	1-17	-	-
Refuge Assurance	3.3	0	21	1	21.00	1-5	-	
NatWest Trophy	4	1	14	0	-	-	-	
Benson & Hedges Cup								
Other First-Class	7	2	17	0	-	-	-	
Other One-Day								
ALL FIRST-CLASS	41	7	164	2	82.00	1-17	-	-
ALL ONE-DAY	7.3	1	35	1	35.00	1-5	-	

D.W. RANDALL - Nottinghamshire

Opposition	Venue	Date	Batting	Fielding	Bowling

BRITANNIC ASSURANCE

Derbyshire	Trent Bridge	April 26	6 & 23	1Ct
Worcestershire	Worcester	May 3	6 & 87	
Leicestershire	Leicester	May 15	120 & 11	3Ct
Warwickshire	Edgbaston	May 19	5 & 17	3Ct
Northants	Trent Bridge	May 23	37	1Ct
Derbyshire	Derby	May 26	12 & 88	3Ct
Kent	Tunbridge We	June 2	178 & 6	
Surrey	Trent Bridge	June 20	24 & 26	1Ct
Sussex	Trent Bridge	July 7	34 & 9	
Lancashire	Southport	July 25	0 & 68	

Middlesex	Trent Bridge	July 28	70 & 56	1Ct	
Essex	Southend	Aug 4	34 & 36 *		
Somerset	Weston	Aug 8	0 & 0		
Lancashire	Trent Bridge	Sept 12	0 & 24	1Ct	
Yorkshire	Trent Bridge	Sept 18	10		

REFUGE ASSURANCE

Yorkshire	Trent Bridge	April 22	54 *	
Lancashire	Trent Bridge	April 29	14	
Worcestershire	Worcester	May 6	12	
Middlesex	Lord's	May 13	30 *	1Ct
Surrey	Trent Bridge	May 20	9 *	
Derbyshire	Derby	June 10	21	
Kent	Canterbury	June 17	49	
Essex	Southend	Aug 5	9	1Ct

NATWEST TROPHY

Northants	Northampton	July 11	56

BENSON & HEDGES CUP

Essex	Chelmsford	April 24	25	
Leicestershire	Trent Bridge	May 1	6	1Ct
Scotland	Glasgow	May 8	7	
Northants	Trent Bridge	May 12	2	
Essex	Chelmsford	May 30	16	
Worcestershire	Trent Bridge	June 13	39	

BATTING AVERAGES - Including fielding

	Matches	Inns	NO	Runs	HS	Avge	100s	50s	Ct	St
Britannic Assurance	15	28	1	987	178	36.55	2	5	14	-
Refuge Assurance	8	8	3	198	54 *	39.60	-	1	2	-
NatWest Trophy	1	1	0	56	56	56.00	-	1	-	-
Benson & Hedges Cup	6	6	0	95	39	15.83	-	-	1	-
ALL FIRST-CLASS	15	28	1	987	178	36.55	2	5	14	-
ALL ONE-DAY	15	15	3	349	56	29.08	-	2	3	-

BOWLING AVERAGES
Did not bowl

J.D. RATCLIFFE - Warwickshire

Opposition	Venue	Date	Batting	Fielding	Bowling

BRITANNIC ASSURANCE

Essex	Edgbaston	June 9	27 * & 22	
Derbyshire	Derby	June 16	38 & 25	
Yorkshire	Sheffield	June 20	9 & 16	1Ct
Kent	Edgbaston	June 23	28 & 43	
Somerset	Taunton	July 4	7 & 16 *	
Surrey	The Oval	July 7	15 & 19	1Ct
Hampshire	Edgbaston	July 28	81 * & 46	1Ct
Sussex	Eastbourne	Aug 4	61 & 8	
Gloucs	Bristol	Aug 8	75 & 7	2Ct
Leicestershire	Edgbaston	Aug 18	15 & 14	
Worcestershire	Worcester	Aug 23	29 & 4	
Somerset	Edgbaston	Sept 7	6 & 20	1Ct
Glamorgan	Edgbaston	Sept 12	41 & 0	1Ct
Lancashire	Old Trafford	Sept 18	17	

OTHER FIRST-CLASS

New Zealand	Edgbaston	May 30	29 & 43
Sri Lanka	Edgbaston	Aug 29	5 & 14

BATTING AVERAGES - Including fielding

	Matches	Inns	NO	Runs	HS	Avge	100s	50s	Ct	St
Britannic Assurance	14	27	3	689	81 *	28.70	-	3	7	-
Other First-Class	2	4	0	91	43	22.75	-	-	-	-
ALL FIRST-CLASS	16	31	3	780	81 *	27.85	-	3	7	-

BOWLING AVERAGES
Did not bowl

M.P. REA - Ireland

Opposition	Venue	Date	Batting	Fielding	Bowling

NATWEST TROPHY

Sussex	Downpatrick	June 27	5

R | PLAYER RECORDS

OTHER FIRST-CLASS

Scotland	Edinburgh	Aug 11	22 & 21 *	

BATTING AVERAGES - Including fielding

	Matches	Inns	NO	Runs	HS	Avge	100s	50s	Ct	St
NatWest Trophy	1	1	0	5	5	5.00	-	-	-	-
Other First-Class	1	2	1	43	22	43.00	-	-	-	-
ALL FIRST-CLASS	1	2	1	43	22	43.00	-	-	-	-
ALL ONE-DAY	1	1	0	5	5	5.00	-	-	-	-

BOWLING AVERAGES

Did not bowl

D.A. REEVE - *Warwickshire*

Opposition	Venue	Date	Batting		Fielding	Bowling

BRITANNIC ASSURANCE

Opposition	Venue	Date	Batting		Fielding	Bowling
Yorkshire	Edgbaston	May 3	29		2Ct	1-6 & 2-2
Northants	Northampton	May 15	202 *		1Ct	3-26
Notts	Edgbaston	May 19	34 & 26		1Ct	
Worcestershire	Edgbaston	May 26	21 & 49 *		2Ct	0-21
Northants	Edgbaston	June 2	5 & 0			
Middlesex	Lord's	June 6	12 & 31 *		2Ct	0-37
Essex	Edgbaston	June 9	33 *			
Derbyshire	Derby	June 16	25		3Ct	
Yorkshire	Sheffield	June 20	30 & 42 *			0-24
Kent	Edgbaston	June 23	30 & 59 *		2Ct	1-16
Somerset	Taunton	July 4	4		2Ct	3-47 & 0-19
Surrey	The Oval	July 7	11 & 17			2-64 & 0-43
Lancashire	Coventry	July 18	78			
Glamorgan	Swansea	July 25			1Ct	0-28
Hampshire	Edgbaston	July 28	12 *		3Ct	3-58
Sussex	Eastbourne	Aug 4	30 & 7 *		1Ct	0-28 & 1-31
Gloucs	Bristol	Aug 8	1 & 20		1Ct	3-46 & 0-9
Leicestershire	Edgbaston	Aug 18	1 & 31			4-42 & 2-51
Worcestershire	Worcester	Aug 23	27 & 25			2-60 & 1-85
Somerset	Edgbaston	Sept 7	58 & 81 *		1Ct	0-26
Glamorgan	Edgbaston	Sept 12	68 * & 45		1Ct	0-13
Lancashire	Old Trafford	Sept 18	121 *			

REFUGE ASSURANCE

Opposition	Venue	Date	Batting	Fielding	Bowling
Northants	Edgbaston	April 29	17 *	1Ct	1-45
Yorkshire	Edgbaston	May 6		1Ct	3-29
Worcestershire	Worcester	May 27	11		1-45
Middlesex	Lord's	June 3	5		
Essex	Edgbaston	June 10	28		0-12
Derbyshire	Derby	June 17	31		
Kent	Edgbaston	June 24	25		1-32
Surrey	The Oval	July 8	25	3Ct	4-36
Glamorgan	Edgbaston	July 15	28		1-28
Notts	Edgbaston	July 22	41		0-43
Hampshire	Edgbaston	July 29	1		0-36
Sussex	Eastbourne	Aug 5	22		0-20
Somerset	Weston	Aug 12	18 *		0-55
Lancashire	Old Trafford	Aug 26	0		1-31

NATWEST TROPHY

Opposition	Venue	Date	Batting	Fielding	Bowling
Hertfordshire	St Albans	June 27	36 *		0-20
Yorkshire	Headingley	July 11	0		0-42

BENSON & HEDGES CUP

Opposition	Venue	Date	Batting	Fielding	Bowling
Glamorgan	Edgbaston	April 24	14		0-26
Kent	Canterbury	May 8	12	1Ct	1-52
Worcestershire	Edgbaston	May 10	6		1-70
Gloucs	Bristol	May 12	29 *		2-27

OTHER FIRST-CLASS

For MCC

Opposition	Venue	Date	Batting		Fielding	Bowling
Worcestershire	Lord's	April 17	39			0-40

For Warwickshire

Cambridge U	Fenner's	April 26	102 *		3Ct	0-9 & 3-34
Sri Lanka	Edgbaston	Aug 29	5 & 1			2-46 & 0-29

OTHER ONE-DAY

Opposition	Venue	Date	Batting	Fielding	Bowling
Surrey	Harrogate	June 13	13	2Ct	
Yorkshire	Harrogate	June 15	2	2Ct	
Surrey	Hove	Sept 3	42		2-53

BATTING AVERAGES - Including fielding

	Matches	Inns	NO	Runs	HS	Avge	100s	50s	Ct	St
Britannic Assurance	22	34	11	1265	202 *	55.00	2	5	23	-
Refuge Assurance	14	13	2	252	41	22.90	-	-	5	-
NatWest Trophy	2	2	1	36	36 *	36.00	-	-	-	-
Benson & Hedges Cup	4	4	1	61	29 *	20.33	-	-	1	-
Other First-Class	3	4	1	147	102 *	49.00	1	-	3	-
Other One-Day	3	3	0	57	42	19.00	-	-	4	-
ALL FIRST-CLASS	25	38	12	1412	202 *	54.30	3	5	26	-
ALL ONE-DAY	23	22	4	406	42	22.55	-	-	10	-

BOWLING AVERAGES

	Overs	Mdns	Runs	Wkts	Avge	Best	5wI	10wM
Britannic Assurance	319.4	93	782	28	27.92	4-42	-	-
Refuge Assurance	83.1	5	412	12	34.33	4-36	-	-
NatWest Trophy	20	2	62	0	-	-	-	-
Benson & Hedges Cup	41	4	175	4	43.75	2-27	-	-
Other First-Class	58	17	158	5	31.60	3-34	-	-
Other One-Day	10	0	53	2	26.50	2-53	-	-
ALL FIRST-CLASS	377.4	110	940	33	28.48	4-42	-	-
ALL ONE-DAY	154.1	11	702	18	39.00	4-36	-	-

C.C. REMY - *Sussex*

Opposition	Venue	Date	Batting	Fielding	Bowling

BRITANNIC ASSURANCE

Opposition	Venue	Date	Batting	Fielding	Bowling
Gloucs	Hove	June 16	4 *		0-54 & 1-37

REFUGE ASSURANCE

Opposition	Venue	Date	Batting	Fielding	Bowling
Leicestershire	Leicester	June 10	12 *		0-34
Yorkshire	Hove	June 17	7		2-45
Hampshire	Hove	July 1			
Notts	Trent Bridge	July 8	1		
Gloucs	Swindon	July 15	2	1Ct	0-23
Warwickshire	Eastbourne	Aug 5	11	1Ct	

NATWEST TROPHY

Opposition	Venue	Date	Batting	Fielding	Bowling
Glamorgan	Cardiff	July 11	1		0-30

OTHER FIRST-CLASS

Opposition	Venue	Date	Batting	Fielding	Bowling
Cambridge U	Hove	June 30			4-63 & 0-70

OTHER ONE-DAY

Opposition	Venue	Date	Batting	Fielding	Bowling
Zimbabwe	Hove	May 13	0 *		
Yorkshire	Harrogate	June 14	3		1-38
Kent	Hove	Sept 2	16		0-32

BATTING AVERAGES - Including fielding

	Matches	Inns	NO	Runs	HS	Avge	100s	50s	Ct	St
Britannic Assurance	1	1	1	4	4 *	-	-	-	-	-
Refuge Assurance	6	5	1	33	12 *	8.25	-	-	2	-
NatWest Trophy	1	1	0	1	1	1.00	-	-	-	-
Other First-Class	1	0	0	0	0	-	-	-	-	-
Other One-Day	3	3	1	19	16	9.50	-	-	-	-
ALL FIRST-CLASS	2	1	1	4	4 *	-	-	-	-	-
ALL ONE-DAY	10	9	2	53	16	7.57	-	-	2	-

BOWLING AVERAGES

	Overs	Mdns	Runs	Wkts	Avge	Best	5wI	10wM
Britannic Assurance	17	0	91	1	91.00	1-37	-	-
Refuge Assurance	16.4	0	102	2	51.00	2-45	-	-
NatWest Trophy	10	1	30	0	-	-	-	-
Other First-Class	37	6	133	4	33.25	4-63	-	-
Other One-Day	15	2	70	1	70.00	1-38	-	-
ALL FIRST-CLASS	54	6	224	5	44.80	4-63	-	-
ALL ONE-DAY	41.4	3	202	3	67.33	2-45	-	-

P. RENDELL - *Somerset*

Opposition	Venue	Date	Batting	Fielding	Bowling

OTHER ONE-DAY

Opposition	Venue	Date	Batting	Fielding	Bowling
Sri Lanka	Taunton	Sept 3		2Ct	2-46

BATTING AVERAGES - Including fielding

	Matches	Inns	NO	Runs	HS	Avge	100s	50s	Ct	St
Other One-Day	1	0	0	0	0	-	-	-	2	-

PLANER RECORDS

PLAYER RECORDS

R

| ALL ONE-DAY | 1 | 0 | 0 | 0 | 0 | - | - | 2 | - |

BOWLING AVERAGES

	Overs	Mdns	Runs	Wkts	Avge	Best	5wI	10wM
Other One-Day	11	1	46	2	23.00	2-46	-	
ALL ONE-DAY	11	1	46	2	23.00	2-46	-	

G.D. REYNOLDS - *Dorset*

Opposition	Venue	Date	Batting	Fielding	Bowling

NATWEST TROPHY

Glamorgan	Swansea	June 27	60		

BATTING AVERAGES - Including fielding

	Matches	Inns	NO	Runs	HS	Avge	100s	50s	Ct	St
NatWest Trophy	1	1	0	60	60	60.00	-	1	-	-
ALL ONE-DAY	1	1	0	60	60	60.00	-	1	-	-

BOWLING AVERAGES
Did not bowl

S.J. RHODES - *Worcestershire*

Opposition	Venue	Date	Batting	Fielding	Bowling

BRITANNIC ASSURANCE

Lancashire	Old Trafford	April 26	72		
Essex	Worcester	May 19	1 & 5 *	1Ct	
Warwickshire	Edgbaston	May 26	2	4Ct	
Yorkshire	Worcester	June 2	13	3Ct	
Surrey	The Oval	June 16	4	2Ct	
Sussex	Worcester	June 20		9 *	
Middlesex	Lord's	June 30	26	2Ct	
Gloucs	Worcester	July 7	55	1Ct,2St	
Somerset	Worcester	July 18		2Ct	
Glamorgan	Abergavenny	July 21		2Ct	
Derbyshire	Derby	July 25	0	5Ct,1St	
Kent	Canterbury	July 28	94 & 0 *	3Ct,1St	
Leicestershire	Leicester	Aug 4		1Ct,2St	
Lancashire	Kid'minster	Aug 8	22	3Ct	
Hampshire	Worcester	Aug 11	33 *	3Ct	
Northants	Worcester	Aug 18	44 * & 28 *	6Ct,1St	
Warwickshire	Worcester	Aug 23	96 & 30 *	5Ct	
Notts	Trent Bridge	Aug 29	50 *	4Ct	
Gloucs	Bristol	Sept 7	7 *	3Ct,1St	
Somerset	Taunton	Sept 12	6 & 34 *	3Ct	
Glamorgan	Worcester	Sept 18	0 & 22	6Ct	

REFUGE ASSURANCE

Somerset	Taunton	April 22		5Ct,1St	
Derbyshire	Derby	April 29	2	0Ct,1St	
Essex	Worcester	May 20			
Warwickshire	Worcester	May 27		2Ct	
Yorkshire	Worcester	June 3	2	3Ct	
Surrey	The Oval	June 17	35 *		
Sussex	Worcester	June 24	0	1Ct	
Middlesex	Lord's	July 1	16		
Gloucs	Worcester	July 8			
Lancashire	Old Trafford	July 15	12	1Ct	
Kent	Canterbury	July 29	1 *	1Ct	
Leicestershire	Leicester	Aug 5		1Ct	
Hampshire	Worcester	Aug 12	26		
Northants	Worcester	Aug 19			
Glamorgan	Swansea	Aug 26	23 *	0Ct,1St	

NATWEST TROPHY

Suffolk	Bury St Ed's	June 27		1Ct	
Somerset	Taunton	July 11			
Northants	Northampton	Aug 1	2	2Ct	

BENSON & HEDGES CUP

Gloucs	Bristol	April 24	1	1Ct	
Kent	Worcester	May 1	8	1Ct	
Glamorgan	Worcester	May 30		3Ct	
Notts	Trent Bridge	June 13		1Ct	
Lancashire	Lord's	July 14	5		

OTHER FIRST-CLASS

MCC	Lord's	April 17	19	2Ct	

OTHER ONE-DAY

Hampshire	Scarborough	Sept 2	22	0Ct,1St	
For Yorkshiremen					
Yorkshire	Scarborough	Sept 6	66 *	1Ct	

BATTING AVERAGES - Including fielding

	Matches	Inns	NO	Runs	HS	Avge	100s	50s	Ct	St
Britannic Assurance	21	24	10	653	96	46.64	-	5	59	8
Refuge Assurance	15	9	3	117	35 *	19.50	-	-	14	3
NatWest Trophy	3	1	0	2	2	2.00	-	-	3	-
Benson & Hedges Cup	5	3	0	14	8	4.66	-	-	6	-
Other First-Class	1	1	0	19	19	19.00	-	-	2	-
Other One-Day	2	2	1	88	66 *	88.00	-	1	1	1
ALL FIRST-CLASS	22	25	10	672	96	44.80	-	5	61	8
ALL ONE-DAY	25	15	4	221	66 *	20.09	-	1	24	4

BOWLING AVERAGES
Did not bowl

K.G. RICE - *Devon*

Opposition	Venue	Date	Batting	Fielding	Bowling

NATWEST TROPHY

Somerset	Torquay	June 27	0		0-34

BATTING AVERAGES - Including fielding

	Matches	Inns	NO	Runs	HS	Avge	100s	50s	Ct	St
NatWest Trophy	1	1	0	0	0	0.00	-	-	-	-
ALL ONE-DAY	1	1	0	0	0	0.00	-	-	-	-

BOWLING AVERAGES

	Overs	Mdns	Runs	Wkts	Avge	Best	5wI	10wM
NatWest Trophy	6	0	34	0	-	-	-	
ALL ONE-DAY	6	0	34	0	-	-	-	

I.V.A. RICHARDS - *Glamorgan*

Opposition	Venue	Date	Batting	Fielding	Bowling

BRITANNIC ASSURANCE

Leicestershire	Cardiff	April 26	3 & 119		0-9
Somerset	Cardiff	May 3	16 & 16	1Ct	0-22 & 0-68
Gloucs	Bristol	May 15	32 & 1	2Ct	
Sussex	Hove	May 19	118 *	2Ct	2-27 & 0-14
Kent	Swansea	May 23	21		0-34
Northants	Northampton	June 9	25 & 109	1Ct	0-30
Hampshire	Southampton	June 16	164 *		1-32
Somerset	Bath	June 20	21		
Yorkshire	Cardiff	June 23	38		0-19
Surrey	Cardiff	June 30	0 & 14		0-10
Gloucs	Swansea	July 4	41		
Leicestershire	Hinckley	July 7	14 & 68 *	1Ct	0-13
Worcestershire	Abergavenny	July 21	41 & 43		0-31
Warwickshire	Swansea	July 25	11 & 65 *		
Middlesex	Lord's	Aug 4	80 & 9		0-22
Essex	Southend	Aug 8	111 & 118 *	1Ct	0-32 & 2-63
Notts	Worksop	Aug 11	127		
Derbyshire	Cardiff	Aug 29	0		

REFUGE ASSURANCE

Leicestershire	Cardiff	April 29	59	4Ct	1-23
Kent	Llanelli	May 13	55		2-28
Sussex	Hove	May 20	31		3-37
Lancashire	Colwyn Bay	May 27	77		1-42
Essex	Ilford	June 3	0		0-31
Northants	Northampton	June 10	45		0-45
Hampshire	Bournemouth	June 17	8		1-38
Surrey	Cardiff	July 1	34 *	2Ct	0-14
Warwickshire	Edgbaston	July 15	31		1-20
Somerset	Neath	July 22	36		1-76
Derbyshire	Swansea	July 29	22	1Ct	1-27
Middlesex	Lord's	Aug 5	35		
Notts	Trent Bridge	Aug 12	54		2-32

329

R | PLAYER RECORDS

Worcestershire	Swansea	Aug 26	3	1Ct	1-18

NATWEST TROPHY

Dorset	Swansea	June 27	118		2-55
Sussex	Cardiff	July 11	74 *		2-43
Middlesex	Lord's	Aug 1	9		0-16

BENSON & HEDGES CUP

Warwickshire	Edgbaston	April 24	21	1Ct	3-38
Gloucs	Cardiff	May 1	28		1-41
Worcestershire	Worcester	May 8	25		0-59
Kent	Swansea	May 12	27	1Ct	0-30
Worcestershire	Worcester	May 30	3		1-32

BATTING AVERAGES - Including fielding

	Matches	Inns	NO	Runs	HS	Avge	100s	50s	Ct	St
Britannic Assurance	18	28	5	1425	164 *	61.95	7	3	8	-
Refuge Assurance	14	14	1	490	77	37.69	-	4	8	-
NatWest Trophy	3	3	1	201	118	100.50	1	1	-	-
Benson & Hedges Cup	5	5	0	104	28	20.80	-	-	2	-
ALL FIRST-CLASS	18	28	5	1425	164 *	61.95	7	3	8	-
ALL ONE-DAY	22	22	2	795	118	39.75	1	5	10	-

BOWLING AVERAGES

	Overs	Mdns	Runs	Wkts	Avge	Best	5wI	10wM
Britannic Assurance	137	26	426	5	85.20	2-27	-	-
Refuge Assurance	69.5	1	431	14	30.78	3-37	-	
NatWest Trophy	26	0	114	4	28.50	2-43	-	
Benson & Hedges Cup	51	1	200	5	40.00	3-38	-	
ALL FIRST-CLASS	137	26	426	5	85.20	2-27	-	-
ALL ONE-DAY	146.5	2	745	23	32.39	3-37	-	

R.B. RICHARDSON - World XI

Opposition	Venue	Date	Batting	Fielding	Bowling

OTHER FIRST-CLASS

India	Scarborough	Aug 29	65 & 42	1Ct	

BATTING AVERAGES - Including fielding

	Matches	Inns	NO	Runs	HS	Avge	100s	50s	Ct	St
Other First-Class	1	2	0	107	65	53.50	-	1	1	-
ALL FIRST-CLASS	1	2	0	107	65	53.50	-	1	1	-

BOWLING AVERAGES
Did not bowl

N.A. RIDDELL - Durham

Opposition	Venue	Date	Batting	Fielding	Bowling

NATWEST TROPHY

Lancashire	Old Trafford	June 27	16		

BATTING AVERAGES - Including fielding

	Matches	Inns	NO	Runs	HS	Avge	100s	50s	Ct	St
NatWest Trophy	1	1	0	16	16	16.00	-	-	-	-
ALL ONE-DAY	1	1	0	16	16	16.00	-	-	-	-

BOWLING AVERAGES
Did not bowl

D. RIPLEY - Northamptonshire

Opposition	Venue	Date	Batting	Fielding	Bowling

BRITANNIC ASSURANCE

Yorkshire	Headingley	April 26		4Ct	
Derbyshire	Northampton	May 3	17		
Warwickshire	Northampton	May 15	36 & 6	2Ct	
Notts	Trent Bridge	May 23	55	1Ct	
Warwickshire	Edgbaston	June 2	2 *		
Middlesex	Luton	June 23	17 & 5	1Ct,2St	

Somerset	Taunton	June 30		1Ct	
Surrey	The Oval	July 4	9		
Yorkshire	Northampton	July 7	34 * & 16	1Ct	
Kent	Northampton	July 18	7	2Ct	
Sussex	Northampton	July 21	44 *	1Ct	
Gloucs	Cheltenham	July 25	6 & 31	2Ct	
Hampshire	Bournemouth	Aug 4	0 & 5	0Ct,1St	
Derbyshire	Chesterfield	Aug 8	12 & 0	3Ct	
Lancashire	Northampton	Aug 11	34	1Ct,2St	
Worcestershire	Worcester	Aug 18	14 & 26 *	2Ct,1St	
Gloucs	Northampton	Aug 23	34 & 41 *	3Ct	
Essex	Northampton	Aug 29	50		
Essex	Chelmsford	Sept 7	18	2Ct	
Leicestershire	Leicester	Sept 12	6 & 109 *	2Ct	

REFUGE ASSURANCE

Leicestershire	Leicester	April 22		1Ct	
Warwickshire	Edgbaston	April 29	3 *		
Kent	Northampton	May 27	6		
Middlesex	Northampton	June 24	3		
Somerset	Taunton	July 1	3	1Ct	
Yorkshire	Tring	July 8	17	0Ct,1St	
Essex	Chelmsford	July 15	3 *		
Sussex	Well'borough	July 22	26		
Notts	Trent Bridge	July 29	0		
Hampshire	Bournemouth	Aug 5		1Ct	
Lancashire	Northampton	Aug 12	6 *	1Ct	
Worcestershire	Worcester	Aug 19		1Ct	

NATWEST TROPHY

Staffordshire	Northampton	June 27			
Notts	Northampton	July 11	1 *		
Worcestershire	Northampton	Aug 1	2		
Hampshire	Southampton	Aug 15	7	1Ct	
Lancashire	Lord's	Sept 1	13	1Ct	

BENSON & HEDGES CUP

Leicestershire	Leicester	April 24	1 *		
Essex	Northampton	May 8	27		
Scotland	Northampton	May 10	9	1Ct	
Notts	Trent Bridge	May 12	7	1Ct	

OTHER FIRST-CLASS

Cambridge U	Fenner's	April 14	22		

BATTING AVERAGES - Including fielding

	Matches	Inns	NO	Runs	HS	Avge	100s	50s	Ct	St
Britannic Assurance	20	27	6	634	109 *	30.19	1	2	28	6
Refuge Assurance	12	9	3	67	26	11.16	-	-	5	1
NatWest Trophy	5	4	1	23	13	7.66	-	-	2	-
Benson & Hedges Cup	4	4	1	44	27	14.66	-	-	2	-
Other First-Class	1	1	0	22	22	22.00	-	-	-	-
ALL FIRST-CLASS	21	28	6	656	109 *	29.81	1	2	28	6
ALL ONE-DAY	21	17	5	134	27	11.16	-	-	9	1

BOWLING AVERAGES
Did not bowl

A.R. ROBERTS - Northamptonshire

Opposition	Venue	Date	Batting	Fielding	Bowling

BRITANNIC ASSURANCE

Notts	Trent Bridge	May 23	5		1-27 & 0-57
Gloucs	Cheltenham	July 25	0 & 0	1Ct	2-123

BATTING AVERAGES - Including fielding

	Matches	Inns	NO	Runs	HS	Avge	100s	50s	Ct	St
Britannic Assurance	2	3	0	5	5	1.66	-	-	1	-
ALL FIRST-CLASS	2	3	0	5	5	1.66	-	-	1	-

BOWLING AVERAGES

	Overs	Mdns	Runs	Wkts	Avge	Best	5wI	10wM
Britannic Assurance	63	14	207	3	69.00	2-123	-	-
ALL FIRST-CLASS	63	14	207	3	69.00	2-123	-	-

PLATER RECORDS

■ B. ROBERTS - *Derbyshire*

Opposition	Venue	Date	Batting	Fielding	Bowling
BRITANNIC ASSURANCE					
Notts	Trent Bridge	April 26	46		
Northants	Northampton	May 3	44	2Ct	
Lancashire	Derby	May 15	8 & 0	2Ct	
Somerset	Taunton	May 19	37 & 4		
Yorkshire	Chesterfield	May 23	49 & 124 *	2Ct	
Notts	Derby	May 26	15 & 7	4Ct	
Surrey	The Oval	June 6	17		
Warwickshire	Derby	June 16	86	1Ct	
Leicestershire	Leicester	June 20		1	
Gloucs	Derby	June 30	2 & 59		
Sussex	Hove	July 4	47	1Ct	
Lancashire	Liverpool	July 7	4 * & 1 *	2Ct	
Essex	Colchester	July 18	56 & 26	1Ct	
Hampshire	Portsmouth	July 21	7 & 0		0-3
Worcestershire	Derby	July 25	18 & 0	1Ct	
Kent	Chesterfield	Aug 4	100 *	4Ct	
Northants	Chesterfield	Aug 8	34 & 56 *		0-23
Middlesex	Derby	Aug 18	27 & 48 *		
Essex	Derby	Aug 23	13 & 7	1Ct	
Glamorgan	Cardiff	Aug 29	5	1Ct	
Yorkshire	Scarborough	Sept 7	31 & 44 *		
Leicestershire	Derby	Sept 18	15	1Ct	
REFUGE ASSURANCE					
Sussex	Hove	April 22			
Worcestershire	Derby	April 29	9	1Ct	
Northants	Northampton	May 6	15		
Yorkshire	Headingley	May 13	53		
Somerset	Taunton	May 20			
Notts	Derby	June 10	26 *		
Warwickshire	Derby	June 17	9		
Surrey	The Oval	June 24	13		
Gloucs	Derby	July 1	5 *	1Ct	
Lancashire	Old Trafford	July 8	28		
Leicestershire	Knypersley	July 15	77 *	1Ct	
Hampshire	Portsmouth	July 22	10	1Ct	
Glamorgan	Swansea	July 29	23		
Kent	Chesterfield	Aug 5	11 *	1Ct	
Middlesex	Derby	Aug 19			
Essex	Derby	Aug 26	45		
Notts	Derby	Sept 5			
Middlesex	Edgbaston	Sept 16	21		
NATWEST TROPHY					
Shropshire	Chesterfield	June 27	14 *		
Lancashire	Derby	July 11	31	1Ct	
BENSON & HEDGES CUP					
Sussex	Derby	April 24			
Somerset	Taunton	May 1	4		
Min Counties	Wellington	May 10	46		
Middlesex	Derby	May 12	5 *	1Ct	
OTHER FIRST-CLASS					
Cambridge U	Fenner's	April 18	12 & 33		1-16 & 1-0
New Zealand	Derby	June 2	25		1-10
OTHER ONE-DAY					
India	Chesterfield	July 16	8	1Ct	

BATTING AVERAGES - Including fielding

	Matches	Inns	NO	Runs	HS	Avge	100s	50s	Ct	St
Britannic Assurance	22	35	7	1038	124 *	37.07	2	4	23	-
Refuge Assurance	18	14	4	345	77 *	34.50	-	2	5	-
NatWest Trophy	2	2	1	45	31	45.00	-	-	1	-
Benson & Hedges Cup	4	3	1	55	46	27.50	-	-	1	-
Other First-Class	2	3	0	70	33	23.33	-	-	-	-
Other One-Day	1	1	0	8	8	8.00	-	-	1	-
ALL FIRST-CLASS	24	38	7	1108	124 *	35.74	2	4	23	-
ALL ONE-DAY	25	20	6	453	77 *	32.35	-	2	8	-

BOWLING AVERAGES

	Overs	Mdns	Runs	Wkts	Avge	Best	5wI	10wM
Britannic Assurance	7	0	26	0	-	-	-	-
Refuge Assurance								
NatWest Trophy								
Benson & Hedges Cup								
Other First-Class	12	5	26	3	8.66	1-0	-	-

Other One-Day

ALL FIRST-CLASS	19	5	52	3	17.33	1-0	-	-	
ALL ONE-DAY									

■ M.J. ROBERTS - *Bucks & Minor Counties*

Opposition	Venue	Date	Batting	Fielding	Bowling
NATWEST TROPHY					
Notts	Marlow	June 27	17 *		
BENSON & HEDGES CUP					
Middlesex	Lord's	April 24	57	1Ct	
Sussex	Marlow	May 1	121		
Somerset	Taunton	May 8	7		
Derbyshire	Wellington	May 10	31		
OTHER FIRST-CLASS					
For Minor Counties					
India	Trowbridge	July 11	85 & 1		

BATTING AVERAGES - Including fielding

	Matches	Inns	NO	Runs	HS	Avge	100s	50s	Ct	St
NatWest Trophy	1	1	1	17	17 *	-	-	-	-	-
Benson & Hedges Cup	4	4	0	216	121	54.00	1	1	1	-
Other First-Class	1	2	0	86	85	43.00	-	1	-	-
ALL FIRST-CLASS	1	2	0	86	85	43.00	-	1	-	-
ALL ONE-DAY	5	5	1	233	121	58.25	1	1	1	-

BOWLING AVERAGES
Did not bowl

■ M.L. ROBERTS - *Glamorgan*

Opposition	Venue	Date	Batting	Fielding	Bowling
BRITANNIC ASSURANCE					
Lancashire	Colwyn Bay	May 26	13		
REFUGE ASSURANCE					
Sussex	Hove	May 20	12 *		
OTHER FIRST-CLASS					
Oxford U	The Parks	April 14	5 *	1Ct	
Oxford U	The Parks	June 2	14	5Ct	
Sri Lanka	Ebbw Vale	Aug 22	25 & 22	4Ct	

BATTING AVERAGES - Including fielding

	Matches	Inns	NO	Runs	HS	Avge	100s	50s	Ct	St
Britannic Assurance	1	1	0	13	13	13.00	-	-	-	-
Refuge Assurance	1	1	1	12	12 *	-	-	-	-	-
Other First-Class	3	4	1	66	25	22.00	-	-	10	-
ALL FIRST-CLASS	4	5	1	79	25	19.75	-	-	10	-
ALL ONE-DAY	1	1	1	12	12 *	-	-	-	-	-

BOWLING AVERAGES
Did not bowl

■ C.M. ROBERTSON - *Zimbabwe*

Opposition	Venue	Date	Batting	Fielding	Bowling
OTHER FIRST-CLASS					
Yorkshire	Headingley	May 16	18 & 15		
Gloucs	Bristol	May 19	4 & 6	1Ct	
Lancashire	Old Trafford	May 23	125 & 0 *		
OTHER ONE-DAY					
Sussex	Hove	May 13	0	1Ct	
Essex	Chelmsford	May 14	3	1Ct	

R — PLAYER RECORDS

BATTING AVERAGES - Including fielding

	Matches	Inns	NO	Runs	HS	Avge	100s	50s	Ct	St
Other First-Class	3	6	1	168	125	33.60	1	-	1	-
Other One-Day	2	2	0	3	3	1.50	-	-	2	-
ALL FIRST-CLASS	3	6	1	168	125	33.60	1	-	1	-
ALL ONE-DAY	2	2	0	3	3	1.50	-	-	2	-

BOWLING AVERAGES
Did not bowl

J.D. ROBINSON - *Surrey*

Opposition	Venue	Date	Batting			Fielding	Bowling

BRITANNIC ASSURANCE

Opposition	Venue	Date	Batting		Fielding	Bowling
Notts	Trent Bridge	June 20				1-14
Northants	The Oval	July 4				
Warwickshire	The Oval	July 7	11 &	27		0-9
Essex	Chelmsford	Aug 18	0 &	18		1-49 & 1-39
Kent	Canterbury	Sept 7	16		1Ct	1-95 & 2-84
Middlesex	The Oval	Sept 12	72 &	0		0-59
Essex	The Oval	Sept 18	7 &	0		0-44

REFUGE ASSURANCE

Opposition	Venue	Date	Batting	Fielding	Bowling
Northants	The Oval	June 3	4		
Kent	The Oval	July 22	16	1Ct	0-19
Leicestershire	The Oval	Aug 12	13		0-22
Hampshire	Southampton	Aug 26	7		0-22

BENSON & HEDGES CUP

Opposition	Venue	Date	Batting	Fielding	Bowling
Yorkshire	The Oval	May 12	2*	1Ct	2-41

OTHER FIRST-CLASS

Opposition	Venue	Date	Batting	Fielding	Bowling
Oxford U	The Parks	May 16	24		1-69 & 0-14

OTHER ONE-DAY

Opposition	Venue	Date	Batting	Fielding	Bowling
Sri Lanka	The Oval	Sept 2	33	1ct	0-25
Kent	Hove	Sept 4	98		1-54

BATTING AVERAGES - Including fielding

	Matches	Inns	NO	Runs	HS	Avge	100s	50s	Ct	St
Britannic Assurance	7	9	0	151	72	16.77	-	1	1	-
Refuge Assurance	4	4	0	40	16	10.00	-	-	1	-
Benson & Hedges Cup	1	1	1	2	2*	-	-	-	1	-
Other First-Class	1	1	0	24	24	24.00	-	-	-	-
Other One-Day	2	2	0	131	98	65.50	-	1	1	-
ALL FIRST-CLASS	8	10	0	175	72	17.50	-	1	1	-
ALL ONE-DAY	7	7	1	173	98	28.83	-	1	3	-

BOWLING AVERAGES

	Overs	Mdns	Runs	Wkts	Avge	Best	5wI	10wM
Britannic Assurance	118.3	21	393	6	65.50	2-84	-	-
Refuge Assurance	11	0	63	0	-	-	-	-
Benson & Hedges Cup	11	0	41	2	20.50	2-41	-	-
Other First-Class	28	7	83	1	83.00	1-69	-	-
Other One-Day	15	1	79	1	79.00	1-54	-	-
ALL FIRST-CLASS	146.3	28	476	7	68.00	2-84	-	-
ALL ONE-DAY	37	1	183	3	61.00	2-41	-	-

M.A. ROBINSON - *Northamptonshire*

Opposition	Venue	Date	Batting		Fielding	Bowling

BRITANNIC ASSURANCE

Opposition	Venue	Date	Batting		Fielding	Bowling
Yorkshire	Headingley	April 26			1Ct	2-47 & 3-47
Derbyshire	Northampton	May 3	1* &	0*		3-80
Warwickshire	Northampton	May 15	1 &	0		2-91
Middlesex	Luton	June 23	0* &	0*	1Ct	0-46 & 0-0
Somerset	Taunton	June 30				0-62 & 2-76
Surrey	The Oval	July 4		0*		1-57
Yorkshire	Northampton	July 7		0*		1-67 & 0-50
Kent	Northampton	July 18				1-75 & 0-19
Sussex	Northampton	July 21				1-61 & 3-68
Gloucs	Cheltenham	July 25	0* &	0		2-119
Hampshire	Bournemouth	Aug 4	0 &	0		0-60
Derbyshire	Chesterfield	Aug 8			1Ct	3-96 & 1-24
Lancashire	Northampton	Aug 11				1-81 & 1-19
Worcestershire	Worcester	Aug 18	0*		1Ct	2-63 & 2-40
Essex	Northampton	Aug 29				0-75 & 0-69
Essex	Chelmsford	Sept 7	0*			3-73 & 3-89
Leicestershire	Leicester	Sept 12	0 &	1*	1Ct	0-117 & 1-23

REFUGE ASSURANCE

Opposition	Venue	Date	Batting	Fielding	Bowling
Leicestershire	Leicester	April 22			1-8
Warwickshire	Edgbaston	April 29			1-53
Derbyshire	Northampton	May 6			2-23
Kent	Northampton	May 27	0		1-73
Glamorgan	Northampton	June 10			1-34
Middlesex	Northampton	June 24	0*		0-32
Yorkshire	Tring	July 8	0*		0-53
Essex	Chelmsford	July 15			0-46
Sussex	Well'borough	July 22			2-59
Notts	Trent Bridge	July 29			0-34
Hampshire	Bournemouth	Aug 5		1Ct	0-21
Lancashire	Northampton	Aug 12			1-56
Worcestershire	Worcester	Aug 19			2-36

NATWEST TROPHY

Opposition	Venue	Date	Batting	Fielding	Bowling
Staffordshire	Northampton	June 27			1-39
Notts	Northampton	July 11		1Ct	1-46
Worcestershire	Northampton	Aug 1	0*		3-33
Hampshire	Southampton	Aug 15	0	1Ct	3-62
Lancashire	Lord's	Sept 1	3*		1-26

BENSON & HEDGES CUP

Opposition	Venue	Date	Batting	Fielding	Bowling
Leicestershire	Leicester	April 24			0-47
Essex	Northampton	May 8	0*		1-35
Scotland	Northampton	May 10	0*		2-47
Notts	Trent Bridge	May 12	1		1-47

OTHER FIRST-CLASS

Opposition	Venue	Date	Batting	Fielding	Bowling
Cambridge U	Fenner's	April 14			2-24 & 0-18
New Zealand	Northampton	June 16			0-53

BATTING AVERAGES - Including fielding

	Matches	Inns	NO	Runs	HS	Avge	100s	50s	Ct	St
Britannic Assurance	17	16	10	3	1*	0.50	-	-	5	-
Refuge Assurance	13	3	2	0	0*	0.00	-	-	1	-
NatWest Trophy	5	3	2	3	3*	3.00	-	-	2	-
Benson & Hedges Cup	4	3	2	1	1	1.00	-	-	-	-
Other First-Class	2	0	0	0	0	-	-	-	-	-
ALL FIRST-CLASS	19	16	10	3	1*	0.50	-	-	5	-
ALL ONE-DAY	22	9	6	4	3*	1.33	-	-	3	-

BOWLING AVERAGES

	Overs	Mdns	Runs	Wkts	Avge	Best	5wI	10wM
Britannic Assurance	520.1	98	1794	38	47.21	3-47	-	-
Refuge Assurance	88.3	7	528	11	48.00	2-23	-	-
NatWest Trophy	56	5	206	9	22.88	3-33	-	-
Benson & Hedges Cup	38.4	1	176	4	44.00	2-47	-	-
Other First-Class	39	7	95	2	47.50	2-24	-	-
ALL FIRST-CLASS	559.1	105	1889	40	47.22	3-47	-	-
ALL ONE-DAY	183.1	13	910	24	37.91	3-33	-	-

P.E. ROBINSON - *Yorkshire*

Opposition	Venue	Date	Batting		Fielding	Bowling

BRITANNIC ASSURANCE

Opposition	Venue	Date	Batting		Fielding	Bowling
Northants	Headingley	April 26	30 &	22		
Warwickshire	Edgbaston	May 3	1 &	59		
Derbyshire	Chesterfield	May 23	12 &	1	1Ct	
Hampshire	Headingley	May 26	60 &	24	1Ct	
Worcestershire	Worcester	June 2	28			
Kent	Tunbridge We	June 6				
Surrey	Harrogate	June 9	85		1Ct	
Warwickshire	Sheffield	June 20	14 &	28		
Glamorgan	Cardiff	June 23	53* &	21*	1Ct	
Notts	Scarborough	July 4	73*		1Ct	
Northants	Northampton	July 7	58 &	76*		
Middlesex	Uxbridge	July 18	3 &	40	1Ct	
Gloucs	Cheltenham	July 21	49 &	70*	1Ct	
Somerset	Scarborough	July 25	31 &	44	1Ct	1-10
Leicestershire	Sheffield	July 28	7 &	4		

PLANER RECORDS

PLAYER RECORDS

R

Lancashire	Headingley	Aug 4	2 & 11		
Sussex	Eastbourne	Aug 8	59		
Essex	Middlesbr'gh	Aug 11	3 & 39	4Ct	
Lancashire	Old Trafford	Aug 18	70 & 9	1Ct	
Middlesex	Headingley	Aug 23	0 & 72	3Ct	
Derbyshire	Scarborough	Sept 7	150* & 14	2Ct	0-18
Notts	Trent Bridge	Sept 18	62* & 5		

REFUGE ASSURANCE

Notts	Trent Bridge	April 22	4	
Warwickshire	Edgbaston	May 6	22	
Derbyshire	Headingley	May 13	21	
Kent	Canterbury	May 20	17	
Hampshire	Headingley	May 27	26	1Ct
Worcestershire	Worcester	June 3	13	
Surrey	Hull	June 10	22	
Sussex	Hove	June 17	1	1Ct
Northants	Tring	July 8	58*	1Ct
Somerset	Scarborough	July 15	15	1Ct
Gloucs	Cheltenham	July 22	33	
Leicestershire	Sheffield	July 29		
Lancashire	Scarborough	Aug 5	0	
Essex	Middlesbr'gh	Aug 12	14	
Middlesex	Scarborough	Aug 26	11	1Ct

NATWEST TROPHY

Norfolk	Headingley	June 27		
Warwickshire	Headingley	July 11		2Ct
Hampshire	Southampton	Aug 1	7	

BENSON & HEDGES CUP

Hampshire	Southampton	April 24	73*
Combined U	Headingley	May 8	57
Lancashire	Headingley	May 10	0
Surrey	The Oval	May 12	43*

OTHER FIRST-CLASS

Zimbabwe	Headingley	May 16	13	2Ct

OTHER ONE-DAY

Sussex	Harrogate	June 14	24*	2Ct
Warwickshire	Harrogate	June 15	3	
World XI	Scarborough	Sept 1	114	
Essex	Scarborough	Sept 3	26	
Yorkshiremen	Scarborough	Sept 6	25*	

BATTING AVERAGES - Including fielding

	Matches	Inns	NO	Runs	HS	Avge	100s	50s	Ct	St
Britannic Assurance	22	38	7	1389	150*	44.80	1	12	18	-
Refuge Assurance	15	14	1	257	58*	19.76	-	1	5	-
NatWest Trophy	3	1	0	7	7	7.00	-	-	2	-
Benson & Hedges Cup	4	4	2	173	73*	86.50	-	2	-	-
Other First-Class	1	1	0	13	13	13.00	-	-	2	-
Other One-Day	5	5	2	192	114	64.00	1	-	2	-
ALL FIRST-CLASS	23	39	7	1402	150*	43.81	1	12	20	-
ALL ONE-DAY	27	24	5	629	114	33.10	1	3	9	-

BOWLING AVERAGES

	Overs	Mdns	Runs	Wkts	Avge	Best	5wI	10wM
Britannic Assurance	3.3	0	28	1	28.00	1-10	-	-
Refuge Assurance								
NatWest Trophy								
Benson & Hedges Cup								
Other First-Class								
Other One-Day								
ALL FIRST-CLASS	3.3	0	28	1	28.00	1-10	-	-
ALL ONE-DAY								

R.T. ROBINSON - *Nottinghamshire*

Opposition	Venue	Date	Batting		Fielding	Bowling

BRITANNIC ASSURANCE

Derbyshire	Trent Bridge	April 26	11 & 86	
Worcestershire	Worcester	May 3	15 & 48	
Leicestershire	Leicester	May 15	0 & 8	1Ct
Warwickshire	Edgbaston	May 19	41 & 47	1Ct
Northants	Trent Bridge	May 23	30 & 56	
Derbyshire	Derby	May 26	69 & 15	
Kent	Tunbridge We	June 2	2 & 1*	

Surrey	Trent Bridge	June 20	5 & 72	1Ct
Leicestershire	Trent Bridge	June 30	0 & 69*	
Yorkshire	Scarborough	July 4	43	2Ct
Sussex	Trent Bridge	July 7	6 & 52	
Hampshire	Portsmouth	July 18	3 & 7	2Ct
Lancashire	Southport	July 25	0 & 41	3Ct
Middlesex	Trent Bridge	July 28	5 & 2	
Essex	Southend	Aug 4	6 & 26	1Ct
Somerset	Weston	Aug 8	79 & 125*	
Glamorgan	Worksop	Aug 11	46 & 8	
Gloucs	Trent Bridge	Aug 18	123 & 13	1Ct
Worcestershire	Trent Bridge	Aug 29	39 & 45	
Middlesex	Lord's	Sept 7	57 & 105	
Lancashire	Trent Bridge	Sept 12	8 & 23	
Yorkshire	Trent Bridge	Sept 18	220* & 36*	

REFUGE ASSURANCE

Yorkshire	Trent Bridge	April 22	1	1Ct
Lancashire	Trent Bridge	April 29	61	2Ct
Worcestershire	Worcester	May 6	0	
Middlesex	Lord's	May 13	6	
Surrey	Trent Bridge	May 20	2	
Derbyshire	Derby	June 10	116	
Kent	Canterbury	June 17	3	
Somerset	Bath	June 24	12	
Leicestershire	Trent Bridge	July 1	0*	
Sussex	Trent Bridge	July 8	15*	
Hampshire	Southampton	July 15	44	1Ct
Warwickshire	Edgbaston	July 22	63	
Northants	Trent Bridge	July 29	74*	1Ct
Essex	Southend	Aug 5	4	
Glamorgan	Trent Bridge	Aug 12	107*	1Ct
Gloucs	Trent Bridge	Aug 19	6	
Derbyshire	Derby	Sept 5	96	1Ct

NATWEST TROPHY

Bucks	Marlow	June 27	30	1Ct
Northants	Northampton	July 11	61	

BENSON & HEDGES CUP

Essex	Chelmsford	April 24	56	1Ct
Leicestershire	Trent Bridge	May 1	25*	
Scotland	Glasgow	May 8	70*	
Northants	Trent Bridge	May 12	106*	
Essex	Chelmsford	May 30	72*	
Worcestershire	Trent Bridge	June 13	26	

OTHER FIRST-CLASS

Sri Lanka	Cleethorpes	Aug 25	18 & 36	

BATTING AVERAGES - Including fielding

	Matches	Inns	NO	Runs	HS	Avge	100s	50s	Ct	St
Britannic Assurance	22	43	5	1693	220*	44.55	4	8	12	-
Refuge Assurance	17	17	4	610	116	46.92	2	4	7	-
NatWest Trophy	2	2	0	91	61	45.50	-	1	1	-
Benson & Hedges Cup	6	6	4	355	106*	177.50	1	3	1	-
Other First-Class	1	2	0	54	36	27.00	-	-	-	-
ALL FIRST-CLASS	23	45	5	1747	220*	43.67	4	8	12	-
ALL ONE-DAY	25	25	8	1056	116	62.11	3	8	9	-

BOWLING AVERAGES
Did not bowl

A. ROBSON - *Surrey*

Opposition	Venue	Date	Batting	Fielding	Bowling

REFUGE ASSURANCE

Derbyshire	The Oval	June 24			1-37

BATTING AVERAGES - Including fielding

	Matches	Inns	NO	Runs	HS	Avge	100s	50s	Ct	St
Refuge Assurance	1	0	0	0	0		-	-	-	-
ALL ONE-DAY	1	0	0	0	0		-	-	-	-

BOWLING AVERAGES

	Overs	Mdns	Runs	Wkts	Avge	Best	5wI	10wM
Refuge Assurance	7	0	37	1	37.00	1-37	-	
ALL ONE-DAY	7	0	37	1	37.00	1-37	-	

R PLAYER RECORDS

P.M. ROEBUCK - *Somerset*

Opposition	Venue	Date	Batting			Fielding	Bowling
BRITANNIC ASSURANCE							
Gloucs	Taunton	April 26	40				
Glamorgan	Cardiff	May 3	69			1Ct	0-33 & 2-34
Derbyshire	Taunton	May 19	34 *&	6		1Ct	0-4 & 1-23
Sussex	Taunton	May 23	27				2-63 & 0-38
Leicestershire	Leicester	May 26	63 &	23 *			0-32 & 0-1
Gloucs	Bristol	June 2	3			1Ct	
Essex	Bath	June 16					0-26
Northants	Taunton	June 30	60 &	44		1Ct	0-17 & 0-21
Warwickshire	Taunton	July 4	114 *&	90 *			
Worcestershire	Worcester	July 18	201 *&	68			0-20 & 0-8
Middlesex	Uxbridge	July 21	70 &	9			
Yorkshire	Scarborough	July 25	11 &	8		1Ct	1-25 & 1-25
Lancashire	Old Trafford	July 28	26 &	12			0-17
Surrey	Weston	Aug 4	49 &	39		1Ct	
Notts	Weston	Aug 8	0				0-22
Hampshire	Taunton	Aug 18	0 &	19			0-17 & 0-34
REFUGE ASSURANCE							
Worcestershire	Taunton	April 22	39				1-10
Hampshire	Taunton	May 13	1				
Derbyshire	Taunton	May 20	85				0-22
Leicestershire	Leicester	May 27	28				
Gloucs	Bristol	June 3	4				
Kent	Canterbury	June 10	29			1Ct	0-24
Essex	Bath	June 17	0				0-27
Warwickshire	Weston	Aug 12	9				2-48
NATWEST TROPHY							
Devon	Torquay	June 27	43				
Worcestershire	Taunton	July 11	20				0-22
BENSON & HEDGES CUP							
Derbyshire	Taunton	May 1					0-57
Min Counties	Taunton	May 8	13				
Middlesex	Lord's	May 10	8			1Ct	
Sussex	Hove	May 12	91				
Middlesex	Taunton	May 30	17			2Ct	2-13
OTHER FIRST-CLASS							
Oxford U	The Parks	April 18	26				0-8
New Zealand	Taunton	May 16	17 &	6			0-26 & 1-35
OTHER ONE-DAY							
Sri Lanka	Taunton	Sept 3	95				1-30

BATTING AVERAGES - Including fielding

	Matches	Inns	NO	Runs	HS	Avge	100s	50s	Ct	St
Britannic Assurance	16	25	5	1085	201 *	54.25	2	6	6	-
Refuge Assurance	8	8	0	195	85	24.37	-	1	1	-
NatWest Trophy	2	2	0	63	43	31.50	-	-	-	-
Benson & Hedges Cup	5	4	0	129	91	32.25	-	1	3	-
Other First-Class	2	3	0	49	26	16.33	-	-	-	-
Other One-Day	1	1	0	95	95	95.00	-	1	-	-
ALL FIRST-CLASS	18	28	5	1134	201 *	49.30	2	6	6	-
ALL ONE-DAY	16	15	0	482	95	32.13	-	3	4	-

BOWLING AVERAGES

	Overs	Mdns	Runs	Wkts	Avge	Best	5wI	10wM
Britannic Assurance	160.3	37	460	7	65.71	2-34	-	-
Refuge Assurance	19	1	131	3	43.66	2-48	-	
NatWest Trophy	5.2	0	22	0	-	-	-	
Benson & Hedges Cup	14	0	70	2	35.00	2-13	-	
Other First-Class	22	5	69	1	69.00	1-35	-	-
Other One-Day	11	0	30	1	30.00	1-30	-	
ALL FIRST-CLASS	182.3	42	529	8	66.12	2-34	-	-
ALL ONE-DAY	49.2	1	253	6	42.16	2-13	-	

P.W. ROMAINES - *Gloucestershire*

Opposition	Venue	Date	Batting	Fielding	Bowling
BRITANNIC ASSURANCE					
Lancashire	Old Trafford	June 9	12 *		

Yorkshire	Cheltenham	July 21	46		
Northants	Cheltenham	July 25	28		1Ct
Warwickshire	Bristol	Aug 8	1 & 61		1Ct
Kent	Bristol	Aug 11	8 & 21		

REFUGE ASSURANCE

Glamorgan	Bristol	April 22	22	
Hampshire	Southampton	May 6		
Essex	Chelmsford	May 13		1Ct
Warwickshire	Moreton-in-M	May 20	5	
Middlesex	Lord's	May 27	11	
Somerset	Bristol	June 3		
Lancashire	Old Trafford	June 10	45 *	
Leicestershire	Gloucester	June 24	13	
Derbyshire	Derby	July 1	2	
Worcestershire	Worcester	July 8	27 *	
Sussex	Swindon	July 15	47	1Ct
Yorkshire	Cheltenham	July 22	9	1Ct
Surrey	Cheltenham	July 29	0	1Ct
Kent	Bristol	Aug 12		
Notts	Trent Bridge	Aug 19	15 *	
Northants	Northampton	Aug 26	31	

NATWEST TROPHY

Lancashire	Old Trafford	Aug 1	20

OTHER FIRST-CLASS

Cambridge U	Fenner's	May 23	15 *& 95	
India	Bristol	Aug 4	2 & 6	1-30

BATTING AVERAGES - Including fielding

	Matches	Inns	NO	Runs	HS	Avge	100s	50s	Ct	St
Britannic Assurance	5	7	1	177	61	29.50	-	1	2	-
Refuge Assurance	16	12	3	227	47	25.22	-	-	4	-
NatWest Trophy	1	1	0	20	20	20.00	-	-	-	-
Other First-Class	2	4	1	118	95	39.33	-	1	-	-
ALL FIRST-CLASS	7	11	2	295	95	32.77	-	2	2	-
ALL ONE-DAY	17	13	3	247	47	24.70	-	-	4	-

BOWLING AVERAGES

	Overs	Mdns	Runs	Wkts	Avge	Best	5wI	10wM
Britannic Assurance								
Refuge Assurance								
NatWest Trophy								
Other First-Class	6	0	30	1	30.00	1-30	-	-
ALL FIRST-CLASS	6	0	30	1	30.00	1-30	-	-
ALL ONE-DAY								

G.D. ROSE - *Somerset*

Opposition	Venue	Date	Batting			Fielding	Bowling
BRITANNIC ASSURANCE							
Gloucs	Taunton	April 26	85			2Ct	1-46 & 3-64
Glamorgan	Cardiff	May 3					1-50 & 0-23
Derbyshire	Taunton	May 19		31			1-75 & 1-24
Sussex	Taunton	May 23	4 *			2Ct	3-52 & 0-21
Leicestershire	Leicester	May 26	3 *			1Ct	0-85 & 5-52
Gloucs	Bristol	June 2	0			1Ct	4-78
Hampshire	Basingstoke	June 6					3-84 & 2-21
Kent	Canterbury	June 9	8 *				4-59 & 4-55
Essex	Bath	June 16					0-78
Glamorgan	Bath	June 20	97 *				0-35
Northants	Taunton	June 30	33 *&	8		2Ct	1-15 & 1-77
Warwickshire	Taunton	July 4	14			1Ct	1-57
Worcestershire	Worcester	July 18		44 *		1Ct	0-49 & 0-29
Middlesex	Uxbridge	July 21	57 &	10 *			0-11 & 1-43
Yorkshire	Scarborough	July 25	35 &	0			1-41 & 2-41
Lancashire	Old Trafford	July 28	27 &	76		1Ct	2-77
Surrey	Weston	Aug 4	85				0-40 & 2-26
Notts	Weston	Aug 8	60			1Ct	0-37 & 0-26
Hampshire	Taunton	Aug 18	13 &	33 *			1-48 & 0-2
Sussex	Hove	Aug 23	54				2-22 & 2-95
Warwickshire	Edgbaston	Sept 7	41 &	14 *		2Ct	3-49 & 0-54
Worcestershire	Taunton	Sept 12	29 &	36			0-15 & 0-51
REFUGE ASSURANCE							
Worcestershire	Taunton	April 22	41 *				0-54
Hampshire	Taunton	May 13	32				0-49
Derbyshire	Taunton	May 20	5				1-45

PLER RECORDS

PLAYER RECORDS   R

Leicestershire	Leicester	May 27	20		3-36
Gloucs	Bristol	June 3	14	1Ct	0-34
Kent	Canterbury	June 10	29		1-29
Essex	Bath	June 17	20	1Ct	3-33
Notts	Bath	June 24	45	1Ct	2-61
Northants	Taunton	July 1	22 *		2-40
Middlesex	Lord's	July 8		1Ct	1-42
Yorkshire	Scarborough	July 15	6		1-45
Glamorgan	Neath	July 22	148		1-24
Lancashire	Old Trafford	July 29	1	2Ct	1-24
Surrey	Weston	Aug 5	3		1-41
Warwickshire	Weston	Aug 12	37		1-41
Sussex	Hove	Aug 26	7		0-12

NATWEST TROPHY
Devon	Torquay	June 27	110	1Ct	0-11
Worcestershire	Taunton	July 11	16		1-40

BENSON & HEDGES CUP
Derbyshire	Taunton	May 1	64		2-58
Min Counties	Taunton	May 8	26 *		1-31
Middlesex	Lord's	May 10	15		1-47
Sussex	Hove	May 12	14		4-37
Middlesex	Taunton	May 30	12		0-23
Lancashire	Old Trafford	June 13	32		2-44

OTHER FIRST-CLASS
Oxford U	The Parks	April 18	32	1-37
New Zealand	Taunton	May 16	12 * & 59 *	0-33 & 1-74

OTHER ONE-DAY
Sri Lanka	Taunton	Sept 3	2	4-16

BATTING AVERAGES - Including fielding
	Matches	Inns	NO	Runs	HS	Avge	100s	50s	Ct	St
Britannic Assurance	22	26	9	897	97 *	52.76	-	7	14	-
Refuge Assurance	16	15	2	430	148	33.07	1	-	6	-
NatWest Trophy	2	2	0	126	110	63.00	1	-	1	-
Benson & Hedges Cup	6	6	1	163	64	32.60	-	1	-	-
Other First-Class	2	3	2	103	59 *	103.00	-	1	-	-
Other One-Day	1	1	0	2	2	2.00	-	-	-	-
ALL FIRST-CLASS	24	29	11	1000	97 *	55.55	-	8	14	-
ALL ONE-DAY	25	24	3	721	148	34.33	2	1	7	-

BOWLING AVERAGES
	Overs	Mdns	Runs	Wkts	Avge	Best	5wI	10wM
Britannic Assurance	530.4	93	1807	51	35.43	5-52	1	-
Refuge Assurance	113.3	1	610	18	33.88	3-33	-	
NatWest Trophy	14	1	51	1	51.00	1-40	-	
Benson & Hedges Cup	55	6	240	10	24.00	4-37	-	
Other First-Class	41	6	144	2	72.00	1-37	-	
Other One-Day	6	1	16	4	4.00	4-16	-	
ALL FIRST-CLASS	571.4	99	1951	53	36.81	5-52	1	-
ALL ONE-DAY	188.3	9	917	33	27.78	4-16	-	

M.A. ROSEBERRY - *Middlesex*

Opposition	Venue	Date	Batting			Fielding	Bowling

BRITANNIC ASSURANCE
Essex	Lord's	April 26	12	&	1	1Ct	
Kent	Lord's	May 15	50	&	37		
Surrey	Lord's	May 23	122	&	0		
Gloucs	Lord's	May 26	50	&	1	3Ct	
Essex	Ilford	June 2	135			1Ct	
Warwickshire	Lord's	June 6	64	&	19 *		1-58
Leicestershire	Leicester	June 16	15	&	0	2Ct	
Lancashire	Old Trafford	June 20			79	1Ct	0-14
Northants	Luton	June 23	115	&	36	5Ct	
Worcestershire	Lord's	June 30	43			1Ct	
Yorkshire	Uxbridge	July 18	36	&	9	2Ct	
Somerset	Uxbridge	July 21	25	&	7		
Kent	Canterbury	July 25	82	&	14	1Ct	
Notts	Trent Bridge	July 28	74	&	0		
Glamorgan	Lord's	Aug 4	0	&	62		
Hampshire	Bournemouth	Aug 8	84	&	6		
Sussex	Lord's	Aug 11	22	&	37	1Ct	
Derbyshire	Derby	Aug 18	7	&	2	2Ct	
Yorkshire	Headingley	Aug 23	2	&	80		
Notts	Lord's	Sept 7	11	&	20 *		
Surrey	The Oval	Sept 12	28	&	27 *	1Ct	0-2
Sussex	Hove	Sept 18	83				

REFUGE ASSURANCE
Lancashire	Old Trafford	April 22	73		
Essex	Lord's	April 29	16	1Ct	
Kent	Folkestone	May 6	52	1Ct	
Notts	Lord's	May 13	80		
Gloucs	Lord's	May 27	0	1Ct	
Warwickshire	Lord's	June 3	51 *		
Hampshire	Basingstoke	June 10	17		
Leicestershire	Leicester	June 17	18	1Ct	
Northants	Northampton	June 24	50		
Worcestershire	Lord's	July 1	73		
Somerset	Lord's	July 8	16		
Surrey	The Oval	July 15	48		
Glamorgan	Lord's	Aug 5	68	1Ct	
Sussex	Lord's	Aug 12	4		
Derbyshire	Derby	Aug 19	0	1Ct	
Yorkshire	Scarborough	Aug 26	9		
Lancashire	Old Trafford	Sept 5	86		
Derbyshire	Edgbaston	Sept 16	17		

NATWEST TROPHY
Berkshire	Lord's	June 27	3	1Ct	
Surrey	Uxbridge	July 11	48		
Glamorgan	Lord's	Aug 1	48		
Lancashire	Old Trafford	Aug 15	16		

BENSON & HEDGES CUP
Min Counties	Lord's	April 24	4		
Sussex	Hove	May 8	1	1Ct	
Somerset	Lord's	May 10	30		
Somerset	Taunton	May 30	38		

OTHER FIRST-CLASS
Cambridge U	Fenner's	May 3	85 & 2 *	1Ct	1-41
New Zealand	Lord's	May 19	9 & 0	1Ct	

BATTING AVERAGES - Including fielding
	Matches	Inns	NO	Runs	HS	Avge	100s	50s	Ct	St
Britannic Assurance	22	40	3	1497	135	40.45	3	10	21	-
Refuge Assurance	18	18	1	678	86	39.88	-	8	6	-
NatWest Trophy	4	4	0	115	48	28.75	-	-	1	-
Benson & Hedges Cup	4	4	0	73	38	18.25	-	-	1	-
Other First-Class	2	4	1	96	85	32.00	-	1	2	-
ALL FIRST-CLASS	24	44	4	1593	135	39.82	3	11	23	-
ALL ONE-DAY	26	26	1	866	86	34.64	-	8	8	-

BOWLING AVERAGES
	Overs	Mdns	Runs	Wkts	Avge	Best	5wI	10wM
Britannic Assurance	11	3	74	1	74.00	1-58	-	-
Refuge Assurance								
NatWest Trophy								
Benson & Hedges Cup								
Other First-Class	11	2	41	1	41.00	1-41	-	-
ALL FIRST-CLASS	22	5	115	2	57.50	1-41	-	-

A.B. RUSSELL - *Scotland*

Opposition	Venue	Date	Batting	Fielding	Bowling

NATWEST TROPHY
Essex	Chelmsford	June 27	37		

BENSON & HEDGES CUP
Essex	Glasgow	May 1	9		0-9
Northants	Northampton	May 10	0		

OTHER FIRST-CLASS
Ireland	Edinburgh	Aug 11	47		1-23

OTHER ONE-DAY
India	Glasgow	July 14	48		

BATTING AVERAGES - Including fielding
	Matches	Inns	NO	Runs	HS	Avge	100s	50s	Ct	St
NatWest Trophy	1	1	0	37	37	37.00	-	-		-
Benson & Hedges Cup	2	2	0	9	9	4.50	-	-	-	-

R   PLAYER RECORDS

Other First-Class	1	1	0	47	47	47.00	-	-	-
Other One-Day	1	1	0	48	48	48.00	-	-	-
ALL FIRST-CLASS	1	1	0	47	47	47.00	-	-	-
ALL ONE-DAY	4	4	0	94	48	23.50	-	-	-

BOWLING AVERAGES

	Overs	Mdns	Runs	Wkts	Avge	Best	5wI	10wM
NatWest Trophy								
Benson & Hedges Cup	2	0	9	0	-			
Other First-Class	6	1	23	1	23.00	1-23	-	-
Other One-Day								
ALL FIRST-CLASS	6	1	23	1	23.00	1-23	-	-
ALL ONE-DAY	2	0	9	0	-			

M.J. RUSSELL - *Oxford University*

Opposition	Venue	Date	Batting	Fielding	Bowling
OTHER FIRST-CLASS					
Hampshire	The Parks	May 3	4	1Ct	
Leicestershire	The Parks	May 23	4		
Glamorgan	The Parks	June 2	2		
Notts	The Parks	June 6			

BATTING AVERAGES - Including fielding

	Matches	Inns	NO	Runs	HS	Avge	100s	50s	Ct	St
Other First-Class	4	3	0	10	4	3.33	-	-	1	-
ALL FIRST-CLASS	4	3	0	10	4	3.33	-	-	1	-

BOWLING AVERAGES
Did not bowl

R.C. RUSSELL - *Gloucestershire & England*

Opposition	Venue	Date	Batting			Fielding	Bowling
CORNHILL TEST MATCHES							
New Zealand	Trent Bridge	June 7	28			3Ct	
New Zealand	Lord's	June 21	13			2Ct	
New Zealand	Edgbaston	July 5	43	&	0		
India	Lord's	July 26				6Ct	
India	Old Trafford	Aug 9	8	&	16 *	2Ct	
India	The Oval	Aug 23	35			3Ct,1St	
TEXACO TROPHY							
New Zealand	Headingley	May 23	13			1Ct,1St	
New Zealand	The Oval	May 25	47 *			1Ct	
India	Headingley	July 18	14				
India	Trent Bridge	July 20	50			0Ct,1St	
BRITANNIC ASSURANCE							
Somerset	Taunton	April 26	12	&	18	3Ct	
Glamorgan	Bristol	May 15	33	&	0	2Ct	
Middlesex	Lord's	May 26			1	3Ct	
Somerset	Bristol	June 2	120			2Ct	
Sussex	Hove	June 16	98			2Ct	
Derbyshire	Derby	June 30	2	&	15	1Ct	
Yorkshire	Cheltenham	July 21	16			3Ct	
Notts	Trent Bridge	Aug 18	79	&	103 *	4Ct	
Worcestershire	Bristol	Sept 7	76				
Sussex	Bristol	Sept 12	31			1Ct	
Hampshire	Southampton	Sept 18	23	&	24	6Ct	
REFUGE ASSURANCE							
Glamorgan	Bristol	April 22	28			2Ct,1St	
Hampshire	Southampton	May 6					
Essex	Chelmsford	May 13	62			0Ct,1St	
Warwickshire	Moreton-in-M	May 20	7			1Ct	
Middlesex	Lord's	May 27	17				
Somerset	Bristol	June 3	13			1Ct	
Derbyshire	Derby	July 1	5				
Sussex	Swindon	July 15	2			1Ct	
Yorkshire	Cheltenham	July 22	12			1Ct	

Notts	Trent Bridge	Aug 19	45	

Opposition	Venue	Date	Batting	Fielding
NATWEST TROPHY				
Lincolnshire	Gloucester	June 27		0Ct,1St
Kent	Bristol	July 11		2Ct
Lancashire	Old Trafford	Aug 1	12	1Ct
BENSON & HEDGES CUP				
Worcestershire	Bristol	April 24	10	
Glamorgan	Cardiff	May 1	46 *	4Ct
Kent	Canterbury	May 10		
Warwickshire	Bristol	May 12	20	

BATTING AVERAGES - Including fielding

	Matches	Inns	NO	Runs	HS	Avge	100s	50s	Ct	St
Cornhill Test Matches	6	7	1	143	43	23.83	-	-	18	1
Texaco Trophy	4	4	1	124	50	41.33	-	1	2	2
Britannic Assurance	11	16	1	651	120	43.40	2	3	27	-
Refuge Assurance	10	9	0	191	62	21.22	-	1	6	2
NatWest Trophy	3	1	0	12	12	12.00	-	-	3	1
Benson & Hedges Cup	4	3	1	76	46 *	38.00	-	-	4	
ALL FIRST-CLASS	17	23	2	794	120	37.81	2	3	45	1
ALL ONE-DAY	21	17	2	403	62	26.86	-	2	15	5

BOWLING AVERAGES
Did not bowl

K.R. RUTHERFORD - *New Zealand*

Opposition	Venue	Date	Batting			Fielding	Bowling
CORNHILL TEST MATCHES							
England	Lord's	June 21	0				0-18
England	Edgbaston	July 5	29	&	18	2Ct	
TEXACO TROPHY							
England	Headingley	May 23	0				
England	The Oval	May 25	0 *				
OTHER FIRST-CLASS							
Worcestershire	Worcester	May 12	4	&	26 *	3Ct	0-25 & 0-27
Somerset	Taunton	May 16			46 *		0-13 & 0-62
Middlesex	Lord's	May 19	68 *	&	2	1Ct	0-26
Northants	Northampton	June 16	42 *			1Ct	0-1
Combined U	Fenner's	June 27	21	&	38		
Essex	Chelmsford	June 30	42	&	40 *		0-24
OTHER ONE-DAY							
D of Norfolk	Arundel	May 6	32 *				0-7
Ireland	Downpatrick	May 9	13 *				
Ireland	Belfast	May 10	2				3-38
Leicestershire	Leicester	June 14	19			1Ct	

BATTING AVERAGES - Including fielding

	Matches	Inns	NO	Runs	HS	Avge	100s	50s	Ct	St
Cornhill Test Matches	2	3	0	47	29	15.66	-	-	2	-
Texaco Trophy	2	2	1	0	0 *	0.00	-	-	-	-
Other First-Class	6	10	5	329	68 *	65.80	-	1	5	-
Other One-Day	4	4	2	66	32 *	33.00	-	-	1	-
ALL FIRST-CLASS	8	13	5	376	68 *	47.00	-	1	7	-
ALL ONE-DAY	6	6	3	66	32 *	22.00	-	-	1	-

BOWLING AVERAGES

	Overs	Mdns	Runs	Wkts	Avge	Best	5wI	10wM
Cornhill Test Matches	3	0	18	0	-	-	-	-
Texaco Trophy								
Other First-Class	39	3	178	0	-	-	-	-
Other One-Day	11	1	45	3	15.00	3-38	-	
ALL FIRST-CLASS	42	3	196	0	-	-	-	-
ALL ONE-DAY	11	1	45	3	15.00	3-38	-	

PLAYER RECORDS S

Z.A. SADIQ - *Derbyshire*

Opposition	Venue	Date	Batting	Fielding	Bowling
BRITANNIC ASSURANCE					
Leicestershire	Derby	Sept 18	0		

BATTING AVERAGES - Including fielding

	Matches	Inns	NO	Runs	HS	Avge	100s	50s	Ct	St
Britannic Assurance	1	1	0	0	0	0.00	-	-	-	-
ALL FIRST-CLASS	1	1	0	0	0	0.00	-	-	-	-

BOWLING AVERAGES
Did not bowl

I.D.K. SALISBURY - *Sussex*

Opposition	Venue	Date	Batting	Fielding	Bowling
BRITANNIC ASSURANCE					
Surrey	Hove	April 26		1Ct	3-89 & 0-26
Kent	Folkestone	May 3	30 * & 5 *		0-135 & 1-20
Hampshire	Southampton	May 15	37 & 19		2-159
Glamorgan	Hove	May 19	3 & 10 *		0-57
Somerset	Taunton	May 23	5		0-66
Lancashire	Horsham	June 2	15 & 0 *		2-46
Gloucs	Hove	June 16	3 *	3Ct	3-62
Worcestershire	Worcester	June 20		1Ct	5-32
Derbyshire	Hove	July 4	68	1Ct	2-49
Notts	Trent Bridge	July 7	0 *	3Ct	1-28 & 1-86
Surrey	Guildford	July 18	21	1Ct	2-84 & 1-77
Northants	Northampton	July 21	0 *		0-36
Hampshire	Arundel	July 25	0		2-108 & 2-69
Middlesex	Lord's	Aug 11	40 *	1Ct	3-115 & 1-60
Somerset	Hove	Aug 23	3 & 30 *		0-80 & 0-5
Leicestershire	Leicester	Aug 29	6		1-87 & 5-79
Gloucs	Bristol	Sept 12	0 & 0	2Ct	1-103
Middlesex	Hove	Sept 18	18 * & 0		2-38
REFUGE ASSURANCE					
Derbyshire	Hove	April 22		1Ct	1-29
Surrey	Hove	April 29			3-40
Glamorgan	Hove	May 20			3-36
Leicestershire	Leicester	June 10			2-21
Yorkshire	Hove	June 17	3 *		0-36
Worcestershire	Worcester	June 24	0	1Ct	0-50
Notts	Trent Bridge	July 8	0	1Ct	0-33
Northants	Well'borough	July 22		1Ct	
Middlesex	Lord's	Aug 12			0-19
Somerset	Hove	Aug 26	7		0-32
NATWEST TROPHY					
Ireland	Downpatrick	June 27			0-19
Glamorgan	Cardiff	July 11	2 *	1Ct	0-47
BENSON & HEDGES CUP					
Derbyshire	Derby	April 24			0-32
Somerset	Hove	May 12	2		1-60
OTHER FIRST-CLASS					
New Zealand	Hove	May 26			1-55 & 1-80
Sri Lanka	Hove	Sept 5			0-103 & 0-41
OTHER ONE-DAY					
Zimbabwe	Hove	May 13	0		4-25
Yorkshire	Harrogate	June 14	14 *		0-44
Kent	Hove	Sept 2	0	1Ct	3-59

BATTING AVERAGES - Including fielding

	Matches	Inns	NO	Runs	HS	Avge	100s	50s	Ct	St
Britannic Assurance	18	23	10	313	68	24.07	-	1	13	-
Refuge Assurance	10	4	1	10	7	3.33	-	-	4	-
NatWest Trophy	2	1	1	2	2*	-	-	-	1	-
Benson & Hedges Cup	2	1	0	2	2	2.00	-	-	-	-
Other First-Class	2	0	0	0	0	-	-	-	-	-
Other One-Day	3	3	1	14	14*	7.00	-	-	1	-
ALL FIRST-CLASS	20	23	10	313	68	24.07	-	1	13	-
ALL ONE-DAY	17	9	3	28	14*	4.66	-	-	6	-

BOWLING AVERAGES

	Overs	Mdns	Runs	Wkts	Avge	Best	5wI	10wM
Britannic Assurance	535.1	103	1796	40	44.90	5-32	2	-
Refuge Assurance	52	2	296	9	32.88	3-36	-	
NatWest Trophy	17	3	66	0	-	-	-	
Benson & Hedges Cup	17	0	92	1	92.00	1-60	-	
Other First-Class	66	10	279	2	139.50	1-55	-	-
Other One-Day	28.3	3	128	7	18.28	4-25	-	
ALL FIRST-CLASS	601.1	113	2075	42	49.40	5-32	2	-
ALL ONE-DAY	114.3	8	582	17	34.23	4-25	-	

G. SALMOND - *Scotland*

Opposition	Venue	Date	Batting	Fielding	Bowling
OTHER ONE-DAY					
India	Glasgow	July 14	0		

BATTING AVERAGES - Including fielding

	Matches	Inns	NO	Runs	HS	Avge	100s	50s	Ct	St
Other One-Day	1	1	0	0	0	0.00	-	-	-	-
ALL ONE-DAY	1	1	0	0	0	0.00	-	-	-	-

BOWLING AVERAGES
Did not bowl

N.F. SARGEANT - *Surrey*

Opposition	Venue	Date	Batting	Fielding	Bowling
BRITANNIC ASSURANCE					
Kent	Guildford	July 21		3Ct	
Gloucs	Cheltenham	July 28	1	2Ct	
REFUGE ASSURANCE					
Kent	The Oval	July 22		3Ct	
Gloucs	Cheltenham	July 29	22		
OTHER FIRST-CLASS					
India	The Oval	Aug 1	18	1Ct,1St	
OTHER ONE-DAY					
Sri Lanka	The Oval	Sept 2			

BATTING AVERAGES - Including fielding

	Matches	Inns	NO	Runs	HS	Avge	100s	50s	Ct	St
Britannic Assurance	2	1	0	1	1	1.00	-	-	5	-
Refuge Assurance	2	1	0	22	22	22.00	-	-	3	-
Other First-Class	1	1	0	18	18	18.00	-	-	1	1
Other One-Day	1	0	0	0	0	-	-	-	-	-
ALL FIRST-CLASS	3	2	0	19	18	9.50	-	-	6	1
ALL ONE-DAY	3	1	0	22	22	22.00	-	-	3	-

BOWLING AVERAGES
Did not bowl

G.P. SAVIN - *Oxfordshire*

Opposition	Venue	Date	Batting	Fielding	Bowling
NATWEST TROPHY					
Kent	Oxford	June 27	23		0-35

BATTING AVERAGES - Including fielding

	Matches	Inns	NO	Runs	HS	Avge	100s	50s	Ct	St
NatWest Trophy	1	1	0	23	23	23.00	-	-	-	-
ALL ONE-DAY	1	1	0	23	23	23.00	-	-	-	-

S	PLAYER RECORDS

BOWLING AVERAGES

	Overs	Mdns	Runs	Wkts	Avge	Best	5wI	10wM
NatWest Trophy	12	0	35	0	-	-	-	-
ALL ONE-DAY	12	0	35	0	-	-	-	-

K. SAXELBY - *Nottinghamshire*

Opposition	Venue	Date	Batting			Fielding	Bowling
BRITANNIC ASSURANCE							
Surrey	Trent Bridge	June 20	0	&	8		0-42
Sussex	Trent Bridge	July 7	5			2Ct	1-44 & 1-29
Somerset	Weston	Aug 8	6	&	20	1Ct	1-55
Glamorgan	Worksop	Aug 11			3		4-92 & 0-47
REFUGE ASSURANCE							
Yorkshire	Trent Bridge	April 22					2-49
Worcestershire	Worcester	May 6	6*				1-54
Middlesex	Lord's	May 13					1-51
Surrey	Trent Bridge	May 20					2-44
Derbyshire	Derby	June 10					1-53
Somerset	Bath	June 24	6*				1-51
Leicestershire	Trent Bridge	July 1				1Ct	1-27
Sussex	Trent Bridge	July 8					0-49
BENSON & HEDGES CUP							
Scotland	Glasgow	May 8					2-39
OTHER FIRST-CLASS							
Oxford U	The Parks	June 6					0-10

BATTING AVERAGES - Including fielding

	Matches	Inns	NO	Runs	HS	Avge	100s	50s	Ct	St
Britannic Assurance	4	6	0	42	20	7.00	-	-	3	-
Refuge Assurance	8	2	2	12	6*	-	-	-	1	-
Benson & Hedges Cup	1	0	0	0	0	-	-	-	-	-
Other First-Class	1	0	0	0	0	-	-	-	-	-
ALL FIRST-CLASS	5	6	0	42	20	7.00	-	-	3	-
ALL ONE-DAY	9	2	2	12	6*	-	-	-	1	-

BOWLING AVERAGES

	Overs	Mdns	Runs	Wkts	Avge	Best	5wI	10wM
Britannic Assurance	89	19	309	7	44.14	4-92	-	-
Refuge Assurance	53.5	0	378	9	42.00	2-44	-	
Benson & Hedges Cup	11	3	39	2	19.50	2-39	-	
Other First-Class	2	0	10	0	-	-	-	
ALL FIRST-CLASS	91	19	319	7	45.57	4-92	-	-
ALL ONE-DAY	64.5	3	417	11	37.90	2-39	-	

M. SAXELBY - *Nottinghamshire*

Opposition	Venue	Date	Batting			Fielding	Bowling
BRITANNIC ASSURANCE							
Leicestershire	Leicester	May 15	11	&	18*		0-39 & 0-30
Warwickshire	Edgbaston	May 19	32*	&	13	2Ct	0-11
Northants	Trent Bridge	May 23	42				1-71 & 0-23
Derbyshire	Derby	May 26	6	&	14		1-21
Hampshire	Portsmouth	July 18	0	&	51		1-31 & 0-4
Lancashire	Southport	July 25	13	&	8		0-30
Gloucs	Trent Bridge	Aug 18	11*	&	13	1Ct	
REFUGE ASSURANCE							
Middlesex	Lord's	May 13	20				0-33
Surrey	Trent Bridge	May 20				1Ct	1-15
Derbyshire	Derby	June 10	34				1-24
Kent	Canterbury	June 17	25			1Ct	2-48
Somerset	Bath	June 24	19				0-45
Leicestershire	Trent Bridge	July 1				1Ct	0-20
Hampshire	Southampton	July 15	24				1-39
Northants	Trent Bridge	July 29	5				
Glamorgan	Trent Bridge	Aug 12	28*			1Ct	
Gloucs	Trent Bridge	Aug 19	24*			1Ct	0-10
Derbyshire	Derby	Sept 5	9				1-25

NATWEST TROPHY
Bucks	Marlow	June 27		41	1Ct

BENSON & HEDGES CUP
Essex	Chelmsford	May 30		0

OTHER FIRST-CLASS
Cambridge U	Fenner's	June 16	30* &	73		0-10

BATTING AVERAGES - Including fielding

	Matches	Inns	NO	Runs	HS	Avge	100s	50s	Ct	St
Britannic Assurance	7	13	3	232	51	23.20	-	1	3	-
Refuge Assurance	11	9	2	188	34	26.85	-	-	5	-
NatWest Trophy	1	1	0	41	41	41.00	-	-	1	-
Benson & Hedges Cup	1	1	0	0	0	0.00	-	-	-	-
Other First-Class	1	2	1	103	73	103.00	-	1	-	-
ALL FIRST-CLASS	8	15	4	335	73	30.45	-	2	3	-
ALL ONE-DAY	13	11	2	229	41	25.44	-	-	6	-

BOWLING AVERAGES

	Overs	Mdns	Runs	Wkts	Avge	Best	5wI	10wM
Britannic Assurance	56.4	8	260	3	86.66	1-21	-	-
Refuge Assurance	40	0	259	6	43.16	2-48	-	
NatWest Trophy								
Benson & Hedges Cup								
Other First-Class	5	1	10	0				
ALL FIRST-CLASS	61.4	9	270	3	90.00	1-21	-	-
ALL ONE-DAY	40	0	259	6	43.16	2-48	-	

C.W. SCOTT - *Nottinghamshire*

Opposition	Venue	Date	Batting		Fielding	Bowling
OTHER FIRST-CLASS						
Oxford U	The Parks	June 6				
Cambridge U	Fenner's	June 16		67*	1Ct	
Sri Lanka	Cleethorpes	Aug 25	13* &	31		

BATTING AVERAGES - Including fielding

	Matches	Inns	NO	Runs	HS	Avge	100s	50s	Ct	St
Other First-Class	3	3	2	111	67*	111.00	-	1	1	-
ALL FIRST-CLASS	3	3	2	111	67*	111.00	-	1	1	-

BOWLING AVERAGES
Did not bowl

R.J. SCOTT - *Hampshire*

Opposition	Venue	Date	Batting			Fielding	Bowling
BRITANNIC ASSURANCE							
Kent	Canterbury	April 26	0	&	1*		1-15 & 2-41
Essex	Southampton	May 23			7*		0-13
Sussex	Arundel	July 25	13	&	16	1Ct	0-21
Warwickshire	Edgbaston	July 28	4	&	0		
Middlesex	Bournemouth	Aug 8	71			2Ct	0-24 & 2-5
Worcestershire	Worcester	Aug 11	17	&	15	1Ct	0-38 & 0-8
REFUGE ASSURANCE							
Kent	Canterbury	April 29	0				2-36
Gloucs	Southampton	May 6	12				
Yorkshire	Headingley	May 27	1				2-39
Leicestershire	Leicester	June 3	4				0-31
Middlesex	Basingstoke	June 10	0				0-7
Glamorgan	Bournemouth	June 17	61				
Lancashire	Old Trafford	June 24					
Essex	Southampton	July 8	7				
Notts	Southampton	July 15	55			1Ct	0-34
Derbyshire	Portsmouth	July 22	76				0-3
Warwickshire	Edgbaston	July 29	47				
Northants	Bournemouth	Aug 5	70			2Ct	0-13
Worcestershire	Worcester	Aug 12	53				2-8
BENSON & HEDGES CUP							
Yorkshire	Southampton	April 24	47				
Surrey	The Oval	May 1	7				0-56

PLANER RECORDS

PLAYER RECORDS

S

BATTING AVERAGES - Including fielding

	Matches	Inns	NO	Runs	HS	Avge	100s	50s	Ct	St
Britannic Assurance	6	10	2	144	71	18.00	-	1	4	-
Refuge Assurance	13	12	0	386	76	32.16	-	5	3	-
Benson & Hedges Cup	2	2	0	54	47	27.00	-	-	-	-
ALL FIRST-CLASS	6	10	2	144	71	18.00	-	1	4	-
ALL ONE-DAY	15	14	0	440	76	31.42	-	5	3	-

BOWLING AVERAGES

	Overs	Mdns	Runs	Wkts	Avge	Best	5wI	10wM
Britannic Assurance	36.4	5	165	5	33.00	2-5	-	-
Refuge Assurance	30.4	0	171	6	28.50	2-8	-	
Benson & Hedges Cup	11	0	56	0	-	-	-	
ALL FIRST-CLASS	36.4	5	165	5	33.00	2-5	-	-
ALL ONE-DAY	41.4	0	227	6	37.83	2-8	-	

T.J.A. SCRIVEN - Buckinghamshire

Opposition	Venue	Date	Batting	Fielding	Bowling
NATWEST TROPHY					
Notts	Marlow	June 27	1		1-73

BATTING AVERAGES - Including fielding

	Matches	Inns	NO	Runs	HS	Avge	100s	50s	Ct	St
NatWest Trophy	1	1	0	1	1	1.00	-	-	-	-
ALL ONE-DAY	1	1	0	1	1	1.00	-	-	-	-

BOWLING AVERAGES

	Overs	Mdns	Runs	Wkts	Avge	Best	5wI	10wM
NatWest Trophy	12	0	73	1	73.00	1-73	-	
ALL ONE-DAY	12	0	73	1	73.00	1-73	-	

A.C. SEYMOUR - Essex

Opposition	Venue	Date	Batting	Fielding	Bowling
BRITANNIC ASSURANCE					
Hampshire	Southampton	May 23	10 * & 0		
Gloucs	Ilford	June 6	4 *		
OTHER FIRST-CLASS					
Cambridge U	Fenner's	May 16	28 & 89	1Ct	
OTHER ONE-DAY					
Zimbabwe	Chelmsford	May 14	6	1Ct	

BATTING AVERAGES - Including fielding

	Matches	Inns	NO	Runs	HS	Avge	100s	50s	Ct	St
Britannic Assurance	2	3	2	14	10 *	14.00	-	-	-	-
Other First-Class	1	2	0	117	89	58.50	-	1	1	-
Other One-Day	1	1	0	6	6	6.00	-	-	1	-
ALL FIRST-CLASS	3	5	2	131	89	43.66	-	1	1	-
ALL ONE-DAY	1	1	0	6	6	6.00	-	-	1	-

BOWLING AVERAGES
Did not bowl

J.H. SHACKLETON - Dorset

Opposition	Venue	Date	Batting	Fielding	Bowling
NATWEST TROPHY					
Glamorgan	Swansea	June 27			0-44

BATTING AVERAGES - Including fielding

	Matches	Inns	NO	Runs	HS	Avge	100s	50s	Ct	St
NatWest Trophy	1	0	0	0	0	-	-	-	-	-

ALL ONE-DAY	1	0	0	0	0	-	-	-	-	-

BOWLING AVERAGES

	Overs	Mdns	Runs	Wkts	Avge	Best	5wI	10wM
NatWest Trophy	12	1	44	0	-	-	-	-
ALL ONE-DAY	12	1	44	0	-	-	-	-

A.H. SHAH - Zimbabwe

Opposition	Venue	Date	Batting	Fielding	Bowling
OTHER FIRST-CLASS					
Yorkshire	Headingley	May 16	10 & 20		2-46
Gloucs	Bristol	May 19	185		1-44
Lancashire	Old Trafford	May 23			1-57 & 1-46
OTHER ONE-DAY					
Sussex	Hove	May 13	21		1-36
Essex	Chelmsford	May 14	0		0-20

BATTING AVERAGES - Including fielding

	Matches	Inns	NO	Runs	HS	Avge	100s	50s	Ct	St
Other First-Class	3	3	0	215	185	71.66	1	-	-	-
Other One-Day	2	2	0	21	21	10.50	-	-	-	-
ALL FIRST-CLASS	3	3	0	215	185	71.66	1	-	-	-
ALL ONE-DAY	2	2	0	21	21	10.50	-	-	-	-

BOWLING AVERAGES

	Overs	Mdns	Runs	Wkts	Avge	Best	5wI	10wM
Other First-Class	75	17	193	5	38.60	2-46	-	-
Other One-Day	17	1	56	1	56.00	1-36	-	
ALL FIRST-CLASS	75	17	193	5	38.60	2-46	-	-
ALL ONE-DAY	17	1	56	1	56.00	1-36	-	

N. SHAHID - Essex

Opposition	Venue	Date	Batting	Fielding	Bowling
BRITANNIC ASSURANCE					
Middlesex	Lord's	April 26	34 *		0-12 & 1-33
Leicestershire	Chelmsford	May 3		2Ct	2-54 & 0-42
Worcestershire	Worcester	May 19	35 *	1Ct	
Hampshire	Southampton	May 23	19 * & 0		0-25
Gloucs	Ilford	June 6	15 & 14 *		
Warwickshire	Edgbaston	June 9	75 *		
Kent	Maidstone	June 4	63		
Derbyshire	Colchester	July 18	42 & 4 *	3Ct	
Lancashire	Colchester	July 21	125 & 26	2Ct	0-28 & 0-46
Leicestershire	Leicester	July 25	2 & 48	2Ct	
Sussex	Chelmsford	July 28	55 & 89		0-15
Glamorgan	Southend	Aug 8	1 & 46	1Ct	0-23
Yorkshire	Middlesbr'gh	Aug 11	3	4Ct	
Surrey	Chelmsford	Aug 18	27 & 55 *	2Ct	
Derbyshire	Derby	Aug 23	55	1Ct	
Northants	Chelmsford	Sept 7	26 & 43	1Ct	
Kent	Chelmsford	Sept 12	20 & 0	1Ct	1-1 & 0-43
Surrey	The Oval	Sept 18	42	2Ct	3-91
REFUGE ASSURANCE					
Warwickshire	Edgbaston	June 10		1Ct	
Lancashire	Colchester	July 22		1Ct	
Sussex	Chelmsford	July 29	31		
Notts	Southend	Aug 5	8		
Yorkshire	Middlesbr'gh	Aug 12	31		
Derbyshire	Derby	Aug 26	9 *		
OTHER FIRST-CLASS					
For TCCB U25 XI					
India	Edgbaston	Aug 15	39 & 0		0-41
OTHER ONE-DAY					
Yorkshire	Scarborough	Sept 3	16		1-4
Hampshire	Scarborough	Sept 4	10		0-6

S — PLAYER RECORDS

BATTING AVERAGES - Including fielding

	Matches	Inns	NO	Runs	HS	Avge	100s	50s	Ct	St
Britannic Assurance	18	27	7	964	125	48.20	1	6	22	-
Refuge Assurance	6	4	1	79	31	26.33	-	-	2	-
Other First-Class	1	2	0	39	39	19.50	-	-	-	-
Other One-Day	2	2	0	26	16	13.00	-	-	-	-
ALL FIRST-CLASS	19	29	7	1003	125	45.59	1	6	22	-
ALL ONE-DAY	8	6	1	105	31	21.00	-	-	2	-

BOWLING AVERAGES

	Overs	Mdns	Runs	Wkts	Avge	Best	5wI	10wM
Britannic Assurance	106.2	18	413	7	59.00	3-91	-	-
Refuge Assurance								
Other First-Class	5	0	41	0	-	-	-	-
Other One-Day	2.2	0	10	1	10.00	1-4	-	
ALL FIRST-CLASS	111.2	18	454	7	64.85	3-91	-	-
ALL ONE-DAY	2.2	0	10	1	10.00	1-4	-	

B.K. SHANTRY - Shropshire

Opposition	Venue	Date	Batting	Fielding	Bowling
NATWEST TROPHY					
Derbyshire	Chesterfield	June 27	4 *		2-47

BATTING AVERAGES - Including fielding

	Matches	Inns	NO	Runs	HS	Avge	100s	50s	Ct	St
NatWest Trophy	1	1	1	4	4*	-	-	-	-	-
ALL ONE-DAY	1	1	1	4	4*	-	-	-	-	-

BOWLING AVERAGES

	Overs	Mdns	Runs	Wkts	Avge	Best	5wI	10wM
NatWest Trophy	10	1	47	2	23.50	2-47	-	
ALL ONE-DAY	10	1	47	2	23.50	2-47	-	

N. SHARDLOW - Wiltshire

Opposition	Venue	Date	Batting	Fielding	Bowling
NATWEST TROPHY					
Surrey	Trowbridge	June 27	6	1Ct	

BATTING AVERAGES - Including fielding

	Matches	Inns	NO	Runs	HS	Avge	100s	50s	Ct	St
NatWest Trophy	1	1	0	6	6	6.00	-	-	1	-
ALL ONE-DAY	1	1	0	6	6	6.00	-	-	1	-

BOWLING AVERAGES
Did not bowl

C. SHARMA - World XI

Opposition	Venue	Date	Batting	Fielding	Bowling
OTHER FIRST-CLASS					
India	Scarborough	Aug 29			0-39 & 0-30
OTHER ONE-DAY					
Yorkshire	Scarborough	Sept 1	28		0-35

BATTING AVERAGES - Including fielding

	Matches	Inns	NO	Runs	HS	Avge	100s	50s	Ct	St
Other First-Class	1	0	0	0	0	-	-	-	-	-
Other One-Day	1	1	0	28	28	28.00	-	-	-	-
ALL FIRST-CLASS	1	0	0	0	0	-	-	-	-	-
ALL ONE-DAY	1	1	0	28	28	28.00	-	-	-	-

BOWLING AVERAGES

	Overs	Mdns	Runs	Wkts	Avge	Best	5wI	10wM
Other First-Class	13	0	69	0	-	-	-	-
Other One-Day	5	0	35	0	-	-	-	-
ALL FIRST-CLASS	13	0	69	0	-	-	-	-
ALL ONE-DAY	5	0	35	0	-	-	-	-

S.K. SHARMA - India

Opposition	Venue	Date	Batting	Fielding	Bowling
CORNHILL TEST MATCHES					
England	Lord's	July 26	0 & 38		1-122 & 2-75
TEXACO TROPHY					
England	Headingley	July 18			2-57
England	Trent Bridge	July 20			1-50
OTHER FIRST-CLASS					
Hampshire	Southampton	July 4			0-34 & 1-79
Kent	Canterbury	July 7	13 *	1Ct	0-37 & 0-11
Min Counties	Trowbridge	July 11			1-43 & 1-47
Leicestershire	Leicester	July 21	23 *	1Ct	1-41 & 0-52
Surrey	The Oval	Aug 1	15		0-29 & 0-7
TCCB U25 XI	Edgbaston	Aug 15			1-57 & 1-24
Glamorgan	Swansea	Aug 18	9		1-23 & 0-48
World XI	Scarborough	Aug 29	34 *		1-91 & 2-53
OTHER ONE-DAY					
League CC	Sunderland	June 28	6		4-25
Scotland	Glasgow	July 14			1-27
Derbyshire	Chesterfield	July 16	8 *		0-51

BATTING AVERAGES - Including fielding

	Matches	Inns	NO	Runs	HS	Avge	100s	50s	Ct	St
Cornhill Test Matches	1	2	0	38	38	19.00	-	-	-	-
Texaco Trophy	2	0	0	0	0	-	-	-	-	-
Other First-Class	8	5	3	94	34 *	47.00	-	-	2	-
Other One-Day	3	2	1	14	8 *	14.00	-	-	-	-
ALL FIRST-CLASS	9	7	3	132	38	33.00	-	-	2	-
ALL ONE-DAY	5	2	1	14	8 *	14.00	-	-	-	-

BOWLING AVERAGES

	Overs	Mdns	Runs	Wkts	Avge	Best	5wI	10wM
Cornhill Test Matches	48	5	197	3	65.66	2-75	-	-
Texaco Trophy	21	1	107	3	35.66	2-57	-	
Other First-Class	179	31	676	10	67.60	2-53	-	-
Other One-Day	32	3	103	5	20.60	4-25	-	
ALL FIRST-CLASS	227	36	873	13	67.15	2-53	-	-
ALL ONE-DAY	53	4	210	8	26.25	4-25	-	

K. SHARP - Yorkshire

Opposition	Venue	Date	Batting	Fielding	Bowling
BRITANNIC ASSURANCE					
Warwickshire	Sheffield	June 20	22 * & 8		
Glamorgan	Cardiff	June 23	53 * & 24		
Notts	Scarborough	July 4	17	1Ct	
Northants	Northampton	July 7	40 *		
Gloucs	Cheltenham	July 21	38		
Sussex	Eastbourne	Aug 8	42		
Essex	Middlesbr'gh	Aug 11	42 & 16		
Lancashire	Old Trafford	Aug 18	5 * & 9 *		
REFUGE ASSURANCE					
Worcestershire	Worcester	June 3	71		
Surrey	Hull	June 10	0	1Ct	
Sussex	Hove	June 17	34		
Gloucs	Cheltenham	July 22	9 *	2Ct	
Leicestershire	Sheffield	July 29	26 *	1Ct	
Lancashire	Scarborough	Aug 5	37		
Essex	Middlesbr'gh	Aug 12	30		

PLAYER RECORDS S

NATWEST TROPHY
Norfolk　　　　Headingley　　June 27　　　　　　　　2Ct

OTHER FIRST-CLASS
India　　　　　Headingley　　June 30　　　　　　　2

OTHER ONE-DAY
Sussex　　　　Harrogate　　June 14　　37 *
Warwickshire　Harrogate　　June 15　　34
Yorkshiremen　Scarborough　Sept 6

BATTING AVERAGES - Including fielding

	Matches	Inns	NO	Runs	HS	Avge	100s	50s	Ct	St
Britannic Assurance	8	12	5	316	53 *	45.14	-	1	1	-
Refuge Assurance	7	7	2	207	71	41.40	-	1	4	-
NatWest Trophy	1	0	0	0	0	-	-	-	2	-
Other First-Class	1	1	0	2	2	2.00	-	-	-	-
Other One-Day	3	2	1	71	37 *	71.00	-	-	-	-
ALL FIRST-CLASS	9	13	5	318	53 *	39.75	-	1	1	-
ALL ONE-DAY	11	9	3	278	71	46.33	-	1	6	-

BOWLING AVERAGES
Did not bowl

S. SHARP - *Minor Counties*

Opposition	Venue	Date	Batting	Fielding	Bowling

BENSON & HEDGES CUP
| Sussex | Marlow | May 1 | 11 * | | 0-26 |
| Derbyshire | Wellington | May 10 | 0 | 1Ct | |

BATTING AVERAGES - Including fielding

	Matches	Inns	NO	Runs	HS	Avge	100s	50s	Ct	St
Benson & Hedges Cup	2	2	1	11	11 *	11.00	-	-	1	-
ALL ONE-DAY	2	2	1	11	11 *	11.00	-	-	1	-

BOWLING AVERAGES

	Overs	Mdns	Runs	Wkts	Avge	Best	5wI	10wM
Benson & Hedges Cup	3	0	26	0	-	-	-	-
ALL ONE-DAY	3	0	26	0	-	-	-	-

R.J. SHASTRI - *India*

Opposition	Venue	Date	Batting	Fielding	Bowling

CORNHILL TEST MATCHES
England	Lord's	July 26	100 & 12		0-99 & 0-38
England	Old Trafford	Aug 9	25 & 12		1-50 & 0-39
England	The Oval	Aug 23	187	2Ct	1-29 & 0-86

TEXACO TROPHY
| England | Headingley | July 18 | 23 * | 1Ct | 1-40 |
| England | Trent Bridge | July 20 | 33 | | 1-52 |

OTHER FIRST-CLASS
Yorkshire	Headingley	June 30	53 *	1Ct	0-5 & 1-54
Kent	Canterbury	July 7			0-37
Min Counties	Trowbridge	July 11	105	1Ct	1-43
Surrey	The Oval	Aug 1	8	1Ct	2-80
Gloucs	Bristol	Aug 4	5 & 133	1Ct	0-36
TCCB U25 XI	Edgbaston	Aug 15	4		1-11

BATTING AVERAGES - Including fielding

	Matches	Inns	NO	Runs	HS	Avge	100s	50s	Ct	St
Cornhill Test Matches	3	5	0	336	187	67.20	2	-	2	-
Texaco Trophy	2	2	1	56	33	56.00	-	-	1	-
Other First-Class	6	6	1	308	133	61.60	2	1	4	-
ALL FIRST-CLASS	9	11	1	644	187	64.40	4	1	6	-
ALL ONE-DAY	2	2	1	56	33	56.00	-	-	1	-

BOWLING AVERAGES

	Overs	Mdns	Runs	Wkts	Avge	Best	5wI	10wM
Cornhill Test Matches	95.5	6	341	2	170.50	1-29	-	-

Texaco Trophy	22	0	92	2	46.00	1-40	- -
Other First-Class	103.3	24	266	5	53.20	2-80	- -
ALL FIRST-CLASS	199.2	30	607	7	86.71	2-80	- -
ALL ONE-DAY	22	0	92	2	46.00	1-40	- -

D. SHAW - *Berkshire*

Opposition	Venue	Date	Batting	Fielding	Bowling

NATWEST TROPHY
| Middlesex | Lord's | June 27 | 36 | | |

BATTING AVERAGES - Including fielding

	Matches	Inns	NO	Runs	HS	Avge	100s	50s	Ct	St
NatWest Trophy	1	1	0	36	36	36.00	-	-	-	-
ALL ONE-DAY	1	1	0	36	36	36.00	-	-	-	-

BOWLING AVERAGES
Did not bowl

K.J. SHINE - *Hampshire*

Opposition	Venue	Date	Batting	Fielding	Bowling

BRITANNIC ASSURANCE
Kent	Canterbury	April 26			1-70 & 2-48
Surrey	The Oval	May 19			0-75 & 1-55
Essex	Southampton	May 23			2-56 & 2-52
Yorkshire	Headingley	May 26		1Ct	4-52 & 0-50
Gloucs	Gloucester	June 20			0-6
Lancashire	Old Trafford	June 23			0-22 & 0-15

BENSON & HEDGES CUP
Yorkshire	Southampton	April 24			0-53
Surrey	The Oval	May 1	0		4-68
Lancashire	Old Trafford	May 8			0-13
Combined U	Southampton	May 12			0-33

OTHER FIRST-CLASS
| Oxford U | The Parks | May 3 | 24 * | | 2-51 |

BATTING AVERAGES - Including fielding

	Matches	Inns	NO	Runs	HS	Avge	100s	50s	Ct	St
Britannic Assurance	6	0	0	0	0	-	-	-	1	-
Benson & Hedges Cup	4	1	0	0	0	0.00	-	-	-	-
Other First-Class	1	1	1	24	24 *	-	-	-	-	-
ALL FIRST-CLASS	7	1	1	24	24 *	-	-	-	1	-
ALL ONE-DAY	4	1	0	0	0	0.00	-	-	-	-

BOWLING AVERAGES

	Overs	Mdns	Runs	Wkts	Avge	Best	5wI	10wM
Britannic Assurance	129.4	17	501	12	41.75	4-52	-	-
Benson & Hedges Cup	32.2	1	167	4	41.75	4-68	-	
Other First-Class	27	13	51	2	25.50	2-51	-	
ALL FIRST-CLASS	156.4	30	552	14	39.42	4-52	-	-
ALL ONE-DAY	32.2	1	167	4	41.75	4-68	-	

D.H. SHUFFLEBOTHAM - *Cambridge Univ*

Opposition	Venue	Date	Batting	Fielding	Bowling

OTHER FIRST-CLASS
Northants	Fenner's	April 14	16 *		0-26
Warwickshire	Fenner's	April 26	24		0-76 & 1-29
Middlesex	Fenner's	May 3	1		0-50 & 0-17
Gloucs	Fenner's	May 23	25 * & 29		1-65 & 0-37
Notts	Fenner's	June 16	4 *		0-38 & 0-37
Kent	Fenner's	June 20		16	
Sussex	Hove	June 30	0 & 6	1Ct	1-36 & 0-25
Oxford U	Lord's	July 4			3-60

S   PLAYER RECORDS

BATTING AVERAGES - Including fielding

	Matches	Inns	NO	Runs	HS	Avge	100s	50s	Ct	St
Other First-Class	8	9	3	121	29	20.16	-	-	1	-
ALL FIRST-CLASS	8	9	3	121	29	20.16	-	-	1	-

BOWLING AVERAGES

	Overs	Mdns	Runs	Wkts	Avge	Best	5wI	10wM
Other First-Class	139	20	538	6	89.66	3-60	-	-
ALL FIRST-CLASS	139	20	538	6	89.66	3-60	-	-

A. SIDEBOTTOM - *Yorkshire*

Opposition	Venue	Date	Batting			Fielding	Bowling
BRITANNIC ASSURANCE							
Northants	Headingley	April 26	16	&	31		1-67
Warwickshire	Edgbaston	May 3	38	&	19	1Ct	3-54
REFUGE ASSURANCE							
Notts	Trent Bridge	April 22	1				1-22
Derbyshire	Headingley	May 13				1Ct	2-18
Surrey	Hull	June 10	3*				1-29
Northants	Tring	July 8					2-21
Somerset	Scarborough	July 15					0-25
Gloucs	Cheltenham	July 22					0-27
Lancashire	Scarborough	Aug 5	2			1Ct	0-33
Essex	Middlesbr'gh	Aug 12	8*			1Ct	1-22
Middlesex	Scarborough	Aug 26					0-33
NATWEST TROPHY							
Norfolk	Headingley	June 27					0-21
Warwickshire	Headingley	July 11				1Ct	1-20
Hampshire	Southampton	Aug 1	1			1Ct	1-35
BENSON & HEDGES CUP							
Hampshire	Southampton	April 24					0-37
Combined U	Headingley	May 8	9*			2Ct	1-41
Lancashire	Headingley	May 10	2				1-35
Surrey	The Oval	May 12					1-43
OTHER FIRST-CLASS							
India	Headingley	June 30					0-46 & 0-23
OTHER ONE-DAY							
Yorkshiremen	Scarborough	Sept 6					1-13

BATTING AVERAGES - Including fielding

	Matches	Inns	NO	Runs	HS	Avge	100s	50s	Ct	St
Britannic Assurance	2	4	0	104	38	26.00	-	-	1	-
Refuge Assurance	9	4	2	14	8*	7.00	-	-	3	-
NatWest Trophy	3	1	0	1	1	1.00	-	-	2	-
Benson & Hedges Cup	4	2	1	11	9*	11.00	-	-	2	-
Other First-Class	1	0	0	0	0	-	-	-	-	-
Other One-Day	1	0	0	0	0	-	-	-	-	-
ALL FIRST-CLASS	3	4	0	104	38	26.00	-	-	1	-
ALL ONE-DAY	17	7	3	26	9*	6.50	-	-	7	-

BOWLING AVERAGES

	Overs	Mdns	Runs	Wkts	Avge	Best	5wI	10wM
Britannic Assurance	44	9	121	4	30.25	3-54	-	-
Refuge Assurance	69	7	230	7	32.85	2-18	-	-
NatWest Trophy	34	8	76	2	38.00	1-20	-	-
Benson & Hedges Cup	40.1	7	156	3	52.00	1-35	-	-
Other First-Class	16.5	2	69	0	-	-	-	-
Other One-Day	8	2	13	1	13.00	1-13	-	-
ALL FIRST-CLASS	60.5	11	190	4	47.50	3-54	-	-
ALL ONE-DAY	151.1	24	475	13	36.53	2-18	-	-

N.S. SIDHU - *India*

Opposition	Venue	Date	Batting			Fielding	Bowling
CORNHILL TEST MATCHES							
England	Lord's	July 26	30	&	1		
England	Old Trafford	Aug 9	13	&	0		
England	The Oval	Aug 23	12				
TEXACO TROPHY							
England	Headingley	July 18	39				
England	Trent Bridge	July 20	23				
OTHER FIRST-CLASS							
Yorkshire	Headingley	June 30	61	&	3		
Hampshire	Southampton	July 4	6	&	58*		
Leicestershire	Leicester	July 21	25	&	6		
Gloucs	Bristol	Aug 4	31	&	142		
TCCB U25 XI	Edgbaston	Aug 15	13	&	108*		
Glamorgan	Swansea	Aug 18	54	&	76*	1Ct	
OTHER ONE-DAY							
League CC	Sunderland	June 28	17				
Scotland	Glasgow	July 14	50				
Derbyshire	Chesterfield	July 16	0			1Ct	

BATTING AVERAGES - Including fielding

	Matches	Inns	NO	Runs	HS	Avge	100s	50s	Ct	St
Cornhill Test Matches	3	5	0	56	30	11.20	-	-	-	-
Texaco Trophy	2	2	0	62	39	31.00	-	-	-	-
Other First-Class	6	12	3	583	142	64.77	2	4	1	-
Other One-Day	3	3	0	67	50	22.33	-	1	1	-
ALL FIRST-CLASS	9	17	3	639	142	45.64	2	4	1	-
ALL ONE-DAY	5	5	0	129	50	25.80	-	1	1	-

BOWLING AVERAGES
Did not bowl

M.L. SIMMONS - *Berkshire*

Opposition	Venue	Date	Batting	Fielding	Bowling
NATWEST TROPHY					
Middlesex	Lord's	June 27	30		

BATTING AVERAGES - Including fielding

	Matches	Inns	NO	Runs	HS	Avge	100s	50s	Ct	St
NatWest Trophy	1	1	0	30	30	30.00	-	-	-	-
ALL ONE-DAY	1	1	0	30	30	30.00	-	-	-	-

BOWLING AVERAGES
Did not bowl

P.V. SIMMONS - *Durham*

Opposition	Venue	Date	Batting	Fielding	Bowling
NATWEST TROPHY					
Lancashire	Old Trafford	June 27	14		0-28

BATTING AVERAGES - Including fielding

	Matches	Inns	NO	Runs	HS	Avge	100s	50s	Ct	St
NatWest Trophy	1	1	0	14	14	14.00	-	-	-	-
ALL ONE-DAY	1	1	0	14	14	14.00	-	-	-	-

BOWLING AVERAGES

	Overs	Mdns	Runs	Wkts	Avge	Best	5wI	10wM
NatWest Trophy	4	0	28	0	-	-	-	-
ALL ONE-DAY	4	0	28	0	-	-	-	-

D.P. SIMPKINS - *Wiltshire*

Opposition	Venue	Date	Batting	Fielding	Bowling
NATWEST TROPHY					
Surrey	Trowbridge	June 27	18		0-29

PLERER RECORDS — S

PLAYER RECORDS

S

BATTING AVERAGES - Including fielding

	Matches	Inns	NO	Runs	HS	Avge	100s	50s	Ct	St
NatWest Trophy	1	1	0	18	18	18.00	-	-	-	-
ALL ONE-DAY	1	1	0	18	18	18.00	-	-	-	-

BOWLING AVERAGES

	Overs	Mdns	Runs	Wkts	Avge	Best	5wI	10wM
NatWest Trophy	6	2	29	0	-	-	-	-
ALL ONE-DAY	6	2	29	0	-	-	-	-

P.R. SLEEP - *World XI*

Opposition	Venue	Date	Batting	Fielding	Bowling
OTHER FIRST-CLASS					
India	Scarborough	Aug 29	42		2-47 & 1-63
OTHER ONE-DAY					
For Rest of the World					
England XI	Jesmond	Aug 2	35 *	1Ct	0-28
England XI	Jesmond	Aug 3			4-34

BATTING AVERAGES - Including fielding

	Matches	Inns	NO	Runs	HS	Avge	100s	50s	Ct	St
Other First-Class	1	1	0	42	42	42.00	-	-	-	-
Other One-Day	2	1	1	35	35 *	-	-	-	1	-
ALL FIRST-CLASS	1	1	0	42	42	42.00	-	-	-	-
ALL ONE-DAY	2	1	1	35	35 *	-	-	-	1	-

BOWLING AVERAGES

	Overs	Mdns	Runs	Wkts	Avge	Best	5wI	10wM
Other First-Class	19	1	110	3	36.66	2-47	-	-
Other One-Day	16	0	62	4	15.50	4-34	-	
ALL FIRST-CLASS	19	1	110	3	36.66	2-47	-	-
ALL ONE-DAY	16	0	62	4	15.50	4-34	-	

G.C. SMALL - *Warwickshire & England*

Opposition	Venue	Date	Batting	Fielding	Bowling
CORNHILL TEST MATCHES					
New Zealand	Trent Bridge	June 7	26		2-49 & 1-14
New Zealand	Lord's	June 21	3	1Ct	1-127
New Zealand	Edgbaston	July 5	44 * & 11 *		0-44 & 1-56
TEXACO TROPHY					
New Zealand	Headingley	May 23			1-43
New Zealand	The Oval	May 25		1Ct	1-59
India	Trent Bridge	July 20	4		1-73
BRITANNIC ASSURANCE					
Yorkshire	Edgbaston	May 3	0		4-40 & 1-29
Northants	Northampton	May 15	55	1Ct	3-72 & 0-34
Notts	Edgbaston	May 19	0 & 0		2-34 & 1-39
Northants	Edgbaston	June 2	24 & 0		1-44
Derbyshire	Derby	June 16	8	1Ct	0-44
Glamorgan	Swansea	July 25			0-47 & 1-62
Gloucs	Bristol	Aug 8	24 & 5		5-57 & 1-39
Leicestershire	Edgbaston	Aug 18	16 & 10 *	1Ct	1-34 & 0-36
Worcestershire	Worcester	Aug 23	5 * & 12		6-94 & 0-61
Somerset	Edgbaston	Sept 7	7 & 10		0-58 & 1-18
Glamorgan	Edgbaston	Sept 12	2 & 4		0-44 & 0-14
Lancashire	Old Trafford	Sept 18	30		
REFUGE ASSURANCE					
Northants	Edgbaston	April 29		1Ct	0-27
Yorkshire	Edgbaston	May 6			0-41
Gloucs	Moreton-in-M	May 20	1		0-50
Worcestershire	Worcester	May 27			1-22
Middlesex	Lord's	June 3			0-28
Derbyshire	Derby	June 17	4 *		1-53
Glamorgan	Edgbaston	July 15	4		0-17
Notts	Edgbaston	July 22			0-29
Leicestershire	Edgbaston	Aug 19			3-20
Lancashire	Old Trafford	Aug 26			0-3

NATWEST TROPHY

Hertfordshire	St Albans	June 27	0			0-21
Yorkshire	Headingley	July 11	8			0-37

BENSON & HEDGES CUP

Glamorgan	Edgbaston	April 24	1			4-22
Kent	Canterbury	May 8	22			4-38
Worcestershire	Edgbaston	May 10	5			2-36
Gloucs	Bristol	May 12			1Ct	1-27

BATTING AVERAGES - Including fielding

	Matches	Inns	NO	Runs	HS	Avge	100s	50s	Ct	St
Cornhill Test Matches	3	4	2	84	44 *	42.00	-	-	1	-
Texaco Trophy	3	1	0	4	4	4.00	-	-	1	-
Britannic Assurance	12	18	2	212	55	13.25	-	1	3	-
Refuge Assurance	10	3	1	9	4 *	4.50	-	-	1	-
NatWest Trophy	2	2	0	8	8	4.00	-	-	-	-
Benson & Hedges Cup	4	3	0	28	22	9.33	-	-	1	-
ALL FIRST-CLASS	15	22	4	296	55	16.44	-	1	4	-
ALL ONE-DAY	19	9	1	49	22	6.12	-	-	3	-

BOWLING AVERAGES

	Overs	Mdns	Runs	Wkts	Avge	Best	5wI	10wM
Cornhill Test Matches	104	27	290	5	58.00	2-49	-	-
Texaco Trophy	32	1	175	3	58.33	1-43	-	
Britannic Assurance	321.4	78	900	27	33.33	6-94	2	-
Refuge Assurance	62.3	3	290	5	58.00	3-20	-	
NatWest Trophy	15	1	58	0	-	-	-	
Benson & Hedges Cup	44	4	123	11	11.18	4-22	-	
ALL FIRST-CLASS	425.4	105	1190	32	37.18	6-94	2	-
ALL ONE-DAY	153.3	9	646	19	34.00	4-22	-	

B. SMITH - *Leicestershire*

Opposition	Venue	Date	Batting	Fielding	Bowling
BRITANNIC ASSURANCE					
Glamorgan	Hinckley	July 7	15 *	1Ct	
REFUGE ASSURANCE					
Worcestershire	Leicester	Aug 5	10		
Surrey	The Oval	Aug 12	10		
Warwickshire	Edgbaston	Aug 19	29		
Kent	Leicester	Aug 26	6		
OTHER FIRST-CLASS					
Oxford U	The Parks	May 23	4		

BATTING AVERAGES - Including fielding

	Matches	Inns	NO	Runs	HS	Avge	100s	50s	Ct	St
Britannic Assurance	1	1	1	15	15 *	-	-	-	1	-
Refuge Assurance	4	4	0	55	29	13.75	-	-	-	-
Other First-Class	1	1	0	4	4	4.00	-	-	-	-
ALL FIRST-CLASS	2	2	1	19	15 *	19.00	-	-	1	-
ALL ONE-DAY	4	4	0	55	29	13.75	-	-	-	-

BOWLING AVERAGES
Did not bowl

C.L. SMITH - *Hampshire*

Opposition	Venue	Date	Batting	Fielding	Bowling
BRITANNIC ASSURANCE					
Kent	Canterbury	April 26	16 & 52	1Ct	
Sussex	Southampton	May 15	35	2Ct	0-0
Surrey	The Oval	May 19	71 & 84		0-9
Essex	Southampton	May 23	128 & 31		
Yorkshire	Headingley	May 26	28 & 58	1Ct	
Leicestershire	Leicester	June 2	80 *		
Somerset	Basingstoke	June 6	25 & 73 *		
Glamorgan	Southampton	June 16	48 & 39 *		
Gloucs	Gloucester	June 20			
Lancashire	Old Trafford	June 23	25 & 53 *		0-8
Notts	Portsmouth	July 18	85 & 46 *	1Ct	

S PLAYER RECORDS

Derbyshire	Portsmouth	July 21	57 & 2			
Sussex	Arundel	July 25	132 * & 61	1Ct		
Warwickshire	Edgbaston	July 28	18 & 29	1Ct		
Middlesex	Bournemouth	Aug 8	31	1Ct	0-0 & 3-35	
Worcestershire	Worcester	Aug 11	5 & 12		0-22	
Somerset	Taunton	Aug 18	1 & 88	1Ct	0-2	
Surrey	Southampton	Aug 23	43 & 111			
Kent	Bournemouth	Aug 29	32 & 53	2Ct		
Glamorgan	Pontypridd	Sept 7	1 & 25 *			

REFUGE ASSURANCE
Kent	Canterbury	April 29	47 *	
Gloucs	Southampton	May 6	89	
Somerset	Taunton	May 13	25	
Lancashire	Old Trafford	June 24		
Sussex	Hove	July 1	3	
Essex	Southampton	July 8	22 *	
Derbyshire	Portsmouth	July 22	30	2Ct
Warwickshire	Edgbaston	July 29	0	
Worcestershire	Worcester	Aug 12	21	
Surrey	Southampton	Aug 26	0	

NATWEST TROPHY
Leicestershire	Leicester	June 27	52	
Essex	Chelmsford	July 11	106	
Yorkshire	Southampton	Aug 1	30	1Ct
Northants	Southampton	Aug 15	0	1Ct

BENSON & HEDGES CUP
Yorkshire	Southampton	April 24	44		
Surrey	The Oval	May 1	3		
Lancashire	Old Trafford	May 8		1Ct	
Combined U	Southampton	May 12	154 *	1Ct	0-2

OTHER FIRST-CLASS
Oxford U	The Parks	May 3	148	3Ct	2-21
India	Southampton	July 4	24 & 36		

BATTING AVERAGES - Including fielding
	Matches	Inns	NO	Runs	HS	Avge	100s	50s	Ct	St
Britannic Assurance	20	35	7	1678	132 *	59.92	3	12	11	-
Refuge Assurance	10	9	2	237	89	33.85	-	1	2	-
NatWest Trophy	4	4	0	188	106	47.00	1	1	2	-
Benson & Hedges Cup	4	3	1	201	154 *	100.50	1	-	2	-
Other First-Class	2	3	0	208	148	69.33	1	-	3	-
ALL FIRST-CLASS	22	38	7	1886	148	60.83	4	12	14	-
ALL ONE-DAY	18	16	3	626	154 *	48.15	2	2	6	-

BOWLING AVERAGES
	Overs	Mdns	Runs	Wkts	Avge	Best	5wI	10wM
Britannic Assurance	22	8	76	3	25.33	3-35	-	-
Refuge Assurance								
NatWest Trophy								
Benson & Hedges Cup	1	0	2	0	-	-	-	-
Other First-Class	6	1	21	2	10.50	2-21	-	-
ALL FIRST-CLASS	28	9	97	5	19.40	3-35	-	-
ALL ONE-DAY	1	0	2	0	-	-	-	-

D.M. SMITH - Sussex

Opposition	Venue	Date	Batting	Fielding	Bowling

BRITANNIC ASSURANCE
Hampshire	Southampton	May 15	5 *		
Essex	Chelmsford	July 28	3 & 15	1Ct	
Warwickshire	Eastbourne	Aug 4	18 & 4		
Yorkshire	Eastbourne	Aug 8	29 & 37		
Middlesex	Lord's	Aug 11	42		
Kent	Hove	Aug 18	6 * & 71		
Gloucs	Bristol	Sept 12	52 & 0		
Middlesex	Hove	Sept 18	32 & 10	1Ct	

REFUGE ASSURANCE
Essex	Chelmsford	July 29	0	1Ct
Warwickshire	Eastbourne	Aug 5	18	1Ct

BENSON & HEDGES CUP
Somerset	Hove	May 12	3	1Ct

OTHER FIRST-CLASS
Sri Lanka	Hove	Sept 5	0 & 29	

OTHER ONE-DAY
Kent	Hove	Sept 2	14	1Ct

BATTING AVERAGES - Including fielding
	Matches	Inns	NO	Runs	HS	Avge	100s	50s	Ct	St
Britannic Assurance	8	14	2	324	71	27.00	-	2	2	-
Refuge Assurance	2	2	0	18	18	9.00	-	-	2	-
Benson & Hedges Cup	1	1	0	3	3	3.00	-	-	1	-
Other First-Class	1	2	0	29	29	14.50	-	-	-	-
Other One-Day	1	1	0	14	14	14.00	-	-	1	-
ALL FIRST-CLASS	9	16	2	353	71	25.21	-	2	2	-
ALL ONE-DAY	4	4	0	35	18	8.75	-	-	4	-

BOWLING AVERAGES
Did not bowl

D.M. SMITH - Hertfordshire

Opposition	Venue	Date	Batting	Fielding	Bowling

NATWEST TROPHY
Warwickshire	St Albans	June 27	39		0-12

BATTING AVERAGES - Including fielding
	Matches	Inns	NO	Runs	HS	Avge	100s	50s	Ct	St
NatWest Trophy	1	1	0	39	39	39.00	-	-	-	-
ALL ONE-DAY	1	1	0	39	39	39.00	-	-	-	-

BOWLING AVERAGES
	Overs	Mdns	Runs	Wkts	Avge	Best	5wI	10wM
NatWest Trophy	1	0	12	0	-	-	-	
ALL ONE-DAY	1	0	12	0	-	-	-	

G. SMITH - Warwickshire

Opposition	Venue	Date	Batting	Fielding	Bowling

BRITANNIC ASSURANCE
Sussex	Eastbourne	Aug 4	30	1Ct	3-36 & 1-45

REFUGE ASSURANCE
Essex	Edgbaston	June 10	5	2-20
Derbyshire	Derby	June 17		2-37
Sussex	Eastbourne	Aug 5		0-8

OTHER ONE-DAY
Surrey	Hove	Sept 3		1-38

BATTING AVERAGES - Including fielding
	Matches	Inns	NO	Runs	HS	Avge	100s	50s	Ct	St
Britannic Assurance	1	1	0	30	30	30.00	-	-	1	-
Refuge Assurance	3	1	0	5	5	5.00	-	-	-	-
Other One-Day	1	0	0	0	0		-	-	-	-
ALL FIRST-CLASS	1	1	0	30	30	30.00	-	-	1	-
ALL ONE-DAY	4	1	0	5	5	5.00	-	-	-	-

BOWLING AVERAGES
	Overs	Mdns	Runs	Wkts	Avge	Best	5wI	10wM
Britannic Assurance	26.5	3	81	4	20.25	3-36	-	-
Refuge Assurance	11	0	65	4	16.25	2-20	-	-
Other One-Day	9.1	2	38	1	38.00	1-38	-	-
ALL FIRST-CLASS	26.5	3	81	4	20.25	3-36	-	-
ALL ONE-DAY	20.1	2	103	5	20.60	2-20	-	-

PLAYER RECORDS

I. SMITH - *Glamorgan*

Opposition	Venue	Date	Batting	Fielding	Bowling
BRITANNIC ASSURANCE					
Somerset	Cardiff	May 3	56 & 16		0-19 & 1-43
Gloucs	Bristol	May 15	19 & 14	1Ct	
Sussex	Hove	May 19	66		0-49
Kent	Swansea	May 23	66		
Lancashire	Colwyn Bay	May 26	10 & 112*		0-19
Hampshire	Southampton	June 16	0		0-27
REFUGE ASSURANCE					
Gloucs	Bristol	April 22	46		0-17
Leicestershire	Cardiff	April 29	35	1Ct	
Kent	Llanelli	May 13	39*		
Sussex	Hove	May 20	33*		
Lancashire	Colwyn Bay	May 27	6		
Essex	Ilford	June 3	8		
Hampshire	Bournemouth	June 17	2		
Warwickshire	Edgbaston	July 15	10		
Somerset	Neath	July 22	6	1Ct	
NATWEST TROPHY					
Sussex	Cardiff	July 11	22	1Ct	1-20
BENSON & HEDGES CUP					
Gloucs	Cardiff	May 1	0		
Worcestershire	Worcester	May 8	21	1Ct	
Kent	Swansea	May 12	9		
Worcestershire	Worcester	May 30	2		
OTHER FIRST-CLASS					
Oxford U	The Parks	April 14	17 & 18*		0-24

BATTING AVERAGES - Including fielding

	Matches	Inns	NO	Runs	HS	Avge	100s	50s	Ct	St
Britannic Assurance	6	8	1	293	112*	41.85	1	2	1	-
Refuge Assurance	9	9	2	185	46	26.42	-	-	2	-
NatWest Trophy	1	1	0	22	22	22.00	-	-	1	-
Benson & Hedges Cup	4	4	0	32	21	8.00	-	-	1	-
Other First-Class	1	2	1	35	18*	35.00	-	-	-	-
ALL FIRST-CLASS	7	10	2	328	112*	41.00	1	2	1	-
ALL ONE-DAY	14	14	2	239	46	19.91	-	-	4	-

BOWLING AVERAGES

	Overs	Mdns	Runs	Wkts	Avge	Best	5wI	10wM
Britannic Assurance	33	3	157	1	157.00	1-43	-	-
Refuge Assurance	2	0	17	0	-	-	-	-
NatWest Trophy	4	0	20	1	20.00	1-20	-	-
Benson & Hedges Cup								
Other First-Class	6	0	24	0	-	-	-	-
ALL FIRST-CLASS	39	3	181	1	181.00	1-43	-	-
ALL ONE-DAY	6	0	37	1	37.00	1-20	-	-

I.D.S. SMITH - *New Zealand*

Opposition	Venue	Date	Batting	Fielding	Bowling
CORNHILL TEST MATCHES					
England	Trent Bridge	June 7	2*	2Ct	
England	Lord's	June 21	27		
TEXACO TROPHY					
England	Headingley	May 23	17*	1Ct	
England	The Oval	May 25	25*	1Ct	
OTHER FIRST-CLASS					
Worcestershire	Worcester	May 12	2		
Middlesex	Lord's	May 19	34		
Warwickshire	Edgbaston	May 30		2Ct	
Combined U	Fenner's	June 27		1Ct	
OTHER ONE-DAY					
Ireland	Downpatrick	May 9		2Ct	
Ireland	Belfast	May 10	19		1-8

BATTING AVERAGES - Including fielding

	Matches	Inns	NO	Runs	HS	Avge	100s	50s	Ct	St
Cornhill Test Matches	2	2	1	29	27	29.00	-	-	2	-
Texaco Trophy	2	2	2	42	25*	-	-	-	2	-
Other First-Class	4	2	0	36	34	18.00	-	-	3	-
Other One-Day	2	1	0	19	19	19.00	-	-	2	-
ALL FIRST-CLASS	6	4	1	65	34	21.66	-	-	5	-
ALL ONE-DAY	4	3	2	61	25*	61.00	-	-	4	-

BOWLING AVERAGES

	Overs	Mdns	Runs	Wkts	Avge	Best	5wI	10wM
Cornhill Test Matches								
Texaco Trophy								
Other First-Class								
Other One-Day	2	0	8	1	8.00	1-8	-	
ALL FIRST-CLASS								
ALL ONE-DAY	2	0	8	1	8.00	1-8	-	

M. SMITH - *Combined Universities*

Opposition	Venue	Date	Batting	Fielding	Bowling
BENSON & HEDGES CUP					
Lancashire	Fenner's	May 1	4*		0-57
Yorkshire	Headingley	May 8	4*		2-46
Surrey	The Parks	May 10	15*		0-53
Hampshire	Southampton	May 12	7*	1Ct	1-49

BATTING AVERAGES - Including fielding

	Matches	Inns	NO	Runs	HS	Avge	100s	50s	Ct	St
Benson & Hedges Cup	4	4	4	30	15*	-	-	-	1	-
ALL ONE-DAY	4	4	4	30	15*	-	-	-	1	-

BOWLING AVERAGES

	Overs	Mdns	Runs	Wkts	Avge	Best	5wI	10wM
Benson & Hedges Cup	40	2	205	3	68.33	2-46	-	
ALL ONE-DAY	40	2	205	3	68.33	2-46	-	

M.J. SMITH - *Scotland*

Opposition	Venue	Date	Batting	Fielding	Bowling
BENSON & HEDGES CUP					
Notts	Glasgow	May 8	7		0-45

BATTING AVERAGES - Including fielding

	Matches	Inns	NO	Runs	HS	Avge	100s	50s	Ct	St
Benson & Hedges Cup	1	1	0	7	7	7.00	-	-	-	-
ALL ONE-DAY	1	1	0	7	7	7.00	-	-	-	-

BOWLING AVERAGES

	Overs	Mdns	Runs	Wkts	Avge	Best	5wI	10wM
Benson & Hedges Cup	10	0	45	0	-	-	-	
ALL ONE-DAY	10	0	45	0	-	-	-	

N.M.K. SMITH - *Warwickshire*

Opposition	Venue	Date	Batting	Fielding	Bowling
BRITANNIC ASSURANCE					
Yorkshire	Edgbaston	May 3	83*		1-36
Northants	Northampton	May 15	8	1Ct	0-17 & 1-22
Notts	Edgbaston	May 19	6 & 14	1Ct	1-82 & 2-76
Worcestershire	Edgbaston	May 26	33 & 0		0-0 & 0-34
Middlesex	Lord's	June 6			0-15
Essex	Edgbaston	June 9	30*		0-35
Worcestershire	Worcester	Aug 23	20 & 20		0-33

S PLAYER RECORDS

REFUGE ASSURANCE

Northants	Edgbaston	April 29		1Ct	1-34
Yorkshire	Edgbaston	May 6			
Gloucs	Moreton-in-M	May 20	5	1Ct	0-46
Worcestershire	Worcester	May 27			2-39
Middlesex	Lord's	June 3	10		0-26
Essex	Edgbaston	June 10	10		0-40
Surrey	The Oval	July 8	12		0-35
Hampshire	Edgbaston	July 29	38 *		3-36
Sussex	Eastbourne	Aug 5	16	2Ct	2-41
Somerset	Weston	Aug 12	21		1-59
Leicestershire	Edgbaston	Aug 19			
Lancashire	Old Trafford	Aug 26	10		2-43

NATWEST TROPHY

Yorkshire	Headingley	July 11	52		0-41

BENSON & HEDGES CUP

Kent	Canterbury	May 8	11		1-43
Worcestershire	Edgbaston	May 10	30 *		0-20
Gloucs	Bristol	May 12		1Ct	

OTHER FIRST-CLASS

Cambridge U	Fenner's	April 26	47	2Ct	1-25 & 0-18
New Zealand	Edgbaston	May 30	24 & 41		1-63
Sri Lanka	Edgbastpn	Aug 29	1 & 43		0-60 & 0-19

OTHER ONE-DAY

Surrey	Harrogate	June 13	23		1-46
Yorkshire	Harrogate	June 15		1Ct	2-52
Surrey	Hove	Sept 3	13	1Ct	

BATTING AVERAGES - Including fielding

	Matches	Inns	NO	Runs	HS	Avge	100s	50s	Ct	St
Britannic Assurance	7	9	2	214	83 *	30.57	-	1	2	-
Refuge Assurance	12	8	1	122	38 *	17.42	-	-	4	-
NatWest Trophy	1	1	0	52	52	52.00	-	1	-	-
Benson & Hedges Cup	3	2	1	41	30 *	41.00	-	-	1	-
Other First-Class	3	5	0	156	47	31.20	-	-	2	-
Other One-Day	3	2	0	36	23	18.00	-	-	2	-
ALL FIRST-CLASS	10	14	2	370	83 *	30.83	-	1	4	-
ALL ONE-DAY	19	13	2	251	52	22.81	-	1	7	-

BOWLING AVERAGES

	Overs	Mdns	Runs	Wkts	Avge	Best	5wI	10wM
Britannic Assurance	109.5	20	350	5	70.00	2-76	-	-
Refuge Assurance	67.3	3	399	11	36.27	3-36	-	
NatWest Trophy	8	0	41	0	-	-	-	
Benson & Hedges Cup	15	0	63	1	63.00	1-43	-	
Other First-Class	68	17	185	2	92.50	1-25	-	-
Other One-Day	21	2	98	3	32.66	2-52	-	
ALL FIRST-CLASS	177.5	37	535	7	76.42	2-76	-	-
ALL ONE-DAY	111.3	5	601	15	40.06	3-36	-	

P.A. SMITH - *Warwickshire*

Opposition	Venue	Date	Batting	Fielding	Bowling

BRITANNIC ASSURANCE

Northants	Edgbaston	June 2	23 & 41		1-63
Middlesex	Lord's	June 6	0 *		2-46
Essex	Edgbaston	June 9	2		
Lancashire	Coventry	July 18	82 & 7 *		2-37
Glamorgan	Swansea	July 25	14 *		0-17
Hampshire	Edgbaston	July 28	85 * & 5		0-11 & 1-16
Sussex	Eastbourne	Aug 4	2 & 13		2-30 & 3-45
Gloucs	Bristol	Aug 8	4 & 21	1Ct	0-31 & 0-26
Leicestershire	Edgbaston	Aug 18	22 & 2		1-25 & 0-11
Somerset	Edgbaston	Sept 7	4 & 75		5-48 & 0-17
Glamorgan	Edgbaston	Sept 12	117 & 0		3-43 & 0-31
Lancashire	Old Trafford	Sept 18	1		

REFUGE ASSURANCE

Northants	Edgbaston	April 29			0-17
Middlesex	Lord's	June 3	2		0-12
Essex	Edgbaston	June 10	2		0-6
Surrey	The Oval	July 8	9		1-8
Notts	Edgbaston	July 22	19		0-21
Hampshire	Edgbaston	July 29	26		
Sussex	Eastbourne	Aug 5	11		3-34
Somerset	Weston	Aug 12	33		1-38
Leicestershire	Edgbaston	Aug 19			0-26

BENSON & HEDGES CUP

Glamorgan	Edgbaston	April 24	13		0-15

OTHER ONE-DAY

Surrey	Hove	Sept 3	6		0-42

BATTING AVERAGES - Including fielding

	Matches	Inns	NO	Runs	HS	Avge	100s	50s	Ct	St
Britannic Assurance	12	20	4	520	117	32.50	1	3	1	-
Refuge Assurance	9	7	0	102	33	14.57	-	-	-	-
Benson & Hedges Cup	1	1	0	13	13	13.00	-	-	-	-
Other One-Day	1	1	0	6	6	6.00	-	-	-	-
ALL FIRST-CLASS	12	20	4	520	117	32.50	1	3	1	-
ALL ONE-DAY	11	9	0	121	33	13.44	-	-	-	-

BOWLING AVERAGES

	Overs	Mdns	Runs	Wkts	Avge	Best	5wI	10wM
Britannic Assurance	148.5	34	497	20	24.85	5-48	1	-
Refuge Assurance	29	1	162	5	32.40	3-34	-	
Benson & Hedges Cup	5	0	15	0	-	-	-	
Other One-Day	10	0	42	0	-	-	-	
ALL FIRST-CLASS	148.5	34	497	20	24.85	5-48	1	-
ALL ONE-DAY	44	1	219	5	43.80	3-34	-	

R.A. SMITH - *Hampshire & England*

Opposition	Venue	Date	Batting	Fielding	Bowling

CORNHILL TEST MATCHES

New Zealand	Trent Bridge	June 7	55		
New Zealand	Lord's	June 21	64 & 0		
New Zealand	Edgbaston	July 5	19 & 14	2Ct	
India	Lord's	July 26	100 * & 15		
India	Old Trafford	Aug 9	121 * & 61 *	1Ct	
India	The Oval	Aug 23	57 & 7 *		

TEXACO TROPHY

New Zealand	Headingley	May 23	128		
New Zealand	The Oval	May 25	5	2Ct	
India	Headingley	July 18	6		
India	Trent Bridge	July 20	103		

BRITANNIC ASSURANCE

Sussex	Southampton	May 15	181		
Surrey	The Oval	May 19	114 * & 1		
Yorkshire	Headingley	May 26	15 & 51 *		
Leicestershire	Leicester	June 2	1		
Glamorgan	Southampton	June 16	153		
Derbyshire	Portsmouth	July 21	2 & 37		
Northants	Bournemouth	Aug 4	0	1Ct	
Somerset	Taunton	Aug 18	58 & 13 *		
Kent	Bournemouth	Aug 29	9 & 74	1Ct	0-5
Glamorgan	Pontypridd	Sept 7	42 & 14 *	3Ct	
Gloucs	Southampton	Sept 18	8 & 124	2Ct	

REFUGE ASSURANCE

Kent	Canterbury	April 29	22		
Gloucs	Southampton	May 6	85		
Somerset	Taunton	May 13	51	1Ct	
Yorkshire	Headingley	May 27	44	1Ct	
Leicestershire	Leicester	June 3	0		
Glamorgan	Bournemouth	June 17	122	1Ct	
Sussex	Hove	July 1	24	2Ct	
Notts	Southampton	July 15	77		
Derbyshire	Portsmouth	July 22	83		
Northants	Bournemouth	Aug 5	9		

NATWEST TROPHY

Leicestershire	Leicester	June 27	35	1Ct	
Essex	Chelmsford	July 11	59		
Yorkshire	Southampton	Aug 1	27	1Ct	
Northants	Southampton	Aug 15	20		

BENSON & HEDGES CUP

Surrey	The Oval	May 1	132		
Lancashire	Old Trafford	May 8	45 *		
Combined U	Southampton	May 12	8 *		

PLADER RECORDS

PLAYER RECORDS

S

OTHER FIRST-CLASS

Oxford U	The Parks	May 3	44		1Ct

OTHER ONE-DAY

Worcestershire	Scarborough	Sept 2	6		1Ct
Essex	Scarborough	Sept 4	14*		1Ct

BATTING AVERAGES - Including fielding

	Matches	Inns	NO	Runs	HS	Avge	100s	50s	Ct	St
Cornhill Test Matches	6	11	4	513	121*	73.28	2	4	3	-
Texaco Trophy	4	4	0	242	128	60.50	2	-	2	-
Britannic Assurance	11	18	4	897	181	64.07	4	3	7	-
Refuge Assurance	10	10	0	517	122	51.70	1	4	5	-
NatWest Trophy	4	4	0	141	59	35.25	-	1	2	-
Benson & Hedges Cup	3	3	2	185	132	185.00	1	-	-	-
Other First-Class	1	1	0	44	44	44.00	-	-	1	-
Other One-Day	2	2	1	20	14*	20.00	-	-	2	-
ALL FIRST-CLASS	18	30	8	1454	181	66.09	6	7	11	-
ALL ONE-DAY	23	23	3	1105	132	55.25	4	5	11	-

BOWLING AVERAGES

	Overs	Mdns	Runs	Wkts	Avge	Best	5wI	10wM
Cornhill Test Matches								
Texaco Trophy								
Britannic Assurance	0.3	0	5	0	-	-	-	-
Refuge Assurance								
NatWest Trophy								
Benson & Hedges Cup								
Other First-Class								
Other One-Day								
ALL FIRST-CLASS	0.3	0	5	0	-	-	-	-
ALL ONE-DAY								

S. SMITH - *Ireland*

Opposition	Venue	Date	Batting	Fielding	Bowling

NATWEST TROPHY

Sussex	Downpatrick	June 27	15		

BATTING AVERAGES - Including fielding

	Matches	Inns	NO	Runs	HS	Avge	100s	50s	Ct	St
NatWest Trophy	1	1	0	15	15	15.00	-	-	-	-
ALL ONE-DAY	1	1	0	15	15	15.00	-	-	-	-

BOWLING AVERAGES
Did not bowl

T.S. SMITH - *Hertfordshire*

Opposition	Venue	Date	Batting	Fielding	Bowling

NATWEST TROPHY

Warwickshire	St Albans	June 27	15	1Ct	0-57

BATTING AVERAGES - Including fielding

	Matches	Inns	NO	Runs	HS	Avge	100s	50s	Ct	St
NatWest Trophy	1	1	0	15	15	15.00	-	-	1	-
ALL ONE-DAY	1	1	0	15	15	15.00	-	-	1	-

BOWLING AVERAGES

	Overs	Mdns	Runs	Wkts	Avge	Best	5wI	10wM
NatWest Trophy	12	1	57	0	-	-	-	-
ALL ONE-DAY	12	1	57	0	-	-	-	-

M.C. SNEDDEN - *New Zealand*

Opposition	Venue	Date	Batting	Fielding	Bowling

CORNHILL TEST MATCHES

England	Trent Bridge	June 7	0	2Ct	1-54
England	Lord's	June 21	13*		1-72
England	Edgbaston	July 5	2 & 21*		3-106 & 1-32

OTHER FIRST-CLASS

Somerset	Taunton	May 16			4-79 & 1-49
Middlesex	Lord's	May 19	0*		5-63 & 1-22
Warwickshire	Edgbaston	May 30	2	1Ct	2-69 & 0-32
Derbyshire	Derby	June 2			4-55

OTHER ONE-DAY

D of Norfolk	Arundel	May 6			2-42
MCC	Lord's	May 7	8*		3-28
Ireland	Downpatrick	May 9			2-27
Ireland	Belfast	May 10			1-4
Leicestershire	Leicester	June 14		1	1-32

BATTING AVERAGES - Including fielding

	Matches	Inns	NO	Runs	HS	Avge	100s	50s	Ct	St
Cornhill Test Matches	3	4	2	36	21*	18.00	-	-	2	-
Other First-Class	4	2	1	2	2	2.00	-	-	1	-
Other One-Day	5	2	1	9	8*	9.00	-	-	-	-
ALL FIRST-CLASS	7	6	3	38	21*	12.66	-	-	3	-
ALL ONE-DAY	5	2	1	9	8*	9.00	-	-	-	-

BOWLING AVERAGES

	Overs	Mdns	Runs	Wkts	Avge	Best	5wI	10wM
Cornhill Test Matches	101	30	264	6	44.00	3-106	-	-
Other First-Class	130.5	26	369	17	21.70	5-63	1	-
Other One-Day	45	9	133	9	14.77	3-28	-	
ALL FIRST-CLASS	231.5	56	633	23	27.52	5-63	1	-
ALL ONE-DAY	45	9	133	9	14.77	3-28	-	

N.J. SPEAK - *Lancashire*

Opposition	Venue	Date	Batting	Fielding	Bowling

BRITANNIC ASSURANCE

Gloucs	Old Trafford	June 9	30		
Hampshire	Old Trafford	June 23	6	1Ct	
Northants	Northampton	Aug 11	5 & 0	1Ct	

OTHER FIRST-CLASS

Zimbabwe	Old Trafford	May 23	138 & 74	1Ct	
Oxford U	The Parks	June 16	61		
Sri Lanka	Old Trafford	Sept 8	43 & 52		1-26

BATTING AVERAGES - Including fielding

	Matches	Inns	NO	Runs	HS	Avge	100s	50s	Ct	St
Britannic Assurance	3	4	0	41	30	10.25	-	-	2	-
Other First-Class	3	5	0	368	138	73.60	1	3	1	-
ALL FIRST-CLASS	6	9	0	409	138	45.44	1	3	3	-

BOWLING AVERAGES

	Overs	Mdns	Runs	Wkts	Avge	Best	5wI	10wM
Britannic Assurance								
Other First-Class	5	0	26	1	26.00	1-26	-	-
ALL FIRST-CLASS	5	0	26	1	26.00	1-26	-	-

M.P. SPEIGHT - *Sussex*

Opposition	Venue	Date	Batting	Fielding	Bowling

BRITANNIC ASSURANCE

Surrey	Hove	April 26	50* & 75*	2Ct	
Kent	Folkestone	May 3	12 & 22	3Ct	
Hampshire	Southampton	May 15	7 & 3	1Ct	

S — PLAYER RECORDS

Glamorgan	Hove	May 19	60 & 131	
Somerset	Taunton	May 23	73 & 83*	
Lancashire	Horsham	June 2	11 & 21	
Gloucs	Hove	June 16	0* & 59	1Ct
Worcestershire	Worcester	June 20	60*	
Derbyshire	Hove	July 4	43	
Notts	Trent Bridge	July 7	55 & 30	1Ct
Surrey	Guildford	July 18	108 & 0*	1Ct
Northants	Northampton	July 21	2 & 13	2Ct
Hampshire	Arundel	July 25	37 & 24	
Warwickshire	Eastbourne	Aug 4	22 & 11	
Yorkshire	Eastbourne	Aug 8	14 & 53	
Middlesex	Lord's	Aug 11	52	
Kent	Hove	Aug 18	14 & 1	1Ct
Somerset	Hove	Aug 23	2 & 11	1Ct
Leicestershire	Leicester	Aug 29	45 & 53	
Gloucs	Bristol	Sept 12	34 & 13	
Middlesex	Hove	Sept 18	33 & 12	

REFUGE ASSURANCE

Derbyshire	Hove	April 22	77	
Surrey	Hove	April 29	18	
Glamorgan	Hove	May 20	26	
Leicestershire	Leicester	June 10	21	1Ct
Yorkshire	Hove	June 17	24	
Worcestershire	Worcester	June 24	15	
Hampshire	Hove	July 1	21	1Ct
Notts	Trent Bridge	July 8	2	
Gloucs	Swindon	July 15	60	1Ct
Northants	Well'borough	July 22	32	1Ct
Warwickshire	Eastbourne	Aug 5	20	
Middlesex	Lord's	Aug 12	16*	
Somerset	Hove	Aug 26	21	

NATWEST TROPHY

| Ireland | Downpatrick | June 27 | | 1Ct |
| Glamorgan | Cardiff | July 11 | 4 | 1Ct |

BENSON & HEDGES CUP

Derbyshire	Derby	April 24	71	
Min Counties	Marlow	May 1	40	1Ct
Middlesex	Hove	May 8	43	
Somerset	Hove	May 12	6	

OTHER FIRST-CLASS

| Cambridge U | Hove | June 30 | | 1Ct |
| Sri Lanka | Hove | Sept 5 | 5* & 21 | |

OTHER ONE-DAY
For D of Norfolk

| New Zealand | Arundel | May 6 | 0 | |

For Sussex

| Zimbabwe | Hove | May 13 | 76 | |
| Yorkshire | Harrogate | June 14 | 30 | |

BATTING AVERAGES - Including fielding

	Matches	Inns	NO	Runs	HS	Avge	100s	50s	Ct	St
Britannic Assurance	21	39	6	1349	131	40.87	2	11	13	-
Refuge Assurance	13	13	1	353	77	29.41	-	2	4	-
NatWest Trophy	2	1	0	4	4	4.00	-	-	2	-
Benson & Hedges Cup	4	4	0	160	71	40.00	-	1	1	-
Other First-Class	2	2	1	26	21	26.00	-	-	1	-
Other One-Day	3	3	0	106	76	35.33	-	1	-	-
ALL FIRST-CLASS	23	41	7	1375	131	40.44	2	11	14	-
ALL ONE-DAY	22	21	1	623	77	31.15	-	4	7	-

BOWLING AVERAGES
Did not bowl

![black bar]

D.M. STAMP - Norfolk

Opposition	Venue	Date	Batting	Fielding	Bowling

NATWEST TROPHY

| Yorkshire | Headingley | June 27 | 18 | | |

BATTING AVERAGES - Including fielding

	Matches	Inns	NO	Runs	HS	Avge	100s	50s	Ct	St
NatWest Trophy	1	1	0	18	18	18.00	-	-	-	-
ALL ONE-DAY	1	1	0	18	18	18.00	-	-	-	-

BOWLING AVERAGES
Did not bowl

![black bar]

J. STANWORTH - Lancashire

Opposition	Venue	Date	Batting	Fielding	Bowling

REFUGE ASSURANCE

| Hampshire | Old Trafford | June 24 | | | |

OTHER FIRST-CLASS

| Zimbabwe | Old Trafford | May 23 | | 1Ct | |
| Oxford U | The Parks | June 16 | | 2Ct | |

BATTING AVERAGES - Including fielding

	Matches	Inns	NO	Runs	HS	Avge	100s	50s	Ct	St
Refuge Assurance	1	0	0	0	0	-	-	-	-	-
Other First-Class	2	0	0	0	0	-	-	-	3	-
ALL FIRST-CLASS	2	0	0	0	0	-	-	-	3	-
ALL ONE-DAY	1	0	0	0	0	-	-	-	-	-

BOWLING AVERAGES
Did not bowl

![black bar]

M.G. STEAR - Berkshire

Opposition	Venue	Date	Batting	Fielding	Bowling

NATWEST TROPHY

| Middlesex | Lord's | June 27 | 5* | | 1-39 |

BATTING AVERAGES - Including fielding

	Matches	Inns	NO	Runs	HS	Avge	100s	50s	Ct	St
NatWest Trophy	1	1	1	5	5*	-	-	-	-	-
ALL ONE-DAY	1	1	1	5	5*	-	-	-	-	-

BOWLING AVERAGES

	Overs	Mdns	Runs	Wkts	Avge	Best	5wI	10wM
NatWest Trophy	9	0	39	1	39.00	1-39	-	
ALL ONE-DAY	9	0	39	1	39.00	1-39	-	

![black bar]

R.D. STEMP - Worcestershire

Opposition	Venue	Date	Batting	Fielding	Bowling

BRITANNIC ASSURANCE

| Yorkshire | Worcester | June 2 | 3* | 1Ct | 1-32 |
| Surrey | The Oval | June 16 | 0* | | 0-13 & 0-78 |

REFUGE ASSURANCE

| Yorkshire | Worcester | June 3 | 1 | | 0-28 |
| Surrey | The Oval | June 17 | 3* | 1Ct | 0-37 |

BENSON & HEDGES CUP

| Notts | Trent Bridge | June 13 | | | 0-38 |

BATTING AVERAGES - Including fielding

	Matches	Inns	NO	Runs	HS	Avge	100s	50s	Ct	St
Britannic Assurance	2	2	2	3	3*	-	-	-	1	-
Refuge Assurance	2	2	1	4	3*	4.00	-	-	1	-
Benson & Hedges Cup	1	0	0	0	0	-	-	-	-	-
ALL FIRST-CLASS	2	2	2	3	3*	-	-	-	1	-
ALL ONE-DAY	3	2	1	4	3*	4.00	-	-	1	-

BOWLING AVERAGES

	Overs	Mdns	Runs	Wkts	Avge	Best	5wI	10wM
Britannic Assurance	45	14	123	1	123.00	1-32	-	-
Refuge Assurance	12	0	65	0				
Benson & Hedges Cup	8	1	38	0				

PLAYER RECORDS

ALL FIRST-CLASS	45	14	123	1	123.00	1-32	- -
ALL ONE-DAY	20	1	103	0	-	-	- -

F.D. STEPHENSON - *Nottinghamshire*

Opposition	Venue	Date	Batting	Fielding	Bowling
BRITANNIC ASSURANCE					
Derbyshire	Trent Bridge	April 26	18 & 12		0-92 & 0-9
Worcestershire	Worcester	May 3	13 & 12*		2-112
Leicestershire	Leicester	May 15	0 & 13*		0-98 & 4-33
Warwickshire	Edgbaston	May 19	15 & 12		3-69 & 3-69
Northants	Trent Bridge	May 23	11		0-23 & 0-52
Kent	Tunbridge We	June 2	4 & 1*	1Ct	2-77 & 6-84
Surrey	Trent Bridge	June 20	9 & 2		2-66
Leicestershire	Trent Bridge	June 30	121		1-53 & 2-36
Yorkshire	Scarborough	July 4	4*		0-23
Hampshire	Portsmouth	July 18	10 & 88*		2-78 & 0-26
Lancashire	Southport	July 25	8 & 18	1Ct	1-127 & 1-44
Middlesex	Trent Bridge	July 28	8 & 44*		2-33 & 5-82
Essex	Southend	Aug 4	2 & 4		2-105 & 0-30
Somerset	Weston	Aug 8	34		2-89
Gloucs	Trent Bridge	Aug 18	0 & 0	1Ct	3-66 & 3-94
Worcestershire	Trent Bridge	Aug 29	25 & 30		3-72 & 0-51
Middlesex	Lord's	Sept 7	7 & 20	1Ct	2-89
Lancashire	Trent Bridge	Sept 12	24 & 51	1Ct	1-131
Yorkshire	Trent Bridge	Sept 18	95		0-4 & 1-30
REFUGE ASSURANCE					
Yorkshire	Trent Bridge	April 22	42		1-28
Lancashire	Trent Bridge	April 29	23		1-48
Worcestershire	Worcester	May 6	3		1-41
Middlesex	Lord's	May 13	5*	1Ct	3-29
Surrey	Trent Bridge	May 20			0-21
Derbyshire	Derby	June 10	6		2-43
Kent	Canterbury	June 17	9		4-28
Somerset	Bath	June 24	34		2-34
Leicestershire	Trent Bridge	July 1		1Ct	3-21
Sussex	Trent Bridge	July 8	32		1-48
Hampshire	Southampton	July 15	14		0-43
Warwickshire	Edgbaston	July 22	4		0-29
Northants	Trent Bridge	July 29	2		0-19
Essex	Southend	Aug 5	26*		3-28
Glamorgan	Trent Bridge	Aug 12			1-40
Gloucs	Trent Bridge	Aug 19		1Ct	1-28
Derbyshire	Derby	Sept 5	7		1-49
NATWEST TROPHY					
Bucks	Marlow	June 27	29		0-12
Northants	Northampton	July 11	4		2-40
BENSON & HEDGES CUP					
Essex	Chelmsford	April 24	22*		1-49
Leicestershire	Trent Bridge	May 1	10		1-39
Scotland	Glasgow	May 8	5		2-49
Northants	Trent Bridge	May 12	2		3-33
Essex	Chelmsford	May 30	25*		1-34
Worcestershire	Trent Bridge	June 13	98*		1-45
OTHER FIRST-CLASS					
Sri Lanka	Cleethorpes	Aug 25	27* & 65		1-34 & 0-17
OTHER ONE-DAY					
For Rest of World					
England XI	Jesmond	Aug 2	0		1-41
England XI	Jesmond	Aug 3			0-17
For World XI					
Yorkshire	Scarborough	Sept 1	15		2-52

BATTING AVERAGES - Including fielding

	Matches	Inns	NO	Runs	HS	Avge	100s	50s	Ct	St
Britannic Assurance	19	33	6	715	121	26.48	1	3	5	-
Refuge Assurance	17	13	2	207	42	18.81	-	-	3	-
NatWest Trophy	2	2	0	33	29	16.50	-	-	-	-
Benson & Hedges Cup	6	6	3	162	98*	54.00	-	1	-	-
Other First-Class	1	2	1	92	65	92.00	-	1	-	-
Other One-Day	3	2	0	15	15	7.50	-	-	-	-
ALL FIRST-CLASS	20	35	7	807	121	28.82	1	4	5	-
ALL ONE-DAY	28	23	5	417	98*	23.16	-	1	3	-

BOWLING AVERAGES

	Overs	Mdns	Runs	Wkts	Avge	Best	5wI	10wM
Britannic Assurance	592.4	90	2047	53	38.62	6-84	2	-
Refuge Assurance	123	11	577	24	24.04	4-28	-	-
NatWest Trophy	17	3	52	2	26.00	2-40	-	-
Benson & Hedges Cup	66	4	249	9	27.66	3-33	-	-
Other First-Class	18	4	51	1	51.00	1-34	-	-
Other One-Day	25.4	3	110	3	36.66	2-52	-	-
ALL FIRST-CLASS	610.4	94	2098	54	38.85	6-84	2	-
ALL ONE-DAY	231.4	21	988	38	26.00	4-28	-	-

J.P. STEPHENSON - *Essex*

Opposition	Venue	Date	Batting	Fielding	Bowling
BRITANNIC ASSURANCE					
Middlesex	Lord's	April 26	14 & 59	1Ct	0-7
Leicestershire	Chelmsford	May 3	35		1-16
Worcestershire	Worcester	May 19	4 & 6*	2Ct	0-10
Hampshire	Southampton	May 23	2 & 4*	1Ct	
Middlesex	Ilford	June 2	16 & 31		0-36
Gloucs	Ilford	June 6	1 & 35*		0-33
Warwickshire	Edgbaston	June 9	85		0-25 & 0-7
Somerset	Bath	June 16	202* & 63*		
Kent	Maidstone	June 4	67		0-38
Derbyshire	Colchester	July 18	1 & 4	1Ct	
Lancashire	Colchester	July 21	21 & 60		0-11
Leicestershire	Leicester	July 25	7 & 131*	2Ct	
Sussex	Chelmsford	July 28	14 & 45	2Ct	
Notts	Southend	Aug 4	46 & 32*	1Ct	
Glamorgan	Southend	Aug 8	63 & 65	2Ct	
Yorkshire	Middlesbr'gh	Aug 11	62	2Ct	
Surrey	Chelmsford	Aug 18	7 & 36		
Derbyshire	Derby	Aug 23	11		
Northants	Northampton	Aug 29	76 & 82	1Ct	1-40
Northants	Chelmsford	Sept 7	0 & 76		0-17
Kent	Chelmsford	Sept 12	11		0-18 & 0-9
Surrey	The Oval	Sept 18	51		1-116
REFUGE ASSURANCE					
Kent	Chelmsford	April 22	5		
Middlesex	Lord's	April 29	5		
Leicestershire	Leicester	May 6	38*		
Gloucs	Chelmsford	May 13	23		0-15
Worcestershire	Worcester	May 20	9		
Glamorgan	Ilford	June 3		1Ct	
Warwickshire	Edgbaston	June 10		2Ct	1-20
Somerset	Bath	June 17	1		1-3
Hampshire	Southampton	July 8	28		
Northants	Chelmsford	July 15	66		
Lancashire	Colchester	July 22	109		
Notts	Southend	Aug 5	50		
Yorkshire	Middlesbr'gh	Aug 12	4	1Ct	1-35
Derbyshire	Derby	Aug 26	3	1Ct	
NATWEST TROPHY					
Scotland	Chelmsford	June 27			
Hampshire	Chelmsford	July 11	44		1-24
BENSON & HEDGES CUP					
Notts	Chelmsford	April 24	0		
Scotland	Glasgow	May 1	4*		2-14
Northants	Northampton	May 8			3-22
Notts	Chelmsford	May 30	4	1Ct	2-44
OTHER FIRST-CLASS					
Cambridge U	Fenner's	May 16	58	1Ct	0-1
New Zealand	Chelmsford	June 30	147		1-52 & 0-15
For TCCB U25 XI					
India	Edgbaston	Aug 15	116 & 41*	1Ct	1-18 & 0-16
OTHER ONE-DAY					
Zimbabwe	Chelmsford	May 14	105		3-26
For England XI					
Rest of World	Jesmond	Aug 2		1Ct	0-20
Rest of World	Jesmond	Aug 3	7		0-21
For Essex					
Yorkshire	Scarborough	Sept 3	57		3-42
Hampshire	Scarborough	Sept 4	18		1-31

S — PLAYER RECORDS

BATTING AVERAGES - Including fielding

	Matches	Inns	NO	Runs	HS	Avge	100s	50s	Ct	St
Britannic Assurance	22	37	7	1525	202*	50.83	2	12	14	-
Refuge Assurance	14	12	1	341	109	31.00	1	2	5	-
NatWest Trophy	2	1	0	44	44	44.00	-	-	-	-
Benson & Hedges Cup	4	3	1	8	4*	4.00	-	-	1	-
Other First-Class	3	4	1	362	147	120.66	2	1	2	-
Other One-Day	5	4	0	187	105	46.75	1	1	1	-
ALL FIRST-CLASS	25	41	8	1887	202*	57.18	4	13	16	-
ALL ONE-DAY	25	20	2	580	109	32.22	2	3	7	-

BOWLING AVERAGES

	Overs	Mdns	Runs	Wkts	Avge	Best	5wI	10wM
Britannic Assurance	96	22	383	3	127.66	1-16	-	-
Refuge Assurance	11	0	73	3	24.33	1-3	-	
NatWest Trophy	4	0	24	1	24.00	1-24	-	
Benson & Hedges Cup	20	0	80	7	11.42	3-22	-	
Other First-Class	27	6	102	2	51.00	1-18	-	
Other One-Day	27	0	140	7	20.00	3-26	-	
ALL FIRST-CLASS	123	28	485	5	97.00	1-16	-	-
ALL ONE-DAY	62	0	317	18	17.61	3-22	-	-

M.E. STEVENS - *Berkshire*

Opposition	Venue	Date	Batting	Fielding	Bowling
NATWEST TROPHY					
Middlesex	Lord's	June 27			

BATTING AVERAGES - Including fielding

	Matches	Inns	NO	Runs	HS	Avge	100s	50s	Ct	St
NatWest Trophy	1	0	0	0	0	-	-	-	-	-
ALL ONE-DAY	1	0	0	0	0	-	-	-	-	-

BOWLING AVERAGES
Did not bowl

A.J. STEWART - *Surrey & England*

Opposition	Venue	Date	Batting	Fielding	Bowling
CORNHILL TEST MATCHES					
New Zealand	Trent Bridge	June 7	27	2Ct	
New Zealand	Lord's	June 21	54 & 42	2Ct	
New Zealand	Edgbaston	July 5	9 & 15	1Ct	
TEXACO TROPHY					
New Zealand	Headingley	May 23	33	1Ct	
New Zealand	The Oval	May 25	28		
BRITANNIC ASSURANCE					
Sussex	Hove	April 26	77 & 15	1Ct	
Lancashire	The Oval	May 3	70 & 54*	1Ct	
Hampshire	The Oval	May 19	17 & 100*		
Worcestershire	The Oval	June 16	7* & 55	1Ct	
Somerset	Weston	Aug 4	24* & 0	4Ct	
Leicestershire	The Oval	Aug 11	3		
Essex	Chelmsford	Aug 18	53 & 11		
Hampshire	Southampton	Aug 23	72 & 27*	2Ct	
Lancashire	Blackpool	Aug 29	23*	1Ct	
Kent	Canterbury	Sept 7	1	3Ct	
Middlesex	The Oval	Sept 12	0 & 47	2Ct	0-32
Essex	The Oval	Sept 18	2 & 51	2Ct	
REFUGE ASSURANCE					
Sussex	Hove	April 29	64		
Lancashire	The Oval	May 6	125		
Notts	Trent Bridge	May 20	10		0-4
Northants	The Oval	June 3	20		
Worcestershire	The Oval	June 17	0	1Ct	
Gloucs	Cheltenham	July 29	3		
Somerset	Weston	Aug 5		1Ct	
Hampshire	Southampton	Aug 26	36	2Ct	
NATWEST TROPHY					
Wiltshire	Trowbridge	June 27			
Middlesex	Uxbridge	July 11	48	1Ct	
BENSON & HEDGES CUP					
Lancashire	Old Trafford	April 24	31		
Hampshire	The Oval	May 1	76		
Combined U	The Parks	May 10	84*	1Ct	
Yorkshire	The Oval	May 12	76		
Lancashire	Old Trafford	May 30	67		
OTHER FIRST-CLASS					
Oxford U	The Parks	May 16	24	1Ct	
India	The Oval	Aug 1	82 & 22	1Ct	
OTHER ONE-DAY					
Warwickshire	Harrogate	June 13	20		
Warwickshire	Hove	Sept 3	36	2Ct	
Kent	Hove	Sept 4	52		

BATTING AVERAGES - Including fielding

	Matches	Inns	NO	Runs	HS	Avge	100s	50s	Ct	St
Cornhill Test Matches	3	5	0	147	54	29.40	-	1	5	-
Texaco Trophy	2	2	0	61	33	30.50	-	-	1	-
Britannic Assurance	12	21	6	709	100*	47.26	1	7	17	-
Refuge Assurance	8	7	0	258	125	36.85	1	1	4	-
NatWest Trophy	2	1	0	48	48	48.00	-	-	1	-
Benson & Hedges Cup	5	5	1	334	84*	83.50	-	4	1	-
Other First-Class	2	3	0	128	82	42.66	-	1	2	-
Other One-Day	3	3	0	108	52	36.00	-	1	2	-
ALL FIRST-CLASS	17	29	6	984	100*	42.78	1	9	24	-
ALL ONE-DAY	20	18	1	809	125	47.58	1	6	9	-

BOWLING AVERAGES

	Overs	Mdns	Runs	Wkts	Avge	Best	5wI	10wM
Cornhill Test Matches								
Texaco Trophy								
Britannic Assurance	5	0	32	0		-	-	
Refuge Assurance	0.1	0	4	0		-	-	
NatWest Trophy								
Benson & Hedges Cup								
Other First-Class								
Other One-Day								
ALL FIRST-CLASS	5	0	32	0		-	-	
ALL ONE-DAY	0.1	0	4	0		-	-	

C. STONE - *Dorset*

Opposition	Venue	Date	Batting	Fielding	Bowling
NATWEST TROPHY					
Glamorgan	Swansea	June 27	25		2-44

BATTING AVERAGES - Including fielding

	Matches	Inns	NO	Runs	HS	Avge	100s	50s	Ct	St
NatWest Trophy	1	1	0	25	25	25.00	-	-	-	-
ALL ONE-DAY	1	1	0	25	25	25.00	-	-	-	-

BOWLING AVERAGES

	Overs	Mdns	Runs	Wkts	Avge	Best	5wI	10wM
NatWest Trophy	12	2	44	2	22.00	2-44	-	
ALL ONE-DAY	12	2	44	2	22.00	2-44	-	

D.B. STORER - *Lincolnshire*

Opposition	Venue	Date	Batting	Fielding	Bowling
NATWEST TROPHY					
Gloucs	Gloucester	June 27	0		

BATTING AVERAGES - Including fielding

	Matches	Inns	NO	Runs	HS	Avge	100s	50s	Ct	St
NatWest Trophy	1	1	0	0	0	0.00	-	-	-	-

PLAYER RECORDS

ALL ONE-DAY	1	1	0	0	0	0.00	-	-	-	-	

BOWLING AVERAGES
Did not bowl

A.C. STORIE - *Scotland*

Opposition	Venue	Date	Batting	Fielding	Bowling
BENSON & HEDGES CUP					
Northants	Northampton	May 10	8		
Leicestershire	Leicester	May 12	19		
OTHER FIRST-CLASS					
Ireland	Edinburgh	Aug 11	32	1Ct	

BATTING AVERAGES - Including fielding

	Matches	Inns	NO	Runs	HS	Avge	100s	50s	Ct	St
Benson & Hedges Cup	2	2	0	27	19	13.50	-	-	-	-
Other First-Class	1	1	0	32	32	32.00	-	-	1	-
ALL FIRST-CLASS	1	1	0	32	32	32.00	-	-	1	-
ALL ONE-DAY	2	2	0	27	19	13.50	-	-	-	-

BOWLING AVERAGES
Did not bowl

A.W. STOVOLD - *Gloucestershire*

Opposition	Venue	Date	Batting	Fielding	Bowling
BRITANNIC ASSURANCE					
Somerset	Taunton	April 26	4 & 74		
Glamorgan	Bristol	May 15	7 & 19		
BENSON & HEDGES CUP					
Worcestershire	Bristol	April 24	8		
Glamorgan	Cardiff	May 1	1		
Kent	Canterbury	May 10			
Warwickshire	Bristol	May 12	5		

BATTING AVERAGES - Including fielding

	Matches	Inns	NO	Runs	HS	Avge	100s	50s	Ct	St
Britannic Assurance	2	4	0	104	74	26.00	-	1	-	-
Benson & Hedges Cup	4	3	0	14	8	4.66	-	-	-	-
ALL FIRST-CLASS	2	4	0	104	74	26.00	-	1	-	-
ALL ONE-DAY	4	3	0	14	8	4.66	-	-	-	-

BOWLING AVERAGES
Did not bowl

P.M. SUCH - *Essex*

Opposition	Venue	Date	Batting	Fielding	Bowling
BRITANNIC ASSURANCE					
Leicestershire	Chelmsford	May 3		1Ct	3-118 & 1-29
Middlesex	Ilford	June 2	27		0-41
Gloucs	Ilford	June 6			0-34
Somerset	Bath	June 16			0-29
Derbyshire	Colchester	July 18	0 *	1Ct	2-36 & 1-7
Lancashire	Colchester	July 21	13 *		1-57 & 0-24
Notts	Southend	Aug 4	2 *		1-5 & 1-56
Glamorgan	Southend	Aug 8			1-43 & 1-73
Yorkshire	Middlesbr'gh	Aug 11	2		3-34 & 2-39
Northants	Northampton	Aug 29			1-57
REFUGE ASSURANCE					
Sussex	Chelmsford	July 29		2Ct	2-43
Yorkshire	Middlesbr'gh	Aug 12	5		0-35
Derbyshire	Derby	Aug 26		1Ct	0-28

OTHER FIRST-CLASS						
Cambridge U	Fenner's	May 16			0-27 & 2-6
OTHER ONE-DAY						
Yorkshire	Scarborough	Sept 3			2-32
Hampshire	Scarborough	Sept 4	6 *		0-22

BATTING AVERAGES - Including fielding

	Matches	Inns	NO	Runs	HS	Avge	100s	50s	Ct	St
Britannic Assurance	10	5	3	44	27	22.00	-	-	2	-
Refuge Assurance	3	1	0	5	5	5.00	-	-	3	-
Other First-Class	1	0	0	0	0	-	-	-	-	-
Other One-Day	2	1	1	6	6 *	-	-	-	-	-
ALL FIRST-CLASS	11	5	3	44	27	22.00	-	-	2	-
ALL ONE-DAY	5	2	1	11	6 *	11.00	-	-	3	-

BOWLING AVERAGES

	Overs	Mdns	Runs	Wkts	Avge	Best	5wI	10wM
Britannic Assurance	252.3	58	682	18	37.88	3-34	-	-
Refuge Assurance	20	0	106	2	53.00	2-43	-	-
Other First-Class	20.1	9	33	2	16.50	2-6	-	-
Other One-Day	20	1	54	2	27.00	2-32	-	-
ALL FIRST-CLASS	272.4	67	715	20	35.75	3-34	-	-
ALL ONE-DAY	40	1	160	4	40.00	2-32	-	-

D. SURRIDGE - *Hertfordshire*

Opposition	Venue	Date	Batting	Fielding	Bowling
NATWEST TROPHY					
Warwickshire	St Albans	June 27	3 *	1Ct	3-61

BATTING AVERAGES - Including fielding

	Matches	Inns	NO	Runs	HS	Avge	100s	50s	Ct	St
NatWest Trophy	1	1	1	3	3 *	-	-	-	1	-
ALL ONE-DAY	1	1	1	3	3 *	-	-	-	1	-

BOWLING AVERAGES

	Overs	Mdns	Runs	Wkts	Avge	Best	5wI	10wM
NatWest Trophy	12	0	61	3	20.33	3-61	-	
ALL ONE-DAY	12	0	61	3	20.33	3-61	-	

I.G. SWALLOW - *Somerset*

Opposition	Venue	Date	Batting	Fielding	Bowling
BRITANNIC ASSURANCE					
Gloucs	Taunton	April 26	7 *		0-1 & 1-57
Glamorgan	Cardiff	May 3	31 *	2Ct	2-117 & 0-57
Derbyshire	Taunton	May 19	0		3-89 & 1-51
Sussex	Taunton	May 23			1-62 & 0-28
Leicestershire	Leicester	May 26			1-47 & 1-16
Gloucs	Bristol	June 2	10		0-43
Hampshire	Basingstoke	June 6		2Ct	0-24 & 2-54
Kent	Canterbury	June 9		1Ct	2-59
Essex	Bath	June 16			1-140
Glamorgan	Bath	June 20			2-63
Northants	Taunton	June 30		9	1-84 & 0-76
Warwickshire	Taunton	July 4	32		
Worcestershire	Worcester	July 18		1Ct	1-84 & 1-69
Middlesex	Uxbridge	July 21	11 *		1-100 & 0-66
Yorkshire	Scarborough	July 25	3 * & 12 *	1Ct	2-71 & 0-35
Lancashire	Old Trafford	July 28	16 & 0	2Ct	3-88
Surrey	Weston	Aug 4	11		1-83 & 2-74
Notts	Weston	Aug 8	27		1-33 & 0-46
Hampshire	Taunton	Aug 18	0 *		1-37
Warwickshire	Edgbaston	Sept 7	14 *	1Ct	0-26 & 0-23
Worcestershire	Taunton	Sept 12	4 & 0	1Ct	0-88 & 0-51
REFUGE ASSURANCE					
Worcestershire	Taunton	April 22	6 *		1-47
Hampshire	Taunton	May 13			0-24
Derbyshire	Taunton	May 20			0-38
Leicestershire	Leicester	May 27			0-20

S PLAYER RECORDS

Gloucs	Bristol	June 3	19		
Kent	Canterbury	June 10	0*		0-12
Essex	Bath	June 17	3		0-32
Notts	Bath	June 24	3*		1-35
Northants	Taunton	July 1	1		1-19
Middlesex	Lord's	July 8			2-44
Yorkshire	Scarborough	July 15	31		0-25
Glamorgan	Neath	July 22		1Ct	
Lancashire	Old Trafford	July 29	7*		1-41
Surrey	Weston	Aug 5	8*		0-28

NATWEST TROPHY
Devon	Torquay	June 27			0-12
Worcestershire	Taunton	July 11		1Ct	0-57

BENSON & HEDGES CUP
Derbyshire	Taunton	May 1			0-45
Min Counties	Taunton	May 8			2-32
Middlesex	Lord's	May 10	0		0-9
Sussex	Hove	May 12		1Ct	1-55
Middlesex	Taunton	May 30	18		0-26
Lancashire	Old Trafford	June 13	8	1Ct	1-40

OTHER FIRST-CLASS
Oxford U	The Parks	April 18		1Ct	1-12
New Zealand	Taunton	May 16			2-52 & 0-68

OTHER ONE-DAY
For Yorkshiremen
Yorkshire	Scarborough	Sept 6		0-48

BATTING AVERAGES - Including fielding
	Matches	Inns	NO	Runs	HS	Avge	100s	50s	Ct	St
Britannic Assurance	21	17	7	187	32	18.70	-	-	11	-
Refuge Assurance	14	8	5	77	31	25.66	-	-	1	-
NatWest Trophy	2	0	0	0	0	-	-	-	1	-
Benson & Hedges Cup	6	3	0	26	18	8.66	-	-	2	-
Other First-Class	2	0	0	0	0	-	-	-	1	-
Other One-Day	1	0	0	0	0	-	-	-	-	-
ALL FIRST-CLASS	23	17	7	187	32	18.70	-	-	12	-
ALL ONE-DAY	23	11	5	103	31	17.16	-	-	4	-

BOWLING AVERAGES
	Overs	Mdns	Runs	Wkts	Avge	Best	5wI	10wM
Britannic Assurance	642.1	150	2042	31	65.87	3-88	-	-
Refuge Assurance	69	2	365	6	60.83	2-44	-	
NatWest Trophy	13	0	69	0	-	-		
Benson & Hedges Cup	45.5	3	207	4	51.75	2-32	-	
Other First-Class	47	11	132	3	44.00	2-52	-	-
Other One-Day	8	0	48	0	-	-		
ALL FIRST-CLASS	689.1	161	2174	34	63.94	3-88	-	-
ALL ONE-DAY	135.5	5	689	10	68.90	2-32	-	

R.G. SWAN - *Scotland*

Opposition	Venue	Date	Batting	Fielding	Bowling

NATWEST TROPHY
Essex	Chelmsford	June 27	26		

BENSON & HEDGES CUP
Essex	Glasgow	May 1	11		
Notts	Glasgow	May 8	53		
Northants	Northampton	May 10	44		
Leicestershire	Leicester	May 12	40		

OTHER FIRST-CLASS
Ireland	Edinburgh	Aug 11	9		

BATTING AVERAGES - Including fielding
	Matches	Inns	NO	Runs	HS	Avge	100s	50s	Ct	St
NatWest Trophy	1	1	0	26	26	26.00	-	-	-	-
Benson & Hedges Cup	4	4	0	148	53	37.00	-	1	-	-
Other First-Class	1	1	0	9	9	9.00	-	-	-	-
ALL FIRST-CLASS	1	1	0	9	9	9.00	-	-	-	-
ALL ONE-DAY	5	5	0	174	53	34.80	-	1	-	-

BOWLING AVERAGES
Did not bowl

J.F. SYKES - *Durham*

Opposition	Venue	Date	Batting	Fielding	Bowling

NATWEST TROPHY
Lancashire	Old Trafford	June 27	4		1-16

BATTING AVERAGES - Including fielding
	Matches	Inns	NO	Runs	HS	Avge	100s	50s	Ct	St
NatWest Trophy	1	1	0	4	4	4.00	-	-	-	-
ALL ONE-DAY	1	1	0	4	4	4.00	-	-	-	-

BOWLING AVERAGES
	Overs	Mdns	Runs	Wkts	Avge	Best	5wI	10wM
NatWest Trophy	6	0	16	1	16.00	1-16	-	
ALL ONE-DAY	6	0	16	1	16.00	1-16	-	

PLAYER RECORDS

T

C.J. TAVARE - *Somerset*

Opposition	Venue	Date	Batting	Fielding	Bowling
BRITANNIC ASSURANCE					
Gloucs	Taunton	April 26	18	2Ct	
Glamorgan	Cardiff	May 3	120 *		0-1
Derbyshire	Taunton	May 19	64 & 9		0-43
Sussex	Taunton	May 23	28	1Ct	0-12
Leicestershire	Leicester	May 26	88	1Ct	
Gloucs	Bristol	June 2	30 & 1 *		
Hampshire	Basingstoke	June 6			
Kent	Canterbury	June 9	82	1Ct	
Essex	Bath	June 16	78 *		0-86
Glamorgan	Bath	June 20			
Northants	Taunton	June 30	39	1Ct	
Warwickshire	Taunton	July 4	23		
Worcestershire	Worcester	July 18	54 & 10		
Middlesex	Uxbridge	July 21	57 & 61	1Ct	0-20
Yorkshire	Scarborough	July 25	14 & 0		
Lancashire	Old Trafford	July 28	17 & 84 *		
Surrey	Weston	Aug 4	38 & 4		
Notts	Weston	Aug 8	96	1Ct	
Hampshire	Taunton	Aug 18	66 & 64		
Sussex	Hove	Aug 23	219	3Ct	
Warwickshire	Edgbaston	Sept 7	10 & 2	1Ct	
Worcestershire	Taunton	Sept 12	18 & 5	3Ct	
REFUGE ASSURANCE					
Worcestershire	Taunton	April 22	3		
Hampshire	Taunton	May 13	9	1Ct	
Derbyshire	Taunton	May 20	7		
Leicestershire	Leicester	May 27	26	1Ct	
Gloucs	Bristol	June 3	4		
Kent	Canterbury	June 10	11		
Essex	Bath	June 17	5		
Notts	Bath	June 24	86	1Ct	
Northants	Taunton	July 1	56		
Middlesex	Lord's	July 8	72 *		
Yorkshire	Scarborough	July 15	8	1Ct	
Glamorgan	Neath	July 22	10	2Ct	
Lancashire	Old Trafford	July 29	17		
Surrey	Weston	Aug 5	41		
Warwickshire	Weston	Aug 12	54	1Ct	
Sussex	Hove	Aug 26	12		
NATWEST TROPHY					
Devon	Torquay	June 27	162 *		
Worcestershire	Taunton	July 11	99 *		
BENSON & HEDGES CUP					
Derbyshire	Taunton	May 1	47 *		
Min Counties	Taunton	May 8	29	1Ct	
Middlesex	Lord's	May 10	93		
Sussex	Hove	May 12	5	1Ct	
Middlesex	Taunton	May 30	49		
Lancashire	Old Trafford	June 13	10		
OTHER FIRST-CLASS					
Oxford U	The Parks	April 18	83		
New Zealand	Taunton	May 16	156	1Ct	
OTHER ONE-DAY					
Sri Lanka	Taunton	Sept 3	5 *		

BATTING AVERAGES - Including fielding

	Matches	Inns	NO	Runs	HS	Avge	100s	50s	Ct	St
Britannic Assurance	22	30	4	1399	219	53.80	2	11	15	-
Refuge Assurance	16	16	1	421	86	28.06	-	4	7	-
NatWest Trophy	2	2	2	261	162 *	-	1	1	-	-
Benson & Hedges Cup	6	6	1	233	93	46.60	-	1	2	-
Other First-Class	2	2	0	239	156	119.50	1	1	1	-
Other One-Day	1	1	1	5	5 *	-	-	-	-	-
ALL FIRST-CLASS	24	32	4	1638	219	58.50	3	12	16	-
ALL ONE-DAY	25	25	5	920	162 *	46.00	1	6	9	-

BOWLING AVERAGES

	Overs	Mdns	Runs	Wkts	Avge	Best	5wI	10wM
Britannic Assurance	17.2	0	162	0	-	-	-	-
Refuge Assurance								
NatWest Trophy								
Benson & Hedges Cup								
Other First-Class								
Other One-Day								
ALL FIRST-CLASS	17.2	0	162	0	-	-	-	-
ALL ONE-DAY								

C.W. TAYLOR - *Middlesex*

Opposition	Venue	Date	Batting	Fielding	Bowling
BRITANNIC ASSURANCE					
Notts	Trent Bridge	July 28	13		0-45 & 0-15
Yorkshire	Headingley	Aug 23	0 *		1-46 & 5-33

BATTING AVERAGES - Including fielding

	Matches	Inns	NO	Runs	HS	Avge	100s	50s	Ct	St
Britannic Assurance	2	2	1	13	13	13.00	-	-	-	-
ALL FIRST-CLASS	2	2	1	13	13	13.00	-	-	-	-

BOWLING AVERAGES

	Overs	Mdns	Runs	Wkts	Avge	Best	5wI	10wM
Britannic Assurance	47.5	7	139	6	23.16	5-33	1	-
ALL FIRST-CLASS	47.5	7	139	6	23.16	5-33	1	-

J.P. TAYLOR - *Staffordshire*

Opposition	Venue	Date	Batting	Fielding	Bowling
NATWEST TROPHY					
Northants	Northampton	June 27	5		0-92

BATTING AVERAGES - Including fielding

	Matches	Inns	NO	Runs	HS	Avge	100s	50s	Ct	St
NatWest Trophy	1	1	0	5	5	5.00	-	-	-	-
ALL ONE-DAY	1	1	0	5	5	5.00	-	-	-	-

BOWLING AVERAGES

	Overs	Mdns	Runs	Wkts	Avge	Best	5wI	10wM
NatWest Trophy	12	0	92	0		-	-	
ALL ONE-DAY	12	0	92	0	-	-	-	

L.B. TAYLOR - *Leicestershire*

Opposition	Venue	Date	Batting	Fielding	Bowling
BRITANNIC ASSURANCE					
Derbyshire	Leicester	June 20			0-18 & 0-16
REFUGE ASSURANCE					
Northants	Leicester	April 22	0		0-34
Glamorgan	Cardiff	April 29	0 *		3-34
Essex	Leicester	May 6			0-41
Lancashire	Old Trafford	May 20			1-65
Hampshire	Leicester	June 3			1-35
Notts	Trent Bridge	July 1			1-35
BENSON & HEDGES CUP					
Northants	Leicester	April 24			1-32
Notts	Trent Bridge	May 1			1-34
Scotland	Leicester	May 12			3-65

BATTING AVERAGES - Including fielding

	Matches	Inns	NO	Runs	HS	Avge	100s	50s	Ct	St
Britannic Assurance	1	0	0	0	0	-	-	-	-	-
Refuge Assurance	6	2	1	0	0 *	0.00	-	-	-	-
Benson & Hedges Cup	3	0	0	0	0	-	-	-	-	-
ALL FIRST-CLASS	1	0	0	0	0	-	-	-	-	-
ALL ONE-DAY	9	2	1	0	0 *	0.00	-	-	-	-

T | PLAYER RECORDS

BOWLING AVERAGES

	Overs	Mdns	Runs	Wkts	Avge	Best	5wI	10wM
Britannic Assurance	9	1	34	0	-	-	-	-
Refuge Assurance	46	2	244	6	40.66	3-34	-	-
Benson & Hedges Cup	29.4	1	131	5	26.20	3-65	-	-
ALL FIRST-CLASS	9	1	34	0	-	-	-	-
ALL ONE-DAY	75.4	3	375	11	34.09	3-34	-	-

M.S. TAYLOR - *Norfolk*

Opposition	Venue	Date	Batting	Fielding	Bowling
NATWEST TROPHY					
Yorkshire	Headingley	June 27	0		0-32

BATTING AVERAGES - Including fielding

	Matches	Inns	NO	Runs	HS	Avge	100s	50s	Ct	St
NatWest Trophy	1	1	0	0	0	0.00	-	-	-	-
ALL ONE-DAY	1	1	0	0	0	0.00	-	-	-	-

BOWLING AVERAGES

	Overs	Mdns	Runs	Wkts	Avge	Best	5wI	10wM
NatWest Trophy	4	0	32	0	-	-	-	-
ALL ONE-DAY	4	0	32	0	-	-	-	-

N.R. TAYLOR - *Kent*

Opposition	Venue	Date	Batting			Fielding	Bowling
BRITANNIC ASSURANCE							
Hampshire	Canterbury	April 26	0	&	6		
Sussex	Folkestone	May 3	57	&	20		
Middlesex	Lord's	May 15	12	&	91	2Ct	
Glamorgan	Swansea	May 23	106				
Notts	Tunbridge We	June 2	1	&	21		
Yorkshire	Tunbridge We	June 6	124 *				
Somerset	Canterbury	June 9	9	&	5		0-29
Warwickshire	Edgbaston	June 23	25	&	28		1-19
Essex	Maidstone	June 4	6				
Northants	Northampton	July 18	97	&	36	1Ct	
Surrey	Guildford	July 21	69	&	26		0-1
Middlesex	Canterbury	July 25	152 *	&	3		
Worcestershire	Canterbury	July 28	64 *	&	73	1Ct	
Derbyshire	Chesterfield	Aug 4	18	&	12	1Ct	0-8
Leicestershire	Dartford	Aug 8	18	&	32		
Gloucs	Bristol	Aug 11	22				
Sussex	Hove	Aug 18	61	&	70 *		
Hampshire	Bournemouth	Aug 29			0	1Ct	
Surrey	Canterbury	Sept 7	204	&	142	1Ct	
Essex	Chelmsford	Sept 12	56	&	86	1Ct	
REFUGE ASSURANCE							
Essex	Chelmsford	April 22	58			1Ct	
Hampshire	Canterbury	April 29	95				
Middlesex	Folkestone	May 6	28				
Glamorgan	Llanelli	May 13	27			1Ct	
Yorkshire	Canterbury	May 20	35			1Ct	
Northants	Northampton	May 27	73			1Ct	
Somerset	Canterbury	June 10	59				
Notts	Canterbury	June 17	28			1Ct	
Warwickshire	Edgbaston	June 24	18				
Surrey	The Oval	July 22	26				
Derbyshire	Chesterfield	Aug 5	78				
Gloucs	Bristol	Aug 12	37				
Leicestershire	Leicester	Aug 26	52				
NATWEST TROPHY							
Oxfordshire	Oxford	June 27	13 *				
Gloucs	Bristol	July 11	0			1Ct	
BENSON & HEDGES CUP							
Worcestershire	Worcester	May 1	8				
Warwickshire	Canterbury	May 8	90				
Gloucs	Canterbury	May 10	19				
Glamorgan	Swansea	May 12	19				

OTHER FIRST-CLASS

Cambridge U	Fenner's	June 20	120		
India	Canterbury	July 7	107 *	1Ct	

OTHER ONE-DAY

Sussex	Hove	Sept 2	30	1Ct	1-30
Surrey	Hove	Sept 4	25		

BATTING AVERAGES - Including fielding

	Matches	Inns	NO	Runs	HS	Avge	100s	50s	Ct	St
Britannic Assurance	20	35	4	1752	204	56.51	5	10	8	-
Refuge Assurance	13	13	0	614	95	47.23	-	6	5	-
NatWest Trophy	2	2	1	13	13 *	13.00	-	-	1	-
Benson & Hedges Cup	4	3	0	117	90	39.00	-	1	-	-
Other First-Class	2	2	1	227	120	227.00	2	-	1	-
Other One-Day	2	2	0	55	30	27.50	-	-	1	-
ALL FIRST-CLASS	22	37	5	1979	204	61.84	7	10	9	-
ALL ONE-DAY	21	20	1	799	95	42.05	-	7	7	-

BOWLING AVERAGES

	Overs	Mdns	Runs	Wkts	Avge	Best	5wI	10wM
Britannic Assurance	21	5	57	1	57.00	1-19	-	-
Refuge Assurance								
NatWest Trophy								
Benson & Hedges Cup								
Other First-Class								
Other One-Day	6	0	30	1	30.00	1-30		-
ALL FIRST-CLASS	21	5	57	1	57.00	1-19	-	-
ALL ONE-DAY	6	0	30	1	30.00	1-30	-	-

N.R. TAYLOR - *Dorset & Middlesex*

Opposition	Venue	Date	Batting	Fielding	Bowling
BRITANNIC ASSURANCE					
Hampshire	Bournemouth	Aug 8	0	1Ct	3-44
REFUGE ASSURANCE					
Kent	Folkestone	May 6			1-47
Notts	Lord's	May 13	4 *	1Ct	0-34
Warwickshire	Lord's	June 3			1-16
Sussex	Lord's	Aug 12			1-38
Yorkshire	Scarborough	Aug 26	5 *		0-46
NATWEST TROPHY					
For Dorset					
Glamorgan	Swansea	June 27	7		0-55
BENSON & HEDGES CUP					
For Minor Counties					
Middlesex	Lord's	April 24			2-26
Sussex	Marlow	May 1		1Ct	0-37
Somerset	Taunton	May 8			2-50
Derbyshire	Wellington	May 10	3		3-52
OTHER FIRST-CLASS					
For Minor Counties					
India	Trowbridge	July 11	0		1-87

BATTING AVERAGES - Including fielding

	Matches	Inns	NO	Runs	HS	Avge	100s	50s	Ct	St
Britannic Assurance	1	1	0	0	0	0.00	-	-	1	-
Refuge Assurance	5	2	2	9	5 *	-	-	-	1	-
NatWest Trophy	1	1	0	7	7	7.00	-	-	-	-
Benson & Hedges Cup	4	1	0	3	3	3.00	-	-	1	-
Other First-Class	1	1	0	0	0	0.00	-	-	-	-
ALL FIRST-CLASS	2	2	0	0	0	0.00	-	-	1	-
ALL ONE-DAY	10	4	2	19	7	9.50	-	-	2	-

BOWLING AVERAGES

	Overs	Mdns	Runs	Wkts	Avge	Best	5wI	10wM
Britannic Assurance	14	5	44	3	14.66	3-44	-	-
Refuge Assurance	34.5	0	181	3	60.33	1-16	-	-
NatWest Trophy	10	0	55	0	-	-	-	-
Benson & Hedges Cup	41	5	165	7	23.57	3-52	-	-
Other First-Class	23	2	87	1	87.00	1-87	-	-
ALL FIRST-CLASS	37	7	131	4	32.75	3-44	-	-
ALL ONE-DAY	85.5	5	401	10	40.10	3-52	-	-

PLANER RECORDS...

PLAYER RECORDS

T

G.A. TEDSTONE - *Gloucestershire*

Opposition	Venue	Date	Batting	Fielding	Bowling
BRITANNIC ASSURANCE					
Essex	Ilford	June 6	13	1Ct	0-1
Lancashire	Old Trafford	June 9	6	1Ct	
Hampshire	Gloucester	June 20			
Leicestershire	Gloucester	June 23	23	1Ct	
REFUGE ASSURANCE					
Lancashire	Old Trafford	June 10	1 *		
Leicestershire	Gloucester	June 24	25		
OTHER FIRST-CLASS					
Zimbabwe	Bristol	May 19	23	2Ct,1St	
Cambridge U	Fenner's	May 23	23	4Ct	

BATTING AVERAGES - Including fielding

	Matches	Inns	NO	Runs	HS	Avge	100s	50s	Ct	St
Britannic Assurance	4	3	0	42	23	14.00	-	-	3	-
Refuge Assurance	2	2	1	26	25	26.00	-	-	-	-
Other First-Class	2	2	0	46	23	23.00	-	-	6	1
ALL FIRST-CLASS	6	5	0	88	23	17.60	-	-	9	1
ALL ONE-DAY	2	2	1	26	25	26.00	-	-	-	-

BOWLING AVERAGES

	Overs	Mdns	Runs	Wkts	Avge	Best	5wI	10wM
Britannic Assurance	2	1	1	0	-	-	-	-
Refuge Assurance								
Other First-Class								
ALL FIRST-CLASS	2	1	1	0	-	-	-	-
ALL ONE-DAY								

S.R. TENDULKAR - *India*

Opposition	Venue	Date	Batting	Fielding	Bowling
CORNHILL TEST MATCHES					
England	Lord's	July 26	10 & 27	1Ct	
England	Old Trafford	Aug 9	68 & 119 *	2Ct	
England	The Oval	Aug 23	21		
TEXACO TROPHY					
England	Headingley	July 18	19		
England	Trent Bridge	July 20	31		0-10
OTHER FIRST-CLASS					
Hampshire	Southampton	July 4	32 & 58 *		
Kent	Canterbury	July 7	92 & 70	1Ct	
Min Counties	Trowbridge	July 11	65		0-3
Leicestershire	Leicester	July 21	30 & 25 *	1Ct	0-9
Gloucs	Bristol	Aug 4	13 & 47		3-79 & 0-6
TCCB U25 XI	Edgbaston	Aug 15	39 & 30 *		0-40 & 0-24
Glamorgan	Swansea	Aug 18	68		0-5
World XI	Scarborough	Aug 29	23 & 108		0-70 & 0-32
OTHER ONE-DAY					
League CC	Sunderland	June 28	19		0-16
Scotland	Glasgow	July 14	10 *	1Ct	0-9
Derbyshire	Chesterfield	July 16	105 *		

BATTING AVERAGES - Including fielding

	Matches	Inns	NO	Runs	HS	Avge	100s	50s	Ct	St
Cornhill Test Matches	3	5	1	245	119 *	61.25	1	1	3	-
Texaco Trophy	2	2	0	50	31	25.00	-	-	-	-
Other First-Class	8	14	3	700	108	63.63	1	5	2	-
Other One-Day	3	3	2	134	105 *	134.00	1	-	1	-
ALL FIRST-CLASS	11	19	4	945	119 *	63.00	2	6	5	-
ALL ONE-DAY	5	5	2	184	105 *	61.33	1	-	1	-

BOWLING AVERAGES

	Overs	Mdns	Runs	Wkts	Avge	Best	5wI	10wM
Cornhill Test Matches								
Texaco Trophy	1	0	10	0	-	-	-	-
Other First-Class	79	12	268	3	89.33	3-79	-	-
Other One-Day	9	2	25	0	-	-	-	-
ALL FIRST-CLASS	79	12	268	3	89.33	3-79	-	-
ALL ONE-DAY	10	2	35	0	-	-	-	-

V.P. TERRY - *Hampshire*

Opposition	Venue	Date	Batting	Fielding	Bowling
BRITANNIC ASSURANCE					
Kent	Canterbury	April 26	107 & 17	2Ct	
Sussex	Southampton	May 15	40	1Ct	
Surrey	The Oval	May 19	8 & 0	1Ct	
Essex	Southampton	May 23	14 & 12		
Yorkshire	Headingley	May 26	23 & 18	2Ct	
Leicestershire	Leicester	June 2	7	2Ct	
Somerset	Basingstoke	June 6	64 & 6		0-19
Glamorgan	Southampton	June 16	52 & 25 *	2Ct	
Gloucs	Gloucester	June 20			
Lancashire	Old Trafford	June 23	15 & 0		
Notts	Portsmouth	July 18	0	2Ct	
Warwickshire	Edgbaston	July 28	119 * & 19 *	1Ct	
Northants	Bournemouth	Aug 4	165	1Ct	
Middlesex	Bournemouth	Aug 8	31	1Ct	
Worcestershire	Worcester	Aug 11	40 & 42		
Somerset	Taunton	Aug 18	96 & 59		
Surrey	Southampton	Aug 23	8 & 6	1Ct	
Glamorgan	Pontypridd	Sept 7	36 & 8	3Ct	
Gloucs	Southampton	Sept 18	1 & 46	2Ct	
REFUGE ASSURANCE					
Kent	Canterbury	April 29	9	2Ct	
Gloucs	Southampton	May 6	6		
Somerset	Taunton	May 13	113 *	1Ct	
Yorkshire	Headingley	May 27	56		
Leicestershire	Leicester	June 3	2		
Middlesex	Basingstoke	June 10	4		
Glamorgan	Bournemouth	June 17	2	2Ct	
Lancashire	Old Trafford	June 24			
Sussex	Hove	July 1	25		
Essex	Southampton	July 8	52	1Ct	
Notts	Southampton	July 15	3	1Ct	
Warwickshire	Edgbaston	July 29	53		
Northants	Bournemouth	Aug 5	84		
Worcestershire	Worcester	Aug 12	17	4Ct	
Surrey	Southampton	Aug 26	56		
NATWEST TROPHY					
Leicestershire	Leicester	June 27	21		
Essex	Chelmsford	July 11	76		
Yorkshire	Southampton	Aug 1	16	1Ct	
Northants	Southampton	Aug 15	24		
BENSON & HEDGES CUP					
Yorkshire	Southampton	April 24	15		
Surrey	The Oval	May 1	24	2Ct	
Lancashire	Old Trafford	May 8	7	1Ct	
Combined U	Southampton	May 12	134		
OTHER FIRST-CLASS					
Oxford U	The Parks	May 3	112		
India	Southampton	July 4	5 & 11	3Ct	
Sri Lanka	Southampton	Sept 12	120		
OTHER ONE-DAY					
For MCC					
New Zealand	Lord's	May 7	4		
For Hampshire					
Worcestershire	Scarborough	Sept 2	95	2Ct	
Essex	Scarborough	Sept 4	1		

BATTING AVERAGES - Including fielding

	Matches	Inns	NO	Runs	HS	Avge	100s	50s	Ct	St
Britannic Assurance	19	31	3	1084	165	38.71	3	4	21	-
Refuge Assurance	15	14	1	482	113 *	37.07	1	5	11	-
NatWest Trophy	4	4	0	137	76	34.25	-	1	1	-
Benson & Hedges Cup	4	4	0	180	134	45.00	1	-	3	-
Other First-Class	3	4	0	248	120	62.00	2	-	3	-
Other One-Day	3	3	0	100	95	33.33	-	1	2	-
ALL FIRST-CLASS	22	35	3	1332	165	41.62	5	4	24	-
ALL ONE-DAY	26	25	1	899	134	37.45	2	7	17	-

T PLAYER RECORDS

BOWLING AVERAGES

	Overs	Mdns	Runs	Wkts	Avge	Best	5wI	10wM
Britannic Assurance	1	0	19	0	-	-	-	-
Refuge Assurance								
NatWest Trophy								
Benson & Hedges Cup								
Other First-Class								
Other One-Day								
ALL FIRST-CLASS	1	0	19	0	-	-	-	-
ALL ONE-DAY								

D.R. THOMAS - *Norfolk & Minor Counties*

Opposition	Venue	Date	Batting	Fielding	Bowling
NATWEST TROPHY					
Yorkshire	Headingley	June 27	5		
BENSON & HEDGES CUP					
For Minor Counties					
Somerset	Taunton	May 8	49*		0-29
Derbyshire	Wellington	May 10	14		1-24
OTHER FIRST-CLASS					
For Minor Counties					
India	Trowbridge	July 11	27		0-65

BATTING AVERAGES - Including fielding

	Matches	Inns	NO	Runs	HS	Avge	100s	50s	Ct	St
NatWest Trophy	1	1	0	5	5	5.00	-	-	-	-
Benson & Hedges Cup	2	2	1	63	49*	63.00	-	-	-	-
Other First-Class	1	1	0	27	27	27.00	-	-	-	-
ALL FIRST-CLASS	1	1	0	27	27	27.00	-	-	-	-
ALL ONE-DAY	3	3	1	68	49*	34.00	-	-	-	-

BOWLING AVERAGES

	Overs	Mdns	Runs	Wkts	Avge	Best	5wI	10wM
NatWest Trophy								
Benson & Hedges Cup	16	3	53	1	53.00	1-24	-	
Other First-Class	15	1	65	0	-	-	-	
ALL FIRST-CLASS	15	1	65	0	-	-	-	
ALL ONE-DAY	16	3	53	1	53.00	1-24	-	

J.G. THOMAS - *Northamptonshire*

Opposition	Venue	Date	Batting	Fielding	Bowling
BRITANNIC ASSURANCE					
Yorkshire	Headingley	April 26		1Ct	1-45 & 3-47
Warwickshire	Northampton	May 15	30 & 14*		2-84
Notts	Trent Bridge	May 23	5	1Ct	1-41 & 0-54
Warwickshire	Edgbaston	June 2	9	1Ct	0-29 & 4-53
Leicestershire	Northampton	June 6			2-74 & 0-12
Glamorgan	Northampton	June 9	0*		7-75 & 0-68
Middlesex	Luton	June 23	0 & 5		0-40 & 0-38
Somerset	Taunton	June 30	48		2-76
Gloucs	Northampton	Aug 23	0 & 5		0-58 & 1-59
Essex	Northampton	Aug 29			0-60 & 1-49
Essex	Chelmsford	Sept 7	15	4Ct	3-64 & 1-72
REFUGE ASSURANCE					
Leicestershire	Leicester	April 22			3-27
Warwickshire	Edgbaston	April 29			0-37
Derbyshire	Northampton	May 6	9		1-39
Kent	Northampton	May 27	1		0-46
Surrey	The Oval	June 3	0		3-21
Glamorgan	Northampton	June 10	0*		0-42
Middlesex	Northampton	June 24	2		0-20
Somerset	Taunton	July 1	19*		1-38
Gloucs	Northampton	Aug 26	4	1Ct	2-43
NATWEST TROPHY					
Staffordshire	Northampton	June 27		1Ct	1-21
BENSON & HEDGES CUP					
Leicestershire	Leicester	April 24			2-59

Essex	Northampton	May 8	3		0-48
Scotland	Northampton	May 10	32		0-52
Notts	Trent Bridge	May 12	0	1Ct	4-45
OTHER FIRST-CLASS					
Cambridge U	Fenner's	April 14	13* & 8	2Ct	1-47 & 0-26

BATTING AVERAGES - Including fielding

	Matches	Inns	NO	Runs	HS	Avge	100s	50s	Ct	St
Britannic Assurance	11	11	2	131	48	14.55	-	-	7	-
Refuge Assurance	9	7	2	35	19*	7.00	-	-	1	-
NatWest Trophy	1	0	0	0	0	-	-	-	1	-
Benson & Hedges Cup	4	3	0	35	32	11.66	-	-	1	-
Other First-Class	1	2	1	21	13*	21.00	-	-	2	-
ALL FIRST-CLASS	12	13	3	152	48	15.20	-	-	9	-
ALL ONE-DAY	14	10	2	70	32	8.75	-	-	3	-

BOWLING AVERAGES

	Overs	Mdns	Runs	Wkts	Avge	Best	5wI	10wM
Britannic Assurance	288.2	49	1098	28	39.21	7-75	1	-
Refuge Assurance	59	3	313	10	31.30	3-21	-	
NatWest Trophy	10	2	21	1	21.00	1-21	-	
Benson & Hedges Cup	39	0	204	6	34.00	4-45	-	
Other First-Class	17	2	73	1	73.00	1-47	-	
ALL FIRST-CLASS	305.2	51	1171	29	40.37	7-75	1	-
ALL ONE-DAY	108	5	538	17	31.64	4-45	-	

K.O. THOMAS - *Essex*

Opposition	Venue	Date	Batting	Fielding	Bowling
OTHER FIRST-CLASS					
New Zealand	Chelmsford	June 30	2		0-76 & 0-5

BATTING AVERAGES - Including fielding

	Matches	Inns	NO	Runs	HS	Avge	100s	50s	Ct	St
Other First-Class	1	1	0	2	2	2.00	-	-	-	-
ALL FIRST-CLASS	1	1	0	2	2	2.00	-	-	-	-

BOWLING AVERAGES

	Overs	Mdns	Runs	Wkts	Avge	Best	5wI	10wM
Other First-Class	18.2	3	81	0	-	-	-	-
ALL FIRST-CLASS	18.2	3	81	0	-	-	-	-

J. THOMPSON - *Wiltshire*

Opposition	Venue	Date	Batting	Fielding	Bowling
NATWEST TROPHY					
Surrey	Trowbridge	June 27	7		0-40

BATTING AVERAGES - Including fielding

	Matches	Inns	NO	Runs	HS	Avge	100s	50s	Ct	St
NatWest Trophy	1	1	0	7	7	7.00	-	-	-	-
ALL ONE-DAY	1	1	0	7	7	7.00	-	-	-	-

BOWLING AVERAGES

	Overs	Mdns	Runs	Wkts	Avge	Best	5wI	10wM
NatWest Trophy	8	0	40	0	-	-	-	
ALL ONE-DAY	8	0	40	0	-	-	-	

N.E. THOMPSON - *Ireland*

Opposition	Venue	Date	Batting	Fielding	Bowling
OTHER ONE-DAY					
New Zealand	Downpatrick	May 9	2		1-23
New Zealand	Belfast	May 10	8	1Ct	1-35

PLAYER RECORDS

BATTING AVERAGES - Including fielding

	Matches	Inns	NO	Runs	HS	Avge	100s	50s	Ct	St
Other One-Day	2	2	0	10	8	5.00	-	-	1	-
ALL ONE-DAY	2	2	0	10	8	5.00	-	-	1	-

BOWLING AVERAGES

	Overs	Mdns	Runs	Wkts	Avge	Best	5wI	10wM
Other One-Day	17	0	58	2	29.00	1-23	-	
ALL ONE-DAY	17	0	58	2	29.00	1-23	-	

S.A. THOMSON - *New Zealand*

Opposition	Venue	Date	Batting	Fielding	Bowling
OTHER FIRST-CLASS					
Somerset	Taunton	May 16	4 *		1-104
Sussex	Hove	May 26	3 *		1-52
Northants	Northampton	June 16	4 *		0-65 & 1-97
Combined U	Fenner's	June 27	1 * & 20	3Ct	0-19 & 0-14
Essex	Chelmsford	June 30		2Ct	2-84
OTHER ONE-DAY					
D of Norfolk	Arundel	May 6			0-58
MCC	Lord's	May 7	5		0-40
Ireland	Downpatrick	May 9	1 *		0-30
Leicestershire	Leicester	June 14	25		1-42

BATTING AVERAGES - Including fielding

	Matches	Inns	NO	Runs	HS	Avge	100s	50s	Ct	St
Other First-Class	5	5	4	32	20	32.00	-	-	5	-
Other One-Day	4	3	1	31	25	15.50	-	-	-	-
ALL FIRST-CLASS	5	5	4	32	20	32.00	-	-	5	-
ALL ONE-DAY	4	3	1	31	25	15.50	-	-	-	-

BOWLING AVERAGES

	Overs	Mdns	Runs	Wkts	Avge	Best	5wI	10wM
Other First-Class	106.2	18	435	5	87.00	2-84	-	-
Other One-Day	40.5	6	170	1	170.00	1-42	-	
ALL FIRST-CLASS	106.2	18	435	5	87.00	2-84	-	-
ALL ONE-DAY	40.5	6	170	1	170.00	1-42	-	

G.P. THORPE - *Surrey*

Opposition	Venue	Date	Batting	Fielding	Bowling
BRITANNIC ASSURANCE					
Sussex	Hove	April 26	9 & 23 *		
Lancashire	The Oval	May 3	27		0-46
Hampshire	The Oval	May 19	2 & 18		
Middlesex	Lord's	May 23	16		
Derbyshire	The Oval	June 6	58 *		
Yorkshire	Harrogate	June 9		44	
Worcestershire	The Oval	June 16		0	
Notts	Trent Bridge	June 20	20	2Ct	
Glamorgan	Cardiff	June 30	40 * & 4	1Ct	
Northants	The Oval	July 4	15 *		
Warwickshire	The Oval	July 7	9 & 3	1Ct	
Sussex	Guildford	July 18	33 & 79		
Kent	Guildford	July 21	42	1Ct	0-23
Gloucs	Cheltenham	July 28	0 & 0	2Ct	
Somerset	Weston	Aug 4	9 & 86		
Essex	Chelmsford	Aug 18	0 & 0	1Ct	
REFUGE ASSURANCE					
Sussex	Hove	April 29	53		
Lancashire	The Oval	May 6	11		
Notts	Trent Bridge	May 20	0		
Northants	The Oval	June 3	2		
Yorkshire	Hull	June 10	46 *		
Worcestershire	The Oval	June 17	55		
Derbyshire	The Oval	June 24	27		
Glamorgan	Cardiff	July 1	11 *		

Warwickshire	The Oval	July 8	35		
Middlesex	The Oval	July 15	41	1Ct	
Kent	The Oval	July 22	69 *		
Gloucs	Cheltenham	July 29	11		
Somerset	Weston	Aug 5	42		
Leicestershire	The Oval	Aug 12	85	1Ct	
Hampshire	Southampton	Aug 26	26		
NATWEST TROPHY					
Wiltshire	Trowbridge	June 27	15 *	1Ct	
Middlesex	Uxbridge	July 11	16		
BENSON & HEDGES CUP					
Lancashire	Old Trafford	April 24	8		1-30
Hampshire	The Oval	May 1	50 *		
Combined U	The Parks	May 10	8		0-15
Yorkshire	The Oval	May 12	14		
Lancashire	Old Trafford	May 30	9		
OTHER FIRST-CLASS					
Oxford U	The Parks	May 16	46 * & 2 *	1Ct	1-30
For TCCB U25 XI					
India	Edgbaston	Aug 15	18 & 5		
OTHER ONE-DAY					
Warwickshire	Harrogate	June 13	0		
Sri Lanka	The Oval	Sept 2	63		0-15
Warwickshire	Hove	Sept 3	30		0-21
Kent	Hove	Sept 4	78		

BATTING AVERAGES - Including fielding

	Matches	Inns	NO	Runs	HS	Avge	100s	50s	Ct	St
Britannic Assurance	16	24	4	537	86	26.85	-	3	8	-
Refuge Assurance	15	15	3	514	85	42.83	-	4	2	-
NatWest Trophy	2	2	1	31	16	31.00	-	-	1	-
Benson & Hedges Cup	5	5	1	89	50 *	22.25	-	1	-	-
Other First-Class	2	4	2	71	46 *	35.50	-	-	1	-
Other One-Day	4	4	0	171	78	42.75	-	2	-	-
ALL FIRST-CLASS	18	28	6	608	86	27.63	-	3	9	-
ALL ONE-DAY	26	26	5	805	85	38.33	-	7	3	-

BOWLING AVERAGES

	Overs	Mdns	Runs	Wkts	Avge	Best	5wI	10wM
Britannic Assurance	9	1	69	0	-	-	-	-
Refuge Assurance								
NatWest Trophy								
Benson & Hedges Cup	7	0	45	1	45.00	1-30	-	
Other First-Class	14	6	30	1	30.00	1-30	-	
Other One-Day	7	1	36	0	-	-	-	
ALL FIRST-CLASS	23	7	99	1	99.00	1-30	-	-
ALL ONE-DAY	14	1	81	1	81.00	1-30	-	

P.W. THRELFALL - *Sussex*

Opposition	Venue	Date	Batting	Fielding	Bowling
OTHER FIRST-CLASS					
Sri Lanka	Hove	Sept 5			2-44 & 3-45
OTHER ONE-DAY					
Zimbabwe	Hove	May 13	17 *		3-40
Kent	Hove	Sept 2	0 *		1-55

BATTING AVERAGES - Including fielding

	Matches	Inns	NO	Runs	HS	Avge	100s	50s	Ct	St
Other First-Class	1	0	0	0	0	-	-	-	-	-
Other One-Day	2	2	2	17	17 *	-	-	-	-	-
ALL FIRST-CLASS	1	0	0	0	0	-	-	-	-	-
ALL ONE-DAY	2	2	2	17	17 *	-	-	-	-	-

BOWLING AVERAGES

	Overs	Mdns	Runs	Wkts	Avge	Best	5wI	10wM
Other First-Class	30	8	89	5	17.80	3-45	-	-
Other One-Day	20	0	95	4	23.75	3-40	-	
ALL FIRST-CLASS	30	8	89	5	17.80	3-45	-	-
ALL ONE-DAY	20	0	95	4	23.75	3-40	-	

T | PLAYER RECORDS

M.J. THURSFIELD - Middlesex

Opposition	Venue	Date	Batting	Fielding	Bowling
BRITANNIC ASSURANCE					
Essex	Ilford	June 2			1-24 & 0-21
OTHER FIRST-CLASS					
New Zealand	Lord's	May 19			0-41 & 1-44

BATTING AVERAGES - Including fielding

	Matches	Inns	NO	Runs	HS	Avge	100s	50s	Ct	St
Britannic Assurance	1	0	0	0	0	-	-	-	-	-
Other First-Class	1	0	0	0	0	-	-	-	-	-
ALL FIRST-CLASS	2	0	0	0	0	-	-	-	-	-

BOWLING AVERAGES

	Overs	Mdns	Runs	Wkts	Avge	Best	5wI	10wM
Britannic Assurance	17	4	45	1	45.00	1-24	-	-
Other First-Class	25	7	85	1	85.00	1-44	-	-
ALL FIRST-CLASS	42	11	130	2	65.00	1-24	-	-

J.K. TIERNEY - Devon

Opposition	Venue	Date	Batting	Fielding	Bowling
NATWEST TROPHY					
Somerset	Torquay	June 27	0		0-62

BATTING AVERAGES - Including fielding

	Matches	Inns	NO	Runs	HS	Avge	100s	50s	Ct	St
NatWest Trophy	1	1	0	0	0	0.00	-	-	-	-
ALL ONE-DAY	1	1	0	0	0	0.00	-	-	-	-

BOWLING AVERAGES

	Overs	Mdns	Runs	Wkts	Avge	Best	5wI	10wM
NatWest Trophy	11	2	62	0	-	-	-	-
ALL ONE-DAY	11	2	62	0	-	-	-	-

H.P. TILLEKARATNE - Sri Lanka

Opposition	Venue	Date	Batting	Fielding	Bowling
OTHER FIRST-CLASS					
Glamorgan	Ebbw Vale	Aug 22	30 & 5	1Ct,1St	
Notts	Cleethorpes	Aug 25	0 & 22	2Ct	
Warwickshire	Edgbaston	Aug 29	109 * & 29 *	1Ct	
Lancashire	Old Trafford	Sept 8	44	2Ct,1St	
Hampshire	Southampton	Sept 12	10 & 100	1Ct	
OTHER ONE-DAY					
Surrey	The Oval	Sept 2	45	1Ct	
Somerset	Taunton	Sept 3	23		

BATTING AVERAGES - Including fielding

	Matches	Inns	NO	Runs	HS	Avge	100s	50s	Ct	St
Other First-Class	5	9	2	349	109 *	49.85	2	-	7	2
Other One-Day	2	2	0	68	45	34.00	-	-	1	-
ALL FIRST-CLASS	5	9	2	349	109 *	49.85	2	-	7	2
ALL ONE-DAY	2	2	0	68	45	34.00	-	-	1	-

BOWLING AVERAGES
Did not bowl

S.P. TITCHARD - Lancashire

Opposition	Venue	Date	Batting	Fielding	Bowling
OTHER FIRST-CLASS					
Zimbabwe	Old Trafford	May 23	15 & 80		
Oxford U	The Parks	June 16	22		
Sri Lanka	Old Trafford	Sept 8	11 & 1		

BATTING AVERAGES - Including fielding

	Matches	Inns	NO	Runs	HS	Avge	100s	50s	Ct	St
Other First-Class	3	5	0	129	80	25.80	-	1	-	-
ALL FIRST-CLASS	3	5	0	129	80	25.80	-	1	-	-

BOWLING AVERAGES
Did not bowl

C.M. TOLLEY - Worcestershire & Comb U

Opposition	Venue	Date	Batting	Fielding	Bowling
BRITANNIC ASSURANCE					
Gloucs	Worcester	July 7	29		0-7 & 0-20
Somerset	Worcester	July 18		1Ct	1-84 & 2-66
Derbyshire	Derby	July 25	16		
Kent	Canterbury	July 28	4 & 0		0-29 & 1-25
Lancashire	Kid'minster	Aug 8	28 *		0-41 & 1-39
Hampshire	Worcester	Aug 11	2	1Ct	0-15
REFUGE ASSURANCE					
Gloucs	Worcester	July 8			1-26
Lancashire	Old Trafford	July 15	1 *		1-20
Hampshire	Worcester	Aug 12	1		
NATWEST TROPHY					
Somerset	Taunton	July 11			0-32
BENSON & HEDGES CUP					
Lancashire	Fenner's	May 1	77		0-26
Yorkshire	Headingley	May 8	6	1Ct	0-38
Surrey	The Parks	May 10	14		0-43
Hampshire	Southampton	May 12	74		0-62

BATTING AVERAGES - Including fielding

	Matches	Inns	NO	Runs	HS	Avge	100s	50s	Ct	St
Britannic Assurance	6	6	1	79	29	15.80	-	-	2	-
Refuge Assurance	3	2	1	2	1 *	2.00	-	-	-	-
NatWest Trophy	1	0	0	0	0	-	-	-	-	-
Benson & Hedges Cup	4	4	0	171	77	42.75	-	2	1	-
ALL FIRST-CLASS	6	6	1	79	29	15.80	-	-	2	-
ALL ONE-DAY	8	6	1	173	77	34.60	-	2	1	-

BOWLING AVERAGES

	Overs	Mdns	Runs	Wkts	Avge	Best	5wI	10wM
Britannic Assurance	88	14	326	5	65.20	2-66	-	-
Refuge Assurance	14	0	46	2	23.00	1-20	-	
NatWest Trophy	6	0	32	0	-	-		
Benson & Hedges Cup	38	6	169	0	-	-		
ALL FIRST-CLASS	88	14	326	5	65.20	2-66	-	-
ALL ONE-DAY	58	6	247	2	123.50	1-20	-	

T.D. TOPLEY - Essex

Opposition	Venue	Date	Batting	Fielding	Bowling
BRITANNIC ASSURANCE					
Middlesex	Lord's	April 26		1Ct	2-79 & 0-42
Worcestershire	Worcester	May 19			4-67 & 1-44
Hampshire	Southampton	May 23	23	1Ct	0-53 & 0-3
Somerset	Bath	June 16			1-48
Kent	Maidstone	June 4		1Ct	0-60
Leicestershire	Leicester	July 25	23 & 2	1Ct	3-69 & 0-22
Sussex	Chelmsford	July 28	7 *	1Ct	3-36 & 2-34

PLACE RECORDS

REFUGE ASSURANCE

Opposition	Venue	Date	Batting	Fielding	Bowling
Kent	Chelmsford	April 22	3 *		0-38
Middlesex	Lord's	April 29	10		2-37
Leicestershire	Leicester	May 6	1 *	1Ct	0-49
Gloucs	Chelmsford	May 13		1Ct	0-51
Worcestershire	Worcester	May 20	0		1-39
Glamorgan	Ilford	June 3		1Ct	2-23
Warwickshire	Edgbaston	June 10			1-27
Somerset	Bath	June 17			2-22
Hampshire	Southampton	July 8	2		1-32
Northants	Chelmsford	July 15			1-34
Sussex	Chelmsford	July 29	0		2-43
Notts	Southend	Aug 5	2		1-45
Yorkshire	Middlesbr'gh	Aug 12	4		0-48

NATWEST TROPHY

Scotland	Chelmsford	June 27			0-32
Hampshire	Chelmsford	July 11		2Ct	0-66

BENSON & HEDGES CUP

Notts	Chelmsford	April 24			1-16
Scotland	Glasgow	May 1			0-35
Northants	Northampton	May 8		1Ct	0-25
Notts	Chelmsford	May 30	10 *		0-25

OTHER FIRST-CLASS

Cambridge U	Fenner's	May 16	0	1Ct	2-25 & 1-29
New Zealand	Chelmsford	June 30	23 *		2-57 & 1-45

OTHER ONE-DAY

Zimbabwe	Chelmsford	May 14			0-29
Yorkshire	Scarborough	Sept 3	0 *	1Ct	1-15
Hampshire	Scarborough	Sept 4	1		1-19

BATTING AVERAGES - Including fielding

	Matches	Inns	NO	Runs	HS	Avge	100s	50s	Ct	St
Britannic Assurance	7	4	1	55	23	18.33	-	-	5	-
Refuge Assurance	13	8	2	22	10	3.66	-	-	3	-
NatWest Trophy	2	0	0	0	0	-	-	-	2	-
Benson & Hedges Cup	4	1	1	10	10 *	-	-	-	1	-
Other First-Class	2	2	1	23	23 *	23.00	-	-	1	-
Other One-Day	3	2	1	1	1	1.00	-	-	1	-
ALL FIRST-CLASS	9	6	2	78	23 *	19.50	-	-	6	-
ALL ONE-DAY	22	11	4	33	10 *	4.71	-	-	7	-

BOWLING AVERAGES

	Overs	Mdns	Runs	Wkts	Avge	Best	5wI	10wM
Britannic Assurance	178	25	557	16	34.81	4-67	-	-
Refuge Assurance	93.5	2	488	13	37.53	2-22	-	
NatWest Trophy	18	0	98	0	-			
Benson & Hedges Cup	31	2	101	1	101.00	1-16	-	
Other First-Class	45	8	156	6	26.00	2-25	-	-
Other One-Day	18	1	63	2	31.50	1-15	-	
ALL FIRST-CLASS	223	33	713	22	32.40	4-67	-	-
ALL ONE-DAY	160.5	5	750	16	46.87	2-22	-	

G.T.J. TOWNSEND - *Somerset*

Opposition	Venue	Date	Batting	Fielding	Bowling

BRITANNIC ASSURANCE

Sussex	Hove	Aug 23	0 & 0 *	2Ct	
Warwickshire	Edgbaston	Sept 7	15 & 6	1Ct	

OTHER ONE-DAY

Sri Lanka	Taunton	Sept 3	77		

BATTING AVERAGES - Including fielding

	Matches	Inns	NO	Runs	HS	Avge	100s	50s	Ct	St
Britannic Assurance	2	4	1	21	15	7.00	-	-	3	-
Other One-Day	1	1	0	77	77	77.00	-	1	-	-
ALL FIRST-CLASS	2	4	1	21	15	7.00	-	-	3	-
ALL ONE-DAY	1	1	0	77	77	77.00	-	1	-	-

BOWLING AVERAGES
Did not bowl

A.J. TRAICOS - *Zimbabwe*

Opposition	Venue	Date	Batting	Fielding	Bowling

OTHER FIRST-CLASS

Gloucs	Bristol	May 19	1	2Ct	0-30 & 3-43
Lancashire	Old Trafford	May 23		3Ct	1-44 & 0-69

OTHER ONE-DAY

Sussex	Hove	May 13	0		2-42
Essex	Chelmsford	May 14	8 *		0-45

BATTING AVERAGES - Including fielding

	Matches	Inns	NO	Runs	HS	Avge	100s	50s	Ct	St
Other First-Class	2	1	0	1	1	1.00	-	-	5	-
Other One-Day	2	2	1	8	8 *	8.00	-	-	-	-
ALL FIRST-CLASS	2	1	0	1	1	1.00	-	-	5	-
ALL ONE-DAY	2	2	1	8	8 *	8.00	-	-	-	-

BOWLING AVERAGES

	Overs	Mdns	Runs	Wkts	Avge	Best	5wI	10wM
Other First-Class	84	22	186	4	46.50	3-43	-	
Other One-Day	22	0	87	2	43.50	2-42	-	
ALL FIRST-CLASS	84	22	186	4	46.50	3-43	-	
ALL ONE-DAY	22	0	87	2	43.50	2-42	-	

T.M. TREMLETT - *Hampshire*

Opposition	Venue	Date	Batting	Fielding	Bowling

BRITANNIC ASSURANCE

Leicestershire	Leicester	June 2	25 *		3-33 & 0-16
Somerset	Basingstoke	June 6	3 *		
Glamorgan	Southampton	June 16	14 *		0-19 & 0-80
Gloucs	Gloucester	June 20			0-9
Lancashire	Old Trafford	June 23		1Ct	0-6 & 0-13
Worcestershire	Worcester	Aug 11			3-61 & 0-22
Kent	Bournemouth	Aug 29	78		1-46 & 1-44
Glamorgan	Pontypridd	Sept 7	23		0-29 & 2-15

REFUGE ASSURANCE

Kent	Canterbury	April 29	18		1-22
Yorkshire	Headingley	May 27	2 *		2-19
Leicestershire	Leicester	June 3			2-28
Lancashire	Old Trafford	June 24			2-43
Essex	Southampton	July 8			2-43
Worcestershire	Worcester	Aug 12			3-22
Surrey	Southampton	Aug 26	21		2-33

OTHER ONE-DAY
For MCC

New Zealand	Lord's	May 7			2-50

For Hampshire

Worcestershire	Scarborough	Sept 2			2-24
Essex	Scarborough	Sept 4			1-16

BATTING AVERAGES - Including fielding

	Matches	Inns	NO	Runs	HS	Avge	100s	50s	Ct	St
Britannic Assurance	8	5	3	143	78	71.50	-	1	1	-
Refuge Assurance	7	3	1	41	21	20.50	-	-	-	-
Other One-Day	3	0	0	0	0	-	-	-	-	-
ALL FIRST-CLASS	8	5	3	143	78	71.50	-	1	1	-
ALL ONE-DAY	10	3	1	41	21	20.50	-	-	-	-

BOWLING AVERAGES

	Overs	Mdns	Runs	Wkts	Avge	Best	5wI	10wM
Britannic Assurance	120.5	30	393	10	39.30	3-33	-	-
Refuge Assurance	45	2	167	12	13.91	3-22	-	
Other One-Day	28.5	3	90	5	18.00	2-24	-	
ALL FIRST-CLASS	120.5	30	393	10	39.30	3-33	-	-
ALL ONE-DAY	73.5	5	257	17	15.11	3-22	-	

T	PLAYER RECORDS

B.W.D. TREVELYAN - *Oxford University*

Opposition	Venue	Date	Batting	Fielding	Bowling
OTHER FIRST-CLASS					
Glamorgan	The Parks	June 2	0	2Ct	
Notts	The Parks	June 6			
Cambridge U	Lord's	July 4			

BATTING AVERAGES - Including fielding

	Matches	Inns	NO	Runs	HS	Avge	100s	50s	Ct	St
Other First-Class	3	1	0	0	0	0.00	-	-	2	-
ALL FIRST-CLASS	3	1	0	0	0	0.00	-	-	2	-

BOWLING AVERAGES
Did not bowl

H.R.J. TRUMP - *Somerset*

Opposition	Venue	Date	Batting	Fielding	Bowling
BRITANNIC ASSURANCE					
Hampshire	Basingstoke	June 6			0-24 & 0-46
Glamorgan	Bath	June 20			0-11
Middlesex	Uxbridge	July 21		1Ct	1-91 & 0-89
Lancashire	Old Trafford	July 28	1 & 4 *	1Ct	3-58
Notts	Weston	Aug 8	4		3-61 & 1-56
Sussex	Hove	Aug 23	0	1Ct	1-49
Warwickshire	Edgbaston	Sept 7	2		0-16 & 0-19
REFUGE ASSURANCE					
Warwickshire	Weston	Aug 12			0-43
Sussex	Hove	Aug 26	0		2-30

BATTING AVERAGES - Including fielding

	Matches	Inns	NO	Runs	HS	Avge	100s	50s	Ct	St
Britannic Assurance	7	5	1	11	4 *	2.75	-	-	3	-
Refuge Assurance	2	1	0	0	0	0.00	-	-	-	-
ALL FIRST-CLASS	7	5	1	11	4 *	2.75	-	-	3	-
ALL ONE-DAY	2	1	0	0	0	0.00	-	-	-	-

BOWLING AVERAGES

	Overs	Mdns	Runs	Wkts	Avge	Best	5wI	10wM
Britannic Assurance	164	41	520	9	57.77	3-58	-	-
Refuge Assurance	14	0	73	2	36.50	2-30	-	-
ALL FIRST-CLASS	164	41	520	9	57.77	3-58	-	-
ALL ONE-DAY	14	0	73	2	36.50	2-30	-	-

D. TUCKWELL - *League C.C. XI*

Opposition	Venue	Date	Batting	Fielding	Bowling
OTHER ONE-DAY					
India	Sunderland	June 28	17	1Ct	

BATTING AVERAGES - Including fielding

	Matches	Inns	NO	Runs	HS	Avge	100s	50s	Ct	St
Other One-Day	1	1	0	17	17	17.00	-	-	1	-
ALL ONE-DAY	1	1	0	17	17	17.00	-	-	1	-

BOWLING AVERAGES
Did not bowl

P.C.R. TUFNELL - *Middlesex*

Opposition	Venue	Date	Batting	Fielding	Bowling
BRITANNIC ASSURANCE					
Essex	Lord's	April 26	7 *		1-68 & 1-35
Surrey	Lord's	May 23	14 * & 1	1Ct	1-57 & 0-0
Gloucs	Lord's	May 26		1Ct	3-68 & 4-111
Essex	Ilford	June 2			0-54 & 2-73
Warwickshire	Lord's	June 6	11 *		2-111
Leicestershire	Leicester	June 16	37		0-15 & 2-39
Lancashire	Old Trafford	June 20			3-90
Northants	Luton	June 23	8	1Ct	3-80 & 5-57
Worcestershire	Lord's	June 30	3		0-25 & 1-68
Yorkshire	Uxbridge	July 18	10		2-67 & 3-49
Somerset	Uxbridge	July 21			3-140 & 1-96
Kent	Canterbury	July 25			0-69 & 1-35
Notts	Trent Bridge	July 28	12 & 5 *	1Ct	2-104 & 3-86
Glamorgan	Lord's	Aug 4	4 *		1-67 & 2-48
Hampshire	Bournemouth	Aug 8	28 * & 12	1Ct	6-79
Sussex	Lord's	Aug 11	3 * & 0 *		3-85
Derbyshire	Derby	Aug 18	10 & 5		0-38 & 1-29
Yorkshire	Headingley	Aug 23	37 & 5	1Ct	2-41 & 0-50
Notts	Lord's	Sept 7		1Ct	4-69 & 0-93
Surrey	The Oval	Sept 12	23 *		1-103 & 2-90
REFUGE ASSURANCE					
Glamorgan	Lord's	Aug 5			0-45
Sussex	Lord's	Aug 12	0 *		1-40
Lancashire	Old Trafford	Sept 5			0-57
NATWEST TROPHY					
Glamorgan	Lord's	Aug 1			2-22
BENSON & HEDGES CUP					
Min Counties	Lord's	April 24			1-42
Derbyshire	Derby	May 12	7 *		0-36
OTHER FIRST-CLASS					
For MCC					
Worcestershire	Lord's	April 17	12		0-13
For Middlesex					
Cambridge U	Fenner's	May 3	36	1Ct	1-36 & 3-57
New Zealand	Lord's	May 19			1-64 & 4-76
OTHER ONE-DAY					
For MCC					
New Zealand	Lord's	May 7		1Ct	0-42

BATTING AVERAGES - Including fielding

	Matches	Inns	NO	Runs	HS	Avge	100s	50s	Ct	St
Britannic Assurance	20	20	9	235	37	21.36	-	-	7	-
Refuge Assurance	3	1	1	0	0 *	-	-	-	-	-
NatWest Trophy	1	0	0	0	0	-	-	-	-	-
Benson & Hedges Cup	2	1	1	7	7 *	-	-	-	-	-
Other First-Class	3	2	0	48	36	24.00	-	-	1	-
Other One-Day	1	0	0	0	0	-	-	-	1	-
ALL FIRST-CLASS	23	22	9	283	37	21.76	-	-	8	-
ALL ONE-DAY	7	2	2	7	7 *	-	-	-	1	-

BOWLING AVERAGES

	Overs	Mdns	Runs	Wkts	Avge	Best	5wI	10wM
Britannic Assurance	948.5	254	2389	65	36.75	6-79	2	-
Refuge Assurance	23	0	142	1	142.00	1-40	-	
NatWest Trophy	12	2	22	2	11.00	2-22	-	
Benson & Hedges Cup	18	0	78	1	78.00	1-42	-	
Other First-Class	88	27	246	9	27.33	4-76	-	-
Other One-Day	11	1	42	0			-	
ALL FIRST-CLASS	1036.5	281	2635	74	35.60	6-79	2	-
ALL ONE-DAY	64	3	284	4	71.00	2-22	-	

D.R. TURNER - *Wiltshire*

Opposition	Venue	Date	Batting	Fielding	Bowling
NATWEST TROPHY					
Surrey	Trowbridge	June 27	18		

PLANER RECORDS

BATTING AVERAGES - Including fielding

	Matches	Inns	NO	Runs	HS	Avge	100s	50s	Ct	St
NatWest Trophy	1	1	0	18	18	18.00	-	-	-	-
ALL ONE-DAY	1	1	0	18	18	18.00	-	-	-	-

BOWLING AVERAGES
Did not bowl

G.J. TURNER - *Oxford University*

Opposition	Venue	Date	Batting		Fielding	Bowling
OTHER FIRST-CLASS						
Glamorgan	The Parks	April 14	5			1-52 & 0-21
Somerset	The Parks	April 18	0			1-41
Hampshire	The Parks	May 3	59		1Ct	2-148 & 2-61
Surrey	The Parks	May 16	34 &	3	2Ct	1-54 & 0-53
Leicestershire	The Parks	May 23	51 &	9		0-72
Glamorgan	The Parks	June 2	13		1Ct	0-78
Lancashire	The Parks	June 16	48			3-100
For Combined U						
New Zealand	Fenner's	June 27	14 &	26	1Ct	0-76 & 0-63
For Oxford U						
Cambridge U	Lord's	July 4	36			

BATTING AVERAGES - Including fielding

	Matches	Inns	NO	Runs	HS	Avge	100s	50s	Ct	St
Other First-Class	9	12	0	298	59	24.83	-	2	5	-
ALL FIRST-CLASS	9	12	0	298	59	24.83	-	2	5	-

BOWLING AVERAGES

	Overs	Mdns	Runs	Wkts	Avge	Best	5wI	10wM
Other First-Class	212.2	39	819	10	81.90	3-100	-	-
ALL FIRST-CLASS	212.2	39	819	10	81.90	3-100	-	-

I.J. TURNER - *Hampshire*

Opposition	Venue	Date	Batting		Fielding	Bowling
BRITANNIC ASSURANCE						
Sussex	Southampton	May 15	1		1Ct	1-13 & 2-60
Surrey	The Oval	May 19				0-45 & 2-60
Essex	Southampton	May 23			1Ct	0-48 & 0-18
Yorkshire	Headingley	May 26	0 *			1-63 & 1-19
OTHER FIRST-CLASS						
Oxford U	The Parks	May 3		14		2-98
OTHER ONE-DAY						
Essex	Scarborough	Sept 4			1Ct	2-44

BATTING AVERAGES - Including fielding

	Matches	Inns	NO	Runs	HS	Avge	100s	50s	Ct	St
Britannic Assurance	4	2	1	1	1	1.00	-	-	2	-
Other First-Class	1	1	0	14	14	14.00	-	-	-	-
Other One-Day	1	0	0	0	0		-	-	1	-
ALL FIRST-CLASS	5	3	1	15	14	7.50	-	-	2	-
ALL ONE-DAY	1	0	0	0	0		-	-	1	-

BOWLING AVERAGES

	Overs	Mdns	Runs	Wkts	Avge	Best	5wI	10wM
Britannic Assurance	108.2	28	326	7	46.57	2-60	-	-
Other First-Class	40	11	98	2	49.00	2-98	-	-
Other One-Day	8	0	44	2	22.00	2-44	-	
ALL FIRST-CLASS	148.2	39	424	9	47.11	2-60	-	-
ALL ONE-DAY	8	0	44	2	22.00	2-44	-	

R.J. TURNER - *Cambridge University*

Opposition	Venue	Date	Batting		Fielding	Bowling
BENSON & HEDGES CUP						
For Combined Universities						
Lancashire	Fenner's	May 1	12 *		2Ct	
Yorkshire	Headingley	May 8	12 *			
Surrey	The Parks	May 10	25 *		0Ct,1St	
Hampshire	Southampton	May 12	0			
OTHER FIRST-CLASS						
Northants	Fenner's	April 14	21		1Ct	
Derbyshire	Fenner's	April 18	18 &	0		
Warwickshire	Fenner's	April 26	12 &	28	2Ct	
Middlesex	Fenner's	May 3	26 &	34	1Ct,1St	
Notts	Fenner's	June 16	32 &	0	0Ct,1St	
Kent	Fenner's	June 20	22 &	35	0Ct,1St	
For Combined U						
New Zealand	Fenner's	June 27	5 &	10	2Ct	
For Cambridge U						
Sussex	Hove	June 30	38 &	14	1Ct	
Oxford U	Lord's	July 4		7	1Ct,1St	

BATTING AVERAGES - Including fielding

	Matches	Inns	NO	Runs	HS	Avge	100s	50s	Ct	St
Benson & Hedges Cup	4	4	3	49	25 *	49.00	-	-	2	1
Other First-Class	9	16	0	302	38	18.87	-	-	8	4
ALL FIRST-CLASS	9	16	0	302	38	18.87	-	-	8	4
ALL ONE-DAY	4	4	3	49	25 *	49.00	-	-	2	1

BOWLING AVERAGES
Did not bowl

R.C. TURPIN - *Devon*

Opposition	Venue	Date	Batting	Fielding	Bowling
NATWEST TROPHY					
Somerset	Torquay	June 27	4		

BATTING AVERAGES - Including fielding

	Matches	Inns	NO	Runs	HS	Avge	100s	50s	Ct	St
NatWest Trophy	1	1	0	4	4	4.00	-	-	-	-
ALL ONE-DAY	1	1	0	4	4	4.00	-	-	-	-

BOWLING AVERAGES
Did not bowl

R.G. TWOSE - *Warwickshire*

Opposition	Venue	Date	Batting		Fielding	Bowling
BRITANNIC ASSURANCE						
Derbyshire	Derby	June 16		1		1-82
Yorkshire	Sheffield	June 20	15			0-9
Kent	Edgbaston	June 23	51 &	12	2Ct	
Worcestershire	Worcester	Aug 23	9 &	0	1Ct	1-10
REFUGE ASSURANCE						
Northants	Edgbaston	April 29				
Yorkshire	Edgbaston	May 6				
Gloucs	Moreton-in-M	May 20	13		1Ct	0-14
Essex	Edgbaston	June 10	4			
Derbyshire	Derby	June 17	9			2-11
Kent	Edgbaston	June 24	5			1-35
Surrey	The Oval	July 8	40			1-29
Notts	Edgbaston	July 22	30 *			2-50
Hampshire	Edgbaston	July 29	5			0-47
Sussex	Eastbourne	Aug 5	1 *			
Somerset	Weston	Aug 12				0-21
Lancashire	Old Trafford	Aug 26	6			2-38

T	PLAYER RECORDS

NATWEST TROPHY
Hertfordshire	St Albans	June 27	1		1Ct	

BENSON & HEDGES CUP
Kent	Canterbury	May 8	2		1Ct	0-4
Worcestershire	Edgbaston	May 10	17		1Ct	0-12
Gloucs	Bristol	May 12				

OTHER FIRST-CLASS
New Zealand	Edgbaston	May 30	64 & 21		1-44
Sri Lanka	Edgbaston	Aug 29	64 * & 4		1-40

OTHER ONE-DAY
Surrey	Harrogate	June 13	36 *	
Yorkshire	Harrogate	June 15	2	
Surrey	Hove	Sept 3	8 *	2Ct

BATTING AVERAGES - Including fielding
	Matches	Inns	NO	Runs	HS	Avge	100s	50s	Ct	St
Britannic Assurance	4	6	0	88	51	14.66	-	1	3	-
Refuge Assurance	12	9	2	113	40	16.14	-	-	1	-
NatWest Trophy	1	1	0	1	1	1.00	-	-	1	-
Benson & Hedges Cup	3	2	0	19	17	9.50	-	-	2	-
Other First-Class	2	4	1	153	64 *	51.00	-	2	-	-
Other One-Day	3	3	2	46	36 *	46.00	-	-	2	-
ALL FIRST-CLASS	6	10	1	241	64 *	26.77	-	3	3	-
ALL ONE-DAY	19	15	4	179	40	16.27	-	-	6	-

BOWLING AVERAGES
	Overs	Mdns	Runs	Wkts	Avge	Best	5wI	10wM
Britannic Assurance	26	2	101	2	50.50	1-10	-	-
Refuge Assurance	45.4	3	245	8	30.62	2-11	-	
NatWest Trophy								
Benson & Hedges Cup	3	0	16	0	-	-		
Other First-Class	27	10	84	2	42.00	1-40	-	-
Other One-Day								
ALL FIRST-CLASS	53	12	185	4	46.25	1-10	-	-
ALL ONE-DAY	48.4	3	261	8	32.62	2-11	-	

PLAYER RECORDS

U

S.D. UDAL - *Hampshire*

Opposition	Venue	Date	Batting		Fielding	Bowling
BRITANNIC ASSURANCE						
Sussex	Arundel	July 25			1Ct	4-144 & 2-12
Warwickshire	Edgbaston	July 28	9			0-66 & 2-93
Worcestershire	Worcester	Aug 11		0*		1-95
Surrey	Southampton	Aug 23	0 &	28*	1Ct	1-87 & 0-9
Kent	Bournemouth	Aug 29				0-80 & 3-70
Glamorgan	Pontypridd	Sept 7	28			2-56 & 1-34
REFUGE ASSURANCE						
Warwickshire	Edgbaston	July 29		2*		1-20
Worcestershire	Worcester	Aug 12			1Ct	2-36
OTHER FIRST-CLASS						
Sri Lanka	Southampton	Sept 12	14			2-15 & 4-139
OTHER ONE-DAY						
Worcestershire	Scarborough	Sept 2		0*		1-42
Essex	Scarborough	Sept 4				1-25

BATTING AVERAGES - Including fielding

	Matches	Inns	NO	Runs	HS	Avge	100s	50s	Ct	St
Britannic Assurance	6	5	2	65	28*	21.66	-	-	2	-
Refuge Assurance	2	1	1	2	2*	-	-	-	1	-
Other First-Class	1	1	0	14	14	14.00	-	-	-	-
Other One-Day	2	1	1	0	0*	-	-	-	-	-
ALL FIRST-CLASS	7	6	2	79	28*	19.75	-	-	2	-
ALL ONE-DAY	4	2	2	2	2*	-	-	-	1	-

BOWLING AVERAGES

	Overs	Mdns	Runs	Wkts	Avge	Best	5wI	10wM
Britannic Assurance	191.3	35	746	16	46.62	4-144	-	-
Refuge Assurance	15	0	56	3	18.66	2-36	-	
Other First-Class	47	11	154	6	25.66	4-139	-	-
Other One-Day	19	0	67	2	33.50	1-25	-	
ALL FIRST-CLASS	238.3	46	900	22	40.90	4-139	-	-
ALL ONE-DAY	34	0	123	5	24.60	2-36	-	

V	PLAYER RECORDS

W.M. VAN DER MERWE - *Oxford Univ*

Opposition	Venue	Date	Batting	Fielding	Bowling
BENSON & HEDGES CUP					
For Combined Universities					
Lancashire	Fenner's	May 1	10		2-42
Yorkshire	Headingley	May 8	27		2-34
Surrey	The Parks	May 10	14		2-50
Hampshire	Southampton	May 12	4	1Ct	1-53
OTHER FIRST-CLASS					
Glamorgan	The Parks	April 14	1	2Ct	0-43 & 0-24
Somerset	The Parks	April 18	18 *		1-44
Hampshire	The Parks	May 3	84	2Ct	0-77 & 0-9
Leicestershire	The Parks	May 23	24 & 39 *		1-52
Notts	The Parks	June 6			1-69
Lancashire	The Parks	June 16	56 *		
For Combined U					
New Zealand	Fenner's	June 27	24 & 14	2Ct	0-28 & 0-30
For Oxford U					
Cambridge U	Lord's	July 4	50		0-23

BATTING AVERAGES - Including fielding

	Matches	Inns	NO	Runs	HS	Avge	100s	50s	Ct	St
Benson & Hedges Cup	4	4	0	55	27	13.75	-	-	1	-
Other First-Class	8	9	3	310	84	51.66	-	3	6	-
ALL FIRST-CLASS	8	9	3	310	84	51.66	-	3	6	-
ALL ONE-DAY	4	4	0	55	27	13.75	-	-	1	-

BOWLING AVERAGES

	Overs	Mdns	Runs	Wkts	Avge	Best	5wI	10wM
Benson & Hedges Cup	42.4	7	179	7	25.57	2-34	-	
Other First-Class	131	27	399	3	133.00	1-44	-	-
ALL FIRST-CLASS	131	27	399	3	133.00	1-44	-	-
ALL ONE-DAY	42.4	7	179	7	25.57	2-34	-	

R.N.R. VARTAN - *Hertfordshire*

Opposition	Venue	Date	Batting	Fielding	Bowling
NATWEST TROPHY					
Warwickshire	St Albans	June 27	10	1Ct	

BATTING AVERAGES - Including fielding

	Matches	Inns	NO	Runs	HS	Avge	100s	50s	Ct	St
NatWest Trophy	1	1	0	10	10	10.00	-	-	1	-
ALL ONE-DAY	1	1	0	10	10	10.00	-	-	1	-

BOWLING AVERAGES
Did not bowl

D.B. VENGSARKAR - *India*

Opposition	Venue	Date	Batting	Fielding	Bowling
CORNHILL TEST MATCHES					
England	Lord's	July 26	52 & 35	1Ct	
England	Old Trafford	Aug 9	6 & 32		
England	The Oval	Aug 23	33	2Ct	
TEXACO TROPHY					
England	Trent Bridge	July 20	54	1Ct	
OTHER FIRST-CLASS					
Yorkshire	Headingley	June 30	47 *		
Hampshire	Southampton	July 4	21		
Kent	Canterbury	July 7	50 * & 83 *		
Leicestershire	Leicester	July 21	80		
Surrey	The Oval	Aug 1	55	1Ct	
TCCB U25 XI	Edgbaston	Aug 15	54		
World XI	Scarborough	Aug 29	3 & 25 *		
OTHER ONE-DAY					
League CC	Sunderland	June 28	28	2Ct	
Derbyshire	Chesterfield	July 16	28		

BATTING AVERAGES - Including fielding

	Matches	Inns	NO	Runs	HS	Avge	100s	50s	Ct	St
Cornhill Test Matches	3	5	0	158	52	31.60	-	1	3	-
Texaco Trophy	1	1	0	54	54	54.00	-	1	1	-
Other First-Class	7	9	4	418	83 *	83.60	-	5	1	-
Other One-Day	2	2	0	56	28	28.00	-	-	2	-
ALL FIRST-CLASS	10	14	4	576	83 *	57.60	-	6	4	-
ALL ONE-DAY	3	3	0	110	54	36.66	-	1	3	-

BOWLING AVERAGES
Did not bowl

VENKATAPATHY RAJU - *India*

Opposition	Venue	Date	Batting	Fielding	Bowling
OTHER FIRST-CLASS					
Hampshire	Southampton	July 4	18		0-28 & 0-56
Kent	Canterbury	July 7	4		1-27 & 1-41
Min Counties	Trowbridge	July 11	33 *		0-67 & 1-58
Leicestershire	Leicester	July 21	3		1-62 & 4-73
Surrey	The Oval	Aug 1	7		1-64 & 0-52
Gloucs	Bristol	Aug 4	40 *		
OTHER ONE-DAY					
League CC	Sunderland	June 28	37 *		0-40
Scotland	Glasgow	July 14			3-22
Derbyshire	Chesterfield	July 16	1		1-46

BATTING AVERAGES - Including fielding

	Matches	Inns	NO	Runs	HS	Avge	100s	50s	Ct	St
Other First-Class	6	6	2	105	40 *	26.25	-	-	-	-
Other One-Day	3	2	1	38	37 *	38.00	-	-	-	-
ALL FIRST-CLASS	6	6	2	105	40 *	26.25	-	-	-	-
ALL ONE-DAY	3	2	1	38	37 *	38.00	-	-	-	-

BOWLING AVERAGES

	Overs	Mdns	Runs	Wkts	Avge	Best	5wI	10wM
Other First-Class	182.3	41	528	9	58.66	4-73	-	-
Other One-Day	33	3	108	4	27.00	3-22	-	

PLETER RECORDS

W

V.DE C. WALCOTT - *League C.C. XI*

Opposition	Venue	Date	Batting	Fielding	Bowling
OTHER ONE-DAY					
India	Sunderland	June 28	0		2-37

BATTING AVERAGES - Including fielding

	Matches	Inns	NO	Runs	HS	Avge	100s	50s	Ct	St
Other One-Day	1	1	0	0	0	0.00	-	-	-	-
ALL ONE-DAY	1	1	0	0	0	0.00	-	-	-	-

BOWLING AVERAGES

	Overs	Mdns	Runs	Wkts	Avge	Best	5wI	10wM
Other One-Day	11	2	37	2	18.50	2-37	-	
ALL ONE-DAY	11	2	37	2	18.50	2-37	-	

A. WALKER - *Northamptonshire*

Opposition	Venue	Date	Batting	Fielding	Bowling
BENSON & HEDGES CUP					
Notts	Trent Bridge	May 12	5		0-39

BATTING AVERAGES - Including fielding

	Matches	Inns	NO	Runs	HS	Avge	100s	50s	Ct	St
Benson & Hedges Cup	1	1	0	5	5	5.00	-	-	-	-
ALL ONE-DAY	1	1	0	5	5	5.00	-	-	-	-

BOWLING AVERAGES

	Overs	Mdns	Runs	Wkts	Avge	Best	5wI	10wM
Benson & Hedges Cup	11	1	39	0	-	-	-	
ALL ONE-DAY	11	1	39	0	-	-	-	

C.A. WALSH - *Gloucestershire*

Opposition	Venue	Date	Batting	Fielding	Bowling
BRITANNIC ASSURANCE					
Somerset	Taunton	April 26	26 & 0	1Ct	6-112 & 0-31
Glamorgan	Bristol	May 15	19 * & 31		4-62 & 5-48
Middlesex	Lord's	May 26	16		0-59 & 1-25
Somerset	Bristol	June 2			2-43 & 1-53
Essex	Ilford	June 6			0-60 & 1-8
Lancashire	Old Trafford	June 9	33 *		0-66
Sussex	Hove	June 16	9	1Ct	2-40 & 2-79
Hampshire	Gloucester	June 20			
Leicestershire	Gloucester	June 23		12	1-97
Derbyshire	Derby	June 30	1		4-32 & 2-86
Yorkshire	Cheltenham	July 21	63 *		2-70 & 0-46
Northants	Cheltenham	July 25	12		3-41 & 8-58
Warwickshire	Bristol	Aug 8	8		2-86 & 2-51
Kent	Bristol	Aug 11	55	2Ct	4-117
Notts	Trent Bridge	Aug 18	29 & 18	1Ct	2-44 & 2-41
Northants	Northampton	Aug 23	31		1-63 & 4-101
Worcestershire	Bristol	Sept 7	18		0-83 & 1-24
Sussex	Bristol	Sept 12	63		2-45 & 2-46
Hampshire	Southampton	Sept 18	20	1Ct	3-51 & 1-93
REFUGE ASSURANCE					
Hampshire	Southampton	May 6			3-30
Essex	Chelmsford	May 13			0-42
Warwickshire	Moreton-in-M	May 20			2-14
Middlesex	Lord's	May 27	1		1-22
Somerset	Bristol	June 3		1Ct	1-14
Lancashire	Old Trafford	June 10	12		1-46
Leicestershire	Gloucester	June 24	0		0-38
Derbyshire	Derby	July 1	15 *		0-19
Worcestershire	Worcester	July 8			1-28
Sussex	Swindon	July 15	11		1-33
Yorkshire	Cheltenham	July 22			0-16
Surrey	Cheltenham	July 29		1Ct	2-29

Opposition	Venue	Date	Batting	Fielding	Bowling
Kent	Bristol	Aug 12			3-28
Notts	Trent Bridge	Aug 19	23		0-15
Northants	Northampton	Aug 26	14	1Ct	3-36
NATWEST TROPHY					
Lincolnshire	Gloucester	June 27			2-16
Kent	Bristol	July 11			6-21
Lancashire	Old Trafford	Aug 1	7		2-69
BENSON & HEDGES CUP					
Glamorgan	Cardiff	May 1	1		2-32
Kent	Canterbury	May 10			0-12
Warwickshire	Bristol	May 12			0-30
OTHER FIRST-CLASS					
India	Bristol	Aug 4	0		2-45 & 0-16

BATTING AVERAGES - Including fielding

	Matches	Inns	NO	Runs	HS	Avge	100s	50s	Ct	St
Britannic Assurance	19	19	3	464	63 *	29.00	-	3	6	-
Refuge Assurance	15	7	1	76	23	12.66	-	-	3	-
NatWest Trophy	3	1	0	7	7	7.00	-	-	-	-
Benson & Hedges Cup	3	1	0	1	1	1.00	-	-	-	-
Other First-Class	1	1	0	0	0	0.00	-	-	-	-
ALL FIRST-CLASS	20	20	3	464	63 *	27.29	-	3	6	-
ALL ONE-DAY	21	9	1	84	23	10.50	-	-	3	-

BOWLING AVERAGES

	Overs	Mdns	Runs	Wkts	Avge	Best	5wI	10wM
Britannic Assurance	583.1	98	1961	70	28.01	8-58	3	1
Refuge Assurance	103.5	6	410	18	22.77	3-28	-	
NatWest Trophy	31	4	106	10	10.60	6-21	1	
Benson & Hedges Cup	23	2	74	2	37.00	2-32	-	
Other First-Class	28	9	61	2	30.50	2-45	-	
ALL FIRST-CLASS	611.1	107	2022	72	28.08	8-58	3	1
ALL ONE-DAY	157.5	12	590	30	19.66	6-21	1	

WAQAR YOUNIS - *Surrey*

Opposition	Venue	Date	Batting	Fielding	Bowling
BRITANNIC ASSURANCE					
Derbyshire	The Oval	June 6			4-77 & 0-16
Yorkshire	Harrogate	June 9	1 *		3-56
Notts	Trent Bridge	June 20			3-29 & 0-86
Northants	The Oval	July 4			6-36
Warwickshire	The Oval	July 7			7-73 & 4-55
Sussex	Guildford	July 18	1 *		3-65 & 0-45
Gloucs	Cheltenham	July 28	1 *	1Ct	2-69 & 0-36
Somerset	Weston	Aug 4			3-80 & 0-31
Leicestershire	The Oval	Aug 11	10 *		4-72 & 2-41
Essex	Chelmsford	Aug 18	11 * & 1		3-51 & 0-64
Hampshire	Southampton	Aug 23	13 *	1Ct	6-66 & 2-132
Lancashire	Blackpool	Aug 29			2-65
Middlesex	The Oval	Sept 12	4 *	1Ct	3-91
Essex	The Oval	Sept 18	14	1Ct	0-21
REFUGE ASSURANCE					
Northants	The Oval	June 3		1Ct	2-23
Yorkshire	Hull	June 10			2-34
Worcestershire	The Oval	June 17		1Ct	3-27
Derbyshire	The Oval	June 24			3-41
Glamorgan	Cardiff	July 1			1-17
Warwickshire	The Oval	July 8	1 *	1Ct	1-41
Middlesex	The Oval	July 15			4-27
Kent	The Oval	July 22			5-26
Gloucs	Cheltenham	July 29	0 *		1-38
Somerset	Weston	Aug 5			3-39
Leicestershire	The Oval	Aug 12			3-43
Hampshire	Southampton	Aug 26			3-40
NATWEST TROPHY					
Wiltshire	Trowbridge	June 27			3-23
Middlesex	Uxbridge	July 11			2-39
BENSON & HEDGES CUP					
Lancashire	Old Trafford	May 30	4		2-55
OTHER ONE-DAY					
Warwickshire	Hove	Sept 3			3-31

W PLAYER RECORDS

Kent	Hove	Sept 4	13*		1-57

BATTING AVERAGES - Including fielding

	Matches	Inns	NO	Runs	HS	Avge	100s	50s	Ct	St
Britannic Assurance	14	9	7	56	14	28.00	-	-	4	-
Refuge Assurance	12	2	2	1	1*	-	-	-	3	-
NatWest Trophy	2	0	0	0	0	-	-	-	-	-
Benson & Hedges Cup	1	1	0	4	4	4.00	-	-	-	-
Other One-Day	2	1	1	13	13*	-	-	-	-	-
ALL FIRST-CLASS	14	9	7	56	14	28.00	-	-	4	-
ALL ONE-DAY	17	4	3	18	13*	18.00	-	-	3	-

BOWLING AVERAGES

	Overs	Mdns	Runs	Wkts	Avge	Best	5wI	10wM
Britannic Assurance	422	70	1357	57	23.80	7-73	3	1
Refuge Assurance	82.2	1	396	31	12.77	5-26	1	
NatWest Trophy	24	5	62	5	12.40	3-23	-	
Benson & Hedges Cup	11	0	55	2	27.50	2-55	-	
Other One-Day	20	3	88	4	22.00	3-31	-	
ALL FIRST-CLASS	422	70	1357	57	23.80	7-73	3	1
ALL ONE-DAY	137.2	9	601	42	14.31	5-26	1	

D.M. WARD - *Surrey*

Opposition	Venue	Date	Batting			Fielding	Bowling
BRITANNIC ASSURANCE							
Sussex	Hove	April 26	38	&	18*	1Ct	
Lancashire	The Oval	May 3	36			1Ct	
Hampshire	The Oval	May 19	129*	&	23		
Middlesex	Lord's	May 23	46			3Ct,1St	
Derbyshire	The Oval	June 6	37*			1Ct	
Yorkshire	Harrogate	June 9	71			1Ct	
Worcestershire	The Oval	June 16	21			3Ct	
Notts	Trent Bridge	June 20	154*			3Ct	
Glamorgan	Cardiff	June 30	29			2Ct,1St	
Northants	The Oval	July 4	4*			2Ct	
Warwickshire	The Oval	July 7	126	&	15	1Ct	
Sussex	Guildford	July 18	40	&	36*	2Ct	
Kent	Guildford	July 21	48			1Ct	
Gloucs	Cheltenham	July 28	5	&	45		
Somerset	Weston	Aug 4	18	&	43		
Leicestershire	The Oval	Aug 11	33			2Ct	
Essex	Chelmsford	Aug 18	0	&	11	3Ct	
Hampshire	Southampton	Aug 23	191				
Lancashire	Blackpool	Aug 29	16*				
Kent	Canterbury	Sept 7	263				
Middlesex	The Oval	Sept 12	75	&	6		
Essex	The Oval	Sept 18	58	&	208		
REFUGE ASSURANCE							
Sussex	Hove	April 29	7			1Ct	
Lancashire	The Oval	May 6	17*				
Notts	Trent Bridge	May 20	34			1Ct	
Northants	The Oval	June 3	7				
Yorkshire	Hull	June 10	22			2Ct	
Worcestershire	The Oval	June 17	27*			2Ct	
Derbyshire	The Oval	June 24	25			2Ct	
Glamorgan	Cardiff	July 1	5				
Warwickshire	The Oval	July 8	0			0Ct,1St	
Middlesex	The Oval	July 15	60			1Ct	
Kent	The Oval	July 22	4			1Ct	
Gloucs	Cheltenham	July 29	51			3Ct	
Somerset	Weston	Aug 5	27				
Leicestershire	The Oval	Aug 12	6				
Hampshire	Southampton	Aug 26	102*				
NATWEST TROPHY							
Wiltshire	Trowbridge	June 27				1Ct	
Middlesex	Uxbridge	July 11	11			3Ct	
BENSON & HEDGES CUP							
Lancashire	Old Trafford	April 24	18				
Hampshire	The Oval	May 1	38			3Ct,1St	
Combined U	The Parks	May 10	33*			1Ct,1St	
Yorkshire	The Oval	May 12	46*				
Lancashire	Old Trafford	May 30	10				
OTHER FIRST-CLASS							
Oxford U	The Parks	May 16	181			6Ct,1St	

India	The Oval	Aug 1	20	&	28		

OTHER ONE-DAY

Warwickshire	Harrogate	June 13	40	2Ct
Warwickshire	Hove	Sept 3	27	
Kent	Hove	Sept 4	26	

BATTING AVERAGES - Including fielding

	Matches	Inns	NO	Runs	HS	Avge	100s	50s	Ct	St
Britannic Assurance	22	31	7	1843	263	76.79	6	3	26	2
Refuge Assurance	15	15	3	394	102*	32.83	1	2	13	1
NatWest Trophy	2	1	0	11	11	11.00	-	-	4	-
Benson & Hedges Cup	5	5	2	145	46*	48.33	-	-	4	2
Other First-Class	2	3	0	229	181	76.33	1	-	6	1
Other One-Day	3	3	0	93	40	31.00	-	-	2	-
ALL FIRST-CLASS	24	34	7	2072	263	76.74	7	3	32	3
ALL ONE-DAY	25	24	5	643	102*	33.84	1	2	23	3

BOWLING AVERAGES
Did not bowl

T.R. WARD - *Kent*

Opposition	Venue	Date	Batting			Fielding	Bowling
BRITANNIC ASSURANCE							
Hampshire	Canterbury	April 26	21	&	11	1Ct	0-41
Sussex	Folkestone	May 3	13	&	0	4Ct	1-6
Middlesex	Lord's	May 15	0	&	13	2Ct	0-15
Glamorgan	Swansea	May 23	3	&	7		1-52
Surrey	Guildford	July 21	10	&	88		0-1
Middlesex	Canterbury	July 25	0				0-22
Worcestershire	Canterbury	July 28	1	&	18	1Ct	0-6 & 2-48
Derbyshire	Chesterfield	Aug 4	124	&	5		
Leicestershire	Dartford	Aug 8	14	&	0*	1Ct	0-5
Gloucs	Bristol	Aug 11	82			1Ct	
Sussex	Hove	Aug 18	64	&	12	3Ct	0-3 & 0-26
Leicestershire	Leicester	Aug 23	14	&	29	1Ct	
Hampshire	Bournemouth	Aug 29	175	&	8		0-0
Surrey	Canterbury	Sept 7	55	&	10		
Essex	Chelmsford	Sept 12	79	&	7		
REFUGE ASSURANCE							
Essex	Chelmsford	April 22	13				
Hampshire	Canterbury	April 29	24				
Middlesex	Folkestone	May 6	24				1-17
Glamorgan	Llanelli	May 13	0				
Yorkshire	Canterbury	May 20	37			1Ct	
Northants	Northampton	May 27	71				
Surrey	The Oval	July 22	14				1-17
Worcestershire	Canterbury	July 29	45				
Derbyshire	Chesterfield	Aug 5	80				
Gloucs	Bristol	Aug 12	3				
Leicestershire	Leicester	Aug 26	0				0-44
NATWEST TROPHY							
Gloucs	Bristol	July 11	47				
BENSON & HEDGES CUP							
Worcestershire	Worcester	May 1	94			2Ct	
Warwickshire	Canterbury	May 8	1				
Gloucs	Canterbury	May 10	60*				
Glamorgan	Swansea	May 12	36				
OTHER ONE-DAY							
Sussex	Hove	Sept 2	67				1-23
Surrey	Hove	Sept 4	41				0-20

BATTING AVERAGES - Including fielding

	Matches	Inns	NO	Runs	HS	Avge	100s	50s	Ct	St
Britannic Assurance	15	28	1	863	175	31.96	2	5	14	-
Refuge Assurance	11	11	0	311	80	28.27	-	2	1	-
NatWest Trophy	1	1	0	47	47	47.00	-	-	-	-
Benson & Hedges Cup	4	4	1	191	94	63.66	-	2	2	-
Other One-Day	2	2	0	108	67	54.00	-	1	-	-
ALL FIRST-CLASS	15	28	1	863	175	31.96	2	5	14	-
ALL ONE-DAY	18	18	1	657	94	38.64	-	5	3	-

PLAYER RECORDS

W

BOWLING AVERAGES

	Overs	Mdns	Runs	Wkts	Avge	Best	5wI	10wM
Britannic Assurance	53	6	225	4	56.25	2-48	-	-
Refuge Assurance	14	0	78	2	39.00	1-17	-	
NatWest Trophy								
Benson & Hedges Cup								
Other One-Day	14	0	43	1	43.00	1-23	-	
ALL FIRST-CLASS	53	6	225	4	56.25	2-48	-	-
ALL ONE-DAY	28	0	121	3	40.33	1-17	-	

S.J.S. WARKE - *Ireland*

Opposition	Venue	Date	Batting	Fielding	Bowling
NATWEST TROPHY					
Sussex	Downpatrick	June 27	22		
OTHER FIRST-CLASS					
Scotland	Edinburgh	Aug 11	4 & 100 *	1Ct	
OTHER ONE-DAY					
New Zealand	Downpatrick	May 9	23		
New Zealand	Belfast	May 10	44		

BATTING AVERAGES - Including fielding

	Matches	Inns	NO	Runs	HS	Avge	100s	50s	Ct	St
NatWest Trophy	1	1	0	22	22	22.00	-	-	-	-
Other First-Class	1	2	1	104	100 *	104.00	1	-	1	-
Other One-Day	2	2	0	67	44	33.50	-	-	-	-
ALL FIRST-CLASS	1	2	1	104	100 *	104.00	1	-	1	-
ALL ONE-DAY	3	3	0	89	44	29.66	-	-	-	-

BOWLING AVERAGES
Did not bowl

S.N. WARMAN - *Lincolnshire*

Opposition	Venue	Date	Batting	Fielding	Bowling
NATWEST TROPHY					
Gloucs	Gloucester	June 27	3		

BATTING AVERAGES - Including fielding

	Matches	Inns	NO	Runs	HS	Avge	100s	50s	Ct	St
NatWest Trophy	1	1	0	3	3	3.00	-	-	-	-
ALL ONE-DAY	1	1	0	3	3	3.00	-	-	-	-

BOWLING AVERAGES
Did not bowl

A.E. WARNER - *Derbyshire*

Opposition	Venue	Date	Batting	Fielding	Bowling
BRITANNIC ASSURANCE					
Notts	Trent Bridge	April 26	11		2-78 & 0-14
Somerset	Taunton	May 19	1 & 1		2-30 & 1-34
Yorkshire	Chesterfield	May 23	1 & 10		2-90 & 1-32
Notts	Derby	May 26	8 & 1	1Ct	3-64 & 0-72
Surrey	The Oval	June 6	17		0-36 & 0-30
Warwickshire	Derby	June 16			0-9 & 0-66
Leicestershire	Leicester	June 20		2	2-72
Essex	Colchester	July 18	0 & 2		1-76
Hampshire	Portsmouth	July 21	0		1-63 & 3-75
Worcestershire	Derby	July 25	4 & 5 *		3-109
Northants	Chesterfield	Aug 8	24	1Ct	2-68 & 2-96
Essex	Derby	Aug 23	4 & 0		3-56
Glamorgan	Cardiff	Aug 29	59		2-53
Yorkshire	Scarborough	Sept 7	10 *		1-43 & 2-64
REFUGE ASSURANCE					
Worcestershire	Derby	April 29	5	1Ct	1-28
Northants	Northampton	May 6	13 *		2-34
Yorkshire	Headingley	May 13	5		0-28
Somerset	Taunton	May 20	4		0-26
Notts	Derby	June 10			1-39
Warwickshire	Derby	June 17	6		0-35
Surrey	The Oval	June 24	11 *		0-56
Lancashire	Old Trafford	July 8			1-57
Leicestershire	Knypersley	July 15			3-18
Glamorgan	Swansea	July 29			2-26
Kent	Chesterfield	Aug 5		1Ct	0-59
Middlesex	Derby	Aug 19			1-20
Essex	Derby	Aug 26			1-36
Notts	Derby	Sept 5		1Ct	2-41
Middlesex	Edgbaston	Sept 16	28 *		2-35
NATWEST TROPHY					
Shropshire	Chesterfield	June 27			4-39
Lancashire	Derby	July 11	1 *		1-45
BENSON & HEDGES CUP					
Sussex	Derby	April 24		1Ct	3-47
Min Counties	Wellington	May 10	16		3-31
Middlesex	Derby	May 12	7		2-48

BATTING AVERAGES - Including fielding

	Matches	Inns	NO	Runs	HS	Avge	100s	50s	Ct	St
Britannic Assurance	14	19	2	160	59	9.41	-	1	2	-
Refuge Assurance	15	7	3	72	28 *	18.00	-	-	3	-
NatWest Trophy	2	1	1	1	1 *	-	-	-	-	-
Benson & Hedges Cup	3	2	0	23	16	11.50	-	-	1	-
ALL FIRST-CLASS	14	19	2	160	59	9.41	-	1	2	-
ALL ONE-DAY	20	10	4	96	28 *	16.00	-	-	4	-

BOWLING AVERAGES

	Overs	Mdns	Runs	Wkts	Avge	Best	5wI	10wM
Britannic Assurance	393.3	67	1330	33	40.30	3-56	-	-
Refuge Assurance	101	0	538	16	33.62	3-18	-	
NatWest Trophy	24	2	84	5	16.80	4-39	-	
Benson & Hedges Cup	33	2	126	8	15.75	3-31	-	
ALL FIRST-CLASS	393.3	67	1330	33	40.30	3-56	-	-
ALL ONE-DAY	158	4	748	29	25.79	4-39	-	

WASIM AKRAM - *Lancashire*

Opposition	Venue	Date	Batting	Fielding	Bowling
BRITANNIC ASSURANCE					
Hampshire	Old Trafford	June 23			2-106 & 1-5
Kent	Maidstone	June 30	1 & 9		3-86 & 2-58
Warwickshire	Coventry	July 18	7 & 32		3-76 & 2-51
Essex	Colchester	July 21	0		0-19
Worcestershire	Kid'minster	Aug 8	14 & 23		0-68
Yorkshire	Old Trafford	Aug 18	8 & 6		0-47 & 1-46
Surrey	Blackpool	Aug 29	17		1-32
REFUGE ASSURANCE					
Leicestershire	Old Trafford	May 20	5		0-32
Glamorgan	Colwyn Bay	May 27	50		2-46
Gloucs	Old Trafford	June 10	37		4-39
Hampshire	Old Trafford	June 24			2-31
Kent	Maidstone	July 1			2-31
Derbyshire	Old Trafford	July 8	7	1Ct	1-59
Worcestershire	Old Trafford	July 15			2-34
Essex	Colchester	July 22	3		1-53
Somerset	Old Trafford	July 29			2-36
Yorkshire	Scarborough	Aug 5	35 *		4-19
Northants	Northampton	Aug 12			0-50
Warwickshire	Old Trafford	Aug 26	31		1-21
Middlesex	Old Trafford	Sept 5	7		0-27
NATWEST TROPHY					
Durham	Old Trafford	June 27		1Ct	2-19
Derbyshire	Derby	July 11	9		4-34
Gloucs	Old Trafford	Aug 1	5 *	1Ct	3-29
Middlesex	Old Trafford	Aug 15	14		1-65
Northants	Lord's	Sept 1			0-35
BENSON & HEDGES CUP					
Surrey	Old Trafford	May 30	2		0-39
Somerset	Old Trafford	June 13	8 *		3-29

W | PLAYER RECORDS

Worcestershire Lord's	July 14	28		3-30

OTHER FIRST-CLASS

Zimbabwe	Old Trafford	May 23	18		1-46

BATTING AVERAGES - Including fielding

	Matches	Inns	NO	Runs	HS	Avge	100s	50s	Ct	St
Britannic Assurance	7	10	0	117	32	11.70	-	-	-	-
Refuge Assurance	13	8	1	175	50	25.00	-	1	1	-
NatWest Trophy	5	3	1	28	14	14.00	-	-	2	-
Benson & Hedges Cup	3	3	1	38	28	19.00	-	-	-	-
Other First-Class	1	1	0	18	18	18.00	-	-	-	-
ALL FIRST-CLASS	8	11	0	135	32	12.27	-	-	-	-
ALL ONE-DAY	21	14	3	241	50	21.90	-	1	3	-

BOWLING AVERAGES

	Overs	Mdns	Runs	Wkts	Avge	Best	5wI	10wM
Britannic Assurance	191	43	594	15	39.60	3-76	-	-
Refuge Assurance	88.1	0	447	19	23.52	4-19	-	-
NatWest Trophy	50.1	3	182	10	18.20	4-34	-	-
Benson & Hedges Cup	31	0	98	6	16.33	3-29	-	-
Other First-Class	13	1	46	1	46.00	1-46	-	-
ALL FIRST-CLASS	204	44	640	16	40.00	3-76	-	-
ALL ONE-DAY	169.2	3	727	35	20.77	4-19	-	-

A. WASSON - India

Opposition	Venue	Date	Batting	Fielding	Bowling

CORNHILL TEST MATCHES

England	The Oval	Aug 23	15		2-79 & 1-94

OTHER FIRST-CLASS

Yorkshire	Headingley	June 30			0-31 & 0-24
Kent	Canterbury	July 7			1-101 & 1-19
Min Counties	Trowbridge	July 11			0-36 & 0-42
Leicestershire	Leicester	July 21			3-76 & 1-56
Surrey	The Oval	Aug 1	8 *		1-81 & 0-19
TCCB U25 XI	Edgbaston	Aug 15			1-74 & 0-18
Glamorgan	Swansea	Aug 18			0-5 & 6-89
World XI	Scarborough	Aug 29	24		1-42

OTHER ONE-DAY

League CC	Sunderland	June 28	10		1-39

BATTING AVERAGES - Including fielding

	Matches	Inns	NO	Runs	HS	Avge	100s	50s	Ct	St
Cornhill Test Matches	1	1	0	15	15	15.00	-	-	-	-
Other First-Class	8	2	1	32	24	32.00	-	-	-	-
Other One-Day	1	1	0	10	10	10.00	-	-	-	-
ALL FIRST-CLASS	9	3	1	47	24	23.50	-	-	-	-
ALL ONE-DAY	1	1	0	10	10	10.00	-	-	-	-

BOWLING AVERAGES

	Overs	Mdns	Runs	Wkts	Avge	Best	5wI	10wM
Cornhill Test Matches	37	5	173	3	57.66	2-79	-	-
Other First-Class	170.3	19	713	15	47.53	6-89	1	-
Other One-Day	7	0	39	1	39.00	1-39	-	-
ALL FIRST-CLASS	207.3	24	886	18	49.22	6-89	1	-
ALL ONE-DAY	7	0	39	1	39.00	1-39	-	-

S.N.V. WATERTON - Lancashire, Oxfordshire & Minor Counties

Opposition	Venue	Date	Batting	Fielding	Bowling

BRITANNIC ASSURANCE

Notts	Southport	July 25	3	4Ct	

NATWEST TROPHY

For Oxfordshire

Kent	Oxford	June 27	0	0Ct,1St	

BENSON & HEDGES CUP

For Minor Counties

Middlesex	Lord's	April 24	6	1Ct	

BATTING AVERAGES - Including fielding

	Matches	Inns	NO	Runs	HS	Avge	100s	50s	Ct	St
Britannic Assurance	1	1	0	3	3	3.00	-	-	4	-
NatWest Trophy	1	1	0	0	0	0.00	-	-	-	1
Benson & Hedges Cup	1	1	0	6	6	6.00	-	-	1	-
ALL FIRST-CLASS	1	1	0	3	3	3.00	-	-	4	-
ALL ONE-DAY	2	2	0	6	6	3.00	-	-	1	1

BOWLING AVERAGES

Did not bowl

S.L. WATKIN - Glamorgan

Opposition	Venue	Date	Batting	Fielding	Bowling

BRITANNIC ASSURANCE

Leicestershire	Cardiff	April 26	21 * & 5		0-94 & 1-60
Somerset	Cardiff	May 3			0-84
Gloucs	Bristol	May 15	1 & 10		2-55 & 3-51
Sussex	Hove	May 19		1Ct	2-66 & 2-94
Kent	Swansea	May 23	1		4-77 & 0-27
Lancashire	Colwyn Bay	May 26	25 *		2-84
Northants	Northampton	June 9	3	1Ct	0-93 & 0-66
Hampshire	Southampton	June 16			4-84
Somerset	Bath	June 20			2-53
Yorkshire	Cardiff	June 23			0-38 & 1-46
Surrey	Cardiff	June 30	3 *	1Ct	1-36 & 1-33
Gloucs	Swansea	July 4	19 *		1-23
Leicestershire	Hinckley	July 7	2		2-53 & 0-34
Worcestershire	Abergavenny	July 21			1-93 & 1-109
Warwickshire	Swansea	July 25	10 *	1Ct	1-94 & 0-36
Middlesex	Lord's	Aug 4	9 & 0 *	1Ct	1-85 & 2-47
Essex	Southend	Aug 8	7		3-72 & 2-102
Notts	Worksop	Aug 11	0		1-79 & 2-45
Derbyshire	Cardiff	Aug 29	8		3-39
Hampshire	Pontypridd	Sept 7	5 & 3		2-100 & 0-18
Warwickshire	Edgbaston	Sept 12	0 & 15 *		5-100 & 4-48
Worcestershire	Worcester	Sept 18	19 & 4		3-124 & 2-47

REFUGE ASSURANCE

Gloucs	Bristol	April 22		1Ct	1-24
Kent	Llanelli	May 13			1-48
Sussex	Hove	May 20			0-28
Essex	Ilford	June 3	1 *		0-19
Northants	Northampton	June 10			1-37
Hampshire	Bournemouth	June 17			2-46
Surrey	Cardiff	July 1		1Ct	2-18
Warwickshire	Edgbaston	July 15		1Ct	5-23
Somerset	Neath	July 22	28		0-71
Derbyshire	Swansea	July 29	2 *		2-29
Middlesex	Lord's	Aug 5	1		1-67
Notts	Trent Bridge	Aug 12			0-27
Worcestershire	Swansea	Aug 26	0		2-33

NATWEST TROPHY

Dorset	Swansea	June 27			2-56
Sussex	Cardiff	July 11			3-18
Middlesex	Lord's	Aug 1	6 *		0-28

BENSON & HEDGES CUP

Warwickshire	Edgbaston	April 24	2 *		0-35
Worcestershire	Worcester	May 8	1 *		0-45
Kent	Swansea	May 12	6		1-51
Worcestershire	Worcester	May 30	5		1-32

OTHER FIRST-CLASS

For MCC

Worcestershire	Lord's	April 17	14		4-83

For Glamorgan

Sri Lanka	Ebbw Vale	Aug 22	1 & 2 *	1Ct	3-92 & 1-48

BATTING AVERAGES - Including fielding

	Matches	Inns	NO	Runs	HS	Avge	100s	50s	Ct	St
Britannic Assurance	22	22	7	170	25 *	11.33	-	-	5	-
Refuge Assurance	13	5	2	32	28	10.66	-	-	3	-
NatWest Trophy	3	1	1	6	6 *	-	-	-	-	-

PLANER RECORDS

PLAYER RECORDS | **W**

Benson & Hedges Cup	4	4	2	14	6	7.00	-	-	-
Other First-Class	2	3	1	17	14	8.50	-	-	1	-
ALL FIRST-CLASS	24	25	8	187	25*	11.00	-	-	6	-
ALL ONE-DAY	20	10	5	52	28	10.40	-	-	3	-

BOWLING AVERAGES

	Overs	Mdns	Runs	Wkts	Avge	Best	5wI	10wM
Britannic Assurance	731.1	118	2489	61	40.80	5-100	1	-
Refuge Assurance	88.3	5	470	17	27.64	5-23	1	
NatWest Trophy	35	5	102	5	20.40	3-18	-	
Benson & Hedges Cup	44	7	163	2	81.50	1-32	-	
Other First-Class	65	19	223	8	27.87	4-83	-	-
ALL FIRST-CLASS	796.1	137	2712	69	39.30	5-100	1	-
ALL ONE-DAY	167.3	17	735	24	30.62	5-23	1	

Benson & Hedges Cup	7	7	1	174	50	29.00	-	1	-
Other First-Class	1	1	0	48	48	48.00	-	-	-	-
ALL FIRST-CLASS	19	23	2	754	138	35.90	1	4	8	-
ALL ONE-DAY	26	24	8	539	90	33.68	-	2	5	-

BOWLING AVERAGES

	Overs	Mdns	Runs	Wkts	Avge	Best	5wI	10wM
Britannic Assurance	503.2	120	1572	47	33.44	5-65	3	-
Refuge Assurance	99	0	562	22	25.54	5-46	1	
NatWest Trophy	46	3	181	6	30.16	3-14	-	
Benson & Hedges Cup	62.4	3	261	12	21.75	4-58	-	
Other First-Class	5	2	6	0	-	-	-	-
ALL FIRST-CLASS	508.2	122	1578	47	33.57	5-65	3	-
ALL ONE-DAY	207.4	6	1004	40	25.10	5-46	1	

M. WATKINSON - *Lancashire*

Opposition	Venue	Date	Batting	Fielding	Bowling
BRITANNIC ASSURANCE					
Worcestershire	Old Trafford	April 26	0 *		1-96 & 0-19
Surrey	The Oval	May 3	46	2Ct	1-113
Sussex	Horsham	June 2	51	1Ct	3-26
Gloucs	Old Trafford	June 9		4	0-33
Middlesex	Old Trafford	June 20	37		4-61
Hampshire	Old Trafford	June 23		41 *	3-54 & 0-10
Kent	Maidstone	June 30	0 & 66		1-38 & 1-32
Derbyshire	Liverpool	July 7	4 & 63		1-56 & 1-47
Warwickshire	Coventry	July 18	14 & 5		1-53 & 0-38
Essex	Colchester	July 21	45	1Ct	0-19 & 0-64
Notts	Southport	July 25	47	1Ct	0-36 & 1-129
Somerset	Old Trafford	July 28	96		3-29 & 5-97
Yorkshire	Headingley	Aug 4	33 & 1		2-29 & 3-94
Worcestershire	Kid'minster	Aug 8	4 & 7		0-85
Yorkshire	Old Trafford	Aug 18	138		2-24 & 5-105
Surrey	Blackpool	Aug 29	0		0-13
Notts	Trent Bridge	Sept 12	4	1Ct	3-34 & 1-73
Warwickshire	Old Trafford	Sept 18		2Ct	5-65
REFUGE ASSURANCE					
Middlesex	Old Trafford	April 22	7		1-50
Notts	Trent Bridge	April 29	33 *	1Ct	0-41
Surrey	The Oval	May 6	3 *		1-61
Gloucs	Old Trafford	June 10	23		3-22
Hampshire	Old Trafford	June 24			
Kent	Maidstone	July 1	33 *	1Ct	2-37
Derbyshire	Old Trafford	July 8	8		2-42
Worcestershire	Old Trafford	July 15	15 *		4-30
Essex	Colchester	July 22	1		0-47
Somerset	Old Trafford	July 29	11 *		2-57
Yorkshire	Scarborough	Aug 5	31	2Ct	0-47
Northants	Northampton	Aug 12	6 *		1-32
Warwickshire	Old Trafford	Aug 26	22		5-46
Middlesex	Old Trafford	Sept 5	10		1-50
NATWEST TROPHY					
Durham	Old Trafford	June 27			0-45
Derbyshire	Derby	July 11	5	1Ct	0-31
Gloucs	Old Trafford	Aug 1	90		3-14
Middlesex	Old Trafford	Aug 15	43		1-62
Northants	Lord's	Sept 1	24 *		2-29
BENSON & HEDGES CUP					
Surrey	Old Trafford	April 24	23		0-31
Combined U	Fenner's	May 1	3		2-51
Hampshire	Old Trafford	May 8	40		0-20
Yorkshire	Headingley	May 10	43 *		3-31
Surrey	Old Trafford	May 30	4		4-58
Somerset	Old Trafford	June 13	11		1-33
Worcestershire	Lord's	July 14	50		2-37
OTHER FIRST-CLASS					
Zimbabwe	Old Trafford	May 23	48		0-6

BATTING AVERAGES - Including fielding

	Matches	Inns	NO	Runs	HS	Avge	100s	50s	Ct	St
Britannic Assurance	18	22	2	706	138	35.30	1	4	8	-
Refuge Assurance	14	13	6	203	33*	29.00	-	-	4	-
NatWest Trophy	5	4	1	162	90	54.00	-	1	1	-

W. WATSON - *New Zealand*

Opposition	Venue	Date	Batting	Fielding	Bowling
OTHER FIRST-CLASS					
Warwickshire	Edgbaston	May 30			2-67 & 0-57
Combined U	Fenner's	June 27		17 *	1-26 & 0-27

BATTING AVERAGES - Including fielding

	Matches	Inns	NO	Runs	HS	Avge	100s	50s	Ct	St
Other First-Class	2	1	1	17	17 *	-	-	-	-	-
ALL FIRST-CLASS	2	1	1	17	17 *	-	-	-	-	-

BOWLING AVERAGES

	Overs	Mdns	Runs	Wkts	Avge	Best	5wI	10wM
Other First-Class	54	10	177	3	59.00	2-67	-	-
ALL FIRST-CLASS	54	10	177	3	59.00	2-67	-	-

M.E. WAUGH - *Essex*

Opposition	Venue	Date	Batting	Fielding	Bowling
BRITANNIC ASSURANCE					
Middlesex	Lord's	April 26	34 & 0	2Ct	2-21 & 0-17
Leicestershire	Chelmsford	May 3	43	2Ct	2-76
Worcestershire	Worcester	May 19	166 *	1Ct	0-63 & 0-21
Hampshire	Southampton	May 23	125 & 39		1-33
Middlesex	Ilford	June 2	39 & 59 *		0-69
Gloucs	Ilford	June 6	204	1Ct	0-17
Warwickshire	Edgbaston	June 9	103		0-7 & 0-24
Somerset	Bath	June 16	0 & 73 *		0-38
Kent	Maidstone	June 4	3		
Derbyshire	Colchester	July 18	126		
Lancashire	Colchester	July 21	0 & 58		
Leicestershire	Leicester	July 25	69 & 31	1Ct	0-4
Sussex	Chelmsford	July 28	103 * & 11	1Ct	0-12 & 0-0
Notts	Southend	Aug 4	30	2Ct	
Glamorgan	Southend	Aug 8	66 & 14	1Ct	0-11 & 0-40
Yorkshire	Middlesbr'gh	Aug 11	207 *	1Ct	
Surrey	Chelmsford	Aug 18	0 & 79 *	1Ct	
Derbyshire	Derby	Aug 23	61	1Ct	
Northants	Northampton	Aug 29	1 & 16	1Ct	1-96
Northants	Chelmsford	Sept 7	44 & 36	2Ct	5-37 & 0-87
Kent	Chelmsford	Sept 12	169	1Ct	0-21 & 1-37
REFUGE ASSURANCE					
Kent	Chelmsford	April 22	50		0-32
Middlesex	Lord's	April 29	44	1Ct	0-25
Leicestershire	Leicester	May 6	84		
Gloucs	Chelmsford	May 13	1		
Worcestershire	Worcester	May 20	4		
Glamorgan	Ilford	June 3	12		2-19
Warwickshire	Edgbaston	June 10	60		1-18
Somerset	Bath	June 17	3		0-32
Hampshire	Southampton	July 8	17		0-7
Northants	Chelmsford	July 15	53		1-42
Lancashire	Colchester	July 22	111		0-45
Sussex	Chelmsford	July 29	28		

W | PLAYER RECORDS

Notts	Southend	Aug 5	7		0-20
Yorkshire	Middlesbr'gh	Aug 12	19	1Ct	3-37
Derbyshire	Derby	Aug 26	59		2-40

NATWEST TROPHY

Scotland	Chelmsford	June 27		1Ct	0-17
Hampshire	Chelmsford	July 11	47		

BENSON & HEDGES CUP

Notts	Chelmsford	April 24	16		1-25
Scotland	Glasgow	May 1	62		
Northants	Northampton	May 8	8 *	2Ct	
Notts	Chelmsford	May 30	4		

OTHER FIRST-CLASS

New Zealand	Chelmsford	June 30	63		0-24 & 0-16

OTHER ONE-DAY

Zimbabwe	Chelmsford	May 14	0	1Ct	0-22
For World XI					
Yorkshire	Scarborough	Sept 1	17		1-27
For Essex					
Yorkshire	Scarborough	Sept 3	0	1Ct	1-9
Hampshire	Scarborough	Sept 4	30		0-11

BATTING AVERAGES - Including fielding

	Matches	Inns	NO	Runs	HS	Avge	100s	50s	Ct	St
Britannic Assurance	21	32	6	2009	207 *	77.26	8	7	18	-
Refuge Assurance	15	15	0	552	111	36.80	1	5	2	-
NatWest Trophy	2	1	0	47	47	47.00	-	-	1	-
Benson & Hedges Cup	4	4	1	90	62	30.00	-	1	2	-
Other First-Class	1	1	0	63	63	63.00	-	1	-	-
Other One-Day	4	4	0	47	30	11.75	-	-	2	-
ALL FIRST-CLASS	22	33	6	2072	207 *	76.74	8	8	18	-
ALL ONE-DAY	25	24	1	736	111	32.00	1	6	7	-

BOWLING AVERAGES

	Overs	Mdns	Runs	Wkts	Avge	Best	5wI	10wM
Britannic Assurance	183	33	731	12	60.91	5-37	1	-
Refuge Assurance	52	1	317	9	35.22	3-37	-	
NatWest Trophy	5	1	17	0	-	-	-	
Benson & Hedges Cup	6	0	25	1	25.00	1-25	-	
Other First-Class	8	0	40	0	-	-	-	
Other One-Day	20	0	69	2	34.50	1-9	-	
ALL FIRST-CLASS	191	33	771	12	64.25	5-37	1	-
ALL ONE-DAY	83	2	428	12	35.66	3-37	-	

S.D. WEALE - Oxford University

Opposition	Venue	Date	Batting	Fielding	Bowling
OTHER FIRST-CLASS					
Glamorgan	The Parks	April 14	7 *		0-31
Somerset	The Parks	April 18			0-14
Surrey	The Parks	May 16	13		0-36 & 0-51
Lancashire	The Parks	June 16		0	1-119
Cambridge U	Lord's	July 4	4 *		

BATTING AVERAGES - Including fielding

	Matches	Inns	NO	Runs	HS	Avge	100s	50s	Ct	St
Other First-Class	5	4	2	24	13	12.00	-	-	-	-
ALL FIRST-CLASS	5	4	2	24	13	12.00	-	-	-	-

BOWLING AVERAGES

	Overs	Mdns	Runs	Wkts	Avge	Best	5wI	10wM
Other First-Class	50	8	251	1	251.00	1-119	-	-
ALL FIRST-CLASS	50	8	251	1	251.00	1-119	-	-

J. WEAVER - Shropshire

Opposition	Venue	Date	Batting	Fielding	Bowling
NATWEST TROPHY					
Derbyshire	Chesterfield	June 27	0	2Ct	

BATTING AVERAGES - Including fielding

	Matches	Inns	NO	Runs	HS	Avge	100s	50s	Ct	St
NatWest Trophy	1	1	0	0	0	0.00	-	-	2	-
ALL ONE-DAY	1	1	0	0	0	0.00	-	-	2	-

BOWLING AVERAGES
Did not bowl

P.N. WEEKES - Middlesex

Opposition	Venue	Date	Batting		Fielding	Bowling
BRITANNIC ASSURANCE						
Somerset	Uxbridge	July 21			1Ct	2-115
Sussex	Lord's	Aug 11	51 &	2		1-68
REFUGE ASSURANCE						
Lancashire	Old Trafford	April 22				0-21
Yorkshire	Scarborough	Aug 26	29 *		1Ct	0-36
Derbyshire	Edgbaston	Sept 16			1Ct	2-35
BENSON & HEDGES CUP						
Minor Counties	Lord's	April 24				0-27
OTHER FIRST-CLASS						
New Zealand	Lord's	May 19	22		2Ct	0-28 & 1-53

BATTING AVERAGES - Including fielding

	Matches	Inns	NO	Runs	HS	Avge	100s	50s	Ct	St
Britannic Assurance	2	2	0	53	51	26.50	-	1	1	-
Refuge Assurance	3	1	1	29	29 *		-	-	2	-
Benson & Hedges Cup	1	0	0	0	0		-	-	-	-
Other First-Class	1	1	0	22	22	22.00	-	-	2	-
ALL FIRST-CLASS	3	3	0	75	51	25.00	-	1	3	-
ALL ONE-DAY	4	1	1	29	29 *		-	-	2	-

BOWLING AVERAGES

	Overs	Mdns	Runs	Wkts	Avge	Best	5wI	10wM
Britannic Assurance	54	8	183	3	61.00	2-115	-	-
Refuge Assurance	16	1	92	2	46.00	2-35	-	
Benson & Hedges Cup	7	1	27	0	-	-	-	
Other First-Class	26	9	81	1	81.00	1-53	-	
ALL FIRST-CLASS	80	17	264	4	66.00	2-115	-	-
ALL ONE-DAY	23	2	119	2	59.50	2-35	-	

A.P. WELLS - Sussex

Opposition	Venue	Date	Batting		Fielding	Bowling
BRITANNIC ASSURANCE						
Surrey	Hove	April 26	44 * &	16	1Ct	0-39
Kent	Folkestone	May 3	69 &	13		
Hampshire	Southampton	May 15	0 &	22 *	1Ct	
Somerset	Taunton	May 23	18 &	23		
Lancashire	Horsham	June 2	33 &	0	1Ct	
Gloucs	Hove	June 16	8 &	22		0-17
Worcestershire	Worcester	June 20	59 *		1Ct	
Derbyshire	Hove	July 4		18		
Notts	Trent Bridge	July 7	23 &	25		
Surrey	Guildford	July 18	0 &	42	1Ct	
Northants	Northampton	July 21	21 &	102 *		1-88
Hampshire	Arundel	July 25	53 &	32		
Essex	Chelmsford	July 28	19 &	14	1Ct	
Warwickshire	Eastbourne	Aug 4	0 &	144 *		
Yorkshire	Eastbourne	Aug 8	42 &	4		
Middlesex	Lord's	Aug 11	9			
Kent	Hove	Aug 18	78 &	36		
Somerset	Hove	Aug 23	2 &	14		
Leicestershire	Leicester	Aug 29	109 * &	43	2Ct	
Gloucs	Bristol	Sept 12	5 &	27		
Middlesex	Hove	Sept 18	6 &	50	1Ct	
REFUGE ASSURANCE						
Derbyshire	Hove	April 22	57			
Surrey	Hove	April 29	86 *			

PLAYER RECORDS   W

Opposition	Venue	Date	Batting	Fielding	Bowling
Leicestershire	Leicester	June 10	2		
Yorkshire	Hove	June 17	6	1Ct	
Worcestershire	Worcester	June 24	34		
Hampshire	Hove	July 1	44*		
Notts	Trent Bridge	July 8	98		
Gloucs	Swindon	July 15	17		
Northants	Well'borough	July 22	2		
Essex	Chelmsford	July 29	6		
Warwickshire	Eastbourne	Aug 5	0		
Middlesex	Lord's	Aug 12	30		
Somerset	Hove	Aug 26	31		

NATWEST TROPHY

Ireland	Downpatrick	June 27			
Glamorgan	Cardiff	July 11	85		

BENSON & HEDGES CUP

Derbyshire	Derby	April 24	53		
Min Counties	Marlow	May 1	0		
Middlesex	Hove	May 8	74	1Ct	
Somerset	Hove	May 12	23		

OTHER FIRST-CLASS

New Zealand	Hove	May 26	86		
Cambridge U	Hove	June 30	137 & 27*	1Ct	2-25
Sri Lanka	Hove	Sept 5	96 & 20	2Ct	

OTHER ONE-DAY

For Duchess of Norfolk's XI

New Zealand	Arundel	May 6	16		

For Sussex

Yorkshire	Harrogate	June 14	5	1Ct	
Kent	Hove	Sept 2	5		

BATTING AVERAGES - Including fielding

	Matches	Inns	NO	Runs	HS	Avge	100s	50s	Ct	St
Britannic Assurance	21	39	6	1245	144*	37.72	3	5	9	-
Refuge Assurance	13	13	2	413	98	37.54	-	3	1	-
NatWest Trophy	2	1	0	85	85	85.00	-	1	-	-
Benson & Hedges Cup	4	4	0	150	74	37.50	-	2	1	-
Other First-Class	3	5	1	366	137	91.50	1	2	3	-
Other One-Day	3	3	0	26	16	8.66	-	-	1	-
ALL FIRST-CLASS	24	44	7	1611	144*	43.54	4	7	12	-
ALL ONE-DAY	22	21	2	674	98	35.47	-	6	3	-

BOWLING AVERAGES

	Overs	Mdns	Runs	Wkts	Avge	Best	5wI	10wM
Britannic Assurance	29	4	144	1	144.00	1-88	-	-
Refuge Assurance								
NatWest Trophy								
Benson & Hedges Cup								
Other First-Class	10	4	25	2	12.50	2-25	-	-
Other One-Day								
ALL FIRST-CLASS	39	8	169	3	56.33	2-25	-	-
ALL ONE-DAY								

■ C.M. WELLS - *Sussex*

Opposition	Venue	Date	Batting	Fielding	Bowling

BRITANNIC ASSURANCE

Opposition	Venue	Date	Batting	Fielding	Bowling
Surrey	Hove	April 26	37		1-59 & 1-16
Kent	Folkestone	May 3	14 & 0		2-67
Hampshire	Southampton	May 15	22 & 25		2-73
Glamorgan	Hove	May 19	1 & 94*		1-90
Somerset	Taunton	May 23	99* & 6*		1-72
Lancashire	Horsham	June 2	0 & 13		0-16
Gloucs	Hove	June 16	55		2-59
Worcestershire	Worcester	June 20			0-41
Derbyshire	Hove	July 4	51		0-58
Notts	Trent Bridge	July 7	5 & 44		1-20 & 3-48
Surrey	Guildford	July 18	0		1-47 & 0-21
Northants	Northampton	July 21	42 & 6	1Ct	0-42 & 0-10
Hampshire	Arundel	July 25	107 & 6		0-18 & 0-31
Essex	Chelmsford	July 28	0 & 21		1-44 & 0-37
Warwickshire	Eastbourne	Aug 4	40 & 19		0-43
Yorkshire	Eastbourne	Aug 8	0 & 15		1-76
Middlesex	Lord's	Aug 11	1	1Ct	0-14 & 0-2
Kent	Hove	Aug 18	41* & 42*		0-80
Somerset	Hove	Aug 23	4 & 2	1Ct	0-111

REFUGE ASSURANCE

Derbyshire	Hove	April 22	8		0-41
Surrey	Hove	April 29	5		0-34
Glamorgan	Hove	May 20	14		0-21
Leicestershire	Leicester	June 10	16		0-30
Yorkshire	Hove	June 17	2		1-17
Worcestershire	Worcester	June 24	29		1-21
Hampshire	Hove	July 1	1	1Ct	2-30
Notts	Trent Bridge	July 8	25		0-45
Gloucs	Swindon	July 15	9		0-17
Northants	Well'borough	July 22	6	1Ct	0-28
Essex	Chelmsford	July 29	28		0-27
Warwickshire	Eastbourne	Aug 5	64		0-17
Middlesex	Lord's	Aug 12	10		1-28
Somerset	Hove	Aug 26	3		2-28

NATWEST TROPHY

Ireland	Downpatrick	June 27			1-6

BENSON & HEDGES CUP

Derbyshire	Derby	April 24	36*		0-44
Min Counties	Marlow	May 1	33		0-30
Middlesex	Hove	May 8	59		1-45
Somerset	Hove	May 12	101		0-71

OTHER FIRST-CLASS

New Zealand	Hove	May 26	8 & 113*	2Ct	0-22 & 0-20

OTHER ONE-DAY

For Duchess of Norfolk's XI

New Zealand	Arundel	May 6	2		0-39

BATTING AVERAGES - Including fielding

	Matches	Inns	NO	Runs	HS	Avge	100s	50s	Ct	St
Britannic Assurance	19	31	4	812	107	30.07	1	4	3	-
Refuge Assurance	14	14	0	220	64	15.71	-	1	2	-
NatWest Trophy	1	0	0	0	0		-	-	-	-
Benson & Hedges Cup	4	4	1	229	101	76.33	1	1	-	-
Other First-Class	1	2	1	121	113*	121.00	1	-	2	-
Other One-Day	1	1	0	2	2	2.00	-	-	-	-
ALL FIRST-CLASS	20	33	5	933	113*	33.32	2	4	5	-
ALL ONE-DAY	20	19	1	451	101	25.05	1	2	2	-

BOWLING AVERAGES

	Overs	Mdns	Runs	Wkts	Avge	Best	5wI	10wM
Britannic Assurance	366	67	1195	17	70.29	3-48	-	-
Refuge Assurance	106.5	6	384	7	54.85	2-28	-	-
NatWest Trophy	9	6	6	1	6.00	1-6	-	-
Benson & Hedges Cup	42	4	190	1	190.00	1-45	-	-
Other First-Class	8	1	42	0		-	-	-
Other One-Day	10	1	39	0		-	-	-
ALL FIRST-CLASS	374	68	1237	17	72.76	3-48	-	-
ALL ONE-DAY	167.5	17	619	9	68.77	2-28	-	-

■ V.J. WELLS - *Kent*

Opposition	Venue	Date	Batting	Fielding	Bowling

BRITANNIC ASSURANCE

Opposition	Venue	Date	Batting	Fielding	Bowling
Notts	Tunbridge We	June 2	2 & 20	1Ct	
Yorkshire	Tunbridge We	June 6	4		
Warwickshire	Edgbaston	June 23	5 & 25	3Ct	
Lancashire	Maidstone	June 30	9 & 11		
Leicestershire	Leicester	Aug 23	40 & 28	1Ct	5-43 & 0-29
Hampshire	Bournemouth	Aug 29	58 & 9		2-29 & 1-8
Surrey	Canterbury	Sept 7	50 & 11	3Ct	4-126
Essex	Chelmsford	Sept 12	34 & 46		0-22

REFUGE ASSURANCE

Lancashire	Maidstone	July 1	13	1Ct	
Worcestershire	Canterbury	July 29	16		
Leicestershire	Leicester	Aug 26	7*		0-5

NATWEST TROPHY

Oxfordshire	Oxford	June 27	100*		

OTHER ONE-DAY

Sussex	Hove	Sept 2	18	1Ct	
Surrey	Hove	Sept 4	107		

W PLAYER RECORDS

BATTING AVERAGES - Including fielding

	Matches	Inns	NO	Runs	HS	Avge	100s	50s	Ct	St
Britannic Assurance	8	15	0	352	58	23.46	-	2	8	-
Refuge Assurance	3	3	1	36	16	18.00	-	-	1	-
NatWest Trophy	1	1	1	100	100*		-	1	-	-
Other One-Day	2	2	0	125	107	62.50	1	-	1	-
ALL FIRST-CLASS	8	15	0	352	58	23.46	-	2	8	-
ALL ONE-DAY	6	6	2	261	107	65.25	2	-	2	-

BOWLING AVERAGES

	Overs	Mdns	Runs	Wkts	Avge	Best	5wI	10wM
Britannic Assurance	85	19	257	12	21.41	5-43	1	-
Refuge Assurance	1	0	5	0	-	-	-	-
NatWest Trophy								
Other One-Day								
ALL FIRST-CLASS	85	19	257	12	21.41	5-43	1	-
ALL ONE-DAY	1	0	5	0	-	-	-	-

◼ M.J. WESTON - *Worcestershire*

Opposition	Venue	Date	Batting			Fielding	Bowling
BRITANNIC ASSURANCE							
Essex	Worcester	May 19	0	&	14		0-23
Warwickshire	Edgbaston	May 26	6	&	11	1Ct	
Yorkshire	Worcester	June 2	3				
Surrey	The Oval	June 16	6	&	38*		
Middlesex	Lord's	June 30	2				
REFUGE ASSURANCE							
Somerset	Taunton	April 22					0-22
Essex	Worcester	May 20	90			2Ct	2-33
Warwickshire	Worcester	May 27	15				1-12
Yorkshire	Worcester	June 3	4				0-36
Surrey	The Oval	June 17	5				0-15
Middlesex	Lord's	July 1	7				0-30
Gloucs	Worcester	July 8	4				1-26
Lancashire	Old Trafford	July 15	31				
Kent	Canterbury	July 29	6				0-26
Leicestershire	Leicester	Aug 5					1-27
Hampshire	Worcester	Aug 12	6				0-32
Northants	Worcester	Aug 19	3*				1-20
NATWEST TROPHY							
Suffolk	Bury St Ed's	June 27	40			1Ct	0-20
Somerset	Taunton	July 11	98				
Northants	Northampton	Aug 1	14			1Ct	
BENSON & HEDGES CUP							
Warwickshire	Edgbaston	May 10	36			1Ct	
Glamorgan	Worcester	May 30	25				1-21
Notts	Trent Bridge	June 13	99*				
Lancashire	Lord's	July 14	19				
OTHER FIRST-CLASS							
New Zealand	Worcester	May 12	3	&	7		1-32 & 0-19
OTHER ONE-DAY							
Hampshire	Scarborough	Sept 2	19				0-18

BATTING AVERAGES - Including fielding

	Matches	Inns	NO	Runs	HS	Avge	100s	50s	Ct	St
Britannic Assurance	5	8	1	80	38*	11.42	-	-	1	-
Refuge Assurance	12	10	1	171	90	19.00	-	1	2	-
NatWest Trophy	3	3	0	152	98	50.66	-	1	2	-
Benson & Hedges Cup	4	4	1	179	99*	59.66	-	1	1	-
Other First-Class	1	2	0	10	7	5.00	-	-	-	-
Other One-Day	1	1	0	19	19	19.00	-	-	-	-
ALL FIRST-CLASS	6	10	1	90	38*	10.00	-	-	1	-
ALL ONE-DAY	20	18	2	521	99*	32.56	-	3	5	-

BOWLING AVERAGES

	Overs	Mdns	Runs	Wkts	Avge	Best	5wI	10wM
Britannic Assurance	7	1	23	0	-	-	-	-
Refuge Assurance	62	0	279	6	46.50	2-33	-	-
NatWest Trophy	4	0	20	0	-	-	-	-
Benson & Hedges Cup	6	1	21	1	21.00	1-21	-	-
Other First-Class	14	2	51	1	51.00	1-32	-	-

Other One-Day	6	1	18	0	-	-	-	-
ALL FIRST-CLASS	21	3	74	1	74.00	1-32	-	-
ALL ONE-DAY	78	2	338	7	48.28	2-33	-	-

◼ J.J. WHITAKER - *Leicestershire*

Opposition	Venue	Date	Batting			Fielding	Bowling
BRITANNIC ASSURANCE							
Glamorgan	Cardiff	April 26	32	&	31*		
Essex	Chelmsford	May 3	31	&	15		
Notts	Leicester	May 15	43	&	13	3Ct	
Lancashire	Old Trafford	May 19	8	&	107*		
Somerset	Leicester	May 26	89	&	18	1Ct	
Hampshire	Leicester	June 2	6	&	62	1Ct	
Northants	Northampton	June 6	35	&	3		
Middlesex	Leicester	June 16	42*	&	0		
Derbyshire	Leicester	June 20	116			1Ct	
Gloucs	Gloucester	June 23	37			2Ct	
Notts	Trent Bridge	June 30	43	&	83		
Glamorgan	Hinckley	July 7	94	&	45		
Essex	Leicester	July 25	8	&	34		
Yorkshire	Sheffield	July 28	23	&	38*		
Worcestershire	Leicester	Aug 4	16	&	62		
Kent	Dartford	Aug 8	6	&	0		
Surrey	The Oval	Aug 11	20	&	23	3Ct	
Warwickshire	Edgbaston	Aug 18	16	&	13		
Kent	Leicester	Aug 23	0	&	100	1Ct	
Sussex	Leicester	Aug 29	16	&	42		
Northants	Leicester	Sept 12	28	&	92		
Derbyshire	Derby	Sept 18	65	&	20		
REFUGE ASSURANCE							
Northants	Leicester	April 22	32			1Ct	
Glamorgan	Cardiff	April 29	72				
Essex	Leicester	May 6	44				
Lancashire	Old Trafford	May 20	34			1Ct	
Somerset	Leicester	May 27	83				
Hampshire	Leicester	June 3	0				
Sussex	Leicester	June 10	53*				
Middlesex	Leicester	June 17	4				
Gloucs	Gloucester	June 24	31				
Notts	Trent Bridge	July 1	4			1Ct	
Derbyshire	Knypersley	July 15	12				
Yorkshire	Sheffield	July 29	25			1Ct	
Surrey	The Oval	Aug 12	8				
Kent	Leicester	Aug 26	20			2Ct	
NATWEST TROPHY							
Hampshire	Leicester	June 27	24				
BENSON & HEDGES CUP							
Northants	Leicester	April 24	46				
Notts	Trent Bridge	May 1	7			1Ct	
Scotland	Leicester	May 12	46				
OTHER FIRST-CLASS							
Oxford U	The Parks	May 23	124*			1Ct	
India	Leicester	July 21	61	&	7*	1Ct	
OTHER ONE-DAY							
New Zealand	Leicester	June 14	9				
For Yorkshiremen							
Yorkshire	Scarborough	Sept 6	10				

BATTING AVERAGES - Including fielding

	Matches	Inns	NO	Runs	HS	Avge	100s	50s	Ct	St
Britannic Assurance	22	42	4	1575	116	41.44	3	7	12	-
Refuge Assurance	14	14	1	422	83	32.46	-	3	6	-
NatWest Trophy	1	1	0	24	24	24.00	-	-	-	-
Benson & Hedges Cup	3	3	0	99	46	33.00	-	-	1	-
Other First-Class	2	3	2	192	124*	192.00	1	1	2	-
Other One-Day	2	2	0	19	10	9.50	-	-	-	-
ALL FIRST-CLASS	24	45	6	1767	124*	45.30	4	8	14	-
ALL ONE-DAY	20	20	1	564	83	29.68	-	3	7	-

BOWLING AVERAGES
Did not bowl

PLAYER RECORDS

W

B.H. WHITE - *Wiltshire*

Opposition	Venue	Date	Batting	Fielding	Bowling
NATWEST TROPHY					
Surrey	Trowbridge	June 27	0		

BATTING AVERAGES - Including fielding

	Matches	Inns	NO	Runs	HS	Avge	100s	50s	Ct	St
NatWest Trophy	1	1	0	0	0	0.00	-	-	-	-
ALL ONE-DAY	1	1	0	0	0	0.00	-	-	-	-

BOWLING AVERAGES
Did not bowl

C. WHITE - *Yorkshire*

Opposition	Venue	Date	Batting			Fielding	Bowling
BRITANNIC ASSURANCE							
Northants	Headingley	April 26	9	&	9	1Ct	
Warwickshire	Edgbaston	May 3	1	&	6		0-6 & 1-40
Kent	Tunbridge We	June 6					0-33
Surrey	Harrogate	June 9	2				5-74
Notts	Scarborough	July 4				1Ct	2-99
Northants	Northampton	July 7	38	&	29 *		0-39
Middlesex	Uxbridge	July 18	12	&	0	1Ct	0-59 & 1-38
Notts	Trent Bridge	Sept 18					0-66 & 0-65
REFUGE ASSURANCE							
Notts	Trent Bridge	April 22	26 *				
Warwickshire	Edgbaston	May 6	30 *				0-26
Derbyshire	Headingley	May 13				1Ct	
Kent	Canterbury	May 20	20 *				2-49
Northants	Tring	July 8					2-56
Somerset	Scarborough	July 15				1Ct	1-34
BENSON & HEDGES CUP							
Hampshire	Southampton	April 24	17 *				
Combined U	Headingley	May 8	1				
Surrey	The Oval	May 12				1Ct	1-31
OTHER FIRST-CLASS							
Zimbabwe	Headingley	May 16	9	&	12 *	1Ct	2-12 & 2-40
India	Headingley	June 30					0-37
OTHER ONE-DAY							
Sussex	Harrogate	June 14				2Ct	1-42

BATTING AVERAGES - Including fielding

	Matches	Inns	NO	Runs	HS	Avge	100s	50s	Ct	St
Britannic Assurance	8	9	1	106	38	13.25	-	-	3	-
Refuge Assurance	6	3	3	76	30 *	-	-	-	2	-
Benson & Hedges Cup	3	2	1	18	17 *	18.00	-	-	1	-
Other First-Class	2	2	1	21	12 *	21.00	-	-	1	-
Other One-Day	1	0	0	0	0		-	-	2	-
ALL FIRST-CLASS	10	11	2	127	38	14.11	-	-	4	-
ALL ONE-DAY	10	5	4	94	30 *	94.00	-	-	5	-

BOWLING AVERAGES

	Overs	Mdns	Runs	Wkts	Avge	Best	5wI	10wM
Britannic Assurance	122	12	519	9	57.66	5-74	1	-
Refuge Assurance	24.1	0	165	5	33.00	2-49	-	
Benson & Hedges Cup	9	0	31	1	31.00	1-31	-	
Other First-Class	37	11	89	4	22.25	2-12	-	
Other One-Day	9	1	42	1	42.00	1-42	-	
ALL FIRST-CLASS	159	23	608	13	46.76	5-74	1	-
ALL ONE-DAY	42.1	1	238	7	34.00	2-49	-	

M.R. WHITNEY - *World XI*

Opposition	Venue	Date	Batting	Fielding	Bowling
OTHER FIRST-CLASS					
India	Scarborough	Aug 29		1Ct	2-51 & 3-46

BATTING AVERAGES - Including fielding

	Matches	Inns	NO	Runs	HS	Avge	100s	50s	Ct	St
Other First-Class	1	0	0	0	0	-	-	-	1	-
ALL FIRST-CLASS	1	0	0	0	0	-	-	-	1	-

BOWLING AVERAGES

	Overs	Mdns	Runs	Wkts	Avge	Best	5wI	10wM
Other First-Class	27	5	97	5	19.40	3-46	-	-
ALL FIRST-CLASS	27	5	97	5	19.40	3-46	-	-

P. WHITTICASE - *Leicestershire*

Opposition	Venue	Date	Batting			Fielding	Bowling
BRITANNIC ASSURANCE							
Glamorgan	Cardiff	April 26	11			6Ct	
Essex	Chelmsford	May 3	0			1Ct	
Notts	Leicester	May 15	2 *				
Sussex	Leicester	Aug 29	11 *	&	4	2Ct	
Northants	Leicester	Sept 12	11	&	0	4Ct	
REFUGE ASSURANCE							
Northants	Leicester	April 22	38			1Ct	
Glamorgan	Cardiff	April 29	2			2Ct	
BENSON & HEDGES CUP							
Northants	Leicester	April 24	7 *			1Ct	
Notts	Trent Bridge	May 1	45			1Ct	
Scotland	Leicester	May 12				2Ct	

BATTING AVERAGES - Including fielding

	Matches	Inns	NO	Runs	HS	Avge	100s	50s	Ct	St
Britannic Assurance	5	7	2	39	11 *	7.80	-	-	13	-
Refuge Assurance	2	2	0	40	38	20.00	-	-	3	-
Benson & Hedges Cup	3	2	1	52	45	52.00	-	-	4	-
ALL FIRST-CLASS	5	7	2	39	11 *	7.80	-	-	13	-
ALL ONE-DAY	5	4	1	92	45	30.66	-	-	7	-

BOWLING AVERAGES
Did not bowl

P. WICKREMASINGHE - *Sri Lanka*

Opposition	Venue	Date	Batting	Fielding	Bowling
OTHER FIRST-CLASS					
Notts	Cleethorpes	Aug 25			1-63 & 3-95
Sussex	Hove	Sept 5	17		0-41 & 2-30
Lancashire	Old Trafford	Sept 8	0		0-11 & 0-11
OTHER ONE-DAY					
Surrey	The Oval	Sept 2	12	2Ct	0-45
Somerset	Taunton	Sept 3	24 *	1Ct	0-45

BATTING AVERAGES - Including fielding

	Matches	Inns	NO	Runs	HS	Avge	100s	50s	Ct	St
Other First-Class	3	2	0	17	17	8.50	-	-	-	-
Other One-Day	2	2	1	36	24 *	36.00	-	-	3	-
ALL FIRST-CLASS	3	2	0	17	17	8.50	-	-	-	-
ALL ONE-DAY	2	2	1	36	24 *	36.00	-	-	3	-

BOWLING AVERAGES

	Overs	Mdns	Runs	Wkts	Avge	Best	5wI	10wM
Other First-Class	79	17	251	6	41.83	3-95	-	-
Other One-Day	18	2	90	0			-	-

W PLAYER RECORDS

ALL FIRST-CLASS	79	17	251	6	41.83 3-95 - -
ALL ONE-DAY	18	2	90	0	- -

K.I.W. WIJEGUNAWARDENE - *Sri Lanka*

Opposition	Venue	Date	Batting	Fielding	Bowling
OTHER FIRST-CLASS					
Glamorgan	Ebbw Vale	Aug 22		1Ct	2-30 & 2-79
Warwickshire	Edgbaston	Aug 29		1Ct	2-82 & 2-31
Lancashire	Old Trafford	Sept 8		2Ct	0-16 & 0-5
Hampshire	Southampton	Sept 12	0	2Ct	1-75
OTHER ONE-DAY					
Surrey	The Oval	Sept 2	1		0-39
Somerset	Taunton	Sept 3			0-50

BATTING AVERAGES - Including fielding

	Matches	Inns	NO	Runs	HS	Avge	100s	50s	Ct	St
Other First-Class	4	1	0	0	0	0.00	-	-	6	-
Other One-Day	2	1	0	1	1	1.00	-	-	-	-
ALL FIRST-CLASS	4	1	0	0	0	0.00	-	-	6	-
ALL ONE-DAY	2	1	0	1	1	1.00	-	-	-	-

BOWLING AVERAGES

	Overs	Mdns	Runs	Wkts	Avge	Best	5wI	10wM
Other First-Class	87.3	13	318	9	35.33	2-30	-	-
Other One-Day	18	1	89	0	-	-	-	-
ALL FIRST-CLASS	87.3	13	318	9	35.33	2-30	-	-
ALL ONE-DAY	18	1	89	0	-	-	-	-

P. WIJETUNGA - *Sri Lanka*

Opposition	Venue	Date	Batting	Fielding	Bowling
OTHER FIRST-CLASS					
Glamorgan	Ebbw Vale	Aug 22			2-40 & 2-85
Notts	Cleethorpes	Aug 25			0-29 & 0-13
Sussex	Hove	Sept 5	5 *	1Ct	1-40 & 1-15
Lancashire	Old Trafford	Sept 8		1Ct	4-133 & 2-83

BATTING AVERAGES - Including fielding

	Matches	Inns	NO	Runs	HS	Avge	100s	50s	Ct	St
Other First-Class	4	1	1	5	5*	-	-	-	2	-
ALL FIRST-CLASS	4	1	1	5	5*	-	-	-	2	-

BOWLING AVERAGES

	Overs	Mdns	Runs	Wkts	Avge	Best	5wI	10wM
Other First-Class	129.4	24	438	12	36.50	4-133	-	-
ALL FIRST-CLASS	129.4	24	438	12	36.50	4-133	-	-

D.J. WILD - *Northamptonshire*

Opposition	Venue	Date	Batting	Fielding	Bowling
BRITANNIC ASSURANCE					
Warwickshire	Northampton	May 15	17 & 0		0-42
REFUGE ASSURANCE					
Leicestershire	Leicester	April 22	0		
Warwickshire	Edgbaston	April 29	0		
Derbyshire	Northampton	May 6	48*		
Surrey	The Oval	June 3	10		3-8
Glamorgan	Northampton	June 10	4		
Middlesex	Northampton	June 24	8		0-31
Yorkshire	Tring	July 8	19		2-26
Essex	Chelmsford	July 15	20		1-36
Notts	Trent Bridge	July 29	2		0-24
Hampshire	Bournemouth	Aug 5	16*		0-23

Lancashire	Northampton	Aug 12	0		2-31
Worcestershire	Worcester	Aug 19		1Ct	0-6
Gloucs	Northampton	Aug 26	15		2-58
BENSON & HEDGES CUP					
Leicestershire	Leicester	April 24	0		
Essex	Northampton	May 8	0		0-20
Scotland	Northampton	May 10	15		0-13
OTHER FIRST-CLASS					
Cambridge U	Fenner's	April 14	20 & 43		1-32

BATTING AVERAGES - Including fielding

	Matches	Inns	NO	Runs	HS	Avge	100s	50s	Ct	St
Britannic Assurance	1	2	0	17	17	8.50	-	-	-	-
Refuge Assurance	13	12	2	142	48*	14.20	-	-	1	-
Benson & Hedges Cup	3	3	0	15	15	5.00	-	-	-	-
Other First-Class	1	2	0	63	43	31.50	-	-	-	-
ALL FIRST-CLASS	2	4	0	80	43	20.00	-	-	-	-
ALL ONE-DAY	16	15	2	157	48*	12.07	-	-	1	-

BOWLING AVERAGES

	Overs	Mdns	Runs	Wkts	Avge	Best	5wI	10wM
Britannic Assurance	12.5	4	42	0	-	-	-	-
Refuge Assurance	44.4	0	243	10	24.30	3-8	-	-
Benson & Hedges Cup	8	2	33	0	-	-	-	-
Other First-Class	9	2	32	1	32.00	1-32	-	-
ALL FIRST-CLASS	21.5	6	74	1	74.00	1-32	-	-
ALL ONE-DAY	52.4	2	276	10	27.60	3-8	-	-

P. WILLEY - *Leicestershire*

Opposition	Venue	Date	Batting	Fielding	Bowling
BRITANNIC ASSURANCE					
Notts	Leicester	May 15	30 & 1		0-0 & 2-40
Lancashire	Old Trafford	May 19	43		1-43 & 2-54
Somerset	Leicester	May 26	15 & 29	1Ct	1-23 & 0-4
Hampshire	Leicester	June 2	42 & 23	1Ct	0-25
Northants	Northampton	June 6	34 & 20*		0-1
Middlesex	Leicester	June 16	5 * & 11		0-14
Derbyshire	Leicester	June 20	4		0-0 & 2-7
Gloucs	Gloucester	June 23	8		0-25 & 0-2
Notts	Trent Bridge	June 30	73 * & 2		1-15 & 0-24
Glamorgan	Hinckley	July 7	4 & 0*		1-60 & 2-69
Essex	Leicester	July 25	7 & 1	2Ct	0-0
Yorkshire	Sheffield	July 28	47 & 18*	1Ct	1-29
Worcestershire	Leicester	Aug 4	7 & 79		1-96 & 0-59
Kent	Dartford	Aug 8	61 & 10		2-94 & 1-29
Surrey	The Oval	Aug 11	1 & 3		0-60
Warwickshire	Edgbaston	Aug 18	46 & 51*	3Ct	
Kent	Leicester	Aug 23	14 & 25	1Ct	0-84
Sussex	Leicester	Aug 29	112 & 35	1Ct	1-61 & 1-30
Northants	Leicester	Sept 12	0 & 30		0-12 & 1-56
Derbyshire	Derby	Sept 18	1 & 0		
REFUGE ASSURANCE					
Northants	Leicester	April 22	5		0-5
Lancashire	Old Trafford	May 20	18	1Ct	2-39
Somerset	Leicester	May 27	52		2-33
Hampshire	Leicester	June 3	68*		0-25
Sussex	Leicester	June 10	4	1Ct	1-44
Middlesex	Leicester	June 17	39	1Ct	2-58
Gloucs	Gloucester	June 24	1	2Ct	2-12
Notts	Trent Bridge	July 1	41		0-17
Derbyshire	Knypersley	July 15	24		0-45
Yorkshire	Sheffield	July 29	7	1Ct	0-25
NATWEST TROPHY					
Hampshire	Leicester	June 27	72*	2Ct	1-54
BENSON & HEDGES CUP					
Northants	Leicester	April 24	49		0-36
OTHER FIRST-CLASS					
Oxford U	The Parks	May 23	177		1-4 & 1-29
India	Leicester	July 21	5 & 76		1-42
OTHER ONE-DAY					
New Zealand	Leicester	June 14	4		1-21

PLATER RECORDS — W

PLAYER RECORDS

BATTING AVERAGES - Including fielding

	Matches	Inns	NO	Runs	HS	Avge	100s	50s	Ct	St
Britannic Assurance	20	37	6	892	112	28.77	1	4	10	-
Refuge Assurance	10	10	1	259	68 *	28.77	-	2	6	-
NatWest Trophy	1	1	1	72	72 *	-	-	1	2	-
Benson & Hedges Cup	1	1	0	49	49	49.00	-	-	-	-
Other First-Class	2	3	0	258	177	86.00	1	1	-	-
Other One-Day	1	1	0	4	4	4.00	-	-	-	-
ALL FIRST-CLASS	22	40	6	1150	177	33.82	2	5	10	-
ALL ONE-DAY	13	13	2	384	72 *	34.90	-	3	8	-

BOWLING AVERAGES

	Overs	Mdns	Runs	Wkts	Avge	Best	5wI	10wM
Britannic Assurance	377.4	101	1016	20	50.80	2-7	-	-
Refuge Assurance	58	0	303	9	33.66	2-12	-	
NatWest Trophy	12	2	54	1	54.00	1-54	-	
Benson & Hedges Cup	11	0	36	0	-	-	-	
Other First-Class	44	18	75	3	25.00	1-4	-	-
Other One-Day	11	3	21	1	21.00	1-21	-	
ALL FIRST-CLASS	421.4	119	1091	23	47.43	2-7	-	-
ALL ONE-DAY	92	5	414	11	37.63	2-12	-	-

N.F. WILLIAMS - *Middlesex & England*

Opposition	Venue	Date	Batting	Fielding	Bowling
CORNHILL TEST MATCHES					
India	The Oval	Aug 23	38		2-148
BRITANNIC ASSURANCE					
Essex	Lord's	April 26	26		3-69 & 1-26
Kent	Lord's	May 15	18		7-61 & 2-67
Surrey	Lord's	May 23	40 & 18		2-57
Gloucs	Lord's	May 26	0 & 50 *		0-32 & 0-10
Essex	Ilford	June 2			2-58 & 1-57
Warwickshire	Lord's	June 6	17	1Ct	0-77 & 0-12
Leicestershire	Leicester	June 16	1		0-34 & 2-49
Lancashire	Old Trafford	June 20			1-53
Northants	Luton	June 23	14		2-23 & 0-12
Worcestershire	Lord's	June 30	49 *		3-27 & 0-28
Yorkshire	Uxbridge	July 18	2		3-55 & 4-43
Somerset	Uxbridge	July 21	22		0-45 & 0-38
Kent	Canterbury	July 25	8	1Ct	0-49 & 3-65
Notts	Trent Bridge	July 28	14 & 3		0-34 & 1-46
Glamorgan	Lord's	Aug 4	17 & 1	1Ct	5-59 & 1-30
Sussex	Lord's	Aug 11	9 & 55 *		1-69
Derbyshire	Derby	Aug 18	5 & 3		1-56 & 0-39
Notts	Lord's	Sept 7		1Ct	3-41
Sussex	Hove	Sept 18	18		1-9
REFUGE ASSURANCE					
Lancashire	Old Trafford	April 22			4-49
Essex	Lord's	April 29			2-33
Kent	Folkestone	May 6			0-51
Notts	Lord's	May 13	3		1-30
Gloucs	Lord's	May 27			1-44
Warwickshire	Lord's	June 3		1Ct	1-22
Hampshire	Basingstoke	June 10			2-29
Leicestershire	Leicester	June 17		1Ct	2-55
Northants	Northampton	June 24			1-39
Worcestershire	Lord's	July 1		4Ct	0-17
Somerset	Lord's	July 8	12		1-39
Surrey	The Oval	July 15	1		1-42
Glamorgan	Lord's	Aug 5	9 *		1-33
Sussex	Lord's	Aug 12	11 *		1-32
Derbyshire	Derby	Aug 19			1-27
Lancashire	Old Trafford	Sept 5	10 *		0-32
NATWEST TROPHY					
Berkshire	Lord's	June 27			0-67
Surrey	Uxbridge	July 11			0-42
Glamorgan	Lord's	Aug 1			0-38
Lancashire	Old Trafford	Aug 15			0-72
BENSON & HEDGES CUP					
Min Counties	Lord's	April 24	1 *		1-27
Sussex	Hove	May 8			2-45
Somerset	Lord's	May 10	22 *		2-52
Derbyshire	Derby	May 12	28		3-37
Somerset	Taunton	May 30	4		3-40

OTHER FIRST-CLASS

Cambridge U	Fenner's	May 3	20	3-35 & 0-5

BATTING AVERAGES - Including fielding

	Matches	Inns	NO	Runs	HS	Avge	100s	50s	Ct	St
Cornhill Test Matches	1	1	0	38	38	38.00	-	-	-	-
Britannic Assurance	19	22	3	390	55 *	20.52	-	2	4	-
Refuge Assurance	16	6	3	46	12	15.33	-	-	6	-
NatWest Trophy	4	0	0	0	0	-	-	-	-	-
Benson & Hedges Cup	5	4	2	55	28	27.50	-	-	-	-
Other First-Class	1	1	0	20	20	20.00	-	-	-	-
ALL FIRST-CLASS	21	24	3	448	55 *	21.33	-	2	4	-
ALL ONE-DAY	25	10	5	101	28	20.20	-	-	6	-

BOWLING AVERAGES

	Overs	Mdns	Runs	Wkts	Avge	Best	5wI	10wM
Cornhill Test Matches	41	5	148	2	74.00	2-148	-	-
Britannic Assurance	469.1	88	1430	49	29.18	7-61	2	-
Refuge Assurance	112	4	574	19	30.21	4-49	-	-
NatWest Trophy	41	3	219	0	-	-	-	-
Benson & Hedges Cup	54	7	201	11	18.27	3-37	-	-
Other First-Class	19	5	40	3	13.33	3-35	-	-
ALL FIRST-CLASS	529.1	98	1618	54	29.96	7-61	2	-
ALL ONE-DAY	207	14	994	30	33.13	4-49	-	-

R.C.J. WILLIAMS - *Gloucestershire*

Opposition	Venue	Date	Batting	Fielding	Bowling
BRITANNIC ASSURANCE					
Glamorgan	Swansea	July 4		1Ct	
Worcestershire	Worcester	July 7	0 & 1	2Ct	
Northants	Cheltenham	July 25	44 *	7Ct	
Surrey	Cheltenham	July 28	0	5Ct,1St	
Warwickshire	Bristol	Aug 8	2	3Ct,1St	
Kent	Bristol	Aug 11	0 *	2Ct	
Northants	Northampton	Aug 23	35 *	2Ct,2St	
REFUGE ASSURANCE					
Worcestershire	Worcester	July 8		1Ct	
Surrey	Cheltenham	July 29		3Ct	
Kent	Bristol	Aug 12		1Ct	
Northants	Northampton	Aug 26			
OTHER FIRST-CLASS					
India	Bristol	Aug 4	50 *	5Ct	

BATTING AVERAGES - Including fielding

	Matches	Inns	NO	Runs	HS	Avge	100s	50s	Ct	St
Britannic Assurance	7	7	3	82	44 *	20.50	-	-	22	4
Refuge Assurance	4	0	0	0	0	-	-	-	5	-
Other First-Class	1	1	1	50	50 *	-	-	1	5	-
ALL FIRST-CLASS	8	8	4	132	50 *	33.00	-	1	27	4
ALL ONE-DAY	4	0	0	0	0	-	-	-	5	-

BOWLING AVERAGES
Did not bowl

R.G. WILLIAMS - *Northamptonshire*

Opposition	Venue	Date	Batting	Fielding	Bowling
BRITANNIC ASSURANCE					
Warwickshire	Northampton	May 15	8 & 9		0-38
Leicestershire	Northampton	June 6			0-19
Glamorgan	Northampton	June 9	34		1-42 & 3-51
Middlesex	Luton	June 23	4 & 11	1Ct	4-94
Somerset	Taunton	June 30			3-64 & 0-54
Surrey	The Oval	July 4	0		1-65
Yorkshire	Northampton	July 7	69 & 2		2-99 & 0-6
Kent	Northampton	July 18	96	1Ct	1-28 & 0-67
Gloucs	Cheltenham	July 25	47 & 0		2-42
Hampshire	Bournemouth	Aug 4	16 & 13		3-82
Derbyshire	Chesterfield	Aug 8	9 & 4		1-41 & 0-9
Lancashire	Northampton	Aug 11	11 * & 10 *	1Ct	1-57 & 0-16

W PLAYER RECORDS

Gloucs	Northampton	Aug 23	1 & 15		1-73 & 0-13
Essex	Northampton	Aug 29	21 *	1Ct	4-99 & 0-8
Essex	Chelmsford	Sept 7	0 & 12 *	2Ct	2-64
Leicestershire	Leicester	Sept 12	1 & 89		1-27 & 1-7

REFUGE ASSURANCE

Glamorgan	Northampton	June 10	1 *	1Ct	1-34
Middlesex	Northampton	June 24	1		
Somerset	Taunton	July 1	1		1-31
Yorkshire	Tring	July 8	35		0-36
Sussex	Well'borough	July 22	6	1Ct	1-63
Notts	Trent Bridge	July 29	20		1-35
Hampshire	Bournemouth	Aug 5	34 *		0-29
Lancashire	Northampton	Aug 12	1 *		0-45

NATWEST TROPHY

Staffordshire	Northampton	June 27		1Ct	1-32
Notts	Northampton	July 11	9 *		1-39
Worcestershire	Northampton	Aug 1	6	1Ct	3-86
Hampshire	Southampton	Aug 15	44	1Ct	1-61
Lancashire	Lord's	Sept 1	9		1-26

BENSON & HEDGES CUP

Notts	Trent Bridge	May 12	17

OTHER FIRST-CLASS

New Zealand	Northampton	June 16	73 & 11 *	0-39

BATTING AVERAGES - Including fielding

	Matches	Inns	NO	Runs	HS	Avge	100s	50s	Ct	St
Britannic Assurance	16	24	4	482	96	24.10	-	3	6	-
Refuge Assurance	8	8	3	99	35	19.80	-	-	2	-
NatWest Trophy	5	4	1	68	44	22.66	-	-	3	-
Benson & Hedges Cup	1	1	0	17	17	17.00	-	-	-	-
Other First-Class	1	2	1	84	73	84.00	-	1	-	-
ALL FIRST-CLASS	17	26	5	566	96	26.95	-	4	6	-
ALL ONE-DAY	14	13	4	184	44	20.44	-	-	5	-

BOWLING AVERAGES

	Overs	Mdns	Runs	Wkts	Avge	Best	5wI	10wM
Britannic Assurance	417.3	116	1165	31	37.58	4-94	-	
Refuge Assurance	47	0	273	4	68.25	1-31	-	
NatWest Trophy	51	5	244	7	34.85	3-86	-	
Benson & Hedges Cup								
Other First-Class	15	3	39	0	-	-	-	
ALL FIRST-CLASS	432.3	119	1204	31	38.83	4-94	-	
ALL ONE-DAY	98	5	517	11	47.00	3-86	-	

S. WILLIAMS - *Wiltshire*

Opposition	Venue	Date	Batting	Fielding	Bowling
NATWEST TROPHY					
Surrey	Trowbridge	June 27	11		

BATTING AVERAGES - Including fielding

	Matches	Inns	NO	Runs	HS	Avge	100s	50s	Ct	St
NatWest Trophy	1	1	0	11	11	11.00	-	-	-	-
ALL ONE-DAY	1	1	0	11	11	11.00	-	-	-	-

BOWLING AVERAGES
Did not bowl

A. WINCHESTER - *Oxford University*

Opposition	Venue	Date	Batting	Fielding	Bowling
OTHER FIRST-CLASS					
Hampshire	The Parks	May 3	0 *		0-50 & 0-31

BATTING AVERAGES - Including fielding

	Matches	Inns	NO	Runs	HS	Avge	100s	50s	Ct	St
Other First-Class	1	1	1	0	0 *	-	-	-	-	-
ALL FIRST-CLASS	1	1	1	0	0 *	-	-	-	-	-

BOWLING AVERAGES

	Overs	Mdns	Runs	Wkts	Avge	Best	5wI	10wM
Other First-Class	13	0	81	0	-	-	-	-
ALL FIRST-CLASS	13	0	81	0	-	-	-	-

A.R. WINGFIELD DIGBY - *Dorset*

Opposition	Venue	Date	Batting	Fielding	Bowling
NATWEST TROPHY					
Glamorgan	Swansea	June 27	23 *		0-60

BATTING AVERAGES - Including fielding

	Matches	Inns	NO	Runs	HS	Avge	100s	50s	Ct	St
NatWest Trophy	1	1	1	23	23 *	-	-	-	-	-
ALL ONE-DAY	1	1	1	23	23 *	-	-	-	-	-

BOWLING AVERAGES

	Overs	Mdns	Runs	Wkts	Avge	Best	5wI	10wM
NatWest Trophy	12	0	60	0	-	-	-	-
ALL ONE-DAY	12	0	60	0	-	-	-	-

J.R. WOOD - *Hampshire*

Opposition	Venue	Date	Batting	Fielding	Bowling
BRITANNIC ASSURANCE					
Kent	Canterbury	April 26	17		
Notts	Portsmouth	July 18	11	1Ct	
REFUGE ASSURANCE					
Middlesex	Basingstoke	June 10	18		
BENSON & HEDGES CUP					
Yorkshire	Southampton	April 24	43 *		

BATTING AVERAGES - Including fielding

	Matches	Inns	NO	Runs	HS	Avge	100s	50s	Ct	St
Britannic Assurance	2	2	0	28	17	14.00	-	-	1	-
Refuge Assurance	1	1	0	18	18	18.00	-	-	-	-
Benson & Hedges Cup	1	1	1	43	43 *	-	-	-	-	-
ALL FIRST-CLASS	2	2	0	28	17	14.00	-	-	1	-
ALL ONE-DAY	2	2	1	61	43 *	61.00	-	-	-	-

BOWLING AVERAGES
Did not bowl

M.C. WOODMAN - *Devon*

Opposition	Venue	Date	Batting	Fielding	Bowling
NATWEST TROPHY					
Somerset	Torquay	June 27	1	1Ct	1-50

BATTING AVERAGES - Including fielding

	Matches	Inns	NO	Runs	HS	Avge	100s	50s	Ct	St
NatWest Trophy	1	1	0	1	1	1.00	-	-	1	-
ALL ONE-DAY	1	1	0	1	1	1.00	-	-	1	-

BOWLING AVERAGES

	Overs	Mdns	Runs	Wkts	Avge	Best	5wI	10wM
NatWest Trophy	12	3	50	1	50.00	1-50	-	-
ALL ONE-DAY	12	3	50	1	50.00	1-50	-	-

PLAYER RECORDS

P.B. WORMWALD - *Shropshire*

Opposition	Venue	Date	Batting	Fielding	Bowling
NATWEST TROPHY					
Derbyshire	Chesterfield	June 27	16		1-24

BATTING AVERAGES - Including fielding

	Matches	Inns	NO	Runs	HS	Avge	100s	50s	Ct	St
NatWest Trophy	1	1	0	16	16	16.00	-	-	-	-
ALL ONE-DAY	1	1	0	16	16	16.00	-	-	-	-

BOWLING AVERAGES

	Overs	Mdns	Runs	Wkts	Avge	Best	5wI	10wM
NatWest Trophy	5.1	1	24	1	24.00	1-24	-	
ALL ONE-DAY	5.1	1	24	1	24.00	1-24	-	

T. WREN - *Kent*

Opposition	Venue	Date	Batting	Fielding	Bowling
BRITANNIC ASSURANCE					
Worcestershire	Canterbury	July 28		1Ct	2-78 & 1-17
Leicestershire	Dartford	Aug 8	1	1Ct	0-18
Sussex	Hove	Aug 18			0-74 & 0-39
Surrey	Canterbury	Sept 7	5 *& 1 *		1-128
Essex	Chelmsford	Sept 12	16 & 0		2-135
REFUGE ASSURANCE					
Leicestershire	Leicester	Aug 26			1-31
OTHER ONE-DAY					
Sussex	Hove	Sept 2	0 *		2-18
Surrey	Hove	Sept 4		1Ct	1-49

BATTING AVERAGES - Including fielding

	Matches	Inns	NO	Runs	HS	Avge	100s	50s	Ct	St
Britannic Assurance	5	5	2	23	16	7.66	-	-	2	-
Refuge Assurance	1	0	0	0	0	-	-	-	-	-
Other One-Day	2	1	1	0	0 *	-	-	-	1	-
ALL FIRST-CLASS	5	5	2	23	16	7.66	-	-	2	-
ALL ONE-DAY	3	1	1	0	0 *	-	-	-	1	-

BOWLING AVERAGES

	Overs	Mdns	Runs	Wkts	Avge	Best	5wI	10wM
Britannic Assurance	122	14	489	6	81.50	2-78	-	
Refuge Assurance	6	0	31	1	31.00	1-31	-	
Other One-Day	17	1	67	3	22.33	2-18	-	
ALL FIRST-CLASS	122	14	489	6	81.50	2-78	-	
ALL ONE-DAY	23	1	98	4	24.50	2-18	-	

A.J. WRIGHT - *Gloucestershire*

Opposition	Venue	Date	Batting	Fielding	Bowling
BRITANNIC ASSURANCE					
Somerset	Taunton	April 26	25 & 37	1Ct	
Glamorgan	Bristol	May 15	3 & 5	2Ct	
Middlesex	Lord's	May 26	24 *& 8	1Ct	
Somerset	Bristol	June 2	4	1Ct	
Essex	Ilford	June 6	92		
Lancashire	Old Trafford	June 9	15		0-7
Sussex	Hove	June 16	17 & 45 *	2Ct	
Hampshire	Gloucester	June 20	9		
Leicestershire	Gloucester	June 23	51 *& 2		
Derbyshire	Derby	June 30	3 & 44		
Glamorgan	Swansea	July 4	19		
Worcestershire	Worcester	July 7	13 & 5	2Ct	
Yorkshire	Cheltenham	July 21	78	1Ct	
Northants	Cheltenham	July 25	112	2Ct	
Surrey	Cheltenham	July 28	2 & 45	1Ct	
Warwickshire	Bristol	Aug 8	4 & 4	1Ct	

Kent	Bristol	Aug 11	16 & 9		
Notts	Trent Bridge	Aug 18	2 & 0		
Northants	Northampton	Aug 23	11 & 4	2Ct	
Worcestershire	Bristol	Sept 7	21 & 72	1Ct	
Sussex	Bristol	Sept 12	3	2Ct	
Hampshire	Southampton	Sept 18	19 & 19	2Ct	
REFUGE ASSURANCE					
Glamorgan	Bristol	April 22	30	1Ct	
Hampshire	Southampton	May 6			
Essex	Chelmsford	May 13	20	1Ct	
Warwickshire	Moreton-in-M	May 20	40	2Ct	
Middlesex	Lord's	May 27	58	1Ct	
Somerset	Bristol	June 3	17	4Ct	
Lancashire	Old Trafford	June 10	68		
Leicestershire	Gloucester	June 24	0	1Ct	
Derbyshire	Derby	July 1	17		
Worcestershire	Worcester	July 8	24		
Sussex	Swindon	July 15	3		
Yorkshire	Cheltenham	July 22	57		
Surrey	Cheltenham	July 29	21	2Ct	
Kent	Bristol	Aug 12	3		
Notts	Trent Bridge	Aug 19	21 *		
Northants	Northampton	Aug 26	50	1Ct	
NATWEST TROPHY					
Lincolnshire	Gloucester	June 27	92	1Ct	
Kent	Bristol	July 11	45		
Lancashire	Old Trafford	Aug 1	4	1Ct	
BENSON & HEDGES CUP					
Worcestershire	Bristol	April 24	97		
Glamorgan	Cardiff	May 1	10		
Kent	Canterbury	May 10	15		
Warwickshire	Bristol	May 12	15		
OTHER FIRST-CLASS					
Cambridge U	Fenner's	May 23	44 & 58	2Ct	
OTHER ONE-DAY					
For MCC					
New Zealand	Lord's	May 7	8	1Ct	

BATTING AVERAGES - Including fielding

	Matches	Inns	NO	Runs	HS	Avge	100s	50s	Ct	St
Britannic Assurance	22	36	3	809	112	24.51	1	4	21	-
Refuge Assurance	16	15	1	429	68	30.64	-	4	13	-
NatWest Trophy	3	3	0	141	92	47.00	-	1	2	-
Benson & Hedges Cup	4	3	0	122	97	40.66	-	1	-	-
Other First-Class	1	2	0	102	58	51.00	-	1	2	-
Other One-Day	1	1	0	8	8	8.00	-	-	1	-
ALL FIRST-CLASS	23	38	3	911	112	26.02	1	5	23	-
ALL ONE-DAY	24	22	1	700	97	33.33	-	6	16	-

BOWLING AVERAGES

	Overs	Mdns	Runs	Wkts	Avge	Best	5wI	10wM
Britannic Assurance	0.5	0	7	0	-	-	-	-
Refuge Assurance								
NatWest Trophy								
Benson & Hedges Cup								
Other First-Class								
Other One-Day								
ALL FIRST-CLASS	0.5	0	7	0	-	-	-	-
ALL ONE-DAY								

J.G. WRIGHT - *New Zealand*

Opposition	Venue	Date	Batting	Fielding	Bowling
CORNHILL TEST MATCHES					
England	Trent Bridge	June 7	8 & 1		
England	Lord's	June 21	98		
England	Edgbaston	July 5	24 & 46		
TEXACO TROPHY					
England	Headingley	May 23	52		
England	The Oval	May 25	15		
OTHER FIRST-CLASS					
Worcestershire	Worcester	May 12	8 & 99		

W   PLAYER RECORDS

Middlesex	Lord's	May 19	54 & 18		
Sussex	Hove	May 26	10 * & 82		
Warwickshire	Edgbaston	May 30	51 & 2 *	1Ct	
Northants	Northampton	June 16	31		1Ct
Essex	Chelmsford	June 30	121		

OTHER ONE-DAY

Ireland	Downpatrick	May 9	49
Ireland	Belfast	May 10	44
Leicestershire	Leicester	June 14	62

BATTING AVERAGES - Including fielding

	Matches	Inns	NO	Runs	HS	Avge	100s	50s	Ct	St
Cornhill Test Matches	3	5	0	177	98	35.40	-	1	-	-
Texaco Trophy	2	2	0	67	52	33.50	-	1	-	-
Other First-Class	6	10	2	476	121	59.50	1	4	2	-
Other One-Day	3	3	0	155	62	51.66	-	1	-	-
ALL FIRST-CLASS	9	15	2	653	121	50.23	1	5	2	-
ALL ONE-DAY	5	5	0	222	62	44.40	-	2	-	-

BOWLING AVERAGES
Did not bowl

N.P.G. WRIGHT - *Hertfordshire*

Opposition	Venue	Date	Batting	Fielding	Bowling

NATWEST TROPHY

Warwickshire	St Albans	June 27	17

BATTING AVERAGES - Including fielding

	Matches	Inns	NO	Runs	HS	Avge	100s	50s	Ct	St
NatWest Trophy	1	1	0	17	17	17.00	-	-	-	-
ALL ONE-DAY	1	1	0	17	17	17.00	-	-	-	-

BOWLING AVERAGES
Did not bowl

S. WUNDKE - *League C.C. XI*

Opposition	Venue	Date	Batting	Fielding	Bowling

OTHER ONE-DAY

India	Sunderland	June 28	3	1Ct	3-41

BATTING AVERAGES - Including fielding

	Matches	Inns	NO	Runs	HS	Avge	100s	50s	Ct	St
Other One-Day	1	1	0	3	3	3.00	-	-	1	-
ALL ONE-DAY	1	1	0	3	3	3.00	-	-	1	-

BOWLING AVERAGES

	Overs	Mdns	Runs	Wkts	Avge	Best	5wI	10wM
Other One-Day	11	0	41	3	13.66	3-41	-	
ALL ONE-DAY	11	0	41	3	13.66	3-41	-	

PLAYER RECORDS

G. YATES - *Lancashire*

Opposition	Venue	Date	Batting	Fielding	Bowling
BRITANNIC ASSURANCE					
Notts	Trent Bridge	Sept 12	106		0-6 & 2-69
Warwickshire	Old Trafford	Sept 18			1-42
OTHER FIRST-CLASS					
Zimbabwe	Old Trafford	May 23	2 *		1-88 & 0-26
Oxford U	The Parks	June 16			0-52 & 0-4
Sri Lanka	Old Trafford	Sept 8	42 & 15 *	1Ct	4-94 & 0-39

BATTING AVERAGES - Including fielding

	Matches	Inns	NO	Runs	HS	Avge	100s	50s	Ct	St
Britannic Assurance	2	1	0	106	106	106.00	1	-	-	-
Other First-Class	3	3	2	59	42	59.00	-	-	1	-
ALL FIRST-CLASS	5	4	2	165	106	82.50	1	-	1	-

BOWLING AVERAGES

	Overs	Mdns	Runs	Wkts	Avge	Best	5wI	10wM
Britannic Assurance	51	12	117	3	39.00	2-69	-	-
Other First-Class	116	26	303	5	60.60	4-94	-	-
ALL FIRST-CLASS	167	38	420	8	52.50	4-94	-	-

R.S. YEABSLEY - *Devon*

Opposition	Venue	Date	Batting	Fielding	Bowling
NATWEST TROPHY					
Somerset	Torquay	June 27	2		0-77

BATTING AVERAGES - Including fielding

	Matches	Inns	NO	Runs	HS	Avge	100s	50s	Ct	St
NatWest Trophy	1	1	0	2	2	2.00	-	-	-	-
ALL ONE-DAY	1	1	0	2	2	2.00	-	-	-	-

BOWLING AVERAGES

	Overs	Mdns	Runs	Wkts	Avge	Best	5wI	10wM
NatWest Trophy	12	0	77	0	-	-	-	
ALL ONE-DAY	12	0	77	0	-	-	-	

I. YOUNG - *Durham*

Opposition	Venue	Date	Batting	Fielding	Bowling
NATWEST TROPHY					
Lancashire	Old Trafford	June 27	0		0-47

BATTING AVERAGES - Including fielding

	Matches	Inns	NO	Runs	HS	Avge	100s	50s	Ct	St
NatWest Trophy	1	1	0	0	0	0.00	-	-	-	-
ALL ONE-DAY	1	1	0	0	0	0.00	-	-	-	-

BOWLING AVERAGES

	Overs	Mdns	Runs	Wkts	Avge	Best	5wI	10wM
NatWest Trophy	6.1	0	47	0	-	-	-	
ALL ONE-DAY	6.1	0	47	0	-	-	-	

THE BULL
UNDER 19
SERIES

ONE-DAY INTERNATIONALS

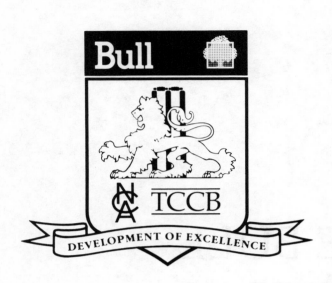

HEADLINES

England v Pakistan

Bull Computer Under 19 Internationals

● As part of the Development of Excellence programme, sponsored by Bull Computers, the England Under 19s contested a full series of Test Matches and One-Day Internationals with Pakistan Under 19s

● The one-day series was shared one match each, England winning impressively by 76 runs at Lord's but coming unstuck two days later at The Oval

● After the opening Test at Northampton had been spoilt by rain, England gained a decisive victory in the second match at Headingley, Darren Gough, Jeremy Hallett all bowling effectively as Pakistan collapsed to 78 all out in their second innings. Jonathan Crawley had earlier made a determined 84, one of two innings in the series that marked him out as a young batsman of immense promise.

● Although the young Pakistani batsmen were at their very best in the third match at Taunton, England salvaged a draw thanks principally to 110 from nightwatchman Dominic Cork. The third Test series of the summer, this time at junior level, had been won and a generation of up and coming youngsters had gained valuable experience.

ENGLAND vs. PAKISTAN

at Lord's on 8th August 1990
Toss : England. Umpires : A.A.Jones and N.T.Plews
England won by 76 runs

ENGLAND

A.P.Grayson	c Zahid Fazal b Athar Laeeq	3
P.C.L.Holloway	c Moin Khan b Naeem Khan	32
J.P.Crawley	run out	0
M.Keech	c Zahid Fazal b Athar Laeeq	7
K.A.Butler	run out	77
J.A.North	run out	2
W.M.Noon *+	c Moin Khan b Athar Laeeq	51
D.Gough	c Shahid Hussain b Naeem Khan	12
J.C.Hallett	b Athar Laeeq	5
D.G.Cork	not out	1
A.A.Barnett		
Extras	(lb 14,w 9,nb 5)	28
TOTAL	(55 overs)(for 9 wkts)	218

PAKISTAN

Rashid Mehmood	b Hallett	16
Tariq Mehmood	c Cork b Hallett	7
Masroor Hussain	lbw b Cork	36
Zahid Fazal	lbw b Barnett	39
Naseer Ahmed	lbw b Cork	1
Moin Khan *+	run out	2
Shahid Hussain	lbw b Gough	0
Naeem Khan	b Cork	0
Mushahid Afridi	b Cork	23
Athar Laeeq	not out	10
Ataur Rahman	c Noon b Hallett	0
Extras	(lb 6,w 2)	8
TOTAL	(42.2 overs)	142

PAKISTAN	O	M	R	W		FALL OF WICKETS	
						ENG	PAK
Athar Laeeq	11	1	40	4	1st	6	8
Ataur Rahman	11	3	21	0	2nd	6	28
Mushahid Afridi	11	0	54	0	3rd	25	86
Naeem Khan	11	0	44	2	4th	85	98
Shahid Hussain	11	1	45	0	5th	180	106
					6th	195	106
ENGLAND	O	M	R	W	7th	198	106
Hallett	7.2	1	26	3	8th	210	141
Gough	8	2	31	1	9th	218	141
Cork	9	0	24	4	10th		142
North	7	0	37	0			
Barnett	11	5	18	1			

ENGLAND vs. PAKISTAN

at The Oval on 10th August 1990
Toss : England. Umpires : D.J.Constant and B.Leadbeater
Pakistan won by 23 runs

PAKISTAN

Rashid Mehmood	c Noon b Irani	38
Mujahid Jamshed	c Noon b Hallett	2
Shakeel Ahmed	lbw b Barnett	39
Masroor Hussain	lbw b Cork	2
Naseer Ahmed	c Irani b Cork	77
Tariq Mehmood	c & b Barnett	20
Moin Khan *+	c Noon b Hallett	1
Mushahid Afridi	run out	8
Athar Laeeq	c Keech b Cork	26
Maqsood Rana	not out	1
Ataur Rahman		
Extras	(b 1,lb 2,w 3)	6
TOTAL	(55 overs)(for 9 wkts)	220

ENGLAND

P.C.L.Holloway	run out	60
M.Keech	c Maqsood Rana b Athar Laeeq	32
J.P.Crawley	c Moin Khan b Rashid Mehmood	8
K.A.Butler	b Mushahid Afridi	3
R.Irani	c & b Rashid Mehmood	4
A.P.Grayson	c Moin Khan b Athar Laeeq	10
W.M.Noon *+	b Maqsood Rana	28
D.Gough	not out	17
J.C.Hallett	c Moin Khan b Athar Laeeq	0
D.G.Cork	c Moin Khan b Athar Laeeq	3
A.A.Barnett	b Maqsood Rana	0
Extras	(lb 15,w 17)	32
TOTAL	(52.4 overs)	197

ENGLAND	O	M	R	W		FALL OF WICKETS	
						PAK	ENG
Hallett	11	2	39	2	1st	9	65
Gough	11	0	49	0	2nd	74	79
Irani	11	2	31	1	3rd	81	106
Cork	11	0	68	3	4th	88	121
Barnett	11	2	30	2	5th	126	128
					6th	127	167
PAKISTAN	O	M	R	W	7th	145	172
Maqsood Rana	9.4	1	35	2	8th	218	173
Ataur Rahman	11	1	35	0	9th	220	192
Athar Laeeq	10	1	33	4	10th		197
Mushahid Afridi	11	2	39	1			
Rashid Mehmood	11	1	40	2			

TEST MATCHES

ENGLAND vs. PAKISTAN

at Northampton on 18th, 19th (no play), 20th, 21st August
Toss : Pakistan.   Umpires : B.Dudleston and B.J.Meyer
Match drawn

PAKISTAN

Rashid Mehmood	st Noon b Roberts	76	(2) c Roberts b Gough	0	
Mujahid Jamshed	c Holloway b Barnett	98	(1) c Roberts b Hallett	7	
Shakeel Ahmed	c Crawley b Roberts	10	(6) c Noon b Barnett	5	
Zahid Fazal	b Barnett	7	b Grayson	73	
Tariq Mehmood	lbw b Roberts	3	(3) c Noon b Gough	24	
Naseer Ahmed	c Grayson b Gough	57	(5) c Noon b Barnett	4	
Moin Khan *+	c Crawley b Barnett	1	(7) not out	49	
Shahid Hussain	b Gough	34	(8) c Crawley b Grayson	0	
Athar Laeeq	not out	3	(9) b Gough	2	
Maqsood Rana			(10) not out	1	
Ataur Rahman					
Extras	(lb 7,nb 2)	9	(b 4,lb 2)	6	
TOTAL	(for 8 wkts dec)	298	(for 8 wkts)	171	

ENGLAND

A.P.Grayson	b Athar Laeeq	18
P.C.L.Holloway	lbw b Athar Laeeq	96
J.P.Crawley	lbw b Shahid Hussain	93
M.Keech	b Shahid Hussain	10
K.A.Butler	c Tariq b Athar Laeeq	43
A.R.Roberts	st Shakeel b Shahid Hussain	33
W.M.Noon *+	b Ataur Rahman	16
J.C.Hallett	c Shakeel b Maqsood Rana	1
D.Gough	lbw b Maqsood Rana	8
D.G.Cork	c Tariq b Shahid Hussain	13
A.A.Barnett	not out	4
Extras	(b 3,lb 7,w 1,nb 6)	17
TOTAL		352

ENGLAND	O	M	R	W	O	M	R	W
Gough	13.1	3	45	2	13	1	53	3
Hallett	13	1	64	0	6	1	25	1
Cork	14	1	59	0	1	0	5	0
Barnett	34	14	69	3	16	4	25	2
Roberts	22	6	54	3	11	1	57	0
Grayson					4	4	0	2

PAKISTAN	O	M	R	W	O	M	R	W
Maqsood Rana	20	2	67	2				
Ataur Rahman	19.3	0	72	1				
Athar Laeeq	31	8	90	3				
Shahid Hussain	49	20	66	4				
Rashid Mehmood	18	3	47	0				

FALL OF WICKETS

	PAK	ENG	PAK	ENG
1st	156	42	1	
2nd	173	97	23	
3rd	184	218	45	
4th	189	231	68	
5th	206	300	100	
6th	213	304	122	
7th	280	309	122	
8th	298	321	162	
9th		344		
10th		352		

ENGLAND vs. PAKISTAN

at Headingley on 28th, 29th, 30th August 1990
Toss : Pakistan.   Umpires : J.W.Holder and D.O.Oslear
England won by 9 wickets

PAKISTAN

Mujahid Jamshed	lbw b Cork	15	c Noon b Cork	4	
Rashid Mehmood	c Noon b Gough	7	b Cork	3	
Tariq Mehmood	c Noon b Cork	24	c Holloway b Hallett	11	
Zahid Fazal	c Keech b Gough	32	lbw b Cork	1	
Shakeel Ahmed	lbw b Cork	64	c Noon b Hallett	9	
Naseer Ahmed	lbw b Gough	0	c Crawley b Cork	0	
Moin Khan *+	not out	114	c Noon b Hallett	6	
Shahid Hussain	c Butler b Cork	0	lbw b Hallett	29	
Athar Laeeq	lbw b Gough	1	c Grayson b Hallett	4	
Naeem Khan	c Noon b Roberts	5	b Gough	1	
Ataur Rahman	c & b Gough	6	not out	1	
Extras	(b 1,lb 6,nb 2)	9	(b 5,lb 4)	9	
TOTAL		277		78	

ENGLAND

A.P.Grayson	c Moin Khan b Naeem Khan	11	c Zahid Fazal b Ataur Rahman	9
P.C.L.Holloway	c Moin Khan b Ataur Rahman	8	not out	20
A.A.Barnett	c Rashid b Ataur Rahman	0		
J.P.Crawley	c Moin b Shahid Hussain	84	(3) not out	5
K.A.Butler	b Naeem Khan	10		
M.Keech	lbw b Naeem Khan	22		
A.R.Roberts	c Shakeel b Athar Laeeq	17		
W.M.Noon *+	lbw b Ataur Rahman	25		
J.C.Hallett	not out	55		
D.Gough	c Moin b Shahid Hussain	36		
D.G.Cork	lbw b Zahid Fazal	45		
Extras	(b 1,lb 7,nb 4)	12		0
TOTAL		325	(for 1 wkt)	34

ENGLAND	O	M	R	W	O	M	R	W
Gough	27.2	4	106	5	12	5	18	1
Hallett	3	0	21	0	11.3	4	33	5
Cork	24	8	73	4	15	7	18	4
Barnett	20	8	47	0				
Roberts	12	4	23	1				

PAKISTAN	O	M	R	W	O	M	R	W
Naeem Khan	39	12	81	3	4.1	1	15	0
Ataur Rahman	32	10	79	3	5	1	19	1
Athar Laeeq	35	7	105	1				
Shahid Hussain	29	17	36	2				
Rashid Mehmood	1	0	4	0				
Zahid Fazal	1.4	0	12	1				

FALL OF WICKETS

	PAK	ENG	PAK	ENG
1st	15	19	4	20
2nd	37	19	13	
3rd	48	25	15	
4th	117	42	35	
5th	117	99	36	
6th	157	132	38	
7th	159	175	55	
8th	182	187	67	
9th	193	246	76	
10th	277	325	78	

ENGLAND vs. PAKISTAN

at Taunton on 7th, 8th, 9th, 10th September 1990
Toss : Pakistan.   Umpires : B.Dudleston and K.J.Lyons
Match drawn

PAKISTAN

Mujahid Jamshed	c Noon b Cork	2
Tariq Mehmood	c Keech b Hallett	106
Shakeel Ahmed	c Hallett b Cork	190
Zahid Fazal	c Noon b Barnett	99
Masroor Hussain	c Keech b Barnett	74
Naseer Ahmed	not out	21
Moin Khan *+	not out	52
Shahid Hussain		
Ataur Rahman		
Athar Laeeq		
Naeem Khan		
Extras	(b 2,lb 10,w 2,nb 3)	17
TOTAL	(for 5 wkts dec)	561

ENGLAND

A.P.Grayson	c Moin Khan b Athar Laeeq	43	run out	1	
P.C.L.Holloway	c Moin Khan b Athar Laeeq	38	c Zahid Fazal b Ataur Rahman	4	
J.P.Crawley	b Ataur Rahman	41	b Ataur Rahman	34	
K.A.Butler	c Moin Khan b Ataur Rahman	19	(5) b Athar Laeeq	29	
M.Keech	c Naseer b Shahid Hussain	87	(6) c Shakeel b Ataur Rahman		
A.R.Roberts	c & b Naeem Khan	30	(7) not out	24	
W.M.Noon *+	c Naseer b Shahid Hussain	24	(8) lbw b Naeem Khan	1	
J.C.Hallett	lbw b Shahid Hussain	5	(9) c Shakeel b Athar Laeeq	19	
D.Gough	lbw b Zahid Fazal	3	(10) not out	19	
D.G.Cork	b Ataur Rahman	9	(4) c Naeem b Athar Laeeq	110	
A.A.Barnett	not out	20			
Extras	(b 12,lb 17,w 6,nb 10)	45	(b 10,lb 9,nb 3)	22	
TOTAL		364	(for 8 wkts)	269	

ENGLAND	O	M	R	W	O	M	R	W
Cork	37	8	104	2				
Gough	23	2	100	0				
Butler	2	0	13	0				
Hallett	27	7	101	1				
Barnett	35	10	111	2				
Roberts	39	6	120	0				

PAKISTAN	O	M	R	W	O	M	R	W
Athar Laeeq	31	10	81	2	23	10	50	3
Naeem Khan	20	1	46	1	21	5	57	1
Ataur Rahman	31	4	71	3	26	4	71	3
Shahid Hussain	54	16	113	3	31	10	55	0
Zahid Fazal	11	4	16	1	5	2	9	0
Moin Khan					2	0	8	0

FALL OF WICKETS

	PAK	ENG	ENG	PAK
1st	2	91	5	
2nd	229	100	16	
3rd	332	148	55	
4th	483	173	127	
5th	494	242	204	
6th		311	240	
7th		323	243	
8th		326	244	
9th		332		
10th		364		